A SAILOR'S ODY

A SAILOR'S ODYSSEY

The Autobiography of
ADMIRAL OF THE FLEET
VISCOUNT CUNNINGHAM of HYNDHOPE
K.T. G.C.B. O.M. D.S.O.

New Introduction by
Admiral Sir Jock Slater G.C.B. L.V.O. D.L.

With 16 *Maps*
and
48 *Photographs*

To

MY STAFF IN THE MEDITERRANEAN

to whom I owe so much
for
their never failing support
loyalty and undefeated spirit
in those difficult
and memorable days
of the Second World War.

Copyright © Andrew Cunningham 1951

First published in Great Britain in this edition in 2022 by
Seaforth Publishing,
A division of Pen & Sword Books Ltd,
47 Church Street,
Barnsley S70 2AS

www.seaforthpublishing.com

British Library Cataloguing in Publication Data
A catalogue record for this book is available from the British Library

ISBN 978 1 3990 9295 1 (PAPERBACK)
ISBN 978 1 3990 9296 8 (EPUB)
ISBN 978 1 3990 9297 5 (KINDLE)

All rights reserved. No part of this publication may be reproduced or transmitted in any form or by any means, electronic or mechanical, including photocopying, recording, or any information storage and retrieval system, without prior permission in writing of both the copyright owner and the above publisher.

The right of Andrew Cunningham to be identified as the author of this work has been asserted by him in accordance with the Copyright, Designs and Patents Act 1988.

Pen & Sword Books Limited incorporates the imprints of Atlas, Archaeology, Aviation, Discovery, Family History, Fiction, History, Maritime, Military, Military Classics, Politics, Select, Transport, True Crime, Air World, Frontline Publishing, Leo Cooper, Remember When, Seaforth Publishing, The Praetorian Press, Wharncliffe Local History, Wharncliffe Transport, Wharncliffe True Crime, White Owl and After the Battle.

Printed and bound in Great Britain by CPI Group (UK) Ltd, Croydon, CR0 4YY

LIST OF ILLUSTRATIONS

Andrew Browne Cunningham

Professor D. J. Cunningham and A.B.C., September, 1900

H.M.S. *Martin*, July, 1901

W Beach, Gallipoli, 1915; A 'Beagle' class destroyer in the Dardanelles

Spring exercises in the Atlantic, March, 1934

H.M.S. *Coventry* and Third Destroyer Flotilla, Leghorn, 1934; H.M.S. *Coventry* and destroyers, Gulf of Corinth, 1935

Admiral Esteva and A.B.C., Malta, January, 1940

Italian salvoes off Calabria, July 9th, 1940; The *Malaya* comes through a forest of Italian bombs

British destroyer off Calabria, July 9th, 1940; Italian cruiser in retreat, Calabria, July 9th, 1940

H.M.S. *Warspite* entering Grand Harbour, Malta; The *Warspite* at sea

Ordeal of the *Illustrious*: January 10th, 1941

On bridge of *Warspite*: before Battle of Matapan

Tobruk, 1941

On board H.M.S. *Phoebe* after evacuation of Crete

At the British Embassy, Cairo

Rear-Admiral Vian's action with Italian fleet, March 22nd, 1942

Algiers, December, 1942

Conference at Gen. Eisenhower's villa, Algiers, May, 1943

Operation 'Husky', Sicily landing, July 10th, 1943

On board H.M.S. *Aurora Pantellaria*, June 9th, 1943

His Majesty's visit to Algiers, June, 1943

Landing craft under repair: Malta, July, 1943

LIST OF ILLUSTRATIONS

Surrender of the Italian fleet, September 10th, 1943

Salerno, September 11th, 1943

The Italian surrender, September 29th, 1943

General Sir John Dill and A.B.C.: Teheran, November, 1943

At the Quebec Conference, September, 1944

Malta Conference, January, 1945, on way to Yalta

V.E. Day, May 8th, 1945; V.J. Day, August 15th, 1945

At home at Bishop's Waltham

My wife and myself with friends in the garden at Bishop's Waltham

Prince Philip unveiling the bust of Cunningham in Trafalgar Square, April 1967

The funeral of Admiral Cunningham on the flight deck of HMS *Hampshire*

LIST OF MAPS

Defences of the Dardanelles, March, 1915	Page	67
Gallipoli Landings, 1915	,,	71
The Mediterranean, 1939	,,	204–5
Eastern Mediterranean, June, 1941–November, 1942	,,	228–9
The Action off Calabria, 9th July, 1940	,,	261
Air Attack on Italian Fleet at Taranto, 11th November, 1940	,,	285
One Day's Work, Eastern Mediterranean, 27th November, 1940	,,	292–3
Battle of Matapan, 10.15 p.m., 28th March, 1941	,,	328
Battle of Matapan, 10.30 p.m., 28th March, 1941	,,	331
Evacuation from Greece, 24th–30th April, 1941	,,	355
Battle of Crete, 20th May–1st June, 1941	,,	381
The Mediterranean, October, 1942–October, 1943	,,	484–5
Invasion of Sicily, 10th–31st July, 1943	,,	549
Invasion of Italy, 9th September, 1943	,,	567
The East Indies and Pacific	,,	632–3
The Effect of Malta Upon the Land Campaigns in Libya	Facing ,,	670

NEW INTRODUCTION
by Admiral Sir Jock Slater GCB LVO DL

I AM delighted that Seaforth Publishing has chosen to reprint *A Sailor's Odyssey* which my great uncle, Andrew Cunningham, wrote with the stalwart help of his old destroyer friend, Captain Taprell Dorling ('Taffrail') and published in 1951. Since then a number of biographies have been written and indeed the Navy Records Society has published two volumes of *The Cunningham Papers – Volume One: The Mediterranean Fleet, 1939–1942* in 1999, and *Volume Two: The Triumph of Allied Sea Power, 1942–1946* in 2006. His detailed and fascinating autobiography has undoubtedly stood the test of time and as many of the generation involved in Cunningham's life are no longer with us, a reprint is most welcome.

Three of Cunningham's great nephews, Sir John Cunningham, Dr Sandy McKendrick and I have decided that any proceeds from this new edition should be shared between the Royal Navy and Royal Marines Charity and King Edward VII Hospital; the latter paying tribute to Cunningham's distinguished father, Professor D J Cunningham (of Cunningham's *Textbook of Anatomy* fame).

I look back on the many weekends I spent with the Cunninghams at the Palace House in Bishops Waltham as a young naval officer in the late '50s and early '60s and the privilege I enjoyed of hearing, at first hand, my uncle's forthright views on so many topics, not least the Royal Navy. I just wish that I had been able to record them. Shrewd and perceptive, little escaped his sharp comments delivered with a penetrating gaze but often with a twinkle in his eye. Moreover, he had the most engaging habit of enjoying mischievous, boyish pranks to keep us all on our toes. He was great fun to be with, very good company and surprisingly modest.

I often reflect on what made him the best of destroyer captains. Without a doubt it was first class seamanship, fine ship handling, tough, uncompromising discipline and an aggressive fighting spirit. He was clearly greatly respected in command but I suspect feared by those who did not meet his high standards and expectations.

Later, as a commander-in-chief, he showed uncanny foresight, incredible stamina, supreme courage, leadership of the highest order and he was resolute in adversity. Behind this was shining honesty, deep humanity and wise counsel. In writing his memoirs seventy years ago, he was, of course, not able to comment on how much his operational decisions were affected by the sterling work of the intelligence agencies not least Bletchley Park. That material was then classified. The hugely significant victory at Matapan in 1941, for example, was the first major Royal Navy operation of the Second World War to be based on SIGINT, and in this case the source was the Italian naval Enigma. But the absence of this material does not in the least detract from either the accuracy or the vividness of the narrative.

One of the many signed photographs in Cunningham's study in the Palace House was one from Winston Churchill inscribed: 'to the Great Admiral of the

Mediterranean'. Although he much admired Cunningham's offensive spirit and willingness to take risks, it is said that the Prime Minister was not initially keen to appoint him as First Sea Lord when Sir Dudley Pound died, as he was uneasy that, unlike others, Cunningham might prove less malleable; however, the Royal Navy was in no doubt that Cunningham was the right man to lead the Service at such a critical time. In the event, he proved highly influential but was not fully at ease in the corridors of power and found the administration burdensome and irritating which must have been trying for the Naval Staff. Furthermore, Cunningham clearly found the Prime Minister a real challenge to satisfy; that said, there was obviously a deep respect on both sides and Churchill must have known that Cunningham was a hard taskmaster and leading the Senior Service with great ability; moreover, there was an admirable rapport amongst the Chiefs of Staff.

Cunningham was buried at sea off the Nab Tower on 18 June 1963. He lay in state in the Chapel of HMS *Nelson*, the naval barracks, and was then taken through the streets of Portsmouth on a gun carriage drawn by sailors, preceded by a double Royal Marines band. Crowds had assembled to pay their respects. With members of my family, I processed behind the coffin down to south railway jetty in the dockyard where HMS *Hampshire*, the County-class destroyer, was preparing to sail. Admiral of the Fleet Sir Caspar John, the First Sea Lord, led the pall-bearers including members of the Board of Admiralty; and Lord Carrington, the First Lord of the Admiralty, led senior mourners in the procession.

To this day, I can see the scene on the flight deck of *Hampshire* as the Chaplain of the Fleet and the Senior Church of Scotland Chaplain conducted the funeral service. The wind was strong and the sea rough with low, threatening clouds racing across the sky. As the coffin slipped into the sea, the ship fired a nineteen-gun salute. I knew we were all saying farewell to one of Britain's greatest fighting admirals who had dedicated his life to the service of his country through the Royal Navy he loved and led with such distinction.

Admiral Jock Slater
First Sea Lord 1995–98

PREFACE

I ALLOWED myself to be persuaded into setting down this record of my life somewhat against my own will and judgment. My main reasons for yielding to the suggestion were because I wished to do justice to those under whom I served and from whom I learnt so much in my earlier years at sea, and also to pay a deserved tribute to those many whom I later had the honour and privilege to command in the Mediterranean and elsewhere. Further, before memory became dimmed by the passage of time, I was anxious to describe what I saw of the part played by the Royal Navy in the two great wars of the present century which lasted in all for more than ten years.

I do not claim that this book provides any serious contribution to history. But it so happened that during my naval service of nearly fifty years my ways have sometimes impinged upon events that are historic, while in later times circumstances ordained that I should become associated with many of those in whose hands history was being shaped.

In describing the years of war I have kept as closely as possible to those matters with which, and in which, the Navy was primarily concerned and engaged. Moreover, as nearly as may be, I have tried to concentrate upon that portion of the Navy with which I happened to be serving. It has naturally been impossible altogether to exclude mention of the other Services, and I trust that I have sufficiently emphasized the fact, often forgotten, that success in war cannot be attributed to any single Service. Each one is helpless without the closest and most loyal co-operation with the other two. This applies equally to our two great Sea Services. In war the Royal and the Merchant Navies have always been interdependent and indivisible.

I wish cordially to thank the Lords Commissioners of the Admiralty for permitting me to make use of certain official records and documents without which this book could hardly have been written, and in particular to say how greatly I am indebted to the invaluable help and advice of those of the Historical Section of the Tactical and Staff Duties Division of the Admiralty Naval Staff, as well as to the Librarian and staff of the Admiralty Library. I should add that on grounds of security I have been requested to paraphrase some of the messages and telegrams quoted; but that this has in no way altered their sense or substance.

PREFACE

My sincere thanks are due to many old friends who at various times have helped to remind me of details which would have been forgotten with the impact of more modern events. Among these I must mention Admiral of the Fleet Sir Algernon Willis; Admirals J. H. Godfrey and Sir John Edelsten; Rear-Admiral R. M. Dick; Captain (S) A. P. Shaw, who for years served as my Secretary afloat and ashore; and Captain Manley L. Power.

In conclusion I am deeply grateful to my friend and old flotilla-mate of forty years ago, Captain Taprell Dorling ('Taffrail'), for his collaboration and the continuous and valuable help and stimulation without which this volume would not have been completed. I am greatly indebted to Bip Pares for the accurate and painstaking care with which she has drawn the charts.

The services of Mary Bishop, who has transcribed what at times has been a complicated and heavily corrected manuscript, have been most helpful.

Cunningham of Hyndhope

ADMIRAL OF THE FLEET

THE PALACE HOUSE,
 BISHOP'S WALTHAM,
  HAMPSHIRE.

New Year's Day, 1950.

CHAPTER I

I

IN the early hours of January 7th, 1883, there was a certain amount of ado at 42 Grosvenor Square, District of Rathmines, in the Union of South Dublin in the county of Dublin. I was being brought into this troublous world as the third child of Professor and Mrs. Daniel John Cunningham. I had been preceded by a sister and a brother, and was followed in due course by another brother and sister. My parents thus produced three sons and two daughters, or, in poker terms, a 'full house sons up'.

Though born in Ireland I am a Scot. Being a grandson of the manse on both sides I am also respectably connected with the Kirk of Scotland. My earliest known ancestor, a Cunningham, was ordained Minister of Ettrick in 1641 and ejected for nonconformity in 1662. It was his eldest son, James Cunningham, who owned a small sheep farm and house of Hyndhope in the parish of Kirkhope in Selkirk County. His second son was Alexander Cunningham, well known as a historian.

My paternal grandfather was the Very Reverend Doctor John Cunningham, born at Paisley in 1819. Educated at the Universities of Glasgow and Edinburgh, he graduated at the former. I have no knowledge of his undergraduate career; but since he won a gold medal for Moral Philosophy at Glasgow, which is in the possession of my elder brother, it would seem he was a distinguished student. Licensed by the Presbytery of Paisley in 1845, he was ordained to Crieff in August of the same year. A year later, on December 23rd, 1846, he married Susan Porteous Murray, only daughter of William Murray, banker, of Crieff, whose portrait gives the impression that he was a man of virile and forceful personality. There were seven children of the marriage: William Murray, October, 1847; Jane, January, 1849; Daniel John, April, 1850; Susan Porteous Murray, September, 1852; Eliza Yeats, June, 1854; Margaret, April, 1856; John, August, 1857. Eliza and John died in infancy. Daniel John was my father.

I hardly knew my grandfather, who died when I was only ten; but I well remember his cheerful sense of fun. My grandmother, on the other hand, I recall as a tall, stately person of whom we children rather stood in awe, for she, by contrast was a disciplinarian. My grandfather used to prompt us on Sundays when we had to recite collects, psalms and hymns to my grandmother.

My grandfather was evidently a man of determined character who held decided, and sometimes unorthodox, views which he did not hesitate to carry into effect. When, for instance, in 1867, he insisted upon introducing a harmonium into his parish church, the 'Crieff Organ Case', as it was called, considerable excitement and controversy was created in Scottish ecclesiastical circles. But he stuck to his guns, though many were scandalized. Again, when one fine Sunday, after a spell of bad weather, he dismissed his congregation and advised them to go into the fields and gather in the harvest, his action was severely criticized by certain of his professional brethren. A good debater with a gift of ready repartee, he had a keen sense of humour and loved a fight. He certainly held very advanced views, and it was little wonder, when he was nominated Moderator of the Church of Scotland in May, 1886, objections were raised to his election by some of those present. A year later, in 1887, the Very Reverend John Cunningham was appointed Principal of St. Mary's College, the centre of the Theological Faculty at St. Andrews University, a post which he held until his death in 1893 at the age of 74.

My grandfather took a very active part in the affairs of the Church, and was largely responsible for carrying through legislation known as 'The Cunningham Act' by which it was made legal for any congregation in the Church of Scotland to elect to a vacant charge a minister of any Presbyterian Church in Scotland, England or Ireland. It was described as an Act of great statesmanship, and one of the first steps towards union. He became a D.D. of the University of St. Andrews in 1860; an LL.D. of Glasgow University in 1886; and an LL.D. of Trinity College, Dublin in 1887.

Daniel John Cunningham, my father, was born at Crieff in April, 1850, and received his schooling at Crieff Academy. Articled at an early age to a business firm in Glasgow, his principal duty during his boyhood consisted of tying up parcels; a proficiency he retained through life. It may well be that his early business training was responsible for the legibility of his bold and distinguished handwriting. However, the firm to which he was apprenticed failed, so he returned to Crieff to wait for an appointment to another firm in India which a relative had promised to obtain when a vacancy occurred.

Some chance incident or meeting often determines a life career. So it was with Dan Cunningham, as he was known to his friends, for during this period of waiting he saw a good deal of a young man of his own age, a medical student. It was this association which aroused his interest and made him decide to study Medicine. His father agreed to pay his expenses for a trial term, and thus it was that he became a medical student at Edinburgh University. Returning for the holidays with a medal, it was decided he should continue his medical course, his father agreeing to help with the money. This allowance, all of which was eventually repaid, supplemented by fees derived from coaching, enabled my father to complete the course and graduate with first class honours in 1874. Two years later, when he took the degree of M.D., he was awarded a gold medal for his thesis.

After graduating, my father was appointed as an assistant and demonstrator in the Anatomical Department of the University by Professor Turner (later Sir William Turner, K.C.B.), the eminent professor of that subject. My parent evidently possessed his father's self-confidence and determination, for I have seen a copy of a letter, written while he was still an undergraduate, in which he applied for the vacant Professorship of Anatomy at the University of Otago, New Zealand. Not unnaturally, he failed to secure the appointment.

In 1879 he married Elizabeth Cumming Browne, eldest daughter of the Reverend Andrew Browne, Minister of the parish of Beith, Ayrshire. At first life was not at all easy, for soon after the young couple returned from their honeymoon it was announced that the Glasgow Bank, in which my father's savings were invested, had failed. But Professor Turner and his father-in-law each came to the rescue with £100, which tided them over their immediate difficulties.

In 1882 my father applied for and obtained the Chair of Anatomy at the Royal College of Surgeons in Ireland, and within two years became Professor of Anatomy at Trinity College, Dublin. This position he held for twenty years before being recalled to Scotland to succeed Sir William Turner as Professor of Anatomy at Edinburgh University, of which Sir William had been elected Principal.

My parent was a strenuous worker. He often set out for Trinity College at 7.30 in the morning, was away all day, and on his return in the evening usually worked in his study until well after midnight. We children saw little of him except in the summer holidays, though he would sometimes spend half-an-hour before we went to bed telling us stories, usually about animals, or reading to us. He was very popular, not only with his University colleagues and students, but with everyone he met. He did not confine himself strictly to the routine duties of his Chair. While in Dublin he wrote his *Manual of Anatomy*, and edited a text-book on the same subject to which many well-known anatomists, who had all been pupils of Sir William Turner, made contributions. Both these books, which have been carried on by his successors, have passed through many editions, and, I understand, are still standard works. He also wrote many scientific papers and memoirs, which were published in various scientific journals. He was certainly one of the leading anatomists and anatomical teachers of his day.

In Dublin my father had many outside interests and activities. Keenly interested in animals, he was Honorary Secretary of the Royal Zoological Society of Ireland, of which he later succeeded Lord Roberts as President. There was a Council meeting at the Zoo every Saturday morning—preceded by an excellent breakfast—to which we boys were sometimes taken. The Zoo was one of our chief delights in Dublin, and during the meeting we wandered round the animals. Being great friends with all the keepers we were allowed to see and do things not permitted to the ordinary public.

My father was also Secretary, and later a Vice-President, of the Royal

Dublin Society. In 1892 his organizing ability was recognized when he was appointed with Dr. Bernard, afterwards Archbishop of Dublin and later Provost of Trinity, to carry out the arrangements in connection with the Tercentenary of Trinity College in 1892. He also served on a Viceregal Commission to enquire into the condition of the inland fisheries in Ireland. In 1900 he was a member of the Royal Commission appointed to enquire into the care of the sick and wounded during the South African War, and acted on a War Office Committee which reported on physical standards for candidates for commissions and recruits. A Fellow of the Royal Society, he served on the Council of that body, and while still in Ireland received the honorary degrees of M.D. and D.Sc. from the University of Dublin; D.C.L. from Oxford; and LL.D. from the Universities of St. Andrews and Glasgow.

My father always said that his twenty years in Dublin were the happiest of his life, and when in 1903 he resigned his Chair at Trinity to return to Edinburgh to succeed Sir William Turner as Professor of Anatomy, the Chairman at a farewell dinner—where he was presented with a silver loving cup—said they all

> recognize how much the genius and enthusiasm of Professor Cunningham has done for practically every scientific movement that has taken place in Dublin in the last twenty years, and the splendid work he has done for the University and Medical School.

Many people remembered my father in Dublin. In May, 1941, when I was in the Mediterranean, I had a letter from Doctor Temple Smith, written from the Transvaal:

> I remember your father, my old Master the Professor of Anatomy, T.C.D., coming up to my brother and me on the platform at Waterloo and saying, "You two are surely my boys——" and he then asked me to keep an eye on his young son, who was going out to Simonstown to join his first ship.

I remember this incident. My mother and father had come over from Ireland to see me off. It was in May, 1899, and I was going to Southampton to take passage in R.M.S. *Norman* to join the cruiser *Fox* on the Cape Station.

To complete this brief survey of my father's life, he was Professor of Anatomy in Edinburgh University from 1904 until his death in 1909. His time was very fully occupied. Appointed Dean of the Medical Faculty soon after going to Edinburgh administrative affairs were added to the duties of his Chair. Then, in 1905, he was responsible for the initiation of regular post-graduate medical courses, which now take such a prominent place in medical education. His death at a time when his enthusiasm and mental faculties were still unimpaired, though for some months his physical powers had been gradually failing, was referred to as "a calamity to the University and to science".

II

Dublin was a good place for young people, we had a very happy childhood. My mother, whom we all adored, was a wonderful manager with a very sweet temperament. Though she could be stern at times when we deserved it, she made us very happy. Sometimes she even stood between us and the justifiable wrath of my father. To be strictly truthful we boys were rather intimidated by our male parent, probably because we saw so little of him. Our Irish cook's threat, "I'll tell the Doctor on yez", usually reduced my elder brother and myself to order and discipline. When we ran wild in Ann's kitchen or raided her larder she threatened all sorts of dire penalties; but never carried them out, not even when I once sullied her face with the blacking brush. She covered up many of our peccadilloes. I remember her with great affection.

We had wonderful holidays. Every summer we went to the country for two months, and several times during the early years to St. Andrews, where we picked up the rudiments of golf on the children's links. My father's chief recreation was fishing, and later he used to take a beat on a salmon river in Ireland, so that we gradually came to know the remoter parts of Connemara, Kerry and other places. At that period we boys did not take willingly to fishing, and were merely taken out to look on and to gaff the salmon.

My father's scientific reading inclined him to think that German was the most important foreign language. Accordingly, we had a succession of German nurses and governesses, most worthy women to whom we were a great trial. German was always the language of the nursery, and up to the age of nine I spoke it with equal facility to English.

In 1891 I was sent to Mr. T. V. Morley's school in Dublin. Up till that time we had been taught by a governess, a wonderful teacher called Miss Harford, to whom I can never be sufficiently grateful for the grounding she gave me. However, I disliked Morley's school when I went there, and do not think I learnt much. My father evidently thought the same, for after two or three terms I was sent to Edinburgh Academy as a day boy, living with two aunts, my mother's sisters, at 28, Palmerston Place.

I found the Academy pretty tough going at first, even in the 'Geits', the name given to the Junior School. However, I soon got used to it, and after two terms was moved into the lowest class of the Senior School, where I found myself with boys a good deal older than myself.

At this period I had given little thought to my future; but had always been interested in boats and the sea. What put it into his head I do not know; but it came as a surprise when I had a telegram from my father, "Would you like to go into the Navy?" The idea appealed to me quite a lot, so, egged on by my aunts, I replied, "Yes. I should like to be an Admiral."

At that time Edinburgh Academy was just starting a 'Navy Class', and it caused considerable disappointment when my father took me away and sent me to Mr. Foster's, Stubbington House, Fareham, a school which specialized in preparing boys for the Navy. I was given a prize at the end of my last term at the Academy, nobody being more surprised than myself. The book which I still possess, was *Roman Life in the days of Cicero*; not wildly exciting reading for a boy of ten.

I spent nearly three years at Stubbington, and thoroughly enjoyed it. We were well looked after and very well fed. Old Montague Foster was a great character. He himself took us in Scripture and some other subjects, and the time in class was punctuated by orders to Sergeant Budd to go and cut a switch from a hedge wherewith to stimulate the laggards. Mrs. Foster, who lived to well over ninety, was very good to all the boys.

One supposes that the teaching given at Stubbington was really cramming. We were required to perform prodigious feats of memory, such as memorizing the dates of all important events from the landing of Julius Cæsar to the accession of James I. I can still remember much of what I learnt there, and the older masters were wizards at driving knowledge into the heads of the unintelligent. On one occasion the history master, one Vip Isaacs—'Vip', I may add, being the short for 'Viper'—said to me in withering tones, "what an extraordinary thing so clever a father should have such an idiot for a son!"

Mathematics came fairly easily to me. I liked mathematical problems and was pretty good at Euclid. On the other hand I could not abide Latin, French and English, and was quite useless at them. I never found I had to work really hard. In fact I have always been lazy. I carried my ease at mathematics right through the *Britannia* when I got there, and at the half-term examinations, which were in mathematics only, I was fairly well up the list.

I was mediocre at games, though I played soccer for the first eleven at Stubbington several times. I started by playing it in the *Britannia*; but gave it up almost at once because there were many others in my term so much better than myself. Then I took to hockey. Cricket failed to interest me.

At the end of the autumn term of 1896 the Navy Class at Foster's went to London to take the Civil Service Examination for the Navy. I passed fairly easily, top of the Stubbington House batch and fourteenth out of sixty-five in order of merit of the accepted entry.

III

I joined H.M.S. *Britannia* on January 15th, 1897, eight days after my fourteenth birthday. Very soon the whole sixty-five of us were divided into four classes, and one made the acquaintance of the other cadets with whom one was destined to work for the next fifteen months.

Life in the *Britannia* has been described in the reminiscences of so many naval officers that I need hardly go into it again. The instruction was mainly technical—mathematics as applied to navigation; some rather indifferently-taught French; a little naval history at the hands of Hamilton Williams— otherwise 'Badger Bill'—and of course, steam, signals, and seamanship in all its branches. Seamanship was by far the most popular, and in 1897 sail in the Navy had not entirely given way to steam. There was still a 'Training Squadron' of four corvettes, or 'screw cruisers' as they were officially termed; with sailing brigs serving as tenders to the boys training ships at Portsmouth and Plymouth, and quite a number of sailing corvettes, sloops and gunboats, with, of course, engines, on foreign stations. So in the *Britannia* we were still taught the elements of sail seamanship, with practical work in the tender *Wave* moored in the river, and a week's cruise at sea in the sloop *Racer*.

We were well fed and exercised; but I played few games and devoted myself to the 'blue' boats, in which I spent every hour I could. Later on, when we became moderately proficient, we were allowed to go sailing in the six rather heavy and sluggish sailing cutters. The work was not really hard, and I was able to devote the winter evenings to acquiring a certain proficiency at chess.

Years later, after the Battle of Matapan, March 28th, 1941, I had a nice message from some of my old term-mates of the *Britannia* sent by Admiral Sir Charles Little, who later sent me some of their letters. These served to remind me that I went by the name of 'Meat Face' as a cadet, and that I acquired some reputation as an amateur pugilist. As one of my term-mates wrote—"I well remember his [my] love of a scrap."

Another remembered the private Sunday afternoon fights with bare fists in a little quarry, and a 'homeric fight' of mine with Charles Clement Swift, which ended in a draw with us both covered in blood, my blood. Why we came to fisticuffs—with most of our term cheering us on—I certainly cannot remember. I do not think I was particularly quarrelsome as a boy.

Our time at Dartmouth was broken into during the summer of 1897 by attending the Naval Review at Spithead to commemorate Queen Victoria's Diamond Jubilee. All the cadets were taken to Spithead in a naval tug called the *Seahorse*, the *Racer*, and an ancient store-ship called the *Wye*. Very rough and ready arrangements were made for the reception of a large number of boys, and I particularly remember the difficulty of retrieving one's own boots from over a hundred similar pairs thrown together in a pile after being cleaned.

We were very impressed at seeing the Queen passing through the lines of the Fleet in the Royal Yacht *Victoria and Albert*, and the ships' companies cheering and bands playing as she went by. What with a brilliantly fine day, all the ships dressed overall with flags and painted in the old-time colouring of yellow masts and funnels, white upperworks, black hulls, and salmon-coloured waterlines divided from the black by narrow white ribands, it was a sight not easily forgotten. The senior cadets, in the *Racer*, manned yards as the Queen went past. This was noted by one of the newspaper correspondents who wrote that he trusted the 'young gentlemen' were not kept aloft during the whole of the Royal progress through the Fleet, which took about two hours.

One remembers we were allowed ashore one afternoon, and myself being much impressed by meeting Admiral Henry James Raby, a gallant old veteran of 69 who was a friend of one of my family, and had been awarded the Victoria Cross as a commander for bravery in bringing in a wounded man under heavy fire at Sebastapol on June 18th, 1855. When the V.C. was instituted in 1856 he was one of the earliest to be gazetted, and was the first officer actually to be decorated by Queen Victoria at the first presentation in Hyde Park on June 26th, 1857. Rumour had it that when Her Majesty pinned the decoration on his chest she fastened it right through his coat and skin and that the intrepid sailor did not blink an eyelid. He died in 1907; but I well remember him ten years earlier.

In command of the *Britannia* in 1897 was Captain the Hon. A. G. Curzon-Howe, who had the reputation of being one of the politest and most punctilious officers in the Navy. He was strict, also. Mrs. Curzon-Howe lived on board with their small son. We all loved her. Many were the kindnesses she did us.

The Commander was Christopher Cradock, who as a Rear-Admiral fought and died gallantly at the battle of Coronel seventeen years later. One remembers him as always being immaculately dressed, with a pointed, neatly-trimmed dark beard, which reminded one of Sir Francis Drake. George Trewby, who afterwards rose to Flag Rank, was our term lieutenant. Our Naval Instructor, the Reverend N. B. Lodge, was the best teacher I ever had.

But enough of those early days in the *Britannia*. Our term passed out in April, 1898, and I was tenth on the list.

I note from the passing certificate, which I still possess, that we had been examined in the following rather formidable list of subjects for boys of fifteen: Religious Knowledge; Algebra; Geometry; Plane Trigonometry, Practical and Theoretical, and its application to useful problems in Navigation, Surveying, etc.; Spherical Trigonometry, and its application to simple Astronomical problems; Navigation, *Practical and Theoretical*, so far as to determine a Ship's position both by Dead Reckoning and Observation according to the ordinary daily practice at Sea; Protracting Geometrical and Nautical Problems; the construction of Charts and their use in the practice of Navigation; the use of the Sextant, Azimuth Compass, Barometer, Thermometer, etc., and the principles of their construction; Elementary Physical Science; French and Drawing, Naval History; Geography and Astronomy; Drawing, Freehand and Mechanical.

By this same certificate Mr. Cunningham was reputed to have shown 'good' proficiency in the use of the Sextant and Artificial Horizon, and to have paid 'much' attention to the various branches of study. He was entitled to a First Class Certificate in Mathematics (1,171 marks out of a possible 1,500); a Second Class in French and Extra subjects (510 marks out of 750); and a First Class in Seamanship (616 marks out of 700).

Mr. Cunningham could *swim*, and his conduct in the *Britannia* had been 'Very Good'.

Mr. Cunningham was satisfied. Having obtained seven months 'Sea Time' on leaving the *Britannia*, he would serve one month at sea as a Naval Cadet, and would be rated a Midshipman without further examination on June 15th, 1898.

I still wonder to what extent my examiners perjured themselves, or who testified to my 'Very Good' conduct. Those that mattered can never have heard about my occasional bare-fisted battles ashore on Sunday afternoons.

Before leaving the *Britannia* we had been asked where we should like to be sent on going to sea, though it was by no means certain that we could go where we wished. I had no particular ideas on the subject; but it so happened that one of my best friends in the *Britannia*, Henry Archer Colt, was anxious to go to the Cape of Good Hope and West Africa Station, so I elected to go with him if possible. We knew the squadron out there was a small one, and the idea of seeing something of the wilds of Africa rather appealed to us. I think, too, we thought there might be a chance of active service in some punitive expedition or another. A Naval Brigade had taken part in the Benin expedition only the year before.

I went home on leave to Dublin and thought no more about it. Then, considerably to my surprise, both Colt and myself were appointed to the cruiser *Fox* on the Cape Station. I was ordered by the Admiralty to take passage to Cape Town in R.M.S. *Norman*, of the old Union Steam Ship Company, sailing from Southampton on May 21st, 1898.

My father and mother came over from Ireland to see me off. We spent one night in London, and as a parting treat my father took us to see the new play, just put on, *The Belle of New York*. My parents were both rather scandalized at the dress, or rather undress, of some of the ladies; but I thoroughly enjoyed it. I embarked in the *Norman* next afternoon, and was delighted to find Henry Colt already on board and in the same cabin as myself.

CHAPTER II

I

WE cadets were rather lost in the old *Norman*, the first big mail steamer we had ever been in. The ship was very full, and among the passengers were the new Commander-in-Chief of the Cape Station, Vice-Admiral Sir Robert Hastings Harris; his flag captain, Reginald Prothero; his secretary and flag lieutenant. There was also a theatrical company and a number of music hall artistes, including Mr. and Mrs. Dutch Daly. He was a famous comedian of those days. Another distinguished passenger was Cecil Rhodes, who of course had his special private table in the dining saloon.

I had promised to write a sort of diary letter to my mother, which she preserved among various others. Our voyage lasted seventeen days, of which my letter covered only the first four. After that I found other things to do. Here are a few extracts, written with all the naïveté of youth. I was only fifteen and four months.

Saturday.—After starting from Southampton we did absolutely nothing but walk up and down, but at last the bugle went for dressing for dinner. Neither Colt nor I dressed. We could not find our places anywhere so we sat ourselves down at Cecil Rhodes' table to the great surprise of the head waiter who tried to turn us out and fetched some official to turn us out but Cecil Rhodes made him let us stay.

We did not sit there again!

Sunday.—We awoke at 8 a.m. and found we had slept thro' the coffee and biscuits and that we were in the Bay of Biscay. I was all right, but Colt succumbed to the motion of the ocean. . . . Colt and I sit beside the 3rd officer (Mr. A. W. Pearse) who is a ripping chap with a very fierce face but very nice. . . . There are some very peculiar passengers on board.

We very soon entered into all the games and competitions, and lost what little money we had in betting on the ship's daily run. I eventually found myself in the final of the chess tournament, the other finalist being Cecil Rhodes. I had difficulty in getting him to play it off, as he always fobbed me off by asking if I had learned the moves yet? However, one afternoon I played and beat him after a fierce struggle. There was still one game and it was two or three days before I eventually got him to the post. Finally we played again after dinner and I had his queen in four moves, which finished it. I think he had dined well.

All through this voyage, though we did not realize it, we were under the steely eye of Captain Prothero. He was a most intimidating man, nearly six feet tall and immensely broad, with a heavy, jet-black beard. We heard later he was known as 'Prothero the Bad'. The flag lieutenant warned us when Colt started smoking on the upper deck in full view of him.

We arrived at Cape Town after a seventeen-day passage and heard that the *Fox* was up the East Coast and not expected back for several weeks. So we were taken to the flagship *Doris*, at Simonstown. She was a 5,600 ton second class cruiser, and even for those days was a most uncomfortable ship for midshipmen, let alone for those lowest of God's creatures the naval cadets. There were twenty-nine of us in the gun-room originally intended for fifteen at the most, and we had our meals in three relays. The food was most indifferent, and because of the high prices prevailing ashore most of the things worth eating went down on our 'extra' bills. Our pay as cadets was one shilling a day, plus a compulsory allowance of £50 a year, or £4 3s. 4d. a month, paid to the Admiralty by our people. The sub-lieutenant of the gun-room, L. A. B. Donaldson, was very severe but also very just. He took a great deal of trouble in taking us boys round the ship and showing us the ropes.

We were greatly relieved when our proper ship, the *Fox* arrived on July 2nd, and we transferred to her. She was smaller than the *Doris*, 4,360 tons, but from our point of view was infinitely more comfortable. There were only eight of us all told in the gun-room, of whom four were midshipmen. I had been 'rated' a midshipman, with an increase in pay of ninepence a day on June 15th, 1898. The certificate for the *Doris*, signed by the redoubtable Captain Prothero, stated that Mr. Cunningham had conducted himself "with sobriety and attention to his duties. Has kept a log". In those days, the captain had to 'insert in his own handwriting the conduct of the officer, including the fact of his Sobriety, if deserving of it'.

The captain of the *Fox* was Frank Hannam Henderson, one of three naval brothers, all of whom rose to Flag rank. The ship had no commander, and the first lieutenant and executive officer was F. C. Gibbons, who was rather a kindly man. There followed a year of almost complete enjoyment. The *Fox* was stationed on the East Coast, with headquarters at Zanzibar, for which she sailed soon after we joined. It was long before the days of refrigerators and bakeries on board H.M. Ships, and after three days at sea, when our fresh meat and bread were expended, we were on salt pork and salt beef on alternate days with ships' biscuits.

My principal duty at sea was as assistant, or 'tanky', to the navigator, Lieutenant Henry L. Dicks. We had no regular naval instructor, and Dicks used also to take us in navigation and pilotage, at which we became quite proficient. He became entitled to the 3d. a day, automatically deducted from our slender pay of 1s. 9d. for the naval instructor. It was an iniquitous system which began in the early eighteenth century whereby midshipmen in seagoing ships, or rather their parents, had each to provide £25 a year to pay instructors hired by the captain. The sum was reduced to 3d. a day, or £4 11s. 3d. a year, I believe, when naval instructors became regular officers. It has now been abolished. But it always rankled with us that young and miserably-paid subordinate officers who were expected to appear and behave as officers, and had some responsibility, should be made to pay for their schooling in professional subjects. All the regular naval instructors I served with, and some of them were chaplains as well and drew full pay as N.I.'s and half the pay of chaplains, pouched 3d. a day from each midshipman and said no more about it. Dicks, however, had other ideas. Every quarter he would solemnly hand to each of us a small bag of rupees representing our accumulated three-pennies. He never thought he earned it; but his instruction in practical navigation was excellent and lasting. To us, of course, an extra £1 2s. 9d. a quarter was something for which to be thankful.

In harbour I was usually in charge and running a sailing cutter on alternative weeks. I never lost the love of sailing I acquired in the old *Fox*.

Except for the Zambesi gunboats, the stern-wheelers *Herald*, *Jackdaw* and *Mosquito*, which never left their river, and the barque-rigged gunboats *Partridge* and *Sparrow*, we were the only ship on the East Coast of Africa. We visited most of the ports—Lamu; Mombassa; Kilindini, where they were starting to build the Uganda railway; many of the islands; Mozambique; Delagoa Bay; and Chinde, at the mouth of the Zambesi, where our captain disembarked and went up-river to inspect the gunboats. It was all intensely interesting to a boy of fifteen, and here and there, where there were British residents and links, I managed to put in quite a lot of golf.

While we were at Zanzibar I began to lose weight rather rapidly, not that I ever had much to lose. It was probably because of the heat and the unsuitable food. I went to the staff surgeon, one Patrick Handyside, who happened to have been one of my father's students and had been asked by him to keep an eye on me. The treatment prescribed was one glass of port after lunch and another after dinner! What effect this had upon my weight I do not recollect; but while it lasted my work during the afternoon was not distinguished by much clear-headedness.

It was before the days of wireless. Except for cables at the ports we visited we were completely out of touch with the flagship at the Cape or the Admiralty in London. Subject to a rather elastic programme our captain had more or less a roving commission, and was monarch of all he surveyed. Gunnery and torpedo exercises hardly disturbed our routine. The *Fox* had four torpedo-tubes, and we solemnly fired torpedoes once a quarter after taking all precautions that they did not run amok. Once a quarter, too, a few rounds were fired by all the guns at a flag on a cask at a range of not more than 2,000 yards. Nobody cared very much whether the shots fell near or wide of the target.

It was a free and joyous existence, particularly for midshipmen, and greatly were we disappointed when, at the end of a year, the *Fox*, which had been three years on the station, was ordered home, and we learnt that we three remaining mids., G. H. Lang, H. A. Colt and myself, were to be sent back to the *Doris*. This was in May, 1899.

In the *Doris*, we went back to the old conditions of overcrowding in the gun-room, with bad food and a generally unhappy time. I was soon promoted to a cutter and learnt a lot about rough weather sailing in the stormy conditions of False Bay. Captain Prothero insisted on the midshipmen sailing their boats in every kind of weather, and at times would even lay up the steamboat specially provided for work during the south-easterly gales. Many a cutter was washed up on the beach to leeward of the anchorage, and the midshipman and crew left there to bring off the boat when the weather moderated.

We did one short cruise up the East Coast, but our life was not a happy one. Donaldson had been promoted. We suffered from unpleasant sub-lieutenants, nowhere to go or to sit, few recreations, and nothing to occupy our minds but an hour or two a day of indifferent instruction which we all did our best to avoid.

By the time we got back to Simonstown, war with the Boers seemed probable, and we talked of little else. The general idea was that a Naval Brigade would be landed as infantry, so long route marches became the order of the day. We wore white uniform dyed with coffee, and sailors' straw hats with a coffee-coloured cover, the idea being that the wearing of this head-gear would prevent the Boer marksman from recognizing the officers.

The South African War started on October 12th, 1899, and the Boer commandos soon crossed the frontier and invested Mafeking and Kimberley. Their main thrust, however, was in Natal. We had very few troops in Natal or Cape Colony, while our army field guns were easily outranged by the Boer artillery. The cruiser *Terrible*, Captain Percy Scott, arrived at Simonstown from Portsmouth, on October 14th, and her sister ship the *Powerful*, Captain Hedworth Lambton, homeward bound from China, at about the same time. A Naval Brigade of about 350 officers and men from the *Doris*, *Monarch*, *Terrible* and *Powerful*, consisting of 290 marines and two small field guns, manned by 53 sailors, was landed at Simonstown on October 20th. It reached Stormberg on the 23rd but was withdrawn because of the Boer advance.

Captain Scott, meanwhile, was improvising field mountings for the *Terrible's* long range 12-pounders, and was thinking of even larger guns. General White was holding Ladysmith, in Natal, and on October 25th, finding he had no artillery capable of keeping the Boer siege guns in check, telegraphed asking if the Navy could send him some long range 4·7's, which was done.

Another Naval Brigade, with a strength of about 400 all told, half of them being marines, was landed on November 19th, and joined Methuen three days later for the relief of Kimberley. The Naval Brigade took with them four of Scott's long 12-pounders mounted in Simonstown Dockyard. Captain Prothero was in command. The *Terrible* went round to Durban, where her Naval Brigade joined the Natal Field Force.

Captain Prothero, several lieutenants, and most of the senior midshipmen had gone to the front, while the ship's company was very depleted. Life on board was indeed dull. The ship was partially filled up again by drafts from home, and two or three new midshipmen joined, mostly fortunate people whose fathers' influence had succeeded in getting them out of the seat of war.

News of our Naval Brigade filtered through, and we heard of the battle of Belmont on November 24th, of Graspan the next day, and the heavy casualties suffered by the Navy. Commander Ethelston of the *Powerful*, Major Plumbe and Midshipman Huddart, both of the *Doris* were killed, while Captain Prothero was severely wounded. In all the Naval Brigade had 15 killed and 79 wounded.

Two 4·7's on field carriages, one manned by sailors and the other by marines, were landed soon afterwards. They were under the command of Commander W. L. Grant of the *Doris*, and did fine work.

In a letter to my mother of January 2nd, 1900, I mentioned having heard that Lord Roberts was coming out to South Africa. He was a friend of my father's, so I wrote:

> I hope Dad informed him that he could have me as his personal aide-de-camp free gratis and for nothing except 5s. a day and my grub, also one horse, which I consider would be a very modest reward for my valuable services, don't you think so?

I was itching to get to the front, and in a letter of January 22nd, 1900, railed because a midshipman junior to me had been lucky enough to land. And in a letter to my brother of January 30th:

> I am fearfully sick at present at not getting up to the front. It is enough to make a saint swear to see these people about a year junior to you and only about two months on the Station going up and you sitting down here doing absolutely nothing.

I seemed doomed to staying put in the *Doris*, and felt most disgruntled and unhappy. There was a war on fairly close, and most of my messmates were at the front. I also longed for some excitement.

Then, early in February, my chance came, a very outside chance. Captain Prothero had returned to the ship after a spell in hospital, and a new major of Marines, Major Peile, had come out from home to replace Major Plumbe, killed in action at Graspan. I heard one morning that he was leaving for the front at 5 p.m., so tackled him at once. He was a kind-hearted man, and said that if I could get permission I might come along as his A.D.C.

I decided there was no time to forward my request through the usual Service channels, but that I must beard the ogre in his den. So after lunch I went along to the captain's cabin, passed the sentry with some excuse, opened the door and found Captain Prothero asleep in an arm-chair.

I was terrified and shaking; but made a noise and woke him up. He glared a bit and looked very fierce; but I managed to stammer out my request.

All he said was: "Want to go to the front, do you, boy?"

"Yes, sir, please."

"Wait outside while I write a note," he growled.

I retired. Then he rang and sent for me.

"Take that ashore and give it to the Secretary," he said, giving me a letter. I should say that the Admiral and his staff lived ashore at Admiralty House.

The upshot was that I was in the train with Major Peile at 5 p.m.

I always regard this bearding of 'Prothero the Bad' as the bravest deed of my life!

All the same, I had got what I wanted. That was something for a midshipman just turned sixteen with a war going on just over the horizon.

II

Cronje with 4,000 Boers had surrendered at Paardeberg on February 28th. As we went north by train to join up with the Naval Brigade serving with Lord Roberts's army, which was about to advance on Bloemfontein, we passed Cronje's train filled with Boer prisoners on its way south. I cannot remember exactly where we detrained; but after a week's trek with a convoy of ox-waggons we joined the Naval Brigade the day after the fight at Poplar Grove and on the eve of Lord Roberts's advance.

There followed four days very hard slogging, and to avoid the main heat of the day we marched from 2 a.m. to 9 a.m. and from 3 p.m. till 10 p.m. It was pretty tough going. We did 34 miles in the first 26 hours. Then Major Peile's groom caught me a horse that was roaming in the veldt and I rode during the last two days. It was not a very good horse, being blind in one eye, and I always had to start it 90 degrees from the direction in which I wished to go. The poor beast was quickly discarded when it was suspected of having glanders. Incidentally, I was no great horseman. Writing to my father a little later, I told him I was doing a great deal of riding and said: "I can't ride but I can stick on which is just as good." In the same letter I mentioned that I had been out on a wood-chopping party with Mr. Ernest

Lowe, Gunner R.N.—"He and I tried wrestling on horseback and pushed each other off on opposite sides—he came down on his head but I came down in a sitting position." Lowe, for his services in South Africa was one of the first four officers to be awarded the purely naval Conspicuous Service Cross (now the Distinguished Service Cross) when it was instituted by King Edward in June, 1901.

We arrived at Bloemfontein without any fighting so far as we were concerned, and camped on the outskirts of the town. I think the Boers, stimulated by Roberts's very rapid march, were in full retreat. A rather dull time in camp was only relieved by the inspection of the Naval Brigade by Lord Roberts on March 22nd. He made a very fine speech, saying that every soldier realized how greatly the Navy had helped the Army, and hoping we should still be with him when he entered Pretoria. After the inspection, to my horror, the Field-Marshal asked for me, and I was pushed out to the front to shake hands. As a great friend of my father's in Dublin, I had met him many times at the Zoo. My father had also written to him asking if he could work it for me to be sent to the front. His efforts were unnecessary. I had already worked it for myself through Captain Prothero.

On May 11th Roberts and his army moved north upon Pretoria, the Naval Brigade going with them, with the exception of two 12-pounder guns left behind to assist in the defence of Bloemfontein. To my intense disgust I was one of the two midshipmen left with them.

"I have had very bad luck all thro' that old pig Bearcroft who has left me behind here," I wrote to my mother on May 13th. "There was really no necessity for anyone being left with these two guns at all. All the other guns have been fighting while we have been waiting for orders to move which never came."

The 'old pig Bearcroft' was Captain John E. Bearcroft, Royal Navy, commanding the Naval Brigade.

A dull time followed. I had a small pony, and used to ride daily into Bloemfontein for orders. That was the only recreation. Before very long, however, I brought back an order to our lieutenant in command that I was to proceed at once and join the main body of the Naval Brigade. On May 26th I wrote to my mother:

> I am off to Kroonstad by next train which is a goods by the way. I am quite well and in perfect health.

I heard later, that one evening Lord Roberts had ridden into the Naval Brigade camp and asked for me. Finding I had been left behind he ordered Captain Bearcroft to have me sent up at once. I do not think my acquaintance with Lord Roberts did me much good in the end, as I afterwards had good reason to appreciate that I was highly unpopular with Captain B. Probably he thought I had used influence to circumvent his wishes.

However, I set off from Bloemfontein in a goods train, sitting on top of the goods in a truck with a lot of soldiers. The Army was nearing Pretoria, so we had over 300 miles to travel. We went very slowly. It took us thirty-six hours to reach Kroonstad, and at the Zand River we did seven miles in thirteen hours! As I see from a letter to my mother, it was bitterly cold at night and I was nearly frozen. How I fed myself I cannot remember; but the soldiers were always generous and ready to share.

At Kroonstad I found the Naval Brigade had moved on a fortnight before, so I followed on to railhead, which was at a place called Roodevaal. Here I found Major Marchant and a party of marines waiting for ammunition. It arrived next day, so I went on with them, trekking. We did about twenty miles a day, and in four days arrived at Viljoens Drift and crossed the Vaal, camping about two miles from Vereeniging. Next day, June 2nd, we put the ammunition on a railway truck and started for Johannesburg, arriving about midnight.

Next morning we heard the naval guns were only six miles ahead, and at 8 o'clock, when I had just managed to get a fire alight on the platform and was frying myself a bit of bacon, who should ride in but the paymaster, who said the guns had started at 7 that morning and were going nineteen miles that day. My chances of picking them up looked rather slender; but after having my breakfast I decided I would try to catch them up on foot, which was rather an undertaking. It meant a twenty-five mile march, carrying my food, blankets and equipment. Luckily I fell in with two soldiers who had acquired, I did not ask how, a flat cart and a small Boer pony. They gave me a lift. We drove until we foundered the pony. So off I went on foot again, and after a couple of hours' walking found the Naval Brigade at about 5 p.m. camped seven or eight miles from the outer forts of Pretoria. I was ordered to join the two 12-pounders under the orders of Lieutenant E. P. C. Back, who was afterwards killed as captain of H.M.S. *Natal* when that ship was blown up at Cromarty by an internal explosion on December 31st, 1915. I had had rather a wearing journey lasting just a week, and was only just in time.

The battle for Pretoria began next morning, June 4th, we having started off at 6.30 a.m. After marching about fourteen miles we expected to come into action at 'Six Mile Drift', about six miles south-west of the town. To quote from my letter to my mother of June 6th:

> We crossed the Drift about 11.30 without any opposition, though we heard General French pounding away at the Boers with the R.H.A., and the Boers at him from their forts. We saw their shells bursting on the ridge in front of us. Then we went on for about two miles farther and the 4·7's came into action, leaving us behind the ridge. . . . In about a quarter-of-an-hour's time Commander de Horsey was hit through the ankle, and

one of our mules was hit in the shoulder and had to be finished off. Then, as the bullets began to fly from Boer snipers, we moved back a little, where we stayed for about half-an-hour, and all the time the bullets were coming over our heads. But the worst was yet to come. Hearing that a party of Boer snipers in a kopje on the right were making it pretty hot for the 4·7's, we moved forward to another position to shell them out, and did so. Suddenly there came a whirr and a scream, and then a bang. A Boer shell had burst among four horses and broken one's leg. Then the fun began. We were on the skyline, and they weighed in and shelled us with three or four guns. The R.A. had come up on our right; but they could not stand it, so they limbered up and away. But we stuck there and fired away. One shell burst in front of the gun and I moved to another. One burst in front of the other, throwing dust all over us. Then the guns became the safest place as shells hardly ever burst in the same place; but I was sent back to bring up our ammunition waggon, where it was worse than ever. The shells were bursting among the waggons and all the troops behind the range, and there was a fearful scramble to get away. I was nearly run over dozens of times. However, I managed to bring our waggon up, and our 4·7's silenced the Boer guns. Then one of General Hamilton's A.D.C.'s came riding up with orders and we moved out to the kopje from which we had driven the Boers to cover the advance of the infantry. We got rather a hot cross fire from the snipers on the left. However, we shelled them out and knocked down the wall on top of the kopje to the right. On examination afterwards the trench behind the wall was found covered with blood. At sunset the infantry rushed the whole line of kopjes.

That, with the pardonable exuberance of a sixteen-year-old midshipman under fire for the first time, was what I wrote in 1900. Looking back on it I doubt if the Boers were putting up a really serious resistance. There was plenty of rifle fire and bullets flicking about, but nothing really much in the way of shelling.

Pretoria, the capital of the Transvaal, was occupied by Lord Roberts on June 5th.

The Naval Brigade had had a gruelling time. The men were dirty, with their clothing mostly in tatters. Many officers and men had been invalided with enteric and dysentry, and some had died. All that remained at the front at this period were about 14 officers, 100 sailors and 70 marines, all manning guns.

The Naval Brigade camped to the north-east of the town, and soon afterwards the 12-pounders were sent to a place called Edendale. It must have been fairly close to the front line, for at intervals we saw parties of Boers riding about in the valley below. We were holding a defensive position about twelve miles from Pretoria, and with us were the 85th Field Battery and the Warwicks and Yorkshires.

On June 10th Lord Roberts started his widespread battle against Botha at Diamond Hill, about twenty miles east of Pretoria. The object of this action was to push the Boers back from the capital, and eventually to round up the enemy between Roberts's army, Buller's force which was advancing from Natal, and French's cavalry.

As I wrote to my mother on June 14th:

> Since my last letter we have been chasing Brother Boer out towards Middleburg, trying to round them up and surround them. On Friday last we shifted our camp, in fact the whole 11th Division did, to a place called Silverton about eight miles from Pretoria, and stayed there till Monday morning when we started and marched about eight miles and did absolutely nothing, though fairly heavy firing was going on all around us. We started at about six next morning and marched till about 10.30, when we came across a farm with oranges and any amount of forage. Finding the good lady's husband had been away for the last six months fighting against us, we commandeered the forage for the mules and the oranges for ourselves. Then we started lunch, and had not been sitting down ten minutes when a most inconsiderate Brigadier-General came up and ordered us to move on. I think he really ought to have considered the fact that we were at lunch. We then moved on about three miles when a Boer gun had the impudence to chuck four shells at us. They missed us altogether, and two fell among the R.F.A. whom they could not see, but nobody was hurt. We then came into action and fired between thirty and forty rounds meeting with no response, so stayed there for about an hour and a half and then got an order to join the Guards' Brigade. The sun was setting as we came up with them. There was a row going on between our infantry and the Boers. Rifle shots and volleys and artillery were all banging away together, and a few stray bullets came whistling round us, but not at all close. In the night John Boer fled and left nothing behind, so it was a complete victory. I picked up a few bits of scrap iron and lead in the morning (bits of shells) which will look fairly well in Lizzie's museum— if she will have them. Don't tear up or throw away this stamp as it will be fairly valuable with the Transvaal postmark on it, but give it to Lizzie or Jack . . ."

After this little episode, we moved back to Edendale, where we remained more or less quiescent until July 24th.

The caterer of our mess was a Victorian (Australian) naval lieutenant called Colquhoun, a great forager. The orders against looting were very strict; but Colquhoun generally managed to get the Boer housewives to part with geese, chickens, ducks, butter, eggs and so on, so we lived well. Colquhoun was one day on horseback cornering a likely-looking pig when Lord Roberts rode up; but the Field-marshal tactfully looked the other way. He also knew the Australian troops. As the army advanced they used to be sent out to drive in the sheep and cattle for provender. It was no unusual thing for a flock of sheep to be driven right over the Naval Brigade camp on its way to the Commissariat Department. By the time the flock had passed two or three fat sheep would invariably have been caught, killed, skinned and hung up.

On July 24th we trekked on with the army in the drive to Belfast, just over 100 miles east of Pretoria, via Elands River, Bronkers Spruit, Hartebeestefontein, Brugspruit, Olifants River, Middleburg, Pan, and Wonderfontein. We had a pretty gruelling time trekking across country, and at one period were attached to, and following hard on, the heels of the cavalry, just as though we were the R.H.A. It was a strange sight to see our mule teams trotting along with the guns and ammunition waggons, and the sailors, some of them barefooted, running alongside, and every now and then jumping on a gun-carriage or a waggon for a lift. We naturally got left behind a few miles, and on one occasion reached the place for the night bivouac to see the cavalry lines neatly laid out before us. But they were in some turmoil, as the guns of Botha's rear-guard were pitching shells into the middle of them. We quickly unlimbered and drove the Boer guns off, and I believe earned the gratitude of the horse soldiers.

We reached Belfast on about August 25th. It was held in force by the Boers, and on the 26th and 27th occurred the battle of that name, where Botha managed to slip through our fingers. As I wrote to my mother on the 31st:

> We were wakened by the Boer shells bursting around. We shelled them all the day with a few intervals and they shelled us and also sniped us. No one was hit and we were given credit for silencing two guns. Next day was Sunday and all was peace until about 8 a.m. and then we shelled a gun. In the evening we started for Machadodorp, and about a quarter-of-an-hour after starting a real good battle began, and though we did not fire a shot we were under heavy fire for over an hour. The whole of the next day we shelled 'Long Tom', the Boer 6-inch. . . .

This was the time, I remember, when we only achieved the necessary range by putting the guns on an incline and so cocking up the muzzles.

We camped near Machadodorp for some time. In the light of present knowledge, I think it was to let our supplies come up.

Some time previously I had heard that my father had been appointed a member of the Royal Commission to come out to South Africa to investigate the medical arrangements. On September 5th, while at a place called Waterval Onder, on the line about forty miles east of Belfast, I received an order, again emanating from Lord Roberts, that I was to go back to Pretoria to see my father, so off I went in an empty goods train and arrived without incident. I met my parent in the hall of the Raadzaal, where the Commissioners were sitting, he already having accused the Marquis of Graham, the present Duke of Montrose, of being me!

There was some discussion as to whether it would be in accordance with the Geneva Convention for me, a combatant, to live in the hospital train in which the Commission was living and moving around the country. However, Lord Justice Romer, the president, who should have known, settled it in my favour. I spent a week in great comfort before leaving to pick up the guns which were advancing with the army towards Komati Poort, on the border of Portuguese East Africa. On the way I joined up with two army officers doing the same thing—Major Baden-Powell of the Scots Guards, and Captain Pat Bolton, Irish Guards. Baden-Powell, a pioneer balloonist, was a brother of Lord Baden-Powell. We travelled mostly by goods train, with many stops on the way. One of these was at a pleasant, small hotel at Crocodile Poort. It was dreadfully hot, so we bathed in the river, two of us going in and the third watching on the bank with a loaded rifle.

While travelling we heard that the vanguard of the army had already reached Komati Poort, and 60 or 70 miles short of that place we came up with Lord Kitchener, who was travelling by train with an escort of two or three companies of Guards and some sappers, who were mending the broken bridges as they went along. I was very kindly welcomed in the Guard's mess, where I lived for about ten days. Twenty-five miles short of Komati Poort a special train was sent there to take on Lord Kitchener. I hastily interviewed Lieutenant Walter Cowan, his naval A.D.C., and was allowed to go in it. I sat in a corner of a guard's van, with Lord Kitchener in the middle in an armchair. At the time I thought him a most forbidding-looking man.

Cowan, with whom I was to serve later, was already a by-word in the Navy. At the age of 29 he had probably seen more active service and collected more medals than many Admirals.

Anyhow, I joined up with the Naval Brigade 12-pounders at Komati Poort that evening, and we spent a few weeks in comparative idleness except for washing to our heart's content in the river. It was an interesting place. The Great Crocodile River marked the boundary between the Transvaal and Portuguese East Africa, and there were miles upon miles of arms of all kinds which the retreating Boers had been forced to lay down before they crossed the border. There were also miles of railway rolling stock, most of the engines and trucks in very bad condition.

Kruger had fled the country. The big battles were over, and it was now more or less a matter of blockhouses and rounding up small raiding parties of Boers. I was not sorry when, at the end of September, 1900, the Naval Brigade were ordered back to their ships. After more than seven months of it I was tired of the war—day after day of hard marching and very little real fighting. I was only seventeen.

The Naval Brigade had had a hard time. On one occasion our 12-pounders covered 90 miles in nine days, while the 54 miles from a place called Kaapmuiden to Komati Poort was done in four days, a pretty good record considering the very difficult country and the bad climate. Grant's two 4·7's, too, had been in all the actions, and had marched over a thousand miles, once covering 250 miles in fifteen consecutive days. One march of 37 miles was done in thirteen hours. The men were splendid. We were a small contingent; but for a period of nine months no man was brought before the commanding officer—"for any crime, neglect of duty, slackness, or any other offence whatsoever."

Reading that official eulogy I was glad to realize that no one in authority had 'seen' our occasional commandeering of livestock, fruit, vegetables and other produce.

We collected a train from the disused rolling stock and loaded up the 12-pounder guns and the sailors. A driver was the difficulty; but after some delay we commandeered a guardsman reputed to have driven a soda-water bottling plant. Off we went amid cheers from everyone, only to come to a dead stop after 3 miles. The man stoking the engine could not keep steam. The boiler tubes had not been cleaned for months. Luckily, we had a stoker petty officer and four stokers who had been serving as stretcher-bearers. They were put on the job; took the front off the boiler of our ancient locomotive; and swept the tubes with brushes made from telegraph wires. This did the trick and we set off again, after wasting half-a-day and having to remain stopped all night. Next morning we started off again at daylight and made good progress. We had done about twenty-five miles of our journey when our driver failed to obey the signals and charged full speed down a hill into a station called Hector Spruit. He crashed into a train standing in the junction, completely wrecking two vans which were bringing proper engine-drivers to Komati Poort. They all jumped clear except two, who were unfortunately killed.

It took our guns' crews all the afternoon to clear the wreckage. We had become a little tired of our guardsman driver, so commandeered one of the regular ones, put our own stokers on to firing the boiler, and reached Pretoria without further incident. Here we were joined by the main body of the Naval Brigade, and travelling only by day until we were in Cape Colony, arrived at Simonstown in due course.

I rejoined the *Doris* and found that much of my own gear that I had sent down from the front had been purloined, including, greatly to my annoyance, twenty of the solid gold discs which Kruger had struck when he ran out of regular coinage. Given the option of staying on the Station or going home I chose the latter, and a few days later, in the middle of October, sailed from Cape Town in the transport *Lake Erie*.

Before leaving I had to collect my back pay from the Dockyard Cashier at Simonstown. It included, of course, five shillings a day field service allowance for the whole time I had been landed. However, I was greatly surprised when I was handed a bag of a hundred golden sovereigns, which was not a very wise method of paying a young man of seventeen. Naturally, I lost about £25 of it playing poker and other games of chance on the way home, which no doubt was experience well bought!

From the purely Service point of view I doubt very much if the Boer War did me much good. All the same, one could never regret it. For one thing, one saw many miles of South Africa walking on one's own feet, or occasionally riding a pony or travelling about in goods trains. Also, it was grand experience for a boy of seventeen to have to live in considerable discomfort, and to have to fend for his men and himself in all sorts of unfamiliar conditions inseparable from active service ashore in a strange country. It taught one responsibility and self-reliance; living, so to speak on one's wits, and making do on improvisation. It also brought one into close contact with the Army, which was most useful in the years that were to come. Above all, it caused one to realize the cheerfulness and endurance, and the many other sterling qualities, of that versatile and adaptable person the British sailor.

CHAPTER III

I

AFTER a few weeks leave in Dublin, where my people were living at 43 Fitzwilliam Place, I was appointed to H.M.S. *Hannibal*, one of the eight battleships of the Channel Squadron. I joined her at Portsmouth on my eighteenth birthday, January 7th, 1901. Here I found Henry Colt, who had already been my shipmate in the *Fox* and *Doris*. Lieutenant H. L. Dicks, too, who had been the navigator of the *Fox*, was serving in the same capacity in my new ship. Among the midshipmen who joined us a month or two later was J. A. G. Troup, who had served ashore with the *Terrible's* guns in Natal and in July, 1900, had also landed during the Boxer troubles in North China. Our naval instructor, one recollects, was a large-bearded man, Maurice A. Ainslie. He went by the nickname of the 'Wombat', though why I cannot imagine. My dictionary tells me a wombat is an Australian marsupial mammal about the size of a badger.

Queen Victoria died at Osborne on January 22nd, and on February 1st the coffin was taken on board the Royal Yacht *Alberta* at Cowes. Escorted by eight destroyers, and followed by the *Victoria and Albert* carrying King Edward VII and the other Royal mourners, the *Osborne*, and the Kaiser's *Hohenzollern*, the *Alberta* steamed slowly through the long lines of British and foreign warships assembled in the Solent. It was a most impressive spectacle which I shall never forget—a dark, lowering afternoon with occasional shafts of wintry sunlight, and all the ships 'manned' by long rows of silent seamen with guards and bands on their quarterdecks. Ensigns and jacks were at half-mast, and these, with the red tunics of the Royal Marine Light Infantry, and the conspicuous white hull and yellow funnels of the *Hohenzollern*, provided the only real splashes of bright colour. The whole fleet fired minute guns and the bands played the funeral march as the *Alberta* and the yachts moved slowly on to Portsmouth. One heard afterwards that King Edward noticed that the Royal Standard of the *Victoria and Albert* was also at half-mast, and asked the reason. "The Queen is dead, your Majesty," came the reply. "The King of England lives," was the answer, and the Royal Standard was mastheaded.

Vice-Admiral Sir Harry Rawson was in command of the Channel Squadron when I joined the *Hannibal*; but in April, 1901, he was relieved by Rear-Admiral A. K. Wilson, who had won the Victoria Cross at the battle of El Teb, in the Soudan, in February, 1884. Nicknamed 'Tug', he came to us with a reputation for toughness, which he certainly did not belie. A few days after joining he signalled 'Out Bower Anchor' in the middle of the dinner hour, and while on passage to Gibraltar sent the whole squadron to 'Night quarters' at 4.15 in the morning. We regarded it as most unfair. Night quarters was usually a matter for some days of deliberation and preparation, and was invariably staged at 10 p.m. and followed by a large supper of beer, sardines and raw onions in the wardroom.

We stayed at Gibraltar for about six weeks, lying outside the breakwater. Only the two flagships, the *Majestic* and *Magnificent*, went inside the mole. I there acquired the experience of running one of those fine boats, a 56-foot picquet boat, in frightful weather. Often weatherbound, we midshipmen from the ships outside lived as best we could in the gun-rooms of the two flagships until the weather moderated.

I spent only about seven months in the *Hannibal*; but I enjoyed my time in her. We were a very happy gun-room, and the mess itself was palatial compared with our poky, overcrowded little dungeon in the *Doris*. I think we were rather ill-disciplined. One of the gun-room scuttles of the *Hannibal* opened on to the platform of the port accommodation ladder, and this method of departure and arrival was greatly used by those young gentlemen who, for one reason or another, wished to avoid being seen by the Officer of the Watch going to or returning from the shore.

In July, 1901, I was sent to the *Martin*, brig, tender to the *St. Vincent*, the boy's training ship at Portsmouth. At that time sail was dying hard, and every boy joining the Navy was not only given sail training in his training ship, but was sent for six weeks or more to a brig or sloop to gain experience at sea. Whether or not it outlived its usefulness I can give no opinion, but sail training certainly produced lads unsurpassed for smartness, alertness and physique. The feats of agility aloft performed by these boys of fifteen and sixteen in the brigs would amaze anyone today and provide an excellent draw for Navy Week.

Our captain in the *Martin*, Lieutenant and Commander Samuel Montagu Agnew, was a thoroughgoing sailor who handled his brig as though she were a high-powered, twin-screw steamship. I remember he had some claim to fame for creasing his trousers athwartships instead of the usual fore and aft. For the rest, he was sardonic and sarcastic, and it was seldom that any drill ended without both midshipmen having their leave stopped for the rest of the commission. However, a polite application for leave next day was never refused. All was forgiven and forgotten.

It was said, I do not know with what truth, that Agnew's career had been blighted by his sarcasm at the expense of his senior officer. To a signal inquiring why his ship had washed clothes triced up to dry at an improper time he was reputed to have replied—"Because they are wet!"

Brig time was a grand time for midshipmen. We had cabins. There were only two of us, and when we had had a little experience we were allowed to handle the ship ourselves. My time in the *Martin* ended all too soon for me.

We spent most of our time at Portland, and at the end of the brig season towards the end of October all the brigs and sloops from there sailed round to Portsmouth to lie up for the winter. Custom decreed that they made a race of it, and the start was allowed at midnight. At that time it was flat calm, without a breath of wind under the land, but our captain, not to be deterred, kedged the *Martin* out of Portland harbour.

All next day and night we beat against a fitful easterly breeze, and 8 a.m. the following morning found us anchored in a thick fog off St. Catherines, Isle of Wight. At noon the fog cleared and a fresh south-westerly breeze sprang up. We weighed and made sail, and with stun'sails set both sides boomed past Bembridge Ledge and arrived at Spithead. There, to our mortification, we saw our sister ship, the *Seaflower*, at anchor and already sending down her upper masts and yards. She had met the naval tug *Seahorse* off the Needles and had been towed up the Solent. Not to be outdone, Agnew signalled and asked permission to proceed up harbour under sail. It was approved, and an hour later saw us made fast to our buoy off Haslar Creek, no mean feat of seamanship.

I remember one slight contretemps while entering Portsmouth harbour, the entrance to which is very narrow. It was blowing fresh and we were coming in under reefed topsails, keeping close to the shore so as to luff up to our buoy on the other side. We were towing a boat alongside, when one of the steamers from Ryde tried to cut in between us and the shore. She could not manage it, so ran into us and nearly squashed our boat. The men in it jumped for their lives, five on board us and one into the steamer. As we collided our anchor caught in the stays of the steamer's mast and brought it down with a crash. It also tore a great hole in her side and brought down her ensign staff. "This," as I wrote to my mother, "shows the difference between two feet of oak and one inch of steel."

Leaving the *Martin* at the end of October, 1901, I was appointed to the *Diadem*, Captain Henry Leah, a big four-funnelled cruiser. After a week or two with the Channel Squadron we were sent to Chatham, a dreary place for a midshipman. However, I was busily engaged in working up for my seamanship examination, which was due to take place on the following January 7th, my nineteenth birthday.

The system of entering cadets at that time, and their age of entry, cannot have been properly worked out, for at the end of their service as midshipmen it produced some very unfair results. We had, I think, to serve three and a half years before attaining the rank of acting sub-lieutenant, though the regulations also laid down that we must have reached the age of 19. In my term quite a number of us had completed the necessary service before becoming 19, which meant we had to wait, some of us for nearly six months. I was fairly fortunate in only having to wait three weeks; but even so I lost a considerable number of places on the seniority list.

My seamanship examination took place on board the old battleship *Repulse* at Chatham on January 7th, 1902, and I succeeded in passing with a first-class certificate.

Thus I shed my midshipman's patches, assumed the single stripe of an acting sub-lieutenant, which was duly 'wetted'; changed into plain clothes; bade farewell to the old *Diadem*; and went on twelve days' leave before joining the Royal Naval College, Greenwich, for courses in navigation and pilotage.

II

One's performance in the examinations at Greenwich and after the courses in gunnery and torpedo at Portsmouth, determined one's position and seniority on the list of sub-lieutenants, and had a profound effect on one's career. I very soon found I was handicapped through practically never having been under a proper naval instructor during my time at sea, whereas many of my contemporaries had had their noses to the grindstone under good instructors for a full three and a half years. Service ashore in South Africa had had a disturbing effect. I was terribly backward. However, though I cannot claim to have worked very hard at Greenwich, which was a good deal too close to London and all its attractions for a young man fresh from the sea, I managed to obtain just sufficient marks to be awarded a 'star', which meant one stayed on at Greenwich for a further advanced course. Realizing that nothing short of a miracle could obtain me a first-class certificate, I am afraid I took things rather easily. As miracles do not often happen I was hardly surprised when I finished the 'Navigation' course, though it included also such other subjects as mathematics, statics, hydrostatics, physics, magnetism and electricity, marine surveying, the steam engine, and French, with a second-class certificate.

The pilotage course followed after summer leave, and on October 15th I went up to London to be examined at the Hydrographic Department at the Admiralty. I was bitterly disappointed when my examiners gave me a second-class, for pilotage was a subject in which I was much interested, and had received an excellent grounding from Lieutenant Dicks, the navigator of the *Fox*.

I had a further disappointment at this time. All the survivors of the midshipmen of the *Doris* who had been to the front in South Africa—one had been killed, and a number had died of enteric—were 'noted for early promotion'. My name was omitted from the list, though I had served longer ashore than any of them. Thinking that a mistake had been made my father wrote to the Admiralty, only to receive a chilly reply to the effect that Captain Bearcroft had not recommended me. Facing Their Lordships with Bearcroft's glowing certificate made no difference. It has always been a mystery to me; but perhaps the personal interest Lord Roberts always took in me had something to do with it.

We left Greenwich in October, and migrated to the Royal Naval College, just inside the dockyard gates at Portsmouth, for our courses in gunnery and torpedo. The building had originally been part of the old Royal Naval Academy established by an Order-in-Council of 1729—"for the better education and training of up to forty young gentlemen (per annum) for H.M. Service at sea". Closed down as such in 1837, it was later used for a limited number of senior officers and mates, then for acting sub-lieutenants. After my time, and until it was bombed out during the war, it became H.M.S. *Dryad*, the Navigation School for embryo Lieutenants (N), popularly known as the 'Wreckers Rest' or 'Retreat'.

We lived here, went down each morning to the *Excellent* steps, and were ferried across the harbour to Whale Island otherwise H.M.S. *Excellent*, the Alma Mater of naval gunnery, for the day's work. Here everything possible was done to make miserable the lives of the sub-lieutenants. We were chivvied and bullied. Maybe we deserved it; but I cannot believe it was necessary or that it did us any good. Being shouted at on parade, or for some minor fault, merely made me feel mutinous. I was glad to get away from the detestable place on March 13th, 1903, with a 'second-class' in gunnery, and a certificate awarded at the end of our courses stating that I had conducted myself with sobriety but that my general conduct was not satisfactory. This smudge on my character was quite unjustly bestowed; but fully in keeping with the general atmosphere that then prevailed at Whale Island, which was harsh and inhuman.

I believe my bad certificate was due to the following incident. At the end of the examination we had to return all the leather equipment and gaiters with which we had been issued to a hut on the parade ground. After a good lunch about six of us set out to do this. We found the hut locked and nobody inside, as there should have been. Not wishing to be delayed and to miss the boat to the mainland, we threw the gear in through the open window. One of the party, making insufficient allowance for a good lunch, broke a window, while an inkpot was upset, and the hut generally in a mess when the storekeeper returned. So all of us were served out with these unfavourable certificates. I afterwards heard that with the exception of myself they all complained and managed to get them altered. I never heard of this, so my certificate as originally written is one of my proudest possessions.

We next went to the *Vernon* for a six weeks' course in torpedo. Here conditions were far more human. The instruction was good, we learnt a lot, and I managed to achieve a 'one'. Thus, on March 14th, 1903, I became a fully-fledged sub-lieutenant. Though the two 'ones' and three 'twos' I had obtained in my exams did not entitle me to any early promotion, they enabled me roughly to keep my position on the list of sub-lieutenants. In due course I was sent my commission signed by Admirals Sir John Fisher and John Durnford, and countersigned by His Majesty King Edward VII.

III

After about a month's leave I was appointed as sub-lieutenant to the battleship *Implacable* in the Mediterranean, travelling to Gibraltar in the *Renown* as one of several sub-lieutenants as passengers, and on from there to Malta in the cruiser *Vindictive*. It took us nearly a month, and we spent three rather dismal weeks at Gibraltar loafing around with nothing to do.

I was pleased at going to the *Implacable*. She was commanded by my old captain in the *Doris*, Reginald Prothero, and though he was exacting to serve under I already had proof that he was not really so intimidating as he looked. The commander was Edward Boyle, who had been one of our watchkeepers in the *Doris*.

The *Implacable* was considered a crack ship. Captain Prince Louis of Battenberg had just left her, and her officers and midshipmen had all been hand-picked. I am not suggesting that I was specially chosen. Far from it. I found there were definite disadvantages in joining a ship of that sort. For an example, everyone was such an expert at one game or another that the average or below the average performer never had a look in.

The ship was in a curious state. I think she was a very good ship; but was in the process of changing from a kind-hearted method of discipline to one which was rather rigid and irksome. The officers and men did not enjoy it, and nor did I. I found myself mate of the messdeck, a position of no responsibility with very little to do. I did not keep watch at sea and not often in harbour.

Prothero was getting old and very crotchety. It was always a dangerous matter to be a witness at captain's defaulters, the witnesses often getting as much and sometimes more in the way of punishment than the delinquent. On my first occasion, after giving evidence about a man who had been brought before me as officer of the watch for some misdemeanour or other, the captain glared at me and said: "Your conduct, boy, has been most reprehensible!" in what manner was never disclosed.

He had shaved his beard; but with his heavy black jowl he was even more intimidating than he had been three years before. A previous kind-hearted captain and commander had allowed each midshipman a chest-of-drawers in addition to his sea chest. At the first Sunday rounds I attended Prothero's horny eye fell upon the chests-of-drawers in the flat where the midshipmen lived. He blazed with anger. "When I was a midshipman I lived in my chest and sometimes bathed in it, too!" he exclaimed. "Throw those damned things overboard, commander!"

The gun-room was rather high-toned, and I found difficulty in living up to its standard. We dressed for dinner every night, an unheard-of practice in a gun-room in those days, and one which, observing the midshipmen's stiff white evening shirts growing even dingier and dirtier during a cruise, I was not sure was a good one.

After about six months in the *Implacable* I heard there was a vacancy for a sub-lieutenant in the destroyer *Locust*. It was true that the gingerbread was not all gilt, as the *Locust's* captain, Lieutenant A. B. S. Dutton, had a bad name among sub-lieutenants and had kicked one or two out of his ship. However, I was tired of having no real responsibility and too little to do, so asked Commander Boyle if he would ask Captain Prothero to apply for me to go. I have the feeling that they were both glad to see the last of me, as I got the job right away. I left the *Implacable* on September 17th, 1903.

So began my long years in destroyers. Many a time have I blessed the notion which caused me to apply for that vacancy in the *Locust*.

Life in that ship was not altogether easy. The sub-lieutenant was the first lieutenant, so to speak, and was responsible for the discipline, general efficiency and cleanliness. Lieutenant Dutton had been given command very young because of his ability and efficiency. He set a very high standard and was not easy to please, but thrust responsibility upon his sub-lieutenant. One heard all about it if things went wrong or were not up to the mark.

The *Locust*, a 30-knot destroyer of 300 tons built by Lairds in 1896, with a crew of 58 and mounting a couple of 18-inch torpedo-tubes, a single 12-pounder and five 6-pounder guns, had four large funnels with the engines between the boilers. She burnt coal, and two of the funnels were fairly well aft. We were painted white, and when steaming, cinders were vomited on to our spotless quarterdeck. Destroyers of those days were delicate craft, and it took a lot of work to keep them running and efficient. It was harder still to keep them clean, and Dutton always insisted upon the corticene decks being as white as a hound's tooth and all the brightwork being polished and shining. I remember that our funnels and upperworks were grey, ours being painted with a special grey wash made from a recipe the secret of which was known only by our Chief Stoker. He was like one of the witches in *Macbeth* over her cauldron when he boiled it up while murmuring incantations.

When we were away on a cruise each destroyer was attached to a battleship, and was looked after like one of the big ship's own boats. I remember several interesting cruises, usually to the Greek islands in the Ægean, which I came to know well. One operation I afterwards turned to good account was a night destroyer attack on the battlefleet in the harbour of Port Itea in the Gulf of Patras. It was a difficult and most unusual job for the destroyers, as the battleships had put the harbour into a state of defence and had altered the seamarks by anchoring launches with searchlights in them some way off the shore hoping we should think they were on some of the outlying islands. So we did. It was rather a hair-raising experience; but the destroyers managed to avoid all the dangers, got safely into the harbour and fired their torpedoes, most of them being caught up in the battleships' nets.

After about three months, to my great regret, Dutton left the *Locust* to go as first lieutenant of the *Britannia* at Dartmouth. He gave me a certificate that gladdened my heart.

Dutton's relief was Lieutenant F. R. Wrottesley, and a few weeks after his arrival the *Locust* paid off and we turned over to a newer ship of the same class, the *Orwell*, which had been under repair for about eighteen months after losing her bow in collision with the cruiser *Pioneer*. On joining her I had my first lesson in dealing efficaciously with undesirable official correspondence. The *Locust* had a crack pulling whaler which had always done well in regattas. We asked to take her with us to the *Orwell*, which was refused by the dockyard Admiral. So while the two ships lay alongside each other the gunner and I changed the boats. Shortly afterwards a letter arrived through the usual official channels asking why the *Locust* had returned a brand-new whaler to the boat slip. This caused Wrottesley some perturbation, so I volunteered to deal with the matter. I put the letter on the wardroom fire and we heard no more about it!

I had a few more pleasant months in the *Orwell*, with plenty to do and always trying to go one better than the other destroyers, when, on March 31st, 1904, I was promoted to lieutenant. I stayed on for a couple of months and then was ordered home, spending a few weeks in the *Banshee* and *Coquet* on passage to Malta and on to Gibraltar. From here I took passage home to Portsmouth in the *Hannibal*, arriving without incident.

I shall always remember my sub-lieutenant's time in Mediterranean destroyers. Our Captain (D), in the depot ship *Egmont*, was John Michael de Roebeck, and among the destroyer captains were Edwyn Alexander-Sinclair, Sir Douglas Brownrigg, Valentine Phillimore, Godfrey Paine, Cecil Foley Lambert, and Arthur Macrorie, all of whom made names for themselves.

I was left on leave for about three weeks, and spent it in Edinburgh, my father having become Professor of Anatomy at Edinburgh University. My family lived at 18 Grosvenor Crescent.

IV

At the end of June, 1904, I was appointed to H.M.S. *Northampton*. A so-called cruiser, she was a barque-rigged, two-funnelled vessel of about 8,000 tons completed in 1878. Her original trial speed had been about 14 knots. In 1904 the *Northampton*, with her two tenders the *Cleopatra* and *Calliope*, cruised round the ports of the United Kingdom and enlisted boys for the Navy. As she was lying at Campbeltown, in Kintyre, I did not have far to travel.

Attired in frock coat and sword, as laid down in the King's Regulations and Admiralty Instructions, I duly reported myself at about 10.30 a.m. to the commander, Frederick Godfrey Bird, whom I had met before as first lieutenant of the *Diadem* and knew as a rather dour officer.

"Come on board to join, Sir," said I.

"Very well, Mr. Cunningham," said he, giving me an unpleasant look. "Go below. Take off your sword. You're officer of the day."

I obeyed orders, giving little heed to the fact that the sails on all three masts were hanging loose for drying. Just before noon I heard a shout from the commander—"Mr. Cunningham. Furl sails."

"Aye, aye, sir," said I, saluting, and trying to look cool, calm and collected, though considerably taken aback. Having just come from destroyers I had forgotten most of my sail drill, and tried valiantly to recollect what I had learnt in the *Martin*, which had only two masts. However, collecting the chief bosun's mate to tell me more or less what to do with the third mast, I went to the bridge and gave my orders. Together we made not too bad a job of it, though it was nothing compared with the mad rush in the *Martin*. The lads in the *Northampton* scrambled aloft and laid out on the yards rather like a lot of ploughboys.

The days of sail were over. I never saw the old *Northampton* spread her wings on passage, and was told that if she did, she invariably flew up into the wind.

Life was not unpleasant. We had nearly 300 boys on board and a fairly large ship's company. There were two lieutenants for watchkeeping duties, myself and another; but we had nothing whatever to do with the boys' instruction. All this seemed to be arranged by the Captain, A. J. Horsley, and several warrant officers.

After I had been in the *Northampton* about a couple of months, however, the Admiralty, not by any means too soon, ordained that the system of training new entries in all ships and establishments was to be altered. In future, lieutenants were to be in charge of the boys and their instruction, and one officer was to be specially detailed to organize it. To my great satisfaction Captain Horsley appointed me to this latter job, which took me off watchkeeping in harbour and gave me more work than I could comfortably tackle. It also put me in rather an invidious position *vis-à-vis* the commander, who had nothing to do with the boys' instruction and was not allowed to interfere; but must produce the instructors from the ship's company. As I naturally chose his best men, Commander Bird was not at all pleased. It was a strenuous job; but I enjoyed every minute of it.

However, the *Northampton* was long out-of-date as a training ship, and in November, 1904, it was decided to turn her over to the more modern cruiser *Hawke*, completed in 1892. We went round to Chatham, and were soon busily employed getting the new ship ready. A new Training Squadron was also formed and put under the command of the Commander-in-Chief,

North America and West Indies, Vice-Admiral Sir Day Hort Bosanquet It was to consist of the *Hawke*, carrying direct-entry boys, or Northampton riggers', as they were called; the *St. George* and *Edgar*, with boys from the training ships; and the *Isis* and *Highflyer*, with naval cadets. Captain Horsley, in the *Hawke*, who was senior officer, was ordered to take the squadron to the West Indies and join the Commander-in-Chief at Prince Rupert's Bay, Dominica.

Halfway across the Atlantic our navigator went down with measles, and I was detailed to take on. Captain Horsley was very anxious about meeting the Commander-in-Chief and anchoring the squadron together on a line of bearing from the flagship. So, much to the disgust of the other captains, we practised the manœuvre all the way over, though without letting go anchors, of course. With me as an amateur Christopher Columbus, we found Dominica and Prince Rupert's Bay, with the flagship *Ariadne* at anchor. Then, in spite of all our practise, we made a complete botch of the anchoring.

After a day or two at Dominica the *Hawke* parted company and made independently for Bermuda, calling for a few days at Antigua on the way. Here, I remember, the hospitable inhabitants plied us with red and green bitters in the club, considerably to our detriment. We eventually arrived at Bermuda with an epidemic of measles on board. So all the boys, in charge of myself and another lieutenant with a doctor in attendance, were landed on Ports Island and accommodated in an establishment which had been used for Boer prisoners-of-war. No better way of training could have been invented, and while the ship was fumigated and disinfected we kept the lads busy from early morning until late at night.

The training in the *Hawke* was much better organized than in the *Northampton*. We had four divisions each of 60 to 70 boys with a lieutenant in charge. I was still in charge of the instruction as a whole and had a division; but except at sea kept no watch or 'day on'. Among the other divisional lieutenants was C. R. Samson, who afterwards became one of the Navy's first airmen.

I look upon this period of my service as one of the happiest and most satisfying. I still hold the opinion that every young lieutenant should do at least a year in the training service. To teach, one has to learn how.

In July, 1905, Captain Horsley was relieved by Captain F. S. Miller, well known as having written *Notes on Handling Ships*. He enthused new life and new ideas into the training, and we lieutenants learnt much from him as officers of the watch. It was a real pleasure to watch him handling the *Hawke*.

We were rather looked down upon by the other training-ships. Our boys, entered direct from the shore, were considered to be uncouth and half-trained. They averaged about six months older; but their general physique was not thought to be so good as the lads who had been fed and drilled for a year or so in one of the stationary training ships or establishments. In these days of rationing it is almost unbelievable; but each of the boys was allowed half-a-pound of beef a day more than the others, this to build them up.

The truth, of course, was that you could pick as husky a lot from the *Hawke* as from any of the other ships. Indeed, in that year, 1905, we thrashed the cutters' crews of them all, finishing up at Queenstown by running right away from the crack crew of the *Black Prince* which had won the training-ship cup for which we were not allowed to compete.

However, this busy and interesting time could not last for ever, and in May, 1906, the *Hawke* paid off. I was not appointed to recommission, probably because Their Lordships in their wisdom thought I ought to have a change from boys' training.

After three weeks' welcome leave with my family in Edinburgh I was appointed to the cruiser *Scylla* for the summer manœuvres, 1906. It was one of the first trade exercises in which merchant ships took part by pretending to be sunk or captured. The only remarkable thing about it was that the little *Scylla*, which was quite slow as cruisers went even in those days, did more damage to trade than all the rest of the commerce destroyers put together. She was well placed at the entrance to the Channel some way out from Ushant.

v

From the *Scylla* I was appointed straight to the *Suffolk*, Captain Rosslyn Wemyss, which was commissioning for the Mediterranean. She was one of the modern 'County' class cruisers, of 9,800 tons, 22 knots, and armed with fourteen 6-inch guns. She was a good ship for those days, with a particularly fine and experienced West Country crew. I found among them about sixty of my old 'Northampton riggers', and most of them in my division. I was delighted at the chance of carrying on their education.

The *Suffolk* was a very happy ship. Everyone liked the captain and the commander, though the latter, Bingham Powell, was thought a little eccentric. I found as first lieutenant my late captain in the *Locust*, A. B. S. Dutton, who had come from the *Britannia* at Dartmouth bringing a hand-picked lot of midshipmen with him.

The *Suffolk* was a good ship. Greatly to my content I was put in charge of the boat sailing; the instruction of the ordinary seamen and boys; and, when Dutton decreed it, of the instruction of the midshipmen as well. What with all this, also my duties as a watchkeeper, I was kept busy.

Rosslyn Wemyss, whose intimates called him 'Rosy', was an unusual captain. He wore a monocle, and under an air of complete insouciance, concealed shrewdness with a very alert mind and a mass of professional knowledge.

On one occasion, when I was doing duty as navigator—I know not why—I had made some error in my calculations for the noon position. He looked over my shoulder in the charthouse, at once put his finger on the spot, and said in his most polite manner, "Here, Cunningham. This is where you've gone wrong."

It was true. I had. Together we corrected the mistake.

Rosy Wemyss had a charming way of treating his officers and was always most courteous and polite. But if the occasion arose he could be fiery-tempered and severe, though never unjust. Well endowed, he was a good mixer and knew everybody. He owned a villa at Cannes, which was a great magnet to the *Suffolk*.

The Mediterranean cruiser squadron then consisted of the *Leviathan*, flagship of Rear-Admiral the Hon. Hedworth Lambton; the *Carnavon*, *Lancaster* and *Suffolk*. Admiral Lord Charles Beresford was the Commander-in-Chief of the Mediterranean Fleet, and he had issued an edict for complete silence on all occasions. Following the precedent of the Royal Yacht, all orders, even by midshipmen in their boats, had to be given by signs, with, on occasion, somewhat peculiar results. Ships companies were not allowed to cheer the success of their shipmates in sporting events; but must only show their appreciation by clapping. It was all rather stupid and unnecessary, and I once had a personal rebuke from the Commander-in-Chief for making too much noise in the *Suffolk's* picquet boat when the cutters I had trained for the obstacle race carried all before them. The rather rude signal left Captain Wemyss quite unmoved, and we duly celebrated the victory in his cabin.

The *Suffolk* was a very sporting ship and carried off all the cutter races and most of the others in the yearly fleet regatta. She was also far ahead in the annual sports. We had a crack cutter and crew and were ready to take on anyone at any time. We all made a fairly steady income by backing them against other ships. The only occasion I ever saw that boat beaten was by the *Argyll*, which had a cutter specially built on the Clyde to race in America. After a ding-dong race of 3 miles the *Argyll's* boat won by half a length, and £658 went out of the pockets of the Mediterranean Fleet into those of the Channel Fleet.

The usual routine of a commission in the Mediterranean continued—fleet exercises, gunnery and torpedo practises, cruises to Greece, the Dalmatian coast, Italy, and the south of France. We were one of the ships detailed to escort King Edward and Queen Alexandra during their cruise in the Mediterranean in the *Victoria and Albert* during the spring of 1907. Joining the Royal Yacht at Toulon, Their Majesties went to Cartagena to visit the King of Spain, and then on to Minorca, Malta and Naples, where they disembarked to meet the King of Italy at Gaeta. They went home overland. One heard that the King's foreign visits occasioned a good deal of fluttering in European diplomatic dovecotes, particularly in Germany.

Gunnery was coming into its own. So far as I can remember we still had competitive gunlayers' tests to try out the individual efficiency of the gunlayers and the drill of the guns' crews, while we also carried out battle practice at medium ranges with the guns controlled as they would be in action. In one of these practices I was one of the officers detailed to go on board each of the firing ships in turn to work a complicated instrument which produced some sort of a graph. What exactly it was supposed to do I cannot remember; but in his report on the instrument the representative of the Inspector Target Practice reported, "The extreme ingenuity of this instrument rather blinds one to its absolute uselessness", a remark which could truthfully have been applied to quite a number of the gunnery appliances of those days. We still had a lot to learn.

And so the time passed happily and busily until, in April, 1908, the *Suffolk* was ordered home to pay off, which we did at Devonport on the 27th. At my request Captain Wemyss promised to do his best to get me the command of a destroyer, the job I had set my heart upon. I had four years seniority as a lieutenant, which at that period was regarded as the minimum for a command.

I went off to Edinburgh on leave. My brother Alan had finished with Woolwich and had obtained his commission in the Royal Artillery in 1906. His battery was stationed at Piers Hill, in Edinburgh, so I saw quite a lot of him. My eldest brother, John, who was a doctor, had joined the Indian Medical Service in 1905 and was out in India. My father had become Dean of the Faculty of Medicine in Edinburgh University; but was in very poor health. Nobody quite seemed to know what was the matter with him.

And so I awaited news of my new appointment with considerable anxiety. I knew that Captain Wemyss had some pull at the Admiralty and would do his best for me. All the same, I imagined my lack of seniority might tell against me, and that I might be sent to a battleship or cruiser. If this happened it would probably mean that I should have to wait another two years before I achieved my ambition, a command of my own.

The long official envelope from the Admiralty arrived one morning early in May. I tore it open. I was appointed to H.M.S. *Hecla*, at Portsmouth, for H.M. Torpedo Boat No. 14, in command.

I knew, of course, that torpedo boats numbers 1 to 36 had originally been designed as 'coastal destroyers'. They were brand new, 26-knotters driven by turbines and completely oil fired. Round about 270 tons, they carried two 12-pounder guns and three torpedo-tubes. In every way, except for size, they compared favourably with the existing 30-knot destroyers, which had the disadvantage of burning coal and being much more difficult to keep clean.

I was delighted at the prospect.

CHAPTER IV

I

I JOINED Torpedo Boat 14 in the Tidal Basin at Portsmouth on May 13th, 1908. Thereafter I was to serve continuously in command of torpedo craft until November 4th, 1919.

We lay alongside our sister ship, T.B. 13, commanded by Paul Whitfield. Being strictly superstitious I felt quite glad my number was 14. In truth, T.B. 13 was not a very lucky ship.

We belonged to the Reserve Fleet, one of a large number of older destroyers and new torpedo boats manned with nucleus crews. Our depot ship at Portsmouth was the *Hecla*, dating from 1878, which was commanded by Captain John Nicholas who was also Captain (D) of the whole flotilla.

A few days after I joined we were ordered to Campbeltown with the destroyer *Kangaroo*, Commander Hubert S. Cardale, and were told to rendezvous with her at Spithead at 9 a.m. I left harbour independently; but found no *Kangaroo* at the rendezvous. I waited for an hour and then became rather flurried, wondering if I had come to the right place. Then, steaming about, I lost myself, in spite of what I thought was a fair knowledge of navigation, and only discovered my whereabouts on the chart by reading the name on the East Ryde Middle buoy.

However, T.B. 13 appeared and was followed at 11 a.m. by the *Kangaroo*, and we set off through the Solent and Needles Channel on our way west. Our reduced crews did not allow us to steam continuously, so we anchored for the night in Falmouth. The next day it was blowing hard from the westward with a heavy sea, so we got no farther than Penzance. When the weather moderated we steamed on round Land's End for Milford Haven.

The captain of the *Kangaroo* did not believe in long sea passages, so we spent the next night in Lough Carlingford. There the two torpedo boats were ordered to Belfast to complete with oil fuel from Messrs. Harland and Wolff's stocks. Glad to be quit of the *Kangaroo*, we made an early start and arrived soon after noon. The captain of T.B. 13 and myself went to call on the Manager of Harland and Wolff's. We found him at lunch, and were told he had no oil fuel and had never had any, so that was that. However, we arrived at Campbeltown the next afternoon, and found there our depot ship *Hecla* and between 20 and 25 destroyers of the 4th (Portsmouth) flotilla. We anchored close to the steamer pier. We had light anchors and the holding ground was very poor. It came on to blow hard two nights later and both torpedo-boats started to drag. I managed to raise steam and get away; but T.B. 13 started her career of misfortune by dragging ashore and being left more or less high and dry at low water. Luckily she did not damage herself. One lived and learned.

We spent the summer at Campbeltown, varied by cruises up the Clyde to various ports. But it was usually gunnery or torpedo exercises in the forenoon and afternoon, followed by a rush into harbour in time for a round of golf. We came south in September to lie up in Fareham Creek, Portsmouth harbour, with only such trips to sea as the duties of the port required or for gunnery or torpedo exercises. During one of these gunnery expeditions I fired about a dozen 12-pounder practise projectiles into Bembridge, and was rather intimidated by the subsequent Court of Enquiry. However, I came out of it unscathed, as it appeared that the target ship had towed the target too close inshore.

It was in August, 1908, I remember, that Captain Reginald Tyrwhitt, of Harwich Force fame during the war of 1914-18, became our Captain (D) in the small cruiser *Topaze*. It was a much better arrangement than having the Captain (D) in a depot ship which did not take her flotilla to sea.

I cannot remember when it happened, but at one time when our Portsmouth torpedo-boats completed to full crews and went to Rosyth for the periodical exercises, our senior officer was Commander Richard Faulkner Herbert Hartland Mahon, in T.B. 13. He was ordered to anchor all the torpedo-boats about twenty of us all told, in such and such a position off the Beamer Rock, just above the Forth Bridge. Mahon completely missed the berthing line at his first attempt, and then went round in a wide circle with all his flock following and missed it again. Round we went again. This was too much for the captain of one of the Chatham boats, T.B. 6, commanded by an irrepressible character called Owen. Halfway round on our third attempt we heard the rapid ringing of T.B. 6's bell, and Owen's stentorial voice shouting through a megaphone, "Last lap! Last lap!" We laughed, but Mahon, who was anything but popular, was not at all amused.

In the summer of 1909 we completed to full crew and assembled off Oban for combined fleet exercises. I took no part in them, as my brother telegraphed from Edinburgh to say that my father was dying. I was temporarily relieved and went home. My father died on June 23rd, 1909.

After three weeks in Edinburgh dealing with family matters consequent on my father's death I rejoined T.B. 14 at Portsmouth. I did not stay in her for long, for very soon I was promoted to the command of the 30-knot, coal-burning destroyer *Vulture*. Personally I thought her distinctly inferior to T.B. 14, and complained to Captain Tyrwhitt that I had been given an Irishman's rise. He was rather annoyed. However, as the result of an exchange in destroyers between Portsmouth and Devonport, I was soon given command of the *Roebuck*. Although a coal-burner she was a beautiful little ship—fast, handy, economical on fuel, with captain's quarters which were palatial compared with those to which I had been accustomed. My cabin in the

Vulture had been very small and cramped, and in T.B. 14 I had had no cabin at all, merely one of the four bunks in the wardroom. Alas, I only spent three months in the *Roebuck*. She developed boiler trouble and had to be paid off on December 16th, 1910.

This left me in something of a predicament. I had been in destroyers for more than two and a half years, and rumours were flying around that the pundits at the Admiralty had ordained that after two or three years in command young officers must go back to a big ship. I hated the idea, so asked Captain (D), who by that time was Mortimer L'Estrange Silver, if he would mind putting in a word for me. I fancied one of the 'River' class, which, though still in the Reserve Fleet flotillas manned by nucleus crews, were better ships than the old 30-knotters. Captain Silver, who was a kindly man, said he would do what he could.

So I went on leave and awaited my fate. My eldest brother was home from India and was working in London preparatory to going out there again. My mother had taken a flat in London to be near him, so it was there that I went.

II

Early on January 8th, 1911, the letter with the Admiralty stamp arrived, and I found to my delighted amazement, that I was appointed in command of the *Scorpion*, one of the latest ocean-going destroyers which had only been completed three months. A ship of about 900 tons, she mounted one 4-inch gun and three 12-pounders, with a couple of 21-inch torpedo-tubes. She had a speed of 27 knots, and was one of a class of sixteen such ships fitted for burning coal, but driven by turbines. At the time I did not realize what I was soon to appreciate, and that was that coal and turbines made an extraordinarily bad mixture.

The Admiralty had rather vacillated about the design of the new destroyers, and quite naturally. In 1908 they had started building the twelve large destroyers of the 'Tribal' class, with speeds of 33 knots and more, driven by turbines and burning oil fuel. But oil came from abroad, whereas coal was home-produced. We had no great oil reserves in Great Britain or abroad; no tanks in which to keep the fuel; and insufficient tankers in which to bring it home. A complete switch-over to oil fuel meant heavy initial expense. Worried by this problem, and the huge cost, the sixteen destroyers of the 'Beagle' class completed in 1910–11, of which the *Scorpion* was one, were coal-burning.

Thereafter, when the storage arrangements had been made, all destroyers were fitted to burn oil, which had tremendous advantages, particularly in small ships. It produced greater speed for the same weight of fuel, and enabled full speed to be obtained in a matter of minutes by switching on the extra sprayers. It did away with the laborious task of shovelling the coal into the furnaces, and thus reduced the stoker complements. It allowed ships to 'oil' at sea, and, above all, did away with the ordeal of coaling ship—which robbed all the crew of their rest immediately on returning to harbour. An hour or two alongside a tanker or a jetty and the job of refuelling was done and the ship ready for sea again with hardly a man having to lift a finger.

To revert, however, to the *Scorpion*. She belonged to one of the Home Fleet flotillas, and I knew at once life was not going to be a bed of roses. The Commodore was Sir Robert Arbuthnot in the light cruiser *Boadicea*, and he had the reputation throughout the Service of being a rigid disciplinarian. He was as strict and exacting to himself as he was to those serving under him. All the same, if I could stay the course I was supremely lucky to get such a fine ship. I had only six years seniority as a lieutenant, and all the other big destroyers were commanded by commanders or senior lieutenants. (The specific rank of lieutenant-commander for a 'two-and-a-half striper', otherwise a lieutenant of over eight years seniority, did not come in until early in 1914. Before that time a lieutenant commanding his own ship was known as a 'lieutenant and commander'.)

I joined the *Scorpion* at Harwich on the afternoon of Saturday, January 11th, relieving Lieutenant R. G. Stone, and spent the rest of the day settling in and trying to make myself acquainted with masses of orders, instructions and memoranda. I had hardly started my Sunday rounds next morning when I was ordered to repair on board the *Boadicea*. The Commodore had already been round the flotillas in his barge and had detected mud on the *Scorpion's* port anchor!

This was my first meeting with the redoubtable Sir Robert; but he was rather apologetic and pleasant when he realized I had only joined the afternoon before. It was the first and last time I was in trouble with him.

I eventually learnt to like and admire him, and he taught me a lot about discipline. Strict though he was, he expected, as I have said, nothing of one that he was not fully prepared to put up with himself. He was a stickler for correct uniform as laid down in the regulations. We were expected to wear stiff white shirts with stiff cuffs in the daytime, and uniform ties of exactly the right width, which I believe was two inches. Coming into harbour after three or four days of gruelling weather at sea, the men must be properly dressed and spotless. Sea-boots were not allowed unless seas were actually breaking over the deck, and if the Commodore saw a destroyer captain bringing his ship into harbour wearing a muffler instead of a clean white collar, the offender was usually ordered to 'repair on board' for a dressing-down. Sir Robert Arbuthnot was not liked in the flotilla, though most people had a grudging admiration for him. The harsh discipline imposed would not answer in these enlightened days.

All the same, he was very good to me. Someone at the Admiralty had ordained that all officers aspiring to the command of destroyers must pass examinations in navigation, gunnery, torpedo and signals. The order was made retrospective. Having already been in command for three years I ignored it, until finally Their Lordships sent an official letter to the Commodore saying I was to take the exams. Sir Robert sent for me and showed me the Admiralty order.

"You'd better try and pass the examinations," he said. "But it doesn't matter if you pass or not. You won't leave the *Scorpion*!"

So on April 12th, 1911, I lightheartedly presented myself at the Navigation School at Portsmouth. After doing various papers and undergoing *viva-voce* examinations in chart work, tides, buoyage and so on, I was made to take a ship out of Portsmouth harbour. She was the torpedo gunboat *Dryad*, about the same size as the *Scorpion*, which I had taken in and out of far more ticklish places. I was amused. I passed the exam, but do not think the three navigating officers were precisely pleased with me. As for the examinations in gunnery, torpedo and signals, I conveniently 'forgot' them, and so did the Admiralty.

King Edward VII had died on May 6th, 1910, and King George V's Coronation took place on June 22nd, 1911. The Review at Spithead took place two days later. It was another magnificent array, the third great naval spectacle I had witnessed at Spithead since joining the Navy fourteen years before. With the destroyers and attendant ships the British warships alone stretched over 26 miles. We had present 42 battleships, new and old; 4 battle-cruisers; 30 armoured cruisers, as they were then called; 37 protected cruisers; 8 scouts, afterwards re-armed and re-classed as light cruisers; 15 torpedo-gunboats; 68 destroyers; 12 torpedo-boats; 8 submarines; and 7 depot ships. There were also many foreign men-of-war.

There followed another period of hard training from Harwich. In a cycle of four weeks the destroyers would go to sea each Monday at noon and stay out till Thursday night for three weeks in succession. On Fridays and during the fourth week we did harbour drills. In the intervals we coaled and tried to keep our ships clean. Weather made no difference. Whether it was a thick fog or a gale of wind we still went to sea, even though we could do nothing in the way of gunnery or torpedo exercises, night attacks, steaming without lights, tactics, taking each other in tow, or any of the other exercises or evolutions that Sir Robert thought would be good for us. It was no wonder that the flotilla became known as the 'Outer Gabbard Yacht Club', so-called from the Outer Gabbard lightship, well out in the North Sea, which was our usual rendezvous by day and by night. It was a hard life; but we learnt a lot.

Spring and summer brought cruisers and exercises with the Home Fleet. War with Germany was already looking up over the horizon, and in the summer of 1911 occurred the Agadir business, when the Kaiser was being truculent over Morocco and sent the gunboat *Panther* to Agadir to 'protect' German interests. There was uneasiness in Europe, and France was genuinely alarmed. Our relations with Germany were also rather strained.

We were with the fleet at Cromarty at this time, and rumour had it that the Admiralty had lost the run of three German flotillas. We destroyers were accordingly put on to patrolling at night at the entrance to the Moray Firth. Our strict orders from the Commander-in-Chief were not to provoke an incident; but we had private orders from the Commodore to open fire on any ship without lights looking like a destroyer that tried to come through our patrol line. Luckily, perhaps, no German destroyers came our way.

I very well remember another incident. Returning up Channel from Portland one dark night in November the Commodore thought fit to reverse the order of the divisions, so that, for the good of their souls and exercise in station keeping, the junior officers were leading and the commanders bringing up the rear. Only our red and green side-lights were being shown. Approaching the Straits of Dover, with a strong south-westerly wind and heavy sea under our tail, I was in the charthouse when I suddenly heard the wheel go hard over. Gaining the bridge the first thing I saw was a double topsail over the top of the bridge dodger. I was in time to reverse the wheel and to put the telegraphs to full speed; but no more. The *Fynn*, a three-masted wooden sailing ship, rammed us on the bulkhead between the engine-room and after boiler-room. There was an almighty shock, followed by a succession of crashes as the *Fynn's* jiboon cleared everything the starboard side of our deck and knocked down our after funnel. Badly dented, our only hole was a 3-foot vertical rip on the bulkhead between the after boiler-room and the engine-room. We were left wallowing, with the water only being kept under by the circulators after it had reached the bottom of the turbines.

The *Fynn*, meanwhile, drifted to leeward with all her headgear gone. I put the searchlight on her, to see her heel over and capsize. We lowered the whaler and picked up five of her six men. The other poor fellow went overboard, and was never seen again. I heard afterwards that twenty feet of the *Fynn's* bow dropped off, which was a good advertisement for the sturdy build of the *Scorpion*.

The flotilla, including my next astern, the divisional commander, steamed majestically on, completely oblivious to the fact that anything untoward had happened. Then the *Renard* came back and towed us into Sheerness. It was a nasty, sticky night.

There was a Court of Enquiry; but the Admiralty paid up without any fuss. We had not a leg to stand upon. The *Fynn* had been beating down Channel, and there was no doubt that the *Scorpion's* officer of the watch had mixed up her red port light with those of the column of destroyers on his starboard hand. Who was held to blame I do not know, but it took three to four months, and a good deal of the taxpayers' money, to repair us in Chatham

Dockyard. We rejoined the flotilla in the spring of 1912 in time for the cruise and usual exercises.

And so it went on, hard work and much sea time, and, under the eagle eye of Sir Robert Arbuthnot, eternal vigilance. Nothing escaped him. Our every little fault or failing was noted, and corrected. He held, and very properly, that the captain was responsible for everything that happened in his ship. It is a sound principle.

Among other things, he insisted upon physical fitness. Each and every officer, no matter what his rank or seniority, was expected to walk ten miles at a stretch once a month. Some may have cheated; but we conformed by walking to Ipswich on Saturday forenoons, having a good lunch at the 'Great White Horse', one of Pickwick's inns, for 2s. 6d. and then returning by 'bus.

Then Sir Robert brought all the ships' companies into the physical fitness test. They landed, 95 per cent of them at a time, under arms, and were expected to cover five miles in an hour. It sounds easy; but what with fat sailors and thin sailors; fat stokers and thin stokers—some slightly asthmatic and many with boots that did not fit, it was amazing to see a ship's company straggling in with some of the officers carrying four and six rifles apiece. The ship that failed had to repeat the operation. Looking back on it, I don't know that it did much good. What with plenty of sea-time and regular coaling ship, men had enough physical exercise without learning to become high-speed infantrymen.

In July, 1912, Sir Robert Arbuthnot left us, greatly to my chagrin. His departure coincided with a complete reorganization of the Home flotillas. New destroyers were rapidly coming into service, and it was decided to have four flotillas, each of twelve destroyers, in full commission with the Home Fleet, apart, of course, from the nucleus crew flotillas at Portsmouth, Devonport and Chatham. There would be a Commodore in over-all command in a light cruiser, and he would not command a flotilla of his own, as Arbuthnot had done. Our new Commodore was Cecil Foley Lambert, whom I had met in the Mediterranean as captain of the *Albatross* during my time in the old *Orwell*. A destroyer officer of note, he was a worthy successor to Arbuthnot, with a reputation for toughness that was nearly as great. His manner was invariably brusque. In the Mediterranean he always had a soft-boiled egg for his breakfast, as he said it was the only thing the Maltese servants could not finger! One morning at breakfast in the wardroom his newly-joined sub-lieutenant timidly asked him at breakfast, "Would you mind passing the salt sir, please," to receive the sharp reply, "What are the bloody servants for?"

Our new Captain (D) in the light cruiser *Boadicea* was E. S. Carey. Reinforced by four of the 'Beagle' class from the 2nd Flotilla, we were made up to sixteen all told and became the 3rd Flotilla.

And so it went on, hard training varied by fleet exercises in all weathers until there was little that any of us did not know about the North Sea in all its moods.

In February, 1913, Captain Carey went sick and after about six weeks was relieved by Captain Cecil H. Fox, a fine destroyer officer, a most pleasant man and a good disciplinarian.

It was at about this time that we happened to be lying in one of the large basins in Chatham Dockyard. On the opposite side lay the battleship *Triumph*, which was paying off. Her captain was Commander Thomas J. S. Lyne, an old friend of mine who had joined the Navy as a bluejacket boy, and, as a Warrant Officer in command of Torpedo Boat No. 60, had been specially promoted to lieutenant for improvising sail after his ship fractured her propeller shaft and sailing her into Saldanha Bay. (Incidentally, Lyne was subsequently promoted to captain in 1918, being the first ranker in modern times to reach that rank, and retired under the age clause of the regulations in 1925. He is now Rear-Admiral Sir Thomas Lyne, K.C.V.O., C.B., D.S.O.). Anyhow, I went to see Lyne, and he, knowing that paint, or the lack of it, was always a difficulty in destroyers, said I could have any paint I wanted and could get away. This was far too good a chance to be missed, so I told our storekeeper, a most excellent Stoker Petty Officer. During the dinner-hour one day he boarded the *Triumph* with about a dozen stokers, and came away with each man bearing a large drum of paint or enamel. He had not gone far on his way round the basin to the *Scorpion* when he was stopped by a dockyard policeman.

"What's going on here?" the constable demanded, very suspicious.

The Stoker Petty Officer was a man of ready wit. "That's all right, sergeant," said he without batting an eyelid. "It's like this. These men are all in the rattle. They're defaulters."

"Defaulters?" said the policeman. "How d'you mean."

"Yesterday these chaps were painting the *Scorpion's* funnels," he was told. "They dropped paint all over the upper deck, so as a punishment the captain ordered that they should each spend their dinner-hour carrying a drum of paint round the basin. I'm in charge of 'em to see there's no shirking."

"Huh!" the constable grunted. "Your captain must be a very funny man."

'Funny isn't the word for it," the Stoker Petty Officer returned. "He's a proper tiger, I give you my word!"

S'o all through the dinner-hour the procession continued with pauses to collect paint from the *Triumph* and unload it in the *Scorpion*. We did well out of that transaction.

Our work and training continued until, in September, rumours began to spread about that the 'Beagles' were to be sent to the Mediterranean. Sure enough orders soon came for us to disperse to our home ports to fit out with awnings and other hot-weather gear. Before we left all the commanding officers were sent for by the Commodore, Lambert. He told us that we had had such a gruelling three years in the North Sea that we might all go out to the Mediterranean in our ships; but that he would only allow us to remain there for a year. After that we should be sent home to command the new destroyers that would then be commissioning for service at home.

Most of us were delighted with the idea of the Mediterranean even for a short spell; but thus it came about that all Commodore Lambert's most experienced North Sea destroyer captains were caught in the Mediterranean on the outbreak of war in August, 1914. Some of them came home; but there, personally, I was to remain, still in command of the *Scorpion*, until January, 1918.

CHAPTER V

I

WE arrived in the Mediterranean in November, 1913. Commander G. R. L. Edwards, in the *Wolverine*, took the whole flotilla of sixteen of us out to Malta, and there turned over to Commander Osmond J. Prentis, who was to be our Commander (D) until Captain C. P. R. Coode became Captain (D) in the *Blenheim* at the end of February, 1914. We were all very sorry to see Edwards go. His overwhelming sense of humour; his cheerfulness and unorthodox methods in getting a job done, had endeared him to us all.

Prentis was a large, burly man, and the *Scorpion*, being commanded by one of the most junior captains in the flotilla, was put into the *Wolverine's* sub-division. This was the start of a great partnership between our two ships which lasted until the *Wolverine* went home in 1917. With others, Prentis was killed on his bridge by a shell from a Turkish gun during our minesweeping operations off Gallipoli in April, 1915. I shall deal with this later in more detail; but we much admired Prentis's persistence in maintaining the object. At times, when we were being literally plastered with shells from the Asiatic batteries, he held on to his signal to slip sweeps, turn and run out of the Straits until it seemed almost madness. Prentis's successor in the *Wolverine* was Adrian St. Vincent Keyes, who had been a term-mate of mine in the *Britannia*.

The Mediterranean Fleet was under the command of Admiral Sir Archibald Berkeley Milne, and consisted of the battle-cruisers *Inflexible*, flagship, *Indomitable*, and *Indefatigable*; the four armoured cruisers *Defence*, *Duke of Edinburgh*, *Black Prince* and *Warrior* under the command of Rear-Admiral E. C. T. Troubridge; four smaller cruisers *Dublin*, *Gloucester*, *Chatham* and *Weymouth*; and our flotilla of sixteen 'Beagle' class destroyers.

Malta as usual was very gay, with dances, at homes, picnics and everything else. But I disliked the social whirl, and spent most of my spare time playing golf and sailing. In the spring of 1914 we went for a cruise to the Italian coast, and March found the whole fleet at Naples. My mother and her two sisters were spending the winter there, and knowing something of the place through previous visits I was able to show them some of the sights.

Our new Captain (D), C. P. R. Coode, who joined the flotilla in February, was a man of strong character who demanded, and obtained, a very high standard. We liked him, particularly as he allowed no one to bully us but himself. He very soon turned his attention to the matter of coaling, in which, to tell the truth, we had not been greatly interested. Regarded as a periodical and laborious penance which had to be undergone somehow, thirty or forty tons an hour from a collier was regarded as sufficient.

Coode, however, started fierce competition. War, he realized, was soon coming, and in our flotilla rapid coaling made all the difference in the time we could spend at sea. The results and order of merit were published each month in flotilla orders, and the rules were strict enough. Times and averages were worked out from the first hawser being secured on board the collier to the last hawser being cast off. There was no disputing the referee, the signal boatswain of the *Blenheim*, who lived with a telescope glued to his eye.

My excellent and experienced ship's company took to the work with enthusiasm, and the *Scorpion* was soon in the first two or three in the monthly records. Our chief rival was the *Harpy*, commanded by Gerald Dickens. Thanks to this peace-time competition some quite astonishing performances were put up during the war. The undisputed record was the *Scorpion's*, 120 tons an hour from a collier, every pound of which had to be shovelled into two-hundredweight bags by hand, hoisted on board, and emptied into our bunkers. Ninety to a hundred tons an hour was quite common in the flotilla; but it required minute organization and a buoyant ship's company. Our total complement was just short of 100, and every officer and man had to pull his bit.

Between March and the outbreak of war in August, 1914, the flotilla visited Corfu, the Ægean Islands and the Eastern Mediterranean. Beyond the fact that the *Scorpion* was inspected at Port Said in June the day after coaling hard all the previous afternoon, I remember few details. I protested to Captain Coode; but he was adamant. We had to work half the night and from early dawn to get the ship even tolerably clean and tidy. Coode made allowances, no doubt; but I think he did it to put us on our mettle.

Towards the end of July the flagship *Inflexible*, with the *Indefatigable*, *Warrior*, *Black Prince*, *Chatham*, *Dublin*, *Gloucester*, *Weymouth* and fourteen destroyers were at Alexandria. War had started to boil up, and on July 28th we hurriedly sailed for Malta, arriving there on the 30th. The warning telegram had arrived, and we at once filled up with coal and stores. Then, on a peaceful Sunday afternoon—it must have been on August 2nd—when most of the men were ashore on leave, we had sudden orders to raise steam with all despatch.

We sailed next day at about noon, to patrol for a short time outside Malta. War had not been declared; but we were all ready, with warheads on the torpedoes and ammunition up for all the guns.

Orders to start hostilities against Germany did not reach the Commander in-Chief until 1.15 a.m. on August 5th, and ourselves a little later.

II

After patrolling off Malta we returned thither, filled up with coal, and sailed again at once, my half of the flotilla—eight destroyers—being ordered to patrol the entrance to the Adriatic to watch for the Austrian fleet. Italy had declared her neutrality, and orders that the Italian coast was not to be approached within six miles, coupled with conflicting wireless signals as to whether or not we were at war with Austria, seemed to make our Adriatic patrol a singularly unprofitable undertaking. All the time we were expecting a collier in an adjacent Greek harbour, Port Vathi in the island of Ithaca; but no collier appeared.

We heard various wireless reports of the *Goeben* and *Breslau*, and were expecting them to break through into the Adriatic. Rear-Admiral Troubridge's four armoured cruisers were to the southward of us, and on the evening of the 6th the excitement began. The *Goeben* and *Breslau* had sailed south from Messina, and were being shadowed by the *Gloucester*. After rounding the toe of Italy they steered north-easterly towards the Adriatic. The *Dublin*, with the two destroyers *Beagle* and *Bulldog* were coming at full speed from Malta to intercept.

That night we joined Admiral Troubridge's four cruisers, and soon after midnight—August 6th–7th—we all altered course to the south and went on at 19 knots, which was about the cruisers' full speed. We heard later that this was because the *Goeben* and *Breslau* had altered course to the south-east, making for Cape Matapan. We were steering to cut them off, and during the night had a signal from the *Defence* saying that the squadron would probably be in action at 6 a.m., which thrilled us to the marrow.

Meanwhile, thanks to the non-arrival of our collier at Port Vathi, Ithaca, destroyer after destroyer kept dropping off through lack of coal and had to go and anchor in some Greek harbour or another until a collier turned up. It was exasperating. By daylight the *Scorpion* had no more than 55 tons left, the most of any; but only three of us were left in company.

It was at about daylight that we had another signal to say that Admiral Troubridge had decided to abandon the chase. I will not comment on this decision. It later formed the subject of a court-martial; but even at that time we all wondered what had happened to our battle-cruisers. We heard later they were steaming towards Malta from the west at very moderate speed!

The four armoured cruisers and we three destroyers steamed into a bay in the south of the island of Zante, where we arrived at 10 a.m. on August 7th. Here the destroyers were ordered to coal alongside the cruisers.

After this most disappointing episode the destroyers gathered at Port Vathi, Ithaca, where our collier had at last arrived. She had correctly been ordered to Port Vathi; but instead of going to the place of that name in

Ithaca, on the west coast of Greece, had gaily gone to Port Vathi, in Samos, some 350 miles away as the gull flies in the Ægean off the coast of Asia Minor! Someone had blundered badly.

And whoever had chartered that wretched ship as a wartime collier for men-of-war, let alone for destroyers, deserved to suffer death by slow strangulation. A foreigner, and commanded by a foreigner, she was an ancient tramp steamer without steam winches and nothing more than a couple of hand cranes, each capable of lifting about half-a-ton, to each hold. One remembers that her captain, a paunchy, oleaginous, dark-skinned fellow, came up to Captain Coode, who was in the *Wolverine*, with a sweet smile and explained in broken English with much gesticulation that the Admiralty had chartered his noble steamer to coal the Mediterranean destroyers for the whole period of the war. Coode, who was a master of nautical invective, told the gallant gentleman to think again. His ship would not be required for any naval purpose whatsoever. That same night a wireless signal went home to the Admiralty announcing in forthright terms what Captain (D) thought of the Admiralty's arrangements for coaling his destroyers. We never saw that collier again.

After completing our coaling, we destroyers joined up with the *Defence* alone for an operation by the French fleet against the Austrian fleet in the Adriatic, it apparently now having been definitely decided that we were at war with Austria. As we saw it, a part of the Austrian fleet was blockading the coast of Montenegro near Scutari, and the French Admiral's idea was to take his battleships into the Adriatic and up the Italian coast by night without lights, and then to cross the Adriatic and sweep down from the north. Admiral Troubridge in the *Defence*, with some French cruisers and we destroyers, was to close the trap from the southward.

Most of the night of August 14th–15th, we were kept in a state of alarm by flotilla after flotilla of French destroyers, of which we had no information whatsoever, passing us to starboard. They were lucky not to be fired upon. When daylight came the whole horizon was covered with French tricolours. We could only just see the topmasts of the main fleet of some twelve battleships and several cruisers over the horizon; but they had all hoisted their largest ensigns at the masthead. It was certainly a most inspiring sight. However, the trap only closed on one small Austrian cruiser called the *Zenta*, and two or three torpedo craft. The latter escaped inshore; but the *Zenta* was soon brought to a standstill by salvos from the French dreadnoughts *Courbet* and *Jean Bart*. She refused to surrender, and in a few minutes burst into flame and blew up. Rear-Admiral Troubridge asked the French Admiral, Boué de Lapeyrère, if he might send in his destroyers to save the swimming Austrians; but was told it was "now too late". It was not a very glorious victory, and we were not sorry when we heard later that most of the *Zenta's* crew had managed to escape ashore.

A few hours later we parted company with the French and steamed down the west coast of Greece and through the Ægean to the entrance to the Dardanelles, up which it was now confirmed that the *Goeben* and *Breslau* had passed on their way to Constantinople. We got there on August 7th, and from then until October 31st, when Turkey came into the war against us, we had as dreary a time as any I have ever experienced. Half the flotilla was recalled for more active work in Home Waters; but to my regret, at the time, the *Scorpion* was one of those destroyers chosen to remain in the Mediterranean.

We patrolled the entrance to the Dardanelles, two days on and two off, boarding and inspecting all steamers entering or leaving. We had no really sheltered anchorage for coaling or resting. When the wind was northerly we anchored the south side of Tenedos island, and vice versa. It was very unusual for our notice for steam to be longer than two hours, and coal-fired boilers did not require the periodical four-day 'boiler clean' required by the oil-burners. Life was dreary indeed until our depot ship, the *Blenheim*, arrived from Malta to look after us; but presently we started collecting quite a fleet— the six 'River' class destroyers from China, *Chelmer*, *Colne*, *Garry*, *Ribble*, *Usk* and *Wear*; three old French destroyers; some of our own submarines and two or three French ones.

We rarely got ashore, and even when we did there was nothing to do. To while away the time some of our more literary-minded people started a monthly paper called *The Tenedos Times*, which was typed and issued monthly from Captain (D)'s office. It had three editors, each in his own way of considerable ability—Gerald Dickens, captain of the *Harpy* and a grandson of the novelist, Charles Dickens; J. B. Waterlow, first lieutenant-commander and flotilla gunnery officer of the *Blenheim*, later killed as commander of the cruiser *Black Prince* at Jutland; and R. T. Amedroz, captain of the *Grasshopper* who was very talented with his pencil. I am not competent to judge the merit of our newspaper; but everyone contributed something and it provided much amusement.

III

On September 21st, Vice-Admiral Sackville H. Carden, who was Admiral Superintendent of Malta Dockyard, was ordered to assume command of the squadron off the Dardanelles with his flag in the *Indefatigable*. He had also the *Indomitable*, with two French battleships, the British light cruisers *Dublin* and *Gloucester*, and the destroyers and other ships already mentioned.

War was declared against Turkey on October 31st; but forty-eight hours beforehand information was received that a Turkish ship was being fitted out as a minelayer in a small port called Vourlah, in the Gulf of Smyrna. The

Wolverine and *Scorpion* were sent to deal with the matter, and we duly arrived off the entrance to Vourlah at daylight. Sure enough at the head of the bay was a fine yacht of about 500 tons. Whether or not she was a minelayer I do not know; but she certainly had two guns mounted. As war had not been declared we retired to seaward and asked for instructions by wireless, to be ordered to make her surrender or destroy her. So back we went into the bay, and the *Wolverine* signalled for someone to come out and talk. A Turkish lieutenant came out in a four-oared boat.

The conversations apparently did not go well, for the Turk left the *Wolverine* in a hurry and when halfway ashore waved his hand. Instantly the supposed minelayer broke into flames forward and aft, and we helped the conflagration with a few well-placed rounds of lyddite. The *Scorpion's* first shell burst at the base of the funnel, which caused it to take wings and land on the roof of a house, which promptly collapsed. It was a pity that our first instructions were not more precise, for it would have been an easy matter to cut her out and bring her away when we first entered the harbour. As it was, a battery of horse artillery clattered on to the jetty as we made our departure, though we were apparently out of range and they did not open fire.

An amusing incident happened at another small place where the *Mosquito* went for some purpose or another and sent her whaler ashore. A Turkish officer came riding full pelt down the jetty, pulled up suddenly, and shot gracefully over the bows of his charger head first into the sea, whence he was retrieved by the *Mosquito's* whaler.

There was a long-range bombardment of the outer Dardanelles forts at daylight on November 3rd. Admiral Carden with the *Indefatigable* and *Indomitable* took on the forts on the tip of the Gallipoli peninsula, and the French battleships those on the Asiatic side. We claimed to have done considerable damage, to have demoralized the Turks and blown up a magazine; but in the light of after events I think we erred on the side of optimism.

War with Turkey made little difference to the destroyer patrol off the Dardanelles, except that it was tightened up by the addition of either the *Dublin* or *Gloucester*. One did not steam within range of the batteries by day without good reason; but the Turks adopted a live and let live policy, and seldom opened fire. When they did, it was not very dangerous.

The weather that winter was certainly a sharp surprise to those who had regarded the Ægean as an area of warmth and calm seas. Strong south-westerly winds with a fairly heavy sea nearly always prevailed, though occasionally we had three or four days of north-easterly blizzards with sleet and snow, as bad, and as bitterly cold, as anything I ever saw in the North Sea. It was difficult to keep one's accurate patrol position day and night with a visibility of no more than 25 yards, and some destroyers had narrow escapes of running ashore. At long intervals destroyers were sent to Kondia, the bay next to Mudros, in Lemnos, for 48 hours rest; but it was not until early December that the *Scorpion* and some of the other destroyers were ordered to Malta for ten days' relaxation and refit and the fitting of voice-pipe fire control to our guns. The respite was very welcome, though needless to remark both officers and men ran a bit wild. The palm went to the sub-lieutenant of the *Grasshopper*, an irrepressible young man, who drove round the island half one night shooting at dogs with a service revolver. His prank made him most unpopular with the authorities.

However, our stay at Malta was all too short, and we were back at Tenedos with the Christmas mail and in time for another spell of the dreary and monotonous patrolling.

Towards the end of January came rumours of a naval attack on the Dardanelles. The 'River' class destroyers were fitted out as minesweepers, and very soon, as more and more ships began to appear, the rumours became a certainty.

The *Indefatigable* and *Indomitable* had gone home, and Vice-Admiral Carden's flag was now flying in the *Inflexible*, fresh from the battle of the Falklands. The *Agamemnon* appeared, with the old battleship *Vengeance*, flying the flag of Rear-Admiral John de Robeck, second in command, and the *Albion, Cornwallis, Irresistible* and *Triumph*. There were four French battleships under Admiral Guépratte, the *Suffren, Bouvet, Charlemagne* and *Gaulois*, and later on we were also joined by the battleships *Lord Nelson, Canopus, Ocean, Swiftsure, Majestic* and *Prince George*, the two last well over twenty years old.

The idea, as we understood it, was to be a step-by-step advance with the forts being silenced by gunfire from the battleships as we progressed. The 'River' class destroyers were to sweep ahead of the bombarding ships, while our flotilla hovered around making themselves generally useful. It sounded just too easy; but few of us in the destroyers had all that touching faith in naval gunnery.

The great day arrived on February 19th, and at 9.50 a.m. a fleet of twelve great ships started bombarding the outer forts at both sides of the Dardanelles from a range outside that of the Turkish guns. The morning was flat calm with hardly a breath of wind, and the spectacle, as I remember it, was immensely impressive. The shooting appeared to be fairly good. The forts seemed to be hit repeatedly, and made no reply. Then, at about 2 p.m., when de Robeck was ordered to take in his five old battleships and finish them off at close range, they suddenly came to life and opened fire, though without much result. I cannot remember the exact time; but the French ships, making clouds of smoke, went in to support. The battle went on until nearly sunset, when all ships were recalled by Vice-Admiral Carden in the *Inflexible*. De Robeck came out flying a signal "Permission to continue the action"; but it was not approved.

The net result of a considerable expenditure of ammunition was precisely nothing, apart, perhaps, from killing a few Turks. Really to knock out the forts it was necessary to get direct hits on the guns or their mountings.

I remember that just before sunset that evening we were thrilled by the appearance of a large ship on the horizon. She closed, and at first we took her for one of the dummy battleships, which the Admiralty had produced to hoodwink the Germans. But when she came nearer we saw she was the real thing, the brand-new *Queen Elizabeth* with her 15-inch guns.

The next day the weather broke, and further operations were held up by a gale. On February 25th, however, when the weather had moderated, the modern guns in the forts at each side of the entrance were successfully knocked out by deliberate fire at 12,000 yards by the *Queen Elizabeth*, *Agamemnon*, *Irresistible* and *Gaulois*, with other ships observing from the flank. During the afternoon the battleships closed in to short range and just hammered the forts to pieces. On our side only the *Agamemnon* was hit, with trifling casualties.

That evening the trawlers entered the Straits and began their sweeping. The destroyers went in to cover them, and I remember that by daylight next morning, the 26th, we had swept a wide channel about four miles up from the entrance and had found no mines. It was on this day, I think, that landing parties of seamen and marines from the battleships were put ashore by destroyers to complete the destruction of the guns at Sedd-el-Bahr, near Cape Helles on the Gallipoli peninsula, and at two forts near Kum Kale, on the Asiatic shore opposite. The landing parties were not seriously opposed, and got back to their ships with a loss of nine killed and wounded, having destroyed with explosives, or found disabled, nearly fifty guns of various sizes. This was the occasion when the *Irresistible's* marines got as far as Krithia, a village 4 miles from Sedd-el-Bahr at the foot of the steep hill called Achi Baba, which dominated the peninsula. It was the only time our troops ever reached that village.

The minesweeping continued, and some of the older battleships steamed up into the swept area and bombarded the inner forts at long range. The guns in the forts made no effective reply; but the bombarding ships were somewhat annoyed by mobile howitzers well concealed on either shore. At first, in the destroyers, when we were fired at, we instinctively moved quickly and thought the ship was certain to be hit. But in a very short time we came to realize that the percentage of hits to rounds fired was very small. The sailors became strangely phlegmatic. I remember a Leading Torpedo-man called Love sitting on the upper deck reading a Wild West thriller in the sun. A shell from a big Turkish gun landed quite close with the usual heavy explosion and upheaval of spray and smoke. Love looked up and remarked: "Another redskin bit the dust," and calmly resumed his reading.

We attended on ships bombarding from inside the Straits during the day, occasionally firing at field guns or any other likely targets, and at night went up to cover the trawlers while they swept the mines, or tried to. It was interesting to watch the big ships in action. Johnny Turk, who could not resist the far larger target of a battleship, seldom fired at us, and from a distance of a few cables we could watch shell bursting and literally rattling on the battleship's armoured sides.

Bad weather, with a strong north-easterly gale, heavy rain and low visibility again held up operations inside the Straits until March 1st, when the bombardment was resumed by six battleships engaging the inner defences. This was the day, I remember, when our whaler had been sent ashore to destroy a fishing-boat in Morto Bay, just east of Sedd-el-Bahr. They were pouring paraffin into her to set her on fire, when down the valley leading to the beach came a considerable body of Turks, about a battalion. With the flash of our first gun at a few hundred yards they turned and bolted like rabbits. We put several shell in among them as they sped.

That night the light cruiser *Amethyst*, with our Captain Coode on board, went up towards the Narrows in support of the destroyers and sweepers. At about 11 p.m., when the whole party were within 3,000 yards of Kephez Point, about eight miles from the entrance and just short of the Narrows and the lines of Turkish mines, they came under the rays of a searchlight. More lights came on, and the minefield batteries on each side of the Straits promptly opened fire. The trawlers had to slip their sweeps and retire. Steaming ahead, the destroyers made all the smoke they could, firing all they knew at the gun flashes and searchlights. The action went on for half-an-hour. Shell pitched all around the trawlers; but by some miracle they got away undamaged.

Covering the sweepers was distinctly nasty, and all sorts of Turkish guns let us have it. Occasionally there was a heavy sort of splodge in the water with a sound quite unlike that of an ordinary shell. Some people said that the Turks were loading their ancient muzzle-loaders with the huge, spherical stone shot, samples of which we later found at Sedd-el-Bahr. All the same, as the days went on, the morale of the Turks improved, and so did their shooting.

The trawlers, with their sweeps running, were far too slow to make appreciable headway against the strong current. Once lit up by the searchlights they became sitting targets at a range of about a mile for every enemy gun that would bear, and more guns were being mounted every day. Moreover the trawlers were manned by ex-fishermen who, quite naturally, were unaccustomed to facing heavy gunfire in their helpless and practically motionless little ships.

The task was repeated night after night, but never with success. Really fast sweepers might have done the job; but the trawlers were much too slow. We were faced with a sort of stalemate. It seemed that until the minefield batteries could be expurgated, they could prevent minesweeping in the Narrows. The batteries could not be knocked out by long-range or indirect gunfire from the ships. They must come close enough inshore to obliterate the shore artillery with every gun they had; but could not accomplish this until the mines were cleared. I believe that as early as March 3rd, Rear-Admiral de Robeck, commanding the inshore squadron, had reported that in his opinion the Straits could not be forced unless one shore or the other were occupied.

On the night of March 10th–11th, the trawlers were ordered to steam up past Kephez Point, to turn, pass their sweeps, and come down with the current. They were to be supported by the old battleship *Canopus*, the *Amethyst* and destroyers.

The *Canopus* went in first and shot up the five searchlights seen to be at work from just below the minefield. She came under heavy but rather wild fire; but for all the good she did she might have been firing at the moon. The lights were extinguished now and then for a few minutes, and then came on again. After this bombardment there was a pause of two hours to give the Turks the idea that operations had ceased for the night. Then seven trawlers steamed up in line ahead, and by great good luck managed to get past Kephez Point, turn, and pass their sweeps while a searchlight was temporarily doused. The leading pair caught mines almost at once, and a trawler was blown up and sunk. The instant the explosion was heard ashore the whole area became bathed in the glare of searchlights almost as bright as daylight, and every shore gun that would bear opened fire. The *Amethyst* and destroyers did their utmost to shoot out the searchlights; but without success. There was nothing for it but to call the operation off.

The same scheme was tried the next night, March 11th–12th, though this time without a battleship in support, as some people thought that the presence of a big ship merely warned the enemy of what was coming. It was no more successful than before.

Orders were now given that the trawler crews were to be stiffened up by regular naval personnel. Each trawler was to have a commissioned officer, in command, with a junior officer, a petty officer and a signalman. There were plenty of volunteers, and the sweeping was ordered to be carried out regardless of cost. "The turning of the corner at Chanak," Vice-Admiral Carden had been told by the Admiralty, "may decide the whole operation and produce consequences of a decisive character upon the war. . . ." This was obvious enough to everyone on the spot, but in the meanwhile everything depended upon the clearing of a channel through the Kephez minefield.

And so, on the night of March 13th–14th, the battleship *Cornwallis* entered the Straits and spent one hour from midnight pounding the searchlights and minefield batteries. At 2 a.m. the *Amethyst* and destroyers closed in and engaged, and at 3 a.m. seven trawlers, accompanied by five picquet boats provided with explosive creeps, steamed up in single line. The enemy was fully awake. Two brilliant searchlights were illuminating the approach. The Turks allowed the sweepers to get into the middle of the minefield on their way up, contenting themselves by firing an occasional single gun. Then the searchlights went out for a moment, and flashed on again. It was evidently a prearranged signal, for at once every gun opened fire.

Followed by a storm of shell the trawlers held on to the turning point, which was roughly a mile above Kephez Point, then swung round and tried to pass their sweeps. They had pressed on with the greatest gallantry; but had already suffered severely. Two had had their entire working crews killed or wounded. Hit by every sort of shell from 6-inch downwards, minesweeping kites were demolished, sweep wires cut, and winches smashed. Only two were fit for sweeping, and they got several mines. I believe no trawlers were actually sunk; but four were put out of action. Lieutenant-Commander J. B. Waterlow, of the *Blenheim*, was in command of all the sweepers that night. Lieutenant-Commander E. G. Robinson, a class and term-mate of mine in the *Britannia*, from the *Vengeance*, commanded one of them. 'Kipper' Robinson, as he was known to his friends, had his trawler hit 84 times. On three separate and distinct occasions in the Dardanelles he greatly distinguished himself and was awarded the Victoria Cross, besides being specially promoted to the rank of commander.

When the sweepers went up, the *Amethyst*, which was an unarmoured, 3,000-ton light cruiser, remained on the edge of the minefield to fire on the searchlights and cover the retirement. At about 4 a.m. she was hit by a large shell which burst near the stokers' bathroom, where the men of the middle watch were washing before going below to turn in. The ship was badly knocked about, and had 24 killed and 36 wounded.

I have rather concentrated on the minesweeping, which at that time was our major responsibility. But on March 4th, under cover of the *Wolverine*, *Scorpion* and one battleship, about 300 marines were put ashore on Kum Kale, on the Asiatic shore at the entrance to the Dardanelles, to cover a demolition party of sailors under 'Kipper' Robinson who were to make certain that all the guns in Orkanie Fort were destroyed. This they succeeded in doing. The Turks, however, had been reinforced and the landing party became involved in stiff fighting, in which they were outnumbered and incurred heavy casualties. During this battle we closed the mouth of the Mendere River, just to the east of Kum Kale, located and shelled a battery that was firing shrapnel at our men ashore, and attended also to the Turkish snipers. Most of our landing party got back; but some were cut off from the landing-place, and in the evening we saw them coming back along the shore, being badly shot up. After dark the *Wolverine* and *Scorpion* were ordered to send in their whalers to bring off any survivors. Our whaler went in in charge of Mr. W. W. Thorrowgood, Gunner (T), who had spent several hours sharpening a service cutlass to a razor edge, and was further armed with two revolvers. When they reached the beach they found a nasty little sea, which made things rather difficult. The gunner ordered the crew over the side into the water to hold the boat off the shore. One weak vessel demurred, whereupon Thorrowgood seized and flung him into the sea, which clinched the argument!

Our boat pulled twice into the shore under heavy rifle fire and brought off two officers and eleven men, of whom two were wounded. She searched the beach for two hours. It was a gallant piece of work which won Thorrowgood the Distinguished Service Cross and his eight seamen Distinguished Service Medals.

The trawlers having been failures as minesweepers it was decided to fit out our destroyers. We had the old pattern A sweep with 9-foot kites, and could sweep at 14–15 knots, or faster if the danger of parting the sweep was accepted. It did not take us more than a week or two to become efficient.

Meanwhile, we did not seem to be getting any nearer our objective of forcing the Straits. On March 16th, Vice-Admiral Sackville Carden's health broke down, and Vice-Admiral John de Robeck took over the command. In point of fact, Rosslyn Wemyss, my old captain in the *Suffolk*, was Rear-Admiral in charge at Mudros and senior to de Robeck. With characteristic magnanimity he volunteered to serve under de Robeck's orders.

Transports with troops on board were already arriving at Mudros. A full-scale landing was clearly contemplated.

IV

On March 18th came the great naval attack on the forts in the Narrows, in which something like eighteen battleships were engaged. Since our division of destroyers was anchored off Tenedos, we saw nothing of the action.

However, I have never understood why we, the eight 'Beagle' class destroyers, which were fully efficient as fast minesweepers, were not used on that day. Half of us spent it lying at anchor, and, with the distant thunder of guns in our ears, champing with impatience. Captain Coode, who had been put in charge of the minesweeping, later told me he had only guaranteed clear water up to limits which were far short of where some of the bombarding battleships went. If we had been used we might have helped to prevent the loss through mines of the *Irresistible*, *Ocean* and *Bouvet*, and the heavy damage to the *Inflexible*. Instead of that we spent the afternoon playing bridge, listening to the bombardment and intercepting wireless reports as to the progress of the action. It was exasperating, to say the least.

In the evening we were ordered to shift berth to make way for the *Inflexible*, which had been mined and badly damaged, to anchor in shallow water. Soon afterwards she appeared, with her forecastle nearly level with the water and the ship's company mustered aft on the quarterdeck.

A little later we weighed and proceeded, to spend the night in the Straits looking for the *Irresistible* and *Ocean*, which had been mined and abandoned, but had not been seen to sink. Not a trace of them could be found. Both these old battleships had gone to the bottom.

The negligible results achieved and losses sustained in this action put an end to the purely naval attempts to force the Dardanelles. If guns alone had provided the defence, the battleships might have forced their way through the Narrows by accepting casualties. But the primary defence was ten lines of nearly 400 mines between Kephez and Chanak, while the mines which caused the losses on March 18th had been laid by a small Turkish vessel called the *Nousret*. Four were swept up; but the rest remained undiscovered and unsuspected for ten days. These mines thus played what Mr. Winston Churchill afterwards called "a recognizable part in the history of the Great War".

In December, 1914, Submarine B.11, commanded by Lieutenant Holbrook, successfully passed under the mines in the Narrows, and torpedoed the old Turkish cruiser *Messudieh* lying in the bay between Nagara and Kephez. It was a most gallant effort, which earned Holbrook the Victoria Cross. Later, it was decided to send submarines right through into the Sea of Marmora in connection with our impending landing, the main idea being to prevent Turkish reinforcements being sent to Gallipoli by sea. The *Scorpion* was indirectly mixed up in one or two of these adventures.

On April 17th Submarine E.15, Lieutenant-Commander Theodore S. Brodie, ran ashore in Kephez Bay near Fort Dardanos. Brodie was killed and most of his crew captured, and reconnaissance from the air showed that the boat was in the hands of the Turks. Then came the task of destroying her, so that she could not be used against us. The first attempt was made by bombardment by a battleship, which was inaccurate and unsuccessful. Then one of our submarines was sent up to torpedo E.15, but though torpedoes were fired, they failed to hit. Next, the *Scorpion* was sent up that same night to destroy E.15 with a torpedo, and we had on board Lieutenant-Commander Charles G. Brodie, twin brother of the Brodie of E.15. It was a tragic duty for him.

We lay a mile or two inside the entrance waiting for the light to get right. We were having our evening meal when we heard 'bump-bump-bump' alongside, so hurriedly rushed on deck, thinking it was a mine. There, nosing down the side, was a torpedo. We sent Mr. Thorrowgood, the Gunner (T), away in the dinghy to deal with it, and in the darkness astern heard sounds of frantic hammering coupled with much lurid language. Thorrowgood, who feared nothing, returned in triumph with the torpedo, from which he had already extracted the pistol. It was B.2's torpedo fired that afternoon at E.15, and had drifted down with the current.

Then up we went in the darkness and failed to find E.15, though we steamed some miles above her reported position and got heavily fired upon from all directions for our trouble. The failure of the Turks to hit the destroyers always surprised me. One felt very naked and vulnerable with shell plopping and bursting in the sea in all directions.

As a final effort to destroy E.15 Lieutenant-Commander E. G. Robinson, 'Kipper' Robinson, was put in charge of two picquet boats fitted with torpedoes in dropping gear. The *Scorpion* was again sent up in support, and once more

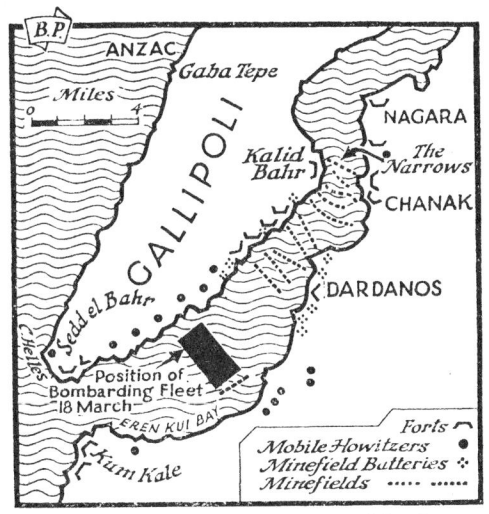

DEFENCES OF THE DARDANELLES, March 1915

the Turkish fire was very heavy. One of the picquet boats was sunk; but the other found and fired at E.15 and claimed to have hit her. Robinson's party came back in triumph having picked up the crew of the sunken picquet boat. It was this exploit with the others I have mentioned, that earned Robinson the Victoria Cross, and well he deserved it.

I say the picquet boat 'claimed' to have hit E.15 for the following reason. On the night of May 12th, seventeen days after the landing, the old battleship *Goliath* was sunk in Morto Bay, just to the east of Sedd-el-Bahr, by a 33-knot, 600-ton Turkish destroyer manned by Germans. At the time this happened the *Wolverine* and *Scorpion* were patrolling in Eren Keui Bay, on the Asiatic side of the Straits. We intercepted a wireless signal in German saying that a *linienschiffe*—battleship—had been sunk and that the destroyer responsible was retiring.

We raced up to the Narrows to cut her off, intercepting other wireless signals on the way, one of them urgently demanding that the searchlights should be extinguished. We reached Kephez Bay, where I suddenly had a signal by shaded lamp from the *Wolverine*, Lieutenant-Commander Adrian Keyes—"Submarine in sight to starboard. Am about to ram". Next I saw a boil of white water under the *Wolverine's* tail as she went full speed astern. And there, full in the glare of the Turkish searchlights, in surface trim and apparently undamaged, was E.15. Then the heavens opened up with guns of every calibre, and we came out of it in a hurry.

Keyes was an ex-submarine officer. What had happened was that he had just taken the submarine for a German U-boat, of whose arrival in the Dardanelles there were plenty of rumours. Then, just in time, he recognized E.15. She was ashore in about 2½ fathoms and had been stripped. In the hasty look we had at her in the intermittent rays of the searchlights we saw no signs of the disintegration that would have been caused by a direct hit from a torpedo. This, of course, does not rule out underwater damage from Robinson's torpedo attack. I believe that the destroyer responsible for sinking the *Goliath* did not return through the Narrows; but gave it up as a bad job, went out of the Straits, and got to Smyrna.

For one reason or another the purely naval attack on March 18th had failed, and preparations were in hand for an amphibious assault on the peninsula. We destroyers were still kept hard at it—minesweeping, patrolling, interfering with the Turkish working parties that we could hear improving the defences and digging trenches at night. Their labours were often interrupted by the sudden glare of a searchlight from seaward followed by a burst of gunfire from everything we had.

As the Greeks had now been prevailed upon to let us use the fine harbour at Mudros, we got a little more rest in harbour and could occasionally let our boiler fires die out. Fresh food was short, and as often as not we were on 'Bare Navy', of which the staple ingredients were bully beef and biscuit. I remember on one occasion embarking Vice-Admiral John de Robeck, George Hope, captain of the *Queen Elizabeth*, and some of the staff, to take them along the peninsula to see what work the Turks were doing to their defences. As lunch-time drew near I became rather fussed, and sent down to enquire what we had to offer the distinguished party. I found we were at our lowest ebb. All we had was a bully beef and rice cottage pie—we had no potatoes—and a rice pudding made, of course, with condensed milk. However, at the right time I asked John de Robeck if he would like his lunch now, and was immensely relieved when he replied: "That's all right, Cunningham. We've brought our food with us. We'll eat it in the chart-house."

That night on our return to Mudros the *Scorpion* was ordered to anchor near the *Queen Elizabeth*, and I was invited to dinner with the Vice-Admiral. We were to sail at 7 a.m. next morning. Just before we weighed the Vice-

Admiral's barge came alongside with a large box for me, which on being opened produced chickens, loaves of bread, butter and all manner of things that I cannot remember now. I heard afterwards that during a quiet interval on board the *Scorpion* de Robeck had penetrated to our galley and talked to the cooks, who had told him, with perfect truth, that we were almost as bare as Mother Hubbard's cupboard.

After this incident we became rather better off in the way of fresh bread, meat and vegetables. Can one wonder how greatly John de Robeck was liked and admired for this and many other little acts, of kind thoughtfulness?

CHAPTER VI

I

By about the middle of March, 1915, Mudros had become the scene of great activity, though we destroyers did not see much of it. Large transports filled with troops were constantly arriving, and then returning to Egypt to be re-stowed for the assault. Great camps for British, Australian, New Zealand, Indian and French troops were set up on shore.

To us in the destroyers who every night patrolled the intended landing beaches and heard the enemy driving in stakes, putting in barbed wire, and digging trenches, the delay was just asking for trouble. There was no doubt that the Turks had been thrown off their balance by the naval bombardment of March 18th, and to give them several weeks for defensive preparations seemed to us to be most unwise. I know that Captain Coode took good care that what his destroyers saw and heard each night was duly represented in the highest quarters; but, as it afterwards appeared, no preparations had been made for landing the troops under fire, and it was an operation which required the most intricate organization. One heard that the guns were in one transport, the ammunition in another, the vehicles in a third, and the machine-guns somewhere else. All the troops and their voluminous stores and equipment had to be disembarked, re-sorted and re-embarked before they could take part in an opposed landing. Mudros offered none of the necessary facilities. The only place where these necessary preparations could be carried out was Alexandria.

However, it is no part of my business to go into the details of an operation which has already been fully described and investigated. I shall confine myself to what we saw from a destroyer of the great combined operation that was launched on April 25th.

To nine of the 'Beagle' class destroyers was given the task of sweeping for mines inside the Straits so as to allow battleships to come up on the right flank of the Army landed on the Gallipoli peninsula. These heavy ships were to smother the Turkish defences and any counter-attacks with their gunfire to facilitate the advance of our troops. The minesweeping destroyers were the *Wolverine*, Commander O. J. Prentis; the *Scorpion*, commanded by myself; *Mosquito*, Lieutenant-Commander A. M. Lecky; *Renard*, Lieutenant-Commander L. G. B. A. Campbell; *Grampus*, Lieutenant-Commander R. Bacchus; *Pincher*, Lieutenant-Commander H. W. Wyld; *Rattlesnake*, Lieutenant-Commander P. G. Wodehouse; *Racoon*, Lieutenant-Commander A. G. Muller; and *Grasshopper*, Lieutenant-Commander R. T. Amedroz. Our sweeping was carried out under the general command of Commodore

A. W. Heneage, who was in the battleship *Agamemnon*, Captain H. A. S. Fyler, which had also the task of dealing with any enemy guns that interfered with us.

Other destroyers were detailed to embark troops from the transports lying offshore, and to land them in the long strings of transports' lifeboats which they had in tow. Two others were to support the assault on De Totts battery, about a mile inside the Straits from Sedd-el-Bahr.

Dawn on April 25th found the *Scorpion* patrolling in the entrance to the Straits, and as the sun rose over the mountains to the eastward and a sea that

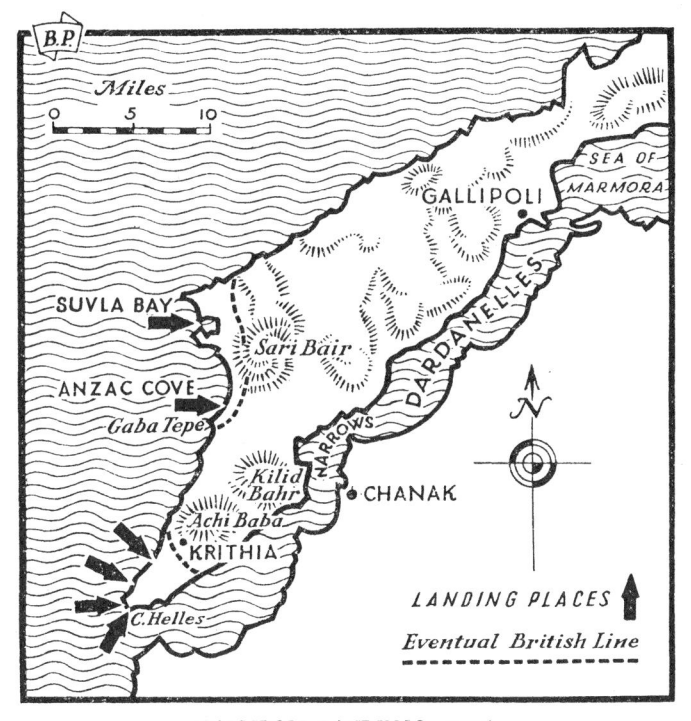

GALLIPOLI LANDINGS, 1915

was flat calm and burnished like a mirror, the spectacle was truly wonderful. Destroyers crammed with troops and boats in tow; trawlers with three boats secured each side; picquet boats with more long tows of boats, were all converging on their allotted beaches. Farther afield were numbers of transports, with a great fleet of battleships and cruisers shelling the beaches as they gradually closed in. The Turkish gunfire in reply did not appear very heavy. Some big stuff was coming down from the direction of the Narrows, though most of the shooting I saw was medium calibre, slow and ill-directed.

I remember watching the six-funnelled French cruiser *Jeanne d'Arc* and the five-funnelled Russian *Askold*, popularly known as 'the packet of Woodbines', blazing away as they supported the landing of the French troops at

Kum Kale on the Asiatic side. I was particularly interested in the rafts, each carrying a 'seventy-five', towed close behind the boats landing the French infantry, and remarked at the time how much quicker they were getting their supporting artillery ashore than the British. What with movement everywhere afloat, the continual roar of gunfire, and the huge clouds of smoke and dust kicked up by shell exploding ashore, it was all intensely exciting to watch.

After three or four sweeps for mines we destroyers lay off the beaches ready to do anything required of us, though for some incomprehensible reason we had the strictest orders not to open fire in support of the Army. I have never discovered who was responsible for this extremely stupid edict, for many excellent opportunities were missed of directly helping the landing by destroyers, so close inshore that they could even see the Turks bobbing up and down in their trenches. The *Scorpion* herself lay stopped for a considerable time off V Beach, near Sedd-el-Bahr, 500 yards off a trench full of the enemy firing on our troops, and unable to do anything. We could see our infantry lying flat on their faces on the beach under withering fire, and every now and then one or two men dashing out to cut the wire in front of them, only to be quickly shot down. It was a tragedy and a mortifying situation for a well-gunned destroyer; but a few days later it was discovered that destroyers really could shoot, both rapidly and accurately, and an order that should never have been given was rescinded. Plenty of bullets came whistling overhead as we lay close inshore; but I do not think they were particularly fired at us. Beyond a few holes in our engine-room cowls and rather conspicuous three funnels we had no damage.

We had little trouble with our first day's sweeping, probably because most of the enemy guns were concentrating on trying to repel the landing. One gun, however, which appeared to be an 8-inch, was very annoying. It fired a shrapnel with a heavy bursting charge of powder, and the loud explosion and heavy black cloud caused it to be known as the 'wrath of God'. It sprinkled us liberally; but did little or no damage.

The second day's sweeping was not so pleasant. During the night a battery had been established behind a ridge on the Asiatic shore, and those in charge of it had a very good idea of the principles involved in applying deflection. Rumour had it they were the *Breslau's* guns served by the *Breslau's* sailors, for they were certainly 4·1's and fired a salvo of five shell. They put up some good shooting, and that day a destroyer was hit every time we made a sweep. My turn came early, for a shell pitched between the legs of the gunlayer of the 4-inch gun on the forecastle, though fortunately it did not burst until it reached the mess-deck below. The stoker petty officer in charge of the fireparty arrived on the bridge and informed me that the mess-deck was on fire, to which I coldly replied, "Then put it out." As we were sweeping at the time there was little else I could say. As a matter of fact there was no fire; but most of the seamen were able to get new kits free, gratis and for nothing, as their lockers were wrecked. Apart from that we had a few small holes in the side where bits and pieces had gone out. The *Blenheim*, our depot ship, patched them up in an hour or two and we were back on the job again the same afternoon.

The third day was particularly galling. We started passing the sweeps well inside the Straits and a good deal higher up than before. We were working in pairs, and no sooner had we formed up to pass the wires, than the 4·1 battery opened fire. The *Wolverine* had just secured her end of the wire and the *Scorpion* was opening out, with the ships about seventy yards apart, when we were straddled by a salvo. Two shell fell over the *Scorpion*, two between the two ships, and the fifth on the *Wolverine's* bridge. It burst against the pedestal of the starboard engine-room telegraph, and instantly killed Commander Prentis, the senior officer of the sweeping destroyers, an R.N.R. midshipman and the coxswain.

On one of the other days spent in sweeping, the *Racoon* was hit in one of her boilers, while the *Mosquito* had heavy casualties. It was not very pleasant paddling along at about 12 knots against a two- or three-knot current, tied by the tail to another destroyer and being fairly constantly straddled by the salvos from those high-velocity guns. We swept up a number of mines, and whenever one came to the surface, our defence against the shore batteries, the *Agamemnon*, turned and legged it out of the Straits. So we destroyers were left to rely on our own gunfire, an opportunity of which we took full advantage.

After a few days the situation ashore was pretty clear to us. Our army was ashore, certainly; but it had only a toe-hold on the peninsula, and rumour, correct for once, told us that we had neither the reserves of men nor ammunition to exploit the initial landings. Minesweeping by day soon ceased as a serious operation, probably because the right flank was not advancing as expected. Also it was becoming expensive in destroyers.

A month or so passed in patrolling, attending on the battleships bombarding, and carrying troops here, there and everywhere. The army had advanced a little; but the dominating height of Achi Baba was nearly as far away as ever, and we had failed to take the village of Krithia, in the foothills. The Turks were putting up a stout resistance.

Reports of the arrival of German submarines now became frequent, and on May 25th, while we were patrolling off Y Beach, on the western side of the peninsula, we saw the *Triumph*, which was steaming slowly in circles with her torpedo-nets out, torpedoed off Gaba Tepe, about six miles away to the northward. We cracked on to full speed and arrived in time to see the *Triumph* roll over and sink. We picked up a man or two; but the *Chelmer*, Lieutenant-Commander Hugh T. England, had already rescued the bulk of the ship's company. The old battleship *Majestic* came out to Cape Helles on the evening of May 26th and anchored close inshore. She was surrounded by transports with destroyers patrolling to seaward; but even these precautions were useless. At dawn on the 27th the *Scorpion* was rushed out of her anchorage to go to the *Majestic's* assistance. She had been torpedoed at anchor. It was certainly a fine performance on the part of the U-boat commander. However, the loss of the *Triumph* and *Majestic* put an end to battleships being always on hand to provide fire support for the army. From now on it was decided to use destroyers for this purpose, and to keep the battleships and cruisers in reserve in protected anchorages.

It has to be remembered that in those days asdics had not been invented and destroyers had no means of detecting submarines unless they actually saw the periscope. Moreover, we carried no depth-charges. Some of the schemes set forth for dealing with enemy submarines if they penetrated the harbour defences were fantastic in the extreme. One idea, which emanated from the *Blenheim*, was for an armed whaler to be kept in readiness. In it were a number of elongated canvas bags, and the blacksmith with his 40-lb. sledge hammer. On a periscope being sighted the whaler went off in chase, and a man in her bows slipped a bag over the top of the periscope, thus blinding the German gentleman with his eye glued to the eyepiece below. If the bag project failed, believe it or not, the blacksmith was directed to smash the top of the instrument with his hammer! Like little Audrey, we laughed and laughed!

The *Wolverine*, whose new captain was Adrian Keyes, whom I have already mentioned and who had been acting as beachmaster at Y Beach, and the *Scorpion*, were detailed for fire support on the left flank of the Helles front. In cases of necessity the battleship *Exmouth* and the cruiser *Talbot* lay at anchor at short notice at Kephalo Bay, in the island of Imbros. There followed six months of great activity. We worked 48 hours on and off, one destroyer being always on the flank and the other at two hours notice in Kephalo. When an operation was in progress both destroyers, and sometimes the *Exmouth* and *Talbot* as well, were brought out to bombard.

What it really came to was that the destroyers were used as mobile batteries, and the army was very glad to have us. Our supporting gunfire was mostly indirect, which produced many new problems which had not been catered for by the gunnery experts and could only be solved by experiment. A permanent spotting officer, Lieutenant Gordon Seath of the Royal Marines, with a few naval signal ratings, lived ashore in a hole in the side of a cliff. Spotting from the most advanced post in the front line, they signalled the necessary corrections. Occasionally we had an aeroplane to spot our gunfire. At night a light was shown on the left extreme of our front line trench as an aiming mark.

The firing procedure was fairly simple. We laid three buoys, from each of which we were registered on all the enemy batteries, trenches and other likely targets. The object was to flummox the inevitable Turkish battery which soon came into being to deter us. It worked, for it was no unusual experience for us to open fire from one buoy, and to see the enemy guns busily plastering one of the two others. We were hit now and then, though no one was seriously damaged.

Some neat problems in naval bombardment had to be taken in our stride, though I fear our rough and ready methods would have failed to obtain the approval of the pundits at Whale Island. On one occasion I remember fire being called for on an entirely new target. Discovering that the range and flat trajectory of the 4-inch gun did not allow the new target to be engaged without hitting the top of a cliff occupied by our troops, we solved the difficulty by cutting the charges in half with a knife and using the gun as a howitzer. It was a most unorthodox proceeding; but certainly produced the answer. We made a wireless signal to the *Blenheim* informing her, and the next day with the mail there arrived a range-table for half charges for the 4-inch B.L. gun made out by Lieutenant-Commander J. B. Waterlow, a gunnery officer after my own heart, to whom we were always heavily indebted for his invaluable assistance. For him nothing was ever too much trouble.

June 28th was perhaps our greatest day on the left flank. The army planned to advance the flank, and while the *Talbot*, screened by the *Racoon*, *Beagle*, *Basilisk* and *Bulldog*, came out to bombard the enemy batteries, the *Scorpion* and *Wolverine*, reinforced by the *Renard*, were detailed to deal with the enemy trenches running down to the sea. We fired deliberately for nearly two hours, and for ten minutes before zero hour as rapidly as possible. I believe we wrecked the Turkish trenches, for the troops in that part of the line advanced unopposed. We had many opportunities of firing on the flying Turks over open sights. About two minutes before zero hour our 4-in gun had become so hot that it refused to run out after recoiling. The run-out contact failed to make by about four inches. It was no time for our fire to fall off, so we short-circuited the contact with a piece of wire. How Whale Island would have solved the problem I do not know.

The army, I think, had gained all their immediate objectives, but were nervous of being counter-attacked that night before they had consolidated and had re-registered their batteries on the new enemy defences. I remember getting a signal to say they were entirely dependent on our fire. The *Talbot* and her destroyers had withdrawn after the attack, and also the *Renard*. The *Wolverine* went in to re-ammunition. So the *Scorpion* stood in at sunset to within 600 yards of the front line, and anchored in 30 fathoms. After dark we put both searchlights on the area in front of our advanced trenches to detect any signs of movement on the part of the enemy. I had my evening meal, and went peacefully to sleep in my clothes on the settee in the chart-house.

At about midnight I was awakened by a thud and several heavy books falling upon me from the rack overhead. Then came the sub-lieutenant's voice through the voice-pipe from the bridge—John G. Nicolas, who was lost in the *Narbrough* in 1918. "Captain, sir," he said, "things are getting pretty hot up here."

They certainly were. I dashed on to the bridge. The Turks were making a deliberate attempt to shoot out our searchlights before launching their attack. Never have I known the air more thick with rifle and machine-gun bullets, and almost immediately both searchlights were shot out. The petty officer leading torpedo-man at the after light crawled up on to the bridge and reported it out of action. He had been shot through the stomach; but happily recovered.

The bottom shelved rapidly, so we dragged the anchor into deeper water, weighed it, and repaired the lights. Almost immediately we had an S O S from our front-line trench to say that the Turks were massing in front of it. Using the light in our trench as an aiming mark and throwing off by using deflection, we filled the gully in front of our trench with lyddite from every gun we had. The Turkish attack collapsed, and it was later reported there were between 300 and 400 dead in front of our trenches at dawn.

We had no killed, but several wounded, and the action aroused the greatest enthusiasm among the ship's company. In memory of it they sent the balance of the canteen surplus on finally paying off to Pearson's Holiday Fund to provide an outing for children on June 29th, the anniversary.

On being relieved by the *Wolverine* we returned to Mudros to fill up with ammunition, having expended nearly all our outfit. On July 1st, greatly to my surprise, I heard I had been promoted to the rank of commander. As I had served no more than three years and three months as a lieutenant-commander I considered myself very fortunate.

II

Large and small monitors, together with four old cruisers specially 'bulged' against torpedo attack—the *Theseus*, *Endymion*, *Grafton* and *Edgar*—were all on the scene by about the end of June, and with their arrival the fire support of the destroyers rather diminished in importance. However, the army liked the destroyers. They could lie close inshore, and their reply to any sudden call for gunfire was immediate and often devastating. By this time our 4-inch gun had fired between three and four thousand rounds, and was rapidly becoming a smooth-bore.

Our work continued, though it had become quite obvious to us that so far as the operations ashore were concerned, we had reached a condition of stalemate. The Suvla operations in August were designed to end this, and to draw away the Turkish troops from the critical area a simultaneous heavy attack was arranged on their positions at Helles. Rear-Admiral D. R. L.

Nicholson hoisted his flag in the *Scorpion* for the operations at Helles. I do not think much ground was made ashore. The Turks had also contemplated an attack and their trenches were full of men. There was fierce fighting with heavy casualties on both sides; but no concrete results.

The results of the Suvla operation are too well-known to be described here; but the failure caused the most bitter disappointment in the fleet. It was so obvious that the whole affair had been mishandled, and that with more dash, enterprise and leadership we might have been successful. No one believed that reinforcements would now be forthcoming to undertake any fresh offensive.

For the operations at Suvla we used 'X' lighters for the first time. Popularly known as 'beetles', they were motor-lighters designed to carry 500 soldiers and specially sent out from England. Of very shallow draught, bullet-proof, fitted with ramps in the bows and capable of a speed of about 5 knots under their own power, they were the forerunners of the landing craft used in the Second World War. After Gallipoli they were finally sent back to Malta, and were used again, *faute de mieux*, to supply the army during General Wavell's first Libyan offensive in December, 1940.

In the midst of our other occupations we had a turn or two on the north flank at Suvla, though there was very little going on. The claims of Salonika were coming to the front, and it looked as though Gallipoli would suffer.

During these months many interesting people took passage in the *Scorpion*, among them General Sir Ian Hamilton, whom we all liked very much. Particularly do I remember the French General Gouraud, who took passage to Helles with a very large staff on a very rough day. All the staff were seasick; but the General did not turn a hair. With his large brown beard and bright eyes Gouraud was a striking figure, vivacious and full of energy as one well could see. Unfortunately our lack of knowledge of each other's language prevented our having any sustained conversation.

In December, 1915, the evacuation of Gallipoli was finally decided upon, first Suvla and Anzac, and later Helles, at the tip of the peninsula. General Davies, in command at Helles, asked that the *Scorpion*, *Wolverine* and *Renard* should be sent back to him, so back we went. A holding attack, in which we played our part, was staged at Helles for the Suvla and Anzac evacuations, which took place the nights of December 18th–19th and 19th–20th. The weather was quite calm, and the withdrawals from both places were successful. The next morning the *Scorpion* and one of the bulged cruisers were detailed to take various army officers up to the Anzac and Suvla beaches to spy out the land and to see what had been left behind. We had some excellent shooting. Numbers of Turks were down on the beaches carrying off the abandoned stores, and we created havoc among them.

The much more ticklish operation of evacuating Helles had yet to come.

The weather had worsened, and at that time of the year it was hardly to be expected that we should get even one calm night. The preliminary stage of this withdrawal started on December 29th, and the final embarkation of the last 17,000 men and 40 guns from Helles was timed to take place, weather permitting, on the night of January 8th–9th, 1916.

I need not go into details; but on January 7th the Turks started a furious artillery attack on both our flanks at Helles. It lasted for three hours, and could only be the prelude to a general attack upon our positions. During the afternoon the Turkish trenches could be seen bristling with bayonets, with their officers trying to make the men leave the trenches. It was an anxious moment; but only in one place did the attack develop, and there it was crushed by the withering gunfire from a battleship, three cruisers, several monitors, and the *Wolverine*.

The night of the final evacuation was an anxious one. We lay off the flank waiting to open fire with all we had if the Turks attacked, knowing that all the time a big operation was in progress in dead silence and without a light showing. Our anxiety grew soon after midnight when the wind and sea rose from the south-west and we realized how the difficulties of embarkation would be enhanced. Still, all remained silent. Then a sudden explosion took place at Helles. Immediately red Verey lights went up all along the line of the enemy trenches, and our orders came to open fire. This all the ships did with a will. We knew the army was away. By 5.30 a.m. the last man was off the peninsula. Whereas a loss of thirty to forty per cent had been expected, the evacuation had been carried out with the loss of one sailor killed.

So ended the Dardanelles campaign, a failure but a very gallant one. Many were the lessons learnt and put to good use in the last war.

Thus also ended any close patrol in and outside the Straits, for the enemy soon mounted guns which kept us at a respectable distance. A large minefield was laid, and the destroyers patrolled outside it. Life was dull indeed. We spent three days on patrol in all sorts of weather, followed by two days coaling and resting at Mudros. After all our months of action and excitement it was a dreary anti-climax.

CHAPTER VII

I

AFTER the evacuation of Gallipoli in January, 1916, most of the troops were sent to Egypt and Salonika. Enemy submarines were already active in the Mediterranean, and as there were many good natural harbours which might be used by German U-boats intending to prey upon the crowded transport route between Egypt and Salonika, it became necessary to institute some sort of a watch over the whole of the Turkish coast of Asia Minor from the Dardanelles to Syria.

Thus it came about that in March, 1916, a change of environment came for the *Scorpion* and *Wolverine* when they were detached to form part of a force operating in the Dodecanese under Captain Frank Larken, in the *Doris*, who had his headquarters at Maltizana, in the island of Stampalia, or Astypalea as it is called in many maps. Most of the bays and inlets on the mainland which might be used by U-boats were mined, usually with narrow channels left open which could be used by destroyers, trawlers and smaller craft. Our main task was to keep a watchful eye on the 150 miles of the transport route between Rhodes and Nikaria, for which purpose we patrolled among the islands known as the Sporades by day, and along the transport route by night.

After about a month of this the *Doris* was relieved by the *Edgar*, Captain Douglas L. Dent, who established his headquarters farther north in the Greek island of Mytilene. I was ordered to open a minor base in the excellent harbour of Port Laki, in Leros, about 120 miles to the southward. With the *Scorpion* and *Wolverine*, three trawlers, eleven drifters and a collier under my orders, I was given more or less a roving commission. I was told to open up sick quarters in Leros and to make local contracts for the supply of beef, bread and vegetables. For the rest, our orders were to patrol from Samos in the north to Rhodes in the south; to investigate the Turkish bays and inlets on the mainland; to sink or capture any Turkish craft found which might be useful for communicating with the outside world; and to shell any villages that fired upon us. It promised to be an interesting job, as indeed it proved to be.

An intelligence system had been established under Professor J. L. Myres (now Sir John Myres) who had been given a commission as a Lieutenant-Commander, R.N.V.R. Myres, a distinguished scholar, an anthropologist and ethnologist, spoke Greek like a native. He had travelled extensively in Greece, Asia Minor and Crete, and had conducted excavations in Cyprus. He was Wykeham Professor of Ancient History, and a Fellow and, later,

Librarian of New College, Oxford. With his many Greek contacts and friends among the local fishermen he was of the greatest assistance to us, though his Greek sympathies by no means made him popular with the Italian governors and officials in the Dodecanese.

On the day of our arrival at Leros I called on the Italian governor at 9 a.m. I was accompanied by Professor Myres, having previously intimated my requirements by letter. The governor had assembled some of the local Greeks who might be able to supply our needs. Early though it was, we sat round a table in the local council house drinking coffee and sipping the sweetest and stickiest of liqueurs.

Thanks largely to Myres, who interpreted, the contracts for provisions were not difficult to arrange, though the *Scorpion's* coxswain, who acted as the ship's steward, insisted upon the loaves of bread being 2 lbs., to facilitate serving out the rations. The Greeks, on the other hand, wanted loaves of one kilo., or 2·2 lbs., which would have greatly complicated the coxswain's accounts. However, the Greek contractor eventually agreed to our demand if we would provide him with a weight of exactly 2 lbs. Returning on board I told the Chief Engine Room Artificer to produce one, and said what it was for. All day long came the sounds of hammering, filing and muttered objurgation from our little workshop. In the evening the Chief E.R.A. came to me with a flat slab of highly-polished steel. "There you are, sir," he said in triumph, "and I'll be blistered if the ruddy Greeks'll be able to carve any chunks out of that!" The coxswain also surprised me by refusing to allow any bullock to be weighed until twelve hours after it had been killed. Though I did not know it at the time, I believe that an animal loses about 20 per cent in weight some hours after being slaughtered. There was no doubt that, through their many visits to Athens and the Ægean, the British sailors mistrusted all Greeks as robbers and rascals.

We had some little difficulty with the sick quarters. We chose a pleasant, nicely-situated house on rising ground. Unfortunately the owner, a lady, had different views, took to her bed and refused to move. However, that problem was solved by a party of Italian soldiers removing her, bed and all. She troubled us no more.

Our collier was a great help. Her master was a full-time co-operator named Hill. We used her double bottoms to store water, which had to be brought 10 miles by trawler. She baked bread for us, and we used her small workshop for repairs. The drifters always lay alongside her in harbour. Incidentally, the making good of defects and all repair work for the three trawlers, eleven drifters and later two picquet boats, not to mention our two destroyers, was undertaken by the Chief Engine Room Artificers and Engine Room Artificers of the *Scorpion* and *Wolverine*. They were masters of improvisation and kings among men.

The issue of orders was particularly difficult. We had no typewriter, and my staff consisted of one junior midshipman. Ships had to have at least one copy of all orders, which had to be written in hectograph ink and duplicated by means of a tray of jelly. We had no refrigerator or means of procuring ice, and the midshipman had to use the greatest ingenuity in getting the jelly cool enough, in a temperature round about 85 degrees, to peel off all the copies we required. One slip and the whole operation had to be repeated. It was not until some years later that the Admiralty allowed a typewriter to every destroyer.

Our work was most interesting, and some of our operations were as exciting as any I have experienced. Acting on intelligence received, we would enter some likely harbour peacefully and quite unopposed, only to be heavily fired upon as we came out. Two picquet boards were soon supplied to deal with the smaller harbours at night. We destroyed many Turkish caïques which might have been carrying supplies to U-boats; but of submarines or their depots we found no trace at all.

Some of the harbours with narrow entrances were strenuously defended, and the Turks used all manner of firearms, including some ancient weapons that fired a heavy leaden bullet about half-an-inch in diameter. It was very soon found that the protective mattresses round our bridges offered no resistance to close-range rifle fire, so the *Blenheim* supplied us with steel plating, which was loopholed. Unfortunately they took several hours to put in place, and when once up navigation had to be done entirely by eye, as the standard compass became quite useless.

Two exciting forays stick in my memory.

On the first occasion we had decided to search a narrow harbour with a village called Kujak at its head, inside the Gulf of Mandelyah—Mendalia in most atlases. A picquet boat was to be sent in at night, covered by the *Scorpion's* gunfire if it became necessary. At 11 p.m. the picquet boat entered the harbour and was duly fired upon from both sides, to which she replied with her Maxim. However, before she got within half-a-mile of the village she found herself in very shallow water which was not shown on the chart, and bumped heavily on an obstruction which was found to be a large drain-pipe running right across the harbour. Here was a pretty predicament. The picquet boat could not turn because of the shoal water. Nor did it seem possible at first to take her out stern first over the drain-pipe. However, the rifle fire had diminished to some extent, and by throwing coal overboard and moving all possible weights forward to lighten the stern, the boat's crew succeeded in easing her gradually back over the obstruction. Her propeller and rudder were damaged, and her exit from the harbour was hastened by heavy rifle fire from both sides of the entrance. She was lucky to get away with it.

Nothing whatever was gained by this expedition and no caïques were found. With our bridge protected by steel plating we tried to enter next morning to shoot up the village, only to be received by heavy rifle fire from both sides of the entrance at ranges of less than 100 yards. The village escaped retaliation because it was round a bend and the heavy rifle fire did not allow our guns to be manned.

On the second occasion we had received information that caïques communicating with the islands were constantly using the little harbour of Gumishlu, on the Budrum peninsula on the north side of the Gulf of Kos. We decided upon another picquet boat expedition at night with the *Scorpion* covering. I was in the picquet boat; but by bad luck our approach was given away by the flaming funnel, and we were received with heavy rifle fire as we steamed through the narrow entrance. The coxswain was shot through the back, and as he fell his convulsive movement of the wheel nearly ran the boat ashore. I took over the helm and nearly did the same. However, we just succeeded in scraping clear, and going on found one caïque which we destroyed with explosive. Our final retreat through the entrance was again fiercely contested.

I made up my mind that the *Scorpion* should take a hand in the business, so at daylight next morning closed the harbour with the intention of bombarding the village at close range. On arriving within about 600 yards of the entrance she was greeted with heavy rifle fire and had three men of the 4-inch guns crew wounded. I considered that the reason for this obstinate defence needed investigation, so we withdrew a little and rigged the steel plates around the bridge. Then, with the upper deck cleared of men, and riflemen manning the bridge loop-holes and mess-deck scuttles, we again steamed for the entrance. Navigational difficulties rather slowed up our approach.

A great battle with rifles took place as we moved through the entrance. Particularly heavy fire came from a small rocky promontory on our starboard hand. Our sailors, who could see the Turks dodging and lying behind rocks and bushes replied with vigour at ranges of fifty yards and less. Bullets whizzed through the air and banged incessantly on the bridge plating, which effectively prevented any further casualties.

Nothing was found in the harbour to justify this resistance, though we heard later that at the time of our visit a party of Turkish troops were in the village collecting taxes in kind. The camels for removing the grain were later discovered behind a hill, many being destroyed by gunfire. The village itself was also bombarded.

The *Wolverine* also had various exciting incidents and many stubborn rifle battles; but I can recollect no details. Adrian Keyes, her captain, was a regular fire-eater, one of those officers who was never prepared to beat a retreat while he still had a whole skin.

We had little trouble with our patrolling trawlers and drifters, manned by fishermen. Indeed, they were so intense on patrol that sometimes they had to be restrained. One drifter skipper was so certain that the caïque he had intercepted was carrying forbidden goods that he took her to Kos, unloaded the whole of her cargo on the jetty, and found precisely nothing!

We did have a slight contretemps with one trawler. The naval authorities, with a complete lack of knowledge of the ways of fishermen, had promoted a drifter skipper to command a trawler. This started a minor mutiny, and very soon the trawler's engineer was hauled before me for not obeying orders. Greatly indignant his defence went something like this.

"He's nowt but a herrin' lugger mon," he said, pointing at the skipper. "It's ma opeenion there's too much Bible bangin' aboard this ship. Thaat mon said that if he sunk a German submarine he'd stop and pick the muckers up!"

I cannot remember how we settled the dispute.

I do not know what effect our operations had on the safety of the Egypt-Salonika transport route; but I do not recollect a single steamer being attacked by a U-boat in our area during the four months we were there.

However, my time on this particular work was finished, for in July the *Scorpion* was suffering from faulty wrapper plates and was ordered home for refit. I took her to Plymouth and turned her over to the dockyard, and thus, for the time being, I was deprived of my good ship. I had a fortnight's leave, and was hurried out again to the Mediterranean to take temporary command of the *Rattlesnake*.

II

My first job after joining the *Rattlesnake* was to form part of the fleet employed in seizing Salamis and the Piræus in September, 1916. The fleet assembled at Milo—a number of French battleships, with our battleship *Glory*; cruisers; minesweepers and a dozen destroyers, my division of four 'Beagles' and eight French. We lay at Milo for about a fortnight before the actual operation started, with two destroyers patrolling outside. Compared with our experience the duty of the destroyers could hardly be called strenuous. We did one day on patrol, one day at four hours' notice, followed by four days 'repos' in harbour.

We sailed for the Piræus on the night of August 31st. Commodore Heneage had charge of the minesweeping operations, which in general were to sweep a channel from seaward into Salamis Bay, there to sweep out the bay as an anchorage for the fleet, and to lay net protection. The minesweeping inside the bay was carried out under my orders with a force of the four British destroyers and some trawlers.

We were at action stations as we steamed through the entrance. The situation was evidently pretty tense, for as we went in we could see the guns of the defences manned and their muzzles following us as we moved. However, nobody opened fire, so all was well.

The trawlers made a botch of sweeping out the anchorage. Their sweeps kept breaking and getting snarled up, and at 2 p.m. it was perfectly obvious that the area would not be thoroughly swept by the time the fleet arrived an hour later. I made a wireless signal to this effect to the French Commander-in-Chief, D'Artige de Fournet; but had his reply to the effect that he did not care and was coming in up to time. So I ordered the four destroyers to pass their sweeps, and we swept round the anchorage at 18 knots, just managing to cover it in time to slip out of the way as the first French dreadnought entered. No mines were found. The fleet looked fine as they came in a single line at high speed. There were about eight battleships, with the ancient *Glory* pelting along at the tail end of the procession doing her best to keep up.

The French then got busy and seized the Greek fleet lying off the dockyard and all the merchant ships in the Piræus; but we took no part in this. We stayed for several days, doing nothing but hearing reverberations of the acute situation on shore. Then it was decided to reduce the British destroyers to two, and as I saw little prospect of anything interesting to do in Greece I elected to take myself off.

The *Scorpion* came out again early in October. I found her in Mudros on the other side of the collier from which the *Rattlesnake* was coaling. Except for the engineer officer, Mr. Richards, she had new officers and mainly a new crew. Many of the men were of the 'conscript' type who had joined for 'hostilities only'.

I was very glad to be back in my old quarters, though I knew none of the officers except Mr. Richards, who was promoted from Chief Artificer Engineer to Engineer Lieutenant in 1917 and was later awarded the O.B.E. He was a grand little man from Pontypool who, by his conversation, appeared to be a very red socialist. Down below in his department he was a veritable dictator. The new first lieutenant was one of the early mates, and the acting sub-lieutenant was R. V. Symonds-Tayler, who had been a midshipman in one of the picquet boats during the landing at Gallipoli and was awarded the D.S.C. He was a fine officer who has since attained high rank in the Service.

We put in a short time on the Dardanelles patrol, a soul-destroying occupation nearly out of sight of the coast along which we had steamed with impunity such a short time before. We left after the remarkable experience of being rammed from right ahead by our next astern, the *Wolverine*. She had mistaken a fixed light on Cape Niger for our stern light, and both officers of the watch put their helms the wrong way. We were badly holed from the forecastle to the keel, though fortunately most of the men got out. Luckily the lower mess-deck was occupied by the old hands of stokers of the last commission. The hatch to their mess-deck had been cut in half by the *Wolverine's* bow; but they escaped with the greatest sangfroid by climbing up the jagged edges of the plates. The ship was badly damaged.

We limped back to Mudros, where we were temporarily patched up by the repair ship. A Court of Enquiry was held on board the *Blenheim*, the President being an ex-navigator, with two other navigators as members. After sitting the best part of the day and consuming a number of Captain Coode's excellent cocktails, the Court finally delivered the remarkable finding: "There is no evidence to show how this collision occurred." Captain (D) was furious, and both officers of the watch took it in the neck, which they thoroughly deserved.

We sailed by ourselves for Malta, where the dockyard made an excellent repair in just over a month. We were then engaged for many months on escort duty.

Occasionally one became stuck with a slow convoy of ships of half-a-dozen different nationalities, and an escort made up of British, French, Italians and Japanese. The Japanese sent eight of their destroyers to the Mediterranean and had taken over and manned two of ours. They looked most efficient and kept their men permanently at action stations. However, I found that the Japanese could not stand punching into a heavy sea at any speed, and when it was blowing at all they were usually miles astern at daybreak.

I remember one amusing incident when we passed a convoy at sea of even more nationalities than usual. The senior officer of the escort was in the sloop *Hydrangea*, which had strings of flags in the International Code flying from all her available halliards. We deciphered it. It was addressed to some Italian merchant ship and read:

"YOU ARE A BLOODY FOOL."

How it read in Italian I would not know. Maybe the sanguinary epithet means nothing to them.

It was at the end of May, 1917, that Captain Coode left us to go home to the Admiralty as Director of Operations (Foreign). I was desperately sorry to see the last of him. I had come to know him well, and he was a tower of strength behind one. He was relieved as Captain (D) first by Captain F. Clifton Brown, and then, in September, by Captain George Chetwode.

I spent most of that year escorting convoys in the Mediterranean, and since I never lost a single ship I suppose I was moderately successful. At the time I put it down to my insistence on exact station-keeping by the escorting destroyers. I had thought out the problem and had written out various suggestions, the bulk of which had been embodied in Fleet Orders. Looking back, I am not so sure that my ideas were quite so important as I thought then. The immunity of my convoys was probably due to sheer luck.

During the summer of 1917 I was offered the appointment of Commander (D) of all the destroyers based upon Malta. I would work directly under the Commodore of Patrols, but should still take my ship to sea. However, I turned it down. My thoughts were directed homewards, as I felt that the really active periods in the Mediterranean were finished. Moreover, the 'Beagle' class, of which the *Scorpion* was one, were being gradually withdrawn from the Mediterranean and replaced by smaller, oil-fired destroyers.

By October, Captain Coode was well in the saddle at the Admiralty, so I wrote to him asking if he could get me a ship under Commodore Tyrwhitt in the Harwich Force, or with Admiral Roger Keyes at Dover. I knew and admired both these officers, and was aware that with them there would be plenty of action and no boredom. In reply I soon had a letter from Coode saying he would do what he could and that, in the meanwhile, he had put the *Scorpion* high on the list for relief and return to England.

We finally sailed from Malta at the end of December full of mails and passengers for England. The latter included a wireless warrant officer, the Governor's A.D.C., and a small Scottish terrier belonging to a young lady in Malta that someone asked me to take home and deliver to quarantine. The young lady, whose name I did not know, had either gone or was shortly going home. Many years later I made the discovery that her name was Miss Nona Christine Byatt. We were married in 1929.

We called at Gibraltar and embarked more passengers and mails, sailing on alone in the face of rather a threatening weather forecast. It was breezing up in the evening as we rounded Cape St. Vincent, and by midnight it was blowing as hard as I have ever seen it in the Atlantic with an enormous toppling sea. At about 4 a.m. next morning I groped my way along the swaying upper deck and down to the wardroom, which was a sickening sight. There was about a foot of dirty water washing about over the deck. The stench was appalling, and most of our passengers, who were camping out on the settees or in arm-chairs since there were not enough cabins to go round, were dead to the world. The table had capsized with its legs in the air, and in it the A.D.C. was asleep with the water lapping all over him. Miss Byatt's Scottie, who was a wise dog, had climbed on top of the A.D.C., the only tolerably dry island in a disturbed sea. The motion was horrible, a sort of combined pitch and roll, with the propellers occasionally coming clean out of the water and shaking the whole stern of the ship as though it might drop off. It was wholly disconcerting. I retired in haste.

With the cold, wintry dawn it was blowing as hard as ever. The upper deck presented a scene of devastation. All our five boats had been washed overboard, the upper deck had been practically cleared of all its lockers, hawser reels and lighter fittings, and the after funnel was leaning over at an angle of about 15 degrees. I seriously considered putting into the Spanish port of Ferrol for shelter; but off Cape Vilano the wind took off a little and on we went. The weather prevented us from finding out how much coal we had left, and we finally reached Plymouth with only nine tons remaining. Securing fore and aft between two buoys without a boat was something of a problem, and as it was Sunday afternoon no one seemed anxious to help. However, we eventually managed it, and never was I more pleased at getting into harbour and having a good night's rest.

The *Scorpion* finally paid off on January 21st, 1918, and I left her with deep regret after seven years and three weeks. I am not unduly sentimental. Ships are expendable; but the *Scorpion* was a staunch little vessel. I knew all her particular idiosyncrasies, all her dents and patches, almost every bolt and rivet. Even now I think I could find my way blindfold along her upper deck. In the long time I was in her we had many memorable experiences in peace and in war, and I had as shipmates some quite wonderful officers and men. During the Second World War many of these old friends wrote to me. In a time of stress and tribulation their letters reminding me of the *Scorpion* in her heyday and wishing me luck were a great encouragement and inspiration.

I have often reflected how curiously history repeats itself. When I left the Mediterranean as a young commander in 1917 I knew it very well. Malta, the Adriatic, Greece, Crete, and a multitude of lovely islands in the Ægean were all old friends. I served in the Mediterranean again between the wars. Little did I imagine how the accumulated knowledge was to be of service to me years later in a position of far greater anxiety and responsibility.

CHAPTER VIII

I

AFTER leaving the *Scorpion* in January, 1918, I went on leave and stayed with my mother in Edinburgh. I had little doubt of being appointed to another destroyer, and had high hopes of being sent to one of the flotillas at Harwich or to the Dover Patrol.

On February 8th I had a telegram from the Admiralty, ordering me to go to Inverness, where I should be told of my appointment. I caught the 1 p.m. train that day, arrived at Inverness, and went to the Station Hotel. A Lieutenant-Commander, R.N.V.R., arrived and he told me I was appointed temporarily to the *Ophelia* in command in place of her captain who was sick. I knew she was a war-built destroyer of the usual type belonging to the 14th Flotilla. Though somewhat consoled that the appointment was only temporary, the Grand Fleet was not what I wanted.

He also informed me that the *Ophelia* was at Port Edgar, in the Firth of Forth, so my journey north was a complete waste of time, and next morning I returned to Edinburgh. I finally joined my new ship at Port Edgar on February 11th.

I was not a bit impressed by her appearance. By our Mediterranean standards she was dirty, and the men slack and slovenly. I do not know if it was altogether their fault. At that time the Grand Fleet destroyers were in a state of staleness with their officers and men in the last stage of boredom. Most of them had spent over three years at Scapa Flow, with very few amenities. They did fairly long spells at sea, often in vile weather, with most infrequent clashes with the enemy. The opportunities for exercise and recreation in harbour were virtually non-existent, while compared with our *Blenheim* in the Mediterranean the Grand Fleet depot ships were futile and seemed to look upon their destroyers as a nuisance. They were not all out to help us.

Much more could have been done to keep the men interested. No doubt the weather at Scapa was worse than that in the Mediterranean, but both Scapa and Mudros suffered from the same lack of amenities ashore, football grounds, canteens, cinemas, and so on. I soon came to feel that a great deal of the inertia and boredom was due to not keeping the men busy enough. Each destroyer worked her own routine, and I noticed that in harbour some of them did not turn to until well after 9 a.m.

I spent only six weeks in the *Ophelia* with the Grand Fleet; but am pleased to recollect that I persuaded Captain Godfrey to adopt a standard routine in the 14th Flotilla which started things going at a reasonably early hour in the morning

After a week or two in the Firth of Forth we went to Scapa, from where we did several trips to sea as part of the escort to a division of battleships covering a Norwegian convoy. The weather was usually atrocious, heavy gales alternating with thick fog.

During the last fortnight of March I began to get wind of some operation pending in the south. Officers would disappear from the flotillas, and a ship or two would suddenly sail for no apparent reason. This, of course, was the blocking expedition at Zeebrugge and Ostend, and though I did not know that, I began to feel anxious lest I should not get a ship in the south in time to take part in whatever operation was to take place. Captain Coode was at the Admiralty, and I had already heard from him that the Harwich Force flotillas were full up; but that Roger Keyes, who was now Vice-Admiral, Dover Patrol, had promised me the first vacancy under his command. On March 28th, I had a signal that I was appointed to the *Termagant*, in the Dover Patrol. Both Captain Godfrey and the Commodore of the Grand Fleet Flotillas asked me to stay on. However, I was not anxious to remain, and succeeded in getting the Commodore's consent to my leaving the *Ophelia* without relief.

I reached London the next day and went straight to the Admiralty to ask the whereabouts of the *Termagant*. I learnt she was refitting at Hull, so I had had another futile and unnecessary journey all because of the extreme secrecy practised in wartime. In my opinion it was much overdone; the height of absurdity if the new commanding officer of a ship could not be told, by coded message or otherwise, where his vessel was situated!

However, I went back to Hull with my baggage to find that the *Termagant* was to spend another seventeen days under refit. What with the dirt and noise the ship was uninhabitable, so I made my home at the local club. It was there I had my first experience of an air raid, when five or six Zeppelins came over at night. There was a great deal of noise and firing; but the bombs did little damage.

II

The *Termagant* was one of the four destroyers building for the Turks at the outbreak of war and taken over by us on completion early in 1916. She was considerably longer than the contemporary British destroyers, and had the imposing armament of five 4-inch guns. In point of fact one could never bring more than four of them into action simultaneously, and two of the four had small arcs of fire. All the same she had the good speed of 32 knots and had comfortable accommodation. She was classed as a flotilla leader, though when it suited the authorities she reverted to a destroyer, which meant that she escorted convoys by day and patrolled at night.

Our refit at Hull ended on about April 17th, and we steamed down the buoyed swept channel to Sheerness at 30 knots. I had arranged for the ammunition, war-heads for the torpedoes, and so on to be waiting for us, so we embarked them at once and sailed again that evening. We anchored in the Downs that night, and reached Dover at 7 next morning. On reporting myself I was disappointed to discover that I was already too late to take any really interesting part in the operation which was pending.

The Dover Patrol, I soon discovered, was very different from the Grand Fleet. The proximity and enterprise of the German destroyers kept it lively. The raid on Zeebrugge took place on April 23rd, soon after our arrival at Dover. With two other destroyers the *Termagant* was detailed to escort the 15-inch monitors to their bombarding position close to Dutch territorial waters not far from the entrance to the Scheldt. Soon after leaving Dover we ran into thick fog, which persisted. On the evening of the 22nd, the monitors anchored in their supposed bombarding positions. Since the shooting was to be entirely indirect without any spotting the positions must be literally exact, and I wondered how on earth they could fix their precise location with sufficient accuracy in a thick fog. However, after anchoring I was told to steam half-a-mile on such-and-such a bearing to find a Dutch navigational buoy, and sure enough there it was. I discovered later that they had Captain H. P. Douglas of the Hydrographic Department on board, and that he was responsible for this fine piece of navigation. The monitors fired deliberately through most of the night, and now and again one heard the burst of a shell fired back by the enemy's big guns. They were using sound ranging. Nothing came very close to us; but in any case I saw little of the business as I spent the night half-a-mile or so to the eastward arguing with a Dutch Admiral in a small torpedo-boat on the question of whether or not the monitors were firing from inside Dutch territorial waters.

After the Zeebrugge operation the *Termagant* was stationed at Dunkirk, which I much preferred to Dover. There was always more chance of action, and one was relieved of the rather monotonous duty of escorting troop transports from Folkestone and Dover to Calais and Boulogne. The Commodore at Dunkirk was Hubert Lynes, who had commanded one of the light cruisers at Harwich and was, I believe, well known as an ornithologist. The second blocking operation against Ostend was to be carried out under his orders, and as it was then being planned I got him to promise to ask for the *Termagant* to be given a front seat. Unfortunately, because of the delay in launching it, the date finally chosen clashed with the *Termagant's* boiler cleaning period, so we took no part in it. Shortly afterwards, Lynes was relieved by Commodore Frank Larken, an old friend who had been captain of the *Doris* in the Ægean and under whom the *Scorpion* had worked on the Asia Minor coast patrol. I easily persuaded him to ask for the *Termagant* to spend most of her time at Dunkirk.

Two divisions of destroyers were always kept at Dunkirk; one of four British destroyers, and the other of four French and two British, though always under British command. All the other T.B.D's were based on Dover. There were three patrols in the Straits on dark nights, and two during the periods of moonlight. The Harwich Force provided the third, or western patrol on dark nights. The eastern patrol was provided from Dunkirk, the other Dunkirk division being anchored in the Roads at immediate notice for steam. All the destroyers at Dover, except those with defects or boiler cleaning, were at immediate notice at night.

By day all the Dover destroyers, except flotilla leaders, escorted troop transports to France. At Dunkirk one division went up harbour and secured inside the docks, and the other lay at half-an-hour's notice in the Roads if not on patrol. Usually a patrol of one large and one small monitor, with a division of destroyers, patrolled the mine-net barrage off Ostend and Zeebrugge. It was a dull job, as the 12-inch monitors could hardly make two knots against a contrary tide.

We were periodically disturbed in the docks by the attentions of a 15-inch long-range German gun. For those days Dunkirk also had a pretty hot time from aircraft, though the bombs were hardly comparable with those of the last war.

Towards the end of May, while out with one of the 15-inch monitors patrolling the net barrage and having a thoroughly dull time, I suddenly spotted heavy firing close inshore and saw four German destroyers shooting at some of our seaplanes. The destroyers were steaming out from the land steering north-easterly. I was in charge of the destroyers, so we made off towards the enemy at full speed, at the same time reporting to the senior officer in the monitor what we had seen and my intention to engage. We had no reply, and rapidly drew away. There were lots of flashing from the monitor, the *Terror*, which my yeoman of signals said he thought was our recall. As we were closing the enemy fast I considered it was by no means the time to break off, so paid no attention to the *Terror's* signals and soon passed out of sight.

When about 9,000 yards from the Germans they were reinforced by five more destroyers from the north-east. We opened fire. It was fairly rough with a fresh north-easterly wind. We were washing down with spray flying everywhere; but allowing for that I have never seen anything to equal the wretched shooting of the *Termagant* and our three others. The German commander helped us all he could by forming his nine boats in line abreast at right angles to our line; but even so we could not hit them. Nor did they hit us, though their salvos certainly appeared to be better controlled than ours. Then another four enemy destroyers appeared from the north-east, making thirteen in all.

By this time Dover and Dunkirk were becoming excited and all sorts of wireless signals were coming through. One of my destroyers, too, had fired away practically all her ammunition, so I thought it best to break off the action. This we did by turning away after firing a few torpedoes through the enemy's line, again without result. Altogether it was a most unsatisfactory affair. To be 5,000 yards off the enemy and unable to hit them was exasperating and a poor reflection on our gunnery, though I believe we did get one hit on the German leader.

After this distressing episode I sought and obtained permission for my sub-division to do some 1-inch aiming rifle practise to exercise the fire control and the gunlayers, though I never had the opportunity of seeing if it improved the shooting. The truth was, of course, that the Dover destroyers were so desperately hard-worked that they had no time for firing practises or exercises. As an example, my opening experience of the Dover Patrol was eighteen consecutive nights at sea with the men at action stations practically the whole time.

Coming back from this unsatisfactory battle we met the *Terror*, and there followed an acrimonious exchange of signals with the senior officer. He wished to know my reasons for chasing the enemy without his permission and when he had made the recall no less than six times. Many effective replies occurred to me; but I contented myself with the statement that his signal had been incorrectly read, and that I had made the signal enemy in sight six times without eliciting any reply. All the same, the senior officer was by no means satisfied. He reported my undisciplined conduct to Commodore Larken, who made very light of it.

It was clear by this time that the second operation for blocking Ostend had been a complete failure. It had taken place in thick weather on the night of May 9th–10th, and because of the difficulty in seeing his exact position before entering, Commander Godsal, the *Vindictive*'s captain, had had to turn her bow into the eastern breakwater instead of the western, as planned. Consequently the prevailing easterly tide together with the sudden release of the pent-up water in the large flushing basin washed the *Vindictive* to one side. She was no obstacle, so another attempt was decided upon.

One morning I was suddenly sent for by the Vice-Admiral Roger Keyes, who asked if I would like to have another try at blocking Ostend. He thought the previous failure was partly due to inexperience in ship handling, and had selected me because he said he wanted an officer used to that sort of thing. He told me I could choose my own officers, and that Chatham would supply the volunteer ship's company. I naturally felt highly complimented; though I very well realized that after two abortive attempts the third would be no picnic.

I did not hesitate.

III

To make a really good job of it, the Admiralty had chosen the old battleship *Swiftsure*. I cannot imagine why she was not detailed before; but it may be that it was considered that an armoured ship was now needed as a battery of 6-inch guns had been mounted at Ostend since the *Vindictive's* attempt. An old cruiser, commanded by an ex-submarine officer, an excellent man, was also told off to assist.

The plan was for the *Swiftsure* to enter between the breakwaters; to put her helm hard over and ram the western arm; after which it was hoped the tide would swing her across the channel. The cruiser would follow in; ram the *Swiftsure* in the stern, and help to push her right across the entrance. Both ships would then sink themselves with the demolition charges in their bottoms. Success all depended upon finding the entrance. As a preliminary I wanted a fireship put alongside the western, or up-tide, arm of the breakwater to light us on our way. Being built of wood it could probably have been set ablaze. However, this was not approved, and instead it was arranged to have an endless chain of coastal motor-boats from the entrance to half-a-mile out to sea, which would give us our position exactly.

I set about selecting the officers. My first choice was my own first lieutenant in the *Termagant*, a magnificent man, Wilfred Joe Williams, promoted from warrant rank for exceptional ability. Lieutenants Aubrey B. Fanshawe and Ronald E. C. Dunbar, both fine officers with long experience of Dover, were the other two. Dunbar was a navigator, and quite imperturbable. I tried hard to get Symonds-Tayler, who had been with me in the *Scorpion*, but he was in one of the Harwich Force destroyers from which he could not be released. The engineer officer, whose name escapes my memory, but who undoubtedly had one of the toughest jobs in the whole party, was another fine officer whose cheerfulness never left him.

As the *Swiftsure* was being prepared in the dockyard at Chatham we were all sent there to the barracks. It amused us to hear that the general opinion amongst the *Termagant's* ship's company was that the first lieutenant and myself had been thrown out of the ship for being too severe with the sailors. All we had been trying to do was to introduce some of the Mediterranean discipline, cleanliness and efficiency in a ship in which they were sorely needed.

For the *Swiftsure* we had a fine ship's company from Chatham Barracks. They were all volunteers, and many of them had been in the previous raids on Zeebrugge or Ostend. One of them, a petty officer called Reed, had steered the *Vindictive* on both occasions, and hoped to steer the *Swiftsure* in a third. However, the doctors interfered for some reason or another, and Reed was removed from us. The crew were a wild lot; but ready for anything, and how they worked.

The ship took a lot of preparation. All the unnecessary gear and stores had to be removed and sent ashore. The conning tower and exposed positions had to be heavily sand-bagged; explosives placed in the double bottoms and the leads run, with dynamo exploders fitted in cases the dynamos failed. There were a hundred and one details to be thought out and jobs to be done, including the mounting of machine-guns and Stokes mortars and the placing of special Dover flares on the quarter-deck. These were flares invented by Brock which turned night into day, and were used by the patrol drifters in the Straits of Dover with the idea of detecting submarines on the surface and forcing them to dive into the minefields. We were only to use them as a last resort, for once they went out one was left completely blinded. Among other things the arrangements for the escape of the ship's company required the most careful consideration and organization. We had no intention of finishing the war in a German prison camp.

All these arrangements took time, and it was nearly three weeks before we were ready to go down the Medway to Sheerness. We took the *Swiftsure* to sea for a full-power trial, and were pleased to find that she could still knock up about 18 knots all out. We had a slight contretemps when the engine-room telegraphs failed while returning to harbour. We had, of course, been reducing speed for entering; but failed to notice that our reductions were not receiving any attention from below. To officers habituated to destroyers 17 knots or so was nothing remarkable. We produced quite an imposing spectacle booming into Sheerness, and only just managed to get a chain of messengers organized in time to go full speed astern at the buoy. I had visions of overshooting it and crashing halfway up the Medway to Chatham.

Then, when everything was ready, and the operation was within two or three days of being carried out, it was suddenly cancelled. We were bitterly disappointed, and from being all keyed-up with suppressed excitement we all felt very flat. Roger Keyes realized our mortification, for he came on board, addressed the ship's company, and gave us the reasons. First and foremost, the Germans had ceased to use the canal from Ostend as a means of getting the U-boats to and from their base inland at Bruges. Second, they had laid a big minefield off Ostend which it was improbable the *Swiftsure* could penetrate.

So there it was. The expedition was definitely off, so we took the ship back to Chatham, handed her over to the dockyard, and returned to our ships at Dover.

I still think it a pity the *Swiftsure* operation never came off.

I returned to the *Termagant*.

IV

By September our hopes of early peace were high. Victory was in the air. The Army was doing great work in France, and on the Belgian coast the Germans were less aggressive and more on the defensive. By the middle of October it became evident that they were already preparing to retire from Ostend and Nieuport. Indeed, they might have actually gone, though no one knew for certain.

This doubt apparently prevailed at a Council ashore with the King of the Belgians, whereupon Roger Keyes became rather impatient and said he would go and see. At that time the Vice-Admiral was living on board the *Douglas*, Commander Roger Rede, at Dunkirk so as to be ready for any emergency. But the *Douglas* was a new flotilla leader. There were orders that she was not to be unduly risked, so all the Vice-Admiral's trips to sea were made in the *Termagant*.

On October 16th he embarked, and in company with two other destroyers we proceeded for Ostend. We met with no opposition, and it was a peculiar and rather thrilling experience to be steaming through waters where no British or French ships had ventured for four years. About two miles short of the heads of the breakwater a four-oared fishing boat appeared, pulling furiously towards us, the men waving to us to stop and shouting "Mines" at the top of their voices. We did stop; but Roger Keyes was not to be deterred from going into the harbour. We lowered the motor-boat, which, like all destroyer motor-boats of that period, immediately broke down. So he set off in a whaler and had a tumultuous welcome ashore and was well kissed by an exultant populace, men and women, young and old. However, the Germans had not fully evacuated Ostend, and the explosion of a land mine caused the Belgian authorities to press the Admiral to hasten his departure. He had learnt what he had come for.

Meanwhile the German batteries up the coast towards Zeebrugge had tumbled to the fact that British destroyers were taking liberties off Ostend, and opened up with some heavy stuff.

Roger Keyes re-embarked in the whaler, and we set off for home pursued by a battery of 12-inch guns. One shell fell close under our forefoot, and the resultant splash came down on the lath and canvas structure which covered the bridge. This collapsed, to leave the Admiral, Captain (D), myself, the flag lieutenant, coxswain and signalman struggling beneath the wreckage and soaked to the skin by the ton or so of sea water that had descended from on high. Roger Keyes' reaction to this incident was to put his head over the bridge-dodger and shout to one of the gun's crew to bring him a piece of the shell. He wanted to find out the calibre of the gun that had fired it.

Soon after the Vice-Admiral had disembarked at Dunkirk we had a signal telling us to be ready to sail again that afternoon and to have a Belgian flag ready. We had no such thing on board; but my signalmen got busy with all the black, yellow and red bunting they could beg, borrow or steal, and managed to get the flag finished just as the King and Queen of the Belgians came on board with Sir Roger Keyes. We sailed at about 4 p.m. with the home-made banner at the masthead, the ships' companies of the big monitors in their bombarding positions cheering as we steamed past.

It was practically dark when we reached Ostend and Their Majesties with the Vice-Admiral went ashore. They had an enthusiastic reception when they entered the town at about 5.50 p.m. As the King and Queen had a dinner-party that night they decided to save time by returning in a coastal motor-boat at about 38 knots, so we went back alone. On arrival we found that our passengers had not turned up, and were just about to sail again to find them when the C.M.B., which had broken down, limped into harbour. I fear the dinner-party could not have started much before midnight.

Two days later the *Termagant* was ordered to Ostend, where Roger Keyes was living on board the *Douglas*. We were to take him on to Zeebrugge, but arrived off Ostend just in time to see a small monitor blow up on a mine. This minefield, the same one which had baulked the *Swiftsure*, had already claimed two other victims, so it was decided to be too dangerous for the *Termagant* to steam on up the coast. The trip to Zeebrugge was therefore made in two C.M.B.s, and the commanding officer of the *Douglas*, Roger Rede, and myself were invited to join the party. On the way our boat punctured a small hole in herself by hitting a baulk of floating timber.

Reaching Zeebrugge we found, to our disappointment, that a French motor-launch, flying an enormous tricolour, had arrived before us. However, we landed and explored the mole, keeping a sharp look-out for booby traps. Wilfred Tomkinson, the Captain (D), who pulled at a steering-wheel hanging temptingly out of a wrecked seaplane, was taken severely to task.

It was nearly dark when we started back with all the party crammed into one C.M.B., a pretty tight fit. It was a beautiful calm moonlight night, and as we approached Ostend at dead low water I noticed various black, globular objects flicking past. Roger Keyes, who was carrying on an animated conversation in French with a French officer looked up and said to the C.O. of the C.M.B., "You damned young fool! You're in the minefield," and then calmly carried on with his conversation. As Roger Rede and I were sitting on the business end of the C.M.B.'s torpedoes our feelings may be imagined.

November 11th came, and with it the Armistice. The *Termagant* was sent to Boulogne to bring back Admiral Sir Rosslyn Wemyss, the First Sea Lord, who was the British Naval Representative at the signature of the Armistice in Marshal Foch's special train drawn up in the Forest of Compiegne. The Admiral and his staff arrived on board the *Termagant* at 6 a.m. the day afterwards, and we sailed for Dover at once. After steaming some distance it was discovered that Wemyss' suit-case containing his copy of the Armistice terms had been left behind in Paris. Worse, much worse, the Admiral's razor had also gone astray. He shaved with mine, while his Naval Assistant, Captain J. P. R. Marriott, and the staff occupied themselves by keeping out of the First Sea Lord's sight. Wemyss was normally imperturbable; but when his personal arrangements went wrong his language could be blistering.

v

Peace descended upon Dover, and left us rather bored after so much excitement. It was difficult to accustom ourselves to the new routine.

The *Termagant* was chiefly employed in taking the great ones over to France or bringing them back. Among others we took His present Majesty; the Duke of Connaught, with whom I did a three-day trip in Belgium; and Lord Beatty, to whom we were glad to show a sample of Dover weather in the shape of a south-westerly gale. We had another gale, a real snorter from the south-eastward when we brought Lloyd George to Dover from Boulogne. I advised him not to sail that night as landing was very doubtful, but he was not to be deterred. During the whole of a frightful passage of about five hours he lay on my bunk reading the *Daily Chronicle*. It was so bad in Dover harbour that we could not go alongside anywhere, so we anchored under the lee of the breakwater and a harbour launch was sent off for the Prime Minister. With the *Termagant* rolling nearly gunwales under it was a job to transfer him. However, we put our Welsh gunner and four sailors into the launch, and conducted the Prime Minister to the gangway. I said good-bye and told him that when I said 'Go' he was to step forward and let go everything. I waited until the downward roll, gave the word, and he obeyed orders, to be fielded neatly by the gunner and the four sailors and put into the cabin. I admired his courage in a difficult situation, for the weather was really dreadful. In any sort of bad weather Dover harbour is one of the worst in the world.

Like many another ship at that period the *Termagant* was hard hit by the Spanish 'flu. At one time we had no more than twenty-six men fit for duty out of a total of about 150. All the wardroom cooks and stewards were smitten, though this did not defeat the first lieutenant, Williams. He picked out a young leading seaman and two A.B.'s and personally instructed them in the art of cookery and stewarding. Williams was able to cope with every emergency.

The young leading seaman, E. G. Buckingham, had been rated before he had a badge for three years good conduct. He stayed with me for eighteen years as my coxswain. An excellent seaman with a remarkable flair for old-time rope work, which had largely been forgotten, he became a fine boat

G

sailor and a very faithful friend. His retirement to pension in 1936, when I had reached the rank of Vice-Admiral, was a great loss.

Early in 1919 my time in the *Termagant* was drawing to an end. I had applied for a destroyer abroad, and on March 1st was appointed to the *Seafire*, destined for China. One of the 'S' class completed in 1918, she was a slightly smaller though faster ship than the *Termagant*. She was at the destroyer base at Port Edgar, in the Firth of Forth, and wishing to take Leading Seaman Buckingham with me, I applied to the Commodore of the Royal Naval Barracks, Portsmouth, his depot, asking to be allowed to do so, pointing out that the *Seafire* was a Devonport ship. I had a very curt reply telling me it was quite irregular for a Portsmouth rating to be sent to a Devonport ship, and that my request could not be granted. Considering this to be nothing more nor less than a piece of obstructionist red tape I made up my mind to get round it. My opportunity came when I was left to act as Captain (D) at Dover for a few days, so I went to the office, ordered Buckingham's papers to be closed in the *Termagant* and transferred to the *Seafire*, and obtained a railway warrant for his journey to Port Edgar. It was highly unorthodox; but that was the last I ever heard of it, and Buckingham remained with me through many ships and appointments before he finally left the Service three years before the outbreak of the Second World War.

So ended my time in the Dover Patrol. I shall always count myself fortunate in having served there, and under the command of Sir Roger Keyes. A great fighter and fearing nothing, he had outstanding qualities as a leader; above all, that asset which counts so much in war—the burning desire to get at the enemy at all times and by any means.

He lies, as I am sure he would wish, in the Cemetery at Dover, surrounded by many of those who lost their lives in actions fought by ships of the Dover Patrol in two great maritime wars. Across the English Channel are Zeebrugge, Ostend, Dunkirk, Calais, Boulogne, and other places of historic memory. From that pale shadow on the horizon which is the French coast, German heavy guns in the Second World War flashed and thundered against Dover and the convoys passing under the white cliffs, and German aircraft were set out to ravage England.

It is fitting that that burial ground of sailors, and the tall Naval War Memorial on the summit of the cliff, should overlook a sepulchre of far nobler proportions where in the course of centuries a host of other seamen have fought and died—the heaving windswept waste, and the shoals and swirling eddies of the Straits of Dover.

CHAPTER IX

I

THE *Seafire*, as I have said, had originally been earmarked for China, a station which I had never seen and on which I had always been keen to serve. However, my chances of getting there were blighted—and for ever —when, in the final allocation of the post-war fleet early in 1919, it was decided to break with tradition and to abolish for the time being any idea of a destroyer flotilla in the Far East. The alteration, no doubt, was dictated by economy.

I joined the *Seafire* at Port Edgar, and we soon found ourselves detailed for service in the Baltic, where there were more complications, particularly in regard to the newly-recognized independent states of Estonia, Latvia and Lithuania.

The Admiralty, too, had their own perplexities. Because of the rapid demobilization, there was difficulty in finding crews for foreign service. Early in March, when we sailed for the Baltic, the *Seafire* was between one-fifth and two-fifths short of her proper complement, which made a great difference when any real work had to be done. Our force was under the command of Rear-Admiral Walter Cowan, in the light cruiser *Curaçoa*. Commander F. Burges Watson, in the flotilla leader *Shakespeare*, was Senior, Officer, Destroyers, and my division consisted of the *Seafire*; *Scotsman*, Lieutenant-Commander Delorest J. D. Noble; *Scout*, Lieutenant-Commander E. F. Fitzgerald; and *Sea Bear*, Lieutenant-Commander Henry M. Coombs.

We called first at Oslo, where the *Curaçoa* delivered some millions of pounds worth of gold bullion, and then went on to Copenhagen. After a week or so there, having an entente with the friendly Danes, male and female, the *Curaçoa*, with the *Seafire* and *Scotsman* in company, sailed for Libau, the port of the newly-established republic of Latvia. We struck a thick fog on the way; but this did not delay the Admiral, who maintained a steady 22 knots regardless of navigational dangers and minefields.

The situation in the Baltic States was curious. Latvia, like Estonia and Lithuania, had originally been Russian; but had been invaded and overrun by the Germans during the war. By the Treaty of Brest-Litovsk in March, 1918, Russia had renounced her sovereign rights in all three provinces. Latvian national units which had been formed in 1915 fought with the Russian army; but after the treaty of Brest-Litovsk fought against the Bolsheviks. It was left to a territorial militia of pro-German leanings organized by the Baltic Barons to restore order, Riga being liberated in May, 1918, after more than four months of Bolshevik rule. Latvian patriots approached the Entente

Powers, and the *de facto* recognition of the National Council by Great Britain and her allies led to the proclamation of the Latvian Republic on November 18th, 1918. By this time the Russian and German imperial armies, the Bolshevik troops who followed them, and lastly the irregular guerilla soldiery of the adventurer Bermondt, had pretty well completed the ruin of a formerly prosperous country.

At the time of our arrival at Libau, Britain was providing the Latvian Army with arms and munitions. Occupying the country, however, was a large German Army under General von der Goltz, which included many units, indistinguishable from German troops, formed by the Baltic Barons, the big landowners, who wished Estonia and Latvia to become Baltic Duchies in union with Prussia. They were fiercely opposed to the new Latvian Government and were supported by von der Goltz as far as he was able without actually breaking the Armistice with the Entente. The Russian Bolshevik armies, meanwhile, who were opposed to everyone, including the British, were operating in Estonia, and had invaded Latvia from the north. Here then were the materials for all sorts of trouble.

II

We spent several peaceful and unexciting weeks at Libau, after which I was ordered to take the *Seafire* to Windau, a small port on a river about sixty miles to the northward. The harbour was protected by two long breakwaters with ample quay space, and was not far from the front line where the Bolsheviks were being held.

We lay alongside, and it was a curious and saddening experience. The inhabitants were destitute and practically starving, though many of them had a considerable number of British golden sovereigns in their possession. The appearance of the children was pitiable, lean, ragged little scarecrows with pale faces and sunken eyes who gathered abreast of the ship holding out their bony arms and crying plaintively, "Mister! Mister! Please bread!" It took our kind-hearted sailors no time at all to improvise a soup kitchen on the jetty. Practically all of our rations went into it; but we had the satisfaction of knowing that for the three or four days we were there the small people were tolerably well fed.

Just after our lunch one day one little boy came navigating himself down the river on a small ice floe. Coming alongside, the urchin sent up the usual pathetic cry for bread. This was too much for our Gunner (T), a large soft-hearted Irishman called Michael O'Leary who rushed below to the wardroom pantry and reappeared on deck with the remains of the rice pudding we had had for the midday meal and a large spoon. The youngster anchored his ice floe and, in less than no time put away about three pounds of food. Soap, too, had not been seen for months, and the women were loud in their gratitude for the few bars of 'King's yellow' that we handed out to them. Our store-rooms would have been denuded if we had stayed much longer at Windau.

We sailed on the fourth day, and immediately on leaving the river ran into thick fog. The swept channel to Libau between the minefields and the coast was no more than three miles wide with various abrupt twists and turns, so we obtained permission by wireless to remain at anchor for the night and to move on when the weather cleared. We arrived at Libau next day, and on reporting myself on board the *Curaçoa* I found the delay was not at all to the taste of Walter Cowan. He did not consider that fog should deter destroyers, while I could only insist that I had taken a reasonable and seamanlike precaution in unfamiliar waters. We parted in some disagreement. Narrow water practice, as at Dover, was apparently not the same as that carried out by the Grand Fleet with the whole of the North Sea at its disposal.

While refuelling next morning I was ordered to take the *Seafire* into the naval harbour at Libau to hasten the movement of a merchant ship which was laden with arms for the Lettish army. Trouble was evidently brewing. The merchant ship's engines had broken down, and the Admiral wanted her moved into the outer harbour and away from any chance of being seized or interfered with.

The port of Libau consisted of an outer port, enclosed by breakwaters, leading to two good inner harbours. That to the northward was the naval harbour, consisting of several large basins approached by a narrow channel spanned by a swing bridge. It was opened when a ship blew four blasts on her syren. The commercial harbour was up a river, and was a long, narrow waterway with wharves on the town side and the entrance rather obstructed by sandbanks.

We steamed into the naval harbour and secured astern of the merchant ship carrying the arms. I sent our engineer officer, Engineer Lieutenant-Commander J. W. Baguley, to enquire about the repairs. He returned with the report that she would not be ready until the next afternoon.

Well behind the jetty alongside which the *Seafire* lay was a large barracks in which were housed a considerable number of German soldiers. Behind the barracks was a tract of pine forest. The Germans crowded round the ship, and had to be pushed back by our sentries.

Next morning I was sitting in my cabin talking to Charles Little, the captain of the *Cleopatra* and my class-mate in the *Britannia*, who had sailed up in his galley. The officer of the watch suddenly appeared to say that a man from the shore wished to see me. A large unkempt, wild-looking, fierce-eyed customer with a bushy black beard was ushered into my cabin. After much animated conversation, part Latvian, part my almost wholly-forgotten

German, with a few scraps of almost incomprehensible English, the whole accompanied by much gesticulation, we gathered that the Latvian G.H.Q., a mile or so away in the forest, had been attacked and captured by the Germans. Something had to be done, and that quickly, so I decided to go and see for myself while Charles Little set off in his boat to report to the Admiral.

As the black-bearded one and myself walked through the forest we came upon German soldiers staggering back with beds, pots and pans, chickens and loot of every sort. We hurried on, and presently came to a large house in a clearing. It was burning fiercely, and beside it a battalion of German troops were forming up to march off. Several Latvian officers, who had been roughly handled and their coats torn off, rushed up and began to explain just what had happened. After much excited and voluble conversation I gathered that the headquarters had been set ablaze after all the senior officers had been arrested and the records removed. By the time I had learnt this the troops had already marched off to the strains of a blaring brass band. There was nothing that I could do at the moment; but it was obviously no time for a ship full of arms to be lying alongside the jetty.

I rushed back hot-foot, determined to tow her out if necessary. However, our engineer officer, stout fellow, had been even better than his word, and the ship was practically ready. We cast off, and I ordered her to follow me down the narrow canal. I was in some doubt as to whether the swing bridge would open to my siren, and had visions of landing a party to take over the mechanism and shoot any Germans who resisted. But all went well. We reached the outer harbour without incident. There I was met with a signal from the Admiral to take the *Scotsman* under my orders, and for the pair of us to proceed at once into the commercial harbour and embark any members of the Latvian government with whom we could make contact. I gathered a 'putsch' was in progress, an armed movement by the Baltic Barons with the help of von der Goltz's troops to capture the Latvian government and replace it with one of their own. The situation was ticklish and dynamic. A couple of destroyers against the whole of von der Goltz's army seemed pretty tall odds, though of course there were our cruisers in the outer harbour.

The *Seafire* and *Scotsman* entered the narrow harbour stern first so as to be pointing the right way if we had to come out in a hurry. We secured alongside the wharf abreast of a very large building. It was the Custom House, and around it we saw considerable German activity which quickly died away when the destroyers appeared. Then started a series of farcical incidents which I can never look back upon without amusement.

The first thing was to dislodge the machine-gun parties at the ends of the wharf. Our guns were already manned, and a polite message was sent to the Germans to say that if they did not remove their machine-guns immediately they would be blown away. They went. A little later a German officer in need of medical attention was brought on board the *Scotsman*. It seemed that he had been ordered to seize the Custom House, a mission that was defeated by our sudden arrival. So mortified was he at his failure that he decided to commit suicide by shooting himself with his revolver. He had made an extremely bad job of it, and had merely chipped a bit of skin from the side of his head. He was treated with a few inches of plaster from the *Scotsman's* medical chest and sent ashore again.

Then a couple of the deposed Latvian ministers, not very important ones, succeeded in getting on board. We accommodated the Minister of Commerce in our small charthouse, where he promptly seized upon my typewriter and busied himself in producing inflammatory pamphlets. We heard that the Prime Minister, M. Uhlmanis, and other ministers had taken refuge with the British Mission, of which a Major Keenan, former resident in the Baltic States, was the head.

All that day and well on into the night the situation remained very tense. Soon after dark two Latvian trawlers, secured close under our bows, attempted to remount their guns which had been removed under the terms of the Armistice. We were not aware what this portended; but seeing no reason why the Baltic Barons should exercise sea power under our very noses we ordered the trawlers to cease their operations forthwith or be sunk. They made little objection.

During the evening meal I was informed that a German officer wished to see me. I went on deck to find a truculent young Baltic Baron armed to the teeth and in German uniform. His instructions were to ask my permission to search the Custom House. We had no orders to take any part in events on shore, so permission was given subject to our visitor being accompanied by a British officer. At the same time he was warned there was to be no fighting on pain of the destroyers' guns opening fire.

I sent Lieutenant-Commander Noble, captain of the *Scotsman*, to take part in the search, and he took with him a petty officer armed with a loaded revolver. Noble told me afterwards that, accompanied by a party of German soldiers, they made an exhaustive peregrination of the extensive cellars and storerooms tunnelled under the huge building. In one dark passage, where the search party evidently expected to find something, Noble told the petty officer to be on the alert. The petty officer drew his pistol and promptly let it off by mistake, fortunately without hitting anyone. This naturally caused a commotion. The Germans seemed anxious to shoot or bayonet someone; but Noble passed it off airily by waving his hands and repeating the only word of German he knew—"Nichts! Nichts!" The search continued.

Meanwhile, as Noble had not returned after about two hours I began to feel anxious, so went to the Custom House to see what had happened. The German sentries outside made half-hearted efforts to stop me; but telling them to go somewhere else in the best German at my command I pushed my way past them and tracked down the search party. I found them in an upstairs room, having rounded up five men and one old woman, who were about to be interrogated. The young ruffian in charge had opened the proceedings by sitting down at a table and putting two loaded pistols in front of him, this intimidation being rather spoilt by loud laughter from Noble. However, the search party discovered nothing. The prisoners were liberated, and so we went back on board and to bed. They had been searching for the missing members of the Latvian Government.

After we had been alongside a day or two the British Government sent a first secretary in the Diplomatic Service to help in dealing with the situation at Libau. He lived on board the *Seafire*. He made a bad start with his arrival, which was after midnight. Our sentries on the jetty had been warned to look out for him, and as luck would have it he was first halted by one of the *Scotsman's* sailors. This sentry ascertained his business, and shouted out to the *Seafire's* sentry, "Here's your bloke!"

Instead of treating it as a joke, our compulsory guest became extremely ruffled. His dignity was offended. However, received by our officer of the watch he was shown down to his cabin, vacated by one of our officers for his especial benefit, and having told the officer of the watch to call him with tea at 8 a.m. turned in. After breakfast next morning he complained to me of the extreme rudeness of the sentry and intimated that he considered the man should be severely punished. After listening to his lengthy complaint I told him, perhaps somewhat tersely, that he was extremely fortunate not to have been called something far more colourful, and left it at that. I fear he was a dissatisfied man, and thought little of the Royal Navy.

Admiral Cowan was well in charge of the situation, and of course was in touch with the British Government by wireless. All his messages to the Germans, in the shape of General von der Goltz, were transmitted through us. They were frigidly polite, always firm and sometimes acrimonious. Von der Goltz did not appear to realize that we were dictating terms, not discussing them.

We had established a line of naval sentries on the jetty about twenty-five yards out from the *Seafire* and *Scotsman*. Ten yards farther afield was a line of Germans, who tried to restrain the crowd of people flocking down to the jetty to see what was going on. The inhabitants had heard, of course, that British warships were on the spot. Not all the mob could be restrained. Now and then small boys or girls dodged through the line of Germans and came to one or other of the destroyers. Invariably they were given a large slice of bread and jam or anything else we had. One day during the dinner hour a small girl who had acquired something was making her way back through the German sentries when one of them knocked her flying with a box on the ear. I heard a roar of anger and sounds of commotion on deck, and arrived there just in time to find the ships' companies of both destroyers swarming over the rails fully determined to do battle with the German sentry and to heave him into the river. They would have done it; steel helmet, rifle and all, if we had not been able to reduce them to order and discipline. An incident of that sort might easily have provoked fighting and bloodshed.

One morning I was aroused by the noise of loud hammering and sawing. I went on deck to see a large force of carpenters erecting a high wooden barricade on the jetty abreast of the destroyers. I sent for the German officer in charge and demanded to know the reason, and he, most politely, told me that the general had heard we were being troubled by the populace and that the palisade was being built to ensure our privacy. He informed me that there would be a door in it with a sentry on duty. The Germans were obviously annoyed by our fraternization with the people, and the stream of inflammatory propaganda compiled by the Minister of Commerce in our charthouse may have had something to do with it.

It took them about two days to finish their barricade complete with an armed sentry to control entrance and exit. I went out and asked the officer if the job was quite finished. He assured me that it was, and that now we should have no further trouble with the crowd.

The jetty was a long one, so the *Seafire* and *Scotsman* immediately shifted berth to other billets outside the confines of the barricade, where, as before, we were soon being visited by the people with their children. We waited with interest for the explosion, which came within the hour. An enormous red staff car drove at full speed on to the jetty. It contained a general, I believe von der Goltz himself, who stood up in the car berserk with rage and started shouting and waving his arms in the air. He addressed no remarks to us. What he roared to his staff was anybody's guess.

After another day or two the excitement died down and the Latvian Government again took over the reins of office. I am not certain how the situation was cleared up; but I think Admiral Cowan's firmness and tact in a delicate situation finally persuaded von der Goltz that his support of the Baltic Barons was unprofitable.

We left the commercial harbour for the outer harbour, and soon afterwards the *Curaçoa* and two destroyers sailed on up the coast for Reval, the principal port of Estonia. It was by no means certain what portion of the Bolshevik fleet at Kronstadt was efficient. However, they might come out to do battle, and in any case were a greatly superior force to ourselves. So on the way to Reval and again after our arrival there we spent several days at sea practising the tactics to be adopted if we met them. To those who knew Walter Cowan and his great fighting record, it will be no surprise to learn that his tactics consisted chiefly of closing the enemy at full speed and engaging with every gun and torpedo that we had.

However, we had no further excitement, for towards the end of April, 1919, the Admiralty had succeeded in manning some of the 'V' and 'W' class destroyers with full crews, and they were sent out to relieve us. I was particularly sorry to leave Sir Walter Cowan's command; but it was really time. Our reduced crews had been kept hard at it, and, quite naturally, were uneasy about their turn for demobilization, though they had entered into the spirit of things and had given no trouble at all. We sailed for England in company with the *Curaçoa*, her steering gear having been damaged through the explosion of a mine.

III

Soon after reaching home, and having had our complements adjusted, we were sent to Harwich to relieve a division of other destroyers that had been sent abroad. Our duties were to run the mails and correspondence for one of the Inter-Allied Commissions in Germany, the one dealing with the disposal of the German merchant fleet and fishing vessels. The headquarters were at Hamburg, where the cruiser *Coventry* was lying.

One of the four destroyers remained at Hamburg, and the other three took turns at running the mail every four days. It was not very arduous, as the trip from Harwich was usually made in a night at 30 knots. However, the navigation in the approaches to the Elbe and going up the river was very tricky. The tides and currents were strong, and the place was a maze of shoals and sandbanks. Towards the end of our time our duties were varied by visits to Bremenhaven, on the Weser; to watch three large liners thought to be trying to get away to sea.

In November, came orders for my division to pay off, for which we took the *Seafire* to Devonport. I was sorry to see the last of her, for we had a good lot of officers and men and had enjoyed some quite amusing times together. She was a fine seaboat and fast in all weathers—33 knots 'all out' when it was not blowing. To me she seemed to have most of the qualities required by a destroyer—speed, a fair gun and torpedo armament, and a reasonably inconspicuous silhouette. Compared with their contemporary destroyers the 'S' class were faster and less expensive to build, and far more rapidly turned out. Some of them were completed in six months. I was to remember the *Seafire* and her qualities many years later when the then First Sea Lord asked for my views as to the best means of producing a rapid extension in our destroyer building programmes. The craft then produced were the well-known 'Hunt' class, which are now classed as frigates.

After paying off the *Seafire* I reported to the Admiralty to discover what the future held. I met with rather a frosty reception and was told nothing. I was not even allowed an interview with the Naval Assistant to the Second Sea Lord, responsible for commanders' appointments. So I climbed a flight of stairs and presented myself in the office of my old friend, Captain C. P. R.

Coode, who was still the Director of Operations, Foreign. After listening to what I had to say he made some pungent remarks about the Second Sea Lord's office and told me to lunch with him, when he would have some news. We met at the Royal Thames Yacht Club, where he told me an appointment in command of a destroyer would be along very shortly, and that meanwhile I was to go on leave.

In Edinburgh I settled down to the first real leave I had had since the outbreak of war. On the morning of January 1st, 1920, an official letter from the Admiralty arrived by the first post. However, I was not curious about my next appointment and put it aside to be opened in the evening when I came back from golf. I opened it just before dinner, to find I had been promoted to the rank of captain. It was a real surprise. I had only done four-and-a-half years as a commander and was still about a week under the age of thirty-seven. I was the junior promotion of the batch, and in those days, five-and-a-half or six years as a commander was by no means unusual.

CHAPTER X

I

I WENT to London to the Admiralty to interview the Naval Secretary to the First Lord, who arranges captains' appointments. He told me what I had been pretty sure of already, that there was no prospect of employment for some time.

In the summer my whole family, with the exception of my brother, Alan, in Singapore, took part of Bamburgh Castle, in Northumberland. We were a large party—my mother; my eldest sister, who in 1908 had married Doctor Edwin Bramwell, a distinguished Edinburgh physician, and their six children; my eldest brother, home from India with his wife and two children; my youngest sister and myself. It was a great family reunion in most pleasant surroundings, the first for many years.

It was at Bamburgh that I received my first appointment as captain, to the Naval Inter-Allied Commission of Control in Germany as President of Sub-Commission 'C'. I knew that this meant I should be in charge of the destruction of Heligoland; but little else. I took passage to Heligoland at the end of September, 1920, and relieved Captain Leonard L. P. Willan, who had been there for a year.

The Commission consisted of Naval and temporary Royal Marine elements, the Navy being represented by the President, myself; Surgeon Commander Leonard Warren; and Paymaster Lieutenant Charles H. S. Leicester as secretary. The temporary Royal Marine party consisted of Brigadier-General Knox, in charge of the technical personnel and representing the Civil Engineer-in-Chief at the Admiralty; a Colonel Warren; a Major whose name I cannot recall; and Captains Hamilton and Dutton, all civil engineers with temporary rank in the Royal Marines. There were also a number of civil engineer personnel of foreman grade with temporary rank as sergeants. It was necessary, of course, that all our people should be in uniform.

The actual work of destruction was carried out by two or three thousand German workmen under the superintendence of our technicians. Though our late enemies were supposed to produce the plans for demolition, they were largely made by our own officers, men of great experience and ability. Most of them had taken part in the construction of Rosyth dockyard. There were also 200 German police, ostensibly to protect the Commission against the workmen. In point of fact the workmen were very friendly, and we got on much better with them than with the 'politzei'.

Most of our officers and other ranks had their wives with them, and those of the officers who wished it were quartered in a small hotel.

The Heligolanders themselves were very friendly. Among the older men there were still to be found pensioners who had served in the Royal Navy before the island had been handed over to the Germans in 1890. The people were of Frisian extraction and had no liking for the Germans. This was hardly surprising, as on the outbreak of war they had been evacuated willy-nilly to Hamburg. They were a fine, sturdy race and grand seamen, undeterred by any weather. They made their living by lobster and other fishing, and fleecing the hordes of German tourists who used to flock to the island during the summer. They were most anxious to be given their independence, and I feel that the decision after the Second World War to keep the inhabitants off the island and turn it into an R.A.F. bombing target was hurriedly taken and a mistake.

On the whole life was pretty dull. There was little room to walk about. The Brigadier-General and I visited the work every morning, which was only a walk of a mile-and-a-half. However, I learnt a lot about explosives and demolitions, which stood me in good stead later on.

The winter was most trying, with gales nearly all the time and the spray flying in sheets right over the island. It was a grand sight to stand on the red cliffs and watch the great breakers rolling in from the westward to burst on the rocks below. But even in the winter we managed to take exercise. Brigadier-General Knox, who was an athlete of some distinction, organized badminton in the unused Kursal. During the summer we used a concrete tennis court laid out in the old German gymnasium.

My German opposite number, the Reichscommissar, was an exceptionally nice man with a gift for languages. He had originally been a silk merchant in Chefoo, North China, and had many British friends. He was equally fluent in German, English or French, though I very soon noticed that when a French Admiral or General visited Heligoland his French mysteriously vanished and an interpreter had to be provided.

The demolition of the fortifications, which it had been anticipated would take five years, progressed rapidly. Certain modifications to the original plan had to be allowed, the Germans being permitted to maintain their Biological Institute, which was more or less an international concern devoted to the study of bird migration and the habits of fish and lobsters.

By the middle of 1921 it was evident that it had become a waste of money and personnel to keep the large establishment of Sub-Commission 'C' in being. So we proposed that it should be withdrawn in October, and that the work of demolition, to be completed in another twelve months, should be supervised by periodical visits of officials from the Civil Engineer-in-Chief's Department at the Admiralty. This was accepted, and in the autumn we were taken home in a cruiser. We were not sorry to see the last of Heligoland. Another winter there would have been dismal indeed.

In spite of the doubts that have sometimes been expressed as to whether or not the fortifications and harbour at Heligoland were effectually demolished after the war of 1914–18, I can most confidently assert that they were. The breakwaters could never again have been used, even as foundations. The eastern one, a structure on steel piles, was practically removed, the piles being drawn piecemeal like teeth. The big western breakwater, built up of large caissons filled with concrete, was blown apart with a succession of charges of two to three tons of explosive. Such photographs of Heligoland that I have seen since the end of the Second World War, indicate that the new breakwater had been built inside the remnants of the old and that the harbour had been much reduced in size. Ashore, on the island itself, every subterranean structure was blown in and demolished, and in most cases the roof was collapsed. Heligoland was as honeycombed with hewn-out tunnels and caverns as is the rock of Gibraltar today.

The truth is that with modern equipment, and a sufficiency of labour and material, no place can be demolished permanently.

II

By the time I returned to England in October, 1921, the shape of things to come was well advanced so far as the Navy was concerned. Apart from the cruiser squadrons abroad there were to be two main fleets, one in the Mediterranean, and the other, the Atlantic Fleet, at home, each with their quota of battleships, cruisers and destroyers. On application at the Admiralty, however, I was told there was no further appointment for me in the immediate future; but that I might do a course in the spring to brush up my technical knowledge. So after reminding the Naval Secretary that I was first and foremost a destroyer officer, I went on leave to Edinburgh.

In February, 1922, I was appointed to Portsmouth for what was known as the 'Senior Officers' Technical Course', where we attended lectures at the gunnery, torpedo, signal and anti-submarine schools, and so forth, and were brought up-to-date in all the technical developments inaugurated during the war. I found it most useful, for things had changed greatly, and having served practically continuously in destroyers there was much which was entirely new to me. I did not complete the course for in April, as luck would have it, I was appointed, greatly to my satisfaction, Captain (D) of the 6th Destroyer Flotilla.

It was true that the Sixth was only a reserve flotilla, manned with two-fifths complements. Nevertheless it was a step in the right direction, as it would lead, all being well, to the command of a fully-manned flotilla in one of the main fleets. We also came under the orders of Rear-Admiral (D), at that time Michael H. Hodges, who flew his flag in the light cruiser *Coventry*.

I joined the flotilla leader *Shakespeare* at Portsmouth, to find that my eight destroyers were distributed at Portsmouth, Devonport and Chatham with crews too reduced to steam them to Port Edgar, which was to be our base. My first task was, therefore, to persuade the Commanders-in-Chief at the three Home Ports to lend us sufficient men to take our ships north. After about a month's importunity I finally got the flotilla together and took them to Port Edgar.

Once there we were far from idle. So far as our fuel allowance and reduced crews permitted we went constantly to sea for exercises. There was another reserve flotilla at Port Edgar under the command of Captain John C. Hodgson, a well-known destroyer officer. On one occasion, by reducing half the destroyers to two or three ratings each, we made up a flotilla nearly fully-manned, and went north to Invergordon for exercises with the Atlantic Fleet and the other destroyers. Hodgson went in his leader and so was in command; but I embarked as his staff officer. The Atlantic Fleet at that time was commanded by Admiral Sir John de Robeck, my old acquaintance of Dardanelles days. However, it was the first time I had met his Chief of Staff, that tall, good-looking, imposing and rather intimidating officer, William Wordsworth Fisher, who went by the name of 'The Great Agrippa'.

Time passed pleasantly enough in these activities from Port Edgar, especially as I was so close to my home in Edinburgh. But I was delighted when, in December, 1922, I was appointed to relieve Captain A. K. Betty as Captain (D), 1st Flotilla, which though it belonged to the Atlantic Fleet, had been temporarily detached to the Mediterranean for service in Turkish waters.

Just before Christmas I crossed to Calais and left for Istanbul—Constantinople—by the Simplon Express, an interesting but quite uneventful journey across Europe. On arrival I had great difficulty in finding out anything about the whereabouts of the First Flotilla, the only certain thing being that they were not at Istanbul. I put up in a most indifferent hotel, and was not at all sorry when the flotilla arrived in a few days and I took over the command.

My new ship was the flotilla-leader *Wallace*, a fine little vessel with a great turn of speed completed by Thornycrofts' just after the war. There did not seem to be very much for the flotilla to do. We anchored as a rule in the northern part of the Bosphorus about fifteen miles from Istanbul, and exercised periodically in the Black Sea.

After this long interval it is waste of time to write of the long and complicated dealings with Turkey after the First World War—the armistice of November, 1918, followed by the occupation of the Dardanelles and Constantinople by Allied ships and troops; the dissention among the Allies; the landing of the Greek Army at Smyrna in May, 1919, and its drive into Asia Minor; the Turkish nationalist activity under Mustafa Kemal Pasha which brought into being a new Turkish government over all territories not under Allied occupation; and the final annihilation of the Greek army which brought the Allies face to face with the victorious Turks on the Asiatic shore of the Dardanelles which had been proclaimed a neutral zone by the Allies. We were perilously close to another war, and at one time, when Ismet Pasha looked like trying to ferry the Turkish army across the Bosphorus, we planned an operation in which the flotilla was to steam up and down the narrow strait at 30 knots. The heavy wash would have wrecked and destroyed the boats, most of which were berthed in tunnels.

It was by no means an idle time for me. I was busy getting to know the officers and men of the flotilla, and working up the ships according to my own ideas. It was probably a painful experience for some who needed a shake-up, and on occasion I may have been rather outspoken in my strictures. In fairness, however, it has to be said that there was a good deal of uncertainty and discouragement among the officers. We were no longer the first Naval Power. The Washington Treaty of February, 1922, had whittled the Royal Navy and scrapped many ships. Because of this shrinkage many officers had become redundant and were in the process of falling under the 'Geddes axe'. One-third of the captains were removed from the active list at a blow, with many commanders, lieutenant-commanders, lieutenants and sub-lieutenants.

To my mind this drastic pruning showed a great lack of foresight and understanding on the part of those responsible, particularly in the case of the younger officers. Many of them, who had expected to remain in the Service until the usual age for retirement on pension, were thrown out into the world on miserable pittances at an age at which it was difficult, if not impossible, to make a new start in life. There were numerous cases of extreme penury and hardship, which did not encourage parents to spend money on putting their sons into a profession which treated them so harshly. The 'Geddes axe' was one of the greatest injustices, and incidentally the worst advertisement, the Royal Navy ever suffered. I think the Admiralty, in the shape of the Second Sea Lord's Department, deserve full credit for the smoothness of our naval demobilization after the Second World War, and for the fact that the hardship and injustice of another drastic 'axe' were successfully avoided.

But I have digressed.

The 3rd Destroyer Flotilla, commanded by Captain Frank Forester Rose, very well-known in the destroyer world, was also in the Constantinople area. One night, in conjunction with them, we carried out an attack on the battleship *Iron Duke*, the flagship of Admiral Sir Osmond de B. Brock, the Commander-in-Chief, in the Sea of Marmora. The incident remains in my mind because the movements of the flotillas, which of course were working without lights, were co-ordinated by radio-telephony. This apparatus was afterwards discarded in the fleet, and most mistakenly, because, I believe, of the difficulty of making a record of what was said!

After about three weeks in the Bosphorus we were sent through the

Marmora to join up with the force anchored in the Dardanelles just above the Narrows between Chanak and Nagara. I had gazed upon this same scenery from the distance eight years before in the *Scorpion*, and it was most interesting to see it from the other end—the hills and gullies of the Gallipoli peninsula which we had finally been compelled to evacuate after such heavy fighting; the Narrows which we had failed to penetrate because of the minefields and batteries. Here we came under the command of the Rear-Admiral, First Battle Squadron, John D. Kelly, a great character and fine seaman and another friend from Dardanelles days when he had commanded the cruiser *Dublin*.

However, my short period of service in this area soon came to an end, for at the beginning of March, 1923, the 1st Flotilla was ordered home to pay off and recommission for further service with the Atlantic Fleet. After another short visit to Constantinople we sailed for England by way of Malta and Gibraltar and dispersed to our Home Ports, the *Wallace* going to Portsmouth.

III

After recommissioning we went north to Port Edgar for working up, and then joined up with the Atlantic Fleet. We carried out the usual strenuous training from Scapa Flow, Invergordon and the Firth of Forth—tactical and strategical exercises; night attacks and massed day attacks on the heavy ships; screening the battle fleet at sea against submarines, with, of course, the usual gunnery and torpedo exercises and harbour drills. Our activities at sea were greatly curtailed by the fuel allowance, which was drastically restricted; but every minute underway was spent in some exercise or another. Our leaders were not allowing us to sit back and be idle because it was peace.

I had an excellent lot of commanding officers, keen and experienced in destroyer work, and I do not think the 1st Flotilla was behindhand in anything. It was a time of change. Asdics for the detection of submarines under water were just being supplied to destroyers, and although we were not so fitted we were rather proud of being the first destroyers to be supplied with gyro compasses.

It should have been a period of greater transition and development as a result of the lessons learnt during the First World War. But the Navy, like the other Services, was sorely handicapped by the popular anti-war and economy campaigns, and the steady reduction in the annual estimates. Aircraft were coming into their own and people, retired Admirals among them, were beginning to ask—"What is the good of battleships?" Heavy ships cost millions, and what use were they if they could be bombed and sunk by cheaper aeroplanes?

This being a personal record, I need hardly go into the details of the Washington Treaty which, among other limitations, brought a ten years 'holiday' in the building of capital ships. It was worse still when this was followed in 1923 by the Government's edict that no major war was to be expected for ten years. People were pinning their faith to collective security under a League of Nations to which not all the nations subscribed. The United States of America was the most notable abstainer. The Navy, meanwhile, most of whose ships had seen hard service during the war, was beginning to suffer from senile decay.

Starting in a small way, the Navy had been using and developing seaplane-carriers since 1914. To the best of their limited capacity these ships and their seaplanes did good work in the First World War.

The Navy was already coming to regard aircraft as an integral part of its armament, so much so that in 1918 certain battleships and battle-cruisers carried land aircraft mounted on their turrets with short runways built out to the muzzles of the guns. At best it was a cumbrous expedient; but with the ships steaming into the wind the aircraft could take off. Once in the air, however, they must either come down in the sea, where they would probably be lost, or else make for a shore aerodrome. These 'planes were primarily intended for artillery observation.

The next development came with aircraft-carriers designed to accompany the fleet at sea, and equipped with wheeled aircraft of special naval type to serve as advanced reconnaissance and striking forces. Hence the *Argus*, a $20\frac{1}{2}$-knot ex-passenger ship, which I believe had been fitted with a full-length flight deck before the end of the 1914–18 war, and was to all intents and purposes a mobile aerodrome complete with hangars and runway. She was closely followed by the *Furious*, one of Lord Fisher's so-called 'light' cruisers originally armed with 18-inch guns and designed for service in the Baltic; and the *Eagle*, an ex-battleship building for the Chilean Navy, both of which were in the process of conversion at the end of 1918. The Navy was slowly feeling its way.

In April, 1918, however, for reasons which I need not go into, the old Royal Naval Air Service and the Royal Flying Corps had been merged into the Royal Air Force under control of the Air Ministry. In 1923, when I was serving in the *Wallace* with the Atlantic Fleet, air co-operation with the fleet at sea was still in embryo, though naval flying had existed for about twelve years. Our aircraft-carrier was the *Argus*, which embarked her complement of fighter or reconnaissance aircraft 'as requisite' from the R.A.F. Base at Leuchars, in Fifeshire. For co-operation with the Navy the R.A.F. also maintained a base for flying boats at Calshot, and various flights of torpedo-carrying and artillery observation aircraft at Gosport.

From start to finish the control of the Naval Air Arm by the Air Ministry was a ghastly failure which militated against the vital air efficiency of the Navy. As the Air Estimates also were ruthlessly shorn, the Naval Air Arm became a sort of Cinderella, starved, neglected and nearly forgotten. It was not until 1937, after a severe and protracted struggle on the part of the Admiralty when Admiral of the Fleet Lord Chatfield was First Sea Lord, that ship-borne aircraft again came under the full operational and administrative control of the Royal Navy with whom they would work in war. It was only just in time.

IV

By the spring of 1923, when I rejoined the Atlantic Fleet with the *Wallace* and First Flotilla, there had been changes in the destroyer command. Rear-Admiral Michael Hodges had been succeeded by Rear-Admiral Arthur Waistell, who in April went to the Admiralty as Assistant Chief of the Naval Staff. He was relieved as Rear-Admiral (D) by Rear-Admiral George H. Baird, an appointment of which we heard with some trepidation. Our hearts rather sank, for our new Admiral was a well-known character and reputed to be tough and a stern disciplinarian with no compassion whatever for those who failed to satisfy his rigid sense of duty. But we found, greatly to our surprise, that he was not altogether the man he had been painted. Perhaps his service in the Mediterranean as Commodore of Patrols during the later stages of the war had softened him, for we found him human and full of understanding, though not suffering fools gladly. He could be terse and even rude when necessary, as on the occasion when his dinner-table, just laid for a party was inadvertently washed out with a hose through the open skylight.

At first there were three fully-commissioned destroyer flotillas with the Atlantic Fleet, with another two flotillas in reserve at Port Edgar. By September, however, the number of fully-commissioned flotillas had been increased to five, which meant that Rear-Admiral (D), who flew his flag in the *Coventry*, had sixty-three destroyers under his command, a large number. In September, 1923, indeed, apart from a very large number of ships of all classes in reserve, we maintained in full commission in seagoing fleets and squadrons all over the world 13 battleships; 2 battle-cruisers; 31 light cruisers; and 63 destroyers, which figures cause one to think nowadays. I do not think that Argentina, Chile or Guatemala would have dared to make passes at British colonial possessions in 1923, when we still had a respectable seagoing fleet!

People certainly appreciated the Royal Navy in those days. 'Hurrah cruises', or visits to the large ports of Great Britain were the fashion. The idea was excellent, though the process was rather wearing to the senior officers. In the summer of 1923 the First Flotilla visited Newcastle-on-Tyne, where the hospitality of the citizens was unbelievably kind. We did what little we could to return the hospitality; but could never repay it all, or the wealth of warm feeling or friendliness. It was overwhelming.

Our later visit to Douglas, Isle of Man, was something of a fiasco. There we were regarded as part of the amenities for the attraction of visitors, rather like a fun fair. They came on board in their hundreds. We did our best to entertain them, and show them round the ships. They left us with our decks dirty; littered with cigarette ends, empty ice-cream cartons and the grisly and gummy remains of shrimps and other edibles in paper bags cast or crammed into odd holes and corners, even the working parts of guns.

We went to our Home Ports for Christmas leave, and then reassembled at Portland with the whole fleet before voyaging south through the Bay of Biscay, with exercises all the way. En route to Gibraltar the First Flotilla visited Cadiz, where we had a hectic time.

Our next port was Gibraltar, where we rejoined the fleet. Immediately on arrival I was called upon to enquire into an incident which had occurred in a destroyer of the Second Flotilla, where the coxswain, returning from leave one night, was attacked and thrown over the jetty. One enquiry had already been held, and though there was strong suspicion against two seamen of that destroyer there did not seem to be any evidence that would convict in a court-martial. The Commander-in-Chief, Sir John de Robeck, and our own Rear-Admiral (D), could not tolerate the perpetrators of such a gross breach of discipline going unpunished, so I was detailed to carry out an exhaustive enquiry on board the actual destroyer. I demanded the assistance of an accountant officer, and Rear-Admiral Baird detailed his own Secretary, Paymaster Lieutenant-Commander A. P. Shaw. This was the first time I came into contact with this most able officer who afterwards became my Secretary, and to whom I am heavily indebted for fourteen years of devoted service from 1932 until I finally left the Admiralty in 1946.

But to resume about the enquiry, we sat for ten days and examined nearly every one of the 120 men of the destroyer. The necessary evidence was collected and two men were brought to trial, one being convicted and sent to penal servitude and the other acquitted. One amusing incident occurred as we took evidence. It came to light that the coxswain who had been thrown into the sea was nicknamed 'the Grocer'.

"Why this peculiar nickname?" I asked an old petty officer who was not giving much away.

"I couldn't rightly say, sir," said he, looking puzzled.

"Was the previous coxswain called by this name?" I demanded.

"Oh, no sir!" the petty officer replied at once. "He weren't called no names. He was the heavyweight boxing champion of the Atlantic Fleet!"

After a few days a troupe of ballet ladies we had seen at Cadiz arrived to give their performance at Gibraltar. It was extremely popular, and the officers of the First Flotilla decided they must have a gala night to mark their appreciation and the renewal of the Cadiz acquaintance. The commanding officers took one stage box to which I was bidden, and the first lieutenants the one opposite. The second lieutenants, who called themselves 'The Middle Class Union', because they came between the first lieutenants and the sub-lieutenants, occupied the whole of the front row of stalls. The wardroom messman had been told to produce a bouquet which I was to hand to the leading lady, rather an old hag.

When the performance started I observed with a slight sinking feeling that Rear-Admiral (D) was seated in the fourth row of the stalls. However, all went well until the moment came for me to present the bouquet. The wardroom messman, a Maltese had done his job only too well, and had brought an enormous structure of flowers which contained a good deal of earth as well. As I leant out of the box to present it it burst into fragments, showering bits and pieces on to an astonished drummer and cellist below. The audience cheered wildly. However, the leading lady gripped what remained of the bouquet and put it behind the wings. Then she tripped off into the Salome ballet, in which Salome goes mad. She was gallivanting around pulling her maniac grimaces when a loud sailor's voice came from the back of the theatre, "Coo! She's seen R.A. (D)." This fairly brought the house down. Not even his best friend could have called Jock Baird a handsome man.

These were not all our activities. We were constantly at sea for practices, and in March carried out strategical exercises with the Mediterranean Fleet, after which we sailed for our Home Ports, the *Coventry* and all the destroyers calling at Ferrol on the way. In the Bay of Biscay we ran into a howling north-easterly gale in which we rolled our decks under and took in water everywhere. Even the battleships were rolling heavily, and I heard one of my sailors remark that he reckoned they would have to postpone the final of the petty officers' billiard handicap—the cynical contempt of the small ship sailor for his contemporary in a battle-wagon!

During the ensuing leave period Rear-Admiral Baird, who incidentally was a very sick man, told me I should be relieved in May. I protested, as I had hoped to do two years and was thoroughly enjoying my time as Captain (D). But it was no use. My service in a reserve flotilla was counted in, and as usual during peace it was difficult to provide all captains with adequate sea time. However the pill was sweetened when I was told that I was to be appointed as Captain in Charge, Port Edgar, the destroyer base on the South Queensferry side of the Firth of Forth. I was pleased not to be parted altogether from destroyers.

After the leave period our cruise took us to Portrush, in Northern Ireland, and then back to Liverpool and Manchester. We were the only flotilla to visit

Manchester. Rear-Admiral Baird came with us, and flew his flag in the *Warwick*. We had an interesting journey up the Ship Canal. The destroyers had to arrange to lower their topmasts while passing under the nine bridges, and it was a sight savouring of old-time seamanship to see the topmasts dipped on passing under a bridge and rehoisted immediately afterwards. We thoroughly enjoyed our visit to Manchester, where the Lord Mayor and citizens were as kind and hospitable as the people of Newcastle-on-Tyne the year before.

The *Wallace* had to go to Portsmouth with defective turbines, and it was there, in May, 1924, that I was relieved by Captain Kenneth MacLeod.

Rear-Admiral Baird, whom we all greatly admired, was suffering from an incurable affliction, of which he was aware. On August 11th, 1924, on board the *Revenge*, he was knighted and invested with the K.C.B. by the Commander-in-Chief of the Atlantic Fleet, Admiral Sir Henry Oliver, on behalf of the King. This honour was gazetted on August 29th, three days before Baird was relieved as Rear-Admiral (D) in the *Coventry* by Rear-Admiral A. P. Addison.

CHAPTER XI

I

I BECAME captain in charge of Port Edgar base, or H.M.S. *Columbine*, in October, 1924. On the south side of the Firth of Forth, upstream of the bridge and close to South Queensferry, it had originally been a small fishing harbour, little more than an area of mud which dried out at low water enclosed by two stone breakwaters. Port Edgar was taken over by the Admiralty for use as a destroyer base just before the First World War, the little harbour being dredged and wooden piers or jetties erected for the accommodation of about thirty-six destroyers. Oil fuel, electric power and fresh water were laid on to all the jetties, and the necessary workshops, power station, drill sheds, barracks and canteens erected ashore. In course of time the disused fishing harbour became a first-class advanced base for destroyers which certainly proved its utility.

By the autumn of 1924 the use of Port Edgar, except as a safe and comfortable berth for the Atlantic Fleet flotillas during their periodic visits to the Forth, had rather lapsed. Most of the repairs to destroyers were carried out in the Royal Dockyards. The Atlantic Fleet flotillas had also been reduced to three—twenty-seven destroyers—in full commission, with one reserve flotilla at Port Edgar.

As captain in charge at Port Edgar I had a small corrugated iron house with two reception and four bedrooms overlooking the pens, where, as a bachelor, I lived in great comfort. When the Atlantic Fleet flotillas were away there was little to do, particularly as the ship's company had been so reduced that it comprised little more than a spare crew for a destroyer and a few artisan ratings, perhaps four hundred in all.

Port Edgar was part of the Atlantic Fleet, so to speak; but in some ways came under the ægis of Commanding Officer, Coast of Scotland, who lived at Admiralty House at Inverkeithing and was also Admiral Superintendent of Rosyth Dockyard. When I joined Rear-Admiral Sir Reginald Tyrwhitt held this appointment. I was greatly contented, for I knew him well through my earlier service in destroyers. In June, 1925, he was relieved by Vice-Admiral Sir Walter Cowan, another old friend. As neither of these distinguished officers cared much for speaking at public functions I was fairly often roped in as their deputy on my side of the Forth.

In the spring of 1925 considerable numbers of boys were being entered for the Navy, principally, it was said, to make up the numbers necessary to provide the large crews for the *Nelson* and *Rodney*, then under construction. An officer from the Admiralty came to Port Edgar and recommended that five hundred boys should be sent to us for a sort of post training service course. I welcomed the idea, but was uncertain how the Commander-in-Chief, Atlantic Fleet, Admiral Sir Henry Oliver, would regard an innovation which poached on his preserve, so I took the precaution of obtaining a copy of the report and sending it to the Commodore of Home Fleet Destroyers.

The scheme suggested included a month's cruise in the Reserve Flotilla, then commanded by Captain John Tovey, now Admiral of the Fleet Lord Tovey, an old and valued friend who had served with great distinction in destroyers during the 1914–18 War, particularly at Jutland.

The scheme went ahead at full pressure, and gave us all as much to do as we wanted.

Soon afterwards the Atlantic Fleet arrived and we discovered to our horror that the Commander-in-Chief had not been consulted by the Admiralty and that all the arrangements had been made without his knowledge. Tovey and I became regarded with deep suspicion, and were lined up before an enquiry held by the Chief of Staff and Commodore (D). Needless to say we defended ourselves with vigour, and when I asked the Commodore what had happened to the copy of the report I had sent him he produced it from his pocket. He had not forwarded it to the Commander-in-Chief. This put an abrupt end to the proceedings. All the same, the Commander-in-Chief's staff were left with a very sore feeling about the whole business, as they considered their authority had been overridden. Not so Sir Henry Oliver, who came and inspected the organization and expressed himself as completely satisfied. A year later, when I said good-bye to him on board his flagship he was most complimentary about the training.

My time at Port Edgar was largely uneventful. The general strike of 1926 affected us very little, though I was put in charge of the security of the port of Leith with a considerable force of seamen and marines from the battleship *Royal Sovereign*, reinforced by a few hundred students from Edinburgh University. Nothing untoward happened.

In March, 1926, Sir Walter Cowan was told he was shortly to be appointed Commander-in-Chief, America and West Indies Station. In a charming letter he asked me to come as his Flag captain and Chief Staff Officer. I jumped at it. The small glimpse I had had of the West Indies in 1905 made me very willing to go there again, added to which I was delighted at the idea of serving with a man for whom I had so great an admiration.

Before going abroad, however, I had to retire to a nursing home to let the doctors have a try at sorting out my inside, which had been giving me a deal of trouble for the last year or so. This I did in March, and after following a false scent the surgeons removed my appendix. Time was short, and I had to join my next ship swathed in bandages, not a pleasant prospect for a West Indian summer.

While I was in the nursing home my mother died. It was not unexpected, for she had been failing for some time. But the breaking of the link which held the family together was a great blow to us all, and I was glad to be going abroad. My recollections of her are all very happy ones. Her unfailing kindness, cheerfulness, sound common sense and ability to see the humour in almost any situation endeared her to everyone who knew her.

II

The flagship of the North America and West Indies Station, the cruiser *Calcutta*, arrived at Portsmouth in April to pay off and recommission with a new ship's company. So great was the popularity of the station that three or four times the number of men required came forward to man her. We had a completely volunteer crew, and as captain I was able to take thirty specially selected boys from Port Edgar with their divisional lieutenant. I also took Commander H. M. Maltby from Port Edgar, a man whom the sailors loved and respected, so we got off with a good start.

I commissioned the ship early in May and took her to Bermuda. Sir Walter Cowan was to follow in June. On arriving at Bermuda we berthed inside the dockyard. I reported myself to the Commander-in-Chief, Vice-Admiral Sir James Fergusson, and made the acquaintance of his wife and four daughters.

The next few weeks were spent working up the *Calcutta* and being initiated into the mysteries of staff work by the Secretary to the Commander-in-Chief and the Staff Officer Operations. It was my first experience of working with a trained staff, and some of my early minutes on the documents placed before me filled them with consternation. The weeks passed pleasantly enough with dinner parties at Admiralty House and Government House; but most pleasant of all were the supper picnics in the grounds of Admiralty House with Lady Fergusson and her daughters, while the Admiral had a stag party. We used to spread out our meal near the gravestone of one Francis, a midshipman, whom rumour said had been knifed by the Admiralty House butler in the early nineteenth century for undue familiarity with a housemaid.

However, Bermuda was uncomfortably hot, and we were glad enough when Sir Walter arrived and we could set off on a cruise.

In those days there were four small 'C' class cruisers and a couple of sloops on the North America and West Indies Station. The squadron's principal duties were showing the flag, keeping in touch with the Royal Canadian Navy, and answering calls from any of the West Indian islands in the event of civil disturbances. The station was so vast that the Commander-in-Chief could never hope to visit it all during the term of his appointment. It included both the east and the west coasts of North America and the whole of the

Caribbean, and, later on, when the 'North' was dropped out of our title, we had both coasts of South America as well.

I am convinced that the policy of showing the flag, particularly in South America, was extremely valuable. Not only were the authorities most affable and hospitable wherever we went; but our visits were warmly welcomed by the British communities in all foreign states. It certainly did good for the White Ensign to be seen in every port, though in course of time being entertained and entertaining in return became something of a bugbear. We literally had no time to ourselves. Visits to ports in the United States, too, did good in ensuring that at least a few British officers made the acquaintance of some of the United States Navy.

On our first cruise we went straight to Halifax, and experienced for the first time the wonderful Canadian hospitality. After a short visit we then sailed for Newfoundland. We fished the rivers running into Hawke Bay and Hare Bay, and wonderful fishing it was. Even those who had never cast a fly had a try at it, though the black fly and clouds of mosquitoes at night soon eliminated all but the most ardent. A call at St. John's completed our Newfoundland cruise.

Our next ports of call were Quebec and Montreal. I was greatly interested in the approaches to Quebec and the passage up the river. The currents and shoals of the St. Lawrence are notorious, and as we steamed through the narrows with their fierce tides we could not help wondering how Saunders, in 1759, managed to get his fleet and the transports containing Wolfe's army up to Quebec. He owed much to James Cook, later famous as the navigator, who I believe took a round-about northern passage. Anyhow, the French defenders were uncomfortably surprised when the fleet appeared. Vaudreuil the governor wrote: "The enemy have passed sixty ships of war where we dare not risk a vessel of 100 tons by night or day."

We went on to Montreal, where berthing in a basin with a 6-knot current running past the entrance was something of an experience. I was grateful for my practice at that sort of entry at Port Edgar. It was after entering the basin at Montreal on one occasion, and watching the *Capetown*, commanded by a distinguished ex-navigating officer enter after us and bump his stem hard against the wall and fracture it, that the Commander-in-Chief said to me: "There you are, Cunningham. When you get an ex-gunnery officer as captain his ship never hits the target; an ex-torpedo officer loses all his torpedoes, and an ex-navigator always hits the wall!"

Montreal was known as the sailors' Mecca. They loved it, and were made most welcome by the hospitable Canadians. Practically everyone in the ship had a hat-peg with some family ashore, while the officers were made honorary members of every club and of at least three or four golf clubs. Even there we had the greatest difficulty in paying for our caddies, and though there was prohibition one became an honorary member of at least half-a-dozen lockers in the dressing-room, each with its bottle of whisky. There were no official functions at Montreal. All these had been cleared off at Quebec, for which we were duly grateful. Montreal was so popular that in organizing cruises for the squadron we always tried to arrange for every ship to spend seventeen or eighteen days there during the summer.

On that first cruise we also visited Charlottetown, Prince Edward Island. My chief recollection of this place is of an enormous dance in the town hall to which all and sundry had been invited. They turned up in every imaginable garb, one young man in shorts and a football jersey. I heard the Lieutenant-Governor say to the Commander-in-Chief: "I guess, Admiral, he's come *pre*pared to *per*spire."

Having handled a squadron of battle-cruisers Sir Walter was not particularly interested in handling a squadron of light cruisers. When I first approached him with the chart of an anchorage, and asked when he would take charge of the squadron for anchoring, he said: "Can't you do it?" Having been a Captain (D) and used to handling destroyer flotillas I assured him that I could. "All right," said he. "You carry on. I'll stay on the after shelter deck and gallop the flag lieutenant." This he did to some effect; but he 'galloped' the navigating commander as well. The Admiral would allow no signal, not even the one to 'Anchor instantly', to remain at the masthead. It had to be hoisted close up and immediately hauled down.

It was the custom for the ships in northern waters to visit ports in the United States during the summer. Though always most interesting, these visits were not much sought after. The Americans were always charmingly hospitable, but it meant a perpetual round of official entertainments which brought a considerable strain on the officers, particularly the Admiral and captains.

This year, on our first cruise, we visited Philadelphia, where there was some sort of exhibition. We had an interesting entry and passage up the Delaware River to the Navy Yard.

An American officer, Lieutenant-Commander Alan Kirk, had been detailed to attend on the Admiral as liaison officer. Under Kirk's auspices we made our round of official calls on the Governor, the Admiral of the Navy Yard, the Mayor and so on. We visited the exhibition at some length, and on the way back to the ship, without the least warning, were shown into a large hall in which some thousands of the American Legion were holding a meeting. The Admiral was called upon to say a few words, which he did most manfully and was cheered to the echo. Sir Walter was always at his best when called upon to speak at a moment's notice.

We were taken to Princeton University where, after lunch and a speech or two, we saw the football match between the University and the Navy. The Naval Academy was in quarantine because of an epidemic of measles, so we and a few American naval officers were the only representatives of the

Navy. Under the able leadership of Alan Kirk we did our best to out-shout the regimented and well-drilled legions of the University. It was a poor best. Most of us thought that American football was a poor edition of our English 'Rugby'. Walter Cowan, however, was delighted. "There's no nonsense about this game," he said. "You don't have to wait till a man's got the ball before you scrag him."

We all thoroughly enjoyed our Philadelphian visit, though we were never out of uniform and could rarely relax. Alan Kirk was a tower of strength and greatly liked by everyone. I corresponded with him at Christmas every subsequent year until I met him again as a Rear-Admiral during the Second World War. He was one of the Naval Commanders during the invasion of Sicily in 1943, and Naval Commander during the American landing in Normandy the next year.

We got back to Bermuda at the end of September, 1926, and settled down to the usual base routine with harbour drills, exercises at sea and squadron competitions. The *Calcutta* proved to have a grand ship's company, and with Maltby as commander we were well in the lead in all activities. My thirty selected boys from Port Edgar were in the forefront of everything. My staff duties took me over to Admiralty House on Clarence Cove, Hamilton Island, two or three mornings a week. It was about two miles away as the gull flies, and I invariably sailed over in my galley, which kept my hand in.

The small dockyard port at Ireland Island, Bermuda, could accommodate four medium sized cruisers alongside; but though excellent in fine weather was supposed to be unsafe in a hurricane. In fact the Station Orders laid it down that at the approach of a hurricane all ships should leave the port and either go to sea or anchor in the Great Sound, the large and commodious anchorage between Ireland and Hamilton Islands. Having read accounts of experiences of ships anchored in the Great Sound during a hurricane, of how in a visibility of less than twenty-five yards they had to steam at 12 knots to their anchors and never knew if they were dragging, I personally doubted the wisdom of this injunction. My opinion was soon to suffer a nasty jolt.

It was on October 21st, I think, that reports came through of a hurricane in the West Indies moving as usual for the coast of Florida. Later news showed it was turning north earlier than expected. The captain of the *Capetown* and myself happened to be dining that evening at Admiralty House, and there we discussed the reports that the hurricane might pass close to Bermuda the next day. On returning on board I held a meeting with the *Capetown's* captain—an eminent navigating officer; our squadron navigating officer; and the master-attendant of the dockyard, a lieutenant-commander who had been passed over for promotion; but, as I had very good reason to know, a skilful navigator of excellent judgment and a sound meteorologist. In the light of reports from Washington the two senior experts held that the centre of the storm would pass 300 miles north of Bermuda next afternoon, and that though we should have strong gales there was no cause for alarm. The master-attendant, on the other hand, maintained that the centre of the hurricane would strike Bermuda, and how right he was. I inclined to the opinion of the two seniors, especially as no hurricane had visited Bermuda in October for over a century.

When I was called at five o'clock next morning it was blowing a full gale from the south-eastward. All we could do was to ride out the storm where we lay. I had never experienced a real hurricane, and was to receive many shocks. The Bermuda islands are surrounded by reefs, rather like the low rim of a saucer with its centre represented by the lagoon. The heavy seas broke heavily over the reefs and filled up the lagoon, with the consequence that the wharves and jetties in the dockyard, normally about five feet above sea level, were very soon awash. We were lying alongside in a basin roughly three hundred yards square. The fierce wind was blowing us on to the jetty, and before long the heavy wooden dockyard fenders were riding clear of the top of the jetty and completely useless. A heavy sea was sweeping in through the narrow entrance, and the ship was rolling deeply, grinding and shuddering against the solid masonry. To add to our other troubles the visibility was practically down to zero because of the torrential, driving rain. The *Capetown* in the inner basin, more sheltered, was rather better off.

At about 12.15 there came a lull, followed by a flat calm. We knew what this portended. The barometer showed the centre of the storm was right on top of us, and that presently the wind would blow with increased violence from the opposite direction. We spent the interval getting out fresh hawsers, and eventually had forty parts of wire hawser to the shore. We had had to let go the starboard anchor underfoot to bring some of the bow hawsers in through the hawse-pipe and secure them to the bitts.

At 1.30, sure enough, it came on to blow much harder than before from the north-west. The strength and noise of the wind were unbelievable, and we were told afterwards that the anemometer ashore registered 138 miles an hour and then gave up the ghost. A tin hut abreast of the ship took wings and vanished. I saw our wireless aerial, four single strands of wire, disappear like a cloud to leeward. I clawed my way forward to the forecastle to see how the hawsers were standing the strain, and arrived just in time to see them snapping like string. The bollards were too close to the edge of the jetty, and the ship, listed by the wind, brought a tremendous upward pull which was more than the hawsers could bear. Then the stern wires carried away, and off sailed the *Calcutta* across the basin. I had visions of the ship ending her days on the very jagged-looking breakwater to leeward. However, the anchor underfoot was slowly bringing her head to wind, and by dint of going full speed ahead on both engines we succeeded in avoiding the breakwater and crashing her on top of one of the round stone structures at the entrance to the basin. Two plates in the flare of the forecastle were stove in; but it was better than being broadside on to the rubble.

The commander, Maltby, and about fifty sailors leapt ashore and secured the ship with dockyard berthing wires. Two young officers swam down with grass hawsers from the berth we had just left so unwillingly, so that we were able to pass wire hawsers across and were pretty well safe again. Maltby, dressed only in a pair of bathing trunks and an old monkey jacket, was an odd sight. It was in the midst of all this excitement that a signalman rushed up to him with a pad, "There will be no tennis at Admiralty House today," the signal read. As if that were not enough, the paymaster commander, oblivious in his cabin to all the wild happenings on deck, sent Maltby a message asking if it would be convenient to pay the boys! The commander's language, I fear, was beyond redemption.

Henry Bradford Maltby was a fine seaman with a wonderful way with men. His memory for all their home affairs was prodigious, and it was quite an experience to see him walking along the upper deck asking one man about the latest addition to his family, another for the lastest news of an ailing wife, or a boy for news of his mother. The men loved and respected him. He was lost at sea as Commodore of a North Atlantic convoy in the Second World War, a fine and gallant officer and a great loss to the Service.

At about 6 p.m. the storm took off sufficiently to allow us to haul back to our original berth. We were sadder but wiser men, speaking, that is, for the captain. The *Capetown* had sustained no more than minor damage; though at the height of the hurricane she had pulled the steel bollards on the jetty to which she was secured, together with masses of solid concrete, clean away. She had had an unhappy time in finding anything really substantial to which to secure.

Our minds, however, were diverted to others. Two of our ships, the *Curlew*, a cruiser, and the *Valerian*, a single-screw sloop, had been due to arrive at Bermuda that morning. We were in wireless touch with the *Curlew*, and knew she was about a hundred miles south of Bermuda. Her weather was dreadful; but she was in no danger. Not so with the *Valerian*, a ship of 1,250 tons. She had reported herself as five miles south of Bermuda at 8 a.m. on October 22nd, and having looked at the Narrows found it nothing but a seething cauldron of sea and spray. The visibility was down to almost nothing, and none of the navigational marks could be seen. She did not attempt to enter; but turned to the south-eastward to face the storm. That was the last we ever heard of her. She was called again and again. There was no reply.

Meanwhile a signal of distress asking for immediate assistance had come in from a steamer to the south-east of Bermuda. The Admiral had ordered the *Curlew* to proceed to her rescue. I need not go into details; but when we had no answer from the *Valerian*, the *Curlew* was ordered to search for her, and the *Capetown* was sent to sea at daylight next morning, October 23rd, to assist. The *Calcutta* was temporarily *hors-de-combat*.

Meanwhile the squadron navigating officer and myself tried to assemble some data to fix the point at which the search should start. By great fortune we hit upon the right spot, and the *Capetown* picked up a Carley float with twenty-nine of the *Valerian's* survivors. The rest of her officers and men had gone down with their ship when she capsized at about 1.30 p.m. on October 21st, very soon after the wind had chopped round to the north-west.

The subsequent court martial on the *Valerian's* survivors, on which I sat as President, threw little light on the cause of her loss. It appeared she was overwhelmed by the terrific wind, and an enormous sea from the opposite direction. My own opinion, however, is that she touched one of the outlying reefs and that capsized her. Not a vestige of the ship or her equipment was ever recovered.

The court martial, while completely exonerating the survivors, brought out the wonderful *sangfroid* of the ship's company in a desperate situation, and the great gallantry and devotion shown by the engine-room personnel and Sub-Lieutenant Ronald Summerford, who lost his life while trying to evacuate the men from the engine and boiler rooms. A memorial to those lost in the *Valerian* was set up in the dockyard church at Bermuda.

The Admiralty naturally asked why the ships in the dockyard basins had not gone to sea or anchored in Great Sound before it was too late. However, their Lordships eventually agreed with our view that a dockyard port which could not be used in any weather was hardly worthy of the name. Various improvements for the berthing of ships were put in hand; bollards being replaced well inshore, and large hawsers and special fenders being provided for ships lying alongside.

III

With the Commander-in-Chief on board we sailed from Bermuda on January 3rd, 1928, and arrived at Nassau after a bad passage of five days. We called at Gun Cay, the headquarters of the rum-running industry only sixty miles from the Florida coast, and while the *Calcutta* lay off I sailed into the inner lagoon in a cutter to see what was going on. It was interesting to see the denizens of this lagoon and their decrepit-looking schooners laden with gallon cans of strong liquor. We went alongside one, and a more depraved-looking set of ruffians I never saw. I had some difficulty in preventing them from passing a couple of cans into the cutter. There were two fast motor-boats used for ferrying the liquor to the mainland, and an American coastguard motor-boat ready for sea at a moment's notice to chase any rum-runner that made a break for it. As it did not appear that any international law was being contravened we took no action.

We stayed some days at Nassau, and then went on to Kingston, Jamaica, where we took part in the reception of the Duke and Duchess of York, their present Majesties, who arrived in the *Renown*. Life, with its spate of official dinners and receptions, was very strenuous. What I enjoyed most was dinner with the Duke and Duchess on board the *Renown* at which the Admiral and I were the only guests. We had to leave rather early, as we had to go on to a dance given in our honour by the Jamaica Club. I have rarely seen anything done so well, with masses of people, a dancing floor built outside on the lawn, a sit-down supper on the tennis lawn and champagne flowing like water. I did not get away until 4.30 a.m. after refusing kippers, bacon and eggs and more champagne.

We were particularly gratified when the Duke and Duchess found time to come on board the *Calcutta* and inspect our sailors.

The *Renown* sailed, and our next ports of call were St. Lucia, Georgetown (British Guiana), Trinidad, Grenada, St. Vincent, Barbados and Antigua before returning to Bermuda early in March. At every place we visited we had the usual dinners, dances and receptions on shore, and gave a dance or afternoon party on board to return the hospitality of the inhabitants.

Of all the islands Antigua interested me most, as I particularly enjoyed visiting the old dockyard at English Harbour, which had been used by Nelson in 1784-87 as captain of the *Boreas* and Senior Officer in the Leeward Islands. As we passed through the old gates we went back nearly a century and a half at the sight of all the old apparatus of sailing ship days, the storehouses, careening berths, and anchors laid out for warping in and out of harbour. There was also the house on the hill overlooking the little harbour where William IV lived in 1787 when, as Prince William Henry, he was captain of the *Pegasus* and a friend of Nelson. Great sums of money must have been spent in fortifying the surrounding heights. All the batteries were overgrown; but the guns were still there if one chose to look for them in the thick bush. The death roll from yellow fever must have been prodigious. I visited the old cemetery, which contained stones and memorials bearing sixty to a hundred names on each. I was shocked, as the graveyard was utterly uncared for; a mass of tangled vegetation and most of the graves little more than heaps of broken rubble. We thought that a great country like ours could have spent a little money in keeping it tidy and decent.

At Trinidad and Barbados Sir Walter and I spent some days ashore at Government House. At Trinidad we stayed with Sir Horace and Lady Byatt, where I made the acquaintance of Miss Nona Byatt, Sir Horace's sister, and discovered that it was her 'scottie' that I had brought home from Malta in the *Scorpion* in 1917. Government House was run rather like a hotel. Our host and hostess could not have been kinder. There were five guests staying in the house and three in a cottage in the grounds, and one just drifted in and said what meals one required. We enjoyed surf riding and bathing, and were introduced to the West Indian dishes of swordfish pie and crab back stew. I liked the latter until I discovered it was made of the large and ugly land-crabs I had seen scuttering around; then I was not so certain.

At Barbados we stayed at Government House with that most kind and hospitable Irish couple Sir William and Lady Robertson, he from Limerick and Dublin and she from County Cork. We got back to Bermuda early in March having been lavishly entertained wherever we went. People were genuinely delighted to see us, and no one can be more hospitable than the people in the West Indies. We did what little we could to return their kindness.

We were at Halifax, Nova Scotia, for the first few days of July, and then went on to various unsophisticated places in Newfoundland for the salmon fishing—White Bear River, St. George's Bay, and Hawke Bay. But we had a definite job to do. The cruiser *Raleigh* had gone ashore on Point Amour, on the Labrador side of the Strait of Belle Isle, in August, 1922, and had become a total loss. The ship was fast on the rocks, and a Canadian professor who often made the voyage through the Straits had written to the Admiralty suggesting that the wreck should be blown up, as the sight of it lying there apparently undamaged caused much derision among his American fellow passengers at the expense of the Royal Navy. So we had been ordered to destroy her, and were given an unlimited allowance of depth-charges to do so.

We anchored in Forteau Bay, Labrador, our first sight of the *Raleigh* having shown us how right the professor was. Except for the absence of guns and a rusty side the ship looked quite undamaged. The winter ice had pressed her hard up on the rocky shore; but on surveying her I found 2 fathoms of water on the landward side and no less than 5 fathoms to seaward. One supposes that the distance from a port with the necessary appliances, or the lateness of the season, prevented any effort to salve her at the time. Her destruction proved a tough proposition. She was very strongly built; but by blowing our way down to the magazines and putting the charges there we finally made a complete job of it. When we left her the bow and stern were off and the port side blown right out. She looked like a wrecked tank, quite unrecognizable as once having been a ship.

After this we spent a fortnight at Hare Bay on the north-east coast of Newfoundland, where the Admiral and I went about eight miles up the Ariége River, and camped in the same place that the officers of the *Cordelia* had used about thirty years before. That it was a good fishing spot was shown by the fact that I caught six salmon while my coxswain was pitching my tent. As I wrote to my aunt: "The most extraordinary thing about the camping was the absolute silence, no sounds except for the birds, and very few of them, and the occasional plop of a leaping salmon. The birds stole the food off your plate if you weren't looking. One night we were visited by a bear,

I

or at least we found his tracks in the mud about ten yards from my tent. On one occasion when the cook had gone off into the forest to chop wood he came face to face with a moose, and hastily abandoned his operations—— A mattress of spruce twigs made a wonderfully comfortable bed—— The total bag of salmon for the whole fishing season by all on board was 366, of which I got 41—— We are now (August 10th) bound for St. John's. Civilization again: dinners, dances, receptions——"

After a few days at St. John's, Newfoundland, we went up to Quebec for forty-eight hours and on to Montreal for seventeen days, where the people were as charming and hospitable as ever. After further brief visits to Newfoundland and Halifax, Nova Scotia, October 1st found us at St. John, New Brunswick. While there the Admiral and several of us dined with the Ancient and Honourable Artillery Company of Massachusetts, they having elected to hold their annual dinner in New Brunswick because of the absence of prohibition there. They all came from Boston, about three hundred of them, and appeared in their old-time uniforms. It was a gargantuan meal of many courses and the more speeches, and I was informed that the drink bill alone for the visit of the 'Ancients' to St. John ran into something like the equivalent of £6,000 quite apart from food, accommodation and other entertainments. No wonder they were received with open arms, and that St. John was given over to revelry. We went on to St. Andrews, New Brunswick, and anchored in the river which formed the boundary between Canada and the United States. It was a lovely little place, and I never saw more beautiful colouring than the autumn crimson of the maple leaves or the bright scarlet of the rowan berries.

This year, 1927, Boston and Washington had been chosen for visits of the Commander-in-Chief in the *Calcutta* accompanied by the *Cairo*, Captain J. A. G. Troup. We were most hospitably received at both places. There was the usual full round of entertainment for officers and men, and at Boston the city gave us a huge luncheon at which the American Admiral proposed the toast of the visitors. In a most friendly way he made great play with the Battle of Bunker Hill, and said he had taken care to berth the *Calcutta* in a billet from which we should have a good and continuous view of the monument commemorating that battle. But Sir Walter Cowan, who by this time had been promoted to full Admiral, and was always at his best when speaking on the spur of the moment, gave rather better than he got. He alluded to the fight off Boston between the *Chesapeake* and *Shannon*, and the banquet prepared by the Bostonians for the captured British officers which never came off. It brought the house down.

We steamed up the Potomac to Washington by night with the *Cairo* close astern, approaching the Navy Yard at 8 a.m., to find the *Mayflower*, the President's yacht, with the President on the bridge, just going alongside. There was an amusing scene on the bridges of both cruisers as the captains and officers hurriedly shifted into full-dress coats and cocked hats over ordinary trousers and sea-boots. Gold-laced trousers were more than we could manage.

We were again provided with a liaison officer of the United States Navy. He certainly did his job. The first day, October 17th, was spent in an interminable series of official calls upon the American Army and Navy authorities; the Secretaries for War and the Navy; the British Minister, in the absence of the Ambassador on leave, and many others. All of these calls were punctiliously returned, and for two days we lived in an atmosphere of guards and bands.

On the second day Sir Walter, his personal staff and myself visited President Coolidge at the White House, and on the third morning we laid a wreath on the tomb of the Unknown Warrior at Arlington. We spent five hectic days at Washington and were literally never out of uniform. Except for a large dinner given on board by the Commander-in-Chief we never lunched or dined in the ship. It seemed to be the custom for rich American ladies to give semi-official dinners and dances in our honour. At one of these entertainments a large tray of cocktails was handed round before we sat down. Our flag lieutenant-commander, E. H. Kitson, took one and was about to toss it down when the American liaison officer broke in with a very loud whisper—"Kitson! Kitson! Don't drink that. This woman's bootlegger is bum!"

All our officers and men were lavishly entertained with luncheons, dinners, dances, sight-seeing tours, theatres, race meetings, golf, tennis and football matches, and the United States Marine Corps took complete charge of our Royal Marines. Perhaps one of the most successful entertainments was the dance given by the ships' companies of the *Calcutta* and *Cairo* to 900 American sailors and their girl friends. Both ships were rigged out to allow of dancing almost anywhere on the upper decks, the music of the Royal Marine band being relayed by loudspeakers.

Our visit to Washington was a most pleasant though gruelling experience, and we were glad to be back in the comparative quietness of Bermuda at the end of October. "I am feeling the consequences of too much high living," I wrote at the time. "What with this and the sticky hot weather I am busy manufacturing excuses for not going to dances. I had quite enough of them in Washington to last me for some time."

Entertaining and being entertained is all very well; but a few days of high-pressure official engagements and entertainment from 9.30 a.m. one morning until 3 or 4 a.m. the next makes the average naval man long to get away to sea. Courtesy visits to foreign ports and 'Showing the Flag' cruises do a great deal of good; but they are among the most strenuous exercises I know and ruinous to the digestion.

IV

The Admiralty had decided to relieve the 'C' class cruisers abroad by the slightly larger and newer 'D's'. The 'C's' were all badly in need of long refits, and so far as the *Calcutta* was concerned we were badly overcrowded as a flagship. Accordingly the *Calcutta* was ordered home in November to pay off at Chatham and turn over to the *Despatch*. We arrived on December 4th, and did not at all appreciate the frost and snow after the sun of Bermuda. The *Despatch* was commissioned, and having made very few changes among the officers and ship's company we sailed from England on December 20th, 1927, and set off down Channel on our way to Bermuda via the Azores. I have never known a worse trip.

Four hundred miles west of Ushant we ran into a full-blooded westerly gale, and were hove to for nearly two days with the ship continually under water. Never since I had brought the *Scorpion* home from the Mediterranean ten years before had I seen such huge seas. The *Despatch* stood up to it fairly well; but the weight of water on her light forecastle caused it to subside,, and it had to be shored up from the keel upwards. Her stern wagged up and down about four feet, and made one wonder when it might break off. We struggled on when the weather moderated and passed the Azores on Christmas Day, having, as we thought, lashed and secured everything on the upper deck. Two days later we ran into another howling gale from the northward. This brought the wind and sea right abeam, and various fittings on the upper deck were smashed or washed overboard. At 2 a.m. the ship suddenly gave a violent shudder, tipping all the officers out of their bunks aft. The engines were stopped, and when re-started the horizontal tail-wagging was so violent that they had to be stopped again. It was found that the port propeller was the cause, so we steamed on on the starboard engine only and reached Bermuda on December 31st. A strong wind was blowing, and with one tug and a propeller out of action I anticipated difficulty in getting alongside the dockyard wall. So before passing through the channel in the reefs to the dockyard I decided to try the port propeller once more. Apparently there was little the matter with it. Later, when we went into dock, we found that the edge of the propeller blades near the boss had been driven flat for a depth of about six inches. We came to the conclusion that a large, steel wash-deck locker had lodged on it on being washed overboard, had jammed there for a time, and then been shaken free again before our arrival.

While in England I had been to the Admiralty and had had an interview with the First Sea Lord, Admiral of the Fleet Sir Charles Madden. He told me that the Government attached so much importance to showing the flag in South America that two of our four cruisers were to be there fairly constantly, only visiting Bermuda for exercises. I pointed out that they would become rather inefficient at gunnery and so on; but he replied that this must be accepted as being of less importance than flag showing. At the same time the whole of South America was added to our station, which now, on paper, extended as far as the South Pole.

It was therefore decided that the Commander-in-Chief in the *Despatch* should inaugurate the extension of our station by a cruise to the west coast of South America, visiting as many states as time permitted. Our itinerary included Nassau; Belize, British Honduras; Puerto Barrios, Guatemala; Jamaica; the Panama Canal; Guayaquil, Ecuador; Callao, Peru; Coquimbo, Valparaiso, Antofagasta in Chile; the Panama Canal again; Puerto Cabello, Venezuela; and then back to Bermuda by way of Trinidad, Barbados and Antigua. This long trip, which took us just over three months—January to April, 1928—was a most exacting one·for the Commander-in-Chief and his staff. Except at sea we had no rest at all from a long series of official functions. Luckily the distance between ports was considerable, which gave us several days of complete rest to recover from a succession of busy days and late nights.

I cannot hope to write fully of this most interesting cruise, so must confine myself to a few of the high-lights. At Puerto Barrios the Admiral and staff, thirteen other officers and fifty ratings were the guests of the government and taken 200 miles by special train to Guatemala City and heavily entertained. The Admiral and I actually stayed with the British Minister, Sir Archibald Clark Kerr, now Lord Inverchapel. We were taken to call on the President, a very mild-looking man remarkable for not having imprisoned anyone for his political opinions. Guatemala City is a lovely spot 4,000 to 5,000 feet up on a plateau, with cold nights and beautiful clear and sunny mornings when one could see half-a-dozen volcanoes smoking in the distance.

After Jamaica and the passage of the Panama Canal our next port of call was Guayaquil, the port of Ecuador right on the Equator and about sixty miles up a muddy river. I have never seen so many mosquitoes. When they were disturbed in clouds as we furled the awnings on leaving they put a number of our signal boys on the sick-list. Perhaps, being young, they were the most succulent. We had the usual official entertainments, and punctuality is not an Ecuadorian virtue. At one dinner to which we were bidden we were kept standing for a full forty-five minutes while a band played both National Anthems several times over.

At the Peruvian port of Callao, our next stopping-place, we usually rolled heavily at our anchor. The entertainments took the usual form and were for the most part held at Lima, some twenty miles inland and connected by a wonderful broad motor road.

During our stay the Admiral and I were taken in an 'autocarrell'—an ordinary six cylinder Hudson car with railway wheels—up into the Andes. The railway was a wonderful feat of engineering, and passed over slender-looking bridges spanning hideously deep gorges and in and out round the spurs of the precipitous mountains. We only went up to 11,500 feet; but at that time, before I had done any long-distance flying, I found it was quite enough for me. Any exertion was most unwelcome. The cattle lived in the mountains, and we were told that they ran a milk train every morning into Lima. It descended by gravity down gradients that were terrifying to us. If I had been the driver of that milk train I should have made very certain of my brakes before attempting the journey.

After Callao, Coquimbo, in Chile, was a rest cure. There were one or two official receptions; but we managed to get in a little exercise in the way of tennis.

We reached Valparaiso early on a Saturday morning in March, and were at once whirled into the usual official calls, and return calls, with a pre-arranged programme that occupied every moment of the days, and a good deal of the nights, of our eight-day visit. It was more strenuous even than Washington, which is saying a lot. I think we were the first British warship to visit Valparaiso since the First World War, and the welcome we received alike from the Chileans and the British community was overwhelming. They went out of their way to see that every man on board had cause to remember his visit.

There were race meetings, picnics, luncheons, cricket and football matches, sight-seeing tours, receptions, dinners, dances and I cannot remember what else. Every officer and man was fully occupied. The Admiral and I visited the local cavalry regiment, the Pieto Curassiers. Sir Walter, being a keen horseman, was absolutely in his element, and we listened to a long and technical discussion between him and the colonel of the regiment as to how much a horse should carry and eat on active service. I do not know what result was arrived at; but on leaving the Admiral was presented with a lance with the regimental pennon. We also visited a division of the Chilean Army in camp. They were a tough-looking crowd of men who marched past doing the goose-step, being German-trained. We were entertained with champagne, beer and speeches, and after a visit to the large local landowner on the way, with more liquid refreshment, reached the ship just in time to change into the appropriate garments for a dinner given by the British Consul General followed by a ball given by the British community. After an exhausting day I finally flopped into bed at 4 a.m. next morning.

We had one day's respite, with no more than some tennis in the afternoon and an evening reception, and the next morning the Admiral, myself and about ten officers and two hundred ratings set off in a special train for Santiago, the capital of Chile, just over 100 miles away. The Admiral and staff called on the President; and the President inspected our sailors drawn up in front of the palace. After this they marched past, with the populace cheering enthusiastically.

The men were then taken to the Sporting Club and given a large meal, followed by another at 5 p.m. at the British Club, after which they returned to Valparaiso by train. The officers were accommodated in the Union Club at Santiago and one of the large hotels. I was put up in the Club in the most princely suite I ever inhabited, and trembled to think what the annual subscription might be. There followed a dinner and a ball given by the British community. I finally got to bed at 3 a.m. and had to catch the 8 o'clock train back to Valparaiso. It was here I met a Chilean lieutenant, Peña by name, who had served with me in the *Scorpion* years before, and had retired and was now associated with the nitrate industry.

After a couple more days of official and unofficial engagements we sailed for Antofagasta, almost completely exhausted after eight days of entertainment and quite glad to get to sea. As I wrote at the time, the Chileans were overjoyed at seeing us. I have never met such friendly people. They were charmed with our little Admiral, who made some very good speeches, and were much impressed by the bearing of our men. There is no doubt that British sailors are among our best ambassadors, and it is good to see that these goodwill visits to South American ports are being continued.

Much the same round of entertainment was repeated at Antofagasta. The Admiral, however, had rather worn himself out and was unwell when we arrived, so I had to deputize for him.

Antofagasta is a fine port built in connection with the railway to export the nitrate, and the Intendente, or Governor, took us up country to visit a nitrate 'officina'. It was just a town, built in the middle of an area of what looked like dried-up mud, and very complete with its hospitals, canteens, dance halls, cinemas and so on. Between 2,000 and 3,000 men were employed, and when one area was worked out, in twenty-five years or so, the whole town was moved on to another spot. We went all over the works and had the process of extracting the nitrate explained and demonstrated. Finally we visited the hospital, which had an English matron, and she invited the Intendente and myself to visit the maternity wards, a peculiar job for an unmarried naval officer. I rather blenched, though not the Intendente, and together we paraded through two large wards full of expectant mothers and others whose expectations had already been realized. Next day we attended a mounted gymkhana staged in our honour by a cavalry regiment. I had to make a speech about horses and horsemanship, about which I knew little except by hearsay from the Admiral; but the Chilean colonel was so pleased that he gave me another lance to present to Sir Walter.

On the way north again we spent two days in the Panama Canal Zone, mostly taken up with lunches and dinners with the American authorities, and then went on to Puerto Cabello, Venezuela. It was not much of a place; but we were driven out to the capital of the province, Valentia, to lunch with the local Governor. We also met President Gomez, a fine-looking old man and a strict disciplinarian. Some students who had demonstrated against his régime were at that moment imprisoned at Puerto Cabello and working daily on making roads. This soon cured their discontent.

So, after further visits to Trinidad, Barbados and Antigua, we ended our South American cruise and returned to Bermuda. It undoubtedly did good in showing the White Ensign in places and countries where it was rarely seen, and our reception everywhere was outstandingly cordial, particularly by the British communities. The friendliness of the people was most marked, and we heard no claims to British Honduras or to British dependencies in the Antarctic. I wonder if one of His Majesty's ships would receive so cordial a reception now? I believe she would, and am convinced that a cruiser or two in South American waters would be of the greatest value to our trade. For us the cruise was very exacting. But it was thoroughly instructive, and opened the eyes of both officers and men to the wealth and possibilities of those countries in South America.

We arrived at Bermuda towards the end of April. Our time on the station was drawing to a close, and I was expecting to be relieved in about July. Vice-Admiral Sir Cyril Fuller had already been appointed to relieve our Admiral in August.

Our packing-up was rudely interrupted on July 2nd by a wireless signal informing us that the *Dauntless*, newly arrived on the station, was ashore off Halifax and in a bad way. We hurriedly embarked the Admiral and all the available salvage gear, and steamed north at 24 knots in fine weather. Things were looking grim for the *Dauntless* when we first saw her, and I never thought she would take the sea again. It was blowing up from the south-west, and she was pounding heavily in the swell and holed in the engine-room and one boiler-room, listing over and covered with escaping oil fuel. To seaward in the clear water we could see the huge boulders over which she had drifted. If it came on to blow a gale we thought she must break her back.

We got a salvage company underway and ordered up salvage floats from an American port at a price which to me seemed frightful, 8,000 dollars a day. The Admiral, however, refused to haggle. Luckily the weather remained fine, and a large floating crane from Halifax was able to remove guns, torpedo-tubes, funnels, and everything that could be moved from the *Dauntless*. The Salvage Master, a Canadian 'Bluenose' skipper, was splendid. The thought of that 8,000 dollars a day going to the Americans just infuriated him and caused him to work like a madman.

The *Despatch* had to sail on July 12th for Bermuda to meet Admiral Fuller. The compressed air arrangements for helping to float the wreck were by no means completed; but it was decided to take advantage of our great towing power and to have a try at plucking the *Dauntless* off before we left. She had a tug forward and another aft with the *Despatch* pulling in the middle. High water was at 3 p.m. and we all tugged together. We gradually worked up speed. Our hawsers came twanging and thrumming out of the water under the heavy strain. We watched them in anxiety; but after a little hesitation the *Dauntless* bumped over the obstructions to seaward and slid off into clear water, afloat once more. At this very moment the American salvage floats were towed through the entrance, too late to be of any use. The Salvage Master became delirious with joy.

We sailed for Bermuda at once, arriving on July 13th. Our remaining few days were spent in farewell parties and turning over to the new Commander-in-Chief and his staff.

We had had a memorable commission in the *Calcutta* and *Despatch*, and I was very sorry to leave the *Despatch* and her magnificent ship's company. On the whole, however, I had had more than enough of the endless round of ceremonial visits and all the social concomitants of luncheons, receptions, dinners and dances. I felt it was high time to get back to the Navy and bring myself up-to-date in the latest developments. In the West Indies one was very much out of it.

We sailed for Liverpool in the Pacific Steam Navigation Company's *Aroya*, and arrived on August 4th, dispersing to our several destinations.

It was a sorrowful moment when I parted from Sir Walter Cowan. When we started in the *Calcutta*, and having known him in the Baltic and at Rosyth, my feelings towards him were those of respectful admiration. But having served with him for more than two years in the much more intimate appointment of Flag Captain and Chief Staff Officer I had come to regard him also with real affection. I do not think that in the whole of that period we ever had a serious disagreement. He taught me a lot. His ideals of duty and honour were of the highest, and never sparing himself he expected others to do the same. We all knew his reputation as a fighting sailor, and of his unbounded personal courage. Nothing ever daunted him. His views on men and things in general were always refreshing, though sometimes unorthodox. To say that he inspired us is no exaggeration. Hasty he undoubtedly was; but if in his haste he unjustly hurt people's feelings or wounded their susceptibilities he was at pains to make amends at the earliest possible moment.

I have spent no happier years at sea than when serving with Sir Walter in the *Calcutta* and *Despatch*. It was the beginning of a friendship which has strengthened with the years and which I greatly cherish.

CHAPTER XII

I

I WENT to the Admiralty and reported myself in the Naval Secretary's office, though with little hope of getting a sea-going command for some time. As a bachelor shoregoing appointments had little appeal for me; but before coming home I had decided to make the best of it and to ask for Shotley, the large training establishment at Harwich. However, that appointment had already been filled, and I was asked if I would like to take the course at the Army Senior Officers School at Sheerness.

I understood that the course was designed to test the fitness of majors and lieutenant-colonels for command of their units. Captain R. B. Ramsay, an ex-submarine officer, was the other naval officer appointed, and together we joined at the end of September, 1928. We listened to many lectures on military subjects, to say nothing of being instructed in the double entry method of keeping accounts, which made me all the more appreciative of the fact that the Navy possessed an accountant branch. We did exercises on the ground in the surrounding country, and established defensive positions on the Detling ridge in deep snow. I do not know that the course itself was of any great value to a naval officer; but one certainly acquired a nodding acquaintance with the problems involved in Army supply. The value of living in a mess for three months with officers of another service was, of course, incalculable. It mattered little how we naval officers acquitted ourselves; though there was some satisfaction in showing that we also knew how to 'reeve a ration' from the home depot to the front-line trench, and to provide the troops with their greatcoats on a cold night after the battle.

Towards the end of the year I again enquired at the Admiralty about future employment, and learned rather to my horror that I was to be nominated for the next year's course at the Imperial Defence College. I felt some alarm because I had never undergone a staff course, and was largely ignorant of staff organization in a big fleet. Also, after two years in the West Indies I was considerably out-of-date.

The I.D.C. had been in existence for some years. Its admirable object was to bring together senior officers of the Royal Navy, Army and Royal Air Force, with officers from the Dominions, and to train them for higher command in a knowledge of each other's problems. Instruction was also given in foreign affairs and economics, and the course was attended by senior Civil Servants from the Foreign Office, and practically all the Ministries. The whole course was designed to broaden the mind and to get the students thinking on subjects outside their own particular service. The Commandants were appointed in turn from the Royal Navy, Army and Royal Air Force, and the instructing staff was drawn from all three Services. Students were supposed to be specially selected for the course, and this method was rigidly adhered to by the Army and the R.A.F. In the case of the Navy, however, it was sometimes the custom to take who was best available, a bad practice which occasionally resulted in the naval students being of an inferior calibre to their military confrères. However, I should not complain as otherwise I do not think I should have been selected.

I look on my year at the I.D.C. as one of the most interesting and valuable I have ever spent. It was mostly new ground to me, and at times the going was hard. But the expert staff officers were always ready to help one out. I learnt a lot, and the association with the Civil Servants, with their views and ideas that were entirely new to me, was particularly valuable.

Besides the most fascinating lectures and addresses the course took us on many interesting expeditions. We visited tank schools, gas schools, naval establishments at Portsmouth and elsewhere, R.A.F. stations, experimental establishments and many others. One most informative trip was to the 1914–18 battlefields in France under the guidance of General Sir A. Montgomery Massingberd. His astounding memory, the way without notes or a map he could point out prominent features of the battle areas and could name all the commanders engaged, were matters of wonder to us all. At Le Cateau the General even knew the names of some of the platoon commanders.

While at the I.D.C. in 1929, I had my first flight in an aeroplane, which came as the result of an argument with a fellow student about the defence searchlights of London. He volunteered to take me up to see for myself, and we took off from Worthy Down one night for a four-hour flight over London. It was a chilly and rather dull proceeding watching London's searchlights through a hole in the floor of the aircraft; but it interests me to remember that my fellow student and pilot was Wing Commander Charles Portal, now Marshal of the Royal Air Force Viscount Portal of Hungerford. Many if not most of the students rose to high command in the Second World War and among the instructors were my old friends Gerald Dickens—now Admiral Sir Gerald —and James F. Somerville—the late Admiral of the Fleet Sir James Somerville.

It was during the course that I renewed my acquaintance with Miss Nona Byatt, home from Trinidad with her brother, Sir Horace, who had been relieved as Governor. We became engaged to be married in October. Towards the end of the course I was informed that I should be appointed in command of the *Rodney* in the Atlantic Fleet in the middle of December. We decided to get married about the same time and before the Atlantic Fleet sailed early in January, 1930, on the spring cruise to Gibraltar. I had many complimentary messages on my courage in taking on a wife and the largest battleship in the Navy at the same time.

I joined the *Rodney* at Portsmouth on December 21st, and after a week in trying to acquire some knowledge of the intricacies of this large vessel, went on leave. We were married from Sir Horace Byatt's house at Bishop's Stortford on December 22nd.

11

To one who had never commanded anything larger than a small cruiser the *Rodney* appeared enormous. This, and her odd bridge arrangements, gave me some qualms at first about handling her in narrow waters. But beyond the remoteness of the stem and a majestic dilatoriness in answering her helm and propellers, I eventually found her little different from the smaller ships to which I had been accustomed.

She had only been in commission for two years, and I was the third captain. We had a fine, experienced crew from Devonport; but they were due to change in the following April, 1930. The commander was Robert L. Burnett—now Admiral Sir Robert—a man with a good hold and an excellent way with the men. He intimated that when the previous captain informed him he was coming as commander, he, Burnett, had been told that the ship had already as many brains as were needed and that was why he had been selected.

To me it appeared that there were far too many executive officers on board, no fewer than nineteen lieutenant-commanders and lieutenants. This may have been necessary because of the armament; but it certainly resulted in work which should have been done by a midshipman or petty officer being consigned to a lieutenant. This meant that those in the lower ranks had little chance of exercising responsibility. Moreover, this host of officers had very little practice in watchkeeping at sea. At the outset of a passage we had to select four to keep all the watches during the trip.

At the end of 1929 the Atlantic Fleet consisted of the battleships *Nelson*, *Rodney*, *Barham* and *Malaya*; the battle-cruisers *Renown*, *Repulse* and *Tiger*; the aircraft-carriers *Furious* and *Argus*; the cruisers *Vindictive*, *Frobisher*, *Canterbury* and *Comus*; and two destroyer flotillas with Commodore (D) in the cruiser *Centaur*. The older battleships *Empress of India* and *Marlborough* which had special complements largely made up of boys under training, were also attached. The Commander-in-Chief, with his flag in the *Nelson*, was Admiral Sir Ernle, now Lord, Chatfield. He had not only been closely associated with Lord Beatty in the battle-cruisers and the Grand Fleet during the 1914–18 war; but had held many important appointments including that of Controller to the Navy. In the Navy he had a reputation second to none.

Rear-Admiral Dudley Pound, with his flag in the *Renown*, was in command of the battle-cruisers. He was an officer of untiring energy and forcefulness.

We spent about a week at Portland, during which we rode out a full gale and saw a small steamer drift past us and go ashore on the breakwater without being able to help. Boatwork was impossible. The target-towing sloop *Snapdragon*, with the two target tugs *St. Genny* and *St. Cyrus*, had already sailed for Gibraltar, and were caught by this same gale at sea. One heard later that the wind was 70 to 80 miles an hour, with squalls approaching 100. There was a very heavy sea, and at 7.45 p.m., 32 miles north-west of Ushant, the little *St. Genny* was struck and completely overwhelmed by a large wave. The *St. Cyrus* following some distance astern with her steering gear broken down, managed to pick up five survivors struggling in the water, and only found them through the calcium flares on the lifebuoys. In this distressing occurrence three officers and twenty men lost their lives.

We sailed from Portland when the weather moderated, the *Rodney* being detailed to lead the fleet out of harbour. A moderate breeze was still blowing, and try as I could I found I could not turn the ship towards the narrow entrance, while the *Nelson*, three cables distant, swung steadily and easily. As we were keeping the fleet waiting I was not surprised at receiving a tart signal from the Commander-in-Chief who then led out himself. Working the engines to turn the ship much too fast for the depth of water is a mistake that has been made by many besides myself. Fortunately I retrieved my reputation on going alongside the mole at Gibraltar.

As usual we had a strategical exercise on passage and were never idle for a moment. But the weather was bad most of the way out; and before reaching Gibraltar we had another heavy gale which strained and damaged some of our destroyers. The war-built destroyers of the 'V' and 'W' classes were beginning to feel their age.

Our time at Gibraltar was made very pleasant for me by the arrival of my wife. She had many friends in the Rock, dating from the time when she had kept house for her brother who was Colonial Secretary there in 1914. She stayed with a friend who had a most comfortable house in the Library Ramp, and in the intervals of going to sea for exercises and gunnery and torpedo practices we made many excursions into Spain, conducted by Miss Cookie Smith, our hostess, and on Sundays organized picnics for some of the *Rodney's* young officers. The quantities of food put away by some of the midshipmen was amazing.

In February, the *Rodney* and a submarine flotilla visited Algiers. We arrived off the port early one morning and were boarded by a French pilot rather the worse for wear. He was suffering from what might be called a heavy hangover. It was clear that the unorthodox arrangement of the *Rodney's* bridge so far aft quite confused him, so he most willingly concurred in our going in stern first through the breakwater, fully believing that it was our normal method of procedure. Our visit was pleasant enough, though we had to undergo the usual round of official lunches and dinners. Algiers is certainly a beautiful city, though squalid enough in parts. It made little impression on me at the time, and certainly I never thought how well I should come to know it in '42 and '43.

On sailing we made a rendezvous with the rest of the Atlantic Fleet for exercises with the Mediterranean Fleet. One remembers that at the time there was considerable controversy in the Navy about the wisdom, or otherwise, of fighting a fleet action at night. Sir Ernle Chatfield was a believer in night fighting and was all for investigating the problems. He was certainly of the opinion that a well-handled and well-trained fleet could stand up to night attacks by destroyers, and lost no opportunity of trying out new tactics. In the Atlantic Fleet the great protagonist of night action was the Rear-Admiral, 1st Battle Squadron, in the *Barham*, the Hon. Reginald Aylmer Ranfurly Plunkett-Ernle-Erle-Drax, an officer of great energy and attainments. I always remembered his remark after I had shown him round the *Rodney*. "Cunningham, on no account allow yourself to become entangled in the technicalities of this great ship."

Our principal exercise with the Mediterranean Fleet was designed to test some of the problems connected with night fighting. Unfortunately it never came to pass. The fleets did not make contact, as the Flag Officer commanding the other side was no believer in heavy ship engagements after dark. The two fleets then anchored at Palma, Majorca, where we had conferences on the exercises, sailing races and inter-ship and squadron reunions.

The Atlantic Fleet returned to Gibraltar, where we became busily engaged in getting off the fleet competitions and sports. Burnett, the commander, besides being the leading light in the theatrical party, was a physical training expert and athlete of repute, so the *Rodneys'* went all out. We won the battleships boxing; but were beaten by one point by the *Tiger* in the fleet boxing. In the tugs-of-war in the sports there were only four teams in it, the *Rodney's* light and heavy seamen and light and heavy marines. The marines, coached by Mr. A. V. Vickery, Gunner, Royal Marines, won both events. They went on to the Royal Tournament at Olympia later in the year to beat the crack teams from the Navy, Army and Air Force.

We sailed for home early in April. During the passage opportunity was taken one evening during the dog watches of exercising taking in tow. The *Rodney* took the *Nelson* in tow. The towed ship always provides the hawser, and when the order came to slip, we held on to our end of the hawser to make it easier for the *Nelson* to heave in. Her chain cable snapped at the sixth shackle, so there we were left in the middle of the Atlantic with 450 feet of her heavy cable at the end of another 900 feet of six and three-quarter-inch wire.

If anyone wants a good exercise in seamanship, let him try to recover cable weighing forty to fifty tons hanging from right aft when the only machinery capable of dealing with that weight, the capstan, is right forward.

In the event, after a tussle lasting six hours we had the hawser inboard with six links of the *Nelson's* cable on the quarterdeck. Then the *Nelson's* wire parted on the capstan and we lost the lot. It was an exciting moment to see the heavy wire surging from side to side as it rushed aft. Fortunately everyone sprang clear and not a man was hurt.

The *Rodney's* full complement was around about 1,300 officers and men, and at Devonport there was considerable difficulty in providing her new complement of ratings. It took nearly every man in the barracks to scratch up the necessary numbers, a sad reflection on the numerical strength in personnel to which the Navy had been allowed to shrink. The Navy Estimates had been drastically shorn; many still good ships that would have been of the greatest use in war were being scrapped; building programmes were retarded; and from a total personnel of 101,800 on April 1st, 1928, the numbers borne were reduced to 93,650 in 1931 and 91,840 in 1932. This was the lowest figure since 1897, when ships were smaller, far less complicated, and carried fewer men.

We were sorry to see the last of our fine ship's company; but luckily there were few changes among the officers. These latter were as good as could be picked anywhere, and in addition to the commander, R. L. Burnett, many of them achieved distinction in the last war. In particular I might mention Lieutenant-Commander George E. Creasy, our first lieutenant-commander and torpedo officer, and Lieutenant-Commander Geoffrey N. Oliver, the gunnery officer. Both had fine war records and are now Flag Officers.

With our new crew we left Devonport early in May and went to Portsmouth to embark the Commander-in-Chief, Sir Ernle Chatfield, and to hoist his flag. Sir Ernle had been appointed Commander-in-Chief, Mediterranean, in place of Sir Frederick Field, who was coming home as First Sea Lord. The *Nelson* was remaining at Portsmouth to complete her docking and to embark the new Commander-in-Chief Atlantic Fleet, Admiral Sir Michael Hodges. We collected the rest of the fleet and proceeded to Invergordon. It was a new and valuable experience to be captain of the temporary fleet flagship, and I welcomed the opportunity of getting to know Sir Ernle Chatfield better and seeing him at work at close quarters. However, he did not stay long, and after rather less than three weeks went back to Portsmouth to turn over to his relief. A 14-oared cutter, with every oar manned by a lieutenant and the commander acting as coxswain, pulled him ashore.

Invergordon in May is always delightful, and on this occasion my wife came up and stayed in the local hotel. We had many a fishing expedition when my duties in the *Rodney* permitted. We had not yet found a permanent house. A search round the neighbourhood of Plymouth had disclosed nothing very attractive that suited us. Moreover, though the *Rodney* was a Devonport-manned ship, she had always to dock and refit at Portsmouth, so where best we should look for a home to enable me to see as much as possible of my wife was rather a problem. Finally we rented a small house at Rowlands Castle some twelve miles north-east of Portsmouth, and here my wife retired when the Atlantic Fleet went north to Scapa Flow in the beginning of June.

On June 8th, the fleet dispersed for individual cruises. We had already been informed that we were required to take a Parliamentary delegation to Iceland later in the month for the millenary of the Icelandic Althing, alleged to be the oldest parliament in the world, so we did not go far afield. We went first to Portrush, on the border of Derry, by Antrim, and not far from the Giant's Causeway. We were made very welcome indeed.

We reached Rothesay on June 16th, and on the 21st our Parliamentary delegation joined the ship and we sailed for Reykjavik at 1 p.m. Our passengers were Lord Lamington, Lord Newton and Lord Marks, with Sir Robert Hamilton, Liberal Member for Orkney and Shetland and Mr. Rhys Davies, Labour Member for West Houghton. Captain Taprell Dorling, Royal Navy, an old destroyer friend, and Mr. H. Warhirst, a photographer of repute, represented *The Times*, and Mr. Kingsley Martin, now Editor of the *New Statesman* was the special correspondent of *The Manchester Guardian*. Kingsley Martin was an interesting man with advanced views and rather out of the common run of people usually met by naval officers. I have no doubt he broadened our outlook.

We spent a week at Reykjavik, where there were also the French cruiser *Suffren*; the Norwegian *Tordenskjold*; the Danish *Niels Juel* carrying the King and Queen of Iceland and Denmark; and the Swedish *Oscar II* with the Crown Prince of Sweden. A number of liners brought Icelanders from America; Norwegian and British tourists; and students from all the Scandinavian countries. Iceland's normal population was 107,000, and some 27,000 other people flocked there for the millenary celebrations, including 500 Icelanders from Canada and United States.

It has to be recorded, I fear, that practically every nation except ours sent valuable presents to commemorate the occasion. As the President of the Althing said in addressing the representatives of foreign Parliaments: "Great and remarkable nations have sent to our country some of their most distinguished sons to take part in our festival. Some have sent us princely presents; others have sent their largest battleships——" I believe our lack of imagination was afterwards rectified by the Foreign Office which sent a standard pattern silver presentation inkstand!

Being June it was broad daylight all night, the sun just dipping behind the mountains for an hour or two around midnight. The Icelanders never seemed to go to bed in summer, probably because they are said to hibernate all through the winter. Except for a day's fishing I was beset by official visits, lunches, dinners, and ceremonies, some of which went on till the small hours of the morning, and most of them with interminable speeches to which we sat and sat and tried to listen and look intelligent. Since nearly all were in languages other than our own it was a little difficult. Quite the best speech of the whole visit was made by one of the American delegates. He had been amply entertained, and the time was close upon midnight when he shambled to his feet to make the twentieth speech of the evening. He swayed to and fro, beaming; said 'Gentlemen', and then abruptly subsided. We sympathized, and applauded.

I had, of course, to pay my respects to the King and Queen of Iceland and Denmark on board the *Niels Juel*, which I was commanded to do at 4 o'clock on the afternoon of their arrival. Their Majesties were most charming and friendly.

King Christian came on board the *Rodney* later the same day, sat in my cabin talking for about half-an-hour, and then asked if he could walk round the ship's company. Though he wore Danish naval uniform, he was of course an Honorary Admiral in the Royal Navy, a Knight of the Garter and a G.C.B. He was a very tall man, and when I asked him to sign the visitors' book on the rather low table in the flat outside my cabin, he went down on both knees to do so, greatly to the surprise of Buckingham, my coxswain; the Marine sentry; and all the rest of us who were present. I should have thought of providing a chair.

The King's visit was closely followed by that of the Crown Prince of Sweden, who sat and talked to me for three-quarters of an hour mostly about his sons, of whom he was very proud. His first wife, of course, was Princess Margaret of Connaught.

The celebrations lasted three days, and took place on the plain of Thingvellir, thirty miles out from Reykjavik along one of the worst roads I have ever experienced. Here, for the time being, 20,000 people lived in a large encampment of 4,200 tents, pitched here and there in veritable towns wherever room could be found for them. Nothing was forgotten. There was a post and telegraph office, shops, many booths and restaurants, all under canvas and provided with running water piped from the neighbouring streams and waterfalls. A tent was provided for me; but I positively refused to leave my comfortable cabin to live in what I imagined would be considerable discomfort.

I went out to Thingvellir for the day of the main celebrations. The scenery was magnificent—a great plain bordered on all sides by mountains, some of which were extinct volcanoes which thousands of years before had poured forth lava to form this gigantic and very thick plateau. In places the crust had subsided to leave deep gullies and fissures bordered by sheer cliffs, and carpeted by lush grass with streams wandering through them. Here and there were deep pools of icy blue water, so clear that the bottom could be seen at 40 feet. In the midst of this plain was the great sheet of placid blue water called Thingvallavater. From the flanks of many of the mountains it was curious to see the vapour of many geysers rising vertically into the still air, for all the world like the smoke of distant heath fires.

The main ceremonies, which included formal meetings of the Althing, a religious service with some wonderful singing by massed choirs of men and women, took place at the old 'Logberg', or Law Rock, in a picturesque gorge near a river and waterfall at the spot where laws were proclaimed when the Vikings first came to the country and inaugurated the annual Parliament in A.D. 930. Incidentally, a representative from the Isle of Man would not allow that the Althing was the oldest Parliament in the world. The House of Keys, he averred, was considerably more ancient. There was much speech-making by the delegates of each and every nation present, and with the masses of people, the students with their banners and coloured caps, and the Icelandic women in their picturesque national dress with velvet skull caps with their long fair hair done in two looped-up pigtails, the scene was most colourful.

It had been arranged by our Parliamentary delegation not to take top-hats and morning coats. Lord Lamington had joined the party at the last moment, and was unaware of this decision. On the occasion of ceremony he appeared in traditional morning coat and top-hat when all the others were in lounge suits. Rhys Davies, the Welsh M.P. for West Houghton, excitedly seized Dorling, *The Times* special correspondent, by the arm: "Captain, Captain!" he exclaimed. "Look at our bloody black-leg!"

After several more official functions and dinners, including an afternoon reception on board the *Rodney* attended by about 350 people, we fired a farewell salute of twenty-one guns and sailed for Holyhead at 10.30 p.m. on July 1st. We had enjoyed our visit to Iceland, though undoubtedly it had been strenuous. Because it was daylight all night and time mattered little to our hosts, I, personally was rarely in bed before 2 or 3 a.m. Even so it seemed slightly indecent to retire with the sun well over the horizon.

Except for a very thick fog coming round the north of Ireland and down the Irish Sea on the way to Holyhead, our passage home was uneventful. I found a sense of tranquillity in the thought that because the bridge was so far aft we could not possibly see any fishing craft or vessel before we hit it, nor be aware of her presence unless she was using her whistle. I doubt whether the young officer stationed in the eyes of the ship with a telephone shared my peaceful feelings. It was long before the days of radar.

We landed our passengers at Holyhead, and arrived at St. Mary's, in the Scillies, on July 6th. Here we spent four days practising hard for the sailing regatta, which was to be held at our next port of call, Falmouth. Having always rather fancied myself as a boat-sailer, and in teaching others to sail, I was determined that the *Rodney* should do well. We met the other heavy ships of the Atlantic Fleet off Falmouth on July 11th. The sailing regatta lasted five days, and the *Rodney* acquitted herself nobly, winning various of the more important races and being very well-placed in others. For two days there was considerable sea and a wind amounting almost to a gale in which the smaller boats like galleys, gigs and whalers had a bad time. One capsized, and several more were swamped or dismasted. In one race I lost my foremast in the galley when well in the lead, and struggled on with the mainmast stepped amidships. The commander's face on my return to the ship was a picture, as he had urged me to take a spare mast and I had declined.

After a four-day visit to Lyme Regis we finally arrived at Devonport on July 23rd, and remained there giving summer leave until September 9th.

III

In September I was informed that I should only be allowed to remain one year in the *Rodney* and that I should be relieved in December, 1930. I was extremely disappointed; but with many captains and too few ships in full commission to go round sea-time had to be shortened to give them all a turn. I could appreciate the difficulty of the Admiralty in getting every captain to sea in a big ship where his capabilities could be tried out and an assessment made from sufficient data to determine whether he was fit for promotion to Flag rank. I knew that the *Rodney* was due for a refit at Portsmouth towards the end of the year, and that her autumn cruise would probably be my last in command.

Sailing from Plymouth Sound we joined up with the rest of the Atlantic Fleet in the Channel and steamed to Invergordon, carrying out exercises all the way. Off the Isle of Wight we were 'attacked' by aircraft, and in the North Sea by the battle-cruisers, submarines and destroyers. Invergordon was supposed to be blockaded and *in extremis*, and it was our job to relieve it. What was the result of our various 'battles' I cannot remember; but as we spent most of our time in action stations I have no doubt we all learnt a great deal.

We reached Invergordon on September 12th, and from there spent a strenuous time exercising in the Cromarty Firth, with firings, tactical exercises, day and night attacks by destroyers and the like.

On September 29th we said good-bye to the fleet and went south to Portsmouth, where we remained until the third week in November in dock and refitting. It was now that I was able to appreciate the joy of having a home at Rowlands Castle. This work being completed, the gunnery experts from Whale Island, H.M.S. *Excellent*, took the opportunity of carrying out blast trials with the 16-inch guns. It had been found that the bridges of the *Nelson* and *Rodney* were quite untenable with the after turret on its extreme after training and the guns at considerable elevation. It was not surprising. With the turret and guns in the position described it was possible from the bridge to see quite ten feet down the bore of the nearest gun. Consequently the after-training of the turrets had been arbitarily reduced, which was a disadvantage. Whale Island had now closed in the bridge with special plate glass windows with very small panes.

After a fake start because of thick weather the trial took place south of the Isle of Wight on November 25th. Unfortunately it was a complete failure. The bridge was indeed untenable through bits of flying plate glass from the completely shattered windows. The bridge structure was also damaged, so we went on to Plymouth to exchange the dockyard wall at Portsmouth for that at Devonport where the damage was repaired during the Christmas leave period.

On December 15th I left the *Rodney* after relief by Captain Roger Bellairs. I was sorry to go, more particularly as during my year in command we had spent less than six months away from a dockyard port and I had no prospect of getting to sea again before I reached the top of the captain's list. Indeed, there seemed little prospect of any employment at all except courses at Portsmouth on the Royal Naval College, Greenwich. Actually, I was not anxious for immediate employment, as I was again having trouble with my inside. So I went to Edinburgh at once and had the necessary operation, returning to our house at Rowlands Castle in March, 1931. It was there that I was informed by the Naval Secretary to the First Lord that I should be appointed Commodore of the Royal Naval Barracks, Chatham, early in July.

CHAPTER XIII

BEING Commodore of one of the Royal Naval Barracks, the depots at the three Home Ports, is a highly responsible position. Though one rather loses touch with the sailors as individuals, one lives right in the midst of the big personnel problems and the manning of ships. Under the local Commander-in-Chief one is responsible for the drafting of crews, and even reliefs for individuals, to ships of every sort. Problems of advancement and welfare and the general well-being of the sailors, with that of their wives and families, become one's constant care. For all this one has to be in closest touch with those Admiralty departments which deal with personnel.

I did not appreciate being so detached from the men and their daily lives and perplexities. Because we were dealing with large numbers the general barracks administration was rather a soulless machine. Perhaps it was necessary; but everything was done by regulation and precedent, and to my mind insufficient allowance was made for the special circumstances of any individual.

The commander appointed soon after I joined the Royal Naval Barracks at Chatham was Eustace Rotherham, a live wire if ever there was one. He was an excellent disciplinarian and an officer who had the respect and liking of all law-abiding men. He would undoubtedly have reached the higher ranks of the Service if his health had not given way some years later.

The Commander-in-Chief at the Nore was my old friend Admiral Sir Reginald Tyrwhitt. Our first social engagement at Chatham, however, was not a success. We had received and accepted an invitation to dine at Admiralty House soon after our arrival. At about eight o'clock one evening, when I had just returned from London after visiting the Admiralty on duty, the telephone rang violently and an agitated flag lieutenant enquired if we were not coming to dinner. I replied that we were coming on the date for which we had been invited, the next night. After some argument I looked up the date in my diary and found that the mistake was mine. It was too late to go then. I spent next morning making agonized apologies for my stupidity; but the Commander-in-Chief took it very lightly. Lady Tyrwhitt, however, ordained that as a penance we must attend her garden party that afternoon, which we did, to have our legs unmercifully pulled. I feel that few Commanders-in-Chief and their ladies would have taken the wrecking of their dinner party with such good-humoured placidity, especially one arranged on purpose to introduce us to all and sundry.

Life at Chatham was very pleasant. We had a very charming official house in the barracks with its own garden and tennis court, while above all I had enough work to keep me fully occupied. We had brought with us a

Scottish maid who had been with us since we were married, a most efficient and kindly soul prepared to turn her hand to anything and a great stand-by in any emergency. A very soft-hearted woman, she allowed herself to become unduly distressed by the tall and exaggerated yarns spun by my boat's crew of the poor sailors being drafted abroad and leaving their wives and families behind them. On one occasion, looking out of an upper window, she saw our guard for the Cenotaph Service in London, one hundred strong, doing their morning practice march with the band. Exclaiming: "They'rre all going on drrraft, puir lads!" she burst into floods of tears and required all the consolation we could give her.

However, before long our peaceful existence at Chatham was to suffer a severe jolt. A Committee examining methods of reducing the country's expenditure had been sitting for some time, and among other economies they recommended a reduction in the pay of the Services. The Atlantic Fleet, after giving summer leave, had arrived at Invergordon on its customary autumn cruise on September 11th, 1931. A day later the Admiralty communicated in Fleet Orders reductions in pay and allowances to take effect from October 1st. I shall not go into the details of a period which is best forgotten; but in many cases the cuts in pay meant considerable hardship.

Looking back on the results and writing from my own personal views and experiences at the time, I have no doubt that many of the officers had fallen out of touch with, and were mostly ignorant, of, the problems and difficulties affecting the men in their home lives. This applied particularly to the senior officers and the officers in big ships. In the destroyers, where officers lived at close quarters with the men and knew them much better, the ship's company was usually a happy family and no trouble occurred. The reason for this detachment in the bigger ships was not self-evident; but it may have been that the officers were so immersed in *matériel* and 'instrumentalisms of every kind', as Mr. Winston Churchill once called them; so engaged in the pressure of constant exercises and practices, that the human factor was neglected. In short we had excellent technicians but few real leaders of men.

Before I became acquainted with the precise details of the cuts in pay, and knew only that cuts were to be made, it was my opinion that they would be accepted, though with considerable discontent. I had the greatest faith in the discipline of the men and loyalty to their officers; but rather overlooked the fact that the mutiny at Invergordon was against the Government decision to cut the pay.

At Chatham we were told that an explanatory letter was coming from the Admiralty which could be read to the ships' companies. In the event it did not arrive until too late, and I had to borrow a copy from a ship just returned from the East Indies! Having read it, I put it away. I could discover nothing in it which could possibly affect the explosive situation in which we now found ourselves—the much-publicized news that the Atlantic Fleet at Invergordon had mutinied against the reductions in pay. A mutiny it certainly was. It has no other name.

Then, and then only, were undertaken the investigations into the home life and financial circumstances of the sailors which should have been examined before the rash announcements of the pay cuts were officially promulgated to the Fleet. We were all to blame. No officers in command of ships, least of all those in command of shore establishments with large bodies of men, could acquit themselves of blame for being unacquainted with the subject and their failure to make representations to higher authority.

At Chatham, where we hastily made arrangements for closing the stable door after the horse had bolted, the men were restive. However, only one incident took place, when a rating mounted a chair and started to make an inflammatory speech which came to an abrupt termination when the chair was quickly whipped from beneath him by a regulating petty officer. Personally I did not expect trouble. The *Repulse*, then with the Atlantic Fleet, had just recommissioned at Chatham, taking over 1,000 ratings from the barracks. Her ship's company, so we heard, were giving no trouble at Invergordon, which was an indication that the mutiny had not been organized at Chatham. Outside the barracks, on 'The Lines', there were meetings of various bodies, the Association of Young Sailors' Wives and so on. They were usually attended by Commander Rotherham in plain clothes; but never came to anything.

All the same it could not be overlooked that the men were labouring under a grievance which was not without some justification. I invited everyone who wished to come and see me and state his case. I spent day after day in interviews, and saw something like 500 men in all. It was pathetic to learn how many of them lived on the border line of poverty, in many cases through their own foolishness in becoming caught up in the rapacious hire-purchase system. I remember one case of an able seaman whose daughter much wished to learn the piano. Instead of sending her, as a normal person would, to learn from a teacher, he or his wife acquired a grand piano on the instalment plan and got in the teacher at so much a lesson. Heaven only knew where he stored the piano in his small house. At the same time there were many cases of young married men with children who were thrifty and managed to make good on the reduced pay; but it left them with little or no margin for illness or other emergencies or the cheapest of amusements.

At Chatham we were fortunate indeed in having a Commander-in-Chief with a great and well-deserved reputation, and a man whom the sailors trusted implicitly. A wise and firm signal from Sir Reginald Tyrwhitt and his frequent presence in the barracks walking through on his way to the dockyard had a very calming effect.

As to the happenings in the Atlantic Fleet at Invergordon I can offer no opinion. However, there were previous warnings of the pay cuts and probable discontent in the *Rodney* and other ships, that I have often wondered if the fleet had immediately gone to sea and, then, after a day or two, have dispersed to other ports, the tragic mutiny at Invergordon would not have been averted. At the moment the Mediterranean Fleet was dispersed, and all was well. It has also seemed curious to me that in the barracks and instructional establishments, where large numbers of men were concentrated and one might have expected the trouble to be most acute, little or nothing happened.

The upshot, as everyone knows, was that the Government rescinded part of the cuts in pay; the ships of the Atlantic Fleet were withdrawn to their Home Ports; and the Admiralty ordered a full and exhaustive enquiry at Portsmouth, Plymouth and Chatham into the sailors' circumstances. The Commanders-in-Chief at each of the ports sat as presidents, and the Admiralty was represented. The reports of the three enquiries were practically identical, and stated so far as I remember that the pay of the sailors could not stand the drastic reductions ordered in the first instance without reducing many of them to penury.

In the end an overall cut of not more than 10 per cent was imposed. The ringleaders in the trouble were ordered to be discharged to barracks, and in November twenty-four men were discharged from the Royal Navy—'services no longer required'. The active discontent died away, though the repercussions continued for some time later.

The incident undoubtedly left a smear on the Navy which was only fully wiped away in the last war. Yet the loyalty of the men was never really wanting. Those who did mutiny at Invergordon were incited to do so by a few loud-voiced agitators, and there is no denying that the whole business of reducing the pay was sadly mishandled and mis-timed.

One can only remember the events of the autumn of 1931 with sorrow and certain feelings of responsibility. The only good that came out of this unhappy period was to drive it home that the Navy as a whole was paying too much attention to *matériel* and far too little to the personnel and its welfare. The Geddes 'axe'; the wholesale scrapping of still useful ships, and the reduction of officers and men to a dangerous minimum; the constant juggling with pay and allowances in the interests of economy, all had their effect. The sailors had come to believe, not without justification, that the pundits in Whitehall knew nothing of the manner in which they lived, and that though their officers were in sympathy with them they were powerless. I need not labour these points.

The Commanders-in-Chief were ordered to send in suggestions for improving the conditions of service for the men. After much discussion a document of nearly a hundred pages was sent in from the Royal Nava

Barracks at Chatham. Many of the recommendations were adopted at once, and others more gradually.

My Secretary, Paymaster Lieutenant-Commander A. P. Shaw, and myself worked for a time on a scheme of central drafting and removing once and for all the iron curtain which still exists between Portsmouth, Devonport and Chatham. Why, we thought, should a warship be manned entirely from one or other of these ports? Why should not the crew, most of whom were specialists or highly-skilled technicians, be drawn from all three? A central system, we thought, would simplify drafting, and ensure fairer proportions of sea service and shore service, and service at home and abroad.

In the end however, we abandoned the idea. Nobody seemed to want it. The fact was that most of the married men made their homes in the neighbourhood of their depots at Portsmouth, Chatham and Devonport. If a Devonport man was serving in a ship which refitted at Chatham, for instance, it would mean a long and expensive railway journey to see his wife and family. The scheme we suggested all depended upon the railways granting free travelling facilities to naval ratings at all times, whether on duty or on leave, in return for an annual *per capita* contribution. I still think the idea of central drafting and mixed ships' companies is a sound one, and that in these days of nationalized railways the scheme deserves consideration.

Various other suggestions were put forward for improving the training of the men of the Fleet. Sail training was put forward, and a committee sat at the Admiralty taking evidence from senior and other officers. Though as a keen boat-sailer the idea was attractive to me, I did not think it was sound. It struck me as being on a par with a suggestion that before driving a taxicab a man should first learn to ride a horse. Moreover, with our small margin of men, we in the Royal Naval Barracks very well knew how we had to scrape and contrive to man or recommission a ship. I could not see how the men or the time were to be found for including sail training into the already overloaded curriculum. Another practical objection was who was to command and sail the training ships? Already near the end of my service as a captain I was one of the last few officers who had ever been in a sailing ship at sea. Anyone much junior to me would have required some years sail training himself before being turned loose in command.

I was called upon to give evidence before the committee, and found as a fellow witness Captain John Tovey. The last time we had given evidence together was about the training of boys at Port Edgar in 1925, though on that occasion we were more in the position of prisoners in the dock. Tovey's views were much the same as mine, and I think the committee were somewhat surprised. In the end, they recommended that sail training should be started.

In the second volume of his autobiography, *It Might Happen Again*, published in 1947, Lord Chatfield has described how perturbed he was on becoming First Sea Lord in January, 1933, to find that a scheme for the revival of sail training had already been approved by the Admiralty. The money to build one 10,000-ton barque, £85,000, was included in the Navy Estimates, and the annual cost of her maintenance was estimated at £22,500. The scheme allowed for the eventual building of four such ships, and as these could not possibly provide training for all the ordinary seamen and boys then joining the Navy, the final suggestion was that it should be confined to petty officers and leading seamen, which would have been sheer waste of time.

Lord Chatfield, in common with many other Flag Officers who had started their careers under sail, was much opposed to the idea, and for many good reasons. There was the question of expense, which had to be subtracted from the already attenuated funds allowed to the Navy for new fighting ships. Moreover, there were no serving officers and petty officers who had ever handled, or even served in, square-rigged vessels, and they, like their crews, would have to learn their job through bitter experience. "I felt," Lord Chatfield wrote in his book, "that the whole proposal was playing with fire; and a disaster, such as happened to training ships even in the old days, would be only too probable." No doubt he was thinking of the *Eurydice*, which capsized and sank off Dunnose, Isle of Wight, in a sudden squall in March, 1878, with a loss of about 300 lives, and the *Atlanta*, which was lost during a hurricane in the West Indies in February, 1880, with a death roll of 280. Both of these vessels were training ships commanded and officered by men experienced in the art of sail.

So Lord Chatfield, on becoming First Sea Lord in 1933, insisted that every penny the Navy could get must be used for fighting efficiency, and for training officers and men in the ships and with the weapons with which they might have to fight, how soon nobody knew. He was glad to rid himself and the Service of the nightmare and incubus of sail training, which could have done nothing to increase the efficiency of the Navy in the war which broke out some six-and-a-half years later. How right he was.

Lord Chatfield, or Admiral Sir Ernle Chatfield as he was then, had been relieved as Commander-in-Chief, Mediterranean, by Admiral Sir William Wordsworth Fisher in November, 1932. Some time before taking up this appointment Sir William and Lady Fisher paid a visit to Admiralty House, Chatham. My wife and I were asked to dinner with the Commander-in-Chief, and after dinner I was firmly placed alongside Admiral Fisher. We had a long conversation, and I remembered we disagreed on various points. It was not until some days later that Sir Reginald Tyrwhitt told me that Admiral Fisher had been looking for a Chief of Staff to accompany him to the Mediterranean. Somebody else was offered that appointment.

In the spring of 1932 I had been informed by the Admiralty that in due course I should be promoted to Rear-Admiral and retained on the active list, so my natural anxiety about the future was set at rest. I was actually promoted on September 24th of that year, after having served as a captain for the then unprecedented period of twelve years and nine months. The time spent on the captain's list had been getting longer since the war, and I was promoted at the peak. However, it did not greatly signify. It was all good experience, and there was always more active employment as a captain than as a Rear-Admiral. Also I was still under the age of fifty, which was young as promotion went in those days.

CHAPTER XIV

I

Though I was now a Rear-Admiral, I was allowed to remain on as Commodore of the Royal Naval Barracks at Chatham until February, 1933, when I went on half-pay. We first took a house at Gullane, East Lothian, where we spent a pleasant month playing-golf and meeting relations and friends from Edinburgh. In April, I was appointed for a Technical Course at Portsmouth, so we rented the Old Manor House at Fareham, a fine old house with a good garden. It has now fallen into the hands of the Civil Engineer-in-Chief's Department of the Admiralty, and, like many another old building, its glory has departed.

I need not describe the Technical Course, for which I went daily into Portsmouth. It was designed to bring us up-to-date in the latest developments. When we visited the Gosport Air Station a number of young pilots of the Royal Air Force and the Fleet Air Arm were waiting to take us up for flights. Thinking that a naval pilot, a lieutenant R.N., would have a better idea of the value of a Rear-Admiral than a young man in the R.A.F., I selected one of the former. We had an interesting flight except for a sudden drop of 800 feet which the young man thought I would like to experience. He was quite in error. On landing I was told that I had chosen the pilot who had been in trouble in China for flying between the masts of a cruiser!

From the Technical Course we passed on to the Tactical Course, held in what used to be the old War College in Portsmouth Dockyard, with my friend Captain J. A. G. Troup as Director. I found this course of the greatest value. One became acquainted with the latest ideas and thought on fleet tactics, besides hearing a few lectures on the subject which were very much to the point. Most of our time, however, was taken up with exercises on the tactical table, where, in conditions made as realistic as possible in such artificial surroundings, we learnt to handle fleets and squadrons. At the end of this course I was informed that I was to be appointed Rear-Admiral (D), Mediterranean Fleet, in the New Year, 1934. It was the one appointment I would have chosen above all others.

II

My appointment was to take effect from January 1st, 1934, so the last months of 1933 were spent in collecting my staff. My secretary, Paymaster Lieutenant-Commander A. P. Shaw, of course was to come. The Signal

Andrew Browne Cunningham.

Pretoria, September 1900. Professor D.J. Cunningham and A.B.C.

H.M.S. *Martin*, July 1901.

W. Beach, Gallipoli 1915. One of the first artificial harbours. H.M.S. *Scorpion* in the background.

A "Beagle" class destroyer in the Dardanelles.

Spring exercises in the Atlantic, March 1934. A battleship in heavy weather.

"We struck a full gale from the north-west…" H.M.S. *Boadicea*. Note the other destroyer visible under her bows.

H.M.S. *Coventry* and Third Destroyer Flotilla at Leghorn, 1934.

H.M.S. *Coventry* and destroyers in the Gulf of Corinth, 1935.

Malta, January 1940. The French Admiral Esteva and A.B.C.

Italian salvoes off Calabria, July 9th 1940.

H.M.S. *Malaya* comes through a forest of Italian bombs.

A British destroyer off Calabria, July 9th 1940.

An Italian cruiser in retreat. Calabria, July 9th, 1940. A close miss aft.

H.M.S. *Warspite* entering the Grand Harbour, Malta, December 20th 1940.

Warspite at sea.

School suggested Lieutenant-Commander D. O. Doble as Squadron Signal and Wireless Telegraphy officer and flag lieutenant-commander, and I concurred. The Admiralty also informed me it was intended to appoint Commander Charles E. Lambe and Lieutenant-Commander Antony W. Buzzard, respectively, as Squadron Torpedo Officer and Staff Officer, Operations. I did not know the officers in question so had no comment to make; but it was not long before I realized my good fortune in having two such outstandingly able officers on my staff.

Our passages were booked to Malta by a P. & O. leaving Tilbury about December 20th, and I went north early that month to take leave of my family in Edinburgh. Just as we were coming south again I went down with tonsillitis, missed the P. & O. and spent Christmas in bed. However, by dint of supreme exertions on the part of Doble we managed to catch the Blue Train across France in time to embark in the same P. & O. at Marseilles.

We arrived at Malta at 8 p.m. on New Year's Eve, and no one came on board to welcome us. The New Year's Eve festivities had considerably hampered my predecessor's flag lieutenant in his ardour to meet us. The date and time of our arrival, however, had become known to many of my old friends among the Maltese. There are no more loyal and faithful retainers, and when we landed at the Custom House we were welcomed by a line of ex-stewards, cooks, dghaisa men and others who had known me in the *Scorpion* seventeen years before.

I took over from my predecessor, Rear-Admiral F. F. Rose, next morning. This operation took about twenty minutes. I have never believed in protracted turns-over. If one does it in detail and at length one is only wasting the time of one's successor, who is always itching to get down to his new job. We also took over the Rose's house, the Casa Pieta, in Guardamangia. It was as good a small house as could be found in Malta, with several large rooms and a big garden with a tennis court. It was on the side of a hill overlooking Pieta Creek and out to sea down Sliema Creek. From the balcony one could watch the entry and departure of all destroyers, though at too great a distance for detailed criticism.

The Rear-Admiral (D)'s command at that time consisted of three modern flotillas, the First, Third and Fourth, each of eight destroyers and a flotilla leader.

Destroyer training and tactics at that time were still very much influenced by the war of 1914–18. The massed and simultaneous attack upon an enemy's battle-fleet by three, four or more flotillas during a fleet action in daylight still held pride of place as the most important function of destroyers, accompanied, of course, by every conceivable method of search and attack by night. New methods were constantly being evolved and tried out, and much time and thought were devoted to simplifying and accelerating the difficult and all-important task of reorganizing and regrouping flotillas for a night attack after they had suffered casualties in an action by day. Apart from this there were the usual destroyer functions of screening the heavy ships and beating off hostile destroyer attacks, anti-submarine work and scouting. Destroyers are truly maids of all work, so our hands were full and the days not long enough to fit in everything.

I need hardly go into details; but personally I was doubtful if massed daylight attacks by flotillas would ever eventuate. No potential enemy seemed to possess a line of battleships to serve as a target. However, massed attacks were unsurpassed for the training of the Captains (D), and the divisional and sub-divisional leaders, in handling their units at high speed in tight corners. Large numbers of destroyers steaming at full speed in confined areas provided just that element of risk which is essential in the training of good destroyer officers. Quick thinking and initiative were essential. Laggards in either respect soon showed up.

The Commander-in-Chief was Admiral Sir William Fisher, whom I knew only slightly. Truth compels me to say that at first I found him very difficult o get on with. Later, when I came to know him better, I conceived the greatest admiration for him, and realized that for some months after one had joined his flag his attitude of aloofness and the odd things he said were intended to try out and test the newcomer.

The Mediterranean Fleet at this time consisted of the four battleships *Queen Elizabeth*, *Revenge*, *Resolution* and *Royal Sovereign*, with the first-named as fleet flagship; the First Cruiser Squadron, *London*, *Sussex*, *Devonshire* and *Shropshire*; Third Cruiser Squadron, *Delhi*, *Despatch*, *Dauntless* and *Durban*; with the aircraft-carrier *Glorious*, relieved after a few months by the *Furious*. The *Coventry*, my flagship as Rear-Admiral (D), was commanded by Captain H. E. Horan, and the three destroyer flotillas by Captain C. F. Harris, relieved in February, 1934, by Captain H. T. Baillie-Grohman; Captain J. W. S. Dorling, and Captain F. G. H. Dalrymple-Hamilton. The destroyers also had a depot ship, the *Sandhurst*, Captain G. H. Creswell.

Within a fortnight of my taking over we sailed on our winter cruise, the *Coventry* and destroyers being spread out over the French and Italian ports in North Africa. We visited Bizerta with two destroyers and had a quieter time than I expected. The Vice-Admiral in command there was Comte de la Borde, a striking-looking man who spoke excellent English, and was a proficient aviator, a keen yachtsman and polo player. He and his charming wife did their utmost to make our visit a pleasant one, and, what is unusual in French official circles, kept the entertainments as informal as possible. At the official dinner he gave the evening ended with progressive table tennis. I was also well beaten in a single by the French Admiral, though I rather fancied myself at the game. However, mess dress and gold-laced trousers are not best suited for violent exercise.

Towards the end of 1942, when we landed in North Africa, de la Borde gained notoriety by refusing to obey Darlan's orders to bring the French fleet from Toulon to Algiers, and had to destroy it when the Germans marched in. For this he was later tried and condemned to death by a court in France, and his wife and family appealed to me to write to the President asking for a reprieve. This I did. He was reprieved, though I doubt if my letter had much to do with it. A large petition asking for clemency had also been organized in France. De la Borde is still in prison. He was, I suppose, a supporter of Vichy, though I never detected any anti-British bias in his behaviour. He was undoubtedly a fine man and a great sailor, though rigidly obstinate.

Towards the end of January the First Flotilla went home to refit and recommission, while the rest of us made a rendezvous with the Third Cruiser Squadron off Cape Bon in torrential rain which lasted most of the day. It had been planned to attack the battle fleet on its return passage to Malta, and the attack duly took place at about 8 p.m. It was not a success, and we were rather startled by the Commander-in-Chief ordering it to be repeated in the morning watch. Two night exercises in one night were unusual; but it woke everyone up and the second attack was successful.

We spent February in Malta, where life was rather a social whirl. But I was glad of the chance to renew my acquaintance with the island and many old friends in every walk of life. The Maltese peasants have all the charm belonging to those who live close to nature, and in our long walks about the island my wife and I made many new friends.

I must not give the impression that the time was entirely spent in social activities. The destroyers were constantly at sea carrying out gunnery, torpedo and anti-submarine practices. The preliminary orders for the spring exercises of the combined Home and Mediterranean Fleets had also arrived, and the staffs were busily engaged in digesting them. Contrary to the usual custom the Commander-in-Chief did not call a conference of Flag Officers to consider the exercise orders. Instead, he ordered each Flag Officer to prepare an appreciation and then talked it over with him.

Shorn of much of its detail, the general idea of the exercises was that the Home Fleet, Blue, was to escort an expeditionary force in transports from a position near the Azores for the mythical occupation of a port on the Atlantic coast of Spain or Portugal. This intention had become known to Red, the Mediterranean Fleet, which was to sail from Gibraltar with the object of destroying the Blue Convoy and escort before it could reach its destination.

There are only two ports on the Atlantic coast of Spain and Portugal supposed to be suitable for Blue's purpose—Arosa Bay, in Spain, and Lisbon, in Portugal, about two hundred and fifty miles to the southward. Our task, Reb's, was by no means easy, as Blue's possible approach course covered an area of many hundreds of square miles. We had two aircraft-carriers; but it was more than likely that the bad weather of early spring in the open Atlantic would rule out any air reconnaissance. If this were so it meant that the enemy would have to be found by surface forces, which would necessitate a great dispersion of our available cruisers and destroyers.

On examining the problem all the junior Flag Officers in our fleet considered that the enemy would use the most southerly route and make for Lisbon. Not so the Commander-in-Chief, who maintained he would steer a more northerly course for Arosa Bay. We left Malta early in March for Gibraltar, and had a bad passage with a north-westerly gale and heavy sea which did considerable damage to the boats and upperworks of the destroyers as they plugged against it. After a few days at the Rock patching up our injuries we sailed again to the westward during the night of March 10th–11th.

Except in destroyers and aircraft the Blue force was superior to our own. With all the circumstances in mind our Commander-in-Chief decided not to depend upon the possibility of aircraft reconnaissance; but fully to cover Blue's line of approach to Arosa Bay with all his available cruisers and destroyers, apart from those required for screening his battleships. With the ships stationed about twelve miles apart, this lookout line would sweep westward during the day and retire eastward during the night. If the Blue battle-fleet were sighted sufficient destroyers were to shadow it, while the remainder searched for and attacked the convoy somewhere in the vicinity.

Off Cape St. Vincent we struck a full gale from the north-west with a correspondingly heavy sea. For twenty-four hours we were making slowly to the northward, practically hove to. I had considerable anxiety for the destroyers, which were obviously having a bad time. Some were reporting severe straining and cracks across their upper decks; but on the whole I decided they were making as good, if not better weather, than the *Coventry*, which, with her low freeboard, was taking in green seas overall and pitching horribly. The sea was practically dead ahead. We carried on, though the delay meant we were twenty-four hours late in reaching the spot from which the cruiser and destroyer sweep to the westward was to be started.

At daylight on March 13th, the two Blue battle-cruisers were sighted and reported by one of our submarines at the southern end of our patrol line. They were on the direct route from the Azores to Lisbon. They were shadowed by a division of our destroyers. Our Commander-in-Chief made no alteration in his plans, and a few hours later a cruiser at the northern end of the lookout line reported the Blue battle-fleet steering the most northerly course it could if making for Arosa Bay. All the remaining destroyers turned northward to shadow and report. The Blue battle-cruisers, between two hundred and three hundred miles to the southward, had obviously made a feint to lure us in that direction.

In the late afternoon of March 13th, Sir William Fisher—Red Commander-in-Chief—realized that the Blue battle-cruisers could not rejoin the Blue battle-fleet before dawn next morning. At the same time the Blue battle-fleet had been located, and he—Sir William—saw it was possible for him to make contact soon after midnight. He therefore decided to bring them to action, realizing that the advantage of surprise would favour him, and that it was improbable he would have another opportunity of engaging a superior enemy in such favourable conditions. He steamed to intercept.

The *Coventry*, with a flotilla of destroyers we had managed to collect, was also in touch with the Blue battle-fleet, and shortly before 1 a.m. on March 14th we were ordered to attack from astern, which we did. The glare of searchlights and star-shell with other visible signs of battle gave our Commander-in-Chief a chance of correcting his final position. Bearing down on Blue at full speed with his battle-squadron on a line of bearing, his ships came simultaneously into action at a range of 7,000 yards.

These bold and masterly tactics not only put an end to the exercise; but settled once and for all the much-debated question as to whether or not British heavy ships could and should engage in night action against corresponding enemy units. At Jutland, it will be remembered, night action had deliberately been avoided. From now on it became an accepted principle that a highly-trained and well-handled fleet had nothing to lose and much to gain by fighting at night.

It is true that we did not have to contend with enemy destroyers. They were many years older than ours, most of them dating from the war of 1914–18 and just after. Unable to face the gale, they had been forced to run for shelter. The Blue Commander-in-Chief had no reason to suppose that our destroyers had made any better weather of it than his own, and was therefore at a disadvantage. Also he was committed to carrying out an operation, that of escorting a convoy over 800 miles of sea in the face of an undefeated though inferior enemy, which in actual war might have been considered unjustifiable. Because of the foul weather neither Commander-in-Chief was able to use air reconnaissance from the carriers.

Sir William Fisher was greatly pleased with the performance of his destroyers, for which I take little credit as I had been with them for only three months. But to me they had certainly shown excellent seamanship in very bad weather, and a high degree of training, efficiency and proper initiative whenever their chance came. I felt very proud of them.

A curious incident, and one which might have had disastrous results, occurred on the night of the fleet battle. The weather had moderated and all ships were darkened and without navigation lights. The *Coventry*, leading a flotilla, was following hard after the enemy fleet at 19 knots. From the bridge I suddenly saw that appeared to be a motor-boat right ahead coming at us at high speed. It was a destroyer's wash. She was retiring out of action, also at 19 knots, on what appeared to be an exactly opposite course. She was very close, and a combined speed of approach of 38 knots, or something like

K

sixty feet a second, does not give one much time to think. I immediately shouted "Hard 'a port!" using the old helm orders, which had been altered a month or two before. Horan, the *Coventry's* captain, realizing my error, immediately followed my order with the correct one, "Hard 'a starboard!" The helmsman, getting two contrary orders, did nothing, which was about the best thing he could have done. The destroyer, which was the *Delight*, passed down the *Coventry's* starboard side at a distance of three yards, no more. A big wave washed over the upper decks of both ships, after which the *Delight* passed through the line of destroyers astern of us and vanished into the night. It was a very narrow shave of a serious collision.

III

After a pleasant interlude at Gibraltar, where we discussed the exercise, held the inter-fleet competitions and met many friends, the two fleets parted, the Home Fleet for the United Kingdom and we for a cruise along the French Riviera. The *Coventry* and the Fourth Flotilla, Captain Dalrymple-Hamilton, visited the small port of Ste. Maxime in the Gulf of Ste. Tropez, where we were made very welcome by the French Authorities and the British residents. We did not escape a number of official engagements, and at the Maire's dinner party I had to make a speech in French. I had never shone in that language, and it was written out for me by Mrs. Dalrymple-Hamilton. I much doubt if it was understood.

The *Coventry* and Third Flotilla, next visited Leghorn. (Incidentally, I can never understand why we do not use the much better-sounding Italian name 'Livorno'.) The senior Italian naval officer there, a Rear-Admiral, was also commandant of the Naval Academy. He was a pleasant, knowledgeable man with some acquaintance of English. Among the official visitors to the ship was the local Fascist boss, who was received by a Royal Marine guard. The marines had the greatest difficulty in keeping straight faces as the black-shirted visitor strutted importantly round the ranks flapping his arm up and down in the Fascist salute. He was taken into my cabin and we conversed in bad French, Commander Charles Lambe acting as my interpreter. Suddenly to my astonishment, just after I had put the question: "How long have you been stationed at Leghorn?" our visitor leapt to his feet, hurried out of my cabin past the guard who had no time to present arms, ran down the ladder, jumped into his boat and cast off. Lambe afterwards confessed that in error he had translated my question with "You've been here long enough!"

We inspected the Naval Academy, and certainly the Italians appeared to give their young officers a good training which ended in an extensive cruise in a sailing training ship. According to our ideas the discipline was unnecessarily harsh, imprisonment in a cell being awarded for quite minor offences. The

Italian Navy was always royalist, and such conversation as I had with the more senior officers disclosed considerable resentment with the Fascist régime, particularly because two Fascist officials, in the guise of physical training experts, had recently been appointed to the staff presumably to keep an eye on what went on and to indoctrinate the cadets in the Fascist creed. On parting the Admiral presented me with a copy of his history of the 1914–18 war which, as it is in Italian, I have never been able to read.

We were back at Malta by the end of April, and there is no pleasanter place in May before it gets too hot. My wife and I entertained modestly at the Casa Pieta, getting to know the younger officers of the flotillas. Our drawing-room was large enough to hold a reasonably-sized dance, though it was hard going on the marble floor. As there was a sub-lieutenant who played the pipes we often finished up with reels on the tennis court. Cocktail parties were much the fashion. Personally I have always detested them, and we neither gave nor attended them. However, our house was generally full of young men, even at times to the extent of a young officer sharing the dog's bedroom. My sister's daughters came out in turn and stayed with us. They made excellent companions for my wife, and for them Malta provided a radical change from Edinburgh. Malta was not all gaiety. The flotillas were always much at sea exercising, and the Commander-in-Chief never believed in allowing the fleet to relax.

The end of June saw us off again for the first summer cruise to the Greek islands, carrying out the usual exercises on passage. Actually they were never usual in the ordinary sense of the word. They always had some novel or unorthodox features which added greatly to their interest and value. The *Coventry's* itinerary took her to several places well-known to me of old— Platea, Ithaca, Argostoli, Corfu, Suda Bay and Navarin. As there was little else to do, my staff and I used to climb all the adjacent hills at each anchorage. At Ithaca we visited the Cyclopean ruins on the hill top, and wondered how the huge stones had been transported there. At Argostoli Horan and I were taken for a motor drive round the island by the Greek Governor, in the course of which we were entertained to tea and speeches at a town on the east side of the island. Tea consisted of brandy, tea, grapes and a cake tasting strongly of goat.

At Corfu I was joined by my wife, and we made many expeditions. One remembers the Archilleion palace, built for the Empress Elizabeth of Austria, and later owned by William II of Germany, an extraordinary example of the Kaiser's taste, or the lack of it, in pictures and statuary, and Paleocastiza, where we climbed to the monastery at the top of the hill to be refreshed with grapes by the monks. Afterwards we regaled ourselves with crayfish and wine at the inn down below on the bay. I recollect, too, the cricket match against the local inhabitants, which most of the town turned out to watch. It was a great change and very pleasant, though rather hot.

My wife went off in a Greek steamer to Athens, there to take ship back to Malta. On the way through the Corinth Canal she had a signal from Lady Fisher, who was cruising in the Commander-in-Chief's yacht, the sloop *Bryony*, asking her to join the *Bryony* at the Piræus, and go on to Navarin.

The *Coventry* went to Suda Bay in Crete, where the flag lieutenant-commander and myself climbed to the top of the adjacent mountain. The day was oppressively hot, and as we did not take the orthodox route but went straight up the going was very rough. We arrived at the mountain village parched with thirst; but were unable to take advantage of the offers of iced beer made by the local innkeeper in American-English as we had forgotten to bring money. We all but exchanged Doble's gold wrist-watch for a bottle or two.

The fleet assembled at Navarin for the regatta, and here to my surprise I found my wife as Lady Fisher's guest in the *Bryony*. The destroyer regatta aroused the greatest enthusiasm, and in the end was won by the Fourth Flotilla by a short head from the Third. The *Coventry* competed in the cruiser's regatta. Having come near to winning it the year before Horan was determined to make certain of it this year. For some time past most things had taken a secondary place to regatta practice. He left nothing to chance, even to organizing my wife into following down every race in the bows of the barge and providing her with a flag in the *Coventry*'s colours to wave at critical moments. Horan's zeal was rewarded. The *Coventry* won handsomely, an excellent performance against eight other cruisers of which four were 10,000 ton 'County' class with complements of around 700. Ours was just over 400.

From Navarin we returned to Malta for a short visit for storing and docking before starting off on the second summer cruise in the Adriatic. We sailed on August 29th, and four days later arrived at the excellent anchorage of Bakar Bay in Yugoslav territory just south of Fiume and on the railway to the interior. My wife arrived a day or two later after a tedious journey through Italy, and we put up at the local inn, notable for the hordes of fleas and even more noisome insects which infested the beds and were only partially kept at bay with Keatings.

We had heard a lot of the good fishing in Yugoslavia so decided to make an expedition, and took the train to the small town of Ogulin. Here we were met by the proprietor of the local hotel and whisked straight off to a river where we caught a few trout and returned to the hotel after dark.

The hotel was almost unbelievably primitive, though the house was scrupulously clean and the food good and simple. The staff never knocked on one's bedroom door before entering, and on the first day the proprietor himself, anxious to get us on the river, burst in upon us to find my wife in a state of considerable undress. So far from being abashed and retreating in confusion he carried on an animated conversation while she completed her toilet. Next morning the two maids came marching in with our breakfast to find me bathing in a basin. It seemed quite the accepted thing.

The proprietor, Herr Rude Bergleitner, in spite of bursting into ladies' bedrooms, was a most courtly and helpful man and had been a sergeant in the old Austrian army. He came fishing with us every day and did ghillie for my wife, besides cooking our lunch on a wood fire beside the river. His fish or bits of pork or veal impaled on twigs and grilled and liberally basted with olive oil were delicious. With this, and grapes, and mugs of coffee and good black bread from the nearest cottage we were well looked after. However poor the cottagers would always produce bread and would never take payment.

We spent five days in this lovely spot, and the scenery was not unlike the Highlands of Scotland, except that the valleys were far wider and beautifully green. It was the greenness of it all that so appealed to us after the aridity of Malta. But with all this glorious meadowland, where in England one would have seen cattle in their hundreds, the beasts grazing were very few and not good cattle at that. This was partly explained by the fact that cattle, oxen and cows, pulled all the country carts, as in Italy.

Our next visit was to Lussin Piccolo, the Italian island off the approaches to the Gulf of Fiume. It was an anchorage not unlike a Norwegian fiord with a narrow entrance which, by the appearance of the batteries on each side, was heavily fortified. As it was a daylight passage of no more than a few hours my wife and several of the officers' wives came with us. It was a pleasant enough place with good hotels designed to attract tourists; but at the time of our visit it was out of the season and like being at Brighton in November.

After a week we moved on to Ljubac Bay, an anchorage in Yugoslavian territory not far from the Italian port of Zara. Ljubac Bay was a wild and desolate spot rather like a Shetland voe, with a narrow and twisting entrance and an anchorage that was completely landlocked. It was practically uninhabited; but this did not prevent several of our young wives from arriving by way of Zara, and camping on a headland near the ship. I never ceased to wonder at the enterprise and initiative of these young women. They were intrepid. If the *Coventry* could visit a place, however unsophisticated, so could they. They put up with every sort of discomfort and the most peculiar forms of transport, colliers, coasters and goodness knew what, to see something of the country and catch an occasional glimpse of their husbands. They were determined young women, and always cheerful.

At Ljubac I took a party in my barge into an inner fiord. On one side, bounded by steep cliffs, we saw a line of piles running out into the water. We followed them and found a narrow entrance between tall cliffs which opened out into a broader river, up which we steamed about four miles and went alongside a pier at a sizeable village. Our arrival out of the blue soon collected a considerable crowd. Then appeared the local police, who, determined to show their importance, demanded our passports. They spoke no English, and we could do nothing but gesticulate. But we had no passports, so the flag lieutenant-commander, with great presence of mind, handed them the old blue-covered Navy List which was always kept in the barge. They could not read a word of it and regarded it upside down; but honour was satisfied. After some smiles and considerable saluting our *bona fides* were established. I have sometimes wondered if an international incident would have been created if our whole party had been locked up for the night.

We made another trip up the river, walking six miles beyond the spot where we could safely take the boat. It was lovely country, though desolate and uninhabited, and the fish were completely disinterested in anything we had to offer.

September 24th saw us at Dubrovnik, a place I had visited in 1907 when it was called by the Italian name of Ragusa. My wife rejoined me here, and we stayed in an excellent though very expensive hotel. Dubrovnik is probably the most beautiful city on the Dalmatian coast with many old buildings dating from the fifteenth century and earlier, and fortifications built by the Venetians with most of the walls and bastions still intact. However, it had become a very popular seaside resort for the people of Central Europe and was very crowded. The romantic setting was rather spoilt by the shorts and pyjamas in which the women visitors seemed to spend most of the day.

From Dubrovnik we made an expedition inland by car to a place called Durmitor, about one hundred and thirty miles away, which was said to have a wonderful lake full of trout and on which the fishing was reserved for crowned heads—and apparently visiting British naval officers. It was a wonderful drive, up and down over several mountain ranges, and the place when we arrived was exquisitely beautiful, with the lake lying at the foot of a 9,000-feet mountain with a snow-capped peak and the lower slopes densely wooded. It was flat calm without a ruffle on the water, so the fishing was poor; but the reflection of the mountain in the lake was unforgettable.

We spent the night in the local inn. We had thought that the hotel at Ogulin was primitive; but this one beggared description. Our party consisted of two married couples and two single men, and the bedroom situation was difficult. We were shown three single rooms and one double with a doorless single room leading off it. My wife and I took the double room and the flag lieutenant-commander was unanimously voted into the room off ours. But he blenched, and the matter had to be settled by a rearrangement of the beds in the other rooms. Washing accommodation there was none, and the only lavatory was outside at the top of a high pole and was approached by a ladder, why I never discovered. The food was abundant though unusual. We dined on meat balls and pancakes, and breakfasted on pancakes, hard-boiled eggs and the scum off boiled milk. We fished most of the second day but caught nothing, and drove back to Dubrovnik by moonlight.

Split saw us next, and here the whole Mediterranean Fleet assembled for the regatta. All the wives moved on here, though I saw little of mine as I was too engaged in sailing. I was fortunate enough to win the Commander-in-Chief's cup and came near to winning another.

Split was an interesting place, with plenty to see, and perhaps the most of all was the remains of Diocletian's palace. He renounced the imperial crown in A.D. 303 and lived there till his death. The huge size of the palace, which originally covered nine and a half acres, shows that the emperor retired with a tolerable competence.

At the end of the week I saw my wife off to Malta in a Yugoslav cargo steamer, she occupying the chief mate's cabin. A good selection of hair oils and male garments, which he had neglected to move, were at her disposal.

From Split the *Coventry* and one division of destroyers moved on to a small township called Rogiznica, chiefly devoted to fishing so far as one could see. We had hardly arrived when we heard the news of the murder of King Alexander of Yugoslavia at Marseilles. Soon afterwards came a signal from the Commander-in-Chief directing the senior officers at the ports among which the fleet had been distributed to call on the local authorities to convey to them the deep sympathy of the British fleet.

I arranged to call on the local town council at 10 a.m., and as my barge rounded the point into the inner harbour we saw the village literally draped with long black streamers, and all the names over the shops and inns blotted out with black strips. At the landing place a dense crowd of women and children were present on our arrival. We were met by three officials dressed in black from head to foot and were led through a lane of weeping women to the council room. I had never seen anything like it, except perhaps as a child when I had watched the departure of an Irish emigrant train from a Galway station.

The council room was large and seemed to be furnished with no more than three red plush chairs; but it was densely crowded with what looked like the entire male population of the village. I made my little speech of condolence, which was interpreted by the only English-speaking resident. Then the head of the council replied. He was a small, insignificant-looking man with a clever face; but he certainly possessed the gift of eloquence. He roused his audience to something between frenzy and national enthusiasm, and had most of them in tears. Every now and then his speech was punctuated by savage shouts from some who could not restrain themselves. When he had finished I was closely examined as to what I knew about the King's assassination, they themselves knowing nothing but the bare facts. They were particularly anxious to know who the murderer was, and of what nationality. Although the wireless news had told us he was believed to be a Croat, this was a

Croatian village. With the people already worked up to a frenzy, I thought it best to keep that bit of information to myself.

The Commander-in-Chief himself had to go to Belgrade as one of the British representatives at the King's funeral, the others being the Duke of Kent and General Braithwaite. One hundred British seamen marched in the funeral procession. Sir William Fisher's great presence, and the sympathy he so well expressed in the many speeches he made in fluent French, made a great impression on the Yugoslavs. At Split he had said to the Ban, or Mayor: "You can organize almost everything, but you cannot organize grief like this." Those words were passed from mouth to mouth and finally came to the ears of the British Minister at Belgrade. I visited Split four years later in the *Hood*, and was told that when they heard of Fisher's death—June 24th, 1937—they held a solemn mass in the Roman Cathedral, an unprecedented honour for a heretic and a foreigner.

Later on in the cruise the *Coventry* and Fourth Flotilla visited the Yugoslav port of Kotor (Cattaro), with the great Mount Lovechen towering in the background. The island of Vis (Lissa) and the whole of the Dalmatian coast are famous in British naval history as the scene of the operations and exploits of Captain Sir William Hoste who was Senior Officer, Adriatic, from 1809 to 1814, when we were still at war against the French. It was one of the post-Trafalgar, pre-Waterloo side-shows against the French, strangely reminiscent of the Allied campaign against the Germans in Yugoslavia and the Dalmatian Islands in 1943–45, that is very often forgotten.

If a digression may be permitted, Hoste, writing from H.M.S. *Bacchante* before Cattaro on January 5th, 1814, described how the French garrison of that fortress had capitulated to the *Bacchante* and *Saracen* after a cannonade lasting ten days. The operation was entirely naval with the help of a few Montenegrin irregulars of doubtful value. A naval brigade had been landed, and naval guns sent on shore. One of the shining lights of the expedition was Captain John Harper, commanding the *Saracen*. As Hoste wrote in his despatched: "Two 18-pounders and two mortars were got up the range of mountains before Cattaro, to the astonishment of friends and foes; and what was deemed impracticable by the French General was accomplished in ten days."

However, the visit of the *Coventry* and Fourth Flotilla to Kotor, or Cattaro, in 1934 coincided with the funeral of King Alexander at Belgrade. Several officers and myself attended the requiem mass in the local church, a simple and beautiful service with the church packed and a large crowd outside. There was a dummy bier in the nave with the schoolchildren and their teachers drawn up in front of it, and the service soon had the little girls in tears. The music and singing were impressive, and the priest roused his congregation with what appeared to be a politico-religious sermon, at the end of which all the people shouted "Slavah!" The ceremony gained additional solemnity from the dull reports of the minute guns fired by the *Coventry* and Yugoslav flotilla leader *Dubrovnik*.

This ended our visit to the Dalmatian ports. We returned once more to the daily round and common task at Malta.

Once again, in the *Hood* in 1937, I was to visit this fascinating country with its simple-hearted and charming people, and to experience their deep friendship for the British people and their admiration for all things British. One looks back on those visits with feelings of real nostalgia. Will the Royal Navy ever again be able to experience the whole-hearted and kindly welcome they invariably received from the Yugoslavs in every walk of life, or will vile and insidious propaganda continue to estrange two peoples who have so very much in common?

CHAPTER XV

I

ALTHOUGH at Malta for ten weeks during the late autumn and winter, the ships were never idle, and were constantly at sea for exercises and practices. The Commander-in-Chief, however, thought that the ships' companies might become stale with too much Malta and its fleshpots, so one evening he sent for Captain Guy D'Oyly Hughes, commanding the 1st Submarine Flotilla, and myself, and instructed us to devise exercises to be sprung upon a ship or ships at any hour of the day or night. This we gladly did, and during the next two months a ship never knew when she was going to be called upon to do something unusual which required initiative and imagination. The same applied to the battleships and cruisers.

Manoel Island, near which the destroyers and submarines lay at their moorings, was particularly suitable for this sort of exercise, though often they took place much further afield. The ships' companies, I might add, entered into the proceedings with great zest and gusto and a fierce competitive spirit. Among the exercises we carried out for the destroyers were landing all sorts of equipment, and setting up wireless stations and mounting guns and searchlights ashore. Some of the destroyers carried a Diesel dynamo in a compartment on the upper deck, which I considered made it eminently suitable for landing and running ashore. The first young lieutenant (E) told to do it scratched his head and said the job would take forty-eight hours, working day and night. When it came to the point he had it ashore in four hours running a searchlight.

The winter cruise started at the end of January, 1935. The *Coventry* and the Third and Fourth Flotillas, with the depot ship *Sandhurst*, went to the Gulf of Patras, on the west coast of Greece. Meanwhile the First Flotilla had been permanently detached to China, and their reliefs, a flotilla of the much older 'V's' and 'W's', had not arrived.

We paid a short visit to Patras, and then moved over the north side of the Gulf, the *Coventry* and Fourth Flotilla anchoring in Itea Bay, and the *Sandhurst* and Third Flotilla in an anchorage three or four miles further south.

Thirty-one years before, when I was sub-lieutenant of the destroyer *Locust*, the Mediterranean Fleet put Itea into a state of defence and the destroyers had been ordered to make a night attack on the fleet. I have described that episode earlier in this book. I determined to repeat that excellent exercise in one way or another, so ordered each of my forces to put their anchorages into a state of defence. They both had a chain of small islands to seaward which were admirably suited to this purpose, and all hands set to with a will. By nightfall nearly every island off both anchorages had its quota of guns, searchlights and dynamos mounted, and its small garrison.

Each force attacked the other's defences in boats after dark and some Homeric combats took place on the rocks and in and around the guns and searchlights. In the midst of the battle, too, some further excitement was caused by the arrival of the local mail steamer which filched a 'boom defence' of Carley floats bodily from its moorings. It was all good sport, and the sailors greatly enjoyed themselves.

The two anchorages were separated by a range of fairly high hills, and another day we landed all available men, some 1,200 on each side, for mountain warfare. No arms were carried, and the only missiles allowed were the wild asphodel bulbs, which grew there in profusion. There was some fine manœuvring over terribly rough ground, and when I arrived in the front line a full-scale battle was in progress with the air full of bulbs about the size of large onions. The captain of the *Sandhurst*, a classical scholar, had made himself a sling as used by the ancient Greeks and was outranging the 'enemy' by a full thirty yards. In spite of the heavy fire there were no casualties except a black eye or two, though the medical officer of one force who established his dressing-station near a wild bees' nest was last seen in hasty and disorderly retreat. The local authorities and inhabitants enjoyed it as much as the sailors and later sent us in a bill for £200 for 'damage to crops'. No one had seen any crops. None would have grown in the arid, stony country where the battle took place; but we had to pay up and look pleasant.

February saw us back in Malta, and here we found the new First Flotilla in their old 'V's' and 'W's'. Destroyers age rapidly; but in spite of the fact that they were in ships fifteen years old the officers and men were in good heart and fully determined to prove that they were as good, if not better, than the more modern flotillas. And well they did it. Captain H. T. Baillie-Grohman in the *Keppel* was Captain (D) and among the commanding officers were Commander B. A. W. Warburton-Lee in the *Witch*; Commander Stephen Arliss, *Wild Swan*; Commander Lord Louis Mountbatten, *Wishart*; Commander G. N. Oliver, who had been our gunnery officer in the *Rodney*, in the *Veteran*; Lieutenant-Commanders Mervyn Thomas, *Whitshed*, and W. G. A. Robson, *Worcester*.

The year's programme of exercises and cruises was somewhat dislocated by the decision that a substantial part of the Mediterranean Fleet was to go home for the Naval Review at Spithead in June in connection with the celebration of His Majesty King George V's Jubilee. The combined fleet exercises, however, were to be held as usual, and early in March the Mediterranean Fleet assembled at Gibraltar.

This year the feature was to be an offensive by the Mediterranean Fleet against trade in the Atlantic, the defence of which was to be undertaken by the Home Fleet. Aircraft were to be used on both sides, though the preponderance was on the side of the defence. The operational area was to the southward of the approaches to the Straits of Gibraltar and included the Canary Islands.

The exercises were highly interesting and instructive and provided plenty of opportunities for initiative on the part of junior officers. Certain old lessons. which we had been apt to forget were re-learnt.

After the exercises both fleets returned to Gibraltar for the usual discussions and the interchange of civilities. Here I took leave of the *Coventry, Sandhurst* and Third Flotilla, all of whom were going home to refit. I returned to Malta with two flotillas with my flag in the *Blanche*, my headquarters being established ashore on Manoel Island from which I conducted the affairs of the destroyers.

The time passed as usual with exercises, and in preparation for the Jubilee Review at Spithead. There was some controversy as to how the Rear-Admiral (D), with his staff and office, were to get home. I was fully prepared to go in a destroyer; but she could not have accommodated my staff. It was finally decided that we should all go in the cruiser *Despatch* ahead of the fleet. My wife went home overland to be present at the review, and the *Despatch* reached Portsmouth at the end of May and I rejoined the *Coventry*.

My brother Alan at that time was in command of the artillery brigade stationed at Portsmouth. He had a small house in Portchester, and as he was away for about a month my wife and I took it from him. It made a very convenient *pied-à-terre*.

The Fleets assembled at Spithead on July 13th and 14th, 157 British warships in all with various liners, yachts and fishing vessels. The concentration, which included eleven heavy ships and eighteen cruisers was imposing enough, though nothing to compare with the Review in July 1914, when we had at Spithead more than sixty battleships and battle-cruisers and fifty-five cruisers of all types and ages.

The review followed the usual pattern of these spectacles, though I believe it was the first occasion on which civilian guests were allowed on board while the Royal Yacht steamed through the lines.

Her progress took about one-and-a-half hours, and as she secured to her buoy over a hundred aircraft of the Fleet Air Arm roared overhead in formation and came dipping down in salute in a long glide. It was a beautiful day and the spectacle was impressive.

All the Flag Officers had the honour of dining with His Majesty that evening, and on the morrow the fleet went to sea for exercises in the presence of the King in an area south-east of the Isle of Wight.

King George V's Jubilee Review was a memorable event, for it was the last time His Majesty was at sea with the Fleet that he knew and loved so well.

II

The *Coventry*, completed in 1918, had seen much hard service. She was an old ship beginning to show signs of decrepitude, so it was decided to relieve her as Rear-Admiral (D)'s flagship by the slightly larger and more modern *Despatch*, in which I had already served with Sir Walter Cowan in America and the West Indies.

When the Mediterranean Fleet returned to its station my staff and myself remained behind to commission and bring on the *Despatch*, my new flag captain being Guy L. Warren, an old friend of Dover Patrol days. Certain alterations and additions were required, chiefly to the bridge and offices. I had the greatest difficulty in persuading the Controller's Department at the Admiralty that they were really necessary, and to give them a reasonable priority. However, we got away at last and reached Malta towards the end of July.

Our few weeks there passed quickly. Like everyone else, we were watching and attempting to assess the situation that was arising in Europe because of Mussolini's obvious designs on Abyssinia and the completely futile contortions of the League of Nations in trying to persuade him to abandon the venture. To us in the Mediterranean Fleet it seemed a very simple task to stop him. The mere closing of the Suez Canal to his transports which were then streaming through with troops and stores would effectually have cut off his armies concentrating in Eritrea and elsewhere.

It is true that such a drastic measure might have led to war with Italy; but the Mediterranean Fleet was in a state of high morale and efficiency, and had no fear whatever of the result of an encounter with the Italian Navy. The Regia Aeronautica was of course an unknown quantity; but we were not at all disposed to attach too much weight to its ability to affect the issue. As the war was to prove we were right.

The move of the fleet to Alexandria was decided upon as a wise precaution. Malta was entirely without air defence, and the presence of the fleet there, within about sixty miles of the airfields in Sicily, might have proved too great a temptation to the Italians.

About a week before the fleet sailed I was sent for by Sir William Fisher to his office in Admiralty House. I found him greatly incensed. He handed me a document, which I recognized as an appreciation of the situation by the Chiefs of Staffs Committee in London, and pointed out two or three paragraphs which I was to read. I did so, and found they contained a very pessimistic, not to say defeatist, view of the Mediterranean Fleet's capacity to deal with the Italians. It was obviously this that had angered the

Commander-in-Chief, and I must say I agreed with him. We had some discussion, which he closed by rising to his feet and saying in his most impressive manner: "Cunningham, I have sent a signal to Their Lordships telling them I disagree with every word of this pusillanimous document. The Mediterranean Fleet is by no means so powerless as is here set out."

Those words would have expressed the feelings of every man if he had been told that the Mediterranean Fleet was not considered strong enough to meet the Italians.

A few days later we sailed eastward. On completion of the exercises on passage the bulk of the fleet was turned over to the Vice-Admiral, Second in Command, Sir Charles Forbes, to take on to Alexandria, and the Commander-in-Chief in the *Resolution*, and myself in the *Despatch*, went on to Port Said. We secured in the outer port on September 2nd.

The object of this separation was to get away from fleet routine and distractions for a short time to enable us to draw up plans for possible war. My staff, which was then the second largest on the station, joined in with the Commander-in-Chief's, and together they drew up skeleton plans of operations against the Italians. It was a busy time.

Most nights I dined with the Commander-in-Chief, and we had discussions after dinner in which his Chief of Staff, Rear-Admiral R. H. T. Raikes; his flag captain, John H. D. Cunningham; and his Captain of the Fleet, William J. Whitworth, all participated. The talks were most enlivening, and few factors in the international situation were left unexplored. Sir William Fisher usually advanced some novel and unorthodox view, more often than not with the sole object of trying out the reactions of his listeners. We managed to get in some exercise, for each afternoon, in spite of the great heat, the Commander-in-Chief, his Chief of Staff, the Captain of the Fleet and myself played three or four sets of tennis ashore.

Many Italian transports were using the Canal, those coming south filled with troops and stores, and a few empty coming north. As they passed close across the bows of the *Resolution* and *Despatch* we were in a good position to count them. The troops generally cheered and shouted "Duce! Duce!" on passing, and for our benefit. One day during the dinner-hour a large transport crammed with two or three thousand soldiers arrived, all cheering defiantly at our two ships. As they passed they broke into the Fascist anthem 'Giovinezzia'; but were considerably put out by the loud shouts of "Encore!" from the hundreds of sailors on the forecastles of the *Despatch* and *Resolution*. It is impossible to describe the withering contempt the British bluejacket can put into his applause if he dislikes the entertainment or entertainer, and on this occasion their sarcastic shouts penetrated even the thick hides of the Italians.

The *Resolution* and *Despatch* rejoined the fleet at Alexandria on September 15th. The Mediterranean was being steadily reinforced from all over the world—the aircraft-carrier *Courageous*; the Second and Fifth Destroyer Flotillas, the Second Submarine Flotilla and two minesweeping flotillas from the United Kingdom; the cruisers *York* and *Exeter* from South America; the *Berwick* and minelaying cruiser *Adventure* from China. The Battle Cruiser Squadron, a squadron of cruisers, and a destroyer flotilla from home were sent to Gibraltar, while the East Indies squadron, destroyers from China and the cruiser *Diomede* from New Zealand, concentrated at Aden. The Second Destroyer Flotilla, from the Home Fleet, presently went on to the Red Sea, and in November was sent to Bombay to refit. At the same time Alexandria was being put into a state of defence.

From the point of view of the destroyers our most valuable reinforcement was the new depot ship *Woolwich*, under the command of Captain Eustace Rotherham. Under his energetic rule and guidance the *Woolwich* was soon to prove herself invaluable. There were few destroyer repairs she would not undertake, and her engineers, artificers, artisans, indeed, all her officers and men, were animated by a great spirit. Destroyers seldom have a good word to say for their depot ships; but they were all loud in their praise for the *Woolwich*.

As the time passed at Alexandria we followed the fluctuations of the situation with particular interest. Abyssinia was invaded during the first week in October; but it did not appear to bring us any nearer to, or further from, war. Such sanctions as were imposed upon Italy were perfectly futile for the purpose for which they were intended. A child would have been aware that only the stopping of Italy's oil fuel would have had any effect.

Meanwhile, as already described, a large and imposing fleet had been concentrated at Alexandria, and by constant exercises at sea, squadrons, flotillas and individual ships were making sure of their efficiency in case they were called upon. Apart from the Home Fleet flotilla at Gibraltar, there were now five flotillas under my command in the Mediterranean. At Alexandria we had two Mediterranean flotillas, the Third and Fourth, with the Fifth, from the Home Fleet. There were two others at Malta, the First, of 'V's and 'W's, and the Nineteenth, formed from destroyers in reserve, under the command of Captain Philip Vian, for whom I had specially asked. His flotilla included six 'V's and 'W's, and three ships of a much older vintage, the *Torrid*, *Thruster* and *Rowena* completed in 1916–17. However, as all these last three normally worked with the Anti-Submarine School at Portland, they were expert at their particular job of hunting U-boats.

All these flotillas were constantly at sea exercising and filling in any gaps there might be in their readiness for war. One such gap appeared to me to be in torpedo fire against fast targets, so we made considerable study of the subject and overcame some of the very difficult problems involved.

It was known to all the Flag officers that if war came it was not the intention of the Commander-in-Chief to wait tamely at Alexandria or anywhere else. The moment the flag fell he was determined to strike at the Italians on their very doorstep. We had planned an operation for the night following the declaration of war which involved a sweep by a strong force of destroyers and cruisers up the east coast of Sicily and into the southern entrance of the Straits of Messina. We were to bombard harbours and port installations, and generally to make ourselves obnoxious. As the senior Rear-Admiral of the force detailed I was to be in command of the operation, though I had heard that Sir William Fisher intended to be on board one of the cruisers.

This operation was tried out at sea, and it was perfectly clear that no Italian ships at sea between the east coast of Sicily and the toe of Italy proper could possibly escape the net. Simultaneously with these rehearsals for the real thing the whole fleet also practised meetings at sea with the Italian battle-fleet.

Anti-submarine exercises against our own submarines were continuous, and brought to light the fact that in the neighbourhood around Alexandria detection of submarines was extremely difficult. Our anti-submarine forces had Asdics; but their utility was largely rendered nugatory by the varying densities of the sea-water in different layers. This was caused by the outpouring of fresh water from the mouths of the Nile. It was a problem which was never really solved.

All these exercises convinced me that the *Despatch* was not fast enough to operate with modern destroyers. I mentioned this to the Commander-in-Chief and suggested I should go to a newer cruiser, as otherwise I should be in the unenviable position of leading my forces from the rear. He fully agreed, and ordered my flag to be shifted to the *Galatea*, one of the new 'Arethusa' class, $32\frac{1}{4}$ knot, cruisers which had just arrived on the station. Though not so suitable as the *Despatch* from the point of view of accommodation for the staff, she had the necessary speed and modern armament and equipment.

By this time, October, 1935, my own personal affairs were beginning to assume some importance in my mind. My relief, James Somerville, my class- and term-mate in the *Britannia*, had already been appointed and would probably relieve me in January. Also the lease of our house in Malta expired at the end of the year. The situation, however, was by no means definite. The Commander-in-Chief's time was also up; but had been extended indefinitely, and I did not think I should leave before he did. Moreover, my successor, Somerville, had to be relieved in his appointment of Director of Personal Services at the Admiralty. The consequent moves involved an officer on Vice-Admiral Sir Charles Forbes' staff and he was being held temporarily, so matters were rather complicated, particularly so far as family affairs were concerned.

On October 17th, the Commander-in-Chief suffered a grievous blow when he had news that his son Nevil had been killed in a flying accident.

Sir William was never outwardly emotional, and we could only imagine what he felt.

It so happened that a large ship of the Italian Lloyd Triestino Line, the *Ausonia*, lay in Alexandria harbour, not far from the *Queen Elizabeth*. Soon after 8 a.m. on October 18th, fire broke out in her boiler room, and seeing the flames and smoke our minds leapt to the possibility that she might be carrying explosives, and that there might be an explosion as disastrous as that in Halifax harbour in 1915.

It was as well that the fleet was prepared for any emergency. Boats from the *Queen Elizabeth* were rushed over to rescue the passengers and crew, and with parties to deal with the fire. Destroyers got underway to assist, and the *Ausonia* was grounded not far from where she lay, mainly, I think, from the amount of water pumped into her.

Though many believed it at the time, I never thought that the fire was caused deliberately. Nevertheless, the danger was there, and there was no doubt that this sudden emergency, and the need for prompt and energetic action, served its purpose in distracting Sir William Fisher's mind from his own personal sorrow.

Admiral Sir Dudley Pound had been designated as Sir William Fisher's relief as Commander-in-Chief, and volunteered to come out as Chief of Staff. His offer was gladly accepted, and on his arrival at the end of October he took over his new duties and Rear-Admiral Raikes became Rear-Admiral, Alexandria.

Time passed, and our expectations of war with Italy fluctuated with the action, or rather the lack of action, by the League of Nations. It was exasperating enough. Had we stopped the passage of Italian transports through the Suez Canal, and the import of oil fuel into Italy, the whole subsequent history of the world might have been altered. However, it was no business of ours to question why.

There being no dock at Alexandria capable of taking any ship larger than a 'C' class cruiser, and the marine growth at Alexandria being more luxuriant than anything we had experienced before, the cruisers were being sent to Malta one by one to dock. The *Galatea's* turn came early in January, 1936. I had expected to shift my flag and remain at Alexandria while the ship was absent; but was ordered by the Commander-in-Chief to go in her. This I was glad enough to do, as it enabled me to visit the two destroyer flotillas stationed at Malta and to see my wife. I found them all in excellent order. After about a fortnight the *Galatea* returned to Alexandria, and as we no longer had a house in Malta my wife came on in a Norwegian steamer.

I was actually at sea in the *Galatea* when we heard of the death of King George V at Sandringham on the night of Monday, January 20th, 1936 It came as a profound shock, and seemed to mark the passing of a definite epoch. We all felt a sense of personal loss, and that the Navy in particular had greatly suffered by the death of a King who had its interest truly at heart and knew and loved it so well after having spent a substantial part of his life afloat.

The fleet at Alexandria was now of an imposing size, and the harbour was very crowded. However, the tension over the Abyssinian business appeared to be dying away, and the necessity for maintaining this great concentration of ships at Alexandria was doubtful. In March, Sir Dudley Pound relieved Sir William Fisher as Commander-in-Chief, and after many farewell functions, including a dinner given by the Flag Officers and captains of the fleet, from which he was pulled back to his flagship by a galley's crew of Admirals escorted by a cutter manned by captains, our fine Commander-in-Chief sailed for home.

I can never forget his departure next morning in the *Queen Elizabeth*, with the great silk Admiral's flag at the main, and the tall figure of Sir William Fisher himself prominent on the fore turret. The *Queen Elizabeth* steamed slowly through the lines on her way to sea, the guards and bands in all the ships being paraded and the sailors 'manning ship'. I have never heard cheers more hearty nor heart-felt. We were losing a friend, and a great commander.

In the roll of those distinguished Admirals who trained the Fleet between the two World Wars, and maintained and cherished its fighting efficiency and well-being, William Wordsworth Fisher must take a high place, perhaps the highest. I, personally, owe more to him that I can ever hope to express, and in my two years of close contact with him as Commander-in-Chief in the Mediterranean I recognized him as an oustanding leader and a great man. Responsibility meant nothing to him, and beneath a rather aloof exterior he had the greatest human understanding, and the softest and kindest of hearts, as many the wife of a young officer or a sailor came to realize. He was not easy to know at the outset. He had no great sense of humour and little time for fools and laggards; but during his service as an Admiral had a great influence upon the Royal Navy and was an inspiration to those who served with him. He died as Commander-in-Chief, Portsmouth, on June 24th, 1937, at the age of sixty-two, a great loss to the Navy and to the country that he served so well.

My relief, James Somerville, arrived three weeks after the Commander-in-Chief's departure and reigned in my stead. There was a big farewell dinner in the *Woolwich* after which my wife and I spent three days in Cairo before sailing for home. There were few commanding officers of destroyers who were not on the platform at Alexandria when we left. I felt most deeply this final severance from the destroyer service, with which, except for a few short intervals, I had been intimately connected since 1908.

We embarked in the P. & O. *Viceroy of India* at Port Said. We arrived at Tilbury in mid-April to be welcomed by a blinding snowstorm. Reporting at the Admiralty I met with a kindly reception; but was rather dashed when I was told by the Naval Secretary to the First Lord that I must expect no further employment until 1938. Such is the way of life in the Navy, where many are called and few chosen.

We retired to Hampshire, to live at an hotel in Botley while looking for a house. In a few weeks we found the Palace House, Bishops Waltham, and though, with the prospect of two years half-pay we were rather giving hostages to fortune, we took it on a long lease and it is now ours. Our living there has been intermittent, but we have never regretted our decision.

In the meadow within sight of our windows are the ruins of the old Palace originally built by Henry de Blois, Bishop of Winchester, in the twelfth century and extended in the fourteenth. Except for the seven years from 1551 to 1558 it remained in the hands of the bishops until destroyed during the Civil War. It was here, in 1182, that the barons met Henry II and granted the supplies for the Second Crusade, here also, in 1194, that Richard I held a council before his last expedition to France. It was frequently visited by royalty, and the wills of Henry II and William of Wykeham were both dated at Waltham, where Wykeham spent his last days. Cardinal Beaufort in his will bequeathed to Queen Margaret his "blue bed of gold and damask" at his palace at Waltham "where the Queen used to lie when she was at that palace, and three suits of arras from the same room". It was frequently visited by Henry VIII and Wolsey, and during his reign was described as "a right ample and goodly Maner Place moted about, and a praty Brooke renning hard by it". It was totally destroyed during the Civil War after a gallant defence by 200 cavaliers, who were forced to surrender to the parliamentarians on April 9th, 1644. "Waltham House in Ashes," a royalist wrote two days later. Bishop Curll, living there at the time, is said to have escaped, disguised and in a dung cart. For some time after that anyone who required stone for building helped himself from the ruins, which, with the site, passed into private ownership in 1869. The ruins are still imposing, though little is left but the shell of the west wing. But it must have been a magnificent establishment in its time, complete with granary, bake-house, brew-house, fishponds and much else, and hunting for the bishops in Waltham Chase, which was amply stocked with deer.

The house we occupy is more modern. Part of it dates from the fifteenth century, though it was altered in the seventeenth, eighteenth and nineteenth centuries. Its chief attractions are the garden and the view of the ruined palace. I sometimes find myself meditating over the centuries of history which that fine old ruin has seen, and the great men who once lived and ruled there.

CHAPTER XVI

I

THOUGH the summer and autumn of 1936 found us fully employed in getting our new house and large garden into order, I was rather appalled at the prospect of doing two whole years outside the Navy. In a fighting service ideas and methods are in a constant and rapid state of progression, and in two years there was bound to be a considerable advance in technique.

Among other things, the fight of the Navy for the control of its own Air Arm was just being launched, and the Tactical, Technical and War Courses, which Rear-Admirals were allowed to attend, were not for Vice-Admirals, to which rank I had been promoted on July 22nd, 1936. So taking it all in all I could see that after two years I should probably be greatly out of touch with the most modern naval developments. However, I was allowed copies of most of the Admiralty Fleet orders. These, with frequent visits to my friends at Portsmouth, and not least to the Commander-in-Chief, Sir William Fisher, was all I had to keep myself up-to-date with naval affairs. Fortunately this period of almost complete severance was to be greatly curtailed.

Early in 1937 an important committee was set up by the Admiralty to study the ventilation of His Majesty's Ships and to make recommendations for its improvement. Subsidiary objects were to study and suggest improvements in the accommodation and messing, with particular reference to messing on the cafeteria system. Finally the committee was to investigate the effect of the newly-introduced 'A' cordite on the men employed in ships' magazines. It was suspected of having a poisoning effect, as some of those handling it had been temporarily knocked out.

The committee consisted of the distinguished scientist, Professor Sir Leonard Hill; a scientist from the Royal Naval College at Greenwich; a representative from the Department of the Director of Naval Construction at the Admiralty; and a representative of the Medical Director-General of the Navy. I was appointed as chairman, and Commander Hon. Oswald Cornwallis was secretary.

This work kept me busy and interested. We met two or three times a week at the Admiralty, and for the rest paid many visits to H.M. Ships and merchant ships, including the *Queen Mary* and many newly-built vessels. It was on board the new American cruiser *Chester* that we studied the cafeteria system of messing in force in the United States Navy. We interviewed many representatives of firms who had their own particular systems of ventilation, and also carried out experiments in the magazines of H.M. Ships. We also had to investigate the problem of getting rid of gases after an explosion in a confined space, and carried out explosion trials in a specially-built structure at Chatham. Certainly I learnt how ignorant I was on those aspects of naval life, except perhaps in regard to accommodation and messing.

During these months big events were taking place around us. The Civil War had broken out in Spain; but at home, at the end of the year, all our thoughts were subordinated to the abdication of King Edward VIII.

My wife and I were among those fortunate enough to be present in Westminster Abbey for the Coronation of His present Majesty on May 13th, 1937. The ceremony with all its pageantry was impressive; but it was a most exhausting day. Called at 5 a.m. we were in our seats soon after 7.30, and though the actual ceremony was over soon after 2 p.m., the transport arrangements had gone awry and we did not get away until 7.30. It was lucky we had taken with us some portable provender in the shape of milk tablets, cheese biscuits, raisins and chocolates, though we had nothing to drink.

The Coronation Naval Review at Spithead, which we were invited to attend in S.S. *Vandyck*, took place on May 20th. We spent an enjoyable and comfortable twenty-four hours on board, and met many old friends including Sir Walter Cowan, whom we were delighted to see. The ship was quite crowded with M.P.s and other privileged people, among them about twenty Admirals, mostly retired, and ranging in age from eighty-six to my own. I need not describe the review, which followed the same pattern as the others. Other Coronation festivities which we attended included the Court Ball at Buckingham Palace and the ball given at Portsmouth by the Navy to the visiting foreign warships.

To our bitter regret the Commander-in-Chief at Portsmouth, Admiral Sir William Fisher—'W.W.' as he was always known in the Service—died on June 24th. We attended the funeral at Portsmouth, which included a simple but very moving service on the quarterdeck of his flagship, Nelson's old *Victory*. The remains were buried at sea near the Nab Tower. We had lost a trusted friend and the Navy an outstanding leader.

It was at about the same time, through my visits to the Admiralty on the work of the committee, that I heard that Vice-Admiral Sir Geoffrey Blake, commanding the Battle Cruiser Squadron and Second in Command Mediterranean Fleet had had to be taken to Bighi Hospital at Malta.

A few days later I was offered this important command temporarily while Geoffrey Blake was ill. I naturally leapt at the opportunity. The Admiralty were anxious that I should get out quickly, so a week later, having hurriedly collected such effects as I thought I should require for two or three months, I was on my way overland to Marseilles. There I embarked in a ship of the Khedivial Line for Malta, arriving at 7 a.m. on July 15th.

I was met by Blake's flag-lieutenant, James Munn, a young officer I had known well in the *Coventry*. In spite of his persuasions I went on board the *Hood* at once, whereby I was not at all popular as they had hoped

I would not appear before 8.30. The captain, indeed, was still in his bath, for which no one could blame him. To one who had spent most of his life in small ships my quarters in the *Hood* were palatial, large and airy cabins on the deck above the quarterdeck with great windows instead of the ordinary portholes. Even my cabin in the *Rodney* was small in comparison.

My next two days were spent in the usual round of official calls. I was very kindly received by the Commander-in-Chief, Admiral Sir Dudley Pound, who gave me his views as to what he considered were the duties of the Second-in-Command. He was strongly of the opinion that the latter should freely express his views to the Commander-in-Chief, especially if he felt there was anything wrong in the fleet or if he disagreed with any of the Commander-in-Chief's actions. I held exactly the same opinion, and though there were few questions upon which we ever disagreed I did not hesitate to say what I thought.

I took the earliest opportunity of visiting Geoffrey Blake in hospital. He certainly looked a very sick man, and the doctors said he could not even be sent home in safety before August. It seemed as though my temporary appointment would last four or five months at least, so I cabled to my wife to let our house at Bishops Waltham if she could and come out and join me in the Mediterranean.

At that period the Battle Cruiser Squadron consisted of the *Hood* and *Repulse*, though the Vice-Admiral was also in charge for administrative purposes of the aircraft-carrier, the *Glorious*, and the fleet repair ship *Resource*. He was further in general charge of the training of the personnel, and what with one thing and another I very soon found I had a full-time job.

The flag captain in the *Hood* was Captain Arthur F. Pridham, a gunnery expert of note who had lately been in command of the *Excellent*, the cradle of all naval gunnery. However, his specialization in gunnery had not impaired his ability in ship handling, and it was a pleasure to see him bring the great 42,000-ton *Hood* stern first into her tight berth in Bighi Bay. Captain John H. Godfrey, a widely-read and most able officer, commanded the *Repulse*.

As my appointment was only temporary I naturally took on Blake's secretary and staff, a most efficient body of officers all of whom later served with distinction in the Second World War. I thought that perhaps the flag lieutenant, James Munn, might not wish to stay on with a different Admiral and would prefer to go home with Blake. So I told him I was very willing to retain him if he liked, and gave him twenty-four hours to think it over. Inside that period he came and said he would like to remain, adding with some *naïveté*—"After all, sir, there must be many worse jobs than being your flag lieutenant!" He could not understand why I was so amused. He proved, as I knew he would, an exceptional flag lieutenant, and spared no pains in guiding my unwilling footsteps through all the social mazes.

My wife let our house with unexpected ease and was on her way out by the end of July, so added to my other activities I had to find somewhere to live. Eventually I fixed on a flat in a new block close to our former house in Pieta Creek. The plumbing was indifferent, the water heating system did not work, and the sandflies were terrible; but apart from that it was good as Maltese flats went. The rooms were spacious enough and one could live with the rather sparse furniture. I left the engagement of maids to my wife. I did not feel that my technique was up to it. She arrived early in August and we spent a very pleasant three weeks. We were very busy with social engagements of all sorts; but managed to fit in various bathing picnics and visits to the old haunts we knew so well. The speed of my new motor barge as compared with that of the *Coventry* made these jaunts far less protracted, and permitted us to go further afield by water.

The fleet was to leave Malta at the end of August for a cruise to Argostoli, in the Greek island of Cephalonia, and the Dalmatian coast. Sir Dudley Pound had never visited Yugoslavia, and I spent an hour or two during our last few days in Malta drilling him in the correct method of inspecting a Yugoslav guard of honour, and in correcting his pronunciation of the phrase "*Pomez Bog Junaci*"—"God be with you, my children"—which has to be shouted before the guard is inspected. Lady Pound had very kindly invited my wife to accompany her in the Commander-in-Chief's yacht, the sloop *Aberdeen*, so she reached the Dalmatian coast before I did.

After exercising hard on passage the fleet spent a few days at Argostoli reviewing and discussing the exercises we had carried out. I need say nothing about them, except that they clearly demonstrated the danger of letting an aircraft-carrier loose by herself. For the purpose of flying aircraft off and on she must steer a course into the wind as well known to the enemy as to her own fleet, with the consequences that, alone and isolated, she was in great danger of being snapped up. The antidote, of course, was for the carrier to operate in line with the fleet and under its protection, though at that time this was anathema to all captains of aircraft-carriers. Hard experience and losses under war conditions quickly altered their point of view. Under the heavy umbrella of the fleet's anti-aircraft fire they were also much less liable to damage through bombing or torpedo attack.

After Argostoli the fleet separated and sailed for their various destinations on the Dalmatian coast, the *Hood* arriving at Split on September 1st. On paying the customary official calls I found that the Ban, or Governor, and most of the other officials were much the same as when I had been there two years before. They gave us a most cordial welcome, and on my intimating that I wished to spend a few days fishing up country agreed to cut down the official entertainments to a minimum. I found my wife established in one of the local hotels after having enjoyed an excellent time at Dubrovnik and elsewhere in the *Aberdeen*. They had also visited the island of Mljet, claimed by the local inhabitants to be the island on which St. Paul was shipwrecked, presumably because of verse 27 Chapter 27, in the Acts of the Apostles—"But when the fourteenth night was come, as we were being driven up and down in Adria, about midnight the shipmen deemed that they drew near to some country." The Maltese, naturally, refuse to allow the claim.

We drove inland for a short spell of fishing. We were a party of four, my wife, myself, the flag lieutenant, and a commander on my staff. We reached our destination during the afternoon, a fairly large village called Livno where the inhabitants were mostly Mohammedans. The accommodation and meals were quaintly primitive; but the landlady fired our fishing ardour by producing two trout of about 4 lb. each for our dinner. We fished next day in a lovely spot where the river ran through a valley between low hills beautifully turfed and carpeted with autumn crocuses. We could drive where we liked along the smooth turf along the river bank. The fishing was fairly good, and among many small fish my wife and I caught one or two good-sized ones. We cooked them for lunch on hot stones accompanied by mushrooms gathered round about. We stayed only a short time in this beautiful spot and left after breakfast on the third day. The landlady produced our bill with some trepidation, and when it was translated from the local dinars into pounds sterling we found it was only £4 for the four of us. We paid cheerfully, and our hostess was so relieved at not having to argue, which was apparently the usual custom, that she insisted on our having two rounds of plum brandy on the house.

We returned to Split to find official affairs rather complicated by the arrival of a Roumanian warship and the fact that it was King Peter's birthday two days later. The celebrations, indeed, started on the night of our return, and we were expected to take part. The illuminations that night were simple but striking, the summits of all the mountains around, about 9,000 feet high, being outlined by chains of thousands of bonfires, and further bonfires on some of the slopes picking out the letters P. II. It was a fine sight which lasted too short a time. Early next morning I attended services of thanksgiving in the Roman Catholic cathedral and the Orthodox church, and for the next two or three days of our visit we just went from one official party to another.

I paid a farewell visit to the Ban and we fell on each other's necks. He was such a nice man and all the people were charming and friendly. Another pleasant touch was when, on our return from the fishing trip, I found a letter waiting for me from our landlord at Ogulin three years before, Herr Rude Bergeleitner, the polite ex-sergeant in the Austrian army. In it he wrote that he had read of our arrival in the local press and that we were intending to fish, so sent us a dozen flies tied by himself and suitable for the rivers in the part of the country in which we now were. It was a kindly thought, and typical of others.

At the last official dinner of all many of the speeches, particularly one by the Roumanian Minister, showed clearly how delighted everyone was that Great Britain was in the process of rearming.

I saw my wife off to Venice and the *Hood* sailed next morning after a wonderful eight days. Nothing could have exceeded the friendliness of the people and the welcome they gave to the officers and men.

Our next port of call was Malta, preparatory to doing a tour of duty on the Spanish coast.

II

The Spanish Civil War had been raging for more than a year without any very definite advantage to either side. Speaking generally, Franco controlled the west and south coasts of Spain with a part in the north, while the government forces held the east coast with the great ports of Valencia and Barcelona. Franco also held Majorca, though the government were in possession of Minorca.

Franco had declared a blockade of the east coast ports, though as neither side had been accorded belligerent rights his blockade was not recognized by the British Government. However, considerable efforts were made by the Franco forces to enforce it, partly by spasmodic and rather futile operations carried out by surface ships based on Cartagena; but principally by aircraft operating from the aerodromes in Majorca. Attracted by the enormous profits to be made by running cargoes into the ports of one side or the other certain British shipowners were operating whole lines of steamers to break the blockade. They were constantly getting into trouble, and for the past nine months or so it had been customary to maintain a British squadron and a Flag Officer at Palma, Majorca, drawn sometimes from the Home and sometimes from the Mediterranean Fleet. It was the Flag Officer's rather difficult and unsavoury task to see that British shipping was not unnecessarily molested, particularly outside Spanish territorial waters. It was for this duty that the *Hood* was about to sail.

In the autumn of 1937 another rather sinister development had arisen, and this was when British ships on the Spanish coast, indeed in other parts of the Mediterranean, were being sunk without warning, apparently torpedoed by submarines. The Spaniards claimed the submarines were Spanish, though actually there was no doubt they were Italian. At the Nyon Conference of September, 1937, in which Italy was invited to participate but did not attend, the British and French governments quickly came to an agreement for routeing all merchant traffic in the Mediterranean, and for patrolling the routes with a large number of destroyers and flying-boats with orders to counter-attack any submerged submarine.

On the return of the *Hood* to Malta I embarked in the Commander-in-Chief's flagship, the *Barham*, and accompanied him to Oran to meet the

French Admiral in the Mediterranean, Esteva, to arrange to implement the agreement arrived at at the Nyon Conference. A conference was held on board the *Barham* on our arrival, and we very soon decided upon the necessary measures. This was my first meeting with Admiral Esteva, whom I afterwards came to know very well. He was a small, very alert-looking man with a square-cut beard turning grey. A bachelor and very austere, he was rather a trial to his staff from the extremely early hour at which he insisted on starting work. They called him 'the monk'. He spoke English very well and was all out to co-operate.

At the end of our talks I returned to Malta in a destroyer, and the Commander-in-Chief himself initiated the Nyon patrols on the Spanish coast. So far as the British contribution was concerned the Mediterranean Fleet was reinforced by destroyers from the Home Fleet, while two squadrons of flying-boats from Coastal Command of the Royal Air Force were stationed at Arzeu, near Oran, with the submarine depot ship *Cyclops* to look after them. When the patrols were instituted they had an immediate and beneficial result. The submarine attacks on merchant ships ceased abruptly. Mussolini's piratical and puny efforts at sea to assist the Spanish Nationalists were quickly and effectually scotched.

Early in October we sailed from Malta in the *Hood* to relieve the Commander-in-Chief. We went first to Arzeu, where I met Sir Dudley Pound for an hour to glean all the latest information, and to see the flying-boats at work.

The *Hood* next visited Gibraltar and Tangier, most of my time there being spent in interviewing people about the Spanish Civil War and the newly-established Nyon patrols. Next we moved on to Palma, Majorca, where the command was exercised by the Spanish Admiral Francesco Morena and much of my time was taken up in visiting him and remonstrating about the high-handed treatment of some British merchant ship or another. We made Palma our headquarters, with periodical visits to Valencia and Barcelona to visit the British consuls and the British minister, and to allay the fears of the latter. Almost every day we spent at Palma squadrons of Italian S.79's roared overhead to bomb Valencia or Barcelona, though when we lay off these ports the bombers never came, so the inhabitants were glad of our arrival.

It was not an enlivening duty. One's only relaxation was an occasional walk ashore, with periodical visits to Admiral Morena. However, he was a weak man with little real control over the Italian and few Spanish aircraft supposed to be acting under his orders. The British consul at Palma, Alan Hillgarth, who accompanied me on these visits was a very live wire. Curiously enough I had known him before as a midshipman in the *Wolverine* in the Dardanelles, where he had been very badly wounded by one of the large leaden bullets fired by a Turkish rifleman.

The first week in November found us back in Malta just in time to take part in the festivities attendant on the arrival of the French Commander-in-Chief, Admiral Abrial, in the cruiser *Algérie* to return the earlier visit of our Commander-in-Chief to Toulon. We had three or four days of hectic lunching, dining and dancing, my contribution being an official lunch in the *Hood*. The French were all very pleasant. Most of them spoke English, and I think they enjoyed themselves.

Meanwhile, our domestic arrangements were causing us some bother. My appointment was only a temporary one, and from the excellent reports from home we all expected that Geoffrey Blake would be out again by December. So my wife had taken a small flat and enticed my brother's daughter to come out and stay with her. My car had been sent out from home, and as soon as I was relieved we intended to go home overland through Italy and France. Sir Dudley Pound had promised to send us, car and all, to Naples. Having no great facilities ashore, all our entertainment was done on board the *Hood*, which was well suited for it. It culminated in a large dinner on St. Andrew's night, when we had two eightsome reels going at one time in my dining-cabin. The ships' band played themselves to the point of exhaustion.

Soon afterwards I was informed that my appointment was made permanent as Geoffrey Blake had retired. He was another serious loss to the Navy, and undoubtedly one who would have risen to the very top.

Now we had the problems of getting our goods and chattels out from England and of finding a house. It was not an easy matter. The Casa Pieta which we had had during my time in the *Coventry* had quite spoiled us for most Maltese houses. However, my turn for the coast of Spain came round again, and sailing early in the New Year, 1938, we arrived at Palma on January 8th. This time we found an Italian Admiral there, and had to entertain him. He was a pleasant man, and not, I think, a confirmed Fascist. He came from Piedmont, and his sympathies were more royalist than anything.

The Civil War in Spain did not seem to have advanced any nearer towards a decision. The Republicans and Nationalists seemed to be carrying out a good many bombing raids on each other's cities, though we saw little of it. The arrival of the *Hood* invariably put a stop to any bombing in her vicinity. Considering the number of raids, however, the damage seemed insignificant. In Valencia and Barcelona one had to go and look for it. There was a recrudescence of sinkings by submarines, which caused me to pay several visits to my Spanish confrère. If he got wind of it in time he usually went to sea; but I caught him several times. I was not at all sorry when an Admiral from the Home Fleet relieved me at Palma on February 3rd and the *Hood* returned to Malta.

Our house-hunting came to an abrupt termination. On visiting the Commander-in-Chief I was told that I should probably be appointed Deputy Chief of the Naval Staff at the Admiralty in the autumn. I felt rather horrified at the prospect, feeling I was quite unsuited for the appointment through lack of staff experience. Naturally, I would have greatly preferred to complete my time in the *Hood*. However, it was not to be. The *Nelson*, with the Commander-in-Chief, Home Fleet, Admiral Sir Roger Backhouse, arrived at Malta on February 14th. I knew he was First Sea Lord designate, and when we dined at Admiralty House I was given the opportunity of a long private talk with him. I explained that I felt quite unsuitable for the appointment of D.C.N.S.; that I had practically no staff training, and was not good at expressing myself on paper. It was all to no purpose. Sir Roger just smiled, and said in his usual charming way that he wanted me to come. So that was that. Instead of taking houses in Malta we began to think of going home again.

In the meanwhile I had much else to consider. The international situation looked ominous. Hitler, having bludgeoned the Austrians into including the Austrian Nazis in the government, obviously had designs on that country. Italy could not be depended upon to take any action against Germany, so we were preparing for eventualities.

We were to carry out the usual spring exercises with the Home Fleet, and sailed for Gibraltar during the first week in March, exercising hard all the way. This year, 1938, there was to be no big strategical exercise between the Mediterranean and Home Fleets, merely a number of smaller ones, in one of which I was in command of one side and James Somerville, who was Rear-Admiral commanding the Mediterranean Fleet destroyer flotillas, the other. In this particular exercise I shifted my flag from the *Hood* to the *Repulse* at sea. Though it was a flat calm the swell was very heavy, and we had many exciting moments while embarking and disembarking, and in returning to the *Hood* during moonlight. Had I realized the height of the swell, which looked nothing from our bridge, I should never have attempted it.

The exercise, which I need not describe, was very interesting, and once more I learnt the unwisdom of one's aircraft-carrier operating apart from the fleet.

Back in Gibraltar again I dined with the Commander-in-Chief, Home Fleet, Sir Roger Backhouse, and had a talk with the First Sea Lord, Admiral of the Fleet Sir Ernle Chatfield, who had come out for the exercises. He was very much concerned about Hitler's designs upon Austria, and in truth it did not require much perspicacity to realize what was going to happen.

While at Gibraltar I was beguiled into attending the races. Before setting out my invaluable secretary, Paymaster Captain A. P. Shaw, handed me a card on which were set down all the expected winners, and also a double. I backed them all, and as every single one came off I returned to the *Hood* considerably richer and with a rather more tolerant view of racing than I usually have.

After this the *Hood* went back to the Spanish coast. Little had changed, though Franco's people now seemed quite confident of winning. Their blockade on the coast had been somewhat relaxed, probably because of the sinking of one of their large 8-inch-gun cruisers, the *Baleares*, off Cartagena by government torpedo craft. Rumour had it that the sinking was largely due to an ex-torpedo rating of the Royal Navy who embarked in one of the government destroyers and succeeded in making the torpedoes run straight. A rear-admiral and more than 600 officers and men were lost, while some 400 were rescued by the British destroyers *Kempenfelt* and *Boreas*.

The successes of Franco's forces on land were causing considerable perturbation in Valencia and Barcelona. The British Minister had now retired to a villa at Caldetas, a small town about twenty-five miles north of Barcelona, and we spent some time lying off the place to give him the comfort of our presence. Plans were also put in train for the evacuation of the British communities in Valencia and Barcelona if the worst came to the worst. Barcelona had suffered a severe bombing during our absence; but although they said they had buried some two thousand dead the actual damage done was not impressive. The people were taking it all with remarkable stoicism, and going about their business quite calmly. The Rambla, as usual, was crammed with stalls with every imaginable spring flower, a lovely sight. I was able to buy the better part of the contents of a whole stall for the equivalent of about half a crown. Palma, Majorca, too, was a pleasant spot in the spring. The export of almonds being one of the island's main industries there was pink almond blossom everywhere.

Our turn of duty finished, we went on to Golfe Juan, arriving for a ten-day visit on April 22nd. Here I met my wife. We decided to get away as soon as possible and tour Provence by car, and a lovely three days we enjoyed, visiting Aix, Arles, Nîmes and Avignon. We thought little of the celebrated wine, Chateau des Papes, sold at Avignon. We got back in time to attend the large party given by the officers of the *Hood* to all and sundry who had entertained them. We thoroughly enjoyed our time on the Riviera, and were sorry to sail for Malta with a visit to Corsica on the way.

My wife was expected to arrive in Malta before me. However, as she and a friend, a Russian lady, elected to pass through Rome on the same day as Hitler arrived, I thought it more probable they would be locked up. Actually they had considerable trouble both in Rome and Naples and were treated with grave suspicion. During their short stay in each city their luggage was taken away from the station and stored in a public lavatory. I never thought my wife would be suspected of carrying bombs to blow up Hitler or Mussolini!

The *Hood* called at St. Florent, a small bay in the north of Corsica and one of the anchorages used by the English fleet during Nelson's operations against Bastia in 1794. When the mayor came off to call he brought a letter written to one of his ancestors by Lord Hood on the subject of provisions for the fleet and the supply of arms to the local Maquis of those days. I put in a couple of days trying to catch trout; but though the rivers were magnificent they were largely devoid of fish. Little wonder. We were afterwards given to understand that the improvident local inhabitants dynamited the rivers to supply trout to the towns on the Riviera.

On arrival at Malta we had some backwash from the Anglo-Italian conversations in April by the news that we were to be visited by an Italian squadron at the end of June and our government wished them to be well entertained. Most of us in the Mediterranean were sceptical about the results achieved by these same conversations. Nobody was prepared to trust anything that Mussolini said or signed, and one had only to regard the reception given to Hitler when he visited Italy a week or two later to realize which way the wind really blew. As our merchant ships were being bombed almost daily by Italian bombers in and outside the Spanish ports it was not easy to work up cordiality. Added to this our visit to the Dalmatian coast in 1938 had had to be cancelled because the Yugoslavs were afraid of unfavourable comment by the Italians and Germans if they held out the hand of friendship to a considerable number of British warships in their ports and harbours.

However, orders were orders, and the fleet set out to give the visitors a good time which, in Latin countries, can be interpreted as one official entertainment after another without respite. Sir Dudley Pound, wishing to be particularly cordial, asked the Italian Commander-in-Chief to bring his wife and two daughters. We were to put up one of the two daughters, a tall order in a flat about the size of a large dog kennel. Fortunately none of these ladies appeared.

The Italian squadron duly arrived, the battleships *Conte di Cavour* and *Giulio Cesare* with four destroyers under the command of Admiral Riccardi. The two battleships were fine examples of old ships modernized, and the work had been most skilfully done. They had been rearmed with ten 12-inch guns and a good anti-aircraft armament. Some sixty feet had been added to their length and this, with modern boilers and machinery, gave them a reputed speed of 26 or 27 knots as against the 21.5 when they were completed in 1915.

Entertainment of all sorts went on unceasingly. We lunched on board the *Conte di Cavour* with Admiral Riccardi, and came to the conclusion that he must have embarked the whole catering staff and band from one of the best hotels in Rome, so distinguished was his entertainment. Afterwards he took us round his palatial and highly decorated private apartments, and took some pride in pointing out a book, *The Life of Nelson*, which always lay on a table by his bedside. His subsequent actions during the war rather showed that he had not greatly profited by his nightly reading.

I gave a large dinner-party to forty-five in the *Hood* preparatory to a dance in the Commander-in-Chief's flagship, the *Warspite*. Decked out with palms, gladioli and carnations, the quarterdeck looked very fine, and the dinner was a great success. On the whole we liked Admiral Riccardi and the senior officers, who were most courteous and pleasant. The younger officers, however, were ill-mannered and boorish. At the *Warspite's* dance my wife's Russian friend, who spoke fluent Italian, asked a young Italian officer who seemed to be doing a lot of standing about, if she could find him a partner. "No," said he. "I prefer to choose my own!"

A cruise to Grecian waters was substituted for our visit to Dalmatia, and the *Hood* and *Repulse* arrived at Corfu early in July. We found His Majesty the King of Greece in residence there and paid our duty calls. One Sunday morning he came and walked round the *Hood*. Corfu can be very torrid in the summer, and in the process of our tour round the ship we all got very hot and exhausted and had to revive ourselves in my cabin. The King dined with me that night and saw the cinema, and as he did not finally leave until nearly 2 a.m., it is to be presumed he was not bored. He struck me as rather a solemn and serious-minded man; but made himself very interesting and pleasant. I was to see a great deal more of him later. At Corfu we visited all the old haunts I knew so well, and paid a further call on the King in his lovely villa.

July 10th found the whole Mediterranean Fleet at Navarin for the annual sailing regatta. It was a poor place for it, for what little breeze there was proved fitful and erratic. As I expected, the *Hood* cleared the board in the sailing races. With her four cutters, three galleys and two whalers she was amply provided with sailing boats. Apart from the regatta we spent rather a boring fortnight at Navarin with little to do but walk. However, my time was nearly up and I was very busy packing.

The day before sailing I went for a long walk with Sir Dudley Pound. He spoke very frankly in giving me his views, and later, at the Admiralty, I found the knowledge of how he was thinking of the greatest value. I did not see him again until I took over from him as Commander-in-Chief, Mediterranean, in June, 1939.

The fleet was turned over to me in the *Hood* for the passage back to Malta, and for three days I kept them hard at it, trying out several of my own ideas in the way of exercises. The *Hood* spent only four days at Malta before sailing for my last tour of duty on the Spanish coast. The *Repulse*, after collecting most of the 3.7-inch field-guns from the fleet, went to Haifa, where the Arabs were in revolt and we, as usual, were woefully short of troops.

At our end of the Mediterranean the Spanish situation had gone far in Franco's favour; but there was little for us to do. We did not even have to protest at the bombing of British ships. The government at home seemed to have acquiesced in the bombing of any British merchant vessel daring enough to try and reach any Spanish government port, and all we had to do was to bring off the British communities if necessary. At Valencia we did embark some refugees and crews of sunken British ships.

By August 20th we were back in an empty Grand Harbour at Malta, and I found my wife all packed up and ready to leave. Two days later I turned over to my relief, Vice-Admiral Geoffrey Layton, and on the 24th embarked in the P. & O. for Marseilles. I had received a letter from the Admiralty instructing me to take up my new appointment at D.C.N.S. on October 17th. I felt slightly disappointed, as my original appointment to the Admiralty was not supposed to take effect until November. However, it was not for me to cavil.

From Marseilles we travelled home overland, and from London went straight on to the Palace House at Bishop's Waltham.

CHAPTER XVII

I

ADMIRAL SIR ROGER BACKHOUSE took up his appointment as First Sea Lord on August 10th, 1938. Admiral of the Fleet Lord Chatfield laid down his office after more than five years service during which he earned the gratitude of the entire Service and of the country. He had fought hard against great difficulties and frustrations to maintain the fighting efficiency and well-being of the Navy, and had put in hand a comprehensive building programme to modernize and bring the fleet to the necessary strength for the test which so obviously lay ahead.

After a hard struggle he had retrieved the Fleet Air Arm for the Navy, and the Service again stood high in the estimation of the country. He had not succeeded in all he attempted. Short-sighted and parsimonious governments had refused to give him all for which he asked, and there were still wide gaps in our armour after years of unenlightened popular belief in the efficacy of 'Collective Security' under a League of Nations which did not include the United States, and unilateral disarmament which caused many of our still useful ships to be scrapped while permitting other nations to build. A succession of naval treaties which could only be considered disastrous in their effect had caused the Navy to be whittled to the bone, particularly in its building and replacement programmes and the number of its personnel.

It was fortunate indeed that Lord Chatfield's wise guidance on defence matters was not to be lost, for early in February, 1939, on his return from a visit to India to enquire into the problem of Indian defence, he became Minister for the Co-ordination of Defence with a seat in the Cabinet.

For the first few days after our arrival at Bishops Waltham towards the end of August, our time was occupied in nothing more important than putting our house in order and arranging to grow flowers and vegetables in the garden. Then my attention was again drawn to the Navy by the receipt of a letter from the new First Sea Lord. Evidently regarding war as more or less inevitable, he was greatly worried by the shortage of destroyers, and asked if I could put forward any suggestions for a comparatively rapid increase in their numbers. He also informed me that there might be considerable difficulty in getting a large destroyer building programme included in the Navy Estimates and agreed to by Parliament.

In 1918-19, when serving in the *Seafire*, I had been much impressed by the ships of that same 'S' class of which sixty-nine had been ordered in 1917. They appeared to possess most of the qualities required by torpedo craft—a displacement of about 1,000 tons; an armament of three 4-inch guns and two double torpedo-tubes; a speed of about 33 knots; good endurance; good seaworthiness in bad weather; fair habitability, and an inconspicuous silhouette. They were also moderately cheap and rapidly built, some, I believe, having been completed in six months. More than fifty of these useful craft had remained at the end of the First World War, but later had been relegated to the reserve, where, through false economy, the men and money were not available for their upkeep and maintenance. They had gradually rusted away and been disposed of as scrap metal. No more than ten remained in service in 1939.

In my reply to Sir Roger Backhouse I mentioned all this, and suggested that a design of small destroyer of about 1,000 tons, more or less on the lines of the 'S' class, should be put in hand at once. The chief requisite, I said, was that when the design was finally decided upon, the new ships should be completed rapidly and in large numbers. I also specified that they should have long seagoing endurance from the point of view of the fuel carried and its economy in use, together with a good anti-aircraft armament.

This, I think, was the genesis of the well-known 'Hunt' class destroyers. They did not entirely come up to our expectations for convoy work in the open Atlantic. But for general service in the more limited waters like the North Sea, English Channel and Mediterranean they were invaluable during the Second World War, particularly for anti-submarine work. They were in great demand. Every Commander-in-Chief wanted them, and all the forty of these little ships that were built gave yeoman service. To avoid hurting the susceptibilities of Parliament the first twenty were originally included in the Navy Estimates as 'fast escort vessels'.

Meanwhile events in Europe were moving apace. Hitler had already seized Austria, and was now demanding the Sudetenland from Czechoslovakia. On September 15th, the Prime Minister had flown to Munich and gone on to Berchtesgaden by train. The negotiations are ancient history and none of my business; but the British and French governments accepted Hitler's demands and forced them upon the Czechs. A week later Mr. Chamberlain again flew to Germany for his meeting with Hitler at Godesberg, when new and more exacting demands were produced by the Fuehrer. The situation was critical.

Again, I need not go into details, but on September 24th I received a message to come at once to the Admiralty for duty. On reporting myself to the First Sea Lord I was ordered to help the Deputy Chief of the Naval Staff, Admiral Sir William James. It did not seem to me to be an easy task, while the D.C.N.S. did not appear to be in any need of assistance. He seemed to have a complete mastery of the situation as it affected the Navy, and the speed with which he wrote and dictated minutes on every conceivable subject excited my admiration. However, as D.C.N.S. designate, it gave me an excellent insight into my own duties in the future.

I was told also to study the war plans, and on sending for them I found they consisted of no more than plans for the despatch of the fleet to the Far East. Apart from this there were no plans at all. At the time I was most surprised; but on mature consideration I feel that the only pre-war plans that can be made at the Admiralty are those for the strategical disposition of the fleet. The detailed planning of offensive or defensive operations *must* be left to the man on the spot, the Commander-in-Chief, after he has been informed by the Admiralty what forces will be at his disposal. During the course of the war the Admiralty must, of course, formulate broad plans to meet the general strategical requirements of the Chiefs of Staff in London, work out the forces required, and suggest them to the Commander-in-Chief afloat. Only the Admiralty can make the necessary forces available. But detailed planning must be left to the local Commander-in-Chief without interference.

On September 28th, orders were issued for the mobilization of the fleet. Though plenty of deficiencies soon became apparent this operation passed off smoothly, and the Navy was as ready as it could be. As everyone knows the crisis terminated in the much-criticized Munich agreement of September 30th. When the tension relaxed and the fleet resumed its normal routine I returned to the Palace House to resume my interrupted leave.

I finally took up my new appointment as Deputy Chief of the Naval Staff on October 17th, and after a week with my predecessor sitting beside me and holding my hand, was left to my own devices.

II

I had known the First Sea Lord, Sir Roger Backhouse, who was now my immediate superior as Chief of the Naval Staff, for many years and had a great liking and respect for him. He was a man of great personal charm, outstanding ability and a prodigious worker. Every morning at the Admiralty he would be dictating at his desk at 9 a.m., and it was seldom that he left before 8 p.m. He could never be induced to take a real rest or a holiday. He really had little use for a staff and preferred to do everything, even to the smallest details, himself. In this respect he wanted knowing, and many were the friendly arguments I had when trying to persuade him to unload some of his heavy burden on to me. I had a great triumph when he turned over to me all matters in connection with the Civil War in Spain. Having spent many months on the spot dealing with the situations as they arose, I probably had a good deal more knowledge of affairs there than he had. But with all his dislike of using his staff for the purpose for which it was intended, Sir Roger Backhouse was a fine man with whom to work, and could be very firm and outspoken in the Defence Committee and the Cabinet.

The principal task confronting the Admiralty at that period was pressing on with the rearmament programme in all its forms. New problems of one sort or another arose nearly every few days. We had greatly to increase the number of officers and men at relatively short notice, and to arrange for the rapid modernization of our ageing and out-of-date capital ships. We had to consider and arrange for the arming of merchant vessels and the conversion of anti-submarine vessels, besides searching for new types which could be converted into anti-submarine craft. Other important questions were the industrial capacity of the country to provide new ships, guns, ammunition and war stores of every sort and kind; the defence of ports against air and other attack; air raid shelters at the dockyard ports; the fitting of certain French destroyers with our asdics for the detection of submarines; and the hurrying on of radar, or 'radio location' as it was first called, for installation in His Majesty's ships. In the autumn of 1938 this all-important invention was still in its infancy at sea. I seem to remember that only two ships, the *Rodney* and the cruiser *Sheffield*, had been fitted and were trying it out with most promising results.

There was much to be done before the Navy could be considered ready for war, and all these many questions, added to the fairly frequent meetings of the Deputy Chiefs of Staff and other committees, kept me very busy. I rarely left the Admiralty before 8 p.m. Incidentally, I had taken a flat in Westminster for use during the week; but generally managed to get away to the Palace House on Saturday afternoon, returning to London on Sunday night or early on Monday morning.

The anti-aircraft defences of the ports presented a particularly stubborn problem. There was a woeful shortage of A.A. guns and every other sort of equipment, and very little had to go a long way. There were also serious divergencies of opinion between the three Services as to the necessity for providing defences for particular ports. The Navy naturally wanted the fleet bases given a high priority, whereas the Army and Royal Air Force were not so greatly interested.

Malta, provided an outstanding example of this clash of opinion. By 1935 it had about twelve anti-aircraft guns, with searchlights in proportion, and during the Abyssinian crisis of that year the number of guns had been increased to twenty-four with the appropriate searchlights. The guns were old 3-inch weapons. The Navy wished the island to have first-class A.A. defence, with plenty of guns and fighter aircraft. The R.A.F experts considered Malta to be incapable of defence against the scale of air attack that might be expected from the aerodromes in Sicily, a bare sixty miles away. The Army accepted the R.A.F. views, so both were unwilling to consider what they thought was waste of money and material on defending a fleet base that so obviously could not be utilized if Italy came into the war against us. How wrong they were. The strange thing was that the First Lord could get little support for the Navy's view in the Committee of Imperial Defence.

A Committee of the Chiefs of Staff, with the Secretary of the Committee Imperial Defence, Colonel Ismay—now General Lord Ismay—in the chair, was continually sitting on this question of port defences. Finally, at the end of July, 1939, after I left the Admiralty to return to the Mediterranean, increased A.A. gun defences for Malta were approved. But the island certainly did not possess anything like its full quota of A.A. guns when Italy went to war in June, 1940, and had no fighter aircraft allowed by establishment. The four Gladiator fighters that were there, in crates in the dockyard, were spares for the Fleet Air Arm in the aircraft-carrier, and had nothing to do with the Royal Air Force. The guns had to be increased and fighters sent out *after* Italy became a belligerent. The surprising thing is that Malta was able to hold out as it did; though if at the outset the Army and R.A.F. had seen eye-to-eye with the Navy as regards the defence of our principal naval base in the Mediterranean, its ordeal would have been considerably lighter.

The much-discussed Anglo-German Naval Agreement of 1935 contained a clause which allowed Germany, while normally only building up to sixty per cent of the British submarine strength, to build up to one hundred per cent in exceptional circumstances. Early in December the Germans informed us they intended to invoke the terms of this clause. This caused considerable concern to the Government and the Admiralty, and it was decided to send a naval mission to Berlin to try to dissuade the Germans from taking a step which could only have unfortunate repercussions. I was nominated as head of this mission, and my companions were Captain Victor Danckwerts, the Director of Plans; a commander from Plans Division; and Mr. C. G. Jarrett, a Principal from the Secretary's Department at the Admiralty.

We flew from Croydon and arrived in Berlin the same evening, and it is worth remembering that a Swedish aircraft took us to Amsterdam, and a Dutch aircraft from there to our destination. On arrival at the Tempelhof aerodrome we were welcomed by our Naval Attaché, Captain (the late Vice-Admiral Sir) Thomas Troubridge and driven to the Adlon Hotel, where accommodation had been provided. Berlin was under snow, though this did not seem to hamper anyone's activities. My suite was expensively and garishly decorated in red plush and gilt. Last time I had been in Berlin in 1920 only the very wealthy could afford to stay at the Adlon. A young German officer rejoicing in the good old Scottish name of Davidson, and was indeed of Scottish descent, was attached to me as a sort of flag lieutenant for the visit. He was a fine lad whose chief ambition was to command a destroyer, and I have often wondered what happened to him during the war.

We dined that night with Captain Troubridge and got outselves as far as possible into the picture, and at 9.30 next morning presented ourselves at the German Admiralty, where we were received by Admiral Raeder, a fine-looking man who made us a pleasant speech of welcome. After I had replied we went into conference, the leading man on the German side being

Admiral Schniewind. We conferred until 1 p.m.; but though the Germans gave the impression of great friendliness we soon realized we were up against a blank wall. Our arguments that there were no special circumstances justifying the application of the 100 per cent clause for submarines, and the unfortunate impression the application would make on public opinion in Great Britain, had no effect at all. They entertained us to lunch at the Kaiserhof Hotel, with Raeder presiding. During the meal I attacked him on the subject, using particularly the argument of the effect upon public opinion at home. Eventually he promised that he would telephone to Hitler that afternoon, give him the substance of our conversation, and ask his decision. Personally I had little hope that the Fuehrer would budge an inch; but it was worth trying.

After lunch Schniewind and the rest of the German delegates drove us out to Potsdam to see Frederick the Great's summer palace *Sans Souci*. I had seen it before; but it is always worth a visit. I was to see it again in happier times. On our return I had a message from Raeder that Hitler would not consent to any alteration in his plan to build submarines, so that was that.

We dined that night with the British Chargé d'Affaires, Sir George Ogilvie-Forbes, a fellow Scot. Among others we met State Counsellor Baron von Weisacker, a charming man who had been Admiral Scheer's flag commander at the battle of Jutland. Another guest was Baron Marschal von Bieberstein, son of the man who had won Turkey away from us in the war of 1914–18.

Our mission having failed there was nothing further to keep us in Germany. We flew back to London next morning, this time in a German 'plane. In those days it was still quite an event to breakfast in Berlin and lunch in London. Before leaving the Adlon, the manager and two clerks had appeared in my suite with the visitors' book, and asked if I would honour them by signing it. He had turned over to a blank page and indicated that I should sign it in the middle, which I did. The opposite page also bore only one signature, that of a well-known cinema actor. Such is fame.

Our complete lack of success in trying to persuade the Germans to be reasonable was only another incentive for pushing on with our rearmament with all possible speed. The more Hitler was 'appeased' the more truculent and grasping he became. It was quite clear that war could not be long delayed, and that Britain would be dragged into it.

III

January and February, 1939, passed with everyone at the Admiralty hard at it, though towards the end of February, for no reason that I could see, there was some relaxation in tension in international affairs.

We were very busy over the Navy Estimates for presentation to Parliament early in March. They were the largest on record in peacetime, £147,779,000, this huge total being brought about by the years of false economy and neglect to which the Navy had been subjected. No fewer than two hundred warships of all types were under construction, and since 1935 the production of guns and armour had gone up 500 per cent, and fire control and director gear by 900 per cent. Included in the building programme were two capital ships, the *King George V* and *Prince of Wales*; one aircraft-carrier; four cruisers; sixteen destroyers; and twenty-two escort vessels—twenty of the latter being the little ships of the 'Hunt' class already mentioned. The personnel was also being increased by 14,000 to a total of 133,000, while the Naval Reserves were being expanded and new divisions of the R.N.V.R. formed at Southampton, Hull and Cardiff.

During February the Navy suffered a crushing blow when Admiral Sir Reginald G. H. Henderson, the Third Sea Lord and Controller, became seriously ill and had to leave his post at the Admiralty. This most versatile and talented officer had given outstanding service during the First World War, particularly at the Admiralty during our life and death struggle against the Kaiser's U-boats. In the years between the wars he had held a variety of appointments. He had commanded aircraft-carriers as a captain, and had served as Rear-Admiral, Aircraft Carriers. Better perhaps than anyone else, he realized the trials and perplexities of the Fleet Air Arm when working under the virtual control of the Air Ministry, and the fatal inefficiency of depriving the Navy of full command of what was rapidly becoming one of its principal weapons. No wiser choice could have been made when Henderson was brought back to the Admiralty as Controller in April, 1934. Described by Lord Chatfield as "that remarkable man", and "a brilliant officer full of imagination, resource and initiative", he was one of the key-men in our naval rearmament. Besides this he had largely been instrumental in the replacement of our old capital ships, cruisers and destroyers. Relieved as Controller by Rear-Admiral Bruce A. Fraser—now Admiral of the Fleet Lord Fraser—on March 1st, Sir Reginald Henderson's death on May 2nd was a loss the Navy could ill afford, particularly at this time of crisis.

On February 14th I was summoned to an investiture at Buckingham Palace, where the honour of Knighthood was conferred upon me by His Majesty the King, and I was invested with the insignia of a Knight Commander of the Most Honourable Order of the Bath.

A month later on March 14th, the country was electrified by the news that German forces had marched into Czechoslovakia. It was at this most critical junction that it became obvious to us all that the health of the First Sea Lord was none too good. As First and Principal Naval A.D.C. to the King, Sir Roger Backhouse attended the Court on March 15th. He looked terribly ill and it was his last appearance in public. After rallying a little he came to the Admiralty for an hour or two one afternoon, and later had papers sent to him with his stenographer attending at his bedside every morning. But to our grieved concern he showed no signs of recovery.

His illness produced a difficult situation for me. As his deputy the greater part of his work descended on my shoulders, on top of my own full-time work as D.C.N.S. Fortunately the senior of the Sea Lords, Admiral Sir Charles Little, the Second Sea Lord, had himself been D.C.N.S., and his advice and help was invaluable. I struggled on as best I could for two or three weeks, with more and more of my time being taken up by the numerous committee meetings brought about by the critical situation abroad. This was also the moment chosen by the French President to visit Great Britain, and as the First Sea Lord's representative I was much involved in official and time-wasting functions. All this extraneous work on top of the ordinary work of two offices was more than one man could cope with in the time available, so I got Vice-Admiral Charles Kennedy-Purvis, President of the Royal Naval College at Greenwich, up to the Admiralty to take the routine work as D.C.N.S. off my hands. An officer of great ability and much experience of Admiralty routine he fitted smoothly into the rather complicated organization. The greatly-reduced height of papers and dockets in my 'in' basket at once became manifest.

The Government did nothing about Czechoslovakia. Indeed, there was nothing they could do. The time for effective intervention had long since passed. However, in so far as it was possible the defence preparations were again speeded up. Rumours and alarmist telegrams poured in from many sources, and it was not at all easy to steer a middle course between keeping the Navy in a state of reasonable preparedness, and giving way to what the panic-mongers demanded. The Navy could not take measures that were at variance with the government policy of waiting and seeing.

On April 4th a highly alarmist telegram arrived to the effect that an air attack on the fleet had been planned and was imminent. At the Admiralty we were most sceptical about its authenticity: but after consultation with the Foreign Office it was decided to order Commanders-in-Chief to take precautions. This resulted in the anti-aircraft guns of the ships of the Home Fleet at Portsmouth and elsewhere being manned during the night. Unfortunately, as it turned out, that night had also been chosen for the launching of the Royal Naval Film Corporation on board the aircraft-carrier *Ark Royal*. It was a large gathering attended by the First Lord and most of the Admiralty with, of course, a number of press representatives to ensure good publicity. I also should have been present had I not been kept in London by the prevailing tension.

In his speech at the end of the entertainment Lord Stanhope, the First Lord, inadvertently mentioned that the A.A. guns of the fleet were manned in case of an air attack. This caused a furore in the press, and I spent a hectic night at the Admiralty warding off tenacious press reporters clamouring for more information. Next day, of course, we discovered that the alarmist telegram was only a scare, so things reverted as nearly as possible to normal. The whole naval situation was most unsatisfactory. Though the crisis persisted, no steps could be taken to prepare the Navy for war at an early date except those minor measures which could be put in force without being seen and advertised by all and sundry.

On Good Friday, April 7th, just as I was sitting down to lunch at home at Bishop's Waltham, I was called to the telephone. I was required to return to London at once to see the Foreign Secretary. It was a matter of urgency. The Italians had invaded Albania. The seriousness of the news was accentuated to me by the knowledge that some of the ships of the Mediterranean Fleet, in fulfilment of a long-planned programme arranged as usual between the Foreign departments of the two countries, were at that moment distributed on visits to various Italian ports.

It has to be observed that on pages 274–276 of *The Gathering Storm*, the first volume of his memoirs of the Second World War, Mr. Winston Churchill severely criticizes the dispositions of the Mediterranean Fleet at the time when Italy invaded Albania. After mentioning the dispersal of the Fleet and saying that three of its battleships "were lolling about inside or outside widely-separated Italian ports", he writes: "At the very time that the Fleet was suffered to disperse in this matter, *it was known* that the Italian Fleet was concentrated in the Straits of Otranto and that troops were being assembled and embarked for some serious enterprise." (The italics are mine.)

Mr. Churchill appears to have based the assumption that the Italian project was known to us beforehand on his belief, after twenty-five years experience in peace and war, that the British Intelligence Service was the finest of its kind in the war.

The facts as I know them are these. It was the policy of the British Government to spare no effort to remain friendly with Italy, and the itinerary of the Mediterranean Fleet, with the visits of certain of its ships to Italian ports, the first for a considerable time, had, as already mentioned, been arranged long beforehand through the usual diplomatic channels. I must state categorically that Italy's intention was *not* known at the Admiralty, and that, to the best of my belief, neither the Foreign Office nor the Government was aware of it. There were, I believe, indications that something was brewing; but at the time an Italian army was still fighting in Spain. Moreover, ever since the barbaric conquest of Abyssinia, the Fascist cry had been "Corsica, Tunis, Nice!"

In 1939 our intelligence about anything inside Italy was sparse, almost non-existent. We had no subterranean access to Italian secret documents or decisions, and were as surprised as anybody when Mussolini risked incurring the severe displeasure of the Vatican by invading Albania on Good Friday.

It is my firm belief, too, that the intended invasion was also kept secret from the Germans.

All the available evidence goes to show that in writing as he did Mr. Churchill was not fully acquainted with the facts.

However, on reaching London I joined Lord Stanhope, the First Lord, and we went over to the Foreign Office where we had an interview with Lord Halifax. Sir Robert Vansittart was present. It was decided, of course, to order our ships to leave Italian ports forthwith.

The next morning, or it may have been on Easter Sunday, I was sent for by the Prime Minister to 10 Downing Street. He had Lord Chatfield with him. He wished to know the destination and future disposition of the Mediterranean Fleet, and after some discussion it was decided that it should assemble south of Malta. Such cruisers as were already in Malta were to sail for Alexandria, while the rest of the fleet should enter Malta, re-fuel and complete with stores, and in due course sail for Alexandria also, avoiding any appearance of undue haste or urgency.

The international situation was going from bad to worse. Conscription was announced by the Prime Minister on April 27th, and the dictators rejected President Roosevelt's message asking them to give an assurance that they would undertake no further aggression. The British government had also given guarantees to Poland, Roumania and Greece, though what possible help we could give to the two first-named countries in the event of their being attacked it was difficult to see.

At the end of April we were again busy with the French, when a delegation from their Ministry of Marine came over for talks on defence matters.

Meanwhile Sir Roger Backhouse's condition did not improve. It was clear that he would be unfit to come back to the Admiralty for at least several months. So it was arranged that if his return to duty were long delayed the Commander-in-Chief, Mediterranean, Admiral Sir Dudley Pound, should be brought home as First Sea Lord. I was told that if this came to pass I would go out and relieve Sir Dudley.

On May 9th it was decided to offer the post of First Sea Lord to Sir Dudley, and at the same time I was offered that of Commander-in-Chief, Mediterranean, with the acting rank of Admiral. Naturally I accepted with alacrity. A relief had to be found for me, and after some signalled consultation with Sir Dudley Pound, Rear-Admiral Tom Phillips was appointed. He finally relieved me as D.C.N.S. on Mary 23rd, when I was able to get away and make my own personal arrangements.

To anticipate, Sir Roger Backhouse died on July 15th. A prime seaman and organizer, he was a man of strong personality and great heart, a firm and loyal friend to those who knew him. Men loved him for his simplicity of character and great modesty. He shunned the limelight of newspaper publicity, and one remembers the somewhat grudging diffidence with which he once allowed his photograph to be taken for press purposes, and his remark: "Why take me? I'm not a thing of beauty." He never spared himself. Indeed, it is probably true that he overworked himself to illness and death. He had few interests outside the Royal Navy, in which he served for forty-nine years. No man is indispensable: but 'R. B.' as he was always known in the Service, was one of those officers it could ill afford to lose, particularly at a time of emergency.

IV

We were fortunate in being able to let our house at Bishop's Waltham and our London flat almost at once, though I found that the seven or eight days allowed to get packed up, pay a flying visit to Edinburgh, extract my secretary from his job at the Admiralty, and select a flag lieutenant were all too short. My tried and trusted mentor Paymaster Captain A. P. Shaw of course came as Secretary, and as Flag Lieutenant I chose Lieutenant Walter A. Starkie, a young officer already highly thought of in the Service who was just completing two years as a term officer at the Royal Naval College at Dartmouth. He joined me in the Mediterranean two or three months later.

It was something of a wrench to leave the Palace House so soon after returning there. We had always been keen gardeners, and the place was looking lovely, with all the tulips in bloom and the orchard a riot of bluebells and narcissi which we never knew existed. However, there could be no real regrets in view of where I was going. I left London on May 31st for Marseilles, where I found the cruiser *Penelope* waiting to take me to join the Mediterranean Fleet at Alexandria. At Marseilles there were no official calls. As time was important the French Admiral met me at the station and drove me to the port, where I said good-bye and embarked. We sailed at once.

I felt a great joy in being at sea again steaming at high speed in perfect weather to what I have always considered is the finest appointment the Royal Navy has to offer. I probably knew the Mediterranean as well as any naval officer of my generation. Of my forty-one years seagoing service since leaving the *Britannia*, I had spent about ten-and-a-half years there in eight different ships, a goodish slice of a lifetime.

My hurried trip in the *Penelope* was fully occupied in replying to the literally hundreds of letters of congratulation that had flooded in upon me on my appointment being made public. Some of those I most valued came from sailors who had been my shipmates years before in the *Scorpion* and other ships. I was greatly touched at their writing to me, and by the kind thoughts and good wishes of everyone. With the international situation as explosive as it was, and the probability of war just over the horizon, I knew that my task would be difficult. To have so much goodwill from so many people was a great help and an encouragement for the future.

ATLANTIC
FRANCE
GER
PORTUGAL
SPAIN
Venice
Genoa
Toulon
ITA
CORSICA
Ro
MAJORCA
Nap
SARDINIA
MEDITER
Gibraltar
Bizerta
Algiers
Oran
Tunis
Pantella
Casablanca
MOROCCO
ALGERIA
TUNISIA
Tripo
MEDITERRANEAN 1939
COASTLINES
ALLIED
NEUTRAL
Miles 0 100 200 300 400
TRIPOL
LIBY
Bip Pares

NY
U·S·S·R
HUNGARY
RUMANIA
BLACK SEA
YUGOSLAVIA
BULGARIA
ADRIATIC
ALBANIA
Istanbul
Taranto
Salonika
DARDANELLES
TURKEY
GREECE
AEGEAN
Corfu
LY
Athens
C. Matapan
RHODES
Suda Bay
CYPRUS
Beirut
ALTA
CRETE
A N E A N
Haifa
PALESTINE
Port Said
Derna
Tobruk
Alexandria
Benghazi
Bomba
Bardia
SUEZ
CANAL
Cairo
NIA
CYRENAICA
EGYPT
RED SEA
AN DESERT

CHAPTER XVIII

I

THE *Penelope* arrived at Alexandria during the afternoon of June 5th, and after anchoring Sir Dudley Pound and I exchanged official calls. His flag was struck at sunset. I dined with him that evening on board the *Warspite*. While he put me into the Mediterranean picture, I did my best to give him an idea of what was going on at home, particularly at the Admiralty. We were up early next morning, he to take off in a flying boat at 4 a.m., and myself to see him off.

Except for the *Warspite* the fleet was at sea. I joined her officially at 9 a.m., and we sailed to join the Fleet. This operation accomplished with the usual ceremony on the change of flags, we carried out some exercises and returned to harbour.

The Mediterranean Fleet at this period consisted of the *Warspite*, fleet flagship, with the *Barham*, *Malaya* and *Ramillies*, of the 1st Battle Squadron, under the command of Vice-Admiral Geoffrey Layton in the *Barham*. The 1st Cruiser Squadron, under Rear-Admiral J. H. D. Cunningham in the *Devonshire*, included also the *Sussex* and *Shropshire*. The 3rd Cruiser Squadron, *Arethusa*, *Penelope* and two ships of the 'Delhi' class, was commanded by Rear-Admiral H. R. Moore in the first-named, while there were three destroyer flotillas with Rear-Admiral J. C. Tovey in the *Galatea* as Rear-Admiral (D). There was one aircraft-carrier, the *Glorious*, Captain Guy D'Oyly-Hughes, together with the *Woolwich* and *Maidstone*, the destroyer and submarine depot ships, with one flotilla of submarines and another of motor torpedo-boats.

Sir Dudley Pound's Chief of Staff, Commodore A. U. Willis, had consented to remain with me. I had known him before when he was squadron torpedo officer on the staff of the Rear-Admiral (D), Home Fleet, and again as a most successful captain of the *Nelson* and the *Vernon*. I was aware that he was one of the cleverest and most able men in the Service of his seniority; but what an exceptionally brilliant officer he was I did not realize until I met him now. It did not take me long to discover how very fortunate I was to have him as my Chief of Staff. Full of imagination and new ideas, most painstaking and thorough in all he undertook, a good and firm disciplinarian, I found our views coincided on nearly every subject.

The Captain of the Fleet, C. E. Hotham, and the Captain of the *Warspite* Victor Crutchley, I had known for many years. Crutchley had earned the Victoria Cross for gallantry in the *Vindictive* during the attempted blocking of Ostend in May, 1918, and had since commanded many ships. With my able Secretary, Paymaster Captain A. P. Shaw, and the temporary Flag Lieutenant, Michael Seymour, we were a very happy party in the dining cabin.

As befitted an important command all the rest of my staff were first-class officers, and all distinguished themselves in the war that was soon to overtake us. Of those that were already in the *Warspite*, or joined soon afterwards, some were to serve with me for four years. I would mention in particular Commanders R. M. Dick, Geoffrey Barnard, T. M. Brownrigg and M. L. Power.

As the Fleet lay in Egyptian waters the official calls were far more onerous than usual. Quite apart from receiving and returning the calls of all Flag Officers and Captains, I had to visit numerous Egyptian officials. I spent two days hard at it, and even then had not finished. Our situation in Alexandria, an Egyptian port, was rather anomalous. Though we made full use of it as a fleet base, with all that it implies, it was really in charge of an official of the Egyptian Government. He, however, was a retired British naval officer, Vice-Admiral Sir Gerald A. Wells. He made all things easy for us, and he and his charming family entertained bountifully in the Port House close by the landing jetty. It became a regular port of call for officers going ashore and returning to their ships.

I found the fleet in great fettle and obviously in a high state of efficiency. Continual exercises at sea and in harbour kept us all busy. On the whole Alexandria was popular enough with officers and men. The officers had plenty of golf, tennis and social activities, and though there was a serious shortage of recreation grounds the men found ample amusement ashore. They also had an excellent Fleet Club accommodated in the old Greek hospital, and run on the lines of Claridge's Club which had been such a success during the Abyssinian crisis. Here they could obtain most of the amenities they needed at very reasonable prices.

While full use was still being made of the dockyard at Malta for docking and refitting ships, we were using Alexandria as our base because of Italian aggression against Albania. Alexandria, however, would have to take the place of Malta in the event of war, and there was much that it lacked before it could be considered even partially adequate as a naval base. The anti-aircraft defences were feeble, and though an aerodrome was contemplated for the accommodation of the aircraft of the Fleet Air Arm when landed, it was not yet in existence. Our preparations went steadily forward, and among other measures we acquired a complete wharf with deep-water berths and a range of storehouses which gradually became filled with masses of naval stores and spare parts. Repair and docking facilities were meagre, though small repairs could be undertaken in the workshops of the Khedivial Line, while their Gabbari dock could take ships up to the size of 'C' class cruisers.

Before I left the Admiralty consideration had been given to sending out to Alexandria the floating dock from Portsmouth, which was capable of taking battleships, and within a few months this wise step was in hand. Moving the floating dock from Malta was impossible because of its indifferent condition. Another problem was the question of magazines for the stowage of spare ammunition, of which there were none. However, approval was given shortly afterwards for their construction among the sand dunes to the west of the town.

During the third week in June the *Warspite* sailed for Port Said, where, with Vice-Admiral Arthur E. F. Bedford, I walked round the naval establishments and inspected the batteries for the protection of the entrance to the Suez Canal. They were most inadequate, and consisted of old 6-inch guns, and not many of them.

We left for Haifa the same night, where I met the District Commissioner and Brigadier (now General Sir Alfred) Godwin-Austen, commanding the 14th Infantry Brigade. Palestine, though in the throes of the Arab rebellion, still kept up the appearance of being under civil control. I had arranged to fly to Jerusalem to visit the High Commissioner, Sir Harold MacMichael, and the General Officer Commanding, Lieutenant-General (now General Sir Robert) Haining. On the short trip to the aerodrome at Haifa our procession of cars was preceded by a lorry filled with armed troops, while more soldier motor-bicyclists were around us. We took off in two small 'planes, myself in one and the Chief of Staff and flag lieutenant in the other, and arrived at the Jerusalem airfield, about eight miles out, after a flight of about fifty minutes. Here we were met by General Haining and the senior Air Officer. We had the same armed procession, and as it was not wise to go through the city, the General took us to various vantage points to see it. Looking down from the Mount of Olives it was most interesting to glimpse many of the places mentioned in the Bible, including Gethsemane and Golgotha. We lunched with the High Commissioner, and afterwards had official talks with him and the General. Returning to the airfield at 3 p.m. we flew back to Haifa, embarked at once and sailed for Alexandria.

The *Warspite* was due to visit Malta for docking early in July, the date of our arrival being put forward by a message from the Admiralty telling me I had to pay a special visit to Istanbul early in August. This suited me very well, as my wife had let our house, booked her passage by P. & O., and was due to reach Malta on July 10th. I was glad the house at Bishop's Waltham and the flat in London were off our hands, for apart from these I had an official residence in Malta, and a house I had taken over from Sir Dudley Pound at Alexandria. We arrived at Malta on July 8th, and the routine business of landing the Commander-in-Chief (myself) and installing him in his official residence, and his staff in the Castille, was soon accomplished.

Admiralty House is in Strada Mezzodi, which in the past decade had become greatly overcrowded. Some not very high-class flats pressed in on the house on three sides, and on the other the huge Auberge de France had been turned into a school and was very noisy. One could see nothing of the harbour, except from the roof, and even then the view was very restricted. Sir Dudley Pound had put forward plans for a new house outside Valetta overlooking the Grand Harbour, and they had all but been approved. However, when I was at the Admiralty and knew I was coming out as Commander-in-Chief, I discussed the matter with the Civil Lord, Colonel J. J. Llewellin. Neither of us thought that the time was appropriate for spending money on new residences, so I agreed not to raise the question; but asked that the house should be slightly modernized and refurnished.

I had known the old building for years and had a great affection for it. In the old days of the Knights of St. John it had first been the Auberge d'Avignon, and then the house of the Captain of the Galleys. Collingwood and many other distinguished Admirals had lived there, and I was quite ready to overlook the disadvantages of its surroundings. The furnishing, however, was a different matter. Out-of-date was the mildest description, with armchairs and sofas of an ancient Service pattern and supremely uncomfortable. So my wife was allowed to go ahead and refurnish the public rooms at Admiralty expense with, of course, new carpets, covers and curtains. They may have suffered a little during the war; but anybody who has visited Admiralty House, Malta, during the last few years can judge what degree of success she made of it. To me, a mere man, it was very lovely.

The rooms were well-shaped and lofty, some of them with cedar beams painted in cream and gold, others with painted ceilings. But whoever had done the electric lighting had the imagination of a cockroach. The house was wired like a battleship with great naval type switches and plugs, and ugly electric light shades like jampots hanging on long leads from the middle of the ceilings, sometimes from the centre of a painting. In my office, for instance, the electric light emerged from the centre of Britannia's stomach! The Dockyard officials were rather disgusted when we made them repair this vandalism. Immediately my wife arrived on July 10th she got right down to all the alterations and additions. The result was well worth the trouble.

Meanwhile the international situation overwhelmed everything. It appeared no less tense than when I was at home. Hitler was pursuing his now well-known technique over Danzig, and it seemed only a matter of time before he made a move against Poland. Tension was in the air, and late in July the First Sea Lord sent out Captain J. G. L. Dundas of Plans Division, with a long informatory letter to bring us up-to-date with what was happening. It appeared there were many indications of preparedness in Germany for a coup after August 15th, probably connected with Danzig. As it was evident that words alone carried no conviction with Hitler, it had been decided to commission the Reserve Fleet on July 31st for two months. At the same time an idea had got about that Hitler would not rush things, and that a state of tension might last for two years or more. This meant, of course, that the Admiralty must still work to its long-term policy of reliefs, commissioning new ships, etc., and could not pursue the short-term policy of placing the existing fleet on a war basis.

The situation as regards Inter-Allied War Plans was not at all satisfactory. The British would have liked to set up an Inter-Allied War Council with the French to keep the grand strategy constantly under review. This, however, was resisted by the French military authorities. Meetings on a lower level between local British and French Commanders were taking place and were undoubtedly a step in the right direction; but it by no means followed that the action proposed had the approval of the respective Governments.

So far as we in the Mediterranean were concerned, we had the problem of Italy if she came into the war against us. There was an idea in political circles at home that Italy could be knocked out at the outset. It was a fallacious belief. Italy could only be knocked out by the defeat of her armies, or by intensive bombing from the air, neither of which were possible at the beginning of the war. It remained for the Navy to do the job; but how? Was it seriously imagined that the fleet would move slowly along Italy's extensive coast bombarding towns and cities on their way? Such a process might affect Italian morale; but the material damage done would not be great. Added to that we might lose a battleship or two by torpedoes, mines, or bombs, for the Italian submarine fleet and air force were by no means negligible. It was pointed out to me that any losses incurred by us would have great propaganda value to the enemy, and would greatly influence Japan in her decision whether or not to enter the war. Another erroneous idea was that we should defeat Italy by conquering Libya, which might also lead to the loss of Italian East Africa and Abyssinia.

My considered opinion, which was strongly expressed at the time, was that if Libya were completely cut off and the Italians there were kept fighting, it was most likely that Libya, Eritrea, Abyssinia and Italian Somaliland would be out of the war in about six months. I further believed that the surrender of the Italian army in Libya, coupled with naval attacks on the Italian coast in places where material damage could be done, would have a great moral effect and might well cause the Italians to lose heart and think they had had enough. It seemed to me to be the only plan which showed any hope of success for us and our Allies in the early stages of the war. I had never heard of any alternative. I went on to point out that the extra forces required to make operations effective against Italy's communications with Libya were not great. All that was needed was sufficient aircraft to ensure 10 per cent reconnaissance in the Eastern Mediterranean, together with fighters and more guns to give Malta some degree of security.

I was strongly averse to holding back battleships from bombarding the Libyan and Sicilian coasts when circumstances demanded because our battle-fleet might eventually be required in the Far East against Japan. To my mind the policy was a mistaken one. Wherever battleships went in the Mediterranean they were within range of air attack and liable to damage. I felt, too, that in spite of the submarine danger, they were safer at sea than in such a poorly defended harbour as Alexandria, and that they should be used to the full in attacks on the enemy coasts with a view to causing material and moral damage. Such attacks might well result in forcing the enemy fleet to sea, which was what we should welcome.

I most strongly deprecated curtailing our offensive operations because battleships might be required later in the Far East. It would not only be most damaging to the morale of our men; but might also give rise to the same sort of outcry at home as was heard about the Grand Fleet in the First World War.

No. Our only policy against Italy was to cut off her supplies, interfere with her communications, bombard her ports, destroy her submarines, and later on, when our military build-up was complete, to conquer Libya and the Italian colonies in East Africa. If, as a result of these operations, the Italian fleet were forced to come out to give battle we should welcome the meeting.

I also had the impression that our requests for increased air defence for Malta and Egypt in the shape of fighters were not likely to be realized because of the pressing needs elsewhere. Neither were we to get any increase in anti-aircraft gun defence except a few guns sent to Alexandria at the expense of Malta. As I wrote at the time, August 1st, 1939: "I think more fighters for Egypt and a fighter squadron for Malta are both urgent. I consider that Malta should have priority, because there are none at all there, and Malta has no means of taking the offensive in the air either by intercepting enemy bombers, or by attacking aircraft in Sicily on the ground. Malta is of immense value to us, and everything possible should be done to minimize the damage that Italian bombers may do to it." In this same letter I pointed out the serious lack of A.A. guns at Malta and Alexandria.

On July 27th, the French Commander-in-Chief, Admiral Ollive, arrived at Malta to confer with me in our combined action in the event of war with Italy, the visit being made in the guise of an official visit to the new British Commander-in-Chief, Mediterranean. I had hoped he would come quietly by air, which would have cut out a lot of the official entertainments. However, he came in the battleship *Provence* escorted by four destroyers, which necessitated the usual spate of calls, receptions, luncheon parties and dinners.

Admiral Ollive, blessed with a large moustache and a great sense of humour, was very much liked by us all, and our conferences were most useful. He was a tough customer, and we found that the French were thinking on much the same offensive lines as ourselves. The Admiral produced the outlines of a series of naval operations against Genoa, Savona and other ports in the Gulf of Genoa which he hoped to carry out in the first twenty-four hours after war was declared against Italy. He also had a plan for a further operation against Palermo. In short, we were in complete agreement, and decided to co-ordinate our respective attacks on the Italian seaboard to force the dispersion of their fleet and the Regia Aeronautica.

Among many other official entertainments, which included luncheon and the 'thé dansant' on board the French flagship, I gave a big dinner in Admiral Ollive's honour at Admiralty House. Afterwards we sat on the roof and listened to the Commander-in-Chief's orchestra, very fine performers. It was then that the proceedings were considerably enlivened by one of the old sofas collapsing under the combined weights of my wife and the Chief of Staff. As neither of them were heavy-weights, it was a fair indication that my requests for the renewal of the furniture at Admiralty House was neither premature nor unreasonable.

The French squadron spent only two days at Malta, and after an affectionate farewell with Admiral Ollive, the *Warspite* and four destroyers, *Cossack*, *Zulu*, *Maori* and *Nubian*, sailed for Turkish waters on July 30th.

Before sailing I had arranged for my wife and a niece Hilda Bramwell, my sister's youngest daughter, who was coming out to join her, to embark in the Commander-in-Chief's yacht, the *Aberdeen*, with Alexandria as their final destination. On the way, under the appearance of a pleasure cruise, they were to visit various small ports and anchorages in Southern Greece, the western end of Crete, and the islands of Kithera and Antikithera which lay between. The officers of the *Aberdeen* were directed to make quick surveys of these anchorages with a view to their use by British tankers in the event of war with Italy. The distance between Alexandria and the Italian coast made the refuelling of small ships a necessity in the event of any prolonged operation, and the use of Malta or oiling at sea might not be possible because of the expected attentions of the Regia Aeronautica. The information gained by the *Aberdeen* during this cruise proved highly useful to us in 1940.

II

Steaming through the Dardanelles, we were met at the other end of the Sea of Marmora by two very smart-looking Turkish destroyers which escorted us to the anchorage in the Bosphorus. This was the old one, which the British fleet used to know so well, off the Palace of Dolmabaghcheh, residence of two Sultans of Turkey, and just ahead of the Turkish battle-cruiser *Yavuz*, the old German *Goeben* that we had chased into the Dardanelles so many years before.

We had a most strenuous visit ahead of us. The programme arranged by the Turks showed little respite in the ceaseless round of official entertainments, which included luncheons, dinners, balls, regattas, football and cricket matches almost without a break, and a visit for myself and my staff to Ankara at the invitation of the Chief of the General Staff, Marshal Fevzi Tchakmak.

The receiving and returning of calls went on all the first day. Wherever we went there was a guard and band. At one embarrassing moment, having changed into mufti to lunch with our Ambassador, Sir Hughe Knatchbull-Hugessen, I found myself in the awkward predicament of having to inspect a large guard with what dignity I could muster dressed in a palm beach suit.

We were royally entertained. Everyone seemed genuinely pleased to see us, and the sailors were well looked after, being taken out to some of the big houses on the Bosphorus. The British Ambassador set a very high standard in his entertainment for 300 sailors. The basis of it was 1,200 bottles of beer and a troupe of dancing girls, both of which were most popular.

I cannot hope to describe our progress wherever we went driven at breakneck speed through the narrow streets with horns blaring, followed by another car with five plain clothes policeman, and the police holding up all the traffic. Nor can I mention all the functions: a dinner and dance at the Pera Palace Hotel given by the Vali of Istanbul from which I retired exhausted at 2 a.m.; my having next morning to place a huge wreath on the monument to Mustapha Kemal in Taxim Square in the presence of a dense and enthusiastic crowd after having walked through the lines of the Turkish guard and our own guard from the *Warspite*. The wreath, about six feet high and very weighty, had to be mounted on an easel. I could not possibly have lifted it, so motioned to the Embassy kavasses to do it for me and I just patted it into place. The kavasses were magnificent in scarlet frock coats and much gold braid.

Then there was a lunch on board the *Yavuz* with the Turkish Commander-in-Chief, where the language question made the going somewhat difficult though our hosts were very kind and thoughtful; followed by a trip up the Bosphorous for about a hundred British and Turkish officers in a ferry steamer; followed by tea with the French Ambassador and his wife; then a quiet dinner on board the *Warspite* with our Naval Attaché and his wife; followed at ten o'clock by a ball at the British Embassy, where I was introduced to all the Ambassadors and their wives, including von Papen, the German. It was a magnificent affair with the mass of uniforms in a lovely setting from which I eventually got away at 1.30 a.m. for an early start to Ankara.

We left the ship in my barge at 7.45, the Chief of Staff, Commander R. M. Dick, the flag lieutenant, two Turkish liaison officers and myself, and after steaming about ten miles to the aerodrome were received by the usual galaxy of Admirals, Generals, and civil representatives, and a large guard and band. We were struck by the tough look of the Turkish soldiers who were magnificent-looking men, and also the high proportion of them with red hair and blue eyes, mountaineers, I believe. Taking off in a very comfortable four-engined aircraft we reached the aerodrome at Ankara at 10 a.m., to be received by the Principal Under Secretary of State, the Minister of National Defence and a crowd of other officers and officials representing the Marine, Air and the General Staff, with the Military Governor of Ankara and the Commandant of the garrison, an enormous guard and band, and some dozens of photographers and pressmen. Driven to the Ankara Palace Hotel we were given accommodation for changing into full dress for the official visits.

Our first duty was to write our names in the President's book, after which we drove on and called on Marshal Tchakmak, a fine looking man with a great air of command and an inscrutable face. Though I had no particular desire to confer officially with him, I had a few points in which I thought it as well he should be instructed, and I did not think it was likely he would have invited me to Ankara just to pay a social visit. However, as he contented himself with pleasant nothings and showed no signs of talking business, I began to suspect that that was indeed the idea. We next called on the Minister of Defence, a colourless nonentity and in the Marshal's pocket, and finally on the Minister of Foreign Affairs, Mr. Saragoglu. He was a very different type, a real live wire by whom I was greatly impressed.

He spoke excellent French, and through Commander Dick, an expert in that language, we got on very well. He asked me at once if official conversations with the Marshal had been arranged, and was surprised and perturbed when I replied in the negative, adding I was quite ready to talk to the Marshal if he wished it. He said he would telephone at once to Marshal Tchakmak and tell him he was to hold official talks with me after lunch, and, I suspect telephoned also to the President to get his support. As I saw it they were divided among themselves, and the Marshal had been difficult to control since Kemal's death. It was certainly difficult to get on friendly terms with him. He absolutely declined to talk officially to any foreign officer unless he was of high rank. A previous British mission had completely failed to get any response.

All these gentlemen returned my call at my suite in the hotel, after which we went to the luncheon given in our honour by the Marshal, a large party of about a hundred including M. Saragoglu and about forty generals. Sitting on the right of the Marshal I found talking with him very difficult. Apart from his own language he spoke only German and my German had almost left me. Noticing this, the Foreign Minister directed one of my Turkish liaison officers, who spoke good English, to sit behind and between us and to interpret. We then got on famously, though the poor Turkish lad lost his lunch.

After lunch we called on the President, General Ineunu, a charming little man who spoke broken English learnt in the last year. He was almost embarrassingly cordial, seizing my hand in both of his while saying haltingly how pleased he was to see us. I was greatly taken with him, and it was difficult to believe that this friendly, quiet little man was the tough General Ismet Pasha who had thrashed the Greeks in Asia Minor and had made things so uncomfortable for us at Chanak in 1922. After coffee we left and went back to the Marshal for an official talk lasting about forty minutes.

I do not think he was too pleased. He was not forthcoming in any way, and his naval views, with those on what should be done in the event of war with Italy, were crude in the extreme. In the short time available I gave him a little lecture on sea power in the Eastern Mediterranean, which I hope he absorbed, though I doubt it. It was quite clear to me that it was desirable to hold further staff talks with the Turks, especially on naval matters; but that the head of any mission must be a senior officer who could talk to the Marshal with full authority and on equal terms.

We flew back to Istanbul that same evening, to arrive on board the *Warspite* just in time to change for a big dinner party to the principal Turkish naval officers and their wives, followed by a ball for four hundred. They were both very successful. Somewhat jaded and weary I finally got to bed at about 2.30 a.m.

We allowed ourselves a little relaxation next morning, when four of us visited St. Sophia, the great church of the Byzantine Emperors built by Justinian in the sixth century, and converted into a mosque after the capture of Constantinople by the Turks in 1453. Most of the wonderful mosaics, of religious subjects, were then destroyed or covered with a thick layer of plaster. In 1847–48 the building was repaired by an Italian architect, and the mosaic figures that remained were exposed to view. The Sultan of that period, Abd-ul-mejid, a broad-minded man with an artistic eye, came to see one of the most beautiful mosaics, a representation of the Virgin and Child. Realizing that it would offend susceptibilities in a Moslem place of worship, the Sultan studied it for some time and then said with a sigh: "Cover it if it must be. Only the eye of God shall see it, and God shall say when it shall be seen again." Covered it was; but permission was given for a layer of matting to be placed over the mosaics before the plaster was applied.

In 1935, Mustapha Kemal gave orders that St. Sophia was no longer to be used as a mosque and that the mosaics were to be uncovered and restored. The work was still being done when we visited it and was in charge of an American, Professor Whitamore, whose whole heart and soul were in the project. He took us round personally and what he told us was most interesting and fascinating.

A final luncheon party on board the *Warspite*, and an enormous soirée given by the Turkish Admiral at a big hotel on the Bosphorus, with alternate libations of whisky and soda and champagne closed our visit. Returning to the *Warspite* at about 2.30 a.m. in my barge in the brilliant moonlight I found on board a photograph of the Turkish Admiral in a gilt frame, a case of wine and 2,000 Turkish cigarettes, presents from the Turkish Navy. I could hardly refuse these gifts, so hastily got up a case of port, which the Turks loved, and sent it over to the *Yavuz*.

"Tens of thousands of Turks gathered along the shores of the Bosphorus and the Sea of Marmora to cheer the British battleship *Warspite* and four destroyers as they sailed for Cyprus after an official visit of five days," said the *Daily Telegraph*. The date was August 6th, and we were escorted by the same two destroyers who had brought us in.

We were all somewhat exhausted mentally, physically and gastronomically after such a ceaseless round of entertainment; but were cheered by the knowledge that at this end of the Mediterranean we had the warm-hearted friendship of these fine people. Our mission had been an important one, and from what we heard later it undoubtedly did a lot of good.

III

Cyprus was to be our next stop, where the fleet in turn were to carry out bombardment and anti-aircraft practices. On the way, however, we had arranged to carry out an important exercise in which the whole fleet was to be engaged in the mock attack on, and defence of, Italian convoys from the home country going to Libya and Tripolitania. Curiously enough the Italians had been trying out exactly the same problem a short while before, with the ships representing the British working from Rhodes. We were unable to discover what conclusions they reached; but as their battleships from Taranto had been constantly off the coast of Cyrenaica we hoped that this disposition had proved satisfactory from their point of view.

Our own exercise was most instructive and interesting and gave us much food for thought. It was also useful for discovering how the ships' companies would stand up to the torrid conditions in the engine-and boiler-rooms and between decks in very hot weather for forty-eight hours with all watertight doors and side scuttles closed and ventilation at a minimum. Our old ships were not originally designed for work in such conditions, and in one of them there were eight cases of heat-stroke. It was little to be wondered at. There were temperatures of 130 degrees in the boiler-rooms. Even on deck it was almost unbearable, and in those days few British men-of-war had modern air-conditioning.

Our visit to Cyprus was mainly for exercises, and we were back in Alexandria on August 15th. There I found my wife and niece, full of their cruise in the *Aberdeen*.

Shortly after arrival I had a long and informative letter from Sir Dudley Pound, the First Sea Lord. His best news was that a heavy scale of anti-aircraft defence for Malta, which we had been pressing for, had been approved. The island was to have a hundred and twelve guns, though this might take some little time to accomplish as at the moment both Malta and Gibraltar were being bled to provide a respectable A.A. defence for the fleet base at Alexandria.

Though partly reassured in my fears of restrictions upon the use of the battle-fleet, matters were not entirely as I wished. An embargo was also placed on any sea or air bombardment as an initial operation on the outbreak of war, the Government having decided that until our enemies did something to give us a free hand in the way of reprisals, we must not do anything which would alienate public opinion, particularly in the United States, or enable our enemies to charge us with having started the killing of civilians. I was not greatly perturbed about this. It was obvious that within a day or two of the outbreak the enemy would give us ample justification.

The First Sea Lord was most pessimistic as to how long the aircraft-carrier *Glorious* would last in the confined waters of the Mediterranean when war came. She would become the target for many shore-based aircraft. However, he agreed that while she was still afloat there was a lot to be said for her aircraft attacking the Italian fleet at Taranto. With this latter suggestion I fully concurred, though I felt much more optimistic about the life of the carrier. In my opinion ships moving at high speed and with full freedom of manœuvre were not easy targets. As it was amply proved later, it required special aircraft in overwhelming numbers to put a carrier out of action.

The international situation was very grave, and it was difficult to see how war with Germany could be avoided. The short-term policy of having the fleet ready for hostilities had been accepted, and it was certainly time. War with Italy was not so likely. Personally, I inclined to the opinion that Mussolini would want to see how things went before committing himself. Hitler, as is well known, invaded Poland on September 1st. This was followed by Mussolini's declaration that Italy would not take the initiative in warlike operations, so the situation was still uncertain.

During the last days of August and the early days of September the fleet was holding the squadron regattas in Alexandria harbour. It was actually while standing on the foremost 15-inch turret of the *Malaya* watching the finish of a race that I was handed the signal stating that Great Britain had declared war upon Germany.

There was little to be done. So far as possible all our preparations had been made. As I wrote to an aunt, I never expected when war was declared to have nothing to do but go ashore and have tea with my wife.

We received the signal "Winston is back", i.e. at the Admiralty, on the evening of September 3rd with considerable satisfaction.

CHAPTER XIX

I

THE torpedoing of the *Athenia* on the evening of September 3rd came as no surprise to us. It merely showed that the Germans were running true to form, and made it all the more galling that we could do nothing to help. Nevertheless, it was undoubtedly wise at first not to trust Mussolini and to lay ourselves open by reducing the Mediterranean Fleet.

Convoy for merchant shipping was instituted almost at once throughout the Mediterranean. We thought it a waste of effort, and considered that strong patrols and anti-submarine measures in the Straits of Gibraltar would have been more economical and sufficient to keep out the German U-boats. We established patrols south of Cape Matapan and the Straits of Otranto to discourage the carriage of contraband by neutral shipping; but our contribution to the war at this stage was disappointingly small.

By the end of September I had come to the conclusion that the Italians would keep us guessing as long as possible, and that nothing short of the concentration of sufficient military and air forces in Egypt and Tunisia to make an attack upon Libya a certain success would make them show their hand. In this connection the security of Malta was of prime importance. I was therefore mortified to learn that if Italy did enter the war it was apparently the intention to postpone any offensive against Libya until we were secure against Germany in the west.

Our position *vis-à-vis* the Turks was far from clear. We were told to hold conversations with them; but I was personally doubtful if they wanted to converse, and was perfectly certain if they did that they would demand deliveries of war material already very scarce with us.

Less than a month after the outbreak of war the well-trained and highly efficient Mediterranean Fleet started gradually to melt away. It was only to be expected, as our ships were contributing nothing to the war at sea. Nevertheless, it was disappointing indeed to see a smooth-running machine broken up and dispersed. The first to go was the 1st Cruiser Squadron and some destroyers, followed by the battleships and *Glorious*. At the end of October the *Warspite* was called for and I was left without a flagship.

The departure of all these ships left about five hundred sailors' wives and children stranded at Alexandria, some of them none too well off. My wife and niece, Hilda Bramwell, with all the officers' wives they could collect, at once set to work to help them and were soon fully occupied with projects for the welfare of the women and children.

The going of the *Warspite* left me with the decision as to where the

Commander-in-Chief, Mediterranean, should establish his headquarters. It had to be either Alexandria or Malta, and both had their advantages. In Alexandria I should be in close touch with the Army and Air Commanders-in-Chief, who had their headquarters in Cairo, and to whom I paid weekly visits to concert policy and measures. At Alexandria, however, accommodation would have to be found ashore for my staff, and a complicated system of communications established. In Malta, of course, the long-standing organization was perfect. I myself favoured Alexandria for the reasons given, but the Admiralty decided that Malta would be better, another reason being that we should be in close touch with the French.

Vice-Admiral Geoffrey Layton, originally in command of the 1st Battle Squadron and Second-in-Command, Mediterranean Fleet, went home in the *Manchester* to take command of a cruiser squadron, leaving me with Rear-Admirals John C. Tovey and H. R. Moore. Tovey's command as Rear-Admiral (D) was reduced to five Australian destroyers, manned by the most stout-hearted of ships' companies, but in old ships of a 1918 vintage. In consequence, Tovey was rather downcast. All the same I felt quite sure that a war on the scale we were now witnessing could not leave the Mediterranean an area of complete calm. The German successes on the continent were bound to have their effect upon Mussolini, and in saying farewell to the officers and men of the *Warspite* I told them I was sure I should see them back in the spring.

We moved to Malta at the beginning of November, and as Admiralty House was still in process of alteration we went for a time to the Casa Pietà, where we had lived before. We borrowed it from Tovey, who remained at Alexandria.

I had another long letter from the First Sea Lord early in November which gave me a good picture of the trend of naval affairs at home and how the anti-submarine war and the air war were progressing. I learnt all the then known details of the loss of the *Royal Oak* in Scapa Flow, a tragic incident; but one in which one could not help admiring the skill and courage of Prien, the German submarine commander. For the first time, too, I heard of the German magnetic mine. Like countless others, I asked myself why we had no immediate countermeasures to this most effective weapon. We ourselves had used magnetic mines in 1918. I was glad to hear that Sir Dudley Pound was standing up well to the strain of his heavy responsibility. In my opinion, however, he was still unduly pessimistic about battleships being able to stand up to air attack. To me there was no proof up-to-date that moving ships were in excessive danger, and I remonstrated with him in my reply.

Towards the end of the year the only British naval forces left in the Mediterranean were three small 'C' class cruisers and the handful of Australian destroyers. I could not complain. It was best that every available ship should be used wherever the situation demanded, and in an emergency the Mediterranean could quickly be reinforced. Our situation was one of watching and waiting. We still tried to enforce some form of contraband control without, however, hurting Italian susceptibilities. It was clear that the longer they could be kept out of the war the better.

If the war spread to the Mediterranean or the Balkans the general intentions of our Government were obscure. There were constant comings and goings and minor conferences between ourselves and the Turks, and with General Weygand, commanding the French forces in the Middle East. General Wavell had also been to Ankara, and, without any warning or naval advice beyond that which could be given by our Naval Attaché, had been engaged in important talks.

There seemed to be an idea, held principally by the French, that in the spring of 1940 the Germans would come down through the Balkans. The French held the view that we should forestall them by landing a strong force at Salonika. My share in these talks was to remind and emphasize to all and sundry that the size of any force landed in the Balkans, and its subsequent reinforcement and supply, depended entirely upon shipping and the naval command of the Ægean. Before any troops could be landed, the shipping must be collected and the command of the sea assured. To me it seemed elementary; but so confusing was the situation that early in December I wrote home setting out the situation in the Middle East as we sailors saw it, and asking what was the policy of the Government in certain eventualities. At the same time I warned the First Sea Lord that whereas our naval forces in the Eastern Mediterranean had been reduced almost to nothing, a policy that was undoubtedly the right one, it had not been accompanied by any diminution of the French Navy in the Mediterranean. This, I pointed out, might result in the French demanding the right to lay down the policy and exercise the overall command because the preponderance of naval and land forces in the area were French. The situation was confused and wholly unsatisfactory.

II

To revert to domestic matters, we moved into a much-improved Admiralty House at Malta towards the end of November. By a lucky chance the new furniture had arrived out from England, hardly a priority cargo in war-time, I thought, but welcome all the same. We settled down to the Malta round, with my wife exceedingly busy with the wives and children of the men who had left the station, and my niece hard at it as a cypherer in the office of the Vice-Admiral, Malta. At the end of November we found that my niece and the flag lieutenant, Walter Starkie, had been busy in quite a different direction.

They had become engaged. My wife and I considered it a very suitable arrangement, though we were none too sure of parental approval. In the few months that Starkie had been with us we had discovered what a fine young officer he was, and one who was bound to get on in the Service. Curiously enough he was a direct descendant of that Sir Oliver Starkie, then spelt Starkey, secretary to La Valette, Grand Master of the Knights of St. John during the great siege of Malta by the Turks in 1565, and whose tomb is to be seen in the crypt of St. John's Cathedral at Valetta.

In December I had a visit from Sir Percy Loraine, our Ambassador in Rome. In his opinion Mussolini was merely sitting on the fence waiting to see which way the cat jumped, and we were by no means free from the likelihood of war with Italy. The Italians, he told us, were much upset with the working of the contraband control in relation to their shipping, and the Duce's feelings on the subject were explosive. Loraine's visit was of the greatest value to us and I think not unhelpful to him.

In our quiet and almost peace-time routine the news of the battle between our three cruisers and the *Admiral Graf Spee* on December 13th came as a great stimulus. We also followed with keen interest the doings of the destroyers and submarines that had lately been in the Mediterranean. All these and other actions, however, added greatly to our fretful impatience at being so much out of it.

Early in the New Year, 1940, the Mediterranean was allotted most unwelcome reinforcements in the shape of two armed merchant cruisers, the *Ranpura* and *Antenor*, for contraband control duties. They were much too big for the job, and since both of them could carry considerable cargoes I protested that they would be much better employed elsewhere. They cruised for a few weeks and then left us, unregretted.

At the end of January I had a visit from my old acquaintance of Nyon Patrol days in 1938, the French Admiral Esteva. We held many conferences during his visit and passed the whole Mediterranean situation under review. He stayed at Admiralty House, and was a very pleasant guest. A tough man and highly religious, he rose each morning at 5.15 and went to mass, followed at seven o'clock by a meagre breakfast of coffee, dry toast and an orange, with nothing more until lunch.

We had received information from home which clarified the situation as regards the Balkans, and gave us the intentions of the Government in certain eventualities, and also dwelt with the matter of aid to Turkey. This made it essential to call a conference between the interested parties, i.e. the three Commanders-in-Chief, Middle East, and the French and Turks. Consequently I was called away to Egypt early in February, and as the *Birmingham* was coming home through the Mediterranean the First Sea Lord kindly allowed me to use her as my flagship. It was pleasant to be at sea again for a short time, if only for the passage to Alexandria.

The conferences took place in Cairo, and the general idea appeared to be to land as large a force as possible in Thrace. However, as the bases allotted by the Turks were quite unsuitable we made little progress. It soon became evident that further talks would be necessary, and it was suggested that Weygand and the three Commanders-in-Chief, Middle East, should go to Ankara towards the end of the month. Weygand was still rather set on going to Salonika, and also suggested Dedeagach as an alternative place for landing the troops and their paraphernalia. I, knowing Dedeagach well, pointed out the difficulties, whereupon Weygand asked his French naval colleague, Admiral Esteva, who had arrived literally out of the clouds and unbriefed, to examine the possibilities. Weygand, I found, was very much inclined to wave aside the naval aspects of these problems.

In writing to the First Sea Lord on the results of this conference I pointed out that in my opinion insufficient emphasis had been laid on the necessity for holding the Gallipoli Peninsula and the European side of the Bosphorus if the Turks had to fall back in Thrace. I suggested that unless we held both sides of the Dardanelles and Bosphorus, U-boats and possibly other enemy units would certainly be able to pass in and out of the Black Sea.

We also found the Turks difficult to deal with in other directions. We had been asked by Marshal Tchakmak for the help of officers in connection with the anti-submarine defences of the Dardanelles and Bosphorus. He said later he would welcome a scheme of defence prepared by us; but would not agree to our officers making the necessary reconnaissance. The Marshal had to be told that if he wanted the plan he must allow the reconnaissance. He was not easy to deal with, and the French found the same.

The result of these unsatisfactory negotiations was that by the end of February I was practically staffless at Malta. The staff officers were travelling all over Turkey and Egypt studying the situation on the ground and making recommendations for improving the defences.

In March the abortive Cairo conference was continued in Aleppo in Syria, the Chiefs-of-Staff to the three Commanders-in-Chief, Middle East, conferring this time with the Turkish Deputy Chief-of-Staff and a French representative. The proceedings were protracted, and in the day-to-day messages we received it looked as though the Turks were playing for time. Some even thought that they might simultaneously be negotiating with the Russians. However, when the Chief of Staff, Commodore Willis, returned he told me this was not so. The continual raising of the question of what support would be available to the Turks if Italy became hostile was not intended to delay matters; but to ascertain if in that eventuality we really meant to help Turkey. He thought that the overruling ideas in the Turkish mind were to remain neutral if it were possible to do so, and that they had no intention, in any circumstances, of being taken charge of and told what to do.

The question of overall command was raised, and naturally there were as many opinions as there were delegates. The Turkish idea of the naval command was that it should all be under the Turkish General Staff, whereupon they had politely but quite firmly to be told that they would have to think again on that subject. This confirmed my previous opinion that there would have to be a senior British naval officer attached to the Turkish General Staff to act as the link between it and the Commander-in-Chief, Mediterranean. The officer selected must be so senior that he had direct access to Marshal Tchakmak.

Taking it all in all, however, considerable progress was made, particularly as regards the defences of the Dardanelles, the Bosphorus and Smyrna. The plans for the defences of these areas, drawn up after a month's sojourn in Turkey by Commanders W. P. Carne and Geoffrey Barnard, the Fleet torpedo and gunnery officers on my staff, were accepted with little alteration by the Turkish General Staff.

I had to pay another visit to Alexandria and Cairo during the third week in March to confer with the other Commanders-in-Chief on the general situation and our preparations. I took passage in the *Delhi*, too small to take any of my staff with me and very much slowed down by bad weather on the way back to Malta.

Early in April I had another letter from Sir Dudley Pound. The value of these periodical communications was incalculable. He not only kept me up-to-date on the general naval situation and what was going on in the way of operations; but gave me a good idea of the latest technical developments. On this occasion I learnt that the Admiralty thought they were gradually getting the upper hand of the U-boats, mines and aircraft, especially in the case of the convoys up and down the east coast of England. This was a great advance, as at one time it was in doubt if they could continue to be run. Scapa Flow, too, had been made safe as a fleet base, and the Home Fleet was back there, a great relief to the Commander-in-Chief who must have been severely handicapped by having to operate from the Clyde.

I also had advance information of the intention to force the iron ore traffic from Narvik to Germany outside territorial waters by laying minefields, and that the reactions to this were expected to be violent. I was glad to hear, too, that Vice-Admiral Sir Geoffrey Blake was being brought back to the Admiralty to deal with the foreign side of the naval operations.

As Mussolini's intentions were greatly distrusted it had also been decided to start sending some of the slower-moving craft back to the Mediterranean, together with some submarines from China. The question of sending barrage balloons to Alexandria was being examined, I was relieved to hear. Best of all, I was told that on certain conditions the *Warspite* would return to the Mediterranean. The First Sea Lord finished his letter by writing—"What would I not give for another 100 destroyers," and in that I fully sympathized.

The mining of Norwegian waters took place according to plan; but coincided with what we now know as the long-prepared German invasion of Norway and Denmark. Though we appeared to have been caught on the wrong foot, our naval operations at the outset seemed to be most successful. It is true we had some losses, but the German losses were much heavier. The accounts of the two battles of Narvik made fine reading, and I was glad to see that my late and prospective flagship, the *Warspite*, gave such a good account of herself. I deeply regretted the loss of the gallant Captain Warburton-Lee, of the *Hardy*, one of the best of destroyer officers who had served under my command on several occasions.

To return to Malta, General Weygand passed through early in April on his way to Paris. He was a very alert little man and a real live wire, flying prodigious distances in a day in spite of his age, which was seventy-three. He had a great sense of humour. I asked him why he was going to Paris, and he replied: "The new Prime Minister must have heard I was very old, and sent for me to see if it was true."

By this time our engaged couple, my niece and the flag lieutenant, had decided they would take the plunge towards the end of April. I received the news that, war or no war, both mothers and my other niece, the prospective bride's elder sister, would come out to see the knot properly tied. The wedding took place on April 24th in St. Paul's Anglican Cathedral, with a reception afterwards in Admiralty House.

III

The general situation was steadily deteriorating. The Norwegian operations were going badly, and there were ominous rumblings from Italy. In a letter dated April 29th the First Sea Lord informed me that the Admiralty were attempting to scratch up some sort of a fleet for the Eastern Mediterranean. With all our commitments at home calling for more and more ships I thought it an act of considerable courage. All the same, the prospect of again having a deck beneath one's feet was most exhilarating. The fleet, it is true, would be heterogeneous, though I was in no mood to cavil. The *Ramillies*, escorting Australian and New Zealand convoys in the Indian Ocean, was being rushed to Alexandria. The *Warspite*, *Malaya* and *Royal Sovereign* were also to join us, with an additional cruiser squadron and various destroyers. Some French units were also coming.

My suggestion of a senior naval officer at Ankara had been accepted, the First Sea Lord informed me, and Admiral Sir Howard Kelly was appointed as liaison officer with the Turks. There was never a better choice. In the years that followed he was a tower of strength. His imposing presence, profound knowledge, and complete command of the French language soon caused him to become *persona grata* in the highest Turkish circles.

I decided to join the fleet at Alexandria at the earliest possible moment; but before doing so felt I must go to Bizerta to talk with my French colleague, Admiral Esteva. I went there on April 30th, and after long discussions returned the following night. I gathered it was the French opinion that Italy would not enter the war, at any rate for some time. If hostilities did come, it was their intention to have their two battle-cruisers, *Dunkerque* and *Strasbourg*, with some small cruisers and destroyers, working from Mers-el-Kebir (Oran), with four 8-inch gun cruisers and some destroyers at Toulon to keep things lively in the Gulf of Genoa. I was disappointed to find that they had made no provision for a small, fast force from Bizerta to work on the all-important Italian communications with Libya. We came to an agreement in principle on the area commands of British and French submarines in the Mediterranean.

On May 1st we had the curious spectacle of a British battleship passing Malta escorted by four cruisers and eight destroyers, three of the cruisers being French. Fifteen miles astern of them came three French battleships escorted by two destroyers and a torpedo-boat. They were all on their way to Alexandria. I received a signal from the First Lord telling me that this strong but miscellaneous force was primarily intended as a demonstration to impress the Italians. I replied by expressing the hope that I should not be called upon to conduct operations with such a party. However, it appeared to be the general opinion at home that our reverses in Norway might tempt the Italians to embark on some adventure in the Balkans.

I sailed for Alexandria in a cruiser on May 3rd, the main body of my staff and office following in the fleet repair ship *Resource*. On arrival I hoisted my flag in the *Malaya*, the only British battleship present. The assembled fleet looked imposing enough; but it was mostly French. The French Admiral in command was Vice-Admiral R. E. Godfroy, one of the best type of French naval officers. Highly intelligent and alert he spoke excellent English, having in years past married an English lady, now deceased. He was most eager to co-operate, and we very soon arranged to have some exercises together at sea in the near future.

On May 10th General Weygand, General Wavell and Air Chief Marshal Longmore, the last-named having just arrived to take command of the Royal Air Force in the Middle East, came on board the *Malaya* for a conference. In view of a forthcoming meeting with the Turks we discussed Turkish and Balkan affairs generally; but our deliberations were overshadowed by the news from home, Germany having invaded Holland, Belgium and Luxemburg. Weygand was quite cheerful about it, and told me that it was what the French General Staff had wished for. I only hoped he was right.

The *Warspite* arrived that night, and I moved over to her next day, May 11th. My prophecy when I said good-bye to her ship's company in November

o

had come true, and very glad indeed we all were to be back in our old quarters. I think the men were glad to see us also. There is a cachet about being fleet flagship which extends to the most junior rating on board. Captain Crutchley had left, having been relieved by Captain Douglas Fisher.

The news from home was grave indeed. The Germans seemed to be having things pretty well all their own way, and had already knocked out Holland. We heard with hope of General Weygand's appointment as Commander-in-Chief in France. We all admired him. He radiated energy, youthfulness and confidence, and had a victorious record behind him.

He was absent from our conference with the Turks at Beyrout on May 20th, a long and tedious day that I well remember. We started by air from Alexandria at 5 a.m. and did not get back until 11 p.m. The conference was not very fruitful. With the background of bad news from England Marshal Tchakmak was clearly doubtful of the ability of the French or ourselves to help Turkey, and the opinion we had formed some months before that she would remain neutral at all costs unless directly attacked was amply confirmed.

Meanwhile ships were arriving to reinforce the fleet from all over the world—the battleship *Ramillies*, the Australian cruiser *Sydney*, and the New Zealand cruiser *Leander* with my old flag Captain H. E. Horan in command.

News from Malta was scarce; but a start had been made with evacuating the wives and families of the men who were no longer on the station. It was suggested that my wife should leave; but she firmly decided it was not fit and proper for the Commander-in-Chief's wife to be among the first to go. She had plenty to do in making the necessary arrangements, and Admiralty House was being run as a sort of hostel for lonely naval wives. My wife sent me a letter she had received from Admiral Esteva. His home town was Rheims, and he was a great supporter of the Cathedral, which had just been restored. The city had been heavily bombed and severely damaged, and his sister and brother, the latter desperately wounded in the previous war, had had to be evacuated. In keeping with his character Esteva wrote: "If our house and all our goods are destroyed, we know that many people are to be severely ruined or hurt and that it is an honour to suffer for high ideals of civilization and not agree with the coarse brutality of those criminal Germans anxious to rule the whole earth." Esteva's sentiments were impeccable.

I have not previously mentioned the British Ambassador to Egypt, Sir Miles Lampson, a great big man, shrewd and understanding with great prestige and influence in the country. I liked him, and he was of the greatest assistance in smoothing over many of our difficulties at Alexandria. He presented me to King Farouk on my first arrival.

The tension rapidly increased. Though Mussolini still kept us guessing, nobody thought that war with Italy could be avoided. It was not a question of whether she would enter the war against us; but when.

For that eventuality we continued to prepare at full pressure.

CHAPTER XX

I

AT the end of May I had another letter from the First Sea Lord, dated May 20th, informing me that it was thought Mussolini would hold his hand for another week. One of the reasons given was that the Italian seaplane-carrier *Miraglia* was due to pass through the Suez Canal on the 25th, and was not due at Massawa, in Eritrea, until the 27th.

In regard to our naval air situation in the Mediterranean he wrote, rather ominously: "I am afraid you are terribly short of 'air', but there again I do not see what can be done because, as you will realize, every available aircraft is wanted in home waters. The one lesson we have learnt here is that it is essential to have fighter protection over the fleet whenever they are within range of enemy bombers. You will be without such protection, which is a very serious matter, but I do not see any way of rectifying it."

It certainly was a serious matter, though no more than we expected. We should have to do the best we could without fighter protection.

The whole situation as regards air over the sea, particularly reconnaissance, was causing us grave anxiety. So far back as December, 1939, I had pointed out to the Air Officer Commanding-in-Chief, Middle East, that in any war in the Balkans the sea communications would be of the highest importance, and had asked if he could allow one or more of his bomber squadrons to exercise over the sea with our ships, and had offered him any targets he required. Owing to shortage of squadrons he was unable to agree to my suggestion and I fully accepted his reasons. I knew he was very thin on the ground.

The only aircraft for deep reconnaissance allotted to the fleet were a few flying-boats divided between Malta and Alexandria. They were excellent when there was no opposition; but quite unsuitable for work anywhere near an enemy coast within range of shore-based aircraft.

The news from home continued to become gloomier and gloomier. The French line was burst open, the Belgians had surrendered, and the Germans had appeared at the Channel ports. We heard of the evacuation from Dunkirk. The defeat of the French seemed to be certain, and it was only a matter of days before the hyena Mussolini came in to share the carcass.

The repair facilities at Alexandria had been somewhat improved, though they still fell lamentably short of what was required to maintain a fleet. The large floating dock from Portsmouth capable of taking battleships had arrived and was in its dredged berth inside the coaling basin. Some dockyard workmen had come from Malta, and these, with the repair facilities of the Khedivial Line and those of the Alexandria tramways organization, were all we had at

SARDINIA
Terranova
Cagliari
ADRIATIC
Bari
Durazzo
YUGO SLAVIA
Naples
ITALY
Brindisi
Valona
ALBANIA
Taranto
STRAIT OF OTRANTO
CORFU
GREECE
Trapani
Messina
IONIAN SEA
SICILY
CEPHALONIA
IONIAN Is.
Bizerta
Tunis
C. Bon
Catania
Pantellaria
Augusta
TUNISIA
MALTA
C. Matapan
KITHERA
EASTERN M
Tripoli
Benghazi
TRIPOLITANIA
CYRENA
Sirte
El Agheila
0 50 100 200
Miles
LIBYAN DESE
Bip Pares
JUNE 1941-N

TERRITORIES
Axis
Axis Occupied
United Nations
Neutral
NAVAL BASES & PORTS
Axis
British
LGARIA
Istanbul
EGEAN SEA
TURKEY
Smyrna
DODECANESE
SCARPANTO
RHODES
KASO
CHANNEL
Heraklion
CRETE
CYPRUS
Famagusta
SYRIA
Beyrut
Haifa
PALESTINE
DITERRANEAN
Tobruk
Bardia
Mersa Matruh
El Alamein
ALEXANDRIA
Port Said
SUEZ CANAL
AFRIKA KORPS
BR. 8TH. ARMY
EGYPT
EMBER 1942

Alexandria. There were minor repair facilities at Port Said and Suez. Reserves of ammunition were low and mostly in the Suez Canal area, while the anti-aircraft defence of the port was provided by twenty-four anti-aircraft guns and a few searchlights.

I was still perturbed about the safety of Malta. It had no fighters, and the full scale of anti-aircraft defence had not arrived. I was doubtful how the island would stand up to bombing, with the possibility of parachute troops and other aerial visitors. It was no more than sixty miles from Sicily. I was not so anxious about seaborne attack. Malta had originally been armed with 9·2-inch guns, one or two of which had been modified to equal the range of any ship's guns which could be brought against them. To these had now been added the two 15-inch guns of the monitor *Terror*, which was incorporated in the defences.

Meanwhile the three Commanders-in-Chief were ordered to prepare an expedition to occupy Crete and Milos. A message received by me in May ran: "If Greek territory is attacked by Italy, expeditions to Crete are to start immediately without further reference to London or Paris. If, however, war with Italy breaks out on any other issue than an attack on Greek soil, no landing of Allied troops on Greek soil is to be made without prior authority."

Four French cruisers had already sailed from Alexandria to Beyrout to be ready to embark troops for this purpose, while we were ready to embark British troops at Port Said. On May 29th I was able to write to Sir Dudley Pound telling him that everything was ready for this move, while two days later I informed the Admiralty that all arrangements were made. The British forces would land in Crete within 24–30 hours of the order being given, and the French within about 50 hours. I should add that we were whole-heartedly in favour of this Cretan project, as the use of Suda Bay for refuelling light craft would greatly facilitate operations against the Italians.

Early in June some misunderstanding appeared to have arisen at the Admiralty in regard to the policy which should be adopted by the fleet in the Eastern Mediterranean in the event of war with Italy. In a message of May 23rd I had informed the Admiralty that our initial object was to secure control of the sea communications in the Eastern Mediterranean and the Ægean, and to cut off Italian supplies to the Dodecanese. I went on to say that this limited object did not envisage cutting the sea communications between Italy and Libya, and that my decision in this respect had been brought about by lack of light naval forces and aircraft; by the fact that a military offensive against Libya was no longer contemplated; and because, if Turkey came into the war on our side, I should have to deal with Italian naval forces in the Dodecanese. I was careful to add that all this did not imply that the Central Mediterranean would be neglected; but that I intended to carry out an early sweep in this direction, with, of course, my heavy ships.

It seems to have been suggested to the Prime Minister that the policy I had suggested was defensive, for on June 5th I had a message from the First Sea Lord: "It has been suggested that the Naval Object as outlined in your message of May 23rd, is purely defensive, but I have never interpreted it as being such, and I know it is your burning desire to make as many opportunities for hitting the enemy hard as your limited forces will permit."

In an Admiralty message of the same date I was requested to signal my exact dispositions and intended movements in the immediate future more fully than had previously been necessary.

In a letter of June 6th, received by me on the 9th, Sir Dudley Pound wrote: "I told the Prime Minister he need have no fears that you would act on the defensive, but he insisted that some telegrams should be sent to all Commanders-in-Chief." The First Sea Lord went on to say that it might be possible to send us the *Illustrious* later on if we felt she would really be of use to us, and that there were many things he would have liked to have sent us before the clash came—"more destroyers, more submarines, more minesweepers and destroyer depot ships, and in particular more fighter aircraft". In this same letter he told me that they were doing all they could to get some Hurricanes sent out to Alexandria; but that he did not think there was any chance of getting fighters sent to Malta as the United Kingdom had got nothing like its appropriate quota.

In replying to this letter on June 9th I said I had rather been taken aback by the signal about the defensive object, and that I hoped that a signal sent on June 6th—which I will mention presently—had cleared up all doubts in the matter.

Nothing was further from our thoughts than to act on the defensive. Broadly speaking, there were two courses of action open to us. One was to remain in harbour or within safe limits in the Eastern Mediterranean, the second to go boldly forth into the Central Mediterranean and test out the air and the submarine risks. We never gave a thought to the strength of the Italian fleet. In various reports the number of their capital ships varied from three to five, rising sometimes to seven. We were perfectly confident that the fleet we had at Alexandria could deal with them if they chose to give battle. On the other hand, if they elected to run, they were the faster ships and we had little chance of overhauling them with our older vessels. Our chief difficulty was how to find the Italian fleet with our almost complete lack of air reconnaissance. This did not seem to be understood by those at home, particularly by the Prime Minister.

It was in the sort of 'prodding' message received by me on June 5th that Mr. Churchill was often so ungracious and hasty. We realized, of course, the terrible mental and physical strain under which he was labouring; but so were we. Such messages to those who were doing their utmost with straitened resources were not an encouragement, merely an annoyance. Moreover, as they implied that something was lacking in the direction and leadership, they did positive harm. If such messages were really necessary, if Commanders-in-Chief on the spot who knew all the risks and the chances were not prepared to get at the enemy on every possible occasion, the recipients ought not to have been in the position they held.

However, the contretemps passed and the situation was finally cleared by my further messages of June 6th. I need not quote them in full; but said, *inter alia*, that our intentions at the outset of hostilities were entirely governed by the necessity of being prepared to occupy Crete at short notice, and that a substantial part of the battle fleet, with cruisers and destroyers, would cover this operation from an area west of Crete. A cruiser would patrol the Kithera Channel, and submarine patrols off Crete would be augmented by others off Augusta, Taranto, the Straits of Otranto, Tobruk, and the Dodecanese. Submarines would also lay mines off Augusta and Cape S. Maria di Leuca, the heel of Italy. I again strongly urged the occupation of Crete, whatever the political situation, as it would give us a fuelling base for operations in the Central Mediterranean and Ægean.

I went on to say that if the Cretan operation were not ordered, it seemed that the operations of the Fleet must unfortunately be governed by Italian action; but that when war became imminent it was my intention that a strong force including battleships should proceed westward to counter any Italian action against Malta or in other directions. This movement might be accompanied by sweeps of the Dodecanese and North African areas, or by anti-submarine hunts south of Crete or in the Kaso and Kithera Channels. If Malta were subjected to seaborne attack we intended to move with the whole fleet to its relief. An attack on Augusta might be the best method of affording relief to Malta; but it was hoped to try out the enemy's air and submarine strength before operating so close to his coasts.

If and when adequate air reconnaissance had been established from Tunisia and Malta, I hoped also to keep a force of cruisers and destroyers working permanently in the Central Mediterranean to prey upon Italian traffic with Libya. Either Malta or a Greek island could be used for fuelling at night.

If Turkey entered the war on our side, operations against the Dodecanese would probably be necessary, and I proposed at the outset to break up the sea communications between the Dodecanese and Italy.

I had to point out that with all these varied commitments I had insufficient destroyers to provide the necessary anti-submarine screen to take the whole of the battle fleet to sea together.

In a message to the First Sea Lord on the same date, June 6th, I said:

> You may be sure that all in the fleet are imbued with a burning desire to get at the Italian fleet, but you will appreciate that a policy of seeking and destroying his naval forces requires good and continuous air reconnaissance, and a means of fixing the enemy when located. I am far from well provided with either requirement, whereas the Italians have both. Indeed

my chief fear is that we shall make contact with little or nothing except aircraft and submarines, and I must get the measure of these before attempting sustained operations in the Central Mediterranean. It must not be forgotten that the fleet base (Alexandria) and repair facilities are exposed to enemy air attack, with very limited fighter protection, and there is no alternative.

On June 8th I had a message from the First Sea Lord in which I was informed that the occupation of Crete could only be carried out if Italy first attacked Greece. Also that the shortage of destroyers and the handicap that it inflicted upon us was fully realized; but that the situation in Home Waters prevented our further reinforcement.

This we could well understand. The Navy had been woefully short of destroyers at the outbreak of war, and up to and including the evacuation from Dunkirk had lost twenty-two, with many more in dockyard hands for repairs from bomb, mine or torpedo damage. We were short of much else, particularly aircraft-carriers, escort vessels and minesweepers. Our aged battleships, not all of them renovated, were not fit to be pitted against heavy bombing, and were really no match for the more modern, well-armed and speedier ships built by some of the foreign powers between the wars.

Out here in the Mediterranean we were also having to contrive and improvise to make bricks with very little straw. To sum up, we lacked aircraft for reconnaissance worst of all, and destroyers and cruisers. The use of Malta could not be relied upon, and Alexandria could not undertake really extensive repairs. We needed ammunition, and many more anti-aircraft guns. Our resources would soon be stretched to the limit, and on the outbreak of war, when the Mediterranean became virtually impassable, our supplies could only be replenished by the convoys running round the Cape of Good Hope.

Another pressing anxiety was the Suez Canal. A stream of Italian ships was passing through it, and when the flag fell it would be difficult to prevent a vessel laden with cement or munitions from blowing herself up and blocking it, for a time at least. The Senior British Naval Officer in the Canal Area had no real powers of delay, and had to invent fictitious reasons for holding up suspicious ships while the Government at home made up its mind. It was useless to ask anything of the Egyptian Government, as they would take no action that might irritate the Italians. On one occasion at least the Egyptian Prime Minister telephoned to Alexandria and ordered the instant release of an Italian vessel which was being delayed by Customs formalities under the Consul General's directions. I do not know why the Italians never attempted to block the Suez Canal or to wreck the port of Alexandria by blowing up a ship. Alexandria was vital for the discharge of stores and munitions for the maintenance of our Armies in the Middle East, even for those brought by the convoys coming round the Cape of Good Hope.

On the 9th I flew to Cairo to meet my Army and Air colleagues. If anything, their headaches were worse than mine. Added to their natural anxiety about possible invasions from the west (Libya), and the south (Eritrea), in both of which areas our forces were outnumbered by about five to one, they were nervous about Jibouti, in French Somaliland, and the Yemen, across the Red Sea from Eritrea, though personally I saw no reason for anxiety about the Yemen with our naval forces in being in the Red Sea. Both my Army and Air colleagues were also complaining strongly about having to deal with two Naval Commanders-in-Chief, i.e. C.-in-C. Mediterranean, and C.-in-C. East Indies, for the Red Sea, and the latter out of touch. I was sympathetic, though at the present juncture I did not really wish the Red Sea to be added to my other operational areas. Before the Abyssinian crisis in 1935 it had formed part of the Mediterranean Station. However, in writing to the First Sea Lord I pointed out the considerations which led me to believe that the Red Sea should again become part and parcel of our domain.

The Red Sea complication was only one of several. All three Commanders-in-Chief, Naval, Army, and Air, had different areas of responsibility. Malta, in particular, was a peculiar case. It did not come into the orbit of the General Officer Commanding-in-Chief, Middle East. In fact I do not believe that the value of Malta to their own operations was ever fully realized in Army circles, except perhaps by General Wavell. Its military importance lay in the fact that it was close to the line of communication from Italy to Libya, and that surface vessels, submarines and aircraft working from the island could do much to cut off the supplies upon which the enemy army in Africa depended.

By June 9th the fleet at Alexandria, on paper, was quite an imposing one. It consisted of the battleships *Warspite*, *Malaya*, *Royal Sovereign*, and *Ramillies*, the latter in the floating dock. We had the 7th Cruiser Squadron: *Orion*, *Neptune*, *Sydney*, *Liverpool*, *Gloucester*; the 3rd Cruiser Squadron: *Capetown*, *Caledon*, *Calypso*, and *Delhi*; some twenty-five destroyers, a mixed bag of the 'D', 'H', 'I', 'J', 'K' and Tribal classes, with the *Stuart* and her four old 'V's' and 'W's', of the Australian flotilla. Of these the four 'K's were sent on to the Red Sea to watch over the Italian destroyers at Massawa. We had a dozen submarines of the 'O' and 'P' class from China, from which station the aircraft-carrier *Eagle* also joined us. With the exception of the fleet repair ship *Resource* and the submarine depot ship *Medway*, we had no other repair or destroyer depot ships.

The French squadron had originally consisted of three battleships, three 8-inch gun cruisers, one 6-inch gun cruiser, and three small destroyers. I had persuaded Vice-Admiral Godfroy that our combined force was unnecessarily large, so two of their battleships had left to return to the Western Mediterranean. That left us with only the battleship *Lorraine*, four cruisers and three destroyers with whom we had had a day at sea manœuvring to get them used to our signal codes.

And so the stage was set.

II

On June 10th the 2nd Destroyer Flotilla and two flying-boats were at sea on a sweep for Italian submarines which might be proceeding to their war stations. I think this movement prevented their project of mining the fleet into Alexandria.

We had news of the Italian declaration of war at 7 p.m., and the fleet at once went to two hours' notice for steam, and the *Ramillies* abandoned her refit. First blood was drawn that night, for at 11.30 the destroyer *Decoy* reported sighting a submarine on the surface, which she attacked. At dawn next morning there was an oil slick on the surface two miles long. Whether or not the submarine was destroyed I do not know.

Preceded by the 7th Cruiser Squadron the *Warspite*, *Malaya*, *Eagle*, and nine destroyers sailed at 1 p.m. on June 11th, the cruisers *Caledon* and *Calypso* joining us during the day. The idea was to steam north-west for Crete, and then along its south coast to a position about eighty miles south of Matapan, with the cruisers sweeping west until dark and an air search ahead of them. The cruisers were then to move south to attack any patrols off Benghazi and Tobruk at first daylight on the 12th. At the same time the French cruisers, under Admiral Godfroy, swept up to the Ægean and off the Dodecanese.

It seemed possible that we, in the Central Mediterranean, might pick up some traffic going to Libya, while there was an outside chance that some of the Italian units might be at sea. It was also essential to try out the Italian air at the earliest possible moment.

But after all we had heard of the Regia Aeronautica we had the curious experience of not sighting a single aircraft, except for one seen by the *Liverpool* and *Gloucester* when they engaged some minesweepers off Tobruk at dawn on the 12th, and were being engaged by the shore batteries in return. As I wrote to the First Sea Lord: "I expected to spend most of the daylight hours beating off heavy bombing attacks on the fleet. Actually the battle squadron never saw a 'plane, though the best part of a day was spent 100 miles off the Libyan coast. . . . This is most encouraging at first sight, but perhaps we should not draw any hard and fast conclusions yet. But the outlook for Red Sea convoys looks distinctly hopeful."

So far as the enemy submarines were concerned, we were not so successful. The cruiser *Calypso* was torpedoed south of the west end of Crete at 2 a.m. on June 12th, and sank at 3.30 with a loss of one officer and thirty-eight ratings. It was a good performance by the submarine, as the cruisers were close astern of a destroyer screen.

The fleet returned to Alexandria on the 14th. We had to make a very cautious entry, as several minefields had been laid by submarines off the harbour during our absence. We were poverty-stricken as regards minesweepers. However, our destroyers took good toll of the unwelcome visitors. We estimated, perhaps optimistically, that two had been destroyed and some others damaged and frightened.

Malta was naturally causing us grave concern. It was being bombed day and night, and the fact that my wife and two nieces were there did nothing to allay my anxiety. As I have said, the anti-aircraft defences were far from complete and there were no fighters, though we were relieved to hear that the Maltese population was standing up well to Italian bombing.

Air Commodore Maynard at Malta sent me a message asking if he might use four spare Fleet Air Arm Gladiator fighters that were in crates in the dockyard for the Mediterranean aircraft-carrier. I gave the most cordial approval, and three of these Gladiators, flown by flying-boat and other pilots inexperienced in flying fighters, did the most gallant work and inflicted loss on the Italian bombers. From all accounts they should have been well sustained by the volume of prayer that went up for their safety from the Maltese whenever they went up to beat off an attack. It is almost unbelievable, but a month or two later a signal was received from some Admiralty department asking why the Commander-in-Chief, Mediterranean had permitted Fleet Air Arm spares to be turned over to the Royal Air Force. I wondered where the official responsible had been spending his war.

There had been a change of Governors in Malta, General Sir Charles Bonham-Carter having gone home to recuperate after a severe illness. He had been relieved by Lieutenant-General Sir William Dobbie, a splendid selection. An Ironside of a man, his profound faith in the justice of our cause and the certainty of Divine assistance made a great impression upon the highly religious Maltese. The calm and complete faith shown in the broadcasts he made nearly every evening contributed immensely towards keeping up the morale of the people.

The Vice-Admiral, Malta (now Admiral Sir) Wilbraham T. R. Ford, was another man in the right place, and a real tower of strength. He played a full and most important part in the organization for the maintenance and defence of the island, and had the unerring knack of overriding each and every difficulty as it arose.

On the fleet's return to Alexandria after its first sweep we were not idle. Destroyers were sweeping for submarines; a cruiser and more destroyers were operating in the Dodecanese; British submarines were on passage through the Ægean to the Dardanelles and Doro Channel, as well as on patrol off Augusta, Taranto and the Straits of Otranto. French submarines were working off Rhodes, Leros, the Straits of Messina and Tripoli. On June 18th it was reported that some fifty Italian U-boats were at sea.

On June 20th an Allied force under Vice-Admiral John Tovey in the *Orion*, with the French battleship *Lorraine*, the cruisers *Neptune* and *Sydney* and four destroyers, sailed to bombard Bardia early next morning. Five other destroyers sailed to sweep along the Libyan coast as far as Tobruk, and as air reconnaissance had reported Italian cruisers and destroyers in that harbour, a force of three British destroyers and the two French cruisers *Suffren* and *Duguay Trouin* left Alexandria as a reinforcement. Bardia was duly bombarded with good results. This was the last operation in which the French participated.

Because of our French squadron we were much concerned with the situation in France, which seemed hourly to be becoming more desperate. Vice-Admiral Godfroy had been full of fight at the outset; but after Pétain asked for an armistice he faded out as a belligerent. This was all the more to be regretted as on June 22nd I had intended to sail with the fleet, including two French ships, to carry out a sweep in force between the south of Italy and Libya. If that achieved no useful result we then intended to carry out a night bombardment of Augusta and a raid of the Straits of Messina. As it was, the whole operation had to be cancelled by the Admiralty as the French were about to sign the armistice.

The French in the squadron with us all had great faith in Pétain and Weygand, and resented their new government being called unconstitutional. They had no use for General de Gaulle. Some of the younger officers and men were all for fighting on. Indeed, there was one complete destroyer's crew who would have been glad to fight under the British flag. Admiral Godfroy I knew as a very honourable man, and whatever happened I had no fears that he would cause me any anxiety or hamper our operations in any way. The men were mostly demanding to go back to France, and towards the end of June I thought there was a chance of the French ships falling peaceably into my hands. If this had happened I was prepared to man the three destroyers and perhaps one 8-inch gun cruiser.

We seemed to be making good headway against the Italian submarines. By post-war records I see that five had actually been sunk in the Eastern Mediterranean since the outbreak of war with Italy, while various others must have been damaged. On one occasion five destroyers under the command of Commander Mervyn Thomas of the *Dainty* were sent out to try and disintegrate the line of submarines that we suspected had been stationed between Crete and the coast of Cyrenaica with the object of intercepting the fleet on its passages to the west. We heard nothing at all of this party for two days until one afternoon Thomas reported his expected time of arrival in Alexandria and requested transport for the survivors of two submarines he had sunk. When he arrived it transpired that he had attacked a third. It was a fine piece of silent service, the ships responsible being the *Dainty* and *Ilex*.

Losses among our own submarines were causing us great anxiety. Three of the ten we had operating, the *Grampus*, *Odin*, and *Orpheus*, had not returned from their patrols, and had to be written off as lost. At the time we had no information as to the cause, but were aware that the Italians had laid extensive minefields off their ports in depths of up to 150 and 200 fathoms. We knew that our young submarine commanders, superbly trained and without thought of danger, would push right in. I did not consider it was fair on them, so gave orders they were not to get inside the 200 fathom line unless in actual pursuit of important enemy units.

Captain S. M. Raw, in the *Medway* in command of the submarine flotilla, was the right man in the right place. Steadfast and imperturbable, he was a good leader, and the submarine officers had the highest opinion of his judgment. He was never daunted by any difficulty. Incidentally, there was an acute shortage of spare submarine ratings, and it was most unlikely that we could get more from England. We called for ex-submarine ratings from the fleet, and if that did not succeed were prepared to call for volunteers and give them a modified course of training in their depot ship, the *Medway*.

On shore, the month of June saw little change in the situation. In spite of their preponderance, the Italians in Libya made no forward move. Indeed, our forward mobile patrols were harrying them to some purpose on the Egyptian frontier, and had even forced a small withdrawal. The R.A.F. bomber squadrons had also gone into action the moment war was declared, and had done considerable damage to dumps, stores and transport behind the Italian lines. They had rather forced the Regia Aeronautica in that region to the defensive.

In his dealings with General Mittelhauser in Syria and General Noguès in Morocco, General Wavell's experience had been much the same as mine with Admiral Godfroy. A determination to fight on when France began to collapse had been replaced by a gradual fading out under the defection of the Pétain government. One could not but admire the calm way in which Wavell accepted these set-backs which so vastly increased his already great difficulties.

Graver and graver became the news from France until, on June 24th, we heard that she had capitulated to Germany and Italy. The next morning, when we were all feeling rather depressed, I was walking up and down the quarterdeck of the *Warspite*. I saw an Admiral's barge approaching, and went to the gangway to receive the Vice-Admiral (D), John Tovey. A smiling figure ran up the gangway and greeted me with: "Now I know we shall win the war, sir. We have no more allies." Such depression as I had vanished. It was impossible to feel downcast in the face of such optimism.

During the last days of June we were still carrying out our anti-submarine sweeps, and it was on the 28th that Commander Mervyn Thomas's destroyers sank the two submarines already mentioned, and probably damaged another. A Sunderland flying-boat had attacked and sunk one more in the Ionian Sea. We were also running a convoy from the Dardanelles and Greek ports to Port Said under the escort of the *Capetown*, *Caledon*, and four destroyers, with two convoys of 13 and 9 knots, respectively, from Malta to Alexandria. To cover these convoys Admiral Tovey was at sea with the 7th Cruiser

Squadron, while further support was provided by the *Royal Sovereign*, *Ramillies*, *Eagle*, and eight destroyers. What happened again emphasized the prime importance of adequate aircraft reconnaissance.

As the result of flying-boats working ahead of the 7th Cruiser Squadron, three Italian destroyers were reported, apparently returning from Libya to Italy. Our cruisers altered course at full speed to intercept, and at 6.30 p.m. on June 28th sighted the enemy about seventy-five miles west-south-west of Cape Matapan steering west at high speed. The cruisers came into action at extreme gun range, and before the Italians were able to escape by superior speed one of them, the *Espero*, was crippled and sunk.

This in itself was a minor incident; but it brought into high relief the paucity of our reserves of ammunition at Alexandria. A tremendous expenditure of 6-inch shell had been necessary to sink this one 1,100-ton destroyer. With the *Liverpool* and *Gloucester* pumping out twelve-gun salvos the ammunition just melted away. Our only reserves near at hand were 800 rounds in the Suez Canal Zone. It being considered impossible at that time to pass slow ammunition ships through the Mediterranean, our next nearest reserve was at Durban, roughly 6,000 miles away. If the 800 rounds in the Canal Zone were shared out among our cruisers which had been engaged on the evening of June 28th, they would have just over 50 per cent of the normal supply in their magazines and shell-rooms. This state of affairs caused us considerable anxiety and prevailed for three weeks.

In writing to the First Sea Lord on June 27th, I said I hoped the French business would soon be settled, and that we should be able to get on with the war. I wrote also:

> I suppose the broad Naval Strategy will require some reconsidering. I hope it will not be necessary to abandon the Eastern Mediterranean: the landslide would be frightful. If the Spaniards leave us alone, I think quite a small force could hold that end, and if the efforts of the Eastern and Western Mediterranean are properly co-ordinated, I feel we can keep the Italians pretty well engaged. . . . Malta is doing very well, I think, and the morale of the Maltese is surprisingly high. . . . Six days ago they were down to the last one of the Gladiator Fleet Air Arm spare aircraft I told them to use. Is it even now too late to get the Air Ministry to send out some fighters? If we had twenty or thirty fighters at Malta ready to operate over the fleet I think we could guarantee to make the Sicilians, anyway, very sorry that Italy had entered the war. I am sure that the provision of aircraft for Malta would make all the difference to our operations both in the Eastern and Western Mediterranean.

In that same letter I suggested that as the 3rd Cruiser Squadron had been reduced to two ships, they should be added to the 7th Cruiser Squadron.

I recommended that the Vice-Admiral (D), John Tovey, should command all the light forces—cruisers and destroyers—and that Rear-Admiral Renouf went to the 7th Cruiser Squadron as Tovey's Second-in-Command with his flag in the *Liverpool*, and administered the cruisers.

One might sum up June, 1940, in the Eastern Mediterranean by saying that we had effectually stopped the Italian communications with the Dodecanese; threatened their communications with Libya; severely frightened their submarines; and put great caution into the hearts of their battle-fleet. If the latter did care to emerge they had a very good chance of being brought to action.

And while the Italian Navy had been shaken, the morale of the men in our Mediterranean Fleet was wonderful. For the Italians they had nothing but a healthy contempt, and were all longing to get at them.

We, who knew and were responsible, were troubled by much. Our ships were old, and we were short of aircraft, destroyers, and minesweepers. We were anxious about Malta and the matter of its supply, also its lack of fighters and anti-aircraft defences. Alexandria, also poorly defended, was a bad substitute as a fleet base. The questions of refits and repairs, the supply of essential stores and ammunition, all added to our burden. There was so much that had to be improvised.

Looking back on those early days of the war against Italy, no less than upon the strenuous months that were to follow, I again realize how much we owed to the magnificent spirit of our officers and men. Their enthusiasm and devotion were beyond all praise. Many times I had reason to thank the system and tradition that produced such fine seamen. No Commander-in-Chief ever had better subordinates. Never was the country better served. It was their outstanding spirit of invincibility in any emergency that enabled them to rise over all our difficulties.

Our ships might be old, and there was much that we lacked. Nevertheless we had our personnel, and, through them, were able to forge a weapon that was as bright and as sharp as highly-tempered steel.

III

On June 17th, before France finally faded out, I had had a message from the First Sea Lord telling me that every effort was being made to keep France in the war, so that the French fleet might continue to operate in the Western Mediterranean even though it might only have the use of the ports in North Africa.

If France made a separate peace, every endeavour would be made to obtain control of the French fleet beforehand, or failing that, to have it sunk.

If this situation arose the protection of our vital Atlantic trade would become a formidable problem unless we could hold the western exit to the Mediterranean, the Straits of Gibraltar. This, with our existing resources, could only be accomplished by moving the British Fleet from the Eastern Mediterranean to Gibraltar. If Spain came into the war the problem would become even more formidable, and the necessity for moving the fleet from the Eastern Mediterranean would be greater still.

It was realized, Sir Dudley Pound continued, there were strong political and military objections to such a step; but our trade in the Atlantic must be the first consideration. The Government had not given a decision one way or the other, but as the withdrawal might have to be made at short notice it was considered desirable that I should be informed so that I could work out the necessary plans. My views were asked for; but it was suggested that part of the fleet should go westward to Gibraltar through the Mediterranean, instead of round the Cape of Good Hope. There was also the question of whether the submarines and their depot ships should be retained in the Eastern Mediterranean, it being assumed that we should continue to defend Egypt with the Army, which would be supplied round the Cape and through the Red Sea. If it were likely that the Army might lose control of the Suez Canal, then we should be prepared to block it.

I replied later the same day, detailing my proposed arrangements for the withdrawal of the Navy, and saying that the possibility had already been considered by General Wavell, and that in this event it was his opinion that Egypt could not be held for long.

Once more I stressed the importance of Malta. If the fleet left the Mediterranean, the morale of the Maltese would collapse, and it would only be a matter of time before the island fell. I concluded by saying: "If the decision is made to let Malta go, and a start is made now, it should be possible to evacuate some quantity of the valuable fleet stores now there and personnel not essential for the defence."

On June 18th I sent a further message to the First Sea Lord saying that my signal of the 17th may have sounded somewhat acquiescent, and that I should like to add some further observations. I said, in so many words, that although I considered it feasible to move the faster portion of the fleet westward from Alexandria through the Mediterranean and the rest through the Suez Canal, the effects of this withdrawal would mean such a landslide in territory and prestige that I earnestly hoped such a decision would never have to be taken. As already pointed out, the Commander-in-Chief, Middle East, considered Egypt would become untenable soon after the departure of the fleet. Added to that Malta, Cyprus, and Palestine could no longer be held, while the Moslem world would regard it as surrender. The prospects of Turkey's loyalty would also be discounted, and even the Italians might be stirred to activity.

I continued by saying I was fully aware of the paramount importance of our Atlantic trade and home defence; but that I felt that with our present forces we should be able to safeguard these in addition to maintaining the Eastern Mediterranean. The Italian battle fleet had so far shown no signs of activity, and from all the indications available to me it did not seem that they were yet considering serious fighting. I was of the opinion that the battleships we had were sufficient to contain the Italian heavy ships with something in hand, and that the route to Malta could be opened when required.

I added that though I suspected it was a shortage of light craft (e.g. destroyers) which was causing most concern at home, I was prepared, if it would be any help, to send one 'R' class battleship round the Cape to join the force at Gibraltar. I felt that even a comparatively small force at Gibraltar would suffice to prevent the Italians from interfering in the Atlantic, particularly if the operations of the Gibraltar detachment were co-ordinated with those of our fleet in the Eastern Mediterranean.

I do not know how near we came to abandoning the Eastern Mediterranean; but if it had come to pass it would have been a major disaster, nothing less.

CHAPTER XXI

I

AT the end of June, 1940, the question of the French squadron at Alexandria had to be settled. Though I had no doubts of the good faith of Vice-Admiral Godfroy, it was impossible for the British fleet in Alexandria to go to sea for operations against the enemy leaving behind in harbour fully efficient units of the French Navy. Immediately we were out of sight they might sail for Beyrout, or even go back to France, where there was no assurance that they would not fall into German or Italian hands and be used against us.

Much the same considerations regarding the units of the main French fleet were in the minds of the authorities at home, and they were about to take action. These French ships were not in the metropolitan ports; but were distributed between the African ports of Mers-el-Keber (Oran), Casablanca and Dakar, the bulk of them being at Mers-el-Kebir.

During the last days of June we became aware that an operation was being planned against the French ships at Oran. An ultimatum was to be given to the French Admiral in command, giving him four alternatives. He might sail his ships to British ports and continue the fight with us; or sail his ships with reduced crews to a British port from which the crews would be repatriated whenever desired; or sail his ships with reduced crews to a French port in the West Indies where they would be demilitarized to our satisfaction, or, if preferred, entrusted to United States jurisdiction for the duration of the war, the crews being repatriated in either case; or, finally, to sink his ships.

If the French Admiral proposed as an alternative that he should demilitarize his ships in the berths they then occupied at Oran, this was acceptable provided it could be effectively carried out in six hours, and would prevent the ships being brought into service for at least a year even with the assistance of a fully-equipped dockyard port.

If all these alternatives were rejected, every effort was to be made by all the means at disposal to destroy the French ships at Mers-el-Kebir, the naval harbour at Oran, but particularly the two battle-cruisers *Dunkerque* and *Strasbourg*. These latter, completed in 1937–38, were ships of 26,500 tons with armaments of eight 13-inch and sixteen 5·1-inch guns. With their speed of $29\frac{1}{2}$ knots they were faster than any battle-cruisers we possessed except possibly the *Hood*.

This operation was entrusted to Vice-Admiral (the late Admiral of the Fleet) Sir James F. Somerville with a force consisting of the *Hood*, the battleships *Valiant* and *Resolution*, the aircraft-carrier *Ark Royal*, two cruisers and eleven destroyers.

On June 29th, I received a signal informing me that it was under consideration to seize the French ships at Alexandria simultaneously with the operation at Oran, the earliest date for which was the morning of July 3rd. I was asked for my views as to the best procedure to be followed to achieve this purpose with the minimum risk of bloodshed and hostilities on the part of the French. Immediately after the operation at Alexandria had been completed, it was stated to be desirable to deal with French ships at Sfax in a similar manner to those at Oran.

That I had strong views on the whole operation goes without saying. To me the idea was utterly repugnant. The officers and men in the French squadron were our friends. We had had many most cordial social contacts with them, and they had fought alongside us. Vice-Admiral Godfroy, moreover, was a man of honour in whom we could place implicit faith. Suddenly and without warning to attack and board his ships, and in the course of it probably to inflict many casualties on his sailors, appeared to me to be an act of sheer treachery which was as injudicious as it was unnecessary.

Violence of this sort would undoubtedly alienate the sympathies of the large French population in Egypt and the Middle East, both highly important to us, and in particular those in the Suez Canal area, whose goodwill and assistance were essential to its operation. Moreover, if those in the French fleet became aware that the forcible seizure of their ships was contemplated it could only result in strong resistance, severe casualties on both sides, and the sinking of their vessels in the most awkward berths. Our ships might also be damaged, which we could ill afford in a fleet by no means too strong *vis-à-vis* the Italians.

It appeared certain to me that the whole question at Alexandria could be settled by negotiation. The French could not go to sea without our consent. The pressure of lack of supplies, pay for the ships' companies, and the urgent wish of his men, particularly the reservists, to go home to France to protect their families, was bound to bring the French Admiral to terms in a short time.

While, of course I cannot pretend to be aware, or to be any judge, of the tense feeling in Great Britain which had prompted so drastic a decision against the French fleet at Oran, it was my considered opinion at the time that it was almost inept in its unwisdom. It would at once add to our enemies, and later on, when the war turned in our favour, as I never doubted it would, and we wanted all the help the French could give us, they might well remember our action against their fleet and the slaughter of their sailors and refuse to help us.

I could not believe that the French would surrender their fleet to the Germans or Italians. The terms of the armistice did not require it, though I believe the Italians demanded that the ships should return to French metropolitan ports. To me it was unthinkable that Admiral Darlan, who had spent all his life and energy in building up the fleet, would tamely deliver it to the enemy. The fact that the main units had already left France and were assembled in African ports seemed to bear out this view. Nothing that has happened in the intervening years has altered my opinion, and some of the views that I expressed in June, 1940, were proved amply true during the landings in North Africa in November, 1942.

I summed up all these arguments in a message sent to the Admiralty on the morning of June 30th:

> I cannot see what benefit is to be derived from forcible seizure of ships in Alexandria, and am most strongly opposed to the proposal. Request urgent consideration of the following points.
>
> 1. Apparently situation at Alexandria is quite different from that elsewhere in Mediterranean. . . .
>
> 2. If ships are to be seized, what is the object? If it is to prevent ships falling into enemy hands, that has already been achieved.
>
> 3. I am convinced that the French would resist most strongly, so that if it is desired to obtain ships for our own use it is unlikely to be achieved by forcible seizure. Such action would be more likely to result in ships being scuttled at their moorings, a harbour filled with wrecks and unnecessary British and French casualties.
>
> 4. Moreover, the effect is likely to be disastrous in the Middle East, particularly in the Suez Canal and at Djibuti, where French co-operation is vitally important, and in Syria, whose friendly attitude is very necessary.
>
> 5. On the other hand, it is quite likely that if things are allowed to go on as they are, the ships may drop into our hands under pressure of lack of pay and food. . . .
>
> 6. However, this appreciation makes no allowance for the repercussions which would follow the use of force at Oran. I am strongly opposed to such action there if it can possibly be avoided. I am not in full possession of the facts, but may remark that the whole of the friendly French element may be alienated, and in particular I would mention the effect in North Africa where friendly attitude may greatly affect naval operations later on.

7. No reports of French ships at Sfax have reached me. Request information. Owing to critical ammunition situation I am unwilling to engage my cruisers in any action except against the enemy.

To this message a reply was received from the Admiralty on July 1st which certainly appeared to be more consistent with the realities of the situation. Briefly, I was told that we should like to obtain the French ships at Alexandria for our own use if it could be done without bloodshed. Personnel who chose to serve on would receive Royal Naval rates of pay and conditions of service, and the others would be repatriated.

If we could not obtain the ships for our use they must be dealt with in one of the following ways, the first being preferable.

First. The ships to remain at Alexandria with skeleton crews, but immediately to be put in a non-seagoing condition, on the understanding that we should only use them if the Germans or Italians broke the terms of the Armistice. The British Government would be responsible for the pay and upkeep of personnel and ships. If Admiral Godfroy insisted that the ships should be demilitarized before he left them I could accept this condition.

Second. The ships were to be sunk at sea.

I was further directed to put these alternatives to the French Admiral at 7 a.m. on July 3rd, laying the emphasis on our desire to keep them in the struggle with us. The hour of seven o'clock was chosen as the action against the French fleet at Oran was timed to take place early on July 3rd. A further message from the Admiralty ordered that my negotiations should be completed before dark on the same day.

As I was receiving all the messages sent by the Admiralty to the Flag Officer, Force 'H', Sir James Somerville, I was also well acquainted with his orders for the operation at Oran. As the details of that unfortunate incident are already well-known, I need not repeat them here.

II

Tuesday, July 2nd, was a day of tense anxiety. It had to be spent in acquainting all the British Flag Officers and captains with what was afoot, and also making preparations for attempting to seize the French ships if the Home Government insisted upon it. I also invited the French Vice-Admiral to visit me at 7 a.m. next morning, an unusual hour which must have caused him to realize that something momentous was about to happen.

Vice-Admiral Godfroy arrived punctually, accompanied by his Chief of Staff, and was piped over the side with our Royal Marine guard and band paraded. I received him, with the usual officers in attendance. Accompanied by my Chief of Staff, Rear-Admiral Algernon Willis, and Commander R. M. Dick, we went below. The meeting took place in my after cabin in the *Warspite*, with all of us sitting in armchairs instead of round a table. The proceedings were entirely formal. We spoke English, except in so far that Commander Dick interpreted if there was any likelihood of misunderstanding. Vice-Admiral Godfroy's demeanour was entirely helpful and cordial, though we could realize, and see, the strain under which he was labouring.

A message from the British Government was read to the Admiral and he was given a copy. It expressed the desire that his ships would fight on with us. He seemed to accept the force of the argument and made no comment, except to say he would have preferred to have this from his own Government.

I then explained that I had been instructed by the British Government to lay before him various proposals for the disposal of the French Squadron, and that I must ask him to accept one or other of them that day. The first proposal was:

> The British Government asks you to put at their disposition the Naval units under your command so that they can continue the struggle against the enemy side by side with the British Navy.
>
> For those who wish to join us the conditions of service and pay will be the same as that of officers, petty officers and men of corresponding rank in the British Navy. Those who do not wish to continue the fight are entirely free to return to France and arrangements will be made as soon as practicable for them to do so.
>
> You are asked to announce these proposals in such a way that they are known to all officers and ships' companies and to make it clear that they are free to make their choice without any constraint.
>
> The British Government guarantees to return to France at the end of the war all ships which have thus taken part with us in the struggle against the enemy.

Admiral Godfroy raised many objections to this alternative, and said he could not possibly accept it without consulting his Government. How, he asked, could their ships fight except under the French flag? The officers and men would be deserters. Furthermore, if he used any of his ships for the war he felt sure that the Germans and Italians would demand an equivalent number of ships of the same class to be handed over to them.

At this stage I pointed out to Godfroy that the terms were good, and that I could, if I wished, communicate them to the French squadron over his head; but naturally preferred not to take this step. Godfroy admitted that he was fully aware of this.

During further discussion, I frequently impressed on Godfroy that surely his object was not only to prevent his ships from falling into the hands of the enemy, but also to preserve them for France. This evidently had a strong effect. However, there seemed to be no prospect of his accepting the conditions outlined.

We passed on to the second proposal:

> If you remain convinced that it is not possible to allow your forces to help the British Navy, the British Government asks you to put your ships in a condition in which they cannot go to sea, and leave on board only skeleton crews sufficient to keep the ships in good order.
>
> In this case the British Government guarantees the pay and supplies for the officers and men thus left on board, and that the ships will only be used if the enemy breaks the terms of the armistice concluded between France, Germany and Italy.

Godfroy brightened up considerably when he read this, and at once intimated that he thought he could accept it. He expressed the desire to have a little time to think it over, and when offered until, say, 1 p.m., said: "Oh, sooner than that." The hour of 11.30 a.m. was agreed to.

The Vice-Admiral was then shown the third proposal:

> If these proposals are neither of them acceptable, the British Government asks you as a third alternative to order your forces in Alexandria to sea in order to sink them outside the port in deep waters.

This evoked no enthusiasm, and when I pointed out that it would in no sense achieve his main object of preserving his ships for France, he agreed to revert to the consideration of the second proposal. He demurred somewhat at the idea of the crews being removed from his ships, and at the back of his mind evidently had strong hopes that the Italians would break the armistice and that he would be able to get into the fight again.

I concluded the meeting, which ended at about 8.30 a.m. by impressing on Godfroy that he must make up his mind by himself and by the end of the morning. I also intimated with all the tact I could muster that it was a case of *force majeure*, and that he could honourably accept either one or other of the three proposals. I added my personal hope that if it could not be the first it would be the second.

Godfroy and his Chief-of-Staff then returned to the French flagship, the 10,000 ton cruiser *Duquesne*.

As a result of this interview we felt distinctly optimistic, and I signalled to the Admiralty saying that the negotiations so far indicated that Vice-Admiral Godfroy was likely to accept the second proposal, that of putting his ships in a condition in which they could not go to sea. I expected his definite answer at noon.

III

All this time I had been aware that Sir James Somerville was already negotiating with the French Admiral Gensoul at Mers-el-Kebir at the other end of the Mediterranean. I was naturally most apprehensive of our success if Somerville was compelled to use force, and the news of it reached Godfroy.

At noon I received his reply to the three proposals in a letter written in French. It came as a bitter disappointment, for he accepted the third alternative, that of sinking his ships. He wrote, in so many words, that it was incompatible with his military duty to allow his ships to fight with ours.

He felt inclined to accept the second proposal if he could recommend it to his superiors, presumably the French Admiralty, who alone could authorize him to disarm his ships in a foreign port under constraint by a foreign authority. If he were forbidden to discuss the matter with his superiors, he was reduced to choosing the third solution, regrettable though it might be for the future, because this and this only, in the conditions that existed, was compatible with their sense of naval honour.

In a separate communication he asked for forty-eight hours grace to make suitable arrangements for the safety and transport of his crews.

I at once replied in an official, personal letter saying I had received his decision with profound regret. I added:

> My instructions leave me with no alternative but to accept your choice to take your ships to sea and to sink them in open waters.
>
> I am prepared to accept the delay of forty-eight hours during which you are making arrangements for the safety and transport of your ships' companies and will gladly facilitate any action you wish taken in this respect.
>
> I am therefore under the painful necessity of asking you to proceed to sea to carry out your purpose at 1200 on Friday, 5th July.

While this appeared to settle the question of the French squadron, most unsatisfactorily it is true, it did not satisfy the desire of the British Government that the squadron should be incapable of action by dark that night. We were also dissatisfied that Godfroy had accepted the third choice, when he had so nearly accepted the second. To us it seemed certain that if his ships could be preserved in a demilitarized condition they would eventually rejoin us or fall into our hands. In either case they would not be lost to France. One more effort had therefore to be made to try and meet all these considerations. One of the principal stumbling blocks was the removal of the majority of the French crews.

So I wrote Godfroy a further letter, a private one to him personally, in which I said I had been casting round in my mind for some solution to the terrible impasse. I understood that he was primarily concerned with the fact that it was incompatible with his duty to remove the crews from his ships. Did not the solution lie in a compromise? If he could make a gesture, which indeed he had already offered to do, it would allow the British Government to realize that his ships would not proceed to sea, and that even now we might prevent a disaster as painful to myself as to him. Would he be prepared to give orders to remove the oil from his ships, and to take the warheads off the torpedoes? The question of the retention or otherwise of the crews could be discussed later. Though he would appreciate that I wrote this appeal personally and privately, it could not affect the measures he would be putting in hand in accordance with his formal decision. I should greatly appreciate Admiral Godfroy's immediate reply.

He agreed to discharge the oil and to remove the warheads without further demur, and by 5.30 p.m. the French ships were already discharging their oil fuel.

All these moves were duly reported to the Admiralty during the afternoon.

All through that day, July 3rd, we lived in a state of painful suspense and anxiety. Reports were coming in from Sir James Somerville's Force 'H' which indicated that the negotiations with the French at Mers-el-Kebir were not having a successful issue. Finally, we became aware that Somerville had been forced to open fire. The tenor of his signals to the Admiralty during that fateful afternoon gave a clear impression of his utter repugnance at having to carry out his drastic orders.

At 8.15 p.m. we received a signal from the Admiralty indicating that they were most dissatisfied with the efforts we had made up-to-date. It read:

> Admiralty note that oil fuel is being discharged by French ships. Reduction of crews, especially by ratings, should however begin at once by landing or transfer to merchant ships, before dark tonight. Do not, repeat NOT, fail.

It is a perfect example of the type of signal which should never be made. Apart from being quite unhelpful, it showed no comprehension whatever of the explosive atmosphere at Alexandria or the difficult conditions in which we were working. It filled me with indignation. Moreover, while ordering us to take action before dark, it was sent off from the Admiralty at a time which was after sunset at Alexandria. As it was impossible to implement it we ignored it completely. At the time I did not believe that signal emanated in the Admiralty, and do not believe it now.

I assembled the Flag Officers on board the *Warspite* that evening and made them aware of the situation. I also told them it was **not** my intention to take action on this latest Admiralty signal, and was happy to find that all of them, without exception, were in complete agreement with me.

Just after I received the Admiralty message to which I took such exception, I received a formal note from Vice-Admiral Godfroy written in French in his own handwriting:

Admiral,

I have just learnt that an ultimatum has been addressed to our Atlantic Fleet by the British Admiralty.

On the other hand my Admiralty has ordered me to sail, though I have demanded to be assured that the order is authentic.

I have replied that sailing is impossible, but that the situation is definitely changing.

So that I may not incur reproach for having discharged oil-fuel after receiving an order to sail, I have stopped the discharge of oil-fuel pending events.

But that changes nothing. I give you my word as to my intentions, which remain unchanged from those which I expressed to you in writing this morning.

The Chief of Staff, Rear-Admiral Willis, went on board the French flagship to reason with Vice-Admiral Godfroy. It was a long and most painful interview; but no amount of persuasion or threats of force made any impression at all upon Godfroy. Having heard of the ultimatum given to the French ships at Mers-el-Kebir, and having received a direct order from his Admiralty to proceed to sea using force if necessary, he now flatly declined to continue discharging oil or to remove any of his men. He further refused to proceed to sea voluntarily and sink his ships in deep water, and asserted that if he were allowed out of harbour he would run for it, though he fully realized this would lead to a battle. Nothing would move him, though he was quite resigned to remaining at Alexandria with his crews on board. He was emphatic in stating that if faced with any demand backed by force he would scuttle his ships in the harbour, at the same time intimating that he would do so in a manner as convenient to us as possible.

After all our negotiations the night of July 3rd found us back where we had started. All that was now in our favour was that we knew Godfroy would not force a fight, and would not in any circumstances hamper us in our operations against the Italians. Nevertheless, in deference to the wishes of the British Government, and the fact that we could not take our fleet to sea before the French squadron was immobilized, the situation could not be allowed to remain uncertain.

Three courses of action were open to us:

1. To attempt to seize the French ships by boarding.

2. To sink them by gun and torpedo fire at their moorings.

3. To face Vice-Admiral Godfroy with a demand to intern or surrender his ships with the result that he would sink them.

We rejected 'one' out of hand, as doubtful of success, the French being now thoroughly on the alert.

We also rejected 'two' as being likely to lead to useless bloodshed on both sides, besides causing the probable sinking of French ships in awkward places in a crowded harbour, with possible damage to our own.

So in signalling a brief account of these events and an appreciation of the situation to the Admiralty soon after midnight on July 3rd–4th, I informed them that I proposed to put the third course of action into operation on the morning of Friday, July 5th. The delay was unfortunate and had to be regretted; but arrangements had to be made for shipping about 4,000 French seamen.

In the small hours of July 4th we retired to bed, much fatigued and worried.

IV

Events moved considerably faster than we anticipated. What happened on board the ships of the French squadron during the night I do not know; but it was evident that Vice-Admiral Godfroy had received a full account of the action against the French ships at Mers-el-Kebir. Just before 7 a.m. on July 4th I was awakened by being given another letter from him, in which he repudiated each and every undertaking he had given, reserved to himself complete liberty of action, and left me in no doubt that he proposed to try and get to sea, if necessary by fighting his way out of harbour.

I went on deck at once, and sure enough the French ships were raising steam. By the appearance of their armaments they were cleared for action. The crisis had come. There now seemed to be no chance of evading what I wished at all costs to avoid, a battle in Alexandria harbour.

We, of course, were not behindhand in our preparations. Where necessary our battleships were kedged round to bring their broadsides to bear. Our destroyers and submarines were warned off to torpedo the French ships at once if they moved from their berths or opened fire.

One chance only remained. I knew it would take the French ships six to eight hours to raise steam and be ready to move, so this short space of time was vouchsafed to us to take what measures we could to induce Vice-Admiral Godfroy to see reason. We decided to appeal to his officers and ships' companies over his head and suborn them from their allegiance to him. It was a most distasteful task; but the only possible thing to do.

Commander Dick's fluent French was again brought into play, and a message was composed addressed to all the French officers and men. In it we set out the helplessness of their situation; our sincere desire not to fight with or kill any of them if they tried to get away; and the generous terms the British Government offered which we assured them could be accepted without loss of dignity or honour. This was flashed several times to every ship, and though we received no acknowledgment we knew very well that their signalmen could and would take it in, and that its purport would be discussed. The same message was written on large blackboards which were taken round the French squadron in boats, so that all the ships' companies could read it.

Every French ship had a British opposite number to look after her, and the captains of those of our ships lying next the French were directed to go on board the vessels for which they were responsible, and to reason with their captains. This measure, combined with the messages, had an excellent effect. It very soon became apparent that not all the officers agreed with Godfroy in his obduracy. Indeed, the captain of the French cruiser lying near the *Neptune* received Captain Rory O'Conor with the greatest cordiality, saying as he went on board: "When I saw the tompions being removed from your guns, I immediately ordered the tompions to be placed in mine." Captain Philip Mack's powers of persuasion won round the French destroyers without much difficulty, while Captain H. T. Baillie-Grohman of the *Ramillies*, boarded the battleship *Lorraine*, and Captain I. B. B. Tower, of the *Malaya* and others, more of the French ships.

During the morning, as we watched, it was interesting to see the leaven gradually working among the French sailors. In most of their ships big meetings were held on the forecastle, in one case on the quarterdeck, and we could usually see ratings haranguing their shipmates. We also noticed the French captains visiting Vice-Admiral Godfroy in the *Duquesne*. The French liaison officer, Commander, now Vice-Admiral Auboyneau, worked tirelessly to bring about a peaceful settlement. One of our staff officers had managed to get through to him by telephone.

The morning passed in suspense. Then, after luncheon, we saw all the French captains go on board Godfroy's flagship. About an hour later he signalled his desire to come on board to see me. During his visit he conducted himself with great dignity, and the upshot of our meeting was that he yielded to overwhelming force. We concluded an immediate agreement on the following terms:

(a) All oil fuel to be discharged from the French ships forthwith.

(b) Ships to be placed immediately in a condition in which they cannot fight.

(c) Discharge of ships' companies to be a matter for further discussion; but it was agreed they should be reduced.

Never in my life have I experienced such a whole-hearted feeling of thankful relief as on the conclusion of this agreement, and the same was felt by every officer and man in our fleet. We had all been desperately anxious to avoid any sort of a conflict with our late Allies. A large share of the credit must go to those of our captains who boarded the French ships and prevailed upon their opposite numbers.

After a short informative message sent off to the Admiralty at about 3.30 p.m., July 4th, I made a more detailed signal later in the day. Though it repeats much of what I have already written, I will quote it in its entirety:

1. Although most undesirable to have a battle in Alexandria harbour, the situation became such that the threat of sinking the French ships at their moorings had to be made.

2. Signals to all ships and personal visits by the British captains were made during this forenoon with the object of influencing the officers and men against useless resistance to overwhelming force.

3. These proved successful as at a post-prandial meeting the captains of the French ships persuaded Godfroy to accept the conditions.

4. Ships are now discharging oil fuel. Tomorrow they will land the obturating pads of all large guns including spares and firing mechanism of small guns together with all warhead pistols. These will be in custody of French Consulate-General with rights of inspection.

5. Godfroy has already requested the Ministry of Marine by signal to make arrangements for the reception of the ships' companies, and I will press for their departure. I am counting on this being hastened by economic pressure and the example of the reservists.

6. With the completion of the above de-fuelling and de-arming measures I shall feel quite free to take the Fleet to sea to continue operations against the enemy.

7. It is assumed that it is not now intended to carry out operations against the few minor French units in Sfax and Susa.

A few hours later I received a personal message from the First Lord and the First Sea Lord:

> After what must have been a most trying and anxious time your negotiations have achieved complete success. We offer you our most sincere congratulations. The Prime Minister also wishes his congratulations to be sent to you.

V

One cannot withold a measure of admiration for Vice-Admiral Godfroy who, throughout this painful episode, and placed in an unprecedented and most difficult situation, conducted himself as an honourable if obstinate man.

In the long and weary months that were to follow he remained on board his flagship and seldom went ashore. The fate of France and the tragedy of Mers-el-Kebir were always in his mind; but no success of the British fleet passed without his letter of cordial congratulation, no loss without his letter of sympathy. I feel sure that in his heart he yearned to be fighting with us.

In a letter of May 2nd, 1941, after our evacuation from Greece, he wrote to me:

> Since we cannot fire our guns during these bombing attacks, we are reduced to watch. It is a pity we can do nothing, because our excellent stereoscopic range-finders would be very valuable at night when hostile aircraft are unlighted by searchlights. But we shall use our small guns and machine-guns against dive-bombers if they seem to fly against us. My thoughts were with you during all these last days we have passed. . . . In spite of the fact that many things are turning more difficult for us here, I try to remain patient in that long ordeal. The idea of your understanding so well our situation helps me.

The crews of Vice-Admiral Godfroy's ships had been reduced by something like 70 per cent. Instead of the deterioration to be expected from enforced idleness his men remained well-disciplined and smart. Many attempts were made by the Free French elements ashore to sow suspicion and discord, and accusations were made that Godfroy was secretly re-embarking the vital parts of the mechanism of his guns that had been landed in accordance with our agreement. On investigation all these accusations were found to be without one scintilla of truth.

After the landings in North Africa in November, 1942, I think Godfroy made a great mistake in remaining too long aloof. Perhaps two-and-a-half years of loneliness and inactivity had produced some sort of fixation in his mind. Neither the persuasions of Admiral Sir Henry Harwood, then Commander-in-Chief, Mediterranean, nor our emissaries from Algiers with pressing letters from myself, were of any avail. The lessons that he could be persuaded, but not coerced, were forgotten. Economic measures taken against his squadron in Alexandria only served to increase his obstinacy.

Finally, but very late in the day, he brought his ships into action with us. I saw him again in Algiers in the spring of 1943, and am glad to know that he now lives in comfortable retirement in the South of France.

CHAPTER XXII

I

It took a few days to get the crews of the French ships reduced to the 30 per cent finally agreed upon; but by July 7th the remainder had been sent away in French transports. We were greatly relieved. Our fleet could now be taken to sea for offensive operations against the Italians without any apprehension of trouble at Alexandria.

I was greatly exercised by the situation of Malta, where the ugly spectre of shortages, if not of actual starvation, was already rearing its head. As I have already pointed out, the Navy had always regarded the island as the keystone of victory in the Mediterranean, and considered it should be held at all costs. It had its first-class dockyard for the refit and repair of the heaviest ships, and was amply stocked with naval stores and ammunition.

The Army and Royal Air Force, however, did not take the same view. Malta they considered, could not be held and defended against continual air attack from Sicily, and possible invasion. This is not to criticize. In 1939 there was not the close understanding and interrelation between the three Services that came into being during the war, and is regarded as natural today. Navy, Army and Air Force were all short of men and material, and each was inclined to regard any particular problem from its own point of view.

Malta is one of the most densely-populated areas in Europe, and its teeming inhabitants had to be fed. In peacetime much of the food and supplies for the civil population arrived in small craft from Italy, Sicily and Tunisia. Heavier items came in larger vessels which did not linger for more than a few hours. It was a sort of hand-to-mouth system, and Malta had no organization or equipment for the rapid handling of heavy bulk cargoes. Moreover, while the Navy and Army had built up and accumulated sufficient supplies in case the island were cut off and virtually besieged, the civil authorities for one reason and another had made no such provision.

We were presented with a pressing and most unpleasant problem, when, within a few weeks of the outbreak of war with Italy, Malta was already beginning to run short.

In consultation with the Governor it was decided as a first step to remove at the earliest possible date all *'les bouches inutiles'* that we could get away. Among these, of course, were my wife and two nieces, and all the wives and children of the naval men who by this time had been scattered to the four corners of the earth. As a result of the Italian bombing there were naturally a large number of others who also wished to find a safer location.

Shipping was available in Malta in the shape of the *El Nil*, a medium-sized passenger liner of the Khedivial Line; the *Knight of Malta*; and an Italian prize, the *Rodi*, which was loaded up with all the Italian prisoners of war who had been brought to the island. It was also decided to bring out in four slow ships a considerable quantity of naval stores badly needed at Alexandria. Two convoys were to be formed, one fast and the other slow, and both were to proceed under cover of the whole fleet.

II

The fleet sailed from Alexandria late in the evening of July 7th, all ships being clear of the harbour by midnight. It consisted of the *Warspite*, *Malaya* and *Royal Sovereign*; the aircraft-carrier *Eagle*; the cruisers *Orion*, *Neptune*, *Sydney*, *Gloucester* and *Liverpool*; with seventeen destroyers. Two submarines were encountered just after our departure, both being attacked by the destroyer *Hasty*, though with what result I cannot say. The rest of the night passed without incident.

Shortly after 8 a.m. on July 8th we had a report from the submarine *Phoenix* to say that at 5.15 a.m. she had sighted two enemy battleships and four destroyers in a position roughly two hundred miles to the eastward of Malta. They were steering south, which led us to suppose they might be covering an important convoy to Libya. The Vice-Admiral, Malta, was thereupon directed to arrange for a flying-boat to shadow this force. Meanwhile we were steering to the north-westward at 20 knots.

This passage of ours was to be a very different matter from our peaceful excursion of the month before. The Italians were becoming active, and throughout July 8th all units of the fleet met with fairly heavy bombing attacks by Italian aircraft from the Dodecanese. The only casualty, but a serious one, was a hit on the *Gloucester*'s bridge, which killed Captain F. R. Garside and seventeen others, and necessitated the ship being steered and fought from the after control position.

Here let me settle once and for all the question of the efficiency of the Italian bombing and general air work over the sea experienced by the fleet in 1940–41. To us at the time it appeared that they had some squadrons specially trained for anti-ship work. Their reconnaissance was highly efficient, and seldom failed to find and report our ships at sea. The bombers invariably arrived within an hour or two. They carried out high-level attacks from about 12,000 feet, pressed home in formation in the face of the heavy anti-aircraft fire of the fleet, and for this type of attack their accuracy was very good. We were fortunate to escape being hit.

In all, during our five days at sea on this occasion, the *Warspite* and the five destroyers with her were attacked thirty-four times in four days, something over four hundred bombs being dropped. Particularly do I remember a most virulent attack on July 12th during our return passage to Alexandria when twenty-four heavy bombs fell along the port side of the ship simultaneously, with another dozen on our starboard bow, all within two hundred yards, but slightly out for line. Other ships had much the same sort of experience. On this day I saw the *Sydney*, which was in company, completely disappear in a line of towering pillars of spray as high as church steeples. When she emerged I signalled: "Are you all right?" to which came the rather dubious reply from that stout-hearted Australian, Captain J. A. Collins, now a Flag Officer in the Royal Australian Navy, "I hope so."

It is not too much to say of those early months that the Italians high-level bombing was the best I have ever seen, far better than the German. Later, when our anti-aircraft fire improved and the trained squadrons of the Regia Aeronautica came to be knocked about by our fleet fighters, their air work over the sea deteriorated. But I shall always remember it with respect. There was some consolation in realizing that there was always more water than ship. Nevertheless, one felt very naked and unprotected.

At 3.10 p.m. on July 8th, a flying-boat from Malta again reported two enemy battleships, six cruisers and seven destroyers steering southward in a position about a hundred miles north-west of Benghazi. An hour later they had swung round to a northerly course. This, coupled with the intensive bombing, rather gave us the impression that the Italians wished to keep us out of the Central Mediterranean, and that the ships reported were, indeed, covering an important convoy to or from Benghazi. We had a chance to cut them off, so it was decided temporarily to abandon the operations in hand, and to move towards Taranto at our best speed to get between the enemy and his base.

The night passed without incident, and at dawn on July 9th, the *Eagle* flew off three aircraft to reconnoitre. However, it was at about 7.30 a.m. that another flying-boat from Malta again reported the enemy fleet to the westward at a distance from us of about a hundred and forty-five miles. They were some fifty miles from Cape Spartivento, on the toe of Italy, and further reports during the forenoon from the flying-boats and the *Eagle's* aircraft showed that an Italian fleet of at least two battleships, twelve cruisers and numerous destroyers was out. They were scattered over a wide area. We were closing them rapidly. At about noon they were ninety miles to the westward.

It was not quite the moment I would have chosen to give battle. They had a large number of cruisers, and we, because the damaged *Gloucester* was not fit to engage in serious fighting, had no more than four, which had little more than 50 per cent of their ammunition remaining. Moreover, the speed of approach was limited by the maximum speed of the *Royal Sovereign*.

However, any opportunity was welcome, and the *Warspite* was soon pushing on in support of our cruisers, which, with no 8-inch gun ships, were heavily outgunned and outnumbered by the Italian.

I will not go into the full details of this action, which has been described at length in my despatch published as a supplement to the *London Gazette* of 27th April, 1948. But it was curious in that it followed almost exactly the lines of the battles we used to fight out on the table at the Tactical School at Portsmouth, a tribute to the nature of the studies and instruction received there. First we had the contact of long-range reconnaissance aircraft; then the exact positioning of the enemy relative to our own fleet by the Fleet Air Arm aircraft from the carrier, and the informative and accurate reports of their trained observers. Next the carrier's striking force of torpedo-bombers went in to attack, though on this occasion, through no fault of theirs, they were not successful. Meanwhile the cruisers, spread on a line of bearing, pushed in to locate the enemy's battle fleet, and finally the heavy ships themselves came into action.

The breeze was in the north-west, with a slight sea and a sky dappled with thin cloud. The visibility was fifteen to twenty miles when, between 2.52 and 3 p.m. the *Orion* and *Neptune* sighted enemy destroyers and cruisers. Vice-Admiral Tovey's four ships were about ten miles ahead of the *Warspite*. About ten miles astern of us came the *Royal Sovereign* and *Malaya* screened by nine destroyers, with the *Eagle* and two more destroyers proceeding to take up a position ten miles east of the *Warspite*. The damaged *Gloucester*, turning back from the cruisers ahead, had been ordered to join the *Eagle*.

At 3.8 the *Neptune*, Captain Rory O'Conor, sighted the Italian heavy ships, and was the first British warship to signal "Enemy battle fleet in sight" in the Mediterranean since the time of Nelson, a great moment for the *Neptune*. Six minutes later a column of four enemy 8-inch cruisers opened fire, and Vice-Admiral Tovey's four ships replied. Meanwhile we had sighted the enemy advanced forces from the *Warspite*, and had opened fire at a range of 26,400 yards on one of the ships engaging our 7th Cruiser Squadron.

The *Orion*, *Neptune*, *Liverpool* and *Sydney*, greatly outnumbered and under very heavy fire, were magnificently handled by Vice-Admiral Tovey, though it required a few salvoes of 15-inch from the *Warspite* to redress the balance when the enemy's preponderance became too pressing.

At 3.30 the enemy turned away under a smoke-screen and fire was checked. The *Warspite*, steaming 24½ knots, turned a complete circle to allow the *Malaya* to catch up. A few minutes later we fired a few salvoes at two cruisers, which were trying to work round to the east to get at the *Eagle*; but the great moment came when at 3.53 the *Warspite* opened fire on the leading enemy battleship at a range of 26,000 yards. Both the Italian battleships replied. They shot well and straddled us at this great range; but the culminating point of the engagement soon came. The *Warspite's* shooting was consistently

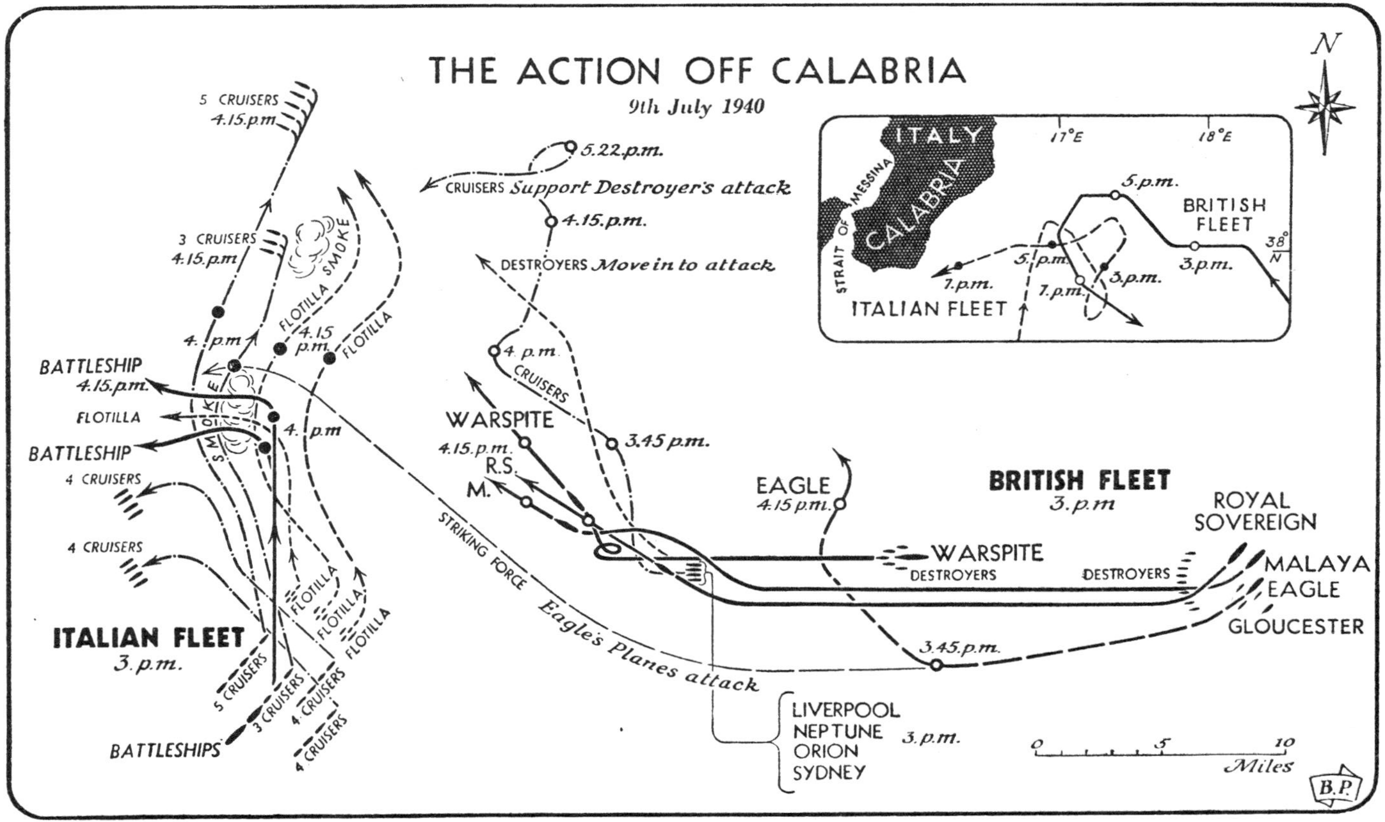

THE ACTION OFF CALABRIA
9th July 1940
N
ITALY
CALABRIA
STRAIT OF MESSINA
17°E
18°E
38° N
BRITISH FLEET
ITALIAN FLEET
5.p.m.
3.p.m.
7.p.m.
5.p.m.
3.p.m.
7.p.m.
5 CRUISERS 4.15.p.m.
3 CRUISERS 4.15.p.m.
5.22.p.m.
CRUISERS Support Destroyer's attack
4.15.p.m.
DESTROYERS Move in to attack
4.p.m.
FLOTILLA SMOKE
4.15 p.m.
FLOTILLA
BATTLESHIP 4.15.p.m.
FLOTILLA
BATTLESHIP
4.p.m
SMOKE
4 CRUISERS
4 CRUISERS
FLOTILLA
FLOTILLA
FLOTILLA
ITALIAN FLEET
3.p.m.
5 CRUISERS
3 CRUISERS
4 CRUISERS
4 CRUISERS
BATTLESHIPS
4.p.m.
CRUISERS
3.45 p.m.
WARSPITE
4.15.p.m.
R.S.
M.
STRIKING FORCE
Eagle's Planes attack
EAGLE
4.15 p.m.
BRITISH FLEET
3.p.m
WARSPITE
DESTROYERS
DESTROYERS
ROYAL SOVEREIGN
MALAYA
EAGLE
GLOUCESTER
3.45.p.m.
LIVERPOOL
NEPTUNE
ORION
SYDNEY
3.p.m.
0 5 10
Miles
B.P.

good. I had been watching the great splashes of our 15-inch salvoes straddling the target when, at 4 p.m., I saw the great orange-coloured flash of a heavy explosion at the base of the enemy flagship's funnels. It was followed by an upheaval of smoke, and I knew that she had been heavily hit at the prodigious range of thirteen miles.

This was too much for the Italian Admiral, my old friend Riccardi, whom I had entertained in the *Hood* in 1938, and who kept *The Life of Nelson* on his bed-table. His ships turned away, and having discharged seventeen salvoes in all, the *Warspite* ceased firing at 4.4, the whole western horizon being overlaid with a thick pall of smoke behind which the enemy became completely hidden. From this time until about 4.40 we, in the *Warspite*, engaged a cruiser at long range which disappeared behind a smoke-screen, and let go a few salvoes of 6-inch at enemy destroyers dodging in and out of the smoke.

Meanwhile, all our destroyers had been sent in to counter-attack, and by 4 p.m. were on the *Warspite's* disengaged bow moving joyously ahead at full speed, dodging the overs from the Italian battleships. A little later some of them were under heavy fire from enemy cruisers, and after a few more minutes, with the 7th Cruiser Squadron, they were engaging enemy destroyers. A few torpedo tracks were seen; but the Italian destroyer attacks were very half-hearted and never pressed home. Whether or not we contacted a submarine trap, I do not know. We saw nothing of any submarines.

One of the *Warspite's* aircraft, flown off during the action, stationed herself over the enemy flagship and kept us informed what was going on. The observer made not a few amusing signals, including one that the enemy fleet was left in considerable confusion, and that all units were making off at high speed to the west and south-west towards the Straits of Messina and Augusta. It was not until 6 p.m., he also told us, that the Italians had sorted themselves out, and in the meanwhile were attacked by their own bombers.

However, to hark back to about 4.40 p.m. I had no intention of plunging straight into the enemy's smoke-screen. We decided to work round to windward and to the northward of it. Some of our destroyers were clear of it by 5 o'clock; but the enemy was out of sight.

Meanwhile the Regia Aeronautica came into action, some hundreds of them. Between 4.40 and 7.25 we endured a series of heavy attacks by large bomber formations. All ships received attention, though perhaps the *Eagle* and *Warspite*, being unmistakable, were rather specially singled out as targets, each being attacked five times. It was most frightening. At times a ship would completely disappear behind the great splashes, to emerge as though from a dark, thick wood of enormous fir trees. I was seriously alarmed for the old ships *Royal Sovereign* and *Eagle*, which were not well protected. A clutch of those eggs hitting either must have sent her to the bottom.

I shall always remember the *Eagle*, Captain A. R. M. Bridge. She played a great part during the approach and subsequent action, and never have there been more skilful or gallant fliers than those young men who manned her seventeen Swordfish; never has better work been done than by those who kept them in the air. Although they did not succeed in hitting a battleship, they hit a cruiser, and carried out a prodigious amount of work between 4 a.m. and sunset. Constant reconnaissance and search, with the launching of two striking forces with that small number of air-crews and aircraft was an astonishing performance. The next day a third striking force was flown off to attack shipping in Augusta, and succeeded in sinking a destroyer.

The action was most unsatisfactory to us. I suppose it was too much to expect the Italians to stake everything on a stand-up fight. Yet, if they had timed their attacks better with all the types of arms they employed they might have given us much trouble. The one 15-inch hit they sustained from the *Warspite* had a moral effect quite out of proportion to the damage. Never again did they willingly face up to the fire of British battleships, though on several subsequent occasions they were in a position to give battle with a great preponderance in force.

By 5.35 our fleet was within twenty-five miles of the coast of Calabria. As there was no hope of re-engaging the enemy before they reached the Straits of Messina we altered course for a position south of Malta. Nothing occurred during the night, and the next morning, July 10th, the *Royal Sovereign* and destroyers were sent in in turn to fuel.

The Vice-Admiral at Malta had been told to delay the sailing of the convoys for Alexandria. However, on hearing that the fleets were engaged he wisely decided that the Italians would be too busy to attend to convoys, so sailed the fast convoy, consisting of the *El Nil*, *Knight of Malta* and *Rodi*, at 11 p.m. on the night of the 9th. It was escorted by four destroyers.

We remained cruising to the southward of Malta until 8 a.m. on the 11th, at which time we were rejoined by the *Royal Sovereign* and destroyers. As I had to get back to Alexandria for an important conference at Cairo I pushed on at 19 knots in the *Warspite* with four destroyers, leaving Rear-Admiral Pridham-Wippell in the *Royal Sovereign*, with the *Malaya*, *Eagle* and remaining destroyers, to bring on the slow convoy.

We had decided to try a more southerly route on our return journey to avoid the bombing we had experienced from the Dodecanese on our way west. We very soon found out our mistake. The inevitable shadowers appeared and called up the bombers from the Libyan airfields, and on July 11th we were heartily bombed until sunset. Rear-Admiral Pridham-Wippell had the same experience, though rather more of it. There was no damage and no casualties. The next day, July 12th, by which time the *Orion* and *Neptune* had gone ahead to join the fast convoy, and the *Liverpool* and *Sydney* had joined the *Warspite*, we had more bombing, and the attacks were rather heavier. With the exception of several casualties in the *Liverpool* through a near miss there was no damage.

Rear-Admiral Pridham-Wippell's party were able to retaliate to some extent against the Italian bombers. Three spare Fleet Air Arm Gladiator fighters from Alexandria had been embarked in the *Eagle* for this very purpose. In normal conditions she carried no fighters, and they could not be struck below. They had to be ranged on the flight deck. Nor had the *Eagle* any fighter pilots. But it so happened that the Commander (Flying), Charles L. Keighly-Peach, was an old fighter pilot, and he and another pilot took up the Gladiators. Keighly-Peach's first effort was not so happy, as he was shot through the thigh by an Italian bomber. Nothing daunted he went up again, and between them the *Eagle's* three fighter aircraft shot down a shadower and two or three bombers.

During the last stage of Pridham-Wippell's journey the Royal Air Force sent out Blenheim fighters which did good work. The Blenheims were normally bombers; but a few had been fitted out as fighters to get the long range.

The attention the Italians paid to the fleet and the slow convoy caused them entirely to overlook the fast convoy carrying the personnel from Malta. For that I was supremely thankful, as my wife and two nieces were on board. Their convoy arrived safely at Alexandria at 9 a.m. on July 13th, the *Warspite* having reached harbour three hours earlier. Knowing we had been in action, they were delighted to see the flagship, though somewhat perturbed to notice she was heeled over. In point of fact she had been purposely listed to examine the bulges to see if they had been damaged by near misses.

I was delighted to get my wife and the two girls out of Malta. Bombed practically every night and often by day, they had not enjoyed it. My wife had chalked up seventy-two raids from the day Italy entered the war until the time she left, a period of twenty-nine days. However, as I wrote home: "The two girls are as fresh as paint. Young Hilda seems to have done extremely well and has taken complete charge of a houseful of women and children in the dockyard area."

The *El Nil*, in which they had travelled, was full of passengers from Marseilles on their way to Egypt. They were bombed at Marseilles, and on arrival at Malta were virtually confined to the ship for nearly a month. The passengers from Malta had been ordered to be on board by 9 a.m. on July 9th, and the ship sailed fourteen hours later, packed with people. Among the passengers was the Bishop of Gibraltar, while the only man on board who knew anything about signalling, and whose services were in constant demand on the bridge, was a chaplain of the Royal Air Force. Their passage was not without incident. One night they were passed by large ships without lights, which were actually ours; but for all they knew might be Italian. There were sundry unexplained bumps at night, some of which shook the ship. They were probably depth charges dropped far away. Captain J. W. A. Waller, Royal Australian Navy, in the *Stuart*, was in charge of the destroyer escort, and took no chances at all. Day or night, on the least suspicion of a submarine contact, he made smoke screens and dropped full patterns of depth charges. As my wife described it when I saw her later, the destroyers were very attentive. After dropping their depth charges they clustered around the discoloured patches in the water for all the world "like terriers, sniffing round a rat-hole". It was a comforting sight.

I finally was able to settle my wife and nieces in a flat about six miles out from Alexandria, where they could hear and see the bombs and gunfire when the raids took place. The Italians, I may say, kept their bombing rigidly to the port. When the Luftwaffe arrived they bombed indiscriminately all over the city, particularly in the Arab quarter teeming with natives and their families.

III

Arrived at Alexandria, we had time to consider our experiences off Calabria.

Several serious implications had arisen, and perhaps the most important was that the 25-year old *Warspite*, which had been largely reconstructed and modernized, was the only ship in the fleet which could shoot at ranges at which the Italian battleships and 8-inch gun cruisers were straddling us comfortably. In writing privately to the First Sea Lord on the day of our arrival I pointed out this fact, and that during this first clash with the Italians neither the *Malaya* nor *Royal Sovereign* crossed the target. "I must have one more ship that can shoot at a good range."

I pointed out, too, that Vice-Admiral Tovey, with his four 6-inch cruisers, had been up against six or seven 8-inch ships and four or five 6-inch cruisers. We also wanted 8-inch cruisers, and I would "dearly like the *York* and *Exeter*", which were 32-knot ships of 8,400 tons armed with six 8-inch.

We needed also an armoured aircraft-carrier like the *Illustrious*, with fighters, an anti-aircraft cruiser like the *Carlisle* and a couple of convoy sloops.

After mentioning the fact that we were bombed throughout most of the operation and had literally to fight our way back to Alexandria, I said that it seemed as though the whole of the Regia Aeronautica were concentrated against our fleets in the Eastern and Western Mediterranean. We were well able to look after the Italian fleet; but I doubted if we could tackle their Air Force as well. "Is anything being done to attack the northern Italian towns? I hope so—if only to draw off some of these birds to the north."

I also stressed the point that it was unjustifiable to take any old battleship into the Central Mediterranean, or to engage the enemy fleet anywhere near their coast in daylight unless the object to be attained were worth losing a battleship.

I apologized for putting forward these demands; but pointed out that our whole position in the Middle East depended almost entirely upon the fleet, and that I wanted to keep it active and able to go anywhere and do anything in conditions of moderate security.

The Italian Navy was soon to have another lesson in the danger of encountering our ships. On July 18th a small squadron consisting of the *Sydney*, Captain Collins, and five destroyers of the 2nd Flotilla under Commander H. St. L. Nicolson, in the *Hyperion*, sailed from Alexandria for the Ægean to intercept any Italian shipping passing to or from the Dodecanese. Four of the destroyers were also to carry out an anti-submarine sweep from east to west along the north coast of Crete, while the *Sydney* with one destroyer in company were to operate against Italian shipping in the Gulf of Athens. At daylight next morning, when Commander Nicolson's destroyers were somewhere off the north-western end of Crete, they sighted two Italian cruisers coming in from the westward. Quite rightly they turned and ran for it, and were very soon under fire with the enemy in full pursuit. The *Sydney* about forty-five miles to the northward, received the *Hyperion's* report of two enemy cruisers, and at once turned south and went on to full speed.

Meanwhile we had intercepted the signals at Alexandria, and I was on tenterhooks. The enemy cruisers might well be 8-inch gun ships, in which case the *Sydney* and her destroyers would be heavily outmatched. All I knew was that the destroyers were being chased, and that Collins, regardless of any odds, was closing them at full speed. After that, dead silence.

It must have been quite two hours later that our feelings of anxiety were changed to those of triumph when the *Sydney* reported she had hit and stopped one of the cruisers, which was badly on fire, and that she was chasing the other to the southward with her, the *Sydney's*, ammunition running low. Though repeatedly hit the second cruiser managed to escape. Destroyers finished off the *Bartolomeo Colleoni*, and were bombed while picking up her 545 survivors, and again during their return to Alexandria, which was not at all to the taste of the Italians. For this fine, brisk action which showed the high efficiency and magnificent fighting qualities of the Royal Australian Navy, Captain Collins was immediately awarded the C.B. by His Majesty, a well-deserved honour. Commander Nicolson received a bar to his D.S.O.

On hearing of this engagement part of the fleet sailed from Alexandria and swept to the north-west, as when last seen the second Italian cruiser was steering south and might be making for Tobruk. She was not sighted; but at dawn on July 20th, six torpedo-carrying Swordfish from the *Eagle* attacked

Tobruk harbour, sent a tanker up in a burst of flame, and sank two smaller ships. The *Eagle's* aircraft had attacked Tobruk earlier in the month, sinking two destroyers and a couple of merchant ships. The second raid on July 20th resulted in the Italians abandoning Tobruk as a supply base for their army and a base for their light naval forces.

IV

During this period in harbour I paid several visits to Cairo to confer with my brother Commander-in-Chief and to acquaint myself with the position ashore.

I learnt that the enemy in the Western Desert were still quiescent; but that they had made a small advance in the Southern Sudan and had captured Kassala, thus cutting the railway line between Gedaref and Port Sudan. This in itself was nothing very serious. Elsewhere in the south the rains prevented operations; but Wavell told us that August would probably see some movement.

Our anxieties over our back-door route through the Red Sea past Eritrea had so far proved unfounded. The convoys were proceeding regularly and practically unscathed, thanks to the excellent work of the Royal Air Force which seemed sufficient to protect them against air attack on that most vulnerable passage. The Italian destroyers and submarines at Massawa were completely lethargic.

As regards the fleet, the air situation was unsatisfactory. The flying-boats working from Malta and Alexandria did their utmost; but were too few in numbers. Reconnaissance over the sea was fitful, and large areas were necessarily left unsearched. Nor were flying-boats the proper type of aircraft for pushing home reconnaissance near the enemy coast or over enemy ports. They were too slow and too vulnerable. It was grossly unreasonable to expect them to expose themselves to attack by Italian fighters in their effort to gather information for the fleet. They behaved with the greatest gallantry; but often returned to Malta with casualties and riddled with bullets.

The Italians, on the other hand, had full knowledge of our movements. Seldom did a unit leave harbour but it was picked up and shadowed by their reconnaissance aircraft, which lost no time in whistling up the bombers.

The fleet had no fighter protection. Long-range fighters there were none, and though the Royal Air Force did their best with their limited resources to give some protection when the fleet was close inshore, it was necessarily very thin. At that time, moreover, fighters did not like operating over the sea.

Of course it was unreasonable to expect fighters to be sent out from

England at this period. The Battle of Britain had started, and the country was fighting for its life. All the same, a few would have made a great difference. Malta, for instance, received none at all until the old aircraft-carrier *Argus* flew in a few from the west on August 12th.

At Alexandria we now had an airfield ashore where the squadrons of the Fleet Air Arm could be landed when the fleet was in harbour. The airfield, small enough, was about eight miles west of the city. When the *Eagle* was not at sea three or four Swordfish worked from an advanced R.A.F. base. Their task was to harry the Italian shipping going to Tobruk or other Cyrenaican ports within their range, and they made a number of fine and fruitful attacks. Our naval air crews at that period had no rest at sea or in harbour. They were a most gallant crowd of young men whom I remember with the greatest admiration.

Towards the end of July I received another letter from the First Sea Lord which contained the welcome news that reinforcements would be sent to the Mediterranean. Among them was to be the *Illustrious*, a new carrier with an armoured flight deck and carrying eight-gun Fulmar fighters. The answer to my requests for better air reconnaissance and long-range fighters was not so satisfactory, though we heard of fighters for the defence of Malta and Alexandria.

The rest of July passed fairly quietly without any further big operations on the part of the fleet, though the cruisers and destroyers were constantly at sea. The Italian reconnaissance continued to improve, and on August 3rd in writing to the First Sea Lord I pointed out:

> Our principal trouble is that we cannot move without our movements being known. . . . They send planes over Alexandria every day, and no force in the last three weeks has been at sea without being discovered and bombed, in some cases very heavily. . . . I shall be very glad when the reinforcements arrive to strengthen our A.A., as there is no doubt that the sailors, expecially those in the destroyers, look a bit askance at going to sea knowing that they will be bombed for perhaps two or three days running. At the same time, they are all in very good heart and cheerful.

In one of the operations to which I have referred the *Liverpool* took a heavy bomb below the bridge which happily failed to explode.

During the early days of August the shape of an operation for the reinforcement of the Mediterranean began to take form under the name of Operation 'Hats'. We were to be sent the battleship *Valiant*, the *Illustrious* and the anti-aircraft cruisers *Calcutta* and *Coventry*. We also became aware that there was a pressing desire on the part of the Prime Minister to send with the ships mentioned a convoy of merchant vessels carrying tanks and motor transport. I was not at all in favour of this, and said so. The presence of merchant ships slowed up the whole operation, and gave the Italians time to concentrate all they had to dispute the dangerous passage through the Sicilian narrows, in which case my vital reinforcements might quite well arrive in a damaged condition. The merchant ships might get through, it is true. On the other hand, they might all be sunk. One could not tell until one tried.

General Wavell, who was in England at the time, also expressed the view that he would sooner have the tanks and motor transport three weeks late than lose a proportion of them. But I could see that the discussion was fierce, as the Prime Minister wished to get the army in Egypt reinforced as soon as possible. He feared an Italian advance might develop very rapidly and anticipate the reinforcements.

In a letter of August 3rd, I told the First Sea Lord of my concern at our submarine casualties. We had lost the *Grampus*, *Odin*, *Orpheus*, *Phoenix* and *Oswald* since the outbreak of war with Italy, the *Oswald* on August 1st. I said there was no doubt that the Italians must have very efficient direction-finding and hydrophones, for as soon as one sent a submarine off an Italian port it was only a matter of time before she was discovered, and sunk. "At the moment," I wrote, "it is not a question of sending them where they will be useful, but where they will be safe." I also expressed my opinion that the 'O', 'P' and 'R' class submarines we had been sent from China, ships with a surface displacement of 1,475 tons, were too large, too old, and with auxiliary machinery that was too noisy, for work in the Mediterranean. I had an idea, too, that the young commanding officers, trained in the turbid waters off the China coast, had not fully grasped the comparative ease with which their large ships could be detected from the air in depths of many fathoms in the clear, translucent waters of the Mediterranean. It meant constant watchfulness. This by no means applied to all of them. Lieutenant-Commander M. G. Rimington, of the *Parthian*, had already proved a thorn in the side of the Italians.

Meanwhile things had started to move on land, and on August 3rd the Italians attacked British Somaliland. Our forces there were too small to hold them, and after a most gallant fighting retreat in which they inflicted severe casualties upon the enemy, our ships of the East Indies Squadron embarked the whole force at Berbera with the exception of the Camel Corps, which was disbanded. The enemy occupation of British Somaliland had naval repercussions. It put the Italians on the southern flank of our vital convoy route through the Gulf of Aden into the Red Sea. However, they made little use of their advantage. The convoys proceeded as regularly and with as little damage as before.

Now we were operating at full stretch the lack of repair and docking facilities at Alexandria was becoming serious. The Admiralty floating dock was the only one which could take a ship of over five hundred feet, and the only one under British control. Moreover, the heavy ships had not been docked for some time before their arrival on the station, and Alexandria was notorious for its rapid marine growth. This, of course, meant loss of speed. The docking of a heavy ship was a large undertaking, necessitating the unloading of all the ammunition. The work was continuously interrupted by air raids. We could not get workmen from Malta, and the principal limitation of the Egyptians was that they would not work on the day of an air-raid or the day after. In writing home about this I pointed out that we had to pass on much of the work to Port Said and Suez, which could only deal with small ships, and that the floating dock at Alexandria might go out of action through bombing on any moonlight night, I hoped without a ship in it. What was to happen when a battleship or cruiser just *had* to refit did not bear thinking about. However, in the moonless period in August it proved possible to get the *Warspite* and *Malaya* docked, which was a great relief to me.

Some of our larger ships were in very poor condition. The *Malaya* was untrustworthy on any operation because of 'condenseritis'. The *Ramillies's* boilers were dying on us, as had the *Royal Sovereign's*. The 8-inch cruiser *Kent* also suffered from chronic condenser trouble, and all these ships required refits. But how?

One of our most important requirements, too, was a destroyer depot ship.

At this period we began to be troubled by low-flying aircraft. One skimmed low over the breakwater one night and dropped two heavy objects with a great splash close to the *Gloucester*. We thought at first they were magnetic mines; but eventually concluded they were torpedoes which went straight into the mud. We discovered no trace of them. Barrage balloons we had none, so once more we were forced to improvise. We erected masts on the breakwater, and every ship was ordered to manufacture a kite and to fly it in harbour when there was sufficient breeze. Woe betide any ship which the Chief of Staff found without her kite flying within half-an-hour of anchoring. To the submarine depot ship *Medway* was entrusted the task of producing kites with explosive charges attached to the kite-wire. Every so often they went off with a shattering report in the air. We hoped that any Italian snoopers from the air or ashore, would report that all our kites carried lethal charges.

The cruisers at sea were also attacked by torpedo-carrying aircraft. They were little danger in broad daylight when they were seen coming in low, miles away; but later they learnt more threatening tactics and gave us some bad frights by attacking in the grey half-light just after sunset.

V

Though the Italians on the Western Desert front as yet showed few signs of serious movement, small-scale fighting was always in progress. To one who had the experience of working with the Army in Gallipoli years before, I was surprised that with a coast road and one flank on the sea the Navy was never asked for assistance. In August, at one of the conferences in Cairo, I offered to knock out some of the Italian positions with heavy guns. This led to the *Warspite*, *Malaya*, *Ramillies* and *Kent*, which had lately joined us, going to sea and bombarding Bardia, a small supply port, and Fort Capuzzo, an Italian strong-point above Sollum.

We made detailed arrangements beforehand with the R.A.F. to give us fighter cover on the return journey to deal with the Italian bombers that would inevitably come after us, while the *Eagle's* fighters also worked from the shore.

Everything went according to plan. Bardia and Fort Capuzzo were subjected to twenty minutes deliberate bombardment from a rain of 15-inch, 8-inch and 6-inch shell, which was a satisfactory spectacle to watch and we hoped had good results. As we expected, the Savoia bombers arrived in considerable force as we steamed east for Alexandria. However, twelve of them were shot down, a heartening sight for the fleet which the sailors thoroughly enjoyed. This was a nasty reversal of fortune for that particular group of the Regia Aeronautica, which had been worrying us at sea. We knew them as the 'Green Mice', from the representation of Mickey Mouse in that colour which they all had painted on their fuselage. They were rather shaken by this set-back.

A week later, on the night of August 22nd–23rd, destroyers shot up the Italian seaplane base at Bomba, to the west of Tobruk, while three Swordfish from the *Eagle* working from an advanced base attacked shipping. The Italians had in the gulf a depot ship, with a destroyer lying alongside one side and a submarine the other. Another large submarine lay astern. The three aircraft were led by Captain Oliver Patch, Royal Marines, who himself torpedoed and sank the large submarine. One each of the remaining two Swordfish attacked the vessels lying alongside the depot ship, which were also sunk. In the excitement and turmoil that followed the depot ship sank also. It was a most daring and gallant effort on the part of our young gentlemen from the *Eagle*.

On August 30th the whole fleet sailed from Alexandria for Operation 'Hats'. In its broad outline it was the plan that our reinforcement should be escorted from the westward to the Sicilian Narrows by Force H. under Sir James Somerville, should pass through the Narrows by night, and join the Mediterranean Fleet between Malta and Pantellaria next morning. The passage was one of considerable risk. The Narrows were thickly mined, and the extent and position of the minefields were unknown to us. Only a week before the destroyer *Hostile* had been lost off Cape Bon. Another point that has to be remembered is that the passage of the fleet into the Central Mediterranean always involved the refuelling of all the destroyers, and usually also a battleship, at Malta. This meant that the rest of the fleet had to spend a day south of Malta while these ships fuelled in turn, and also made it essential that the stocks of oil fuel at Malta should be maintained at high level.

When we sailed for Operation 'Hats' from Alexandria, we took with us the first convoy for Malta of three merchant ships and a tanker. The convoy was heavily bombed south of Crete, and the largest ship, the Federal Steam Navigation Company's *Cornwall*, Captain F. C. Pretty, was hit and set on fire aft. She was also holed below the waterline, while her steering gear, wireless and two guns were put completely out of action. The master and crew acted with great determination. The magazine blew up and the fire spread to one of the holds; but was eventually got under control. Captain Pretty signalled that he could steer his ship with the propellers, maintained his speed and station in the convoy, and arrived safely at Malta two days afterwards. It was a fine feat of seamanship for which the master was awarded a decoration.

It was during this passage, I remember, that at dusk one evening, reconnaissance aircraft from the *Eagle* sighted the Italian fleet, reported as five battleships, about ninety miles to the northward. It was too late for aircraft to make a torpedo attack, and at that distance in darkness the chances of bringing the Italians to action were very small indeed. Our fleet stationed itself to cover the convoy during the night. When our aircraft went up again at dawn nothing could be seen of the enemy.

Suffice it to say that Operation 'Hats' went off as planned. Our reinforcement by the *Valiant*, *Illustrious*, *Calcutta* and *Coventry* not only meant a great accretion to our strength; but gave us a carrier that could keep fighters over the fleet during daylight hours at sea. Moreover, we now had two large ships with R.D.F. or radio direction finding, now known as radar. We had previously to rely upon our own eyesight to spot aircraft coming in to attack, and it was astonishing how keen-eyed some of the sailors became. Now, however, we could rely on a warning when attacking aircraft were still forty or fifty miles away, which was a very welcome let-up for the anti-aircraft guns' crews.

The *Illustrious's* Fulmar fighters came into action at once. The fleet, of course, was being shadowed as usual when it started its passage east, and when Jack Tovey brought his squadron in from the north where he had been patrolling during the night, he also brought his little Italian friend with him. The Fulmars quickly tumbled both of them into the sea to the loud cheers of the ships' companies, who had had just about as much as they could stand of being bombed without retaliation. The tremendous effect of this incident upon everyone in the fleet, and upon the Commander-in-Chief as much as anyone, was indescribable. From that moment, whenever an armoured carrier was in company, we had command of the air over the fleet. By that I do not mean that the bombing attacks ceased. Far from it. But we felt that we now had a weapon which enabled us to give back as good as we were getting, and also gave us vastly increased freedom of movement.

The anti-aircraft cruisers *Calcutta* and *Coventry* were also particularly welcome for giving much-needed protection to our convoys.

During the return passage to Alexandria the fleet split into two divisions, one passing to the north and the other to the south of Crete. At dawn on September 4th, every available aircraft from the *Eagle* and *Illustrious* was sent in to attack the airfields in Rhodes, from which came the aircraft that gave us sleepless nights at Alexandria. They were given a good basting; but it was unfortunate that because of the variable winds the *Eagle* was fifteen minutes late in flying off, which meant her bombers arrived when the Italians were properly alarmed and had fighters in the air. To my great regret four Swordfish were lost with their valuable crews, those skilled and gallant airmen who had done such grand work in the past few weeks. The Navy could ill afford to lose them. They were the cream of the Fleet Air Arm.

Simultaneously with the attack upon Rhodes the *Sydney* shelled the airfield at Scarpanto, the destroyers in company sinking two E-boats.

Rear-Admiral A. L. St. G. Lyster had come out in the *Illustrious* to take command of the Carrier Squadron. His arrival was most timely, and he relieved my staff of all responsibilities in regard to the Fleet Air Arm. At our first interview he brought up the matter of an attack on the Italian fleet in Taranto harbour, and I gave him every encouragement to develop the idea. It had, of course, already been mentioned in my correspondence with Sir Dudley Pound, though to him the operation always appeared as the last dying kick of the Mediterranean carrier before being sent to the bottom. To Admiral Lyster and myself the project seemed to involve no unusual danger.

On September 13th the Italians launched their long-expected offensive in the Western Desert. They advanced cautiously, came down the Halfaya Pass and occupied Sollum, just over the Egyptian frontier, and moved on to Sidi Barrani, where they halted.

There was a disagreement in principle between the Army on the one hand, and the Navy and R.A.F. on the other, as to how the enemy advance should be met. The Army wanted the Italians to come on to Mersa Matruh, some eighty miles further east, where they were all ready to meet them and were confident of giving the invaders a real knock. There was thus some disappointment when Marshal Graziani halted at Sidi Barrani. The Navy and the R.A.F., on the other hand, were all against lightly surrendering territory which brought enemy airfields nearer to Alexandria and other important centres.

R*

However, as it was the Army that was primarily involved they had to have their way, which was only right.

We did our best to help. The Italian advance brought their left flank near to the sea. Destroyers and gunboats bombarded their troop concentrations and other targets almost nightly, and though the damage they did may have been inconsiderable, they kept the enemy awake and on the hop.

The gunboats deserve more than a cursory mention. They were little ships of 625 tons of very shallow draught built in 1915 for service on the rivers in Mesopotamia during the First World War. They were later sent to China for use on the Yangtse and West Rivers. I had gladly accepted the offer of some of these little ships for service in the Mediterranean, as their small size and shallow draught made them difficult targets for bombs or torpedoes, while their two 6-inch guns, though old, were useful weapons. Of these the *Ladybird*, *Aphis* and *Gnat*, later joined by the monitor *Terror* with her pair of 15-inch guns, all gave grand service off the Libyan coast in 1940–41 on the sea flank of the Army. Over long periods they bombarded almost every night, paying particular attention to Bardia and Tobruk as the battle on shore surged to and fro. Of the four ships mentioned only the *Aphis* survived.

But to hark back to September, 1940, the larger ships also were used for bombarding Bardia, and it was during one of these expeditions that the cruiser *Kent* was torpedoed in the moonlight by an Italian 'plane. The torpedo exploded aft near the propellers, and it was with the greatest difficulty that she was towed back to Alexandria by destroyers.

Our bombardments from the sea certainly had some effect, for by September 26th we were able to report that all enemy concentrations had moved inland, and there was practically nothing left to be engaged.

VI

Ashore at Alexandria my wife and two nieces were still in the flat, the two girls fretting because they could get no war work to do although both were trained as V.A.Ds. But a house was a necessity so that we could offer some hospitality to officers, many of whom valued a bed ashore after weeks at sea without any real rest. Matters became crucial when the owner of the flat arrived, and my wife and nieces had to move into an hotel. However, in October the Ambassador and Lady Lampson came to our rescue and kindly offered us the use of the Residency at Alexandria, which they were not using during the war. It was just the house for us, in a fine position five or six miles away from the harbour with good accommodation and a large garden. We gratefully accepted.

My eldest niece eventually found employment as an Occupational Therapist in the hospital we shared with the Army. She received no salary to start with, but later became part of the Army Medical Establishment and served all over Egypt, eventually being awarded the M.B.E. Work for the younger girl, who now saw her husband, my flag lieutenant, W. A. Starkie, fairly frequently, was not so important. Nevertheless, being a trained dietician, she was anxious to do something, and served at the hospital on a committee which superintended the food of the patients. To satisfy all and sundry, Navy, Army and Air Force, wounded and ill, and from all over the world, was no sinecure.

Starkie, meanwhile, was becoming restive, and I agreed with him that it was no time for an officer of his ability and seniority to be serving as a flag lieutenant. So he was appointed as first lieutenant of the destroyer *Juno*, Commander St. John Tyrwhitt, son of my old friend and leader. I knew that with him Starkie would get a good grounding in destroyer work to fit him for a command of his own. He left us in December, his place as flag lieutenant was taken by Lieutenant Hugh Lee, from the *Jervis*.

I wonder whether I was a good prophet, or merely hopeful? In a letter to an aunt in September, 1940, I wrote: "My own opinion is that the war will be brought to a conclusion out here. Perhaps by the collapse of the Italians."

Much was to happen in the three years before we invaded and conquered Sicily in July, 1943, and the first Allied troops landed on the mainland of Europe, at Salerno, in the following September, thereby puncturing what Mr. Winston Churchill referred to as "the soft belly of the Axis".

It was on the same date that Italy collapsed, and on September 11th, 1943, that we had the supreme gratification of accepting the surrender of the Italian fleet at Malta.

CHAPTER XXIII

I

AT the end of September nearly two thousand troops were embarked in the *Liverpool* and *Gloucester* as reinforcements for Malta. Part of the fleet, known as the 'first eleven', the *Warspite, Valiant,* and *Illustrious*, with the cruiser squadron, sailed to escort them. The 'second eleven', of course, were the *Malaya, Ramillies,* and *Eagle*.

Though the Fulmars took their toll of the enemy's shadowers, it did not prevent some heavy bombing. On our second day at sea the reconnaissance aircraft from the *Illustrious* sighted the Italian battle-fleet about 120 miles to the northward. They had four battleships out this time, including the *Littorio* and *Vittorio Veneto*, fine new ships of 35,000 tons armed with nine 15-inch and a speed of 31 knots. After some thought we decided to press on with the main object of landing the toops in Malta, and no more was seen or heard of the Italians.

The operation followed the pattern to which we were now accustomed, and beyond some bombing nothing impeded our return to Alexandria. Meanwhile the demands of Malta for supplies were becoming more and more pressing, and it was decided to run another convoy early in October.

I had another interesting letter from the First Sea Lord on my return to harbour in which he told me of the magnificent work of the R.A.F. fighters in the Battle of Britain, and the enormous amount of shipping and barges the Germans had concentrated between the Scheldt and Havre for the invasion of England. They had also mounted a large number of long-range guns between Calais and Boulogne, and because of these, and owing also to the fact that no fighter cover could be spared for any ships sent to operate on the Belgian or French coasts, the Navy could do little against the invasion fleet.

Personally I was very sceptical about an invasion being attempted. With the Home Fleet in being, besides all the local flotillas, I could not see how the Germans could expect to obtain command of the sea for long enough to pass over the Channel the enormous number of slow and defenceless craft that would be required to make a landing on any scale likely to be successful. Even if the enemy had command of the air, which they showed no signs of obtaining, our ships could still operate. We should have losses; but once among the invasion flotillas our ships would be comparatively safe.

I also received the cheering news that at last the destroyer depot ship *Woolwich* was to be sent out to us, and that I should probably get the *Barham* and four destroyers shortly. This was most welcome, particularly the destroyers.

Ours were greatly overworked and under-rested, and repair facilities for them did not exist.

I had been harassed, and not a little irritated, by a 'prodding' signal received from the Minister of Defence on September 9th in which he seemed to imply that we had been rather backward in our offensive operations against the Italian fleet; but that with the arrival of the *Illustrious* and *Valiant* it was hoped we should do more. I replied at once, saying I hoped it had been made clear to Mr. Churchill that the prerequisite of successful operations in the Central Mediterranean was constant and complete air reconnaissance in that area, in which respect we still fell far short, and that operations of the fleet were drastically curtailed by the number of our destroyers.

It was quite evident to me, as to everyone else on the spot in the Eastern Mediterranean, that our difficulties were not entirely comprehended by those in authority at home. I pointed this out in a strong letter to the First Sea Lord, in which, *inter alia*, I said that about one-third of the destroyers were continually out of action, while the number that remained were quite insufficient for our numerous commitments and fleet operations. We had to use valuable destroyers for escorting numerous slow convoys to Haifa, Port Said and Cyprus, though I had asked several times for some slow escort vessels and had had no reply to my signals.

"I know how difficult it must be to supply these needs from home, and how hard up you are for these craft," I continued. "I would have no objection to having my requests turned down, provided it is clearly understood by those in authority what drastic limitations this imposes on the fleet. At the moment, to carry out any fleet operation, I have to hold up all local operations and wait till I can scrape sufficient destroyers together."

I went on to mention Malta, which by April 1st, 1941, would have to be sent little less than 400,000 tons of supplies. This meant something like two convoys a month, each one involving a complete fleet operation, without counting the bringing back of empty ships. The convoy trips would provide good opportunities for operations against the Italians, though the fleet would be at reduced strength because I lacked destroyers to provide the screen for all the heavy ships at once, and the convoy could not be denuded of escorts. Moreover, to fight an action when hampered with a convoy was not the happiest moment. I again pointed out the inadequacy of the repair facilities at Alexandria, which I felt was not fully realized. Malta could only be used for the repair of a few odd submarines and destroyers. In my mind I had the constant anxiety as to what was to be done with a damaged capital ship, which made me very reluctant to risk them in waters which might be mined without some very good reason. The Italians, I must repeat, were laying mines in depths of up to 200 fathoms.

II

Early in October we ran another convoy to Malta, and as four Italian battleships had been sighted at sea on the previous occasion, this time our whole fleet went out to cover the operation. The convoy reached Malta without incident and without even sighting a hostile aircraft, probably because the weather was bad with heavy thunderstorms. Nor was anything heard of the Italian fleet. We had one misfortune, when the destroyer *Imperial* was damaged on the way in to Malta by a mine laid in 180 fathoms. We were probably lucky to have no other casualties.

We brought another small convoy away from the island, and on the first night out, October 11th–12th, the *Ajax*, Captain E. D. B. McCarthy, which was in the line of cruisers spread to the northward, ran into an Italian flotilla. After a most spirited action at ranges of 4,000 yards and less in moonlight she sank two destroyers and damaged a third, setting her on fire. She then engaged two other ships, which disappeared behind a smoke-screen with some celerity when fire was opened. The *Ajax* did not come off unscathed. Hit seven times in all she sustained considerable damage to her bridge and radar equipment, largely caused by a fire in a storeroom. There was some difficulty in the *Ajax* because of the blinding effect of the flash of her own guns, whereas the enemy were using flashless ammunition with good tracers.

When I heard all the details of this action I signalled to the Admiralty that the *Ajax* had been handled—"with resolution and skill. It is particularly satisfactory that this was the first night shoot of this newly commissioned ship". It was a fine performance, and looked as though the *Ajax* were going to live up to the fine reputation she had already earned in the battle against the *Admiral Graf Spee* off the River Plate.

Next morning a flying-boat from Malta reported that the damaged destroyer was making for harbour in tow of a consort. The *Illustrious* flew off three Swordfish with torpedoes, and it was a quaint sight to see the big Sunderland moving off with the three little chickens under her wing. The *York* was also sent off hot-foot to finish off the cripple.

The towing destroyer slipped and made off at full speed to the northward when our aircraft attacked. When the *York* appeared the crew of the badly-damaged *Artigliere* waved white sheets and garments as a sign of surrender, as well they might. We were within easy range of the Regia Aeronautica, and remembering the bombing of the *Havock* while engaged in picking up the survivors of the *Bartolomeo Colleoni* on July 19th, Captain R. H. Portal was in no mood to stop and lower his boats, which had my complete approval. Instead, he dropped floats under the *Artigliere*'s stern. There was some difficulty in persuading the Italians to take to the water; but when they eventually did so the *York* opened fire and the *Artigliere* blew up.

I made a signal to the Italian Admiralty in plain language giving the position of the rafts with the survivors. They were duly picked up, though I was chided by the authorities for what I thought was a humane action. "In view of feeling of public here suffering under intensive and ruthless attacks," the message read, "it might be well to exclude from future communiqués reference to gallantry of enemy or to compromising our fleet's position for benefit of enemy." I may have been wrong; but on this occasion the Italian destroyers *had* fought well. As for compromising the fleet's position, the *Ajax's* action must already have caused the enemy to be aware of our presence.

Some not very heavy bombing took place during our passage back to Alexandria. We had an American war correspondent on board the *Warspite*, and just before one of the attacks he was sitting typing in the wardroom when enemy aircraft were reported. A young lieutenant went down and told him to hurry up and get on deck so that he could write a good eye-witness story. He was met with the reply: "No, sir. My people want a live story, not a dead correspondent!" Needless to say he was really no safer in the wardroom than anywhere else.

On the night of October 13th–14th, under cover of this operation, aircraft from the *Illustrious* and *Eagle* bombed Leros, in the Dodecanese. Swordfish dropped nearly a hundred bombs on hangars and fuel tanks, and did considerable damage.

In the twilight of the evening before our arrival at Alexandria the fleet was attacked by torpedo 'planes. The heavy barrage put up by the battleships defeated their attackers; but the cruisers were not so fortunate, the *Liverpool* being torpedoed in the bows. The torpedo damage was not really extensive; but the explosion started a fire which spread to the petrol tank. This exploded also, and in my opinion caused part of the contents of the foremost magazine to blow up as well, with the consequence that the *Liverpool's* bows broke away from just before the bridge and remained hanging. The *Orion* took her in tow by the stern, a difficult task with the mangled bows acting as a drogue and a rudder. The tow parted after 100 miles; but on the hawsers being re-passed the damaged bows fell off and the job became easier. However, the night was brilliantly moonlit, and we had some hours of anxiety. There was always the possibility that the Italians would try to finish off the *Liverpool* and perhaps bag the *Orion* as well.

The entry of the battle-fleet into Alexandria at 1 a.m. was most spectacular, of which our American correspondent took full advantage in his despatches. We approached during a heavy air raid, and low-flying aircraft, thought to be carrying torpedoes, had been reported. We made for the shallow water of the Great Pass—the entrance to Alexandria harbour—at high speed, firing a blind barrage on both sides with our guns flashing and the sparkle of bursting shell all over the horizon.

These night attacks had now been fully developed by the Italians. They were nerve-racking and dangerous, particularly as they were thrown in at dusk after our aircraft-carrier had flown on all her fighters for the night. We had no specially-equipped night-fighters. However, we realized how lucky we were that they had not started when we were entirely without radar. The *Illustrious*, so fitted, now picked up the attackers at a good distance and they were met with a heavy barrage at five miles.

Vice-Admiral John Tovey was not out with us on this last occasion. He had been recalled to the Admiralty, and before long we heard of his appointment as Commander-in-Chief, Home Fleet. I was delighted to think of him in this important command, in which I knew he would be highly successful. But he was a great loss to us in the Mediterranean, and to me personally. His advice, outspoken criticism, loyal support, cheerful optimism and imperturbability were a great help. Originally in command of the destroyers, and then as second-in-command of the fleet, and in charge of all cruisers and destroyers, he had proved himself a fine leader who had the confidence of us all.

Rear-Admiral H. D. Pridham-Wippell now became second-in-command and in command of the light forces with the acting rank of Vice-Admiral. A friend of Dardanelles days, and an ex-destroyer officer of great experience and merit, I had the greatest faith in him and confidence in his judgment. In the difficult times through which we were to pass he never failed. His appointment in command of the Battle Squadron was given to Captain H. B. Rawlings, who was promoted to acting Rear-Admiral. He had already proved himself in command of the *Valiant*, and had also served in destroyers in the First World War. Qualifying as a torpedo specialist he had had an interesting and varied career, and for two years had been with a military mission in Poland during the Polish war against the Bolshevists. After commanding various ships, he had been for three years our Naval Attaché in Japan. An officer of great strength of character, he also was a happy selection.

III

Back at Alexandria I found a Turkish delegation headed by Admiral Ulgin, whom I had met at Istanbul in 1939. They made no secret of the fact that they had come to probe our strength. I gave them lunch in the *Warspite*. They had had a most uncomfortable journey from Turkey, so when they had finished their tour I sent them back to Mersin, in Asia Minor, north of Cyprus, in the destroyer *Nubian*.

Ashore there was little change in the Western Desert. The Italians still remained stuck at Sidi Barrani, though there appeared to be some prospect of activity in the Sudan and Abyssinia. I had heard that my brother, Alan

Cunningham, now an acting Lieutenant-General, was on his way out, while towards the end of October the Secretary of State for War, Anthony Eden; General Smuts; General Wavell; Air Chief Marshal Longmore, the A.O.C. in C. Middle East; and General Platt held a conference at Khartoum to discuss an offensive in that region.

Anthony Eden came to Alexandria and lunched with me on board the *Warspite*. It was most interesting to get the news straight from home from one who knew everything and was on intimate terms with Mr. Churchill. Later, after a ceremonial dinner on shore, I carried Mr. Eden off to the Fleet Club, where several thousand sailors gave him a roaring reception. He spoke to them very well and was literally mobbed on the way out, with men thumping him heartily on the back and his hand being snatched and shaken. I think he enjoyed it. The sailors were in great heart.

I made various trips to Cairo to confer with my colleagues and the Secretary of State for War; but my routine at Alexandria was much the same as usual. My wife by this time was well settled in at the Residency, and was starting to fill it with convalescent officers or those needing rest. It did not hold many, but there were few days when she did not have two or three guests. I always slept on board. It was my custom to spend the mornings dealing with paperwork or in visits to ships or establishments. But after lunch I invariably went ashore for a round of golf or a set or two of tennis, returning to the ship at about six o'clock for more work. I made the staff conform to the same routine, as if I sent for a staff officer it was annoying to find he was ashore. On moonless nights I could usually dine at the Residency; but when there was a moon the attentions of the Italian bombers were too pressing, and I remained in the ship.

My military and air colleagues would have preferred the Naval Commander-in-Chief's headquarters also to be in Cairo, so that he and his staff would always be available for consultation. It would certainly have had advantages; but I firmly refused. So long as I had a seagoing fleet and the prospect of meeting the enemy I could not consider leaving it. Tradition, and, in my opinion necessity, demanded that the Commander-in-Chief should be in his flagship sharing as far as possible in the dangers and difficulties of his officers and men.

I met the objections of my colleagues by establishing at the Combined Headquarters at Cairo a section of my staff headed by a young Captain, H. G. Norman—now a Rear-Admiral. He was an officer of great ability and a good mixer, and acted as my additional Chief-of-Staff, also representing the Commander-in-Chief, East Indies. However, my military and air colleagues never ceased to impress upon me, and indeed on the Chiefs of Staff at home, how essential it was that I should leave the fleet and establish myself at Cairo. Fortunately the First Sea Lord backed me up in my refusal.

IV

It was on October 28th that Italy presented the ultimatum to Greece, demanding consent to her occupation of certain strategic points within a few hours. It was a declaration of war and not unexpected, particularly after the dastardly sinking of the little Greek cruiser *Helle* while lying at anchor off the mole at Tinos, in the Cyclades, by an Italian submarine on August 15th. The *Helle* was on a peaceful visit and was dressed with flags in honour of the Feast of the Assumption.

From the naval point of view this news was good and bad. It meant that we could now use Suda Bay in Crete as an advanced base for our operations in the Central Mediterranean. Before this we had, indeed, occasionally stationed tankers in Greek anchorages and used them for refuelling. But the Italians became aware of it, bombed our ships in Greek waters, whereupon the Greeks naturally protested to us and demanded their withdrawal.

On the other hand, with Greece in the war, it was quite certain that we should presently have to send her troops and quantities of war material. This would mean a steady stream of convoys to and fro across the Eastern Mediterranean and the Ægean, all liable to attack by submarines and within easy reach of the Italian airfields in the Dodecanese. This in turn would entail an additional strain upon our already overworked destroyers and escort forces.

So indeed it proved. Sir Arthur Longmore, the Air Officer Commanding-in-Chief, on his own responsibility, sent a fighter squadron to Greece, and was soon ordered to send others. General Wavell was called upon to provide anti-aircraft and other units which he found it equally difficult to spare. Eventually, in March, 1941, we had to turn to our new naval commitment of arranging for the safe transport to Greece of some 58,000 troops with their mechanical transport, full equipment and stores, and their maintenance when there. They went, of course, in merchant ships, which had to be covered and escorted. However, even in November we were beginning to wonder how long our overworked cruisers, destroyers and other light craft would hold together.

I have to pay the warmest tribute to the engineer officers and the men of their departments who kept the smaller ships running and in the fighting line all through the war in the Mediterranean. At no time have those ships been so hardly driven, or their engineering personnel so hardly pushed. They had so largely to improvise. The destroyers, in particular, were continually at sea. Their only rest and opportunity for running repairs came during the brief periods in harbour allowed for boiler cleaning, cut, by my strict orders, to the barest limit of time. We had no destroyer depot ship to take part of the burden, though the fleet repair ship *Resource* did all she could to help. The sum total of repair facilities was quite inadequate, and scattered all over the ports in Egypt. Yet the destroyers and other light craft were kept efficient and running until they were knocked out or damaged in action and could run no more. Those of the engineering department were grand men. Realizing the vital importance of the work they were doing, they would cheerfully take any risks rather than admit their ships could not go to sea. They never let the fleet down, or the Royal Navy.

Crete also had to be provided with defences, airfields and a garrison, and Suda Bay converted into an advanced base for the fleet. The difficulty was there was no proper boom defence, nor was any to be forthcoming for several months.

At 1.30 a.m. on October 29th, the morning after Italy's attack upon Greece, I took the whole fleet to sea. We had four battleships, the two aircraft-carriers, four cruisers and the usual destroyers, and it was my intention to be off the west coast of Crete by dawn on the 31st to cover the passage of ships to Suda Bay and to give battle to the Italian fleet if they came out to interfere. As usual we were sighted, shadowed and reported by the enemy's reconnaissance, though not actually attacked. On November 1st, however, there were heavy air raids on Suda Bay and Canea, the first of many. From now until the end of the first week in December our cruisers and destroyers were hard at it covering and escorting the convoys to the Piræus and Suda Bay. They had no rest.

In the Western Desert, round about Sidi Barrani, the *Ladybird*, now joined by the *Aphis*, constantly bombarded the Italian flank where it came down to the sea. These two little ships managed to make things very lively, and though constantly attacked from the air seemed to bear charmed lives.

v

We had not put away our idea of attacking the Italian fleet at Taranto. Rear-Admiral Lyster, in the *Illustrious*, was carefully making his preparations and training his air crews. To ensure success we required the closest co-operation with the Royal Air Force reconnaissance at Malta, as we were entirely dependent upon them for the latest news of the disposition of the enemy fleet, and if possible photographs of them in harbour. In this respect we were lucky, for by this time the Malta reconnaissance force consisted of Glenn Martins. They were a great advance on the Sunderland flying-boats which, however gallant their crews, were quite unfitted for the job. As I later wrote in my despatch describing the attack on the Italian battleships at Taranto: "The success of the Fleet Air Arm was due in no small degree to the excellent reconnaissance carried out by the Royal Air Force Glenn Martin Flight (No. 431) from Malta, under very difficult conditions and often in the face of fighter opposition."

Our plans were well advanced by the middle of October, and we had wanted to carry out the attack on Trafalgar Day, October 21st. Owing to a fire in the *Illustrious's* hangar, however, the operation had to be postponed. November 11th, when there would be a suitable moon, was chosen. The delay was fortunate. Further reconnaissance and photographs of Taranto showed, after minute examination, that the anchorage was now protected by a balloon barrage and the battleships by nets. This materially altered the method of attack.

It had been intended that both the *Illustrious* and the *Eagle* should take part in the operation; but two days before sailing the *Eagle* developed defects in her petrol system, probably caused by the many near misses she had sustained during a number of heavy bombing attacks. The whole ship's company were bitterly disappointed; but the best that could be done was to embark five of her Swordfish in the *Illustrious*, with eight pilots and eight observers all experienced in night flying, so that at least some of the *Eagle's* fine and efficient airmen could take part in the great venture.

The operation was timed to coincide with the passage of convoys to Suda Bay and Malta, and the passing through the Sicilian Narrows of further reinforcements for the Mediterranean Fleet consisting of the battleship *Barham*, the cruisers *Glasgow* and *Berwick*, and six destroyers.

The *Warspite*, with the *Illustrious, Valiant, Malaya, Ramillies* and destroyers sailed from Alexandria on the afternoon of November 6th, and made to the westward to cover the convoy movements already mentioned. Except for the usual attentions of the Italian shadowers and bombers, which were drastically dealt with by the Fulmars from the *Illustrious*, the fleet arrived off Malta without incident, and the *Ramillies* and destroyers were sent in to fuel in turn.

Our cruisers had joined us by this time and spent the night sweeping to the northward, to rejoin the battle-fleet at 7.15 on the morning of November 10th. Three hours later we met our welcome reinforcements from home, whereupon the fleet proceeded north-eastward to attain a position to the west of the Ionian Islands, which also covered a convoy of four ships leaving Malta for Alexandria. There was an air attack that afternoon which was beaten off by the Fulmars and the bombs dropped at random, and during the next day, the 11th, the Fulmars were again very busy driving off and shooting down shadowers with complete success. One of the most important requirements of the plan was an unobserved approach to the flying-off position, roughly forty miles west of Cephalonia and about one hundred and seventy from Taranto. It was there or thereabouts that the *Illustrious* would have to remain from the time her aircraft flew off for the attack until they returned. On that day, too, she sent an aircraft to Malta to bring out the latest reconnaissance photographs.

These showed five battleships in Taranto, and during the day the permanent R.A.F. reconnaissance that was being kept over the port reported the sixth battleship entering the harbour. So all the pheasants had gone home to roost.

Simultaneously with the attack on Taranto, it had been decided to raid the Straits of Otranto and temporarily to interrupt the Italian communications with Albania. This operation was to be carried out by Vice-Admiral Pridham-Wippell with the cruisers *Orion*, *Sydney*, and *Ajax*, and the destroyers

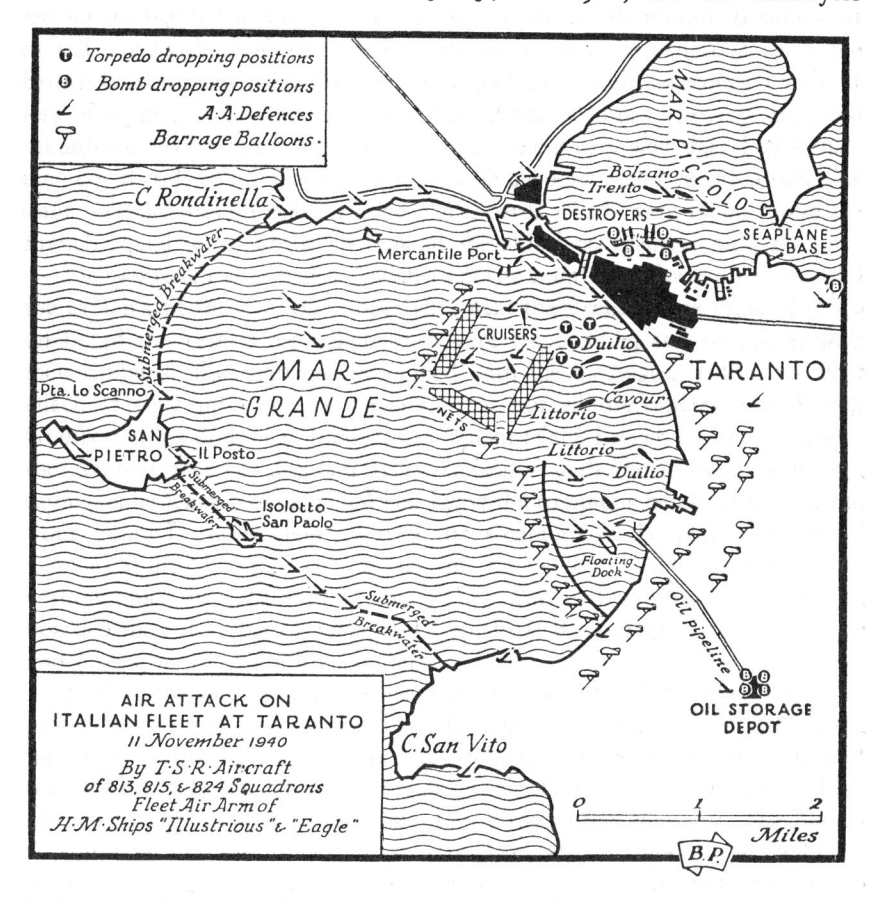

Nubian and *Mohawk*. They parted company with us soon after 1 p.m. on the 11th.

At 6 p.m. Rear-Admiral Lyster in the *Illustrious*, supported by more cruisers and destroyers, was ordered to proceed in execution of previous orders for Operation 'Judgment'. The *Illustrious* carried with her the high hopes and good wishes of the whole fleet, and just before she left I signalled: "Good luck then to your lads in their enterprise. Their success may well have a most important bearing on the course of the war in the Mediterranean." As may be imagined, we spent the night on tenterhooks.

The attack on Taranto has frequently been described, so I need hardly go into all the details. The attack was made in two main waves about one hour apart each of twelve aircraft, preceded by two aircraft dropping flares and bombs along the eastern side of the Mar Grande to silhouette the battleships against the glare and to make it easier for the torpedo aircraft coming in from the south-westward. It was also hoped that these flares and bombs would serve to distract attention from the main attack, as would dive-bombing attacks upon a line of cruisers and destroyers in the Mar Piccolo.

Admirably planned and most gallantly executed in the face of intense anti-aircraft fire, Operation 'Judgment' was a great success. Three of the Italian battleships were badly damaged, photographs taken next day showing two beached and a third sunk by the bows. Two cruisers also seemed to have been damaged in the Mar Piccolo as a result of the bombing attacks.[1] Two of our aircraft and four brave young men failed to return.

The zeal and enthusiasm with which these deliberate and accurate attacks were carried out in comparatively slow aircraft in the face of intense fire cannot sufficiently be praised. It was a great day for the Fleet Air Arm, and showed what they could do when they had their chance. Taranto, and the night of November 11th–12th, 1940, should be remembered for ever as having shown once and for all that in the Fleet Air Arm the Navy has its most devastating weapon. In a total flying time of about six and a half hours—carrier to carrier —twenty aircraft had inflicted more damage upon the Italian fleet than was inflicted upon the German High Sea Fleet in the daylight action at the Battle of Jutland.

The *Illustrious* and Vice-Admiral Pridham-Wippell's party rejoined us at daylight next morning, November 12th. As the *Illustrious* hove in sight I caused a flag signal to be hoisted—"*Illustrious* manoeuvre well executed", which was an under-statement. The air crews were in a state of great jubilation. They clamoured to repeat the operation the same night. I agreed at first when Rear-Admiral Lyster made the suggestion, though I rather felt that when the excitement wore off and the strain of their ordeal began to tell upon the air crews it would be unfair to send them in again. I therefore felt somewhat relieved when a bad weather report automatically put a stop to a second venture.

Meanwhile, Pridham-Wippell and his cruisers and destroyers had enjoyed a riotous night. At about 1.15 a.m. they had come upon a convoy of four merchant ships and two destroyers off Valona. One merchant ship was sunk, two were set on fire and left sinking, and the fourth escaped under cover of smoke. Both the destroyers departed at high speed after one of them had been hit and damaged.

On the morning of November 12th the Italians made strenuous efforts

[1] From subsequent information it was confirmed that of the battleships the *Italia*, hit by three torpedoes, sank; the *Conti di Cavour*, one torpedo, sank; the *Caio Dulio*, one torpedo, sank by the bows; the cruiser *Trento* hit by one bomb which perforated deck and side but failed to explode; two destroyers, damaged by near misses.

to locate the fleet, presumably to make a heavy bombing attack in retaliation. They did not have much luck, for three Cant flying-boats were quickly shot down by the *Illustrious* fighters. The last air battle took place over the fleet, and we saw the large bulk of the Cant dodging in and out of the clouds with three Fulmars diving in after her. There could only be one end, and presently a flaming meteor with a long trail of black smoke fell out of the sky, and splashed into the sea just ahead of the fleet. One could not help feeling pity for the Italian airmen who had undertaken a hopeless task in their unwieldy aircraft.

The cruiser *Berwick* was one of the ships that had reinforced us from the west forty-eight hours before. Her captain was Guy L. Warren, my late flag captain in the *Galatea*. As the Cant fell into the sea he made me a personal signal: "What fine shooting you have in your Greek coverts."

The crippling of half the Italian battle-fleet at a blow at Taranto had a profound effect on the naval strategical situation in the Mediterranean. The enemy promptly moved the rest of their fleet to Naples, whence they could still operate in the Central Mediterranean by coming south through the Straits of Messina; but only under the closer observation of the Royal Air Force reconnaissance from Malta.

It reduced, if it did not altogether abolish, the threat of the enemy fleet interfering with our never-ending succession of convoys to Greece and Crete, and enabled our battleship strength in the Eastern Mediterranean to be diminished. This in turn brought relief to our hard-pressed destroyers, as fewer were now required as an anti-submarine screen for the smaller battle-fleet. Within the next few weeks the *Malaya* and *Ramillies* sailed for home.

Congratulatory messages streamed in from all and sundry, including one from His Majesty which gave the greatest satisfaction to the whole fleet: "The recent successful operations of the Fleet under your command have been a source of pride and gratification to all at home. Please convey my warm congratulations to the Mediterranean Fleet, and in particular to the Fleet Air Arm on their brilliant exploit against the Italian warships at Taranto."

The Air Officer Commanding-in-Chief, Sir Arthur Longmore, came to Alexandria and paid a special visit to the *Illustrious* to congratulate the air crews. This act by an old sailor-airman who had served in the Royal Naval Air Service on its formation some years before the First World War was greatly appreciated.

Taranto, too, provided a much-needed stimulus to those at home, who were having such a difficult time with so great a burden. One might almost draw a parallel with Lord St. Vincent's remark when bearing down on the enemy at the Battle of Cape St. Vincent on February 14th, 1797: "A victory is very essential to England at this moment." The First Sea Lord wrote to me: "Just before the news of Taranto the Cabinet were rather down in the dumps; but Taranto had a most amazing effect upon them."

The fleet was back in Alexandria on November 14th; but not to rest.

Convoys for Greece and Crete were waiting to sail, and during the next two days the bulk of our ships were off again. Some three thousand four hundred troops for the Piræus with their stores were embarked in the *Berwick*, *York*, *Glasgow*, and *Sydney*.

Probably in revenge for Taranto, the Italian aircraft were keeping up continuous attacks upon Alexandria harbour. It did not much matter when the fleet was present, for the Italians would not face the heavy barrage put up by the ships. While we had been away, however, they had been doing pretty much as they liked, even flying low over the harbour in broad daylight. The destroyer *Decoy* had a bomb in her wardroom, fortunately without much damage; but what was really serious was that they had dropped a number of time bombs round the floating dock which went off at intervals three days later. The dock, our only means of repairing underwater damage to large ships, was seriously endangered, and a destroyer being undocked had a narrow shave. But luck was with us in the larger issues. Nevertheless, it convinced me that the anti-aircraft defence organization was really bad. It consisted of a mixture of British and Egyptian manned guns and searchlights, and the question of command was obscure.

I took up the question with the General Officer Commanding Middle East, pointing out that attacking aircraft were apparently not being detected by the radar, and that the fire from the A.A. Batteries ashore was poor and inefficient. The attackers were never illuminated by the defence searchlights, nor, in spite of the many attacks, had any enemy aircraft been shot down. The situation at the moment was that Alexandria harbour was virtually being defended by the fleet when present, and the strain on our guns' crews, who already had long hours of standing to at sea, would become serious unless the shore defences could be made to perform their proper function of defending the fleet at its base. I added that I did not consider that political considerations should be allowed to prejudice this vitally important matter. In making the last observation I referred to the holding back of A.A. batteries and fighters to protect other places in Egypt which had never been threatened.

General Wavell was sympathetic, though of course he also suffered from grave shortages. There was a steady improvement in the defences at Alexandria, though one could never say they were a real deterrent to determined attack. When the fleet was in harbour the volume of gunfire was imposing enough. In its absence at sea the gun defence was quite another matter.

VI

In a letter to the First Sea Lord on November 21st I informed him that apart from running the routine convoys to Malta, Greece, and Crete, I intended again to attack the Italian communications across the Straits of Otranto as soon as I could definitely locate the undamaged vessels of the Italian battle-fleet. I also expressed the opinion that perhaps the Dodecanese were getting ripe for plucking. General Wavell had a unit of the commando type which was to be based in Crete, and it occurred to me that it could probably be used for a small operation in the Dodecanese. In this opinion, as an attack upon Castelorizzo showed later, I was proved to be very wrong.

The situation in Crete was improving rapidly. It had an adequate garrison against anything short of a full-scale invasion, and two airfields, one an existing small one at Heraklion, near the middle of the north coast, and the other at Maleme, west of Suda Bay. Both were being developed and provided with A.A. defence. The monitor *Terror* with her two 15-inch and good armament of smaller guns had been brought from Malta and for a time formed the mainstay of the defence in Suda Bay. We had a fairly efficient boom which would prevent the entry of submarines; but our most pressing need was an adequate net defence against torpedoes. The improvised net defence, which was really nothing more than a dummy, was quite useless, and we very soon had proof of it. On December 3rd the *Glasgow* was hit by two torpedoes dropped at about three thousand yards from their target by two aircraft approaching from the entrance of the bay. By some misfortune the cruisers were surprised, and the enemy was not fired upon until the torpedoes were dropped. This, however, does not detract from the enterprise of the attackers and the excellence of the Italian torpedoes. It was lucky that the *Glasgow*, though badly damaged, was able to return to Alexandria at 16 knots. There she was temporarily repaired and finally left the station for permanent repairs at the beginning of February, 1941.

Although it was unwise for ships to anchor in Suda Bay for long periods, it provided us with a most valuable advanced base, particularly for fuelling cruisers and destroyers.

The Greek Army was doing well against the Italians on the Albanian front, even advancing into Albania. Our squadrons of the R.A.F. were doing grand work in their support, though their absence was greatly felt in the Western Desert, where at this time General Wavell was preparing for his offensive. Nothing as yet had been suggested about naval co-operation on the sea flank for bombardment, or the even more important task of running forward supplies by sea.

As the Italian battle-fleet was now crippled it was decided to send an important convoy from the United Kingdom right through the Mediterranean with supplies for Malta and Alexandria. As usual, it would be brought to the entrance of the Sicilian Narrows covered by Force 'H' from Gibraltar, and met by the Mediterranean Fleet off Malta and taken on to its destination. The occasion was also to be made the opportunity for a number of operations from our end of the Mediterranean; a convoy to Malta; the *Ramillies* and *Kent* to pass into the western Mediterranean; the normal convoys to Greece and Crete; while aircraft from the *Illustrious* and *Eagle* were simultaneously to carry out raids on the Dodecanese and Tripoli, 750 miles apart, a good indication of the measure of control we now enjoyed in the Eastern and Central Mediterranean.

The *Warspite*, *Valiant*, *Illustrious* and destroyers sailed from Alexandria before dawn on November 25th after all the other movements were afoot. We called at Suda Bay to fuel the destroyers and land the commando troops from the Middle East, and then steamed on to Malta to rendezvous with the rest of the fleet and meet the convoy coming in from the westward. While waiting off Malta on November 27th, we intercepted signals which showed that the cruisers of Force 'H' were in contact with the enemy. Listening with envy we soon learnt that the Italians were in full flight towards Sardinia, and rapidly out-distancing our ships, only our cruisers and aircraft from the *Ark Royal* coming into action.

The convoy was met and safely escorted to its several destinations. A feature of this cruise to the Central Mediterranean, and a most unusual one, was that not a single gun was fired by the *Warspite* or any of the ships in company with her throughout the whole of our seven days at sea.

The bad knock the Italians had sustained at Taranto; the fact that we now had efficient air cover over the fleet which resulted in the shooting down of their reconnaissance aircraft and the mauling of their bomber squadrons; the continual and mounting losses inflicted upon the convoys to Tripoli; and the virtual segregation of the garrisons in the Dodecanese, all had their repercussions in Italian naval circles. It was at about this time that the Italian Chief of the Naval Staff, Admiral Cavagnari, was relieved by my late opponent Admiral Riccardi. There was also a crisis in the General Staff, and Mussolini, profoundly disturbed and dissatisfied with the conduct of the campaigns in Albania and Libya, accepted the resignation of Marshal Badoglio, the Supreme Commander of the Italian Army.

VII

Towards the end of November, 1940, I had been greatly concerned to receive information about a project which was being seriously considered at home. This was nothing more nor less than the capture of Pantellaria, the mountainous Italian island of about forty-five square miles some one hundred and fifty miles west-north-west of Malta, and therefore more or less in the Narrows between Sicily and Tunisia. It has a normal population of about nine thousand, and lacks fresh water.

The operation was to be called 'Workshop', and the forces to be employed were some three thousand five hundred specially trained commando troops embarked in the *Glenearn*, *Glengyle*, and *Glenroy*. These were fine cargo passenger liners, diesel-driven, capable of speeds of about nineteen knots, each carrying a number of special landing craft instead of ordinary boats. The whole operation was to be under the command of Admiral of the Fleet Lord Keyes.

It required no detailed examination on my part to dislike the whole idea intensely. I considered it a wild-cat scheme. I had no doubt at all that the island could easily be captured, and held afterwards. But I was frankly aghast at the notion of adding to our already heavy commitments another island in a position still more or less dominated by the enemy. We were having difficulty enough in maintaining Malta. To add to it Pantellaria, with a garrison and its considerable civil population requiring to be supplied also, seemed to me to be the height of unwisdom. Nor could I see what possible use Pantellaria would be to us. True, it possessed a small airfield from which fighters could operate; but to be of any use fighters required petrol, bombs, ammunition and the usual organization for their maintenance. The island, moreover, had no harbour worthy of the name, and would become a mere incubus..

The capture of Pantellaria, so close to Sicily, would undoubtedly have a popular appeal in England and look well in the headlines. It might even cause some despondency in Italian circles. But in my opinion the disadvantages far outweighed any advantage. The Italian garrison had caused us no concern up-to-date, and the small harbour could take nothing more than a few E-boats. Also, although I well knew Lord Keyes' ardent fighting spirit, I felt quite sure that to have an officer of his seniority operating independently within the area of my command would lead to difficulties

All this I set out in signals to the Admiralty, and proposed as an alternative that this force should be used to capture one or more of the Dodecanese Islands. These with their airfields, being on the flank of our convoy routes, were something of a menace, though once occupied by us they would not be so difficult to maintain because they were not under close surveillance from the enemy's main positions.

I found that the First Sea Lord shared my dislike of the 'Workshop' operation, while it did not appear that the other Chiefs of Staff were enamoured of it. During December signals passed backwards and forwards, protesting from us and insistent from home. Finally I was informed that for one reason and another the operation was postponed until the moonless period in January. It was then overtaken by the turn of events and finally abandoned. In the light of what happened later we may consider ourselves fortunate that the expedition against Pantellaria was never launched.

There was something else on my mind during December. I mentioned the action of November 27th between Force 'H' and the Italian fleet, which occurred south of Cape Spartivento, Sardinia. Force 'H' at the time was covering an important convoy of three merchant ships carrying tanks and other mechanical transport for the Middle East, and four corvettes. Two of the cruisers each carried 700 personnel of the Army and Royal Air Force.

I need not go into any particulars of the action, but it led to a Board of

Enquiry. The authorities at home questioned the correctness of placing the safety of the convoy as the first consideration, though it was quite evident that the heavy ships of Force 'H', the *Renown* and *Ramillies*, had no chance of overtaking the flying Italian battleships. I had thought this a most iniquitous action on the part of those at home, especially as the members of the Board of Enquiry were flown out to Gibraltar before the Admiral had sent in his report or even returned to harbour. The First Sea Lord mentioned it in one of his letters, which gave me the chance of a rejoinder. I criticized it severely:

ERN MEDITERRANEAN
ber, 1940

You ask me if I was surprised at the Board of Enquiry on Force 'H's' action south of Sardinia. You will wish me to speak out quite frankly and say that I was very sorry for the decision, more especially as the Board was set up even before Force 'H' had returned to harbour.

The action was an unsatisfactory one. When one is burdened with a convoy one's hands are always tied to a certain extent. Of course the Fleet Air Arm got no hits, although they claimed to have done so, and it is obvious that all the enemy ships had the legs of Force 'H'.

At the time I thought it intolerable that a Flag Officer, doing his utmost in difficult circumstances, should be continuously under the threat of finding a Board of Enquiry waiting for him on his return to harbour if his actions failed to commend themselves to those at home who knew little or nothing of the real facts of the case. Such prejudgment is not the best way to get loyal service.

I might add that the Board of Enquiry came to a decision entirely favourable to the Flag Officer Commanding Force 'H'.

VIII

An important conference was held at Cairo on December 4th, when the final plans were discussed for the coming offensive in the Western Desert, timed to start on the 7th. In conversation with me General Wavell said he would not predict how far our advance would penetrate into Libya; but he was fairly sure he could cut off the desert expert, General Malete, at Nibeiwa Camp, near Sidi Barrani. The rest was anybody's guess. However, he was full of hope, and determined to go all out if the Italians showed signs of making off.

The battle was to be fought under the direction of Lieutenant-General Sir Henry Maitland Wilson (now Field-Marshal Lord Wilson of Libya), a shrewd and imperturbable soldier whom I have always regarded as one of the outstanding military figures of the war; but little publicized. In the subsequent years he was given several difficult and unpleasant tasks, notably Greece, Palestine and Transjordan, Syria, Persia and Iraq, and he invariably made the most of them. A large and cheerful man, 'Jumbo' Wilson was greatly liked by the Navy.

The actual front-line fighting was under the command of General (now Sir) Richard O'Connor, with whom at that time I was unacquainted. During the campaign that followed, his eager, thrusting and offensive spirit, his willingness to take a risk, commanded the enthusiastic admiration of all his naval friends. We thought of his capture later in the Western Desert as a real tragedy.

The Navy took a pleasure in working with these two fine officers, though the naval share in the offensive was not very great, and I would gladly have done more.

We formed an Inshore Squadron of the *Terror*, brought down from Suda Bay, with the three veteran gunboats *Ladybird*, *Aphis*, and *Gnat*. They were reinforced from time to time by the Australian destroyers *Vampire*, *Vendetta*, *Voyager*, and *Waterhen* under Captain H. M. L. Waller, Royal Australian Navy, of H.M.A.S. *Stuart*. At the outset I placed the Inshore Squadron under the command of Rear-Admiral H. B. Rawlings—Rear-Admiral, 1st Battle Squadron—whose only order was to help the Army in every possible way. He was also directed to arrange for supplies to be sent up to the front line by sea. This traffic started as a dribble, grew into a stream, and swelled into a river as the campaign progressed.

It is interesting to remember that at Alexandria we found a couple of the old, self-propelled 'X' lighters, used in the Dardanelles twenty-five years before and then known as 'beetles'. I think they had been shipped there from Malta. The prototypes of our modern landing craft, they were small, unseaworthy vessels of slow speed about the size of Thames lighters. Laden with immediate necessities, they were sent to sea from Alexandria, and in the bad weather one foundered soon after leaving. The other, given up for lost, struggled on, admirably handled by the officer in command. Weathering the storm she finally beached herself in the creek at Sidi Barrani with stores that were badly needed by the troops.

As is well-known, the offensive was a resounding success, and showed Wavell for the really great leader and soldier that he was, one not afraid to take a chance and to make the very most of it when it comes. Sidi Barrani fell, and the Italians were routed. Sollum and Fort Capuzzo were captured on December 16th, and the next day Rear-Admiral Rawlings signalled that he intended to develop the harbour facilities and wireless stations at Sollum and Bardia, and was asking for fixed A.A. defences. Bardia eventually fell on January 5th, 1941.

Meanwhile the *Terror* and the three gunboats did valiant work, giving the Italians on the coast continual sleepless nights before the offensive started, and harrying them day and night in their retreat along the coast roads and over the Halfaya Pass. Shore Artillery, bombing 'planes, torpedo 'planes and E-boats did their utmost to hamper the Navy's operations; but without success. The bombardments continued. The ships had some unusual jobs. At Sollum, for instance, the *Terror* shouldered the task of supplying water for the advancing troops. Simultaneously with the advance, impeded by sand-storms and gales of wind, a stream of small merchant ships and other craft moved to and fro along the coast between Alexandria and the front line. They brought food, water, ammunition and all else, returned with sick and wounded and masses of Italian prisoners, of whom there were thirty thousand by mid-December.

This offensive had one result which, though perhaps hardly noticed at the time, was supremely important. It brought the three Commanders-in-Chief, Naval, Military and Air, closer together, and made them realize that success could only be obtained by continual co-ordination and co-operation; that each Service depended on the others; and that the campaign by sea, land and air was really one. Before this time we had been inclined each to pursue a vague and shadowy object, actually more or less the same; but each Commander-in-Chief using his own arm without much consultation with the others. After this first offensive in Libya, in which perhaps the three Services proved each other, the closest consultation on all important moves became a *sine qua non*. I paid many more visits to Cairo, and Wavell and Longmore often flew to Alexandria to talk to me, sometimes at extremely early hours.

IX

While this satisfactory advance in the Western Desert continued, the main fleet was not idle. The *Warspite, Valiant, Illustrious, Gloucester, York,* and eleven destroyers sailed at 1 a.m. on December 16th to cover convoys, and while thus engaged to carry out the usual crowded programme of operations. Early the next morning aircraft from the indefatigable *Illustrious* bombed Rhodes and other targets in the Dodecanese, while later the same day the whole fleet put in to Suda Bay to fuel. Our intention was to bombard and bomb Valona, the main supply port for the Italian army in Albania, on the night of the 18th, and thus give our Greek friends a helping hand. The 7th Cruiser Squadron, meanwhile, with three destroyers, were to sweep into the Adriatic as far as the line Bari-Durazzo and see what they could pick up.

The weather on the 18th was foul, with high and variable winds, strong squalls and heavy rain. We decided that flying that night would be impossible, so the *Illustrious* was detached at dark. However, we were determined to persist in the operations by the battleships and cruisers, so we pushed on. The decision to leave the *Illustrious* behind was ill-chosen, for at about midnight, when we arrived off Valona, it was a beautiful clear moonlit night and flat calm, though bitterly cold with snow low down on the hills and none of us really prepared for it. I was glad of a balaclava helmet knitted by my wife. The cruisers went ahead and had no luck, sighting nothing. We two battleships fired 100 rounds of 15-inch into Valona. The results could not be seen because of intervening hills, 2,000 feet high, and, without spotting, I am doubtful if we did much damage. However, it must have shaken the Italians, who were taken completely by surprise. Well after the bombardment had ceased searchlight and star-shell were seen in the direction of Saseno Island, that was all.

We then went on to Malta, and as things had been very quiet for some time I decided to take the *Warspite* into the Grand Harbour for a night or two while the destroyers refuelled. I particularly wished to see the dockyard, and to consult with the Vice-Admiral, Sir Wilbraham Ford, and the Governor.

I handed the residue of the fleet over to Rear-Admiral Lyster, in the *Illustrious,* who made excellent use of his time in a cruise towards Pantellaria. On the afternoon of December 21st some of his aircraft found a convoy of three Italian merchant ships escorted by a destroyer about twenty miles east of the Kerkenah Islands, Tunisia, on their way to Tripoli. Nine Swordfish attacked, and one of the merchant vessels was seen to blow up while another sank.

Meanwhile the *Warspite* steamed into the Grand Harbour during the early afternoon of December 20th. It was our first visit since May, and news of our arrival had been spread abroad. As we moved in with our band playing and guard paraded the Barracas and other points of vantage were black with wildly-cheering Maltese. Our reception was touchingly overwhelming. It was good to know that they realized that though the fleet could not use Malta for the time being, we had them well in mind.

I went round seeing all our old friends in the intervals of more official visits. Admiralty House looked very stripped and deserted, and in the hall I was met by my bandmaster and our two Maltese maids, both the latter weeping with emotion and asking if I could not persuade my wife to return.

I went all over the dockyard next morning with the Vice-Admiral and was mobbed by crowds of excited workmen singing 'God Save the King' and 'Rule Britannia'. I had difficulty in preventing myself from being carried around, and had to make more than a dozen impromptu speeches telling all and sundry how greatly the fleet still depended upon them, and congratulating them on the fine way they were working under incessant attack and great difficulties. It was a very moving experience, and once again I realized what a great acquisition we had in Sir Wilbraham Ford. I had several meetings with the Governor, Lieutenant-General (later Sir) William Dobbie, another fine man and a tower of strength. My staff discussed the supply situation. We stayed in Malta about forty hours completely undisturbed by any air attack. It was a most useful visit.

The opportunity had been taken of the presence of the fleet in the Central Mediterranean to pass a convoy and the *Malaya* through the Narrows to the westward. Unhappily one of the escorting destroyers, the *Hyperion*, was mined and badly damaged. She was taken in tow by the *Ilex*; but as dawn found them close to Pantellaria I had to give orders for the *Hyperion* to be sunk.

We rejoined the fleet, and after an uneventful passage reached Alexandria at 3 p.m. on Christmas Eve. Back at our base we learnt that the pursuit of the routed Italian army in Libya was being somewhat hampered by administrative difficulties and what the Americans would call 'logistics', and by the shortage and unreliability of the motor transport. Rear-Admiral Rawlings was making strenuous efforts to get the small harbour of Sollum open to assist army supply problems with a regular service of coasters; but it was a difficult task. Far distant were the days when we possessed the huge organizations for opening up captured and destroyed ports which played so important a part in the later years of the war. In December, 1940, we were learning by experience. We lacked much in the way of material, and still had to contrive and improvise.

On Boxing Day, the three Commanders-in-Chief met in Cairo, and took the decision that the Libyan campaign must have precedence over the two other offensives that were being planned in Abyssinia and the South Sudan, at any rate until the capture of Tobruk. This was the first I had heard of the intended capture of that place and I found it particularly heartening. It had a sizable harbour, which would not only serve as a supply port for

T

the Army, but would be of the greatest utility as a fuelling base for light forces working with the fleet in the Central Mediterranean.

And so the year 1940 ended in high hope. The Navy had a great degree of control in the Central Mediterranean and convoys were passing through both ways. We had carried out offensive strikes in the Adriatic, and were taking a fair and increasing toll of the enemy's convoys to Tripoli, upon which his army in Libya so vitally depended. Malta, though still rather lacking in anti-aircraft defence, was almost back to normal as regards repair work, while the R.A.F. bombers working from the island were dealing heavy blows upon Tripoli. Best of all, the presence of the *Illustrious* gave us as nearly as possible the command of the air over the fleet whenever it went to sea. We had the measure of the Regia Aeronautica, and with the valuable help of the Royal Air Force had drawn its teeth.

On shore the Army had won a fine victory against great odds. The invaders of Egypt had been shattered and hurled headlong back over the frontier with heavy losses in men and material, and now had to look to themselves in Eastern Cyrenaica. Though the Italians still held out at Bardia, it had been by-passed, and afforded only a temporary check to our advance. Actually on New Year's Eve it was being subjected to a softening process by naval bombardment and R.A.F. bombing, and was to fall on January 5th, 1941.

Compared with what had been our situation six months before we felt we had cause for satisfaction.

CHAPTER XXIV

I

In the Mediterranean and Middle East we started the year 1941 on the crest of the wave, while things were improving at home. The Battle of Britain had been won by the Royal Air Force, which certainly made invasion seem more of a gamble than ever. The heavy nightly bombing of our cities and industrial areas, however, was causing much destruction and dislocation, and our losses at sea through U-boat attacks were very serious indeed. From what I learnt from the First Sea Lord it was fully realized that our greatest danger lay in the Battle of the Atlantic. The U-boats were ranging further and further afield. We lacked destroyers and escort craft, while Coastal Command of the Royal Air Force was woefully short of aircraft, particularly aircraft of very long range. Some change in the relations between Coastal Command and the Admiralty was also desirable. Surface forces and aircraft working over the sea and engaged in the anti-U-boat war must work in the closest co-operation and under single control.

I was distressed to see that attacks were being made on Sir Dudley Pound in the Press and in Parliament. To one like myself who had a fair idea of his difficulties and vast responsibilities and the stout-hearted manner in which he was facing up to them, this malicious gossip seemed cruelly and unwarrantably unjust.

The Navy had already incurred considerable losses in Norway, at Dunkirk and elsewhere. Up to the end of 1940, indeed, one battleship, two aircraft-carriers, two cruisers, thirty-seven destroyers and twenty-four submarines had been sunk. Naval responsibilities were vastly increased by the defeat of France and the enemy occupation of the west coast of Europe from the North Cape in Norway to the Pyrenees, which gave them many bases for submarines and aircraft. The Germans had the superiority in the air, and were using aircraft against our shipping in the North Sea, the English Channel and the Western approaches. In the Atlantic the virulent U-boat war was gradually extending, while enemy surface raiders were operating against our trade in the South Atlantic, the Indian Ocean, and even the Pacific. The public could not be told everything; but the Navy was stretched almost to breaking point. I doubt if ever in its long history so tremendous a burden had been imposed upon those who manned its ships or directed its world-wide operation.

To revert to the Mediterranean, the last days of 1940 had found the Army going strong in the Western Desert, though temporarily held up before Bardia while supplies were brought forward. The place was well-fortified and was reputed to have a garrison of about twenty-five thousand.

The assault was fixed for January 3rd, and the battle-fleet had been asked to take a hand and step up the weight of the gunfire from the sea, which hitherto had been given by the *Terror* and the gunboats. Accordingly, the *Warspite*, *Barham*, and *Valiant*, with cruisers and destroyers, sailed from Alexandria on the 2nd, being joined that evening by the *Illustrious*. Our task was to prevent the large accumulation of enemy troops and tanks in the northern third of the area from taking the Australians in the flank while they went in to the attack. Indeed, we had to concentrate our fire on an area surrounded on three sides by our own troops.

At 8 o'clock next morning, with the *Illustrious* fighters overhead to protect us against air attack, and our own Swordfish catapulted off to spot the fall of shot, we were reaching the bombarding position. The Swordfish reported the enemy on the move, and from 8.10 until 8.55 the three battle-ships drenched the area with their twenty-four 15-inch guns. It was not particularly spectacular from the sea, merely the thick clouds of smoke and dust flung up by the bursting shell. What it must have been like to the Italians I cannot imagine; but as all enemy movement ceased I imagine our task was successfully accomplished. One coast defence battery ashore answered our fire and pitched a few shell near us; but beyond this there was no retaliation that I remember.

While at Malta we had unearthed some of the 15-inch shrapnel shell with which the *Queen Elizabeth* had done such execution at Gallipoli in 1915. I made a small bet with the fleet gunnery officer that they would still burst satisfactorily. I lost that wager. When we tried them out the balls inside the shell were all rusted together.

The battleships retired the same afternoon, leaving the *Terror*, *Aphis* and *Ladybird* to continue the supporting fire. I felt a little sorry for them as we moved off, for I knew that when the *Illustrious* fighters departed the *Terror* and her little consorts would have full attention from the enemy bombers and were being left to 'carry the can', as the sailor puts it. Sure enough they did catch it; but being old hands at the game they were able to drive the bombers off for the time being.

I drew the attention of the First Sea Lord to the fine work of the *Terror*, Commander H. J. Haynes; *Ladybird*, Lieutenant-Commander J. F. Blackburn; and *Aphis*, Lieutenant-Commander J. O. Campbell. I wrote that they— "have done splendid work, with the two little gunboats close inshore using everything they have got. The *Terror* has had goodness knows how many torpedoes fired at her by torpedo-bombers; but so far without result. Her guns are worn nearly to the limit of safety, but she can still bowl lobs."

The Australian assault was successful, and on January 5th Bardia fell, and some twenty-five thousand more Italian prisoners were in the bag. The capture of Bardia brought the Army the great relief of a proper water supply, while before long the little port was being used by a succession of small craft running stores of every description for the Army.

It so happened that my promotion to Admiral, and that of Pridham-Wippell, my second-in-command, to Vice-Admiral, synchronized with the bombardment of Bardia, January 3rd. Before that date, we had been 'acting' in those ranks.

II

January 7th found the whole fleet at sea again for an operation called 'Excess'. The main object of this movement was to pass through the Mediterranean from the west a convoy of four large merchant vessels, three of them bound for the Piræus with urgent supplies for our Greek Allies, and the other with an even more important cargo for Malta, which included some four thousand tons of much-needed ammunition. The opportunity was also to be taken to run an oiler to Suda Bay, two merchant vessels laden with supplies, oil fuel and petrol into Malta from Alexandria, and to bring another convoy away. Afterwards, when the convoys were in moderately safe waters, it was intended that the fleet should undertake offensive operations against shipping on the Italian coasts.

One feature out of the ordinary was that on this occasion the cruisers *Gloucester* and *Southampton* and two destroyers, under the command of Rear-Admiral E. de F. Renouf, were to go on ahead through the Sicilian Narrows and take over the convoy from Force 'H' which was bringing it from Gibraltar. They were lucky to get through safely. During their passage west in bright moonlight they were sighted and challenged by a signal station in Pantellaria. Altering course to open that island, both ships cut mines with their paravanes after crossing the 200-fathom line. The whole operation was rather more intricate than usual, with of course, every movement and alteration of course prearranged and carefully synchronized.

In the *Warspite* I carried out my usual routine. I never took my clothes off at sea except for my daily bath, and never left the close proximity of the bridge. I had a sea cabin and bathroom one ladder down, and here I had my meals unless some urgent situation compelled me to have them in the Commander-in-Chief's charthouse on the bridge. The five Commanders on the staff, Dick, Carne, Barnard, Brownrigg and Power, kept watch day and night and conducted the routine movements of the fleet. By day I was practically always on the bridge and if I was not, the Chief of Staff, Rear-Admiral Willis, was there. If things were quiet he would be on the bridge until midnight, when he was relieved by the Captain of the Fleet, Richard Shelley, until 3 or 3.30 a.m. Then I came up, and was always on the bridge at dawn. I was on call, of course, at any time during the night. Everything was reported to me, and I was invariably up for any alterations of course other than the normal zigzags.

Operation 'Excess' started according to plan, and at 4.30 a.m. on January 10th the *Warspite*, *Valiant*, and *Illustrious* with seven destroyers were to the north-west of Malta, steering for the convoy. The day began well. Soon after 7.30, at which time it was dawn, we had a report from the cruiser *Bonaventure*, which was joining us from the west, saying she had sighted two enemy destroyers. Almost simultaneously we sighted gun flashes to the westward, so increased to full speed in case the convoy escort needed support. As we swept on we passed close to the convoy, indeed some of the destroyer screen passed through it. We could just make out the figures of the troops in the merchant vessels, and I wondered at the time if they were thrilled by the sight of these three large ships steaming at full speed to the sound of the guns. It must have been a fine spectacle in the grey light of the morning.

Broad daylight soon after 8 o'clock found us within five or six miles of Pantellaria, with the *Bonaventure* and *Hereward* still firing heavily at close range into a crippled and burning enemy destroyer. The other had escaped. The destroyer blew up, whereupon the battle-fleet turned to follow the convoy.

Then things started to go wrong. I was watching the destroyer screen taking up their new stations, always a fascinating sight to an old destroyer officer, when I suddenly saw a heavy explosion under the *Gallant's* bows. She had been mined, and in water through which the battle-fleet had passed only a short time before. Her bow was blown clean away and she was left helpless. The *Mohawk* took the stern portion in tow, and Rear-Admiral Renouf with the *Gloucester*, *Southampton* and *Bonaventure* was ordered to escort what remained of the *Gallant* into Malta. She reached the island early next morning and was docked, though never repaired. In 1943 she still lay beached on the Marina.

In the meantime the fleet steamed south-east after the convoy, presently to be located and reported by enemy aircraft. A shadower was shot down by the *Illustrious's* Fulmars; but just before 12.30 we were attacked by two Italian torpedo-bombers, which came in low. Their torpedoes passed astern of the *Valiant*. This incident had the unfortunate but natural result of bringing the fighters down from where they were patrolling high over the fleet.

Almost immediately large formations of aircraft were sighted to the northward, and were very soon overhead. They were recognized as German, three squadrons of Stukas. The *Illustrious* flew off more fighters; but neither they nor the patrol already in the air could gain sufficient height to do anything. We opened up with every A.A. gun we had as one by one the Stukas peeled off into their dives, concentrating almost the whole venom of their attack upon the *Illustrious*. At times she became almost completely hidden in a forest of great bomb splashes.

One was too interested in this new form of dive-bombing attack really to be frightened, and there was no doubt we were watching complete experts. Formed roughly in a large circle over the fleet they peeled off one by one when reaching the attacking position. We could not but admire the skill and precision of it all. The attacks were pressed home to point-blank range, and as they pulled out of their dives some of them were seen to fly along the flight deck of the *Illustrious* below the level of her funnel.

I saw her hit early on just before the bridge, and in all, in something like ten minutes, she was hit by six 1,000 lb. bombs, to leave the line badly on fire, her steering gear crippled, her lifts out of action, and with heavy casualties.

The *Warspite* was hit once, on the fluke of the starboard bower anchor. Actually I saw the bomb burst; but fortunately the detonation was incomplete and we suffered no great harm. One of the staff officers who watched it hurtling over the bridge from astern told me it looked about the size of the wardroom sofa.

The *Illustrious* reported herself as badly hit and making for Malta; but it was not until 3.30 p.m. that she was steering more or less steadily in that direction at 17 knots. Meanwhile we remained close to give her what cover we could. Between four and five o'clock, still on fire, she was attacked, with the battleships, by another twenty dive-bombers. My heart sank as I watched her, wondering how with all her heavy damage, she would stand up to it. I need not have worried. As the attacks developed I saw every gun in the *Illustrious* flash into action, a grand and inspiring sight. Moreover, her Fulmar fighters, which had flown on to Malta when their parent ship was damaged, had refuelled and come out again. They managed to shoot six or seven Stukas into the sea and to damage others. The *Illustrious* eventually arrived off Malta at 9.45 p.m. and was taken safely into harbour.

So far as the battleships were concerned, the *Valiant* had one killed and two wounded by splinters.

During the night we withdrew to the eastward, covering the convoy. We had plenty to think about. In a few minutes the whole situation had changed. At one blow the fleet had been deprived of its fighter aircraft, and its command of the Mediterranean was threatened by a weapon far more efficient and dangerous than any against which we had fought before. The efforts of the Regia Aeronautica were almost as nothing compared with those of these deadly Stukas of the Luftwaffe. Moreover, we very well knew that with the *Illustrious* berthed in Malta under their noses, the Germans would spare no effort to knock her out.

However, more trouble was yet to come.

Having seen the *Gallant* into Malta, Rear-Admiral Renouf, with the *Gloucester* and *Southampton*, left the island at 5 a.m. on January 11th to rejoin the fleet to the eastward. Neither ship was fitted with radar, and at 3 p.m. we had a report that they had been attacked by twelve dive-bombers coming in unexpectedly out of the sun, and that both ships were hit. The *Gloucester* was struck through the roof of the director tower by a bomb which failed to explode. Severely damaged, she had nine killed and fourteen wounded. Rear-Admiral Renouf was unfortunate. This was the fourth ship of his squadron to be damaged, though personally he was a lucky man. It was the second time that the cruiser in which he was flying his flag was hit on the bridge structure by a dud bomb.

The *Southampton's* two hits were a different matter. By an unhappy coincidence the attack synchronized with a stand-off by both ships' companies after their strenuous forty-eight hours continuously at action stations. In fact they were at tea. The *Southampton* was hit in the wardroom and the petty officers' mess, so that all those best qualified to lead the fire-fighting and damage control became casualties. She was soon blazing, and shortly after 7 p.m., with the fires completely out of control, the ship had to be abandoned and sunk by a torpedo. The survivors were embarked in the *Gloucester* and the destroyer *Diamond*.

The *Illustrious* was berthed in the Grand Harbour at Malta, and the Constructors department at once went into action to get her repaired. It was hardly to be expected that the Luftwaffe would miss the chance. Day after day she was savagely attacked. There was a particularly heavy raid by seventy aircraft at dusk on January 16th, when the *Illustrious* was hit again, though not seriously damaged. The merchant vessel *Essex* however, which had arrived with the convoy, was hit in the engine-room with a loss of fifteen killed and twenty-three wounded. By some miracle the 4,000 tons of ammunition in her holds was undamaged. In that same raid the cruiser *Perth* was damaged below water by a near miss. Considerable destruction was done in the dockyard, and there were many civilian casualties.

Malta was heavily raided again on the 18th and 19th, more serious damage being done to the bottom plating of the *Illustrious* on the latter occasion by bombs bursting on the bottom close alongside and thus producing a mining effect. The R.A.F. fighters and Fleet Air Arm Fulmars took heavy toll of the attackers, and with the guns of the *Illustrious* constantly in action the dockyard officers and workmen laboured frenziedly to make her temporarily fit for sea again. The undaunted constructors struggled on, and the Chief Constructor, Mr. J. C. Joughin, himself sat in the diving-boat alongside the *Illustrious* to encourage the divers. He was a great man.

On January 19th I informed the Admiralty that the situation was difficult and that Malta was being heavily raided. It was urgently necessary to get the *Illustrious* and large merchant vessels away; but up to the present bad weather had prevented my sending destroyer escorts. I added that this would be done as soon as possible, and that cruisers were assembling at Suda Bay to provide cover in the Central Mediterranean. The *Eagle* was out of action with defective stern glands, and barely enough destroyers could be raised to send two battleships to sea to support the exit of the *Illustrious* and merchant vessels from Malta. The most urgent requirement was more fighter aircraft for Malta, and this matter I was pursuing with the Air Officer Commander-in-Chief, Middle East.

It was obvious to all that if the *Illustrious* was to survive she must be got away from Malta, and get away she did. By dint of superhuman efforts on the part of everyone concerned she slipped to sea on the night of the 23rd, and made for Alexandria at 24 knots. This unexpected turn of speed resulted in her missing the cruiser squadron sent west to escort her, which was perhaps as well, as they were heavily bombed. However, she made contact with the covering battle-squadron, and at noon on January 25th, battle-scarred and triumphant, arrived at Alexandria and came into harbour cheered to the echo by the *Warspite* and other ships as she steamed slowly past.

That *Illustrious* episode stands out as a triumph for British shipbuilding and our Naval Constructors, as well as for those who repaired her at Malta. I sent a message to the Vice-Admiral at Malta expressing our warmest appreciation of the work done under conditions of great difficulty to get the ship away. The men of Malta dockyard deserved all the praise we could give them.

We, for our part, were gratified at receiving a very cordial signal from His Excellency, the Governor of Malta, in which he expressed sympathy for our losses during the recent operations, and the appreciation of the whole island for the efforts made by the Mediterranean Fleet in bringing them supplies.

The *Illustrious* would have to leave the station for extensive repairs. She would not be battleworthy for months; but on January 12th, two days after she had been bombed, the Admiralty took the decision to send us the *Formidable*, then serving in the South Atlantic. She would come to us round the Cape of Good Hope, which meant that we might expect her some time in March.

III

I found plenty to occupy me at Alexandria, and first we disposed of the *Illustrious's* aircraft where they might best help in the war. We left a squadron of Swordfish and twelve Fulmars at Malta, where they were badly needed for offence and defence. Some more Swordfish were sent to Crete, and a flight to the Western Desert to work with the R.A.F. and under the Senior Officer of our Inshore Squadron.

Longmore, the Air Officer Commanding-in-Chief, came to see me soon after our arrival, and together we discussed the new situation brought about by the arrival of the Luftwaffe. As usual, he was very understanding and sympathetic, and promised all the fighter co-operation he could provide. General Wavell, just back from a visit to Athens, also came to see me on January 17th. He told me of the military situation in Greece and elsewhere. Lest it should invite German intervention the Greeks refused direct military assistance; but wanted equipment and supplies of all kinds with squadrons of the Royal Air Force.

Our estimate of the German air strength in the Mediterranean at this period was a hundred dive bombers, one hundred and fifty long-range bombers and fifty reconnaissance aircraft. This considerable strength seemed to indicate that they were contemplating something more important than an attack upon our sea communications. It rather looked as though Hitler, fearing an Italian collapse, intended to come to their assistance by starting large-scale operations in the Mediterranean. Meanwhile, from various reports, we began to suspect the arrival of the Luftwaffe in the Dodecanese, and sure enough the Suez Canal was attacked on the night of January 18th–19th. There were neither damage nor casualties; but the Canal traffic had to be held up for twenty-four hours because of unexploded bombs.

This first attack on the Canal made us rather apprehensive. Except for fast ships, the route through the Mediterranean must be abandoned for the time being. Were the enemy going to try closing our back door also? It was essential that all the convoys coming round the Cape and up the Red Sea with reinforcements and supplies for the Army should use the Canal. Alexandria was the only port in Egypt with the facilities for dealing with a large volume of shipping.

At about this time Colonel Donovan, from the United States, lunched with me on board the *Warspite*. He had been travelling round Europe sizing up the situation and had just come from the Balkans. I found him a most pleasant and interesting man, very much alive. We talked about the naval situation in the Mediterranean, and he offered to send a message to the United States saying they must let us have some fighter aircraft. I did nothing to discourage him.

We had long been considering a commando operation in the Dodecanese. The idea was to take Kaso, the island near Scarpanto off the eastern end of Crete, which would have given us both sides of the Kaso Straits, always the scene of much U-boat and E-boat activity. Furthermore, we intended mounting a gun or two on Kaso to command the airfield at Scarpanto. But for some reason the Chiefs of Staff at home vetoed the operation. We regretted it. As subsequent events showed the occupation of Kaso would have paid a dividend.

However, a little later in January there came an instruction from the Chiefs of Staff at home telling us they had been considering the situation caused by the arrival of the Luftwaffe in the Mediterranean and the refusal of the Greeks of any direct military aid. It was the opinion that an attack should be planned on the Dodecanese, particularly on Rhodes, so as to secure our position in the Ægean. This certainly fell in with my views, though I could not see where the troops or other resources were to come from, especially as they also stressed the importance of capturing Benghazi. For this Dodecanese project the three specially equipped assault ships, *Glenearn*, *Glengyle* and *Glenroy*, were also to be sent out to us.

Meanwhile all was going well ashore. General Platt was advancing in Southern Sudan, and my brother was starting to move south of Abyssinia. In the Western Desert the Army was pausing preparatory to the assault on Tobruk. The Inshore Squadron, now under the command of Captain Harold Hickling, had been giving all possible help in bombarding, evacuating prisoners, landing supplies and so on. On January 19th I was able to report to the Admiralty that in spite of bad weather, the Inshore Squadron in the last ten days had ferried thirty-five thousand Italian prisoners of war to Alexandria, besides supplying stores to Sollum and Bardia at the rate of 500 tons daily and clearing both those harbours for traffic. Preparations had also been made for using the harbour at Tobruk as soon as possible after its capture. A small ship laden with everything necessary for this purpose was kept at Sollum ready to move on when the assault started.

In the event the 6th Australian Division, supported from the sea by the *Terror* and *Ladybird*; Captain Waller, Royal Australian Navy, in the *Stuart*, with the destroyers *Vampire* and *Defender*, broke into the outer defences at Tobruk at dawn on January 22nd, and by midday the town and harbour were in our hands. The port was in fair condition, though considerable damage had been done to the wharves and cranes. However, there were a good number of lighters, while the oil storage was intact and by no means empty. On the 27th we were able to report that Tobruk was open to sea traffic, that the Italian boom defence was 80 per cent efficient, and that there was ample coal and water.

With the Chief of Staff I flew to Tobruk two days later and inspected the harbour and shore defences. It was an interesting visit. The harbour, though fouled by wrecks, had far more sheltered accommodation than I expected. There was ample room for our supply ships. The old Italian cruiser *San Giorgio*, bombed by the R.A.F. and finally destroyed by the Italians, lay sunk near the entrance with much of her hull above water and still smoking. With her heavy armament of four 10-inch guns and eight 7·5s she had been one of the mainstays of the defence against attack from the sea.

Captain Hickling was also in general charge at Tobruk. He and his men had done a remarkable job of work in preparing the harbour for traffic. It was of the greatest value and assistance to the Army.

To digress for a moment. My wife had instituted large sewing and knitting parties at the Residency at Alexandria several mornings a week, and there the wives of officers and ratings turned out woollies for the sailors and garments for the Red Cross. They badly needed sewing machines, and from some source of information known only to herself my wife had heard they were to be had in Tobruk. She mentioned this to Captain H. M. L. Waller, of the *Stuart*, in command of the Australian destroyer flotilla working with the Inshore Squadron, and Waller promised to do what he could.

Landing at Tobruk he was stopped by the Military Police. For fear of wholesale looting nobody was allowed into the town. Waller argued with the man: "I had a hand in helping to capture this place. Surely I can go and have a look at the results of our bombardments!"—"No, sir. I've orders to let no one in," the M.P. replied. "If I let one in we shall soon have the place full of these bloody Australians pinching every mortal thing."

What persuasive blarney Waller used to get his own way I do not know; but some days later a lorry drove up to the Residency at Alexandria and discharged two sewing machines in crates. One, a most imposing-looking piece of machinery by Singer which Waller had labelled 'The Admiral's Model', was rechristened 'Marchesa Graziani' by the ladies.

Hector Macdonald Laws Waller will always remain in my mind as one of the very finest types of Australian naval officer. Full of good cheer, with a great sense of humour, undefeated and always burning to get at the enemy, he kept the old ships of his flotilla—the *Stuart, Vampire, Vendetta, Voyager, Waterhen*—hard at it always. Greatly loved and admired by everyone, his loss in H.M.A.S. *Perth* in the Java Sea in March, 1942, was a heavy deprivation for the young Navy of Australia.

IV

Malta had suffered a series of very heavy air attacks since the arrival of the Luftwaffe, particularly when the *Illustrious* was in the Grand Harbour. But I was greatly heartened by the reports about the dockyard received from the Vice-Admiral, Sir Wilbraham Ford. Although considerably damaged, they expected to be back to 80 to 90 per cent efficiency in two or three weeks.

All through the months that the island was under constant attack I was always amazed at the way the dockyard came to life again after being, as I thought, completely knocked out of action. There seemed to be no limit to the degree to which a damaged dockyard could rehabilitate itself. In this case the Vice-Admiral reported that what was holding him up was lack of labour, which had been badly shaken by the heavy bombing; but was gradually improving. Damage to the electric supply was another obstacle. The docks were not so badly damaged as he had feared, and they were already capable of docking and refitting a cruiser. The *Breconshire*, a merchant vessel, was being converted to carry petrol, and the work to get the more important engineering shops deep underground was being pushed on. In all the troubles to come, Malta dockyard was never completely out of action for very long. The indefatigable and undefeated Admiral Ford, enthusiastically supported by the dockyard officers, always found some way of keeping it working and rapidly repairing the damage and destruction.

The fleet was now restricted in its activities by the lack of an aircraft-carrier; but there was no let-up in the convoy work to the Ægean or along the coast of Libya. Indeed, with the opening of Tobruk as a supply port for the Army our commitments greatly increased.

There had been some changes and additions to the fleet which to some extent eased the strain on the overworked destroyers. We now had the three small anti-aircraft cruisers *Coventry*, *Calcutta* and *Carlisle*, and no convoy was complete without one or the other of them. The new cruiser *Bonaventure* just out from England was also a useful addition, though in her action with the Italian destroyers off Pantellaria she had fired away 75 per cent of her low-angle ammunition, of which there was no reserve on the station and none could be expected till late in February or early March. This restricted her use, though her radar, then more or less a modern development fitted in only the newest ships, made her most useful in company with other units.

Four South African whalers had arrived, the *Southern Floe*, *Southern Isle*, *Southern Maid* and *Southern Sea*, staunch little ships finely manned and commanded; also the *Chakla* and *Fiona*, small passenger vessels from India, splendidly commanded by officers of the Royal Naval Reserve with part Indian crews, who soon showed their worth when running supplies for the Army along the Libyan coast.

Finally, after more than six months of war with Italy, Alexandria now proudly wore a balloon barrage.

The end of January found the Army still going strong. Derna was captured on the 30th, and the advance of Benghazi began. It was entered by the Australians on February 6th, while the armoured forces, by a grand dash across the open desert along the chord of the arc, cut off the retreat of the Italians south of Benghazi. As Mussolini himself said, the 10th Italian Army ceased to exist. This desert variety of the naval manœuvre of crossing the enemy's T greatly delighted the Navy. However, so far as land supply was concerned, this magnificent advance from the borders of Egypt brought the Army to the end of its tether, and gave the Navy the heavy commitment of trying to open the port of Benghazi for the small ships needed to bring forward the petrol, food, ammunition and quantities of miscellaneous stores without which the Army became immobilized.

On February 9th, I signalled to the Inshore Squadron:

The feat of the Army in clearing Egypt and occupying Cyrenaica in a period of eight weeks is an outstanding achievement to which the Inshore Squadron and the shore parties along the coast have contributed in no small measure. I am fully alive to the fact that this result has been made possible by an unbreakable determination to allow no obstacle to stand in the way of meeting all requirements. All officers and men who took part in these operations may well feel proud, as I do, of their contribution to this victory.

Supplying the Army by sea through Benghazi was a problem indeed. It added another two hundred miles to the journey from Alexandria, and Benghazi was actually nearer to the enemy air bases at Tripoli and in Sicily. The breakwater was widely breached and the entrance partially blocked, while the enemy lost no time in laying mines from aircraft. The Army were very anxious that Benghazi should be used as their main supply port; but their resources did not allow of even a reasonable quota of guns to defend the place from any attack from seaward or from the air. The fighter defence was also very meagre. All the same, we did our best to be helpful, and though the Germans started shedding magnetic mines in the harbour on February 13th, we sailed a convoy for Benghazi the next day, with the *Terror* and *Coventry* to help in the defence.

However, the Germans were perfectly well aware of the value of the place to us, and made persistent air attacks with which the defences were totally unable to deal. The German dive bombers were a menace. We had lost the minesweeper *Huntley*, on her way to Derna, on January 31st, and the *Southern Floe* and *Ouse* by mines off Tobruk on February 11th and 20th. A hospital ship, the *Dorsetshire*, had also twice been attacked and damaged by near misses in the Gulf of Sollum.

At Benghazi, at dawn on February 22nd, the *Terror*, fighting back with all she had, was narrowly missed by a bomb which started slow leaks in various compartments. Commander Haynes knew that the Luftwaffe were out to sink his ship, and in reporting his damage to me and asking for fighter cover, which could not be given, ended his signal by saying: "I consider it only a matter of time before the ship receives a direct hit."

I ordered the *Terror*'s withdrawal, and was forced to tell the Army that if Benghazi could not be efficiently defended, we could not use it. They, poor men, could do nothing, as most of their anti-aircraft guns were being withdrawn to be sent to Greece.

The *Terror* sailed for Tobruk at dusk, exploding two acoustic mines on leaving Benghazi which caused further flooding. The next morning, off Derna, she was again heavily dive-bombed and near-missed, her back being broken and her engine-room flooded. A corvette and a minesweeper tried to take her in tow; but she developed a heavy list and finally had to be abandoned. Thus went a gallant ship, twenty-five years old, which had started her fighting career on the Belgian coast in the previous war, and had joined the Mediterranean Fleet from Singapore. Her anti-aircraft guns had been in action at Malta and Suda Bay. Along the Libyan coast on the right flank of the Army, besides softening up the enemy positions with her 15-inch guns, worn practically to smooth-bores, she had acted as a perambulating repair shop, water-carrier, supply ship and much else. Time and time again her guns had provided the only anti-aircraft defence in some newly-occupied harbour. The *Terror's* officers and men had endured much, and might well be proud of their record. I was certainly proud of them.

On February 24th we lost another ship of the Inshore Squadron when the *Dainty*, Commander Mervyn Thomas, was dive-bombed and sunk off Tobruk. Thomas, who had done so well against Italian submarines in the previous June, had recently put up another notable performance by successfully towing a large tanker, torpedoed off the east end of Crete, well over a hundred miles to Suda Bay, though attacked on the way by torpedo bombers.

CHAPTER XXV

I

As the Luftwaffe had arrived in the Dodecanese, we fully expected that one of their next steps would be the dropping of magnetic mines in the Suez Canal. So far as our meagre resources would permit, we had done what we could to combat this new menace by fitting out some of the Canal hoppers with magnetic mine sweeps and by creating a skeleton organization for a watching service.

The first mines were actually dropped on January 30th, 1941, and the Canal had to be closed. It was reopened on February 3rd; but on that day and the two days following a ship was mined, one of them in a very awkward position where she partially blocked the fairway. By cutting down on other commitments the defences were reinforced; but the minelaying continued. There were casualties among the sweeping forces, and the situation became very serious. By February 7th we had accounted for sixteen mines; but there were others. It was estimated that the Canal could not be open for traffic until the 18th, and then only for ships up to 15,000 tons. March 5th was our date for the transit of large warships.

This was particularly galling. Because of the damage to the *Illustrious*, the fleet was hampered in its operations by the lack of an armoured carrier to provide the necessary fighter cover. The *Formidable* was waiting in the Red Sea; but could not join us at Alexandria until the Canal was open. We also wished to get the *Illustrious* and *Eagle* away, the first-named to be permanently repaired in the United States. The *Eagle*, for whose services the First Sea Lord had asked to help in running down the German surface raiders in the Indian Ocean and South Atlantic, was long overdue for a refit. Moreover, with her unarmoured flight deck, she could not be used in the Mediterranean within range of the German dive-bombers.

I flew to the Canal on February 10th and inspected all the defence and clearance arrangements with Vice-Admiral Sir James Pipon, who was Senior Naval Officer, Suez Canal. The organization was rapidly being improved under his able and energetic direction; but the watching for the exact spots where the mines were dropped was very expensive in man-power, and absorbed some three-and-a-half battalions of British troops. It was later well done by Egyptian troops.

There was also some doubt as to how the mines behaved. Twenty-four ships had passed safely over one spot, and the twenty-fifth exploded a mine. It was thought that mines lying in shallow water might be drawn out into the deeper water by the suction of passing vessels. The sweepers being not entirely successful, the method used was to fix the position of the mine when dropped by cross-bearings from the watchers, and then to send down a diver to locate it, both naval and Arab divers being employed. This done the mine was either dragged to one side and rendered harmless, or else blown up where it lay. If it could not be accurately located, the whole area around it was plastered with depth charges, which was most successful.

The really critical business was getting the *Formidable*, *Illustrious* and *Eagle* past the wreck of one ship which lay across the Canal. However, by dredging and pulling the wreck to one side, a passage was eventually cleared. The Canal was actually reopened on February 11th; but it was not until March 10th that the *Formidable* eventually reached Alexandria, having been squeezed through the Canal with literally no more than a few feet to spare on either side. The *Illustrious* went a week afterwards and the *Eagle* later still. For merchant vessels we were well on top of our troubles by the end of March, and it was very seldom that the Canal had to be closed for more than twenty-four to forty-eight hours. Shortage of fighters and of anti-aircraft guns were the root causes of our predicament.

Along the North African coast at Tobruk we were by no means certain that we were not dealing with acoustic mines, as all the ships that had touched them off were diesel-engined. There, up to February 10th, we had only one loss, though other ships had been damaged and our repair resources were badly strained in trying to patch them up. However, Tobruk was open, though not without risk.

Writing to the First Sea Lord on February 10th, I said: "This delay"—i.e. the arrival of the *Formidable*—"is a nuisance, as I want to pass in a Malta convoy." In regard to the German dive-bombers I added: "We are trying some new methods against them. One which looks very promising is to make the destroyer screen put up an umbrella barrage over a particular ship, probably the carrier. I am also going to have twelve fighters in the air over the fleet when we encounter these gentlemen again. I haven't much doubt of the result. Pridham-Wippell's four cruisers kept them at arm's length and inflicted casualties when the *Illustrious* was on passage from Malta."

II

Our attention now became focused upon Greece. The unfortunate death of General Metaxas at the end of January had resulted in a change of opinion on the part of the Greek Government in the matter of direct British assistance, and on February 8th they asked whether they could rely upon our help in the event of a German invasion.

There were definite signs that German strategic ideas were veering to the south and south-east, partly because of the severe set-backs suffered by the Italians, partly because of Syria and the oil resources of Iran lay at the back of Hitler's mind.

The Italians were very feeble partners. Besides having been ignominiously thrown out of Cyrenaica, and being pushed back with heavy losses on both fronts in East Africa, they had not acquitted themselves with credit against the Greeks in Albania. Mussolini, for all his flashing bayonets, was teetering on the brink of a further collapse. The Luftwaffe had already come to his help in the Mediterranean, and now it seemed certain that the Wehrmacht must come also.

It was a few days after the Greek Government's request that the Commander-in-Chief, Middle East, received a new directive from the War Cabinet. Briefly, we had orders that there was to be no offensive beyond the western frontier of Cyrenaica; that Cyrenaica was to be held with the minimum force; that the largest possible land and air forces were to be sent at once to the help of Greece; that we were to press on with our preparations for an attack upon the Dodecanese. We also heard that Mr. Eden, the Secretary of State for War, and General Dill, the Chief of the Imperial General Staff, were on their way out.

This new directive gave Wavell more of a headache than it gave me. I was tolerably certain that the Navy could get all the forces that could be collected to Greece in comparative safety. But Wavell had to decide upon the minimum force necessary to hold Cyrenaica, and to keep his two offensives in East Africa in movement simultaneously with the collection and preparation of an Army for Greece. The problems of the Air Officer Commanding-in-Chief were only slightly less than those of General Wavell. He was poverty-stricken for aircraft in most areas, and now had to decide where they should be reduced to virtual destitution to carry out this new commitment.

The fourth item of the War Cabinet directive, the attack on the Dodecanese, rather led me to think that the authorities at home were living in a land of optimistic dreams. I, personally, was anxious enough to make an attempt in that direction; but with our resources stretched to breaking-point it was painfully obvious that the Navy could do no more. Apart from any offensive against the Italian fleet, we already had on our hands the upkeep of Malta and the supply of the Army in Libya some hundreds of miles from Egypt. Now, with a large increase in the convoys to Greece for the transport and supply of an Army there, it was quite impossible for us to think seriously of yet another expedition to the Dodecanese.

A conference was held at Cairo on the arrival of Eden and Dill on February 19th, and I gave it as my opinion that any forces available could safely be transported to Greece. Wavell, Air Chief Marshal Longmore, Dill and Eden flew to Greece on the 22nd, Captain R. M. Dick accompanying them as my representative. Briefly, the decisions arrived at were that a force of three infantry divisions and one armoured brigade should be sent there with additional squadrons of the Royal Air Force. The ports of disembarkation were to be the Piræus and Volo. There was considerable discussion on the line to be held. Naval and air objections ruled out the port of Salonika, and eventually the Aliakhmon line was decided upon. This was the first feasible position, on the hills west of the Vardar River and along the River Aliakhmon, south of which rises the range of mountains of which Mount Olympus forms part. The probable attitude of the Serbs came under examination. Would they resist if the Germans entered their country? The question was left in doubt.

Further conferences were held in Cairo on the return of Eden and Dill. The decisions were confirmed, and they flew on to Ankara to see if the Turks were inclined to help in the event of a German invasion of Greece. The Turks, however, influenced no doubt by the proximity of the Germans in Bulgaria, decided upon neutrality. Personally, I felt this suited us best. As a neutral, Turkey could not be such a drain on our resources as if she were a belligerent. We had literally nothing to give away, and the Turks knew it.

There has been much discussion and controversy as to whether we were right or wrong in sending troops to Greece. We, the naval element, thought roughly as follows. We were bound by treaty to help Greece if she were threatened, so there was no question at all that it was, politically, the right thing to do. On the other hand, we had serious misgivings if it was correct from the military point of view. We doubted very much if our Naval, Military and Air resources were equal to it. No doubt our opinions were somewhat influenced by the fact that we were in possession of the Libyan coast as far west as Benghazi. From the Navy's point of view this facilitated the supply of Malta and the passage through the Sicilian Narrows, and conditions would be better still if the advance were continued towards Tripolitania. We had no illusions that the help we could send the Greeks would enable them to stem a really serious German invasion. Indeed, when the decision to send troops was finally taken, we started at once to think of how we should bring them out.

At the final meeting in Cairo with Wavell, Eden and Dill, I gave it as my opinion that though politically we were correct, I had grave uncertainty of its military expedience. Dill himself had doubts, and said to me after the meeting: "Well, we've taken the decision. I'm not at all sure it's the right one."

The movement of the Army to Greece started on March 4th, and will be dealt with later.

III

Because we had no armoured aircraft-carrier, the fleet had been considerably restricted during February in its operations in the Central Mediterranean. No convoy with supplies could be run to Malta; but we had gone to sea on February 1st to make a diversion while the Fleet Air Arm from Force 'H' in the Western Mediterranean attempted to torpedo the Lake Tirso dam in Sardinia. Its destruction would have put about half the power supply of the island out of action. We also heard with pleasure of Sir James Somerville's successful bombardment of Genoa, and the Fleet Air Arm's bombing of Leghorn and Pisa. Our cruise in the Eastern Mediterranean was without incident.

Later in February we were able to send two infantry battalions to Malta in cruisers, and to bring out a small convoy.

Towards the end of the month we undertook an operation with the commando troops in Crete against the small Dodecanese island of Castelorizzo, to the east of Rhodes, which we wished to use as an advanced base for motor torpedo-boats. At first all went well, and much to the delight of the inhabitants the island was captured without difficulty. The Italians in Rhodes, however, reacted with most unexpected vigour and enterprise. They bombed the island heavily, and after dark landed troops from torpedo craft. Our communication with the island failed, and we knew nothing of what was going on; but next night had to send two destroyers to evacuate the Commando. It was a disappointing affair and greatly mishandled. As I later wrote to the First Sea Lord:

> The taking and abandonment of Castelorizzo was a rotten business and reflected little credit on anyone—— The Italians were unbelievably enterprising, and not only bombed the island, but bombarded it and landed troops from destroyers. For some reason the Army wireless set did not work, and so we got no information of what was going on. These Commandos we have out here are on a tommy-gun and knuckle-duster basis, and apparently can't defend themselves if seriously attacked. I had sent twenty-five Marines bristling with machine-guns in the *Ladybird*; but some fool ordered them to re-embark. All we can say is that we have learnt a lot from it and won't repeat the mistakes.

At this period, the middle of February, I was becoming increasingly concerned about the scantiness of the Royal Air Force co-operation with the fleet. Air Chief Marshal Longmore always did his best to help; but he lacked the aircraft. Our long-range reconnaissance had never been adequate, in no way comparable with the Italian, while there were no fighters available for the defence of our convoys along the coast of Libya. What it came to was that Longmore was perilously short of squadrons. We, the Navy, had come to the opinion that what was wanted in the Mediterranean was some organization similar to the Coastal Command at home, with aircraft definitely detailed for work with the fleet, and under our operational control. It seemed to me to be self-evident that if such an organization had been found necessary in Home Waters, it was even more so in the confined waters of the Mediterranean.

Air Chief Marshal Longmore came to see me on February 16th, and I showed him the draft of a long message I proposed sending to the Admiralty. He raised no objections, and was fully aware that I was not being critical of him. In spite of his woeful shortage he had always been most co-operative and helpful.

I pointed out to the Admiralty, in so many words, that with the arrival of the Luftwaffe in the Mediterranean our aircraft-carrier could no longer expect the immunity she had enjoyed with only the Regia Aeronautica. Quite apart from the increased risk of damage, it would now be necessary for the carrier to embark more fighters. Space being limited, this could only be done at the expense of the reconnaissance and torpedo-carrying aircraft, with the result that the striking effort of the carrier would be proportionately reduced. Malta and the Ægean convoys were also threatened, and some method of providing fighter protection was urgently needed. The carrier could not be everywhere.

I continued by saying that for the prosecution of the war in the Mediterranean, it was essential to supplement the long-range reconnaissance aircraft working from Malta and Greece, and the squadrons working from the carrier. This could be done by the provision of additional aircraft operating from strategic positions on shore for offensive work, for local reconnaissance, for anti-submarine duties, and for the fighter protection of convoys. The strategic positions where these extra aircraft were needed were Malta, Crete, Cyrenaica, and the Epirus, on the west coast of Greece. The trend of the war, I added, might also necessitate establishing more aircraft for work over the sea in the Northern Ægean, and perhaps also in Turkey.

I went on to say that Malta was already being used in this way with aircraft of the Fleet Air Arm, while a squadron from the damaged *Illustrious* was being sent to Crete, where it was hoped also to send Fleet Air Arm or Royal Air Force fighters before long. Six naval Swordfish were also being maintained in Cyrenaica whenever possible. I concluded by saying that what we needed for the Mediterranean was an organization similar to the Coastal Command of the R.A.F. at home, and the provision of aircraft equipped and trained to work over the sea. We particularly needed long-range torpedo-reconnaissance aircraft, and long-range fighters.

The beginning of March saw all the preparations made for the transport of the Army to Greece, and on the 4th I informed the Admiralty that this would involve continual personnel, mechanical transport, and stores convoys for the next two months. The escort and covering forces for these movements would absorb the whole activity of the fleet, and the destroyers, in particular, would have to be very heavily worked. *Inter alia*, I intended to run a convoy to Malta as soon as possible after the arrival of the *Formidable*. I wished to "make it quite clear" to the Admiralty that the move of this large force to Greece involved considerable risk, and said that if the Germans started an air offensive from Bulgaria against our convoys and the ports of disembarkation, losses must be expected, as our anti-aircraft and fighter defence would be very weak for some time. Nor could surface action by the Italian fleet against our convoys be ruled out. I continued by saying that the Suez Canal was susceptible to acoustic and magnetic minelaying, which was the cause for much anxiety when big troop and mechanical transport movements were just starting. Malta also was having a difficult time, and the strain upon its personnel, particularly upon the fighter pilots, was considerable. I ended:

> I am very conscious that this next two months is going to be an equally critical period in Home Waters, and I represent the situation out here not in order to press my needs; but rather so that their Lordships can strike a just balance with their knowledge of available resources. It would be useless hiding the fact that mine are taxed to the limit, and by normal security standards my commitments exceed available resources. I have, however, considerable hope that all these difficulties can be overcome. We are, I am convinced, pursuing the right policy and the risk must be faced up to.

On March 6th I reported to the Admiralty that the first convoy had sailed for Greece, and that thereafter there would be a convoy every three days. I sent out the measures taken for their protection. Cruisers were also being used as fast transports for personnel.

On March 4th I had received a message from the Admiralty informing me that His Majesty had graciously been pleased to create me a Knight Grand Cross of the Most Honourable Order of the Bath. This was highly gratifying as showing that the work of the Mediterranean Fleet was appreciated; but my remark on hearing of this honour—"I would sooner have had three squadrons of Hurricanes", came from the bottom of my heart. I was thinking of the way our little ships were being pounded on the supply route along the Libyan coast.

Our air situation was really desperate, and I emphasized this in a letter to the First Sea Lord of March 11th, by which time Benghazi had been recaptured by the Germans. I mentioned the loss of the *Terror* on February 23rd, and the *Dainty* off Tobruk on the 24th. In addition we had also lost along the Libyan coast the minesweeper *Huntley* on January 31st, the *Southern Floe* on February 11th, and the trawler *Ouse* on February 20th. Other ships had been damaged.

"We are losing so many small ships on the Cyrenaican coast," I told Sir Dudley Pound. "I hope it will turn out that our policy of helping Greece is the right one. To me it is absolutely right, but I much doubt if our resources, particularly naval and air, are equal to the strain. After our occupation of Benghazi practically all fighters and A.A. guns were moved back. . . . It is unbelievable; but there are only sixteen heavy A.A. guns between Alexandria and Benghazi, and they are all now" (March 11th) "at Tobruk. All the rest have been withdrawn to go to Greece. . . . There seems to be some bad misunderstanding about the state of our Air Force out here. I feel the Chiefs of Staff are badly misinformed about the number of fighter squadrons available. Longmore" (the Air Officer Commanding-in-Chief) "is absolutely stretched to the limit, and we seem to have far fewer than is supposed at home. We are getting sat on by the Germans in Cyrenaica. The figures there are over two hundred German and Italian fighters against thirty of our own. It seems to me that if the fighter situation is not taken in hand drastically and speedily we are heading straight for trouble—not only in Greece; but if the Germans advance in Libya we have no air forces to stop them, and actually very little else either."

I went on to mention Malta, which was in a very bad state: "I have just seen the Air Vice Marshal, who is here to report. He tells me that the Germans are right on top of them. He has only eight serviceable Hurricanes left, and the German fighters are coming over in droves and machine-gunning people in the streets of St. Paul's Bay and other outlying villages. He is being sent six from the shortage here; but that is no good. He ought to have two full squadrons and at once. I am really seriously concerned about Malta. I am running a convoy there in about ten days time; but with their defences in the present state I am quite expecting some of the ships to be damaged. The Grand Harbour and the creeks are also being mined whenever the enemy cares to come. This is a gloomy picture; but someone is misinforming the Chiefs of Staff about the real state of affairs out here. We must have large numbers of fighters rushed out to us if we are to make any headway, and, indeed, they are needed to save what may be a serious set-back."

In that same letter I told the First Sea Lord that the move to Greece was in full swing. We were taking great risks with thin escorts. The Italians were bombing most of the convoys; but the anti-aircraft cruisers were keeping the bombers high, and up-to-date the convoys had run unscathed: "One A.A. cruiser, the *Coventry*, is running with very little bow below water, and the *Carlisle* is running on one shaft only, the other being drawn for repair. But they must just run on while this move to Greece is in progress. The *Greyhound* bagging that submarine in the Kaso Strait" (at the eastern end of Crete) "is a most timely performance. The prisoners said there were six to eight Italian submarines in Leros which are refusing to go to sea."

Incidentally, as the *Carlisle's* damaged propellor shaft could not be dealt with at Alexandria, it was sent to Malta lashed against the topsides of a submarine. The *Coventry* had been torpedoed some weeks before and patched as well as might be.

The task of transporting the troops to Greece, known as Operation *Lustre*, was continued all through March. Those grand little anti-aircraft cruisers *Calcutta*, *Coventry* and *Carlisle*, with the escorting destroyers and other small craft, beat off all air attacks. Though there were some minor casualties among ships proceeding with the convoys but not going to Greece, or in ships returning empty, neither a soldier nor any equipment was lost during the transport to Greece of some sixty-eight thousand troops with their mechanized transport, full equipment and stores which lasted from March 4th to April 24th.

But I anticipate. We had held another conference in Cairo on March 6th, attended by the three Commanders-in-Chief; Mr. Anthony Eden; General Dill; General Smuts and General Pierre van Reynveld, Chief of the South African General Staff. My brother, Lieutenant General Alan Cunningham, fresh from his successes in Somaliland and Abyssinia, was also present, having been picked up by General Smuts on his way. It was the first time I had met that remarkable old man General Smuts, then aged seventy. What most impressed me about him was his youthful energy, his quick grasp of the situation, and his calm wisdom in counsel. He was a great help and a comfort to all three of the sorely-tried Commanders-in-Chief. There was much on our minds, and we had plenty to discuss.

Dill and Eden flew off to Athens again, and were afterwards joined by Wavell. They found things in Greece in a bad way, for the Greeks had not implemented the agreement previously reached. The three divisions they had stipulated should be withdrawn from Macedonia to man the Aliakhmon Line had not been moved, nor yet had they moved the troops from Albania which they had agreed to withdraw for the same purpose. Time was short. The Germans had entered Bulgaria on March 1st. It was only a matter of weeks before they invaded Greece. General Papagos had promised to do his best to scrape up some reserves; but it was fairly obvious that the holding of the Aliakhmon Line, where our British troops were being sent, was now a gamble.

It has been written elsewhere that this was the time we could have reversed our decision about helping the Greeks, and have withdrawn our troops without loss of honour. Maybe that is true. Nevertheless we had encouraged the Greeks in their resistance to the Italians, and it seemed all wrong to desert them now. After consultation with the War Cabinet at home it was decided to continue to give them all the aid in our power.

In March, 1941, when the Italians renewed their offensive, Swordfish squadron (No. 815) from the *Illustrious* moved to Eleusis airfield, near Athens, and thence to an advanced base at Paramythia, at the head of a valley in the Albanian mountains. The Royal Air Force was already operating from there against the Italian shipping plying between Brindisi, Valona and Durazzo, and the Fleet Air Arm used R.A.F. maintenance personnel and transport. During their five weeks sojourn in this bitterly cold climate, which entailed long flights by night over mountainous country, two Fleet Air Arm squadrons (Nos. 815 and 819) sank five Italian merchant ships and seriously damaged five more. At least one laden ammunition ship was blown up. The last raid carried out from Albania was on April 1st, for soon afterwards the Germans advanced into Greece, forcing the naval squadrons to withdraw first to Eleusis and then to Maleme in Crete, and finally, at the end of May, 1941, to Dekheila, in Egypt.

The *Formidable*, as I have already mentioned, was squeezed through the Suez Canal, and finally joined us at Alexandria on March 10th. At once we began to consider the question of a convoy to Malta. Apropos of this convoy, I must risk being tedious by referring to messages which passed between myself and the Admiralty. On March 16th, I sent the following signal for the First Sea Lord:

> Secretary of State informs me that owing to risk to carrier the delivery of Hurricanes to Malta by aircraft carrier has been abandoned.
>
> I hope you may be able to reconsider this, particularly as I wish to run a convoy on 23rd March to Malta, risking the *Formidable* and to a greater extent the convoy, both during the approach and while unloading. This risk will be much accentuated if Malta's fighters have not been reinforced by then with Hurricanes.

On the same date I had the following somewhat tart reply in a personal signal from Sir Dudley Pound.

1. The earliest date of getting Hurricanes to Malta by carrier is 28th March; delivery by this method has at no time been abandoned.

2. Had *Ark Royal* been in *Illustrious*'s place, I am sure you are in no doubt what her fate would have been, but the risk to the carrier is but one of many factors taken into account.

3. I am not sure you fully appreciate events outside the Mediterranean. The Battle of the Atlantic is of supreme importance over all other commitments. The U-boat, mine and aircraft menace is not only on our own coasts but U-boats are already operating in the Freetown area and may be operating off Newfoundland.

In addition there is the surface menace from a pocket battleship at large, one 'Hipper' class 8-inch cruiser at Brest and two enemy battle cruisers in the North Atlantic, against which all the capital ships of Home Fleet and Force 'H' are, with the exception of *Nelson*, employed on convoy escort duty. While the situation lasts, Force 'H' primary duty will be to the westward rather than the eastward.

4. I trust you will disabuse Longmore that the reinforcement of Malta with Hurricanes will become a routine affair, which I suspect he hopes for. Although glad to use carriers as air transports in grave emergency, I feel this is wrong when it can be avoided by looking ahead sufficiently.

I felt constrained to reply, which I did in a personal, and I hope a mollifying, message to the First Sea Lord:

1. I feel I should be failing in my duty if I did not point out our difficulties in the Mediterranean with suggestions for meeting them, but at the same time I fully realize the difficulties you have in the Atlantic; and believe me have no wish to add to your anxiety.

2. The most drastic and early measures are needed to restore the situation at Malta, which alarms me seriously. Enemy air forces operate over the island just as they please.

3. Regarding the use of carriers to reinforce the aircraft at Malta, I am unaware of any opinion expressed by Longmore, but feel you are not fully informed of the Middle East Fighter situation. If we are to avoid getting into grave difficulties, large reinforcements of fighters are urgently necessary. Both the Secretary of State for Foreign Affairs and the Chief of the Imperial General Staff have represented the situation.

4. By looking ahead, it would be possible to dispense with carriers to supply Malta with fighters. The failure to do this has placed us in the present rather grim situation.

The convoy of four ships with stores for Malta left Alexandria on March 19th, and the next morning the battle-fleet with the *Formidable* sailed to cover it. The passage was uneventful, the enemy reconnaissance failing to locate either the convoy or the supporting forces. The battle-fleet turned back on the night of the 22nd, and the convoy reached Malta next morning. They were, however, bombed in harbour, two of the merchant vessels being hit, and the *Bonaventure* and *Griffin* being damaged by near misses.

We were back at Alexandria late on the 24th, and the next day I had a visit from Longmore. We had a long discussion on the general air policy, particularly as regards the support of the convoys going to Greece; both in actual fighter protection and the bombing of enemy aerodromes. I knew very well that Longmore would give us all the help he could. Incidentally, these same convoys were receiving support against possible attack by enemy surface forces from our cruisers based on Suda Bay.

It was there, in the early morning of March 26th, that we had a set-back when the harbour was attacked by six fast explosive motor-boats. The cruiser *York* was severely damaged, and with boiler-rooms and engine-room flooded had to be beached. She had no steam or power for pumping, lighting or working her turrets. The tanker *Pericles* was also hit and holed amidships, though the bulk of her valuable cargo was undamaged. Our only 8-inch gun cruiser was out of action. Once more we had paid the penalty for the inadequate defence of the fleet base.

Six prisoners were picked up on rafts, and it seemed that the explosive motor-boats were sent off from two torpedo-boats, and that the boats were abandoned by their crews before reaching the target. While the Italians on the whole displayed little enterprise and initiative at sea, it always amazed me how good they were at these sort of individual attacks. They certainly had men capable of the most gallant exploits. One remembered that towards the end of the previous war an Italian motor-boat in the Adriatic had torpedoed and sunk the Austrian battleship *Viribus Unitis* in broad daylight.

Before the war was ended we were to suffer further losses of this sort through the brave initiative of individual Italians.

IV

At about this time sickness deprived the Mediterranean Fleet of several of its Admirals. Rear-Admiral Renouf, who had had a most strenuous time, had to go home, and was relieved by Rear-Admiral I. G. Glennie, lately captain of the *Hood*. In the course of a reorganization the latter became Rear-Admiral (D) in command of the destroyers.

Rear-Admiral Frank Elliott, in charge at Alexandria, unfortunately also had to be relieved. He had been very successful in a difficult appointment, and had made himself much liked by the Egyptian officials with whom he came in frequent contact. He was relieved by Acting Rear-Admiral George H. Cresswell, an old destroyer officer. The First Sea Lord also asked me to release Vice-Admiral Lumley Lyster, lately in command of the aircraft-carriers. With his great ability and experience in naval air matters, he was needed at the Admiralty as Fifth Sea Lord. I let him go with great regret, and Captain Denis W. Boyd, of the *Illustrious*, assumed command of the aircraft-carriers with the acting rank of Rear-Admiral. He hoisted his flag in the *Formidable*.

But to me, personally, there was a much greater loss. Rear-Admiral Algernon Willis had literally exhausted himself as Chief of Staff, and himself said that he must be relieved. I was very grieved at losing his services; but I could well see that for his own sake he must have a rest. He had been indefatigable, and hard at it for nearly three years. What the Mediterranean Fleet owed to his great ability and imagination, his outstanding powers of organization and improvisation, it is quite impossible to describe. I owed more to his wise counsel, his unfailing help, and far-seeing mind than I can ever hope to repay. No Commander-in-Chief afloat in time of war, in circumstances of great stress and difficulty, ever had a better friend or a more loyal collaborator.

Willis left us at the end of March. To his bitter regret he missed the Battle of Matapan on the night of March 28th through allowing his successor to go to sea in the *Warspite* on that occasion to gain experience. The destruction of those three Italian cruisers at point-blank range would have been a fitting termination to his service as Chief of Staff to the Mediterranean Fleet. But it was not to be.

As Willis's successor I had been able to secure the services of Captain (now Admiral Sir) John H. Edelsten after some signalled discussion with Sir Dudley Pound, who wished me to take somebody else. But during my short period at the Admiralty as Deputy Chief of the Naval Staff I had watched Edelsten, then Deputy Director of Plans, and marked him down as a very fine officer. I knew also that Sir Roger Backhouse had had the highest opinion of his ability. If Willis had to go, no better man could have been found as his relief.

CHAPTER XXVI

I

By the third week in March, 1941, we knew that the German attack upon Greece could not be much longer delayed. Moreover, from March 25th onwards it was observed that there was a noticeable increase in the enemy's air reconnaissance to the south and west of Greece and Crete, with daily attempts to reconnoitre the harbour at Alexandria. The unusual persistence with which the movements of the Mediterranean Fleet were being watched caused us to believe that some important operation by the Italian fleet might also be intended.

There were various courses of action open to the enemy. They might attack our vulnerable and lightly escorted convoys carrying troops and stores to Greece. They might intend to cover a convoy of their own taking reinforcements to the Dodecanese. It was possible, too, that the Italian fleet might create a diversion to cover a landing in Greece or Cyrenaica, or even an all-out attack upon Malta. Of these possibilities, the first, the attack upon our convoy route to Greece, probably south of Crete, was the most likely.

To prevent this our most obvious course was to have the battle-fleet to the area west of Crete. However, it was practically certain that we should be shadowed and reported by the enemy's air reconnaissance, in which event the Italian fleet would merely defer its operation until we were forced to return to Alexandria to refuel. If we were to have a fair chance of intercepting the Italians we needed tolerably accurate information that they were actually at sea, while it was desirable that we should leave during the early part of the night to avoid being located by aircraft till next morning. If our departure from Alexandria could be kept secret, so much the better. The movements of our convoys in and out of the Ægean were also perfectly well-known to the enemy, so to raise no suspicion it was necessary that their movements should appear normal, while at the same time they must not be exposed to attack.

During the morning of the 27th, one of the flying-boats from Malta reported a force of three Italian cruisers and a destroyer 80 miles east of the south-eastern corner of Sicily steering to the south-eastward, roughly in the direction of Crete. The visibility being bad, the flying-boat could not shadow. There was considerable discussion between my staff and myself as to what the sighting of this Italian cruiser squadron really meant. For cruisers to be in that position and steering that particular course seemed to indicate that some of the Italian heavy ships were also in that neighbourhood, and our lightly-escorted convoys to Greece were certainly a tempting bait.

It so happened that on March 27th only one convoy was at sea. Bound for the Piræus with troops it was to the southward of Crete. It was ordered to steam on until dark, and then to reverse its course. A south-bound convoy from the Piræus was directed not to sail.

I myself was inclined to think that the Italians would not dare to try anything. Later on we noticed some unusual Italian wireless activity, which finally decided us to go to sea after dark and to place the battle-fleet between the enemy and where he supposed our convoys must be. At the same time I bet Commander Power, the Staff Officer, Operations, the sum of ten shillings that we would see nothing of the enemy.

It was fortunate we made up our minds to proceed after nightfall, for at noon and again in the late afternoon the enemy air reconnaissance over Alexandria must have reported a very peaceful-looking fleet lying at its moorings.

I also arranged a little private cover plan of my own. We were aware that the Japanese consul at Alexandria was in the habit of reporting any fleet movements that he observed, though whether or not his information reached the enemy in time to be of any importance to them was another matter. I decided to bluff this gentleman, so went ashore to play golf carrying an obvious suit-case as though I intended to spend the night ashore. The Japanese consul spent most of his afternoons on the golf links. He was unmistakable, indeed a remarkable sight, short and squat, with a southern aspect of such vast and elephantine proportions when he bent over to putt that the irreverent Chief of Staff had nicknamed him "The blunt end of the Axis".

This little plot worked as intended. Retrieving my suit-case, I returned to the *Warspite* after dark and the fleet sailed at 7 p.m.

What the Japanese consul thought and did when he saw the empty harbour next morning was no affair of mine.

II

While leaving harbour the *Warspite* went too close to a mud-bank, which filled the condensers with mud. This had consequences later, as our speed was reputed to be reduced to 20 knots. The night was uneventful as we steamed on to the north-westward at that speed. The *Warspite, Barham, Valiant* and *Formidable* were in company, screened by the destroyers *Jervis, Janus, Nubian, Mohawk, Stuart, Greyhound, Griffin, Hotspur* and *Havock*.

As I have said, the one convoy at sea in the danger area had been ordered to reverse its course at nightfall. Vice-Admiral Pridham-Wippell in the *Orion*, with the *Ajax, Perth* and *Gloucester*, and the destroyers *Ilex, Hasty, Hereward* and *Vendetta*, all of which had been operating in the Ægean, were ordered to be south-west of Gavdo Island at daylight on March 28th.

A dawn air search was flown off from the *Formidable*, and at about 7.40 a.m. one of these aircraft reported four cruisers and some destroyers not far off the position where our four cruisers were supposed to be, so naturally we took them for Vice-Admiral Pridham-Wippell's force. However, just before 8.30, Pridham-Wippell himself reported three enemy cruisers and destroyers to the northward of him. This made it clear that the enemy fleet was at sea, so I cheerfully paid up my ten shillings.

The situation, however, was confused, and it was difficult to estimate from the aircraft reports just how many different enemy forces had been sighted. One report mentioned 'battleships', and it seemed natural enough to us that the Italian cruiser squadrons should be supported by a battle-squadron. On the other hand, we could not be certain. Italian cruisers had constantly been confused with battleships in previous reconnaissance reports.

Pridham-Wippell's cruisers were estimated to be about ninety miles ahead of us, so we increased to the *Warspite*'s full speed, which at that time was no more than 22 knots because of the condenser trouble. Meanwhile Pridham-Wippell had recognized the enemy cruisers he had in sight as ships armed with 8-inch guns. As he wrote: "Knowing that vessels of that class could outrange my squadron and that, having superior speed, they could choose the range, I decided to try to draw them towards our own battle-fleet and carrier."

The Italian cruisers followed him, and at 8.12 opened fire at a range of nearly thirteen miles. It was accurate to start with and seemed to be concentrated on the *Gloucester*, which "snaked the line" to avoid being hit. At 8.29, when the range had dropped by about a mile, the *Gloucester* opened fire with three salvoes from her 6-inch guns, all of which fell short. The enemy altered course to the westward, and at 8.55 ceased firing. Pridham-Wippell swung round to keep touch.

Just before 11 a.m. Pridham-Wippell sighted an enemy battleship to the northward, which immediately opened an accurate fire at a range of 16 miles. Our cruisers turned away under cover of a smoke screen and ran for it at full speed; but had a very unpleasant time, being closely straddled by 15-inch projectiles.

To us in the *Warspite* the situation did not look too good. We knew that the 'Littorio' class battleships were capable of 31 knots, and the night before, because of engine trouble, the *Gloucester* had reported herself capable of no more than 24. There was also another strong enemy cruiser squadron to the northward of Pridham-Wippell. However, the sight of an enemy battleship had somehow increased the *Gloucester*'s speed to 30 knots.

Something had to be done, and the *Valiant* was ordered to go on at her utmost speed to support Vice-Admiral Pridham-Wippell. It had always been my intention to hold back the air torpedo striking force until the enemy battle-fleet was close enough to ensure that if one of their ships were hit, our battle-fleet would be certain of overtaking and destroying her. But in this emergency my hand was forced. The striking force was already in the air, and I ordered the *Formidable* to send them in. Their attack relieved the pressure on Pridham-Wippell; but had the unfortunate effect of causing the enemy battleship to turn away and make off while still some eighty miles distant. This meant there was no chance of bringing her to action during daylight, if at all.

Meanwhile the low speed of the *Warspite* was causing me much annoyance. I knew that the Commander (E) was sick ashore; but was aware that the Fleet

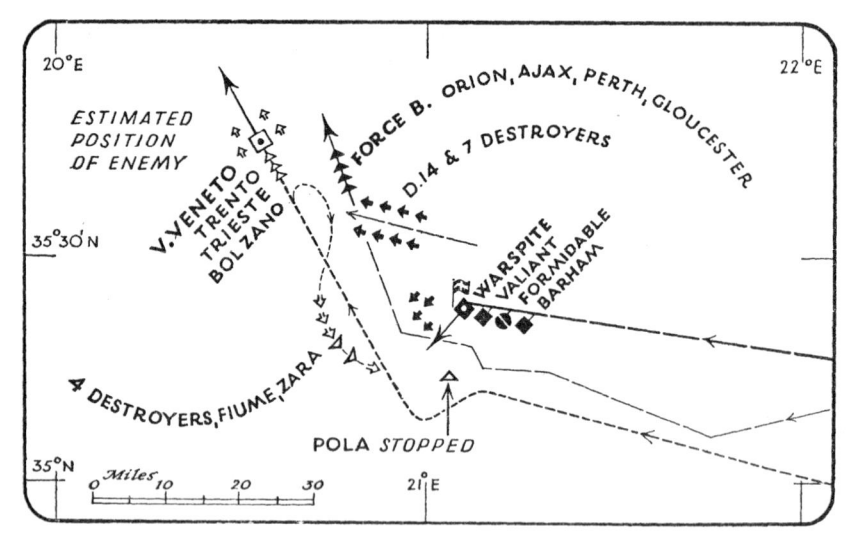

BATTLE OF MATAPAN
10.15 p.m., 28th March, 1941

Engineer Officer, Engineer Captain B. J. H. Wilkinson, was on board. So I sent for him and told him to do something about it. He went below, and in a short time I was gratified to see that the *Valiant*, which had been coming up at full speed from astern, was no longer gaining. We pressed on together.

At this time further considerable delay was caused by the fact that the wind was in the east, from astern. This meant we had to make periodical turns in that direction to allow the *Formidable* to work her aircraft. However, at 11.30 it became so essential for us to hurry on to Pridham-Wippell's support, that the *Formidable* was detached to conduct her flying operations independently, while the battle-fleet went on at full speed. The *Formidable* quickly dropped astern, and it was with some anxiety that we saw her attacked by torpedo-bombers. Our relief can be imagined when she successfully avoided the torpedoes.

At about noon the air striking force returned and reported one probable hit on the battleship, which was the *Vittorio Veneto*. A few minutes later a Royal Air Force flying-boat reported a further enemy force consisting of two 'Cavour' class battleships and some further 8-inch cruisers. The battleship attacked by the Fleet Air Arm was alone except for a destroyer screen; but there was another force of cruisers 20 miles to the south-eastward of her. The air reports showed that all the enemy forces were retiring to the westward.

We sighted our own cruisers at 12.30, and the *Formidable* was ordered to fly off a second striking force to attack the *Vittorio Veneto*, then roughly sixty-five miles ahead.

We settled down to a chase, and it was clear enough that it would be a long one and without reward unless the *Vittorio Veneto* was damaged and slowed up by our aircraft attacks. The pursuit was made even longer as speed had to be reduced to 22 knots to allow the *Formidable* to rejoin and the *Barham* to keep up. But we had one providential piece of good fortune. The easterly wind dropped and it became flat calm with occasional light airs from the westward, which meant that the *Formidable* could carry out all her flying operations from her station in the line.

Just after 3 p.m. one of our aircraft reported the *Vittorio Veneto* still about sixty-five miles ahead and still steering to the westward. The second air striking force went in to the attack, to report three hits and that the *Vittorio Veneto's* speed was down to 8 knots. This excellent news was unduly optimistic, for an hour later our quarry was still 60 miles ahead and going 12–15 knots, which meant she could not be overhauled before dark. A small force of Fleet Air Arm Swordfish from the airfield at Maleme in Crete had also attacked one of the cruiser squadrons and reported a possible hit, while in the course of the afternoon Royal Air Force bombers from Greece came into action with bombing attacks. No ship was hit; but there were several near misses. The attacks gave the enemy a good fright, and were particularly welcome to us as giving the Italians a dose of the medicine we had been enduring for months.

It now became necessary to establish surface touch with the enemy, so at 4.44 p.m Vice-Admiral Pridham-Wippell was ordered to press on at full speed and get into visual touch with the retreating enemy. The destroyers *Nubian* and *Mohawk* were also sent ahead to form a visual signal link between Pridham-Wippell's cruisers and the battle-fleet. The situation was still very confused, for as the afternoon wore on we continued to receive reports showing another enemy force containing battleships to the north-west of the *Vittorio Veneto*. These reports, as we discovered later, were incorrect. The force referred to consisted entirely of cruisers. No other battleship was out.

We now had to signal some plan for the night which was coming on, and decided to form a striking force of eight destroyers under Captain Philip Mack, of the *Jervis*. If the cruisers made contact with the *Vittorio Veneto* the destroyers would be sent in to attack, and if necessary we should follow it up with the battleships. If the cruisers failed to make contact, I intended to work round to the north and north-west and try and catch the *Vittorio Veneto* at daylight next morning. In the meanwhile the *Formidable* was ordered to send in a third aircraft torpedo attack at dusk.

But we needed a clear picture, and at 5.45 the *Warspite* catapulted her own aircraft with the Commander-in-Chief's observer, Lieutenant-Commander A. S. Bolt on board, to try and clarify the situation. By 6.30 we had the first of a series of reports from this highly trained and experienced officer which quickly told us what we needed. The *Vittorio Veneto* was 45 miles from the *Warspite* and making good about fifteen knots to the westward. The Italian fleet had concentrated into a bunch, with the battleship in the middle with two columns of ships on each side of her, one of destroyers and the other of cruisers, with a destroyer screen ahead. From other air reports we still heard of the other force of battleships and 8-inch cruisers to the north-westward.

At about 7.30, by which time it was nearly dark, the third striking force of Swordfish went in to attack, and at the same time Pridham-Wippell reported the enemy ships about nine miles to the north-west. A little later the striking force reported probable hits, though there was no definite information that the battleship had been hit again.

Now came the difficult moment of deciding what to do. I was fairly well convinced that having got so far it would be foolish not to make every effort to complete the *Vittorio Veneto*'s destruction. At the same time it appeared to us that the Italian Admiral must have been fully aware of our position. He had numerous cruisers and destroyers in company, and any British Admiral in his position would not have hesitated to use every destroyer he had, backed up by all his cruisers fitted with torpedo tubes, for attacks upon the pursuing fleet. Some of my staff argued that it would be unwise to charge blindly after the retreating enemy with our three heavy ships, and the *Formidable* also on our hands, to run the risk of ships being crippled, and to find ourselves within easy range of the enemy dive-bombers at daylight. I paid respectful attention to this opinion, and as the discussion happened to coincide with my time for dinner I told them I would have my evening meal and would see how I felt afterwards.

My morale was reasonably high when I returned to the bridge, and I ordered the destroyer striking force off to find and attack the enemy. We settled down to a steady pursuit with some doubts in our minds as to how the four destroyers remaining with the battle-fleet would deal with the enemy destroyer attacks if the Italians decided to make them. At this stage the enemy fleet was estimated to be 33 miles ahead making good about fifteen knots.

Vice-Admiral Pridham-Wippell with his cruisers also had his perplexities. To gain contact with the *Vittorio Veneto*, closely guarded by three cruiser squadrons and some eleven destroyers, was indeed a problem, particularly

A SAILOR'S ODYSSEY 331

as Pridham-Wippell must keep his four ships concentrated in readiness for instant action. In the event he never made contact.

At 9.11 we received Pridham-Wippell's report that an unknown ship lying stopped 5 miles to port of him had been located by radar. We went on after the enemy's fleet, and altered course slightly to port to close the stopped ship. The *Warspite* was not fitted with radar; but at 10.10 the *Valiant* reported that her instruments had picked up what was apparently the same ship 6 miles on her port bow. She was a large ship. The *Valiant* gave her length as more than six hundred feet.

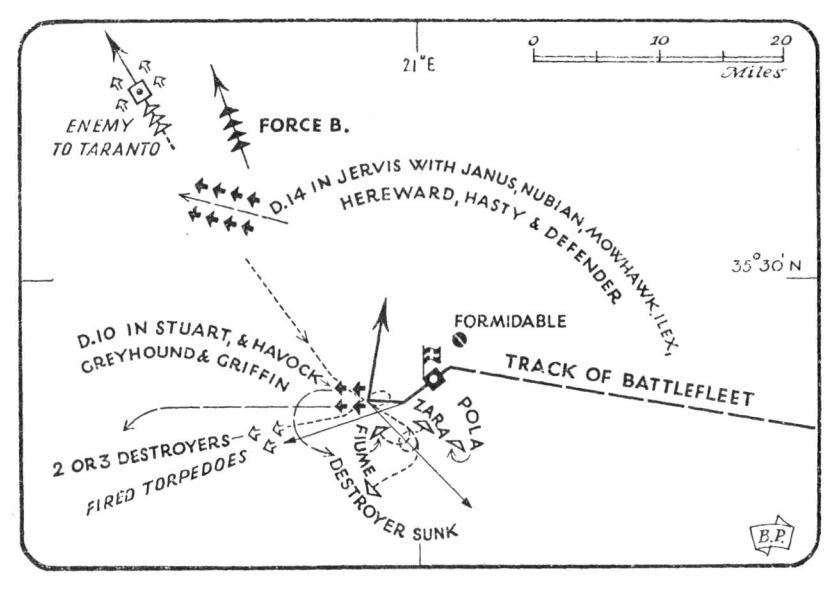

BATTLE OF MATAPAN
10.30 p.m., 28th March, 1941

Our hopes ran high. This might be the *Vittorio Veneto*. The course of the battle-fleet was altered 40 degrees to port together to close. We were already at action stations with our main armament ready. Our guns were trained on the correct bearing.

Rear-Admiral Willis was not out with us. Commodore Edelsten, the new Chief of Staff, had come to gain experience. And a quarter of an hour later, at 10.25, when he was searching the horizon on the starboard bow with his glasses, he calmly reported that he saw two large cruisers with a smaller one ahead of them crossing the bows of the battle-fleet from starboard to port. I looked through my glasses, and there they were. Commander Power, an ex-submarine officer and an abnormal expert at recognizing the silhouettes of enemy warships at a glance, pronounced them to be two 'Zara' class 8-inch gun cruisers with a smaller cruiser ahead.

Using short-range wireless the battle-fleet was turned back into line ahead. With Edelsten and the staff I had gone to the upper bridge, the captain's, where I had a clear all-round view. I shall never forget the next few minutes. In the dead silence, a silence that could almost be felt, one heard only the voices of the gun control personnel putting the guns on to the new target. One heard the orders repeated in the director tower behind and above the bridge. Looking forward, one saw the turrets swing and steady when the 15-inch guns pointed at the enemy cruisers. Never in the whole of my life have I experienced a more thrilling moment than when I heard a calm voice from the director tower—"Director layer sees the target"; sure sign that the guns were ready and that his finger was itching on the trigger. The enemy was at a range of no more than 3,800 yards—point-blank.

It must have been the Fleet Gunnery Officer, Commander Geoffrey Barnard, who gave the final order to open fire. One heard the 'ting-ting-ting' of the firing gongs. Then came the great orange flash and the violent shudder as the six big guns bearing were fired simultaneously. At the very same instant the destroyer *Greyhound*, on the screen, switched her searchlight on to one of the enemy cruisers, showing her momentarily up as a silvery-blue shape in the darkness. Our searchlights shone out with the first salvo, and provided full illumination for what was a ghastly sight. Full in the beam I saw our six great projectiles flying through the air. Five out of the six hit a few feet below the level of the cruiser's upper deck and burst with splashes of brilliant flame. The Italians were quite unprepared. Their guns were trained fore and aft. They were helplessly shattered before they could put up any resistance. In the midst of all this there was one milder diversion. Captain Douglas Fisher, the captain of the *Warspite*, was a gunnery officer of note. When he saw the first salvo hit he was heard to say in a voice of wondering surprise: "Good Lord! We've hit her!"

The *Valiant*, astern of us, had opened fire at the same time. She also had found her target, and when the *Warspite* shifted to the other cruiser I watched the *Valiant* pounding her ship to bits. Her rapidity of fire astonished me. Never would I have believed it possible with these heavy guns. The *Formidable* had hauled out of the line to starboard; but astern of the *Valiant* the *Barham* was also heavily engaged.

The plight of the Italian cruisers was indescribable. One saw whole turrets and masses of other heavy debris whirling through the air and splashing into the sea, and in a short time the ships themselves were nothing but glowing torches and on fire from stem to stern. The whole action lasted no more than a few minutes.

Our searchlights were still on, and just after 10.30 three Italian destroyers, which had apparently been following their cruisers, were seen coming in on our port bow. They turned, and one was seen to fire torpedoes, so the battle-fleet was turned 90 degrees together to starboard to avoid them. Our destroyers were engaging, and the whole party was inextricably mixed up. The *Warspite* fired both 15-inch and 6-inch at the enemy. To my horror I saw one of our destroyers, the *Havock*, straddled by our fire, and in my mind wrote her off as a loss. The *Formidable* also had an escape. When action was joined she hauled out to starboard at full speed, a night battle being no place for a carrier. When she was about five miles away she was caught in the beam of the *Warspite's* searchlight sweeping on the disengaged side in case further enemy ships were present. We heard the 6-inch control officer of the starboard battery get his guns on to her, and were only just in time to stop him from opening fire.

The four destroyers, *Stuart*, Captain H. M. L. Waller, Royal Australian Navy; *Greyhound*, Commander W. R. Marshall-A'Deane; *Havock*, Lieutenant G. R. G. Watkins; and *Griffin*, Lieutenant-Commander J. Lee-Barber, in company with the battle-fleet, were then ordered to finish off the enemy cruisers, while the battle-fleet collected the *Formidable* and withdrew to the northward to keep out of their way. According to their own reports the destroyers' movements were difficult to follow; but they had a wild night and sank at least one other enemy destroyer.

At 10.45 we saw very heavy gunfire, with star-shell and tracer, to the south-westward. Since none of our ships was on that bearing it seemed to us that either the Italians were engaging each other, or that the destroyers of our striking force might be going in to attack. Just after 11 p.m. I made a signal ordering all forces not engaged in sinking the enemy to withdraw to the north-eastward. The objects of what I now consider to have been an ill-considered signal were to give our destroyers who were mopping up a free hand to attack any sizeable ship they saw, and to facilitate the assembly of the fleet next morning. The message was qualified by an order to Captain Mack and his eight destroyers of the striking force, now some twenty miles ahead, not to withdraw until he had attacked. However, it had the unfortunate effect of causing Vice-Admiral Pridham-Wippell to cease his efforts to gain touch with the *Vittorio Veneto*.

Just after midnight the *Havock*, after torpedoing a destroyer and finishing her off by gunfire, reported herself in contact with a battleship near the position where we had been in action. The battleship was Captain Mack's main objective, and the *Havock's* report brought Mack's destroyer striking force back hot-foot from their position nearly sixty miles to the westward. An hour later, however, the *Havock* amended her report to say that it was not a battleship she had sighted, but an 8-inch cruiser. Soon after 3 a.m. she sent a further message reporting herself close to the *Pola*, and, as all her torpedoes had been fired, Watkins asked whether—"to board or blow off her stern with depth-charges."

The *Havock* had already been joined by the *Greyhound* and *Griffin*, and when Captain Mack arrived he took the *Jervis* alongside the *Pola*. That ship was in a state of indescribable confusion. Panic-stricken men were leaping over the side. On the crowded quarterdeck, littered with clothing, personal belongings and bottles, many of the sailors were drunk. There was no order or discipline of any sort, and the officers were powerless to enforce it. Having taken off the crew Mack sank the ship with torpedoes. The *Pola*, of course, was the vessel reported by Pridham-Wippell and the *Valiant* between 9 and 10 the night before as lying stopped on the port side of our fleet's line of advance. She had not been under gunfire or fired a gun; but had been torpedoed and completely crippled by one of the aircraft from the *Formidable* during the dusk attack.

Her sinking at 4.10 a.m. was the final act of the night's proceedings.

Reconnaissance at dawn by the *Formidable's* aircraft, with others from Greece and Crete, failed to discover any trace of the enemy to the westward. As we discovered afterwards, the *Vittorio Veneto* had been able to increase speed and get clear away during the night.

As daylight came on March 29th our cruisers and destroyers were in sight making for the rendezvous with the battle-fleet. Feeling fairly certain in our minds that the *Warspite* had sunk a destroyer in the mêlée the night before, we eagerly counted them. To our inexpressible relief all twelve destroyers were present. My heart was glad again.

It was a fine morning. We steamed back to the scene of the battle to find the calm sea covered with a film of oil, and strewn with boats, rafts and wreckage, with many floating corpses. All the destoyers we could spare were detached to save what life was possible. In all, counting the men from the *Pola*, British ships rescued 900, though some died later. In the midst of this work of mercy, however, the attentions of some German J.U. 88's pointed the fact that it was unwise to dally in an area where we were exposed to heavy air attack. So we were compelled to proceed to the eastward, leaving some hundreds of Italians unrescued. We did the best we could for them by signalling their exact position to the Italian Admiralty. They sent out the hospital ship *Gradisca*, which eventually saved another 160.

An unfortunate mistake in ciphering prevented a Greek destroyer flotilla from being present at the action, in which I feel sure they would have played a gallant part. They were sent through the Corinth Canal to Argostoli with commendable promptitude; but arrived too late for the battle, though they picked up another 110 Italians.

The fleet was subjected to the expected air attack during the afternoon of March 29th. Though broken up by the *Formidable's* fighters it was fairly heavy; the *Formidable* herself being close-missed by several heavy bombs. We reached Alexandria without further incident in the early evening of Sunday, March 30th. On April 1st I caused a special Thanksgiving Service to be held on board all ships for our success off Cape Matapan.

Shortly afterwards I was visited by the Patriarch of the Orthodox Greek Church at Alexandria who offered us his congratulations on the victory which he described not only as a great deliverance; but also a manifestation of God's Power, for which he and his Church offered thanks to Almighty God. After his return to the City he presented the Fleet with a sacred icon of St. Nicholas, the patron saint of sailors and travellers, which was placed in the Chapel precincts of the *Warspite*.

Although the *Vittorio Veneto* had escaped, we had sunk the three 10,000-ton, 8-inch gun cruisers *Zara*, *Pola* and *Fiume*, together with the 1,500-ton destroyers *Alfieri* and *Carducci*. The Italian loss in personnel was about 2,400 officers and men, most of them being caused by our devastating bombardment at close range. The *Fiume* received two 15-inch broadsides from the *Warspite* and one from the *Valiant*; the *Zara* four from the *Warspite*, five from the *Valiant*, and five from the *Barham*. The effect of those six- or eight-gun salvoes of shell, each weighing nearly a ton, cannot be described.

There was considerable jubilation in the fleet at Alexandria. Our sailors felt, and rightly, that they had something back for the days of continual bombing they had endured during their repeated excursions to sea in the Mediterranean.

At Matapan our casualties were happily very light, for we lost only one aircraft with its crew.

Once again, before closing this account of the battle, I must pay a tribute to the magnificent work of the Fleet Air Arm. To quote from my despatch, published as a Supplement to the *London Gazette* of July 31st, 1947:

> ... whatever the result, the gallantry and perseverance of the aircraft crews and the smooth efficiency of deck and ground crews in H.M.S. *Formidable* and at Maleme are deserving of high praise.—An example of the spirit of these young officers is the case of Lieutenant F. M. A. Torrens Spence, Royal Navy, who, rather than be left out, flew with the only available aircraft and torpedo from Elsusis to Maleme and in spite of reconnaissance difficulties and bad communications arranged his own reconnaissance and finally took off with a second aircraft in company and took part in the dusk attack.

III

Looking back on the engagement which is now officially known as the Battle of Matapan, I am conscious of several things which might have been done better. However, calm reflection in an armchair in the full knowledge of what actually happened is a very different matter to conducting an operation from the bridge of a ship at night in the presence of the enemy. Instant and momentous decisions have to made in a matter of seconds. With fast-moving ships at close quarters and the roar of heavy gunfire, clear thinking is not easy. In no other circumstances than in a night action at sea does the fog of war so completely descend to blind one to a true realization of what is happening.

Nevertheless, we could claim substantial results. Those three heavy Italian cruisers with their 8-inch guns were armoured against 6-inch gunfire and always a threat against our smaller and more lightly armed ships. More important still, the supine and inactive attitude of the Italian fleet during our subsequent evacuations of Greece and Crete was directly attributable to the rough handling they had received at Matapan. Had the enemy's surface ships intervened in those operations, our already difficult talk would have been wellnigh impossible.

Admiral Angelo Iachino was in command of the Italian fleet with his flag in the *Vittorio Veneto*. I have read his account of the operation and the night battle, and there is no doubt that he was badly served by his air reconnaissance. This is surprising to us who know how efficient the Italian reconnaissance had been on many other occasions. However, as Admiral Iachino says, the Italian naval co-operation with the air in the tactical field was very imperfect.

It appears that they were relying upon German aircraft reports before the battle, and as the weather was by no means unfavourable it is not easy to understand why their reconnaissance failed. At 9 a.m. on March 28th German aircraft from the Ægean had actually reported one aircraft-carrier, two battleships, nine cruisers and fourteen destroyers in such and such a position at 7.45. This actually was our fleet, which up to that time Admiral Iachino had thought was still safely at Alexandria. However, on plotting the position given, the Admiral convinced himself that his Ægean reconnaissance had mistaken the British fleet for his own, and signalled to Rhodes to this effect. He does not seem to have become aware that the British battle-fleet was at sea until later.

On the evening of the 28th, when the *Pola* was damaged by our air attack, Admiral Iachino's information led him to believe that the nearest British battleship was 90 miles astern of him, something over four hours' steaming. With this in his mind his decision to detach the *Zara* and the *Fiume* to help the crippled *Pola* cannot be questioned. He was originally urged to send destroyers; but finally decided that only a Flag Officer, Rear-Admiral Carlo Cateneo in the *Zara*, who did not survive, could take the responsibility of deciding whether the *Pola* should be taken in tow, or abandoned and sunk.

Instead of being 90 miles astern, the British battle-fleet was roughly half that distance.

The result we know.

Admiral Iachino's book also discloses an extraordinary state of unpreparedness in the technique of night fighting on the part of the Italian Navy. They had not visualized a night action between heavy ships and did not keep their heavy guns manned, which accounts for the turrets of the *Zara* and

Fiume being trained fore and aft when we first sighted them. They had good ships, good guns and torpedoes, flashless ammunition and much else; but even their newest ships lacked the radar which had served us so well, while in the art of night fighting in heavy ships they were no further advanced than we had been at Jutland twenty-five years before.

Admiral Iachino's reception at the hands of the Chief of the Italian Naval Staff, Admiral Riccardi, was chilly. Mussolini, on the other hand, was not unfriendly, and listened with patience to Iachino's complaints about the reconnaissance. The outcome of that interview, and of Matapan, strengthened the Italian resolve to build aircraft-carriers to provide the Navy with its own reconnaissance. I seem to remember that Italy had an uncompleted aircraft-carrier at the time of her surrender in September, 1943.

CHAPTER XXVII

I

THE general situation at the beginning of April, 1941, gave us plenty to think about.

The news from the south was good. In Eritrea, Keren had been captured by General Platt, and Asmara was taken on April 1st, thus opening the way to the Italian naval port at Massawa. Addis Ababa, in Abyssinia, was entered by our troops on April 5th, and Massawa in our hands by the 8th. The Italian destroyers from the latter port were caught by the *Eagle's* Swordfish working from Port Sudan, two being torpedoed and sunk and the third driven ashore and wrecked. So the threat of surface attacks on our convoys in the Red Sea, never really serious, was finally removed. I was glad enough to get back our three destroyers that were working there.

Operation 'Lustre', the transport of the Army to Greece, was going according to plan, though the high-level and dive-bombing attacks on the convoy were becoming heavier and we lost some ships, happily with few casualties. A more serious loss had occurred on March 31st, when the cruiser *Bonaventure*, escorting a convoy from Greece to Alexandria, was torpedoed and sunk by a submarine south of Crete.

There had been a rising in Yugoslavia, and with the young King Peter in the saddle it looked as though the Yugoslavs would resist if the Germans invaded their country. But overshadowing everything else was our position in Cyrenaica. The Germans had attacked from El Agheila, and our troops were in retreat. Looking back on it after all these years it seems as though the High Command in Cairo were taken badly by surprise, and, though well aware of the German concentrations in Libya, the weight and vigour of the enemy attack was entirely unexpected. The Luftwaffe was also present in great strength, both in supporting the German troops and in attacking our bombarding and supply ships.

The news became worse and worse, and at an important conference in Cairo on April 6th, at which General Dill, the Chief of the Imperial General Staff, and Mr. Anthony Eden were both present, it was as bad as it could be. The Germans had attacked Greece and Yugoslavia, and were advancing rapidly in Cyrenaica with our troops retreating and nearing Tobruk. The question on what line the Army should try to stand came up for discussion, and also the important matter of whether or not Tobruk should be held. The Army, having accumulated some months' supplies at Tobruk, was anxious to hold it. I supported the proposal with the idea of keeping the enemy, particularly the Luftwaffe, as far from Alexandria as possible. Air Chief Marshal Longmore agreed for much the same reasons. I further gave it as my opinion that Tobruk could be supplied from the sea.

The situation in the Western Desert became rapidly worse. Our forces were being hurled back, and as additional blows Generals O'Connor and Neame had fallen into the hands of the Germans, while most of our armour was captured at Mechili. It was doubtful indeed where we could stop the enemy. However, in Cairo on April 9th, the firm decision was taken to hold Tobruk. Had I been gifted with second sight and been able to foresee the long tale of ships lost and damaged in supplying the fortress, I very much doubt if I should have been so confident in saying that it could be done.

By April 11th, Tobruk was surrounded. By the 13th it was closely invested and the enemy had pressed on to Sollum, on the Egyptian border 80 miles to the eastward. Except for Tobruk, all our gains in the magnificent winter campaign had gone. We were back from where we had started, and doubtful if we could hold on there. We were fighting an enemy of infinitely superior strength and skill to the Italians. On April 14th, when all else was sombre, there came one little gleam of sunshine. The Germans launched a heavy attack upon Tobruk which, though it penetrated the defence in places, was effectually repulsed.

All this time the ships of our gallant little Inshore Squadron had been doing their utmost to harass and hamper the advancing enemy by bombarding airfields that could be reached from the sea, and by shooting up enemy transport and troop concentrations. They had had a very rough time, with many hair-breadth escapes from the enemy bombing. The supply of Tobruk by sea now became a major responsibility for the Navy. Enemy airfields were close at hand, and the port, together with all the ships approaching it, were mercilessly bombed. Another difficulty was the continual mining of the harbour and its approaches by enemy aircraft. To the everlasting credit of the small force of minesweepers stationed there the channel was kept clear. In spite of all difficulties, about four hundred tons of stores a day were still being landed.

A small band of fighters was maintained on the Tobruk airfield until April 24th; but their losses on the ground were so heavy that they then had to be withdrawn. After that date Tobruk had to rely upon its own resources for air defence. To anticipate, so well was this ground defence organized and conducted, that the enemy found daylight air attacks unprofitable. This was the first example I remember of anti-aircraft guns alone getting the measure of air attacks by day.

With so much going on at once it is difficult to describe events in their strict chronological order; but by the end of the first week in April the news from Greece was worse. The Piræus, the main supply port for the Army, was being heavily attacked by the Luftwaffe. On April 7th the *Clan Fraser*, carrying ammunition, was hit and blown up, badly wrecking the port, setting it ablaze, and destroying most of the facilities for unloading. The cruiser *Ajax* and the anti-aircraft cruiser *Calcutta* were lying in the Piræus at the time, though in spite of the mines dropped in the harbour they managed to make their way to sea. Thereafter, the bombing and minelaying at the Piræus was continued until the port was almost wholly disorganized.

On April 13th the Suez Canal was at last able to take the *Eagle* on her way home. The whole fleet was sorry to see the last of this finely-manned and commanded ship. As she sailed from Port Said I sent her a message:

I very much regret not having had the opportunity to come on board and say good-bye to you all. We are all very sad to see *Eagle* leaving the Mediterranean Fleet, where, at the outset of the Italian war, she bore the brunt of the enemy air attack on the fleet and replied with such good effect. The best wishes of the whole fleet go with her, and we all know that wherever she is stationed her work will be of the same high standard that we have come to expect from her. Good-bye. My grateful thanks for all your good work go with you.

II

The Libyan supply line from Italy now assumed overwhelming importance. Both we and the authorities at home were fully aware that its interruption was vital for the safety of Egypt, though a serious difference of opinion arose as to a practical method of achieving it. So far as my resources permitted I was fully prepared to take all possible measures; but the grave difficulties did not appear to be appreciated in England. Moreover, there was considerable vacillation and no clear-cut opinion as to whether Greece or the Western Desert was to have priority. Signals indicating first one and then the other were constantly being received, and we could not have it both ways.

The most obvious course was to send a naval force to Malta to work against the enemy convoys; but it was equally obvious that with the lack of air cover this force could only work by night. At sea in the daytime it would be at the mercy of the dive-bombers. Good air reconnaissance from Malta was also essential for finding the convoys, while it was vital that the island should have ample supplies of oil fuel. For ships to accomplish their mission during the hours of darkness meant that they must steam at high speed, which meant an increased fuel consumption. Malta was alarmingly short of this precious commodity. Its air reconnaissance was weak, as was the fighter defence. The dockyard was steadily being knocked to bits by enemy bombers.

The submarines working from Malta, some of them the new small 'U' class, had been taking a steady toll of the Libyan convoys; but it was by no means enough. Moreover, because of the incessant bombing Vice-Admiral Ford was also perturbed because the submarine crews were not getting the rest in harbour which was so important if they were to put up a good performance at sea.

I drew the attention of the Admiralty to the situation at Malta, and also pointed out that the island needed some aircraft trained in daylight attacks upon shipping. Many signals on these and kindred subjects passed between the Home Authorities and myself. I felt most strongly that those at home were ignorant of the real state of affairs in the Mediterranean and failed entirely to comprehend our great difficulties.

It was not easy to spare destroyers for Malta, as the services of any ships sent there would be lost to the fleet for a time. Although Matapan might be assumed to have knocked the heart out of the Italian fleet, there was no knowing when it might not be forced to sea by its German masters. We therefore had to keep within call sufficient destroyers to screen the battle-fleet in case it became necessary for us to provide heavy cover for the convoys running to and from Greece. However, as a start, the four destroyers *Jervis*, *Nubian*, *Mohawk* and *Janus* were sent to Malta under the orders of Captain P. J. Mack of the *Jervis*.

A further suggestion from home was that the battle-fleet should bombard Tripoli, the principal supply port for the Axis forces in North Africa, and something over eight hundred miles from Alexandria. This plan did not commend itself to me in any way. I was sceptical about the damage that would be done by even three battleships bombarding at the range at which they would be firing, and I considered the risk to the ships to be completely unjustified. It involved manœuvring in broad daylight within a few miles of one of the enemy's most important air-fields, Castel Benito, near Tripoli, from which we might expect a heavy and continuous attack for some hours while retiring after the bombardment. We had a shrewd idea, too, that there were minefields off Tripoli; but had no knowledge of their position. I was strongly of the opinion that the attack on the port was really the legitimate task of the Royal Air Force, which, according to all accounts, was already devastating Hamburg and other German cities.

I was also offered the old battleship *Centurion* for an attempt to block Tripoli harbour. This I was very willing to try; but the delay in the *Centurion's* arrival in the Mediterranean round the Cape of Good Hope was unacceptable.

Signals passed to and fro, and finally, on April 15th, I received a long message from the Admiralty. I need not quote it in full, but was told thet "drastic measures" were necessary "to stabilize the position in the Middle East", which would interrupt the Axis "communications drastically and for a considerable time." It had therefore been decided "that an attempt must be made to carry out a combined blocking and bombardment, the latter being carried out by blocking ships at point blank range" as they approached the harbour. I was informed that after careful consideration it had been decided that the battleship *Barham* and a 'C' class cruiser should be used for this purpose.

Various details followed, and in the final paragraphs of this extraordinary message, apparently dictated by somebody who appeared to know little of Tripoli, or to have any true realization of our circumstances in the Mediterranean, I was somewhat naïvely informed:

> Rather than damage several ships in a bombardment of doubtful value, the deliberate sacrifice of a ship to achieve something really worth while is considered preferable, although doubtless you will regret this use of *Barham*.

I may say at once that this project filled me not only with regret, but with disquietude. It was received at a moment when we were still busily engaged with the transport of the Army to Greece, and its maintenance. Even then the eventual necessity of evacuation was already in our minds. The Italian fleet might choose to interfere in this operation, and I could not willingly agree to the sacrifice of one of our three battleships. We had also on our hands the maintenance of Malta, upon which all depended, and the supply of the garrison of Tobruk.

We examined the proposal to block Tripoli in all its detail, and came to the conclusion that the chances of effectually sealing the port with the *Barham* in the manner suggested were improbable in the extreme. We reckoned the odds at ten to one against, and never had we heard of a blocking operation, not even at Zeebrugge, which had been successful in the face of enemy opposition.

In my return signal to the Admiralty I pointed out the navigational difficulties. We had mined certain of the approach channels with magnetic mines from aircraft. Other channels were too shallow for a battleship. The *Barham* drew 32 feet of water, and would be unhandy at low speed with less than two feet under her bottom. However skilful her handling, I was unable to see how she could be expected to wedge herself in exactly the right position within point-blank range of the enemy guns with enemy dive-bombers overhead.

Even if the harbour were blocked, the enemy, and I quote:

> will still be able to use Tripoli by lightering inside the reefs which they are already doing. With the good weather season ahead this will at the best only slow up the work of unloading.

I went on to say:

> By this very effort we give the enemy the measure of the desperation of our Cyrenaican situation and even if successful we shall have lost a first-class fighting unit whose loss will provide an inestimable fillip to the failing Italian morale. Partial success or failure will intensify these aspects . . . at worst, if we do not succeed, we lose a most valuable unit which may be almost desperately needed in this or other theatres. Finally I have not taken into account the certain loss of nearly 1,000 officers and men (including many higher gunnery ratings) for whom there is no prospect of getting away and who will be sent on this operation unaware of what they are in for.

I added that I hesitated to raise the air question again; but when I knew what the enemy was able to do to the Piræus and other Greek ports by bombers working from Sicily, and heard of the devastation caused by the Royal Air Force in Kiel and Hamburg, I found it difficult to believe that the blocking operation was justified while this alternative existed. The *Barham* operation relied on one shot in the locker. Intensive air action over a period of one month must wreck the small port of Tripoli, while keeping the enemy under continual strain and loss.

I have seen fit to query Their Lordships' decision for the reasons I have given (I concluded), and request the matter may be considered afresh. In the meantime *Barham* is fortunately due for docking and under this pretext will be de-stored and prepared. I would prefer to attack with the whole battle-fleet and accept the risks rather than send in *Barham* unsupported. . . . Should one of the battleships be seriously damaged in these circumstances I should attempt to use her as a block-ship, removing her ship's company by light craft subsequently.

Meanwhile I received another personal message from the First Sea Lord stating, *inter alia:*

> H.M. Government has given instructions that every possible step must be taken by the Navy to prevent supplies reaching Libya from Italy and by coastwise traffic even if this results in serious loss or damage to H.M. ships. The army's difficulty to stabilize and improve will be increased with every convoy reaching Libya and any coastal transportation of supplies. Failure by the Navy to concentrate on prevention of such movements to the exclusion of everything not absolutely vital will be considered as having let side down.

To this I replied on April 16th saying that I was fully conscious of the necessity for stopping supplies to Libya; but that it could not be considered to the exclusion of all other commitments in the Mediterranean. We had an operation in prospect which included the extraction of three empty supply ships from Malta and sending some 'cucumbers'—magnetic mines—there, while we intended to lay more cucumbers off Benghazi, and to attack the aerodromes at Rhodes. I gave the reasons, and added:

> No less than four operations are in train for next 24 hours including two landings. We are not idle in Libya and nobody out here will say the Navy has let them down.

On April 16th, also, I sent another message to the First Sea Lord, saying that it had been usual that blocking operations of the sort proposed should only be carried out by men who volunteered for such dangerous work.

> Considerations of secrecy and the nature of this operation prevent me calling for volunteers (I continued). To get the *Barham* there at high speed and for her to bombard effectively at least two-thirds of the engine-room ratings and the complete trained turret and guns crews must be on board. These, with the ship's company of *Caledon* (the 'C' class cruiser that was also to be used as a block-ship) will involve an estimated total of over a thousand men. With Castel Benito aerodrome but a few miles away and no foreseen prospect of getting any of these men away, casualties will be very heavy. To send in these men unprepared on this operation, involving certain capture and heavy casualties, will seriously jeopardize, if it does not destroy, the whole confidence of the fleet in the higher command, not only here but at home also.

I was not opposed in principle to a blocking operation, though I deprecated sacrificing a valuable ship. But the method suggested filled me with indignation, apart altogether from the physical difficulties, which were formidable. If it had been a forlorn hope on the part of volunteers I should not have objected; but to let down more than a thousand men, who were bound to sustain heavy casualties and had no chance whatever of getting away, was more than I could stomach.

I hope I have explained the situation fairly. After a further interchange of messages the idea of trying to block the harbour of Tripoli with a fully-commissioned battleship was dropped, and the Admiralty agreed to the alternative forced upon me that the port should be bombarded by the battle-fleet at close range. If a ship were damaged, we should try to run her in to block the harbour. We really did not expect to get away with it without having a ship disabled, either by air attacks or in one or other of the minefields. We were aware that the minefields existed; but whereabouts only the enemy knew. A ship crippled close to the enemy's coast was a ship lost. There was no hope of bringing her away.

Meanwhile, when all these messages were being exchanged, the four destroyers from Malta—*Jervis, Nubian, Mohawk* and *Janus*—under Captain P. J. Mack had enjoyed a signal success. At about noon on April 15th a reconnaissance aircraft from Malta had reported five enemy merchant ships escorted by three destroyers, near Cape Bon, on the coast of Tunisia. They were steaming a southerly course at about nine knots, obviously bound for Tripoli. Most of the Libyan convoys gave Malta as wide a berth as possible to try to avoid being sighted and attacked. They used the shortest sea route between Sicily and the North African coast, and moved on to Tripoli hugging the shore.

Mack sailed from Malta at 6 p.m., judging that if he steamed 26 knots he could reach a position off the Kerkenah Islands well ahead of the convoy. The preliminary movements, the search for the convoy, and the subsequent action, which Mack himself referred to as the "Skirmish off Sfax", are admirably and tersely described in a Supplement to the *London Gazette* of May 11th, 1948, which gives an excellent impression of the thrilling excitement of a high-speed destroyer action at night. It was a fine clear night with a good moon. Here are extracts from the narrative of the *Jervis*:

0158 Sighted ships bearing 170 degrees about six miles.
0159 Made signal 'Enemy in sight to port'.
0207 Able to count five ships in all.
0211 Seven ships counted.
0213 Enemy now seen to consist of five merchant vessels, one large destroyer, two small destroyers.
0220 Opened fire on enemy destroyer bearing 100 degrees, range 2,400 yards.
0222 Enemy hit by pom-pom and 4·7-in. Enemy appeared to return fire with Breda and probably 3·9-in. with flashless cordite.
0225 One merchant vessel on fire.
0227 Checked fire. Destroyer sinking.
　　From now on a general mêleé ensued. Fire was opened with 4·7-in., pom-pom, Breda, 0·5-in. and Hotchkiss at many enemy ships at ranges varying from 50 to 2,000 yards. One merchant ship of about three thousand tons attempted to ram me, but I just crossed his bows in time by going full speed ahead on both engines. . . . One large destroyer passed down the line to starboard and was heavily engaged, hit with the first salvo and set on fire amidships.
0240 Fired one torpedo at large enemy destroyer, probably obtaining a hit aft.
0250 An ammunition ship blew up with an enormous explosion; smoke and flames rose to a height of 2,000 feet and *Jervis* who was 1,500 yards away was showered with pieces of ammunition, etc., weighing up to 20 lbs.; the sea around appeared as a boiling cauldron. Inspection reveals that the ammunition was of German manufacture.

0252 Received a signal from *Nubian* reporting that *Mohawk* had been sunk by torpedo. I ordered *Nubian* to burn masthead light and I proceeded towards her.

0311 A torpedo track passed directly under the bridge, apparently fired from the large destroyer previously engaged, which was stopped and burning and thought to be out of action. Opened fire on this destroyer, scoring several hits, and as the bearing drew too far aft ordered *Janus* to finish her off, which she did.

0320 The situation was now as follows:

One destroyer sunk; two destroyers, four merchant vessels burning fiercely; the fifth merchant vessel (the ammunition ship) sunk; *Mohawk* sunk in about seven fathoms lying on her side with about fifty feet of her forecastle above water. . . .

In this spirited and successful action the convoy and escort were annihilated. The loss of such a fine fighting ship as the *Mohawk* was greatly to be regretted, though such losses by chance torpedoes in a night mêlée were only to be expected. It was fortunate that Commander J. W. Eaton and a large proportion of his ship's company were saved.

Meanwhile other ships had been at work on the Libyan coast. On April 15th the *Gloucester* and *Hasty* successfully bombarded concentrations of enemy motor transport near Capuzzo, while the little *Ladybird* fired upon the aerodrome at Gazala and destroyed five or more aircraft. On this day, too, the *Gnat* arrived at Alexandria with eight direct hits, two on the waterline, sustained during a bombardment near Sollum on April 14th.

III

At 7 a.m. on April 18th the *Warspite*, with the *Barham*, *Valiant*, *Formidable*, *Phoebe*, *Calcutta* and screening destroyers sailed from Alexandria. The *Breconshire* was taken to fuel the destroyers, and also carried much-needed oil and aviation spirit for Malta. From Malta four large merchant vessels were to be brought back to Alexandria. It was the plan for the fleet to approach the island as though covering these convoys in the normal way, and after dark on April 20th to steam south at high speed so as to be in position to bombard Tripoli before dawn next morning. The battleships were to be preceded by destroyers sweeping, while Wellingtons of the Royal Air Force and Swordfish of the Fleet Air Arm were to bomb Tripoli before our bombardment. Naval aircraft from the *Formidable* were to provide flare illumination besides spotting for our gunfire.

The chief difficulty about any bombardment from the sea at night is invariably to get an exact fix of the ships' positions so that the range of the target is accurately known. For this purpose a submarine, the *Truant*, was sent on forty-eight hours ahead to fix herself accurately 4 miles off the harbour entrance. She would show a light to seaward as we approached to serve as a navigational mark.

The timing was perfect. The *Warspite*, *Barham* and *Valiant*, having been joined by the *Gloucester*, circled the *Truant* in line ahead just like rounding a buoy. I heard later from Lieutenant-Commander H. A. V. Haggard, the *Truant's* commanding officer, that they were greatly thrilled as they watched the four ships, completely darkened, passing within fifty yards and then putting over their helms to steer to the westward. The silence was only broken by the rippling sound of our bow waves, the wheeze of air pumps, and the muffled twitter of a boatswain's pipe on the *Warspite's* messdeck.

We passed along the line of the harbour and returned, and from 5 a.m. until 5.45 pumped 15-inch and 6-inch shell into the harbour and amongst the shipping. The *Gloucester's* sixteen gun salvoes must have been particularly effective. It was difficult to see precise results as the previous bombing by aircraft had raised clouds of smoke and dust; but the aircraft reported great damage with five or six ships sunk. We could see for ourselves a fine oil fire burning in the area for which the *Valiant* was responsible. After about twenty minutes the shore batteries woke up. A certain amount of stuff flew overhead; but the shooting was very wild and they hit nothing.

The *Formidable* rejoined, and we made off to the north-east at high speed, girding ourselves for the heavy air attack which we felt certain would follow. But for some reason or another nothing happened. Perhaps the Luftwaffe was too busy elsewhere. Perhaps, as some thought, the wireless station at Tripoli, at which, among other targets, the *Warspite* had been firing, had been put out of action. Anyway, there it was, an anti-climax as pleasing as it was unexpected. My personal fears had ranged from the complete loss of a ship in a minefield to heavy damage to them all through dive-bombing.

The return to Alexandria, where we arrived during the morning of April 23rd, was more or less uneventful. A force under Vice-Admiral Pridham-Wippell, which had been beating up the coast between Benghazi and Tobruk joined us on the way. The usual shadowing aircraft appeared and some were shot down; and a threatened attack by three J.U.88's was broken up by the *Formidable's* Fulmars who shot two of the enemy into the sea.

We had been incredibly fortunate, or perhaps the objects again of Divine favour. I had been totally opposed to the bombardment of Tripoli by the fleet from the outset, and was equally against a repetition of the naval bombardment which seemed to be in the minds of the authorities at home.

I expressed these views to the Admiralty in a message of April 22nd. I need not quote it in full; but I said that our present commitments were already more than we could deal with efficiently. We had got away with the Tripoli bombardment once; but only because the Luftwaffe was elsewhere and we had achieved surprise. It had taken the whole Mediterranean Fleet five days to accomplish what a heavy bomber squadron working from Egypt could probably carry out in a few hours. The fleet had also to run considerable, and in my opinion, unjustifiable risks in an operation which had been carried out at the expense of all other commitments, when those commitments were most pressing. It seemed to me that the Air Ministry were trying to lay their responsibilities on the Navy's shoulders and were not helping as they should on the naval side of the war in the Mediterranean. I instanced Malta, and the latest decision not to send Beaufighters there. This would serve to perpetuate the conditions then existing whereby the enemy could freely move his convoys by day without fear of air attack, whereas even within a few miles of our own coasts our convoys were only free from that danger on dark nights. I pointed out that our increasing losses in the Ægean convoys were attributable, in large measure, to inadequate air support; also that some time before I had proposed the institution of a Coastal Command comparable to that at home for co-operation with the Mediterranean Fleet, and that no reply had been received. I was quite satisfied that the Air Officer Commanding-in-Chief co-operated with me as far as his forces allowed; but they were quite inadequate. I added that I was sending the cruiser *Gloucester* to Malta to back up the destroyers working against the enemy convoys to Libya; but that the fuel situation at Malta was very serious. I intended to try to run in two large tankers during a forthcoming operation. The supply of fuel to the island would continue to be an anxiety until we had a really fast tanker.

The Admiralty replied on April 23rd giving me their ideas as to how the enemy convoys to Tripoli should be attacked by day and by night. If we were to make certain of stopping them, which we must do if we were not to risk losing Egypt, it seemed necessary to have a battleship at Malta. It had been decided to be worth while to expend a battleship to prevent the convoys getting through. I was also informed that the Royal Air Force had offered to maintain at Malta six Blenheims of their specially trained anti-ship squadron, if in return the naval Swordfish squadron from Malta were used for laying magnetic mines at Tripoli. Every endeavour would also be made to send some Beaufighters to Malta to assist in protecting the battleship against dive-bombers at sea.

I was beginning to feel seriously annoyed. This constant advice, not to say interference, in how to run our own business from those who seemed to be unaware of the real facts of our situation did not help us at all. They were a mere source of worry. The last Admiralty message, indeed, completely ignored the grave shortage of fuel at Malta, and that, by basing a battleship there which would always be steaming at high speed when at sea, would involve the expenditure of still more fuel which would have to be replenished in convoys from Alexandria. Moreover we were already stretched to the

The ordeal of the *Illustrious*, January 10th 1941. "At times she became almost completely hidden in a forest of great bomb splashes.... In all, in something like ten minutes, she was hit by six 1,000-lb. bombs, to leave the line badly on fire, her steering gear crippled, her lifts out of action, and with heavy casualties."

The Luftwaffe bomb Malta. H.M.S. *Illustrious*, being alongside the Parlatoria Wharf, is hidden behind the bomb splash in the right background.

On the bridge of the *Warspite*. Before the Battle of Matapan, March 28th 1941. The Commander-in-Chief with Captain John H. Edelsten, the Chief of the Staff designate.

Tobruk, 1941.

Major-General Bernard Freyburg, V.C., with the Commander-in-Chief and Vice-Admiral Sir Henry Pridham-Wippell on board H.M.S. *Phoebe* after evacuation of Crete.

At the British Embassy, Cairo. *From left to right*: A.B.C.; General Sir Claud Auchinleck; Sir Walter Monckton; Emir Mansour Sexth, son of Ibn Saud, King of the Hejaz; Sir Miles Lampson, British Ambassador.

Rear-Admiral Vian's action against the Italian fleet, March 22nd 1942. Italian salvoes falling. Destroyers and a smoke-screen.

Algiers, December 1942. *From left to right*: Admiral Darlan; General Eisenhower; A.B.C.; General Giraud.

General Eisenhower on board *Nelson* at Algiers with Commander-in-Chief and Vice-Admiral Algernon Willis.

A conference at General Eisenhower's villa at Algiers, May 1943. *Standing, left to right*: Air Chief Marshal Sir Arthur Tedder; A.B.C.; General Sir Harold Alexander; Lieut.-General Sir Bernard Montgomery. *Seated:* Mr. Anthony Eden; General Sir Alan Brooke; the Prime Minister; General Marshall; General Eisenhower.

Operation Husky. The landing in Sicily, July 10th 1943. This photograph, taken soon after dawn, shows British troops unloading stores and preparing beach roads.

On board H.M.S. *Aurora* off Pantellaria, June 9th 1943. *Left to right:* Commodore R.M. Dick, Chief-of-Staff to C.-in-C. Mediterranean; A.B.C.; General Eisenhower.

Commodore W.G. Agnew; A.B.C.; General Eisenhower.

His Majesty's visit to Algiers, June 1943. The King's arrival at Maison Blanche aerodrome, near Algiers, June 12th 1943.

The King inspects sailors of the United States Navy (Vice-Admiral H. Kent, U.S.N., immediately behind His Majesty.

limit, and as I still had to reckon with the possibility of engaging the Italian fleet, I was unwilling to deprive our fleet of one of its three battleships. The whole crux of the matter as regards the attack on the enemy convoys to Tripoli lay in proper air support from Malta. This I explained again to the Admiralty in a message of April 26th:

> If we consider that six or even sixteen destroyers can be certain of intercepting Libya convoys without proper air support to enable them to work by day we should be blind to facts. The situation is analogous to that in the English Channel, which has many advantages we have not, and where interception distances are much less. Despite this, enemy vessels seem to pass freely there. The great difficulty of intercepting these convoys is a fact that must be squarely faced, and I therefore feel it wrong to expect much from a few destroyers at Malta.

The Prime Minister entered into this controversy with a long message received by me on April 27th. He informed me there could be no departure from the principle that it was the prime responsibility of the Mediterranean Fleet to sever all communications between Italy and Africa. After mentioning the bombardment of Tripoli, and informing me that the same weight of bombs as we had fired of shell in forty-two minutes, might, by his information, have been dropped by one Wellington squadron from Malta in ten and a half weeks, or by one Stirling squadron in about thirty weeks, he went on to say that I did not appreciate that the primary aim of the Air Force in Malta was to defend the naval base against air attack, in order that our surface craft might operate against enemy convoys.

I need not refer to the rest of the message, to which I did not reply. We were far too busy with our other commitments.

Nevertheless, I had the complete answer.

We fully concurred that our primary responsibility was the severance of all communications between Italy and Africa. There were, however, two other commitments of immediate importance; the evacuation of the Army from Greece which had started on April 24th, and the supply of Malta. These commitments were not exclusively naval. In all cases, particularly against the Libyan convoys, very considerable air support was required.

A high degree of air reconnaissance should have been available, and for weeks on end I had had no knowledge of the whereabouts of the Italian fleet. During the evacuation from Greece only one flying-boat at a time from Malta could be kept on patrol in the Ionian Sea, between the heel of Italy and Greece. This was all the more serious because our battle-fleet was immobilized at Alexandria for the reason that every destroyer we possessed, and we could have done with many more, was actively engaged in the evacuation of the Army from Greece.

Malta, undoubtedly, was the correct strategical base for a fleet, though even so, part of the fleet would have to be maintained elsewhere to cover the convoys in the Ægean and the Army supply line between Alexandria and Tobruk, both of which needed air co-operation. Malta, however, had never been brought up to its established scale of anti-aircraft defence in guns and fighter squadrons, in consequence of which it was dangerous as a base for warships. Very few ships had used the island and its dockyard facilities, and emerged undamaged. With the arrival of the German dive-bombers in Sicily—only 60 miles away—and the increase in minelaying from the air, the hazards had been greatly enhanced.

I could never agree that the primary duty of the Royal Air Force in Malta was to defend the island. In my considered opinion it had the equally important function of making use of the ideally-situated base for offensive air action against the enemy; besides working in close co-operation with our surface ships attacking the convoys to Libya. The Navy, by itself, could only interrupt the Axis communications with Tripoli. It could not stop them.

Repeatedly and consistently, I had stated and re-stated these views over a period of two years. Yet Malta was still being subjected to continual air attack and was held under the thrall of constant observation; while every time the fleet put to sea from Alexandria or anywhere else, we were dogged by shadowing aircraft. From Greece we were trying to evacuate some fifty thousand men with meagre air reconnaissance, and very thin fighter protection around Crete against the attacks of about four hundred German dive-bombers. Along the coast of Libya our convoys were being heavily bombed at sea and in harbour with little or no fighter protection, and our losses were steadily increasing. At Tobruk, we were reduced to sending one ship at a time because there was no fighter protection at all. The eventual arrival of the Luftwaffe in Southern Greece would make our use of Suda Bay precarious, and would greatly complicate the supply of Malta from Alexandria with dive-bombing from Greece, Italy, Sicily and North Africa.

The Navy alone could not save Egypt, or even play its full part, until the air situation was squarely faced. It was doubtful if the weakened Army could hold its position on the Egyptian frontier. In my opinion we should lose Egypt in the course of a few months unless every nerve were strained to increase our air forces, and if this were not done we should lose a great proportion of the fleet in the endeavour to save the situation.

As we saw it, the battle of the Libyan convoys could only be won by the Navy in close partnership with an adequate air force. We urgently needed long-range fighters to give air cover to our convoys in every area; sufficient short-range fighters to give us control of our bases at Malta, Alexandria, Suda Bay and Tobruk; and adequate reconnaissance aircraft to give us the same information of the enemy's movements at sea as the enemy possessed of ours.

The lack of all the air co-operation we needed was in no way due to Air Chief Marshal Longmore, the Air Officer Commanding-in-Chief. He had been the most loyal and understanding colleague with the liveliest grasp of naval problems. The difficulty was entirely one of poor resources. The picture, indeed, was a gloomy one, and if our deficiencies in the air could not be made good, and quickly, I foresaw we should have to face some very unpleasant alternatives in the Middle East.

Why the authorities at home apparently could not see the danger of our situation in the Mediterranean without adequate air support passed my comprehension. However, within about a month the bitter lesson was to be learnt, in Crete.

CHAPTER XXVIII

I

By the middle of April, 1941, the prevailing picture of unrelieved gloom was by no means brightened by the way things were shaping in Greece. Though our Army was being compelled to fall back, the convoys continued to run to the Piræus. The Luftwaffe was taking a hand in the sea battle, and we were beginning to lose valuable ships which we could not replace. The left flank of the Greek position was exposed by the withdrawal of the Yugoslav army to the west. Indeed, everything in Greece was as bad as it could be, and on April 15th, before some of the events described in the last chapter, Wavell and Longmore had been on board the *Warspite* for a conference at which we were forced to the conclusion that the only possible course was to withdraw the British troops from Greece. Wavell flew on to Athens to place the situation fairly before the King of the Hellenes and his government and to obtain their concurrence.

By April 18th all the fighting in Yugoslavia was finished and the Greek army, exhausted by its long struggle, first against the Italians and now against the Germans, was beginning to show signs of disintegration. The King and government agreed to the evacuation of the British forces, now retreating fast. The date for the beginning of the withdrawal was first fixed for April 28th; but this was soon realized to be too far ahead. Retiring under incessant and very heavy air attacks, which were virtually unopposed, our Army was practically immobilized by day, while the roads in the rear upon which our troops depended for their supplies and movement, were severely bombed. Wireless communications were also disorganized by the mountainous nature of the country.

The Royal Air Force, after a most gallant struggle against overwhelming odds, and having lost its airfields as the Army retired, had been forced to leave Greece and to do the best it could from Crete and other bases. No more than a handful of aircraft was left to continue the battle, and it could only provide the thinnest of air cover for shipping in the immediate neighbourhood of Crete. No reinforcements could be sent from the Middle East. The aircraft simply did not exist.

As has been said, the principal port, the Piræus, had been wrecked and disorganized by the explosion of an ammunition ship on April 7th. The German superiority in the air continued to show itself, and on April 21st and 22nd we lost twenty-three ships, including a Greek destroyer and two hospital ships, in Greek waters.

There were good and sufficient reasons for advancing D-day for the start of the evacuation, which was known as Operation 'Demon', to April 24th.

Rear-Admiral H. T. Baillie-Grohman was sent to Greece to work with General Sir Henry Maitland Wilson on the land side. Vice-Admiral Pridham-Wippell, with all the available cruisers and destroyers, was in general charge of the naval operations with his headquarters at Suda Bay, Crete.

The salvage of the cruiser *York*, at Suda Bay, had had to be abandoned because of her further bomb damage, and for service in his beach parties, for communications, and for manning locally requisitioned small craft, etc., Baillie-Grohman was given the whole of the *York's* ship's company with other officers and men sent up from Alexandria. The plan was to embark from a number of beaches to which good roads gave access—Megara, Raphina and Raphtis in the Athens area; and Nauplia and Tolon, Monemvasia, and Kalamata in the Peloponnesus.

For lifting the troops there were four cruisers, the *Orion* (Vice-Admiral Pridham-Wippell's flagship), *Ajax*, *Phœbe*, and H.M.A.S. *Perth*; the three anti-aircraft cruisers *Calcutta*, *Coventry* and *Carlisle*; some twenty destroyers; three sloops: H.M.S.'s *Glenearn* and *Glengyle*, then known as 'Infantry Assault Ships', but later as 'Landing Ships, Infantry' or L.S.I.'s, and provided with special landing craft instead of boats; nineteen medium-sized troop-ships; with various miscellaneous units, including a number of 'A' lighters, the forerunners of the better-known tank landing craft, or L.C.T.s. Under the general direction of Commander K. Michell, in Greece, a number of caïques, motor-boats and local craft were chartered and fitted out for ferrying troops to the ships from the shore. As it happened, hundreds of soldiers owed their escape to the small craft requisitioned in this manner. To save shipping Crete was to be used as a staging post, and it was hoped that the whole evacuation would be completed in three days. Actually it took six.

Operation 'Demon', in which 50,672 troops were withdrawn, was intricate and extraordinarily difficult. Because of the complete enemy command in the air, Baillie-Grohman wisely ordered ships not to approach the chosen beaches until one hour after dark, and to be away, at latest, by 3 a.m. The Navy had to see to it that the ships were at the right beaches at the right time, with sufficient small craft on the spot to ferry off the troops.

The Army, meanwhile, moving mainly by night over unknown roads to the beaches where the ships awaited them, were fighting all the way with no cover against the enemy aircraft which filled the sky, bombing and machine-gunning all they saw. The soldiers were dog-tired, hungry and thirsty; but, as Baillie-Grohman wrote: "The Army organization in rear of the beaches and the discipline of the troops were magnificent; especially considering that they had been fighting a rear-guard action for some weeks, from Salonika almost to Cape Matapan."

On April 24th, D-day, I signalled: "The object is to embark men, if possible, with arms; but no material must be allowed to take precedence to men. Troop-ships with men embarked to sail direct to Alexandria, except 'Glen' ships which must unload at Suda Bay and do a second embarkation. Destroyers to take their troops to Crete, where they will be transferred later."

The services of the *Glenearn* and *Glengyle* were particularly valuable. Their special landing craft, and the independent tank landing craft, though working in the reverse direction to that for which they were intended, undoubtedly made it possible to embark many more troops than would otherwise have been the case.

The merchant vessels and their officers and crews behaved magnificently, their masters never hesitating to take their ships into unfamiliar, unlighted and difficult anchorages, with no navigational marks and often without adequate charts. They acted throughout with the greatest courage, skill and determination. They did not come off scathless.

The Dutch ship *Slamat*, embarking troops at Nauplia on April 27th, should have sailed at 3 a.m.; but rather than leave some troops behind, waited until 4.15. Three hours later she was bombed and set on fire, the destroyers *Diamond*, Lieutenant-Commander P. A. Cartwright, and *Wryneck*, Commander R. H. D. Lane, being sent to her assistance. The *Slamat* sank, the destroyers being dive-bombed while rescuing her survivors. The *Diamond* and *Wryneck* were again bombed early that afternoon; both ships being hit and sunk almost immediately. Only 1 officer, 41 ratings and 8 soldiers were saved from the destroyers, while 500 of the troops from the *Slamat* were lost.

The *Costa Rica* was bombed and sunk this same afternoon, all her troops and crew being rescued by the destroyers *Hero*, *Hereward* and *Defender*. The *Pennland* also was twice bombed, and sunk.

H.M.S. *Ulster Prince*, one of the fast motor-ships of the Belfast Steamship Company used as a troop-carrier, grounded at Nauplia while trying to go alongside a jetty, and was heavily bombed, set on fire, and gutted next day.

The *Glenearn* was twice hit by bombs. The first time she was set on fire; but managed to deal with the blaze, and went on and embarked her quota of troops. Two days later she was hit in the engine-room and completely disabled. She was towed to Suda Bay by the destroyer *Griffin* and eventually on to Alexandria by the sloop *Grimsby*. Both were masterly towing feats by ships ill-adapted for that purpose, particularly in the face of air attack. Incidentally, the *Grimsby* had previously assisted another bombed merchant vessel, the *Scottish Prince*, into Suda Bay. The *Grimsby's* commanding officer, Commander K. T. D'Arcy, was a man of resource.

Other losses there were among the small craft working off the beaches in Greece, but on the whole we had to consider ourselves extremely fortunate.

Baillie-Grohman summed up the situation in his report: "The enemy made no attempt to bomb our evacuation beaches or our ships by night. This may have been partly due to our policy of not permitting ships to reach beaches

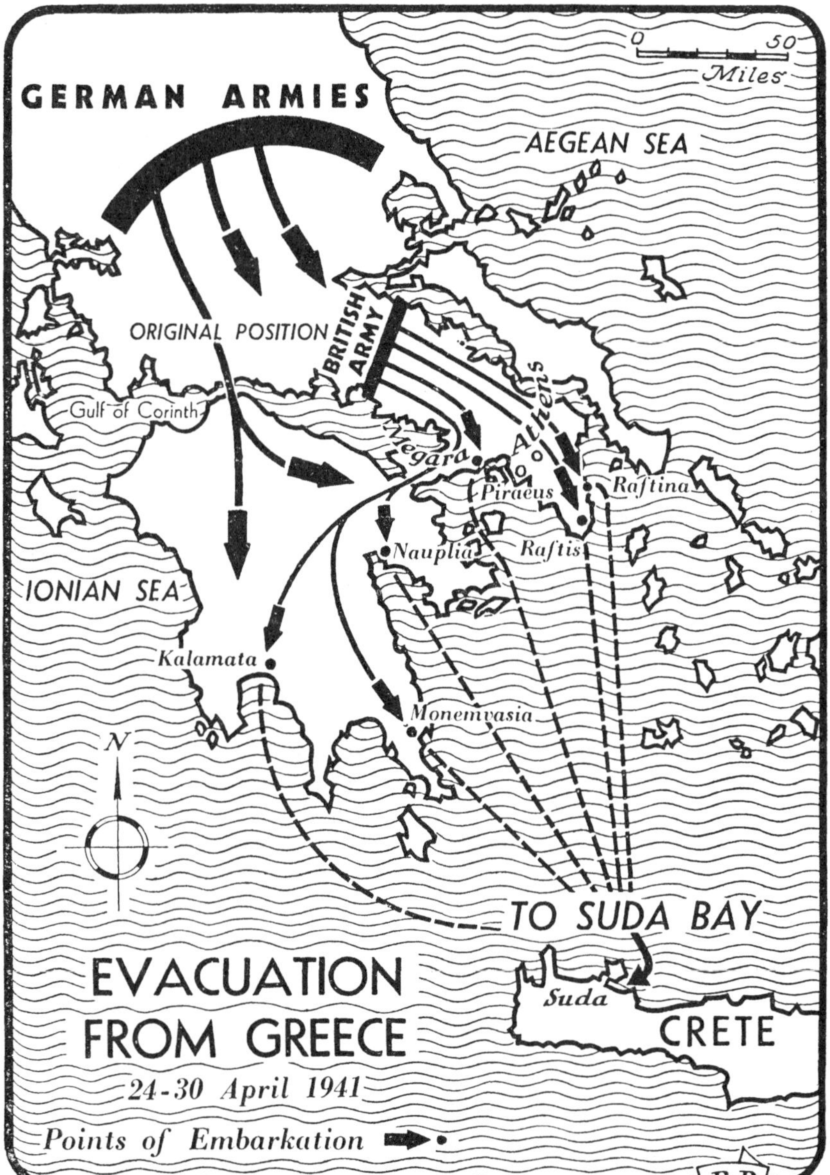
0 50
Miles
GERMAN ARMIES
AEGEAN SEA
ORIGINAL POSITION
BRITISH ARMY
Gulf of Corinth
Athens
Megara
Piraeus
Raftina
Nauplia
Raftis
IONIAN SEA
Kalamata
Monemvasia
N
TO SUDA BAY
Suda
CRETE
EVACUATION FROM GREECE
24-30 April 1941
Points of Embarkation
B.P.

till one hour after dark, and so making it more difficult for the enemy to find the exact beaches in use. Or it may have been due to lack of flares or the enemy's deliberate policy to make use of daylight only. Whatever the reason, our evacuation was certainly very much simplified by the enemy's failure in this respect."

I can agree.

The large convoys taking the troops on from Crete to Alexandria came through without loss, and it has to be remembered that the whole operation was carried out without any cover from the battle-fleet. Every available destroyer was engaged in the actual evacuation, and none was left to take the battle-fleet to sea until the very end, when it was essential to provide cover for the large convoys to Egypt. We owed much to the inertness of the Italian fleet. Had they chosen to interfere, Operation 'Demon' would have been greatly slowed up. At the worst, it might have been interrupted altogether.

We were not completely successful. The enemy made a surprise airborne attack on the Corinth Canal area, seizing the only bridge. This meant that some of our troops who were going to a port in the Peloponnesus had to be diverted to the Athens area, which dislocated the arrangements there. On April 28th, too, a small mobile enemy column occupied the town of Kalamata, in the south, where 8,000 men were to be embarked from the quays. The senior officer in the ships sent there heard that the town and harbour were in enemy hands and abandoned the operation. It was an unfortunate decision, as the destroyer *Hero*, Commander H. W. Biggs, nosing her way inshore, reported soon afterwards that the troops were on the shore south of the town, that evacuation was possible from the beach, and that all firing in the town had ceased. I was told later that a fine counter-attack by some mixed units had driven the Germans out of Kalamata. The *Kandahar*, *Kimberley* and *Kingston* joined the *Hero*, and between them these four destroyers took off 324 troops in their own boats. On the two following nights the *Isis*, *Hero* and *Kimberley* lifted 235 more. But to our great regret some 4,000 British and 2,000 Palestinian and Cypriot troops, with 1,500 Yugoslav refugees, had to be left behind and were forced to surrender.

Rear-Admiral Baillie-Grohman did grand work in the most onerous conditions imaginable. With everything in confusion in a strange country, with the language difficulty and his uncertain communications, with the changing political situation and the uncertainty of arriving at firm figures and dates for the numbers of troops to be embarked and from where, he yet succeeded in producing something like order out of chaos.

I cannot speak too highly of Vice-Admiral Pridham-Wippell's part in this most trying operation. With the scantiest of information, bad communication and meagre resources, he had to provide the ships for Baillie-Grohman's requirements at the shortest notice, and, as was natural, the arrangements were constantly changing. The situation for Pridham-Wippell himself altered almost from hour to hour as reports came through of the ships upon which he was relying for the night's embarkation being bombed and disabled. There could be no certain planning, and new schemes had to be improvised at almost a moment's notice. More than once he had to step into the breach with his own flagship, the *Orion*, and steam at full speed to one of the beaches to help to embark the troops. Moreover, he had a large number of ships working under his orders, and during the early part of the operation was in constant anxiety over fuel. There was none left at Suda Bay until the arrival of the fleet oiler *Brambleleaf* on April 26th.

As I have said a total of 50,672 soldiers were carried away from Greece of whom 500 were lost in the *Slamat*. As at Dunkirk, the losses in equipment, armour, guns, transport, ammunition and stores were very heavy. Also, many of the small craft working off the beaches were lost or had to be destroyed. However, in retrospect, I feel that the episode is one to which the Royal Navy and Merchant Navy can look back with pride. Of the men who were embarked only about 14,000 were brought away from recognized wharves or jetties. All the rest were taken off to the ships from open beaches in landing craft, ships' boats and any other craft that could be collected, a process which was depressingly slow at night. Yet one reads of the merchant ships each lifting up to 3,500 men a night, the cruisers up to 2,500, and the destroyers crammed with anything up to 800 and 850. The seamen did gallant work, and the cruisers and destroyers had already been working at full pressure for weeks.

The King of the Hellenes and the British Minister left Greece in a Sunderland flying-boat on April 23rd and established themselves at Suda Bay. At Kalamata, the destroyer *Defender* embarked 250 soldiers with the Yugoslav Crown jewels in cases.

On April 27th the Germans entered Athens. Just before their arrival we received at Alexandria a poignant message from the Athens wireless station: "Closing down for the last time, hoping for happier days. God be with you, and for you." Then silence.

Baillie-Grohman, with Major-General Bernard Freyberg, commanding the New Zealand Forces, after seeing the last of the troops off the beaches at Monevasia, embarked in H.M.S. *Ajax* at 3 a.m. on April 29th.

II

The defence of Crete now assumed the first importance. After being used as a staging-post for the troops from Greece there was naturally much confusion in the island. In addition to the British troops which had not been sent on to Egypt, there were some 14,000 or 15,000 Italian prisoners of war, and some thousands of Greeks. The King of the Hellenes was also in the island. The troops were in bad shape, weary after their experiences and armed only with light weapons.

Major-General E. C. Weston, Royal Marines, who had arrived in the Mediterranean with the M.N.B.D.O.—Mobile Naval Base Defence Organization—for Suda Bay, was at this time in command in the island. The M.N.B.D.O. was at Haifa, engaged in restowing the ships carrying it, which had been sent out from England round the Cape stowed in a manner which bore no relation to the priority in which all the various items would be used. It arrived at Suda Bay early in May, and its Royal Marines, with their anti-aircraft guns, searchlights, booms, nets, mines and so forth, provided a welcome addition to the defences.

Chiefly because the shipping and escorts were not available to move them to Egypt, General Wavell decided to leave in Crete 16,000 troops who had been evacuated there from Greece to form the garrison. It was also decided to send the Italians to Egypt as soon as the shipping could be found to take them. He entrusted the command in the island to General Freyberg, General Weston retaining command of the Suda Bay area. On the naval side Captain J. A. V. Morse, also of the M.N.B.D.O., was appointed Senior Naval Officer.

It is necessary here to say something of the topography of Crete. The island is 160 miles long east and west, with a width north and south varying between 35 and $7\frac{1}{2}$ miles. A back-bone of high mountains, which can be crossed in no more than a few places, runs nearly its whole length and slopes abruptly down to the sea on the southern side. All the bays and harbours are on the northern coast, an unfortunate fact for us as they could only be reached through the Kaso Straits at the east end of the island, and the Antikithera and Kithera Channels to the west, all of which were in easy range of enemy aerodromes. No port or real anchorage exists on the south coast, while the only country suitable for airfields is on the northern side. We had two airfields, one at Maleme, about 10 miles west of Suda Bay, and the other near Heraklion, a small port about 65 miles to the eastward. There was also a small landing strip at Retimo, about 20 miles east of Suda. From the point of view of defence it would have suited us much better if the island could have been turned upside-down.

It had been decided that the island must be held, and that an attack was inevitable. It was considered most probable that the enemy would not risk a seaborne invasion in the face of our command of the sea; but that the assault would be airborne. Consequently, the defence was mainly centred round the airfields at Maleme, Retimo and Heraklion, and the principal port of supply, Suda Bay. There were some, however, who considered that our command of the sea would be precarious because of the heavy attacks that could be delivered on our ships from the enemy bases nearby, particularly if we lacked fighter cover.

I shall deal later with the battle for Crete and its eventual evacuation.

III

The beginning of May brought no great change over the rest of the Mediterranean theatre. Rommel had been brought to a standstill more or less on the Egyptian frontier, probably through lack of supplies. Tobruk, still in our hands, had sustained another assault by land, and if anything the air attacks were heavier and more frequent because of the absence of any fighter defence. The losses in small ships and mine-sweepers were mounting, and they were hard put to keep the channel clear and to run in the necessary supplies. The little *Fiona*, Commander L. Griffiths, R.N.R., an ex-merchant ship of light draught and small tonnage so valuable for service along the Libyan coast, had been sunk by aircraft off Sidi Barrani on April 18th. The *Chakla*, a similar vessel, was sunk in Tobruk harbour on the 29th. Both these ships had been handled with great skill and gallantry, and the *Chakla's* latest feat had been the towing of the *Desmoulea*, a large disabled tanker, from Suda Bay to Port Said, escorted only by a trawler. Attacked six times on the way by bombers and torpedo aircraft she never broke wireless silence.

These losses were the price we had to pay to the almost complete lack of air cover. At the beginning of May there were no more than thirteen fighters fit for action in the Western Desert.

Our casualties along the Libyan coast at this period decided me in ordering that in future supplies to Tobruk should also be carried in small auxiliary schooners commissioned as H.M. ships; and that a water-tanker and a petrol-carrier were to be run in during the moonless periods. All destroyers or other warships regularly going to Tobruk were to carry stores and bring away personnel; but must be well clear of the port between dawn and dusk. The average daily supply to be aimed at was seventy tons.

The Inshore Squadron had given outstanding service, and on April 30th I had signalled to the Senior Officer:

> It is fully realized by the Air Officer Commanding-in-Chief and myself how great are the difficulties of working the port of Tobruk, and the dangers encountered by ships sailing thereto without adequate fighter protection. Magnificent work is being done by your squadron and the men at Tobruk, and I trust that an end will come soon to the present bleak period.

Malta was also under a minelaying attack from the air of the most virulent kind. I had withdrawn Captain Mack and his three destroyers and replaced them by six destroyers newly sent out from England under the command of Captain Lord Louis Mountbatten. They were the *Kelly*, *Kipling*, *Kelvin*, *Kashmir*, *Jackal* and *Jersey*. Five days after their arrival the *Jersey* was mined and sunk in the entrance to the Grand Harbour while returning from a night sortie in search of enemy convoys. The cruiser *Gloucester* had also been sent to Malta to back up the destroyers; but the mining became so intense that she was often bottled up in the harbour or forced to remain out. When the *Jersey* was mined the *Gloucester* and two destroyers could not enter, and were ordered to Gibraltar to return with a convoy. Passing through the Sicilian Narrows the *Gloucester* exploded a mine in her paravanes; and later the same day was repeatedly attacked by enemy aircraft. She was hit in the stern by a bomb which luckily went right through the ship before exploding, and her speed was not affected. This was the third time she had been hit by a bomb during her year's service in the Mediterranean.

The attention of the enemy's minelaying aircraft was also drawn to Alexandria, where we had mines in the harbour and near the entrance channel known as the Great Pass, though luckily not in it. Other mines landed and exploded ashore, where they caused considerable loss of life and much damage.

We had hoped for a respite for our cruisers and destroyers after the gruelling time they had had during the evacuation of Greece and for weeks before that. There was hardly one of them which was not in urgent need of repair or refit, and, above all, of rest for the ships' companies. Writing to the First Sea Lord on May 3rd I mentioned that Pridham-Wippell and myself had noticed signs of strain among the officers and ratings, particularly in the anti-aircraft cruisers and also in the destroyers. "The former have had a gruelling time ever since the move of the Army to Greece started on March 4th, never a trip to sea without being bombed."

But there was to be no respite. It was essential to bring out tank reinforcements to our hardly-pressed Army in Egypt. A convoy of five large merchant vessels was to be brought through the Mediterranean; a gamble undoubtedly, but well worth trying as the need was great. At the same time we were being sent reinforcements for the fleet, the battleship *Queen Elizabeth*, and the cruisers *Naiad* and *Fiji*. As usual, Force 'H' was to cover the convoy as far as the Sicilian Narrows, and the Mediterranean Fleet would pick it up south of Malta. The code name for the operation was *Tiger*.

For our part we determined to run two convoys into Malta, one consisting of four large merchant ships with supplies, and the other of two large 10-knot tankers carrying in all 24,000 tons of oil-fuel to replenish the dangerously depleted stocks in the island. It was also decided to give Benghazi a pasting with a cruiser and three destroyers as the fleet passed. It was being used by the enemy as a supply port on a small scale.

The Mediterranean Fleet and Force 'H' were both timed to sail on May 6th

We had some difficulty in getting away, as Alexandria had again been mined the day before and all the heavy ships had individually to be taken to sea by a force of sweepers. I remember there was bad visibility because of a duststorm, so that the *Formidable* did not fly off her aircraft. I took to sea with me Admiral Sir Walter Cowan, who had come out with the commandos and was serving in the rank of commander.

After we had been a day at sea the Vice-Admiral, Malta, reported that his harbours were completely mined in, and that the destroyer flotilla there could not sail to join the convoy. All the sweepers that dealt with magnetic mines had also been lost or damaged. This was a sorry business; but having started I was certainly not going to order our convoys for Malta back to Alexandria. So I sent for the Fleet Torpedo Officer, the rather silent, imperturbable and never defeated Commander W. P. Carne, and told him to do something about it. Incidentally, we had a corvette fitted for magnetic minesweeping, the *Gloxinia*, with one of the convoys, though she could never be expected to deal with all the mines. However, in about an hour's time Commander Carne reappeared with a long signal in which the Vice-Admiral, Malta, was directed to blast a channel into Malta with depth-charges, of which, fortunately, there were plenty in store. I do not know if the procedure was strictly orthodox; but the basis of the idea was that a depth-charge dropped every so many yards would countermine or upset the firing mechanism of any magnetic mine in the vicinity of the explosion. The scheme was a triumphant success. Various mines were destroyed in the approaches and a swept channel buoyed. It has to be recorded, however, that when the *Gloxinia*, towing her magnetic sweep, or 'fluffing her tail', as they called it, led the convoy into harbour next day, nearly a dozen more mines went up as she steamed through the breakwater entrance.

When passing Benghazi the *Ajax* and three destroyers were detached to shoot up the port during the night of May 7th–8th. They had great success, for after bombarding the harbour area they later met a convoy of two merchant ships. One, carrying motor transport and ammuniton, blew up, and the second ran ashore and was left well ablaze after several explosions. I afterwards heard lurid tales of motor-lorries hurtling through the air right over the destroyers.

Malta had been having a very bad time. Aware, no doubt, that the sea and air forces from the island formed the spearhead of the attack on their Libyan convoys, the enemy had been bombing the harbour and airfields without mercy, quite apart from the minelaying. The Royal Air Force lowattack Blenheims had come into action against the Axis shipping and were doing good execution, while the Malta submarines were taking a steady and increasing toll. In something like a month at this period, submarines sank eleven ships and damaged another. The *Upholder*, commanded by the late Lieutenant-Commander Malcolm D. Wanklyn, V.C., D.S.O., was responsible for four vessels sunk and a fifth damaged. This gallant officer was awarded the Victoria Cross for his action on May 24th, 1941, when on patrol off Sicily. The *Upholder's* listening gear was out of action and the light was failing; but sighting a south-bound troop convoy heavily escorted by destroyers he went in to attack. After nearly being rammed by a destroyer he fired torpedoes which sank the 18,000-ton liner *Conte Rosso*, crammed with troops. Thirty-seven depth-charges were dropped in the subsequent counter-attack. Lieutenant-Commander Wanklyn perished with his ship off Tripoli in April, 1942, a great loss to the submarine service and to the Royal Navy. In the period April, 1941, to March, 1942, the *Upholder* sank one destroyer; two U-boats; ten merchant ships of which three were large liners of 18,000–19,000 tons; and damaged one cruiser and three more merchant vessels.

In May, 1941, the enemy's retaliation on Malta was severe. Widespread damage was done in the dockyard and its vicinity. Most of the workshops were down to 50 per cent of their normal efficiency, some as low as 25 per cent, while the dry-docks were only operable by hand.

To revert to the *Tiger* convoy, the fleet arrived south of Malta without incident, and five cruisers were detached to join the convoy to the westward and to shepherd it through the Narrows. The *Breconshire*, which had accompanied us, was sent to Marsaxlokk, Malta, to fuel the destoyers in turn. Providence worked in our favour. For the time of year the weather was most unusual, thick with low cloud almost down to our mast-heads. Many enemy craft appeared on the radar scan. They were searching for us; but thanks to the low visibility no attack developed. All that happened was that one of the *Formidable's* Fulmars, cruising above cloud level, tumbled a J.U.88 into the sea. We met the convoy. One merchant vessel had been sunk by a mine in the Narrows. Another had been torpedoed, but was able to proceed. Force 'H' reported themselves as being heavily attacked from the air; but without either damage or casualties. They had taken good toll of the attackers.

The fleet and convoy steamed east for Alexandria, the convoy heavily protected by the three anti-aircraft cruisers, *Carlisle*, *Calcutta* and *Coventry*, and the *Dido*, *Naiad* and *Phœbe*, with their heavy A.A. armaments. The thick weather persisted and no air attack developed until the night of May 10th, when, in a flat calm with a full moon, the enemy came in on the convoy; but were beaten off. They next hit off the fleet, stationed down moon from the convoy, and attacked with both high and low-flying aircraft. The terrific volume of gunfire put up by the four battleships and the *Formidable* was too much for them and the bombing was wild, though some of the destroyers on the screen had near misses.

The 5th Flotilla was detached off Benghazi to give it another bombardment before returning to Malta, and the fleet and convoy arrived safely in Alexandria on May 12th, on which day the faithful little *Ladybird*, after nine months of fine service, under the command of Lieutenant-Commander J. F.

Blackburn, was sunk by dive-bombers at Tobruk. A hospital ship, the *Karapara*, had been deliberately bombed there on May 4th, while three days later we had lost the minesweeper *Stoke*. The supply of Tobruk was still one of our major problems, and two destroyers were being run in there every night with supplies, returning to Alexandria with wounded.

The *Ladybird* was a particularly sad loss. She sank in shallow water and her crew were withdrawn, though I believe the Army continued to man her guns as part of the anti-aircraft defences at Tobruk. We had a signal from the Commanding Officer of the South Staffordshire Regiment, which we passed on: "All ranks of South Staffords having had opportunity of getting to know officers and crew of H.M.S. *Ladybird* and seeing so much of their co-operation in the Western Desert, wish to express their sympathy at the loss of this gallant little ship."

The *Ladybird's* sailors were intensely proud of their ship and her record. I visited some of her wounded in hospital, and was greatly struck by their cheerfulness. Two young men in adjacent beds with only one leg between them made a very deep impression on me. They took their disability in such a fine spirit.

The Admiralty sent us a congratulatory message on the safe arrival of the *Tiger* convoy, which they regarded as a 'memorable achievement'. We did not altogether congratulate ourselves, being fully aware that the success of the operation must be ascribed to the thick and cloudy weather, which, for that time of the year in the Mediterranean, was unprecedented. Unfortunately the apparent ease with which a convoy was brought through from end to end of the Mediterranean caused many false conclusions to be drawn at home, and I think made some people think that we were exaggerating the dangers and difficulties of running convoys and operations of any sort in the face of the vigorous action of the Luftwaffe. Before long the dismal truth was painfully to be brought home to them.

The unloading of the convoy at Alexandria went well, though, as I informed the First Sea Lord, I had cause for dissatisfaction. As every tank was unloaded it went straight into the tank repair shop to have sand and dust filters and other odds and ends fitted. "So there, under one roof, a few hundred yards from *Warspite* at this moment, about a hundred of these valuable tanks are collected and will be there for about fourteen days or longer with German aircraft flying round these parts every night. Why on earth these filters aren't fitted before they are shipped I can't think. The forty-three Hurricanes are just the same, congregated on a nearby aerodrome having filters fitted."

I was disturbed about our shortage of anti-aircraft ammunition, and on May 13th had to inform the Admiralty that since April 20th between one-third and one-half of the main items in the Mediterranean Fleet had been expended. The remaining stocks of 5·25-inch and 4·5-inch were now down to only three-quarters of the outfit required for the fleet, and we knew very well that the enemy's attack upon Crete could not be long delayed and that every ship would soon be in action.

Malta, too, was more on my mind than ever. Thanks to what amounted to the complete air superiority of the enemy, the attacks were almost continuous. On May 15th the Vice-Admiral reported that seven Hurricanes had been lost in three days, most of them with their pilots. The result of the attacks was that no less than twenty-seven Hurricanes, four Beaufighters and two Glenn Martins had been badly damaged on the ground, while one Blenheim had had to be wiped off. Admiral Ford said that the heavy losses were largely due to our aircraft being inferior to the enemy's, and unless the most modern fighters and a few night fighters were sent immediately, Malta was riding for a bad fall and would soon be unable to protect the harbour, shipping or population.

Writing to the First Sea Lord three days later I said:

I was sorry to burden you with our anxieties by signal the other day; but these troubles of ours are very real to us.—We are trying to make headway against an air force which outnumbers ours vastly, and we are short of fleet fighters and look like being short of A.A. ammunition. There is also practically no reconnaissance, whereas the Germans and Italians report us as soon as we put our noses out of port.—We really must get something analogous to a Coastal Command out here. I made a signal about it some six weeks ago, but have so far had no reply.

I have just received the Admiralty telegram about mining the Red Sea and Shatt-el-Arab, and attacks on Red Sea shipping.—While I know we must help them as being the nearest place they can get help from, I don't see in the Admiralty message any realization of the fact that we are still desperately short of minesweeping gear here, and that if we send A.A. sloops away it must be at the expense of our own operations. . . .

With Crete on my mind, and our almost complete lack of shore-based fighter cover for the fleet, I felt great anxiety for the future.

IV

At the beginning of May the Air Officer Commanding-in-Chief, Sir Arthur Longmore, had been ordered home. We thought at first it was only temporary, but it soon became apparent that we were not going to see him again. We most deeply regretted his departure. He was a true comrade and a friend. His early upbringing in the Navy had given him a real understanding of naval problems, and, as I have said, he had been one of the first officers to join the Royal Naval Air Service before the First World War. Out of his meagre resources, and no one at home seemed to realize how desperately meagre they were, he had invariably co-operated to the full and helped us all he could. We felt a great sense of loss when we heard he had gone for good.

The arrival of two new Flag Officers, Rear-Admirals E. L. S. King and I. G. Glennie, gave us the opportunity of rearranging the Flag Officers' appointments. The title of Vice-Admiral, Light Forces, no longer met the requirements of the type of war upon which we were entering, while I considered that a senior Admiral was necessary to command the battle-fleet at sea when I, through force of circumstances, had to remain ashore to keep in close touch with my Army and Air Colleagues. From my flagship at sea I could not collaborate closely with them for the operations that impended.

Accordingly, Vice-Admiral Pridham-Wippell, who had been created a K.C.B. for his fine work at Matapan and in the evacuation of Greece, was appointed in command of the battle-fleet, with his flag in the *Queen Elizabeth*. Rear-Admiral King, in the *Naiad*, commanded the 15th Cruiser Squadron; while Rear-Admiral Rawlings became Rear-Admiral 7th Cruiser Squadron with his flag in the *Orion*. Rear-Admiral Glennie became Rear-Admiral (D), with his flag in the *Dido*, or in the destroyer depot ship *Woolwich* if the *Dido* were required to act as a 'private' ship.

CHAPTER XXIX

I

IT was realized that an attack upon Crete would come just as soon as the enemy was ready, and that the main attack would probably be airborne. This reduced the time factor to the period it took the Germans, no doubt with forced Greek labour, to provide the necessary airfields.

For our part we were not idle, and the necessary steps for putting the island defences into what condition was possible, for organizing and rearming the garrison, and running in supplies of all descriptions were energetically pressed on. The facilities for unloading heavy stores at Suda, the main port, were very poor. There was only one pier alongside of which ships of shallow draught could be berthed. All the larger vessels had to lie at anchor and unload their cargoes into lighters. The harbour, too, was being subjected to increasingly heavy air attacks, and the fighter cover was so thin that serious casualties were caused among the ships and their crews, to say nothing of the unloading teams. However, by the strenuous efforts of the Naval Officer in Charge, Captain J. A. V. Morse, most of the difficulties were overcome. In the period April 29th to May 20th, when the German attack developed, some 15,000 tons of Army stores were off-loaded from fifteen ships. In the course of this eight vessels were sunk or seriously damaged.

On the night of May 15th–16th, the *Gloucester* and *Fiji* landed a battalion of the Leinster Regiment with their full equipment at Heraklion, while two nights later the *Glengyle*, Captain C. H. Petrie, landed seven hundred men of the Argyle and Sutherland Highlanders at Tymbaki, an anchorage on the south coast of Crete, to march over the mountains to Heraklion.

It was the general opinion that the island could be held against airborne only. However, it was expected that the enemy might also attempt a seaborne landing in support. The repulse of this latter assault stood out as the Navy's main function, and it was with this end in view that we made our dispositions. The main difficulty, of course, was that Alexandria was some 440 miles away from the scene of action, while it was impossible to use Suda Bay as a base because of the continuous air attacks. It was hardly to be expected that the Italian fleet would remain passive while an attack upon Crete was in progress, so this made it necessary for us to provide battleship cover off the western end of the island. Apart from this our dispositions provided for three forces of cruisers and destroyers to the south of Crete ready to move into the Ægean round both ends of the island in the event of any threat of seaborne invasion. The obvious policy was not to commit our forces to the northward of Crete during daylight unless enemy forces were known to be at sea, though they were always to move in at night to patrol or sweep to the northward off the areas where landings might be expected.

Shore-based air cover was virtually non-existent, and our carrier, the *Formidable*, Captain A. W. La T. Bisset, could not take part in the operations until May 25th. She had been reduced to no more than four serviceable aircraft because of losses and wear and tear during the bombardment of Tripoli and the more recent *Tiger* convoy. There were no reserves of naval aircraft or flying personnel.

From various indications we expected the attack to take place on May 15th, and on that date Vice-Admiral Pridham-Wippell was on his station to the west of Crete with two battleships and five destroyers, while the three forces of cruisers and destroyers were ready in theirs. After deep consideration I had decided against going to sea personally. It was imperative that I should be in Alexandria in good communication with all the four dispersed forces at sea, and to direct the naval side of the operation as a whole. It was necessary, too, that I should be in the closest touch with my colleagues, the other Commanders-in-Chief. Vice-Admiral Pridham-Wippell, with his great experience and sound and steady judgment, would be representing me in the front line.

However, the enemy delayed his attack, and it became necessary to relieve the battleships already at sea for refuelling at Alexandria. Rear-Admiral Rawlings accordingly hoisted his flag in the *Warspite*, and took her with the *Valiant*, *Ajax* and eight destroyers to relieve Pridham-Wippell in the covering position. The light forces of cruisers and destroyers, which had swept the north coast of Crete on the night of May 16th-17th without result, also returned to Alexandria, topped up with fuel and went off to sea again.

The enemy had begun his operations on May 15th with the heavy bombing of our positions and airfields. At Maleme airfield at this period, under the command of Commander G. H. Beale, were three Gladiators and three Fulmars of the Fleet Air Arm; with three Royal Air Force Hurricanes from Greece, though both aircraft and crews were virtually unfit for flying after weeks of intensive work against the overwhelming strength of the Luftwaffe. Squadron-Leader Howell, however, flew several successful combats. As regards the Fleet Air Arm, two Gladiators and two Fulmars were shot down or written off, so the naval fighter pilots flew the Hurricanes to relieve their R.A.F. comrades. About three days before the final airborne attack by the enemy all three Hurricanes flown by naval pilots took on ten times their number and shot down six of the enemy, all three Hurricanes being damaged or shot down in the process. Commander Beale then sent Lieutenant-Commander Alan Black and Lieutenant (A) R. A. Brabner back in a Sunderland, as there were no more aircraft of any type. Beale himself remained behind with the men to defend the airfield as best they could. After being severely wounded he was captured by the enemy, but is still serving as a Captain. R. A. Brabner subsequently became an M.P., and was unhappily killed in an air crash after he had become Under-Secretary of State for Air.

On writing to a friend for information of this episode, I was told that one of the participants could not feel that Maleme was "worth more than a line or two". I cannot altogether agree. It is an example of grand personal courage on the part of Beale, Brabner, Black and an observer called Sutton under the worst possible conditions which stands out brightly in the gloom of the Cretan affair, and is worthy to be recorded.

On May 20th, after four days of incessant bombing, the German airborne attack started.

II

I do not propose to follow the fighting ashore except in so far as it affected the naval operations. Actually, at the end of the first day, the situation was by no means unfavourable, though part of the airfield at Maleme was in enemy hands.

At Alexandria, on hearing that the assault had started, I gave orders for the various light forces to move up towards Crete, to pass through the Kaso Straits and the Antikithera Channels at dusk, and to establish patrols to the northward of the island. Six Italian motor torpedo boats were met in the Kaso Straits and engaged, retreating after four of them had been damaged. Three destroyers bombarded the aerodrome at Scarpanto; but beyond this nothing happened. Our forces withdrew to the southward of Crete at dawn on the 21st, and all through the day were subjected to heavy air attacks. The *Ajax* was damaged by near misses, and the *Juno*, hit during a high-level attack by Italian bombers, sank in two minutes. One of her magazines blew up. I heard later that Walter Starkie, the *Juno's* first lieutenant and my niece Hilda's husband, had been killed. It was a heavy blow.

No seaborne landing had yet taken place; but long-range air reconnaissance had indicated that groups of small craft escorted by destroyers were steering towards Suda Bay from the northward. Our light forces again patrolled to the north of Crete during the night of May 21st–22nd. If there were no developments, the two groups under Rear-Admirals King and Glennie were directed to work northward on a wide zigzag at daylight on the 22nd to locate enemy convoys.

At 11.30 p.m., the force under Rear-Admiral Glennie, consisting of the *Dido, Orion, Ajax, Janus, Kimperley, Hasty* and *Hereward*, met a large enemy convoy about eighteen miles north of Canea. It consisted of many caïques packed with German troops and several small steamers, escorted by torpedo boats. Our ships had endured much during that day, and as Glennie reported they "conducted themselves with zest and energy", ramming and sinking by gunfire. One of the escorting torpedo boats, after firing torpedoes, was hit by the *Dido* and blown up by the *Ajax*. Radar was invaluable in leading our ships on to new targets, and in a scrambling engagement in the dark which lasted in all for two-and-a-half hours, at least a dozen caïques and three or small steamers were sunk, shattered or blazing. Some four thousand German troops were left to drown, and the first attempted invasion by sea was completely frustrated.

Glennie, however, was now in a difficult predicament. His flagship, the *Dido*, had expended 70 per cent of her anti-aircraft ammunition, and the *Orion* and *Ajax* 62 and 58 per cent respectively. In the face of probable heavy air attack at daylight, the *Dido* herself was in no condition to comply with my orders to join Rear-Admiral King's squadron and sweep northward in search of further prey. Glennie was naturally reluctant to withdraw his own flagship and leave the rest of his squadron to face the air attacks that were certain to come. So, and perhaps rather unfortunately, he retired with all his ships. In the light of what came to pass, the *Orion* and *Ajax*, with the ammunition that remained to them, would have been a valuable reinforcement to Rear-Admiral King. However, Glennie could not foresee that.

At 4 a.m. next morning, the 22nd, Rear-Admiral King's force, now consisting of the cruisers *Naiad* and *Perth*, with the anti-aircraft cruisers *Calcutta* and *Carlisle*, and the destroyers *Kandahar*, *Kingston* and *Nubian*, were off to Heraklion. At daylight, in accordance with my instructions, they started to sweep north-westward in search of further enemy convoys. The squadron was soon located by the enemy and under heavy air attack and fighting back. At 8.30 a.m. a single caïque was sighted ahead. She was carrying German troops, and was sunk by the *Perth* while the *Naiad*, Rear-Admiral King's flagship, engaged large numbers of aircraft. Soon after nine o'clock a small merchant vessel was sighted and the destroyers were ordered to sink her. About an hour later, some twenty-five miles south of the island of Milo, an enemy torpedo boat and more caïques were sighted to the northward. Our destroyers chased, while the two cruisers engaged the enemy destroyer, which retired under a smoke screen. The destroyer *Kingston* came into action, hit and damaged the enemy torpedo boat, and reported sighting a large number of caïques behind the smoke screen. Several caïques full of enemy troops were sunk.

Though in contact with an enemy convoy, Rear-Admiral King considered he would jeopardize his whole force if they stood on to the northward. He was already under very heavy air attack and his anti-aircraft ammunition was beginning to run low. His speed as a squadron was limited to 20 knots, the full speed of the *Carlisle* being no more than 21. Accordingly he broke off the action and steered west for the Kithera Channel to get clear of the Ægean. His situation was extremely difficult; but the decision to retire, I think, was a faulty one. It is probable that the safest place was in amongst the enemy convoy, and retirement could not better the most unpleasant position in which he found himself. Also, the destruction of that large convoy would have justified severe losses. However, it is easy to criticize others when one is not on the spot. Admiral King and his squadron had had a gruelling time. He had been in action with motor torpedo boats two nights before. Without any air cover whatsoever he had been bombed continuously for more than four hours the day previous and had lost the *Juno*. His ships' companies had been on the alert for more than forty-eight hours. Officers and men were under severe strain and tension. Ammunition was running low, and if he had continued the action to the northward he was moving away from any supports. It was a cruel situation; but I have always held that if the enemy is in sight on the sea air attacks or other considerations must be disregarded and the risks accepted. The short engagement, however, undoubtedly turned back the convoy and the troops, and if the latter did ever succeed in reaching Crete they were not in time to influence the course of the battle on shore.

Retiring to the south-west, Rear-Admiral King's squadron was bombed continuously for three-and-a-half hours. The *Naiad* was damaged by near misses. Two of her turrets were put out of action, several compartments flooded, and her speed was reduced to 16 knots. The *Carlisle* was hit, and Captain T. C. Hampton killed. At 1.21 p.m. Rear-Admiral Rawlings' force, consisting of the *Warspite, Valiant,* with the *Dido, Orion, Ajax, Gloucester, Fiji* were sighted coming from the westward through the Kithera Channel.

The battle-fleet, which had been joined by Rear-Admiral Glennie's squadron and the *Gloucester* and *Fiji* during the morning, had been patrolling twenty to thirty miles west of the Kithera Channel where, as Rawlings said, it was "serving a useful purpose by attracting enemy aircraft". The shortage of anti-aircraft ammunition in his cruisers was causing anxiety—the *Gloucester* 82 per cent short; the *Dido*, 75 per cent; *Fiji*, 70 per cent; *Orion*, 62 per cent. However, just before 12.30, when Rawlings heard that the *Naiad* had been badly hit and that King's force needed support, he increased to 23 knots and made the bold decision to enter the Ægean. An hour later the *Warspite*, Rawlings' flagship, was hit by a heavy bomb which wrecked her starboard 4-inch and 6-inch batteries, and thus put half her anti-aircraft guns out of action.

The two forces joined up and turned west to clear the Ægean. Then they were overtaken by a series of misfortunes. The destroyer *Greyhound*, returning from sinking a caïque, was hit by two bombs and sank in 15 minutes. Rear-Admiral King, now the Senior Officer on the spot, ordered the *Kandahar* and *Kingston* to pick up the survivors. Unaware of the shortage of ammunition in the *Gloucester* and *Fiji*, he also directed those two vessels to support while the work of rescue was in progress.

The *Kandahar* and *Kingston*, with the *Greyhound's* men in the water, were subjected to continuous bombing and machine-gun attacks from low-flying aircraft. Some days later, visiting the wounded in hospital in Alexandria, I was told by a young ordinary seaman that he himself had got away in the *Greyhound's* whaler with the first lieutenant and about eighteen men. Seeing an enemy aircraft coming straight at them, the lad went overboard and swam under water. When he came up and looked into the boat every man was dead.

At about three o'clock Rear-Admiral King, who had been informed by Rawlings of the precarious state of the ammunition in the *Gloucester* and *Fiji*, ordered them to withdraw. Half-an-hour later they were sighted coming up from astern at full speed, with their guns still in action. At 3.50 the *Gloucester* was hit by several bombs, set on fire, and completely disabled, with her upper deck a shambles. The *Fiji* reluctantly decided she must leave her, so throwing overboard her Carley floats she made off to rejoin the fleet under continuous air attack.

Thus went the gallant *Gloucester*. She had endured all things, and no ship had worked harder or had had more risky tasks. She had been hit by bombs more times than any other vessel, and had always come up smiling. As she left Alexandria for the last time I went alongside her in my barge and had a talk with her Captain, Henry Aubrey Rowley. He was very anxious about his men, who were just worn out, which was not surprising, as I well realized. I promised to go on board and talk to them on their return to harbour; but they never came back. I doubt if many of them survived, as they, too, were murderously machine-gunned in the water. Rowley's body, recognizable by his uniform monkey jacket and the signals in his pocket, came ashore to the west of Mersa Matruh about four weeks later. It was a long way to come home.

At 4.45 the *Valiant* was hit aft by two bombs during a high-level attack, but suffered no serious damage.

At 6.45 the *Fiji*, Captain P. R. B. W. William-Powlett, which had survived some twenty bombing attacks in the last four hours and was reduced to using practice ammunition, succumbed to an attack by a single M.E. 109 which came out of the clouds in a shallow dive and dropped its bomb close alongside. It blew in the *Fiji's* bottom, and she came to a standstill with a heavy list and her engines crippled. Half-an-hour later another single aircraft dropped three more bombs which hit and exploded over a boiler room. The list increased, and **at 8.15** the ship rolled right over and sank. The two destroyers *Kandahar* and *Kingston*, which were in company, lowered their boats and rafts and withdrew to avoid damage from almost certain air attack, returning after dark to pick up more of the *Fiji's* survivors and finally rescuing a total of 523. They had been subjected to no fewer than twenty-two air attacks between 2.45 and 7.20, and were now very short of fuel. As I wrote in my **despatch:**

Where so much that was meritorious was performed it is almost invidious to particularize, but I feel I must draw the attention of Their Lordships to two outstanding examples. These are the conduct of *Kandahar* (Commander W. G. A. Robson, Royal Navy) and *Kingston* (Lieutenant-Commander P. Somerville, D.S.O., Royal Navy) during the whole period of the operation and, in particular, the rescue of the crews of *Greyhound* and *Fiji* . . . all the rescue work during daylight and was carried out in face of heavy bombing and machine-gunning. The other story is that of the gallantry and devotion of Commander W. R. Marshall A'Deane, Royal Navy, of *Greyhound*, whose self-sacrifice stands out even amongst this record of fine deeds. After the loss of his own ship he was picked up by *Kandahar*. Whilst *Kandahar* was engaged in rescuing the crew of the *Fiji*, Commander Marshall A'Deane dived overboard, in the darkness, to the assistance of a man some distance from the ship. He was not seen again.

For this act of supreme gallantry this brave officer was awarded a posthumous Albert Medal.

Another gallant action of this period was that of Petty Officer A. E. Sephton of the anti-aircraft cruiser *Coventry*. On May 18th this ship had been patrolling south of Crete when news was received that the hospital ship *Aba* was attacked by dive-bombers. The *Coventry* went to her rescue, whereupon the dive-bombers attacked the cruiser, raking her with machine-gun fire. A bullet passed through Sephton's back; but though in great pain he continued to direct the fire at the enemy and refused all help. Carried to the sick-bay after the action, he died next day. Sephton's action may well have saved the *Coventry* and the *Aba*, and for his magnificent example he was awarded a posthumous Victoria Cross.

III

Meanwhile at Alexandria, as the afternoon gave way to evening, and evening to night, our hearts were heavy as the news of our casualties kept coming in. In my office ashore close to the war room where the positions of all our ships were plotted hour by hour on the large-scale chart, I came to dread every ring on the telephone, every knock on the door, and the arrival of each fresh signal. In something less than twelve hours of fighting against the unhampered Luftwaffe we had lost so much, two cruisers and a destroyer sunk, with two battleships and two cruisers damaged. Most of the ships were woefully short of ammunition, and I very well knew the anxiety and physical strain under which their devoted officers and men were working.

During the day, May 22nd, I had signalled to all our ships at sea: "Stick it out. Navy must not let Army down. No enemy forces must reach Crete by sea."

The night patrol to the northward of Crete—to stop any seaborne invasion—still had to be maintained, come what might, so four destroyers were ordered to their beat off Heraklion, and the *Ajax* and *Orion* were directed to join them. In the event the order did not reach the cruisers in time, so they rejoined Rear-Admiral Glennie's force which was returning to Alexandria. The destroyer patrol off Heraklion was without incident.

The 5th Destroyer Flotilla from Malta, under the command of Captain Lord Louis Mountbatten in the *Kelly*, with the *Kashmir, Kipling, Kelvin* and *Jackal*, had joined the battle-fleet during the afternoon, and been sent to see if they could pick up any of the *Gloucester's* or *Fiji's* men. This was later countermanded, and the flotilla was sent to patrol during the night to the northward of Canea and Maleme. They destroyed two caïques full of troops and bombarded the enemy-held airfield at Maleme, retiring at full speed before daylight.

At about 8 a.m. next morning, May 23rd, on their way to Alexandria, and having been twice attacked from the air without damage, the *Kelly*, *Kashmir* and *Kipling* were attacked by twenty-four dive-bombers. The *Kashmir* was hit and sank in two minutes. The *Kelly*, steaming 30 knots under full helm, was hit by a large bomb. She listed heavily over to port and capsized, still moving through the water. After floating upside down for half-an-hour she finally sank. The German aircraft, before leaving, subjected the survivors from both ships in the water to the usual hail of machine-gun bullets. The *Kipling*, Commander A. St. Clair-Ford, at once closed to rescue the survivors and remained on the scene for three hours in the face of six high-level bombing attacks. She picked up 279 officers and men from the water. Between 8.20 a.m. and 1 p.m. she was attacked by forty aircraft which dropped more than eighty bombs; but emerged undamaged. She eventually arrived 70 miles off Alexandria next morning, the 24th, with no oil fuel remaining and had to be towed in.

One reason for all these losses was the disregard of a golden rule which we had long since found essential in all our previous encounters with aircraft, and that was never to detach ships for any particular tasks. The fleet should remain concentrated and move in formation to wherever any rescue or other work had to be done. The detachment of the *Greyhound* was a mistake, as was that of the *Gloucester, Fiji,* and other ships. Together, the fleet's volume of anti-aircraft fire might have prevented some of our casualties.

At Alexandria it had been in our minds to send the battle-fleet to a dawn rendezvous with the 5th Flotilla to support them during their withdrawal. However, on the night of the 22nd we had a report of the 'state' of the close-range anti-aircraft ammunition from Rear-Admiral Rawlings, from which it appeared that his battleships had expended all they had. We knew that the ammunition of the cruisers was at a very low ebb, so all forces at sea were ordered to Alexandria to replenish. Actually a mistake occurred in Rawlings' signal, and whether it was phonetic or just bad writing I do not know. Anyhow, the first copy of the signal shown to the Chief of Staff and myself indicated that the battleships were 'empty' of short-range ammunition, whereas the typed copy distributed next morning had the word 'plenty', which was correct. Whether or not the absence of the battle-fleet really influenced the fate of the *Kelly* and *Kashmir* is open to question. It might well have been that with more ships as targets our losses would have been greater. With our complete absence of fighter cover the Luftwaffe, by sheer weight of numbers, were having it practically all their own way. Perhaps a score of them had been shot down; but gunfire from the best of ships cannot deal with aircraft which an officer who was there likened to a swarm of bees.

The battle ashore in Crete had gone badly. After twenty-four hours heavy fighting the enemy had complete control of Maleme airfield and were able to build up their strength by troop-carrying aircraft. Our forces were being inexorably pressed back towards Suda Bay. Captain Morse, the Naval Officer in Charge, was already beginning to consider plans for evacuation.

During the night of May 22nd–23rd the destroyers *Decoy* and *Hero* embarked the King of the Hellenes, the British Minister and other important personages on the south coast of Crete and sailed for Alexandria. As they passed the battle-fleet Rear-Admiral Rawlings firmly ordered them on to the battleships' screen to prevent them being caught alone by aircraft. This wise precaution was not at all to the liking of His Majesty, as he informed me when I met him at Alexandria.

It had also been decided to try and land reinforcements, and the *Glenroy*, Captain Sir James Paget, with a battalion and some other units, escorted by the *Coventry* and the sloops *Auckland* and *Flamingo*, sailed from Alexandria on the afternoon of the 22nd for Tymbaki, on the south coast of Crete. The destroyers *Jaguar* and *Defender* left at the same time to disembark ammunition badly needed by the Army at Suda Bay on the night of May 23rd–24th, a mission which was successfully accomplished.

Because of the intense scale of air attack south of Crete, however, I consulted General Wavell and at 11.30 on the 23rd ordered the *Glenroy* to turn back. It appeared to be sheer murder to send her on. At about 4 p.m., to my amazement, the Admiralty sent a direct message to the *Glenroy* ordering her to turn north again, and about an hour later sent me a signal urging that her reinforcements be landed if it could be done that night. Of course it was much too late, so I ordered the *Glenroy* back to Alexandria and informed the Admiralty that if she had proceeded north she would have arrived at daylight, the worst possible time for air attacks with the Luftwaffe everywhere. The less said about this unjustifiable interference by those ignorant of the situation the better.

We made another plan to reinforce Crete by the fast minelayer *Abdiel* and destroyers.

Another signal received from the Admiralty on the 23rd also informed me what I already knew only too well—that the outcome of the battle for Crete would have serious repercussions, and that it was vitally important to prevent seaborne expeditions reaching the island in the next day or two, even if this resulted in further losses to the fleet.

I replied to this at some length, pointing out that it did not seem to be realized that the withdrawal of all forces to Alexandria had been forced upon me by the necessity for refuelling and because the anti-aircraft ammunition in practically all the ships was spent. I added that the fleet was operating 400 miles from its base, and that it was impracticable to have any considerable force in the Ægean on the night of the 24th, though the two destroyers landing ammunition at Suda had orders to operate against any attempt at landing near Maleme. A further force of two cruisers and two destroyers would sweep along the north coast of Crete on the night of May 24th–25th, while the *Abdiel* was already on her way to Suda Bay with stores and ammunition for the Army.

The Chiefs of Staff in London had also asked for an appreciation, and I gave it as my opinion that the scale of air attack now made it no longer possible for the Navy to operate in the Ægean or the vicinity of Crete by day. We could not guarantee to prevent seaborne landings without suffering losses which, added to those already sustained, would seriously prejudice the command of the Eastern Mediterranean.

To this the Chiefs of Staff replied that the situation was being allowed to "drag on", and that unless more drastic action could be taken than that I had suggested, the enemy would be able to reinforce the island to a considerable extent. The Chiefs of Staff said that it was essential that the Commanders-in-Chief should concert measures, and that the fleet and the Royal Air Force must accept whatever risk was entailed in preventing any considerable reinforcement from reaching Crete. If air reconnaissance showed enemy movements by sea north of Crete, the fleet would have to operate in that area by day, though considerable losses might be expected. It was added that only experience would show how long the situation could be maintained, and that time was the dominating factor.

I found this message singularly unhelpful. It failed most lamentably to appreciate the realities of the situation. So I replied that:

> It is not the fear of sustaining losses but the need to avoid losses which will cripple the fleet without any commensurate advantage which is the

determining factor in operating in the Ægean. As far as I know, the enemy has so far had little if any success in reinforcing Crete by sea.

I continued by suggesting:

> The experience of three days in which two cruisers and four destroyers have been sunk, and one battleship, two cruisers and four destroyers severely damaged shows what losses are likely to be. Sea control in the Eastern Mediterranean could not be retained after another such experience.

I went on to say that the enemy's supply by sea had not yet come into the picture. In spite of the loss and turning back of his convoys, he was so prolific in the air that for the moment he was able to reinforce and keep his troops supplied by air at will, and that this process was quite unchecked by any air action on our part, while the sight of a constant and unhindered process of J.U. 52's flying into Crete was among the factors likely to affect the morale of our troops. I added that the effect of the recent operations was cumulative, and that the officers, men and machinery were nearing exhaustion. Since the decision to send an Army to Greece at the end of February they had been kept running almost to the limit of their endurance, and now, with their work redoubled, they were faced with an air concentration beside which, I was assured, that in Norway was child's play. I emphasized again that what we needed was better air reconnaissance, which should allow us to keep our forces far enough away by day to avoid serious loss pending the moment when the enemy committed his convoys to their sea voyage, and we went in and destroyed them. I had not received the reinforcements of reconnaissance aircraft I had so earnestly requested. As I was actually writing this message, on May 26th, I had news that the *Formidable* and *Nubian* were both returning to Alexandria with bomb damage.

The aerodrome at Scarpanto was being largely used by the enemy for his air attacks upon Crete. It had therefore been decided to attack it with Fleet Air Arm aircraft from the *Formidable*, which had built up her fighter strength to twelve Fulmars, though some were of doubtful utility. Vice-Admiral Pridham-Wippell in the *Queen Elizabeth*, with the *Barham*, *Formidable* and eight destroyers was given charge of this operation, and sailed from Alexandria at noon on May 25th. Between 5 and 6 a.m. next morning, from a position about a hundred miles south-south-west of Scarpanto, four Albacores and four Fulmars went in to attack. They achieved complete surprise, destroying and damaging various aircraft on the ground. Later in the morning enemy aircraft were continually being detected by radar, and the eight serviceable aircraft that the *Formidable* had left made twenty-four flights and had twenty combats, in the course of which more enemy aircraft were shot down. At 1.20 p.m. while withdrawing, Pridham-Wippell's force was attacked by twenty aircraft which approached from the direction of North Africa. In the dive-bombing attacks which followed the *Formidable* was hit twice and badly damaged, while the *Nubian* had her stern blown off but could still steam 20 knots.

On the night of the 25th–26th, the *Ajax*, *Dido* and three destroyers had again swept along the north coast of Crete, but sighted nothing.

The *Glenroy*, escorted by the *Coventry*, *Stuart*, and *Jaguar* was also on her way to try landing troops at Tymbaki. They were bombed during the morning of May 26th, and at 6.20 p.m. were heavily attacked by dive-bombers and then by low-flying torpedo bombers. The *Glenroy* avoided the torpedoes, but was slightly damaged and had some casualties from near misses and machine-gun fire. Three of her landing craft were holed, and a large dump of cased petrol on the upper deck was set ablaze. To cope with the fire the *Glenroy* had to turn south to bring the wind aft, and one of the landing craft at the davits had to be jettisoned. With eight hundred troops on board and a large cargo of petrol the situation was most unpleasant; but when the flames were mastered the convoy again resumed its course for Crete. However, because of the time lost the troops could not have been landed before daylight in the landing craft that remained, added to which the weather was unsuitable for landing on an open beach. Once more the *Glenroy* had to be turned back.

During the night of May 26th–27th the *Abdiel*, *Hero* and *Nizam* landed troops and stores at Suda Bay. These were the last reinforcements sent into Crete.

We had yet another casualty on May 27th when Vice-Admiral Pridham-Wippell's force, which was covering the return of the *Abdiel* and destroyers, was attacked at about 9 a.m. by fifteen enemy aircraft which appeared from the direction of the sun. The *Barham* was hit by a bomb on 'Y' turret and two of her bulges flooded by near misses. A fire was started and not put out for two hours. At 12.30 I ordered the force back to Alexandria.

IV

To hark back to the fighting ashore, May 23rd had seen the formation of a new defensive line in the Maleme–Canea sector. Very heavy air attacks were being made on our troops, who lacked all fighter cover, while the Germans kept up a steady flow of reinforcements with their troop-carrying aircraft. Captain Morse, as has been said, was already considering plans for evacuation. On the night of the 25th–26th the enemy broke through this new line after several attacks had been repulsed, and on the 26th our troops were compelled to withdraw still further. It was realized that it would not be long until the whole front in that sector collapsed. The situation was better at Heraklion, but this could not affect the main battle.

On May 26th I met General Wavell; Air Chief Marshal Tedder, the acting Air Officer Commanding-in-Chief; General Sir Thomas Blamey, the General Officer Commanding the Australian Forces in the Middle East; and the Rt. Hon. Peter Fraser, Prime Minister of New Zealand. Wavell was under no illusions as to the situation in Crete. Indeed, evacuation was in the air, and General Blamey and Mr. Fraser were full of anxiety as to the fate of the Australian and New Zealand troops fighting desperately in the island.

My view was perfectly clear. I needed no persuasion. It was impossible to abandon the troops in Crete. Our naval tradition would never survive such an action. Whatever the risks, whatever our losses, the remaining ships of the fleet would make an all-out effort to bring away the Army. I had hopes that taking men off the south coast would be less difficult than operating ships in the Ægean in broad daylight. At the same time I told Wavell that with the enemy's complete command in the air the moment might come when, with the terrible losses among the troops during their embarkation and their passage to Alexandria, lives might be saved if they surrendered where they were.

Late on May 26th General Freyberg reported from Crete that the limit of endurance had been reached by his troops at Suda Bay. His small, ill-equipped force could not stand up to the concentrated bombing and attacks by greatly superior numbers they had endured for a week. The only chance of its survival was to withdraw to the beaches on the south coast of the island, hiding by day and moving by night. The force at Retimo was cut off and short of supplies, and Heraklion was apparently surrounded.

It was quite evident that those at home had no idea of what the situation really was, or what the troops in Crete, or the fleet, had already endured, for on May 26th the Prime Minister cabled to General Wavell—"Victory in Crete essential at this turning point of the war. Keep hurling in all you can."

To this, early on the 27th, Wavell replied that the Canea front had collapsed, and that Suda Bay was only likely to be covered for another twenty-four hours, if as long. To land reinforcements might now be considered impossible because of the German command of the air. On the island the troops were being subjected to overwhelming and unopposed air attack which, sooner or later, must drive the stoutest troops from their positions and make administration practically impossible. He feared it must be recognized that Crete was no longer tenable, and that the troops must be withdrawn as far as possible.

A reply came back the same day from the Chiefs of Staff in London to the effect that Crete should be evacuated forthwith, saving as many men as possible without regard to material.

At 3 p.m. on May 27th the fateful decision was taken, and we wearily turned to planning another evacuation with fewer ships, far less resources and in circumstances much more difficult. Our seamen and our ships were worn to the point of exhaustion, and now they were asked for more.

So began that difficult retreat over the mountains to the southern shore of Crete, covered by gallant rear-guard actions on the part of Australians, New Zealanders and Royal Marines.

The first phase of the Battle of Crete was ended, and as I wrote in my despatch:

> That the fleet suffered disastrously in this encounter with the unhampered German Air Force is evident, but it has to be remembered on the credit side that the Navy's duty was achieved and no enemy ship, whether warship or transport, succeeded in reaching Crete or intervening in the battle during those critical days. Nor should the losses sustained blind one to the magnificent courage and endurance that was displayed throughout. I have never felt prouder of the Mediterranean Fleet than at the close of these particular operations, except perhaps, at the fashion in which it faced up to the even greater strain which was so soon to be imposed upon it.

CHAPTER XXX

I

By May 27th, after the decision to evacuate Crete, the troops from the Suda Bay area began wearily to fall back over the mountains to Sphakia, a small fishing village on the south coast of the island. The village and the shingle beach, no more than 200 yards of which could be used by ships' boats, was hemmed in by a rugged escarpment of cliff 500 feet high. The road over the mountains from Suda ended with a series of acute hair-pin bends and terminated abruptly at the cliff edge, from which a narrow zigzag track descended precipitously to the beach below. The ascent took at least two hours.

We had no knowledge of how our troops had fared at Retimo. An aircraft of the Royal Air Force had been sent there to drop a message ordering the garrison to withdraw to Plaka Bay, on the south coast, from where they would be embarked. As the aircraft never returned we could not know if the orders had been received. At Heraklion, farther east, the Army had won its battle and the airfield was still in our hands. This was the only place where the jetties in the harbour were available for the embarkation of about four thousand men.

On the naval side the evacuation had to be undertaken with ships whose officers and men were on the verge of complete exhaustion, physically and mentally. As for the ships themselves, they had been driven hard for more than two months without the occasional two or three days' respite in harbour for boiler cleaning and running repairs. Their machinery had become unreliable, while many were struggling on as best they could after damage by enemy bombing. Moreover, their numbers were depleted. We had already lost two cruisers and four destroyers; while two battleships, our aircraft-carrier, another cruiser and a destroyer were out of action for weeks or months. Another five cruisers and four destroyers had been damaged; but were still able to steam and to fight.

We were not really in favourable condition to evacuate some twenty-two thousand soldiers, most of them from an open beach, in the face of the Luftwaffe. But there was no alternative. The Army could not be left to its fate. The Navy must carry on.

In view of the confusion and uncertainty of the situation in Crete General Wavell sent me a Military Liaison Officer, Major-General J. F. Evetts. His help was invaluable. I was also notified by the Air Officer Commanding-in-Chief that some fighters with long-range tanks would be available to provide some cover for ships; though owing to the distance from our bases the cover would necessarily be meagre and spasmodic. Group Captain C. B. R. Pelly

BATTLE OF CRETE
20 May–1 June 1941

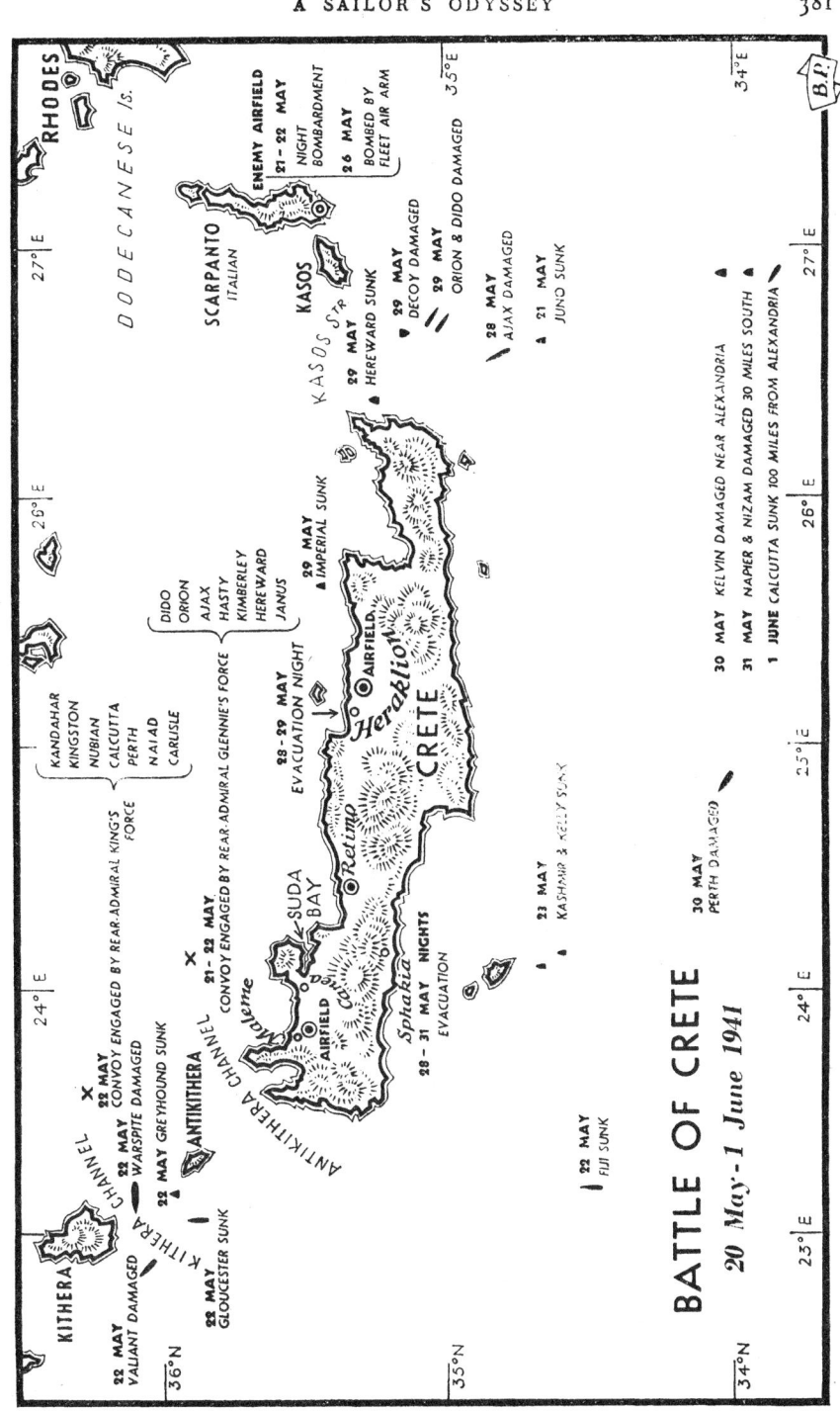

- **KITHERA** — 22 MAY VALIANT DAMAGED
- **KITHERA CHANNEL** — 22 MAY × CONVOY ENGAGED BY REAR-ADMIRAL KING'S FORCE; 22 MAY WARSPITE DAMAGED; 22 MAY GREYHOUND SUNK
- 22 MAY GLOUCESTER SUNK
- **ANTIKITHERA** — 21–22 MAY × CONVOY ENGAGED BY REAR-ADMIRAL GLENNIE'S FORCE
- **ANTIKITHERA CHANNEL**
- **SUDA BAY** — Canea; Maleme AIRFIELD
- **Sphakia** — 28–31 MAY NIGHTS EVACUATION
- 22 MAY FIJI SUNK
- 23 MAY KASHMIR & KELLY SUNK
- Retimo AIRFIELD
- Heraklion AIRFIELD — 28–29 MAY EVACUATION NIGHT
  - DIDO, ORION, AJAX, HASTY, KIMBERLEY, HEREWARD, JANUS
- KANDAHAR, KINGSTON, NUBIAN, CALCUTTA, PERTH, NAIAD, CARLISLE
- 29 MAY IMPERIAL SUNK
- 29 MAY HEREWARD SUNK
- 29 MAY DECOY DAMAGED
- 29 MAY ORION & DIDO DAMAGED
- 28 MAY AJAX DAMAGED
- 21 MAY JUNO SUNK
- **KASOS STR** — **KASOS**
- **SCARPANTO** ITALIAN — 21–22 MAY NIGHT BOMBARDMENT; 26 MAY BOMBED BY FLEET AIR ARM; ENEMY AIRFIELD
- **DODECANESE IS.** — **RHODES**
- 30 MAY PERTH DAMAGED
- 30 MAY KELVIN DAMAGED NEAR ALEXANDRIA
- 31 MAY NAPIER & NIZAM DAMAGED 30 MILES SOUTH
- 1 JUNE CALCUTTA SUNK 100 MILES FROM ALEXANDRIA

was attached to my staff at Alexandria to co-ordinate the fighter protection with the movements of our ships. Pelly was a tower of strength, and under his able management the organization quickly took shape and undoubtedly saved us many casualties.

One of the difficulties with which we had to contend was that we could not get a reasonably correct estimate of the number of troops to be lifted each night. This sometimes resulted in ships not being filled to capacity, while on other occasions insufficient ships were sent to the point of embarkation. All we knew with tolerable certainty was that the total number to be brought away was about twenty-two thousand.

The general plan was as follows. Troops from the Maleme–Suda area were to embark from the beach at Sphakia. Those from the Retimo area, if they could be contacted, were to come off from Plaka Bay. Troops from Heraklion would be taken off from Heraklion harbour, while a small number to the south of Heraklion were expected to make their way to Tymbaki, on the south coast.

Evacuation was invariably to be carried out at night, usually between midnight and 3 a.m. This would allow ships to be as far as possible from the enemy air bases during daylight. Ashore in Crete, the evacuation was to be covered by troops fighting a rear-guard action from Suda Bay to the south coast. Major-General E. C. Weston, Royal Marines, was placed in command of the rear-guard.

II

It had been decided that the main evacuation on the night of May 28th–29th, would be from Heraklion and it was planned to bring off the whole force in one lift. For this purpose a force under Rear-Admiral Rawlings in the *Orion*, with the cruisers *Ajax* and *Dido*, and the destroyers *Decoy*, *Jackal*, *Imperial*, *Hotspur*, *Kimberley* and *Hereward*, sailed from Alexandria at 6 a.m. on the 28th. They were to pass through the Kaso Straits at the eastern end of Crete.

From 5 p.m., when about ninety miles south of the Straits, until dark, the force was subjected to heavy air attacks—high-level and dive-bombing, as well as torpedo attacks. At 7.20 the *Imperial*, Lieutenant-Commander C. A. de W. Kitcat, was narrowly missed by a bomb, though at the time she appeared to be undamaged. At 9 p.m. the *Ajax* had a close miss which started a fire, wounded twenty men, and caused some slight damage to the ship's side. It was unfortunate that exaggerated reports of the damage were given to her captain, and when he signalled them to the Rear-Admiral the *Ajax* was ordered to return to Alexandria.

However, in spite of these mishaps the force arrived off Heraklion at

11.30 p.m., and the destroyers crept into the harbour, went alongside the jetties, ferried the correct quota of troops off to the cruisers, and embarked their own loads with steady efficiency. I was told later that the General in command was somewhat indignant at having to evacuate, as he said he—"had won his battle", which indeed he had, in spite of the constant enemy reinforcements. Severe losses were inflicted on the Germans right up to the time of evacuation.

In all four thousand troops were embarked by 3 a.m. without alarming the enemy, a noteworthy performance, particularly without lights in pitch darkness.

The force sailed at 3.20, and twenty-five minutes later things started to go wrong. The *Imperial's* steering gear failed, obviously having been damaged by her close miss the night before. She narrowly avoided colliding with both cruisers. It could hardly have happened at a more inopportune moment; but as the force must try to clear the Kaso Straits before daylight, it was no time for indecision. Rawlings at once ordered the *Hotspur*, Lieutenant-Commander C. P. F. Brown, to embark the troops and ship's company from the *Imperial*, and to sink her. Easing to 15 knots Rawlings steamed on, leaving the *Hotspur* to her task, which was successfully accomplished by 4.45.

In a book written by the First Lieutenant of the *Hotspur*—Lieutenant-Commander Hugh Hodgkinson—*Before the Tide Turned*—the author gives a graphic description of the feelings of those on board his ship at this time. They were by themselves with nine hundred troops on board, and thinking they would be alone in the Kaso Straits in broad daylight a few miles from the enemy airfields at Scarpanto. They pushed on at full speed. Their relief can be imagined when, in the grey light of the dawn, they saw the shapes of ships ahead of them. Rawlings had waited.

But the delay over the *Imperial* had cost a precious ninety minutes, and it was not until sunrise that the squadron turned south to pass through the Kaso Straits. Fierce air attacks started at 6 a.m. and continued at intervals until 3 p.m., by which time the squadron was within 100 miles of Alexandria.

At 6.25, when the squadron was in the middle of the Kaso Strait, the *Hereward*, Lieutenant-Commander W. J. Munn, who had been my Flag-Lieutenant in the *Hood*, was hit by a bomb which caused her to reduce speed. Once again Rawlings had to make the difficult decision whether to leave her and push on, or to stand by her and expose his ships with the troops on board to even greater risk. As the *Hereward* was seen to be making towards Crete, then only five miles away, Rawlings decided to push on. The *Hereward* was last sighted steaming slowly towards the shore with all her guns in action against the enemy aircraft. She was eventually sunk; but it is satisfactory to know that Italian torpedo-boats saved almost all the troops and the ship's company.

The delay to the squadron also resulted in no contact being made with the fighters sent out to cover its retirement. These aircraft were operating at their extreme range, and could not remain on their stations. It was not until noon that two naval Fulmars made their appearance.

Meanwhile the force was literally fighting its way south against wave after wave of attacking enemy aircraft. At 6.45 a.m. a close miss on the *Decoy*, Commander E. G. McGregor, fractured the turbine feet and reduced the speed of the squadron to 25 knots. A quarter of an hour later another very close miss on the *Orion* imposed a further reduction in speed to 21. At 7.35, Captain G. R. B. Back was severely wounded by an explosive bullet from a dive-bomber, and he died two hours later. Rawlings himself was wounded. At 8.15 the *Dido*, Captain H. W. U. McCall, was hit by a bomb on 'B' turret, and at 9.0 the *Orion* was struck on 'A' turret. Both attacks were made by dive-bombers, and in each case the turrets were put completely out of action. At 10.45 the *Orion* was again attacked by eleven J.U. 87's. A bomb pierced her bridge, wrecked the lower conning-tower, and burst on the stokers' mess-deck. She had nearly, 1,100 troops on board, and the casualties below were very heavy, a total of 260 being killed and 280 wounded. Among others three of the engineer officers were killed, and all normal communications between bridge and engine-room were destroyed. The steering gear was put out of action and three boiler-rooms were damaged, and the *Orion* was out of control until after the steering wheel could be connected and a chain of men organized to pass orders from the emergency conning position to the wheel. Because the oil fuel had been contaminated with sea-water the *Orion's* speed fluctuated between 12 and 25 knots. To make matters worse the devoted ship had also been badly on fire.

That was the last of the dive-bombers; but at 1 p.m., 1.30 and 3.0 there were high-level attacks.

At about 8 p.m. Rawlings brought his shattered squadron into Alexandria, the *Orion* herself with ten tons of fuel and very few rounds of ammunition remaining. I shall never forget the sight of those ships coming up harbour, the guns of their fore-turrets awry, one or two broken off and pointing forlornly skyward, their upper decks crowded with troops, and the marks of their ordeal only too plainly visible. I went on board at once and found Rawlings cheerful but exhausted. The ship was a terrible sight and the mess-deck a ghastly shambles.

While this tragic operation was in progress the four destroyers, *Napier*, *Nizam*, *Kelvin* and *Kandahar*, under Captain Stephen H. T. Arliss of the *Napier*, had been sent to Sphakia, chiefly to land small arms and provisions for the troops ashore; but also to bring off any troops in readiness to embark. They arrived without incident and started the embarkation of 700 men half an hour after midnight, completing the task by 3 a.m. on May 29th, and having also landed badly-needed rations for 15,000. To facilitate the work they had embarked additional whalers at Alexandria. They had only one air attack on the way back, the *Nizam*, Lieutenant-Commander M. J. Clark, being slightly damaged by a near miss. They had the advantage of air cover and were glad to see an enemy aircraft crashed in the sea, probably shot down by an R.A.F. fighter.

III

The next night, May 29th–30th, was to provide the really big effort, and at 9 p.m. on the 28th a force under Rear-Admiral King, in the cruiser *Phœbe*, sailed for Sphakia. The other ships were the *Perth*, *Glengyle*, *Calcutta*, *Coventry*, *Jervis*, *Janus* and *Hasty*.

Major-General Freyberg, commanding the troops in Crete, and Captain Morse, the Naval Officer in Charge, Suda, had established their headquarters in a cave near Sphakia. The portable wireless sets and naval ciphers, sent round from Suda in a motor launch, had been sunk with that ship on May 24th. A second wireless set sent by road was damaged, and the Royal Air Force set at Sphakia was used for outside naval communications.

Our signals from Crete had been rather confusing. Captain Morse had told us that upwards of 10,000 troops would be available for evacuation on the night of the 29th–30th; but an Army message stated that it was unlikely that the troops could hold out until the night of the 30th–31st, and that an "optimistic view" of the fighting troops which could be evacuated would be 2,000; but that there would also be stragglers. We gathered from these signals that the situation in Crete was desperate; but that 10,000 men remained to be taken off, of which only 2,000 would be in formed bodies. It also appeared that the 29th–30th would have to be the last night of evacuation.

General Evetts flew to Cairo and reported to Wavell on the naval situation. After consulting Blamey and Tedder, Wavell sent me a personal message saying it was thought that the cruisers and the 'Glen' ships should not be risked any further; but that the evacuation by destroyers might continue.

A signal was made to the Admiralty setting out the evacuation situation up-to-date, and pointing out that the casualties among the closely-packed troops on board the ships had been heavy. It was not to be expected that on the next day, May 30th, we should get away without equally heavy losses, particularly if the *Glengyle*, with 3,000 men on board, were hit. We further asked if we were further justified in accepting a similar scale of loss and damage to that already incurred to our already weakened fleet. We were ready and willing to continue the evacuation so long as a ship remained, realizing that it was against all the tradition of the Navy deliberately to leave troops in enemy hands.

That same evening, the 29th, we had a reply from the Admiralty ordering the *Glengyle* to turn back, and the remaining ships to carry on. By that time it was too late to recall the *Glengyle*, so Captain Waller in the *Stuart*, with the *Jaguar* and *Defender*, were sent to join Vice-Admiral King. The intention was that they should not carry troops; but would be used as extra cover and for rescuing the troops from any ship which might meet with misfortune. I informed the Admiralty of my intention, which was approved.

During the course of the day one of General Evett's staff interviewed a number of officers who had been brought away from Crete the previous night. From their accounts it seemed that the situation there was by no means so bad as we had been led to believe, so we decided to send four destroyers to continue the evacuation on the night of May 30th–31st.

Meanwhile Rear-Admiral King's force was proceeding to Sphakia, and the only incident that happened during the passage was when a single J.U. 88 dropped a stick of bombs near the *Perth* without doing any damage. The squadron arrived at 11.30 p.m. on the 29th, the cruisers and *Glengyle* anchoring while the *Calcutta*, *Coventry* and the destroyers patrolled to seaward. The anti-aircraft cruisers were not needed to embark troops; but the destroyers closed the beach one at a time to take away their quotas. The troops were ferried off in landing craft from the *Glengyle* with two others brought from Alexandria in the *Perth*. The operation was completed by 3.20 a.m. on the 30th, when the force sailed for Alexandria with 6,000 men. Three motor landing craft were left at Sphakia for use on subsequent nights.

The force was attacked three times during its return passage to Alexandria, the *Perth*, Captain Sir P. W. Bowyer-Smith, being hit and her foremost boiler-room put out of action. More bombs fell very close to the *Perth* and *Jaguar*; but did no further damage. Two or three fighters of the Royal Air Force provided air cover during most of the day, and were successful in driving off dive-bombers, besides shooting down two enemy aircraft and damaging several more.

On the 30th Captain Stephen Arliss in the *Napier*, with the *Nizam*, *Kelvin* and *Kandahar*, sailed from Alexandria to continue the embarkation that night. During their passage to Sphakia the *Kandahar*, Commander W. G. A. Robson, developed a defect and had to return. At 3.30 p.m. the three destroyers that remained were attacked by three J.U. 88's, damage being caused to the *Kelvin*, Commander J. H. Allison, from a near miss which reduced her speed to 20 knots. She also was ordered back, and Captain Arliss went on with the *Napier* and *Nizam*. They arrived off Sphakia at 12.30 a.m. on the 31st, and by 3 a.m., using the landing craft which had been left behind and their own boats, actually embarked the full quota of 1,400 troops originally allotted to the four destroyers, a remarkable performance. Air cover had been provided for the return journey; but from 8.50 until 9.15 a.m. the *Napier* and *Nizam* were attacked by a number of J.U. 88's, and the *Napier* was close-missed and damaged in the engine and boiler-rooms, which reduced her speed to 23 knots. Knowing so well what the men in the ships were enduring, I was depressed at counting up our casualties. However, we could but carry on.

The information from Crete indicated that the rear-guard under Major-General Weston were making a fine fighting and orderly retreat over very difficult country, and on May 30th, Major-General Freyberg, from Sphakia, asked for one last lift of up to 3,000 men on the night of May 31st–June 1st. This was a considerable increase on previous estimates, and the ships for this number were just not available because of our losses and damage. After consulting Wavell we decided to send every possible ship we could; but to inform Freyberg that we should probably be unable to lift more than 2,000. For ourselves we were quite ready to take every man that could be crowded on board. What we had in our minds was the terrible casualties that must ensue if a ship were badly hit and either sunk or severely damaged, while a ship crammed with troops was seriously hindered in fighting back with her anti-aircraft armament.

During the night of the 30th–31st Wavell ordered Major-General Freyberg to return to Egypt. I sent similar instructions to Captain Morse, whose stout-hearted vigour and counsel had been of the greatest value throughout. Both these officers returned to Alexandria in a Sunderland flying-boat, leaving Major-General Weston, Royal Marines, in command in the island.

At 6 a.m. on May 31st Rear-Admiral King in the cruiser *Phœbe*, with the minelayer *Abdiel* and the destroyers *Kimberley*, *Hotspur* and *Jackal* sailed from Alexandria to carry out the final evacuation. That same morning we had a message from Captain Arliss, who was on his way back, saying that there were roughly 6,500 men to come off from Sphakia. Accordingly, Rear-Admiral King was authorised to increase the maximum number of troops to be embarked to 3,500.

Soon afterwards Mr. Fraser, the Prime Minister of New Zealand, with Wavell, Freyberg and Evetts came to see me. As the result of our deliberations it seemed that Rear-Admiral King's five ships would be able to bring off most of the troops assembled at Sphakia, so a message was sent telling him to fill up to capacity. At the same time I informed the Admiralty that I had called a halt after the evacuation that night, and that even if Rear-Admiral King's ships were to suffer no damage in the operation in which they were then engaged, the Mediterranean Fleet would be reduced to two battleships, one cruiser, two anti-aircraft cruisers, one minelayer and nine destroyers fit for service.

At about 8 p.m. I had a message from General Wavell which I was asked to pass on to Major-General Weston in Crete, our naval wireless being the only means of communication. It was a personal message from the Commander-in-Chief to Weston, informing him that that night was the last night on which evacuation could take place, and authorizing the capitulation of any troops who had to be left behind. As the despatch of this message would mean an irrevocable decision to cease the evacuation, we gave it our most careful consideration before finally deciding to send it on. Just afterwards General Blamey, who was perturbed at the small number of Australians so far taken out of Crete, asked for a ship to be sent to Plaka, where he believed a number of troops were assembled. There was no certainty that there were troops at Plaka, and I had to tell him that at this late hour I greatly regretted that it was impossible to alter our plans.

On the way to Sphakia Rear-Admiral King's squadron was attacked three times by aircraft. None of the bombs fell close, and the sight of them being jettisoned on the horizon showed that the fighters of the Royal Air Force were busy. The ships duly reached Sphakia at 11.20 p.m., and having embarked nearly 4,000 men sailed at 3 a.m. on June 1st. Many had to be left behind.

During the night Major-General Weston returned to Egypt in a flying-boat on Wavell's instructions after handing written orders to the senior remaining Army Officer to surrender. It is grievous to have to record that a large proportion of the men left in Crete were those who had fought such a gallant rear-guard action from Suda, including Special Service, or Commando, troops, and to the particular sorrow of their naval comrades, about 1,000 Royal Marines.

The force under Rear-Admiral King had an uneventful return passage to Alexandria; but we were not to escape a final blow. To provide a heavier scale of anti-aircraft defence, the *Calcutta* and *Coventry* were sailed from Alexandria in the early hours of June 1st to join up with the returning ships. At 9 a.m., when about 85 miles north of Alexandria, the *Coventry's* radar picked up aircraft approaching from the northward, and about twenty minutes later two J.U. 88's dived down from the direction of the sun. A stick of bombs from the first aircraft just missed the *Coventry*, Captain W. P. Carne; but two bombs from the second 'plane hit the *Calcutta*, Captain D. M. Lees. Seriously damaged, the *Calcutta* settled fast and sank within a few minutes. The *Coventry* was able to pick up 255 of her ship's company with whom she returned to Alexandria.

The loss of the little *Calcutta* was greatly felt. She had served with the Mediterranean Fleet since September, 1940. She was the only anti-aircraft cruiser without radar; but admirably commanded and with a first-rate ship's company she had a wonderful record of safely-escorted convoys. She was in action practically every time she went to sea, and had served on the Libyan coast, during the passage of many convoys to Greece and the subsequent withdrawal, during the reinforcement of Crete, and the final evacuation. We were sad to think that her gallant and most useful career was now ended.

Early on June 1st I had a signal from the First Sea Lord saying that if there was any reasonable chance of embarking any substantial formed body of men on the night of June 1st–2nd, he thought the attempt should be made.

With the greatest regret I was forced to reply that Major-General Weston had returned with the report that the 5,000 troops remaining in Crete were incapable of further resistance because of strain and lack of food. They had, therefore, been instructed to capitulate, and in the circumstances no further ships would be sent. In later messages to the Admiralty I pointed out that the only ships available were two battleships and five destroyers, all the remainder being either damaged or too slow. Fighter protection was also sparse and irregular. I added that because of the inevitable confusion in Crete the figures given to me for evacuation varied very greatly. Up to May 30th I had hoped that the last trip, that of Rear-Admiral King's force, would result in almost everyone being brought off. On that day, however, the figures had suddenly been increased by 5,000.

Some 16,500 British and Imperial troops were brought safely back to Egypt, and provisions and stores were landed for those who had to be left behind. The 2,000 Royal Marines of the Mobile Naval Base Defence Organization after manning the defences at Suda Bay, fought gallantly with the rear-guard and had to leave half their number behind. I drew the particular attention of the Admiralty to their performance, and said that they had "conducted themselves in a manner worthy of the highest traditions of the Corps".

The Mediterranean Fleet had paid a heavy price in the battle for Crete—the *Gloucester*, *Fiji* and *Calcutta* sunk, with the destroyers *Juno*, *Greyhound*, *Kashmir*, *Kelly*, *Hereward* and *Imperial*. The *Warspite*, *Barham*, *Formidable*, *Orion*, *Dido*, *Kelvin* and *Nubian* were damaged beyond repair on the spot, and would be out of action for some months; while the *Perth*, *Naiad*, *Carlisle*, *Napier*, *Kipling* and *Decoy* would be under repair for some weeks, and the *Havock*, *Kingston* and *Nizam* for a fortnight. Of the grand men of the fleet who had shared our triumphs and adversities for so long well over 2,000 were dead. Such losses would normally only occur during a major fleet action, in which the enemy might be expected to suffer greater losses than our own.

I felt very heavy-hearted. We had been fighting against the strength of the Luftwaffe, and once again it had been borne in upon us that the Navy and the Army could not make up for the lack of air forces. In my opinion three squadrons of long-range fighters and a few heavy bombing squadrons would have saved Crete.

In conclusion, perhaps I may quote the final paragraphs of my covering despatch:

> It is not easy to convey how heavy was the strain that men and ships sustained. Apart from the cumulative effect of prolonged seagoing over extended periods it has to be remembered that in this last instance ships' companies had none of the inspiration of battle with the enemy to bear

them up. Instead they had the unceasing anxiety of the task of trying to bring away in safety, thousands of their own countrymen, many of whom were in an exhausted and dispirited condition, in ships necessarily so overcrowded that even when there was opportunity to relax conditions made this impossible. They had started the evacuation already over-tired and they had to carry it through under conditions of savage air attacks such as had only recently caused grievous losses in the fleet.

There is rightly little credit or glory to be expected in these operations of retreat, but I feel that the spirit of tenacity shown by those who took part should not go unrecorded.

More than once I felt that the stage had been reached when no more could be asked of officers and men, physically and mentally exhausted by their efforts and by the events of these fateful days. It is perhaps even now not realized how nearly the breaking point was reached, but that these men struggled through is the measure of their achievement, and I trust that it will not lightly be forgotten.

So ended the Battle of Crete, and a disastrous period in our naval history—a period of great tension and anxiety such as I have never experienced before or since. It was accentuated by the fact that I had to sit back in Alexandria while great events were taking place, dreading the sound of the telephone bell which was usually the harbinger of more bad news of loss or damage. But with it all there was an intense pride, which was fully justified, that our seamen never flinched in standing up to conditions almost beyond human endurance. At the back of my mind, however, there was the disturbing thought that those at home apparently failed to appreciate what our ships and our men had endured.

In a long letter to the First Sea Lord on May 30th I pointed out, among other matters, the state of fatigue to which our men were reduced after days of constant bombing attack and long periods at sea. Out of the last two months the *Ajax* had spent fewer than ten nights in harbour, and the *Dido* one night in twenty-one. It was the same with most of the other ships, particularly the destroyers.

I ended that letter by referring to my own personal affairs, and said: "It may be that the Admiralty would like a change in command of the fleet out here. If this is so, I shall not feel in any way annoyed, more especially as it may be that the happenings of the last few days may have shaken the faith of the personnel of the fleet in my handling of affairs."

On June 2nd I had the following personal message from General Wavell, which was promulgated to the fleet: "I send to you and all under your command the deepest admiration and gratitude of the Army in the Middle East for the magnificent work of the Royal Navy in bringing back the troops from Crete.— The skill and self-sacrifice with which the difficult and dangerous operation was carried out will never be forgotten, and will form another strong link between our two services.—Our thanks to all and our sympathy for your losses."

IV

The hasty conclusion that ships are impotent in the face of air attack should not be drawn from the Battle of Crete. The struggle in no way proved that the air is the master over the sea. The proper way to fight the air is in the air, which was shown during the last few days when the Royal Air Force was able to provide a certain amount of fighter cover which permitted our ships to continue their tasks comparatively unhindered. If shore-based, long-range fighters cannot reach the area in which the ships must operate, then the Navy must carry its own air with it.

As I had said, a few squadrons of long-range fighters and heavy bombers might have saved Crete; but looking back I sometimes wonder whether the loss of the island was really such a serious matter it seemed at the time. Had we defeated the German attack and held the island the problem of its maintenance and supply would have been extraordinarily difficult. We should undoubtedly have required a large garrison, and though it is true that the defence could primarily have been entrusted to the Greeks, the drain on our slender resources of arms, ammunition and equipment available in the Mediterranean would have been heavy. Moreover, as has already been said, all the ports available for landing supplies were on the north coast within easy reach of enemy airfields. Though it is hardly to be expected that the Luftwaffe could maintain the same scale of attack, for it was obviously massed for the special operation of capturing the island, it is certain that the ports on the north coast could never have been used except at night.

The Royal Air Force would also have had to be maintained in considerable strength in Crete. This would have involved the construction of new airfields. When one considers all the extra equipment and supplies necessary for the R.A.F., to say nothing of maintaining the troops, it is difficult to see how the necessary masses of stores could have been landed on the limited beaches on the south coast of Crete, and have been transported over the mountains to where they were needed.

On the other hand, it is not to be denied that the retention of Crete would probably have done away with much of the difficulty of supplying Malta during the critical phases that were soon to come upon us. It was the German air force in Crete on the flank of our convoy route to Malta that made the maintenance of that island from the east so costly and hazardous.

There is another aspect, the effect of her Balkan campaign upon Germany.

It started on April 6th, 1941, and tied up twenty-seven field divisions, of which no fewer than seven were Panzer divisions, about one-third of the total Panzer strength of the German army. The victory in Crete, moreover, cost the Germans some 22,000 troops, of whom 5,000 were drowned by the Royal Navy, and about 400 aircraft. I have seen it stated that the delaying effect of their attacks upon Greece and Crete not only interfered with Hitler's designs upon Syria and Iran; but eventually proved disastrous in their attack upon Russia. The German army reached the outskirts of Moscow in October, 1941, by which time the early frost had begun to interfere with its movements. Its arrival in front of Moscow five weeks earlier would probably have led to the capture of that city, the importance of which it is difficult to exaggerate.

Our defence of Crete, therefore, may have served its purpose in the overall pattern of the war.

v

The evacuation, however, did not entirely end on June 1st. The *Glengyle* had left three of her landing craft behind at Sphakia, and on the night of June 8th–9th, one of these came ashore near Sidi Barrani with Major Garrett, Royal Marines, 5 other officers and 134 other ranks. They had left Crete on June 1st and had struggled some 230 miles with a minimum of food, water and petrol. When the engine became useless, they finished the journey under a sail improvised of blankets and anything else they could find. It was a gallant feat.

Yet another party of 5 officers and 148 soldiers in, I believe a caïque, reached Mersa Matruh on June 9th, while the *Glengyle's* other two landing craft, carrying in all something over 100 men, reached the Egyptian coast on June 10th and 11th. I have a note to the effect that as late as July 29th the submarine *Thrasher* reported herself as returning to Alexandria with 78 soldiers from Crete.

Moreover, other parties of officers and men of whom I have no record were brought to safety. Resistance to the enemy in Crete did not die out when we evacuated the island. For the next four years the German garrison was to be harassed by guerilla bands. These fighters were Cretans and Greeks backed up by British troops who had remained in the island, or by commando troops specially landed. Sheltered by the inhabitants, living in caves and villages in the fastnesses of the mountains, they descended by night to raid isolated German outposts, attack transport, and to destroy, blow up or burn all they could. To have eliminated the guerilla bands would have required a large-scale expedition. As it was, the Germans had to maintain in Crete a force which was ridiculously out of keeping for simple garrison duty.

Quite soon after the evacuation it was realized that we must do all in our power to sustain these guerilla fighters. There was also the more immediate task of organizing the withdrawal of considerable numbers of British troops in hiding and awaiting help from outside. Hence the *Thrasher* episode. A large share in this work fell upon our submarines, which reconnoitred by periscope in daylight, closed the selected beaches after dark to exchange recognition signals with a reception party ashore, after which commando troops and supplies were sent ashore in rubber dinghies, and other men embarked. It was hazardous work, for these clandestine 'cloak and dagger' expeditions had often to be carried out within half a mile of some German look-out station. The steep, rocky coast, too, was practically uncharted from the point of view of operations close inshore, and the beaches used often consisted of little more than a few yards of rough shingle at the mouth of some precipitous ravine. Moonless nights were normally chosen, and moving in to within 50 or 100 yards of the shore through shallows studded with rocks was dangerous in the extreme, particularly in winter with a heavy sea running, or with the iron-bound coast blanketed in thick mist.

These expeditions became known as the 'Crete ferry trip', and a new phase started in 1943 when motor-launches replaced the submarines.

That, however, is another story.

CHAPTER XXXI

I

WE now had to sort out our ideas, and to consider what could be done with the greatly reduced fleet that remained to us after the operations in Crete. We had the *Queen Elizabeth* and *Valiant*; the *Ajax* and *Phœbe*; the anti-aircraft cruiser *Coventry* with a temporary bow; and seventeen destroyers in various states of effectiveness. Our commitments at the moment were the supply of Tobruk, always a great drain on destroyers and small ships; the interruption of the enemy's supply line to Libya; and the ever-pressing necessity of the maintenance of Malta.

The supply of Tobruk we treated more or less as a matter of routine. Two nights out of three a couple of destroyers ran in stores, and during the moonless periods we sent periodical water and petrol carriers. Captured Italian schooners also made regular trips and had some thrilling adventures. Their small size made them unprofitable targets for enemy aircraft, and as their enterprising captains had possessed themselves, by means legitimate or dubious, of heavy armaments of light anti-aircraft weapons, a low-flying attacker was apt to get more than he bargained for. Every man on board seemed to have acquired his own private A.A. weapon, and sometimes more than one. However, the losses in our small ships were mounting steadily. The sloop *Grimsby* had been sunk by aircraft off Tobruk on May 25th, while the *Auckland* went on June 24th. The Australian destroyer *Waterhen* was bombed and sunk off Sollum on June 29th, while the next day the *Flamingo* and *Cricket* were put out of action. The destroyer *Defender* was sunk on July 11th. The supply of Tobruk by sea was a costly undertaking.

It was not possible to provide a force of surface ships at Malta to prey on the enemy's convoys going to Libya, so this duty had to be left to the submarines and aircraft, and very fine work they were doing. At the beginning of June I had occasion to signal to the Senior Officer Submarines, Malta:

> I wish to express my appreciation of the successes which have been achieved in the last few weeks by you and your command in attacks against the Tripoli convoys. In these times of adversity this work is more than ever important to the Empire's effort. Well done and carry on.

The supply of Malta in quantity had to be shelved for the time being. We had no air cover for any convoys running in supplies. Our aircraft-carrier had been put out of action. Shore-based aircraft could not assist, and the enemy now held the airfields in Crete and along the bulge in the

African coast between Benghazi and Bardia, just over two hundred miles to the southward. To send convoys to Malta from the east was to court disaster. Our experiences in Greece and in Crete had taught us that failure had been brought about by our lack of air protection. The best we could do to supply Malta was to get out two of our minelaying submarines, the *Cachalot* and *Rorqual*, and to start them off on regular trips with what petrol and essential supplies they could carry. It was not very much. As regards petrol, each submarine took sufficient to keep the R.A.F. and Fleet Air Arm aircraft in Malta in operation for about three days.

At the end of May I had sent the Admiralty a long appreciation of our situation consequent on the loss of Crete. I did not mince matters. I started by pointing out that the enemy air bases had been moved forward, and that we might expect a heavier scale of air attack upon Egypt and the Western Desert. It was clear that the fleet would have to face serious loss by day whenever at sea outside the effective range of fighters operating from the shore. We were thus for the moment driven back to the defensive, and our liberty of action was greatly restricted. The immediate repercussions were threefold. The supply and hence the safety of Malta were jeopardized; attacks on the Libyan convoys were made very hazardous; and the route through the Mediterranean was virtually closed.

The answer seemed clear. We had lost the northern flank and were unlikely to regain it. Therefore we must try and get the southern flank. If the Army could reach, say, Derna, a good deal would have been done to ease the situation.

But we must have adequate air forces. The whole object of clearing the southern flank along the Libyan coast was to provide ourselves with airfields for the continual bombing of enemy aerodromes in Crete, Greece and the Ægean, and to make them untenable. With more airfields in Libya our bombers could force the Luftwaffe to the westward and thus relieve the pressure on Egypt and our supply lines to the Western Desert. With a chain of fighter aerodromes cover could be given under which the fleet might operate in the Central Mediterranean in reasonable protection. More airfields would provide striking bases from which bombers and torpedo-carrying aircraft could operate to seaward. This last was of particular importance as providing protection to Egypt against seaborne attack if the fleet should be seriously reduced in strength.

I added that it was understood our air strength was increasing rapidly. If it continued to increase and we acted as suggested we might yet prove that the enemy had made a costly blunder. To continue his present scale of attack, to go on to Cyprus and Syria as he might well intend to do, drew his own air strength increasingly into the Eastern wilderness; but to take advantage of this we must have strength in the air, and immediately.

The lesson of recent events was quite definite and repeated that of France and Norway, which was that military operations in modern war could not be conducted without air forces which would allow at least a temporary air superiority. We now had a chance from Egypt to crush a large portion of the German Air Force if we acted in time, and if His Majesty's Government were prepared to regard the Eastern Mediterranean and Middle East as of importance second only to the defence of Britain. Indeed, it might well be described as an integral part of the defence of Britain since it had drawn off so much scale of attack. I said, and here I quote exactly: "We are on the verge of disaster here for we stand to lose fleet and thus Malta, Cyprus and Egypt unless we act at once (repeat) at once."

I continued by saying that all obstacles must be swept aside somehow and we must have the following: (*a*) a Coastal Command Force of torpedo-bombing aircraft, bombers and reconnaissance aircraft, which could find convoys and sink the enemy and could thus take over the function of carriers. (*b*) Fighter and bomber forces to allow the Army to advance ruthlessly. (*c*) Bomber forces to allow us to strike at the enemy and to smash his aerodromes.

In the Eastern Mediterranean we were unlikely to have to fight more than one-third of the German Air Force. Was it not therefore a supreme chance of discounting his overall superiority? To do it all energy and the best brains of the three Services at home and in the Middle East were needed; but it could be done. "If it is not done," I ended, "our position in Middle and Far East will crumble completely."

II

We soon had more trouble on our hands, this time in Syria, where German penetration had been foreseen for some time. It was not believed that the Vichy French authorities there would make any resistance to the Nazis, and the French General Dentz was avowedly pro-German. The disastrous effect of the German control of Syria was obvious. It would open the Nazi way to the south-east and isolate Turkey, making the Turks more responsive to German pressure. The threat to the Haifa oil-fuel supplies and even to Egypt would be dangerous. It was therefore decided that it was necessary to forestall the Germans, and Wavell had to set to and find a force for the operation. It was quite impossible to estimate how far the French would resist. There might even be elements of the French forces who would come over to our side, though this could not be counted upon. Some Free French troops were available; but the use of these might only exacerbate the bitterness of the fighting.

In the event, the invasion of Syria was launched with a force much smaller than that available for the defence, and when this was realized the French in Syria resisted strongly. General Sir Henry Maitland Wilson was placed in command of the operation.

We were asked to provide support on the sea flank, and from our depleted forces we scraped together the only two effective cruisers, the *Phœbe* and *Ajax*, with the destroyers *Kandahar*, *Kimberley*, *Jackal* and *Janus*. The force was placed under the command of Vice-Admiral E. L. S. King, with headquarters at Haifa.

Fulmar fighters of the Fleet Air Arm were also sent to Palestine to give cover to our ships, and other naval aircraft to Cyprus to act if necessary against the French naval forces at Beirut, or against any attempt to reinforce or supply them. The French forces consisted of two large, fast, well-armed flotilla leaders, three submarines, a sloop and a small patrol vessel. I was in in some doubt as to whether these French units were to be treated as enemies during our advance into Syria, particularly as we did not know what sort of a reception our troops would receive. The question of the attitude of the French squadron at Alexandria towards our incursion into Syria also had to be considered; but Admiral Godfroy gave me his assurance that nothing that happened in Syria would alter our agreement entered into in July, 1940.

Another naval force, consisting of the *Glengyle*, *Coventry*, *Hotspur* and *Isis*, was detailed to embark Special Service troops at Port Said with the object of landing them in Syria on the night of June 7th–8th for the purpose of holding a bridge.

The operation started on June 8th, and I do not propose to follow it in detail. It suffices to say that at first all went well; but French resistance stiffened and heavy fighting developed, which necessitated Wavell having to scrape up reinforcements in all sorts of ways. He was also able to bring in the troops which had been quelling the German-inspired revolt in Iraq. The final results were good, for on July 10th General Dentz asked for an armistice, and a convention was signed five days later.

The naval squadron took a full share in the campaign, supporting the Army with gunfire, and engaging troop concentrations and supply trains. The French naval forces soon gave evidence that they did not intend to remain as quiescent spectators. On June 9th the *Phœbe* was missed by a torpedo from a French submarine, and when the cruisers retired to Haifa the French flotilla leaders *Valmy* and *Guépard* came out and found the *Janus* by herself off Sidon. Hit by a salvo of three shell, the *Janus* was brought to a standstill with her bridge wrecked, and her fire control and a boiler-room out of action. She received two more hits while stopped. The *Jackal*, *Hotspur* and *Isis* appeared on the scene and engaged the French ships, which retired at full speed.

Our retaliation was not long in coming, for on June 13th, Swordfish torpedoed a French merchant ship in Juneh harbour, 8 miles north of Beirut. Two days later, while in close support of the Army, the *Isis* and *Ilex* were bombed and severely damaged. This, with *Janus*, meant that another three of our irreplaceable destroyers were out of action. The French tried to run arms into Syria, and on June 16th aircraft of the Fleet Air Arm from Cyprus torpedoed and sank the flotilla leader *Chevalier Paul*, engaged on this duty, between Cyprus and Syria. On June 22nd another flotilla leader, the *Vauquelin* was damaged during an air attack on Beirut harbour. The other flotilla leader, the *Guépard*, put to sea, and in an indecisive action with our cruisers on the night of the 23rd was hit by a 6-inch shell. June 25th saw the sinking of the French submarine *Souffleur* by the *Parthian* off Beirut, while on July 4th naval aircraft sank a French merchant ship off the Turkish coast.

It was somewhat disappointing to realize that the Fleet Air Arm Fulmars, working from their shore bases in Palestine to give air cover to our ships off the coast, were no match for the French shore-based fighters. It was hardly to be expected, as the Fulmars were primarily intended to work from aircraft-carriers. Nevertheless it came as something of a shock when, as on June 9th, three were shot down and another two badly damaged.

However, our ships, increased when they were available by two more cruisers, operated continually off the Syrian coast in support of the Army, and I think made an important contribution to the success of the short campaign. I was greatly relieved when the armistice of July 10th and the convention five days later put an end to operations which, I must confess, came as an irritating though necessary interlude in the midst of all our other commitments and responsibilities.

British troops in control over the whole of Syria brought a great improvement to our strategical position in the Middle East, and gave us a land frontier contiguous with that of Turkey. There was some trouble with General de Gaulle over the armistice terms, the principal point at issue, so far as I recollect, being the access his Free French agents should be allowed to have with the Vichy troops under General Dentz. De Gaulle became rather wild about it, and at one time wished to denounce the armistice. But Mr. Oliver Lyttelton, who had come out from England as Minister of State, eventually prevailed upon him to see reason.

I was interested, as it seemed necessary that Beirut and other Syrian ports should be under British naval control, to which General Catroux, de Gaulle's representative, agreed. De Gaulle himself appointed a French naval officer to command at Beirut. We got over that by sending Captain J. A. V. Morse, of Suda Bay fame, to Beirut. He handled affairs with his usual forceful tact and urbanity, and was very soon in complete command of everything that was worth controlling.

III

After some pressure from home General Wavell had been induced to undertake a counter-offensive in the Western Desert, though the summer heat in the desert made it undesirable and, as usual, the resources for an offensive were scanty. So far as naval considerations went we welcomed it. The relief of Tobruk would have saved us the constant anxiety of its supply and many losses among our small ships, while the occupation of the airfields along the Libyan coast to provide fighter cover for convoys and the fleet would have allowed us to resume the supply of Malta in spite of the absence of an aircraft-carrier.

The tanks brought out from the United Kingdom in Operation 'Tiger' had been made desert-worthy in the workshops at Alexandria, while those worn out in the retreat were coming back into service. To help in this work the Navy had provided about ninety artificers and blacksmiths. I was told, however, that there had been insufficient time for training the tanks' crews with what, in some cases, were unfamiliar weapons.

But the attempt was decided upon and Operation 'Battleaxe' was launched on June 15th, the principal objective being the relief of Tobruk. No naval forces were engaged. It was decided that all the fighters should be used for the support of the Army, and there were not enough to cover naval forces in addition. It was a sad commentary on the conditions in which in those days our Army was expected to conduct offensive operations. They might indeed have been grateful for the support of naval gunfire along the coast. All we could do to help was to prepare for opening up the little port at Sollum, and to increase the flow of supplies to Tobruk.

At first there was some small success; but then Rommel was found to be in greater strength than was expected. After two or three days heavy fighting the Army had to withdraw to the point from which they had started, with heavy losses of armour. So the supply of Tobruk had to be continued as before.

Early in June the German aircraft started to pay attention to us in Alexandria, and put in a fairly heavy raid on the night of the 7th–8th. Some thirty to forty aircraft took part, most of them dropping mines. The greater number fell ashore, where they caused great havoc and heavy casualties among the civil population. There was no damage in the harbour; but the result was rather disturbing as there was a wholesale exodus and all work in the port and dockyard ceased. It was pathetic to see the Arab families streaming out of Alexandria to the west using every type of conveyance, taxis, lorries, horse wagons, donkey carts and even lone donkeys, piled high with their women, children and poor belongings. Five days later work was still at a standstill, and as I wrote to the First Sea Lord: "If we have many more raids, even on this small scale, I fear that Alexandria will cease to function as a repairing and discharging port." As it turned out I was unduly pessimistic. Having bestowed their families in a safe place most of the men returned to work.

On June 22nd we had the news that Germany had attacked Russia, and found it very satisfactory. It was bound to take some of the pressure off us.

Late in the month we began to send away the ships damaged at Crete, now sufficiently repaired to make the passage to a shipyard. The *Orion* was one of the first to go, on her way to the United Kingdom round the Cape of Good Hope. I made her a farewell signal, mentioning her distinguished record from the outbreak of war to the evacuation of Crete, and congratulating the officers and men on their fine work. The *Warspite* sailed for the transit of the Canal and passage to Bremerton Navy Yard, on the west coast of the United States, by way of Colombo and Singapore. I was grieved at her departure, and was not to see her again in the Mediterranean for two years, and then in very different circumstances. The *Barham* had sailed earlier for repairs at Durban.

When the *Warspite* left us on June 24th I moved ashore, with my office in a building near the Gabbari Docks at Alexandria. It was my intention to move to the *Queen Elizabeth* when the *Barham* returned from her refit and became available as Vice-Admiral Pridham-Wippell's flagship. Meanwhile, he flew his flag in the *Queen Elizabeth*.

There were further suggestions in high places that I should move permanently to Cairo. I was strongly opposed to such a step. As I wrote to the First Sea Lord on June 11th:

> In my opinion, though it might be a convenience to the other two (Commanders-in-Chief) at times, it is quite unnecessary. There wouldn't be a full day's work for me at any time, and I should be totally divorced from the operations of the fleet. The next demand would be for the Commander-in-Chief, East Indies, to come to Cairo too, for the convenience of the soldiers, or is it suggested that there should be an Admiral at Cairo with Commander-in-Chief, Mediterranean and East Indies, operating the two fleets under him? As far as strategy is concerned the co-operation at the present moment is quite good. In other words, in the higher ranks I don't think anything further is necessary . . .

The *Formidable* did not finally sail until July 24th for Port Said and the Cape for permanent repair in the United States. We had some reinforcements during June, the cruiser *Leander*, and the fast minelayer *Latona* which came from England round the Cape in thirty-six days with Oerlikon guns for the fleet, anti-tank guns and other urgent stores. We were also glad to welcome the Australian sloop *Parramatta*, and three minesweepers from South Africa.

June was another great month for our submarines. The small U-class from Malta were continuing to take a steady toll on the enemy shipping on the Tripoli route, besides working off the coasts of Sicily and Italy. The continual bombing of Malta, however, was giving them little rest in harbour and to cheer them up a little I made them a signal:

> The strain of the continuous and arduous duties you are being asked to carry out is fully appreciated, but your fine actions clearly indicate that their necessity is very apparent to you and I am certain that you will carry on with the same ready efficiency.

The larger T-class submarines working from Alexandria were also having great success in the Ægean and off Derna and Benghazi. Apart from destroying two submarines, one Italian and one French, they had sunk eight supply ships or tankers and damaged two more. So great were the opportunities for submarines to inflict heavy losses on Axis shipping in the narrow waters and restricted routes in the Eastern Mediterranean that I asked the Admiralty to send me all that could be spared.

Early in July I had a visit from President Roosevelt's special envoy, Mr. Averill Harriman. He stayed with us at the Residency for two days, and went round all the activities in Alexandria. In one of the trips in my barge looking at the French squadron they went too close to the ammunition barges, and were promptly fired upon by the Royal Marine custodians, luckily without damage. We liked Mr. Harriman very much. He was so obviously out to help.

Changes in the organization and command were upon us early in July. With a view to taking some of the administrative work off Wavell's shoulders, General Sir Robert Haining was sent out from home with the resounding title of Intendant General. He was also to be responsible for our naval supplies and I had to provide him with two or three first-class officers for his staff. As I told him at the time they were sent to prevent him from interfering in our supply arrangements, which were highly satisfactory. Actually it was soon found that a job for such a senior officer really did not exist independently of the Middle East military command, so General Haining went home. The appointment of Mr. Oliver Lyttleton as Minister of State was an excellent innovation. Although he did not come much into the naval picture I could see that he took an immense amount of political work off the shoulders of the General Officer Commanding-in-Chief. He also made a very good chairman of the Middle East Defence Council which was set up shortly after his arrival, and an unbiased chairman of the Commanders-in-Chief Committee.

But these changes were accompanied by a severe blow. Wavell was himself relieved and exchanged positions with the Commander-in-Chief in India, General Sir Claud Auchinleck.

I was desperately sorry to see Wavell go. We had come through a lot together, triumphs and set-backs. We were great friends, and I think trusted each other fully. Though naturally we did not agree on everything, we both knew that the other would go all out to help his opposite number. I had the greatest admiration for Wavell. He was cool and imperturbable when things went wrong, and steadfastly refused to be riled by the prodding messages to which he, like myself, was at times subjected from the authorities at home, and which were, it must be confessed, singularly unhelpful and irritating in times of stress. Wavell was always ready to take a chance. Never once did he have the good fortune to fight with all the resources he really needed. His operations usually had to contain the elements of a gamble. Assuredly he will be recognized by posterity as one of the great Generals thrown up by the war, if not the greatest. He left Cairo at 7 a.m. on July 7th, and I made an early start and was on the airfield at Heliopolis to see him off. Incidentally, I was back in the house at Alexandria for breakfast, such are the advantages of air travel.

As regards the overall command in the Middle East, I have never been a great believer in Supreme Commanders. Among Allies they may be a necessity, and in the case of General Eisenhower the organization was an outstanding success; but I am quite sure that with our own three fighting Services working together, much better results are obtained if the three Commanders-in-Chief are men of the right type determined loyally to support each other to the mutual advantage. After all, the three Services in war are interdependent and largely indivisible. They are all working to a common end, and if this is borne in mind each Commander-in-Chief will always be thinking of how he can assist his two colleagues, and will not wait to be prodded by a Supreme Commander. Under a 'Supremo' the heads of the three Services tend to drift apart. Without one they have to get together, and if they settle and loyally strive after the same object they are bound to get agreement. I hope I can claim that Wavell, Longmore and myself were such a team of three. However, in holding these views I may perhaps be considered old-fashioned and out-of-date.

The 'Supreme Commander' in fact, was an invention of the Americans, and when they themselves were up against the problem of finding one to conduct the final operations against metropolitan Japan, the Army and Navy failed to reach agreement. General MacArthur and Admiral Nimitz were left independent of each other.

IV

After the end of the Syrian campaign in the middle of July and the failure in the Western Desert, all three Services were mainly engaged in repair and re-equipment, with the general build-up of personnel and material after the heavy fighting of the past few months. Reinforcements, with masses of stores and equipment, were coming out from the United Kingdom, the United States and Australia by the back door route up the Red Sea, and the unloading facilities at Suez and other ports in the Canal area were working under ever-increasing pressure. This did not escape the attention of the enemy, who made several heavy air attacks on Port Said and also mined the Suez Canal, causing it to be closed on several occasions. Some damage was caused to shipping, and the Cunard White Star liner *Georgic*, hit by dive-bombers at Suez, was set on fire. Her magazine exploded, and after fouling and slightly damaging the *Glenearn* she drifted ashore and was completely gutted above water.

We had some anxiety when the great liners *Queen Mary*, *Queen Elizabeth*, *Aquitania* and *Ile de France*, with large reinforcements from Australia, were approaching Suez during the third week in July. We decided that only one of these ships should be allowed in the roads at a time, and then only in the day-time when she could be given air protection.

The major problem which confronted all the Commanders-in-Chief was how soon an offensive could be opened in the Western Desert. It was not intended to allow Rommel to sit quietly on the Egyptian frontier. Each Commander-in-Chief had his own good reasons for wishing to push the enemy back out of Cyrenaica.

After the fall of Crete we anticipated that the Germans might try to seize Cyprus as *a pied à terre* for an attempt against Syria. In case they were still thinking about Cyprus the opportunity was taken to reinforce the garrison. The operation started on July 18th and continued until the end of the month, a division of troops, units of the Royal Air Force, with mechanical transport and stores, being carried to the island in cruisers, destroyers, and the fast minelayers *Abdiel* and *Latona*.

The supply of the troops in the Western Desert was constantly with us, with the inevitable toll of losses and damage among our little ships. Hitherto this important work had been carried out by the old Australian destroyers, which we presently reinforced with the *Defender* and *Decoy*. The Tobruk run, as I have said before, was an arduous operation under constant air attack. This entailed continual steaming at high speed, and the twenty-three-year old Australian 'Vs' were literally dropping to bits after much hard work. Indeed, patched up again and again and all in need of extensive refits, they were only kept running by the sheer grit and determination of the officers and men of their engineering departments.

With the enemy front line at Sollum they could be attacked almost as soon as they left Alexandria. So they sailed in daylight, and by nightfall had to be as close as possible to Tobruk, some three hundred miles from Alexandria. Fighter protection was provided as far as possible; but there was usually a period during daylight when they were not covered. Also, to get under fighter cover on the return journey, they had to leave Tobruk at a very early hour in the morning, so the time for unloading was limited. Moreover, the air attacks were by no means restricted to daylight, and at night it was by no means unusual for the destroyers to find enemy aircraft patrolling and waiting for them off the end of the swept channel into Tobruk. If they were sighted by the enemy on moonlit nights the passage could be dangerously unpleasant.

I have already mentioned the loss of the sloops *Grimsby* and *Auckland*, sunk off Tobruk in May and June; the Australian destroyer *Waterhen*, lost off Sollum on June 29th; and the *Defender*, near-missed on July 11th in bright moonlight by a heavy bomb which exploded under her engine-room, flooded her engine and one boiler-room and broke her back. After a most determined effort by the Australian destroyer *Vendetta* to tow her back to Alexandria, the *Defender* had finally to be sunk off Sidi Barrani. The sloop *Flamingo*, too, and the old river gunboat *Cricket* were damaged by near misses.

In July we considered it was asking too much of the same few ships to keep them on this dangerous service week in and week out. It was intensely disliked. Indeed, the jetty at Alexandria alongside of which they loaded their stores for Tobruk was commonly known to the ships' companies as 'the Condemned Cell'. Also, as the Australian destroyers must soon be sent away to refit, we decided that the work should be done by all the destroyers in turn. The minelayers *Abdiel* and *Latona* were used for some of the Tobruk trips; but they were no better than destroyers. Though they could carry 100 tons of stores, the time they could spend at Tobruk did not allow the whole of their cargoes to be unloaded.

The destroyers vied with each other in cutting down the time of unloading, and some remarkable discharging feats were accomplished. Perhaps the *Jervis*, Captain Mack, broke all records. He told me that he was able to get rid of his 50 tons of stores into lighters in twenty minutes.

To help the destroyers some ten or a dozen 'A' lighters, loaded at Mersa Matruh with tanks, mechanical transport and stores, were also used for the run to Tobruk. They too had their losses.

v

By the middle of July Malta was causing us acute anxiety. Except for the limited quantities of essential stores sent in in the minelaying submarines no supplies had reached the island since early in May. Some time before I had suggested to the First Sea Lord that as we in the Eastern Mediterranean seemed to be absorbing most of the attention of the Luftwaffe in the

Mediterranean, it would be a good idea if a convoy were run in to Malta from the west. So in the latter part of July an operation of this nature, Operation 'Substance', was entrusted to Force 'H', reinforced by the *Nelson* and some cruisers, the whole under the command of Admiral Sir James Somerville. Opportunity was also taken to embark troops in the cruisers.

Our part in this was confined to a sortie of the battleships from Alexandria, which steamed west during daylight to try and hoodwink the enemy into believing that the convoy was being met and brought right through the Mediterranean. Two submarines were sent on ahead to make wireless manœuvring signals to the west of Crete, while the battle-fleet returned by night to Alexandria. The subterfuge worked, and had the effect of bringing out the enemy air reconaissance in force.

Though a destroyer was sunk, and a cruiser, another destroyer and a merchant ship were damaged, Operation 'Substance' was a brilliant success. Six large merchant vessels with much-needed supplies reached Malta. A seventh had started; but had gone ashore during a fog at Gibraltar. As luck would have it she was the ship carrying the Royal Air Force personnel to maintain the Beaufighter squadrons in Malta.

Another result of this operation was that the *Breconshire* and six large merchant vessels, immobilized for so long in Malta because they could not be brought east in the face of the menace from the air, were able to make their way to Gibraltar under cover of Force 'H' during its return journey.

The convoy arrived at Malta on July 24th, and just before dawn on July 26th, probably in an attempt to destroy the newly-arrived ships, some fifteen to twenty Italian E-boats, with a few of the explosive craft of the sort that had been used at Suda Bay, attacked the Grand Harbour. The St. Elmo breakwater was hit by torpedoes; but the main attack was beaten off by the harbour defence guns, largely manned by Maltese, in about three minutes. All the enemy craft that escaped were pursued and sunk by our fighters on their way back to Sicily, and a boat was brought into Malta intact with all her crew killed. The successful repulse was hailed with great jubilation.

The Maltese detested the Italians. During the early Italian bombing a petty officer steward, one Talliana, had been left behind at Admiralty House. One morning he brought news to my wife that an Italian bomber had been shot down, adding fiercely that if the Maltese laid hands on the crew they would be lynched then and there. My wife remonstrated, pointing out that the Italians might retaliate against our airmen, and that in any case lynching was against International Law. Talliana regarded her with a pitying sort of expression. "International Law not in Malta, Signora," he said, shaking his head.

To revert to Alexandria, the newly-established Middle East War Council held a meeting in my office on July 19th. I have no doubt we had plenty to discuss, though precisely what it was I cannot remember. General Auchinleck flew home for a short visit. As I wrote to Sir Dudley Pound: "I presume he is going home to explain why the Western Desert offensive must be delayed till November. It's a great pity; but his reasons appear good and sufficient to us out here, unless something happens which radically alters the situation."

Meanwhile I was impressing upon Air Chief Marshal Tedder the crying need for something analogous to the Coastal Command at home with its headquarters at Alexandria. Our relations with the Royal Air Force were not easy, and I think the Army was finding the same. But since the Battle of Crete, on account of which the R.A.F. came in for much undeserved odium and criticism, they had become very touchy and difficult of approach.

What we wanted was more aircraft definitely allocated for fleet co-operation, with personnel specially trained to work over the sea. Both the Italians and the Germans quartered the whole Mediterranean every day, and had a close look into all our ports. We lacked this advantage, and at times I had no information for a week or ten days of what enemy ships were in the Piræus, Suda Bay, or anywhere in the Ægean. It was galling to be bereft of this vital information. It gave us no chance of forestalling any probable enemy movements by sea.

We suggested that the reconnaissance aircraft and the Beaufighters from Malta should form the nucleus of the new force. Although the Air Officer Commanding-in-Chief accepted the suggestion of a Coastal Command in principle, he positively refused to allot aircraft for the sole duty of naval co-operation. There seemed to be an unwillingness to admit that R.A.F. personnel working over the sea required special training, though we, with our long and hardly-bought experience, knew otherwise. Moreover, as the necessity for special training had been conceded at home, it was difficult to see where the difference lay.

Looking back I think the Air Chief Marshal's reason for refusal was chiefly his lack of resources, though that was not the reason he gave. The net result was that we still had to put up with insufficient and largely ineffective air reconnaissance and co-operation.

It was at about this time that we experienced in a touching and very tangible way the gratitude of the Dominion troops to their naval comrades for having brought them away from Greece and Crete. The Australians presented our men with, so far as I remember, some twenty-nine thousand bottles of beer from their stores, a gift that was very much appreciated.

The New Zealanders, on the other hand, made a collection and amassed nearly £900 for naval charities. At a simple little ceremony on board the *Phœbe*, the ship that had brought so many away from Crete, in the presence of Freyburg and his Brigadiers Puttick and Hargiss, with other officers and a detachment of New Zealand troops, I was handed a cheque after a moving and pleasant speech by a New Zealand private soldier, to which of course I replied. Afterwards the troops were entertained to the midday meal by the *Phœbe's* ship's company, while the officers lunched with my wife and myself at the Residency. I think it is true to say that much as the naval sailor liked and admired all the Dominion troops, he had a very special place in his heart for the New Zealanders with whom he was thrown in such very close contact in the Mediterranean.

CHAPTER XXXII

I

THE failure of the June offensive in the Western Desert, Operation 'Battleaxe', and the regretttable but necessary decision that no further advance in that area could be attempted until November, might have been expected to provide a breathing space for our hard-pressed light craft. In point of fact conditions were much to the contrary. It involved us in the problem of supplying Tobruk for much longer than we had anticipated, and the enemy's opposition to this supply was daily becoming more practised, efficient and heavier. The supply of Malta, of course, was always with us; but our chances of contributing towards it while we were without a carrier, and with Cyrenaica and Crete both in enemy hands, were slender. Enemy U-boats had also appeared in some strength, and were operating against our supply routes to Tobruk and Syria.

On the other hand the operations of our submarines from Malta and Alexandria, and aircraft of the Royal Air Force and Fleet Air Arm from Malta, were having the most gratifying results. Each month showed a steady increase in the destruction of the enemy's supplies bound for Libya, and hardly a day passed without a report of a ship or ships sunk or damaged. This happy result was largely brought about by the diminution in the air attacks on Malta, probably because a large proportion of the Luftwaffe had been diverted to Russia.

However, the enemy was fully alive to the importance of interrupting our supplies, and having fairly effectually put an end to supply by the direct way through the Mediterranean, now began to attack our back door route through the Red Sea to Suez. Heavy raids, including minelaying in the Canal, were made over the whole area. There were no fewer than ten in August; Port Said, Ismailia, Port Tewfik and Suez all being bombed. A few ships were damaged; but on the whole the enemy failed to disorganize our supplies. In September the enemy also started using long-range aircraft, Focke Wulf and others, which penetrated some way down the Red Sea attacking our convoys.

At this period masses of war material of all sorts were pouring into Egypt by this route from the United Kingdom and the United States. As I have said before, Alexandria was the only port with good facilities for unloading heavy cargo, which meant that practically all the shipping had to come through the Canal. All the Egyptian harbours and anchorages were greatly congested with ships awaiting their turn, although two or three subsidiary ports had been opened to relieve the crowding at Suez. The defence of all this mass of shipping was far beyond the resources of the Royal Air Force. They were particularly lacking in radar, so the *Coventry* and *Carlisle* had to be sent there to provide the necessary warning and to help in the anti-aircraft protection. Two other cruisers, the *Naiad* and *Galatea*, were sent to provide extra protection for the big liners, crammed with troops, as they approached Suez, while the Fulmar fighters of the Fleet Air Arm were sent to the Red Sea. In spite of all this there were some bitter complaints from the masters of several American ships about their lack of protection against aircraft attack.

This situation again raised the question of command in the Red Sea; in other words, should it come under the Commander-in-Chief, Mediterranean, or the Commander-in-Chief, East Indies. The problem had come up before in 1940, when the Commanders-in-Chief Army and Air had not wished to deal with two separate naval Commanders-in-Chief. For the more pressing reasons given above, however, it was now necessary to settle the matter, and the obvious course was that the Red Sea should be joined to the Mediterranean. It was necessary that all the ports being developed for the supply of the Army in the Middle East, and the so-called 'safe anchorages', should be under the Naval Officer in Charge at Suez, and that the Senior Naval Officer in the Canal Area should be responsible for the calling forward of ships for unloading. Moreover, the Red Sea must be run under its own Senior Naval Officer and have its own forces for the escort and air protection of shipping. I had no wish to assume this extra responsibility; but one-man control was essential. I represented all this to the Admiralty after consulting the Commander-in-Chief, East Indies, so in October the Red Sea again came into my orbit, and Rear-Admiral R. H. C. Hallifax, who had already come out as Senior Naval Officer, Red Sea, and had hoisted his flag at Aden, moved to Suez. It was a much better arrangement altogether.

The attacks of the German long-range aircraft did little damage, though they hit some ships. The enemy themselves suffered considerable losses, on one occasion no fewer than three in a night. The more to deter them I caused a rumour to be passed round that before the survivors of one aircraft could be rescued the crew had been taken by sharks. The Air Officer Commanding-in-Chief protested somewhat, saying that his fighter pilots might also take a dim view of flying over the Red Sea.

As I have said, the matter of the supply of Malta was always with us, though there was little we could do about it from our end of the Mediterranean. However, there was no immediate hurry as the island had received a good-sized convoy in July. Early in September Malta was well reinforced by fighters flown in from carriers from the west under cover of Force 'H', and at the end of the month it was decided to repeat the July operation by sending the *Breconshire* and eight large merchant-vessels to Malta, also under cover of Force 'H'. At the same time the fleet sailed from Alexandria to give the impression that the convoy was coming right through the Mediterranean. As the *Barham* had rejoined after repairs at Durban I had my flag in the *Queen Elizabeth*.

Very careful preparations had been made for the defence of the convoy. Every available long-range fighter in Egypt or elsewhere on the station was sent to Malta, while all the submarines from Malta took up their stations off Naples, Taranto and north of Sicily in case the Italian fleet came out to interfere. Actually it did emerge from Naples and came south; but made off again when Force 'H' went after it.

The operation was highly successful, though the convoy and Force 'H' were subjected to persistent torpedo-bomber attacks. The *Nelson* was torpedoed, and one merchant-vessel, the *Imperial Star*, was torpedoed in the Narrows at night and had finally to be sunk. The other ships got through to Malta. Admiral Somerville, who was again in charge of the operation, attributed the success to the use of a new and hitherto untried route close along the south coast of Sicily. This was the result of a bold suggestion of Admiral Ford's at Malta, and the Malta submarines of the 10th Flotilla had gallantly nosed their way through the minefields to find the route. We returned to Alexandria without apparently having been sighted by the enemy's air reconnaissance, though we had deliberately broken wireless silence to give the impression that we were bound for the Central Mediterranean.

It was after this operation that I became involved in some discussion with Sir Dudley Pound on the subject of publicity. The Mediterranean submarines had been doing such fine work that he was anxious to use it as propaganda. Publicity is anathema to most naval officers, and I was no exception. I could not see how it would help us to win the war. However, the First Sea Lord was receiving some prodding minutes at the time, one of which asserted that the Mediterranean Fleet did not appear to have been doing much fighting since Crete, so it was not surprising that he wished to make public the fact that we were by no means inert. I fear I was not very forthcoming. Indeed, I complained somewhat strongly of a B.B.C. announcement which had stated that an important convoy had passed through the Mediterranean and reached its destination at the very moment that the enemy was known to be using large air forces for searching the Eastern Mediterranean, with other forces waiting to attack. Such waste of enemy effort and immobilization was of particular value to us at a time when freedom from bombing at Suez and in the Red Sea was all important. This was only another example of injudicious publicity from those at home who did not understand the local implications.

However, in regard to publicity about our submarines Admiral Sir Max Horton, Flag Officer, Submarines, came out to visit them. I saw him, of course, and we more or less reached a measure of agreement. Let me make it quite clear that I had nothing but admiration for the gallant and arduous work our submarines had done in conditions of great hazard.

II

Although the submarines and aircraft from Malta were doing good work against the enemy convoys to Libya, the question of using surface ships from the island was always in our minds, particularly since our fighter defence there had been considerably improved and the air attacks were less virulent. Any surface force operating from Malta, however, would have to travel a long way to intercept convoys. To escape the attentions of the aircraft the enemy was now running his ships well to the eastward, some indeed close under the coast of Greece, before making across for Africa. Our chief difficulty was to provide the necessary ships. Although Crete had left us woefully short of cruisers, we could at a pinch provide a couple for Malta. To provide fleet destroyers, the only ones that were any use for the job, was quite beyond our resources with the supply of Tobruk still one of our major commitments.

That the First Sea Lord was also troubled about the interception of the enemy supplies to Africa goes without saying. Late in August I had a signal from him on the subject, in which he said that in spite of the efforts of our submarines and aircraft the number of ships reaching Tripoli pointed to the fact that the enemy must be building up supplies and reinforcements to an extent which might prejudice the success of our offensive when it came off. He raised the question of a surface force at Malta, and, if I agreed with this view, asked how many cruisers and destroyers I considered necessary. He intimated they would have to be provided from the Eastern Mediterranean, and suggested that the anti-aircraft cruisers like the *Naiad* and *Phœbe* might be suitable. He also asked what force of long-range fighter aircraft I considered necessary at Malta to provide the necessary cover for the ships engaged in cutting the enemy's communications.

We also were most anxious to maintain a surface force at Malta, though in replying to this signal, we disputed the assertion that the enemy was building up his supplies and increasing his forces in Libya. All our information went to show that he was having acute difficulty, and was unable to compete with ordinary maintenance, let alone to build up reserves. (A report from very good sources covering the period May 1st to August 20th showed that about 35 per cent of the ships leaving Italy for Libya had been sunk or seriously damaged by submarines and aircraft, and that the German Afrika Korps and Luftwaffe were suffering acutely through lack of fuel and mechanical transport.)

We fully agreed that surface forces should work from Malta; but for the moment action had had to be postponed because of our lack of fleet destroyers. The real crux of the matter was the supply of Malta itself, particularly the supply of oil fuel. We had 30,000 tons there at the time, and it would be unwise to let it drop below 15,000. On that margin we could perhaps run two cruisers and four destroyers for two months, when it would again become necessary to replenish Malta with fast tankers. Furthermore we pointed out that 6-inch gun cruisers were preferable to the 5·25-inch gun 'Naiads' for dealing with the heavy Italian cruisers, if indeed the 'Naiads' were not altogether ruled out because Malta had no reserve of 5·25-inch ammunition.

Though we did not exclude the provision of fleet destroyers for Malta, we pointed out that to do so would cut our destroyer force to the bone. It would mean stopping the refits and dockings which were necessary if they were to be kept in running condition, while we also had to consider the supply of Tobruk and possibly other advanced bases in Cyrenaica in the future. On every one of these trips the ships were attacked from the air, and allowances must be made for casualties. Even as it was, the supply of Tobruk had to be greatly curtailed if the battle-fleet went to sea with its destroyer screen.

We also emphasized that the main value of a surface at Malta would be a deterrent and a delay to the enemy. We might hope to bag a convoy or two; but the enemy could use wide evasive routeing and might always bring a superior force to bear. Too much must not be expected. All the same, the enemy supply would be impeded. As regards air cover, one long-range fighter squadron was considered essential; but we stressed the need for better long-range reconnaissance without which the surface force could operate neither safely nor effectively. Finally, we were unable to provide any ships for Malta until September 30th, by which date we hoped to have relieved an Australian brigade from Tobruk, of which more anon.

Further signals were exchanged late in September, when I had to inform the First Sea Lord that I could no longer provide cruisers for Malta because of commitments in the Red Sea, where air protection had to be provided for the heavy concourse of shipping. However, I offered to supply fleet destroyers for Malta if they could be replaced by 'Hunts', so four of the latter were sailed to join us round the Cape.

Finally, in the third week in October, a force consisting of the cruisers *Aurora* and *Penelope*, and the destroyers *Lance* and *Lively*, were sent out to Malta from the United Kingdom. They were soon to show their worth.

III

I have several times mentioned the supply of Tobruk, and if that fortress was rightly described as 'a running sore' to the enemy, it was something equally painful to the Royal Navy.

During August the destroyers and schooners, with an occasional small merchant vessel, kept up an average supply of stores and ammunition of about one hundred and fifty tons a day, a highly creditable performance. There was no air cover in the port or during the last part of the run, with continual bombing when the enemy became aware that we were unloading at Tobruk at night. The Germans also mounted batteries which fired into the harbour, and though they had little more than a nuisance value the enemy guns demanded periodical attention from our gunboats, cruisers and destroyers. We estimated that the enemy also had four or five U-boats working on the Tobruk route. They used Bardia as a base, and as this place was a repair and maintenance area for the Afrika Korps it also received a share of our bombardments from the sea.

I have mentioned that the *Stuart* and the Australian destroyers of the Tenth Flotilla had largely been used for the supply of Tobruk. The *Stuart* finally sailed for Australia on August 22nd, with one engine completely out of action and the ship seriously in need of a refit. On her departure I signalled to the Australian Navy Board:

We on the Mediterranean Station much regret that H.M.A.S. *Stuart* is to leave us. This gallant ship has achieved an unsurpassed record under the distinguished command of Captain Waller. In all the major operations of the Mediterranean Fleet she has played a leading role and no call for a difficult duty has ever been in vain. To keep this old ship operational and efficient, the work of the engine-room department has been above praise. The departure of the great little ship and her gallant crew is a loss to the Mediterranean Fleet.

Incidentally, the *Vendetta*, the last of the Australian destroyers, left us at the end of October.

In the latter part of August a demand was made for the replacement of one Australian brigade from Tobruk. I was most reluctant to impose this additional strain on the already overworked destroyers, added to which it seriously interfered with the supply organization. However, it appeared that military and political reasons made it necessary. So during the moonless period the fast minelayers *Latona* and *Abdiel* with the destroyers took some 6,000 Polish troops and some thousands of tons of stores into Tobruk, and brought 5,000 Australians away, an outstanding performance on the part of all concerned. During this operation the cruiser *Phœbe* was torpedoed by an aircraft, but was able to reach Alexandria under her own power.

In early September the Royal Air Force tried to extend the air cover over the Tobruk supply route by using the airfield at Sidi Barrani. But after a week or so an advance by the enemy, later discovered to be no more than a reconnaissance in force, led to its abandonment.

In September, too, we started using 'A' lighters, tank landing craft, on the supply run, loading them up with stores, tanks and mechanical transport at Mersa Matruh. Because of their slow speed a great part of their passages were made without air cover, and they had some homeric battles with aircraft. Early one morning, too, three of them fought a fierce engagement with a submarine on the surface, eventually forcing the U-boat to dive. These craft operated until late in October, and were then withdrawn. Out of the ten with which they had started five were sunk; but their work was invaluable. In all they landed at Tobruk 2,800 tons of stores and 55 tanks, besides guns and mechanical transport.

In mid-September, again, when there was no moon, we were once more called upon to replace nearly 6,000 Australian troops in Tobruk with others from Syria. I was much opposed to it. It upset many other arrangements, and was only undertaken under considerable pressure from the Australian Government. In eleven days the minelayers and destroyers ferried some 6,300 troops and 2,100 tons of stores into Tobruk, and brought some 6,000 men away.

In October a final replacement of the Australian troops in Tobruk was demanded of us. I expressed myself as strongly against it, and showed General Blamey the long list of ships sunk and damaged on the Tobruk run. The relief came at a very bad time, and as I wrote to the First Sea Lord it might have serious repercussions in forcing the delay of the Western Desert offensive by two to four weeks. Neither of the other Commanders-in-Chief favoured the idea; but our advice was turned down and General Blamey had his way. The operation started on October 12th and continued until the 26th. It was never quite completed, for on the evening of the 25th on her last trip to Tobruk, the *Latona*, Captain S. L. Bateson, was hit by a bomb in the after engine-room, set badly on fire, and immobilized. She remained afloat for two hours; but her deck cargo of ammunition exploded and the magazine blew up. The *Hero* and *Encounter* took off the passengers and crew, the *Hero* being damaged by a near-miss while alongside. Seven soldiers were lost, together with 4 officers and 26 men of the *Latona*.

In a fortnight about 7,100 troops and an average of 103 tons of stores a day were landed at Tobruk, and some 7,900 men brought back to Alexandria. As usual, the fine work of the destroyers and other ships engaged on the Tobruk run, though largely unrecognized by those who did not know the circumstances, was immeasurable in its importance to the campaign in the Western Desert.

On October 21st the veteran gunboat *Gnat*, Lieutenant-Commander S. R. H. Davenport, which had done such good work in bombarding at Tobruk and elsewhere, was torpedoed by a U-boat and her bows completely blown off. Because of her trim the little ship was unable to steer or make way through the water. No other ship was in company, and for some hours she lay completely helpless, though luckily strong fighter protection was maintained over her all day. Then the *Griffin*, *Jaguar* and some other ships came to the *Gnat's* rescue, and, after sunset she was taken in tow stern first by the *Griffin* for Alexandria, where she eventually arrived. It was a fine performance. We had the idea of making one complete ship out of the stern portion of the *Gnat* and the bows of the *Cricket*; but because of the constructional difficulties it had eventually to be abandoned.

The tale of our losses on the Tobruk run was mounting steadily; but whenever the place is mentioned my mind at once goes back to the Naval Officer in Charge, Captain Frank Montem Smith, D.S.O., R.D., R.N.R., outstanding among gallant men. Except for a few weeks when he had to be withdrawn for illness he was at Tobruk throughout the siege. When he was in hospital at Alexandria I went to see him and offered him command of a ship; but in his quiet voice he firmly replied: "No, sir. I'd like to go back to Tobruk," and so he went.

Unperturbed and unafraid in the midst of the heaviest air attacks, he was always the first man on board any ship hit by a bomb, on fire, or in any other trouble. The first in any post of danger, he set an inspiring example to everyone.

And at Tobruk Smith was killed, the last man leaving after seeing the oil-storage tanks well ablaze when the fortress fell into the hands of the enemy in June, 1942. As a guide to the destroyers coming into Tobruk at night, the green starboard light was always shown in the sunken ship alongside of which they lay to unload. This lantern now rests on Smith's grave.

IV

During these months of preparation for an offensive in the Western Desert further efforts were made by my brother Commanders-in-Chief to induce me to move my headquarters to Cairo. They were most persistent, and even approached the Chiefs-of-Staff at home, enlisting the help of the Minister of State, when he went home for a short visit, to press their point of view. However, I remained obdurate. I could not, and would not, be divorced from the fleet, and as the First Sea Lord backed me up I managed to have my own way.

The question of Royal Air Force co-operation over the sea was still very much in my mind. For over a year I had been pressing the Air Officer Commanding-in-Chief to set up an organization similar to the Coastal Command at home to provide adequate air reconnaissance over the sea, and air cover and air striking forces to make up for the absence of an aircraft-carrier in the event of the fleet having to operate in the Central Mediterranean. While Air Chief Marshal Tedder saw my point of view and was quite sympathetic, he had been unable to do anything because his resources, like ours, were strained almost to breaking point. We wanted aircraft fully trained and accustomed to working over the sea, a highly specialized function, and feeling nothing further would be gained by pursuing the matter locally, I asked the First Sea Lord to take it up at home, and sent Rear-Admiral Boyd, Rear-Admiral (Air), to England to ensure that Sir Dudley Pound was made fully aware of the situation.

After considerable resistance on the part of the Air Ministry agreement was reached in October, and a Naval Co-operation Group, No. 201, was finally set up at Alexandria. It was commanded by Air Commodore L. H. Slatter, whose Senior Staff Officer was Group Captain Scarlett-Streatfield. These two officers were quite splendid, and conditions improved from the moment of their arrival. We had someone on the spot to whom we could refer immediately, while they provided a most convenient channel of communication with the Air Officer Commanding-in-Chief at Cairo.

Although this matter was satisfactorily settled, my frequent conferences with my Military and Air colleagues in Cairo had made me apprehensive about the strength of our Air Force for the coming offensive in the Western Desert. It seemed to me that we were going into action in considerable inferiority. I was given a total figure of 520; but this included the Naval Co-operation Group. As for fighters, I was told we had 192, which included 24 fighters of the Fleet Air Arm. The total figure of aircraft was later amended to 660; but this again included the bombers at Malta, every aircraft of the Fleet Air Arm, and the reconnaissance squadrons. I had no objection to the inclusion of the Fleet Air Arm aircraft. It was our intention to throw everything into the battle. All the same, I did not think they should be included when comparing our strength with the enemy's. They might well have had to be withdrawn at short notice for the naval duties for which they were specially trained and experienced.

Apart from Sicily, Italy, Greece, Crete and the Dodecanese the enemy was estimated to have about 600 aircraft in North Africa, so it did not look as though we should have much, if any, air superiority. However, if the Air Officer Commanding-in-Chief was satisfied, it was not for me to complain.

Apropos of the Fleet Air Arm, we had had Swordfish and Albacores operating in the Western Desert for some time. Because of their specialized sea training in navigation they had made quite a name for themselves as accurate flare-droppers, circling the bombing area with flares after which the Wellingtons made their attacks with bombs. I believe the Germans reported that the British had some helicopters in the Western Desert which were very accurate bombers. These were probably the old Swordfish going up wind.

October saw me frequently in Cairo where the preparations for the Western Desert offensive were being pressed forward. I had little time at sea, though the battle-fleet was out on several occasions under the command of Vice-Admiral Pridham-Wippell. But movements were greatly circumscribed, not so much because of the lack of air cover, as by there being no destroyers to act as a screen. All the destroyers we had were fully occupied with the supply of Tobruk and our various other commitments.

My brother Alan had been selected to command the coming offensive, and he had his headquarters in the desert to the west of Alexandria. The better to ensure that nothing was lacking in the liaison between his headquarters and mine I attached an officer to his staff. This was Captain Guy Grantham, that brilliant and most capable officer who had become available when his ship, the *Phœbe*, was torpedoed.

These last months saw several changes among the Flag Officers. Vice-Admiral E. L. S. King, commanding the 15th Cruiser Squadron, went home to take up an appointment at the Admiralty, and for a time the squadron was under the command of Captain M. H. A. Kelsey, of the *Naiad*, until Rear-Admiral Philip Vian came out from England. I particularly regretted to hear that Vice-Admiral Ford was to be relieved at Malta at the end of the year. However, I felt it was only right, as he had been five years there and ever since the outbreak of war with Italy had had a particularly onerous time, especially after the advent of the Luftwaffe and the intensive bombing of Malta. He was a sterling officer undaunted by any difficulties, of which he had plenty. His courage, unflagging energy and helpfulness provided shining examples to everyone in that hard-pressed island. I was glad to think that his services were not to be lost to the Navy in his new appointment as Commander-in-Chief, Rosyth.

Admiral Ford was eventually relieved at Malta by Vice-Admiral Ralph Leatham, lately Commander-in-Chief, East Indies, on January 1st, 1942.

Rear-Admiral Vian, whom I knew of old, assumed command of the 15th Cruiser Squadron on November 1st. He had a distinguished record of service during the war, and I was delighted to have him with me. He was essentially a fighting sailor, and I regarded his advent as a considerable addition to the strength of the Mediterranean Fleet.

v

On October 18th, the Commanders-in-Chief in Cairo were somewhat startled at receiving a message from the Chiefs of Staff in London. If the forthcoming offensive in the Western Desert resulted in a decisive victory, we were informed that His Majesty's Government were considering exploiting the situation by attacking and capturing Sicily. The bulk of the troops for the operation, to be known as 'Whipcord', was to be drawn from the United Kingdom; but we were directed to start planning our share. I need not go into the details, or mention all the signals that passed to and fro between ourselves and the authorities at home. We were fully aware, of course, of the advantages of capturing Sicily; but the whole idea presupposed the collapse of the Italian morale as a result of a shattering defeat in the Western Desert.

My personal view was expressed in a letter to the First Sea Lord of October 23rd, 1941, when I wrote:

> I can't say I like 'Whipcord'. It seems to me that up-to-date we have failed through not thinking of one object at a time, and I feel that before embarking on another operation we should hold North Africa firmly up to the Tunisian border. I agree that, if we can spare the shipping and forces, the expedition should be in readiness in case of a complete collapse of Italian morale; but it will be very difficult to assess when this has happened — I doubt if the morale of the (Italian) Air Force, mostly officers, will collapse, and heavy air attacks on our convoys from Sardinia, Italy and Sicily—on troop-ships not merely store-ships—might wreck the expedition before it arrived.

I need say no more, for on October 29th, in view of the heavy naval commitment required and the effect on our convoys, Operation 'Whipcord' was abandoned. I felt greatly relieved. I saw little chance of the prerequisites being attained, and was sure that our resources were not up to it.

CHAPTER XXXIII

I

NOVEMBER found us on the eve of the Western Desert offensive, with all three Services busily engaged in preparation. Our first and principal naval task was the replenishment of the supplies in Tobruk, where the replacement of the Australian troops in October had caused the reserves to fall dangerously low. We continued our heavy supply programme with the *Abdiel* and the destroyers, while a few small store carriers were run in to Tobruk when opportunity offered.

During the siege the port of Tobruk had been greatly damaged by the heavy bombing, so we had also to prepare for the rapid improvement of the harbour facilities when the Army advanced, and their use for landing the large quantities of fuel and stores without which the Army could not operate.

We planned various bombardments from the sea in support of the Army, while to provide diversions the whole fleet was to be used to simulate the passage of a convoy through the Mediterranean. We also arranged sham landings behind the enemy front line, with the threat of another pretended landing at Tripoli from Malta. But fleet movements had greatly to be restricted. We did not wish to divert the fighters for our air cover from their main task of the battle in the desert. In retrospect, it seems a pity that the overall fighter strength in the Middle East could not have been augmented during the waiting period. If the battleships with their 15-inch guns could have come into action on the sea flank of the Army I feel that their assistance would have been valuable.

Between November 2nd and 8th, the *Abdiel* and destroyers were engaged in the relief of the Cyprus garrison by fresh troops from Palestine, some fourteen thousand men being carried into the island, the same number taken out. It was rather an unwelcome responsibility at this juncture; but as the U-boats were active it was safer to move the troops in fast warships than in slower merchant vessels.

In the last chapter I described how it had been decided to send two cruisers, the *Aurora* and *Penelope*, and two destroyers, the *Lance* and *Lively*, to Malta from the United Kingdom. They had reached the island on October 21st. On the afternoon of November 8th aircraft from Malta located a convoy of merchant vessels escorted by destroyers off Cape Spartivento, near the toe of Italy. They were steering to the eastward, obviously making for the west coast of Greece before turning south for Libya. Under the command of Captain W. G. Agnew in the *Aurora*, Force 'K', as this Malta squadron was called, sailed immediately. At forty minutes past midnight they duly intercepted a convoy of eight merchant vessels and four destroyers, with another pair of merchant vessels escorted by two destroyers joining from the northeastward. The result was a holocaust for the Italians. In the course of a brisk action nine of the ten merchant ships were sunk, and the tenth, a large tanker, was left ablaze. At least three destroyers were also sent to the bottom. This was a further shattering blow to Rommel's already exiguous supplies. The presence of a surface striking force at Malta was paying an ample dividend, and formed a constant menace to the maintenance of the Axis army in North Africa.

Fighter reinforcements for Malta were flown in from the *Ark Royal* from the west on November 12th. But the next afternoon, on her return journey, the *Ark Royal* was torpedoed by a U-boat 30 miles east of Gibraltar. She was a great loss. In a time of great stress our aircraft-carriers were already far too few.

Submarines and aircraft from Malta had also been playing havoc on the enemy's supply line, and in this connection it is interesting to know the results as revealed by the Italians since the war. Our increased activity in the Central Mediterranean, with cruisers and destroyers working from Malta over a considerable period, not only produced a serious shortage in Italian shipping, but completely disorganized the traffic to Tripoli. The only shipping that sailed came through the Straits of Messina, rounded the toe of Italy, and steered east through the Gulf of Taranto and the Ionian Sea before turning south off the west coast of Greece and making for Benghazi or Tripoli. There were three main reasons for this procedure. In skirting the coast the Italian convoys had fighter protection over a considerable part of their voyage and were out of reach of our air striking forces from Malta. Benghazi was nearer to Rommel's front line; but was too badly damaged to be anything but of minor importance. Tripoli, though constantly bombed by the Royal Air Force from Malta, was still the main supply port for the Axis army in Libya. Moreover, with our cruisers at work the Italians considered they required a covering force of at least one division of cruisers and supporting destroyers for each convoy. They had difficulty in keeping these warships at sea because of the acute shortage of oil fuel.

Figures can be made to prove almost anything; but during the month of October, 1941, almost 63 per cent of the shipping despatched from Italy to Libya was sunk in transit. In November the percentage sunk or damaged was 77, and only 8,400 tons reached its destination, the lowest monthly delivery during the war. December saw 49 per cent of the Libyan tonnage sunk or damaged. It very soon became clear to the Axis that if these conditions continued their campaign in Africa would die through inanition.

However, Malta's strength in fighter aircraft was never really sufficient for its heavy task, and in December, when the Luftwaffe in Sicily was heavily reinforced, this became painfully obvious. Extreme gallantry on the part of the airmen could never make up for the lack of aircraft and the great difficulty of their maintenance. From just over fifty air raids in October and seventy-five in November, the air attacks upon Malta leapt to something like one hundred and seventy-five in December and more than two hundred and seventy-five in January, 1942. In February the number of raids fell to about two hundred and thirty, and this meant 990 tons of bombs, principally on the aerodromes, the Grand Harbour and dockyard. When the city of Coventry was laid waste in October, 1940, it received something just short of 200 tons of bombs. In March, 1942, Malta was to receive 2,170 tons, and in April about 6,730 tons from 5,715 bombers. In that critical month the daily average of bombers over the devoted island was 190.

Kesselring was in Sicily, and it was the German plan to knock out all resistance and reduce Malta to a heap of rubble before trying to occupy the island with airborne troops and a seaborne expedition. It was our intention to frustrate this with every ship we possessed, air cover or none, come what might. Perhaps it was lucky that the seizure of Malta was never attempted; but the project was not finally abandoned until the end of June, 1942, by which time our Army had been driven back to El Alamein, where Rommel had also been forced to a standstill through lack of petrol and ammunition.

From the beginning of the war with Italy up till November, 1942, 17 per cent of all the supplies loaded for the enemy in North Africa was sunk or destroyed. Of this amount lost the Italians attributed 45 per cent to our submarines, 26 per cent to R.A.F. and 11 per cent to naval aircraft, 8 per cent to surface ships, 7 per cent to mines, and the rest to the ordinary perils of wartime navigation.

But I have anticipated. The point I wish to make is that Malta was really the linchpin of the campaign in the Mediterranean. As the island served as the principal operational base for the surface ships, submarines and aircraft working against the Axis supply line to North Africa, its maintenance had a direct bearing on the progress of the battle in Cyrenaica, a fact that is not always appreciated.

NOTE. *For a diagram showing the influence of Malta upon the ebb and flow of the land campaign in Cyrenaica see Appendix.*

II

Our offensive in the Western Desert was timed to start at dawn on November 18th. I remember that the Polish General Sikorski arrived in Egypt a few days beforehand, and we sent him in the *Kipling* to visit the Polish troops in Tobruk. On his return to Alexandria he lunched with me on board the *Queen Elizabeth*, and by luck my brother Alan, who was in command of the Army about to come to grips with Rommel, was also visiting me. I did not see much of Sikorski; but he made a most favourable impression on all of us. Brisk and full of energy he seemed to have a full grasp of the situation and the confidence of his troops.

Our offensive started as planned, and I do not propose to follow the course of the operations which have already been fully described. But briefly our centre and right were to hold on and contain the enemy, while our armour did a left hook from the south and forced the enemy tanks to fight. There was a code word which directed our centre and right to advance, and another for the Tobruk garrison to break out to the south-east. Once the enemy armour was destroyed, and this was all-important, our Army was to press on to Benghazi and beyond. Over-optimistic reports from our armour resulted in the code word being made too soon.

Things went well at the start; but there was stiff opposition with heavy fighting at Sidi Resegh. The Tobruk garrison made their sortie on the 21st and advanced about seven miles; but failed to make contact as the main advance had been held up. Meanwhile we were faced with a heavy programme of supplying the Army by sea. Mersa Matruh needed 600 tons of fresh water a day for the first fortnight, and then 80 tons a day. Tobruk, when relieved and opened up, required 1,100 tons a day of stores and petrol; and Derna and Benghazi, when captured, 200 and 600 tons a day respectively. These quantities may not sound enormous; but the small ships carrying them had to run the gauntlet through an area still dominated by enemy aircraft and infested by U-boats. Twenty German U-boats had entered the Mediterranean in October to stiffen up the failing efforts of their Italian partners.

Our first casualty occurred on November 23rd, when the *Glenroy*, taking the harbour clearance party and lighters to Tobruk, was torpedoed by a U-boat and had to be beached. The troops and naval clearance party were taken on to Tobruk in a destroyer, and the *Glenroy* was eventually towed back to Alexandria.

The fierce fighting by the Tobruk garrison had produced an acute shortage of ammunition, and a supply ship laden with a full cargo, S.S. *Hanne*, was sailed from Alexandria under escort of the Australian sloop *Parramatta*. At 1 a.m. on November 27th the last-named was sunk by a U-boat, no more than twenty of her ship's company being saved; but the *Hanne's* valuable cargo was safely delivered. The *Parramatta* was a great loss. She had a good record of fine service. The little schooner *Maria Giovanni* which had done such excellent work during the siege was lost at about this period, having run ashore in enemy territory outside the Tobruk defences. The *Tiberio* went a month later, capsizing while entering Mersa Matruh for shelter during a heavy gale after her cargo had shifted.

Cruisers and destroyers, meanwhile, had carried out bombardments of Halfaya and Bardia, while I had taken the battle-fleet to sea on November 21st and had proceeded westward until dark in support of the dummy convoy which had sailed from Malta to simulate an attack on Tripoli and thereby, we hoped, to draw off some of the enemy's air strength.

On November 23rd I had a personal signal from the First Sea Lord telling me he had been discussing the situation in the Western Desert with the Prime Minister. Three things were apparent: the enemy's shortage of petrol; his extreme efforts to put petrol into Benghazi; the enemy's air situation was such that it was more than doubtful if he could spare any aircraft for work over the sea near the African coast. . . . The effect of keeping the enemy short of petrol would have such far-reaching results that the First Sea Lord was sure I was considering the possibility of using surface forces for the interruption of enemy traffic to Benghazi during the forthcoming very critical period.

On the same date came a personal signal on the same subject from the Prime Minister in which he said he had asked the First Sea Lord to communicate with me about the vital importance of intercepting surface ships taking reinforcements, supplies and, above all, fuel to Benghazi. "Our information here," the message continued, "is of a number of vessels now approaching or starting. Request has been made by enemy for air protection but this cannot be given owing to the absorption in battle of his African Air Force. . . . I shall be glad to hear through the Admiralty what action you propose to take. Stopping of these ships may save thousands of lives apart from aiding a victory of cardinal importance."

The interception of enemy supplies was naturally a subject which occupied our every waking moment; but the supposition that the enemy's air strength had in any way diminished showed that the usual optimism at home was not based upon any real knowledge of the facts. We, who were in a position to know, had observed no falling off in the enemy's air activity over the sea.

I need hardly quote my replies in full; but to the Prime Minister I answered that I was very much alive to the vital importance of the Benghazi supply route, and that he would already have been informed of my dispositions to meet the situation. Unfortunately the reported absorption of the Luftwaffe in the land battle had not been borne out in practice. A very lively interest was being taken in our movements by the enemy, while our own weakness in air reconnaissance was adding a heavy hazard to the work of our light forces.

In replying to the First Sea Lord I went into rather more detail, pointing out that the matter had been under consideration for a long time, and that orders were already issued for combined action against enemy convoys by cruisers and destroyers from Alexandria working in conjunction with Force 'K' from Malta. The forces were sailing that day. I mentioned the enemy's air reconnaissance, and that the operation would entail the cruisers spending the daylight hours of one day in the Central Mediterranean. It was 'a chancy enterprise', for our ships would have to rely upon our air reconnaissance, which was none too good, to keep them clear of any superior enemy force.

I ended by saying that I felt sure that all these considerations were well known to him, and that I hoped he would be able to explain to the Prime Minister the difficulty of intercepting a convoy by a force based 550 miles from the scene of operations and under constant enemy observation.

Further messages passed between us and the Admiralty, and the First Sea Lord suggested that a further force should be sent to Malta to take turns with Force 'K', one of the forces always being at sea. This, of course, had occurred to us also; but the shortage of fuel had prevented it. However, in view of the overriding necessity of stopping the supplies at that moment I consented to send two more cruisers and two destroyers to Malta, though I had to point out that because of the shortage of oil fuel there we could not hope for more than three sorties each by Force 'K' and this new force.

In the early hours of November 24th two enemy convoys were reported at sea making for Benghazi. Force 'B', consisting of the *Ajax, Neptune, Naiad, Euryalus, Galatea* and four destroyers, the whole under Rear-Admiral Rawlings in the *Ajax*, sailed at 4 a.m. to intercept. Force 'K', in the Central Mediterranean, returned to Malta, refuelled and went to sea again.

At 4 p.m. the same day I sailed from Alexandria with the *Queen Elizabeth, Barham, Valiant* and eight destroyers to be within call if enemy heavy ships put in an appearance.

III

At about 4.30 next afternoon, November 25th, when the battle-fleet was patrolling between Crete and Cyrenaica, I was sitting in my bridge cabin in the *Queen Elizabeth* having tea. I suddenly heard and half-felt the door give three distinct rattles, and thought we had opened fire with our anti-aircraft guns. I went quickly up the one ladder to the bridge, and then I saw the *Barham*, immediately astern of us, stopped and listing heavily over to port. The thuds I had heard were three torpedoes striking her. She had been torpedoed by a U-boat. The poor ship rolled nearly over on to her beam ends, and we saw the men massing on her upturned side. A minute or two later there came the dull rumble of a terrific explosion as one of her main magazines blew up. The ship became completely hidden in a great cloud of yellowish-black smoke, which went wreathing and eddying high into the sky. When it cleared away the *Barham* had disappeared. There was nothing but a bubbling, oily-looking patch on the calm surface of the sea, dotted with wreckage and the heads of swimmers. It was ghastly to look at, a horrible and awe-inspiring spectacle when one realized what it meant.

The destroyers were quickly on the scene, some to hunt the submarine, others to pick up survivors. But though the U-boat had broken surface after firing, and passed so close down the side of the *Valiant* that the guns could not be sufficiently depressed to hit, contact was never made.

About four hundred and fifty survivors were rescued, including Vice-Admiral Pridham-Wippell. But Captain G. C. Cooke, fifty-five other officers and eight hundred and six men lost their lives. It was a most distressing calamity.

I saw many of the rescued later in hospital. Some of them had sustained horrible injuries through sliding down the ship's bottom as she rolled over. The *Barham* had been out of dock for six months, and the barnacles had grown to an enormous size in the warm water of Alexandria.

We discovered later that the U-boat had come right through the destroyer screen.

The First Sea Lord sent us a message of condolence, and when next I wrote to him I said: "We very much appreciated your signal about the *Barham*. She is indeed a heavy loss. We blundered straight on to the submarine. There was no necessity for us to be there any more than anywhere else. . . . It was a most daring and brilliant performance on the part of the U-boat, which fired from a position about two hundred yards ahead of the *Valiant*. If there is anything to be learnt from it, it is that our anti-submarine vessels are sadly out of practice. I am withdrawing the *Otus* (submarine) from operational duty to run her as a 'clockwork mouse'," in other words, for the instruction of anti-submarine ratings.

We spent a very unhappy night. After the day's happening our nerves were all on edge. Large numbers of aircraft kept passing close to us, many of them without any recognition signal to show they were friendly, though I believe they were mostly ours. On one occasion, if not more, I restrained the captain of the *Queen Elizabeth*, Captain Claud Barry, from opening fire at aircraft within six thousand yards of us. I was most unwilling to give away our position by the flashes of gunfire.

The battle-fleet returned to Alexandria next day. Our light forces from Alexandria had had no encounters; but on the afternoon of the 24th the *Penelope* and *Lively* from Malta had intercepted an enemy convoy of two merchant vessels escorted by two destroyers. After a short engagement both the escorts made off and the merchantmen were blown up and sunk.

On the 27th the *Ajax* with Rear-Admiral Rawlings, and *Neptune*, with the destroyers *Kimberley* and *Kingston*, sailed from Alexandria to reinforce Force 'K' at Malta. For the first part of their passage they were accompanied by the *Naiad* and *Euryalus* with two destroyers, which had orders to sweep east along the Cyrenaican coast on their way back to Alexandria. They returned next day without incident.

At the end of November our cruisers and destroyers were still working at full pressure, and in spite of the fact that there was no air cover, we were still running convoys to Tobruk. The garrison there joined hands with the

New Zealanders on the 27th, forming a narrow corridor into the fortress, though the situation there and to the eastward was still very confused with hard fighting. I note that we sent two destroyers to Tobruk on the 28th each carrying 50 tons of ammunition for the Army, and that other large convoys, with lighters for unloading, personnel, stores and a ship laden with the all-precious petrol, sailed from Alexandria on the 30th.

On the same date, as the enemy was reported to be running supplies in destroyers from Navarin, in southern Greece, to Derna, we had three destroyers patrolling 30 miles north of Derna during the night, with two cruisers and two destroyers in support. They did not meet the enemy; but on the way back to Alexandria, while carrying out a submarine sweep, the destroyers were attacked by three torpedo-bombers in broad daylight and the *Jackal* was hit right aft by a torpedo. Though her steering compartment was wrecked, her propellers and shafts were undamaged, and she was able to return to Alexandria at 14 knots. There were no casualties in the *Jackal*; but in the course of the engagement the commanding officer of the *Jaguar*, Lieutenant-Commander J. F. W. Hine, who had done such good work, was killed by the explosion of a shell.

It was on December 1st that the heavy fighting south-east of Tobruk resulted in the corridor being broken by the enemy's capture of Sidi Resegh, and the New Zealanders having to be withdrawn. But there was one slice of luck, for at 3.30 a.m. on the same day, working in conjunction with a Wellington fitted with radar, ships of Force 'K' from Malta sank the Italian merchant vessel *Adriatico* carrying ammunition and supplies to Benghazi. Acting on information received Force 'K' then moved west to intercept a tanker and a destroyer reported near Kerkenah Bank, off Sousse, on the east coast of Tunisia. Force 'K' intercepted these ships at 9.40 a.m. The destroyer, after fighting gallantly, was blown up and sunk, while the tanker, carrying army personnel, with petrol and oil, went up in flame and smoke.

The end of November and the beginning of December saw the peak of our intensive attack on the Axis supply line to North Africa. After that it gradually diminished, partly because of the huge increase in the strength of the Luftwaffe in Italy and the increasing severity of the air attacks upon Malta; but due even more to mishaps to our surface ships working from the island. Earlier in this chapter I have stressed the influence of the offensive from Malta upon the ebb and flow of the campaign in Cyrenaica. Allowing for the time-lag for the accumulation of supplies, it is to be noted that when the Malta offensive was at its height Rommel's army was usually in retreat or hard put to maintain its position due to lack of resources. When Malta was neutralized by German air attack and our surface forces, submarines and aircraft could no longer operate effectively, Rommel was able to build up his supplies and follow it up with an offensive.

It was in December that we were faced with a reduction in our anti-submarine forces by the threatened withdrawal of the 22nd South African Anti-Submarine Group, *Southern Maid*, *Southern Isles*, *Southern Sea*, and *Protea*, under Lieutenant-Commander S. A. Trew, of the South African Naval Service, which had been lent to us for a year. At a period when the U-boats were very active I was reluctant to see these ships go, particularly as they had done such good work on the Tobruk run. I asked for an extension and signalled to the Admiralty:

> The loss of these efficient little ships and experienced crews will be deeply felt. I beg that a request be made to the Union Government, asking that they be allowed to remain in their essential work, which is hand in hand with the fine exploits of the troops of their Dominion ashore.

I am glad to say their time was duly extended.

The supply of Tobruk continued, and so did our losses. On December 6th, H.M.S. *Chakdina*, Commander W. R. Hickey, R.N.R., a small passenger steamer, was torpedoed by an aircraft and sunk almost immediately. About two hundred survivors were rescued, among them prisoners of war, including the German General von Ravenstein. The next day we had the sloop *Flamingo* damaged, also by an aircraft, and H.M.S. *Chantala*, another small passenger steamer commanded by Lieutenant-Commander C. E. I. Gibbs, R.N., was mined in Tobruk harbour after unloading. She sank with her upper deck awash and her back broken.

The enemy started his withdrawal to the westward on December 7th, and the next day Tobruk was relieved after a siege of 242 days. In a signal to the Admiralty on December 11th I gave details of the troops and stores landed and taken away from the fortress by the Navy during the period of its investment, April 12th to December 10th, 1941. Here it is:

Personnel out of Tobruk	34,115
Wounded ,, ,, ,,	7,516
Prisoners of war ,, ,, ,,	7,097
Personnel into Tobruk	32,667
Guns ,, ,,	92
Stores ,, ,,	33,946 tons
Tanks ,, ,,	72
Sheep ,, ,,	108
Naval Casualties:	
Killed and missing	469
Wounded	186

Merchant Naval Casualties:
    Killed and missing 70
    Wounded 55

H.M. Ships sunk: Destroyers 2, Sloops 3, Anti-submarine vessels and minesweepers 7, H.M. Store Carriers and Schooners 7, 'A' lighters 6, Gunboat 1, fast Minelayer 1.
    Total 27

H.M. Ships damaged: Destroyers 7, Sloop 1, Anti-submarine vessels and minesweepers 11, 'A' lighters 3, Gunboats 3, Schooners 1, H.M.S. *Glenroy*.
    Total 27

Merchant vessels sunk: 6 and 1 schooner.

Merchant vessels damaged: 6.

This then was the tale of our achievement and sacrifice in support of the Army, which the soldiers in Tobruk fully realized and appreciated.

A speech by the Prime Minister in the House of Commons on the subject of the supplies at Tobruk made no mention of how the supplies had got there, or the hard time our small ships had had in carrying out this obligation. As I later wrote to Sir Dudley Pound:

> I fear the Prime Minister's speech on the supplies at Tobruk made all out here in the Service very angry. I sent a signal to the Admiralty showing the losses. Do you think that even at this late hour the Admiralty might make a signal recognizing the work of these small ships? It would I think be very well received. I hear the men are a bit sore-hearted at receiving no official recognition of what has been as gallant work as has ever been done . . . I issued a message to the little ships myself, but it is not the same thing.

After the relief of Tobruk the Army's offensive progressed rapidly. Substantial pockets of the enemy still held out at Bardia and Sollum, and these called for periodical bombardments from the sea. But they were by-passed by the Army, and Derna was in our hands by December 21st with Benghazi three days later.

On December 6th we heard the news of the Japanese attack on Pearl Harbour, and within forty-eight hours we were at war with Japan. I have been told in some American circles that it was considered the Japanese had based their tactics for the Pearl Harbour operation upon our attack upon the Italian fleet at Taranto. Be that as it may, it could not be denied that they achieved a noteworthy success by crippling the strength of the United States fleet just at the time when it was most needed. As a result of it the Japanese were able to pursue their practically unhindered campaigns in the Philippines, Malaya and the Dutch East Indies, though, as an offset, and a factor which eventually proved to be decisive, it brought the vast resources of the United States into the struggle on our side. However, we were to suffer many grievous reverses before the strength of our new ally was fully deployed.

The effect upon the Mediterranean Fleet was felt at once. The Australian cruiser *Hobart*, the *Abdiel* and various smaller units left us immediately and sailed for the Far East. This was more than made up for, however, by the return of the *Dido* after being repaired, and the arrival of eight destroyers, with the *Antwerp* and *Malines*, which were small passenger steamers of medium speed, and a group of minesweepers. But the war with Japan inevitably postponed the day when aircraft-carriers could again be sent to the Mediterranean.

IV

December was a month of great activity, during which we concentrated principally upon the interruption of the enemy's supplies, the protection of our own convoys, and the replenishment of the oil-fuel at Malta. All the cruisers and destroyers were engaged upon these tasks. This left no antisubmarine screen for the battle-fleet, which was consequently doomed to inaction.

The work of our surface forces from Malta necessitated extreme measures for maintaining the supply of fuel in the island, and H.M.S. *Breconshire*, Captain C. A. G. Hutchison, a converted merchantman which could carry 5,000 tons of oil-fuel and some petrol, was largely used for this purpose. The lack of a really fast tanker was greatly felt throughout the war in the Mediterranean; but more pressing needs prevented one or two being built. Three years later, when our fleet was sent to the Pacific, one of the first demands was for a fast tanker; but there was none. Both the Germans and the Japanese possessed them; but it was not until after the German capitulation that we acquired a surrendered 22-knot tanker and supply ship too late to be used in the Pacific war.

The various passages of the *Breconshire* to Malta always took the same course. She was escorted from Alexandria by the 15th Cruiser Squadron and destroyers, to be met at sea by Force 'K' from Malta and escorted in. They usually had to run the gauntlet of heavy air attacks, and sometimes had greater excitement still.

After one such trip to Malta from which she returned to Alexandria on December 8th, the *Breconshire* sailed again on the 15th. However, there had been various other incidents during those seven days.

At about 3 a.m. on the 11th the *Farndale*, off the Libyan coast, sighted a submarine on the surface, which fired a torpedo and dived. The destroyer attacked twice with depth-charges, and the U-boat was forced to the surface and made off at 18 knots, to be overtaken and sunk. She was the Italian *Caracciolo* carrying evacuees from Bardia including an Italian General, who was drowned. Some fifty survivors were rescued.

At 2.30 a.m. on December 13th the destroyers *Sikh, Legion* and *Maori*, with the *Isaac Sweers* of the Royal Netherlands Navy, which were coming to Malta from Gibraltar, made contact with two Italian 6-inch gun cruisers and two destroyers off Cape Bon, Tunisia. Commander G. H. Stokes, in the *Sikh*, was the senior officer. Taking full advantage of the dark shadow of the land he led his ships in to the attack, and in the brilliant action that followed both cruisers and one of the destroyers were sunk, while the other was damaged. For this exploit Commander Stokes was awarded the C.B., an unusual distinction for an officer of his rank.

On the same day, following a report that enemy forces were operating in the Ionian Sea, Rear-Admiral Vian's cruisers sailed from Alexandria to intercept. He was to join the cruisers and destroyers from Malta during the night of the 14th–15th. On the 14th enemy forces were reported making northward towards Taranto, and it seemed that the convoy they were covering had also turned back, probably because of our heavy concentration of submarines south of the Straits of Messina, in the Gulf of Taranto, and along the convoy route towards the west coast of Greece. The records show that the submarine *Upright* sank two large merchant ships on the 13th, while the *Utmost* damaged another. On the 14th the *Urge* put two or three torpedoes into the *Vittorio Veneto* which caused serious damage. Rear-Admiral Vian's force had been ordered back to Alexandria, and at midnight on the 14th–15th, when he was about to enter the searched channel off Alexandria, the cruiser *Galatea* was hit by two torpedoes fired by a U-boat and sank almost at once. Some one hundred and fifty officers and men were rescued, but that fine officer, Captain E. W. B. Sim, was unhappily lost.

At 10 p.m. on the 15th Rear-Admiral Vian was off again in the *Naiad*, with the *Euryalus, Carlisle* and seven destroyers, to escort the *Breconshire* with her precious oil fuel to Malta. The *Aurora, Penelope* and six destroyers left Malta next evening, the 16th, to meet Vian and to take the *Breconshire* on.

After dark on the 16th Vian sent the *Carlisle* and two destroyers to the eastward to chatter on their wireless at midnight to give the enemy a false impression of what was happening. However, it was obvious that Vian's force had been sighted and reported by enemy shadowers, for at 11.30 p.m. Italian heavy ships were again reported at sea by our submarines off Taranto.

This placed Vian in rather a serious predicament, so we ordered the Vice-Admiral, Malta, to sail every ship he had to join him, while Vian was told that his primary object was the safety of the *Breconshire* until dark on the 17th, and then, after detaching her to Malta, that he was to attack the enemy with torpedoes.

For me it was galling in the extreme. Part at least of the enemy battle-fleet was at sea, and there was I, fretting and fuming at Alexandria, with my battleships immobilized in harbour through lack of a destroyer screen.

Vian met the Malta detachment at daylight on the 17th and the whole force continued to the westward during the day with the *Breconshire* in company. Shadowed the whole time, he was constantly attacked by high-level and torpedo-bombers, luckily without damage. At 8.25 a.m. enemy heavy forces had been reported to the northward, while a further report at 3.25 p.m. placed them at a distance of about sixty miles in the same direction. Our reconnaissance was unsatisfactory, very few aircraft being available, and at 5.45, in the midst of a heavy air attack, Vian suddenly sighted two Italian battleships and various cruisers and destroyers to the westward, between him and his destination. After detaching the vulnerable *Breconshire* at full speed to the southward Vian boldly closed in to attack, which was the only thing that could be done. Dusk was already coming on, and after firing a few salvoes the enemy battleships drew off to the northward and disappeared in the darkness. I cannot say for certain, but maybe the *Carlisle's* wireless signals at midnight gulled the enemy into believing that our battle-fleet was a few miles astern of Vian's cruisers.

The *Aurora* and other ships met the *Breconshire* and escorted her to Malta, where they arrived on December 18th. In the meantime the *Breconshire* had been sighted from the African coast in the Gulf of Sirte, and the enemy thought a landing was about to take place. This sighting happened to coincide with a surprise attack by our Long-Range Desert Group upon a nearby encampment. As the garrison were all facing out to sea standing by to repel the threatened landing, they were shot to ribbons by the L.R.D.G. before they collected themselves.

As Vian returned to Alexandria at high speed, air reconnaissance from Malta on December 18th showed that Italian battleships had turned about and were remaining in an area about halfway between Malta and Benghazi. This made it evident that the enemy convoys had also turned, and were aiming to arrive at Benghazi and Tripoli during the night. Accordingly after refuelling, the *Neptune*, *Aurora*, *Penelope*, with the destroyers *Kandahar*, *Lance*, *Lively* and *Havock*, sailed from Malta at high speed to try to intercept the convoy off Tripoli. The force was under the command of Captain Rory O'Conor, of the *Neptune*.

At about 0.39 a.m. next morning, when it was blowing hard with a heavy sea, they ran into a minefield about twenty miles east of Tripoli. The *Neptune* exploded a mine in one of her paravanes, and going full speed astern ran into another mine which wrecked her propellers and steering gear and brought her to a standstill. Sheering out to port and starboard the *Aurora* and *Penelope* also exploded mines. The first-named, badly damaged, managed to clear the minefield and was able to reach Malta at reduced speed escorted by two of the destroyers, the *Lance* and *Havock*. The *Penelope*, slightly damaged through the explosion of a mine in her paravanes, stood by to take the *Neptune* in tow when she drifted clear of the field.

At 1 a.m. the *Neptune* exploded a third mine and listed over to port. The *Kandahar*, Commander W. G. A. Robson, entered the minefield to tow or rescue the ship's company, when she also exploded a mine which blew off her stern. The *Penelope*, Captain A. D. Nicholl, was preparing to close to take the *Neptune* in tow when O'Conor signalled to her to keep clear. At about 4 a.m. a fourth mine exploded under the *Neptune*'s bridge. Five minutes later she rolled over and sank. I do not know whether it was then or earlier that Captain Nicholl was faced with the most difficult decision. It was against all naval usage to abandon comrades in distress; but he rightly considered that he would only lose more ships if he entered the minefield to help. Sunrise was close at hand. He was off the enemy's coast, so with a heavy heart he turned back for Malta.

Orders had been given for the *Neptune*'s crew to abandon ship. A heavy sea was running, and the men had to go overboard. Only two Carley floats were available, and some who tried to reach the damaged *Kandahar* by swimming failed in the attempt. According to the sole survivor of the *Neptune*, Leading Seaman J. Walters, only Captain O'Conor, fourteen men and himself remained on a raft at daylight. In the next four days the survivors succumbed one by one, the gallant O'Conor succumbing on December 23rd. At about 4 p.m. the next day Walters was rescued by an Italian torpedo boat.

The *Kandahar*, half under water and gradually sinking, remained drifting all day, unmolested by the enemy. Signals from her were received at Malta, and she was also sighted by friendly aircraft. Vice-Admiral Ford was not the man to lose the chance of saving a destroyer's crew, so after dark the *Jaguar*, Lieutenant-Commander L. R. K. Tyrwhitt, sailed from Malta to find the *Kandahar* by midnight, by which time she should have drifted clear of the minefield, and to be clear by daylight. Though assisted by a Wellington fitted with radar, the *Kandahar* was not actually found until 4 a.m. on December 20th. The sea was still so rough that Tyrwhitt's attempt to go alongside bow to bow had to be abandoned, so the *Jaguar* lay off while the *Kandahar*'s crew swam across, after which the wreck was sunk. I fear that Ford's orders for the *Jaguar* to be away by daylight were not strictly obeyed; but it was a fine piece of work and she got safely back to Malta, having saved eight officers and one hundred and fifty-seven men.

This disastrous episode, which considerably diminished the activities of

Force 'K', the cruisers of which were now reduced to the *Penelope*, because the *Ajax* also was out of action with defects, was exactly the sort of mishap I had feared would happen when the battle-fleet bombarded Tripoli earlier in the year.

v

Meanwhile something very unpleasant had happened at Alexandria. For some time we had suspected that the Italians contemplated an attack on the battleships. We had information that they possessed some sort of submersible explosive motor-boat which could travel on the surface or under water, and was fitted with apparatus for lifting nets which enabled it to pass under the normal defences. On December 18th, I warned the fleet by signal that attacks on Alexandria harbour by air, boat or human torpedo might be expected in calm weather. Besides the boom and the net defence at the harbour entrance, each battleship was surrounded by a floated net as a protection against torpedoes, human or otherwise. Arrangements were also made for patrolling boats to drop small explosive charges at the harbour entrance at regular intervals.

At about 4 a.m. on December 19th I was called in my cabin on board the *Queen Elizabeth* with the news that two Italians had been found clinging to the bow buoy of the *Valiant*. They had been taken on board and interrogated; but had vouchsafed nothing and had been sent ashore under arrest. I at once ordered them to be brought back to the *Valiant* and confined in one of the forward compartments well below the waterline. The boats of all ships were also called away to drop the small charges around them, while the ships' companies were turned out of their hammocks below and chain bottom-lines were dragged along the ships' bottoms.

Just before 6 a.m. when I was on the quarter-deck of the *Queen Elizabeth*, there was a violent explosion under the stern of the tanker *Sagona*, lying close to the *Queen Elizabeth* with the *Jervis* alongside. Both the tanker and the destroyer were badly damaged, the *Sagona* being badly holed aft with her rudder and screws damaged. The *Jervis's* injuries were to keep her in dock for a month.

About twenty minutes later I saw another heavy explosion under the *Valiant's* fore turret, and four minutes after that, when I was right aft in the *Queen Elizabeth* by the ensign staff, I felt a dull thud and was tossed about five feet into the air by the whip of the ship and was lucky not to come down sprawling. I saw a great cloud of black smoke shoot up the funnel and from immediately in front of it, and knew at once that the ship was badly damaged. The *Valiant* was already down by the bows. The *Queen Elizabeth* took a heavy list to starboard.

Three of our boiler-rooms were flooded, and we were unable to raise steam. Our list was compensated by flooding the opposite compartments; but with some thousands of tons of water in the ship the *Queen Elizabeth* was very low in the water. We brought a submarine alongside each side to provide power, and in twenty-four hours were able to provide power for ourselves; but there was a hole about forty feet square under the two foremost boiler-rooms and the ship was out of action.

In spite of the *Queen Elizabeth's* disablement, I continued to occupy my quarters on board. In order to deceive the enemy into believing that we were undamaged, we even went so far as to have a photograph taken for reproduction, we hoped, in the foreign press, showing the ceremony of hoisting the Colours with the guard and band and myself on the quarter-deck and the ship looking completely as usual. How far the enemy was hoodwinked I never discovered, though we were not at all certain that the enemy's reconnaissance aircraft had not evaded our fighter patrol and taken a photograph of the *Queen Elizabeth* with the two submarines alongside. However, we could not conceal the damage to the *Valiant*. After being lightened as much as possible she had to be put into dock. Her damage was worse than expected, extending over about eighty feet including the keel. She would require at least two months for temporary repairs.

Thus our last two remaining battleships were put out of action. It was a heavy blow. As I wrote to the First Sea Lord a few days later:

> We are having shock after shock out here. The damage to the battleships at this time is a disaster, and my chief concern is that it has added so much to your burdens and anxieties... The worst feature is we do not know how they penetrated the boom defence. The prisoners state they came in through the gate when it was opened for the destroyers to enter. This is certainly quite possible; but they must have been prepared to come under, through, or over the net. Charges were being dropped but do not seem to have deterred them, which lends colour to the suggestion that they came through when the gate was open . . . We are now getting concrete blocks on the bottom right across the entrance with a *chevaux de frise* on top up to a 40-foot depth and to the foot of the net. It is costing a lot; but we must have this harbour really secure. . . . The last few days everyone has had the jitters, seeing objects swimming about at night and hearing movements on the ships' bottoms. That must stop.

Very shortly after the damage to the battleships a young engineer officer suggested that if the ships went slow astern with their engines while lying at their buoys or at anchor the rush of water along the ships' bottoms would prevent the fixing of any charges. Thereafter we adopted this procedure when such attacks threatened. It is a pity we did not think of it before.

The attack had been carried out by three human torpedoes, each manned by an officer and one rating. They were embarked in the Italian submarine *Scire* at Leros, and were launched off Alexandria at 8 p.m. on December 18th, waiting about off the entrance until they saw the gate opened. They actually entered the harbour at the same time as the destroyers, one of them nearly being rammed in the process.

The two men of the first torpedo, after fixing the explosive head of their weapon to the propellers of the *Sagona*, divested themselves of their diving dresses, swam ashore, walked through the dockyard and were arrested at the gates. The second pair, found on the *Valiant's* buoy, were sent ashore and then brought back by my orders and incarcerated below. The explosive charges had time fuses, and as the time approached the prisoners became very restive and asked to see the captain. This was allowed; but as they refused to give any information they were hustled below again. On begging to be taken up again they advised Captain Morgan to clear the ship as there was about to be a big explosion. This pair, numbed with cold after several hours immersion, had been unable to clamp the explosive charge to the *Valiant's* bilge keels; but had dropped it on the bottom of the harbour, about fifteen feet below.

The two who damaged the *Queen Elizabeth*, they who were nearly rammed by a destroyer, passed under the nets round the ship and fixed their charge to the bilge keel. Taking off their diving dresses they also swam ashore, and managed somehow to get out of the dockyard and into the town. Here they were delayed for some time through difficulty in cashing an English £5 note. Catching a train to Rosetta, some thirty-five miles to the east at the mouth of the Nile, where they arrived at 8 p.m. on December 20th, they spent the night at an hotel, planning to make their way to a rendezvous where they were to be re-embarked in their submarine on the night of the 21st. As the other crews did not arrive they waited before making their way to another rendezvous three nights later. They made enquiries about trains to Cairo, where it seems they intended to claim protection from the Spanish Consul whom they thought would hide them and help them to escape. However they never got there, for at 3 p.m. on the 23rd they were arrested by a policeman near Rosetta.

We handed all these six prisoners over to the Army, with the request that they were segregated with no communication with the outside world for six months. One cannot but admire the cold-blooded bravery and enterprise of these Italians. Everything had been carefully thought out and planned. Tins of calcium carbide were even found floating in the harbour with which they hoped to ignite the oil fuel released by the explosions.

VI

The loss of the *Prince of Wales* and *Repulse* off Malaya on December 10th, about which I need make no comment, had a profound effect upon our sailors, who rather took the view that these two ships, because of their inexperience of aircraft attacks, should never have been sent out. However, that is not for me to discuss.

But while all the events described were happening in the Mediterranean the Army's offensive was going well. After a pause at Tobruk, Derna was captured on December 19th and Benghazi on the 24th. Benghazi was found in a very bad state indeed, with all the port facilities demolished and the harbour much obstructed and mined. Bad weather delayed the opening; but the port, such as it was, was working on the 31st, when the first convoy sailed from Alexandria. It was understood that the General Officer Commanding the 8th Army intended to continue his advance as soon as possible; but it was entirely dependent on supplies, particularly petrol. An estimate of what was required was 400 tons a day at Benghazi, which would carry the Army as far as Burat. To advance any further would require 800 tons a day. These were prodigious quantities to be put into a devastated port some five hundred miles from Alexandria.

Enemy submarines were still causing heavy losses on the route along the North African coast. Between the 23rd and 28th they sank three merchant vessels, including one of the precious petrol carriers, and damaged another. The corvette *Salvia* was also sunk. At last, however, our counter-offensive against the U-boats met with some success, for we sank three and damaged others.

But what overshadowed everything else in our naval situation was the crippling of our last two battleships, just at the period when we were expecting again to be able to operate in the Central Mediterranean with air cover from the captured aerodromes along the North African coast. The war with Japan made it unlikely that any further force of heavy ships could now be spared for the Mediterranean, and it was difficult to see how the position of ascendancy at sea which we had achieved at such heavy cost could be maintained. For the moment it looked as though we should have to leave it to the Royal Air Force to try if they could dispute the control of the Central Mediterranean with the enemy's fleet.

In reply to a message from the Admiralty on this subject I replied:

> It is considered that the decision on the employment of air forces in maritime operations should provide sufficient aircraft to give us control of the Central Mediterranean, where we have at present no battleship. It is vital that the number of aircraft should be apparent to the enemy

immediately to hide our weaknesses from him, which, if known, would permit him time to establish himself in his objective in such a way that it would be impossible for us to regain our present position.

It is clear that we should not allow our status in the Mediterranean to deteriorate as a result of our efforts to improve the situation in the Far East. It is considered that your signal does not make this position clear.

If we fail to deter the enemy's heavy ships during the next months from establishing control of the Mediterranean, he will achieve reinforcement of his forces in North Africa, be in a position to secure Malta and endanger our Middle East forces. Therefore I urgently request that our policy towards the Far East be subject to the need of security in the Mediterranean.

This security can only be provided by an air force suitable for striking in sufficient numbers.

Our land offensive against the enemy is a further factor in the above considerations. Our return route to Europe can be obtained from North Africa and it is in Europe where we must defeat Germany. For this reason we must consider the retention of control of this theatre as our main objective.

The anxiety that caused us to send this message proved to be only too well-founded. In the event the air striking forces were never able to prevent the Italian fleet from going to sea, while the Axis army in Libya eventually accumulated supplies that nearly allowed Rommel to reach Cairo.

And so the year 1941 closed with our naval forces in the Mediterranean at their lowest ebb. We had started the year with high hopes, and had had some triumphs. But the entry of the German forces into the theatre had been altogether too much for our limited resources, and we had sustained set-back after set-back. Taking an overall view, our lack of air power, and the huge superiority of the Luftwaffe, had dominated the whole situation in the Mediterranean.

But the gloom was not entirely unrelieved. The Army had re-established itself in Cyrenaica, and the all-important task of supplying Malta was thus made easier. (We had not yet realized how precarious was our hold on the Benghazi bulge upon which so much depended.) Furthermore, the enemy was heavily engaged in Russia, which surely must bring some relief in the West. On the other hand, that was again offset by the opening of the war with Japan.

We could only fight on and work on in the hope that when America got fully into her stride we should feel the difference.

CHAPTER XXXIV

I

THE New Year of 1942 found our naval situation in the Eastern Mediterranean depressing in the extreme. There was no reduction in any of our commitments, while our resources to meet them were greatly diminished. The Italian fleet, including their battleships and 8-inch gun cruisers, had shown signs of activity, and we now had no battle-fleet to threaten them if they emerged into the Central Mediterranean. It was thus possible for the enemy to run his convoys to North Africa escorted by a surface force far stronger than anything we could bring against him, though we were fully prepared to take any chance that presented itself of attacking at night.

Because of the heavy bombing of Malta our air reconnaissance was sparse and intermittent, and the air striking force, even if it had been strong enough to have any real effect, was often without the necessary intelligence to enable it to operate in time. The Italian fleet could also make it very risky for running our convoys to Malta with supplies, though as an offset we had the north coast of Libya almost as far as El Ageilha, and could rely upon fighter protection for our shipping nearly as far west as a night's steaming from Malta. However the U-boats were very busy along the Libyan coast, and our anti-submarine forces were so attenuated that submarine hunts and attacks were irregular.

The Army moved on to a line just short of El Ageilha and there halted preparatory to a further advance as soon as the necessary supplies could be accumulated. The Navy, for its part, was feverishly trying to open up the port of Benghazi to allow the supplies to be landed. Our efforts there were greatly hampered by heavy gales and the thorough manner in which the port had been demolished by the enemy.

Early in January the enemy had a striking success in running a large convoy into Tripoli which was not attacked on passage. A strong enemy force including a battleship was sighted by air reconnaissance steering south early on the 4th. It was seen again during the evening. Although the air striking force was sent out from Malta it failed to make contact. This was not surprising, as at that time the island had only one aircraft fit for reconnaissance. The Italian covering force was again sighted early on the forenoon of January 5th, while the convoy of nine merchant vessels was later seen entering Tripoli. The covering force was again sighted by a submarine on the 6th while making for Taranto. The submarine attacked, though without result.

This was a dismal story, and in commenting upon it in a message to the Admiralty I pointed out that because of inadequate air reconnaissance not a single air attack had been made either upon the enemy covering force or the convoy. This unfortunate immunity would dim the enemy's anxiety, and would cause him to become more venturesome. I went on to say that with an enemy escort of that strength our surface forces were powerless to intervene, while air forces trained to operate over the sea were inadequate for sufficient reconnaissance, let alone to provide an efficient striking force. I ended by saying that unless some naval and strong air reinforcements could shortly be provided, I could not see how Malta could be maintained, far less the enemy's supplies to Tripoli be stopped. Nor could a seaborne attack upon Malta be ruled out, particularly in view of the increased scale of air attack to which the island was being subjected, and the inability of the defence to defeat it.

I had a letter from Vice-Admiral Ford dated January 3rd, which gives such a good picture of the state of affairs in Malta at this period that I will quote it at some length. He wrote:

> I've given up counting the number of air raids we are getting. At the time of writing, 4 p.m., we have had exactly seven bombing raids since 9 a.m., quite apart from over a month of all night efforts. The enemy is definitely trying to neutralize Malta's effort, and, I hate to say, is gradually doing so. They've bust a sad number of our bombers and fighters, etc. and must continue to do so. . . . Now we have Libya, and soon I trust Tripoli, I consider Malta must be made stiff with *modern* fighters—Mosquitoes which can fly out from the U.K. on their own and Spitfires from Takoradi if a carrier cannot buzz them off. Guns and stores must come in a submarine beforehand. Just a bit of co-operation between Air and Admiralty and quite simple . . . . The powers at home must give up safety first and send us out the latest if they want to hold Malta and use it as a base. . . . Minesweeping is now difficult, and they appear to be laying them everywhere. Poor *Abingdon*, the only sweeper, and in daylight she got machine-gunned, eight casualties in *Abingdon* alone. I am trying to sweep during the dark hours. . . . Work in the yard is naturally very much slowed up at present as the result of the constant raids. . . . Until we get net defence I shall continue to be worried, especially for Marsamuscetto and the submarines. Nothing really to stop 'em. Why, oh why did not . . . press for my . . . scheme of underground shelters. They would have been finished by now. As I write another bombing raid is just over and at least two more of ours burnt out—damnable to be quite useless. Something must be done at once. How I can unload convoys I cannot think. . . . .

Vice-Admiral Ford, having been relieved by Vice-Admiral Sir Ralph Leatham, was to leave us on January 19th. As he wrote in this same letter: "I want you to know that I have done nothing about leaving this island—i.e.

in asking to go. Much the reverse, as I told the powers I was more than willing to stay on for the duration."

Before Ford left I made him a signal recording our appreciation of the great work he had done during his arduous five years at Malta. I was truly sorry to see his departure. He was a man of many parts, and an inspiration to all who served with him. We all realized how greatly he had contributed to the efficiency of the fleet in keeping ships repaired and running in his much-battered dockyard, and how much he had done for the island and its people. It is no exaggeration to say that he was one of the mainstays of the defence of Malta through one of the most grievous periods of its eventful history.

However, to revert to the question of convoys. While the enemy was engaged in the important operation already mentioned, our light forces were at sea running the *Glengyle* into Malta with precious oil fuel, and bringing the *Breconshire* away. This operation was a complete success. But these two ships, fine and useful though they were, were not sufficient to keep Malta going, so we decided to try to run in four more ships in the middle of January. We did not come off without casualties. Torpedoed by a U-boat on the morning of January 17th, the destroyer *Gurkha* sank soon afterwards, though not before the Netherlands destroyer *Isaac Sweers* towed the wreck clear of blazing oil fuel and succeeded in rescuing practically the whole of the ship's company. We had another loss on January 19th, when the merchant vessel *Thermopylae*, which had developed engine-room defects and had been detached for Benghazi with the *Carlisle* and two destroyers, was hit in a bombing attack pressed home by a single J.U. 88. The ship caught fire, and as she was carrying a large quantity of ammunition had later to be sunk. All but thirty of the passengers and crew were rescued by the *Havock* in difficult conditions.

The other three ships of the convoy reached Malta in safety, and though heavily attacked from the air were successfully berthed.

From the point of view of air reconnaissance and cover this operation was very well conducted. The work of the Royal Air Force 201 Naval Co-operation Group was strikingly efficient and valuable. Very full reconnaissances were flown from Malta and Cyrenaica, while the fighter protection provided from the forward aerodromes in Cyrenaica worked well in difficult conditions. The Malta fighters also did an excellent job in protecting the convoy during its arrival. It showed what could be done with aircraft trained to work over the sea.

However, our satisfaction and hopes of being able to supply Malta with comparative ease were short-lived. The success of these operations depended almost entirely upon our holding the forward aerodromes in Cyrenaica so that the convoys could be protected until well on their way. On January 21st the Afrika Korps started an attack in the El Ageilha area, while three days later we received the unwelcome news from our Naval Liaison Officer with the 8th Army that preparations were being made to evacuate Benghazi, though for the moment they were precautionary only. But it was only too true. On January 25th there came the message: "Army Commander has ordered the evacuation of Benghazi." It was particularly galling. We had just got the port running again, and apart from other stores had actually landed some 3,000 tons of petrol. But there was no help for it. We had to bring away the small craft and the naval personnel, and with the Royal Engineers did our best to demolish the port again. Nevertheless, not everything could be destroyed, and I fear the enemy acquired considerable and valuable supplies.

But to return to the Central Mediterranean. On January 23rd strong enemy forces had again been reported at sea and moving southward. They were escorting a convoy, and once more this movement coincided with our running a cargo of oil fuel into Malta in the *Breconshire*, and bringing out the *Glengyle* and another fast ship, the *Rowallan Castle*. The enemy force included battleships, so that attack on it was left to the air striking force from Malta. They claimed some hits on the convoy. Apart from a certain amount of bombing, which caused no casualties, our operation to Malta and back passed off without incident.

Meanwhile things were going badly in the Western Desert. The main body of troops withdrew from Derna on February 1st, the port was demolished, and the ships and naval base party left for Tobruk. The Army fell back to a line some miles to the west of Tobruk, which meant that the whole of the Cyrenaican hump was again in enemy hands. Any convoys taking supplies to Malta must now pass through the 200-mile gap between Crete on the north and the bulge of Cyrenaica on the south. Enemy aerodromes thus lined each flank of the convoy route, and the future of Malta looked very black indeed.

The air raids on the unfortunate island were daily growing in intensity, and though Force 'K'—*Ajax*, *Penelope* and destroyers—continued to operate from there, it was only a matter of time before they would be forced to leave. The destroyer *Maori*, hit in the engine-room by a bomb at 2 a.m. on February 12th, caught fire, blew up and sank in the Grand Harbour. The submarine base on Manoel Island in Lazaretto Creek was hit by two mines dropped during a daylight raid. Considerable damage was done to the living quarters, while there was mortality among the inmates of the pig farm maintained to eke out the rations. However, we were seriously considering bringing out all the submarines from Malta to Alexandria, as during the day they now had to spend most of their time submerged. This necessarily resulted in insufficient rest between patrols and a loss of efficiency at sea.

On February 7th I had sent a personal message to the First Sea Lord setting out the situation at Malta in all its grim bleakness. I pointed out in so many words the serious effect upon the island caused by our recent reverses in Libya. After all our efforts and sacrifices in supplying Tobruk and in moving Army supplies forward by sea, the withdrawal had come as a bitter disappointment. It was impossible to say how far the retirement would continue, though General Auchinleck realized the need to hold a line as far west as possible and was making every effort to do so. I had always thought that if we held a line near Derna it would be just possible to run convoys to Malta in reasonable safety; but that line had already gone, and as it was thought that the enemy's offensive might continue until May we might find ourselves pushed back to the Egyptian frontier.

I said that we were thus faced with a period during which the passage of convoys to Malta from the east could only be carried out at very great hazard, as there was a long stretch over which no air cover could be provided. At the same time we could provide no surface force to act as a deterrent to the Italian heavy ships, while the scale of air attack upon them was greatly reduced through our loss of the forward aerodromes in Cyrenaica. I also summed up the situation in Malta itself, pointing out that the island had aviation spirit up to about August 1st; but that other supplies would last no longer than June 1st. Moreover, there was only about 5,000 tons of oil fuel remaining there.

In all these circumstances I gave it as my opinion that we must take great risks to keep Malta supplied. We must run in a convoy as soon as possible before the enemy air forces were reorganized and while the enemy was still pre-occupied with his Libyan offensive. I added that unless the risks were considered prohibitive, I intended to sail a convoy which was actually loading and would be ready within a week. If we were unlucky we might well lose the whole convoy. On the other hand we might get a good proportion of the ships through and thus cover our immediate anxiety about the supply of Malta. Meanwhile I was using a submarine, the *Porpoise*, to carry vital stores to the island.

I should mention that it was not at all easy to collect the merchant vessels for a Malta convoy. It all depended upon whether ships of the necessary size and speed were available in the Middle East. In the prevailing circumstances it was quite useless to send ships of less than 15 knots, and these were scarce. Some merchant vessels, all honour to the gallant men who served in them, made the highly hazardous voyage again and again; but their good luck could not hold for ever.

Anyhow, on the afternoon of February 12th the *Clan Chattan*, *Clan Campbell* and *Rowallan Castle*, with the anti-aircraft cruiser *Carlisle* and seven 'Hunt' class destroyers, sailed from Alexandria. Rear-Admiral Vian, with the cruisers *Naiad*, *Dido*, *Euryalus* and eight destroyers, followed in support. The convoy was in two sections, both of which were attacked from the air during the 13th. At 5.30 p.m. the *Clan Campbell*, bombed and hit in the coal bunkers and further damaged by a near miss, had to be detached to Tobruk escorted by two destroyers. Shadowing continued all the next morning, and the convoy was subjected to high-level and dive-bombing attacks from 1.45

to 4 p.m., during which the *Clan Chattan* was hit in the after-hold and caught fire. Completely disabled, she had to be sunk by our own forces.

Meanwhile, after dark on the 13th, three large merchant vessels with H.M.S. *Breconshire* sailed east from Malta escorted by the *Penelope* and six destroyers. This detachment met Rear-Admiral Vian's force at 2.40 p.m. on the 14th, the escorts being exchanged in the midst of a fierce air battle. About half-an-hour later the *Rowallan Castle* was near-missed and had her engines disabled. The destroyer *Zulu* took her in tow; but could not make sufficient speed to have any chance of reaching Malta in safety. From Alexandria I had reluctantly to give orders for the *Rowallan Castle* to be sunk, which was done at 8 p.m. So with the loss of our last merchant ship the attempt to supply Malta had failed.

The *Penelope* and two destroyers returned to Malta, while Vian, with his cruisers, the remaining destroyers, the *Breconshire*, and the empty merchant ships arrived safely at Alexandria. Air reconnaissance disclosed that two enemy forces were at sea trying to locate our damaged ships. This trip involved a colossal expenditure of 5·25-inch anti-aircraft ammunition. After four days of almost continuous action the three cruisers had expended some 3,700 rounds. This caused us considerable anxiety. No more than one and one-third outfits of ammunition for each cruiser remained on the station.

The failure of this convoy to reach Malta produced a very grave situation. The Chiefs of Staff at home, having received messages from General Dobbie, the Governor of Malta, were fully alive to the danger, and on February 27th they signalled to the Middle East Defence Committee giving their views. They pointed out that the most drastic steps were justifiable to retain the island for use as an air staging point and as an impediment to the enemy's reinforcement route. (Incidentally, I am unaware if anyone had suggested abandoning the island. Certainly the Navy had not.) The Chiefs of Staff went on to say that they were unable to supply Malta from the west, and that our chances of doing so from the east depended upon an advance in Cyrenaica. They estimated that the situation in Malta would become dangerous in early May if no convoys had got through. They felt we must aim to be so placed in Cyrenaica by the dark period in April to enable us to run a substantial convoy into Malta, not only to send maintenance necessities; but to build up stocks well above the existing critical level. They suggested a further attempt to run a convoy in March, and enjoined on us that no consideration of risk to the ships themselves need deter us, and that while the operation was in progress it was to be regarded as our primary military commitment—the term 'military', of course, being used in the widest sense.

The opinions of the Chiefs of Staff in London were fully in accordance with the views already held by the Navy. All the same, February was nearly ended, and any advance to capture the Cyrenaica airfields by the dark period in April seemed unlikely in the extreme.

A few days later the Chiefs of Staff at home made a change in the responsibility for Malta. Up to date the Naval and Air Commanders-in-Chief had been responsible for their forces there, whereas the troops in the island came under the command of the Governor, who was also Commander-in-Chief. He worked directly under the Chiefs of Staff in London. The troops in Malta were now placed under the Commander-in-Chief, Middle East, a change which gave us all a share in the responsibility for the island. There could be no confliction of interests in the future as there had sometimes been in the past.

II

The first two months of 1942 saw various changes in the fleet, partly due to the necessity for providing a fleet for the Far East.

The fast minelayer *Abdiel*, which had done such sterling work in Crete, Cyprus and on the run to Tobruk, left us on New Year's Day. I signalled to her: "Good-bye and good luck. You leave the Mediterranean Station with a fine record of arduous and hazardous service well performed of which you may all be proud."

The last Australian-manned destroyers *Napier*, *Nizam* and *Nestor*, under Captain Stephen Arliss, also left us to join the Eastern Fleet, with the Netherlands destroyer *Isaac Sweers*. I was very sorry to lose them, particularly Captain Arliss, a steadfast and stalwart officer who at Crete and since had faced many difficult and dangerous situations with great credit and success. Four more of our veteran Mediterranean destroyers sailed eastward in February, the *Griffin* and *Decoy* to join the Eastern Fleet, and the *Kimberley* for repairs at Bombay. Between December, 1941, and February, 1942, the submarines *Trusty*, *Truant* and *Rover* also left us for the Far East.

But our greatest loss at this period was Rear-Admiral H. B. Rawlings, who struck his flag in the *Ajax* on January 15th, and went home to England for a well-deserved rest. He was a man of many fine qualities, and no failings that I ever discovered. Rather quiet and retiring he never obtruded himself; but was quite fearless in discussion and in expressing his occasionally unorthodox opinions. Full of imagination, he thought in a highly original way, largely, no doubt, as the result of the great knowledge and experience acquired outside the usual naval orbit in Poland and Japan. A man of high ideals, he was quite fearless in action. Highly strung, I feel sure he had difficult moments and had sometimes to drive himself relentlessly; but with his capability of rapid and courageous decision in tight corners he seemed instinctively to do the right thing. With his great sense of humour and very human understanding he was a grand and inspiring leader much liked, respected and trusted by those who served under him. As for me, I have the greatest affection for Rawlings as a friend and a comrade, coupled with admiration for his great qualities as a leader and a fighting seaman.

During the first two months of 1942 we were still running supplies to Tobruk, and had destroyers damaged and two merchant ships sunk by aircraft. The U-boats also were particularly active along the Libyan coast, and the *Kimberley* had been torpedoed off Tobruk on January 12th, but was towed to Alexandria by the *Heythrop* with her stern blown off, while the *Gurkha*, as already mentioned, was sunk by a submarine on the 17th. The 'Hunt' class destroyer *Farndale* was hit by a bomb off the Libyan coast on February 9th, the missile passing through the ship and exploding outside abreast the boiler rooms, both of which were flooded. The *Farndale* reached Alexandria in tow two days later, and without a single casualty.

Enemy aircraft, fully occupied in other directions, were not paying very much attention to the Suez Canal area during January and February, so our shipping through that highly important funnel proceeded unimpeded.

Our submarines from Alexandria and Malta continued to do excellent work. In all during January and February, 1942, they sank three U-boats, one destroyer and eleven merchant vessels, besides damaging another three merchantmen. In the previous September I had signalled to the Admiralty saying that every submarine that could be spared for service in the Mediterranean was "worth its weight in gold" which was almost the literal truth when one considers what was done by the submarines of the 1st Flotilla working under the most able and energetic command of Captain S. M. Raw at Alexandria, and the smaller boats of the 10th Flotilla operating from Malta under the equally fine direction of Captain G. W. G. Simpson. We were lucky to have two such excellent officers in command of the submarine flotillas. Both Raw and Simpson had the trust and affection of the officers and men who served under them, whose welfare was always in their minds. They were tireless in their efforts to keep their flotillas efficient, and the losses their submarines caused to the enemy must be the measure of their success.

Earlier in this book I have mentioned the gallant Lieutenant-Commander M. D. Wanklyn, V.C., D.S.O., and his outstanding work in the *Upholder*. Here I feel I must give a brief account of two other cases of great bravery.

In February the *Thrasher*, Lieutenant H. S. Mackenzie, was on patrol off Crete. On the 16th in broad daylight, she attacked a heavily escorted merchantman entering Suda Bay and sank her with two torpedoes. In return the *Thrasher* was hunted by three patrol craft and two aircraft. Some thirty-three depth-charges were dropped, more accurately than usual; but though severely shaken the *Thrasher* escaped without serious damage. Still close to the enemy coast she surfaced after dark, when it was discovered that two 100-lb. bombs dropped by aircraft were lodged in the forward casing. Lieutenant P. S. W. Roberts and Petty Officer T. W. Gould volunteered to remove them, and set about their dangerous task by the light of an electric torch. The first bomb, lying on the casing, was fairly easily disposed of. The second was inside the casing, and had to be coaxed about twenty feet past various projections with both men inside the casing lying flat on their stomachs, one pulling and the other pushing, before the bomb could be finally dragged clear. The whole operation took fifty minutes, and quite apart from the fact that no one knew when the bomb might explode, the *Thrasher* might have had to dive suddenly, in which case the two men imprisoned inside the casing must have been drowned. Happily no enemy patrol craft appeared. For their outstanding courage both Roberts and Gould were awarded the Victoria Cross.

Early in March, 1942, the submarine *Torbay*, Commander A. C. C. Miers, operating in the Corfu, Taranto and Messina areas, undeterred by narrows and shoals, entered the harbour at Corfu in brilliant moonlight with a flat calm sea in search of four large troopships which he thought had gone there. He went in on the surface at dusk, twice having to dive to avoid patrol craft. After charging his batteries he went on submerged, intending to attack by moonlight. But he saw no signs of any ships through his periscope, so determined to wait until dawn. With the many patrol craft about he described the rest of the night as "fairly harassing". Forced to turn away to avoid being rammed by a patrol vessel he re-entered Corfu roads in daylight. The troopships were not there; but instead Miers torpedoed two supply ships at short range, sinking one and damaging another. This done he had to make his escape. He had some twenty miles to travel to the entrance, so increased to full speed and went deep. He finally withdrew after spending seventeen hours inside an enemy harbour in the most dangerous and difficult conditions. I am glad to say his bravery was also recognized by the award of the Victoria Cross.

In all, during March, our submarines sank five merchant vessels and three U-boats, with another three merchantmen severely damaged. The consistent gallantry and determination of the young officers and crew of our submarines excited my warmest admiration. In spite of their own heavy losses in the Mediterranean since the outbreak of war with Italy—twenty boats sunk up till the end of March, 1942—they never faltered. They, more than any other single arm, played a decisive part in cutting the Axis supply line to Libya, and thus in helping to make possible the eventual advance of the 8th Army to Tripoli and beyond.

CHAPTER XXXV

I

During the month of March, 1942, the enemy stepped up his air attacks in all areas. Malta had a particularly evil time, with great difficulty in keeping the airfields in action. Tobruk was also under heavy attack because of insufficient fighter protection, while early in the month a fairly heavy attack was made upon the Suez Canal area, luckily without causing any interruption in the flow of shipping. So far as the Navy was concerned the problems confronting us were much the same as before, our principal tasks being the interference with the enemy's supply routes, the supply of Malta, and the regular running of ships to Tobruk for the supply and maintenance of the Army.

Information of an enemy convoy about to sail was received early in March; but because of the damage to the airfields at Malta its time of departure was not discovered. When the reconnaissance aircraft were able to get away some five hours late on March 7th, the convoy was not located, probably because the search was too far to the northward. Nor was the convoy sighted on March 8th. On March 9th, however, aircraft from Malta sighted a force of cruisers and destroyers with four merchant vessels roughly two hundred miles south-east by south of Malta steering about north-west, homeward bound. It became clear that the south-bound convoy was well on its way to Tripoli, and this was confirmed a little later when a force of eight destroyers and five merchant vessels were sighted off the African coast steering west for that port. During the afternoon a striking force of Beauforts from Malta attacked the north-bound convoy, and claimed that one cruiser had been hit by a torpedo and set on fire. Further strikes were flown off after dark. The convoy was found; but in one case darkness prevented any attack. In the other only three Wellingtons of the twenty which had taken off attacked with bombs and claimed a possible hit. This was by no means satisfactory.

At Alexandria, more than eight hundred miles to the east, our cruisers and all the available destroyers were brought to short notice when we heard that a cruiser had been torpedoed. Because of the difficulty of providing air cover they were not sailed until 4 a.m. on March 10th, so as to be off Tobruk by dusk and to pass on through the dangerous area to the west under cover of darkness. Rear-Admiral Vian, in the *Naiad*, was in command. No contact was made with any damaged enemy cruiser. However, the opportunity was taken to bring the cruiser *Cleopatra*, which had just come out from England, and the destroyer *Kingston*, away from Malta, and they joined up with Vian for the run back to Alexandria. The *Cleopatra*, incidentally, had had a rude reception at Malta, having been hit by a bomb on the forecastle as she entered the Grand Harbour.

Vian's forces were bombed continually throughout the 11th on its return journey when between Crete and Cyrenaica; but sustained no damage. The luck did not hold, for during the evening the *Naiad* was hit amidships by a torpedo from a U-boat. She assumed a heavy list and sank in twenty minutes, with a death roll of eighty-two. Vian himself and the rest of the officers and men were picked up by the *Jervis*, *Kipling* and *Lively*. As I wrote to the First Sea Lord a few days afterwards: "Such a loss that little *Naiad*. A highly efficient weapon with a ship's company with a grand spirit. The four cruisers were bombed from 9 a.m to 6.30 p.m. without damage, and then to stumble on a submarine was just too sickening. The American liaison officer who was on board and sustained a badly-smashed ankle told me that the behaviour of the ship's company was wonderful when she sank." Captain Guy Grantham, who had returned from acting as Naval Liaison Officer in the Western Desert, was the *Naiad's* captain. Three days later, when Vian hoisted his flag in the *Cleopatra*, he took Grantham with him as his flag captain.

That whole operation was an undoubted success for the enemy, who achieved his object of getting his convoy into Tripoli at small cost, if, indeed, at any cost at all, as the claims of the air striking force from Malta could not be substantiated. I told the Admiralty that the lessons learnt were that Malta must be adequately protected against air attack (by more fighters) if air reconnaissance was to be effective, as the areas covered by Malta's reconnaissance could not be covered by 201 Naval Co-operation Group from Alexandria: that there were insufficient reconnaissance aircraft in the Middle East to ensure effective search in the Central Mediterranean: that more and better-trained Wellingtons were necessary to ensure effective attack on enemy convoys . . . At the same time I emphasized that the available aircraft did all that could be expected of them, the Beauforts being deserving of special credit. But until our reinforcements in aircraft were met we could not hope to stop enemy convoys. In this instance the important south-bound convoy was not sighted until it was off the Tripolitanian coast, and it was not attacked.

In the early hours of March 15th, the *Dido*, *Euryalus* and six destroyers bombarded Rhodes. The force proceeded under fighter cover from Cyprus, and the flour mills, motor repair shops and aircraft hangars were given a heavy shelling. Our aircraft provided good illumination with flares, though because of low cloud it was impossible to estimate the damage. However, several fires were started and the results were thought to be substantial.

On March 19th Captain Philip Mack was relieved by Captain A. L. Poland as Captain (D) of the 14th Destroyer Flotilla.

Mack was a great loss to his flotilla and to the Mediterranean Fleet. He was a first-class destroyer officer who instinctively took the right action on every occasion, and the most difficult and risky operations could safely be entrusted to his experienced direction. Wise in counsel, a gallant and determined leader, he kept not only his own flotilla, but all the destroyers, happy and pleased with themselves, and to him must in great measure be attributed the fact that however sorely tried, whatever their losses, the destroyers always cheerfully set about the task on hand. He radiated good spirits, and in his company it was rarely possible for anyone to be steeped in gloom. Blessed with a keen sense of humour and a great love and feeling for his men he invariably returned to harbour with the tale of some quaint remark made by one of his sailors. At sea, while changing the destroyer screen, the *Jervis* often passed close down the side of the *Warspite*, and Mack's large weatherbeaten face and broad smile acted as a tonic to us all. Everyone was fond of Philip Mack, and went to him for advice if in difficulty or trouble. I am not unduly sentimental; but few men have inspired in me such admiration and personal affection. In all respects he was a grand man and a fine officer, a fighting seaman of the very first quality with the supreme knack of making himself loved, respected and trusted.

After leaving us Philip Mack became Flag Captain to Sir John Tovey, Commander-in-Chief, Home Fleet, in the battleship *King George V* in May, 1942. Promoted to Rear-Admiral in January, 1943, he was killed in an air crash on April 29th while on his way out to join us in North Africa. He would have gone far, and was a great loss to the Service of which he was so fine an example. I personally mourned the passing of one of my greatest friends.

II

In March our thoughts were mainly concentrated on getting a convoy through to Malta. As I have already written, the Chiefs of Staff in London had pointed out that it was a primary military commitment for all three Services. Four ships had been assembled and loaded, one of them being H.M.S. *Breconshire*, officially described as a 'commissioned auxiliary supply ship', which had already made the dangerous passages to Malta and back more often than any other ship. The names of the others, which, with those of the other merchant vessels which carried supplies to beleaguered Malta from east or west, deserve to live in the annals of the Merchant and the Royal Navies. On this occasion they were the *Clan Campbell*, which had been knocked out of the previous convoy through bomb damage, the *Pampas*, and a stout-hearted Norwegian called the *Talabot*.

It had been arranged that all three Services should make special efforts to get the convoy through. The Army was to make a feint advance to threaten the enemy airfields and thus to divert hostile aircraft from attacking the convoy. The R.A.F. was to attack aerodromes in Crete and Cyrenaica to keep aircraft grounded. Fighters were to cover the convoy as far as possible, which they did until 9 a.m. on the 22nd, when they were operating a full three-hundred miles from their base. Number 826 Naval Air Squadron, working with the R.A.F., was to bomb Derna on the nights of the 20th–21st and 21st–22nd to assist in creating a diversion. Air reconnaissance and air striking forces were arranged from Libya and Malta.

The convoy sailed from Alexandria at 7 a.m. on March 20th, escorted by the *Carlisle*, Captain D. M. L. Neame, and six destroyers, the *Sikh*, *Zulu*, *Lively*, *Hero*, *Havock* and *Hasty*. Rear-Admiral Vian, in the *Cleopatra*, with the cruisers *Dido* and *Euryalus*, and the *Jervis*, *Kipling*, *Kelvin* and *Kingston*, left harbour at 6 p.m. It had been arranged that 'Hunt' class destroyers should carry out an anti-submarine sweep between Alexandria and Tobruk the night before the convoy sailed and during daylight on the 20th, after which they were to fuel at Tobruk and join the convoy during the forenoon of the 21st. At 11 a.m. on the 20th, while engaged on the anti-submarine sweep, the *Heythrop* was torpedoed by a U-boat. Taken in tow by the *Eridge*, she sank at 4 p.m. with a loss of fifteen killed or missing. Vian's force and the convoy, which had been joined by five of the six 'Hunts' from Tobruk, met about seventy miles north of Tobruk during the morning of the 21st, and proceeded westward at 12 knots with relays of fighters overhead. A sixth 'Hunt' from Tobruk, delayed by a fouled propeller, joined up in the evening. These six ships—the *Southwold*, *Beaufort*, *Dulverton*, *Hurworth*, *Avon Vale* and *Eridge*—each with their six 4-inch guns—provided a most valuable addition to the anti-aircraft defence of the convoy.

The *Penelope* and *Legion* from Malta joined Vian at 8 a.m. next morning, the 22nd, so the force was complete, well on its way and within about two hundred and fifty miles of Malta. It had already passed the dangerous area between Crete and the hump of Cyrenaica to the southward without attack. This was largely attributable to the successful shelling by the Army of the airfield at Martuba and their threat against Tmimi, some sixty miles west of Tobruk.

But Vian's peaceful progress was soon to be interrupted. On the evening of the 21st the convoy had been reported by German transport aircraft passing from Cyrenaica to Crete, and soon after 5 a.m. on the 22nd, Vian had a report, timed about four hours earlier, from Submarine P.36 to the effect that destroyers and heavier ships were leaving Taranto. This indicated that air attacks might start at any moment, while enemy battleships and cruisers might appear a few hours later. Because of the continual and heavy bombing attacks upon Malta, the air reconnaissance from the island was very thin and the further movements of enemy surface forces were not reported.

The air attacks upon Vian's force and the convoy started at 9.30 a.m. on the 22nd, half an hour after the last fighter patrol had had to leave, and continued with increasing intensity until dusk. In all some one hundred and fifty aircraft were used, torpedo and high-level bombers, shadowers and spotters. The attacks during the morning, confined to a few torpedo shots at long range by Italian aircraft, were not particularly dangerous. The convoy being well protected by an inner screen of cruisers and destroyers, with more destroyers about two miles ahead, the Italians were beaten off by heavy gunfire. It was later in the day, when the German aircraft came into action, that the convoy and escort were hard put to avoid damage.

Vian was determined that come what might the convoy would not turn back; but should, in his own words, "proceed to Malta even if enemy surface forces made contact." The general plan which had been evolved and practised was for the four cruisers and eleven 'Fleet' destroyers to be organized in five divisions. Working semi-independently, they would lay smoke between the enemy and the convoy, and then turn and attack with torpedoes under cover of the smoke-screen if the enemy attempted to break through it. At the same time the anti-aircraft cruiser *Carlisle* and one 'Hunt' class destroyer would lay a smoke-screen across the wake of the convoy, while the remaining five 'Hunts' formed a close escort to the convoy against air attack.

At 12.30 p.m. Vian assumed his organization to fight a surface action on the lines planned, and an hour later, when a shadowing aircraft dropped four red flares ahead of the convoy, he had his first intimation that enemy ships were probably in the vicinity. They were not expected to make contact until 4.30 or 5 p.m. However, at 2.10 p.m. the *Euryalus* reported smoke to the northward, while seventeen minutes later both the *Euryalus* and *Legion* reported ships in that direction, much earlier than expected. Originally thought to be three battleships they were, in fact, two 8-inch cruisers and one 6-inch cruiser with four destroyers. Their range was about twelve miles. It was blowing a strong breeze from the south-east, which was rapidly freshening, with a rough sea and moderate swell.

The Rear-Admiral at once led out to the northward, concentrating by divisions, while the convoy and close escort turned away to the southward. Once clear of the convoy Vian's divisions turned eastward to lay their smoke-screen. The enemy opened fire at 2.36 at very long range, and as they had now been recognized as cruisers, Vian swung round towards them, still making smoke. At 2.56 the *Cleopatra* and *Euryalus* opened fire on a heavy cruiser at a range of about twenty thousand yards; but the enemy turned northward after five minutes and finally drew out of range. One of the Italian cruisers turned back for a few minutes for a sharp exchange of fire with our two cruisers; but turned away at 3.15 to rejoin her consorts. The enemy having gone, Vian steered to rejoin the convoy, and at 3.35 made me a signal saying "Enemy driven off".

We were, of course, intercepting all his signals at Alexandria. So far all was well.

A few Italian high-level bombers had harmlessly attacked Vian's striking force during the short engagement. The whole venom of the German J.U. 88's had been concentrated on the convoy, which made high-level and dive-bombing attacks from 9,000 feet. Thanks to the good shooting of the escort and the excellent handling of the convoy their attacks achieved nothing except to cause a great expenditure of ammunition on our part. The *Carlisle* had already expended one-third of her outfit, while the *Southwold*, one of the 'Hunt' class, reported—"Nine attacks so far. Forty per cent 4-inch ammunition remaining." In the heavy sea and the rising wind the destroyers had been fighting their guns in the most difficult conditions, with their gun crews drenched. The ships were washing down forward and aft. Even the bridges and director towers of the cruisers were swept by heavy spray when they steamed to windward.

Hardly had the Rear-Admiral overhauled the convoy when the *Zulu*, at 4.37, again reported four ships to the north-eastward. At 4.48 we heard Vian's report of one enemy battleship and four cruisers, and at 5.8 he reported that the enemy battleship was accompanied by cruisers and destroyers. The enemy was in two groups, and as we know now the nearest, about nine miles away, consisted of two 8-inch cruisers with a 6-inch cruiser and four destroyers, and the second, at a distance of 15 miles, of the battleship *Littorio*, and four destroyers. They were all steering south-west at high speed to cut off the convoy from Malta.

This was indeed heavy mettle, and put Vian into a very nasty position. He could, of course, get away with the warships if he abandoned his convoy; but his task was to get the merchant ships to Malta regardless of losses. So putting a bold face on it he ordered the convoy to steer to the southward away from the enemy at its best speed, and with his divisions acting as before proceeded to lay a thick smoke-screen between the Italians and the convoy.

For the next two hours, until 7 p.m. the situation was still fraught with danger. My feelings and those of my staff in our offices at Alexandria while the battle was in progress are better imagined than described. Never have I felt so keenly the mortifying bitterness of sitting behind the scenes with a heavy load of responsibility while others were in action with a vastly superior force of the enemy. We could visualize so well what was happening —the Italian battleship and cruisers to the northward; Vian's four cruisers and destroyers laying their smoke-screens and dodging the enemy's 15-inch and 8-inch salvoes; the violent air attacks upon the *Breconshire* and the three merchant ships upon which, for all we knew, the fate of Malta depended; the heavy and rising sea which so greatly hindered the work of the destroyers. We could imagine it all, yet there was nothing we could do to help.

I shall not attempt to describe this very complicated action; but the tactics of Rear-Admiral Vian and his divisional leaders—Captain H. W. V. McCall in the *Dido*; Captain A. L. Poland in the *Jervis*; Captain St. J. A. Micklethwait in the *Sikh*; and Commander H. R. Graham in the *Zulu*—were masterly. While conforming to the general idea they had largely to act on their own initiative. No less gallant was the behaviour of all the commanding officers, officers and men of the ships concerned.

The pall of thick smoke laid by our ships, and constantly added to, spread like a thick blanket over the surface of the sea as it drifted to the north-westward with the wind. The enemy consistently tried to move round this smoke-screen to the westward to get at the convoy to the south. Our ships, dodging out and in of the frayed and tattered edges of the smoke cloud like a pack of snapping terriers, determinedly prevented the Italian movement by engaging with guns and torpedoes as opportunity offered.

No enemy destroyers seem to have taken part in the action. The Italian force engaged consisted of the battleship *Littorio*, with her 15-inch guns, two 8-inch cruisers and one 6-inch cruiser; ours of four weak cruisers and eleven destroyers. Out-gunned though they were, our ships did not hesitate to engage at the moderate ranges of 10,000 to 14,000 yards, or to close in to 6,000 yards to fire torpedoes. We had some casualties. Hit by a 6-inch shell on the bridge, the *Cleopatra*, Vian's flagship, was damaged and sustained some casualties. The *Havock*, near missed by a 15-inch shell, had a boiler badly damaged which reduced her speed to 16 knots. Another 15-inch shell crippled the *Kingston* as she turned to fire torpedoes at a range of 6,000 yards, though she was able to reach Malta under her own steam. The *Euryalus* and *Lively* were hit by shell splinters, though their damage was not serious. The only hit sustained by the Italians was by a medium-sized shell which burst aft in the *Littorio*. Our expenditure of ammunition was heavy; but much of the gunfire was inevitably ineffective, the range being uncertain and the shell splashes being invisible because of smoke, the wild weather and the long range at which most of the action was fought.

Exceptionally fine work was done by Captain Micklethwait and his four destroyers which held off the enemy without other support for nearly half-an-hour, described by Vian as "a remarkable feat"; while Captain Poland, with his four destroyers and the *Legion*, was responsible for the determined and courageous torpedo attack at 6,000 yards which finally caused the enemy to turn back. From the Italian accounts we know that many torpedoes crossed the enemy line, though none hit. The threat was enough.

Our relief at Alexandria was indescribable when we heard that the Italians were withdrawing. To try and take some of the responsibility off Vian I signalled to him that doubtless he had considered dispersing the convoy and letting them make their way to Malta as fast as they could steam. He had anticipated my thoughts and had already done so. At 7.40 p.m. with darkness fast approaching and the convoy not being in sight, he had decided to turn back to Alexandria and to send the convoy on. It was known that the Italians were retiring to the northward, and having failed to make contact with the convoy by day, being driven off, it was unlikely that they would risk a night attack. "The weather was strong south-easterly to east-south-easterly gale, with a rising sea and swell," Vian wrote in his despatch. "Fuel in the 'K' class and 'Hunt' class destroyers was insufficient to allow an extra day to be spent in the central basin west of Benghazi, so it was necessary to get as far east as possible through bomb alley by daylight."

Vian had a difficult passage back to Alexandria in the teeth of the gale, though his ships suffered no damage beyond that caused by the bad weather. He had started off at 22 knots; but soon had to reduce to 18 and then to 15 knots. By dawn on the 23rd only one destroyer, the *Sikh*, was still in company, all the others having dropped astern through the bad weather in which most of them had sustained damage. R.A.F. fighters were over the force throughout most of the day, though working at very long distances from their bases. Enemy shadowers appeared during the morning; but no attacks developed until 4.10 p.m., when eight J.U. 87's came in, concentrating largely upon the damaged *Lively*, which was a mile or so astern because of her action and weather damage. Until dusk sporadic attacks were made by J.U. 88's and torpedo-bombers, though no ships were hit. Speed was increased when the weather moderated, and the *Lively*, unable to steam more than 17 knots, was detached to Tobruk.

Vian, with the rest of the force, was able to increase to 26 knots at dawn on the 24th, and after an early morning attack by two enemy torpedo-bombers which achieved nothing, he arrived at Alexandria at 12.30 p.m.—"honoured", as he says, "to receive the great demonstration that then ensued." Indeed, they had a wonderful reception, being enthusiastically cheered by the crews of all the warships and merchant vessels in the harbour. I went on board the *Euryalus* at once to congratulate the Rear-Admiral on his fine performance, for which he was subsequently created a K.B.E. The condition of the fleet after this action was pretty desperate. Action and weather damage had taken a severe toll of the destroyers, and as I signalled to the First Sea Lord on March 26th no more than two fleet destroyers remained serviceable.

I shall always consider the Battle of Sirte on March 22nd, 1942 as one of the most brilliant naval actions of the war, if not the most brilliant. As told here it sounds easy; but it is against all the canons of naval warfare for a squadron of small cruisers and a handful of destroyers to hold off a force of heavy ships. Nor must the mistake be made of thinking the Italians were inefficient in this action. Our destroyers going in to attack were received by heavy and accurate gunfire, and it was only by the mercy of Providence that many of them were not sunk and still more severely damaged. But the thought of penetrating a smoke-screen to get at the convoy with his heavy ships, knowing that destroyers were waiting to attack him as he emerged on the other side, was too much for the nerves of the Italian Admiral. For any

Flag Officer, however courageous, it must always be a problem. In such circumstances, the odds are always so much on the destroyers.

The determination and team-work of all the ships engaged more than fulfilled the high standard expected of them. This, combined with the fine leadership and masterly handling of his force by Philip Vian, produced a heartening and thoroughly deserved victory from a situation in which, had the roles been reversed, it is unthinkable that the convoy or much of its escort would not have been destroyed.

III

Throughout the whole period the surface actions were in progress the convoy with its close escort was heavily attacked from the air. German J.U. 88 bombers, and Italian and German torpedo-bombers all took a hand. They attacked with resolution and skill; but accomplished nothing, apart from almost exhausting the ammunition of the escorts. This beating off of the heavy air attacks in heavy weather was a severe test of our gunnery and seamanship, as well as the endurance of the ships' companies. Vian told me that at one time, between the two surface actions, the sky over the convoy was black with aircraft and shell bursts. Even at a distance of 8 miles the sound of the 4-inch fire from the *Carlisle* and the 'Hunts' was like continuous pom-pom fire. At least five enemy aircraft were shot down, and others must have been damaged. The defeat of these terrific air attacks was one of the main features of the battle.

The two Malta ships, the *Penelope* and *Legion*, joined the convoy after dark, as did the damaged *Havock* and *Kingston*. The *Carlisle* and the six 'Hunt' destroyers also remained in company. At 7 p.m. Captain Hutchison, of H.M.S. *Breconshire*, the convoy Commodore, had obeyed the operation orders on his own initiative, and had dispersed his four ships on diverging courses to make the best of their way to Malta at full speed, each with a destroyer or two as escort. It was intended that they should reach the island at daylight on the 23rd; but the enforced detour to the south during the action gave the enemy bombers another chance. In spite of the gregale, and a thick and lowering dawn, aircraft appeared at daylight. The ships had to run the gauntlet of the aircraft attacks all the way to the entrance to the Grand Harbour, with the escorts, perilously short of ammunition, opening fire only when immediate danger threatened. Our fighters did good work, though greatly hampered by the weather and the damage caused to the airfields by continual bombing.

The Norwegian *Talabot* and the *Pampas* passed through the breakwater entrance soon after 9 a.m., each accompanied by a destroyer. Both ships had had narrow escapes two hours before, the *Pampas* actually being hit by bombs which failed to explode.

At 9.20 the *Breconshire*, having completed all but eight miles of her dangerous journey, and having survived a score of attacks, was hit in the engine-room and completely disabled. It was blowing a gale with a very heavy sea, and the *Carlisle* prepared to take her in tow while circling round engaging the enemy aircraft which continued to attack. Then the *Penelope* tried to take the *Breconshire* in tow; but all efforts were unsuccessful because of the bad weather and the deep draught of the damaged ship. Drifting towards the shore the *Breconshire* was anchored, and three destroyers remained to cover her.

At daylight the *Clan Campbell*, escorted by the *Eridge* was 50 miles south of Malta. Air attacks soon started, and at 10.30 the *Clan Campbell* was hit by a bomb which was dropped from a height of 50 feet. Her engine-room flooded, and she sank soon afterwards. The *Eridge* saved one hundred and twelve of the *Clan Campbell's* people, a difficult operation which took two and a half hours in the heavy weather prevailing. The *Legion*, ordered to join the *Clan Campbell*, was damaged by a near miss and had to be beached in Marsaxlokk.

While screening the *Breconshire* at anchor, the destroyer *Southwold* was mined and sunk in spite of the most determined efforts to save her. The *Breconshire* was eventually towed into Marsaxlokk during the night of the 24th–25th by the dockyard tug *Ancient*. Hit and set on fire on the 26th, she finally rolled over and sank soon after 11 a.m. on the 27th with part of her side under water. Much of her oil-fuel was afterwards saved by fitting valves to her exposed bottom.

Thus went the indomitable *Breconshire*, a fine ship most ably commanded by Captain C. A. G. Hutchison, who must look back with pride at the outstanding record of his ship during his period in command. Hutchison was a fine seaman and a stern disciplinarian; but inspired by their captain's example the officers and men of the *Breconshire* fought like tigers.

Meanwhile furious air attacks had developed upon Malta. The *Legion* was sunk on the 26th soon after reaching the Grand Harbour from Marsaxlokk. The *Talabot* and *Pampas* were also hit, the first-named having to be scuttled in case the cargo of ammunition should explode and wreck everything in the vicinity. All the holds in the *Pampas* but two were flooded. Apart from the *Breconshire's* oil fuel, only 5,000 tons of the nearly 26,000 tons of cargo which had been carried to Malta at such risk and price was safely unloaded.

The behaviour of all the personnel in the convoy was beyond all praise, as was the good handling of the merchant ships and the excellent work of the masters and of the naval liaison officers on board them. There is no doubt that the defeat of the heavy air attacks on the convoy on March 22nd was due in no small measure to the excellent seamanship and discipline of the men of the Merchant Navy.

IV

March was indeed a month of misfortune. Apart from Malta, we still had Tobruk very much on our minds. The U-boats were again active along the Libyan coast, and the port was under constant air attack. We had two merchant ships damaged, though our worse losses occurred on March 26th, when the destroyer *Jaguar* and the oiler *Slavol* were sunk by submarines.

The *Jaguar*, hit by two torpedoes at 4.45 a.m., sank at once, fifty-three of her ship's company being rescued. All the others were lost, including the commanding officer, Lieutenant-Commander L. R. K. Tyrwhitt. Originally in command of the *Hasty*, which had kept the sea in astonishing fashion, Tyrwhitt was one of the last of the destroyer captains who had been with us at the outbreak of the Italian war. An exceptionally able officer, modest and retiring, he kept himself always in the background. One heard little of him or his ship. Yet when I referred to his record during the past two years I found he had been in every operation of importance and had done consistently fine work. He was a great loss to the destroyer service.

But the heavy air attacks upon Malta gave us the greatest cause for anxiety. The savage increase in their intensity after the arrival of the convoy showed only too clearly that there was no further chance of using surface forces from the island while that scale of attack persisted. The dockyard was a shambles of rubble and twisted girders from shattered buildings, and they were nearly out of oil-fuel. The Vice-Admiral, Sir Ralph Leatham, therefore started getting away all the ships that could steam after patching them up as best he could.

The *Carlisle* and four 'Hunts' sailed for Alexandria on March 25th, and on their arrival I made them a signal: "Well done indeed. I am pleased to see you back." The cruiser *Aurora* and the 'Hunt' class destroyer *Avon Vale*, the latter having been damaged by a near miss and by collision with the *Breconshire*, left Malta for Gibraltar on the 29th; the *Havock* on April 5th; and the *Penelope* on April 8th. To the *Aurora* when she sailed I made a message wishing her ship's company good-bye and good luck, adding:

> At all times a serious threat to the enemy, *Aurora* has proven herself by her efficiency and gallantry in action to be well worthy of the name she bears and those who bore it before.

With the exception of the *Havock*, which unfortunately ran ashore at high speed near Kelibia, south of Cape Bon, and had to be destroyed by her ship's company, who were interned by the French, all these ships reached their destination without further damage. The sailing of these vessels from Malta represented a series of the most determined efforts on the part of both the ships themselves and the dockyard authorities in the face of heavy and continuous air attack. The *Penelope*, Captain A. D. Nicholl, who himself was wounded, had many casualties, including her gunnery officer. Her ship's company never left their guns, and she actually expended her outfit of anti-aircraft ammunition and had to be re-ammunitioned before she could sail.

Some destroyers, too badly damaged to sail, had to remain behind at Malta and were lost. The much-tried *Kingston* was destroyed in dock, and her distinguished captain, Commander Philip Somerville, killed. He was another great loss. The *Kingston's* shattered hull was later used to block the channel between St. Paul's and the main island, which was the end of a fine ship.

And so, to a great extent, the enemy had achieved his purpose. Malta was badly knocked about, though by no means down and out. Twice during the next month or so reinforcements of fighters were flown into the island. The submarines *Parthian, Regent, Rorqual, Porpoise* and *Cachalot* ran in vital supplies, and later the fast minelayer *Welshman* made a hazardous voyage with ammunition. But I anticipate. The point is that Malta held out. Nevertheless, it was a very close thing.

v

The passage of this convoy to Malta in March was the last operation that took place under my direction. In the middle of the month I had a message from the First Sea Lord telling me that it was proposed to send me to Washington to head the Admiralty delegation there. Earlier, at the end of January, Sir Dudley Pound had told me in a letter that during the visit of the Chiefs of Staff to the United States, just ended, they had made great progress in setting up the necessary organization to ensure close co-operation with the Americans. He said: "Before we left we had got a combined Chiefs of Staff combined planning and combined intelligence on a satisfactory footing." I was required to be the representative of the First Sea Lord on the Combined Chiefs of Staff committee.

As may be imagined, I was by no means anxious to go. I disliked leaving the Mediterranean Fleet, particularly at a time when their fortune was at its lowest ebb. I felt quite sure that Admiral Sir Charles Little, who was already in Washington, could fill the post far better than I could ever hope to do. However, I had made it a rule never to question any appointment. So on March 19th I wrote to the First Sea Lord:

> Your signal about Washington came rather as a surprise, although it had been my intention to write to you at the end of this month (two months short of my three years out here) and tell you that, though I was perfectly fit and ready to go on if desired, if you felt that a change was desirable

out here to make it without considering me. I was perfectly ready to go. As you say, there is now no fleet to go to sea in; but counting heads this is still the largest command. The personnel number over 25,000. . . . For the last nine months politico-strategical problems have occupied most of the Commander-in-Chief's time; but as I see it, one of his most difficult jobs is keeping up the morale of the sailors, the seagoing ones, in present circumstances. It is not easy to sit in an arm-chair and send ships out well knowing the time they are going to have until they return to harbour. If one went oneself it would make all the difference.

And so it was arranged. My relief was to be Admiral Sir Henry Harwood, and until he arrived in about two months time Admiral Pridham-Wippell was to be Commander-in-Chief, Mediterranean. I was enjoined to keep my departure as secret as possible as it was not desired to let the enemy know I had gone. This, of course, was a great compliment; but most unwelcome as it prevented me from going round the ships and saying good-bye to the sailors and thanking them for all the wonderful work they had done. However, as the next best thing, I left behind me three messages, one to the Fleet, one to the Merchant Navy, and one to Malta, to be promulgated as soon as the ban was lifted. I need not quote them in full; but I told them of the deep regret with which I laid down the command in the Mediterranean. It had been my greatest pride that throughout the war the Mediterranean Fleet had consistently shown itself the master of the enemy in every branch of naval warfare, whether in the air, against submarines, or in surface fighting. It was this factor that had enabled us during the last two years to impose our will on the enemy to a very high degree, despite his great preponderance in every class of ship and almost overwhelming strength in the air:

> This achievement of the officers and men of the Mediterranean Fleet in some two years of the most strenuous naval fighting on record is one which I greatly treasure, as greatly as I do the privilege of having led the fleet during that period. . . . The enemy knows we are his master on the sea, and we must strain every nerve to keep our standard of fighting so high that this lesson never fails to be borne in upon him. . . . Our world-wide commitments at present mean that we have not at times as large forces as we would like to carry the war to the enemy's front door. This will not always be so, and I look forward to the day when the Mediterranean Fleet will sweep the sea clear and re-establish an age-old control of this waterway so vital to the British Empire. I am confident that that day is not far distant, and meanwhile I wish you all good fortune and God speed.

When I drafted that signal I had no idea that in about seven months I should again be back in the Mediterranean, though at the western end of it.

To the officers and men of the Merchant Navy I sent the message:

> There is probably no theatre of war in which more tenacity and courage has been required of the Merchant Navy than in the Mediterranean. During my tenure of command I have seen innumerable instances of the unobtrusive yet sterling work of the Masters, officers and crews under conditions often of great difficulty and danger. It has been possible to keep an Army and Malta supplied only because the Merchant Navies have surmounted these difficulties. . . . I thank you for your good work which we in the Royal Navy fully appreciate and which we greatly admire.

I sent another message to the Vice-Admiral at Malta, mentioning that the defence of Malta was an epic which had been stressed from many sources; but that I wished to draw attention more to the other aspect, namely, that of the enormous damage done to the enemy for which the submarine, air and surface forces at Malta had so largely been responsible:

> The record (I said) has been magnificent, and I heartily thank every officer and man who has taken part, not forgetting those who have had the less spectacular, but none the less exacting, task of maintaining and bringing back into action our ships and aircraft to the discomfiture of the enemy. . . . The very extent of the success of the forces based on Malta has led to a ceaseless battering of the fortress, but one has only to think of the air effort the enemy is diverting to this purpose to realize that this is but another of the services that Malta is rendering to the Empire.

We spent little time in farewells. The Flag Officers and captains were kind enough to dine me on board the *Queen Elizabeth*, and the platform from which our train left for Cairo was crowded with officers. What I said in looking round those tried and trusted faces and in bidding them farewell I cannot remember. All I can recollect was what was in my heart. I felt poignantly overcome at leaving all my faithful friends and comrades, rather as though I had lost everything. I need not dwell upon it.

From Cairo, on April 3rd, we started for home by air—my wife; Richard Shelley, the Captain of the Fleet, who had been relieved; and my Flag Lieutenant, young Patrick Milligan who had relieved Hugh Lee a month or two earlier when Lee had gone home for a course at the signal school. General Auchinleck, Air Chief Marshal Tedder and Sir Walter Monckton, the acting Minister of State, very kindly came to see us off in our flying-boat. For those days I suppose the journey was reasonably comfortable, though I am not sure that my wife was favourably impressed with her introduction to air travel.

We went by flying-boat to Kartoum, where we spent the night with Major-General Sir Herbert Huddleston, Governor General of the Sudan. We travelled across Africa to Sierra Leone in a land 'plane, spending a night at Genefra and coming down next day for lunch at Kano in Nigeria. We voyaged under the name of Mr. and Mrs. Browne, though as we were usually met on our descents by an A.D.C. and conducted to Government House our incognito did not appear to be impenetrable. After some vicissitudes at Lisbon, where our flying-boat was commandeered for H.R.H. the Duke of Gloucester, we landed at Bristol in a Dutch aircraft and were met by the flag lieutenant to the Board of Admiralty. At Paddington I was surprised and very much touched to find the whole Board of Admiralty assembled to meet us with the exception of the First Sea Lord, who in a note expressed his regret at being absent because of Lady Pound's serious illness. Two days later I was entertained by the Board of Admiralty, a compliment which was as pleasant as unexpected. The Prime Minister did me the honour of being present.

England in war seemed a strange place after my long absence.

CHAPTER XXXVI

I

WE spent about ten days in London, where I had many consultations at the Admiralty and was put into the picture in regard to the work at Washington. There did not seem to be any real urgency in my arrival and many arrangements had to be made. Added to this I had been a long time abroad, and badly wanted some leave and a chance to see my family.

It had been decided to up-grade the Washington appointment. Admiral Sir Charles Little had been there since before the entry of the United States into the war, and had made an unique position and name for himself. Now, however, a larger staff was required to cope with the work of the Combined Chiefs of Staff, and it was decided to appoint a Rear-Admiral as our Admiral's Chief of Staff. I found that Rear-Admiral Wilfred Patterson had already been selected, and though I had never met him I was very willing to have him. A better choice could not have been made. Captain Royer M. Dick, from my staff in the Mediterranean, was to come to Washington as Deputy Chief of Staff.

I shook myself clear of London, and we went first to Wales and then to Edinburgh for short visits to relatives. Finally, we went to a small and very comfortable hotel in Rothiemay, near Huntley, Aberdeenshire, to fish and to spend ten days in perfect peace except for the visit of an officer from the Admiralty who came to collect my views on the question of the French fleet at Alexandria.

Back in London during the third week in May I found myself extremely busy at the Admiralty interviewing anyone who had any ideas of the line we should take in co-operating with the American Navy in Washington. I also became acquainted with the members of the United States delegations in London, and had some most interesting and informative talks in which I learned a lot. We summoned a young nephew of my wife's, Jim Byatt, to spend a week-end with us from his training establishment at Gosport. He was a leading seaman, hoping presently to become a sub-lieutenant R.N.V.R. in the Fleet Air Arm. Our flat was in Buckingham Gate, and people in St. James's Park were edified by seeing an Admiral walking and talking to a young man in bluejacket's uniform. And why not?

Our journey to the United States was constantly being postponed. First there was some difficulty about the 'plane, and then I was anxious to get my position and status over there fixed on a stable basis before I finally left London. Once I got there I knew I might write endless letters which would merely be pigeon-holed. Incidentally, the delay also gave us time to sort out our belongings. The difficulty was to know what to take and what to leave behind in store.

I had lunch with the Prime Minister and Mrs. Churchill at 10 Downing Street, and was invited to Chequers on the following Sunday for dinner and to spend the night. It was a small party of six all told, and after dinner we saw a film. Later I was conducted to the great man's study, where we had a long *tête-à-tête* talk. I found him most fascinating, and though we disagreed on various matters I was in thorough sympathy with his offensive outlook. Two convoys were being run to Malta at the time, one from Gibraltar and the other from Alexandria. We had a long discussion about their chances of getting through. I must have misled Mr. Churchill about the convoy from Alexandria, as I expressed a most optimistic view which was proved completely wrong in the light of what actually happened. The convoy from Alexandria had to turn back, and of the six ships that left Gibraltar only two reached Malta.

It was on my return from Scotland that I had been much surprised to find a personal letter from the Prime Minister informing me that it was his intention to submit my name to the King with the recommendation that His Majesty might be graciously pleased to approve that the dignity of a Baronetcy of the United Kingdom be conferred upon me in the forthcoming list of Birthday Honours.

I have never set much store by titles and I was very wishful of refusing. I went to see the First Sea Lord to ask if I could refuse. I found that Sir Dudley Pound, with great kindness, had been pressing for it, and he also pointed out to me that the men of the Mediterranean Fleet might regard this honour as a tribute to their work during my period in command. So I accepted the dignity with this very much in my mind.

We managed to pay a hasty visit to our house in Bishop's Waltham. It was let, of course, and though the house appeared to be very full of people, it was being fairly well kept. We later discovered that the agent we employed had let the house to a Southsea landlady who had been bombed out and had removed herself and her lodgers to Bishop's Waltham. Hence the large number of people we saw. Our old Scottish maid, to our great sorrow, had died while we were abroad.

June 21st still saw us in London, our air passage being put off from day to day. The Prime Minister had asked me to travel with him by sea; but I had refused. His invitation did not include my wife, and I did not think she would care to fly the Atlantic without me.

Finally we got away on June 23rd and flew from Bristol to Foynes. Here we had an amusing experience as we were about to embark in the flying-boat for the Transatlantic crossing. We were again travelling incognito with a false passport which set us out as Mr. and Mrs. Bissett-Christie, supposedly travelling on government service. The Eire military at Foynes had us in in turn for questioning before we were allowed to embark. The Irish colonel asked my name and business, to which I replied that I was Mr. Bissett-Christie of the Board of Education. "That's curious," said he. "You're down on this paper of mine as a naval officer!" Considerably taken aback I answered: "That must be a clerical error." He grinned and made no further ado, and we were soon on board. We took off at 11 p.m. and had a very comfortable flight, except for the long hiatus between meals. We had had our dinner at 6 p.m.; but the clocks went back six hours during the night, and breakfast was not served until 8 a.m. next morning. An interval of twenty hours between meals does not suit me.

Our flight to New York was non-stop, unusual for those days, and occupied just twenty-five hours. There was more trouble on landing. Our proper passports were sealed up in the Embassy bag and could not be got at, and there we were arriving in the United States with false credentials.

However, the interviewing officials, after pulling my leg for some time, knew quite well who we were, and we were glad to find that the American Navy had sent a 'plane to take us straight on to Washington. So after being bombarded by questions from a horde of pressmen with photographers' flashlights going off all round us we finally got away, to land at Washington at about 10.30 p.m. Here we were met by Admiral Sir Charles and Lady Little, and taken to the Wardman Park Hotel, where they were also staying.

II

The next few days were spent in an unending round of official calls, conducted by Charles Little. I met Mr. Stimson, Secretary for War; Mr. Knox, Secretary for the Navy; General Marshall; Admiral King, and many others. Before leaving, the Littles also gave a large party to enable us to meet the more junior officers and officials. Mr. Churchill, who had arrived in Washington, himself took me to pay my respects to the President by whom I was greatly charmed and impressed.

Before we had left London the news from the Middle East had been most depressing, and our thoughts were much on what was happening out there. In the course of a conversation with the Prime Minister in Washington, we had discussed the question of Tobruk if the Army was pushed right back. I remember telling him that at a meeting of the Commanders-in-Chief in Cairo in January, after the enemy's counter-attack in the El Agheila area, we had come to the firm and unanimous decision that Tobruk should not again be held. I do not recollect the actual discussion; but after the naval losses we had incurred in keeping the fortress supplied for eight months I had a good deal to say on the subject. The general opinion was that Tobruk should not be held. Mr. Churchill regarded the abandonment of Tobruk with scorn, and said it must be held. On June 20th, three days before we left for the United States, Tobruk fell to the enemy with considerable loss of men and valuable material. Bardia, Sollum, Sidi Barrani and Mersa Matruh were occupied by the enemy in turn, and by June 30th our Army had fallen back to the position at El Alamein.

In America we had news that we had lost a considerable part of our armour during the retreat. With remarkable promptitude and generosity the American Chiefs of Staff decided to send out a considerable number of the new Sherman tanks with which one of their divisions had recently been equipped. Their great supply chief, General Somervell, had them loaded in four fast ships, which were on their way to the Middle East round the Cape within a few weeks. When one of these ships was sunk by a submarine he at once loaded up another faster vessel, so that they all arrived at much the same time. I was greatly impressed by such spontaneous and open-handed generosity, which should never be forgotten.

To revert to more mundane topics, however, we did not stay long in the Wardman Park Hotel, which was too expensive for our pockets. Instead we took a flat, or I should say an 'apartment', though as we could only get casual help we had to do most of the chores ourselves. Fortunately we discovered that my new flag lieutenant, a young officer of the R.N.V.R. who had served as a signalman in a trawler, had been excellently brought up and was unsurpassed at washing up and cleaning white shoes. My wife spent most of her days searching for a house; but it was not until well on in July that she found a suitable one. We moved in on August 1st, with rather a curious *ménage*, our staff consisting of Sackett, my chief steward, who had been with me at Chatham; Chief Petty Officer Percy Watts, my coxswain; a Chinese steward, Ah Ping, stranded from a British cruiser; a coloured cook and a coloured maid. The cook was a character. When my wife said she hoped the kitchen would be kept clean, the cook replied: "Mam, cleanliness comes next to Godliness, and I am a Christian woman."

My duties in Washington were not particularly exacting. They consisted principally in keeping in close touch with the Navy Department, and in sharing all our views and troubles. The Chief of Staff, Patterson, was a great success, and very soon established the friendliest relations with his American colleagues. The British Mission was headed by General Sir John Dill, whom, of course, I knew well. He was a most charming man of outstanding character and ability. It was a pleasure to work with him, and I greatly admired his calm and balanced outlook on the war. He was a bosom friend of General Marshall's, and it is quite impossible to over-estimate the value of that friendship to our relations with our great ally. The more I saw of John Dill the more I admired him and valued his staunch comradeship.

I saw a good deal of Admiral Ernest King, my American opposite number.

A man of immense capacity and ability, quite ruthless in his methods, he was not an easy person to get on with. He was tough and liked to be considered tough, and at times became rude and overbearing. It was not many weeks before we had some straight speaking over the trifling matter of lending four or five American submarines for work on our side of the Atlantic. He was offensive, and I told him what I thought of his method of advancing allied unity and amity. We parted friends. It is only fair to say that at the time he was wrapped up in the naval operations in the Pacific against the Japanese in which the United States Navy was having its ups and downs. On the whole I think Ernest King was the right man in the right place, though one could hardly call him a good co-operator. Not content with fighting the enemy, he was usually fighting someone on his own side as well.

General Marshall I liked and admired immensely. One did not need to be long in his company before recognizing his sincerity and honesty of purpose. He could be obstinate enough; but would always listen to another point of view.

General Arnold, head of the Army Air Force, also sat with the American Chiefs of Staff, and a few weeks after my arrival Admiral Leahy, the President's Chief of Staff, took the chair. Leahy was a charming and courteous man who made an excellent chairman, smoothing out difficulties and calming any approaching storm.

The other members of our British Mission were Major General Macready and Air Vice Marshal Sir Douglas Evill.

I also renewed my acquaintance with Lord Halifax, our Ambassador, whom I had not seen since Munich days. It was not long before one realized the unique position that he and Lady Halifax had built up in America. My admiration for him as the very best type of Englishman remains unbounded.

The social side of our work was definitely a burden. Every Friday, after lunching with them, we had a meeting with the American Chiefs of Staff and discussed any questions referred to us from home, or any matters that they wished us to refer to our Chiefs in London. Our own organization was run on much the same lines as the Chiefs of Staffs Committee at home, and we had as Secretary Colonel Dykes, a most able man afterwards unfortunately killed in an air accident. The Americans had adopted a very similar organization, and their Secretary, Brigadier-General Bedell Smith, was an outstanding man full of knowledge with a great flair for getting on with people. He was never taken aback. He possessed a profound sense of humour, and had a ready and witty answer to everything and a wise-crack for each and every occasion.

We at home have our inter-service rivalries and jealousies; but the dislike existing between the American Army and Navy was an eye-opener to me and was carried to extraordinary lengths. I sometimes wondered if it was drilled into the embryo officers at West Point and Annapolis. General Marshall,

Admiral Stark and a few other senior officers were above this constant and acrimonious bickering; but I do not think the same could be said of many others. It was a great pity.

Over and above these engagements we also had a weekly meeting at the British Embassy, when the Ambassador assembled the heads of all the British missions in Washington. The military chiefs gave a short exposition of military affairs, while we heard all about the work and progress of the other missions, economic, shipping and so forth. The meetings provided the means for a most useful exchange of information.

At the time of my arrival in Washington the German U-boats were causing the most serious losses to the Allied shipping up and down the east coast of the United States and in the Caribbean. The reason was undoubtedly the shortage and inexperience of the escort craft and aircraft, while the Americans had nothing analogous to our Coastal Command. The majority of anti-submarine aircraft were Army bombers, which were inefficient for and unaccustomed to work over the sea. Moreover, the Army were quite intolerant of any naval control over their aircraft.

As I wrote to the First Sea Lord on July 31st: "The fact is they are in a mess. The Army have, I believe, demanded that they should conduct the aerial anti-submarine war, and I believe at one time demanded that our Hudson squadron should be put under them." I was asked for my views, and as I told Sir Dudley Pound, "the line I have suggested to them on the main issue is that it really doesn't matter who is the head of their aerial anti-submarine effort provided it is all under one organization and that that organization is under the operational control of the Navy Department."

The Hudson squadron mentioned was one of our highly trained squadrons of Coastal Command, Royal Air Force, sent to help, and to show how anti-submarine work should be carried out in the light of their long experience on the other side of the Atlantic. At the same time we also had a flotilla or two of British anti-submarine vessels working under the American Navy on their east coast.

I remember that soon after our arrival I had to give a big press interview at the Press Club, while a few days later I lunched at the Oversea Press Club. At the latter function I seized the opportunity of implying that all was not well with their anti-submarine organization, and stressed the vital need for an all-out effort against the U-boats, while hinting at the desirability of unity of command in American waters in this particular sphere. I was heavily cross-examined; but hope I came through the barrage of searching questions without discredit. During my talk I was somewhat perturbed to see two or three American Admirals among the company. However, they came up afterwards and told me that I had said what really wanted saying. Several of the newspapers took up the subject in their leaders.

Later in the war the American Navy provided their own anti-submarine aircraft and all was peace. But before the war it was the rule that all aircraft with wheels not fitted for landing on carriers belonged to the Army Air Force, even though they might be called upon to operate over the sea.

III

The American Chiefs of Staff went to England in July to discuss offensive operations which the President had ordered for 1942. In general, the Americans had fixed their eyes on a landing in Northern France as the surest and most rapid method of defeating Germany. Mr. Churchill and the British Chiefs of Staff favoured a landing in North Africa, and did not believe that a cross-channel invasion of Northern France was possible before 1944. It was doubtful if there were sufficient trained troops to undertake the landing, or the shipping or reinforcements to exploit it. Finally, after discussing all the alternatives, the landing in North Africa was decided upon. Thereafter the matter was continually under review between the staffs in both countries, and Mr. Roosevelt decided it should take place by October 30th.

The United States Chiefs of Staff had returned from Great Britain rather dissatisfied. They were not really enthusiastic about the North African operation to be known as 'Torch'. Indeed, on August 12th I wrote to the First Sea Lord saying that this lack of keenness "would not matter a row of pins; but it reacts on 'Torch', for which there are few signs of enthusiasm, and they do not seem to be getting down to it though they pay lip service to the usefulness of the operation. I may be overstressing this; but I feel that at the moment there is not the whole-hearted enthusiasm so necessary to produce success. I am quite sure that King is dead against it, and that he has given it as his opinion that it is of no value to the war effort of the United Nations, and this opinion of his is reflected all through the Navy Department." Admiral King, I think, rather regarded any forces sent to the European theatre as wasted because they were not fighting the Japanese in the Pacific.

This was how I regarded it at the time, and it was certainly difficult to get things moving, though we had considerable discussion on the question of command. Lieutenant-General Eisenhower had already been nominated as Supreme Commander, with Brigadier General Bedell Smith as his Chief of Staff.

The question of the Naval command aroused considerable divergencies of opinion. Broadly speaking there were three points of view:

(a) A Naval Commander-in-Chief under the Supreme Commander of the whole expedition and directing operations alongside the latter in close consultation.

(b) A Naval officer of comparatively junior rank on the staff of the Commanding General.

(c) A Naval officer of high standing on the staff of the Commanding General as his naval adviser or Naval Chief of Staff.

Each of these three arrangements had their own supporters. My own view which I always held was that (a) was the only possible solution.

At the end of July Bedell Smith came to have a heart-to-heart talk with me. He was enthusiastic for the 'Torch' operation; but had little encouragement from the United States Navy Department. As he explained, his reason for coming to see me was to get a naval opinion as to the effect the Allied occupation of North Africa would have upon the Naval and shipping position as a whole. Admiral King apparently had stated that it would have little or no effect, hence Bedell Smith's desire for an independent opinion. I told him that the gain accruing from complete success was just incalculable from every point of view. Among other things Italy was the weak partner in the Axis, and if we could occupy the whole North African seaboard from Egypt to Spanish Morocco, Italy at once lay open to invasion. She was what the Prime Minister later referred to as the "soft under-belly of the Axis". Airfields along the whole stretch of the North African coast would eventually give us dominance in the air, and enable us again to pass convoys through the Mediterranean. I need not go into all the matters we talked about; but we naturally discussed the reactions of the French in Algeria and Tunisia. Incidentally, Bedell Smith told me that both Marshall and Eisenhower were all out for 'Torch'.

Bedell Smith also expressed the view that it was of the greatest importance to have as the Naval Commander-in-Chief an Admiral who was wholeheartedly in favour of the operation. He sounded me as to whether I would take on the appointment. I replied very guardedly. I did not know the views of the British Government or the First Sea Lord. However, I did say that if it was thought that I could be of use I should be proud to serve under an American Supreme Commander. In writing to the First Sea Lord on July 31st I mentioned what had been said during this interview, and told him I did not in any way wish to put myself forward; but if it was thought I could be of use I would be more than willing to serve as Naval Commander-in-Chief.

John Dill also expressed the view to me that I should go as Naval Commander-in-Chief. As for me, I was already sated with the rather detached atmosphere of Washington and my office desk. I really yearned to be up and doing again, though I was not going to thrust myself forward, especially as the First Sea Lord might already have made his own and another selection.

Actually several messages on the subject passed between us. Sir Dudley Pound's first intention had been not to have a Naval Commander-in-Chief.

Three separate commands were involved: the actual command of the naval part of the expedition; the command of the battle-fleet and other ships covering the landings; and the command at Gibraltar, which must inevitably play a great part in launching and providing for an expedition to occupy North Africa. Gibraltar also had commitments in regard to the convoys in the Atlantic, and I think the First Sea Lord was in some doubt about placing it under a Supreme Commander.

To me, however, it was not a practical proposition to expect the Supreme Commander to deal with three separate Naval Commanders, and I urged on Sir Dudley Pound that he must have one Admiral in whom the Supreme Commander could confidently place the command of all the naval part of the expedition, Gibraltar included.

At the end of August General Dill went home to give our Chiefs of Staff the exact progress about 'Torch' in the United States and the views of the American Chiefs of Staff. The situation was not clear, and the preparations were still rather hanging fire. As yet there was no firm decision as to where the forces should land, and delay was being caused by obvious differences of opinion between the United States Army and Navy.

While Dill was at home I consulted my British colleagues on this matter of delay in the preparations for 'Torch'. With their agreement I asked for a discussion on the subject at one of our weekly meetings with the American Chiefs of Staff. The conference room was cleared except for the Chiefs of Staff and representatives, and we had a most interesting and full review of the whole matter, covering also the questions of command and the best places for the troops to land.

The American Chiefs of Staff appeared to be highly nervous of the attitude of Spain, and I was closely examined as to how we were to maintain forces in the Mediterranean if the Franco government came into the war against us. Gibraltar might be besieged, and the whole of the Spanish coast, as well as Spanish Morocco, might be hostile territory. I held the personal view that Franco had already lost his chance of coming into the war with any likelihood of gain. I did not consider that he would now move against any Anglo-American occupation of North Africa. Moreover, if he did, the Spanish coastal cities and towns were notoriously susceptible to the pressure of sea power and to air attack, so the Franco government might get more than they bargained for. Furthermore, if our forces moved with sufficient speed we could seize the north coast of Morocco, and with one side of the Straits of Gibraltar in our hands, I felt sure we could pass our convoys into the Mediterranean. I also expressed the view that if we were bold enough we could go as far east as Tunisia and land at Bizerta. This last suggestion aroused no enthusiasm. The American Navy considered we might be hard pressed even to maintain ourselves as far east as Algiers.

Though no decisions were reached at this particular meeting, the discussion cleared the air and left our American colleagues in no doubt as to what was in our minds.

I had another interview with President Roosevelt early in August, when Admiral King and myself were sent for together. Among other matters the President wanted to know about the heavy losses in the last convoy to North Russia, P.Q.17. It was not very easy to explain, as I had received no details. Nor had Admiral King. But in an interview lasting about twenty minutes we also discussed other more general matters, including the preparations for 'Torch'. When I left the President's office I was hemmed in by the Press. I got away by telling them that Admiral King would tell them everything when he emerged. However, he was the complete sphinx and told them nothing.

Towards the end of August, and in the beginning of September the affairs of 'Torch' brightened and began to take definite shape. It was decided to land inside the Mediterranean at Algiers and Oran, and outside the Mediterranean at Casablanca. I personally thought that Casablanca was a bit of a gamble because of the surf. The number of days in the year in which landing on an open beach is possible in that neighbourhood are very few. However, the decision to land there was a concession to the fear that the Spanish coasts in the Straits might be held against us.

I heard definitely that I was to be the Allied Naval Commander of the Expeditionary Force, A.N.C.X.F. for short.

The command of the Casablanca landing caused some further discussion. Admiral King wanted it to be independent of the main expedition, and under the command of the American Commander-in-Chief, Atlantic. This was an impossible attitude to take up with myself as General Eisenhower's principal Naval adviser, so to speak. King, however, always had a rooted antipathy to placing United States naval forces under British command, though he raised no objection to British forces and units being under United States command whenever he thought it fit and proper. Finally we came to a compromise. The Casablanca force was to be placed under the American Commander-in-Chief, Atlantic, until it passed a certain longtitude, when it became subject to the orders of the Supreme Commander, General Eisenhower. However, the chain of naval command was always a little nebulous, though I always took it that the Casablanca naval force was under me. In the Mediterranean itself there was no question about it.

For the Casablanca landing General Patton was to be in command of the troops and Vice-Admiral H. Kent Hewitt in command of the Navy.

In the middle of September, Vice-Admiral Sir Bertram Ramsay, who had been appointed Deputy Naval Commander, Expeditionary Force, came to Washington to see me, and to meet the American Chiefs of Staff. Long before I knew I was to have anything to do with 'Torch' Ramsay had asked me if I could recommend any good staff officers. I told him to collect any of my Mediterranean staff that were available, and he had acquired Commanders

Geoffrey Barnard and T. M. Brownrigg, both officers of great operational experience and exceptional attainments. He brought the latter to Washington with him, and I remember that my wife and I took Ramsay and Brownrigg out to dine at a well-known restaurant twenty miles out of the city. From the menu one ordered a chump chop and the other steak. Their faces when they were served with gargantuan helpings were worth seeing.

Apart from the actual planning, we had many conferences among ourselves and with the Americans. We had, among other things, to thrash out various tricky questions of command. Ramsay and I were also bidden to the White House one night after dinner and sat talking with the President and Harry Hopkins for nearly three hours. We talked principally of 'Torch' and kindred affairs. It was a fascinating evening, and I hope our optimism impressed the great man. I was much interested in the way in which Harry Hopkins's questions always went to the root of the matter under discussion. He was not to be put off by vague generalities, not that we tried to shirk straight answers; but he wanted facts and definite opinions.

I now had to provide myself with a Chief of Staff, as Wilfred Patterson, to his great disappointment, had to remain in Washington to carry on the naval business on my departure, no relief for me being readily available. It did not take me long to ask the Admiralty for Captain R. M. Dick, whom I knew to be a brilliant officer. He had worked with me for three years and knew me and my methods, or perhaps I should say lack of method. He was much liked by, and got on very well with, the Americans, particularly Bedell Smith, Eisenhower's Chief of Staff. Dick had also been in on the 'Torch' discussions from the very beginning, while as we were about to land in French territory his intimate knowledge of French would be highly useful. He was, of course, very junior for the appointment; but that did not worry me. The First Sea Lord acquiesced at once, and Dick was appointed Chief Chief of Staff with the rank of Commodore.

On September 20th Dick and I flew over to Great Britain in a bomber, not the most comfortable form of transportation, though speedy. We spent about twelve days in England, very busy conferring, planning and so on. I found time to go to Wales for a day to see my two aunts. His Majesty also sent for me. Of course the whole operation 'Torch' was being kept secret; but my connection with it was even more secret and was unknown except to a very few. I was supposed to be in England for consultations in the ordinary line of business.

Early in October I flew back to Washington, this time more comfortably in an American Army 'plane. After clearing off all necessary business I finally left America on October 11th, delighted to be getting away from the hothouse atmosphere of Washington and actively back into the war. Rather to her disgust my wife had to remain in Washington as part of the cover-plan to give the impression that I was returning in due course.

Our flight across the Atlantic was even more uncomfortable than the previous one. It was bitterly cold and the bomber was unheated, and we heard the ice rattling off the wings. On our arrival at Prestwick I found my sponge frozen hard inside my suitcase. It reminded me of the old days on the bridge of a destroyer in the North Sea in mid-winter.

All through our sojourn in Washington affairs in the Middle East were much in our thoughts. We had heard with dismay of the retreat to El Alamein, and the naval exodus from Alexandria. We had mourned the loss of the *Eagle* in a convoy to Malta from the west, a fine old ship which had done an outstanding job during the war and had paid an ample dividend. Our anxiety about Malta grew. We knew how short were the supplies of all sorts in the island, and we entered with even more zest into the preparations for operation 'Torch' which, if successful, would mean the end of Malta's trial and our freedom of the Mediterranean.

CHAPTER XXXVII

I

By the middle of October, 1942, unhindered by any need to return to Washington, I was able really to get down to the more or less detailed arrangements for 'Torch', the Allied landing in North Africa. Time was very short and quite inadequate to give the crews of the landing craft any thorough training; but this had to be accepted.

The actual date of the landing was governed by two factors; the desire to bring early relief to the Russians by the establishment of the 'Second Front', and the need for making the assaults before there was any real deterioration in the weather. We also needed a reasonable time to organize and prepare the various naval and other forces, particularly the merchant shipping. D-day, which had originally been fixed for October 30th, had in mid-September been advanced to November 4th. On September 26th, however, an aircraft on the way to Gibraltar was reported overdue, and soon afterwards the body of a naval officer was washed ashore near Cadiz. He was carrying an official letter for the Governor of Gibraltar giving the date of the operation and saying that General Eisenhower would arrive at Gibraltar two or three days beforehand. Another letter on the body had apparently been opened by the action of sea water. As articles from the crashed aircraft were still coming ashore, the Governor of Gibraltar thought it possible that other documents of a compromising nature might have come into the hands of the Spanish authorities. His warning reached England on September 28th, and D-day for 'Torch' was postponed until November 8th, the latest date when it was considered feasible to land the American troops on the open Moroccan beaches near Casablanca.

By the time I became implicated in the arrangements the naval planning had already reached a certain stage of readiness under the able direction of Admiral Sir Bertram Ramsay. The naval forces and the ships to carry the troops were allocated. So were the necessary convoys for the subsequent build-up of supplies and reinforcements, though because of the continual losses inflicted by the U-boats the actual ships were constantly having to be altered. The ports of departure had been arranged, and the shipping was in process of concentration. Intensive training of the landing craft crews and of a small proportion of troops in amphibious operations was also being carried out at the Combined Training Centre near Inverary in western Scotland. Admiral Sir Bertram Ramsay, who was assisting me, paid many visits of inspection to see the training in progress.

But while all these preliminary arrangements were in train there was little actually on paper in its final form. The Naval plan had not been written, and all the complicated movements and details laid down and co-ordinated in the form of operation orders. This was a monumental task, and as the time available was very limited I decided it required special treatment.

I already had three members of my old Mediterranean staff in London with me—Commodore R. M. Dick, and Commanders T. M. Brownrigg and Geoffrey Barnard. I came to the conclusion that the only way to get the plan written was to augment these three knowledgeable officers with a fourth from my Mediterranean team, Commander M. L. Power, who had written many a plan for us and was a master of clear and concise exposition. At the time he was commanding a destroyer in the Home Fleet. While I knew he would not be particularly pleased to leave his ship I felt he would readily answer the call to come and help. So with the permission of the Admiralty I signalled to Admiral Sir John Tovey, Commander-in-Chief, Home Fleet, asking for Power to be released. He was sent off at once, and after a few days during which he was put into the picture, Dick, Brownrigg, Barnard and Power set to work with eight Wrens, and the necessary documents were completed and printed just in time for issue before the ships sailed. I think Power was responsible for most of the co-ordination, and I believe he dictated for about four days almost without stopping with four Wren stenographers on duty and another four standing off and waiting to come on. Commander L. G. Durlacher, a clever and most able signal officer, wrote the signal orders, which were almost as complicated and detailed as the others. All this preliminary work was done at Norfolk House in St. James's Square, where we worked in the closest contact with the Americans, as well as at the Admiralty.

The operation orders represented a masterly piece of work issued in eight parts. We were not directly concerned with the planning of the American landing near Casablanca. Our orders involved the sailing, routeing, exact timing, and arrival at their respective landing places inside the Mediterranean at Oran and Algiers of two advance convoys of some forty-five ships, to be followed by a main body of more than two hundred vessels with a hundred escorts carrying some 38,500 British and American troops of the first flights with all their impedimenta. Over and above this the orders laid down the movements and duties of all the purely naval forces inside the Mediterranean, which, apart from more than a hundred vessels at Gibraltar, meant another one hundred and seventy-six vessels of all types from battleships and aircraft-carriers to submarines, sloops, corvettes and motor launches.

Gibraltar would be the hinge-pin of the whole operation. To ensure the passage of something more than four hundred ships through the Straits only eight miles wide within a limited period of time was the problem upon which all else depended. The orders provided for this, as well as for the refuelling of smaller vessels at Gibraltar. The whole large-scale movement was extremely complicated, and success depended upon rigid adherence to a time-table.

I was kept very busy in other directions, particularly in meeting people. As I wrote to a relative: "I seem to have spent a week of lunching or dining." I remember dining at 10 Downing Street with two American Generals, and the Prime Minister being full of new ideas for confounding our enemies. Then the conversation switched to the battles of the American Civil War, about which Mr. Churchill's knowledge was amazing. I confided to my relative that I thought him "an extraordinary man!"

I recollect a large luncheon party I gave for the American Admirals and Generals at which Sir Dudley Pound was present, and a dinner in the Painted Hall at Greenwich in which General Smuts was the guest of the Board of Admiralty. These more or less social engagements were rather tiring on top of a full day's work; but they all had a utilitarian purpose.

During this period I naturally saw a good deal of Lieutenant-General Eisenhower. Looking back to the day I first met him I remember being most favourably impressed. I liked him at once. He struck me as being completely sincere, straightforward and very modest. In those early days I rather had the impression that he was not very sure of himself; but who could wonder at that. He was in supreme command of one of the greatest amphibious operations of all time, and was working in a strange country with an Ally whose methods were largely unfamiliar. But as time went on Eisenhower grew quickly in stature, and it was not long before one recognized him as the really great man he is—forceful, able, direct and foreseeing with great charm of manner, and always with a rather naive wonder at attaining the high position in which he found himself. We soon became fast friends, and I can only hope that he had for me some of the great esteem and personal affection I had for him. From the very beginning he set Anglo-American unity and friendship as his aim, and not only on the surface. He left nothing undone to advance it. The staffs were closely integrated, and it was not long before its British and American members ceased to look at each other like warring tom-cats, and came to discover that the nationals of both countries had brains, ideas and drive.

For my part I was quite determined that nothing should stand in the way of this vital unity of thought and purpose, and I hope I and my staff succeeded. At times we were sorely tried. To our way of thinking the Americans are more given than ourselves to calling a spade a spade without troubling to wrap it up in polite verbiage. On the whole our relations with the United States Army were more cordial than with the Navy. I have no greater friends than many United States naval officers; but a few of them had a habit of always being right in their own opinions, which in the light of our considerable war and operational experience was galling in the extreme. I again met Admiral H. R. Stark, 'Betty' to his intimates, for whom I have a great admiration. We became, and remain, firm friends, and I can think of no American who did more for Anglo-American harmony than did Stark during his service in England.

We met and became friends with all the American Generals. Mark Clark, a tall, fine-looking man nicknamed the 'American Eagle' by Mr. Churchill, probably on account of his rather predatory-looking nose, acted as Chief of Staff to Eisenhower before the arrival of Bedell Smith. A most able and energetic officer he was nominated as Deputy Supreme Commander, though at Gibraltar and in the early days at Algiers his duties were more those of a Chief of Staff. Brigadier-General Alfred M. Gruenther, head of the United States Army planners, always timely and original with his wisecracks, was most popular with us all.

Eisenhower also had two American naval officers on his staff, Rear-Admiral B. H. Bieri and Captain Gerauld Wright, who were both excellent officers. I do not exactly know what was their precise function; but it may have been for liaison duties with the American Casablanca force under Rear-Admiral H. Kent Hewitt U.S.N., which itself was under the ultimate command of Admiral Royal E. Ingersoll, Commander-in-Chief, Atlantic Fleet, to whose command all Admiral Hewitt's vessels belonged.

The British General in command of the British First Army, which was to follow up the first landing at Algiers, was Lieutenant-General Kenneth Anderson. A Scot, very direct and outspoken, he was not everybody's man; but I liked and thought a lot of him. His operations in mountainous Tunisia during the rain and mud of the difficult winter of 1942–43 showed him up as a fine fighting soldier. Air Marshal Sir William Welsh was in command of the Royal Air Force, and Lieutenant-General James Doolittle in charge of the United States Army Air Force.

I do not propose to go into any great detail of Operation 'Torch', the British naval share in which is fully set out in my despatch of March 30th, 1943, which, with the reports of Vice-Admiral Sir Harold Burrough and Commodore Thomas H. Troubridge, commanding the Eastern and Centre Naval Task Forces for the attacks upon Algiers and Oran, is printed as a Supplement to the London Gazette of March 22nd, 1949. Very briefly, the Americans were to land at three places in the Casablanca area, while the landings at Oran and Algiers were under the charge of the Royal Navy. Incidentally, Admiral Burrough's force was to consist of 67 warships and 25 merchant vessels, and Commodore Troubridge's of 70 warships and 34 merchant vessels.

Force 'H', consisting of the battleships *Duke of York* and *Rodney*; the battle-cruiser *Renown*; the aircraft-carriers *Victorious*, *Formidable* and *Furious*; the cruisers *Bermuda*, *Argonaut* and *Sirius*, and seventeen destroyers, was under the command of Vice-Admiral Sir Neville Syfret in the *Duke of York*. Rear-Admiral A. L. St. G. Lyster had his flag in the *Victorious*. Force 'H' had the duty of covering both British Task Forces and their 'follow-up' convoys against attack from the sea by Italian or Vichy-French naval forces, while unless strong enemy forces were at sea the *Rodney*, *Furious* and three destroyers were to be detached at 6 a.m. on D-day to join Commodore Troubridge. One cruiser could be sent to reinforce Admiral Burrough at Algiers.

I should add that both the Eastern and Centre Task Forces had cruisers and destroyers for close cover and bombarding, with aircraft-carriers to provide fighter cover for the landings.

II

Reports from North Africa led us to believe that the British were much disliked by the French, whereas there was no such antipathy for the Americans. These reports mostly came from Mr. Robert D. Murphy, the representative of the American State Department in North Africa. So it was decided that the landings were to appear as almost entirely American, and that the first troops to go ashore were to be American so, if possible, to reassure the French that our intentions were entirely pacific. In actual fact this difference in feeling towards the Americans and ourselves was much exaggerated. Those Frenchmen who were anti-Vichy cared not at all whether it was the British or the Americans who had come to help them, and vice versa. Indeed, the hardest resistance of all was to the Americans at Casablanca. The French Navy certainly had cause to dislike us, and in all three ports they resisted energetically to the Allied landings in November, 1942. However, when the fighting died down the reception of both British and Americans was uniformly cordial.

Murphy was in touch with some French Generals and others who were anti-Vichy, and during October these Frenchmen asked for a meeting with American representatives. On October 19th Major-General Mark Clark, Brigadier-General Lemnitzer, Colonel Holmes and Hamblen, with Captain Gerauld Wright, U.S.N., were embarked at Gibraltar by H.M. Submarine P.219, Lieutenant N. L. A. Jewell. The party was landed in folboats on the coast about fifty miles west of Algiers on the night of October 21st–22nd.

I need not describe the dramatic circumstances of this meeting, which was amply publicized soon afterwards; but it was successful. General René Mast, Chief of Staff to General Juin in command of the French Military forces in the Algiers area, informed Clark that with four days' notice he could guarantee that little or no resistance to a landing would be offered by the French Army or Air Force, and that he would guarantee free entry into Bone. No actual changes in the plans for 'Torch' came about as the result of this mission. However, it was very encouraging, and was followed by an arrangement with General Giraud, who had escaped from a German prison in April and was in unoccupied France, to co-operate with the Allies.

But no co-operation could be expected from the French Navy. As I had already discovered from my dealings with Admiral Godfroy at Alexandria, the Navy had been in a peculiar psychological state since the surrender of France. Most of the senior officers regarded Admiral Darlan as their titular leader, and were loyal to Marshal Pétain as the head of the French Government. Moreover, they were embittered against us, the British, because of our attacks upon their ships at Oran and Dakar, while we had also fought against the French in Syria. This could not be overlooked. The French Navy manned most of the coastal defences in North Africa.

It was also highly important that, if possible, the harbour installations and shipping in the ports of Algiers and Oran should not be destroyed before our forces gained control of them, so two enterprises were prepared, one for each port. The idea was for two small ships, the destroyers *Broke* and *Malcolm* at Algiers, and the ex-American coastguard cutters *Walney* and *Hartland* at Oran, both carrying American troops, should rush the harbour defences and land troops to occupy the batteries and key points and to seize all merchant shipping.

Here I may say that the timing of the assault upon the harbour defences at Oran came under fierce criticism from Rear-Admiral A. C. Bennett U.S.N., the officer who was detailed to take charge at Oran after its capture. His method of drawing attention to his disagreement rather illustrated the confusion that existed in some people's minds as to the proper chain of naval command, which was due, no doubt, to Admiral King's intense dislike of putting American naval units under British naval orders. Instead of taking the normal procedure and coming to discuss it with me or Commodore Troubridge, the officer commanding the assault at Oran, Bennett adopted the unusual course of writing direct to General Eisenhower, who very properly sent the letter on to me. While not much caring for the method in which the matter was raised I considered there was something to be said for Bennett's criticisms. The time for the direct assault on the harbour was too rigidly fixed, so the orders were modified to give Commodore Troubridge a free hand as to the moment the attack should be launched.

This is just an instance of the slight friction that arose on one or two points, and usually with the United States Navy. It came, I think, from the American custom of always expecting written orders to be obeyed to the letter. Our Navy, on the other hand, perhaps with the memory of the failures caused by rigidity of orders, always gave the commander a free hand to vary the orders if the circumstances seemed to demand it—the doctrine of trusting the man on the spot.

Nevertheless, these small differences of opinion did not in any way interfere with the steady progress in our preparations. The relations of my staff and myself with our American colleagues hardened into real friendship. The convoys were steadily assembled and the ships loaded, and as much preliminary training was carried out as the short time available permitted. As I have already said, it was all too short to perfect the crews of the landing craft in all their duties.

Nevertheless, I personally felt most optimistic about the whole operation. If we could land sufficient troops at the places we had chosen, I was sure that the French opposition, half-hearted as I expected it to be, would soon collapse. I was not inclined to pay much attention to the numerous bogys that arose to daunt us, such as the infra-red detection of ships; the attitude of Spain; the chances of the operation being disclosed to the enemy by our preparations at Gibraltar, and so on and so forth. There were plenty of these scares, and they grew with every day we waited. There was even one rumour that the Spanish could detect the number of ships passing through the Straits of Gibraltar by measuring the heat given off by their funnels. The bogey of infra-red detection had one unfortunate result; in that when the time came the transports lay off and lowered their landing craft unnecessarily far from the shore. This in its turn made it difficult for the half-trained crews of the landing craft to find the correct beaches in the darkness.

The American landing at Casablanca, of course, was gambling with the weather; but plans were explored for the ships to stand off and on until the weather was suitable, fuelling in turns, at Gibraltar if necessary. If the weather did not moderate, the Casablanca force would proceed through the Straits and land in the Beni Saf-Nemours area between Oran and the eastern border of Spanish Morocco.

For the actual assault General Eisenhower was to establish his headquarters at Gibraltar, and mine were to be there also.

The strain thrown on the resources and organization at Gibraltar was immense. A train of auxiliary craft, tugs, tankers, colliers, ammunition vessels, and special personnel was already on its way in advance convoys early in October, and the berthing space and anchorage were very congested. Commodore W. E. Parry was sent to help the Vice-Admiral at Gibraltar, Sir Frederick Edward-Collins, with the necessary preparations. Parry left Gibraltar before the operation; but in view of the huge number of small craft that would be based there I thought it necessary that they should have a special officer to deal entirely with them. I applied for and secured the services of Captain Geoffrey N. Oliver, whom I had known for years, and in whose outstanding ability and personality I had good reason to have complete confidence. He went to Gibraltar with the rank of Commodore, and his services were invaluable. In the event Gibraltar as a whole stood up well to the superhuman exertions demanded of it. Except in a few very minor respects it filled the position of an advanced base with great success.

Before I left for Gibraltar it was arranged to send the same submarine that had landed General Clark in North Africa to the south coast of France to bring out General Giraud. We confidently hoped that he would bring over the whole of North Africa to our side. Lieutenant Jewell, in H.M. Submarine P.219, later renamed the *Seraph*, accordingly sailed from Gibraltar at 8 p.m. on October 27th, with Captain Gerauld Wright, U.S.N. on board to give the impression that the ship was under American command. The code word for this operation was 'Minerva', and the object was to embark 'King Pin' (General Giraud) off the French Riviera in the small hours of November 6th.

III

My connection with 'Torch' was still being kept a dead secret. Actually it was known to very few people outside the Admiralty, and I was supposed to be in London for consultation before returning to Washington. So on October 28th, in plain clothes, I took the train to Plymouth accompanied by those of my staff who had not flown on ahead to Gibraltar. Admiral Sir Bertram Ramsay stayed in London as Deputy Allied Naval Commander of the Expeditionary Force, and to be our rear link at home. His services in that respect were inestimable. If in the strenuous weeks ahead we wanted anything we signalled direct to Ramsay and he personally arranged it at the Admiralty. This procedure was entirely new. It was found so useful that it was adopted in all subsequent operations of a similar nature.

At Plymouth the Commander-in-Chief, Sir Charles Forbes, saw me off in his barge for the cruiser *Scylla*, Captain I. A. P. MacIntyre, lying in the Sound. Driving through Plymouth to the Millbay Docks I remember being greatly shocked by the wholesale destruction wrought by the German bombers. The devastation was frightful, and it occurred to me that a glimpse of it might have been of service to some of my American friends in peaceful Washington. The *Scylla* sailed at once for Gibraltar. Even the ship's company had no knowledge of where they were bound or what I was doing on board. The better to keep it dark we had arranged for a dummy signal to lie casually on the captain's table intimating that I was bound for the Far East after calling at Gibraltar.

I had had to collect a fresh personal staff. Paymaster Captain A. P. Shaw, my trusted and experienced secretary, had temporarily remained in Washington. In his stead I was fortunate in securing the services of Paymaster Captain H. C. Oswin, who already had considerable secretarial experience. As flag lieutenant I selected Robert Dampier, son of a retired Admiral who lived in our village. He had been called up and done some time as an ordinary seaman in a destroyer before obtaining his commission as a Sub-Lieutenant R.N.V.R. and had served some months in a Free French escort vessel working in the Atlantic. Dampier had a fair knowledge of colloquial French, which he and I were to find most useful.

We arrived at Gibraltar early on November 1st and disembarked. Admiral Edward-Collins had kindly offered to put me up in his very comfortable house, The Mount; also the Chief of Staff, secretary and flag lieutenant, so we were well placed. When he arrived, Eisenhower was accommodated by the Governor, Lieutenant-General Frank Mason-Macfarlane, at the Convent.

We had plenty to do in installing ourselves in our offices in the tunnel burrowed into the Rock. The offices were good enough; but were not pleasant places to work in, being damp and rather airless. However, they were proof against anything short of a first-class earthquake. Eisenhower's offices were on the opposite side of the tunnel to mine. I had another office in the Dockyard from which I could watch the ships assembling and receive the calls of the commanding officers. It was thrilling to be amongst the seagoing Navy again. I felt as though I had been away from it for years instead of only seven months.

The Royal Air Force were also in the tunnel, where we had an excellent combined Naval and R.A.F. operations room. Here also I should mention the outstandingly fine work of the R.A.F. working from the very congested airfield on the North Front.

On the large wall charts in the operations room we anxiously watched the progress of the convoys, now all at sea and coming through the Atlantic. German submarines had lately been very active and the losses of merchant vessels heavy, partly owing to the reduction of escorts which had been withdrawn to protect the 'Torch' convoys. If one of our personnel convoys had been located by a submarine pack the result might have crippled one of the landings. But all went well, and every convoy from Great Britain passed through the Straits without loss.

There were various reasons for this highly successful though rather unexpected achievement. Good routeing, good escort work and handling of convoys entered into it. Additional anti-submarine vessels also patrolled the U-boat transit area in the Bay of Biscay. Heavier surface forces patrolled the Denmark Strait between Iceland and Greenland, and between Iceland and the Faroes, in case any of the German heavy ships in Norway tried to break out into the Atlantic. The demands upon Coastal Command of the R.A.F. were heavy. A considerable proportion of its anti-U-boat force had had to be diverted to the pursuit of blockade-runners and as an assurance against the threat of surface raiders, while the remainder operated in the Bay of Biscay. Bomber Command of the R.A.F. was called upon to help by providing escort to the convoys and together with the Eighth United States Air Force carried out precision bombing of the U-boat bases in the Bay of Biscay and the naval port of Brest.

The defence for the 'Torch' convoys was marshalled in strength. But no imaginable defence could altogether have warded off the concentrated attacks of thirty to forty U-boats. The procession of large convoys converging on the Straits of Gibraltar passed close enough to submarine concentrations; but it is the almost incredible fact that they were not attacked and sustained no casualties.

As we know now the German High Command became aware during October that there were unusually large quantities of shipping and extraordinary activity in many ports in Great Britain and the United States. They realized that a large expeditionary force was about to be sent oversea. Everything pointed to a landing in Africa, and the blow, the Germans calculated, would be directed against Dakar. They made their dispositions accordingly, some sixty German and Italian U-boats being massed around the Azores and Madeira. A convoy bound for Sierra Leone ran into part of this concentration and was very severely handled, thirteen of its ships being sunk in attacks lasting four consecutive nights.

Our convoys remained unscathed, and the enemy was not aware of his mistake until too late. This immunity was largely due to the Allied aircraft which kept the convoy areas clear of enemy shadowers and forced his U-boats to remain submerged.

By November 3rd, the 8th Army had completed its great stroke at El Alamein, and the next day Rommel was in full retreat under heavy land and air attack. By November 5th the 8th Army was advancing all along the front. We were watching Montgomery's drive with intense interest, knowing full well that if 'Torch' were successful it would greatly assist the advance in Libya.

Eisenhower had had rather a perilous flight out from England, and arrived at Gibraltar on the afternoon of the 5th. His reception was a quiet one, and I met him later in our tunnel. Meanwhile we were somewhat perturbed at the lack of any news from Submarine P.219, which was supposed to be picking up General Giraud. This persisted all through the next day.

The convoys and their covering squadrons passed through the Straits on the night of the 6th–7th, and the complete wireless silence indicated that all was well. I remember going to Europa Point, and seeing some of the darkened ships passing. November 7th was a day of anxiety. We heard early that U.S.S. *Thomas Stone*, one of the American 'combat loaders' for the attack upon Algiers had been torpedoed at 5.35 a.m. and stopped. Later reports told us that although disabled she was in no danger except from further attack. She was taken in tow by the destroyer *Wishart*, and enterprising efforts were being made to get her 1,400 troops forward to their objective. Captain O. R. Bennehof, U.S.N., the *Thomas Stone's* captain, took the courageous decision of sending his landing craft and troops off on a journey of 140 miles to their beaches under the escort of the only anti-submarine vessel then available to screen his ship. They arrived some twelve hours late.

On November 7th we also surmised that some at least of the convoys

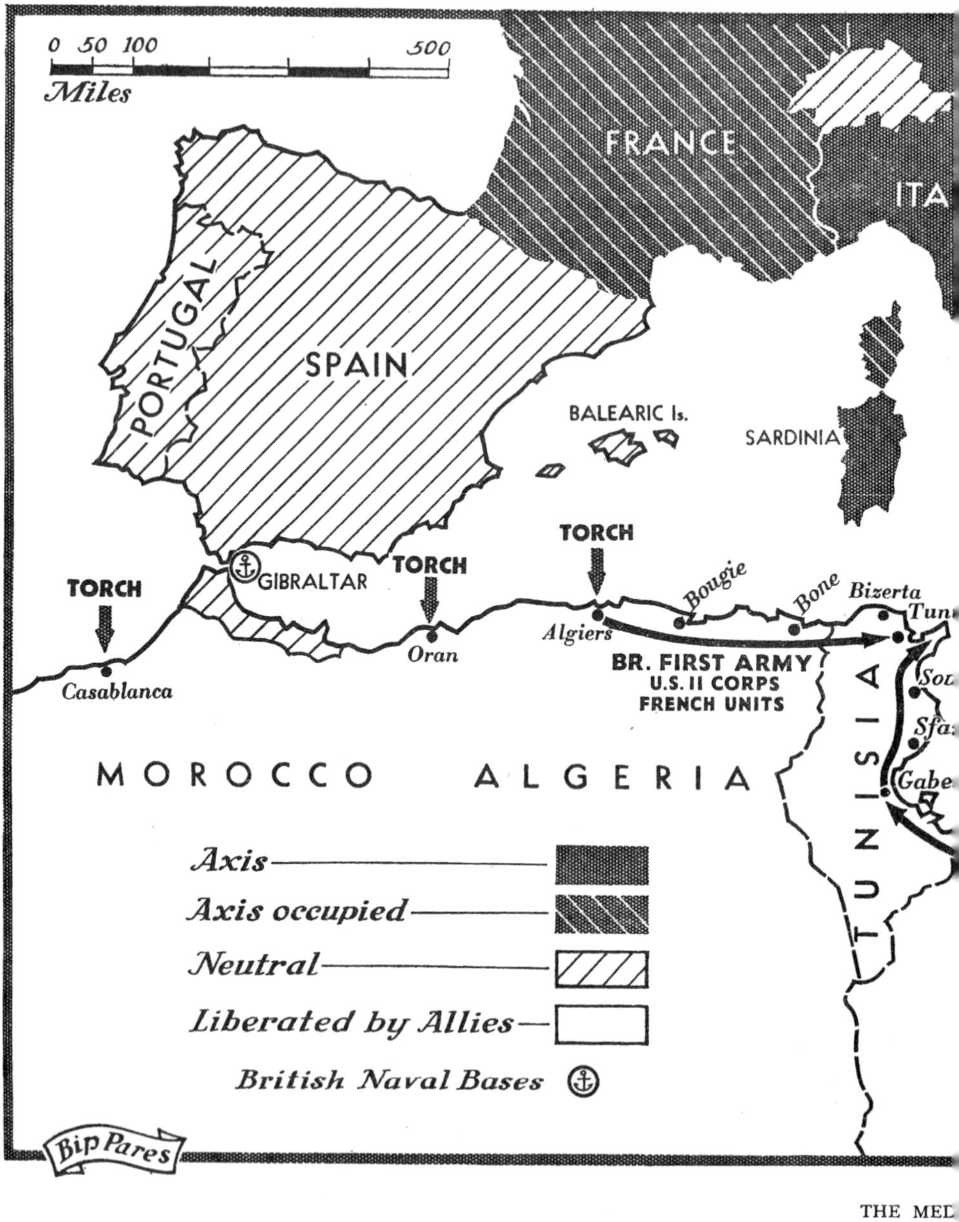

THE MED

October, 194

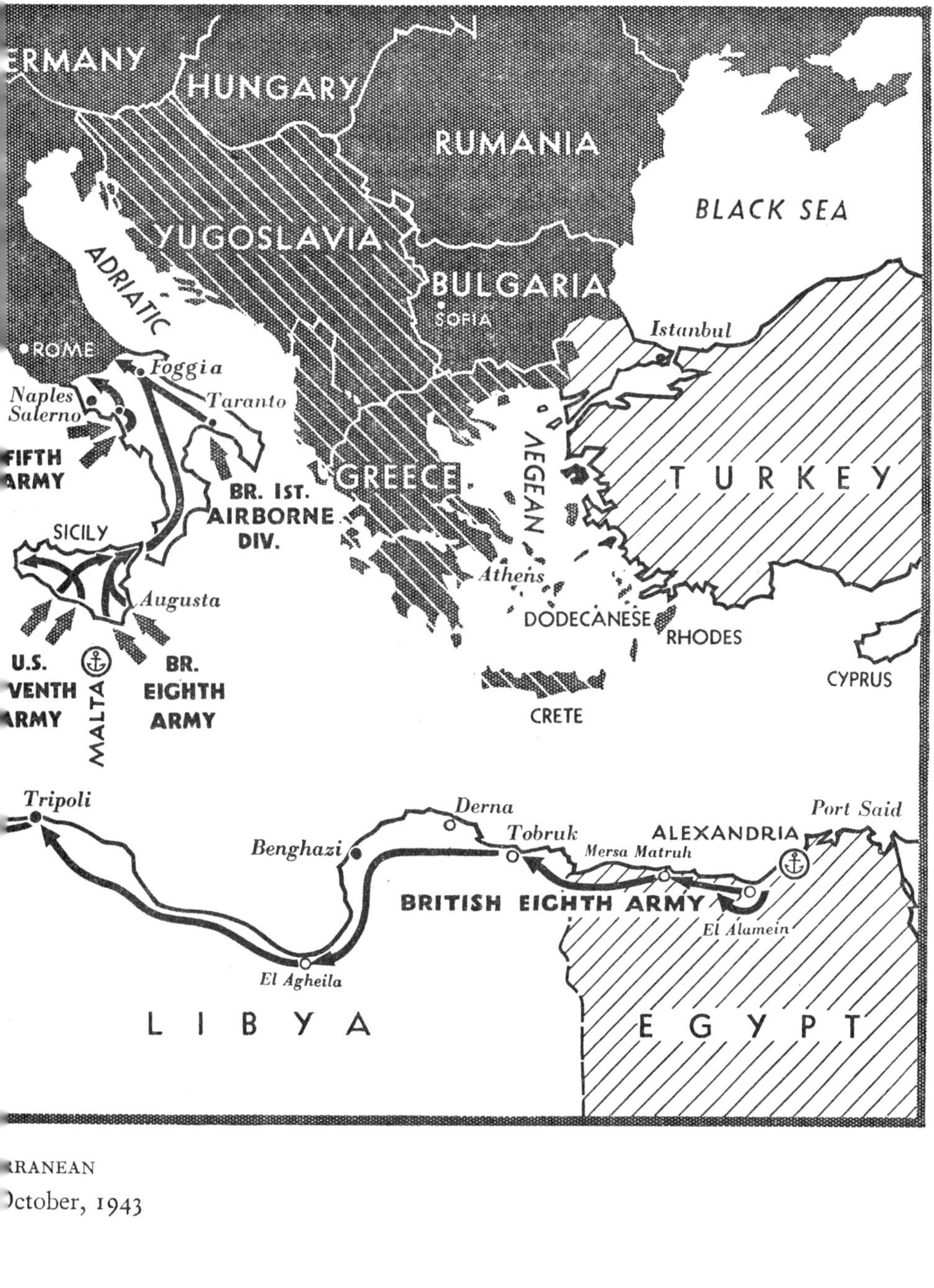

RRANEAN
October, 1943

and covering forces had been sighted by the enemy's air reconnaissance. Indeed, the main Algiers convoy was shadowed during the afternoon. But our intelligence also told us that the enemy thought we were running an extra large convoy to Malta, and were massing their aircraft in Sardinia and Sicily to deliver the usual concentrated attacks.

We were watching the weather closely, particularly that on the Atlantic coast near Casablanca. On November 6th it had looked distinctly unpromising; but on the 7th reports from the American submarine stationed off the coast said that the sea had gone down because of a contrary wind and conditions were more favourable. Just after 5 p.m. Eisenhower sent out the order for the operation to be carried out by all forces.

At last we had news of Submarine P.219 and General Giraud. The General and his party had been safely picked up from a small boat off La Fosette, some twenty miles east of Toulon, at 1.15 a.m. on the 6th. The submarine's wireless had been out of action and she could not at first inform us. A Catalina aircraft was sent out to meet the submarine, and they duly sighted each other on the morning of the 7th. The aircraft landed on the sea. General Giraud with his party and luggage were transferred in folboats, and by 11 o'clock were on their way to Gibraltar.

On his arrival Giraud was taken direct to the office in the tunnel where Eisenhower and Clark went into conference with him. I was not privy to what was going on, and my first inkling that all was not well was seeing Eisenhower come out of his office looking desperately tired and worried. It was about 7.30 and they had been arguing for hours. I took Eisenhower off to dinner at The Mount and he told me of the difficulties that had arisen.

We had hoped that Giraud's influence would unite the many divergent factors in French North Africa and end any opposition to the Anglo-American landing. Instead, he had flatly declined to take any part in the operation except as Supreme Commander of the whole expedition. He also wanted part of the convoys to be diverted to land some sixty thousand men in the south of France. Great soldier though he was, General Giraud had little or no idea of the vast amount of organization and preparation that had gone before the launching of a large amphibious operation like 'Torch', and how utterly impossible it was to alter the objects and the orders when once the expedition was at sea. Giraud's strategical views were also somewhat crude and out-of-date.

Dick, my Chief of Staff, and I both thought that Giraud's demands had naturally been put at their highest at the outset, and that after further consideration he would be more reasonable. After dinner Eisenhower went back to the office for two or three hours more talk with Giraud and Clark. At the end of the discussion the Frenchman was still as stubborn as ever.

Next morning, November 8th, there was a further conference at Government House. The Governor and I both attended and I took Dick with me, being sure that his knowledge of French and of the French would be useful. As we had expected, Giraud finally came off his high horse, and after more talk declared himself willing to co-operate on our terms, which were roughly that he should be recognized as Commander-in-Chief of all the French troops and be in general charge in North Africa.

IV

We had spent all the night of November 7th–8th in the tunnel. The first landings at Algiers and Oran were timed for 1 a.m., and from then on reports kept coming in from the various beaches. Though I cannot go into all the complicated details, I should say that at both places pilotage parties had been detailed to reconnoitre the beaches beforehand. This had been done from submarines working offshore at periscope depth. For the actual operation there were three submarines for the actual beach-finding and to serve as beacons off the landing places in the Algiers area, and another two off Oran. A folboat with a shaded light was stationed 400 yards off each beach to assist in the navigation. Very briefly, the flights of landing craft from the transports were to be led by motor launches to the beacon submarines, where the motor launches were to embark the pilot officers for the penultimate lap of the journey to the folboats. From there the landing craft would push on for the shore.

In the Algiers area there was evidently no resistance worth mentioning as the troops got ashore. The first objectives were soon reached. But the distance away from the shore at which the transports launched their landing-craft, the inexperience through lack of adequate training of the landing-craft crews, coupled with an unexpectedly strong set of the currents which caused the transports to be drifted westward at the rate of four miles an hour, resulted in some units being landed in the wrong places and others becoming badly mixed up.

At one of the beaches a short distance west of Algiers, some landing-craft, starting late, missed their intended beaches and reached a spot two miles eastward of their proper position. Of the six landing-craft in this particular flight four came under heavy fire and were sunk, while the other two were forced to withdraw. It was fortunate indeed that at Algiers there was no determined military resistance on shore.

The French Navy, however, which manned most of the batteries, was by no means so favourably disposed towards us. The entry of the *Broke* and *Malcolm* into Algiers harbour carrying American troops to prevent the sabotage of the harbour installations, and of the French shipping in the port, was fiercely resisted. The *Malcolm*, heavily hit in the boiler-rooms, was forced to withdraw before entering. On her fourth attempt at 5.20 a.m. the *Broke* charged the boom at full speed, entered the harbour, and managed to get alongside a jetty. Her three companies of troops were landed, and the power station and oil installation occupied. Apart from desultory sniping and machine-gun fire things were tolerably quiet until about 8 o'clock, when the French batteries opened fire. By 9.15 more guns had come into action and the *Broke's* position was untenable. Leaving 250 men ashore the ship was forced to withdraw, being heavily hit on the way out of the harbour. Taken in tow by the destroyer *Zetland*, which had been bombarding a battery at Cape Matifu, the *Broke* sank next day in the worsening weather. The men left ashore were rounded up by the French and temporarily made prisoners.

The airfield at Blida, some twenty miles inland from Algiers, surrendered to carrier-borne Martlets at 8.30, and R.A.F. Spitfires from Gibraltar flew in soon afterwards, the airfield being occupied by Allied troops before noon. Maison Blanche aerodrome, east of Algiers, had also been captured by troops by 8.30. By 10 o'clock it was reported serviceable and a squadron of Hurricanes from Gibraltar were landing. The presence of the R.A.F. helped materially to supplement the extremely efficient air support given to the landings by the hard-pressed fighters and squadrons of the Fleet Air Arm working from the carriers.

French resistance stiffened during the morning and early afternoon, and the batteries round Cape Matifu had to be bombed by the Fleet Air Arm and bombarded from the sea before they were all in Allied hands at about 4.30. Meanwhile the wind had freshened from the north-east to raise a considerable sea on some of the beaches. The unloading of stores on the beaches west of Matifu was considerably delayed, and in this sector no fewer than forty-five landing-craft were wrecked. Many more became casualties on the beaches west of Algiers.

At about 5 p.m. Vice-Admiral Burrough had a message from Major-General C. W. Ryder, U.S.A. in command of the troops on shore, which was passed on to us at Gibraltar: "Darlan wishes to negotiate immediately. He will not deal with any Frenchman. Recommend that arrangements for Algiers be presented. Resistance of Navy in isolated batteries has been severe. Resistance of Army has been token."

This was good news, amplified by a further message two hours later stating that General Ryder had had a conference with General Juin who was acting for Admiral Darlan, that all resistance in Algiers had ceased, and that the town was being occupied starting at 7 p.m. General Ryder added that he and Mr. Murphy were conferring with Admiral Darlan at 10 a.m. next morning, November 9th, to fix the definite terms.

The first Axis air attack developed at dusk, a destroyer and two transports being damaged. However, the convoys were proceeding to Algiers Bay during the afternoon, and by dark more Allied troops had been landed and Commodore J. A. V. Morse had been installed as Naval Officer in Charge, Algiers.

At dawn next morning, November 9th, Admiral Burrough's flagship, the *Bulolo*, entered the harbour and berthed alongside in a somewhat spectacular manner. Twice attacked on the way round by J.U. 88's, her engine-room telegraphs had been put out of action. She sailed majestically alongside her jetty at nine knots and was brought up all standing by the shallow water, displacing some masonry in the stone wall ahead. As Burrough wrote in his report: "An enthusiastic reception was given to us by the large crowd assembled on the dock-side and on the road overlooking the harbour."

v

At Oran the landing operations went better, the landing-craft reaching their assigned beaches. The French were taken completely by surprise, and there was no opposition on the beaches. But when the *Walney* and *Hartland* with their troops on board attempted to rush the harbour to prevent sabotage, they met with fierce resistance. The operation failed, both ships being sunk with heavy casualties.

In consequence the harbour was badly damaged by the French before its final capture by the Allies, the floating docks and many ships being sunk, thereby restricting the berthing area and denying their use to us. Our attempt, which was worth while, was foiled by the alertness of the French Navy. It is as well I think, to bear in mind that great achievements in war are seldom brought about without considerable risks to personnel, and that their failure is not in itself proof that the enterprise was faultily conceived or executed. I think the ill success of the *Walney* and *Hartland* was partly due to their use of loud-speakers calling upon the French harbour defences to surrender. We at headquarters knew nothing about their intention to do so. Had we been aware of it, we should have told them to rush the boom and to go about their business as silently as possible.

This attack on the harbour at Oran was carried out by Captain Frederic Thornton Peters, a retired officer, who had been largely responsible for its planning. Though wounded he survived the exploit; but was unhappily killed a few days later when a Catalina in which he was returning to the United Kingdom crashed on landing. For his gallantry at Oran he was awarded the American Distinguished Service Cross and in May, 1943, was posthumously awarded the Victoria Cross "for valour in taking H.M.S. *Walney* into the harbour of Oran in the face of point blank fire in an enterprise of desperate hazard".

Three French destroyers and a submarine chaser from Oran gallantly but foolishly came out and attempted to interfere with the landings. They were engaged by the battle-tried *Aurora* and our destroyers, with the consequence that one French destroyer and the submarine chaser were sunk, another was driven ashore, while the third, on being hit, turned and fled in the direction of Oran. It was highly distasteful for our ships to have to destroy French vessels which should have been fighting with us.

Aircraft of the Fleet Air Arm from the carriers did excellent work by providing fighter patrols over the area, in tactical reconnaissance, and by creating havoc among the French aircraft on Tafaraoui and La Senia airfields. Eighty per cent of the enemy aircraft were put out of action, and the fact that most of the French fighters were destroyed either in the air or in the hangars at La Senia probably deterred such bombers as remained serviceable from taking off and interfering with the landings. Later inspection of the aerodromes showed that the French bombers were bombed up and fuelled, the fighters complete with ammunition and petrol, and the seaplanes at their base at Arzeu, some twenty miles to the eastward of Oran, had their torpedoes in place complete with pistols and ready for immediate action. By the evening of November 8th American Spitfires were operating from Tafaraoui.

Gunfire support had to be given on several occasions by the *Rodney* to keep down the fire from Fort Santon which opened up on the transports and forced them to lie a long way out, thereby delaying the landing. However, the disembarkation of men and stores proceeded all through the 8th and 9th, though somewhat hampered by swell on the last day. Stubborn fighting ashore continued all through the 9th, and that morning the cruisers *Aurora* and *Jamaica* engaged two Vichy destroyers, driving one ashore in flames and forcing the other to retire damaged to Oran where she had to be beached. Early on November 10th, Major-General L. R. Frendendall, the American officer commanding shore, felt himself strong enough to assault the city of Oran. Stiff resistance continued throughout the morning; but by 11 a.m. armoured units had penetrated into the city and the French capitulated by noon.

A landing at Bougie, 100 miles east of Algiers, had been planned for November 9th; but had to be postponed because of the weather. It was eventually carried out unopposed at dawn on the 11th, with the covering force and landing under the orders of Rear-Admiral C. H. J. Harcourt in the cruiser *Sheffield*, with Brigadier A. L. Kent-Lemon as Military Force Commander of the British troops in three transports. Another transport, with R.A.F. stores and petrol, was sent on to Djidjelli, 35 miles east of Bougie, to land troops to capture the airfield; but this was prevented by the heavy swell breaking on the beach.

Axis aircraft were active along the coast, and the delay in our being able to operate the airfield at Djidjelli had far-reaching results. It restricted fighter protection at a time when the ships and the troops landing on the beach east of Bougie were subjected to heavy bombing attacks. The first raid took place at dusk on the day of landing, when the monitor *Roberts* was hit and set on fire, and the *Cathay*, one of the transports, was seriously damaged. She caught fire and sank later. A second transport, the *Awatea*, was also bombed and had to be abandoned after catching fire. At dawn next day, November 12th, a third transport, the *Karanja*, was set on fire, to sink later. There were more air attacks throughout the day, in the course of which the auxiliary anti-aircraft ship *Tynwald* was also sunk. The landing force was virtually without air cover for two days and under heavy air attack; but by early on November 13th R.A.F. Spitfires were operating from Djidjelli, and had the situation well in hand. On the next day, when the shipping at Bougie was again attacked, eleven of the raiders were shot down and others damaged.

An unopposed landing at Bone, 125 miles east of Bougie, took place at 3 a.m. on November 12th, when British commando troops and two companies of infantry were put ashore from the destroyers *Lamerton* and *Wheatland*. Though frequently dive-bombed during the day both these ships escaped damage.

VI

The force of nearly a hundred warships, transports and cargo vessels under the command of Rear-Admiral H. Kent Hewitt, U.S.N. for the landings at three places on the west coast of French Morocco had sailed from the United States between October 23rd and 25th. The thirty-one thousand troops, who had with them two hundred and fifty tanks, were commanded by Major-General George S. Patton.

The expedition was purely American, and I shall not attempt to describe it in any detail; but briefly the Northern Attack Group was to land at Mehdia, for the capture of Port Lyautey, 65 miles north-east of Casablanca. The Centre Attack Group was to be put ashore at Fédala, for the seizure of Casablanca, some 23 miles to the north-east; and the Southern Attack Group at Safi, 110 miles south-westward of Casablanca. These assaults, if successful, would secure the narrow coastal plain at the foot of the Middle Atlas mountains which contained all the important airfields, and through which ran all the principal lines of communication in French Morocco.

The capture of Casablanca, the French naval base and the headquarters of the naval and military forces in Morocco, was the crux of the whole expedition.

As I have said, the landing beaches were open to the Atlantic and success depended largely on the weather. On November 6th, when Admiral Hewitt was nearing his destination, the forecasts from Washington and London for D-day were anything but encouraging: "Surf 15 feet high and landings impossible." The meteorologist with Admiral Hewitt, however, considered the storm was moving too rapidly to have any adverse effect on the beaches, and predicted that the weather would moderate and make landing possible.

Admiral Hewitt had to make a most difficult decision. If he ignored the forecasts from Washington and London and decided to stick to the Casablanca plan he must deploy his forces on November 7th, the eve of D-day. If he attempted the landings in adverse weather the results might be disastrous. If, on the other hand, he adopted the alternative plan of entering the Mediterranean, he might meet a heavy concentration of enemy submarines, and in any case would have to land the troops on the largely unsurveyed beaches between Oran and the frontier of Spanish Morocco. Moreover, if he elected to land there it would have left untouched at the outset a considerable part of the French Army and Navy in North Africa.

The Admiral chose the bolder course, and at midnight on November 6th–7th decided to risk the weather and go for Casablanca. Fortune favoured him. The sea went down, and on November 7th, his large collection of ships was approaching the coast in fair weather with a north-easterly wind and a smooth sea.

The assaults in all three areas were timed to synchronize with those at Algiers and Oran. They succeeded; but only after great difficulties and heavy fighting in which the French Navy and Air Force also put up strong resistance. The heavy covering bombardments by the American warships played an important part in the operations as a whole by neutralizing the fire of the French defences. When the surf rose on November 9th many landing-craft were driven ashore and lost. Others mistook their landing places and were wrecked on rocks, while in some cases there was great confusion on the beaches and the exits could only be used by tracked vehicles because of the soft sand. The American difficulties were much the same as ours inside the Mediterranean, and most of them, like ours, could be ascribed to lack of training. However that had to be accepted. If we could not have landed as we did on November 8th the occupation of French North Africa would have had to be postponed until the spring of 1943. The time available was quite insufficient for the preliminary training that was really necessary.

As I wrote later when all the reports had been examined and the evidence sifted: "No officer commanding a unit will ever be satisfied that he has had adequate preparation and training until his unit is trained and equipped down to the last gaiter button. There are times in history when we cannot afford to wait for the final polish. . . . We could not afford to wait, and the risk of embarking on these large-scale operations with inadequate training was deliberately accepted in order to strike when the time was ripe."

Both the Americans and ourselves still had much to learn in the organization and conduct of amphibious operations.

In concluding this chapter, I should like again to emphasize some of the remarks I made in my official despatch on operation 'Torch'. I wrote that the operation achieved the success it did was due, among other reasons, "to the sound planning and forethought shown in the Naval sphere by Admiral Sir Bertram Ramsay, who made a contribution not easily measured to the smooth running of the seaborne operations," and "to the excellent co-operation which existed through all ranks of the services of both nations, the foundations of which were laid during the period of combined planning at Norfolk House." I mentioned also how much we owed "to the high standard of seamanship and technical efficiency which is mercifully still maintained in the units of the Fleet," and to "the courage, determination and adaptability of the Merchant Navy."

In ending my despatch I felt also that "it should be placed on record that in this most difficult of all types of operation with a number of services involved and despite the difficulties inherent in welding together the systems of command and organization, there reigned a spirit of comradeship and understanding which provided that vital force which brought success to our undertakings. The embodiment of that spirit was exemplified in our Commander-in-Chief, General Dwight D. Eisenhower: we count it a privilege to follow in his train."

I cannot end this chapter without a tribute to my devoted staff. As I wrote from Gibraltar on November 10th after we knew our landings had been successful: "We have had such wonderful luck . . . I don't know how it would have gone without my three old Eastern Meds., though. Dick, Power and Brownrigg have the whole thing on their shoulders, and to a slightly less degree Barnard and Durlacher. They are surprising everyone by their efficiency and capacity. I must say I like working with these Americans. We all get on famously. Roy Dick is surprising even me, and all the High-up Americans think he is a great man."

Some two and a half years later, in May, 1945, when Eisenhower was the Supreme Commander of the Allied Expeditionary Force on the Continent and I was First Sea Lord, I wrote to congratulate him upon the unconditional surrender of Germany.

He replied with great cordiality and friendliness in a letter dated May 10th, 1945. I will not quote all he wrote; but just one passage:

> Incidentally, just the other day someone asked me what particular period I would probably remember longest in this war. The subject was intriguing enough to demand an hour's conversation and out of it I came to the conclusion that the hours that you and I spent together in the dripping tunnels of Gibraltar will probably remain as long in my memory as will any other. It was there I first understood the indescribable and inescapable strain that comes over one when his part is done—when the issue rests with fate and the fighting men he has committed to action.

CHAPTER XXXVIII

I

MEANWHILE, at Gibraltar, we had been fairly satisfied with the way the occupation was progressing at Algiers and Oran; but were having considerable difficulty in obtaining information from Admiral Hewitt's Western Task Force. We knew the landings had taken place and that there had been considerable resistance; but little else. The few signals we received were sparse, and while news from Vichy sources indicated we had had success, they intimated that the French were fighting stubbornly.

Light bombers were sent off from Gibraltar to try to get into touch with the American commanders; but they were either shot down by French fighters, or in some cases were unrecognized by American aircraft. Finally I suggested to General Eisenhower that I should send a fast ship to clear up the situation. The cruiser-minelayer *Welshman* was in harbour preparing for a dash to Malta, and on November 12th she embarked Rear-Admiral Bieri U.S.N. of the General's staff and steamed at high speed to make touch with Admiral Hewitt at Casablanca.

Generals Clark and Giraud had flown to Algiers on the 9th to make contact with the French authorities. As I thought my Chief of Staff, Commodore Dick, would be very useful because of his intimate knowledge of French, he went with them. Captain Gerauld Wright, U.S.N. and Colonel Julius Holmes, of Eisenhower's staff, were also in the party.

They landed at Maison Blanche aerodrome near Algiers just before dusk as a heavy air attack developed on the port and airfield. It was important to get into touch with the American and British military commanders as soon as possible; but after an adventurous drive into the city, with the Axis 'planes attacking and the anti-aircraft guns in action, they found that the American and British Generals, Ryder and Anderson, were out in the city taking what steps they could to ensure the safety of the Allied troops. Algiers itself was in a very disturbed state. Having recovered from the first shock of the landing, the French had come to realize how small an Allied Force, with so comparatively few guns and armoured vehicles, was in possession. French troops were being moved into key positions, and since the Allies had insufficient men to deal drastically with any organized resistance if it broke out afresh, the position was one of extreme delicacy. This, coupled with the urgent need for pushing on east as soon as possible to forestall any German movement in Tunisia, which had even then begun, placed our representatives at a disadvantage in the subsequent negotiations.

The party drove straight to the American Consul General's villa, close to the Hotel St. Georges, which was the French Naval Headquarters closely guarded by French naval ratings. Accommodation for the visitors was arranged in an annexe to the hotel, and in these bedrooms they lived and had their offices. There was an air of secrecy and conspiracy which would not have been out of place in a 'thriller' novel.

Since the American Consul General's house was thought to be wired so that conversations could be over-heard and recorded, the greatest caution had to be observed in all discussions. Mr. Murphy, the representative of the American State Department, who had been conducting negotiations and was also deeply involved in the anti-Vichy movement which had failed after its initial success when General Clark had landed from the submarine on the night of October 21st–22nd, was also suspected by the French. When he arrived at the villa he mentioned the uneasy situation in Algiers; how he and his party had all been arrested when Allied troops did not enter the city in force within a few hours of the first landing; and how a number of British naval ratings and American troops from H.M.S. *Broke* were still imprisoned. Mr. Murphy himself had to be most circumspect. He had been confined to his house and only just released, and was probably still being closely watched. Most important of all, the arrival of General Giraud had not had the rallying effect upon all friendly-disposed Frenchmen for which the Allies had hoped. No officer of any great importance had followed his lead, and he himself was in a precarious position. Moreover, Admiral Darlan was still at liberty, and all the leading French authorities were in a state of bewildered indecision. The fact was that not one of them could be counted upon as being reliably attached to the Allied cause.

This information was disturbing. General Eisenhower had instructed Clark to direct Giraud to use all his influence to stop French resistance to the Allies. Giraud must also urge upon all Frenchmen that their vital interests coincided with ours, and in particular must insist upon all leaders and forces in Tunisia destroying Axis aircraft and resisting Axis occupation.

On that evening of November 9th, therefore, the first need was an immediate conference with Giraud, and he was asked to come secretly to the American Consul's General's villa under cover of darkness. Since discussion in the house was dangerous the meeting was held in darkened cars outside. Some alarm was caused in the course of the discussion when some cars with bright lights drove up. It was feared that Giraud and all the Allied party were about to be arrested. However, nothing happened.

The conference was entirely unsatisfactory. Giraud, though astounded and bewildered at the almost complete lack of support with which he had been received by the French, was still stubbornly insistent that the Allies should carry out their promise of creating him Commander-in-Chief of all the French forces in North Africa, in spite of the fact that he had no following. It had to be reiterated to him that such a step would be folly. It would result in his being Commander-in-Chief in name only, which would only accentuate the hostility of those who had the real power to stop further French resistance to the Allies. Fierce fighting, it has to be remembered, still continued at Oran and at the three American landing places on the west coast of Morocco. General Giraud left the meeting, and at a further conference between the Allied party and Mr. Murphy it was decided to meet Admiral Darlan next morning, November 10th.

The meeting was held at the Hotel St. Georges, Admiral Darlan, Generals Juin and Mendigal, and Admirals Fénard and Battet, with all the Allied representatives, being present. Darlan repeatedly refused to accept the terms of the armistice which included the whole of North Africa, and would not sign them without the authority of Vichy. The atmosphere was electric. A possé of American troops was posted round the hotel. Inside them were the French naval guards, and in the hotel itself a large number of armed French officers. General Clark had ordered that none of the Allied party was to carry arms, so if drastic action had to be taken and French officers arrested things might have become most unpleasant for our representatives inside the building. When Darlan refused to accept the terms and got up to leave it appeared there might be some shooting. General Clark rose and said that as Darlan would not agree to the terms, he must now take his own measures. Our representatives were actually leaving the conference room with the object of taking steps to effect the arrest of all the French officers concerned when Admiral Battet took Colonel Holmes by the arm and asked for five minutes grace. What happened during that anxious five minutes one does not know; but General Clark was called back, and greatly to the relief of all the Allied Officers concerned Darlan announced that he would issue orders to all the military, air and naval forces in North Africa, including Morocco and Tunisia, to cease fighting immediately. There and then he signed the necessary orders, which were sent off by air, while the French commanders were also communicated with by telephone.

Meanwhile General Giraud had asked Darlan to meet him in conference; but Darlan had refused. Finally, however, he consented to do so, and a meeting was arranged for 3 p.m. that afternoon.

At a further conference with Darlan, General Clark asked him to issue an order to the French fleet at Toulon. The result was inconclusive, though Darlan said he had instructed the fleet to be prepared to move at short notice if the Germans entered unoccupied France, and that in no circumstances would the fleet be allowed to fall into German hands.

The definite order for the cessation of fighting had thus been obtained. Nevertheless, a fine political tangle remained. Darlan was in control of all the forces in North Africa in the name of Marshal Pétain, as he had written in his cease-fire orders, while Giraud, to whom the Allies were deeply committed, was no nearer becoming Commander-in-Chief. If he were so appointed, there were signs that none of the local French Generals would obey his orders.

More diplomatic jostling took place that afternoon, November 10th, when Giraud expressed his displeasure that Darlan had been allowed to issue his cease-fire orders. Again Giraud insisted that he should be appointed Commander-in-Chief immediately and the fact publicly announced. This produced another awkward situation, as it would probably cause Darlan to revoke his orders for hostilities to cease. During the afternoon General Clark, with General Giraud and Mr. Murphy, visited Darlan and tried to reach a compromise. The Admiral, having just received word that he had been disowned by Marshal Pétain, was greatly dejected and said he would have to cancel his cease-fire orders.

General Clark thereupon told Darlan that he would not be permitted to revoke his orders, whereupon Darlan said that in those circumstances he must be made a prisoner. Clark replied that this was acceptable to him, and a guard was placed round the house of Admiral Fénard, where Darlan was living. Darlan gave his word of honour that he would remain there, and would not cancel his orders for hostilities to cease. General Juin, who was present, also stated he would issue no revocation order. Clark then tried again to get Darlan to order the French fleet from Toulon to Algiers, to which the Admiral replied that his orders would no longer have any effect; but that he would issue a plea to the French fleet. Clark then left the meeting, and Generals Juin and Giraud tried to work out a compromise.

A little later Admiral Fénard, a friend of Darlan's, told Mr. Murphy that news had been received that the Germans were about to enter unoccupied France and that Darlan said that if this were true and he received verification, he would consider himself free of any further moral obligations and would ignore Marshal Pétain's orders disowning him. Darlan asked that General Clark should visit his house again to discuss matters including the disposition of the French fleet. A further conference between the Allied negotiators and Generals Giraud, Juin, Koetz and Mendigal, the last three being strong Darlan supporters, was held later. The news of the reported German entry into France had a profound effect and greatly helped matters. The French were informed that Darlan was to be asked to hand over the fleet to the Allies.

There were spasmodic air raids during the evening, though as a whole the situation in Algiers was fairly quiet. A message from Oran greatly relieved anxieties, as it stated that Oran had fallen at noon, and that the Allied troops had had an enthusiastic reception. All Allied prisoners there had been released. As regards our prisoners at Algiers, Commodore Dick was obliged to go to Admiral Moreau to demand their instant release. He found them still confined in what was little better than a large cell.

General Clark, accompanied by Commodore Dick, Colonel Holmes and Captain Wright, U.S.N., had another interview with Admiral Darlan that evening, November 10th. In spite of all persuasion and urging, however, Darlan refused to issue any orders to the fleet until he was certain the Germans were moving into Southern France. He said that fighting had already ceased in French Morocco. At this stage of the proceedings General Clark was anxious to take the American guards off Darlan, as it lowered his local prestige and made negotiations very difficult.

The French commanders were still in a state of turmoil and bewilderment, and the Allied representatives felt some anxiety as to the attitude of the French Navy towards our ships and troops which were to be landed at Bougie, Djidjelli and Bone. There was much vacillation on the part of the French Admiral responsible. But the meeting with Darlan was cordial, and this was the first occasion on which the Admiral offered to shake hands with Commodore Dick. Previously, while cordially shaking hands with all the American officers, he had studiously refrained from doing do with Dick, the only British representative. That evening, however, on hearing that Dick was my Chief of Staff and had been with me at Alexandria, he offered to shake hands. As Dick himself wrote:

"The offer, which had been anticipated, was accepted with some reluctance, for obvious reasons. However, the moment was a delicate one in the negotiations, and it seemed best to pocket pride and do so. It was not done, however, without a sharp exchange on the subject of past history, which had a surprisingly good effect. Thereafter Admiral Darlan dealt with the British representative frankly, and, it should be recorded, gave and continued to give every assistance in naval matters."

Admiral Darlan's ignorance of Commodore Dick's official position as my Chief of Staff was natural. It was not until November 9th that it was publicly announced that I was Naval Commander of the Expeditionary Force. The 'past history' mentioned by Dick referred to the British attacks upon the French ships at Oran and Dakar in 1940, which Darlan had neither forgotten nor forgiven.

That night, at Gibraltar, where we had already been informed of the ups and downs of the negotiations, I had a signal from Dick asking for the policy as regards the destination of the French fleet, and suggesting that it should be directed to proceed straight across the Atlantic, stopping at Gibraltar to fuel. He added that there was a likelihood of the fleet's refusing to obey Darlan's orders.

We replied that all efforts should be made to get the French fleet to sail for Gibraltar, and, since Hitler had confirmed the German occupation of Southern France, that Admiral Darlan, General Juin and General Giraud should be urged to telephone at once to Tunis urging Admiral Esteva, the Resident General, to denounce the Axis and to declare for the Allies.

Next day, November 11th, the situation at Algiers was still fluctuating; but, after a further meeting, Darlan made a signal to Admiral de la Borde, Commander-in-Chief of the French fleet at Toulon:

> The protest sent by the Marshal to Marshal Von Runstedt shows that there is no agreement between him and the German General for the occupation of France. The armistice is broken. We have our liberty of action. The Marshal being no longer able to make free decisions, we can, while remaining personally loyal to him, make decisions which are most favourable to French interests. I have always declared that the Fleet would remain French or perish. The occupation of the Southern coast makes it impossible for the Naval forces to remain in Metropolitan France. I invite the Commander-in-Chief to direct them towards West Africa. The American Command declares that our forces will not encounter any obstacles from Allied Naval Forces.
>
> Admiral of the Fleet, François Darlan.

So the Toulon fleet had been 'invited' to sail, though nobody concerned had any belief that it would do so. Darlan himself, when told by Commodore Dick of the dispositions made to cover the French fleet when it moved towards Gibraltar said: "You are more optimistic than I am in making these arrangements. I am afraid they will not come."

Admiral de la Borde's reply to Admiral Darlan's suggestion is said to have been one extremely unparliamentary French word which indicated flat and uncompromising refusal.

The afternoon of November 11th brought a further agreement whereby Admiral Darlan should become the political head in French North Africa, and General Giraud the military commander of all the French forces. This, however, was complicated by the fact that Marshal Pétain had nominated General Noguès, Foreign Minister to the Sultan of Morocco, as Commander-in-Chief, because he said Darlan was a prisoner of war and not available. General Noguès was accordingly summoned to a conference at Algiers the next day, the 12th. The guards were removed from Darlan's house, and a public announcement drawn up for issue emphasizing the need for the unity of all French factions in the common cause. Both Darlan and Juin telephoned to Admiral Esteva, my old friend and Resident General of Tunis, telling him to resist the Germans. I also passed a personal message to Esteva urging him to come in on our side, and saying that assistance would be rushed to him. But it was too late. The Germans were already flying into Tunis, counsels were too divided to resist them, and Esteva himself was a hostage. He replied to Darlan's message: "I have a tutor at my elbow."

More satisfactory work was done at Algiers on November 11th when the French were made to release nearly a thousand British prisoners at Laghouat and Geryville. Most of them were officers and men of the Royal and Merchant

Navies, and they included a large proportion of the crews of the cruiser *Manchester* and the destroyer *Havock*. On this same day, too, broadcasts were made in French stating that Hitler had denounced the armistice, and inviting the French Toulon fleet to sail for Gibraltar and French merchant seamen to take their ships there. Our ships already had orders to receive any French vessels coming over with cordiality.

There was some disappointment on November 12th at Algiers when it was discovered early in the morning that the orders to the authorities in Tunis to resist the Axis had been held up until the arrival of General Noguès. Moreover, the agreement of the previous day about the appointments of Darlan and Giraud had not yet been approved by all concerned. It was, therefore, impossible to make the announcement calling upon all Frenchmen to unite against the Axis. Troops were at once moved in to force obedience to the agreement, and a message was sent to General Eisenhower asking him to come to Algiers. However, on November 12th, the day before Eisenhower's arrival, General Clark and the other Allied representatives met Darlan, Juin, Noguès and other Frenchmen. The conference was stormy. As Commodore Dick described it later: "after a series of dramatic incidents, in which on two occasions the French had to be left to themselves to exchange vituperations, all parties agreed on the original arrangements."

Meanwhile our troops had landed at Bone, Bougie and Djidjelli with little or no opposition. Indeed, in pursuance of Darlan's orders to cease resistance and co-operate with the Allies, they were welcomed by a large number of the French. This, at any rate, removed one of our great anxieties.

However, there was still a fine political tangle at Algiers, and the situation was even more complicated because General de Gaulle, to whom the British were committed, was decidedly unpopular with most of the other French Generals. So it was to clear up the imbroglio that Eisenhower flew to Algiers on November 13th, and I went with him. From the aerodrome at Maison Blanche we drove straight to the Hotel St. Georges, where we had a short preliminary meeting with General Clark and Mr. Murphy and learnt how the land lay. At 2 p.m. we had a full conference with the French, Darlan, Giraud, Noguès, Juin, and Admirals Fénard and Moreau being present. Broadly, Darlan, as I have said, was to be Governor General or its equivalent in French North Africa, while Giraud was to command the French Army. Noguès was to remain Resident General of French Morocco. Eisenhower stressed that the immediate object must be to fight the Germans, and Darlan agreed and went on to mention the reconstruction of France.

I was much interested in meeting Darlan, whom I had not seen before. Naturally I had heard much of him, though generally with a few qualifying and uncomplimentary adjectives. He greeted me most effusively, shook me warmly by the hand, and said: "Thank you for Admiral Godfroy," referring of course, to my dealings with the French fleet at Alexandria. He went on to say that although Admiral de la Borde might not obey his orders, he did not think, he, de la Borde, would allow the Toulon fleet to fall into German hands. I insisted that Darlan should send another message to de la Borde mentioning that the Italian fleet was on its way north, and assuring him of the support of the British fleet. Darlan also told me that he thought that Admiral Godfroy, at Alexandria, would come in with us. We talked of Admiral Esteva at Tunis, who was now a hostage to the Germans.

Once more I bitterly regretted that bolder measures had not been taken in Operation 'Torch', and that we had not landed at Bizerta, as I had suggested. Esteva was a true patriot. He loathed the Germans, and I am quite sure he would have welcomed the Allies. As Resident General in Tunisia he became caught up in events while we were parleying with Darlan, and then it was too late. The French General and Admiral in Tunisia were also sitting on the fence. In a letter written to me in April, 1949, Esteva says that the military and naval commanders in Tunis were under the orders of Vichy and Algiers and that he had no control over them; but I think a stronger character would have ordered them to resist the Germans. However, if one puts oneself in his place one realizes the extremely difficult position in which he found himself. He had a direct order from Marshal Pétain to resist the Allies—but he should also have resisted the Axis.

Esteva was brought to trial before the High Court of Justice in France in March, 1945, and was found guilty of treason and intelligence with the enemy. He was sentenced to imprisonment for life, with loss of military rank and civic rights, national degradation and confiscation of his property. His life was spared because of his successful efforts to preserve the lives of allied nationals at the time of the German invasion. In a recent letter to me from the fortress in which he is still confined Esteva assures me that he worked for us all along the line in Tunisia. I have no reason whatever to disbelieve this statement, and it is true that he wished to remain behind in Tunis when the Axis forces surrendered in May, 1943; but was forced into an aeroplane and taken away. In view of his fine record his sentence was more severe than was expected, and to my mind was cruelly vindictive.

However, to revert to Algiers and November 13th, 1942, the conferences made us very late in starting back to Gibraltar. We arrived there after dark in very thick weather with practically no ceiling. The radio in our Fortress had apparently given up the ghost, as for some hours Gibraltar had been trying to divert us. We eventually picked up some lights, and after milling around for some time at 500 feet and having a dummy run or two at the aerodrome, I being fully aware that the Rock was 1,400 feet high, we made a perfect landing, much to the relief of the reception committee who had been throwing fits since sunset.

The agreement with Darlan aroused the most acrimonious comment in the British and American press, particularly the former. As I wrote a few days later: "I found the General—Eisenhower—rather in despair over our politicians not much liking his dealings with Darlan. They are curious people, always wanting to have it both ways. Of course our obligations to de Gaulle make it difficult for them to justify our dealings with D."

For some time the spate of criticism was a constant thorn in the sides of those who were conducting any negotiations in North Africa, for often it was seized upon by the French as an excuse for not being able to do this or that for the reason that the attacks in the press, in Parliament and in Congress so undermined Darlan's authority that he could not persuade the senior French officers to accept his orders. However, both the President and the Prime Minister supported Eisenhower in the course he had taken. In my view it was the only possible course, and absolutely right. Darlan was the only man in North Africa who could have stopped the fighting and brought the authorities and people of North Africa in to help us in the struggle against the Axis.

It has to be remembered that most of the civil authorities were absolutely loyal to Marshal Pétain, and it was only by bluffing all and sundry into believing that he had Pétain's authority that Darlan was able to impose his will. The bulk of the population was apathetic one way or the other. Except for a few patriotic spirits, people did not wish to be dragged into the war and were definitely unhelpful, particularly when Algiers, Bone and other coastal cities and towns were bombed. Algiers, too, was full of refugees from Metropolitan France who had come there to avoid the misery and beastliness of war, and now it had arrived on their very doorsteps. But there has never been any doubt in my mind that our agreement with Darlan was the right one. It enabled us to get on with our chief task of fighting the Axis, while it also gave us the co-operation of the French Army in North Africa and the use of Dakar and French Equatorial Africa.

We were much less satisfied with the attitude of Admiral Godfroy and his fleet at Alexandria. He was still obstinate in refusing to come in with us.

II

I have already mentioned our landings at Bougie, Djidjelli and Bone on November 11th and 12th. The original plan provided for the rapid advance of the British force to the eastward in an attempt to capture Tunis and Bizerta. General Anderson acted with energy. After occupying the inland towns of Setif and Constantine, November 15th saw him at Tabarka, a small port on the coast some sixty miles from Bizerta. In spite of steadily mounting difficulties from lack of transport, and torrential rain which converted roads and airfields into veritable quagmires for days at a time, the British First Army pushed on and reached Mateur and Djedeida, some twenty and twelve miles respectively from Bizerta and Tunis. But they were too weak for further operations, and had to fall back to a line about thirty-five miles west of Bizerta and Tunis.

To hark back to my own movements, I embarked in the cruiser *Aurora* at Gibraltar on November 15th for visits to Oran and Algiers to see how they were getting on with the clearance and use of the ports. At Oran I went to see the local French Admiral, following up the messenger I sent to tell him of my intended call in ten minutes in case he should clear out before I could pay my visit. He received me frigidly but politely, and I was able to tell him what I wanted. I also saw Rear-Admiral A. C. Bennett, U.S.N., who was having some difficulty in creating order out of chaos. But good work had already been done in clearing the port of wrecks, and a fair number of ships were unloading stores and supplies for the Army, mostly in the outer harbour. I was able to make some advance arrangements for the berthing of Admiral Syfret's heavy ships of Force 'H' at Mers-el-Kebir, the naval port of Oran.

We reached Algiers next day, where some things were good and some bad. I had succeeded in obtaining the services of Commodore J. A. V. Morse, of Suda Bay fame, as Commodore in charge. I knew him to be a forceful officer of great tact and ability, and found, as I expected, that he had established cordial relations with the French port authorities and that unloading from ships was going well; but that there was difficulty in getting the stores away through lack of transport.

A large number of ships were still at anchor in Algiers Bay, their only protection against U-boat attack being an anti-submarine patrol to seaward. The air defence also left much to be desired. By some mischance or want of foresight the Royal Air Force radar warning set had not arrived, not having been given sufficient priority in the loading programme. As late as on December 5th I was to write to the First Sea Lord: "Today, nearly a month after Algiers was taken, the *Alynbank* (an auxiliary A.A. ship) in the Bay still provides the long-range warning. Some short-range sets, however, are working satisfactorily."

Eisenhower moved permanently to Algiers from Gibraltar on November 24th, and I followed the next day. We both had offices on the first floor of the Hotel St. Georges, mine fitted as a bedroom which I used for a night or two though there was no heating or hot water. I found that my staff and that of the Supreme Commander had been competing for the same villa for their respective bosses. Eisenhower was already in it; but he most kindly offered to give it up if I really wanted it. Of course I refused any such thing. There was another house, the Villa Kleine, in the same garden. Indeed, I thought it was the better of the two as it had central heating. It belonged to rich people, and, as I wrote to my relative "is a very modern house with a cocktail bar in the drawing-room. . . . And you should see my bathroom, several steps up to the bath and a basin with cut-glass bottles all round it, some still filled with exotic scents as the lady apparently left in a hurry when the bombing started. The bed is upholstered in blue satin, and alongside the head of it, let into the wall, is the lady's private wireless set. . . . The grounds are very secluded and just lovely, with palms, orange trees, syringas and all manner of flowering shrubs with bougainvillea and masses of rose trees which will soon be in blossom. Watts, my coxswain, is thoroughly enjoying himself and has already planted vegetables. He is looking round for hens." Incidentally, after an expedition of twenty miles into the country Watts came back in triumph with six hens and a cockerel.

So it was here that I settled in with the Chief of Staff, my secretary and flag lieutenant. The only approach was up a winding road and through a single gate heavily guarded by American soldiers who were no respecters of rank. Until we enlisted the help of Major Lee, Eisenhower's military aide-de-camp, we had several hectic experiences with trigger-happy G.I.'s after dark, gruffly demanding our identity and business with the muzzle of a loaded tommy-gun thrust in through the window of the car.

Algiers at that time was no bed of roses. No day passed without an air raid of some sort either on the mass of shipping in the bay, the port or the city itself, the latter chiefly at night. From the verandah outside the villa, which was well up the hill overlooking Algiers and the sea, we had a magnificent view of all that went on, and sometimes it was spectacular enough. However, as I said, adequate air defence in fighters or anti-aircraft guns was still lacking.

The R.A.F. and United States Army Air Force were terribly hampered by the frightful weather. The airfields, dusty in summer, were transformed into virtual swamps by the heavy rain. Great numbers of our aircraft were bogged down and unable to take off, while the enemy, with their all-weather concrete runways, could operate with full freedom. This state of affairs persisted most of the winter until we had the material to weatherproof our runways. Even so aircraft moving off the tracks often became hopelessly stuck in the morass of mud.

Bone, some two hundred and sixty miles east of Algiers, was quite a good port with several excellent berths for unloading, so it naturally became the advanced supply base for the First Army. It also had an airfield with a good runway from which fighters could be operated in most weathers. Being just within range of the enemy's supply route by sea to Bizerta and Tunis, it was also well suited for night operations by cruisers and destroyers. So we decided to keep a small squadron there under the able and energetic command of Rear-Admiral C. H. J. Harcourt. We called it Force 'Q', and it very soon gave the enemy a taste of its mettle, as I shall presently relate.

To be in charge of the port of Bone itself I brought Commodore G. N. Oliver forward from Gibraltar. Again his drive and quiet determination proved him to be a veritable tower of strength in a situation that was always difficult and sometimes dangerous.

The enemy were fully aware of the value of Bone as a supply base for the Army in Tunisia. Moreover, they had every reason to dread the night attacks of our cruisers and destroyers on their own supply line. At the outset, until we could get our own fighters forward, the Germans had the local air superiority, and the savagery of their attacks upon Bone and the shipping there very soon showed us that it was unprofitable to run large personnel ships anywhere east of Algiers. Air attacks upon the port occurred every night and day during November. On the night of the 27th–28th, for instance, there was continuous bombing for five and a half hours during the course of which the destroyer *Ithuriel* was badly hit.

But we soon had our revenge. British submarines were maintaining a continuous and concentrated patrol in the approaches to Tunis and Bizerta. On December 1st an enemy convoy, located by air reconnaissance, was attacked by one of these submarines, which, after inflicting damage, was forced to dive on being counter-attacked by enemy motor torpedo-boats. Force 'Q', consisting of the cruisers *Aurora*, Captain W. G. Agnew; *Argonaut*, Captain E. W. L. Longley-Cook; *Sirius*, Captain P. W. B. Brooking; with the destroyers *Quentin* and H.M.A.S. *Quiberon*, was at sea under the command of Rear-Admiral Harcourt with his flag in the *Aurora*. At about half an hour after midnight on December 1st–2nd these ships fell upon the convoy off the Gulf of Tunis, and for the enemy it was a holocaust. Engaged at point-blank range four supply ships or transports and three destroyers were sunk or set on fire. It was a ghastly scene of ships exploding and bursting into flame amidst clouds of steam and smoke; of men throwing themselves overboard as their ships sank; and motor vehicles carried on deck sliding and splashing into the sea as vessels capsized. What men the enemy lost, what quantities of motor transport fuel, and military supplies were destroyed I do not know; but not one ship of that convoy survived. Our submarines next morning reported large areas covered in debris and thick oil with numbers of floating corpses in lifebelts. We suffered no losses or damage during the action; but on the way back to Bone in the early dawn the *Quentin* was sunk by a torpedo from an enemy aircraft. Most of her crew were rescued by H.M.A.S. *Quiberon* under heavy bombing.

It was in retaliation for this success, no doubt, that the enemy launched a heavy air attack upon Bone before dawn on December 4th, and another which lasted from 8 p.m. on the 4th to 4 a.m. on the 5th. The quays and jetties of the port were congested with shell, petrol and other stores. There were bad fires and explosions with considerable losses of ammunition and valuable material, with fairly heavy casualties. But more and more of the attackers were shot down by our fighters as the airfield became fully operative, while further toll was taken by gunfire from the ships, so that as December wore on the raids became less frequent. All the same, with occasional sharp recrudescences, air raids on Bone continued off and on until the Axis forces in Tunisia surrendered in May, 1943.

I have said that the large personnel ships could not be risked east of Algiers because of the air menace. The Algerian roads were completely inadequate for the huge mass of heavy Army traffic, while the single-line railway from Algiers was execrable with an acute shortage of rolling stock. Partly because of this, partly because transport by sea is always more rapid and economical than transport by road or rail, we had to use coastwise shipping for sending reinforcements and supplies to Bone. The task fell upon the smaller vessels and landing-craft, and convoys escorted by destroyers and other naval craft sailed eastward from Algiers every fourteen days or so until the end of the Tunisian campaign. In one period of seven weeks during the worst of the bombing these little ships discharged some 128,000 tons of supplies at Bone, while about 4,000 tons of food and petrol was reloaded into naval landing-craft, and taken forward to the smaller ports of La Calle and Tabarka to the eastward. All these convoys had to be fought through, and no passage was without incident.

A shuttle service for troops between Algiers and Bone every third or fourth night was undertaken by four small ships of the Royal Navy. Originally fast cross-Channel steamers, they had been requisitioned as Landing Ships Infantry (Medium). They were the *Queen Emma*, *Princess Beatrix*, *Royal Ulsterman* and *Royal Scotsman*, the first-named commanded by an old destroyer friend of mine, the imperturbable Captain George Gibbs, distinguished in the First World War. Carrying between them some 3,300 troops on every trip, these four ships had ferried 16,000 men to Bone by December 5th, an outstanding achievement. By February 13th, 1943, they had carried another 36,000. Always under air attack, and sometimes under U-boat attack as well, their regular voyages were never uneventful. I remember them with great pride and satisfaction. They came through without loss or damage, for which I was thankful. Their hard and devoted service was of the greatest help to the final success of our campaign in Tunisia.

Conspicuously fine work on the run to Bone was also done by the tank-landing ships H.M.S. *Bachaquero*, *Misoa* and *Tasajera*, as well as by the ferry steamer S.S. *Empire Dace*. Most of the petrol and fuel was carried in two small tankers of the Merchant Navy, the *Empire Bairn* and *Empire Gawain*.

III

Meanwhile the matter of the French fleet at Toulon had become critical. Though the Germans had marched into unoccupied France, they had announced they would not occupy the fortified area of Toulon. On the surface, therefore, the position of the French fleet was safeguarded. Admiral Darlan, as already described, had requested Admiral de la Borde to sail his ships to Gibraltar; but had met with blank refusal.

Admiral de la Borde, whom I knew as a fine sailor and a brave man, apparently hated Darlan almost as much as the Germans. The result we all know. As we expected, the Germans broke their promise, and in the early hours of November 27th made a sudden advance and occupied Toulon. To prevent his ships from falling into enemy hands de la Borde was forced to scuttle them, which caused us considerable depression. This was the price France had to pay for dissension in the Navy.

Admiral de la Borde also paid the price for his obstinacy. He was later tried and condemned to death; but a petition for reprieve was successful and the sentence was commuted to imprisonment for life.

I have always felt deeply about the sadness of the fates of Admirals Esteva and de la Borde. I am convinced that their patriotism was never in doubt. Their mistakes arose through wrong thinking at a time of great stress and difficulty and their blind allegiance to Pétain and the German-controlled Vichy government which they considered the constitutional government of France. Like many other Frenchmen they did not seem to understand that the Allied occupation of French North Africa was the first step in the liberation and final salvation of their country from the hated Germans. They suffered for a mistaken loyalty.

Darlan was more successful with the Governor-General in French West Africa, Pierre Boisson, who joined in with us late in November. Boisson had been a poilu in the 1914-18 war and was badly wounded. A thorough patriot and devoted to the interests of his country his only thought was to keep French West Africa intact for France. I saw a certain amount of him from time to time, and formed a high opinion of his straightforward and forceful character.

So the beginning of December found us in a fairly strong position. Though we had come near to occupying Tunisia, we had been forestalled by the German airborne troops. Bad weather and mud was beginning to show that serious winter campaigning there was impracticable without better preparations and organization. But we held the whole of North Africa from Tunisia to well down the West Coast, and with the First Army in Tunisia being built-up and reinforced, and the Eighth Army advancing rapidly from the east, it was only a matter of time before the Axis forces between us were squeezed out or forced to capitulate.

The ports of Algiers, Oran and Casablanca were working well, and reinforcements and masses of military stores were starting to pour in. At Algiers, where the shipping losses were fairly serious through attacks by aircraft and Italian 'limpeteers' with their explosive charges, more and more ships were being accommodated in the port and few in the open bay. Our defence against aircraft, U-boats and mines was improving steadily.

Of course I had my own troubles, not the least of which was when I had news that my wife was crossing to England in a slow convoy which left

New York on November 19th. I was very anxious until I heard of her safe arrival. The French fleet at Alexandria was also on my mind. I sent message after message to Admiral Godfroy asking for his active co-operation; but he too was beset by mingled perplexities, and did not feel himself in a position to move.

The French Navy, indeed, was all at sixes and sevens in its loyalties. I had thought that the German breaking of the armistice and the fate of the Toulon fleet must inevitably cause Godfroy and his ships to come in with us. But it was not to be. As I wrote home on December 1st: "They have now no excuse for remaining inert, except perhaps that so many Frenchmen at the present time appear to have lost all their spirit. Doubtless it will revive; but at the moment the will to fight for their country is completely absent."

Yet, for the first time, we had got ahead of Hitler, and had much for which to be thankful. What with the Russian counter-offensive just starting at Stalingrad, I began to see the shining dawn of final victory gradually creeping up over the hitherto dark horizon.

CHAPTER XXXIX

I

In the last chapter I just touched upon the operations of the British First Army under General Anderson in their first attempts to capture Tunis and Bizertia. During December our troops were still hard at it. The enemy was active and constantly reinforced, and the fighting was bitter. The weather conditions were frightful, with heavy rain every day which converted the countryside and roads into virtual swamps impassable for tanks, guns and heavy transport, and spelt misery for the troops themselves in the glutinous mud. They were fighting among the hills and in the mountains in very difficult country, and the nights were bitterly cold. Reinforcements, chiefly American, were pushed forward; but the bad weather, coupled with the lack of transport and the poor conditions of the roads limited the size of the forces that could be maintained in the fighting line.

It had been hoped to bring off an attack towards the end of December; but after a personal visit to the front and seeing the conditions Eisenhower himself cancelled it. The best that could be done while waiting for better weather was to stabilize the front line some thirty-five miles from Bizerta and Tunis with the left flank on the coast. The work of the First Army and its young troops under General Anderson during the period of cold, rain, mud and fierce enemy activity can only be described as magnificent. Because it was unspectacular, it received little publicity compared with the rapid advance of the Eighth Army from the east.

The pause in Tunisia provided the opportunity for a much-needed reorganization and the building-up of transport and supplies in preparation for an all-out offensive when the weather improved. Another important measure was the improvement of the indifferent airfields by weatherproofing the runways. As I said earlier, they could not be used during the heavy rains because the grass airstrips were converted into bogs. The enemy had all-weather runways, and used them to full advantage. It was vitally necessary that we should have the means of providing air cover over our troops, as well as over the forward ports used for the disembarkation of supplies and reinforcements. Air cover was also necessary for our convoys and the ships operating in the Sicilian Channel.

We, of the Navy, were back to the old and strenuous task that we knew so well from our time in the Eastern Mediterranean—that of ensuring that the flow of our own supplies proceeded unimpeded, while that of the enemy was interrupted.

Very soon after the Allies landed in North Africa the enemy greatly reinforced his U-boats in the Mediterranean. I need not go into figures; but we had sustained considerable losses, particularly of large and valuable ships coming away unescorted from the landing areas. The fast minelayer *Manxman* was torpedoed by a U-boat on December 1st while on her way from Malta to Gibraltar. She was towed to Oran, and then to Gibraltar for repairs. On December 21st, the 24,000 ton P. & O. liner *Strathallan*, with troops and British nurses on board, was also torpedoed off Oran. The ship was set on fire and abandoned, and became a total loss.

On the other hand the enemy submarines were severely punished, thanks largely to the persistent good work of more than a hundred aircraft of Coastal Command and the United States Air Forces working from Gibraltar and North Africa. When the convoys started running regularly and properly escorted our losses were not unduly heavy, though it was seldom they were not attacked during their passage through the Western Mediterranean. Enemy aircraft from the south of France also took a hand, and before our fighter defence was properly organized they also took a toll of our merchant shipping, usually between Oran and Algiers. However, losses through aircraft attacks became progressively fewer, though the U-boats remained a nuisance to the end.

Meanwhile our own submarines were doing excellent work. The *Maidstone* and the 8th Flotilla, commanded by Captain G. B. H. Fawkes, arrived at Algiers early in December, while the 10th Flotilla, Captain G. C. Phillips, was based upon Malta. Three of the boats of these two flotillas were lost during November and December; but the others operated consistently against the enemy's supply line to Tunisia through the heavily mined Sicilian Channel, and off the Italian ports where supplies were shipped. In the last two months of 1942 these fine young men, working in conditions of great hazard in mined areas covered by the enemy's light surface forces and aircraft, sank fourteen merchant vessels, two destroyers, one U-boat and two small craft. Another ten merchant ships, with a cruiser, a destroyer and a torpedo boat, were all damaged. To anticipate, I might add that in the months of January, February, March and April, 1943, they accounted for another fifty-seven merchantmen, one submarine, one torpedo-boat and seven small craft sunk, with another eleven merchant ships and a destroyer damaged. The work of the 8th and 10th Submarine Flotillas was invaluable.

The enemy's main supply line ran from Sicily to Bizerta and Tunis. It involved a short open sea passage of little more than a hundred miles which could be covered in ten hours or less. This convoy route lay roughly two hundred mies from Bone where, as I said in the previous chapter, we maintained a force of cruisers and destroyers known as Force 'Q'. If necessary another handful of cruisers and destroyers could be sent to operate from Malta, which was equidistant from the Axis convoy route.

At the outset the enemy made the passage both by day and by night. Rear-Admiral Harcourt's smashing success against a convoy on the night of December 1st–2nd, however, brought about a temporary change in the enemy's plans, for thereafter he showed a preference for the daylight passage in spite of the risk of air attack. To ensure the safety of this vital convoy route the Axis laid two long minefields, one from the west of Bizerta and the other from near Cape Bon, east of Tunis, both reaching nearly to the coast of Sicily. Through the canal, so to speak, between these two mine barriers the enemy hoped eventually to pass his convoys by night without much risk of attack by our light surface forces.

These minefields certainly added to our difficulties. They had to be avoided, which meant that our ships from Bone or Malta had to steam a circuitous and lengthier course before reaching the enemy's convoy area, which was within easy reach of the enemy airfields in Sicily. We lacked adequate fighter protection, and the consequence in practice was that we had to accept the risk of our cruisers or destroyers being at sea without air cover during daylight either at the beginning or end of their operations, probably both.

We eventually countered this move by using our fast minelayers *Abdiel* and *Welshman*, and the submarine *Rorqual*, to lay lines of mines across and between the two enemy fields, starting as close to the Tunisian coast as possible and gradually working northward, rather like fitting rungs into a ladder. Aircraft from Malta co-operated by laying mines close inshore; but the bulk of the work was done by the *Abdiel*, Captain David Orr-Ewing, and as the minelayers were unescorted, the task was particularly risky. But the risk was worth while. These cross minefields in what the enemy thought was clear water lost him several ships and I remember that one of the first victims was a vessel called the *Ankara*, specially fitted for carrying tanks, which we had often tried to catch from the Eastern Mediterranean but had never succeeded.

All the same, though our submarine and light forces were doing good work, far too many enemy supply ships were making the passage by day, and our air forces seemed to be incapable of dealing with them. I represented this to General Eisenhower and had a meeting with him and General Spaatz, commanding the American Army Air Force, to discuss the question. Spaatz was a grand little man, always ready for anything and a great friend. He undertook to deal with the matter, though at the time I thought he was much underrating the difficulties and very much overrating the ability of aircraft to find and effectually to bomb ships at sea. I tactfully pointed out that it was not so easy as he seemed to think. Operating over the sea required experienced navigators, and the pilots of his military 'planes might have difficulty in knowing their own whereabouts, in discriminating between friend and foe, and so on. But Spaatz brushed my doubts aside, and went off to do the job.

For the next ten days or so we carefully watched the results, and nothing much seemed to be happening to the Axis shipping. Then one morning I had a message asking if General Spaatz could come and see me. Of course I said yes, and in due course he arrived. He walked into my room and opened the conversation by saying: "Admiral, I've just come to tell you that we don't know a darned thing about this business of working over the sea. Will you help us?"

I already held Spaatz in high esteem; but that simple remark of his endeared him to me more than ever. There are not many men who are great enough to acknowledge error. Of course we helped him. That afternoon a young Fleet Air Arm observer whom the Americans nicknamed 'Boy Jones' was detailed to join them, and finally we had ten of our highly-trained observers working with the American bombing squadrons operating over the sea, and Lieutenant-Commander V. G. H. Ramsay Fairfax, a very experienced observer, on Spaatz's staff. I am sure that Spaatz and his fliers would be the first to admit the great value to them of these officers of our Fleet Air Arm. I remember having to pay up several bottles of whisky which I had wagered with Spaatz on the destruction of some particular named vessels.

In the last chapter I said something of our naval responsibility of supplying the left flank of the Army in Tunisia by sea through the port of Bone, and the stores being carried forward in landing-craft to La Calle and Tabarka, just behind our front line. As I have said, Commodore G. N. Oliver, was in charge at Bone. No better man could have been chosen for what was a very trying and difficult job.

By the middle of December Force 'H', under Vice-Admiral Sir Neville Syfret, consisting of the battleships *Nelson*, *Rodney*, one or more aircraft-carriers, and some destroyers was dividing its time between Gibraltar and Mers-el-Kebir (Oran). They provided our heavy cover in case the Italian fleet put in an appearance; but the Italian battleships and cruisers remained quiescent in their harbours.

We had a few air attacks upon Algiers during December which did some slight damage in the harbour area and among the shipping, while in the early hours of the 12th there was a 'limpit' attack upon the shipping in the outer anchorage, which sank one merchant vessel and damaged three more. The sixteen Italians concerned, who had come from a submarine, were captured and made prisoners. Like the others who had made a successful attack at Alexandria, they were not allowed to communicate with the outside world.

Just before the first light of dawn on December 14th, during the return of Force 'Q' to Bone at 26 knots, after one of its night expeditions to the Sicilian narrows, the cruiser *Argonaut*, Captain E. W. L. Longley-Cook, was torpedoed simultaneously in bows and stern by an Italian submarine and severely damaged. She presented an extraordinary sight on arriving at Algiers with portions of her bows and stern blown away, and a tangle of mangled plating reaching well up into the air on her starboard side aft. Though her rudder was missing, her engines and two of her four propellers were still working. Temporary repairs were carried out at Algiers, after which she sailed under her own steam for Gibraltar. There she was docked, before crossing the Atlantic for thorough repairs at the Navy Yard at Philadelphia.

As the services of Captain C. R. McCrum, the Maintenance Captain, were required elsewhere, Captain Longley-Cook became the Captain of the Fleet on my staff while his ship was refitting.

II

On December 24th the apparent tranquillity of the political situation in North Africa was rudely disturbed by the assassination of Admiral Darlan. The facts are well known. A young fanatic named Bonnier de la Chapelle gained access to the Admiral's office in the Palais D'Etè as he was returning after lunch and emptied a revolver into him. The lack of precaution in those around him and the police against such an incident was almost incredible. The French announced that "Darlan was a victim of those who would not forgive him for having again taken up the struggle against Germany at the side of the Allies"; but I do not think there was any truth in this. The ultimate responsibility for the crime was never properly fixed. Many hands were in it, and it was of no service whatever to the Allied cause.

History will doubtless judge Darlan and I will not attempt to anticipate the verdict. Common accounts stamped him as being a traitor to the Allied cause, while the Germans have stated that he was ready to communicate some of our naval movements and secrets. We know that he had a meeting in Paris with Admiral Otto Schultze, Commanding in France, early in December, 1941, while on January 28th, 1942, he met Admiral Raeder at Evry-le-Bourg and some form of co-operation was arranged in certain naval matters.[1] But it is certain that once Darlan made up his mind to throw in his lot with the Allies at the end of 1942, he acted absolutely squarely with us, and was the only man who could have brought North and West Africa in with us. To me, personally, he was invariably most cordial, in fact I lunched with him and his wife at the Palais D'Etè the day before his murder.

I have often speculated as to what he was really doing in North Africa at the time of our landing. It was given out of course, that he was visiting his sick son. But he had been there for about six weeks, an inordinate time for such a visit by a man in his position. Had he an inkling of what was about to happen, and did he wish to be on the winning side?

[1] See *Hitler and his Admirals*. Anthony Martienssen (Secker and Werburg.) pages 245-249.

I do not know; but Darlan was not the only Cabinet Minister to be in North Africa at that time. Mendigal, the French Minister for Air, later told me he actually flew over our 'Torch' convoys on his way there.

There was a large state funeral, with bands and representative detachments from the French Army and Navy, the American Army, and the Royal Navy, the British Army and the Royal Air Force. It started with a long requiem mass in the cathedral, followed by a procession to the chapel where the Admiral's body lay in state. All the leading figures attended, and French, American and British officers filed slowly past the coffin. It was a colourful and impressive display with the mass of different uniforms.

Then we became immersed in a welter of French politics. Who was to be Darlan's successor?

The choice eventually fell upon General Giraud, who was appointed High Commissioner of North Africa. But the appointment did not last long. Giraud was primarily a soldier, and was completely unfamiliar with the devious machinations of French politics. The administrative side of the government did not interest him. His only anxiety was to get the French Army organized and equipped to get on with the fighting.

French politics in Algiers were certainly in a tangle. Most of the leading figures in Algiers were supposed to be on the list for assassination, with Mr. Murphy, the representative of the American State Department, at the top. Mr. Harold Macmillan, who came out before the end of the year as the British Minister Resident at Allied Force Headquarters, told me afterwards that his name was the only one not on the list and that only because he had arrived after Darlan's murder.

I was delighted to have Mr. Macmillan on the spot, as it took me right out of the political business and allowed me to get on with my proper job of running the naval side of the war in the Western Mediterranean. I had always made a point of visiting Eisenhower in his office for about twenty minutes each morning during which we discussed current topics and operations. Later he used to hold a daily meeting of all the heads. At the outset, as the senior British officer with Eisenhower, I inevitably found myself mixed up in politics, an invidious position as I could only give my own personal opinion. I was quite unaware of the views of the British government and was given no guidance.

Macmillan's arrival was a blessing to me, though at first it was not entirely pleasing to the Americans. But in no time at all he made himself indispensable. It was certain that he and Murphy relieved Eisenhower of an immense amount of political manœuvring though of course they could not relieve him of the final responsibility for making decisions.

I had a small dinner-party at my villa on Christmas night. Eisenhower's villa was in the same grounds. Just before my guests were due he asked if he could come and see me. He arrived with them at about 8 p.m., and by order of President Roosevelt presented me with the American Army Distinguished Service Medal. It was quite unexpected, and I was greatly touched at the kind things he said.

III

The year 1943 had a much brighter opening than the one which had just ended. January, 1942, had found us at the lowest ebb of our fortunes. Now, twelve months later: "Far back, through creeks and inlets making, comes silent flooding in, the main."

We had cause to be optimistic. The Eighth Army was moving steadily and inexorably towards Tripoli, driving the Axis forces before it. The Russian offensive at Stalingrad was gathering weight and momentum, and the Germans were in full retreat. We had established ourselves in North Africa, and were gradually building up our strength to defeat the enemy in Tunisia as soon as conditions allowed. After that a whole vista of possibilities for offensive action lay open before us, including knocking Italy out of the war. Meanwhile, in Tunisia, General Anderson's tough First Army, with the French and the Americans, were still having hard fighting, but on the whole were managing to maintain their positions.

Early in the New Year we heard that President Roosevelt, the Prime Minister, and the Chiefs of Staff of both countries were to meet at Casablanca. They arrived there on January 12th and 13th. Eisenhower was summoned to attend, and flew there on the 15th, having a most unpleasant journey. Two of the four engines of his Fortress gave up the ghost, and he finished the flight wearing parachute harness and ready to jump.

A day or two later Sir Dudley Pound, the First Sea Lord, sent for me also. I had an interesting though uneventful flight, and stayed for two nights in General Patton's sumptuous villa. He was a most charming and interesting host. Responsible for the security and other arrangements for the Casablanca Conference, Patton had organized everything on a most lavish scale, including much barbed wire guarded by a swarm of the toughest-looking sentries and military police who checked up on everybody.

I attended a meeting of our Chiefs of Staff and had several conferences with Sir Dudley Pound and his American opposite number, Admiral Ernest King. The latter was in an excellent mood and most amenable and understanding. One night I dined with the President. Mr. Churchill and all the Chiefs of Staff were present, with Mr. Harry Hopkins and young Franklin Roosevelt. I sat on the President's left, and it was fascinating to hear the interplay of conversation between the two great men. We spent most of our time listening.

While at Casablanca I took the opportunity of visiting Rear-Admiral John L. Hall, U.S.N., the Flag Officer in Charge, whom I had met in Washington. He was a fine type of officer of commanding appearance and manner, and most able and splendid in co-operation. He had the port well in hand and running smoothly. I saw some of the installations and the French battleship *Jean Bart*; but lack of time made my visit a very short one.

A number of decisions were taken at the Casablanca Conference, including one very important one affecting the commands. My position was left unchanged, though the First Sea Lord had discussed with me the desirability of extending the sphere of my command to the east to cover the whole of the Mediterranean. It was certainly rather an anomaly that two forces whose operations were directed to the same end, that of interrupting the enemy's supplies to North Africa, should be directed by two Commanders-in-Chief. However, no alteration was made for the time being.

General Sir Harold Alexander, who had been present at the Conference, was nominated to command all the land forces under the Supreme Commander, General Eisenhower. The Eighth Army was to come under the Supreme Commander when it entered Tunisia. Tedder was nominated Commander-in-Chief of the Air Forces in North Africa.

Much was also hoped for the meeting between Generals Giraud and de Gaulle under the auspices of the two great men. These hopes were to prove somewhat illusory. They reached no working agreement. While Giraud, in the eyes of the de Gaullists, was regarded as a reactionary general who, among others, was largely responsible for the collapse of France in 1940, de Gaulle was considered by the opposite faction as something of an upstart who preached much glib nonsense about mechanized warfare and had political views which were dangerously left wing. To unite the pair was like trying to mix oil and water.

One piece of welcome news that we heard at Casablanca was that Tripoli was expected to be in the hands of the Eighth Army in about a fortnight. It was wished to use the port for supplying the army, and much depended upon the condition in which it was left by the enemy. It was on January 23rd that the announcement was made that Tripoli had fallen.

From Casablanca General Marshall and Admiral King came on to Algiers and stayed with Eisenhower. Sir Dudley Pound also came and spent a couple of days with me. I derived much benefit from our conversation, while the First Sea Lord was able to see something of our work at first hand. Generals Sir John Dill and Sir Harold Alexander also came on to Algiers.

Meanwhile I must hark back a little, for a good deal had been happening in naval circles during January.

Bone, as I have already said, was being heavily attacked by enemy aircraft, largely because it was our principal port of supply for the First Army in Tunisia. The port was always a busy one, added to which it provided the base for Force 'Q'. Between December 13th, 1942, and February 1st, 1943, it had sixty-eight red warnings and more than two thousand heavy bombs.

There were particularly heavy daylight air attacks on Bone and the aerodrome nearby on January 1st and 2nd. About a hundred aircraft came over on the 1st, attacking in waves of five. The cruiser *Ajax*, which had only joined Force 'Q' the day before after an extensive refit subsequent to being damaged in the Eastern Mediterranean, was again bombed and severely mauled, necessitating her leaving the station for further repairs. Two merchant ships were also damaged, and the berthing facilities were much hampered by the grounding of stricken ships. Another sharp attack took place next day, when the *Ajax* was near-missed; the minesweeper *Alarm* had her back broken and had to be beached, finally becoming a total loss; while four merchantmen were hit and caught fire. Two of them, which carried petrol, were lost.

Some doubts were expressed as to the wisdom of keeping cruisers and destroyers at Bone; but I had to harden my heart. I made a signal to Rear-Admiral Harcourt, commanding Force 'Q', that I knew he was having an unpleasant time; but that he must stick it out. If our ships withdrew we were playing the enemy's game. I told him improved defences were on the way. A few days afterwards I visited Bone in the destroyer *Lookout*, and returned to Algiers by air.

The anti-aircraft defences were strengthened by the Army at my particular request, while we established a battery at Cape de Garde using the 4·7-inch guns from the damaged destroyer *Ithuriel*. This was to prevent the enemy minelaying in the approaches to Bone, our sweepers having accounted for many mines since we occupied the port. Motor torpedo boats and Swordfish aircraft were also stationed there for anti-shipping strikes, though they had had little luck up-to-date. Night sweeps against enemy shipping in the Sicilian channel were still being carried out by surface vessels from Malta and Bone. There was a scarcity of targets; but on the night of January 17th–18th the *Lightning* and *Loyal* had the good fortune to meet an enemy merchant ship carrying ammunition. She was fired upon, and blew up in smoke and flame.

During January bases for landing-craft were established at Bougie and Djedjelli, Bougie also being used for landing stores for the Army. Philippeville, further to the eastward, was used for the discharge of convoys, and was very busy as the terminus of the tank ferry service from Oran.

Force 'H', consisting of the *Nelson*, *Rodney*, *Formidable* and destroyers, visited Algiers on January 3rd and sailed again at dusk on their return journey to Mers-el-Kebir. Their brief stay was mainly to show the French population that we had large ships operating on their doorstep. Unfortunately, Vice-Admiral Sir Neville Syfret, commanding Force 'H', was found to be suffering from acute appendicitis on January 23rd. He had to be operated upon and sent to a hospital ship. Vice-Admiral Sir Harold Burrough was flown out from England to take over the temporary command.

Little more of general interest occurred during January, except that on the 15th the first of the Women's Services in the shape of twelve officers and six ratings of the Women's Royal Naval Service arrived at Algiers from Gibraltar in the destroyers *Penn* and *Pathfinder*—'the Wren's Special', as they called it. These most useful ladies were the forerunners of the many more Wrens who were presently to join us, and their services were invaluable.

On January 21st I was promoted to Admiral of the Fleet. My Union Flag was hoisted in the *Maidstone* at 8 a.m. on that date. I considered myself extremely fortunate at having been lucky enough to reach the highest rank in His Majesty's Navy.

IV

After the Casablanca Conference the Prime Minister flew on to Cyprus, and then to Adana, where he met the Turks. From there he went on to Cairo. He called at Tripoli on his way home and reviewed the Eighth Army, and on February 4th we were electrified at being informed that he was coming on to Algiers next day. In vain the War Office in London told him it would be extremely dangerous to come, and that there was a plot to assassinate him. Eisenhower was also strongly opposed to the visit, all of which made Mr. Churchill the more determined to have his own way.

He arrived by air early the next forenoon, February 5th, and the most elaborate precautions were taken for his safety. We all met him at the airfield at Maison Blanche, and the official procession with Eisenhower set out for the return journey to Algiers by the ordinary direct route. In the meanwhile the Prime Minister and myself embarked in Eisenhower's special car, a heavily armoured vehicle with bullet-proof windows. Escorted by a couple of jeeps, we drove into Algiers from the north and to my villa by a most circuitous route, Mr. Churchill grumbling and most impatient at the length of the drive.

We lunched at Eisenhower's villa, Giraud, de Gaulle, Noguès, Peyrouton, Boisson and all the senior Frenchmen being present. The Prime Minister was supposed to take off again after lunch on his way home; but decided to remain until after dinner. As a bluff a cavalcade of cars was formed up outside the villa during lunch as though Mr. Churchill's departure were imminent. We were still at the luncheon-table when some consternation was caused by a sudden burst of machine-gun fire just outside the front door. It was only Major Lee, Eisenhower's A.D.C., who had left the table to see that everything was ready. While examining the gun in one of the jeeps he inadvertently fired a burst into the side of the villa. Some days later I asked Lee what the Supreme

Commander had said to him. "That's the worst of it, Admiral," he replied. "He hasn't said a darned thing—yet!"

The dummy procession started and went to the airfield, and a 'plane duly left for Gibraltar. Near midnight we took the Prime Minister to the airfield; but for some reason his aircraft would not function. So we brought the great man back to my house at about 2.30 a.m., he not in the best of tempers. He went straight to bed. We got him away next day flying straight home.

As I wrote to my wife about Mr. Churchill's visit: "You never saw anything like the house. Every type of hanger-on, detectives, valets, secretaries. The Foreign Office was set up in Roy Dick's bedroom!"

Perhaps the most important result of the Casablanca Conference was the decision to proceed with the invasion of Sicily as soon as possible after the defeat of the enemy in North Africa. There had been an inclination in some circles to take Sardinia first. It would have been an easier operation; but the occupation of Sicily, which was nearer Italy with its many airfields within easy reach of Malta and the Sicilian narrows, had many advantages.

Planning started at once in February, and the various commanders were chosen. The operation was to be known as 'Husky', and on the British side Admiral Sir Bertram Ramsay was to command the assaulting squadron, and General Sir Bernard Montgomery the troops. For the Americans, Vice-Admiral H. Kent Hewitt was to command the sea forces and General Patton the troops. The whole operation, of course, was under the ultimate direction of Alexander, Tedder and myself, with Eisenhower as Supreme Commander.

Fierce fighting still continued in Tunisia. In the middle of February the Germans launched a heavy attack in the southern sector, that held by the Americans. Our forces had been somewhat misled by our intelligence, which seemed to indicate that the main attack would come further north. Anyway, the Americans took a hard knock. They fought well enough: but were too thin on the ground and the reserves were insufficient. So back they came with considerable losses.

American officers were much upset about the reverse, as a reverse it undoubtedly was. Some of them had perhaps talked too big, and were consequently humbled. Loose tongues on both sides started to wag, and some bad feeling was engendered between the two Allies. An ignorant and largely malicious controversy arose as to the fighting qualities of the American troops. Doubts were thrown on American courage and skill and willingness to fight, which was grossly unfair. The troops were said to be 'green', which may have been true; but courage they never lacked. They were at much the same stage as were the British a year after they had entered the war, young, inexperienced, and apt to be thrown off their balance the first time they went into action. They very soon learnt.

There was no bickering at Allied Force Headquarters, and Eisenhower quickly took steps to put a stop to it elsewhere. It was his direction that there should be no dissension between Allies, no harsh or unjust criticism of each other's faults and failings. I remember that one evening Eisenhower asked me to dinner at short notice to meet, as he put it, "a bunch of generals". After dinner he spoke out quite frankly as to what was the matter with the American troops. When I left he thanked me for coming and said he was particularly anxious to say exactly what he thought before a British officer. The little incident only increased my admiration for him.

It must have been at about this time that one day when I was in Eisenhower's office he gave me two personal letters to read, one from the President and the other from Harry Hopkins, both starting with "Dear Ike". Eisenhower then said: "I never know how far to go with you Britishers, but just how long will it be before you start calling me Ike?"

"Just half a second," said I, "provided you'll call me Andrew in return."

Eisenhower was, or rather is, an honest and very sincere man. We were the greatest of friends.

In Tunisia the Germans had also attacked the British in the northern sector and had forced a small withdrawal, and during all this fighting ashore, which received scant notice in the English press, the Navy was hard at it fighting the battle of supplies. Vast quantities of stores, ammunition, vehicles and war material of all descriptions was pouring into the North African ports, and on one day, early in February, there were eighty merchant ships, laden or empty, in the port of Algiers alone. To anticipate, the tonnage of shipping into the 'Torch' area since the first landing to March 12th, 1943, reached the colossal total of 8,029,929 tons. Though very few convoys escaped either submarine or aircraft attack the tonnage lost during this period was 385,350 tons, 2·4 per cent of the total, or, if the assault period be excluded, 1·5 per cent of the total. This surely was a striking tribute to the efficacy of our escorts and the aircraft of Coastal Command, R.A.F., to say nothing of the fine sea discipline and fighting qualities shown by the personnel of the Merchant Navies.

On February 1st we were mortified to hear of the loss of the fast minelayer *Welshman*, which was sunk by a submarine with heavy loss of life while on passage from Malta to Alexandria.

I cannot go into details of our constant battle against the U-boats in which, among others, the destroyers *Quentin* (sunk on December 2nd, 1942), *Quiberon*, *Wheatland*, *Easton*, *Bicester* and *Lamerton*; the sloop *Enchantress*; the corvettes *Lotus*, *Starwort* and *Poppy*; the minesweeper *Cadmus* and the trawler *Lord Nuffield*, all had their successes. But I feel I must pay a special tribute to three little ships of the Royal Canadian Navy, the *Ville de Quebec*, Lieutenant-Commander R. E. Coleman; *Port Arthur*, Lieutenant E. T. Simmons; and *Regina*, Lieutenant-Commander Harry Freeland, which accounted for three submarines in twenty-six days, one each. I was glad to congratulate them on this remarkable 'hat trick', and sorry to see the last of them when they left the Mediterranean soon afterwards.

I have already said something of the work of our own submarines operating from Algiers and Malta, and of the great value of their work against the enemy's supply line. Aircraft also did their best during daylight to stop the passage of Axis convoys and ships across the Sicilian straits. They never wholly succeeded, largely because we lacked aircraft of the right type or in sufficient numbers.

I have mentioned the port of Bone and its value, and here, before long, we were able to send a reinforcement of British M.T.B.s and a few of their American counterparts, the P.T. boats, though the former, particularly the 'D' type, were lamentably slow and so full of gadgets and unnecessary amenities that they could hardly fulfil their functions. These craft made war on the German E-boats, and also mined the approaches close in to Tunis and Bizerta.

Towards the end of February the Admiralty finally decided that the anomaly should be brought to an end of forces from Bone and Malta working under different Commanders-in-Chief for the same object of disrupting the enemy's supply line to Tunisia. So just as the Eighth Army was brought under Eisenhower's command when in Tunisia, my area of authority was also extended. I was, therefore, appointed Commander-in-Chief, Mediterranean, again and made responsible for all matters which affected the Mediterranean as a whole, while the distribution of forces between the Western Mediterranean and the Levant was put in my hands. Admiral Sir Henry Harwood, hitherto Commander-in-Chief Mediterranean, who had always been most co-operative and helpful in every way, became Commander-in-Chief, Levant.

My operational area was extended to the eastward and bounded by a line joining the Tunisian–Tripolitanian border, to a position 35 degrees North 16 degrees East, and thence to Cape Spartivento, at the toe of Italy. This brought Malta within my orbit, though until it became possible to supply Malta and the Middle East from the westward Commander-in-Chief Levant remained responsible for their supply.

I have to confess I had considerable personal gratification at having again become Commander-in-Chief, Mediterranean, and at having Malta, for whose succour we had struggled so fiercely in the earlier years, again in the area of my command. If my memory serves me it has only been given to one other officer twice to assume the historic title of Commander-in-Chief, Mediterranean, and then not during war. This was Vice-Admiral Sir Pulteney Malcolm, who was there in 1828–1830, and again in 1833.

I visited Malta at the end of February, flying there in an American Fortress lent me by the Americans. Invariably when I asked Bedell Smith, Eisenhower's Chief of Staff, if he could let me have a 'plane, his reply was the same: "Admiral, the whole of the American Air Force is at your disposal."

Vice-Admiral Sir Ralph Leatham was Acting Governor at Malta, and I stayed with him at San Anton Palace. He had been relieved as Vice-Admiral, Malta, by Vice-Admiral Stuart Bonham-Carter, who was deep in the very hard and intricate work of preparing the island for the leading part it would have to play in the next large-scale operation, the invasion of Sicily.

Harwood came to meet me, and we quickly and amicably settled the details of our new relations to each other. I visited the dockyard and all the naval establishments. The dockyard, under the able administration of Rear-Admiral K. H. L. Mackenzie, was badly knocked about; but was going strong, not only in the upkeep and repair of ships, but also in rehabilitating its own docks, buildings and machine shops. As I wrote to the First Sea Lord, I was most impressed by the way they were overcoming their many difficulties. Except for a little broken glass Admiralty House was quite undamaged, whereas the large house next door, the Auberge de France, had been blown into a heap of rubble.

Shortly afterwards ill-health compelled Harwood to relinquish his appointment. Leatham relieved him temporarily until the arrival of the new Commander-in-Chief, Levant, Admiral Sir John Cunningham.

v

The month of March, 1943, brought several changes in the general organization and commands in the Western Mediterranean.

Vice-Admiral A. U. Willis, my late Chief of Staff in the *Warspite*, took over the command of Force 'H' from Vice-Admiral Burrough on March 4th, with his flag in the *Nelson*. Incidentally Force 'H' spent the first ten days or so of March at Gibraltar, this being brought about because our reconnaissance had temporarily lost sight of some of the German capital ships in northern waters. A sortie into the Atlantic might be contemplated.

Vice-Admiral H. Kent Hewitt, U.S.N. was appointed, under me, to command all the United States naval forces in the Mediterranean. This was a measure I very much welcomed. He set up his headquarters in the St. Georges Hotel next door to mine, and the arrangement of having ourselves and our staffs side by side was most convenient. We worked together like brothers. Hewitt's Chief of Staff was Rear-Admiral Spencer S. Lewis, an excellent officer who later cemented Anglo-American naval relations by marrying an officer of our Women's Royal Naval Service.

Hewitt was a very able officer and a most loyal and wholehearted co-operator. We became the greatest of friends, which persisted all through the years he was Commander-in-Chief of the United States Navy in European waters.

Although convenient to us, Hewitt's presence in Algiers cannot have been the best arrangement for him. As I have mentioned, he had been nominated Naval Commander for the American force detailed for the invasion of Sicily, while his General, Patton, was near Oran. However, they were accustomed to planning some hundreds of miles apart, and no harm seemed to come of it.

Another change which was very welcome from our naval point of view was the appointment of Air Vice-Marshal Sir Hugh Lloyd to command the Royal Air Force units co-operating with the Navy. Having been at Malta in 1941 and 1942 Lloyd was particularly well suited for the work, and was thoroughly acquainted with our naval requirements. His arrival made a great difference to our air effort over the sea. He also provided me, for my own use, with a Beaufighter and a young night-fighter pilot who was resting for a time after a long series of nocturnal operations. The pilot was a most efficient young man, who landed or took off with me at any hour of the day or night, though he did once get a wigging from the group captain at Lukka airfield, in Malta, for the dashing way in which he landed the Naval Commander-in-Chief.

The Beaufighter greatly facilitated my task of visiting the outlying parts of my command, and I could reach Malta in a surprisingly short time. It was at about this period that a considerably overdue action was taken by the provision of an official aircraft, a Dakota, for the Naval Commander-in-Chief, though it was manned by the United States Army Air Force. Nevertheless, I usually preferred to travel by my less comfortable but twice-as-fast Beaufighter.

Our main naval effort during March, in close co-operation with the air, was against the enemy's lines of communication between Sicily and Tunisia. Though night sweeps by our surface forces had no spectacular success, the mere fact of our sending ships to sea for periodical night sweeps dislocated and delayed the enemy convoys, and frequently held them up in both directions. They were further hampered by the necessary wide detours caused by our minefields. It was on the night of March 12th, during one of our sweeps, that we had the misfortune to lose the destroyer *Lightning*, which was hit by two torpedoes from an E-boat. The *Loyal* picked up 170 survivors, including the commanding officer. The *Lightning* was replaced in Force 'Q' by the Polish destroyer *Blyskawica*.

The success of our submarines against Axis shipping—they sank no fewer than seventeen supply and store ships in February and thirteen in March, besides damaging five others—led to increased anti-submarine activity on the part of the enemy. As I said earlier, our submarines were working in conditions of extreme hazard in enemy controlled and patrolled waters. During March we had to deplore the loss of the *Tigris*, *Thunderbolt* and *Turbulent* with their brave crews, which failed to return from patrol. It is difficult to find words with which to extol the gallantry and self-sacrificing fortitude of the officers and men of our submarines in the face of their heavy losses. Their spirit, alike with their courage, was magnificent.

Our naval air squadrons of Swordfish and Albacores from Malta and Bone were operating against the enemy shipping in co-operation with the R.A.F. The pilot of one of these aircraft which crashed into the sea east of Cape Serrat, in Tunisia, reached the shore in his rubber dinghy. On landing he sank into a quicksand from which he was finally rescued by Arabs and taken to their hut. While there he saw some German soldiers passing the door, from which he concluded, and rightly, that he was wrong side of the fighting line. Waiting until dark he started off alone, walked through the German lines and eventually made contact with our troops.

I must say I envied these young gentlemen some of their adventures, and wished that I were taking a more active part in the fighting. The soldier's saying that "War is like a cinema. The best seats are high up and at the back", applied very forcibly to some of us at Algiers.

Bone was still the main target for the enemy's air attacks, though anti-aircraft guns and fighter defence, coupled with radar, greatly reduced their effectiveness. On one occasion our M.T.B.s from Bone laying mines off Bizerta were engaged by E-boats. In the skirmish that ensued one of the enemy craft was stopped and set ablaze, and the two others fired into each other.

Mers-el-Kebir was attacked by limpeteers on the night of March 23rd–24th, when swimmers were reported in the bay. Fire was opened, and one was hit while the other disappeared. We also had our excitements at Algiers, where the air attacks were more frequent than usual. On the night of the 26th the harbour was attacked by eight aircraft. Five circling torpedoes were dropped. One of these hit a merchant ship in the exact spot she had already been torpedoed and finished her as a ship. Another was recovered after striking the detached mole, and the others exploded harmlessly. Of the four which fell in the port area two struck buildings and exploded. Another hit a pier by the Post Office on which was a Bofors gun. The gun's crew, unhurt except by a shower of masonry which did no vital damage, were loud in their indignation. Being torpedoed, they said, was a sailor's job! With the heavy anti-aircraft fire from our many guns, the streams of tracer and the searchlights. it was a noisy and spectacular display as seen from the verandah of my villa.

At Djedjelli the base was coming into operation for the training and maintenance of the stream of landing-craft of all descriptions that were reaching us for, among other purposes, the forthcoming invasion of Sicily.

Once again, with Cyrenaica clear of the enemy, the route to Malta was open from the east. Two convoys from Alexandria reached the island during March and unloaded 28,000 tons of cargo and some 7,500 tons of much-needed oil fuel.

VI

During the last week in March the Eighth Army broke through the Mareth Line and advanced rapidly to the north. The small port of Sfax was occupied on April 10th. There was no water or light, while the dock area and residential district had been badly damaged. The channel was quickly cleared to admit L.C.T.s, and the first convoy arrived from Tripoli on the 14th. Some 14,000 tons of Army stores had been discharged by the end of April.

Sousse, about seventy miles to the northward, was entered on April 12th. The enemy's demolition had failed and the port was little damaged, though the harbour was full of wrecks and the entrance partially blocked. By the 17th sufficient petrol had arrived to enable M.T.B.s to use the port as an advanced striking base, and the first batch of these craft arrived five days later. The enemy was still making desperate efforts to supply his forces in Tunisia by sea, though with the better weather they had the greatest difficulty. Among other small craft they were using a number of Siebel ferries, reasonably fast, shallow-draft vessels like landing-craft with a heavy anti-aircraft armament. The M.T.B.s from Bone and Sousse, with our naval aircraft, were a constant menace to the Axis shipping. Hardly a night passed but they were off Tunis and Bizerta; mining, harrying the patrols, attacking and sinking vessels carrying the stores, ammunition and petrol so badly needed by Rommel's army. It was always a surprise to me how the Italian seamen continued to operate their ships in the face of the dangers that beset them. They were liable to surface, submarine and air attacks throughout the whole of their passage from Sicily, and the fact that they stood up to it should be remembered to their credit.

It was not only at night that our M.T.B.s operated. Provided warships display their proper ensigns before opening fire, it is a perfectly legitimate *ruse de guerre* for them to use the enemy's ensign. Taking advantage of this on my personal instructions, three of the M.T.B.s from Sousse, under the command of that gallant and enterprising young officer Lieutenant P. F. S. Gould, proceeded close up the east coast of Tunisia past Kelibia and rounded Cape Bon in broad daylight, to shoot up two Italian minesweepers, an armed motor-launch, and several aircraft on the beaches. Later they sighted and attacked a merchantman under the escort of two destroyers. In the fierce action which followed the merchantman was hit by a torpedo and was later sunk by aircraft. Our M.T.B.s came under heavy fire from the destroyers and shore batteries, as well as from enemy fighters which came diving down to join in the battle. All our craft were hit, and the brave Gould and several others were killed or died of their wounds. It was a praiseworthy exploit.

The day before this incident I had made a signal to our Light Coastal

Forces to the effect that I was following their excellent work with intense interest. I told them they were contributing greatly to the difficulties of the enemy and the advance of our armies in Tunisia.

I must again say something of the outstanding work of the submarines of the 8th and 10th Flotillas, which was undoubtedly a major contributing factor in the success of the Allied Armies during the desperate eleventh hour attempts of the enemy to reinforce and keep supplied his forces in Tunisia. It may be invidious to mention individual ships when all did so well; but from the time of the 'Torch' landing in November until the last week in April the *Splendid* sank a destroyer and six merchant vessels, including two tankers, besides damaging another destroyer and a merchantman. The *Sahib's* record in the same period was a U-boat and six merchantmen sunk and another damaged. We were greatly distressed when the *Splendid* and *Sahib* were lost off Corsica and the north coast of Sicily on April 21st and 24th respectively.

The record of the *Safari* was also remarkable. From the 'Torch' period to the middle of April she destroyed seven merchantmen, two schooners and some barges alongside a pier, besides damaging another merchant ship. Her really outstanding effort was the sinking of an entire convoy of three ships on April 10th and 11th, one of them being a tanker.

Our destroyers were not idle. At 3 a.m. on April 16th, the *Pakenham* and *Paladin*, on a sweep from Malta, sighted and attacked two large Italian destroyers off Marittimo, at the western end of Sicily. Both the Italians were sunk, though in the course of the engagement the *Pakenham* was hit four times. A shell in the engine-room unfortunately put the ship out of action, and she was set on fire aft. She was taken in tow by the *Paladin*, but had finally to be abandoned and sunk at daylight because of the proximity of the enemy airfields in Sicily. Fighters from Malta beat off enemy air attacks while the survivors were transferred, and the *Pakenham* sank at 6 a.m. having lost nine killed.

Another destroyer incident took place on the night of April 28th–29th when the *Laforey* and *Tartar*, operating from Bone, had a scrimmage with six E-boats and an enemy submarine. The *Laforey* rammed one E-boat and cut her in two, while the others were damaged by gunfire, one probably being sunk.

Even during the first few days of May the enemy was still making desperate efforts to supply his forces in Tunisia. At about midnight on May 3rd–4th the *Nubian*, *Petard* and *Paladin*, working from Malta, fell upon a large merchantman escorted by an Italian torpedo boat off Kelibia, to the southward of Cape Bon. Both were accounted for, the merchant vessel blowing up with a mighty explosion. A ship of around 8,000 tons, she was bound from Naples to Tunis with mechanical vehicles, ammunition, bombs and landmines for the Axis army.

Our destroyers were being used to the limit of their capacity. This was the *Nubian's* twenty-second sortie against enemy shipping since her arrival at Malta in December, 1942. On seven of those nights she had been present at the destruction of one or more supply ships and their escorts.

VII

From Algiers, in the middle of April, I had paid another flying visit to Malta to see the progress of the preparations for 'Husky', the invasion of Sicily. The island would have to provide for the repair and maintenance of a large number of landing-craft, and though the arrangements were in hand, they were not moving as fast as necessary. Most unfortunately, it was at this time that Vice-Admiral Bonham-Carter began to crack up under the heavy strain, and a few days later had to be invalided home. With the consent of the First Sea Lord, I appointed Rear-Admiral Arthur Power, then commanding the 15th Cruiser Squadron working from Malta, to replace him. An officer of fierce energy and outstanding character and ability, Power fully justified his selection and made an important contribution to the success of 'Husky'.

During April I had a very welcome visitor at my villa in the shape of Vice-Admiral Sir Walter Cowan, my old friend and Commander-in-Chief in the West Indies years before. Serving in the rank of commander with Indian mechanized cavalry in the Western Desert, they had been surprised and overrun by Italian armoured vehicles in the early morning, Cowan being captured after expending all his pistol ammunition. He told me in his quiet voice: "If I'd only had a companion and some more ammunition I'd have captured that Italian armoured car." Having been released by the Italians, he was now on his way home.

Walter Cowan stayed with me for six days, and spent much of his time walking round the garden and picking flowers. By the kindness of the French we were also able to send him up to Sidi-bel-Abbes to visit the Foreign Legion, which greatly interested him. He was thrilled at the chance of taking passage home in a cruiser. His age was seventy-one. Still full of warlike energy, he was out again with the Commandos in a few months.

Meanwhile our detailed planning for 'Husky' was not progressing as it should. No definite outline plan for the operation was yet forthcoming. The drawing up of the naval detailed plans for landing some 160,000 Allied troops and large numbers of guns and vehicles, with masses of ammunition and miscellaneous stores, on an enemy coast involved much inter-Service co-ordination and weeks of meticulous and complicated work, and we had not yet been able to make a proper start. Two plans had been accepted and the work begun. Then each in turn was cancelled and the labour went for nothing. We, the Navy, fully aware of the magnitude of our task and of our responsibilities, were becoming exasperated at the delay, and time was drawing on. D-day for 'Husky' had already been fixed for July 10th.

Vacillation in war does not make for success, and constant changes of mind in the method of carrying out a complicated, large-scale operation are a bugbear to those responsible for its conduct. However, I shall have more to say on this important subject in the next chapter.

VIII

By the end of April the stage was set for the final defeat of the Axis army in Tunisia. Rommel, having foreseen the inevitable, had already handed over his command to von Arnim on Hitler's instructions.

The Eighth Army, brought up against the enemy's strongly fortified positions in the mountains just north of Enfidaville, country impossible for tanks, was brought to a standstill after bitter fighting. Ordered to hold on where he was, Montgomery's First Armoured Division was detached and sent to join General Anderson's forces operating in the Goubellat Plain, to the north-west near Medjez-el-Bab.

After a prolonged and bloody struggle the final break-through from the west came between May 6th and 10th—a small force of the French in the extreme north; then the United States 2nd Corps of three divisions making for Bizerta; next the British First Army of three armoured and four infantry divisions driving for Tunis from the direction of Medjez-el-Bab; then a French Corps of two divisions; with Montgomery's Eighth Army of three divisions striking north from Enfidaville.

The Luftwaffe was conspicuous by its absence. It had left the Afrika Korps to its fate. The R.A.F. and the U.S.A.A.F. had it all their own way, and had blown the enemy out of the sky. By May 7th the Axis front was crumbling to pieces in every direction, and our forward troops were into Bizerta and Tunis. Except for isolated pockets of resistance, May 10th saw the Axis horde, routed, utterly demoralized and surrendering, penned into the Cape Bon peninsula with a stream of British armour cutting it off from the south. The rest of the fighting was mostly mopping up.

By May 12th—7.52 a.m. was the official time—all organized enemy resistance came to an end. The whole of Africa was ours. Something like a quarter of a million Axis prisoners and vast quantities of material were in our hands. It was a stupendous victory—just about six months after the Allies had landed in North Africa, and three years after Italy had entered the war and the first fighting in the Western Desert.

It is not for a sailor to express his opinions on fighting ashore; but the end in Tunisia was a fitting culmination to the victorious advance of the Eighth Army from El Alamein, and the stubborn fighting of the First Army

—British, American and French—in the gaunt mountains and morasses of thick mud in the valleys of Tunisia. Even in the later phases of the war I doubt if such achievements were ever surpassed.

And now, after some necessary clearing up, the southern shore of the Mediterranean was open from end to end. Once more, by the use of sea power, the way lay open for us to attack the enemy on his own soil.

IX

I have said little about the work of the Navy in the eventful days of our final victory.

On May 8th, hearing from Army Headquarters that Allied troops were in Bizerta, Commodore Oliver at Bone hoisted his broad pendant in a M.T.B. and proceeded thither accompanied by a motor gunboat. Entering the harbour soon after 10 a.m. they were received with heavy, close-range fire from cannon and machine-guns, and after suffering some casualties and considerable damage both boats were forced to retire. They were lucky to escape. Oliver's broad pendant was eventually hoisted at Fort Koudiat, Bizerta, two days later.

Though it had been expected that the enemy might make a final stand in the Cape Bon peninsula we had visualized that he might, also, try to evacuate some of his forces by sea. Indeed, it was reported that piers and jetties were being built. Our plans for this eventuality were already made. Destroyers and light coastal craft had been scraped up from all over the Mediterranean and the Levant, and strong day and night patrols were instituted in the Sicilian channel and close inshore off the strip of territory that remained to the Axis.

With the great land conflict in progress it was unreasonable to expect fighter protection for our surface forces by daylight. They were attacked, but could deal with their attackers by gunfire. The German air effort over the sea was a waning shadow of what it had been in the days of Greece and Crete.

I remember that some objection was taken by the R.A.F. to the presence of our surface forces in the Sicilian Channel during daylight. They wished to bomb everything they saw afloat. We came to the usual friendly compromise. They could attack anything within five miles of the enemy-held coast, i.e. within range of any shore batteries, and the Navy would take care of the rest.

On May 8th, when we moved all our available destroyers in for a close day and night patrol off the Cape Bon peninsula, I made them a signal, "Sink, burn and destroy. Let nothing pass." I knew most of the destroyer captains. Some of them, and many more of their ships' companies, had endured the agony that our men had had to face during the evacuations from Greece and

Crete two years before. We called the operation 'Retribution', not in any spirit of revenge or because we intended to slaughter defenceless survivors in the water, as the Luftwaffe had done in 1941; but because we hoped, and most earnestly, that those of the enemy who essayed the perilous passage home by sea should be taught a lesson they would never forget.

The work of the destroyers at this juncture did not lack danger and excitement. The patrols had to be maintained in water which had been heavily mined by the enemy and ourselves. There was also the risk that some of our aircraft pilots were untrained in ship recognition, and the five-mile limit meant little to them in their fast-moving craft. One unfortunate incident did occur, though there was a humorous side to it.

To facilitate the recognition of our destroyers their bridge structures were painted red. Two of our 'Hunt' class, the *Bicester* and *Zetland*, finely manned and commanded, and who had already made names for themselves by the efficiency with which they had escorted convoys and punished U-boats, were attacked by American-manned Spitfires.

The *Bicester* was hit by a bomb in the wardroom, though it fortunately lodged in an oil tank without exploding. The *Bicester's* commanding officer, Lieutenant-Commander S. W. F. Bennetts, an ex-submarine officer known to his contemporaries as 'Baron Bicester' and famed for his extensive knowledge of the lesser-used terms of the English language, overheard the American pilots talking on their radio telephones. Tuning in on his own set he chimed in by calling them everything he could lay his tongue to in a most uncompromising way. Even the Americans were surprised. Listening, Bennetts heard the leader say in a voice filled with admiration—"Say. I guess this guy's friendly!" I am unaware of Bennett's retort; but can imagine it.

I cannot go into all the details of 'Retribution', or the 'Kelibia Regatta', as our destroyer officers called it; but in the event no more than a few isolated parties of Germans or Italians tried to escape by sea in motor, sailing and rowing boats, rafts and even rubber dinghys. In all about a thousand prisoners were collected afloat. I have no doubt that the sight of those little grey ships of ours off the coast deterred many more, and, indeed, prevented any organized attempt at evacuation.

On May 13th after the official surrender, I signalled to the ships:

> The campaign in North Africa has concluded with the surrender or destruction of all Axis forces. It is a tribute to the work of our light forces that even in the desperate circumstances in which the enemy found themselves, no real attempt was made to evacuate by sea, and that such few as hazarded the attempt were speedily rounded up by ships on patrol. I have watched with satisfaction the progressively good work performed in harassing the enemy at sea during the last weeks, and in particular the good work in the last phase which has enabled a large number of craft

of different types to work by day and by night in close proximity to an enemy coast without confusion and with a high degree of success. I congratulate you all on a difficult and arduous job well performed.

X

Much remained to be done by the Navy.

The French naval dockyard at Ferryville, near Bizerta, had been systematically bombed by the Allies and the rest sabotaged and blocked by the enemy. The dry-docks could not be used. Bizerta itself was in ruins without electricity, water or drainage, and the Germans had sunk twenty-six ships in the narrow entrance from the Avant Port to the Goulet. In some cases three ships had been scuttled on top of each other, large steamers, destroyers, floating cranes, lighters and harbour craft. Though small coasters and landing-craft could use the port for the supply of the Army and the evacuation of thousands of prisoners of war—1,000 tons of stores a day were being landed by May 14th—the wall of sunken ships presented a complete barrier to larger vessels.

Commodore G. N. Oliver was the British officer in charge, and a team of salvage experts was sent forward by Commodore W. A. Sullivan, U.S.N. to clear the port. They blasted a channel with explosives, and by about the end of May the entry channel was deep enough for 10,000-ton 'Liberty' ships. Commodore Oliver was required for other duties, and on May 20th, Admiral Sir Gerald Dickens, my flotilla-mate in the Dardanelles, had hoisted his flag as Flag Officer in Charge, Bizerta and Tunis. Like so many other senior officers he was serving in the rank of Rear-Admiral.

We set about reorganizing the fleet. In Force 'H' the *Nelson* and *Rodney* were temporarily relieved by the *King George V* and *Howe*, with Rear-Admiral A. W. La T. Bisset in command with his flag in the *King George V*.

Rear-Admiral Cecil Harcourt was appointed in command of the 15th Cruiser Squadron—*Newfoundland, Euryalus* and *Orion*—with his flag in the first-named; while Captain W. G. Agnew, of the *Aurora*, became Commodore in command of the 12th Cruiser Squadron, *Aurora, Penelope, Sirius, Cleopatra* and *Delhi*, with his broad pendant in the *Aurora*.

Embarking at Algiers in the *Newfoundland* on May 22nd I paid a visit to Malta, returning to Algiers on May 26th. I wished to see how the organization for the invasion of Sicily was getting on. I was determined to be there for the actual operation, and as I found 'squatters' in Admiralty House I had them evicted to other quarters to provide accommodation for myself and my numerous staff when the time came.

But the heaviest naval task after the surrender in Tunisia was the clearance of the minefields, so that shipping might pass through the Mediterranean to the Middle East instead of using the passage round the Cape of Good

Hope. This meant shortening the distance by about six thousand miles and a great economy in tonnage.

The approaches to Malta, the Galita and Sicilian Channels, and the whole area to the east of the Cape Bon peninsula were thickly mined. A channel from Sousse to Tripoli must also be swept. In all some six hundred miles had to be cleared in frequent bad weather and strong tides through an area strewn with wrecks. Many of the enemy mines, too, were fitted with explosive anti-sweeping devices which parted sweep wires and occasioned delay. The arduous operation was begun on May 9th by the 12th, 13th and 14th Minesweepers under Captain J. W. Boutwood and Commander L. J. S. Ede, and the channel was swept by June 9th with the loss of one motor minesweeper and damage to H.M.S. *Fantome*. I made a signal congratulating all the officers and men in the fleet-sweepers, trawlers, motor minesweepers and motor-launches concerned, and they richly deserved their further signal of appreciation from the Admiralty on the conclusion of their outstanding achievement.

The first through convoy passed Gibraltar through the Mediterranean on May 17th, rounded Cape Bon on the 21st and arrived at Alexandria on the 26th. The first convoy to reach Malta unopposed since 1940 reached the island on May 24th.

Thus ended the Navy's share in the victory in Tunisia. We had travelled a long way and had endured many vicissitudes and a few triumphs; but all the toil and sacrifice was worth it in the end.

We had much for which to be thankful.

Again I must mention my deep personal gratitude to those who worked behind the scenes, my most loyal and devoted staff whose efforts made all things possible. I have already said something of those who lived with me—'Roy' Dick, my Chief of Staff; 'Tim' Shaw, my Secretary; my Flag Lieutenant, Dampier, or 'Dampie' as he was affectionately called by his many American friends.

I have also mentioned Commanders, later Captains, Geoffrey Barnard, T. M. Brownrigg and M. L. Power, all of whom were concerned with day to day operations and planning, and whose services, as ever, were invaluable. Commander L. G. Durlacher, too, was entirely responsible for the ramifications of our most complicated system of naval communications upon which all else depended. His work was onerous and most exacting, particularly as our methods differed from those of our Allies. Durlacher had to overcome many difficulties; but was always successful. We owed a lot to his great ability, tact and sound common sense. He was also intimately concerned with the planning side of all operations, not merely with the normal day-to-day routine communications over a large area.

There were many others who laboured whole-heartedly in the background, and upon whose work we depended. I cannot mention them all by name. Nevertheless, the names of two officers must go into this record,

Captain (E) L. A. Taylor and Constructor Captain I. E. King, who had to do with the repairs to damaged and disabled ships in dockyards which had largely been shattered by bombing or deliberate and well-calculated enemy sabotage.

Both these fine officers were past-masters in the art of improvisation in the most difficult circumstances, while the imperturbable Captain King was a salvage expert of no mean order and saved many a stricken or sunken ship. Largely by their efforts the ships and landing-craft in the Mediterranean were kept efficient and running at a time when every vessel was of value and we had none to replace casualties. Without the devoted work of Taylor and King and their respective staffs, we should not have been able to do all that we had to do.

Commodore J. A. V. Morse, in charge of the port of Algiers was not actually on my staff, though I naturally saw much of him and his work. Algiers, which was our principal port for the supply of the Army and the repair of ships, was no bed of roses. Morse's conspicuous ability, his drive and energy, quiet imperturbability and charm of manner, coupled with his innate flair for getting the best out of people and getting on with all and sundry, particularly the French and the Americans, were assets of great price which enabled him to succeed where many others might have failed.

As Commander-in-Chief there were many behind the scenes to whom I, and, may I say, the Mediterranean Fleet as a whole, owed more than can be expressed in mere words.

CHAPTER XL

I

WITH the defeat of the Axis in Tunisia all our energies could now be concentrated upon our final preparations for the next great task, the invasion and capture of Sicily. This operation had been decided upon at the Casablanca Conference in January and finally authorized on the 23rd of that month. It was to be the greatest amphibious assault ever undertaken up till that period. Some 160,000 Allied troops, with 14,000 vehicles, 600 tanks and 1,800 guns were to be landed in enemy territory in the face of hostile resistance. This initial landing was to be followed by a stream of reinforcements with huge quantities of stores and war material. Nearly two thousand vessels of all types, warships and merchantmen, were to take part in the first assault. More than three thousand two hundred were to participate in the operations as a whole.

The problem was immensely complicated. I cannot begin to give any indication of what the preliminary organization entailed. A large number of suitable ships had first to be earmarked from all over the world, which was a task for the Ministry of Transport and its American equivalent. The provision of the necessary vessels meant a heavy drain upon Allied shipping resources at a most critical period of the war. The U-boat battle still raged in the Atlantic. Allied losses through submarine action in February, 1943, totalled sixty-three ships of about 360,000 tons. March brought the crisis in the North Atlantic and the peak of the submarine effort. There were one hundred and twelve U-boats at sea, and in all areas we lost one hundred and eight ships of 627,000 tons. Thereafter the U-boat effort started gradually to wane. The months of April and May, 1943, will probably be chosen by historians as the period when the pendulum swung, and the offensive at sea finally passed into the hands of the Allies.

Once earmarked, the ships selected for the invasion of Sicily had to be marshalled into convoys, and the escorts and convoy routes provided and arranged. The exact speed of all convoys must be worked out, so that they arrived at their final destinations at the right time and in the right order. Minesweepers had to precede the ships moving in to the assault, while covering forces of cruisers and destroyers must be on the spot to provide any necessary gunfire during the landing and afterwards. L.S.T.s with landing-craft of all descriptions had to be organized into their flotillas, and their routes and exact timing laid down beforehand. The duties and movement of motor torpedo boats, motor launches and a host of smaller craft, had to be considered and set forth in writing. Anti-submarine and anti-aircraft measures must be provided, and the necessary air cover arranged in close co-operation with the Royal Air Force. There had also to be a strong force of capital ships to give battle to the Italian fleet if it came out to fight.

These matters were only part of the problem. Exact loading tables must be worked out for each and every ship landing troops or their supplies, and the priorities arranged. The complications were endless, and these and many other details involved the closest and most intricate co-operation between the planning staffs of the three Services, Navy, Army and Air, both British and American. It meant weeks, even months of hard work.

As I have said, the invasion of Sicily was finally decided upon on January 23rd. An outline plan was sent out from England soon afterwards, and combined planning headquarters were set up at Algiers on February 10th. This first plan, which was accepted with some minor modifications, envisaged simultaneous assaults in the west and the south-east of Sicily—to the west by the Americans, in the south-east by the British. It was with this broad outline in their minds that our planners set to work.

They soon ran into heavy weather, which perhaps was inevitable when General Sir Harold Alexander, who was to command the Allied troops landing in Sicily, together with Generals Montgomery and Patton, who were to be his subordinate military commanders, were all engaged actively in the field in Tunisia. It was impossible for them to give the plans for Sicily their early and detailed consideration. Moreover, while the planning staffs of the three Commanders-in-Chief—Alexander, Tedder and myself—with that of the Supreme Commander, were in close contact at Algiers, those of the subordinate commanders were widely separated. The staffs of Admiral Ramsay, the Naval Commander of the British assault, and General Montgomery, were at Cairo. Vice-Admiral Hewitt, U.S.N., the American Naval Commander, was at Algiers, while General Patton's planners were near Oran.

At the end of February this first plan was rejected by General Alexander for reasons fully described in his despatch. As he wrote: "I also considered at this time concentrating the efforts of both Task Forces" (British and American) "against the south-eastern corner of the island," though at this stage he rejected this last idea because a port was necessary to the Americans and it seemed essential to ensure the early capture of Palermo.

All the preliminary work of our planners went for nought, and after a series of conferences and discussions another plan was produced. It retained the idea of the British landings in the south-east and the American assault in the west. But Air Chief Marshal Tedder pointed out that the airfield at Ponte Olivo, north of Gela on the south coast of Sicily, was a first-class air base which was left untouched. Unless it were captured for our use our air forces would be working under an intolerable situation. I agreed with Tedder, also pointing out that from the naval point of view the risk of allowing the Luftwaffe to operate from the group of airfields in the south-east of Sicily was unacceptable.

Some further modifications were made and agreed to by General Eisenhower on March 20th, and the work of planning started afresh. Then General Alexander began, to quote his own words, "to consider more and more the dangers presented by the dispersal of our forces," i.e. the British assaulting in the south-east and the Americans in the West. It was difficult, he argued, to estimate the likely scale of enemy resistance, or to what extent the Italians would fight. We had no superiority in numbers, and, to quote the despatch—"such advantages as we enjoyed—the initiative to attack where we chose, command of sea and air, and a certain superiority in equipment, at least over the Italians—would be diminished by dispersion."

General Montgomery shared these views, and in a message of April 24th to General Alexander said: "Planning so far has been based on the assumption that the opposition will be slight and that Sicily will be captured relatively easily. Never was there a greater error. The Germans and also the Italians are fighting desperately in Tunisia and will do so in Sicily."

For myself I cannot see how the dispersion of our assaults would in any way have altered our overwhelming command of the sea.

Anyhow, on April 29th a conference was called at Algiers at which it was proposed that both the British and Americans should assault the south-eastern corner of Sicily—the British around Avola, north of Cape Passero, and the Americans on each side of the Pachino peninsula which terminates in Cape Passero. I at once demurred. Apart from my general conviction that in amphibious operations the landings should be dispersed, I again insisted that it was essential to secure the use of the airfields at the earliest possible moment to safeguard the mass of shipping lying off the beaches. Tedder also entered strong objections from the air point of view. The Eighth Army plan would leave thirteen airfields in enemy hands, far too many for effective neutralization by air action. Unless the airfields could be captured for our own use at the earliest possible opportunity he would be opposed to the whole operation. General Alexander was thus faced, to paraphrase the despatch, with a complete contradiction between the Army view, on the one hand, and that of the Navy and Air Force, on the other.

On April 28th I had written to the First Sea Lord:

> We are arriving at a state of deadlock out here over 'Husky'. As you know, about fourteen days ago the outline plan was produced by us after big difficulties had been overcome. The suggested new plan (I continued), does away altogether with the assaults on the south-west beaches—those whose object was to take the south-west group of aerodromes—and concentrates all the assaults on the south-east beaches.
>
> Personally I think this plan is unsound as it leaves three aerodromes in the occupation of the enemy except for such force as the R.A.F. can put on to them, and we are landing from a mass of shipping a mere thirty

miles off. It also seems to surrender our greatest asset—that of being able to assault the island in numerous places at once at will. . . . Tedder is also absolutely opposed to this new plan.

But the seriousness of it all is that here we are with no fixed agreed plan, just over two months off D-day and the commanders all at sixes and sevens, and even if we do get final agreement someone will be operating a plan he doesn't fully agree with. Not the way to make a success of a difficult operation.

On May 3rd General Alexander decided to recast the whole plan. Briefly, the American assault in the west was cancelled, and the whole weight of the Seventh (United States) Army was to be transferred to the south-east of the island on the immediate left of the Eighth Army. To quote his despatch:

"I decided, in fact, to take a risk on the administrative side rather than the operational risk of dispersion of effort. This was contrary to what had hitherto been regarded as one of the fundamental principles of the operation: that we must capture Palermo at the earliest possible moment if we were to have a hope of maintaining sufficient forces for the reduction of the island. On my new plan the only ports we should be certain of capturing in the first stage would be Syracuse and Augusta, the latter more a naval anchorage than a port, and possibly Catania; the whole of Seventh Army would have to depend on beach maintenance except for such help as it might get from the small port of Licata which—was only rated at a capacity of six hundred tons a day. The risk was, therefore, grave, but there were two factors which brightened the prospect. The first was that there was a reasonable probability of suitable weather in July for beach maintenance. The second was the coming of the D.U.K.W.S.—these ingenious amphibious vehicles—which revolutionized the problem of beach maintenance."

In his despatch General Alexander went on to say that his intention to concentrate his force gave him some concern. Having decided to take a calculated administrative risk for operational reasons, he realized that:

"this risk was unevenly divided and almost the whole of it would fall on the Seventh Army. In other ways also it might well seem that the American troops were being given the tougher and less spectacular tasks: their beaches were more exposed than the Eighth Army's and on some of them there were awkward sand bars, they would have only one small port for maintenance and Eighth Army would have the glory of capturing the more obviously attractive objectives of Syracuse, Catania and Messina, names which would bulk larger in press headlines than Gela or Licata or the obscure townships of central Sicily. Both I and my staff felt that this division of tasks might possibly, on these understandable grounds, cause some feeling of resentment."

General Alexander was aware, from the Tunisian campaign, of General Patton's punctilious and scrupulous sense of duty, and knew that his orders would not be questioned.

"But in the case of so difficult and important an operation and since it might appear that an American Commander was being required to scrap the results of difficult and tedious planning and undertake a heavier burden than he had expected at the order of a British superior, I felt a natural anxiety about American reactions. I wish to place on record here that General Patton at once fell in with my new plan, the military advantages of which were as clear to him as to me, and neither he nor anyone in Seventh Army raised any form of objection. It is an impressive example of the spirit of complete loyalty and inter-Allied co-operation which inspired all operations with which I was associated in the Mediterranean."

On May 8th I wrote to the First Sea Lord:

I think it is well that you should know of the atmosphere here after the acceptance of the final 'Husky' plan. The Admiral (Hewitt) and General (Patton) of the Western Task Force are very sore about it. . . . There is no doubt that the maintenance of three American divisions—is a very tricky problem, involving the supply over beaches and perhaps one small port for some six weeks, 3,000 tons a day and no one really knows whether he can do it or not.

Hewitt has told Patton definitely that he does not think he can, but Patton has taken up the attitude that he has been ordered to land there and he will do it.

I think myself that, barring accidents, it can be done, and I have assured them of all the assistance we can give them.

At last we had the broad outline of a plan upon which to base our detailed organization and arrangements. D-day for the landing in Sicily was timed for a bare two months ahead!

It is not for me, as the Naval Commander-in-Chief concerned, to criticize any military plan, let alone the one that we finally adopted for Sicily. Looking back, I am of the definite opinion that any one of the alternatives would have been equally successful.

It has to be realized that any amphibious operation is merely the opening, under particular circumstances, of a primarily Army battle. It is the function of the Navy and the Air to help the Army to establish a base or bases on the hostile coast from which the military tactical battle must be developed to gain the final object. It is upon the Army's tactical plan that the combined plan must depend; the Navy and the Air Commanders joining with the Army Commander to ensure that the base or bases chosen can be captured without prohibitive loss in their respective elements, and that, when seized, they will fulfil requirements.

If much time is not to be wasted and the more confusion caused it is essential that the responsible Commanders-in-Chief, together with the Task Force Commanders to be responsible for the tactical battle, should meet at the outset to discuss and thrash out the sound basic plan upon which all else depends. It is equally important that when once decided upon, the plan should not be changed save for reasons of exceptional urgency, such as a complete change in the enemy's dispositions or a major strategic upheaval.

This was not so in the case of 'Husky' for the reasons I have stated. The operation was authorized on January 23rd; combined planning headquarters set up on February 12th, and the work started. A new plan was evolved and work began again. Once more the plan was cancelled and preparations came to a standstill. The final firm outline plan was not approved until May 12th, the day before the Axis surrender in Tunisia. This meant that although five months were available for perfecting the plans in all their complicated detail, the heavy task had to be compressed into two months. This resulted in some confusion and unnecessary duplication in the issue of orders. The invasion of Sicily was successful in spite of all the difficulties, and the fears we had entertained about the enemy's use of the airfields and the difficulties of maintaining and supplying the Armies over open beaches never arose to a sufficient extent to cause real anxiety. This was largely due to the dogged persistence with which the American Navy carried on their difficult task of landing men and material over open beaches in bad weather, no less than General Patton's brilliant and rapid campaign which resulted in the capture of the south-western airfields and of 36,000 prisoners, together with the occupation of Palermo for use as a supply port, by July 22nd, twelve days after the landings.

I do not criticize the overhead plan for 'Husky' as eventually carried out. I am perfectly confident that any of the alternative plans would have succeeded. What I do maintain is that the three months delay in the production of the final overhead plan for the operation should never, and need never, have occurred.

II

I must go back to May and June.

Now that the Mediterranean was open, there remained the islands of Pantellaria, Linosa and Lampedusa, all of which had Italian garrisons. Linosa and Lampedusa were unimportant; but Pantellaria, about one hundred and fifty miles west-north-west of Malta, and roughly the size of the Isle of

Wight, is rugged and mountainous with a little harbour, fit only for small craft, in the north-west. It had a sizeable garrison, a small airfield, radar stations, and was reputed to be heavily fortified, though we had noticed that whenever our ships approached it, which was fairly frequently, they had never been seriously engaged.

There were some who classed Pantellaria as a miniature Gibraltar bristling with guns, which it would be impossible to carry by direct assault. They were very averse to any attempt to capture it. I did not share in this opinion. Its value to us during the forthcoming operation was obvious. It lay in a commanding position in the centre of the Sicilian channel, and fighters working from the airfield would be able to provide cover over some of the beaches where we proposed to land in Sicily. At this stage its value to the enemy was doubtful, though in earlier days the airfield had been used by bombers, and the harbour by E-boats, working against our shipping.

In spite of the dismal forebodings of many, Eisenhower decided that Pantellaria should be captured. The plan was to soften up the defences with some days of heavy bombing from the air and bombardment from the sea, and then to assault the island in the small harbour area. Landing was impossible elsewhere. The First British division was allotted to the assault, and the naval arrangements and organization were placed in the capable hands of Rear-Admiral Rhoderick R. McGrigor, who had come out from England to take charge of one of the landings in Sicily and was later to take over the appointment of Flag Officer, Sicily. McGrigor at once set about training and rehearsing the crews of his landing-craft.

While these important matters were being considered we had various distractions which had to be attended to. It had been decided to hold a Victory March at Tunis in which units of the First Army, with representative detachments of the American and French forces which had taken part in the recent victory, should all appear. This took place on May 20th, with the troops marching past, bands playing and General Eisenhower taking the salute. Most of the Allied Commanders were with him—Alexander, Tedder, General Juin, various other French Generals, and myself. Mr. Harold Macmillan and Mr. Murphy were also on the saluting platform.

It was an impressive display, and I was greatly struck by the fine appearance of the men of the British First Army. They were in wonderful fettle—magnificent young men, fit, smart and in great spirits: toughened by their hard fighting and trying winter in the cold and mud. I remarked to Mr. Macmillan who was standing beside me that the very sight of them made one proud to be British.

The Americans and French also looked grand, the French particularly so in their many different uniforms—the Foreign Legion; Chasseurs d'Afrique; Tirailleurs; Zouaves; the Goums in their long, camel-hair robes and slapping sandals. The parade had been timed to last an hour and a half. Actually it

Landing craft under repair in the badly damaged dockyard at Malta, July 1943.

Surrender of the Italian fleet. An Italian battleship under the guns of *Warspite*, September 10th, 1943.

Salerno, September 11th, 1943. U.S. cruiser *Savannah* struck by a radio-controlled bomb.

A little later: U.S.S. *Savannah* badly down by the bows. Ship in foreground is H.M.S. *Abercrombie*.

The Italian surrender. Air Chief Marshal Sir Arthur Tedder; Lieut.-General Mason-Macfarlane; General Sir Harold Alexander; Marshal Badoglio; General Eisenhower; A.B.C.

Marshal Badoglio on board H.M.S. *Nelson*. Malta, September 29th, 1943. The Royal Marine Guard.

Teheran, November 1943. General Sir John Dill and A.B.C. taking exercise in the grounds of the British Embassy.

At the Quebec Conference, September 1944. Sir Hastings Ismay; Sir Alan Brooke; Sir John Dill; A.B.C.

Conference at Malta, January 1945, on the way to Yalta. On left: Admiral King, U.S.N.; General Marshall. *At the top of the table:* General Bedell Smith. *On right from top:* Major-General R.E. Laycock (dark man looking down); Field-Marshal Sir Henry Maitland Wilson; Marshal of the Royal Air Force Sir Charles Portal; Field-Marshal Sir Alan Brooke; A.B.C.; Admiral Sir James Somerville; General Sir Hastings Ismay.

V.E. Day, May 8th 1945. The Prime Minister with the three Chiefs of Staff, General Sir Hastings Ismay and Major-General Sir Leslie Hollies in the garden at 10 Downing Street.

V.J. Day, August 15th 1945. His Majesty with three Chiefs of Staff, at Buckingham Palace.

At home at Bishop's Waltham. Part of the ruins of the old Palace of the Bishops of Winchester in the background.

My wife and myself with friends in the garden at Bishop's Waltham.

A bust of Cunningham. Prince Philip unveiling the bust of Cunningham in Trafalgar Square, April 1967.

Burial at sea. The funeral of Admiral Cunningham on the flight deck of H.M.S. *Hampshire*.

took twice as long as the French had crowded in many more units than their proper allowance. They naturally wished to impress the Tunisian inhabitants, particularly the Arabs.

We all went to lunch with General Juin and afterwards rather unexpectedly, were taken off to call on the new Bey of Tunis, who presented Eisenhower and the rest of us with the highest Tunisian Order, that of Nichan Iftikhar, the 'Order of Glory'. The diplomats, Mr. Murphy and Mr. Macmillan, set out for the palace, but diplomatically lost their way, so did not appear for investiture.

The Sultan of Morocco must have become aware that the Bey of Tunis had decorated the Allied Commanders, for he decided to do the same. General Noguès, the French Resident-General in Morocco was deputed to carry out the investitures, and he arrived at Algiers to do so. The Order with which we were presented was that called 'Ouissam Alaouite', a gorgeous-looking decoration with a bright orange ribbon. Eisenhower was invested with the sash and star. Another sash and a star were placed upon me, after which the supply ran short. So mine were removed and hung upon Tedder, finally coming to rest upon Bedell Smith, the American Chief of Staff. My insignia reached me later.

At the end of May we had an influx of visitors to Algiers. General de Gaulle arrived from England, with General Georges and various French statesmen from elsewhere. They had come to confer with Giraud, and to arrange a set-up embodying all parties willing to unite and fight for the liberation of France.

At the same time Mr. Churchill arrived straight from the Washington Conference, accompanied by General Marshall and General Sir Alan Brooke, Chief of the Imperial General Staff. The Prime Minister and his entourage occupied my villa, and I cleared out and lived on board a cruiser in the harbour with my personal staff. We had many conferences, usually dealing with future objectives after the capture of Sicily, and for clarification of the decisions reached by the Combined Chiefs of Staff in Washington. On most days there were large parties to lunch and dinner at the villa.

Just before the Prime Minister's visit, Admiral Godfroy at Alexandria consented to bring his squadron over to Giraud to fight on the side of the Allies. Later, some of his destroyers came through the Mediterranean to join us, while his cruisers and the battleship *Lorraine* sailed round the Cape of Good Hope to Dakar. In converse with the Prime Minister on this subject I drew his attention to the first verse of the penultimate chapter of Ecclesiastes: "Cast thy bread upon the waters: for thou shalt find it after many days." My innocent remark was rather ill received.

The French authorities came to an agreement by June 3rd, on which date they set up a 'Committee of Liberation' composed of three or four of Giraud's supporters and an equal number of de Gaullists. A lunch was arranged at my villa to celebrate the rapprochement, the Prime Minister, Mr. Eden, Generals Giraud, de Gaulle and Georges, with Mm. Monnet, André Philippe and Massigli all being present, together with various Americans and British. Many speeches were made in French, and all the French parted as friends for the time being.

But it was an uneasy truce. Before long the Committee set up what they called a 'Committee of Epuration' and, very ill-advisedly in my opinion, started to interfere with the French naval command. They played havoc with the Admirals.

Our relations with the French Navy had always been most cordial, and they co-operated in the most friendly spirit in any way they could. Admiral Michelier, in command, was an excellent officer, able, energetic and full of fire. However, he was unpopular with Giraud, while the Americans also disliked him because of the stiff resistance the French Navy under his command had put up to their first landings at Casablanca. At any rate, the Americans were disinclined to take any steps to keep him in office when he was 'epurated' by the committee.

Vice-Admiral Collinet, from Dakar, another fine and able officer, was appointed in Michelier's stead; but he lasted a very short time. Rumour had it that he had demanded a seat on the Committee of Liberation. This was altogether too much for the Generals, who saw the chance of again reducing the Navy to the subordinate service it had been before its emancipation by Darlan. Anyhow, Collinet went back to Dakar and Rear-Admiral Lemonnier succeeded him in command at Algiers. He was an able and most co-operative officer who ever since the landings had managed the French Mercantile Marine in the Allied interest with great success. He was equally successful with the French Navy and when dealing more directly with us.

But to return to Pantellaria, the assault was timed for June 11th, and on the previous days the air forces had poured their bombs upon the island while individual batteries were bombarded by cruisers and destroyers. Two days before the actual assault we staged a sort of dress rehearsal. The aircraft were to bomb heavily, while four cruisers and destroyers were to bombard, the latter from close inshore. The further to test the reactions of the garrison M.T.B.s were also to close the harbour entrance. Eisenhower and myself embarked in the *Aurora* at Bone the night before to witness the operation. We had some difficulty with Mr Churchill who was most anxious to come with us. He remained unconvinced by our argument that his life was far too valuable to the Allied cause to be risked in this unnecessary way. He finally left for home on June 5th, four days before the Pantellaria rehearsal; but I think he still holds it against us that he was not allowed to prolong his visit to see some action, for which he was always a glutton.

Before the Prime Minister flew home he readily assented to my request that he should visit the *Maidstone* to see some of the officers and men of the

Eighth Submarine Flotilla who had been doing such fine work. As usual, he said exactly the right thing to them gathered round him on deck, and afterwards went to the wardroom, where he was soon surrounded by young officers. He chatted and joked with them in his inimitable way, and in the course of conversation one fine young commanding officer with a most distinguished record, innocently remarked: "My submarine, sir, has been adopted by Epping."

The Prime Minister beamed. "Good!" he said. "That's my constituency. I hope they've done you well."

"No, sir," said the young officer. "They've done nothing up to date."

"Huh!" was the reply. "We'll have to see about that."

That afternoon messages went forth to Epping, and any previous shortcomings of Mr. Churchill's constituents were more than amply compensated.

I had never regarded Mr. Churchill as emotional; but when we left the *Maidstone* the tears were streaming from his eyes as he talked of those fine boys walking in the valley of the shadow of death.

Some months later, when I was attending a Chief of Staff's Conference in London with the Prime Minister in the chair, a signal was brought to me saying that this gallant young officer's submarine was missing, presumed lost. I showed it to Mr. Churchill at the end of the meeting, and reminded him of the Epping conversation on board the *Maidstone* at Algiers. His expression changed. He murmured something I did not catch. He was greatly moved.

The Pantellaria rehearsal went off according to plan. The air bombing was an impressive sight, and the reply of the batteries to the fire of the cruisers was wild in the extreme. It looked as though the Italian gun-control arrangements had been knocked out. The reception of the M.T.B.s at the harbour entrance was feeble enough, and had we had a few hundred troops in landing-craft I believe we could have taken the island there and then. General Eisenhower and I were much encouraged, and in the event the island fell easily into our hands on June 11th, white flags being hoisted as the troops started to move shorewards in their landing craft. I need not describe it, as it had full publicity at the time; but the excuse given for surrender, i.e. that water was lacking, was incorrect. The truth was that the Italians, stunned by their defeat in Tunisia, had no stomach for further fighting. They had had enough, though some hours elapsed before all resistance ceased. Lampedusa and Linosa, of no practical value, surrendered to naval forces within twenty-four hours.

The day after Pantellaria surrendered, His Majesty the King, travelling incognito by air as 'General Lyon' came to Algiers on a visit to the fighting men in North Africa. His impending arrival had been kept a secret; but within a few hours it was known all over Algiers, some of the more discerning citizens having recognized him in his car. He was accommodated in a villa, where Eisenhower, Alexander, Tedder and I dined with him that night. His Majesty was most anxious to visit Malta, and pressed the suggestion on me during dinner. I was most favourably inclined to the idea and needed little persuasion. The effect on the Maltese would be immense, and not only on the Maltese, but throughout the whole Empire. Nor did I think that if the proper precautions were taken the risks were prohibitive. So after consultation with the responsible authorities at home and locally the visit was arranged for a week ahead.

The King had an exceptionally heavy programme, and did not spare himself. We felt greatly honoured that he was able to find time to inspect the men of the Sea Services in the port area of Algiers. The *King George V*, *Howe* and two American cruisers were in the harbour, and we managed to assemble a most representative parade. There were about five thousand of our own seamen and Royal Marines; some six hundred of the United States Navy, very smart and well turned-out, and, best of all, about one thousand two hundred officers and men of the Merchant Navy from the merchant vessels in the port.

His Majesty expressed himself as highly pleased and gratified at everything he saw. Himself a seaman, he asked many shrewd questions. He met all the British and American Flag Officers, and visited the United States flagship and the *Howe*. Everybody was delighted to see him. On the Sunday he attended Divine Service in the church we had established in the dockyard, and one night honoured me by dining at my villa. He went to Tunis and Tripoli to visit the Army and the Royal Air Force, and on the evening of June 19th I met him in Tripoli, where we embarked in the battle-tried *Aurora*, Commodore W. G. Agnew, for passage to Malta.

The *Aurora* was escorted by the destroyers *Eskimo*, *Jervis*, *Nubian* and *Lookout*, and the 200-mile voyage passed off without incident. At dawn a large fighter escort was roaring overhead, and soon afterwards we met the sweepers who had been making certain that no mines existed in the approaches to the Grand Harbour. For obvious reasons the visit had been kept a dead secret, but at 5 a.m. the Maltese were informed of His Majesty's impending arrival. It was time enough. The Baraccas and all other vantage points were thick with cheering people as the *Aurora*, flying the Royal Standard, passed through the breakwater at 8 a.m. and moved to her buoys. The King stood on a special platform built in front of the bridge so that all could see him. I have witnessed many memorable spectacles; but this was the most impressive of them all. The dense throngs of loyal Maltese, men, women and children, were wild with enthusiasm. I have never heard such cheering, and all the bells in the many churches started ringing when he landed. Incidentally, we had no ship-sized Royal Standard, and the one flown by the *Aurora* was made and painted on board the *Howe* at Algiers.

The King made an extensive tour of the island, and we all lunched with the Governor, Field Marshal Viscount Gort, at Verdala Palace. It was the first time a Sovereign had landed in Malta since 1911, and the effect on the inhabitants was tremendous. The visit produced one of the most spontaneous and genuine demonstrations of loyalty and affection I have ever seen.

The King did not spare himself, and at 10 p.m. we sailed for the return passage to Tripoli after a busy and most stirring day. His Majesty left us for home on June 25th.

III

Meanwhile the planning for 'Husky' was proceeding steadily. On the British side the final plan involved the launching of the assaults from widely-separated starting points. It was probably the most complicated problem that ever faced a planning staff. Two British divisions and a brigade were to come from Suez in ships; another division from Tunisia in landing-craft with part of it staging at Malta on the way. A Canadian division was to sail from the United Kingdom in two ship convoys, while another British division, earmarked as a reserve, was to wait in the Sousse-Sfax area to be ferried over in landing-craft.

The Seventh, United States, Army used the ports west of Tunis—one division from Algiers, partly in ships and partly in landing-craft; another from Bizerta; another, with an armoured division, from Oran; another from the United States and staging in the Oran area. Two airborne divisions, one British and the other American, were based on Kairouan in Tunisia. Incidentally though Bizerta was devastated, the Americans had set up a highly efficient landing-craft base there. We were also rapidly getting the dockyard at Ferryville into running order for repair work, though the docks were unusable without considerable repair, and the machine tools were buried under the débris of the collapsed buildings.

There was a good deal of discussion as to the situation of the headquarters for 'Husky'. General Alexander's headquarters were originally at Algiers, and later at Carthage, near Tunis, with a small tactical headquarters at Malta. The R.A.F. and U.S.A.A.F. also had their headquarters near Tunis, where Eisenhower had an advanced post. Thus there was considerable pressure brought to bear on the Navy to move there also. I was very much against it. Malta, with its front line position a bare sixty miles from Italy, and its first-class naval communications already in existence, seemed to me to be the ideal place. It would have taken months to establish the necessary communications in the Tunis area or anywhere else. I pressed my view, and though the Air preferred to remain where they were, it was finally decided that Eisenhower, Alexander and myself should be at Malta for the actual operation. Vice-Admiral Ramsay and General Montgomery decided to come there also.

The actual landings on the British side under Ramsay were to be in charge of Rear-Admirals Rhoderick McGrigor, Sir Philip Vian and Thomas

H. Troubridge, while Rear-Admirals Alan G. Kirk, John L. Hall and R. L. Conolly were on the American side under Vice-Admiral Hewitt, U.S.N. This was a fine team of most able and experienced officers.

As I have already pointed out, 'Husky' was a stupendous operation demanding the most exact organization and timing. As D-day approached I detected an inclination in Army circles to make light of it, so I offered a few words of warning and caution. For myself I felt quite certain of success, being sure that the Italians had had enough of fighting and were only longing for some very good reason to make peace. Though our information gave us to believe that the troops in Sicily had been reinforced by another German division, not even the Germans could be everywhere at once to meet our spread-out attacks.

However, there was a good deal of unjustified optimism, particularly in Army circles. In a letter of June 25th to the First Sea Lord I said:

> The soldiers seem to think that they will be landed at the exact spot they expect to be, that the weather will necessarily be perfect, and that naval gunfire will silence all opposition. . . . The weather does not appear to be settling down as it ought to at this time of year. We have just had four days blow in the Malta Channel which would have made any operation impossible. The thought of having, at short notice, to turn back and delay all those ships and landing-craft, over two thousand in all, is a bit hair-raising. However, we have plans for it, and we reckon up to twenty-four hours before 'H' hour it can be done without much confusion.
>
> Against these somewhat pessimistic reflections we can, however, get some favourable facts. I was at the big rehearsal of our American assault this morning, and a feature was the exceptionally good handling of the assault craft, although of course mistakes in timing were made. I only hope the crews of our landing-craft are as well trained.
>
> We seem to be just getting on top of our troubles with regard to having the landing-craft fit for the operation. But it has taken every repair facility in the theatre and practically everything else has had to be laid aside. So I have every hope that in spite of all delays we shall come up to the starting gate in good condition.

We were taking no chances with the Italian fleet in case they came out to fight in defence of their country. Our naval forces had been increased to a strength adequate to the task. Vice-Admiral Willis had gone home with the *Nelson* and *Rodney*; but on June 9th re-hoisted his flag in the first-named at Scapa Flow. Eight days later he sailed for Gibraltar with the *Nelson*, *Rodney*, *Warspite*, *Valiant* and the aircraft-carrier *Indomitable*, escorted by two flotillas of destroyers. He arrived at Gibraltar on June 23rd, the day after the *Howe* and the *King George V* had sailed from there for Mers-el-Kebir. The *Nelson* and *Rodney* later came on to Algiers, and the *Valiant* and *Warspite* proceeded to Alexandria.

For the actual invasion of Sicily Force 'H', under Willis, consisting of four battleships, the aircraft-carriers *Formidable* and *Indomitable*, and the usual destroyer screen, would be cruising in the Ionian Sea. The *Howe* and *King George V* were intended to be kept in reserve at Algiers, while for service with Force 'H', as well as for the bombardment of shore targets in support of the Army, we had Rear-Admiral Harcourt's 15th Cruiser Squadron —*Newfoundland*, *Uganda*, *Orion* and *Mauritius*—and Commodore Agnew's 12th Cruiser Squadron—*Aurora*, *Penelope*, *Cleopatra*, *Euryalus*, *Sirius* and *Dido*.

In the event our fleet was given no opportunity of engaging the Italians, though a few days before the landing Force 'H' appeared to the south-west of Crete as a feint to keep the enemy guessing as to the real location of the assault. On the night of July 11th–12th, too, the night after the landings, the *Howe*, *King George V*, *Sirius* and *Dido*, escorted by destroyers, carried out a short bombardment of Marsala and Marittimo, at the western end of Sicily. This was to simulate another intended landing and to pin down any enemy forces at that end of the island.

IV

On July 3rd I sailed from Algiers for Malta in the cruiser *Uganda* with the bulk of my staff, arriving next day. I had had all the officers and their wives, who had been using Admiralty House as a hostel, cleared to other quarters. I settled in on the ground floor, with the Chief of Staff, Secretary and Flag Lieutenant, while the rest of my numerous staff used the large public rooms on the first floor, where the Vice-Admiral, Malta, was also accommodated.

I had an office in the Lascaris bastion overlooking the Grand Harbour. Power, the Vice-Admiral, Malta, and Ramsay, the Naval Commander for the British landings, also had offices there.

Our actual headquarters, with the combined naval and air operations room with its enormous wall chart, and all the communications staff, were in a tunnel dug from Lascaris through the soft sandstone to the middle of the moat under Valletta. Though slightly better than our dank and dismal cavern at Gibraltar from which we had conducted the North African landings, the Lascaris tunnel was extremely smelly and appallingly hot. No doubt it was sufficiently proof against bombing; but the tunnelling had disturbed the sandflies. The casualties from sandfly fever reached formidable proportions, particularly among the young communication ratings. Not a few of my staff were also stricken.

Malta bustled with activity. In particular, the airfields presented a scene of intense animation packed with aircraft of all types, mainly fighters. The energetic Americans, undaunted by any difficulties, had even bull-dozed, levelled and laid an airstrip on Gozo from which to operate fighters to cover the assaults on their beaches. This caused me to reflect that at a Defence Committee meeting in 1938 I had pressed for airfields in Gozo to extend the defences of Malta. My suggestion met with no response.

The Grand Harbour and the adjacent creeks were gradually filling with ships and landing-craft, and on the large-scale wall chart in our subterranean operations room the coloured lines marked with symbols showed the steady approach of the convoys bringing the assaulting troops. They came from the east and from the west, converging as if along the supporting strands of some huge spider's web upon Malta and about eighty miles of the Sicilian coastline.

Looking at that chart showing the carefully synchronized movements of hundreds of vessels in convoy, all steaming through certain points at their pre-arranged speeds, I often found myself wondering what might happen if things went wrong. We hoped we had the measure of the U-boats and of the Luftwaffe as well; but the movement of this great mass of shipping must be known to the enemy. We had taken every possible precaution in the way of anti-submarine and anti-aircraft protection; but there was always the odd chance that the convoys might be attacked.

I had implicit faith in our planners; but what chaos and confusion might also arise if one single detail in our planning had gone awry? The time available for drawing up, co-ordinating, drafting and issuing the printed operation orders to each and every convoy and naval unit had been short enough; but a single error in calculation, a solitary false figure, might make the difference between success and failure. Mine was the ultimate responsibility for the landing of 160,000 troops and all their varied impedimenta. It is hard to describe one's feelings at such a time; but idle to suggest that one did not feel anxiety on the eve of a great operation. So much depended upon success in this, our first invasion of enemy territory in Europe.

Eisenhower and Alexander arrived in Malta on July 8th and were accommodated by the Governor at Verdala Palace, though Eisenhower had alternative quarters near mine in our rather unsavoury tunnel.

D-day, as I have said, was July 10th, and 'H' hour, when the first troops were to land, was 2.45 a.m.

For some days past the R.A.F. and the U.S.A.A.F., in overwhelming superiority, had been pounding the airfields and defences of Sicily. Lying awake on a quiet night one could sometimes hear the heavy rumble of the bombing. But the weather was on my mind. If it blew up I had visions of what might happen on some of those open beaches in Sicily. I had already told Eisenhower that up till twenty-four hours before zero hour we could reverse the many convoys and delay the assault if the weather became too bad for landing. After that, I had said, whatever happened, the operation must take its course and we must risk the consequences. Actually, between ourselves—the Naval Staff—we had decided that noon on July 9th, was the very last moment we could cancel the assault for next morning.

On the morning of the 9th, when the various convoys from both ends of the Mediterranean were beginning to assemble in their positions eastward south of Malta, the weather started to deteriorate. It came on to blow hard from the north-westward, which was unusual for the time of year, and to

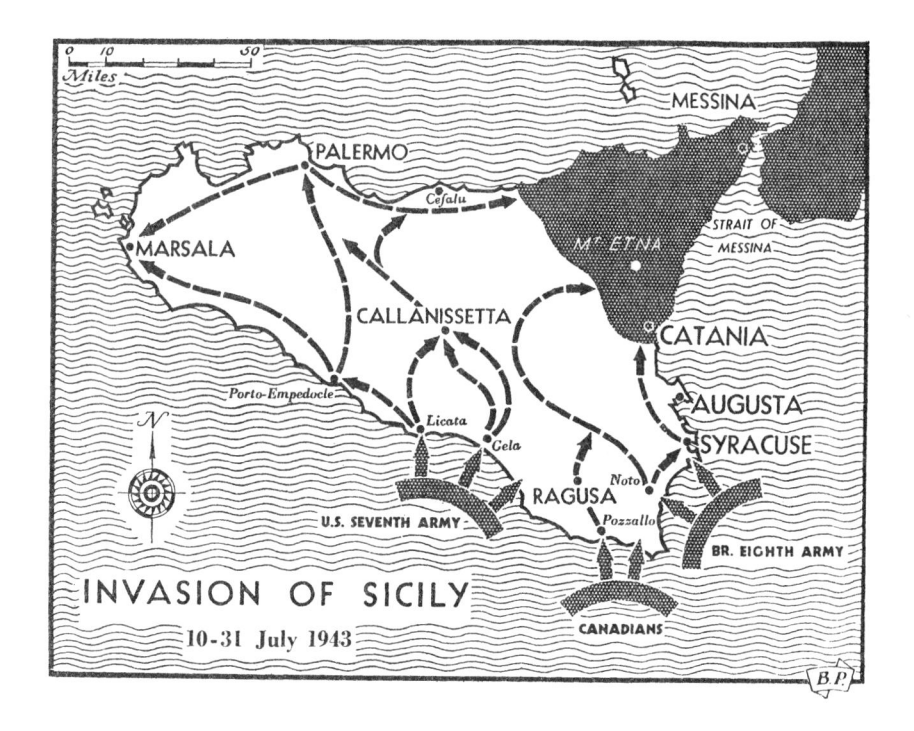

raise a short, choppy sea. Wind and sea rapidly increased until, by early afternoon the weather was really bad. I remember Eisenhower being in my office as the meteorologists brought me their forecasts. On the east side of Sicily, where the Eighth Army was to land under the lee, there was no doubt that the conditions would be favourable. On the south side of the island, however, where the Americans were to be put ashore, conditions would be very difficult. Moreover, punching against the sea then running, it was very doubtful if the many landing-craft of all descriptions, the motor-launches and other small vessels could make their objectives up to time. Some even might be swamped and founder.

On the other hand, if at that late hour we turned the convoys round inevitable confusion would ensue. Our signals might not get through to all the units, so some might go on and some not. Our attempt to land twenty-four hours later might produce a ragged and ill-timed assault. However, those of us with Mediterranean experience knew that with these sudden blows the wind usually took off at sundown, and our meteorologists predicted that this was likely to happen. So with rather fearful hearts we decided to let matters take their course. The landing-craft flotillas from Malta started to sail during the afternoon. Our anxieties were not at all relieved as we watched them literally burying themselves, with the spray flying over them in solid sheets, as they plunged out to sea on their way to their assault positions.

During the later afternoon, for the want of something definite to do, Commodore Dick and I drove out to one of the airfields. It was the last place we should have visited. All the winds of heaven seemed to be roaring and howling round the control tower. We returned to Admiralty House in deep anxiety, and though by about 8 p.m. it was still blowing hard the wind had definitely started to fall. After our evening meal Dick and I went to Delimara Point to see the airborne glider force go by for the support of the Eighth Army landing. They were flying at only three or four hundred feet in pairs of towing aircraft and gliders, sometimes in twos and threes, sometimes in larger groups, with their dim navigation lights just visible. In the pale half-light of the moon they looked like flights of great bats. Occasionally we could hear the drone of engines above the howling of the wind.

As it may be remembered, the airborne attacks, both British and American, were unfortunate. The wind was still blowing at about forty miles an hour when the parachutists were dropped and the gliders slipped over Sicily. Many of the pilots of the transport and towing aircraft were inexperienced in actual operations and navigation. The American airborne troops were dropped in small parties over an area of fifty square miles. Of the one hundred and thirty-four gliders with British troops from Tunisia, nearly fifty came down in the sea, and only twelve reached their correct positions. The occupants of some of our crashed gliders were luckily rescued by destroyers and small craft.

On the night of July 9th the sixty-mile gap between Malta and Sicily became crowded with shipping, and the chart in our operations room criss-crossed with the lines showing the tracks of convoys, squadrons and flotillas converging on the beaches of Sicily. Those many ships showed no lights. There was complete wireless silence. The weather was improving.

At some time after midnight Eisenhower and I turned in in our clothes in our cabins in the Lascaris tunnel. The die was cast. We were committed to the assault. There was no more that we could do for the time being.

I had already sent a message to all ships and naval units taking part. I said:

1. We are about to embark on the most momentous enterprise of the war—striking for the first time at the enemy in his own land.

2. Success means the opening of the 'Second Front' with all that implies, and the first move towards the rapid and decisive defeat of our enemies.

3. Our object is clear and our primary duty is to place this vast expedition ashore in the minimum time and subsequently to maintain our military and air forces as they drive relentlessly forward into enemy territory.

4. In the light of this duty, great risks must be and are to be accepted. The safety of our ships and all distracting considerations are to be relegated to second place, or disregarded as the accomplishment of our primary duty may require.

5. On every commanding officer, officer and rating rests the individual and personal duty of ensuring that no flinching in determination or failure of effort on his own part will hamper this great enterprise.

6. I rest confident in the resolution, skill and endurance of you all to whom this momentous enterprise is entrusted.

Here I must pay a tribute to the young officers of the Royal Naval Volunteer Reserve in command of the landing and other small craft. Many of them were manned by new and inexperienced officers, while before the actual operation there had been a heavy demand for the movement of troops, airmen and vehicles to their staging points or bases for the assault. This involved heavy and continuous running by the landing-craft at times when they should have been exercising, and we had some anxiety that the training would be insufficient and also that the engines might not stand the strain. But on that shocking night of July 9th–10th, thrashing into a strong wind and heavy sea in which several were damaged, they pressed determinedly on for their objectives. Some of them necessarily arrived late; but the great majority reached their appointed beaches with their important cargoes intact. It was greatly to their credit.

At many places along the Sicilian coast the enemy garrisons had been on the alert for weeks. One expected that the Italians might even maintain offshore patrols. But the garrisons, lulled into a sense of security by the wild weather, and believing that no one would attempt a landing in such conditions, allowed their vigilance to relax. Syracuse and Augusta were quite close; but the Italian sailors apparently confined their small craft to harbour and themselves to bed.

CHAPTER XLI

I

THE landings in Sicily have so often been described that it is not my intention to write of them in any detail. I shall merely try to set down how they affected me personally.

There had been strict wireless silence during the night; but just before 5 a.m. on the 10th an intercepted message was brought to me which indicated that some at least of the Royal Marine Commandos, who landed on the left of the Canadians to the west of Cape Correnti—to the south-west of Cape Passero—were safely ashore. I knew that their landing-place, though by no means the worst in the prevailing wind, was very exposed, so greatly cheered, I went into his room in the tunnel and told Eisenhower. From then on reports of successful landings at all points began to pour in, and the opposition did not appear to have been heavy.

During the morning I embarked in the *Abdiel* and visited the beaches. There was still a heavy surf running on the southern beaches at Scoglitti, Gela and Licata, where the Americans had landed. Numbers of landing-craft washed up on the shore showed clearly enough the severe conditions they had encountered. The landing conducted by my old friend Rear-Admiral Alan Kirk had been particularly difficult. He had had a dead lee shore, and I made him a congratulatory signal as the *Abdiel* steamed past. We saw few signs of fighting; merely a few bombs dropping, some enemy troops, probably Italian, retiring, with the occasional rumble of artillery or bombing well inland.

The Armies went ahead fast. The only real anxiety we had was at Gela, where on July 11th the Germans put in a strong counter-attack against the American 1st Division. Hard fighting lasted from 8 a.m. to 4.30 p.m., and at one time enemy tanks penetrated to the beach. The Americans stood fast, and assisted by heavy direct naval gunfire, to which the monitor H.M.S. *Abercrombie* with her 15-inch guns contributed most successfully, the Germans were finally repulsed. General Patton told me later that the situation had been ticklish. He himself had been left far out in front.—"Admiral," he said, "I was no longer in command of an Army; but merely a reconnaissance unit."

The days that followed were full of activity for the Navy. We had to build up the supplies for the Army, land reinforcements, and run anti-submarine and anti-aircraft patrols outside the vast number of merchant vessels lying off the beaches. There were bombardments by cruisers and destroyers in support of the Army, and on one occasion the *Warspite*, my former flagship, shelled Catania with her 15-inch guns. She developed a remarkable turn of speed for her age, having been launched in 1913. I felt bound to make her a signal—"Operation well carried out. There is no doubt that when the old lady lifts her skirts she can run." The journalists called the veteran *Warspite* 'the old lady' for ever afterwards.

There were almost nightly raids on the Straits of Messina by our motor torpedo boats and frequent battles with the E-boats. Also, the invasion of Sicily was a particularly bad period for the enemy submarines in the Mediterranean. Nine Italian and four German U-boats were destroyed between July 11th and August 22nd, M.T.B.s sinking two in the Straits of Messina, one a German and the other an Italian, on two successive nights. Three succumbed on July 12th, one, the Italian *Bronzo*, surrendering intact to the minesweepers *Seaham, Boston, Poole* and *Cromarty* off Syracuse, and being towed to Malta with the White Ensign flying over the Italian tricolour. Thereby hangs a tale.

General Eisenhower had with him two Agency Press correspondents, the one American and the other British, to whom he gave the latest information, he being the arbiter as to what could be published and what not. The messages, in short, did not go through the normal censorship. Unaware of our strict naval rule that the destruction of enemy submarines must on no account be imparted to or mentioned by the Press, particularly in cases where enemy codes and cyphers might have been captured and therefore compromised, Eisenhower in all innocence told his two journalists of the *Bronzo* episode. They promptly, and without our knowledge, published it to the world. The reaction was immediate—a severely-worded signal from the Admiralty demanding to know why this tit-bit of news had been made public contrary to all rules and regulations. Someone was evidently in for trouble. My harassed Public Relations Officer, who dealt with all matters connected with the Press, brought the Admiralty message to my Chief of Staff and finally to me, suggesting we might inform the Admiralty that the Supreme Commander was the real culprit. This we did. General Eisenhower was too large a mouthful even for the Admiralty. We heard no more about it.

I fully realize the value of the Press in wartime; but this was neither the first nor the last occasion on which we found ourselves in trouble. Once, at Algiers, at the request of the Admiralty, I had been prevailed upon to hold a Press conference to say something of the work of the Navy. In the course of this I remarked that I hoped Tripoli would soon be in the hands of the Eighth Army and that the Navy would use the port for running in supplies. I could see no harm in this, as the facts that we had captured Tripoli and were using it could never be concealed from the enemy.

However, the Chiefs of Staff in London took immediate exception to what I said, and issued a peremptory order to all Commanders-in-Chief at home and abroad that in future, whenever they held a Press conference, the gist of what they purposed to say was to be approved by the Chiefs of Staff beforehand. I have to confess I became irritated and retorted by signal that if the Commander-in-Chief himself did not know what he could safely say 'on the record' and what he could not, he was not fit to be Commander-in-Chief.

The result of the order was that I refused to give any further Press conferences, and the Navy, I suppose, lost some publicity. It was quite impossible for me to signal beforehand what I should say when the time came, or what exact answers I should give to the astute and agile questions of thirty or forty British and American gentlemen of the Press avid for news stories. But I should like to say how loyal ninety-nine per cent of them always were, and how carefully they guarded any secrets which were told them 'off the record'.

But in writing all this, I have diverged from my main topic, the assault upon Sicily.

The port of Syracuse was occupied during the evening of our landing, and made a most useful supply port. Augusta was captured before dawn on July 13th after considerable fighting, thus providing the Navy with a most useful protected anchorage suitable for a large number of ships of almost any size. We quickly developed it as a base for our motor torpedo boats.

After his initial check, General Patton made a spectacular march to the north coast in the torrid heat, cleared the western end of the island and made many Italian prisoners, occupied the airfields, and took Palermo on July 22nd. His subsequent advance east along the coastal cliff road towards Messina, which in places had been demolished or rendered temporarily impassable by the retreating Germans, was greatly assisted by three what our American friends call 'end runs', i.e. landing forces behind the enemy's front line. It was a striking example of the proper use of sea power, and Rear-Admiral Lyal A. Davidson, U.S.N. conducted these subsidiary amphibious operations with great skill and energy.

The heaviest opposition put up by the enemy was undoubtedly in front of the British Eighth Army. Progress was slow and Catania was stubbornly defended. The terrain, dominated by the great bastion of Mount Etna in the background, was undoubtedly most difficult, though I thought at the time we might have lessened our difficulties and hastened the advance if we had taken a leaf out of the American book and used our sea power to land troops behind the enemy lines. We had the ships ready at Augusta with commando troops embarked for just such operations, and I was sure that with Rear-Admiral McGrigor, full of fire and energy, in charge, operations of this sort would have been no less successful than those on the north coast. Late in the day, on the night of August 15th–16th, one such landing took place at Scaletta, eight miles south of Messina. It had little result, as the enemy had already retired.

July 19th, on which date the appointment of Admirals Ramsay and Hewitt as the Naval Commanders of the Eastern and Western Task Forces came to an end, saw the virtual end of 'Husky' so far as the landing of the Seventh and Eighth Armies were concerned. Thereafter the support and supply of the troops in Sicily became a routine operation under the Commander-in-Chief, Mediterranean.

Malta was again full of activity, and it was very pleasant to see the island resuming its function as a great base. It was a treat to have the harbour full of ships, and to watch the arrival and departure of cruisers, destroyers and swarms of small craft. Writing home on July 14th I said: "Today as I look out of my office window the Grand Harbour looks as it used to be. Two battleships" (the *Nelson* and *Rodney*) "are lying down below, the first to come into the harbour since I paid a short visit in the *Warspite* in December, 1940. Willis told me he was quite thrilled coming in, and I must say so was I."

One night, I remember, we were treated to a moderate and very noisy air raid, and it was a wonderful experience to see Malta's well-tried air defence going into action. The roar and thunder of the anti-aircraft fire, increased by that of the ships lying in the harbour, had to be heard to be believed. Everything worked like clockwork. Dick and I watched from the roof of Admiralty House. The sky was criss-crossed with streams of coloured tracer and the rays of searchlights, punctuated overhead by the golden sparkle of bursting shell. In a few minutes the whole harbour, dockyard and most of Valetta had disappeared under a pall of white, fleecy smoke, in the thick blanket of which the roof of Admiralty House and the roofs of a few other buildings stood out like islands. To the best of my recollection that raid did no damage.

I paid a visit to the Sicilian coast in the *Abdiel* on July 18th and landed at Augusta. It was a most impressive anchorage, and I found that our M.T.B. lads had set up an excellent headquarters and base for their attacks on the Straits of Messina. All the inhabitants seemed to have deserted their houses and possessions, and the harbour was full of abandoned small craft, mostly sailing vessels and of little use.

I flew back to Algiers on July 25th to attend to routine matters, to be met with the news of Mussolini's downfall, the assumption by the King of Italy of the command of the armed forces, and the appointment of Badoglio as Prime Minister. It was obvious that Italy had started to crack up, and we had already heard that hundreds of the Italian troops in Sicily had thrown away their arms and hastily changed into civilian clothes. However, the end was not yet.

I spent a lot of time in the next few weeks in the air, flying between Algiers, Malta and Eisenhower's headquarters and the Air headquarters, both near Tunis. We held various conferences to decide upon the further moves after Sicily was in our hands. Everyone was anxious to exploit our success at once; but as was to happen so often in subsequent operations the landing-craft necessary for amphibious assaults were all tied down to the task of building up and supplying the Army in Sicily. This effectually ruled out any large operation for the time being. The landing-craft and other small craft were also badly in need of repair and refit after months of hard running. During this period my Beaufighter aircraft fully proved its usefulness in saving valuable time.

Studying the question of future operations led us to the conclusion that while we should invade the toe of Italy across the narrow Straits of Messina, progress would inevitably be slow unless it were accompanied by a major assault further north. The Naples area was favoured. The Combined Chiefs of Staffs concurred, and plans for operation 'Avalanche', the landing in the Gulf of Salerno, were put in train.

The fighting in Sicily continued well into August. Catania fell to the Eighth Army on the 5th, and provided us with another excellent port for supplying the Army. By the second week in August the Germans realized that the game was up and started to pull out. There was no effective way of stopping them, either by sea or air. The passage across the Straits of Messina, no more than three miles, could be made in less than one hour, and was covered by batteries and searchlights on both sides. The Germans sent their troops across by night, which ruled out serious interference by our aircraft. And though our M.T.B.s made almost nightly sallies well into the Straits at great risk to themselves, they could not really interrupt the enemy's traffic.

On August 17th the American forces entered Messina from the east. They were followed in a few hours by the Eighth Army from the south. Thus, after thirty-eight days of fighting, the whole of Sicily was ours.

It was at about this time that I was presented by General Giraud with the Grand Cordon of the Legion of Honour. Commodore Dick, Lieutenant Dampier and myself were asked to lunch at the Palais D'Etè at Algiers. Before the meal, in a most colourful ceremony, with guards of Spahis and other French troops, French sailors and our own sailors, bands, and a number of the leading Frenchmen and French Admirals, I was invested with the sash and star and solemnly kissed on both cheeks by Giraud.

Some weeks later Admiral Hewitt and myself were both made Honorary Members of the Seventh Spahis, and each presented with one of their fine red woollen cloaks lined with white. It is a cherished possession which I have had some difficulty in retaining. My wife's covetous glances are often cast in its direction, for there is no doubt it could well be converted into a garment suitable for a lady.

II

Operation 'Husky', as I have said, was the largest amphibious operation ever carried out up till that time. Before relegating it to the limbo of ancient history, I should like to mention a few matters affecting the part played by the Sea Services which struck me most forcibly at the time.

I was tremendously impressed by the fine spirit, discipline and calm determination of the many officers and men of the Allied Merchant Navies who so greatly contributed to our success. They were our real comrades in arms, undaunted by any difficulty or danger. Dangers there certainly were with the enemy U-boats and minefields, and a great mass of stationary shipping lying off the beaches within easy striking distance of the enemy airfields. One remembers the Hospital Ship *Talamba*, white-painted and brilliantly lit in accordance with the Geneva Convention, which was deliberately and wantonly dive-bombed and sunk three miles off Syracuse on the night of July 10th while actually embarking wounded.

We were much indebted to the gallant young men of the Combined Operations Reconnaissance and Pilotage Parties, the 'C.O.P.P.s', who landed and reconnoitred the landing beaches beforehand in folboats sent in from submarines. Then there were the submarines themselves, the *Unruffled, Unseen, Unison, Unrivalled, Seraph, Shakespeare* and *Safari*, which served as inshore beacons guiding the flights of landing-craft to their beaches in the dark and early morning of July 10th.

As for the landing-craft of many different types, this was their first major operation. Many of their officers and men lacked experience and were new to the sea. Some of them had voyaged across the Atlantic. Quite apart from their rude buffeting during the passage to Sicily, they carried out their various tasks during the landings with a competence and courage that excited my warm admiration. Experienced observers on the spot commented upon the efficiency and initiative with which these craft were handled in the crowded waters off the beaches. There was good reason for the message of congratulation I sent to them and to those responsible for keeping them in repair and running order.

A great feature of the operation were the American D.U.K.W.S—popularly 'Ducks'—now well-known, but then a complete novelty to us. It was amazing to see these ingenious amphibious craft loading stores alongside the ships in a swell, wallowing inshore, and then waddling dripping up the beaches to deposit their cargoes in the dumps inland. Remarkably well handled, they saved much time and effort, as well as traffic-congestion on the beaches.

Our cruisers were frequently in action in support of the Army, and against likely targets on the Italian mainland. The destroyers, as usual, were ubiquitous—bombarding, providing anti-submarine patrols and screens, and helping in the anti-aircraft defence of the crowd of shipping. Among the bombarding ships were our old friends the twenty-eight year old river gun-boats *Aphis* and *Scarab*, which had done such good work along the coast of Cyrenaica. Particularly useful work, as ever, was done by the minesweepers, while during the months of July and August, British submarines in the

Mediterranean sank something like fourteen enemy supply and troop ships, three U-boats, two destroyers and five smaller vessels and auxiliaries.

During the actual operations, and the period covering the transportation of men and material to Sicily from Great Britain and the United States through the U-boat zone in the North Atlantic, the total of Allied merchant shipping lost amounted to 85,000 tons. The Germans claimed 516,830 tons, just about six times too much.

Our British naval losses during the period of the campaign were two submarines, three motor torpedo boats, one motor gunboat and a few landing craft. The aircraft-carrier *Indomitable* was hit by an aircraft torpedo, while the cruisers *Cleopatra* and *Newfoundland* were torpedoed by U-boats. All these three ships, though damaged, reached Malta in safety.

We were gratified to receive a message from General Eisenhower congratulating the Royal and United States Navies, while General Sir Harold Alexander sent me a letter which was ordered to be brought to the notice of all officers and men of the Mediterranean Fleet. He wrote:

> Before leaving Malta for the mainland, I should like to take this opportunity of expressing, on behalf of the Fifteenth Army Group, our admiration for, and gratitude to the Royal Navy and the other naval units you command for the magnificent support and service you have given and continue to give to the troops under my command. It will gratify you to hear what I hear on all sides—namely, unstinted praise for the Senior Service.

In the despatch already quoted in the previous chapter, General Alexander also mentioned the debt which the land operations owed to the sister services. On the Navy:

> fell the weight of what was in some way the most arduous, detailed and vital part of the operation, the actual conveyance of the troops to their objectives. I do not mean merely to point out the obvious: that to invade an island it is necessary to cross the sea; but to evoke to the imagination some picture of the gigantic nature of the task of convoying for such distances, assembling and directing to obscure and unlit beaches in an enemy territory an Armada of two thousand ships and craft. I must mention only in passing the assistance of naval gunfire on the beaches and the silent strength of the covering forces waiting, and hoping, for the appearance in defence of its native soil of that fleet which once claimed to dominate the Mediterranean. It is a theme which can be described only by a naval specialist, and one of which the Royal Navy and the United States Navy are justly proud. . . .

III

After the capture of Messina, preparations for the shore-to-shore landing across the Straits into the toe of Italy were at once put in hand, among them the mounting of a colossal number of guns around Messina to cover the landing. To anticipate, this subsidiary operation, known as 'Baytown', was actually carried out on September 3rd under the energetic command of Rear-Admiral McGrigor. It was preceded by heavy bombardments of the coastal batteries in the Reggio and Cape Pillaro areas by, among other ships, the battleships *Nelson*, *Rodney*, *Warspite* and *Valiant*.

At dawn on September 3rd, under cover of a tremendous volumne of fire from our artillery massed on the Messina side, not to mention that of the *Mauritius* and *Orion*; the monitors *Erebus*, *Roberts* and *Abercrombie*; six destroyers and the two gunboats *Aphis* and *Scarab*, two divisions of the Eighth Army, one British and the other Canadian, set forth in a swarm of landing and other craft.

I had embarked in the destroyer *Tartar* the night before, and was on the spot to watch the assault. Never, since perhaps the time of Gallipoli, had I seen or heard such a bombardment. In point of fact it was really an anti-climax and probably a waste of ammunition. The Italians were not fighting, and the Germans had already pulled out to the north. There was no retaliation except for an occasional ill-aimed shell plopping harmlessly into the middle of the Straits. Indeed, except for the roar and thunder of our vast concentration of artillery it was more like Cowes Week than an assault on enemy territory. Our people called it the 'Messina Straits Regatta'. Nevertheless, it was interesting to see the tank-landing ships and craft disgorging tanks with their bows and ramps well into the olive groves, and troops, guns, vehicles and stores being put ashore from flight after flight of other craft. Having much else to do I only remained on the spot long enough to communicate with McGrigor.

It was a bloodless victory, this, our first landing on the mainland of Europe; but the crews of the landing-craft did excellent work. The Navy had promised the Army to ferry 5,000 vehicles in five days. By working all out, with some of the craft making as many as ten or twelve trips a day, 5,300 vehicles were transported across the Straits in *three* days.

Meanwhile planning had been going forward for the main operation of a landing in the Gulf of Salerno, with Naples and its fine port facilities as the objective. Before going thoroughly into the question I had favoured a landing in the Rome area; but this was finally ruled out because it was far beyond the range of any Allied shore-based fighter aircraft, while heavy German reinforcements were pouring into Italy from the north. Even the Gulf of Salerno was outside the range of all Allied fighters except the most modern American, and they could spend no more than about twenty minutes operating time over the battle area. So we planned to support the landing by the fighters from five aircraft-carriers until airfields ashore could be seized or constructed and the R.A.F. and U.S.A.A.F. fighters could come into action.

At a conference on August 17th between the Supreme Commander and the Commanders-in-Chief, September 9th was fixed as the date for the operation at Salerno, 'Avalanche', and it was decided a few days later that the operational headquarters of all three Commander-in-Chief should be in the Tunis area. Commanders for the landing were to be Admiral H. Kent Hewitt, U.S.N. for the Navy, and General Mark Clark U.S.A. for the Army. The subordinate naval commanders were to be Commodore Geoffrey N. Oliver for the British landing, and Rear-Admiral John L. Hall, U.S.N. for the American.

Rear-Admiral Sir Philip Vian, with his flag in the cruiser *Euryalus*, would command the force of aircraft-carriers, Force 'V'—*Unicorn, Hunter, Stalker, Attacker, Battler*—detailed to furnish fighter cover over the beaches. Vice-Admiral Willis with Force 'H' would provide cover against any enemy interference from the sea. Fighters from his two carriers had also to afford cover over Force 'V', as well as their normal anti-submarine patrols and cover over the battle-fleet.

In the meantime it had become more and more evident that the Italian people were more than anxious to get out of the war. However, Badoglio made no sign. Indeed, he declared his intention of prosecuting the war vigorously. His difficulty, of course, was that he was completely under the thumb of the Germans. At the end of July, with the approval of the combined Chiefs of Staff, Eisenhower broadcast to the Italian people calling upon them to surrender. Though this had a good effect, it produced no overt move from those in authority.

However, on August 17th, information was received from the British Minister in Lisbon that an Italian General, Castellano, had arrived there secretly and wished to enter into negotiations. Having obtained the concurrence of the Combined Chiefs of Staff, at that time conveniently together in Quebec, Eisenhower sent Bedell Smith, his Chief of Staff, and Brigadier Kenneth Strong, his Chief of Intelligence, to Lisbon. They took with them a short list of the Allied demands, though as regards the disposal of the Italian Navy the demands fell far short of what was required. Neither myself nor my Chief of Staff, Commodore Dick, had been consulted.

After a series of melodramatic meetings and incidents which would not have been out of place in a spy story, Bedell Smith and Strong returned with the news that there was a desperate desire to surrender on the part of the Italians. The Germans, however, had infiltrated into all the important posts in the administration of the war and in the country, and the Italians were terrified and completely at a loss how to act. In any case they could not think of capitulation unless it coincided with a large-scale landing by the Allies on the Italian mainland.

For the next fortnight or so negotiations muddled along. It was difficult always to know the *bona fides* of the negotiators on the Italian side, for they were periodically changed. But to cut short a complicated story, terms of surrender were finally signed in Sicily on September 3rd, in a document later known as the 'Shorter Instrument'. Briefly, the terms comprised the complete surrender of the whole of the Italian armed forces, wherever they were, on the evening of September 8th, the night before our landing in the Gulf of Salerno. On that date, at 6.30 p.m. simultaneous announcements of the capitulation would be made by Eisenhower and Badoglio.

Arrangements were also made for an American airborne division to be dropped near Rome to stiffen up the Italian resistance to the Germans. I undertook the responsibility of supplying this force by sea through the small port at the mouth of the Tiber. The American Brigadier General Taylor, commanding the airborne division, went secretly to Rome with a companion to make the necessary arrangements. The story of their adventures, too, read like the wildest fiction, and they were lucky not to be caught and treated as spies. But nothing came of it. The Italians took fright and the airborne operation had to be cancelled.

At this time President Roosevelt, Mr. Churchill and the Combined Chiefs of Staff were in conference at Quebec. We heard little of their deliberations, except that it had been decided to appoint Lord Louis Mountbatten as Supreme Commander, South-East Asia. What caused me grave concern was the news that all was not well with the First Sea Lord, Sir Dudley Pound. Lady Pound had died in July, which had been a heavy blow to him. I now learnt that he was failing, worn out through overwork, I feared. For the time being I heard no more of his condition, except that on arriving in England he had been taken to hospital.

IV

The date for 'Avalanche', the Salerno landing, was drawing near. The decision that the headquarters for all the Commanders-in-Chief for this operation were to be near Tunis had caused the Navy some embarrassment, not to say inconvenience. The communications at Bizerta were quite inadequate to deal with the huge volume of signal traffic pouring into the office of the Commander-in-Chief, Mediterranean, and the telephone system was indifferent and insecure. We therefore decided to have a headquarters ship alongside at Bizerta, and for myself and operations staff to live on board. The routine business would be carried on at Algiers, and I would pay periodical visits to clear up any outstanding points.

In staff matters the Navy has a different system from the Army. It is not our custom for the Commander-in-Chief to delegate operational or other important decisions to anyone except perhaps his Chief of Staff. He deals with them himself, and signs all important orders with his own hand.

So on September 7th I moved to Bizerta with some of my staff. Our headquarters ship was the *Largs*, which was crowded and uncomfortable, particularly in hot weather, though her excellent commanding officer did his best for us.

All was in train for the Italian surrender. The arrangements for the fleet were that they should leave Spezia on the announcement of the capitulation and make for North Africa, where they would be met and escorted to Malta. Another contingent from Taranto would be shepherded to Malta a day or two later. We could not be certain, of course, that the Italian fleet would conform to these arrangements; but as the alternative was falling into the hands of the Germans we hoped they would.

The impending Italian surrender, and the arrangements for their fleet, had been kept a dead secret. All the Press correspondents, the broadcasters, the photographers and the cinematographers were already embarked in their ships to cover the landing at Salerno, so there was nobody available to describe or to photograph the surrender of the fleet, which was a pity. However, when I said *au revoir* to Eisenhower the day before leaving Algiers for Bizerta I mentioned this, and he suggested that Commander Hary Butcher, U.S.N.R., his naval A.D.C., a good photographer, should be present with his selection of cameras. So Butcher was flown to Malta and embarked in the *Warspite*, flying the flag of Rear-Admiral Bisset, before she sailed with the other ships of Force 'H' to cover the Salerno landing.

In the event of the Italian fleet sailing according to expectation, Bisset had sealed orders instructing him to take under his command the *Warspite* and *Valiant* and certain destroyers, including one French and one Greek, to meet the Italians off the North African coast, and conduct them to Malta.

In retrospect I think we may have been too secretive in our dealing with the Press; but we found it hard to believe that the Italians would surrender their fleet without firing a shot. As it was, my harassed Public Relations Officer found himself involved in much personal abuse and acrimonious recrimination which he found it most difficult to counter. Fuel was added to the fire of discontent by a signal from the Admiralty demanding to know why an American naval officer had been the only person permitted to pull off a world 'scoop'. The fact was that not even the P.R.O. had been let into the secret.

I need not go into details of the surrender which has already been fully described; but the three great Italian battleships *Roma*, *Italia* and *Vittorio*

Veneto sailed from Spezia during the later afternoon of September 8th. That night they were joined by cruisers and destroyers from Genoa, and on the morning of the 9th the whole fleet was sighted by our air reconnaissance steaming down the west coast of Corsica in accordance with our instructions. For some reason that was never quite clear to me, though some said the orders were issued by the Germans in the name of the Italian Admiralty, the fleet turned east into the Gulf of Asinara, in the north of Sardinia, instead of making their way south with all despatch. In consequence they were caught by German aircraft and attacked with glider bombs, which resulted in the *Roma* being blown up and sunk with heavy loss of life, including the Commander-in-Chief. The *Italia*, which was also hit and damaged, and the *Vittorio Veneto* with five cruisers and seven destroyers steamed on for the North African coast.

At 6 a.m. next morning, September 10th, the Italians were met by the *Warspite*, *Valiant* and destroyers. The Italian flagship, the cruiser *Eugenio di Savoia*, flying the flag of Admiral Romeo Oliva, who had taken over the command after the death of his Commander-in-Chief, was boarded by Captain T. M. Brownrigg, my Staff Officer, Plans, who had originally been my Fleet Navigating Officer in the *Warspite*. The *Savoia*, leading the Italian line, formed astern of the *Warspite* and *Valiant*, with our destroyers leading the Italian destroyers on each flank.

That afternoon, as they passed Bizerta, with Eisenhower and my Chief of Staff, Commodore R. M. Dick, I went out in the destroyer *Hambledon*, Lieutenant-Commander G. W. McKendrick, to watch them go by. To me it was a most moving and thrilling sight. To see my wildest hopes of years back brought to fruition, and my former flagship the *Warspite*, which had struck the first blow against the Italians three years before, leading her erstwhile opponents into captivity, filled me with the deepest emotion and lives with me still. I can never forget it. I made a signal congratulating the *Warspite* on her proud and rightful position at the head of the line.

The battleships *Andrea Doria* and *Caio Duilio*, with two cruisers and a destroyer from Taranto arrived at Malta on the afternoon of September 10th; the *Warspite* and *Valiant* with the ships under their charge, reaching the island next morning.

Meanwhile, when I knew that the Italian fleet was actually committed to surrender, it seemed to me there was nothing to prevent our occupying Taranto if we moved a squadron there quickly enough. Eisenhower held exactly the same view. The difficulty was to find the troops; but the First British Airborne Division was made available. The troops were to be embarked in cruisers at Bizerta and taken to Taranto at full speed. They were to sail on September 9th; but Eisenhower asked me if I could advance it by one day, to which I replied that if he could produce the troops I could produce the ships. Accordingly the cruisers *Aurora*, *Penelope*, *Sirius*, *Dido*, with the cruiser-minelayer *Abdiel* and the United States cruiser *Boise* embarked the soldiers and their equipment and left Bizerta on the evening of the 8th.

The operation was by no means without risk. We had heard through our intelligence that German E-boats had been sowing mines in the anchorage at Taranto, and though I felt fairly sure that the Italian fleet would not resist, I was not certain about the forts and batteries, which might, of course, have been taken over by Germans. So Vice-Admiral Power, at Malta, was ordered to hoist his flag in the *Howe* and to proceed to Taranto with the *King George V*, a flotilla of destroyers and some minesweepers, in case things went wrong. Boldness was called for, and this I knew Arthur Power would supply in full measure. The Italians knew nothing of our intended arrival, and we could expect no co-operation from them.

After making his rendezvous with the cruisers, Power met the Taranto detachment of the Italian fleet leaving the swept channel on its way to surrender at Malta. Preceded by his minesweepers, he pushed on into Taranto harbour in the late afternoon of September 9th. There was no resistance, and the cruisers began to disembark their troops and stores. But our information about mines was only too true. The troops were actually being landed when the *Abdiel*, swinging to her anchor, struck a mine and sank in a few minutes with heavy loss of life, particularly among the heavily accoutred soldiers. The loss of them, and of a gallant ship which had served us so well for so many months, was greatly to be deplored. However, the rest of the troops were safely landed. They occupied the town, and boldly advanced north into the country, eventually to join up with the Eighth Army.

On September 11th, I flew to Malta to meet the Italian Admiral da Zara, in charge of the Taranto detachment, to give him instructions for the disarmament and disposal of the Italian fleet. Malta was *en fete*, with the people wild with jubilation and many of the streets draped in flags. Among others, the parish priest of shattered Senglea, contiguous to the dockyard and therefore one of the main targets for the air attacks, announced the Italian surrender from his pulpit. He was the undaunted man who calmly walked up and down the main street reciting his office during the worst air raids to give courage and comfort to his people.

Admiral da Zara came ashore at the Custom House and was received with full military honours, and, on my behalf by Commodore Dick. My office in the Lascaris bastion was no more than about sixty steps up a circular stairway; but I thought it advisable that da Zara should see something of what the Axis airmen had done to Malta, and also that the Maltese should see him. Accordingly we had him brought a roundabout way by car. I might add that my Chief of Staff considered his position most invidious, particularly if the Maltese took it into their heads to stone the Italian Admiral.

Da Zara was a pleasant-enough man speaking good English; but as was only natural felt his position keenly. Matters were quickly settled. There was little or no opposition to our proposals. That day, September 11th, I made a signal to the Admiralty: "Be pleased to inform their Lordships that the Italian Battle fleet now lies at anchor under the guns of the fortress of Malta."

Other Italian ships came in to surrender, the battleship *Guilio Cesara*, the seaplane-carrier *Miraglia*, with a number of destroyers, torpedo boats and submarines. So large a force could not be kept at Malta, and on September 14th the *Italia* and *Vittoria Veneto*, with four cruisers and four destroyers, sailed for Alexandria under the escort of the *Howe*, *King George V* and six destroyers.

CHAPTER XLII

I

To keep this narrative more or less on a personal level, I have no intention of trying to describe that complicated operation *Avalanche*, the landing in the Gulf of Salerno, in any great detail. The final object was the occupation of the port of Naples, and the immediate object the capture of a bridgehead and the neighbouring airfields over a front of about forty miles, including the road running through the Plain of Salerno, from Paestum in the south through Battipaglia to the port of Salerno and Vietri sul Mare in the north. It was also hoped to capture the high ground from which Salerno itself and the landing beaches could be overlooked and covered by artillery fire.

General Mark Clark, of the United States Army, was in command of the Fifth Army which carried out the operation, and Vice-Admiral H. Kent Hewitt, U.S.N. the overall Naval Commander. Rear-Admiral John L. Hall, U.S.N. commanded the Southern Attack Force responsible for landing the American Sixth Corps and their supplies over open beaches south of the Sele River near Agropoli, while Commodore G. N. Oliver, of the Royal Navy, with his broad pendant in H.M.S. *Hilary*, had the duty of landing the British Tenth Corps, commanded by Major General Richard L. McCreery, over beaches about three miles south-east of the town of Salerno. The actual landing-places of British and Americans were thus separated by about fifteen miles.

The first waves of assaulting troops touched down on their respective beaches in the early hours of September 9th. The surrender of the Italian armed forces had been broadcast by Eisenhower and Badoglio the evening before; but for some time past, realizing the capitulation was imminent, the Germans had been taking over the defences and disarming and replacing the Italian troops. There was considerable opposition to the first landings; but by sunset on the first day this had been temporarily overcome, the beaches were in our hands, and the Germans had withdrawn.

But the enemy mobile artillery in the hills still dominated our landing-places, and Kesselring was feverishly concentrating all his available troops and armour for the inevitable counter-attack. Moreover, though we did not know it at the time, the enemy had at his disposal a new and potent weapon, the radio-controlled bomb, launched from and directed by aircraft. Though it might not be of much use against troops on shore, it was a menace against ships operating off the coast, and we had no immediate antidote.

On the morning of September 11th, the American cruiser *Philadelphia*, working with the bombarding forces off the American landings south of the

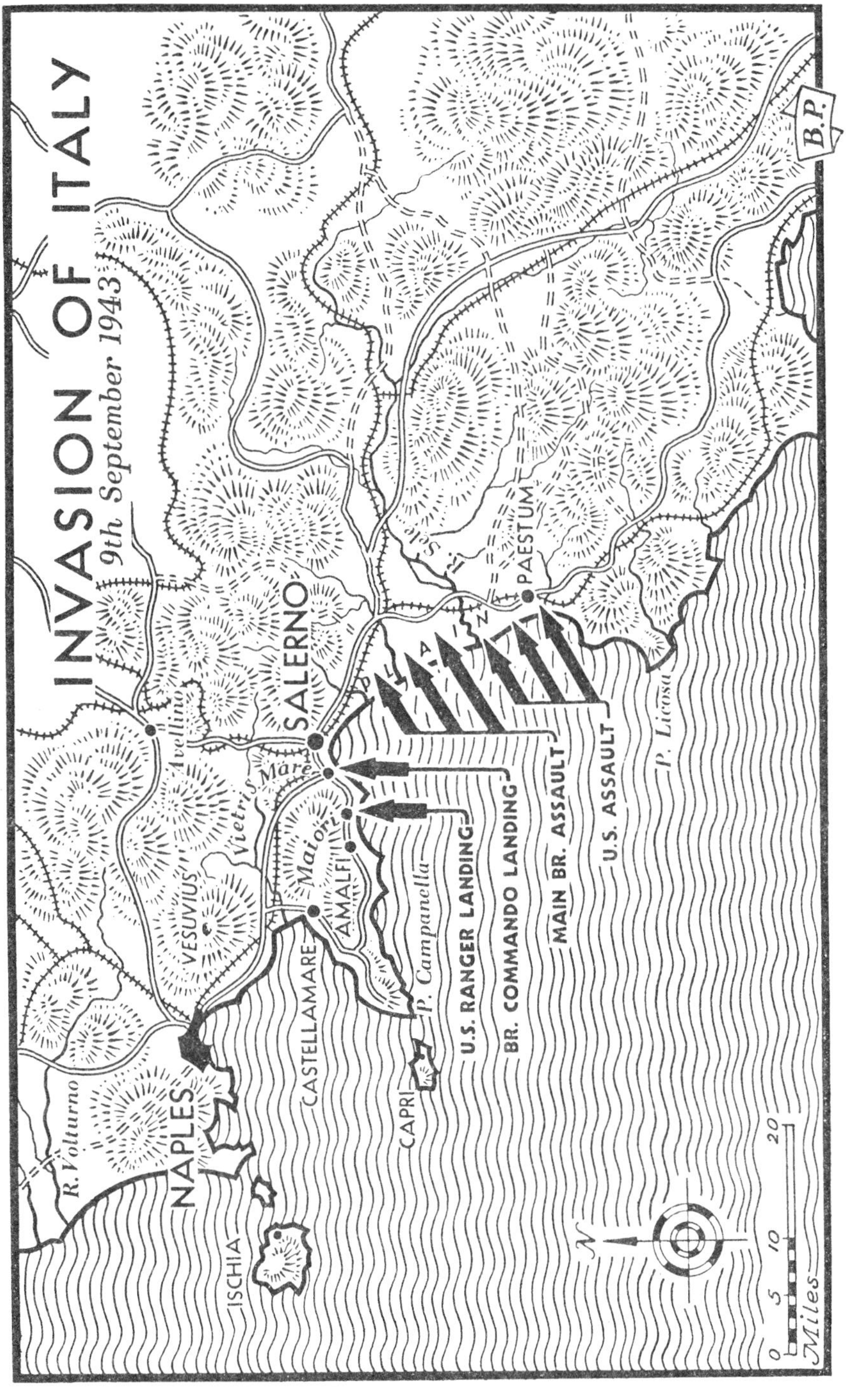

Sele River, was near-missed by one of these new weapons. Though severely damaged, she still continued to operate. Nine minutes later her sister ship, the *Savannah*, was hit. The bomb penetrated a turret and burst deep in the ship, the heavy explosion causing severe structural damage with about one hundred casualties and bad flooding. Those who saw the incident thought the ship was gone; but she remained afloat, and reached Malta for docking for temporary repairs before going on to the United States for refit.

On the night of September 11th–12th the Germans started a series of counter-attacks which nearly ended in disaster. The enemy captured the little town of Battipaglia and continued to advance, striving to drive a wedge to the sea between the Americans in the south and the British to the north. The situation became precarious. The Allies were thin on the ground, and the narrow strips of territory held did not permit our artillery to be deployed and used to its full effect. Irrigation ditches and citrus groves provided serious obstacles to our tanks, while every beach, every dump, each little level area congested with troops, guns, vehicles and stores, was under heavy gunfire. Though the airfield at Montecorvino had been captured, it also was under fire and could only be used for forced landings.

Heavy naval bombardments continued throughout September 12th. Reinforcements of troops were called for from Sicily and North Africa. The cruisers *Euryalus*, *Scylla* and *Charybdis* were rushed to Tripoli to embark others.

The Germans ran true to form. Before dawn on the 13th they bombed the hospital ships *Newfoundland* and *Leinster* lying brilliantly lit out at sea, the *Newfoundland* being sunk with heavy loss of life. That same afternoon the cruiser *Uganda* was hit and seriously damaged by a radio-controlled bomb; but managed to reach Malta.

September 13th, was a critical day ashore. The weight of the German attack came down the Sele River and penetrated to within three miles of the beaches, driving a deep bulge between the British and the Americans.

On September 14th the weight of the enemy attack had forced the Americans to give more ground, and the military situation was critical. Vice-Admiral Hewitt also took a grave view of the naval situation. He was perturbed about the naval losses sustained as the result of direct enemy action, while the military situation had imposed new demands and requirements upon naval ships and craft. Shortly before 3 p.m. Hewitt made me a signal saying that the military situation continued to be unsatisfactory, and asking for heavy air bombardment and naval bombardment by heavy ships behind the enemy positions. Were heavier naval forces available? To this I replied that I would give all the help I could, and that the *Valiant* and *Warspite* were sailing forthwith. The *Nelson* and *Rodney* were also available if required and had been ordered to Augusta.

It was on this day, D + 5, September 14th, that plans were made between

General Clark and Vice-Admiral Hewitt to embark Fifth Army headquarters in H.M.S. *Hilary*. At Clark's request Hewitt ordered all available craft in the assault areas to be ready to transfer troops from the Southern Attack area to the Northern Attack area, or vice versa. The unloading of all merchant ships in the Southern Attack area was also stopped preparatory to possible withdrawal.

Late this afternoon, September 14th, Commodore Oliver was summoned to visit Hewitt's headquarters ship. Oliver, incidentally, had only just parted from Major-General McCreery, commanding the British Tenth Corps, who had not mentioned any important change of plan.

Reaching Hewitt's headquarters ship, Oliver found the naval staff feverishly working out plans for the transfer of the Fifth Army headquarters to H.M.S. *Hilary*; to move units of the British Tenth Corps from the Northern to the Southern Attack area; and units of the United States Sixth Corps in the opposite direction.

Oliver said he would gladly accommodate General Clark and his personal staff in the *Hilary* if necessary; but as the complete staff already ashore numbered nearly two thousand with about five hundred vehicles, it was quite impossible to accommodate them all. Oliver also gave it as his firm opinion that considering enemy opposition and the nature of the beaches for re-embarkation, the operation of transferring troops from one attack area to the other was quite impossible and not to be contemplated. Now that the troops were ashore, he insisted, the only thing that they could do was to stay and fight it out with all the support the Navy could give them in the way of gunfire.

On his return to the *Hilary*, Oliver at once got into contact with General McCreery at his headquarters ashore. McCreery, to put it mildly, was horrified at the proposal to evacuate troops from one attack area to the other. Moreover, General Clark had made no mention of any such idea at that day's meeting. Immediately, at about 10 p.m., McCreery originated a signal addressed to General Clark and Admiral Hewitt stating that no mention had been made at that day's conference of any plan for transferring British units from the Northern Attack area to the Southern, and that he considered there was no question of its taking place.

It was Commodore Oliver's opinion then, as now, and I whole-heartedly agreed with him, that the further progress of the troops depended on our ability to keep the beaches open, and to go on unloading men, guns, ammunition and stores. This, in turn, depended mainly on the security of the flanks of the twenty-mile stretch of coast over which the landings were being made. The beaches and the immediate hinterland were flat; but the flanks, around Salerno in the north and Agropoli in the south, were mountainous. Mobile guns firing from these mountains could dominate the anchorages and stop unloading. A break through to the beaches over the flat ground in the centre near the River Sele would not have had nearly so serious an effect as this gunfire from the mountains, and would have been most vulnerable to naval gunfire on reaching the shore.

I consider that General McCreery and Commodore Oliver displayed most commendable firmness and resolution in adopting the attitude they did. Any evacuation or partial evacuation from one or other of the narrow Allied beach-heads would have resulted in a reverse of the first magnitude—an Allied defeat which would have completely offset the Italian surrender, and have been hailed by the Germans as a smashing victory.

II

On September 15th, when the *Warspite* and *Valiant* reached the vital area, the German attack near the Sele River had been held. Every available ship was bombarding, the battleships coming into action at ranges of up to 21,800 yards. On the morning of the 14th all the available aircraft of the Mediterranean Air Force had been switched on to the bombing of the German concentrations. The heavy and accurate naval gunfire effectively sealed off the enemy thrust from reinforcement, and the bombing helped to convert the spearhead of the German attack into a huddle of men, tanks, guns and vehicles which were mercilessly pounded. By the 16th the military situation was fully stabilized, and the link-up of the Fifth Army and Montgomery's Eighth Army coming up from the south was imminent.

It was during the early afternoon of the 16th that the *Warspite*, after completing her third successful bombardment that day, was hit by a radio-controlled bomb which burst below, to inflict severe damage and many casualties. She was narrowly missed by two others. She managed to struggle out of action at slow speed; but at 3 p.m. the last boiler filled with sea water and all steam failed. The old ship was taken in tow, and after an adventurous passage sideways through the Straits of Messina reached Malta on the 19th. She later went on to Gibraltar, where I walked under her in dry-dock and saw the two enormous cofferdams built on her bottom. I thought she would require an extensive refit before she fought again; but in her damaged condition she was still able to play an outstanding part in bombarding during the Normandy landings in June, 1944. In that same month she was further damaged by a mine on her way from Portsmouth to Rosyth. Temporarily repaired, she was again in action against Brest in August and Le Havre in September. On November 1st she fired her last rounds in action against the German defences at Walcheren. I know of no ship with a worthier fighting record, which started at Jutland on May 31st, 1916. Among my most valued possessions is one of the *Warspite's* bells, which hangs outside my house at Bishop's Waltham and is used to call me from the garden to the telephone.

I have said nothing of Force 'V', Rear-Admiral Sir Philip Vian's force of five escort carriers. It had been the intention to operate the naval fighters only for the first two days of the Salerno assault to assist in providing air cover over the beaches. They actually worked for three and a quarter days, and flew 713 sorties in forty-two hours of daylight. This, for the relatively small number of aircraft concerned, was the limit of their endurance. The few enemy aircraft met was a disappointment; but I had pleasure in congratulating Vian on the excellent work done by his command. The carriers had had little time to work together as a unit before engaging in a major operation of great importance and some hazard. The decision to carry out the landings was founded in the first instance on the cover and protection provided by aircraft of the Naval Air Arm flown originally from the carriers at sea until such time as Montecorvino airfield was captured and made available for them and for other aircraft flown in from Sicily.

On September 17th I visited the operational area in the destroyer *Offa*, and went on board Vice-Admiral Hewitt's flagship, the *Anson*, to discuss the situation. I then went on with Admiral Hewitt to the British landings further north, where we had lunch in the *Hilary* with Commodore Oliver. As ever Oliver was on the crest of the wave—calm, imperturbable, and completely optimistic as to the final outcome.

With the mountains towering in the background, the beaches like ants' nests with men unloading stores and ammunition, and regular streams of boats and landing-craft passing to and fro between the ships and the shore, the scene reminded me vividly of Gallipoli. Cruisers were methodically bombarding the enemy positions, and in the intervals between their salvoes one heard the heavy rumble of artillery from inland. Except for the smoke and dust of bursting shell in the far distance there was little to be seen of the actual battle.

By the 18th the crisis was well past. The enemy was showing signs of retiring and the Allied beach-head was secure.

The assault had come very near to failure, and for a time the situation was precarious. As I wrote later in my report:

> That it succeeded after many vicissitudes reflected great credit on Admiral Hewitt, U.S.N., his subordinate commanders and all those who served under them. That there were extremely anxious moments cannot be denied—I am proud to say that throughout the operation the Navies never faltered and carried out their tasks in accordance with the highest traditions of their Services. Whilst full acknowledgment must be made of the devastating though necessarily intermittent bombing by the Allied Air Forces, it was the Naval gunfire, incessant in effect, that held the ring when there was danger of the enemy breaking through to the beaches and when the overall position looked so gloomy. More cannot be said.

Admiral Hewitt's report on 'Avalanche' included the phrase: "The margin of success in the Salerno landing was carried by the naval gun." Commodore Oliver wrote: "There was not enough space to bring into action all the artillery landed. Naval gunfire filled the gap and undoubtedly saved much time and many casualties in the course of breaking down the enemy's defences and pushing through to the plain of Naples."

The Germans themselves attributed our final success to the devastating effect of the naval gunfire.

At daylight on October 2nd after further fierce fighting, advanced troops of the Allied Army were in Naples, and Rear-Admiral J. A. V. Morse, Flag Officer, Western Italy, disembarked there the same morning. Commodore Oliver arrived in the *Hilary* next day, to note that the devastated city was still under spasmodic shell-fire in the late afternoon. Minesweepers, boom defence vessels, salvage ships, tugs, patrol craft followed, together with the naval port party: "An army of ants to eat their way into the wreckage," as Admiral Morse put it.

The tale of the conversion of the shattered port of Naples into the largest port in the world does not enter into my narrative; but thus ended the Navy's share in the operation known as 'Avalanche', a combined Allied undertaking described by the Prime Minister as "an important and pregnant victory".

III

On September 22nd I sailed from Malta for Taranto in a cruiser to clear up certain uncertainties about the Italian Navy and merchant shipping. My chief trouble was that the soldiers had produced surrender terms—the 'Shorter Instrument' signed in Sicily on September 3rd—without consulting myself or any of my staff. In consequence, various important naval matters had been left unspecified. My main object was to get the Italian mercantile marine, or what remained of it, working in the Allied cause as soon as possible. I also wished to arrange for the smaller vessels of the Italian fleet, destroyers and so forth, to be used for escort work.

We arrived off the swept channel leading to Taranto in a thick fog, and were considerably delayed in getting in. Admiral de Courton, the Italian Minister of Marine, though very downcast, was pleasantly amenable, and we had little difficulty in coming to an agreement. Since at that time there was no recognized Italian government, the agreement was drawn up in the form of a document between Admiral de Courton and myself. Known as 'The Cunningham-de Courton Agreement' it was later signed on my behalf by Rear-Admiral McGrigor.

Admiral de Courton later proved himself to be a strictly honourable man who carried out all that he promised. Incidentally, he told me that the Italian captains who had been unable to get their ships away from Spezia and had scuttled them in harbour had been summarily shot by the Germans.

The British and American Governments were anxious that the full terms of surrender should be signed by Badoglio with some ceremony. I suggested that one of the battleships of Force 'H' at Malta should be the scene of the signing, and Eisenhower asked me to make the arrangements. My first inclination was to hoist my flag in my old ship, the *Rodney*; but on second thoughts I decided that the *Nelson*, Admiral Willis's flagship should be the place of meeting.

Eisenhower, with his Chief of Staff, Bedell Smith; the three Commanders-in-Chief, Alexander, Tedder and myself; Lord Gort, the Governor of Malta; Vice-Admiral Willis, Mr. Macmillan and Mr. Murphy assembled on board the *Nelson* during the forenoon of September 29th. Badoglio, de Courton, Ambrosio, and other Italians had arrived earlier in an Italian cruiser. The Marshal was received by a full guard of Royal Marines, with the whole of the *Nelson's* ship's company on parade. After the reception and introduction we went below to the Admiral's quarters. Eisenhower and Bedell Smith saw Badoglio alone and discussed the terms of surrender. After that, with all of us seated round the large table in the dining-cabin, signatures were put to the document known as 'The Longer Instrument'. What took place during the private conversation between Eisenhower, Bedell Smith and Badoglio I do not know; but again the question of the disposal of the Italian fleet was not properly faced. This omission, greatly to my disgust, had later to be repaired by adding a clause to 'The Cunningham-de Courton Agreement'.

IV

Meanwhile the news from home about the First Sea Lord, Sir Dudley Pound, was increasingly grave. It would be false modesty to suggest that I was not intimately concerned, for more than once he had asked me whether he should not resign and allow me to relieve him. I had always pressed him to stay on.

On September 28th I had received a message from the Prime Minister telling me that a relief for Sir Dudley Pound was under consideration, and asking if I could be spared to come home for consultation. The next day, on board the *Nelson*, I told Eisenhower that it was possible I might be leaving and asked if he had any objection. He answered at once that if I were offered the appointment of First Sea Lord it was my duty to accept.

I flew back to Algiers on September 30th, and on October 1st Vice-Admiral Willis was installed to act as deputy during my absence in England. I flew home.

I have no record of my movements during the next fortnight or so, and the period remains in my memory as a sort of mental whirl in which I visited many places and saw the more people. I reached London on October 1st, and went straight to the Admiralty and saw the First Lord, Mr. A. V. Alexander. I also had interviews with other members of the Board, and made close enquiries both at the Admiralty and from senior officers outside whether it was really desired that I should become First Sea Lord. I knew that the office desk was not my strong suit. My own feeling was that however grieved I might be at leaving the Mediterranean, it was my duty to go to the Admiralty if it were felt throughout the Service that I should go. Apparently it was, for I received assurances on all sides. On October 1st one very distinguished Flag Officer holding an important appointment who had originally been my senior wrote to me on another matter and added spontaneously:

> Now I see that Dudley Pound has gone sick—he has had a long bout in a most trying position, and if he should be unable to go on, I assume that you will, in due course, take his place. . . . That is what the whole Navy would like to see, but I know that you personally would view the suggestion with some distaste! All the same, I think for the good of everyone, you ought to do it if it comes your way.

My wife had come up to London. We were invited to Chequers, and on Sunday, October 3rd, Mr. Churchill asked me into his study where we had a heart-to-heart talk. He expressed his deepest regret at losing Sir Dudley Pound, and asked me if I would take on in his place. I accepted. We had some further conversation as to who should relieve me as Commander-in-Chief, Mediterranean. I suggested Admiral Sir John H. D. Cunningham, then Commander-in-Chief Levant, and his appointment was decided upon. Next morning, when we left Chequers, the Prime Minister insisted upon my inspecting his guard as the First Sea Lord. The announcement of my appointment was made on October 5th.

I took the first opportunity of visiting Sir Dudley Pound in hospital. He was gravely ill, and I knew he was dying. He could not speak; but recognized me and pressed my hand. It was a sad moment. I was at a loss for words.

I flew back to Algiers on October 6th or 7th, having asked my successor, Sir John Cunningham, to meet me there.

The matter which bulked largely in our minds was the question of the islands in the Dodecanese. Kos, Leros and Samos had been occupied by troops from the Middle East after the Italian surrender; but on October 3rd, while I was in England, Kos had been recaptured by the Germans.

I shall describe more precisely what happened in the next chapter; but on October 9th I flew to Tunis for a conference with General Eisenhower and all the Commanders-in-Chief, Mediterranean and Middle East, where it was decided if possible to hold on to Leros and Samos. I flew back to Algiers, and then received a message from the Prime Minister instructing me to go to Cairo to confer on the same subject with Mr. Anthony Eden and others. It was again decided to hold on to Leros and Samos. I flew back to Algiers the same night, and remember both journeys as among the most uncomfortable I ever experienced. I travelled both ways in commercial aircraft, with hard seating and nowhere to put one's feet.

Back at Algiers I started packing up to leave. On October 14th, the eve of my departure, the Supreme Commander staged a march past of Allied soldiers and sailors in my honour at the St. Georges Hotel, the Allied For e Headquarters. I left Algiers by air from Maison Blanche aerodrome on October 15th.

Many were there to see me off—Eisenhower and Tedder; Admirals and Generals, British, American and French; members of my staff; all the more senior officers and officials with whom I had worked. There were many guards of honour, with bands. I was greatly touched. With that peculiar constriction in the throat which comes of deep emotion, I found difficulty in expressing myself when saying farewell to all my faithful friends and comrades. We had passed through troublous times together; but had won through in spite of everything. I was leaving after serving for the second time as Commander-in-Chief of the Mediterranean Fleet, and I knew the Mediterranean better than any other part of the world. I was leaving my beloved ships, and the gallant people who manned them. It was a great wrench.

Perhaps I may be forgiven for quoting the farewell signal made after my flag was struck in H.M.S. *Maidstone* at sunset on October 17th, 1943.

> I leave you all in the Mediterranean with keen regret; but also with pride.
>
> It has been my privilege for the last year to command a great fleet of ships of the Allied nations of every category from battleships to the smallest craft. We may well look back with satisfaction to the work which has been performed. You have caused grievous discomfiture to the enemy. You have carried and protected hundreds and thousands of men and millions of tons of supplies. You have taken a vital part in throwing the enemy out of Africa, in the capture of Sicily, and, finally, in the invasion of Italy and the re-entry of the United Nations to the mainland of Europe. It is a high achievement of which you may well be proud. To you all who have fought and endured with such courage, tenacity and determination, I send my heartfelt thanks and appreciation.
>
> We still have far to go, but I know well that the spirit of our countries

as I have seen it in those whom I have had the honour to command, will carry us through to the day when we can return to enjoy the blessings of the land with the fruits of our labours.

I had arrived in London on Sunday, October 16th, before this message was promulgated, and joined the Admiralty at once.

CHAPTER XLIII

I

My previous experience of the Admiralty had been confined to those few months as Deputy Chief of the Naval Staff in 1938–39 when everything else was overshadowed by our unwearying attempts to prepare the Navy for the war which was inevitably coming, and every few weeks we were stimulated by some new crisis in international affairs. When I joined again in October, 1943, the Admiralty was running on oiled wheels. The foundation of final victory at sea had been well and truly laid. All the difficulties, strains, shortages and disappointment of the earlier years of the war had been staunchly borne by my predecessor, and my task was merely to reap where he had so ably sown.

At the same time, I thought that these same oiled wheels were rather inclined to run in a groove, and the war to be conducted as a matter of daily routine. However, this may be an unfair criticism of a great department. As Commander-in-Chief all my days had been filled with thoughts, my own and others, of how further damage could be inflicted upon the enemy; most of my attention concentrated upon future operations for which I was responsible. The tempo at the Admiralty was much slower, and one was rather appalled by the number of departments and people who had to be consulted before action took place. In our consideration of operations there I thought there was insufficient appreciation of the fact that the strength and quality of the enemy's air force was nothing like what it had been during the first three years of the war. Norway, Greece and Crete seemed to have left a series of scars on the Navy which were not easily forgotten.

I cannot claim to have had any resounding effect on the Admiralty during my service there. I had hoped to bring an atmosphere of greater cheerfulness and optimism into the lives of the naval staff until, some years later, I was informed that within four days of my arrival one of the senior officers had seriously considered asking to be relieved. I have no recollection of what lapse on my part produced this unfortunate desire.

I found myself in considerable disagreement with the types of ships we were intending to build and building. Though the *Vanguard* had been laid down before the future course of the war was clear, I considered her a waste of labour and money. It was doubtful if she would be ready even to take part in the war in the Far East. In cruisers and destroyers, too, there was in my opinion a grave tendency to sacrifice fighting power for endurance, while I thought, and still think, that the destroyers were much too large. They had become carriers of radar and radar ratings; and though they could detect the approach of every type of enemy on the sea, under the sea, and in the air, they could do little about it when in range because of their lack of gun power.

I was in time to have the cruiser designs re-examined; but little could be done about the destroyers, which were too far advanced. In justice, it must be said that the destroyers were good ships for the abnormal sort of war that was being fought in the Pacific—carrying an air war to enemy territory in aircraft-carriers, with battleships and cruisers providing anti-aircraft protection for the carriers, and destroyers as the outer ring fence against aircraft and submarines.

I found a strong team on the naval side at the Admiralty, and several old friends. The Deputy First Sea Lord was Admiral Sir Charles Kennedy-Purvis, whose wise mind, great ability and knowledge of Admiralty departments and methods were invaluable in relieving the First Sea Lord of much of the administrative work. The Second Sea Lord, Vice-Admiral Sir William Whitworth, was an old destroyer friend with a distinguished war record. With his flag in the *Warspite*, he had smashed up the German destroyers in the Ofot Fiord by his bold handling in the second battle of Narvik. Though I was acquainted with the Controller, Vice-Admiral Sir Frederick Wake-Walker, I had never been with him in the same fleet or on the same station. But I was well aware of his brilliant work in countering the magnetic mine early in the war, and of his able and successful shadowing of the *Bismarck* which so greatly contributed to her destruction.

The Fourth Sea Lord, Rear-Admiral F. H. Pegram I knew well from the early war years in the Mediterranean. Rear-Admiral Denis Boyd, late captain of the *Illustrious* and Rear-Admiral, Air, in the Mediterranean, was Fifth Sea Lord. With all his great experience, I could think of no one more capable of handling the complicated affairs of the Fleet Air Arm at the Admiralty.

As Chief of the Naval Staff one was also a member of the Chiefs of Staff Committee, and here I was by no means confident of my ability to make a satisfactory contribution to its deliberations.

My colleagues were General Sir Alan Brooke, the Chairman, and Air Chief Marshal Sir Charles Portal, both men of the highest ability with many years of staff experience behind them, and considerable service on the Committee; Portal for nearly three years. I had an almost complete lack of staff training, and have to confess to an inherent difficulty in expressing myself in verbal discussion, which I have never got over except on certain occasions when I was really roused. I realized I had neither the ability nor knowledge of Brooke and Portal, nor their experience in dealing with members of the Government. Sailors, as Lord Fisher once said, are not remarkable as dialecticians. They are more given to making decisions and acting upon them. Hence I looked forward with some trepidation to the meeting of the Chief of Staffs Committee, with the Prime Minister often present. I was well aware that Mr. Churchill was apt to overawe and bear down lesser beings by the sheer weight of his personality and persuasion. He did not care to be contradicted or thwarted.

However, I was always well briefed by the Vice Chief of the Naval Staff, Vice-Admiral Sir Neville Syfret, who was a tower of strength, a man of great ability and of quick and sound decision with a brilliant war record. His great knowledge and charm of manner made him a delightful comrade. No less helpful was the Director of Plans, my old staff officer, Captain Charles Lambe. As I had realized would happen years before, his outstanding ability had placed him in one of the key positions in the naval and defence staff.

Though well acquainted with the naval situation in the Mediterranean, I was less *au fait* with what was going on at home and in the Far East. The same was true of the battle in the Atlantic.

I do not wish to reiterate facts which are already well known; but July, August and September had been particularly bad months for the German U-boats. No fewer than seventy-one had been sunk, and our shipping losses had steadily diminished. But though definitely on the wane, the submarine menace was never fully countered. With the enemy's development of 'Schnorkel' and his production of U-boats of high submerged speed with greatly improved engines, it remained with us until the very last day of the war in Europe.

The conduct of the submarine campaign at the Admiralty was in the capable hands of my late Chief of Staff in the Mediterranean, Rear-Admiral John Edelsten, who was Assistant Chief of the Naval Staff, U-boat Warfare and Trade. The organization for keeping track of the U-boats, analyzing the intelligence, and checking and cross-checking all the information that came in, was centred in a large room under the Citadel. With no more than a superficial knowledge of the work before I arrived I was amazed at its proficiency. In charge of the organization was Captain C. R. B. Winn, R.N.V.R., a barrister in private life, and his knowledge of the U-boats, their commanders, and almost what they were thinking about, was uncanny. I must not go into details; but every submarine leaving an enemy harbour was tracked and plotted, and at any moment Captain Winn could give the numbers, likely positions and movements of all the U-boats at sea. His prescience was amazing.

The task of translating this knowledge into the appropriate counteraction on our part fell principally onto the broad shoulders of the Commander-in-Chief, Western Approaches, Admiral Sir Max Horton, from his headquarters at Liverpool.

Apart from the anti-submarine war, the operations in Home Waters divided themselves into two distinct forms: those in and around the coastal waters of Great Britain, and those in which the Home Fleet was engaged farther afield.

As regards the coastal work, the English Channel and the southern part of the east coast were the scene of almost nightly actions with the German E-boats, which were briskly engaged by our destroyers, M.T.B.s and M.G.B.s. Within a week of my arrival an action fought off the Brittany coast between our forces and a detachment of heavily-armed German destroyers and E-boats cost us the cruiser *Charybdis*, which was torpedoed and sunk with heavy casualties on October 23rd.

The Home Fleet, under Admiral Sir Bruce Fraser, guarded the northern approaches and the exits to the Atlantic. It had periodical major operations in escorting and covering the convoys to North Russia, one of the most thankless tasks of the war at sea. Our Russian allies, with a lack of sea sense, never seemed to realize the difficulty of conducting convoy operations well beyond the Arctic Circle, or to be particularly grateful for the valuable cargoes of war material from the United States and Britain fought through to Archangel at great risk and the sacrifice of the lives of our seamen.

During summer, when it was light all through the twenty-four hours, the convoys were always subject to continual and heavy attacks by submarines and aircraft, though the inclusion of escort carriers and aircraft with each convoy eventually provided a successful antidote. In winter, with no more than a few hours of half-hearted daylight around noon, the convoys and their escorts had vile weather, with heavy gales, fogs, and blinding snow-storms in which the visibility fell to nothing. With the temperature around zero, guns and deck fittings were rendered unworkable through frozen snow and spray. Moreover, there was always the risk of attack by enemy heavy ships and other surface vessels, stationed in the harbours in north Norway. On September 22nd, the *Tirpitz*, lying behind the nets and booms in the Aaltenfiord, had been disabled in a gallant attack by our midget submarines. But there still remained the battle-cruiser *Scharnhorst*.

Admiral Sir James Somerville was Commander-in-Chief of the Eastern Fleet with his flag ashore at Colombo. He had only one battleship, the *Ramillies*, with a number of cruisers, destroyers and escort vessels. For the time being the task of the Eastern Fleet was not exciting; being merely to secure our sea communications across the Indian Ocean against attacks by surface raiders and submarines, mostly Japanese. Though the Japanese kept some cruisers at Singapore, they were too busy against the Americans in the Pacific to spare large naval forces further west. We were arranging that early in the New Year, 1944, Somerville's fleet should be reinforced by the *Queen Elizabeth*, *Valiant* and *Renown*, and the aircraft-carrier *Illustrious*.

At the Admiralty, I felt rather like a spider sitting in the middle of a web vibrating with activity, though, unlike the spider, it was rarely my task to take direct action. This had to be left to the Commander-in-Chief on the spot.

I must admit to a certain nervousness in dealing with the civil side of the

Admiralty. The First Lord, Mr. A. V. Alexander, I knew well, and our relations were invariably cordial. There were a few occasions on which we disagreed, when I was usually accused of over simplification. We did not keep the same hours of work. The First Lord started rather late in the day according to my ideas, and usually worked into the small hours. I was always at my desk before 9 a.m., and preferred to be in bed by 11 p.m. unless something urgent or important was in hand. I disliked the Government Department habit of not starting before 10 a.m., though if people were forced to live at a distance I suppose there was some reason for it. However, I am reminded that in 1801, when the Earl of St. Vincent was First Lord of the Admiralty at the age of sixty-six, his hours for interviewing all and sundry were from 5 to 7 a.m.!

For the civil servants at the Admiralty I have the greatest admiration, perhaps tempered at times with the impatience of an impatient man. But their knowledge and ability, their logical method of approaching and dealing with all problems, commanded my deepest respect. I retain a feeling of gratitude for their continual tolerance and helpfulness towards one whose methods must at times have filled them with horror.

Our own private affairs were not so comfortable. We had our house at Bishops Waltham, where my wife could always stay, but no accommodation in London. My predecessor had had a bedroom and bathroom in Admiralty House, the First Lord's official residence. Mr. Churchill, when First Lord, had offered Sir Dudley Pound a flat in the Admiralty. The offer, however, had been declined, possibly because of Lady Pound's poor state of health.

So for a time I took over the bedroom in Admiralty House, with my faithful coxswain, Chief Petty Officer Watts, cooking my breakfast on an electric heater. Accommodation in London was very difficult to find, and as my wife was determined to spend most of her time there with me, Mrs. Dalrymple-Hamilton, the wife of my friend Rear-Admiral Frederick Dalrymple-Hamilton, the Naval Secretary, kindly provided a room in their flat whenever my wife was in town.

So the position was not very satisfactory, and we were delighted when the Prime Minister renewed his offer of a flat in the Admiralty. Though not very favourably received by those who had the responsibility for providing office and other accommodation for a greatly swollen establishment, a flat was converted and furnished at the top of Mall House, which had once been the First Sea Lord's official residence; but had been given up between the wars. We entered into residence early in February 1944, and it was a real godsend. Here, with two most efficient Wrens to look after us, we lived for two-and-a-half years with week-end visits to Bishops Waltham.

Soon after I joined the Admiralty there was an amusing incident about the telephone. One Saturday afternoon when I was at Bishops Waltham I was rung up by the Prime Minister's Secretary. Mr. Churchill wished to speak to me on the 'scrambler'. Did I have a scrambler?—No. Why didn't I have a scrambler?

The upshot was that the Prime Minister ordered a scrambler telephone to be put in my house so that he could speak to me before midnight. At about 5 p.m. Post Office Engineers arrived from Southampton and Winchester and started their work. The scrambler, however, was not working until after 1 a.m., and my wife and I were kept out of bed until then. I rang up 10 Downing Street. Mr. Churchill was in bed and asleep.

II

I said earlier that I was well aware of the situation in the Mediterranean; but within comparatively few days of my assuming office at the Admiralty we suffered a grievous disappointment.

Soon after the Italian surrender, we had occupied Kos, Leros and Samos and other islands in the Dodecanese in hope of encouraging the Italian garrisons to hold them against the Germans. The enemy in Greece reacted with vigour, large air reinforcements being sent there from France and Russia. On October 3rd, Kos was recaptured by a surprise assault which at a stroke deprived us of the only airfield from which fighter cover could have been afforded over the naval forces operating in the vicinity. On October 9th, at a conference at Tunis which had been attended by General Eisenhower, all Commanders-in-Chief in the Mediterranean and Middle East, and myself, it was decided to hold Leros and Samos as long as supplies could be maintained.

Our efforts were unsuccessful. The whole story of the naval operations in the Ægean between September 7th and November 28th, 1943, during which we had six destroyers sunk, and two cruisers and two destroyers damaged, has been told elsewhere. I need not repeat it. Very briefly, however, the enemy succeeded in landing in Leros on November 12th, and on the 16th, the slender British garrison was forced to surrender after nearly five days of continuous bombing and hard fighting. Leros was by way of being an Italian naval base; but neither the Italian troops, nor their coast defence or anti-aircraft batteries, made any substantial contribution to the defence. Samos was evacuated a few days later.

It is easy to be wise after the event; but I am still strongly of the opinion that Leros might have been held. However to quote a few paragraphs of the despatch.

> We failed because we were unable to establish airfields in the area of operations. . . . The enemy's command of the air enabled him so to limit the operations and impair the efficiency of land, sea and air forces

that by picking his time he could deploy his comparatively small forces with decisive results. . . . The naval forces engaged on these operations, cruisers, destroyers, submarine and coastal craft, and the small force of aircraft available to 201 (Naval Co-operation) Group all fought hard and did valuable work under particularly trying conditions. They achieved considerable success against the enemy and held off the attack on Leros for some time, but not without heavy casualties to our own forces. . . . Had more aircraft been available, especially modern long-range fighters, and given more luck, the operations might have been prolonged, but after the loss of Kos, if the enemy was prepared to divert the necessary effort, it is doubtful if Leros could have been held indefinitely without our embarking on a major operation for which no forces were available.

III

To revert to the Admiralty.

Admiral of the Fleet Sir Dudley Pound was a dying man, and on October 21st, the anniversary of Trafalgar, he passed away, worn out in the service of his country.

On Tuesday, October 26th, there was a procession from the Admiralty for the Memorial Service at Westminster Abbey, which was attended by the Duke of Gloucester, representing the King, the Prime Minister, members of the Government and most of the notabilities in the country. It was a grey, misty day in keeping with the occasion, and the service in the half-light of the crowded old Abbey was most moving and impressive.

The caskets containing the ashes of the late First Sea Lord and Lady Pound were taken to Portsmouth and lodged on board H.M.S. *Victory*, and on October 27th I attended the funeral at sea. A procession was formed from Nelson's old flagship to the cruiser *Glasgow*, alongside the South Railway Jetty. She slipped and proceeded to sea, and about thirty miles out, off the Nab Tower, the caskets were committed to the sea with the appropriate service and ceremony. It was fitting that Lady Pound's ashes should be committed with those of her husband. She had worked so hard and done so much for the sailors and their wives.

I find it difficult to sum up Dudley Pound's character. With great experience and an immense knowledge of the Navy and all its affairs, he was a tremendous worker and never spared himself. His energy always astounded me, and perhaps he overdid it. In the hottest weather in the Mediterranean he would sometimes dance until the small hours of the morning and be off shooting at 6 a.m.

He had an orderly and logical mind, and in the professional line was a master of detail, which at times led him into trying to do too much himself.

He was not, perhaps, a man of great imagination or insight. Much of his service as a captain and a Flag Officer had been spent in important appointments at the Admiralty, and it is fair to say that his talents lay more in the administrative field than in executive command at sea. Though as Commander-in-Chief in the Mediterranean he kept the fleet in the high state of efficiency in which he found it, it may be that he cannot be numbered among those great Sea Officers who were responsible for training the fleet during that most difficult period of economy and retrenchment between the two World Wars.

Yet, when the war came in September, 1939, it cannot be doubted that Dudley Pound was the right man in the right place. For four most difficult years of trial and disappointment he bore the brunt and responsibility of the war at sea. Fearless and outspoken, he stood like a rock against the waves of adversity. They beat against him in vain, leaving him unshaken and unmoved, even in the face of criticism in Parliament and the press, some of it cruelly unjust and bitter, when the tide of the war at sea was running against us. His many trials left him brave, confident and unperturbed, while planning steadily for the victory that he knew must come. I am glad to think that the dawn of victory was already creeping up over the horizon before he died.

I have no doubts that he made mistakes. Who does not who has great responsibility? There were occasions when I, as Commander-in-Chief, Mediterranean, strongly disagreed with him; but in my experience he never objected to being told. He never courted popularity, and was not one to give his intimacy freely. Moreover, he was not invariably a good judge of character, and his actions were sometimes hasty and unjust. I will mention no names; but undeserved strictures and censures sometimes caused unnecessary bitterness to those at sea.

To me, personally, he was always most kind and considerate, backing me up against opposition in my suggested courses of action when he knew them to be right; satisfying my not infrequent demands for more ships, particularly destroyers, which could ill be spared from the main theatre of the war at sea, the battle of the Atlantic upon which all else depended. In our infrequent meetings during the war, and in our long personal correspondence, he discussed matters in the most frank and intimate way.

I am proud to have served so long under Dudley Pound. To me, through many periods of stress and anxiety, he was always a helpful friend.

IV

It is not my intention to enter into details of the work of the Chiefs of Staff Committee. It would take volumes to set out all their activities. Under the Minister of Defence, Mr. Churchill, they were primarily responsible for the grand strategy of the war. Anything which might affect the running of the war, even in the slightest degree, was referred to them for an opinion, and as a body they had attained a position of considerable importance and independence. This was principally due to Mr. Churchill's close and intimate connection with their work. Anyone criticizing the Chiefs of Staff, no matter how high his position, was likely to find the Prime Minister's heavy guns turned against him.

With the entry of the United States into the war, the work of the British Chiefs of Staff had become a matter for close co-operation with the American Chiefs of Staff. They met as often as necessary, and when apart the British Chiefs of Staff were represented in Washington by senior officers of each Service who put forward the views of their chiefs in London. As already described, I had held this position as the British naval representative for some months in 1942. I had been relieved by Admiral Sir Percy Noble.

In October, 1943, the principal matter under discussion by the Chiefs of Staff was the preparation for the invasion of the Continent. Though the date had not definitely been fixed, it was intended that the operation should take place as early as possible in 1944. We were also preparing for a meeting with our American opposite numbers, and were looking forward to the time when Germany was defeated and we were able to lend all our energies to the overthrow of Japan. In fact there was already a small British naval planning section in Washington conferring with the Americans about our contribution to the war in the Pacific.

Discussion was also taking place as to the overall military commanders for the Allied invasion. It had apparently been thought that the Supreme Command might be given to the Chief of the Imperial General Staff, General Sir Alan Brooke, and no one would have exercised it better. But the fact that the majority of troops fighting on the Continent would eventually be American, and various other reasons, made it expedient that the Supreme Commander should be an American. Sir Alan Brooke stood aside, and the choice seemed to lie between Generals George Marshall and Eisenhower, with the former as the most probable. Aware of Marshall's unique position in the American Chiefs of Staff Committee, I, personally, did not see how he could be spared from Washington.

One of my first tasks was to select the Naval Allied Commander-in-Chief for the invasion. One name stood out above all others for his ability, character and experience, that of Admiral Sir Bertram Ramsay. The Prime Minister cordially accepted the choice, though the final selection of all the commanders was left to the forthcoming conference with the Americans.

The arrangements for the conference with the American Chiefs of Staff went rapidly forward. It was decided we should meet in Cairo, and the President, the Prime Minister, several other Ministers, the Combined Chiefs of Staff and their staffs were to be there by November 21st. Mr. Churchill had decided to go as far as Algiers or Malta by sea, and the battle-cruiser *Renown* was placed at his disposal. We embarked at Plymouth on the 14th and sailed after dark, the party consisting of the Prime Minister; his daughter, Mrs. Oliver; the United States Ambassador, Mr. Winant, and myself. I had met Mr. Winant before on several occasions, and in the close proximity on board a ship I saw a lot of him and had many talks. I conceived a great liking for him, and admiration for his sincere and forthright nature.

I was glad to be on board a ship again, even though a passenger. The weather in the Bay was somewhat boisterous, and our escorting destroyers had difficulty in keeping up. It also reduced the attendance at meals. It was my first trip in the *Renown* and I greatly admired her weatherly qualities at speed.

It was during this voyage, I remember, that I spoke to the Prime Minister of a skeleton plan produced by our staff in Washington for the employment of our fleet in the Pacific. Mr. Churchill later forgot it, and for a very long time, nearly until a conference at Quebec in September, 1944, refused to have anything to do with sending a fleet to the East, except to the East Indies. He required much persuasion.

After a call after dark at Gibraltar and another at Algiers, where we met the new Commander-in-Chief, Mediterranean, Admiral Sir John Cunningham, the *Renown* went on to Malta. John Cunningham met us there also, and I spent a night ashore in Admiralty House. As I wrote to my wife, I had not expected to "sit under Icarus again", Icarus being the painting on the ceiling of the sitting-room on the ground floor usually reserved for the Commander-in-Chief's wife.

We had intended to fly on from Malta. But the weather was bad, so after staying forty-eight hours we sailed in the *Renown* for Alexandria. Immediately on arrival the Prime Minister went straight on to Cairo. I spent the night with Vice-Admiral Willis, now Commander-in-Chief, Levant, and went on next day.

The Mena House Hotel, in the shadow of the Pyramids, had been taken over in its entirety for the conference. A few of the staff were accommodated there; but most of the higher authorities, Combined Chiefs and so on, had offices only in the hotel and were distributed in villas on the road to Cairo. The Prime Minister and President each had their own villas, Mr. Roosevelt having come by battleship to Oran and flown the rest of the way.

The villa, in which Brooke, Portal and myself were housed was quite an imposing-looking building from the outside standing a few hundred yards from the main road in a large garden. It was said to belong to a princess; but if so she had rather scamped the plumbing. However, we were fairly comfortable and well looked after by a sergeant and a number of other ranks of the A.T.S. As I had also brought Chief Petty Officer Watts, with my Royal Marine driver, Kells, and a car, I did not want for attention.

The conference opened on November 22nd, and we attended several plenary sessions with the Prime Minister and President at which General and Madame Chiang Kai Shek were present. Madame, a fascinating figure and beautifully dressed, usually acted as interpreter for her husband, the subject under discussion being action against Japan.

The combined Chiefs of Staff held numerous meetings. Sir John Dill was over from America, and as usual his knowledge of the background in Washington made his wise counsel invaluable.

We discussed the war in all its aspects and phases, and came to full agreement on all matters of moment without any difficulty. There was no dissimilarity of views at this conference. The great men decided that Eisenhower should be Supreme Commander for the invasion of Normandy the next year, the date of which was fixed within limits. I considered that the choice of Eisenhower was a very wise one.

The British were the hosts at this Cairo conference, and everything was done on a lavish scale, though it was difficult to compete with General Patton's hospitality and organization at Casablanca in the previous January.

While we were at Cairo it was learnt that Marshal Stalin had consented to meet the President and Prime Minister, Teheran being named as the place of assembly. So we flew there on November 27th, our British delegation consisting of Mr. Churchill, Mr. Eden, the three Chiefs of Staff, John Dill, Ismay and two or three staff officers. The American team was Mr. Roosevelt, Harry Hopkins, and the United States Chiefs of Staff. Stalin had M. Molotov and Marshal Voroshilov with him.

We, the British, were all housed in the Embassy precincts, the Chiefs of Staff in the house of the Oriental Secretary, a most hospitable man who did his utmost to make us comfortable. But I fear the invasion must have stretched the resources of the Embassy staff to the limit. Our drive from the airfield to the Embassy was almost a major operation, with armoured cars, jeeps and motor bicycles all round us. But such Persians as we saw did not seem particularly interested.

The first plenary session was held on the evening of November 28th at the Russian Embassy. We all took our places round a very large table, and the meeting was largely taken up by complimentary speeches by the Big Three, though there was also an exchange of views in a general way. As this was my first sight of him, I was much interested in watching Stalin. I was impressed; but conceived an instinctive dislike. It would be difficult to put into words exactly what caused my antipathy; but he gave me a feeling of unease and distrust. Nevertheless he was very much all there, and fully a match for the two outstanding personalities with whom he was dealing. He was quick to pick up a point, and never at a loss for a reply without consultation with anyone. He unerringly seized on the weakness in any statement.

Molotov talked a lot and said very little. Voroshilov looked, and I think was, rather stolid and wooden-headed. He was, however, representing the Russian equivalent of our Chiefs of Staff, so Brooke and Portal had a conference with him. So as not to overweight him, Dill and I stood out and walked round the Embassy garden. I do not think anything very much came out of these particular deliberations.

The Teheran conference as a whole was useful. It was the first time the Big Three had got together and exchanged ideas. Though no great decisions may have been made, future operations and their dates were disclosed. In no other way could so much information be obtained about the general trend of the war in Russia. Except at the highest level the Russians were much keener in acquiring information than in imparting it.

Next day the Prime Minister presented the King's Sword of Stalingrad to Marshal Stalin, speaking with his own matchless eloquence. Stalin replied. It was a simple but impressive ceremony, though our young officer handing over the sword was rather outmatched in size by the enormous young Russian receiving it.

Next day, November 30th, was Mr. Churchill's sixty-ninth birthday. As a body, the Chiefs of Staff visited him in his bedroom during the forenoon to wish him many happy returns. We had had the idea of singing "Happy Birthday to you"; but decided it was beyond our capability.

That night the Prime Minister gave a birthday dinner to all the delegates. It was a great party and not without humour. Speeches began early, and the great men excelled themselves. Molotov was in his element. Everybody's health was drunk in turn, and as each health was proposed Stalin rose, marched round the table and clinked glasses. Allied cordiality and unanimity was never at a higher level. Later in the evening I asked Stalin why he had not brought an Admiral with him to represent the gallant Russian Navy. He replied that it was quite unnecessary. He himself was head of the Russian Navy.

I should have said that Stalin spoke no English, though it was said he understood a certain amount. Anyhow, he always spoke through an interpreter, one Pavlov. During the dinner the Marshal rose to speak, and Pavlov, sitting some way down on the other side of the table, rose to interpret. This synchronized with the serving of an ice pudding, a truly monumental erection. When it got as far as Pavlov the waiter tripped and tipped the whole pudding over him. He did not dare to stop interpreting, and stood there declaiming Stalin's eloquent speech while those sitting on each side of him, of whom Brooke was one, did their best to clean him up with their napkins. I pitied poor Pavlov. It was a moving spectacle.

After a final plenary session on December 1st, we started back for Cairo, and on the way the British Chiefs of Staff took the opportunity of entertaining their American colleagues at Jerusalem, which none of the latter had seen. We stayed at the King David Hotel in great comfort, and the next day were shown all the sights in Jerusalem and its vicinity by a most amusing Irish Franciscan father. Next day we flew back to Cairo to finish up the conferences.

While in Teheran all the Chiefs of Staff had wished to drive to the Caspian, a distance of just over a hundred miles. However we were warned against it, and were not encouraged to stray much beyond the Embassy walls. We had been allowed only one valet to two Chiefs of Staff, and I shared with Portal. So I had taken my driver, Marine Kells, in preference to my faithful Watts, because a Royal Marine would know the technique of cleaning R.A.F. buttons. On arrival in Cairo I discovered that Kells, with superb aplomb, had borrowed a car and with Brooke's valet had driven to the Caspian. So they were the only members of the party to see it!

We finished up our work in Cairo in a couple of days and started on our way home. Brooke, Portal and myself wished to pay different visits, so we parted for the time being. I was put down at Algiers, where I spent a day discussing Mediterranean business with John Cunningham. Flying being impossible because of the weather, he sent me on to Gibraltar in the cruiser *Dido*, where I rejoined the others. We flew on home, arriving in England on December 11th.

On his return journey Mr. Roosevelt called at Malta to present the people of that island with the 'Presidential Citation' for their conduct and services during the war and the invasion of Sicily. The Prime Minister went to Tunis; but unfortunately developed pneumonia and had to remain there ill for the next few weeks, afterwards going on to Marrakesh, in Morocco, to recuperate.

It was just after Christmas, in Tunis, that Mr. Churchill had conferences with Generals Eisenhower and Sir Henry Maitland Wilson, newly nominated as Eisenhower's successor as Supreme Commander in the Mediterranean; Admiral Sir John Cunningham; General Sir Harold Alexander; Air Chief Marshal Sir Arthur Tedder and others. The subject under discussion was the landing behind the enemy lines at Anzio to hasten the advance of the Fifth Army in Italy, then engaged in heavy fighting for Monte Camino and the even more formidable Cassino. Of this operation, which took place on January 22nd, 1944, I shall have more to say later.

v

Back to our usual round at the Admiralty, we were greatly cheered by two notable naval successes at the end of the year.

In the early hours of December 26th a large convoy accompanied by its usual quota of destroyers and escort vessels was some fifty miles to the southeastward of Bear Island on its way to North Russia. Cover was being provided by Vice-Admiral Robert Burnett, in the cruiser *Belfast*, in company with the

Norfolk and *Sheffield*. As there was always the chance that the *Scharnhorst* might emerge to attack the convoy, Admiral Sir Bruce Fraser, the Commander-in-Chief, Home Fleet, in the battleship *Duke of York*, with the cruiser *Jamaica* and four destroyers, was about one hundred and eighty miles to the south-south-west. Incidentally, the convoy had persistently been shadowed and reported by U-boats and aircraft, and soon after 3 a.m. the Admiralty had sent a message to the effect that the *Scharnhorst* was probably at sea.

The positions of the convoy and covering forces, nearly one thousand five hundred miles away, were plotted on the large scale charts in the War Room at the Admiralty, and when once wireless silence was broken we intercepted every report and signal. We knew it was blowing a full gale from the south-west with a heavy sea, and that the convoy of nineteen merchant ships was steering roughly east-north-east at 8 knots. We heard Admiral Fraser divert the convoy to the northward, and indicate his own position, course and speed. He also ordered Burnett to report his position, and the senior officer escorts that of the convoy. It was thrilling to watch the chart; to speculate what might happen.

For some hours we waited. Then, at 8.40 a.m., in the grey twilight of the Arctic dawn, the *Belfast's* radar located the *Scharnhorst* $17\frac{1}{2}$ miles to the west-north-west between herself and the convoy, which was then about fifty miles away on roughly the same bearing. Burnett was already steering towards the convoy at 24 knots with his cruisers spread, when at 9.21 the *Sheffield* sighted the *Scharnhorst* at a range of $6\frac{1}{2}$ miles. It was still so dark that the *Belfast* fired star-shell. The *Norfolk*, with her 8-inch guns, opened fire a few minutes later; though neither the *Belfast* nor the *Sheffield*, with their 6-inch, came into action at this stage.

Steaming at 28 to 30 knots the *Scharnhorst* altered course first to the south-east and then to the northward. In the prevailing weather the maximum speed of Burnett's cruisers was no more than 24 knots, and at 10.20, in the half-light, he lost touch with the enemy. There was suspense and anxiety at the Admiralty as we sifted the information and plotted the positions. However, judging correctly that the enemy would try to work round to the northward to make another attempt to attack the convoy, Burnett proceeded to close it. He was presently joined by four destroyers, and before long was zig-zagging about ten miles ahead of the merchant ships.

The *Scharnhorst* was temporarily lost, and Admiral Fraser was in something of a quandary. He knew that because of the weather the enemy had four to six knots advantage in speed over Burnett's cruisers, and also that unless some ship regained touch and shadowed he would have little chance of intercepting with the *Duke of York*. His four destroyers, too, were beginning to run short of fuel.

At the Admiralty we listened, watched and waited with what patience we could muster. There was nothing we could do to help. There were dismal faces.

But Burnett's appreciation had been perfectly correct. He felt confident that the *Scharnhorst* would return to the convoy from the north or north-east. At five minutes past noon he was rewarded when the *Belfast* was again in contact with the enemy by radar. About a quarter-of-an-hour later the great *Scharnhorst* was in sight, and Burnett's three cruisers came into action.

Our suspense at the Admiralty lifted. We knew, and Admiral Fraser knew, that there was now every chance of the *Scharnhorst* being brought to action by the *Duke of York*.

Burnett's four destroyers were ordered to attack with torpedoes; but were unable to do so because of the heavy weather, and the fact that the enemy immediately swung round to retire at high speed to the southward. From that moment the German battle-cruiser was a ship in flight. She abandoned any further attempt to reach the convoy. She was a beaten ship, driven off by three much smaller and weaker opponents, and apparently quite unaware that Admiral Fraser, with the *Duke of York*, *Jamaica* and destroyers, was steaming hard to the eastward to cut her off from her base in Norway.

Burnett's handling of his cruisers and destroyers was masterly. He had been in action for about twenty minutes at ranges of 9,000 to 16,000 yards, during which the *Norfolk* was twice hit by 11-inch shell and the *Sheffield* straddled and peppered with splinters. By 12.40 p.m., however, this phase of the engagement was over, and Burnett, keeping his cruisers in close company, did not attempt to engage; but settled down to shadowing the *Scharnhorst* by radar from just outside visibility distance. He was reporting all the time to Fraser, who was admirably placed for interception.

This continued for the next three hours, until at 4.40 p.m. in the darkness, Fraser and Burnett were in radar contact. Burnett was ordered to fire star-shell, and eight minutes later the *Duke of York* and *Jamaica* were in sight of the enemy and engaged at 12,000 yards.

With the *Scharnhorst* steaming at high speed, the engagement developed into a chase to the eastward with the *Duke of York* in action for the next two hours, the cruisers opening fire whenever they had a chance, and the destroyers gradually gaining ground with the heavy sea on their starboard quarter. During this period the enemy seems to have been hit by at least three 14-inch shell, which eventually reduced her speed. The *Duke of York* was frequently straddled.

At about 6.50, illuminating the target with their own star-shell, four destroyers went in to attack, firing torpedoes at ranges of 1,800 to 3,500 yards. Their attacks were gallantly pressed home, and it seems probable that three torpedoes hit. The *Scharnhorst's* speed was reduced to 20 knots and still diminished, and at 7.1 p.m. the *Duke of York* and *Jamaica* were again in action at 10,400 yards. For the next five minutes the enemy was repeatedly hit, and fires and flashes from exploding ammunition were flaring up throughout the length of her. The *Belfast* joined in this action, and at 7.28, by which time the *Scharnhorst's* speed had dropped to about five knots, the *Belfast* and *Jamaica* were ordered to close and sink her with torpedoes. Hits were probably made as underwater explosions were felt; but the target was completely shrouded in smoke. More destroyers attacked and further torpedoes went home, and at about 7.45 the *Scharnhorst* sank. Thirty-six ratings were rescued.

There was jubilation in Whitehall. The elimination of the *Scharnhorst* was a great weight off our minds and a most timely success, made possible by the excellent dispositions made for the defence of the convoy, the high state of morale and training of the Home Fleet, and the fine way in which all the forces and ships concerned were led and handled.

But as usual Hitler's Navy had shown little of the fighting spirit of the Imperial German Navy of 1914–18. It was rather like the *Admiral Graf Spee* over again. When the *Scharnhorst* made contact with our cruisers the second time she turned and fled for home. She was a ship of great tonnage and high speed, armed with 11-inch guns. Her three opponents were smaller, weaker and slower. In the weather and visibility then prevailing, by all the tenets of naval warfare, she should have been able to brush the *Belfast*, *Sheffield* and *Norfolk* aside, attack the convoy, and have broken away in safety after destroying it. But the will was not there. No wonder Hitler was displeased.

Another episode occurred before the end of the year which showed up the morale of the German Navy in a peculiar light.

The enemy was engaged in running the blockade to the French ports in the Bay of Biscay with a few fast merchant ships. His practice was to send a large force of destroyers about four hundred miles out to escort the blockade runners home. Up to date we had been unable to intercept them.

On the morning of December 27th a Sunderland aircraft of Coastal Command, Royal Air Force, sighted a suspicious ship about five hundred miles west of Finisterre. Other aircraft were diverted to the area, and the vessel, which mounted guns and was a blockade-runner, was bombed and sunk. Her survivors took to the water in boats and rafts.

Immediately on receiving the Sunderland's first sighting message, the cruisers *Glasgow* and *Enterprise* were ordered to sea to intercept the destroyers which we knew would be sent out to bring in the blockade-runner. On examining the instructions I saw that our cruisers were being sent about four hundred miles out to avoid possible air attack. It appeared to me that at this distance their chances of intercepting the enemy destroyers were practically nil. I also felt that in this type of operation air attack must be risked, and that in any case the likelihood of damage from the air was not greatly to be feared. So I had the *Glasgow* and *Enterprise* brought about two hundred miles nearer in.

It was as well that we did so, for soon after daylight next morning, the

28th, Coastal Command aircraft reported eleven enemy destroyers about two hundred miles west of where the blockade-runner had been sunk. They had come out to escort the blockade-runner home; and were steaming westward at 20 knots. By going on to full speed the *Glasgow* and *Enterprise* were able to intercept, and after a running fight in bad weather with both forces steaming hard to the south-east three of the enemy craft were sunk and others probably damaged. It was by no means a one-sided battle, for five of the destroyers were 2,400 tonners of the *Narvik* class each mounting five 5·9-inch guns, the other six being of the 'Elbing' class each with four 4·1s. Against the nineteen 6-inch of our two cruisers, the enemy mounted twenty-five 5·9s and twenty-four 4·1s. The Germans also had their torpedo armaments and an extra five knots speed. Had they remained concentrated and attacked the *Glasgow* and *Enterprise* they might have had a great success. As it was they fled, thereby missing a chance which any British destroyers would have welcomed.

So the year 1943 closed with the Navy in great heart. The U-boat menace appeared to be held, and the enemy's surface forces had been severely handled.

CHAPTER XLIV

I

WE had some reason to feel optimistic in the New Year of 1944.

First, and most important, we had definitely obtained the ascendency over the U-boats. The enemy had lost no fewer than fifty-three during the last quarter of 1943, and they had now largely been withdrawn from the vital area in the Atlantic and were being used with extreme caution. Our merchant ship losses, though still serious, had dwindled.

All the same, we were well aware that the lull was only temporary. The battle was not finally won, and a recrudescence must be expected. In December Admiral Dönitz had referred to the heavy submarine losses, and had gone on to speak of creating what was virtually a new navy, far greater and stronger than anything which had gone before. A month later he returned to the same theme in admitting that we had gained the advantage in submarine defence; but had added that the day would come when we should be offered a first-rate submarine war. "The submarine weapon," he asserted, "has not been broken by the setbacks of 1943. On the contrary, it has become stronger. In 1944, which will be a successful but a hard year, we shall smash Britain's supply with a new submarine weapon."

In the meanwhile, we were engaged with confidence in building up in Britain the Armies and the supplies presently to be used for the invasion of Normandy. The country was rapidly becoming an armed camp. Huge numbers of American troops were being ferried across the Atlantic. Eisenhower had already been nominated as Supreme Commander for the forthcoming operation, with Tedder as his Deputy. Generals Montgomery and Bradley, respectively, would command the British and American Armies, while Admiral Ramsay and Air Chief Marshal Leigh-Mallory were the Naval and Air Commanders-in-Chief.

Further afield the Fifth Army had obtained its lodgment in Italy and was fighting its hard way towards Rome, while in the north Russian forces had penetrated well into Poland. In the Pacific the Americans definitely had the measure of the Japanese, for with the battle of Midway, in June, 1942, and their successful though long drawn-out struggle for Guadalcanal at the end of the year, the offensive had passed into the hands of our Allies.

The elimination of the Italian fleet in the Mediterranean had permitted the reinforcement of the British Fleet under Admiral Somerville in the East Indies for operations against the Japanese.

Though the end was not yet in sight, we had just cause to be hopeful.

II

In Italy, the landing at Anzio, operation 'Shingle', upon which Mr. Churchill had set his mind, was carried out on January 22nd. It did not achieve its expected effect of causing the enemy to withdraw from before Cassino. On the contrary, Kesselring used part of his Rome garrison to isolate the Anzio bridge-head, and for four months our troops there had to be supplied and reinforced by a regular ferry service of landing-ships and craft from Naples, as well as by larger vessels. This absorbed valuable shipping at a time when every available ton was being earmarked and collected for the invasion of Normandy.

The date for this latter operation, known as 'Overlord' was not rigidly fixed, though the detailed planning was already in progress. However, it was realized that it must take place as soon as possible after the end of May, from which time there was usually fine weather in the Channel. Too early or too late a date might leave insufficient time for the preparatory softening by the Royal Air Force and the United States Air Force of the enemy's communication system, key industries and other vital points in Germany, France and the Continent.

Time was also required for the design and final construction of various appliances to ensure the success of our landings. I cannot mention a tithe of them; but among the most ambitious were the artificial harbours to provide sheltered water in any weather conditions. These, the well-known 'mulberries', were to be built of huge concrete caissons towed piecemeal across the Channel and sunk in place. There would be subsidiary piers alongside which ships could lie for disembarking their cargoes, together with all the necessary equipment.

At the outset naval opinion was inclined to be sceptical about the probable efficacy of the 'mulberries', two of which were to be provided, one for the British and the other for the Americans. My own personal view was that it should be possible to make the first landings, and to provide the necessary build-up of reinforcements and supplies, without these artificial harbours. I knew at first hand what had been done in North Africa, Sicily and Italy, and considered that the industrial effort expended in building large numbers of what were virtually concrete ships might more usefully have been employed in other directions.

In the event they were successfully towed across the Channel and sunk in place, though off the American landings, 'Omaha' beach, in water that was much too deep. In the bad weather that occurred a few days after the first landing the caissons sustained considerable damage, partly due to faulty construction. Because their freeing ports were too small to release the heavy volume of water, they filled up and burst outwards. However, the 'mulberries' and their subsidiary piers made a useful contribution to the success of the operation, and were estimated to have accelerated the supplies put ashore by about fifteen per cent.

The provision of sufficient landing and assault ships and craft required continual examination and pressure. It was naturally desired to carry out the first assault on the broadest possible front with the greatest possible number of divisions. This in turn depended upon the number of ships and craft available, for the services of which there were many conflicting claims. The strongest claim of all came from the Pacific, where the American operations against the Japanese consisted almost entirely of a succession of seaborne assaults against one island after another. But the Mediterranean and the East Indies also had claims upon shipping, while for 'Overlord', the Normandy operation, we had to earmark ships of every size and type for the follow-up convoys. We were particularly short of coasters, which were highly important for the build-up.

The Americans in the Pacific placed a high value on naval bombardment in support of amphibious assaults, particularly by battleships, much higher than I thought was really justifiable. Though we provided all the battleship bombardment that was asked for, I considered the demands rather excessive. Here I think I was wrong.

These, and many other arrangements and decisions, gave the Admiralty and the Chiefs of Staff plenty to do during the early months of the year. Each and every suggestion, every new gadget that anyone thought of, proved in time to be essential, and had to be met or provided. I often found myself wondering how we had ever succeeded in any of our enterprises in the Mediterranean with our poor, austerity standards of assault equipment.

In February the German bombers once more started their attacks upon London, though not on nearly so heavy a scale as before. However, sitting one night in my office at the Admiralty I had the curious experience of seeing one of my two windows blown in and the other blown out by a bomb which exploded on the Horse Guards Parade. Lunching with the Prime Minister a day or two later I observed that Number 10 Downing Street also lacked much glass.

My daily routine at this period was as regular as I could make it. I was usually in my office at 9 a.m. or soon afterwards, and until just before 10.30 saw Syfret on current operations, and Edelsten on the previous day's anti-submarine progress. I also interviewed many others who had anything to ask or to tell me. At 10.30 every day except Sunday I attended the Chiefs of Staff meetings in the room connected with the War Rooms built under the Home Office and Air Ministry and entered from Great George Street. Our meetings seldom ended before 1 p.m. All the afternoon until dinner-time I was back at work seeing people, dealing with papers, or attending meetings. I was in my office again after dinner; but unless there was another Chiefs of

Staff meeting or a Defence Committee meeting with the Prime Minister in the chair, I insisted on going to bed at 11 p.m. Mr. Churchill's meetings seldom started before 10 o'clock and usually went on into the small hours.

We usually spent Saturday afternoon and Sunday at Bishops Waltham, but it can be understood how convenient I found it to have a flat in the Admiralty. I was always on the spot, and did not have to go out to a club or to hunt for meals in some restaurant. I can never cease to be grateful to my wife, as well as to the two devoted Wrens, for the way in which I was looked after.

Every Monday evening the Chiefs of Staff had to attend a Cabinet meeting to give an account of the war in their respective spheres during the past week. There were also countless official luncheons, receptions and cocktail parties to meet this personage or that. As they bit into my all too precious time and were always unwelcome, I did my best to avoid them without being impolite.

With all these outside engagements; the mass of papers and dockets in my 'in' tray; the flood of signals from all over the world; and the endless stream of people coming to see me, I found it physically impossible to give real attention to all the matters brought before me. Many unimportant subjects received no more than cursory consideration at my hands, and I had to accept the opinions of the staff without burdening myself with a mass of detail. Fortunately no man was ever better served by more helpful or efficient staff officers.

In the early part of 1944 two questions were causing considerable trouble to the Chiefs of Staff; the strategy in the Mediterranean, and that in the Far East and the East Indies at the end of the war in Europe.

At Teheran we had agreed with the United States Chiefs of Staff that as a support to the landing in Normandy, there should be another landing in the south of France, operation 'Anvil'. The American Chiefs of Staff were very set on this project, while we, the British, were rather against it. Landing in the south of France meant reducing our forces and, to a certain extent closing down on the Italian campaign, while diverting landing-craft and other facilities from Italy.

As the preparations for Normandy, 'Overlord', developed, the opinions of the British Chiefs of Staff hardened more and more against 'Anvil'. Much discussion took place. I cannot claim that I took much part in it. On the whole I was neutral, though when it came to a collective opinion I was at one with my colleagues.

I could quite well understand the point of view of the Americans in wishing to allow nothing to stand in the way of throwing the greatest possible strength into the decisive area, i.e. France. At the same time I realized how disappointing it would be to our people to halt a successful campaign which might well bring us into Austria, which was certainly a political desideratum. At one period in the discussions the United States Chiefs of Staff agreed with their British colleagues that 'Anvil' should not take place; but with such obvious and bitter reluctance that the Prime Minister set himself to bridge over the difference. In the end it was decided early in April that General Maitland Wilson, now Supreme Commander in the Mediterranean, should be directed to prepare for 'Anvil' with a specific target date.

The second question that absorbed much of our attention was the employment of the British Fleet at the end of the war in Europe. During the latter part of 1943 the British planning section in Washington had produced an outline scheme in conjunction with the American planners for the use of the British Fleet in the Pacific, and had also made some calculations as to the strength of the 'Fleet Train' of repair ships, ammunition ships, tankers, storeships, salvage vessels, hospital ships, and so forth to support it. I was wholeheartedly in favour of sending the fleet to join with the American fleet in active operations. The Chiefs of Staff also agreed, for it seemed about the only force that could be spared. The Army and Royal Air Force were already fully occupied.

For some reason which I never really understood the Prime Minister did not at first agree. He seemed to take the view that the fleet would be better employed in assisting in the recapture of our own possessions, Malaya and Singapore, or it may be he was rather daunted, if daunted he ever was, by the huge demands made upon shipping by the provision of the fleet train. He may also have been influenced by the undoubted feeling that prevailed in naval circles in the United States, from Admiral King downwards, that they wanted no British fleet in the Pacific. It was contended by certain American strategists that our fleet would be better employed against the Japanese in Malaya, Borneo and the Dutch East Indies. In the second volume of Robert E. Sherwood's *The White House Papers of Harry L. Hopkins* reference is made to a letter from the United States Ambassador in London, that great friend of this country, Mr. Winant, to Hopkins, in which the Ambassador wrote: "there has seeped into this country through military channels a belief that the British Navy is not wanted in the Pacific".

All this uncertainty led us to consider the middle course of Australian and Empire troops, and the necessary Air, with the British Fleet, going for Amboina in the Moluccas from Northern Australia late in 1944 or early the next year. From there they would operate against the Dutch East Indies and Borneo.

It was not until some months later that the Prime Minister was eventually brought round, as I felt quite sure he would be, to agreeing that the fleet should join the Americans in the Pacific. Meanwhile the Admiralty went steadily on with their preparations. As was only natural, the provision of ships for the fleet train met with strong opposition from Lord Leathers, the Minister of War Transport. Discussions on the subject went on for months, indeed long after the fleet had sailed for the Pacific.

At the end of February Sir William Whitworth became Commander-in-Chief, Rosyth, and his place as Second Sea Lord was taken by Vice-Admiral Willis, who at once found himself thrown straight into the important deliberations on man-power. His clear and incisive mind was never seen to better advantage than in threading the mazes of the readjustment of numbers between the three Services, and later on in producing a scheme and organizing the fair and contented demobilization of the wartime Navy.

In about April the Minister of War Transport received another shock by a demand from the 'Overlord' planners for sufficient ships for the construction of five 'gooseberries', artificial breakwaters formed of sunken ships placed end to end to shelter the beaches under their lee. Two of them were to be merged into the 'mulberries'. It might be thought that with the enormous project of two 'mulberries', the artificial harbours, the 'gooseberries,' were redundant. But the advantage of the latter was that the ships forming them could proceed to their scuttling places mostly under their own steam, and be in position almost at once to provide shelter in the event of bad weather for the assault-craft landing troops and equipment over the open beaches. The towage and sinking of the prefabricated concrete units for the 'mulberries' took much longer.

After much discussion and reluctance the ships for the five 'gooseberries' were found, in all thirty-one British and twenty-three American old merchant ships. The Navy also raked the dockyards and produced a number of veterans, among them the old battleship *Centurion*, the cruiser *Durban*, the old French battleship *Courbet*, and the Dutch cruiser *Sumatra*. I was greatly in favour of the 'gooseberry' project which, on a more limited scale, had been successfully used in the Dardanelles twenty-nine years before. And there is no question that on the Normandy coast these artificial breakwaters were one hundred per cent successful, and saved the situation during the sudden storm that created havoc on the beaches a few days after D-Day.

Eisenhower set up his headquarters for 'Overlord' at Bushy Park, though before the actual assault the operational portions of Shaef—Supreme Headquarters Allied Expeditionary Force—and the headquarters of the Twenty-first Army Group, were set up in the grounds of Southwick Park, about seven miles from Portsmouth, and slightly more from Bishops Waltham. It was a curious camp laid out in the hazel groves, with the branches meeting overhead and completely concealing the large number of caravans, huts and tents. Admiral Ramsay had his headquarters in Southwick Hall nearby. As I spent nearly every week-end at the Palace House, Ramsay almost invariably dined with us on Saturdays during the weeks before D-day, usually bringing his Chief of Staff, Rear-Admiral George E. Creasy, or some other officer with him. So I found myself very well posted in the naval side of the operation. We also saw a good deal of my friend Bedell Smith, Eisenhower's Chief of Staff, and dined with him in his lair in Southwick Park, where he was surrounded by almost every comfort, including a cinema in his caravan.

During the two or three months before the assault the plan of bombing the French communications, and demolishing key bridges and rail centres to isolate the German troops opposing the landings, was very hotly disputed at a high level. It had little to do with me; but the Prime Minister was aware that it would cost many French lives which would naturally embitter the French nation. I need hardly go into all the arguments for and against; but after a system of warnings had been arranged advising the inhabitants to evacuate for the time being the areas chosen for attack, and consultation with the French authorities, Eisenhower had his own way.

Meanwhile British ports were gradually becoming filled with invasion craft of all descriptions. I paid several visits to Portsmouth and Southampton to see the preparations, and to watch troops rehearsing the embarkation and landing, with guns, vehicles and stores being loaded and unloaded. It was all intensely interesting.

For some time past we had heard rumours of Germany's new secret weapon, a pilotless aeroplane or rocket bomb, or some such contrivance. One could not help wondering what would happen if they opened up with it on one of our crowded invasion ports. Every foot of the enemy coast within likely range had been photographed, and all concrete structures for which there was no apparent use heavily bombed. But we were still much in the dark, and never quite knew when some new frightfulness might not develop.

III

To return to purely naval affairs, our intelligence in February and March seemed to indicate that the *Tirpitz*, which had been severely damaged by our midget submarines in Aaltenfiord in the previous September, was sufficiently repaired to proceed to Germany for a full refit. It was not suggested that in her present condition she was anything of a threat to our Russian convoys; but if she reached Germany it would be only a matter of months before she reappeared. The chase and final destruction of the *Bismarck* had shown what tough customers these ships were.

To us at the Admiralty it seemed essential that an attempt must be made to cause further damage and to prevent her moving, and air attack appeared to be the only method. Aaltenfiord was out of range of the heavy bombers of the Royal Air Force, so after much discussion and a full study of the subject the Commander-in-Chief, Home Fleet, was asked to carry out the operation with the aircraft-carriers *Victorious* and *Furious*. The attack took place at dawn on April 3rd under the direction of Vice-Admiral Sir Henry Moore just as the *Tirpitz* was getting underway. It was a complete success, the great ship being hit by fifteen to twenty medium-sized bombs. It was unfortunate that some of the armour-piercing bombs which should have done most damage failed to burst; but her upperworks were wrecked and most of her controls must have been destroyed. Her return to Germany was now probably out of the question. To make quite certain, however, it was decided to repeat the operation. The attempt was made on April 25th; but the attack was prevented by bad weather. However, the operation was not wholly abortive, as the striking force met a convoy of four ships and an escort off Bodo, in the Vest Fiord, and sank the lot.

Some changes in the important naval commands were due at about this time. Before long the most important fleet would be that in the East, while the Home Fleet would decline in importance. Moreover the Admiralty representative in Washington, Admiral Sir Percy Noble, was shortly due to retire and it was necessary to find a suitable relief. The position was very important, and Noble had been most successful. He was popular and highly esteemed by his American colleagues, and his place was difficult to fill. Sir James Somerville seemed to be the very man; but his appointment would mean a new Commander-in-Chief, Eastern Fleet.

After some cogitation I decided to recommend Sir Bruce Fraser for the latter command, and if our strategy for the Pacific should eventually be agreed to, Fraser would go on there. Vice-Admiral Sir Henry Moore would become Commander-in-Chief, Home Fleet. These changes were put up to the Prime Minister for approval; but it was some time before he would agree to any change.

Early in May the Dominion Premiers arrived in London for the Empire Conference. The Chiefs of Staff attended many of their meetings, and gave reviews of what was happening in their respective spheres. I met many old friends. I already knew General Smuts; Mr. Mackenzie King, Canada; and Mr. Peter Fraser, New Zealand. Mr. Curtin, Premier of Australia, was new to me, and though introduced I had no conversation with him. He seemed rather shy of coming to grips on naval matters, and dodged the talk he was supposed to have with the First Lord and myself. However, when we finally understood his views they were very sound. To put it briefly, Australia was vitally interested in the Pacific. While welcoming British forces to use Australia as a base for the war against Japan, Australians were desperately anxious to take their full share in the fighting. They did not wish that their man-power should be relegated to the task of producing for the British and the Americans. This was a point of view with which we were in the most cordial agreement.

I think the Empire Conference was most successful, and I very well remember the dinner at the Royal Naval College, Greenwich, to all the Dominion Premiers. I sat between Sir Firozkhan Noon, Defence Member of the Governor-General's Executive Council, India, and Mr. Clement Attlee, the Deputy Prime Minister. I had much interesting conversation with the latter. The First Lord, Mr. A. V. Alexander, made an excellent speech, and he was followed by Mr. Curtin. Peter Fraser spoke next, and he was very emotional and nearly in tears when he spoke of the Navy's evacuation of the New Zealanders from Crete. My ears burned badly.

IV

Time drew on.

On May 15th there was a final presentation of the plans for 'Overlord' at St. Paul's School in Hammersmith, His Majesty being present. I sat between the Prime Minister and Admiral Stark. All the members of the War Cabinet attended, with Eisenhower and Admirals, Generals and Air Marshals by the score. Never in all my long experience have I seen a conference chamber more crowded with officers and others of high rank. The meeting had naturally been kept a dead secret; but I found myself wondering what might happen if the Germans made a daylight raid in force and landed a bomb on the building. It was not until June 13th that the first V-1, the flying bomb, reached London.

Apart from the weather, the only available dates early in June which could be used for 'Overlord' were the 5th, 6th and 7th, with the 5th as the tentative D-day. We were limited in our choice of dates because we needed a moon for the airborne assaults immediately before the landings; complete darkness for the minesweepers and convoys during the approach; low-water to deal with the beach obstacles; and nearly one hour's daylight before the first landings for the bombardment and bombing of the beach defences.

The naval commands under Admiral Sir Bertram Ramsay had been arranged months beforehand, and it may be convenient to mention them here. Rear-Admiral Sir Philip Vian was to command the British assault, and my friend, Rear-Admiral Alan Kirk, the American. Vian had under him for the three British beaches Rear-Admirals A. G. Talbot, Commodore C. E. Douglas-Pennant, and the well-tried Commodore G. N. Oliver who had done so well at Salerno. Rear-Admirals W. G. Tennant and H. A. Hickling had to do with the towage and placing of the 'gooseberries' and 'mulberries'. The laying of 'Pluto', the pipe-line for petrol across the Channel, was in charge of Captain J. H. Hutchings.

The full story of 'Neptune', which was the naval part of the overall operation known as 'Overlord', and the greatest amphibious operation in history, has been told many times and from many different angles in all its detail. I need not repeat it, but am lucky in having made personal notes during a most eventful period.

On Friday, June 2nd, the Prime Minister sent for the First Lord and myself to come to his map room at 12.45. Once there he blithely informed us that he had arranged with Sir Bertram Ramsay to embark in the *Belfast* with Rear-Admiral Dalrymple-Hamilton for 'Overlord', and that he would be seriously angry with anyone who tried to prevent him. I do not know if he was really in earnest; but remembering his obstinate efforts to witness the bombardment of Pantellaria a year earlier, I replied that I would risk his wrath and said outright that it was absolutely wrong for him to go. He grunted and glared at me. Apparently he had also approached Eisenhower on the same subject, and his request had been refused. To that Mr. Churchill had retorted that while Eisenhower was the Supreme Commander, he was not in administrative control of the Royal Navy, and there was nothing to prevent Winston Spencer Churchill being enrolled as a genuine member of some ship's company. This intransigeance, thank goodness, was finally settled by His Majesty, who wrote telling the Prime Minister that if he went, he, the King, was equally entitled to go as the head of all the three Services. That finished the argument, though I have no doubt Mr. Churchill was bitterly disappointed.

On Saturday, June 3rd, I drove as usual to Bishops Waltham, calling in to see Vian on the way. There had been some doubt as to whether he would be well enough to take part in the assault, and Ramsay and I had decided that G. N. Oliver should take command of the whole British landing if Vian failed. However, I found him in great form and my fears vanished. Ramsay and Creasy, his Chief of Staff, came to supper that evening, and we had a long talk. The weather forecast was none too good, and for the first time I noticed signs of strain in Ramsay. He was extremely anxious about the operation, though he really need not have been. Though the responsibility lay heavily on his shoulders his organization and planning were as nearly perfect as they could be, and I had no doubt that with average conditions of weather he would put the Army ashore in the right place at the right time. As some of the convoys must go to sea earlier than others, the final decision as to the possibility of attacking on June 5th had to be taken at 4 a.m. the day before.

Early in the morning of the 4th I had a message from the Admiralty telling me that the operation was postponed for twenty-four hours. I was not surprised. It was blowing force 5 to 6, and when Ramsay rang me up later he told me there was low cloud over the French coast which would hamper our air operations and bombardment from the sea. I left the Palace House after lunch and called in at Ramsay's headquarters on the way and discussed the situation with him. One or two of the forces already at sea were rather mixed up because of the twenty-four-hour delay, and again the forecast was not good. After a call on the Commander-in-Chief, Portsmouth, Admiral Sir Charles Little, at his house on Portsdown Hill, I walked round his headquarters burrowed under the hill at Fort Southwick, and then drove on to Selsey to see sections of the artificial harbours. I eventually reached London at 7.30 p.m.

Next day, Monday, June 5th, the three Chiefs of Staff had been invited to lunch at 10 Downing Street. The Prime Minister was full of optimism. We attended a Cabinet Meeting at 6.30 p.m. The meteorologists had predicted a few days of fine weather after the present storm blew itself out, so it had been decided that 'Overlord' should be carried out. After the air and naval bombardments the landings were timed for 6.30 and 7.30 next morning. I spent most of that night in the lower War Room at the Admiralty watching the progress of the convoys plotted on the chart. The weather in the Channel was not good, and some of the smaller craft were feeling it and lagging behind, while the engine-room of four tank-landing-craft carrying guns had been swamped. It was a curious repetition of what had happened at the invasion of Sicily, though for 'Overlord' we had many more ships and craft at sea. However, by 1 a.m. on the 6th, there was nothing to show that the enemy had taken alarm. Blowing weather generally seems to favour the attackers and to put the defenders off their guard.

The War Room saw me again early next morning watching the course of the landings, which, so far as the British were concerned, were going well. Unfortunately the Americans had trouble at one beach.

Except for a few concluding remarks I will not attempt to describe 'Overlord', in which I had no operational responsibility. However, Admiral Ramsay's despatch, published as a Supplement to the *London Gazette* of October 28th, 1947, may profitably be read in conjunction with the other accounts.

We, at the Admiralty, held a watching brief. Ramsay had everything under his command during the operation, including the Commanders-in-Chief at Portsmouth, Plymouth and the Nore, who were actually his seniors. It was an arrangement I greatly disliked; but it was necessary that the whole of the naval side of the operation should be under one head. We reverted to normal conditions as soon as possible.

At the Admiralty, of course, we were vitally interested in any attempts to interfere by sea, for the Channel and the anchorages off the beaches were filled with masses of shipping, and a most tempting target. On the afternoon of June 7th the Prime Minister warned me by telephone that he anticipated that Dönitz would order the U-boats to take all risks in attacking our shipping. I replied that we should provide many risks for them to take.

In the event U-boats had started to stream out of the Biscay ports on D-day, travelling at full speed on the surface to reach our Channel convoys. The whole area had been flooded by aircraft of Coastal Command, R.A.F., and from June 7th till the 10th they attacked twenty-three U-boats by day and night, sinking six and damaging more. Another twenty-three U-boats had been attacked by the end of June, of which six were sunk by surface forces working in conjunction with aircraft. Our comparative immunity to submarine attack was principally due to the enthusiastic efficiency of Coastal Command.

There were almost nightly sallies by E-boats from Havre and Cherbourg, and spirited encounters on the part of our M.T.B.s and M.G.B.s. There were also enemy destroyers at Brest, and in the early hours of June 9th the Tenth Destroyer Flotilla operating under the orders of the Commander-in-Chief, Plymouth, made contact with four Germans. After a spirited action two of the enemy were destroyed and the others badly damaged.

But undoubtedly the most serious menace to our shipping in the assault area was the minelaying from E-boats and low-flying aircraft, the latter being particularly difficult to counter. The Germans, with their usual ingenuity, produced two new types of mine, both of which were actuated by the reduction of pressure when a ship passed over them. One of these types could not be swept in any conditions, and the other only in certain conditions of weather. Mines caused a number of casualties.

I may fittingly end my experience of 'Overlord' on June 16th, when I left the Palace House and embarked in the *Arethusa* at Portsmouth at 7.45 a.m. His Majesty came on board a quarter-of-an-hour later and we sailed for France. It was an extraordinary sight crossing the Channel and seeing all the convoys going and coming. We arrived off the British beaches at about noon, the sea being quite rough. The King went ashore to see General Montgomery, and we transferred to the *Scylla*, Vian's flagship, and sailed for 'Gold' beach where our 'mulberry' was being built. We landed after lunch and went to Ouistreham, where we climbed the lighthouse which was being used for spotting the gunfire from our ships and looked down on the positions where the enemy was reputed to be. I wondered why the Germans did not knock down the lighthouse, and the parachute boys spotting from there thought so too. They did not welcome our presence at all. I should add that others were there with me, including Air Chief Marshal Portal and General Ismay.

Re-embarking in the *Scylla* we returned to 'Juno' beach and rejoined the *Arethusa* with the King on board, eventually arriving at Spithead at 8.45 p.m. where we disembarked. It was a most interesting and varied visit, involving, among other things, a good many acrobatic changes of ships and boats in quite a respectable lop. As I remarked to one of my companions, the principal features of the day seemed to be the huge collection of ships, the good organization for the maintenance of small craft, and the prodigious expenditure of naval ammunition.

v

The United States Chiefs of Staff arrived at Euston from Holyhead on the evening of June 9th, and I went to meet them. General Marshall was as charming as ever, and Admiral King as saturnine.

The next few days were greatly occupied with conferences, the principal

topic being operations to assist and accelerate 'Overlord'. The U.S.C.O.S —
if I may so call them, were still anxious to land in the south of France, operation
'Anvil'. We were rather divided on the subject, and the Prime Minister
obstinately against it. The alternative to invading in the south of France
was to retain all the troops in Italy and to push on with the campaign there.
I was not deeply implicated. The considerations were mainly military and
political. It was no debating point for a sailor.

I was much more interested in our future strategy in the Far East, and
what should be the function of the British fleet when it arrived. I understood
that Admiral King had no objection to the Amboina project, though he
would prefer the British and the Australians to go for Surabaya. He seemed
quite determined to keep the Royal Navy out of the Pacific. However, the
settlement of that question lay in the future.

At about 4 a.m. on June 13th I was awakened by an air raid warning and
a little gunfire; but only one aeroplane was reported. There came another
warning later, and the duty captain reported a pilotless aircraft. It was the
first V-1 to fall upon London, and came down in Bethnal Green, where it
destroyed a railway bridge. Thereafter they gave us plenty to think about,
and were much worse than we had been led to suppose. In one fortnight
they had dropped only 100 tons less weight of explosives than in the worst
fortnight of the blitz, and the casualties, though not so heavy, were mounting
steadily. To the average person they were most disturbing. One heard them
coming for so long, and the period between the shutting off of the engine and
the explosion was a time of great suspense and tension. After a few nights of
sticking it out in the flat at the Admiralty, I descended almost nightly to my
cabin under the Citadel, while my wife and the two Wrens went to their
bomb-proof quarters in the Admiralty. The most annoying thing about
the flying bomb was that the worse the weather the more came roaring over.
Our defences were hampered; but the bombs were not.

The question of operation 'Anvil', the landing in southern France to
back up 'Overlord', remained a matter of disagreement between ourselves
and the American Chiefs of Staff until the end of June. The Americans felt
very strongly about it and were supported by President Roosevelt, so in the
end, on June 30th, we bowed to their firmly-expressed wishes.

CHAPTER XLV

I

THE story of those unforgettable days of hard fighting and great battles which followed on to the landing of the Armies in Normandy in June, 1944, is hardly germane to what is essentially a naval story. It is sufficient to say that the Admiralty followed the course of the day-to-day operations with the closest attention, ready always to take immediate measures for further assistance in the way of naval bombardment, increasing the flow of supplies, and so forth. The regular visits of Ramsay, and periodical visits of Bedell Smith, to supper at the Palace House on Saturdays provided me with much valuable first-hand information which was barely touched upon in the summarized daily situation reports.

We suffered considerable losses through the mines I have already mentioned, while the Germans also produced torpedoes of a new type which either moved slowly, or drifted in with the tide, and circled or homed on the ships in the crowded anchorage. They also did some damage. One of the chief factors which greatly accelerated the build-up was Ramsay's wise decision to take the responsibility of beaching the tank-landing ships and coasters and leaving them high and dry at low water. This measure had my cordial approval, as the ships could unload straight into lorries driven out on the hard sand. The constructors had expressed grave doubt if the older type L.S.T.s would stand the strain; but so far as I remember there were no untoward incidents.

Baffled in their attempts to get at our invasion convoys with submarines of the older type, the enemy took to using his Schnorkel boats in the invasion area and round the coasts of Britain. I need not describe the Dutch-invented Schnorkel, or 'Snort' as we now call it, which permits a submarine to remain under water for long periods without having to come to the surface to re-charge the batteries. But these pests crawled submerged along the coasts to reach their patrol positions, where outlying rocks made them very difficult to detect by the radar in surface craft or aircraft. Tide-rips, eddies and wrecks in shallow water also militated against the successful use of asdics. However, during June and July U-boats sank only eight merchantmen in the invasion area and round the coasts of Britain, which was considerably fewer than we had a right to expect. Over the same period twenty-two U-boats were sunk in those areas out of the total of forty-eight destroyed in the northern hemisphere.

This result was not unsatisfactory; but as the Schnorkel boats might be used with increased vigour in the future, and radar was useless and asdic greatly hampered, the Admiralty were forced to ask for and obtain from the War Cabinet a priority to undertake a large programme of mine manufacture. With such stocks as were already available minefields were also laid in the focal areas where the U-boats seemed to congregate. Being essentially defensive, this mine-laying policy did not greatly commend itself to anyone; but it was the best that could be done with the means available. It had some slight success, and, no doubt, a deterrent effect; but the war was ended before our scheme of mine defence was fully complete.

In the Chiefs of Staff Committee we, like Martha, were "troubled over many things". Perhaps the most critical problem for the Navy was a firm decision as to the use of the British fleet at the close of the war against Germany. The Chiefs of Staff, as I have said, favoured its employment in active co-operation with the United States Fleet in the Pacific, the front line in the war against Japan. But it was very difficult to convince Mr. Churchill and other Ministers in the War Cabinet, who inclined to a policy of using our fleet in a more or less subsidiary role in the East Indies, at any rate not in the Pacific proper. The matter of man-power entered into the question. Perhaps, quite naturally, the Government were anxious for considerable reductions in our Fighting Services after the defeat of Germany.

Admiral Fraser had duly been appointed Commander-in-Chief, Eastern Fleet. But he, and also quite naturally, was rather adverse to taking up his appointment until he was aware of how his fleet was to be used. When he went out in August the question was still unsettled. Incidentally, the Eastern Fleet had carried out very successful operations against the Japanese held port of Sabang, north of Sumatra, Surabaya, and the Andaman Islands. I will describe these operations more fully in the next chapter. But the news from that station was not universally good. The floating dock at Trincomalee buckled while the *Valiant* was being docked, seriously damaging the ship and breaking three of her A-brackets. It was a bad business which put the ship out of action for a long time.

There were still large German forces in Norway, and for some months ships and aircraft of the Home Fleet, not to mention our submarines, had been carrying on a successful offensive against the enemy convoys passing up and down the coast. Early in August, too, the fine break-through of the United States Eighth Corps to overrun the Brittany peninsula and to isolate Brest, Lorient and St. Nazaire, with the consequent danger to the enemy of being cut off further south, enabled us to push our naval patrols well into the Bay of Biscay. Destroyers backed up by cruisers had considerable success against the enemy's coastwise traffic. The Germans were feeling the pinch in every direction.

On August 15th the much-disputed operation 'Anvil', re-named 'Dragoon', took place in the south of France, American and a few French troops being landed at four places to the south-west of Cannes under cover of the Allied Navies, which included various units of the French fleet. I will not describe this operation, which was entirely successful, and was designed to capture Toulon and Marseilles, followed by an advance up the valley of the Rhone to link up with the Allied Army already fighting in the north.

Mr. Churchill had persuaded Sir John Cunningham to allow him to witness the landing, which he did from the destroyer *Kimberley*. As one young naval officer wrote in a letter: "The Prime Minister suddenly arrived out of the blue in a destroyer, and we knew nothing of his arrival until it was broadcast throughout the ship. Our men cheered, and looking through glasses as he went past we could see the old boy on the destroyer's bridge smoking a cigar and making his V-sign. It bucked up our men no end." On his return Mr. Churchill told me he was much annoyed because the *Kimberley's* orders kept her too far out!

Arrangements were already in train for a meeting between the President and Prime Minister at Quebec during September, Mr. Churchill, of course, being accompanied by the Chiefs of Staff and many others. Before leaving London, however, we had the excellent news that the Armies were nearing Antwerp. Ramsay and I had both been in some anxiety about the supply of the Army as it advanced. We were in dire need of a port, for the artificial harbour at Arromanches was being used to capacity and was becoming rather clogged up. A suggestion had been made to use airborne forces to capture Calais; but for some reason or another the idea was dropped.

The approaching capture of Antwerp presented a tantalizing picture, though both Ramsay and myself agreed that it must firmly be pointed out to the Army Command that Antwerp lay well inland and about fifty miles up a river still controlled by the enemy. Before the port could be used for shipping the German defences must be cleared.

Our forebodings were pretty well correct. By September 4th, Antwerp was in our hands with its port facilities practically intact. In the pæan of triumph at its capture the clearance of the approaches was not treated as a matter of urgency. For the time being one of the finest ports in Europe was of no more use to us than an oasis in the Sahara desert.

The approaches to the Scheldt and the estuary were studded with minefields. Before any minesweeping could begin the powerful German defences and garrisons on South Beveland and Walcheren, on the north side of the river, must be eliminated. I represented these facts to my colleagues, the other Chiefs of Staff, and I believe that after our arrival at Quebec the Chief of the Imperial General Staff, Alan Brooke, and his American opposite number, General George Marshall, took action with the Army Commanders on the spot.

Suffice it to say that whereas the port of Antwerp was captured on September 4th, South Beveland was not finally overcome by British and Canadian troops until October 30th. On November 1st an amphibious assault was launched on Walcheren, and after very severe fighting with heavy losses the enemy resistance there was eliminated by November 9th. The mine-sweeping started at once; but it was not until November 26th, just about twelve weeks after its occupation, that Antwerp saw the arrival of the first ships carrying much-needed supplies for the Army.

II

The Prime Minister, Mrs. Churchill, the Chiefs of Staff and their staffs left London on September 5th and embarked that evening in the *Queen Mary* at Greenock. It was the first time I had taken passage in one of these monster vessels, and it was difficult to realize one was in a ship and not a hotel. I had a suite with sleeping cabin, two sitting-rooms and three bathrooms, and on leaving my palatial quarters I was always in doubt whether to turn right or left to go forward or aft. I was given the free run of the bridge by the Commodore, that fine man of the sea James Gordon Partridge Bisset, now Sir James, who had first gone to sea as an apprentice in sail in 1898. This gave me a chance of keeping my eye on the escorting cruiser which accompanied us all the way across, and the four destroyers which parted company on the second day out. It said a lot for the steaming qualities of the sixteen-year old cruisers *Kent*, *Berwick* and *Devonshire* which in turn escorted us out and home, that they were able to keep station on the *Queen Mary* at 29 knots and sometimes more.

We had various meetings and discussions with the Prime Minister on the way across, and of course the daily meetings between the Chiefs of Staff. It was very hot and sticky when we got into the Gulf Stream on September 8th, and Mr. Churchill sent for Commodore Bisset and tried to persuade him to alter course into cooler weather. As this would have taken us over the Newfoundland Banks and have caused a deviation from the track laid down by the Admiralty, Bisset very rightly objected. Together we went and convinced the great man that such a course was impracticable. After a fog on September 9th and a diversion to the southward clear of reported U-boats we finally arrived at Halifax on September 10th. At 2 p.m. we left the ship and embarked in the most comfortable special train waiting to receive us. In my sleeping berth the bed was a large double one. High officials of the Canadian railways were on board to see we had all we needed. We set off at once, and while daylight lasted there were crowds at every station to see and to acclaim the Prime Minister. There was no doubt about his popularity.

We reached Quebec next morning to find that the President and Mrs. Roosevelt had already arrived, and the Governor-General, the Earl of Athlone, and the Prime Minister, Mr. Mackenzie King, just arriving. Admiral Sir Percy Noble had also come from Washington. We, the Chiefs of Staff, were soon established in most comfortable quarters in the Chateau Frontenac, my suite of rooms being on the thirteenth floor overlooking the river. I knew Quebec well from my previous visits in the *Calcutta* and *Despatch*, and was delighted to see it and its lovely surroundings again, no more beautiful in the world.

Conferences started at once, interrupted by the inevitable round of engagements. That evening, however, I had a shock when I was handed a cable from my wife telling me that my old aunt in Wales, my mother's sister, was dead. I should miss her badly. Ever since my midshipman's days I had written to her every week, and she to me. She was a woman of great character and courage, and aged though she was I had hoped that her indomitable spirit would have kept her alive to see our final victory. But it was not to be. She was a sad loss to me and all of my family.

The most important matters that had to be discussed between the President and Prime Minister, and the British and American Chiefs of Staff, were the future of the campaign in Italy and what United States troops should be kept there, and also how the British Navy should be employed in the war against Japan. Our first meetings with the United States Chiefs of Staff brought full agreement on all the points that mattered. That night, September 12th, we all dined with the Earl of Athlone at the Citadel, where the President and Mrs. Roosevelt, with the Prime Minister and Mrs. Churchill, were staying. It was a large party, the United States Chief of Staff, Mr. Mackenzie King, and other Canadian Ministers all being present. I sat next to Mrs. Roosevelt, and had much interesting conversation.

Our first plenary meeting with the President, Prime Minister, and the United States Chiefs of Staff took place the next day. Mr. Churchill led off with a good review of the war in general, and, somewhat to the surprise of Brooke, Portal and myself, ended by offering the British main fleet for operations against Japan in the central Pacific in co-operation with the American fleet. Mr. Roosevelt at once replied: "No sooner offered than accepted."

Remembering the Prime Minister's strongly expressed desire that our fleet should be used for the more limited purpose of assisting to regain Singapore, Malaya, North Borneo and other British possessions from the Japanese, I was naturally delighted. I was always convinced that, whatever the difficulties of supply and of providing the ships for the fleet train, the proper place for our battleships and aircraft-carriers was in the central Pacific working in close concert with the Americans. Our final stake in that ocean was fully the equal of theirs. At the same time, I was well aware of Admiral Ernest King's rooted aversion to our fleet operating with the American in its drive towards Japan proper.

And now the die was cast. Mr. Churchill had offered our fleet, and the offer had been accepted!

The plenary meeting on September 13th closed with an address by the President congratulating the Combined Chiefs of Staff on their friendly relations.

These relations became somewhat shattered next day when we met the United States Chiefs of Staff and again raised the question of the British Navy in the Pacific. Admiral King, adamant as ever, hotly refused to have anything to do with it, and tried to persuade us that the President's acceptance of the offer did not mean what had been said. King, having turned his guns on General Marshall, was finally called to order by Admiral Leahy, the President's Chief of Staff, with the remark: "I don't think we should wash our linen in public". King, with the other American Chiefs of Staff against him, eventually gave way; but with a very bad grace.

The atmosphere was less stormy when we met King next afternoon. He was resigned to the use of our fleet in the Pacific; but made it quite clear that it must expect no assistance from the Americans. From this rather unhelpful attitude he never budged.

After a final Combined Chiefs of Staff meeting at which we tied up any loose ends in our report to the President and Prime Minister, the last plenary session was held next morning. It passed off happily; but I was distressed to see how frail the President was looking.

Another whose appearance shocked me was Sir John Dill, who attended all the meetings as head of our military mission in the United States. He looked so ill that I besought him to give up and go home to restore his health; but this he utterly refused to do. This fine soldier and great gentleman died on November 4th. What he did for the Allied cause in Washington is just incalculable. The Americans well recognized his worth, and he was given an official state funeral in Arlington Cemetery and a special citation in Congress, most unusual honours for a foreigner.

To celebrate the end of the Quebec Conference the three Chiefs of Staff had decided to go fishing. So after some trouble in getting away because the Prime Minister wished for a meeting that night, which happened to be a Saturday, we went to the air port, took off in an amphibian, and after an hour's flight landed on a lake in the wilds of Northern Quebec near a large log house belonging to a fish and game club whose president, a Mr. de Carteret, had come specially from Montreal to be our host. In these beautiful surroundings we spent two very happy days, not catching many fish; but enjoying a real rest after our many conferences and other engagements at Quebec. It was a wild spot. On the sand at one bay where I landed in the early light of the morning my guide pointed out the spoor of bears, moose and foxes.

After two days I had to return to accompany the Prime Minister home in the *Queen Mary* from New York. Brooke and Portal, who were flying to England, spent another two days in the wilds.

After one night in Quebec I flew to New York with some others, and embarked in the *Queen Mary* that evening, September 19th. We left the jetty at 7.30 next morning, and the Prime Minister and his party came on board at the quarantine anchorage. Escorted by three American destroyers we sailed soon afterwards. I lunched that day with the Prime Minister; Lord Leathers—the Minister of War Transport, and General Ismay also being present. Mr. Churchill seemed very well and in high spirits, and now thoroughly converted to the use of the British fleet in the Pacific. That is why I mention this particular meal, of soft-shelled crabs and large beefsteaks, because the Prime Minister told Lord Leathers that the fleet train for the Pacific must be done on a handsome scale. If we needed thirty or even forty ships we must have them! Lord Leathers became somewhat pensive.

I need not mention the rest of the voyage, during which I naturally saw much of Mr. Churchill, and had much discussion and some argument. As the only member of the Chiefs of Staff Committee on board I was asked to look over the military portions of his speech for the opening of Parliament. He had rather a habit of making out that the Army was doing nearly all the fighting, so I put in a few amendments.

The Prime Minister was always most interesting, but particularly so when he was able to relax during meals. "Dined with P.M.", I noted in my diary for September 23rd. "Much conversation ranging from the next League of Nations to the South African War, so did not get to bed until 1.30." On another occasion at dinner—Caviare and vodka, lamb chops, sweet and Stilton cheese with the usual liquid embellishments—he talked of 1914-15 when he was First Lord of the Admiralty as a man of forty, and of a galaxy of Admirals, some of whom I had served under in my youth—'Jackie' Fisher; Arthur Knyvet ('Tug') Wilson; Prince Louis of Battenberg; Jellicoe; Beatty and many others.

We had hoped to save a day by landing at Fishguard; but there was a heavy sea running and we had to push on to Greenock, where we arrived at 5.30 p.m. on September 25th and travelled by the night train from Glasgow to London.

III

Back at the Admiralty, the main policy for the Japanese war was now settled so far as the Navy was concerned; but it was a very different matter to make the necessary arrangements to get that policy implemented. To begin with, we had against us the intense feeling of Admiral King and the Navy Department in Washington that the British Fleet was not wanted in the Pacific, and that in that area we must depend entirely upon our own efforts. We could expect no help from the American organization.

Here, however, I must quickly place it on record that the attitude of the

United States Navy in the Pacific was entirely different. Headed by its Commander-in-Chief, Admiral Chester W. Nimitz, the American fleet welcomed ours with open arms and gave us all the help in its power. It was not merely polite language when Nimitz, in January, 1945, directed one of his liaison officers with the British fleet to tell Admiral Fraser—"We will make it" (the combined operations of the U.S. and British fleets) "work regardless of anything." Later, in his own report, Admiral Fraser wrote: "Despite their doubts, the Americans put their trust in us unstintedly, and the generosity and help of all were invaluable to our success . . ." Vice-Admiral Bernard Rawlings, in operational command of our task force in the Pacific, was even more explicit. "It will not," he wrote, "be out of place to remark on the helpfulness of the American authorities both at Manus and Ulithi." (American island bases.) "I trust we did not ask for their assistance until we were faced with problems which frankly seemed beyond us, but whenever we did so appeal it was responded to with the utmost vigour. . . . I have yet to find a more helpful and responsive attitude than that accorded to me by those American authorities responsible for the provision and movements of lifeguard submarines and aircraft . . ." these latter being employed for the rescue of crews of aircraft.

But I anticipate.

At the Admiralty in the autumn and winter of 1944 we had also to overcome the very natural resistance of the Minister of War Transport to letting us have all the ships we needed for the Fleet Train in the Pacific. Shipping was woefully short, and the number of vessels we required was certainly imposing, far exceeding anything that had ever been thought necessary. But with no advanced base, and our main base in Australia over four thousand miles away from the scene of operations, we had, so to speak, to carry our shell on our backs. At one time our fleet train consisted of about a hundred ships of all types—destroyers and submarine depot ships; accommodation and hospital ships; tankers and store-ships; ammunition and victualling store-ships; aircraft repair and store-ships; salvage vessels; water-carriers and distilling ships, a veritable armada. To the mind of one accustomed to the austere standards of the Mediterranean, some of the ships demanded appeared at first to be redundant, though the naval staff assured me that they were all essential. To fight alongside and with the same facilities as the Americans, we had to some extent to adopt their scale of logistics, which was very lavish.

I remember that one of the first demands made on the Admiralty from the Pacific was for a fast tanker of 18 knots or more to accompany the fleet. We had made the same demand from the Mediterranean years before; but even in 1944-45 no such ship was available.

The difficult question of the supply of vessels for the fleet train persisted until late in 1945, and was finally settled to our satisfaction by the Prime

Minister requesting the Chancellor of the Exchequer, Sir John Anderson, to examine and adjudicate.

We had also to obtain the concurrence of the Australian Government to basing our fleet in Australia, and using that great country as our principal source of supply with a miniature Controller's Department of the Admiralty set up out there. The Australians were not too forthcoming at first. They had not yet ceased to supply the Americans. Nevertheless, when our fleet did arrive, nothing could have exceeded the generous assistance that was given, or the overwhelming kindness with which our officers and men were welcomed.

There was also the difficult question of commands. After various exchanges with the Navy Department in Washington, it was settled that the British fleet should come under Admiral Nimitz's command. This, of course, was quite acceptable to us. But to avoid any difficulties about seniorities, it appeared that Fraser would have to exercise his command first from Australia and then from any advanced base that we might be able to set up. He would seldom be able to fly his flag afloat, so a more junior officer had to be chosen as second in command and to command the fleet at sea. The selection of the various officers for the subordinate commands gave little trouble. There were any number of brilliant men with distinguished war records.

While Fraser, of course, was the obvious Commander-in-Chief, I was personally convinced that Vice-Admiral Sir Bernard Rawlings was the right man for service as second-in-command. In the Mediterranean he had shown outstanding powers of leadership and ability to deal with any situation, however difficult. At the same time it was essential that he should be acceptable to Fraser, so on his way out to the East I had asked Fraser to see Rawlings and to signal if he agreed to the appointment. His concurrence came at once.

For the aircraft-carriers, which would provide the main striking force, we chose Vice-Admiral Sir Philip Vian, while two brilliant officers who were completing their service as Assistant Chiefs of the Naval Staff at the Admiralty, Rear-Admirals E. J. P Brind and R. M. Servaes, would command the two cruiser squadrons. Rear-Admiral J. H. Edelsten, from the Admiralty, would be Rear-Admiral, Destroyers.

For the difficult key post in Australia we were fortunate to have available Charles S. Daniel, a man of immense ability who had been Director of Plans at the Admiralty in 1940—41, and was thoroughly *au fait* with all sides of the Admiralty war organization. He became Vice-Admiral (Administration) to the British Pacific Fleet. Rear-Admiral D. B. Fisher was to command the fleet train, a mighty fleet of its own, and Rear-Admiral R. H. Portal was to be in Australia in charge of the Fleet Air Arm. Altogether, our team of Flag Officers was a very strong one.

Within six months of the end of the war in Europe we hoped to have in the Pacific the four battleships of the 'King George VI' class, with five or six armoured carriers and later some of the light fleet carriers as well. These, with eleven cruisers, nine escort carriers, and strong contingents of destroyers, submarines, sloops, frigates, minesweepers and the usual ancillary vessels, would constitute a strong and well-balanced addition to the United States fleet. In particular, we hoped that our armoured carriers would make a good showing against the Japanese Kamikazes, or suicide 'planes, which were causing the Americans considerable anxiety. This, indeed, they did.

IV

In London, ever since June, the flying bombs, the V-1s, had continued to be a menace. By August 14th, the latest date for which I have the figures, they had killed some 5,200 people, wounded 18,000, and destroyed 900,000 houses. Their effect upon morale was noticeable, for whatever the weather they might arrive at any time of the day or night. By early October, however, most of the flying bomb launching-sites had been captured by the advance of the Allied Armies, though the enemy were still launching a few from aircraft, which considerably reduced their accuracy.

The first V-2s, the rocket bombs, were used on August 1st, and by October we were receiving our share of them. Compared with the V-1s, they actually came as something of a relief. They arrived at such a terrific speed that there was no minute or so of anticipation. The first thing one knew was the explosion, when one had either had it or escaped. My wife and I and our little household ceased to use the underground air raid shelters, and slept soundly in our beds in the Archway flat.

In my last chapter I described the sinking of the *Scharnhorst* on December 26th, 1943, and made some mention of our convoys to North Russia. While the *Scharnhorst's* destruction and the disablement of the *Tirpitz* removed the threat of surface attack, the air and U-boat menace was unabated.

The tale of these Arctic convoys would provide a book in itself; but to hark back to the early months of 1944, convoys out or home had been run in January, February, March, April and May, after which they were temporarily suspended because of the need for all our escort forces to be prepared for the Normandy invasion. They were resumed in August, and continued to run until the end of the war in Europe.

Since September, 1942, every convoy had been accompanied by one or more escort-carriers apart, of course, from the normal escort and covering force of heavier ships. With improved radar and weapons, aircraft working from the carriers scored spectacular successes against the U-boats, while their fighters gave far greater protection against air attacks.

In March, 1944, aircraft of the Fleet Air Arm from H.M.S. *Chaser* sank U-boats on three successive days, while in April another three U-boats were despatched in three days by destroyers and aircraft from the *Tracker* and *Activity*. During a return convoy in May the *Fencer's* aircraft sank three U-boats in two days. Successes later in the year were scored by aircraft from the escort-carriers *Vindex* and *Campania*. In all, during 1944, no fewer than twenty-three German submarines were destroyed on the Arctic route—nine directly by naval aircraft; three by naval aircraft in co-operation with surface ships; six by surface vessels; four by long-range aircraft of Coastal Command R.A.F.; and one by a British submarine.

The inclusion of escort-carriers in our Russian convoys paid ample dividends, as they did also in the Atlantic. Our losses in the Arctic convoys, which until V.E. day remained one of our major and most difficult commitments in fulfilment of our pledge to our Russian allies, were greatly diminished.

Little, too little, has been written or said about the work of the Fleet Air Arm, and of the surface escorts and merchant ships as well, in the succession of Arctic operations from August, 1941, onwards. From first to last there were forty-one convoys outward and thirty-six homeward, in which seven hundred and seventy-five merchant ships took part. Eighty-one allied merchant vessels were sunk with a loss of 525 lives. Nineteen of His Majesty's ships, including two cruisers, were lost and another fourteen damaged, with a loss of 2,055 officers and men. Military supplies to the value of £308,000,000 were shipped for North Russia, with another £120,000,000 worth of raw materials, foodstuffs, machinery, industrial plant, medical supplies and hospital equipment. Over and above this the British public contributed £5,260,000 for medical supplies and clothing under the 'Aid to Russia' charity schemes, while the British Government made another grant of £2,500,000.

The severe weather conditions and the ice of the Arctic, particularly in winter, caused as much difficulty and delay to the convoys as did the enemy opposition. If the surface escorts and merchant ships suffered in the heavy gales and the bitter cold, the few hours of wan greyness which passed for winter daylight, the fierce blizzards and snowstorms, and even the salt spray freezing solid as it fell, the young men of the Fleet Air Arm operating from the frozen flight-decks of the carriers took their lives in their hands every time they took off. The conditions in which they worked were indescribable. The aircraft patrols might be flown off in clear weather; but when the time came to land on again with petrol nearly exhausted the carrier herself might be invisible in a lashing snowstorm. This happened many a time, and the number of close shaves in the recovery of these valiant young naval pilots is unbelievable. Many, numbed with cold, had to be lifted out of their cockpits. Their work was beyond all praise.

The smaller surface escorts, too, had much with which to contend. In January, 1944, a little anti-submarine trawler called the *Strathella* lost touch with a convoy bound to Iceland from North Russia in very heavy weather. As R.A.F. aircraft saw nothing of her and no further news was received, she was presumed lost after a week. Five weeks later an American aircraft reported the trawler drifting helpless off the east coast of Greenland. Help was sent, and the crew of twenty-two were rescued in good health after their bitter ordeal.

Russia had much for which to be grateful. In April, 1944, one of our homeward bound convoys brought 3,000 Russian naval officers and men to man British warships transferred to the Soviet Navy. On the last day of October in the same year we sent a special convoy of two fast merchant ships, the *Empress of Australia* and *Scythia*, from Liverpool with about 11,000 Russian ex-prisoners of war liberated by the advance of the Allied Armies on the Continent. These ships, heavily escorted, reached the Kola Inlet on November 6th.

Well might M. Maisky say: "The Russian convoys are a Northern Saga of heroism, bravery and endurance. This Saga will live for ever, not only in the hearts of your people, but also in the hearts of the Soviet people, who rightly see in it one of the most striking expressions of collaboration between the Allied Governments, without which our common victory would have been impossible."

In view of what has happened since, I sometimes wonder if these were merely hollow words. Since 1945 the Soviet Government has done little to acknowledge any indebtedness to its former Allies.

Whilst on the subject of North Russia I am reminded that the *Tirpitz* was finally disposed of by the Lancasters of the Royal Air Force on November 12th. It made little difference to our naval dispositions as she was no longer a fighting unit; but there was always the chance that she might have been got back to Germany. Hit and near-missed by very heavy bombs she now heeled over and capsized.

v

I have already mentioned that the port of Antwerp was not finally open to shipping until November 26th. In the meanwhile the advance of the Allies had been held up, partly through enemy resistance; but principally because of the need of supplies brought about by the lack of ports.

On the extreme south of the Allied line, the American Seventh and the French First Armies, which had landed in southern France in August, and were now operating between Strasbourg and Saarbrucken, were being well supplied through Marseilles, though it was over four hundred miles distant as the crow flies.

The American and British 'mulberries' on the Normandy coast had never really been intended for work during the winter, and the American 'mulberry' had already been partially demolished in the bad weather a few days after the landing. The Biscay ports—L'Orient, St. Nazaire and Bordeaux—were still in the hands of the enemy, so the American First, Third and Ninth Armies, operating roughly between Aachen and Metz, were being supplied through Cherbourg, which had been captured on June 27th and was being used within a month, together with what could be brought over the Normandy beaches, more than three hundred miles away.

Havre and Dieppe had fallen to the Canadian First Army; but at Havre especially the systematic enemy demolitions had rendered the port unusable for months. There were German garrisons in Boulogne, Calais, Dunkirk and Ostend, which had been ordered to hold out to the death. The Canadians were put on to opening up the ports at any cost, and severe fighting had continued on the coast all through September and October. Ostend fell, to provide some 4,000 tons of supplies a day to Montgomery's two Armies in the north. Boulogne and Calais were captured in their turn; but they, with Ostend and what supplies still came over the British 'mulberry' harbour at Arromanches, were insufficient to meet requirements. The battle had stagnated into a battle for supplies. The British Second Army, in Belgium, and the Canadian First Army were living from hand to mouth. Until Antwerp was working to capacity and supplies could be built up, no further advance was possible.

Towards the end of November some discussion arose in the Chiefs of Staff Committee and with Eisenhower about future plans to get the battle moving again. Except in so far as the ports were concerned it was hardly a naval matter; but there was a sharp difference of opinion between Montgomery backed up by Alan Brooke on the one hand, and Eisenhower, on the other.

Briefly, Montgomery favoured a large concentration in the north and a push into the industrial Ruhr after crossing the Rhine. Eisenhower also wished for a push into the Ruhr, another to the south of the Ruhr, with the American and French Armies in the south driving on from Alsace, in other words an advance over the whole line. Montgomery's contention was that there was a decided risk that neither the northern nor the centre offensive would be sufficiently strong and Brooke agreed.

I think I have seen it stated that had Montgomery's plan been accepted, the war would have been finished in 1944. This was not claimed at the time, and is an afterthought on the part of someone who agreed with Montgomery's views. In any case, Eisenhower stuck to his guns, and later, at Malta, in January, 1945, when the President and Prime Minister and their staffs were on their way to a further conference with the Russians at Yalta, there was more discussion between General George Marshall and Alan Brooke on the same subject. The final results fully justified Eisenhower, though it may be that early in December Montgomery was advocating the safer method.

The question also became entangled with the overall command of the Armies in the field. Montgomery wished for a unified command of all the Armies, American, British, Canadian and French. Eisenhower's settlement of this question was that he, personally, commanded all the Armies, with Montgomery commanding in the north and Bradley in the south. I think myself that this, politically, was probably the best solution, though I disagree with any Supreme Commander being in direct operational command of Armies in the field.

However, all these controversies were overshadowed by Runstedt's sudden offensive in the Ardennes which started on December 16th. It is hardly for me to discuss or describe Hitler's last real bid for victory in the West, in which the German advance, backed up by a large number of the fanatical S.S. divisions, overran three American divisions of the First Army holding an eighty-mile front in the centre of the Allied line, and all in that area was confusion and chaos. The enemy thrust finally penetrated to a depth of about forty miles.

Montgomery's immediate dispositions to cover the line of the Meuse were masterly. And very soon, as the situation developed, apart from his own British and Canadian Armies, he was placed in temporary command of the American Ninth and the remainder of the American First Armies north of the bulge.

Further south, the 101st United States Airborne Division was surrounded in Bastogne, close to the northern corner of Luxembourg, and a most important road junction for any German thrust towards Dinant and Namur. Very severe pressure was brought upon the 101st, and they were called upon to surrender. The reply of their gallant commander, Brigadier-General Maxwell D. Taylor, was a model of brevity; the single and expressive word "Nuts!"

General George Patton, commanding the American Third Army, was rushed up from the south through Luxembourg to counter-attack on the southern flank of the German penetration, which reached its maximum near Dinant on Christmas Eve. He went in with three divisions and made a business of it. When he and a convoy of vehicles got through to Bastogne after severe fighting he was asked by Taylor what he had come for!

The 'Battle of the Bulge' set back the Allied plans for the advance into Germany by about six weeks. The Allies had been caught unprepared, and it was undoubtedly the stubborn resistance and magnificent fighting of isolated bodies of American troops in the early days of the German offensive which saved the situation. These troops rose to the crisis. They neither panicked nor lost heart. By the end of the year immense pressure was being brought on the north and the south of the enemy salient, and the Germans, suffering hideous casualties, were gradually being squeezed back to the positions from which they had started.

On the subject of this offensive, Ramsay, who was at S.H.A.E.F. headquarters, wrote me an interesting letter on December 22nd.

> When the attack first developed (he said), the operations staff were pleased and started licking their chops at the prospect of what they were going to do to the Hun. I can't say that I shared this optimism when I saw that only three U.S. divisions were holding an 80-mile front opposite it and that support had to come from the flanks. However, I was told that the Hun divisions were newly formed and not up to much. . . . Since then, what with almost a standstill in the air owing to fog and shocking flying conditions and the throwing in of a large number of S.S. divisions, things have steadily deteriorated, though they might have been very much worse. This is the sort of mix up that the Germans handle quicker and better than ourselves, but I think we should be able to seal off the area and sort it out within the next few days. . . . It may of course rebound to our advantage, as was at first hoped, in which case it should have a bad effect on the German army as a whole. . . . Meanwhile, the French people are pretty anxious about the situation, as one can well understand and sympathize with. It is slightly disturbing when one remembers that in the last war we held the Western Front with nearly two hundred divisions and compares much the same front now being held by about fifty. Should the Hun be able to shorten his eastern front or economize to any large extent in divisions there, or exchange tired divisions for fresh ones, we should feel the draught very severely. However, our air supremacy, when it is able to function, will make up for a great deal of the balance if it should turn against us. . . .

Ramsay went on to say that naval affairs were "going pretty well", though there might be some unpleasant incidents at Antwerp due to V-1s and V-2s, which continued to shower down in somewhat increasing numbers. Even as he was closing his letter a report had come through from Antwerp to say that one of the locks had been slightly damaged by a bomb.

VI

Towards the end of 1944 we had our usual perplexities at the Admiralty.

September had seen the loss of seven Allied merchant ships to twenty-three U-boats sunk in all areas. The corresponding figures for October were one and twelve, and those for November seven and eight.

December, when we lost nine merchant ships to seven submarines destroyed in action and another five through other causes was also rather disappointing. After six months experience in using Schnorkels in coastal waters the U-boats succeeded, for the time being at least, in gaining a certain degree of immunity against air and surface attack. There was a sharp recrudescence of activity in the English Channel, where five merchant ships and a frigate were sunk and another two merchant ships and a frigate damaged, between December 18th and 29th. Midget submarines off the Scheldt and in the Straits of Dover were also difficult to deal with.

We had hoped to have had the first units of the British Pacific Fleet on that station early in December. There was no longer any need to keep a strong force of battleships and fleet aircraft-carriers in the East Indies. Older ships and a squadron of escort carriers were sufficient for the support of any operations there. But Admiral Nimitz asked that before coming into the Pacific the fleet's aircraft should attack Palembang, the centre of the petroleum sector in the south of Sumatra. This was probably a move by the Americans to delay the arrival of our fleet, maybe for logistic reasons. Anyhow, as it was impossible to attack Palembang during December because of the weather, the fleet was delayed until January. Perhaps it was all for the good, as it gave the carriers more time to exchange their older type aircraft for the new Avengers.

At the end of 1944 another conference was in the wind between Mr. Churchill, President Roosevelt and Marshal Stalin. Certainly there were many problems that could best be settled round a table. There were differences of opinion as to where the conference should be held, and Stalin could not be persuaded to come west. However, on Christmas Eve, which was a Sunday, the Prime Minister rang me up at Bishops Waltham and told me the President had suggested meeting at Yalta at the end of January. Would I let him have a report on the place! Beyond the fact that Yalta was in the Crimea I could not enlighten him.

To revert to a personal topic, on December 12th at 5.30 p.m., I attended a meeting of the War Cabinet with the other Chiefs of Staff. After our discussion we met Eisenhower and Tedder in the map-room where the former explained his future intended operations against Germany. Later we all dined with the Prime Minister, and the talk ranged over many subjects. In reply to a short speech by Mr. Churchill, Eisenhower said that after the war he was going to resign and devote himself to the fostering of good relations between his great country and ours. He told us, too, of the almost fabulous sums he had been offered to write a book and newspaper articles.

We did not break up until 1.30 a.m., and as we were leaving the Prime Minister called me alone into the Cabinet room. He first asked if I was of Scottish ancestry, which I was easily able to confirm. He then said he had been looking into the precedence of the various Orders of Knighthood, and asked if I knew anything about the Order of the Thistle. I replied that it was one of the most ancient and honourable of all the Orders, and Scotland's own.

He then said it was his intention to recommend to His Majesty that I should be created a Knight of the Thistle. It was so unexpected that I was rather at a loss for words; but realizing that the honour was even more a compliment to the Navy than it was to me, I thanked him warmly. I could remember no naval officer outside the Royal Family who had ever received this great distinction.

Mr. Churchill was obviously dead tired. After our short talk he drank a cup of soup and turned to a pile of papers on his writing-table. I begged him to stop work and to go to bed. But he would not.

It was thus that my name appeared in the Honours List on New Year's Day, 1945.

CHAPTER XLVI

I

THE New Year of 1945 saw the beginning of the end in Europe and the dawn of victory in the East.

By about the middle of January, after fierce fighting, Runstedt's offensive in the Ardennes had been defeated, and he had been pressed back practically to his starting point. He had suffered some 120,000 casualties, with heavy losses in tanks, guns, aircraft and vehicles. Largely through the Allied bombing, his reserves of oil and fuel for aircraft and mechanical transport were seriously depleted.

The Russian offensive all along the eastern European front which started in January was sweeping all before it.

In October, 1944, British troops had been landed for the liberation of Greece. It is no part of my business to go into any details of the political rivalry which hampered the task of restoring Greek independence, and caused considerable bloodshed. It was a tragedy that British troops and British ships sent to liberate the country and to help to restore law and order should have been drawn into the conflict on the side of the Greek Government through the necessity of dealing with the terrorist minority represented by E.A.M., of which E.L.A.S. was the military combatant force and E.L.A.N. the naval. But if the rebels chose to fight for power I suppose there was no alternative. We were greatly relieved when a settlement of sorts was reached between the Greek Government and E.A.M., which relieved British troops of the unwelcome task of fighting their late allies in what was virtually a civil war.

The Navy suffered a heavy loss in the death of Admiral Sir Bertram Ramsay on January 2nd. Taking off to fly to England in snowy weather his aeroplane stalled and crashed on the airfield. All in it were killed.

Bertie Ramsay had been my friend for years. He was a fine sailor and a magnificent organizer, and a man of the highest integrity with great personal charm of manner. He had retired from the Service before the war when Chief of Staff in the Home Fleet through a difference of opinion with his Commander-in-Chief on a matter of principle. Rejoining the Service at the outbreak of war, he was appointed Flag Officer at Dover and first came into prominence for his magnificent work and organization in evacuating our shattered Army from Dunkirk, a task in which anyone might have failed without discredit. As we have seen, he was responsible for the earlier plannings for the landings in North Africa in November, 1942, while his services as my deputy in England in the course of those operations were invaluable. He was our Naval Commander for the British landings in Sicily in July, 1943, and the overall Naval Commander for the Allied landings in Normandy in June of the next year. For Dunkirk, Sicily and Normandy his name should be remembered.

He was buried in France, and on January 8th I flew to Versailles to be present at the funeral. I walked with Eisenhower in the procession. It was a simple, moving ceremony in the snow-covered cemetery in which all the five who had been in the aircraft were buried at the same time.

Our return journey by air remains in my mind. We ran into snowstorms, and were diverted to Christchurch instead of London. Reaching London by car at about 11.30 p.m. I was met with a message that the Prime Minister wished to see me. I settled with him that Vice-Admiral Sir Harold Burrough should relieve Ramsay as Naval Commander, though at first Mr. Churchill had wished to abolish the appointment. But it was obvious enough that a responsible officer of high rank was still required to deal with the opening up of ports and the supply of the Army by sea. Moreover, it was expected that Emden, Bremen, Hamburg, Kiel and other German ports would soon be in our hands, while we should also have to cope with the eventual surrender and disposal of the German navy and naval establishments.

The Admiralty's principal headache at this period was a renewal of the enemy's submarine activity. Between fifty and sixty U-boats were still operating, their main effort being concentrated inside the Irish Sea, where they sank five merchant ships during January and damaged two more. The Schnorkel boats being difficult to detect either by radar or asdic, all we could do for the moment was to press on with our policy of laying defensive minefields. The new German one-man and two-man submarines, the Bibers and Seehundes, were also becoming a nuisance in the eastern end of the Channel and off the Dutch and Belgian coasts, particularly in the approaches to the Scheldt and Antwerp. However, they were being well dealt with by our patrols. In other areas U-boats of the older type were still fairly widespread, having appeared in the Arctic, off Halifax, and in the western approaches to the Straits of Gibraltar. So the submarine campaign was by no means won, while we were aware that the Germans were mass-producing boats of an even deadlier type of very long range and high under-water speed.

In the Chiefs of Staff Committee the Italian campaign was under constant review, with two conflicting opinions. Ours was to keep as many troops as possible in Italy to persist in the final defeat of the Germans there and the subsequent Allied occupation of Austria; while the United States Chiefs of Staff were anxious to withdraw troops from the Italian theatre to reinforce the Armies in France.

Meanwhile the preparations for 'Argonaut', another conference between the 'Big Three', went on steadily. The plan was for us to meet the Americans in Malta before going on to the Crimea, and President Roosevelt was coming to the island in the American cruiser *Quincy*.

On January 29th we, the three Chiefs of Staff, left Northolt by air in our York. We reached Malta in just under six hours, which for those days was good going. I was put up at Admiralty House by John Cunningham, where James Somerville, from Washington, was also staying. Brooke and Portal, with General Sir Henry Maitland Wilson, Supreme Commander in the Mediterranean theatre, were accommodated by the Governor, Lieutenant-General Sir Edward Schreiber, at San Anton Palace. The three American Chiefs of Staff had already arrived. That night, through some grave mischance, the aircraft bringing out some of the staff, including Brooke's personal assistant, crashed on Lampedusa. It was a sad business.

The Prime Minister arrived by air on the morning of the 30th, and was accommodated in the cruiser *Orion* in the Grand Harbour. Mr. Eden and Mr. Stettinius, the United States Secretary of State, who arrived later, were lodged on board the *Sirius*.

We had offices in the Castille, close to the old naval offices which had been badly damaged during the bombing. Our preliminary meetings with the United States Chiefs of Staff passed off satisfactorily. We discussed all aspects of the war, including the shipping situation, the U-boat campaign, and, among other things, the transfer of air forces from Italy to the Western Front. On February 1st there was disagreement between General Marshall and Brooke on the subject of the conduct and strategy of the campaign in the west. I will not go into the points at issue, already described by Eisenhower in his book;[1] but at the time I thought that Marshall's complaint was not unjustified. I notice in the book that some weeks later Brooke told Eisenhower that he was glad he, Eisenhower had stuck to his plans. At a time when the defeat of Germany was in view by the combined effort and sacrifice of all the Allies, we wanted no disagreement as to how victory should be achieved.

We could not avoid the usual round of official dinners during our short stay at Malta, and one I particularly remember was that given by John Cunningham at Admiralty House, at which the United States Chiefs of Staff; Bedell Smith, Eisenhower's Chief of Staff; Alan Brooke; Maitland Wilson; Admirals Stark and Hewitt; Lord Leathers, and many others were present. The old house looked its best, for my namesake, the Commander-in-Chief, had brought out all the old furnishings that we had left in 1940. It would have delighted the heart of my wife to have seen it, for she was mainly responsible. With Mr. Bellizzi conducting the Commander-in-Chief's string orchestra it was like the old days before the war.

Our American naval friends were much impressed with it all. One Admiral, looking at the tablet in the hall with the names of all the naval Commanders-in-Chief in the Mediterranean dating back to seventeen hundred and something, said to me: "It needs a British Admiral to live up to a place like this." I felt complimented, for here, in Malta, there was antiquity. And there is something

[1] See Eisenhower's *Crusade in Europe* (William Heinemann) pages 404-410.

in tradition as it applies to the Royal Navy. Among the names on that tablet are those of Lord Hood; John Jervis, later the Earl of St. Vincent; Lord Keith; Nelson; Collingwood, and a host of others of lesser repute. In the sixteenth century, during the reign of the Knights of St. John, Admiralty House had been occupied by the Captain of the Galleys.

President Roosevelt arrived in the *Quincy* on February 2nd, and late that afternoon we had a plenary session on board at which the Prime Minister was present. I was quite shocked at the appearance of Mr. Roosevelt, who looked very frail and worn out.

We flew off from Malta just before 1 a.m. on the 3rd, and after a fairly comfortable flight, relieved at times by sucking oxygen, landed at Eupatoria, in the Crimea, at 7.30 a.m. our time, or 9.30 Russian. We were received by M. Molotov and various Russian Admirals and Generals. After a snack in a tent, we drove over the mountains to Alupta, arriving at 2.30 to find ourselves housed in a villa originally belonging to Prince Vorontsov, a sort of Scottish baronial mansion with a Moorish admixture. The house had served as Manstein's headquarters when the Germans were fighting in the Crimea, and had been presented to Manstein by Hitler as a reward for his services. He was so anxious to preserve it that he held on to the last minute when every other house and villa was being blown up, so the Russians got it back more or less intact. The library, which we Chiefs of Staff used as an office, was still filled with books, mostly French. Curiously enough, I found a history of Hampshire with a description of the old Palace at Bishop's Waltham, the ruins of which are in the grounds of my house.

Our villa soon became very crowded, with more and more people constantly arriving. The bathrooms, I remember, were few and far between. But any discomforts that we suffered were as nothing to those of the juniors, who were herded into two sanatoria.

There was a plenary meeting next day, February 4th, at the American villa, which had originally belonged to the Czar. The President, the Prime Minister and Marshal Stalin were all present, and Mr. Roosevelt was requested to take the chair. Stalin asked for an explanation of the operations on the Western Front, which was given by General Marshall. Stalin then spoke about the Russian offensive, and said it had been launched earlier than intended as a comradely counterblast to Runstedt's offensive in the Ardennes. He went on to say that the Allies had only to ask, and the Russian Army would do all in its power to help. Mr. Roosevelt spoke, and was followed by a brilliant discourse from Mr. Churchill. But nobody really took up the point that we had only to ask the Russians for what we needed, so when it came to my turn to speak on the U-boat situation, I finished by telling Stalin that he would make a striking contribution to the war at sea if the gallant Red Army would push on and capture Danzig, where many of the new-type submarines were being built. This suggestion seemed to cause general hilarity, and the Prime

Minister laughed heartily. However, he later congratulated me on saying what I had. The Russians were never very sea-minded.

I need not go into all the matters discussed between the 'Big Three', or at the various meetings between the Chiefs of Staff of the three countries. They are all ancient history, though I recollect that Admiral King still seemed averse to the British fleet operating with the American in the Pacific, in spite of the fact that its co-operation had been asked for by Admiral R. A. Spruance, commanding the United States 5th Fleet, shortly to be employed in the amphibious assault upon Okinawa, in the Ryukyu Islands, the chain of islands between Japan and Formosa. King gave it as a reason that he was still uncertain about General MacArthur's future operations.

Marshal Stalin gave a big dinner to all the visitors, which, though by no means lacking in hospitality and good feeling, was an exhausting function. Molotov had been put in charge of the toasts, which ran into nearly fifty. The Prime Minister was in his usual good form; but the President looked very ill. I sat next to Mr. Stettinius, and immediately opposite me was a saturnine, very Jewish-looking man who I was told was head of the O.G.P.U. I particularly noticed that he listened very carefully to all that was said, and drank all the toasts in lemonade or mineral water. Behind Stalin's chair was a regular giant of a man wearing a black alpaca jacket who occasionally helped with the waiting and sometimes advised the great man what to eat and drink. He may have been Stalin's personal bodyguard; but the next day, unless my eyes deceived me, he appeared in a General's uniform while some group photographs were being taken.

One day we had the chance of visiting Sevastopol, a drive of about three hours over mountainous country. We stopped two or three times to look at the old Crimean battlefields, the Alma, the scene of the charge of the light brigade at Balaklava, Inkerman, and the Redan and the Malakoff. Taken to the Naval Headquarters at Sevastopol we were met by three Russian Admirals and a General, all extremely pleasant. Then a General of Coast Artillery, through an interpreter, gave us a forty-minute talk on the eleven months heroic defence of the fortress by the Russian Army and Navy, and its final recapture by the Russians. It was a gallant feat of arms, and the fighting had been desperate. I had never seen a city so badly knocked about. Hardly a building was intact. On our way back we visited the cemetery where many of our Crimean dead lie buried. It had been held as a strong-point and fought over by both Russians and Germans. Most of the headstones were levelled.

We finally got away from Yalta by air on February 10th, reached Malta that afternoon, and took off again at 1.30 next morning. I spent an uncomfortable night. We flew at 12,000 feet, and I do not know whether my restlessness was caused by a lack of oxygen or a surfeit of Russian hospitality, particularly vodka and caviare. We landed at Northolt at 9.20 a.m. on the 11th, and I was glad enough to drive straight home to Bishop's Waltham with the prospect of a quiet night in bed. I went to London next afternoon, and that evening went into a clinic for an operation on my right eye. It was successful and I was allowed out on bail, though it was not until the 19th that I was back at my desk at the Admiralty with my left eye doing the duty of both.

II

I feel I have not said enough about the work of the Royal Navy in the Indian Ocean during 1944. We had greatly reinforced Admiral Somerville's Eastern Fleet, and in January of that year it had returned to Ceylon with its main base at Trincomalee. It consisted of the battleships *Queen Elizabeth* and *Valiant*, the battle-cruiser *Renown*, the *Illustrious*, two escort carriers, together with a number of destroyers, escort vessels and submarines.

To give a brief summary, there were insufficient escorts to run all the Indian Ocean shipping in convoys. There were about six German U-boats operating from Penang, with a few Japanese submarines also on the prowl. Japanese naval forces were also at Singapore, and there was always the chance that warships or fast raiders might appear in the Indian Ocean. But the submarines were causing serious losses, particularly near Ceylon and around Socotra, Cape Guardafui and Aden in the approaches to the Red Sea. In the first quarter of 1944 we lost some thirty merchant vessels in the Indian Ocean.

Our own submarines and the long-range aircraft of the Royal Air Force were waging a constant war against Japanese shipping in the Straits of Malacca, along the coast of Burma and in the Java Sea. But in April Somerville's Eastern Fleet, which had been reinforced by the French battleship *Richelieu*, the American aircraft-carrier *Saratoga* and two destroyers, with Dutch, Australian and New Zealand units, was off on an offensive mission of its own designed to serve as a diversion to the American offensive in New Guinea. The Japanese naval base at Sabang, in the north of Sumatra, was successfully attacked by aircraft from the *Illustrious* and *Saratoga*, oil tanks being set ablaze, shipping and shore installations badly hit, and aircraft destroyed in the air and on the ground. There was virtually no counter-action on the part of the enemy.

Somerville was again at sea in May when, passing south of the Cocos Islands, he took his fleet to the Exmouth Gulf, in Western Australia, re-fuelled there, and returned to strike Surabaya, in Java, with his carrier-borne aircraft, causing great damage. During June, Port Blair, in the Andamans, was successfully bombed by the *Illustrious's* aircraft, and bombarded from the sea, by a force under Vice-Admiral Sir Arthur Power, Somerville's second-in-command.

Our Eastern Fleet, as it was called in those days, was energetically used in carrying the war into Japanese-held territory.

In August, 1944, Admiral Sir Bruce Fraser, Commander-in-Chief designate of the British Pacific Fleet, relieved Somerville in command. Fraser flew home to England for consultation in October; but was back in Ceylon by mid-November, and on the 22nd became Commander-in-Chief, British Pacific Fleet. Hoisting his flag in the *Howe* on December 2nd he sailed for Australia, and in January, 1945, flew to Pearl Harbour to confer with Admiral Chester W. Nimitz, Commander-in-Chief of the United States Pacific Fleet. On the 15th of that month he reported to Nimitz from Sydney: "I hereby report for duty in accordance with Octagon decision. The British Fleet will look forward to fighting alongside the United States Fleet in whatever area you may assign us." ('Octagon', I should add, was the code-name for the Quebec Conference of September, 1944.)

Vice-Admiral Sir Arthur Power became Commander-in-Chief, East Indies Fleet, on November 22nd, and under his able and energetic direction the offensive continued.

In October 1944, the Navy was supporting the Fourteenth Army in its difficult advance along the Arakan coast of Burma for the final object of recapturing the port of Rangoon.

To anticipate, Akyab was occupied without opposition on January 3rd, 1945, and Ramree Island, some fifty miles down the coast, with its airfield, was in our hands by February 22nd. Very few of the Japanese garrison escaped.

Mandalay was taken by the Army on March 20th, and after further amphibious operations Rangoon was occupied on May 3rd. I had been in some doubt about this latter operation because the difficulties of navigation and the terrain at the mouth of the river greatly favoured the defence; but my pessimism was unfounded.

Meanwhile other ships of the East Indies Fleet, reinforced on occasion by the aircraft-carriers passing through on their way to the Pacific, were repeatedly striking at the Japanese outports and airfields in the Nicobar and Andaman Islands, and the oil refineries in Sumatra. Destroyers were soon carrying out sweeps east of the Andaman and Nicobar Islands and along the Tenasserim coast of Burma to isolate the enemy garrisons and cut off their supplies by sea, while British submarines were ranging all through the Malacca Straits and Java Sea, destroying shipping and laying mines. They had almost incredible adventures during their long cruises in those tropical waters, and the endurance and resource of their young officers and men was beyond all praise.

There was much to be done over a very wide area, and in 1945 all the ships of the East Indies Fleet, particularly a squadron of escort-carriers commanded by Rear-Admiral G. N. Oliver, and the destroyers and small craft, were used to the limit of their capacity.

The greater portion of the Japanese fleet was engaged against the Americans; but the enemy had left some cruisers and destroyers at Singapore. On May 15th an enemy heavy cruiser with a destroyer was sighted and attacked by aircraft in the Straits of Malacca. The nearest surface force consisted of five destroyers of the 26th Flotilla, commanded by my late staff officer, Captain Manley L. Power, in the *Saumarez*, with the *Venus*, *Vigilant*, *Virago* and *Verulam* in company. When the report was received Power at once went on to full speed to intercept. He was in contact with the enemy by radar off Penang at about midnight, and the destroyers went in to attack with torpedoes. Hit eight times, the 10,000 ton *Haguro*, armed with ten 8-inch guns, was sent to the bottom. The destroyer with her was damaged. Our damage and casualties were fortunately light. It was a dashing and smart piece of destroyer work which greatly pleased me.

Another Japanese heavy cruiser, the *Ashigara*, was sunk by the submarine *Trenchant* off Singapore on June 8th. On the last day of July the 10,000-ton cruiser *Takao*, lying at her moorings in the Johore Strait, Singapore, was most gallantly attacked and damaged by Lieutenant I. E. Fraser, R.N.R. and Leading Seaman J. J. Magennis in a midget submarine. They first had to make their way through the enemy minefields, and then to creep along the bottom. Reaching the cruiser there was just room for the submarine to be forced under her bottom, and attaching the explosive charges was a matter of great difficulty Fraser and Magennis faced certain execution if captured, and for their cold-blooded bravery they were both awarded the Victoria Cross.

III

March, 1945, at home saw a further increase in the U-boat activity, their greatest energy being concentrated in British coastal waters; but with a few boats working off Newfoundland and Nova Scotia, with others near Iceland and in the eastern part of the North Atlantic. Our losses during the month in all areas were fifteen merchant vessels, of which twelve were sunk in British waters or the English Channel, three by midget submarines. We were having success against the submarines, for March saw the destruction of no fewer than thirty-four, sixteen by the heavy bombers of the United States Air Force in their attacks on Hamburg, Wilhelmshaven and Bremen. This was all to the good. All the same, the loss of shipping in home waters, most of it engaged in supplying the Army on the Continent, was disquieting.

The Germans were starting to totter. Their final defeat depended upon our maintaining an uninterrupted flow of supplies to the Allies. Accordingly, I started collecting all the destroyers and escort vessels I could lay my hands upon, including six 'Hunt' class destroyers from the Mediterranean. I also gave orders that all refits were to be postponed, and that even ships with only one propeller working were to continue to run. Everything must be sacrificed to holding the U-boats during the next few months.

CHINA
KARACHI
INDIA
BOMBAY
CALCUTTA
CHUNGKING
MANDALAY
ARAKAN
BURMA
HANOI
HONG KO
HAINAN
RANGOON
SIAM
CHINA
SEA
TRINCOMALEE
COLOMBO
CEYLON
ANDAMAN Is.
NICOBAR Is.
INDO CHINA
SAIGON
SABANG
PENANG
MALACCA STR.
MALAYA
LABUAN
BRUNEI
BR. N.
SARAWAK
SINGAPORE
SUMATRA
BORNEO
JAVA
SOERABAJA
NETHERLANDS EAST INDIES
LIMIT OF JAPANESE INVASION
INDIAN OCEAN
N
EXMOUTH GULF
Bip Pares

THE EAST INI

KOREA
TOKYO
JAPAN
N
SHANGHAI
OKINAWA
SAKISHIMA
FORMOSA
PACIFIC
OCEAN
PHILIPPINES
ULITHI
TRUK
PALAU Is.
EQUATOR
MANUS
ADMIRALTY Is.
NEW GUINEA
CELEBES
AMBOINA
TIMOR
DARWIN
CORAL SEA
AUSTRALIA

AND PACIFIC

The Armies were on the move again in February with the object of destroying the Germans west of the Rhine and occupying the western bank of the river. Though there was some difficulty in by-passing the enemy in the Netherlands because the civil population was on the verge of starvation, the operations went well, and by March 6th the Allies were pretty well near the line of the river. On March 7th, after a rapid and spectacular drive, American forces under General C. H. Hodges seized the Ludendorff Bridge over the Rhine at Remagen. It was still more or less intact, and reinforcements were rushed across. My March 23rd, a division of General Patton's Third Army was over the river south of Mainz, and three days later units of General Patch's Seventh Army had made a crossing just south of Worms. Meanwhile, after severe fighting on March 23rd and 24th, Montgomery's Twenty-first Army Group, supported by British and American Airborne Divisions, had forced a crossing of the river in the north near Wesel. In all of these hard-fought operations the Allied Air Forces had played a most important part.

The Rhine was a formidable obstacle, particularly in the north where it was wide and swiftly-flowing, and the enemy could raise the water level and increase the strength of the current by opening the dams along the eastern tributaries. The crossing was not unlike the shore-to-shore landing across the Straits of Messina, for until damaged bridges could be repaired or pontoon bridges built, troops, tanks, guns and supplies had to be ferried over the river.

The Allied Navies had been called upon to assist. Small landing-craft had been sent to the front, some of these vessels, 45 feet long and 14 feet wide, being brought forward by water, though by far the greatest number went by road in tank transporters, with their naval crews and equipment. British landing-craft under the command of Captain P. H. G. James, Royal Navy, did remarkable work during the crossing of the Rhine by Montgomery's Twenty-first Army Group, and were also of great utility for towing sections of pontoon bridges and many other odd jobs. Small naval parties had also been sent forward for the Rhine crossing to prevent the use by the enemy of midget submarines, explosive boats and saboteur swimmers.

On the lower Rhine and the West Scheldt estuary another naval force under Captain A. F. Pugsley, Royal Navy, was responsible for the sea flank of our Armies. Using assault craft they carried out a number of raids against enemy positions which were almost uniformly successful. Naval craft of Pugsley's and James's flotillas took part in the final crossings of the Rhine when the Canadian Army advanced westward into Holland.

Apart from the regular replenishment of the Army by sea, the Allied Navies were also responsible for the working of the ports through which flowed the main stream of supplies. At the end of March about 10,000 tons of stores a day were being landed at Antwerp for the British, and 20,000 tons for the Americans, while the main personnel traffic passed through Ostend and Calais for the British, and Havre for the Americans.

With the crossing of the Rhine in the west, and the rapid advance of the Russians in the east, the end for Germany was very near.

IV

I have already mentioned the measures to deal with the threat of the German U-boats; but our difficulties at the Admiralty during these early months of 1945 lay also in the administrative field. We were trying to carry out two tasks which were largely incompatible; to reduce our naval manpower, and simultaneously to man and supply our Pacific Fleet.

Added to this we had the constant strain of striving against the firm desire of the United States Naval Authorities in Washington to keep our fleet away from the fighting in the Pacific. Some rather injudicious statements on our side, and perhaps some calculated assertions on the part of certain American officers, raised rather a storm in the British press about the implication that our fleet was incapable of operating in the Pacific on terms of comparative equality with the American, particularly in the matter of supply. The controversy was eventually stifled, largely because of a statement by Admiral Nimitz, Commander-in-Chief of the United States Pacific Fleet, intimating that the active co-operation of our fleet would be welcome. Nevertheless, the feeling persisted that we were not wanted, and our request to establish our own advanced base in the Philippines was pronounced impossible.

Here I should say that the ships and men of the Royal Australian Navy had long since worked in close contact with the Americans. They had fought gallantly in many actions.

However, by the end of February, 1945, the British Pacific Fleet had concentrated at Sydney—the battleships *King George V* and *Howe*; the aircraft-carriers *Indomitable*, *Victorious*, *Illustrious* and *Indefatigable*, together with five cruisers and a dozen or more destroyers. Ships of the Fleet Train, with their covering and escort forces, had arrived and were still arriving.

In the middle of March the fleet moved forward to Manus, in the Admiralty Islands, north of New Guinea, where the Americans had established a temporary naval base. They were most co-operative and helpful; but Manus was no health resort. The anchorage was spacious enough; but the torrid heat was enervating. As wrote Rear-Admiral Douglas Fisher, commanding the Fleet Train: "Manus weather is really lousy. It has rained like the devil for four to six hours every day, and latterly it has taken to blowing fairly hard. But the swell in the harbour is our worst enemy, and owing to this it has been really difficult getting the big ships fuelled, and all ships provisioned, ammunitioned and stored. . . . The prospect of having active work ahead is attractive and a great incentive. . . ."

Activity was not long in coming, for on March 18th, Admiral Rawlings' Task Force 57, consisting of the ships already mentioned, sailed north from Manus for Ulithi, another American temporary naval base in the Palau Islands, not far from Yap, between the Caroline Islands and the Philippines. Rawlings had already received a heartening message from Admiral Nimitz: "The British Carrier Task Force and attached units will greatly increase our striking power and demonstrate our unity of purpose against Japan. The U.S. Pacific Fleet welcomes you."

Ulithi was reached on March 20th, and the fleet refuelled from American sources. Two days later Rawlings reported to Admiral Spruance, commanding the American 5th Fleet, that his ships would be ready for duty in the early morning of the 23rd. Admiral Spruance replied: "Welcome T.F.57. Good hunting. . . ."

Task Force 57 sailed from Ulithi at 7.15 on the morning of March 23rd. Hopes ran high. After months of uncertainty, laborious organization and much hard work, our British Pacific Fleet had at last been detailed to play its definite part in the war against Japan. The code word for the operation was 'Iceberg'—the seizure of Okinawa, the most important of that long necklace of the Ryukyu islands stretching in the arc of a circle between Japan and Formosa which provided the enemy with an almost complete chain of airfields covering the Eastern Sea and the southern approaches to Japan. Okinawa had powerful defences and a strong garrison. It lies roughly three hundred and fifty miles from the Japanese mainland. Its airfields were required for carrying the war into the enemy's homeland.

Admiral Spruance was in naval command of the American Fifth Fleet engaged in the operations. Rawlings' Task Force was to support the preparatory air and sea bombardments and the main assaults by guarding their southern flank and neutralizing as continuously and for as long as possible the Japanese airfields in the Sakishima group, roughly two hundred miles to the southwestward.

The destroyers were refuelled from tankers of the Fleet Train, which had been met at sea, and also from both battleships, on the way to the operational area, the work being considerably impeded by a strong north-easterly wind and swell. This completed, Rawlings pushed on at $23\frac{1}{2}$ knots, and at sunrise on March 26th, from a position 100 miles south of their targets, strong fighter sweeps were flown off from Vian's four carriers to attack the airfields on the islands of Ishigaki and Miyako. Bomber strikes were flown off later.

After very severe fighting, the enemy's organized resistance in Okinawa did not finally cease until June 21st. During this period the *King George V* and *Howe*, with Vian's aircraft carriers, the cruisers and destroyers, together with ships of the Fleet Train and their escort and covering forces, were continuously at sea from March 23rd to April 23rd, a period of thirty-two days, and again from May 1st to May 31st, thirty days. The eight-day interval was spent at the American naval base at San Pedro Roads, Leyte in the Philippines, making good defects, fuelling, ammunitioning and storing from ships of Rear-Admiral Douglas Fisher's Fleet Train. Of him, Fisher, Admiral Fraser wrote that his "successful servicing of the Fleet at sea and in harbour has been the admiration of all".

Rawlings gives a little picture of the conditions at Leyte:

> Boats were again very short and quite insufficient for libertymen to be landed. Since the libertymen could not get to the beer, I authorized the beer to be brought to them, the amount available allowing one bottle per day per head. This innovation proved immensely popular—and I have no doubt whatever that it was a great and well-deserved boon in a period of hard work in great heat. . . . The heat and lethargic effect of the climate which being drier was not quite so marked as at Manus, made conditions very trying for personnel employed, between and below decks, on maintenance, boiler cleaning, etc. Much work of this type had to be done at great speed, and personnel concerned did well. Office work, occasioned by the inevitable influx of correspondence after such a long period at sea, was no less trying. There was, in fact, little time for rest or relaxation for officers or ratings during this period, and after a day or two most of us, I feel sure, wished ourselves back at sea again.

I cannot give any adequate impression of the work carried out by the ships under the command of Rawlings and Vian during this total period of sixty-two days spent in alternate air operations against the enemy and refuelling and storing at sea; but in all, air strikes from the British carriers were launched on twenty-one days.

However, after the first series of successful attacks which started on March 26th, the Japanese were not slow to retaliate, particularly with their Kamikazes, or suicide bombers. In the early morning of April 1st, after an enemy aircraft had machine-gunned both the *Indomitable* and *King George V*, an enemy 'plane dived into the base of the *Indefatigable*'s island structure, killing or wounding thirty officers and men and putting the flight deck temporarily out of action. Within a commendably short time her aircraft were again being operated. Shortly afterwards the destroyer *Ulster* was near-missed by a bomb and had to be towed to Leyte. That evening another Kamikaze dived into the *Victorious*, which was under full helm. One wing of the 'plane touched the flight deck, and it spun harmlessly into the sea where the bomb exploded. A similar incident occurred when the *Illustrious* was attacked by a Kamikaze five days later.

On April 12th and 13th, aircraft from the British carriers varied their programme by attacking enemy airfields and other targets in northern Formosa. After more attacks upon the Sakishima group, the British Task Force reached Leyte on April 23rd.

Although it carries this narrative well beyond the surrender of Germany and other events yet to be described, I may as well briefly mention the operations of the British Pacific Fleet until June 7th, when it arrived at Sydney for major replenishment and refitting before co-operating with Admiral W. F. Halsey's Third United States Fleet in its attacks upon the Japanese mainland.

Sailing from Leyte on May 1st, May 4th found the British Task Force 57 back in the operational area off the Sakishima group. By this time the *Illustrious* had been relieved by the *Formidable*, and the cruiser *Argonaut* by the Canadian-manned *Uganda*. The New Zealand-manned *Gambia* took part in both phases of the operations, with the British *Swiftsure*, *Euryalus* and *Black Prince*.

Shortly after noon on May 4th, after the usual air strikes during the morning, Rawlings, with his two battleships, five cruisers and six destroyers, parted company with the aircraft-carriers for a bombardment of the airfields at Miyako, the northernmost of the Sakishima islands. The conditions were excellent, and the attack was decided upon because it was desirable to knock out the anti-aircraft guns ashore, and also because, as Rawlings wrote: "the effect on the morale of ships of the bombarding force would be most beneficial." The runways and A.A. defence area were well hit, and there was no enemy retaliation.

It was shortly before noon on this day that the *Formidable* was hit by a Kamikaze which crashed into the flight deck near the island structure, having released its bomb just before striking. The *Formidable* had eight killed and forty-seven wounded, in addition to which a fire started on deck destroying eleven aircraft. Apart from other damage, the flight deck was holed and indented, and the ship's speed was reduced by a splinter of the armoured deck which passed below to a boiler-room and finally pierced the inner bottom. A few minutes later another Kamikaze landed on the flight deck of the *Indomitable*, Vian's flagship, bounced over the side after doing some slight damage, where the bomb exploded after the 'plane submerged. Within a few minutes another suicider, badly hit, crashed in flames within ten yards of the *Indomitable's* bow. The fires in the *Formidable* were soon under control, and by about 1 p.m. she was capable of 24 knots. On May 6th she was fully operational, which was a very fine effort.

May 9th was another day of incidents. In the late afternoon another suicide 'plane, heavily hit, crashed on to the *Victorious's* flight deck. The resulting fire was soon under control; but the bomb explosion holed the flight deck and did other damage. About five minutes later she was hit by another Kamikaze, which glanced over the flight deck and went overboard, flaming furiously. Apart from other damage this 'plane destroyed four aircraft. It was surprising that in these two attacks the casualties were no more than three killed and nineteen wounded.

A minute later yet another suicider made a pass at the *Victorious*, and then shifted target to the *Howe*, farther ahead. Heavily hit, the aircraft passed over the battleship's quarter-deck and crashed in flames within a hundred yards.

Within eight minutes a fourth Kamikaze approached the *Formidable* and then the *Indomitable*, being engaged by both ships. The attacker then swerved and dived into the after deck park of the *Formidable*. There was a heavy explosion, followed by fire and heavy smoke. Speed had to be reduced for the flames to be dealt with; but they were extinguished within fifteen minutes. One man was killed and a few injured. Six aircraft were burnt out on deck, though another eleven were damaged in the hangar through blazing petrol streaming below after a rivet in the flight deck had been blown out by the explosion.

In spite of their severe experience both the *Victorious* and the *Formidable* continued to operate, though necessarily not at their full efficiency.

I need not mention the many strikes and incidents, the periods of fogs and bad weather, and the occasions when heavy bombs at the rate of seventy-five an hour were embarked by the carriers at sea from a ship of the Fleet Train by the whip and inhaul method. It was on the evening of May 25th that the British Task Force 57 left the operational area after its second spell of service. Calling at Manus on the way, most of the ships reached Sydney during the first week in June for repairs and replenishment before setting forth early in July for attacks upon the Japanese mainland in company with the Third United States Fleet under Admiral Halsey.

Soon after sailing Rawlings received a farewell message from Admiral Spruance, who signalled: "I would express to you, to your officers and men, after two months operations as a Fifth Fleet Task Force, my appreciation of your fine work and co-operative spirit. Task Force 57 has mirrored the great traditions of the Royal Navy to the American Task Forces." To this generous message Rawlings replied that he and all under his command were proud to have been in a position to lend a hand in a crucial operation, and hoped they might continue to do so until final victory.

I shall briefly describe the further operations of the British Pacific Fleet in the next chapter. In the meanwhile, in their first period of service while working under conditions which were wholly unfamiliar, our ships had gained much valuable experience. I have mentioned the Kamikaze attacks in some detail because it had been amply proved that the armoured flight-decks of our carriers enabled them to stand up to heavy punishment and still to continue to operate. Some of the more lightly-armoured American carriers had been set on fire and disabled when attacked in the same way.

As Admiral Fraser wrote in his covering despatch, printed with the reports of Rawlings and Vian in a Supplement to the *London Gazette* of June 1st, 1948:

> Doubt as to our ability to operate in the Pacific manner was somewhat naturally in American minds. This, however, was soon changed. The toll taken by the suicide bombers of the more lightly-armoured American carriers led to an increase in the proportionate effort of our carriers, and the evidence of American eyes that we could support ourselves logistically relieved their anxieties on that score. We have now, I am sure, become not only welcome but necessary in Central Pacific operations.

Fraser paid a justifiable tribute to Rawlings "inspiring leadership, resolution and fine judgment", while Rawlings wrote that the achievements of the carriers "derived directly from the sustained determination and leadership of Vice-Admiral Sir Philip Vian himself, for to him fell the conduct and handling of the Fleet during its most active periods."

At home, in the Admiralty, we were much gratified by the performance of our fleet in the Pacific.

CHAPTER XLVII

I

THE Allied cause suffered a heavy blow in the death of President Roosevelt on April 13th, 1945. I cannot attempt to describe a world figure of immense stature; but we, who had seen a lot of the President in our various meetings, felt we had lost not only a wise ally but a firm and whole-hearted friend of Britain. We remembered how greatly he and America had helped us in the dark days when Britain was fighting alone: his fight against the desire for 'isolationism' among his own countrymen; his 'neutrality patrol' in the Western Atlantic which so greatly curbed the activities of the U-boats in our hour of stress and fell not far short of armed conflict with Germany before war was declared; the fifty destroyers we had been given in the autumn of 1940 in return for sites for the creation of American bases in the West Indies, Bermuda and Newfoundland; the plentitude of financial and military aid so freely granted under 'lend lease'. In retrospect, I find it difficult to see how Britain could have survived without assistance from the other side of the Atlantic before the formal entry of the United States into the war after the Japanese attack upon Pearl Harbour on December 7th, 1941. Indeed, we have so much for which to be everlastingly grateful to the United States of America that it cannot be expressed in words. Much of that gratitude is due to Franklin Delane Roosevelt and his advisers for their wisdom and foresight in bringing home to the mass of their countrymen that after the fall of France, Britain, bleeding and impoverished, stood alone as a buttress against the Nazi domination of the civilized world.

I knew nothing of President Roosevelt as a politician. To me he was a man of great wisdom, charm of manner, humanity and simple kindness. He took a profound interest in the Navy, and in the days of his affliction collected stamps as a hobby and a relaxation. His quiet, unforgettable voice in those 'fireside talks' over the radio must have lifted the hearts of millions all over Britain and the Empire just as they did in America. I think it is right to say that our admiration and affection for the President of the United States of America were second only to the feelings we treasured for our own great leader, Mr. Churchill.

I do not mean to say that Britain and America always saw eye to eye in the conduct of the war when we came to fight as Allies. There were mistakes and hasty judgments on both sides, as perhaps this narrative has shown. Maybe we erred in criticizing the American desire to land in southern France in the summer of 1944, and Eisenhower's strategical conduct of the campaign in the north. On the other hand, we were beset by Admiral King's deeply-rooted aversion to the employment of the British Fleet in the Pacific, while I remember the vexation we were caused by the President's sudden offer to the Russians of one-third of the Italian fleet, which was made without previous consultation with us. In the meanwhile we had to lend Russia the battleship *Royal Sovereign*, four destroyers and four submarines, which we could ill afford.

But in spite of the occasional differences of opinion, the President was always the staunch friend of Britain. I have no doubt that his attitude gave encouragement to other great American leaders like General Eisenhower and Admiral Nimitz, to mention two out of the scores of others, to be equally helpful and friendly.

President Roosevelt wore himself out in the service of his country and her Allies in the greatest of all wars. The last time I saw him at Yalta he was obviously a very ill man. I wish he might have been spared to see the final triumph over Germany and Japan, of which he was one of the principal architects.

II

By the third week in April it was obvious that the war was over so far as Europe was concerned. Everywhere the German armies were breaking up, and by April 18th, the Ruhr pocket was finally eliminated with a total bag of about 325,000 prisoners. The Allied Armies drove on. However, the sequence of further events is so well-known that I need not repeat it. It is sufficient to say that an instrument for the unconditional surrender for all the German armies in Italy became operative at noon on May 2nd, while on May 4th, Montgomery reported that the unconditional surrender of all enemy forces in Holland, north-west Germany and Denmark, including Heligoland and the Frisian Islands, would become effective at 8 a.m. on May 5th. The unconditional surrender of Germany to the Western Allies and Russia was signed at General Eisenhower's headquarters at Rheims at 2.41 a.m. on May 7th, and operations ceased at 11.1 p.m. on May 8th.

The Russians made difficulties by refusing to recognize the signature of Eisenhower's headquarters and wanting it to be signed in Berlin by Marshal Zhukov. Indeed, Stalin did his best to have any announcement of the German surrender postponed until May 9th on the grounds that the fighting on the Russian front continued. This was resisted. The final act of capitulation with the German representative was 'ratified' in Berlin on May 9th with Air Chief Marshal Tedder signing for Great Britain; General Spaatz for the United States; Marshal Zhukov for Russia, and General de Lattre de Tassigny for France.

May 8th, V.E.-Day, was a day of some turmoil in London. At the

Admiralty we held a Board Meeting at noon, the principal business being the drinking of a bottle of Waterloo brandy produced by the First Lord, Mr. A. V. Alexander. At 4.30 p.m. we drove to Buckingham Palace to be present when His Majesty received the War Cabinet and the Chiefs of Staff. We had difficulty in getting there because of the dense throng of excited people round the Queen Victoria Memorial. For the same reason Mr. Churchill, recognized and mobbed by cheering citizens, was very late. The King made an excellent speech of appreciation, and the Prime Minister replied with his voice full of emotion.

I drove to the Air Ministry with Portal and had a cup of tea in his office, and then on to the Ministry of Health, where the Prime Minister, members of the War Cabinet and ourselves had to appear on the balconies. I have rarely seen such a crowd. Whitehall was packed from Trafalgar Square to Parliament Square. The Prime Minister said a few words, to which the mass of people reacted with wild enthusiasm. I was lucky to be able to dine quietly in our flat with my wife and my brother. Buckingham Palace and the Admiralty Arch were floodlit, and what with the noise of fireworks and the cheering crowds in the Mall flocking to Buckingham Palace to shout for the King, the Queen and the Princesses, there was little peace or quietness.

By the King's command the Navy had been ordered to 'splice the mainbrace' with the issue of an extra tot of rum. On the morrow there came a prompt rejoinder from James Somerville, head of the British Admiralty Delegation in Washington:

> Poor B. A. D. can splice no brace,
> Because of rum there is no trace.

James may or may not have been mollified for the lack of this staple item of naval sustenance by his promotion to Admiral of the Fleet.

However, quite apart from the war in the Pacific, we still had plenty to do and to think about at the Admiralty. Our immediate concern had to do with the U-boats still at sea. Hitler had committed suicide on April 30th, Admiral Dönitz being nominated as his successor. At 4.14 p.m. on May 4th the latter had ordered all U-boats to cease hostilities and return to base; but this did not prevent two Allied merchant vessels being sunk on May 7th within a mile of May Island, in the entrance to the Firth of Forth, by one of the new type U-boats with high under-water speed. However, immediately after the German capitulation, the Admiralty ordered the German High Command to give surrender orders to all the U-boats at sea. They were to surface, hoist black flags, report their position in plain language, and to proceed by fixed routes to designated ports and anchorages.

The first U-boat to obey surfaced off the Lizard on May 9th and was shepherded to Portland. On May 10th, U-532, which carried a cargo from Japan of 110 tons of tin, 600 tons of rubber, 8 tons of wolfram, 5 tons of molybdenum, and half-a-ton of quinine, surfaced near the Faroe Islands and was sent to Loch Erribol. Up till May 31st forty-nine U-boats had surrendered at sea, and by mid-September, by which time a fuller inventory was possible, one hundred and fifty-six German submarines had been surrendered to the Allies, and another two hundred and twenty-one had been scuttled or destroyed by their crews. Another eight had been dismantled, while seven others were in Japanese hands.

I will not burden this narrative with any analysis of the causes of the destruction of seven hundred and eighty-one German, eighty-five Italian, and one hundred and thirty Japanese U-boats during the war. The figures, however, which were presented to Parliament by the Admiralty in a White Paper of March, 1946 (Cmd. 6751), are interesting, so I have included them in the form of an appendix.

As the result of the German surrender, the Admiralty, and Admiral Sir Harold Burrough, who had become Allied Naval Commander-in-Chief, Expeditionary Force, on Sir Bertram Ramsay's death, had much on their minds. I can only mention a few of their manifold responsibilities.

Means had to be found of sending food in great quantity into Holland to prevent the starvation of the civil population, and the port of Rotterdam opened up to shipping. The Channel Islands had to be occupied, and about 22,000 Germans removed. In Germany itself Bremen, Wilhelmshaven, Cuxhaven, Hamburg, Kiel and other commercial or naval ports had to be occupied by naval parties and opened up to shipping. The Kiel Canal had to be cleared, and the surrender of Heligoland taken. Units of the German navy must be dealt with, and the naval dockyards, or what remained of them, taken over.

All this entailed a great deal of organization and a heavy drain upon our naval personnel, quite apart from the huge effort of the necessary extensive minesweeping, in which the Germans themselves were made to co-operate. Naval missions and personnel had also to be sent to Denmark and Norway for the same purposes.

All this miscellaneous work was not without incident. Rear-Admiral H. T. Baillie-Grohman, who was Flag Officer, Kiel, reported that V.E.-Day was anything but a public holiday for himself and his staff. Besides a constant influx of refugee ships from the Baltic, he had many interviews with German senior officers and had to cope with 4,000 German troops who landed at Eckernforde from landing-craft unaware that the war had ceased, and full of enthusiasm for continuing it.

Rear-Admiral G. C. Muirhead-Gould, Flag Officer, Wilhelmshaven, landed at my old haunt, Heligoland, on May 11th, and accepted its surrender. The island was devastated by bombing and almost uninhabitable; but a British naval party was left there in charge of a lieutenant-commander. The next day the British lieutenant-commander was forced to place the senior German naval officer under arrest for his obstructive conduct.

Rear-Admiral R. V. Holt, in Denmark, and Rear-Admiral J. S. M. Ritchie, in Norway, also had a wealth of interesting experiences.

Back in London, I was admitted an Honorary Freeman of the Fishmonger's Company, one of the most ancient of the London guilds, on May 14th. According to one book of reference members of these guilds were originally forbidden to wear beards or to play football. The first restriction can no longer apply. Admiral Sir Aubrey Smith, then Master of the Fishmongers, has been very neatly bearded in all the years I have known him.

In the Chiefs of Staff Committee we were discussing the future of the war against Japan. Ever since the previous November strong forces of land-based American Super-Fortresses and carrier planes, had been bombing targets in the Japanese main islands. The raids had increased in violence on Tokyo, Yokohama, Nagoya, Osaka, Kobe, Nagasaki and other cities; on the naval bases and dockyards at Yokusuka, Kure and Sasebo; on oil refineries and aircraft plants. Attacks were being carried out by as many as three hundred to five hundred Super-Fortresses and six hundred to one thousand two hundred carrier aircraft at a time.

Towards the end of this month, in discussing the future of the war against Japan in the Chiefs of Staff Committee, we were glad to find that we could provide a military force of five British or Australian divisions and detachments of the Royal Air Force to co-operate in the great assault on the main Japanese islands that it was hoped to carry out late in 1945. I welcomed this move. It meant that all three Services would then be operating in the main theatre of hostilities.

But political considerations now began to disturb the even progress to complete victory. Japan still remained to be beaten, and the chief feeling in the Chiefs of Staff Committee was one of profound disgust that any political questions should be allowed to be raised while the war was still in progress. The dissolution of the Coalition Government had its effect in that our rulers became so occupied in political strife and argument that it was difficult to get decisions. Germany was already beaten. Japan was at the other end of the world, out of sight and largely out of mind.

The Coalition broke up on May 23rd, and the Conservatives came into power. Mr. Brendan Bracken became First Lord of the Admiralty in place of Mr. A. V. Alexander. Though Mr. Bracken was much occupied with the forthcoming general election during his short term of office, we obtained a satisfactory solution to the question of the Fleet Train in the Pacific. Under the arbitration of Sir John Anderson we were finally able to get all the ships we needed.

On June 11th, I was invited to become an Honorary Bencher of Lincoln's Inn, an honour I was proud to accept, and on the next day I was at the Guildhall when General Eisenhower received the Freedom of the City of London, a most dignified ceremony. Eisenhower's speech in reply greatly moved his audience. Some of them were actually in tears. He spoke again after the subsequent luncheon at the Mansion House, paying a fine tribute to his British colleagues in North Africa, France and elsewhere, and to Britain generally. His sincerity and complete lack of bombast or vanity were impressive. No wonder 'Ike' was so greatly loved by those who knew him.

Meanwhile, as there were many matters to be settled, it had been decided to hold another meeting of the Big Three at Potsdam. We, the three Chiefs of Staff, flew there on July 15th, to find ourselves accommodated in a villa on the shore of a lake, where we were greatly plagued by mosquitoes. Although the area was occupied by the Russians, each delegation had its own zone guarded by its own troops. The lake itself was patrolled by the Russians and one was liable to be fired upon if one ventured upon it. Brooke and Portal, who embarked in one of the boats belonging to the villa to see if there were any fish to be caught, were soon turned back.

I need hardly mention all our conferences and discussions; but at one of our meetings General Marshall told us of the atomic bomb test which had taken place in the New Mexico desert on July 16th, and a few days later informed us that President Truman and Mr. Churchill had agreed to its use against Japan on August 6th. I may say that the question of its use was not referred to the Combined Chiefs of Staff for an opinion, though looking back I think it is fair to say that if we had been consulted we British would have been in favour of using it. The invasion of Honshu, the central island of Japan, defended by some 975,000 regular troops and 7,000,000 of the home guard would have been a very tough proposition involving immense Allied casualties. Moreover, the dropping of an atom bomb and the resulting colossal devastation and casualties, would have given the Japanese a good excuse for surrendering, or any rate a good point upon which to base their surrender.

But looking back and being wise after the event, I think we rather failed to estimate the real significance of the heavy bombing attacks already being made upon Japan by shore-based and ship-borne aircraft. Admiral Halsey's powerful American fleet with its carriers, and the British Pacific Fleet, were operating practically unmolested off the Japanese coast—bombing and bombarding. Hardly a Japanese city was out of range of the swarming Allied bombers; no coastal town was immune from shelling. With all these devastating attacks, and Russian action in Manchuria, I think Japan would have surrendered without either invasion or the use of the atom bombs. I consider now that it was a pity and a mistake that we ever dropped them.

During our ten days near Potsdam I managed to pay visits to Berlin and Kiel. I need not describe the truly frightful destruction in the capital, but at Kiel the harbour seemed full of floating cranes, lighters, tugs and floating docks, sufficient to have provided Portsmouth, Plymouth and Chatham. The U-boat shelters were intact, and we saw one with about a dozen midget submarines and masses of parts. Every portion of the dockyard seemed to be littered with prefabricated parts of submarines. The *Hipper* was in dock, slightly damaged by our bombing, though more so by her own crew with depth-charges. The *Admiral Scheer* was capsized, and there were many other warships and numbers of merchant ships, mostly damaged. At the torpedo works at Eckernforde we saw a captured film of Dr. Walther's experiments with a 27-knot submarine of a special type with streamlined hull and very fast under water, and turbines as well as Diesel and electric propulsion. We then saw Dr. Walther himself, who demonstrated his fuel called 'Engelin', which I understand consisted of oxygen derived by the decomposition of hydrogen peroxide by a platinum process. I was supremely thankful that the war had ended when it did, and that no more than a handful of the new type U-boats had been completed. With their high submerged speed, they would have presented a serious problem for our convoy escorts.

There was a final dinner at the Prime Minister's house near Potsdam, attended by President Truman, Generalissimo Stalin, M. Molotov, Mr. Eden and many others, including the Chiefs of Staff of the three countries, and Field Marshals Alexander and Montgomery. We had the usual long list of speeches and toasts. We flew back to England on July 25th, myself with a few mementoes in the shape of what I hoped was a piece of Hitler's marble-topped desk from his shattered room in the Chancellery in Berlin; a handful of Iron Crosses and medals picked up from among the rubbish on the floor of another room; together with two books from one of the palaces at Potsdam, one a wild west novel with the book-plate of the ex-Crown Prince, and the other a signed copy of a book by Lord Charles Beresford presented to William II by the author.

At noon on July 26th, the day after our arrival, we realized there had been a landslide in the general election. Mr. Churchill and his party were out, and that evening Mr. Attlee was called upon to form a Government. We said farewell to Mr. Churchill next day. He was quite cheerful, though rather overcome with emotion when the time came to say good-bye.

On August 9th, after I had been away from London for a few days fishing in Scotland, I had a charming letter from Mr. Churchill starting "My dear Andrew", and going on to say that he had been granted the privilege of sending in his Resignation List of Honours. It was his "earnest desire that my three great friends the Chiefs of Staff should receive some recognition on my initiative of the work we have done together in these long and anxious years." He therefore hoped he might submit my name to the King for a Barony. I accepted.

I had seen a great deal of Mr. Churchill in many different environments and circumstances during my service as First Sea Lord and before. We had not always seen eye to eye, and had had our occasional disagreements and arguments. But never for a moment could I lose my profound admiration and respect for that most remarkable and courageous Englishman who by his energy, obstinacy and sheer force of character led Britain and her people through the greatest perils the country ever experienced. Who could forget his words over the radio, that speech of his when he told us he had nothing to offer but blood and sweat and tears? He was so pugnacious, so valiant, so filled with the spirit of offence, so unhesitant of risk if there was something to be gained, so ready to support anyone who took risks for some great object. He hated that hideous motto 'Safety First', which has always been anathema to me.

In a letter to him soon after he left office, I told Mr. Churchill that I could never forget the kindness and consideration he had shown to me when I first joined the Chiefs of Staff Committee as something of a novice, and how privileged and honoured I felt in having worked under him. I said, too, how very deeply I regretted that what, to me, was a most proud association, had not been permitted to continue until the end of the war.

Those words were not written in mere politeness; but from the bottom of my heart. I still think it was a calamity that a general election, with all its artificiality and political rancour, was forced upon us at the time it was. It divided our united country into two political camps at a period when victory was already in sight, and we needed all the strength and wise counsel we had at our disposal to accomplish the most difficult task of reconstruction after a devastating six years of hostilities.

III

To revert to the Far East, large American forces had landed on the island of Luzon, in the Philippines, on January 9th, 1945, and on July 5th General MacArthur announced that the whole of the islands had been liberated.

On May 1st, Australian troops, with small forces of Netherlands East Indies troops, had landed at Tarakan Island, off the north-east coast of Borneo, after bombardments and air attacks by the American 7th Fleet and ships of the Royal Australian Navy. On June 10th there were more Australian and American landings on the west coast of Borneo at Labuan and Brunei Bay. The airfield at Labuan was captured, and the troops entered Brunei town on June 13th. On the 20th of the same month Australian troops landed unopposed in Sarawak to capture the Seria oilfields, while on July 1st, after fifteen days of naval and air bombardment, Australian and Dutch troops were put ashore at Balikpapan, on the east coast of Dutch Borneo. Borneo was rapidly overrun by the Allies, and before long all the Japanese airfields and one of the richest sources of oil supply in the Netherlands East Indies were in our hands.

Similar progress had been made in New Guinea, where the Japanese concentrations were being hemmed in, while farther to the west ships of the

British East Indies Fleet were still hard at work. Between July 5th and 10th they were carrying out extensive minesweeping operations in the approaches to the Malacca Straits, while air attacks and bombardments from the sea were carried out on enemy installations in the Nicobar Islands. Carrier-borne aircraft were also attacking airfields in north-west Sumatra.

As Admiral Power wrote to me:

> As regards current operations, they are designed for training minesweepers and our fighter aircraft by going right over the enemy's waters. We are having considerable success in knocking their aircraft about, destroying locomotives and a few small ships, and at the same time keeping them guessing.[1] G. N. Oliver is just off on another run. . . . The number of aircraft we destroy is small, but when taken as a percentage of the total number of Japanese aircraft in S.E.A.C.,[2] it is very appreciable. I hope . . . the naval aircraft will have written off thirty per cent of the available Japanese aircraft. . . . . I am sure we can get shipping through the Singapore passages, even if they decide to fight and still occupy the island, when we possess the Straits of Malacca. I trust we shall not atomize Singapore in our haste to possess the place.

On July 24th, 25th and 26th, the British East Indies Fleet continued its offensive operations by shelling and bombing Japanese troop concentrations on the west coast of Malaya. Heavy damage was reported.

As regards the British Pacific Fleet, a force of cruisers and destroyers with two aircraft-carriers, under the command of Rear-Admiral E. J. P. Brind, bombarded and bombed the Japanese base at Truk, in the Caroline Islands, on June 14th and 15th.

On July 6th Rawlings' Task Force, consisting of his flagship, the *King George V*; Vian in the *Formidable*, with the *Victorious* and *Implacable*; the cruisers *Newfoundland*, *Black Prince*, *Euryalus*, H.M.N.Z.S.s *Achilles* and *Gambia*, H.M.C.S. *Uganda*; and five destroyers including one Australian, joined up with Admiral Halsey's Third United States Fleet for the assaults upon Japan. In their first attack on July 17th, 1,500 aircraft from the Allied carriers raided Tokyo, doing immense damage. That same night the battleships, including the *King George V*, shelled Hitachi and Sukegawa, on the coast some eighty miles north-east of Tokyo. After pressing home its attacks during bad weather the Allied fleet turned its attention to destroying the Japanese fleet. There were carrier-borne air strikes against the naval base at Yokosuka, in Tokyo Bay, on July 18th, in the course of which twelve warships were sunk and nine others, including the battleship *Nagato*, severely damaged.

Between July 23rd and 30th there were further heavy air attacks from the sea on the Japanese naval base at Kure, in the Inland Sea, and other cities

---

[1] Commanding the escort carriers.   [2] South-East Asia Command.

and targets along the enemy coast from Osaka to Nagoya. Long-range bombers from Okinawa co-operated. Apart from the other damage to airfields, shore establishments and oil refineries, these attacks provided the knock-out blow for the remnants of the Japanese fleet. Of the twelve battleships with which they had started the war eleven had been sunk and the other damaged. Fifteen of their twenty aircraft-carriers had been destroyed and four heavily damaged. Of eighteen heavy cruisers sixteen had been sunk and two damaged. Of twenty-two light cruisers twenty had been sunk and another damaged. There had been equal mortality among the destroyers and lighter craft, while in the fortnight ending July 23rd five hundred and fifty-six enemy aircraft were destroyed.

On the night of July 29th–30th Hamanatsu, on the south coast of Honshu, was bombarded for three and a quarter hours by American and British warships, with the ships, at one period, no more than three-quarters of a mile from the shore.

The first atomic bomb was dropped on Hiroshima on August 6th, and the second on Nagasaki on August 9th. On this latter date American and British warships bombed and shelled Kamaishi, on the north-east coast of Honshu. Their last attacks on the Japanese mainland were made in the early hours of August 15th, shortly before the cease fire order. Japan had accepted the Allied demand for unconditional surrender. August 15th, 1945, was V.J.-Day. The war was ended. Some of our ships which took part in the final operations against Japan had been continuously at sea for fifty-five days, all of them for more than forty.

On August 27th, Admiral Sir Bruce Fraser signalled to the Admiralty that our ships had anchored in Japanese waters, and by the 30th a large Allied Fleet had concentrated in Sagami Bay, near Tokyo. Admiral Nimitz was present with his flag in the battleship *South Dakota*, and Admiral Fraser in the *Duke of York*, he having been delegated to sign the formal instrument of surrender on behalf of Great Britain.

Most of the ships present were naturally American; but apart from his own flagship Fraser had with him in Japanese waters, Rawlings' *King George V*; the aircraft-carrier *Indefatigable*; Rear-Admiral Brind, in the *Newfoundland*, with the *Shropshire* and *Hobart* of the Royal Australian, and *Gambia* of the Royal New Zealand, Navies; the British destroyers *Wager*, *Whelp*, *Barfleur*, *Wrangler*, *Wakeful*, *Troubridge*, *Termagant*, *Tenacious*, *Terpsichore*, *Quality*, *Wizard*; the Australian destroyers *Warramunga*, *Nizam* and *Napier*; the escort carriers *Speaker* and *Ruler*; and eight escort vessels, together with ships of the Fleet Train.

The Japanese surrender was signed on board Admiral Halsey's flagship, the battleship *Missouri*, on September 2nd.

I need not describe the re-occupation of Hong-Kong by a British naval force under Vice-Admiral Harcourt on August 30th, and the subsequent surrender of the Japanese forces in Malaya, the Netherlands East Indies, British and Dutch Borneo, Burma, New Guinea and many outlying islands.

But after the first Japanese blow against the United States Fleet at Pearl Harbour in December, 1941; the enemy's occupation of the Philippines, Borneo, Malaya, the Netherlands East Indies, and his virtual destruction of the slender British, Dutch and United States naval forces in those areas, it is interesting to realize what made it possible for the Allies to achieve the victory against Japan in the face of initial disasters of such magnitude.

I would refer my readers to a masterly report by Fleet Admiral Chester W. Nimitz submitted to the Secretary of the Navy when he relinquished his appointment as Chief of Naval Operations of the United States Navy in December, 1947.[1]

> Naval forces (he wrote), have always played a vital and often deciding role in warfare by invading adjacent areas to project their pressure on enemy territory. . . . The development between World Wars I and II of naval aviation provided naval forces with a striking weapon of vastly increased flexibility, range, and power. . . . It spearheaded our Pacific attack. First, it swept the sea of all naval opposition. Then it became the initial striking weapon in the capture of Guam, Saipan, and Iwojima—the advanced bases from which long-range bombers were able to strike the vital centres of the Empire. Finally—our Navy—participated directly in the destruction of those vital centres on Okinawa and the home islands by gunfire and bombing; in spite of the concentration of Japanese airpower our Navy made possible the success of our gallant land forces. . . . In all these operations the employment of air-sea forces demonstrated the ability of the Navy to concentrate aircraft strength at any desired point in such numbers as to overwhelm the defence at the point of contact. These operations demonstrate the capability of naval carrier-based aviation to make use of the principles and mobility and concentration to a degree possessed by no other force. . . .

In short, as Admiral Sir Herbert Richmond wrote in his book *Statesman and Sea Power*: "Sea power did not win the war itself: it enabled the war to be won."

I know it may be foolish to envisage any future war fought in the same conditions as the last; but Admiral Nimitz clearly demonstrates that, in any operations against enemy territory far oversea, aircraft from carriers, which after all, are only highly mobile airfields, must still provide the spearhead of the assault in the absence of convenient bases for the operation of shore-based bombers of long range.

It has to be remembered, too, that Britain is not self-supporting in the

[1] Printed in *Brassey's Naval Annual*, 1948.

way of food, fuel and raw materials, which have to be carried by sea. The U-boats of 1939-45 were finally defeated by the combination of surface forces working in conjunction with shore-based and ship-borne aircraft. If war should come again, we might be faced with another U-boat campaign against our essential merchant shipping.

These, then, are two of the reasons why, in a world that is troubled, Britain still requires a Navy, and the Navy its Air Arm.

CHAPTER XLVIII

I

It was hard to realize that the War was really ended, though I was supremely thankful. Mentally tired after all the years of activity with no real respite, I felt rather like Collingwood when he was kept in the Mediterranean for five years after Trafalgar, and had a longing for his home in Northumberland. "Tell me how do the trees which I planted thrive?" he asked his wife in a letter. "Is there shade under the three oaks for a comfortable summer seat? Do the poplars grow at the walk, and does the wall of the terrace stand firm?" Like him I had a longing for a quiet life in my small house in the country.

Alan Brooke had already told me he intended to go at the end of the year, and I felt I should put in the few months necessary to start the sorting out of the Navy from a war to a peace footing, to arrange my successor, and then retire into private life. Meanwhile, there was plenty of work to be done.

The news of the complete Japanese surrender had come through just after midnight on August 14th–15th, and at the Chiefs of Staff meeting next morning we ordered a detachment of the British Pacific Fleet under Vice-Admiral Harcourt to proceed to Hong-Kong. I may say that the Americans by no means approved of our action in this matter, though the United States Chiefs of Staff did not actually say so. There was considerable delay in getting the surrender signed at Hong-Kong, though this mattered little. Harcourt, who acted throughout in accordance with Government instructions, took full charge on arrival with his squadron and installed himself with complete success as Military Governor.

On August 15th, the Prime Minister and members of the Cabinet, with the three Chiefs of Staff, went to Buckingham Palace to congratulate His Majesty on the final victory. That night was again very noisy with the streets full of people; but the illuminations were very lovely. We went to the roof of the Admiralty to see them, and it gave me quite a thrill to see the floodlit figure of Nelson in Trafalgar Square towering high over London. It was the only illuminated statue as far as we could see.

On Sunday, August 19th, the three Chiefs of Staff had the honour of driving behind Their Majesties in a state landau for the Thanksgiving Service at St. Paul's. The service was impressive with beautiful music, and the sermon was preached by the Archbishop of Canterbury. We drove back as we went, and had some conversation with the King and Queen and the Princesses on the steps of Buckingham Palace. The King was amused when I ventured to point out the unseamanlike arrangements of the state landau, there being no method of slipping the tow in case of necessity.

Meanwhile Admiral H. R. Stark, known to his friends as 'Betty', had left us to go home, his time being up as Commander-in-Chief of the United States Naval Forces in European waters. He was relieved by Admiral H. Kent Hewitt, my friend of the Mediterranean.

I was desperately sorry to lose Stark. In the last two years we had become the closest of friends, working together without any trace of a disagreement. He is a great friend of Britain, and while with us all his efforts were directed, and with outstanding success, to seeing that no ill-feeling marred the harmonious relations between the Royal and the United States Navies working together over this side of the Atlantic. Stark's task of smoothing over Admiral King's abrupt methods was sometimes invidious and difficult; but his courtesy and honesty of purpose could never be withstood. I am glad to say that our personal friendship grows closer with the years, and we still keep up a regular correspondence.

We gave him what I hope was an adequate send-off after the valuable work he had done in this country. The Board of Admiralty dined him in the old Painted Hall at Greenwich, and the Prime Minister and Foreign Secretary both attended and spoke. After dinner Stark and myself were mobbed by young officers, Wrens included, striving for autographs. I had had enough of it after fifty or sixty signatures when I heard a Canadian voice behind me demanding just one more. I turned. It was a Canadian midshipman. "Hullo, Canada," I asked. "And where do you come from?"

"Hamilton, sir," said he.

I knew perfectly well of Hamilton, Ontario; but to pull his leg I asked: "And where's Hamilton?"

"Gosh!" he replied, regarding me with a pitying smile. "Where's London?"

Three days later I went to Southampton to see Stark embark in the *Queen Mary*. A crowd of officers were there to wish him farewell, with a band and guards from all the three Services. We saw him on board the ship, after which he came ashore and dined quietly with my wife and myself at the Palace House. I drove him back afterwards, and said a final good-bye on board, unhappy at his departure. He was a great friend and ally.

II

Now began a period of difficulty and worry, and we very soon came to realize how much easier it was to make war than to reorganize for peace. We had a new Prime Minister and Minister of Defence in the shape of Mr. Attlee, and many new members of the Government, to deal with. We were fortunate in having Mr. A. V. Alexander at the Admiralty with his long experience of that office.

There was naturally great pressure to release huge numbers of men from all the Services all over the world, though without much thought how they were to be brought home. Fortunately the demobilization schemes were ready and were put into action at once. But in the event they were found too slow, and matters were not at all easy. We still had heavy commitments, which did not diminish as time went on. Forces had had to be provided for Germany, the Middle East, Italy, Greece, Malaya and many other areas. All the Dominions naturally wanted their men back as soon as possible, and the amount of shipping for trooping purposes was nothing like sufficient for all the moves which everybody wished to be carried out with first priority. Indeed we were soon at the game which, I think of necessity, every government must play, of trying to have our cake and to eat it.

In some matters the Americans were none too easy to deal with, and their ideas about the bases they required in the future seemed to show little faith in the efficiency of the United Nations organization set up at San Francisco. This latter organization, and its contemplated commitments in the future, also gave the Chiefs of Staff plenty to think about.

We were no less busy at the Admiralty. We had to crystallize our views about the post-war Fleet; to decide which ships already building should be completed and which should be cancelled; and to assess the minimum manpower we should require. With the large growth in the Naval Air Arm, the proportion of men on shore was bound to be greater than before the war, and this raised the matter of the minimum manpower required for the Fleet as a whole. It would require a book in itself to deal even briefly with all the problems that came under review. For months there was little or no relaxation in the tempo at the Admiralty.

In September we suffered a great loss in the sudden death of Admiral Sir Frederic Wake-Walker, the Third Sea Lord and Controller, and Commander-in-Chief designate for the Mediterranean. He was a great Controller, able, energetic and full of ideas. Possessing great vision he always looked ahead, and his mind was full of schemes for averaging off the work in the shipyards in the lean years that were to come and for the betterment of the technical branches of the Navy. He was inclined to be impatient and did not suffer fools gladly; but the Navy owes him a lot.

Wake-Walker's untimely death brought various changes in the Flag Officers' appointments at home and abroad in the months that followed. Sir Algernon Willis was offered, and accepted, the command in the Mediterranean, and was relieved as Second Sea Lord by Sir Arthur Power. He, in turn, was relieved as Commander-in-Chief, East Indies, by Vice-Admiral Sir Arthur Palliser, the latter being replaced as Fourth Sea Lord by Vice-Admiral Douglas Fisher, who had commanded the Fleet Train in the Pacific with such conspicuous success. Vice-Admiral Charles Daniel became Third Sea Lord and Controller, and Sir Neville Syfret, Commander-in-Chief, Home Fleet, in place of Sir Henry Moore, who became Head of the British Naval Mission in Washington towards the end of 1945, and later Naval Representative of the British Chiefs of Staff on the Military Staff Committee of the Security Council of U.N.O.

On September 27th, on the occasion of Their Majesties' visit to Edinburgh, I was installed as a Knight of the Thistle in the Chapel of that Order in St. Giles' Cathedral. Later, in the presence of Their Majesties and all the Knights, I handed over the *Warspite's* White Ensign to St. Giles' Cathedral, while Captain Ford, of the *Queen Mary*, presented the Red Ensign of that fine ship. These were the first flags of the sea to take their places among the tattered old Colours of the famous Scottish regiments.

Honours such as I had never dreamed of poured in upon me. In June, 1945, the honorary degree of LL.D had been conferred upon me by Edinburgh University, of which I was elected Lord Rector in the October following. In September, I received the Freedom of Hove, the home town of the *King Alfred* establishment which had trained so many fine young officers of the Royal Naval Volunteer Reserve during the war. During November, in company with Field Marshal Sir Harold Alexander, I was accorded the Freedom of Manchester, and was greatly touched by the warm-hearted welcome of the people of that great city. The list until the end of 1945 was completed by the conferment of the honorary degrees of LL.D. from the Universities of Cambridge and Birmingham, while in the summer of 1946 these honours were followed by a D.C.L. from Oxford University, and the LL.D. from the Universities of Leeds and Glasgow. This list has since been added to by the honorary degree of LL.D. from the Universities of Sheffield and St. Andrews.

I felt overwhelmed and somewhat bewildered at all this great kindness; but realized that these compliments were not so much personal to me, as a tribute to the Royal Navy and to those thousands of fine officers and men I had had the honour to command during the six years of war.

On November 21st I went to the House of Lords to be introduced. Admirals of the Fleet Lord Chatfield and the Earl of Cork and Orrery honoured me by being my supporters. I had asked Admiral of the Fleet Lord Keyes to oblige me in that capacity; but he was too ill.

Roger Keyes died on December 26th, a great figure who did a lot for the Navy. He was full of the offensive spirit, and I look back to the time I spent under his command in the Dover Patrol during the First World War with vivid recollection. After a memorial service with full naval honours in Westminster Abbey he was buried in the Zeebrugge portion of the cemetery at Dover, a fitting resting-place for a great sailor and leader of the little ships who had blocked Zeebrugge and had held the Straits against the enemy.

We spent Christmas, 1945, at Bishop's Waltham, and on my arrival I found a parcel there from the United States Ambassador, John Winant, addressed: "To my Admiral, Andrew Cunningham." Inside was a fine old silver tankard and a Christmas card, thanking me for my help to 'Ike', my services to the cause, and a speech I had made at Cambridge. At the conferment of degrees at that University, Winant, though he was a graduand, refused to speak and left it to me, and I had opened with some very deserved complimentary references to him.

The tankard is one of my most cherished possessions. It was the gift of a great man and a real friend and admirer of Britain.

III

The names of the three Chiefs of Staff, Alan Brooke, Portal and myself, appeared in the New Year's Honours List of 1946 on our elevation to the rank and dignity of Viscounts. Telegrams and letters of congratulation came pouring in, and I was glad to realize that my naval friends took the honour as a compliment to the Navy.

Portal had left, and Tedder had joined the Chiefs of Staff Committee on appointment as Chief of the Air Staff. We survivors missed Portal, for the three of us had been together for well over two years and had drawn very closely together. We had had our disagreements; but I cannot remember one that we were not able to compose among ourselves.

Charles Portal is an exceptional man, eminently able, calm and not easily to be roused, and redoubtable and most lucid in argument. When I first met him as a fellow student at the Imperial Defence College years before, I realized he was destined to rise to the top of his Service. He and I had many a difference of opinion; but it never engendered any hard feelings. I shall always treasure his friendship and admire his great qualities. Fortunately he is still young enough for his outstanding abilities to be of great service to the country.

Our labours altered little, and on the whole the work became more intricate as the aftermath of the war sorted itself out. The Chiefs of Staff and their staffs were fully occupied with the problems of Greece and the Netherlands; the affairs of U.N.O.; the disposal of the former Italian colonies; our own post-war defence organization and the strength and composition of the armed forces.

At the Admiralty my chief private thought was how soon I could get away; but the selection of my relief and making him available was not at all easy. After many consultations with the First Lord and enquiry into the opinions of many senior officers, Sir John Cunningham was decided upon. Perhaps I should say that we are not related. But his appointment meant the whole series of reliefs already indicated, and these, with the delays caused by overlapping and the necessary leave periods, meant that I could not hope to get away until late in May.

Sir John Cunningham's forthcoming appointment as First Sea Lord was announced on March 1st.

Our purely parochial difficulties at the Admiralty were largely concerned with the reductions in naval personnel and our many naval commitments abroad, all of which absorbed men. A new pay code was also being evolved by discussions between the three Services and the Treasury. At the time agreement was reached the new rates of pay appeared reasonable. But the ratings had counted on the inclusion of the 'war service increment' as a permanent part of their new rates, and were not content when this was discovered not to be so. The senior ratings were also disgruntled, partly because of the levelling up of the rates of pay between the seniors and juniors. Other inequities were also brought to light which could be set down to trying to pay all the Services the same rank for rank, although the conditions in which they served were completely different. It was put forward by the senior ratings, with some justice, that in the Navy alone of all the Services, the family man had two establishments to maintain except during his short periodical visits to the Royal Naval Barracks at one or other of the Home Ports. This was the exception in the Army or the Royal Air Force in peace time.

After long discussion with the Commanders-in-Chief at the Home Ports some easement was arranged; but had the Board of Admiralty been given more time for the study of the new rates of pay before they were rushed through and announced, it is probable that difficulties would never have arisen.

The weeks went by with some new problem thrown up by the war relative to the future defence of the country being referred almost daily to the Chiefs of Staff Committee. Our recommendations for the future defence organization were received with favour and adopted with minor modifications, and the defence arrangements in the various areas for which we were responsible slowly took shape. At the Admiralty, too, the pressure of work was unabated.

February, 1946, was a month of considerable activity for me personally. Early in the month I was approached by the City authorities and asked if I would accept the Freedom of the City of London, and with it the presentation of a Sword of Honour. Only one answer was possible to the offer of this outstanding honour, which of course included Alan Brooke and Portal, so the ceremony was fixed for early in June.

In February, too, the French General Juin, whom of course I knew well from our time in Algiers, paid an official visit to England. Before he came we were informed that he had been deputed by the French Government to invest the Chiefs of Staff with the Grand Cross of the Legion of Honour. I had already received this decoration from General Giraud in Algiers, so I was to receive the Médaille Militaire, a most unusual and distinguished award which can only be conferred upon non-commissioned officers and men of the Army and Air Force, and equivalent ranks in the Navy, for gallantry in war, and, as an exception, to Generals and Admirals for long and distinguished service in war. I believe I share with Mr. Churchill the distinction of being one of the two living foreigners who possess this decoration. It is one that I particularly prize after close association with the French forces in the Mediterranean and my friendship with so many distinguished Frenchmen. The investiture took place at the French Embassy.

A few days later I travelled north to Edinburgh to receive the freedom of the city with which my family had been connected for so many years.

At about this time the Deputy First Sea Lord, my old and valued friend Admiral Sir Charles Kennedy-Purvis, became ill, and we never saw him again at the Admiralty. To my great sorrow he died in May. His services at the Admiralty during the last years of the war cannot be over-estimated. Working away unobtrusively, rather in the background, he took a prodigious amount of work off the shoulders of the already overburdened First Sea Lord. With his great ability and knowledge, his wisdom, tact and quiet manner, he solved many a complicated problem without worrying his chief. He was very much missed, though as reductions were taking place in the Admiralty staff his place was not filled.

Though the matter had little to do with us, we were much concerned in February with a mutiny in ships of the Royal Indian Navy at Bombay and Karachi. The causes were rather obscure to us at home; but ships of the East Indies Squadron had to be sent there. I made the strict proviso that if there was any shooting to be done, it should only be carried out on the direct orders of the Indian authorities. I did not intend it to be said later that the brutal British Navy had fired on the poor Indian sailors. However, the arrival of the *Glasgow* and one or two smaller ships at Bombay and their calm and resolute demeanour had a very quietening effect, and the trouble died away. The mutiny subsequently formed the subject of an enquiry by two or three legal luminaries and Vice-Admiral Wilfred Patterson. The conclusions reached were sensible. However, matters were boiling up in India, and the government decided to send out a Cabinet Delegation in an attempt to reach a settlement. Mr. Alexander, the First Lord, was one of its members, and during his absence the Prime Minister assumed responsibility for the Admiralty.

During March the visit of Their Majesties and the Princesses Elizabeth and Margaret to South Africa for an extended tour of the Union was under discussion. I was asked if it would be possible for the Royal Party to go in the *Vanguard*, which was then completing. I welcomed the opportunity of the King travelling in our latest battleship, and of South Africa seeing something of the Navy, so after obtaining the Prime Minister's consent it was arranged.

I paid another visit to Manchester during March to address the Luncheon Club of that city on the subject of the Navy. I was able to combine it with a short visit to Eaton Hall where the Dartmouth cadets had their war quarters, and also with a visit to Belfast to be present when the new aircraft-carrier *Eagle* was launched from Messrs. Harland and Wolff's shipyard by Her Royal Highness, the Princess Elizabeth. I crossed from Liverpool in the new 'battle' class destroyer *Solebay*, a fine enough ship which seemed to carry every mortal weapon and gadget except guns. I noted at the time that—"these 'Battles' fulfil my worst expectations. An erection like the Castle Rock, Edinburgh, on the bridge. They call it a director, and all to control four guns firing a total broadside of about 200 lbs. We must get back to destroyers of reasonable size and well-gunned."

Princess Elizabeth was received with great enthusiasm and cheering, and performed the launching ceremony with great charm and dignity. Her speech at the luncheon afterwards was excellent. Altogether her visit to Northern Ireland was a great success. I flew back to London during the afternoon, arriving in less than two hours.

At the end of March I fell into the hands of the doctors, and was sentenced to six weeks in bed at Haslar Hospital. This, with the First Lord away in India, was awkward, so I intimated to the Prime Minister that if he thought it advisable I would leave the Admiralty at once. Mr. Attlee decided otherwise. I do not think my absence was of much consequence. The new Second Sea Lord, Vice-Admiral Sir Arthur Power, and the Vice-Chief of the Naval Staff, Vice-Admiral Rhoderick McGrigor, carried the burden with great efficiency. At the same time I was not cut off from what went on at the Admiralty. Budgets of papers were sent down to me, and I had constant visits from my Secretary, the devoted Captain (S) A. P. Shaw, and my Naval Assistant, Captain Sir Charles Madden. I also had a bedside telephone through the Commander-in-Chief's exchange in Portsmouth, and could get on to the Admiralty at once, and they to me. I was very well looked after, and had a pleasant room overlooking a lawn and trees and lots of standard roses. I was even provided with masses of books and papers and free cigarettes by, I believe, the Red Cross. As I have never smoked, the cigarettes were passed on to someone more in need of them. But it was boring indeed to be tied by the leg and inactive. My wife's daily visits were a joy and an alleviation. It was a blessing that Bishop's Waltham was so close.

I was back at the Admiralty by the middle of May, very glad to be on the move again after so long in bed, though somewhat slow on my feet. My date of relief had been fixed for June 6th.

I resumed my duties on the Chiefs of Staff Committee. Alan Brooke, who normally took the chair, was away touring the various theatres of war for consultation with the Commanders-in-Chief. I declined to replace Tedder who had been chairman during Alan Brooke's absence. I had such a short time to go, and was very busy clearing up arrears of work and preparing to turn over to Sir John Cunningham.

Late in May I was presented with the United States Navy Distinguished

Service Medal. Mr. Winant, the United States Ambassador, had originally intended coming to Haslar for the ceremony; but he had to return to the United States. The presentation was actually made by my old friend Admiral H. Kent Hewitt in London in the presence of Admiral Leahy and other American naval officers, all of whom wore the British Orders that had been conferred upon them. I greatly appreciated the kind things that were said when the medal was presented, and remembered Christmas Day, 1942, at Algiers, when General Eisenhower presented me with the Army D.C.M. by order of President Roosevelt. How much had happened in the three and a half years that lay between.

On June 5th I was granted a parting audience with His Majesty at Buckingham Palace, and also took leave of the Chiefs of Staff Committee with deep feeling and a great sense of loss. Alan Brooke was back from his journeying, and said many nice things to which I was quite unable to reply with adequacy. Parting from one for whom I had a profound admiration and personal affection was a great sorrow. Straight, absolutely honest and outspoken, he was outstandingly able in his difficult and most responsible position. Though impulsive at times, he always spoke out fearlessly and fluently against what he knew to be wrong. Generous almost to a fault, Alan Brooke was always actuated by the highest motives, and was a very charming companion. Jealousy in any shape or form did not enter into his composition. I am no judge of his capability as a fighting soldier; but feel that had it come his way in the later stages of the war he would have been one of our most brilliant commanders in the field. His long services to the country during war as Chief of the Imperial General Staff and on the Chiefs of Staff Committee were immeasurable.

I was also sorry to part from General Lord Ismay, who had been Chief of Staff to the Minister of Defence for six years, and the Deputy Secretary and Secretary of the Committee of Imperial Defence in the years before the war. He always gave us the wisest and more valuable help, and was a master at producing a composed decision from points of view that were often diametrically opposed.

Major General Sir Leslie Hollis, Royal Marines, Senior Assistant Secretary in the office of the War Cabinet from 1939 to 1946; Major General Sir Edward Jacob, Military Assistant Secretary to the War Cabinet over the same period, and their most efficient staff, I shall always remember with gratitude. Their experience and wise counsel was invaluable.

On June 6th I left the Admiralty for the last time and drove to Bishop's Waltham. It was painful to part from so many tried and trusted friends, naval and otherwise, and I was at a loss for words when saying good-bye. However, it was not quite the end, for on June 8th I was again in London for the Victory March. To take our places on chairs to the right of the Royal saluting base in the Mall, Alan Brooke, Portal and myself had to go there by car. Great difficulty had been experienced by those making the arrangements to find a car large enough to take the three of us. It was even suggested that Alan Brooke and I should go together with Portal following in another car. But we were determined to be together, and I even suggested making a special body for a car in one of the dockyards. However, a suitable vehicle was eventually found, and after a short preliminary procession we reached the saluting base, where the King, the Queen and the Royal Family arrived soon afterwards. Mr. Churchill and the Prime Minister came together.

I need not describe the Victory March through London. It was a fine and moving spectacle. My mind instinctively went back to Tunis in May, 1943, and the magnificent bronzed and battle-hardened young men I had seen marching past there. We had come a long and troublous way.

On June 10th the three wartime Chiefs of Staff drove in procession to the Guildhall in state landaus to receive the Freedom of the City of London. Our wives went with us. It had been arranged that if it were raining the ladies should go in closed cars. But they decided otherwise. Wet or fine, in spite of new hats and smart clothes, they were determined that nothing should prevent them driving in state landaus with their husbands. Fortune favoured us. It was an exacting and memorable occasion; but I hope we came through the ceremony and speeches at the Guildhall and at the subsequent luncheon at the Mansion House without discredit. But I was aware that Portal's speech in the Guildhall put mine completely in the shade. The Swords of Honour from the City of London which reached us later were weapons of an old-fashioned type of magnificent workmanship in beautiful scabbards and cases of green shagreen. Mine is one of our greatest treasures.

John Cunningham, my successor, had most kindly refused to take up his residence in the Admiralty Archway Flat until all these ceremonies and our various farewell functions were ended, so we were able to carry them out in great comfort.

We drove down to Bishop's Waltham on June 11th, though even that was not quite the end. A few days later, in the list of Birthday Honours, Alan Brooke and myself were awarded the Order of Merit. Portal had already received this honour on leaving the Chiefs of Staff Committee early in the year; and on June 24th Alan Brooke and I were granted an audience with the King at Buckingham Palace when His Majesty invested us.

Though I was glad to get away from the Admiralty, and the prospect of a complete rest was most pleasing, I cannot pretend that it was not a great wrench to cease all active participation in the affairs of the Navy. Half a century is a long time, and it was a few months short of fifty years since I had joined the *Britannia* at Dartmouth as a small cadet, little realizing what I was in for. None of my forbears had been at sea.

I had had wonderful experience and seen a good deal of the world, particularly the Mediterranean, and had abundant memories of association with some great public characters and thousands of fine men in the Royal Navy. It had been a period of great change and transition, and I had served in ships of nearly every type, including one of the old-time brigs. I had even seen muzzle-loading guns afloat, and the period when naval actions were expected to be fought at a mile and less. I had had experience of active service ashore in South Africa as a midshipman, and afloat in the two World Wars.

I have little to regret. Fortune favoured me at every turn. How else could one of such limited attainments have reached so far? I realize I have been lucky, and can think of others more talented and industrious than myself who fell by the wayside through sheer force of circumstance, not through any fault of their own. I am not, and never was, an expert in any of the technical subjects, or what Mr. Churchill once called the 'instrumentalisms', of the Navy, which used to be one of the surest roads to advancement in peace. I think I was fortunate in obtaining command while still a young man, for it taught me much of what I know about sailors. After all, it is the men who win battles. I owe a great deal, too, to the fine example of the officers under whom I served, particularly in destroyers and later. Their names have been mentioned; but they, and others like them, were responsible for grafting the improved technique of an entirely new Navy on to the imperishable tradition of service and self-sacrifice of the old. The fighting spirit was never lacking.

I have no profound philosophy of life to propound. As perhaps I have shown, I have always been inclined to rebel and to speak out against decisions that I felt to be wrong. Otherwise, I think I have usually taken things as I found them, and tried to make the best of them.

And now, living fairly close to Portsmouth, we are not entirely out of touch with the Navy. Many old naval friends are good enough to come and see us, and we hear much of what goes on. Our house, which we have now been able to purchase, our garden, our dogs, a cat, our geese and poultry, keep us occupied. For the rest, we have many more calls upon our time than we could ever hope to fulfil, even if we wished to, and one is conscious of a growing distaste of being disturbed in the even tenor of our way by exacting engagements and functions. We live very contentedly with our 'roses in December'.

I may close my autobiography with some lines from a poem by James Graham, Marquis of Montrose, 1612–1650, which have hung over my desk for many years:

> He either fears his fate too much
> Or his deserts are small,
> That dares not put it to the touch,
> To gain or lose it all.

Finally, to the end of my life, I shall remain convinced that there is no Service or profession to compare with the Royal Navy.

In 1638, John Holland wrote what he called his first *Discourse of the Navy*. I should like to quote a few lines of his, which are as true today as they ever were:

> If either the honour of a nation, commerce or trade with all nations, peace at home, grounded upon our enemies' fear or love of us abroad, and attended with plenty of all things necessary either for the preservation of the public need or thy private welfare, be things worthy thy esteem (though it may be beyond thy shoal conceit), then next to God and the King give thy thanks for the same to the navy, as the principal instrument whereby God works these good things to thee. As for honour, who knows not (that know's anything) that in all records of late times of actions chronicled to the everlasting fame and renown of this kingdom, still the naval part is the thread that runs through the whole wooft, the burden of the song, the scope of the text?

APPENDIX I

U-BOAT CASUALTIES: GERMAN, ITALIAN AND JAPANESE

The following totals were produced by a joint Anglo-American investigation after the war with access to enemy records. They were published in a White Paper (Cmd. 6751) presented to Parliament in March, 1946. Fractional figures are accounted for by the credit for sinkings of particular U-boats being attributed to more than one of the causes shown, though for each submarine destroyed only one 'kill' has been awarded. The term 'British' refers to all British, Dominion, Imperial and Allied forces, other than American, under British operational control, while 'American' indicates all United States and Allied Forces, except British, Dominion and Imperial, working under the operational control of the United States.

(*The tables which follow are reproduced by permission of the Controller of H.M. Stationery Office*)

GERMAN U-BOAT CASUALTIES

CAUSE	BRITISH								AMERICAN					
	1939	1940	1941	1942	1943	1944	1945	*Total*	1942	1943	1944	1945	*Total*	*Grand Total*
Ships	6	10½	25	27½	48	57	34½	208½	5½	11	10½	11½	38½	247
Shore-Based Aircraft	—	½	3	25½	83	51	34	197	10½	32	3	3	48½	245½
Ship-Borne Aircraft	—	1	—	1½	1	10½	1	15	—	23	6	—	29	44
Ship and Shore-Based Aircraft	—	2	1	3½	7	9	1½	24	1½	3	3	½	8	32
Ship and Ship-Borne Aircraft	—	—	—	—	2	5	—	7	—	1	5	—	6	13
Submarines	1	2	1	2	5	6	2	19	—	—	1	1	2	21
Bombing Raids	—	—	—	—	—	8½	12½	21	—	1	13½	27½	42	63
Naval Mines Laid by Shore-Based Aircraft	—	—	—	—	1	9	6	16	—	—	—	—	—	16
Naval Mines Laid by Ships	2	2	—	3	1½	2½	5½	16½	—	—	—	—	—	16½
TOTAL	9	18	30	63	148½	158½	97	524	17½	71	42	43½	174	698

Total destroyed above	698
Other causes	59½
Unknown causes	23½
TOTAL	781

ITALIAN U-BOAT CASUALTIES

CAUSE	BRITISH 1940	BRITISH 1941	BRITISH 1942	BRITISH 1943	BRITISH Total	AMERICAN 1942	AMERICAN 1943	AMERICAN Total	Grand Total
Ships	10	8	8	9	35	—	2	2	37
Shore-Based Aircraft	2	1	3	2	8	1	1	2	10
Ship-Borne Aircraft	1	—	—	—	1	—	—	—	1
Ship and Shore-Based Aircraft	2	1	1	1	5	—	—	—	5
Submarines	2	4	7	5	18	—	—	—	18
Bombing Raids	—	—	—	1	1	—	1	1	2
TOTAL	17	14	19	18	68	1	4	5	73

Total destroyed above 73
Other causes 3
Unknown causes 9
                    —
TOTAL 85

JAPANESE U-BOAT CASUALTIES

CAUSE	BRITISH 1941	1942	1943	1944	1945	Total	AMERICAN 1941	1942	1943	1944	1945	Total	Grand Total
Ships	—	2½	1	2	—	5½	—	5½	13	36	11	65½	71
Shore-Based Aircraft	—	—	—	—	—	—	—	1	1	1	2	5	5
Ship-Borne Aircraft	—	—	—	—	—	—	1	—	—	3	5	9	9
Ship and Ship-Borne Aircraft	—	—	—	—	—	—	—	—	1	1	—	2	2
Ship and Shore-Based Aircraft	—	½	½	—	—	1	—	1½	1½	—	—	3	4
Submarines	—	1	1	1	—	2	—	5	3	7	8	23	25
Naval Mines	—	—	—	—	—	1	—	—	—	1	2	3	4
TOTAL	—	4	2½	3	—	9½	1	13	19½	49	28	110½	120

Total destroyed above   120
Other causes   5
Unknown causes   5
                        ———
TOTAL   130

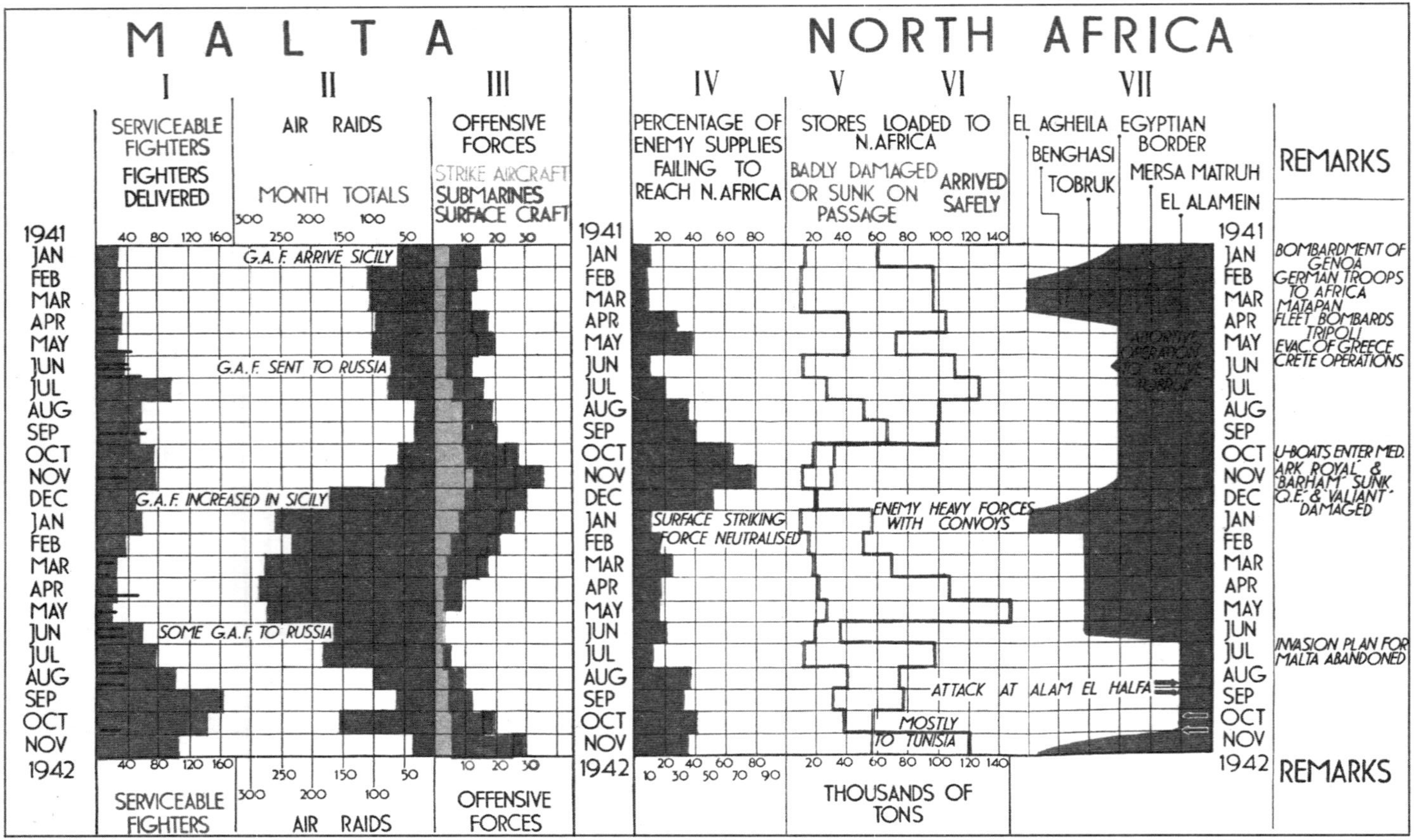
MALTA
I
SERVICEABLE FIGHTERS
FIGHTERS DELIVERED
II
AIR RAIDS
MONTH TOTALS
III
OFFENSIVE FORCES
STRIKE AIRCRAFT
SUBMARINES
SURFACE CRAFT
G.A.F. ARRIVE SICILY
G.A.F. SENT TO RUSSIA
G.A.F. INCREASED IN SICILY
SOME G.A.F. TO RUSSIA
NORTH AFRICA
IV
PERCENTAGE OF ENEMY SUPPLIES FAILING TO REACH N.AFRICA
V
VI
STORES LOADED TO N.AFRICA
BADLY DAMAGED OR SUNK ON PASSAGE
ARRIVED SAFELY
THOUSANDS OF TONS
SURFACE STRIKING FORCE NEUTRALISED
ENEMY HEAVY FORCES WITH CONVOYS
MOSTLY TO TUNISIA
VII
EL AGHEILA
BENGHASI
TOBRUK
EGYPTIAN BORDER
MERSA MATRUH
EL ALAMEIN
ATTACK AT ALAM EL HALFA
1941
JAN
FEB
MAR
APR
MAY
JUN
JUL
AUG
SEP
OCT
NOV
DEC
JAN
FEB
MAR
APR
MAY
JUN
JUL
AUG
SEP
OCT
NOV
1942
REMARKS
BOMBARDMENT OF GENOA
GERMAN TROOPS TO AFRICA
MATAPAN
FLEET BOMBARDS TRIPOLI
EVAC. OF GREECE
CRETE OPERATIONS
U-BOATS ENTER MED.
'ARK ROYAL' & 'BARHAM' SUNK
'Q.E.' & 'VALIANT' DAMAGED
INVASION PLAN FOR MALTA ABANDONED

APPENDIX II

THE WAR IN THE MEDITERRANEAN:

JANUARY, 1941–NOVEMBER, 1942

I am indebted to Captain W. A. Adair, O.B.E., Royal
Navy, for the following notes, and the interesting series
of graphs which accompany them.

1. When Italy came into the war in June 1940, the Mediterranean was at once closed to our merchant ships, and thereafter convoys, almost without exception, were restricted to those needed to keep Malta going. Apart from one or two convoys in 1941, all the supplies for the Middle East land battle had to be sent round the Cape. This meant that more shipping was required, and that supplies took much longer to reach our forces. The only compensating advantage was that over 99 per cent of the supplies which left the United Kingdom reached the Middle East in safety.

2. The land battle in the Western Desert turned out to be largely a matter of logistics. Whichever side succeeded in building up the biggest force of tanks and aircraft, petrol and reserves, was able to advance until its lines of communication with its base were stretched to the limit. The opponent, working on shorter and shorter lines of communication, was able to build up reserves quicker, and in due course halted the advancing army. This see-saw went on until November, 1942, when the Eighth Army broke out of its position at Alamein, and thereafter never looked back.

3. It was thus the Navy's duty, and the term includes, of course, the Maritime Air Forces, to reduce the amount of supplies which reached the enemy in North Africa, thereby turning the balance in favour of our Desert Army.

4. Events proved that our success or otherwise in dealing with the enemy's supply line to North Africa varied in almost direct proportion to the amount that our own Naval and Air Forces could be based on Malta. It was thus of major, if indirect, interest to the soldiers and airmen fighting in Cyrenaica to ensure that Malta was kept supplied and operational. One feels that this fact was not always widely appreciated.

5. The diagram shows, month by month, how the fortunes of both sides rose and fell during the period from January, 1941, to November, 1942.

6. Looking at the diagram, from left to right. The first graph shows the average number of operational R.A.F. fighters at Malta, and in black horizontal lines, the numbers of fighters which were flown off aircraft carriers to Malta. The chief point is the very low level at which we started, while although the numbers were built up to over eighty in July, 1941, these were soon whittled

away by the increasing numbers of enemy air raids, until in March, 1942 we had only twenty operational fighters in the island. It was not until June of that year that the input into Malta began to overtake the waste.

7. The second graph shows in blue the monthly totals of air raids on Malta. The chief items of interest here are that 1941 started off with the establishment of the German Air Force in Sicily, with a resultant increase in the number of raids. Then, in June, came the withdrawal of part of the German Air Force for the Russian war; next, the re-inforcement of the G.A.F. in December, followed by an increasing offensive which did not weaken until June, 1942. The similarity in the nature of graphs I and II is noticeable.

8. The third graph shows the offensive forces based on Malta; in stone-colour, strike aircraft, both R.A.F. and Naval; in red, submarines; and in blue, surface ships. These forces reached a maximum in November and December, 1941, when four cruisers, four destroyers, fourteen submarines, forty-five R.A.F. and seventeen Naval strike aircraft were operational. After the heavy air attacks in the succeeding months, the nadir was reached in April, 1942, when the surface striking force had been neutralized, and there were only four submarines, three R.A.F. and two Naval strike aircraft operational at Malta. In the following month even the submarines had to be withdrawn and did not return until August, 1942.

9. The fourth or centre graph shows the proportion of stores loaded for the enemy forces in North Africa which failed to reach their destination. These figures and those of the next two graphs are obtained from enemy sources. Here again it is noticeable that the kill varies very closely with the forces, particularly the surface forces, based on Malta.

10. The fifth and sixth graphs are shown on the same base, the first giving the monthly tonnage of enemy stores loaded for North Africa which never arrived, and the second, the corresponding tonnage which arrived safely.

11. Finally on the right is shown how the British Army fared territorially in the North African campaign.

12. The graphs show the cause and effect of what happened in the Mediterranean. January, 1941, saw the Desert Army advancing, but as will be seen from the second line, the German Air Force had arrived in Sicily. There were so few fighters in Malta that no surface striking force could be based there, and the submarines and strike aircraft from Malta could only take small toll of the enemy supplies. Accordingly the enemy was able to send German reinforcements and build up supplies in Libya, and soon after our Desert Army reached El Agheila it was pushed back to the Egyptian border. This retreat was further hastened by the War Cabinet decision to send all available land and air forces to Greece.

13. The next phase started in April, 1941, and covered the operations in Greece and Crete. At first we were able to base surface forces on Malta, and so the toll on enemy supplies rose sharply. At the end of May, however, all available Naval forces had to be sent to assist in the Crete operations, and at once our killings on the supply route fell.

14. At the end of the Crete operations the Mediterranean Fleet was reduced to a force of two battleships, two cruisers and twelve destroyers undamaged, so while we were still licking our wounds after Crete, and with the new

commitment of maintaining Tobruk on our hands, we could spare no surface striking forces for Malta.

15. The next phase started in October, 1941, by which time the Mediterranean Fleet had been reinforced, and the Navy had flown off large fighter reinforcements to Malta. A surface force could be spared for that island, and at once, for the first time, more enemy supplies were sunk than arrived safely. The result can be seen on the right-hand line—when the Army attacked they were able to relieve Tobruk and once again drive back the enemy out of Cyrenaica.

16. The German High Command had, however, fully appreciated the importance of their sea lines of communication in the land battle for North Africa, and accordingly the German Air Force in Sicily was reinforced with the object of driving the Royal Air Force out of the sky over Malta. Concurrently they despatched twenty German U-boats into the Mediterranean for the first time, and as a result of these two actions we were temporarily unable to challenge the enemy's control of the central Mediterranean. Malta went through a very thin time and the enemy pushed the Eighth Army back to Tobruk. One convoy was fought through to Malta in March, 1942, against attack by the Italian battle-fleet, but unfortunately although the convoy reached the island almost intact, there were few operational fighters available, and the entire convoy was sunk by air attack in the harbours of Malta before more than a fraction of the stores had been unloaded.

17. During the next month air attacks on the island were so heavy that all offensive forces had to be withdrawn. The only bright spot from our point of view was that while the German Naval Authorities appreciated the value of Malta they could not persuade their Military colleagues of the same point, and so, fortunately for us, no invasion of Malta was attempted.

18. In the next period will be seen the obvious result of the last phase. The enemy was able to build up supplies in North Africa, and in June, 1942, the Eighth Army was pushed right back to El Alamein.

19. The last phase opens in July 1942. A great effort was made to reinforce Malta, and between June and August, two convoys were fought through from the west and a hundred and ninety-five fighter reinforcements were flown off carriers. The enemy air raids on Malta diminished owing to the increased opposition they received, and this in turn meant that submarines could return to the island. Once again will be seen the rising toll on enemy supplies. In July too, the enemy finally decided to abandon the invasion of Malta. From that month onwards Rommel was operating over very long lines of communication, and at the same time was getting less and less in the way of supplies. In October, the proportion of supplies the enemy lost in transit again reached 40 per cent for the first time that year, and so far as petrol was concerned the loss was 67 per cent. The result is well known. When Field Marshal Montgomery with the Eighth Army, supported by the Desert Air Force, attacked at Alamein at the end of October, after ten days' hard fighting Rommel was forced to retreat at full speed to El Agheila.

20. If the effect of the attack on the enemy's sea communications be doubted, some short extracts from Field Marshal Rommel's diary may be

quoted. He had been given a directive to attack at Alam el Halfa in August, to defeat the Eighth Army, and then to drive on and capture the Suez Canal.

21. On 29th August, Rommel reported that owing to the non-arrival of the petrol and ammunition promised, he would undertake the attack only with the object of defeating the Eighth Army at Alamein. He says in his war diary: "The further objectives in my directive are not obtainable. Even the limited objective is only possible if the Air Force can lend me 1,000 tons of petrol."

22. On 2nd September, four days later, after the commencement of the battle, he says: "The non-arrival of petrol requested, which was the condition laid down for the successful carrying out of even limited operations forbids the continuation of the attack." After referring to the loss of petrol tankers he continues: "These circumstances force the panzer army to suspend the offensive; the Army will therefore fall back slowly under enemy pressure to the starting line, unless the supply and air situations are fundamentally changed."

23. To summarize, during the period from the start of the Italian war to November, 1942, 17 per cent of all the supplies loaded for the enemy in North Africa were lost. Of this overall loss the enemy attributes 45 per cent as being due to submarines, 11 per cent to Naval and 26 per cent to R.A.F. aircraft, 8 per cent to surface ships and 7 per cent to mines.

24. It is often said that figures can be made to prove anything, but it is claimed that the diagram shows that the ships, submarines and strike aircraft based on Malta contributed materially to the victories in the Western Desert. Further, it is clear that had it been possible to spare more fighters for Malta, large losses in ships, men and material would have been avoided.

INDEX

I—GENERAL

In most cases the ranks of officers and others mentioned in the Index are those held at the time

Aachen, France, 619
Aaltenfiord, Norway, 580
—— penetrated by midget submarines, 600
Abd-ul-mejid, Sultan of Turkey, 215
Abrial, French Admiral, 187
Abyssinia, 210, 307
—— Mussolini's designs, 173
—— Mediterranean Fleet move to Alexandria, 174
—— Italian transports use Suez Canal, 174
—— Battle Cruiser Squadron sent to Gibraltar, 175
—— East India Squadron concentrate at Aden, 175
—— Destroyer Flotilla go to Red Sea, 175
—— Fleet ready to strike at Italians, 175
—— invaded, 175
—— futile sanctions against Italy, 175
—— enemy activity, 280
—— campaign held up, 297
Abyssinian successes, 320
'A' Cordite Committee, 180
Achi Baba, 61, 73
Acoustic mines along N. African coast, 312
Adair, Capt. W. A., R.N.: The War in the Mediterranean, 671-4
Adana, Turkey, visited by Mr. Churchill, 518
Addis Ababa, Abyssinia, entered, 338
Addison, Rear-Admiral A. P., 118
A'Deane, Commander W. R., 372
Aden, 629
—— Gulf of, vital convoy route, 269
Adlon Hotel, Berlin, 197
'Admiral's Model, the', a sewing machine, 308
Admiralty House, Bermuda, 121
—— —— Chatham, 154
—— —— Clarence Cove, Hamilton Island, 124
—— —— Inverkeithing, 119
—— —— Malta, 208-9 *et seq.*; its antiquity, 627
—— running on oiled wheels in a groove, 577
Adriatic patrolled, Aug. 1914, 56
—— offensive strikes, 298
Ægean, 90
—— naval command of, 220
—— position to be secured, 307
Aeroplane, first flight in, 139
Afrika Korps left to its fate, 528

Agadir incident, 49-50
Agnew, Capt. W. G. (later Commodore), 419 505, 531, 547
—— Commander Samuel M., 33, 34
Agropoli, 569
Ah Ping, Chinese steward, 465
Ainslie, Maurice A., 32
Air attack on convoys by Wellingtons unsatisfactory, 447
—— cover, lack of, responsible for heavy naval losses, 359
—— Force at Tobruk withdrawn, 339
—— Force strength for Western Desert offensive causes apprehension, 416
—— Force strength in Crete, 367
—— Forces do good work, 455
—— Ministry, 114
—— —— not helping naval war in Mediterranean, 348
—— protection for Mediterranean Fleet lacking, May 1940, 227, 350-1
—— reconnaissance sparse and intermittent, Jan. 1942, 438; causes striking Italian successes, 438-50
—— reconnaissance efficient and valuable to fleet, 440
—— strength, necessity for superiority, 395-6
—— —— of Luftwaffe in the Mediterranean, 306
—— striking force pays ample dividends, 420; without necessary intelligence to have effect, 438
—— situation unsatisfactory, 267
—— superiority of the Germans, 299
Airborne Divisions on the Continent, 634
Aircraft carrier, danger if left to herself, 183, 188
—— carrier flight decks withstand heavy punishment, 639
—— carriers designed, 114
—— —— shortage of, June 1949, 233
—— for fleet co-operation urged and turned down, 406
—— greatly inferior in numbers causes anxiety, 319
—— massed by enemy in Sardinia and Sicily, 486
—— menace on many coasts, 321
—— regarded as integral part of naval armament, 114
—— strength of enemy in N. Africa, 416

677

INDEX

Aircraft used at Combined Fleet exercises, 1935, 171-2
Airfields in Sicily, a serious problem, 535
Aix, France, visit to, 189
Akyab occupied, 630
Albacore air squadrons, 524; make name for themselves, 416
Albania, invaded by Italy, 201
—— Italian communications interrupted, 285
—— Greek Army successes against Italians, 289
—— Mussolini dissatisfied with campaign, 290
Alarmist telegram of air attack on Fleet, April 1939, 200-1
Alexander, A. V., First Lord, 574, 581, 643, 654, 659
—— Field-Marshal Sir Harold, 516, 535, 536; dispatches concerning Sicilian invasion, 537-8; 540, 545; sets up H.Q. at Malta, 548; thanks Allied Navies, 558-9; 573, 589, 647, 656
—— of Yugoslavia, H.M. King, murder of, 167; funeral 168-9
—— -Sinclair, Capt. Edwyn, 39
Alexandra, H.M. Queen, 43
Alexandria, 55, 70, 207, 233, 235-6, 301
—— imposing fleet concentration over Abyssinian invasion, 175
—— a strong base, 207-8
—— desire for increased air defences, 211, 217, 231, 288
—— squadron regattas, 1939, 217
—— sailors' wives and children stranded, 218
—— balloon barrage, 223, 309
—— repair facilities improved, 227
—— arrival of large floating dock, 227
—— bad substitute as a fleet base, 240
—— Italians bomb port only; Luftwaffe indiscriminately, 265
—— fighters for defence promised, 268, 306
—— bombed daily, 268
—— repair and docking facilities serious, 269-70, 277
—— fleet attacked by torpedo planes, 279
—— enemy attempts to reconnoitre harbour, 325
—— Japanese consul hoodwinked, 326
—— heavy air raid, 399
—— Italians penetrate boom defence, 433-5
Algeria, French reactions if N. Africa invaded, 469
—— conditions on land inadequate, 506
Algiers, 159, 471, 475, 477, 478, 501, 503, 507, 519, 545
—— landings at, 487
—— airfields captured, 487
—— a very disturbed state, 494, 495
—— raided daily, 504
—— 'limpet' attack, 512
—— French politics in a tangle, 514
—— visited by Mr. Churchill, 518
—— colourful ceremony, 556
—— Bay, 503

'A' Lighters, losses, 404; in action on run to Tobruk, 413
Aliakhmon Line, Greece, a gamble to hold, 315, 320
Allied Air Forces play important rôle, 634
—— Armies, spectacular drive in Europe, 634-5
—— Force H.Q., Algiers, 519
—— invasion of Continent preparations, 585-7
—— Merchant Navies' part in Sicilian campaign, tributes, 557-8
—— Navies thanked for co-operation in Sicilian campaign, 558
—— —— help in Rhine crossing, 634
—— —— total daily supplies to Armies 634-5
Allison, Commander J. H., 386
Alma battlefield visited, 628
Alphonso XIII, King of Spain, 43
Alsace, 619
Alupta, Crimea, 627
Amboina, 598, 606
Ambrosio, Italian, 573
Amedroz, Lt.-Commander R. T. 58, 70
American Civil War, 476
Ammunition reserves in Mediterranean low, 230; great naval shortage, 443
Amphibious operation, the largest in history, 556-8
Ancient and Honourable Artillery Company of Massachusetts dine in Canada, 130
Andaman Islands attacked, 608
Anderson, General, 477, 494, 502, 509, 515, 528
—— Sir John, 615, 645
Anglo–German Naval Agreement, 1935, 197, 198
—— –Italian relations, 1938, 190-1
Ankara, 214, 224, 315
Annapolis, Maryland, U.S.A., 466
Anofagasta, Chile, courtesy visit to, 133; nitrate mines visited, 135
Antarctic dependencies, 136
Antigua, visits to, 128, 133, 136
Anti-aircraft defences, clash of opinions, 196-7; 268
—— guns, great shortage, 319
—— cruisers keep bombers high, 319
—— ammunition, a shortage causes heavy naval losses, 369-74
Antikithera Island, Crete, surveyed as anchorage, 1939, 212; 358, 368
Anti-Submarine School, Portland, 175
—— vessels, conversion of, 196; sadly out of practice, 425
—— war, forms of, 579-80
Anti-submarine craft (British) under American Navy, 467
Antwerp captured, 609; approaches to not treated as urgent, 609, 610; 618, 619; supplies landed, 634-5
Anzac, 77

INDEX

Anzio, Italy (Operation 'Shingle'), landing at, 589, 595
Arabs in revolt, 1939, 208
Arbuthnot, Sir Robert, 48, 49, 51
Archangel, 580
Arctic convoys to N. Russia, 580; temporarily suspended, 616; total losses, 617; weather conditions, 617; a 'Northern Saga of heroism', 618
Ardennes, Rundstedt's offensive, 620, 624, 627
Argentina, 115
Argostoli, Ionian Island, courtesy visits to, 163, 183
Argyle and Sutherland Highlanders at Tymbaki, Crete, 366
Ariége River, Newfoundland, 129-30
Arles, France, visit to, 189
Arliss, Commander (later Captain), Stephen, 171, 384, 386, 444
Armed forces, post-war strength and composition problems, 657
Armies (British):
    First Armoured Division in Tunisia, 528
    First Army in N. Africa, 502-3; receives little publicity, 509; maintain position, 515, 516; stubborn fighting in Tunisia, 528-9; in Tunisian Victory march, 540
    First Division, 540
    Second Army in Belgium, 619
    Eighth Army, push forward, 515, 516; break through Mareth Line, 525; occupy Sfax, 525; enter Sousse, 525; advance from El Alamein, 528; 537; assault on Sicily, 549; in Sicily, 554, 556; invade toe of Italy, 559; in Italy, 570
    Fifteenth Army Group thank Allied Navies, 558-9
    Tenth Corps in Italy, 566, 569
    Twenty-first Army Group, 599, 634
    14th Infantry Brigade, 208
    85th Field Battery, R.A., 26
Army requirements at close of war, 655
—— reverses in Tunisia, feeling between Allies, 519, 520
—— Senior Officers' School, Sheerness 138-9
—— supplies by Navy through Benghazi, 310
Arnold, General, head of U.S. Army Air Force, 466
Arosa Bay, Spain, 159, 160
Arromanches, 609, 619
Artificial breakwaters (gooseberries), construction of, 599
—— harbours for invasion of Normandy, 595-6, 599; used to capacity, 609, 619
Artillery observation air base at Gosport, 114
Arzeu, seaplane base, N. Africa, 186, 490
Asdic hampered by Schnorkel boats, 607-8, 625
Asdics, supply of, 113; utility rendered nugatory, 176
Asinara, Gulf of, 563

Asmara, Eritrea, captured, 338
Association of Young Sailors' Wives, 151
Astypalea Island, 79
Athens, 80, 306; conference at, 320; Germans occupy, 1941, 357
—— Gulf of, 266
Athling Parliament, Iceland, millenary celebrations, 144-6
Atlantic Fleet appointment, 113, 119-20, 139
—— trade situation, 241-2
Athlone, Earl of, 610, 611
Atomic bomb:
    test, 646
    agreement to its use against Japan, 646
    dropped on Hiroshima and Nagaski, 650
Attlee, Rt. Hon. Clement R., M.P., 602, 654, 660, 662
Auberge de France, Malta, 209
Auchinleck, Gen. Sir Claude, 401, 406, 460
Augusta, Sicily, 237, 263, 537; Allied landing, 551; captured, 554, 555
Atlantic and Mediterranean Fleets in night exercises, 142
—— —— —— —— combined exercise, 1935, 171-2
—— Battle of the, of supreme importance, 321-2
—— Fleet, 110; reduction of flotillas, 119; in 1929, 140; mutiny due to pay reductions, 150-1
Austria bludgeoned, 188; occupation of in view, 625
Australian troops:
    in South African war, 28
    6th Australian Division break into Tobruk, 307
    capture Benghazi, 309
    in Crete, 379, 388
    troops at Tobruk replaced, 413, 414
    in the Pacific, 648
    Air Force, 645
Australian Navy Board, signal to, 412
—— Government's generous assistance to Royal Navy, 615
'Autocarrell', a motor car with railway wheels, 133-4
Avenger aircraft in the Pacific, 622
Avignon, France, visit to, 189
Avola, Sicily, 536
Azores, 159, 160

Bacchus, Lt.-Commander R., 70
Back, Lieut. E. P. C., R.N., 25
—— Capt. G. R. B., R.N., 384
Backhouse, Admiral Sir Roger, 188, 193, 194, 195; illness, 199-200; death of, 203; 324
Baden-Powell, Major, 29
'Badger Bill' (*see* Williams, Hamilton)

INDEX

Badoglio, Italian Marshal, resigns, 290; 555, 561; broadcasts Italian surrender, 566
Baguley, Engineer Lt.-Commander J. W., 101
Baillie-Grohman, Capt. (later Rear-Admiral) H. T., 158, 171, 253, 353, 354, 356–7, 644
Baird, Rear-Admiral George H., 115, 116, 117, 118
Bakar Bay, Yugoslavia, 164
Balaklava battlefield visited, 628
Balikpapan, Dutch Borneo, liberated, 648
Balkans, Germans expected through, 220; situation clarified, 221; 225
Baltic, service in the, 99, 100–6
Bamburgh Castle, Northumberland, 108
Barbados, visits to, 128, 133, 136
Barcelona, 185, 186, 187, 189
Bardia bombarded, 236–7, 422
—— bombed, 271, 274, 412
—— fall of, Jan. 1941, 295
—— by-passed by British forces, 298
—— supplies brought forward, 299
—— assault on, 300
—— falls, 300–1; battle fleet's help, 300–1
—— Navy supply stores, 307
—— enemy occupy, 465
Bari-Durazzo, Italy, 296
Barnard, Commander (later Captain) Geoffrey, 207, 223, 301, 332, 471–2, 475; praised, 493; 532
Bastogne, Luxembourg, 620
Bateson, Capt. S. L., 414
Battenberg, Prince Louis of, 37, 613
Battet, French General, 496
Battipaglia, Italy, 566, 568
'Battle' class destroyers, 660
Battle of Britain, 268, 276, 299
—— of the Atlantic the greatest danger, 299
'Battle of the Bulge', 620–1
Battlefields of 1914–18 in France visited, 139
Battleships, use of questioned, 113–14
B.B.C., injudicious publicity of submarine successes, 410
'Beagle' class destroyers, 51, 52, 54, 65, 70, 83, 86
Beale, Commander G. H., 367, 368
Beamer Rock, 46
Bearcroft, Capt. John E., R.N., 24, 35
Beatty, Admiral of the Fleet Earl, 97, 140, 613
Beaufort, Cardinal, 179
Beauforts attack enemy convoy, 447; special credit, 448
Bedford, Vice-Admiral Arthur E. F., 208
Beetles ('X' lighters), forerunners of landing craft, 77 (*see also* 'X' lighters)
Before the Tide Turned, 383
Beirut, 397, 398
Beith, Ayrshire, 11
Belfast, N. Ireland, visit to, 660
—— Transvaal, S.A., 28
Belgium, King Albert of, 95; lands at Ostend, 1914, 96
—— invaded, 225
Belgrade, King Alexander of Yugoslavia's funeral, 168–9

Belize, British Honduras, courtesy visit to, 133
Bellairs, Capt. Roger, R.N., 148
Bellizzi, Mr., 626
Belmont, Battle of, 22
Bembridge, firing projectiles into causes Enquiry, 46
Benghazi, 235, 259, 307, 362
—— captured, 309
—— persistent enemy air attacks, 310
—— magnetic mines laid, 344
—— port shot up with success, 361, 362
—— badly damaged, 420
—— supplies for Army, 422, 438
—— captured, 428, 436
—— evacuated by British, Jan. 1942, 441
Benin expedition, 17
Beni-Nemours, N. Africa, 480
Bennett, Rear-Admiral A. C., U.S.N., criticizes assault on Oran, 479; 503
Bennehof, Capt. O. R., U.S.N., 483
Berbera, force embarked, 269
Beresford, Admiral Lord Charles, 43, 647
Bergleitner, Herr Rude, 165, 184
Berlin, mission to, fails, 197–8
Bermondt, guerilla leader, 100
Bermuda, 41, 121; hurricane, 124–5; 128, 129, 131, 132, 133, 136
Bernard, Dr., Archbishop of Dublin, 12
Bethnal Green receives first V-1 to fall on London, 606
Betty, Capt. A. K., 111
Beyrout, conference at, May 1940, 226; French cruisers ready to embark troops, 230
Bibers (midget submarines), 625
Bieberstein, Baron Marschal von, 198
Bieri, Rear-Admiral B. H., U.S.N., 477, 494
Bighi Bay, Malta, 182
Biological Institute. Heligoland, 109
Bird, Commander Frederick G., 40
Birmingham University confers hon. degree LL.D., 656
Biscay, Bay of, patrolled by anti-submarine craft, 482
—— U-boat bases bombed, 482
—— naval patrols penetrate well in, 608
Bishop, Mary, 8
Bishop's Stortford, 140
—— Waltham (*see* Palace House)
Bisset, Capt. (later Rear-Admiral) A. W. La T., 367, 531, 562
—— Commodore (now Sir) James G. Partridge, 610
Bizerta, Tunisia, 470, 502, 545, 561
—— visit to, 158
—— no provision for French base, 225
—— failure to land, 501
—— Axis lay long and cross minefields, 511
—— occupied, 528
—— Navy's effort to enter, 529
—— Germans scuttle twenty-six ships, 531
—— in ruins, 531
Black, Lt.-Commander Alan, 367, 368

Blackburn, Lt.-Commander J. F., 300, 362-3
Blake, Vice-Admiral Sir Geoffrey, illness of, 181, 182; retirement, 187; 223
Blamey, Gen. Sir Thomas, G.O.C. Australian Forces, 378, 385, 388; calls for replacement of troops at Tobruk, 414
Blida airfield, Algiers, captured, 488
Bloemfontein, Orange Free State, S.A., 23, 24, 25
Blois, Henry de, Bishop of Winchester, 179
Board of Enquiry. Operation by Force 'H', Nov. 1940, vindicated, 291-4
Bodo, Vest Fiord, 601
Boisson, Pierre, Governor-General French W. Africa, 507 518
Bolt, Lt.-Commander A. S., 330
Bolton, Capt. Pat, 29
Bomba, Italian seaplane base shot up, 271
Bombay, 659
Bombing of cities at home causes dislocation, 299
Bone, N. Africa, unopposed landing, 491; 498, 500, 502
—— value as supply base, 504
—— attacks by enemy, 505, 516-17, 524
—— tonnage supplies, 506
—— total troops ferried and landed, 506
—— naval reinforcements, 521
Bonham-Carter, Gen. Sir Charles, 236
—— Vice-Admiral Stuart, 522, 527
Borde, Comte de la, C.-in-C. French Fleet, Toulon, 158, 159, 499
—— assured of support of British Fleet, 501
—— refuses to sail his ships to Gibraltar, 506
—— detests Darlan, 507
—— scuttles his ships, 507
—— sentenced to life imprisonment, 507
Bordeaux, Biscay port, 619
Borneo, employment of British Fleet, 598
—— captured, 648
—— Japanese surrender, 651
Bosanquet, Vice-Admiral Sir Day Hort, 41
Bosphorus, narrow straits occupied, 112
—— arrival at, Aug. 1939, 212
—— necessity of holding, 222, 223
Boston, U.S.A., visit to, 130
Botha, General, 27, 28
Botley, Hampshire, 179
Bougie, N. Africa, unopposed landing, 490, 491; 498, 500
—— landing craft base established 517
Boulogne 96, 97, 98; captured, 619
Boutwood, Capt., R.N., 532
Bowyer-Smith, Capt. Sir P. W., R.N., 386
Boxer rising, N. China, 32
'Boy Jones', a Fleet Air Arm observer, 512
Boyd, Capt. (acting Rear-Admiral) Denis, 323, 416, 578
Boyle, Commander, 38
Boys training for the Royal Navy, 119-20
Brabner, Lieut. R. A., 367-8
Bracken, Brendan, First Lord of the Admiralty, 645

Bradley, Gen., G.O.C. American Forces for invasion, 594, 620
Braithwaite, Gen., 168
Bramwell, Dr. Edwin, 108
—— Mrs. 108
—— Hilda, 163, 212, 216, 218, 220, 221; weds, 224; 257, 264, 274
Brassey's Naval Annual, 651 *fn.*
Bremen, 625, 644
Bremerhaven, visit to, 106
Bremerton Navy Yard, U.S.A., 400
Brest, bombed, 482
—— enemy destroyers at, 605
—— isolated by U.S. Eighth Army Corps, 608
Brest-Litovsk, Treaty of, 99
Bridge, Capt. A. R. M., R.N., 263
Bridge structure of destroyers painted red, 530
Brind, Rear-Admiral E. J. P., 615, 649, 650
Brindisi, 321
Bristol, 461
British and Americans closely integrated, 476-7
—— anti-submarine vessels work under U.S. Navy, 467
—— Carrier Task Force, 636
—— East Indies Fleet, 269, 649
—— Fleet, its employment at end of war in Europe, 598; divided views, 608
—— Honduras, courtesy visit to, 133, 136
—— Intelligence Service sparse concerning Italy, 201-2
—— midget submarine exploit, 631
—— Pacific Fleet, first units, 622; 629-30; operations, 635-40; 646, 649, 653
—— Somaliland attacked by Italians, 269
—— Task Force 57 in the Pacific, 636-40
Brittany peninsula overrun by U.S. Forces, 608
Brock, Admiral Sir Osmond de B., 112
Brodie, Lt.-Commander Charles G., 66
Bronkers Spruit, S.A., 28
Brooke, Gen. Sir (later Viscount) Alan, 541, 578, 585, 586, 588, 589, 609, 611, 612, 619; disagrees with Gen. Marshall, 626; 653, 657, 660, 661; receives Freedom of London, 662; awarded Order of Merit, 662
Brooking, Capt. P. W. B., 505
Brown, Lt.-Commander C. P. F., 383
—— Capt. Clifton F., R.N., 85
Browne, Elizabeth Cumming (*see* Cunningham, Mrs. D. J.)
—— Rev. Andrew, 11
Brownrigg, Capt. Sir Douglas, 39
—— Commander (later Capt.) T. M., 207, 301, 472, 475; high praise, 493; 532, 563
Bruges, 94
Brugspruit, S.A., 28
Brunei Bay, Borneo, 648
Buckingham, Leading Seaman E. G., 97, 98, 145
Budd, Sergt., 14
Budrum peninsula, 82

Bunker Hill, Battle of, 130
Burat, 436
Burmese coast, 629
Burnett, Commander (now Admiral Sir) Robert L., 140, 142, 143, 589, 590, 591
Burrough, Vice-Admiral Sir Harold, 477, 488, 489, 517, 522, 625, 644
Butcher, Commander H., U.S.N.R., 562
Buzzard, Lt.-Commander Antony W., 157
Byatt, Sir Horace, 128, 139, 140; Colonial Secretary at Gibraltar, 1914, 141
—— Lady, 128
—— Jim, 462
—— Miss Nona Christine, 86, 128, 139 (*see also* Cunningham, Viscountess)

Cadiz visited by Royal Navy, 116
Cairo, conferences: Jan., 1938, 222; June, 1940, 233; July, 1940, 267; August, 1940, 271; on Western Desert offensive, Dec., 1940, 294; Dec., 1940, 297; Feb., 1941, 314; March, 1941, 320; April, 1941, 338; preparations for invasion of Continent, Nov., 1943, 585-7
Calabria, coast of, 263
Calais, 90, 98, 111, 609, 619; supplies landed, 634-5
Callao, Peru, courtesy visit to, 133
Calshot, flying boat base, 114
Cambridge University confers honorary degree of LL.D., 656
Campbell, Lt.-Commander J. O., 300
—— Lt.-Commander L. G. B. A., 70
Campbeltown, Kintyre, 39, 45, 46
Canadians land in Sicily, 552
—— invade toe of Italy, 559
Canadian troops in action, 609
—— First Army in France, 619, 620
—— Army advance into Holland, 634
Canea, heavy enemy air raids, 283
—— patrol, 373
Cannes, troops land near under cover Allied Navies, 609
Canterbury, Archbishop of, 653
Cape St. Vincent, rough seas, 86, 160, 161; battle of 1797, 287
—— Bon, Tunisia, naval exercises, 159; action off, 430; large minefields, 511; 525; enemy penned in, 528
—— de Garde, 517
—— Guardafui, Somaliland, 629
—— Helles, Dardanelles, 73
—— Matapan, Greece 57, 353
—— Matifu, Algeria, bombarded and bombed, 488
—— Niger, 84
—— Passero, Sicily, 536
—— Pillaro area, bombarded, 559

—— Serrat, Tunisia, 524
—— Spartivento, Sardinia, 259; enemy fleet flee, 291; enemy convoy sunk, 420
—— Town, S.A., 19
—— Vilano, 86
Captain of the Galleys, Malta, 209, 627
Capuzzo, enemy transport bombarded, 346
Cardale, Commander Hubert S., 45
Carden, Vice-Admiral Sackville H., 58, 59, 60, 63, 65
Carey, Capt. E. S., R.N., 51, 52
Caribbean, the, 122
Carne, Commander (later Capt.) W. P., 223, 301, 361, 388
Caroline Islands, 636
Cartagena, 43, 185
Carteret, Mr. de, 612
Carthage, Tunis, 545
Cartwright, Lt.-Commander P. A., 354
Casablanca, French ships in, 243; 471, 474, 477; American landing, 480, 492; 494, 507
—— Conference, Jan., 1943, 515-6; decisions, 519, 534-5; 542
Casa Pieta, Malta, 157, 163, 187, 219
Caspian, a drive to the, 589
Cassino, Italy, 589; enemy withdraw, 595
Castel Benito, near Tripoli, important enemy airfields, 341, 344
Castellano, Italian General, 560
Castelorizzio, comments, 317
Castelorizzio Island, Dodecanese, a disappointing operation, 289, 316
Castle Rock, Edinburgh, 660
Catania, Sicily, 537; bombarded, 552; 554, 556
Cateno, Italian Rear-Admiral Carlo, 336
Catroux, General, 398
Cattaro, Yugoslavia, courtesy visit to, 168
Cavagnari, Italian Admiral, 290
'C' class cruisers recalled, 132
Cephalonia, 284
Ceylon, 629
Chamberlain, Neville, 202
—— flies to Munich, 194
—— flies to Godesberg, 194
—— agreement at Munich criticized, 195
Chanak, 63, 66, 113
Channel Islands relieved, 644
Chapelle, Bonnier de la, 513
Charlottetown, Prince Edward Island, visit to, 123
Chasseurs d'Afrique in Tunis victory march, 540
Chatfield, Admiral Sir Ernle (now Lord), 115, 140, 142, 143, 153-4, 188; retires, 193; wise guidance on defence, 193; Minister for Co-ordination of Defence, 193; 199, 656
Chatham, 35, 40, 50, 51, 52, 92, 93, 94, 111; Commodore, R.N. Barracks, 148, 149-56, 153, 646
Chequers, visit to, 463
Cherbourg, 605, 619

INDEX

Chetwode, Capt. George, R.N., 85
Chiefs of Staff Committee study defences, 197; 584-5; congratulated on friendly relations, 612
Chile, 115; courtesy visit to, 133, 134-5
—— British Club, 135
—— Sporting Club, 135
—— President of, courtesy visit to, 134
—— Union Club, 135
Chilean Navy, 114
Chinde, Mozambique, 20
Churchill, Rt. Hon. Winston, 66, 150, 275, 281, 461, 477, 574, 578-9, 581-2, 583, 584-5, 586, 587, 588, 596, 597, 601, 602, 604, 606, 625, 626, 641, 647, 648, 662
—— criticizes disposition of Mediterranean Fleet, 201; the facts, 201-2
—— 'Winston is back', 217
—— messages concerning Mediterranean Fleet often ungracious and hasty, 231-2
—— disagreement concerning slow arrival of reinforcements, 268-9
—— hoping for more offensive operations by E. Mediterranean Fleet, and reply thereon, 277
—— lays down responsibility of Mediterranean Fleet, to which no reply is sent, 350
—— on importance of intercepting enemy surface ships and reply thereon, 423
—— speech on supplies at Tobruk causes anger in the Navy, 428
—— entertains and unintentionally misled, 463
—— in Washington, 464, 465, 468
—— favours landing in N. Africa, 468
—— refers to Italy as 'soft under-belly of the Axis', 469
—— his knowledge of American Civil War, 476
—— support for agreement with Admiral Darlan, 502
—— at Casablanca, 515; Cyprus, 518; Adana, Turkey, 518; Tripoli, 518; Algiers, 518-19, 541, 542
—— reviews Eighth Army, 518
—— a glutton for action, 542
—— anxious to see Pantellaria bombarded, 542
—— at Quebec Conference, 561, 611-13
—— develops pneumonia at Tunis, 589; recuperates at Marrakesh, 589
—— on use of British Fleet after war in Europe ended, 598, 608
—— desire to watch Normandy invasion frustrated, 603
—— witnesses landing of troops in south of France, 609
—— weather in Gulf Stream trying, 609
—— reviews war in general, 611
—— offers British main fleet for operations against Japan, 611

—— relaxation periods, 613
—— at Yalta Conference, 619, 622
—— mobbed and cheered, 643
—— agrees on use of atom bomb, 646
—— Mrs., 463, 610, 611
Civil servants at the Admiralty, 581
Clair-Ford, Commander A. St., 373
Clarence Cove, Hamilton Island, 124
Clark, General Mark (the 'American Eagle'), 477, 478, 486, 494, 495, 496, 497, 498, 500, 560, 566, 569
—— Lt.-Commander M. J., 385
Coalition Government dissolved, 645
Coastal Command, R.A.F., and the Admiralty, change of relations desirable, 299
—— —— heavy demands, 482
—— —— persistent good work, 510
—— —— enthusiastic efficiency, 604
Cocos Islands, 629
Coleman, Lt.-Commander R. E., R.C.N., 520
'Collective Security', unenlightened belief in its efficacy, 193
Collinet, Vice-Admiral, 542
Collingwood, Admiral Lord, 209, 627, 653
Collins, Capt. J. A., R.A.N., 259, 266
Colombo, 580
Colquhoun, Lieut., R.N., 27,
Colt, Henry Archer, 17, 18, 19, 21, 32
Combined Naval command, divergent opinions, 468-9
—— Training Centre, near Inverary, Scotland, 474
—— Operations Reconnaissance and Pilotage Parties praised, 557
'Commissioned auxiliary supply ships', outstanding services, 449
'Committee of Epuration' plays havoc with admirals, 542
—— of Liberation set up by French at Algiers, 541-2
Compiègne, Forest of, 96
'Condemned Cell, the', Alexandria, 404
Connaught, H.R.H. the Duke of, 97
—— H.R.H. Princess Margaret of, 145
Connemara, Galway, 13
Conolly, Rear-Admiral R. L., U.S.N., 546
Conscription announcement, 1939, 202
Conservative Government defeated, July 1945, 647
Constantine occupied, 502
Constantinople, 58, 111, 113
Convoy duties, 85, 89, 90, 91
—— to N. Russia, 580; successful naval action, 589-92; 616-8
Coode, Capt. C. P. R., R.N., 54-5, 57, 62, 64, 70, 85, 86, 89, 106-7
Cook, James, navigator, 122
Cooke, Capt. G. C., R.N., 425
Coolidge, President, U.S.A., 130, 131
Coombs, Lt.-Commander Henry M., 99
Copenhagen, visit to, 99
Coquimbo, Chile, courtesy visit to, 133, 134

Corfu, Ionian Island, courtesy visit to, 163, 164; 191; entered by submarine, 446
Corinth Canal area, surprise enemy airborne attacks, 356
Cork and Orrery, Admiral of the Fleet Earl of, 656
Cornwallis, Commander Hon. Oswald, 180
Coronation Naval Review, Spithead, 1937, 181
Corsica, visit to, 189
County Cork, 129
Courton, Admiral de, 572, 573
Coventry, bombing of, 421
Cowan, Lieut. (later Admiral Sir) Walter, R.N., 29, 99, 101, 104, 105, 106, 119, 120, 121, 123, 124, 128, 130, 131, 133, 134, 135, 137, 173, 361, 527
Cradock, Rear-Admiral, 16
Creasy, Lt.-Commander (later Admiral Sir George), 143, 599
Cresswell, Capt. (later Rear-Admiral) G. H., 158, 323
Crete:
Western ports surveyed as anchorage, 212
preparations to occupy, 230
to be occupied if Greece attacked by Italy, 1940, 233
defence of, 283, 357
improved situation, 289
enemy air reconnaissance, 325
thin fighter protection against 400 German dive bombers, 350
used as a staging post, 353
troops form a garrison, 358
topography of, 358
heavy enemy bombing, 367
air force virtually wiped out, 367
German airborne attack, 368
seaborne landing frustrated, 368-74
battle ashore goes badly, 374
the King evacuated, 374
heavy enemy air attacks, 374
reinforcements for Army, 374-5
Admiralty fails to realize situation, 375-6
Maleme-Canea sector defence line, 377
forces cut off at Retino, 378
Canea front collapses, 378
evacuation, 378-90, 395-6
British Army win battle of Heraklion, 380
dispatch on battle 389-90
effect of Balkan campaign upon Germany, 392
battle proved disastrous to Germany, 392
German designs upon Syria and Iran interfered with, 392
'ferry trips', 393
evacuation of New Zealanders, 602
Crieff, 9, 10
—— Academy, 10
'Crieff Organ Case', 10
Crocodile Poort, S.A., 29
Cromarty, Scotland, 25
—— Firth, 147
Cronje, Boer General, surrenders, 23

Cross Channel steamers (see Landing Ships, Infantry, Appendix IV)
Crusade in Europe, 626 fn
Cruiser designs re-examined, 578
Cruisers and destroyers, fighting power sacrificed, 577-8
Cruises: Greek islands, 38; to South America, 133-7; French and Italian ports in N. Africa 158-9; to Argostoli island and Dalmation coast, 183; the Riviera, 162, 189; to Grecian waters, 163-4, 191; sailing regatta at Navarin, 191
Crutchley, Capt. Victor, R.N., 206, 226
'Cunningham Act, The', 9
Cunningham-de Courton Agreement, The, 572, 573
Cunningham, Lt.-General Alan (brother), 44, 108; in command of Artillery Brigade, Portsmouth, 172; 280; advance south of Abyssinia, 307; in Cairo, 320; commands offensive in Western Desert, 417, 421
—— Alexander, 9
—— Professor Daniel John (father), 9-12, 13, 28, 35, 44, 46
—— Mrs. D. J. (mother), 11, 13, 18, 47, 54, 88, 108; death of, 121
—— Daniel John (uncle), 9
—— Eliza Yeats (aunt), 9
—— James, 9
—— Jane (aunt), 9
—— Very Rev. Dr. John (grandfather), 9; Moderator of the Church of Scotland, 9; Principal of St. Mary's College, 9; university degrees, 9
—— Mrs. John (grandmother), 9
—— John (uncle), 9
—— John (eldest brother), 44, 47, 108
—— Admiral Sir John Henry Dacres, 174, 206, 522, 574, 586, 589, 609, 626, 657-8, 660, 662
—— Margaret (aunt), 9
—— Susan Porteous Murray (aunt), 9
—— William Murray (uncle), 9
—— of Hyndhope, Viscount Andrew (see also under Letters)
—— early days, 9-35
—— promotions, 39, 44, 76, 107, 110, 120, 154-5, 176, 202, 301, 518
—— engagement, 139; marriage, 140
—— a social engagement not a success, 149
—— offered temporary command Battle Squadron, 181
—— Deputy Chief of Naval Staff, 188-9, 195
—— studies war plans and is surprised, 195
—— acting Chief of Naval Staff, 200
—— receives congratulations, 255
—— chided for humane action, 279
—— First Sea Lord, 574
—— mobbed by officers and men, 654
—— enters House of Lords, 656
—— concludes fifty years' naval service, 662-3

Cunningham, Viscountess, marriage, 140; at Gibraltar, 141; 143; 144, 154, 159; at Corfu, 163; Navarin races, 164; Bakar Bay, Yugoslavia, 164-5; Ogulin, 165; Ljubac Bay, 165; Dubrovnik, Dalmatian coast, 166-7; Dumitor, 166; Malta, 167, 182-3, 191, 209, 212; Spithead Jubilee Review, 1935, 172; Porchester, 172; at Bishop's Waltham (*see* Palace House); coronation of H.M. King George VI, 181; 177, 178, 184; Venice, 185; Naples, 189; treated with suspicion in Rome, 189; 191, 208, 209, 212, 216, 217; looks after wives and children at Malta, 220, 226; helps in welfare work, 218, 220, 221; 257; Alexandria, 264, 274; 265; looks after convalescent officers, 281; institutes sewing and knitting parties, 307-8; leaves Alexandria, 460; 463; in Washington, 465, 472; leaves Washington in slow convoy, 507-8; 581, 582, 597, 606, 611, 616, 626, 660
Curll, Bishop, 179
Curtin, John, Australian premier, on use of Australian troops, 601-2
Curzon-Howe, Capt. the Hon. A. G., 16
—— Mrs., 16
Cuxhaven, 644
Cyclopean ruins, Ithaca Island, visited, 163
Cyprus, visit to, 216; slow convoys to, 277; 397; garrison reinforced, 403; relieved by fresh troops, 419; visited by Mr. Churchill, 518
Cyrenaica occupied in eight weeks, 310
—— further offensive held up, 314
—— British troops in retreat, 338
—— desperate situation, 343
—— aim to oust enemy, 403
—— ebb and flow of campaign, 426
—— good fighter protection for Navy, 440
—— clear of enemy, 524
Czar of Russia, 627
Czechoslovakia invaded by enemy, 199; British Government remains impotent, 200

'D' class cruisers, 132
'D' for 'Torch', 474
Daily Chronicle, 97
Daily Telegraph, 216
Dakar, W. Africa, 541, 542
—— French ships in, 243
—— Germans anticipate Allied landing, 483
—— British attack on French ships, 479, 498
—— use of port by Allies, 502
Dalmatia, Yugoslavia, courtesy visit to, 183; proposed visit of Mediterranean Fleet cancelled, 190

Dalrymple-Hamilton, Capt. (later Rear-Admiral) F. G. H., 158, 162, 581, 603
—— Mrs. 162, 581
Dampier, Lieut. Robert ('Dampie'), R.N.V.R., 481, 532, 556
Danckwerts, Capt. Victor, 197
Daniel, Vice-Admiral Charles S., 615, 655
Danzig, Hitler's technique, 209; its capture discussed at Yalta, 627-8
D'Arcy, Commander K. T., 356
Dardanelles, 58-78, 111, 113
—— necessity of holding, 1940, 222, 223
—— convoys from, 238
Darlan, French Admiral, 159, 245, 479, 488, 495-9, 542
—— becomes Governor-General of French N. Africa, 500
—— on Italian Fleet moving north, 501
—— assassinated, 513
—— state funeral, 513-4
Dartmouth, 15
—— cadets' war quarters, 659
Davenport, Lt.-Commander S. R. H., 414
Davidson, a young German officer, 197
—— Rear-Admiral Lyal A., U.S.N., 554
Davies, General, 77
—— Rhys, 144, 146
Dedeagach, Ægean Sea, French suggest landing forces 222
de Gaulle, General Charles, 237, 502, 516, 518, 541, 542
—— wished to denounce Syrian armistice, 398
—— unpopular with French generals, 500
Delagoa Bay, Mozambique, 20
Delaware River, U.S.A., 123
Demobilization schemes, 655, 658
Denmark invaded, 224; enemy surrenders 642; 645
Dent, Capt. Douglas L., 79
Dentz, French General, 396
Derna, 395
—— supplies for Army, 422, 426
—— captured, 428; Dec., 1941, 436
—— British troops withdraw, 441
—— bombed, 450
Derry by Antrim, 144
Destroyers considered too large, 577-8
—— fitted to burn oil, 47-8
—— shortage of, 193
—— hard-pressed, 287
—— losses up to Dunkirk evacuation, 233
—— fighting power sacrificed for endurance 577
Detling ridge, defensive exercises, 138
Devonport, 51, 106, 110, 143, 147, 153
Diamond Hill, S. A., 27
Dick, Commodore (later Rear-Admiral) Royer M., 8, 207, 213, 214, 246, 253, 301, 314, 462, 472, 475, 486; high praise, 493, 494, 497; shakes hands with Darlan, 498; 499; describes stormy conference, 500; 518, 532, 555, 556, 560, 563, 564
Dickens, Admiral Sir Gerald, 55, 58, 139, 531

Dickens, Charles, 58
Dicks, Lieut. Henry L., R.N., 19, 20, 32
Dieppe, 619
Dill, Field-Marshal Sir John, 314; 314–15; 315; 320; 338–9, 465, 469, 470, 516, 587, 588; his death, 612
Dinant, Belgium, 620
Diocletian's, palace visited, 167
Discourse of the Navy, 664
Dispatches (*see under* Letters)
Djibuti, 245
Djidjelli, N. Africa, landing at, 490, 491; 498, 500; landing craft base established, 517; 524
Dobbie, Lt.-General (later Sir) William, Governor of Malta, 236, 296, 297, 305, 443
Doble, Lt.-Commander D. O., 157
Dodecanese, 79
—— Italian air base, 258, 263
—— unsuccessful attempt, 289
—— enemy garrisons segregated, 290
—— bombed, 296
—— Luftwaffe arrives, 306
—— commando operation, 306
—— an attack out of the question, 314
Dolmabaghcheh, Palace of, 212
Dominica, 41
Dominion troops show gratitude to Royal Navy, 406–7
Donaldson, Sub.-Lieut. L. A. B., 19, 21
Dönitz, German admiral, on heavy submarine losses, 594
—— orders U-boats to take all risks, 604; 643
Donovan, Col., U.S.A., 306
Doolittle, Lt.-General James, U.S.A. Air Force, 477
Dorling, Capt. Taprell, R.N., 8, 144, 146
—— Capt. J. W. S., R.N., 158
Douglas, Capt. H. P., R.N., 90
—— Isle of Man, visited by Royal Navy, 116
—— Pennant, Commodore C. E., 602
Dover, 90, 91, 96, 97, 98
—— Patrol, 86, 89, 90
—— Straits of, midget submarines in, 622
10 Downing Street, London, lacks glass through enemy bombers, 596; 604
D'Oyly-Hughes, Capt. Guy, R.N., 206
Drake, Sir Francis, 16
Dublin, county of, 9, 32, 129
Dubrovnik, courtesy visit to, 166, 183
D.U.K.W.S. ('Ducks') first used in invasion of Sicily, 537, 557
Dunbar, Lieut. Ronald E. C., 92
Dundas, Capt. J. G. L., 209
Dunkirk, 90, 91, 95, 98, 619
Durazzo, 321
Durban, Natal, S.A., 22, 239
Durlacher, Commander L. G., 475; praised, 493; 532
Durmitor, hotel accommodation lacks description, 166–7
Durnford, Admiral John, 36
Dutton, Lieut. (later Capt.) A. B. S., R.N., 38, 39, 42, 108

Dutch East Indies:
 Japanese campaign unhindered, 429
 employment of British Fleet, 598

E.A.M., terrorist minority in Greece, 624
East Africa, heavy Italian losses, 314
East Indies, 630, 659
—— British Fleet's rôle, 608
—— British Fleet reinforced, 594
—— claims upon shipping, 596
—— Indies Squadron concentrate at Aden, 175
Eastern Fleet, 580, 629–30
—— successful operations against Japanese, 608
Eastern Mediterranean Fleet operations, 230–576
E-boats, nightly actions, 580, 605
Eckenforde torpedo works, Germany, 647
Ecuador, courtesy visit to, 133
Ede, Commander L. J. S., 532
Edelsten, Admiral Sir John, 8, 324, 331, 332, 579, 596, 615
Eden, Rt. Hon. Anthony, M.P., at Khartoum, 281; Alexandria, 281; Cairo and Athens, 320; Cairo, 314, 338–9; Greece, 314–15; Ankara, Turkey, 315; 575, 587, 626, 647
Edendale, S. Africa, 26, 27
Edinburgh, 107, 156, 157, 203
—— Academy, 13, 14
—— University, 10; confers honorary degree of LL.D., 656
Edward VII, H.M. King, 24, 32, 36, 43; death of, 49
—— VIII, H.M. King, abdicates, 181
Edward-Collins, Admiral Sir Frederick, 480, 482
Edwards, Commander G. R. L., 54
Egypt, 79
—— desire for increased air defences, Aug., 1939, 211
—— military and air forces, 218
—— serious differences over safety unappreciated in England, 340
—— Navy unable to save it alone, 350
—— tank reinforcements, 360
Egypt-Salonika transport route protected, 83
Eisenhower, General Dwight D., U.S.A.: 471, 474, 494, 514, 515, 516, 535, 536, 543, 562, 563, 573, 575, 585, 594, 600, 602, 622, 626, 641, 642, 661
—— nominated Supreme Commander, 468; appointed 587, 589
—— favours N. African landings, 469
—— his aim Anglo-American unity, 476
—— H.Q. at Gibraltar, 480, 482
—— confers with General Giraud, 486
—— 'a privilege to follow in his train' 493
—— in despair over politicians, 502

INDEX

Eisenhower moves to Algiers, 500, 503
—— postpones an attack, 509
—— opposes Mr. Churchill's visit to Algiers, 518
—— on dissension between the two Allies, 519-20
—— takes salute at victory march, Tunis, 540
—— invested with Tunisian Order, 541
—— invested with Moroccan Order, 541
—— H.Q. at Malta, 545, 548
—— gives news to Press and Admiralty objects, 553-4
—— broadcasts to the Italian people, 560
—— broadcasts Italian surrender, 566
—— H.Q. set up for invasion of France, 599
—— refuses request of Mr. Churchill to watch Normandy invasion, 603
—— diverse views with Montgomery, 619-20
—— receives Freedom of City of London, 645-6
El Agheila, Cyrenaica:
  Germans attack from, 338
  British troops await supplies, 438
  attacked by Afrika Korps, 440; 464
El Alamein:
  Army retreat to, 421
  British fall back to, 465
  retreat to, 473
  Eighth Army strike, Nov., 1942, 483
  victorious advance, 528
E.L.A.N., naval and military combatant forces for Greece, 624
El Teb, Soudan, 32
Elands River, S. Africa, 28
Elbe, tricky approaches to, 106
Eleusis airfield, Athens, 321
Elizabeth, H.M. Queen, 653, 656, 659, 661
—— H.R.H. Princess, 653, 659, 660, 661
Elliott, Rear-Admiral Frank, 323
Emden, 625
Empire Conference, May 1943, 601
Enfidaville, Tunisia, 528
Enemy convoy damage, 505
—— convoys dislocated between Sicily and Tunisia, 523
—— penned into Cape Bon peninsula, 528
—— surrender in N. Africa, May 1943, 530
—— submarines suffer in the Mediterranean, 553
—— use Siebel ferries, 525
—— unsuccessful attempt to escape by sea from Tunisia, 529-30
England, Lt.-Commander Hugh T., 73
England, preparations for invasion of, 276
English Harbour, Antigua, 128
Eren Kui Bay, 67
Eritrea, 210, 211, 234, 267, 338
Esteva, French Admiral, 186, 221, 222, 225, 226; asked to denounce Axis, 498, 499; hostage of Germans, 501; found guilty of treason, 501
Estonia, 99
Ethelston, Commander, 22

Eupatoria, Crimea, 627
Europe, events move apace, 194
Evetts, General J. F., 380, 385, 386
Evill, Air Vice-Marshal Sir Douglas, 466
Evry-le-Bourg, 513
Exercises; attacked by 'aircraft', 147
—— in night attacks, 157-8
—— surprises by day and night, 170-1
Exmouth Gulf, W. Australia, 629
Explosive trials at Chatham, 181

Fairfax, Lt.-Commander V. G. H. Ramsay, 512
Falmouth, 45; regatta, 146
Fanshawe, Lieut. Aubrey B., 93
Fareham Creek, Portsmouth, 46
Faroe Islands, 644
Farouk, King, 226, 230-1, 232
Fascist régime disliked by Italian Navy, 163
Fawkes, Capt. G. B. H., R.N., 510
Fédala, French Morocco, landing by American troops, 491-2
Fénard, French Admiral, 496, 497, 500
Fergusson, Vice-Admiral Sir James, 121
—— Lady, 121
Ferrol, Spain, 86; visited by Royal Navy, 117
Ferryville dockyard near Bizerta, bombed by Allies, 531; gets into running order, 545
Field, Sir Frederick, First Sea Lord, 143
Fighting power of cruisers and destroyers sacrificed for endurance, 577
First World War, 1914-18:
  preparations, 55
  Adriatic patrolled, 56
  Italy declares neutrality, 56
  German ships sail south, 56
  Austrian Fleet attacked, 57
  —— —— blockades coast of Montenegro 57
  Turkey declares war, 58
  Dardanelles campaign, 58-78
  Zeebrugge blockade, 90
  German destroyers attacked, 91-2
  Ostend, attempted blockade, 92, 93-5
  Armistice signed, 96
  lessons learnt, 113
Firth of Forth, 89, 113
Fisher, Lord, 63, 114, 578, 613
—— Capt. (later Vice-Admiral) Douglas R.N., 226, 332, 615, 635, 637, 655
—— Nevil, killed in flying accident, 176-7
—— Admiral Sir William Wordsworth, 111, 154, 158, 160, 161, 168, 170, 174, 176-7; farewell at Alexandria, 178; a great loss, 178, 181
—— Lady, 154
Fishmongers' Company bestows Honorary Freedom, 645

688   INDEX

Fitzgerald, Lt.-Commander E. F., 99
Fiume, courtesy visit to, 164
Fleet alarmist telegram of imminent air attack, 200-1
—— Air Arm (*see also* Royal Navy): 264, 321, 346
—— —— retrieved, 193
—— —— Gladiators in crates at Malta, used by R.A.F., 236
—— —— Admiralty enquires why, 236
—— —— Gladiators bombard Bardia, 236-7
—— —— most devastating weapon, 286
—— —— receive congratulations, 287
—— —— Fulmars take heavy toll, 304
—— —— losses in Crete, 367
—— —— attack Scarpanto, 376
—— —— gratifying results from Malta, 408
—— —— in the Red Sea, 409
—— —— render good service in N. Africa, 488, 490
—— —— their value, 512
—— —— and convoys to N. Russia, 617-18
—— —— why it is required, 651-2
—— bases, defence of, 196
—— Club, Alexandria, 207, 281
—— exercises, 1935, 171-2
—— in commission, 115
'Fleet Train' for repair of ships, opposition to, 598; 613, 614-15 in the Pacific, 635, 636, 639, 645
Fleets, Mediterranean and Atlantic formed, 110
Florida, 124
Flying and rocket bombs (V-1 and V-2), London casualties, 616
—— boat base at Calshot, 114
—— bomb (V-1) reaches London, 602
—— in the Navy, early days, 114-15
—— boats unsuitable for work required, 227
Foch, Marshal, 96
Focke Wulf long-range aircraft attack convoys, 408
Folkestone, 90
Forbes, Admiral of the Fleet Sir Charles, 174, 176, 481
Force 'B', 424
—— 'H', protects important convoy, 289; contact with enemy, 290; vindicated at Board of Enquiry, 1940, 291-4; 301, 316; orders for duty westwards, 322; operation 'Tiger', 360-3; heavily attacked, 362; helps convoy to Malta, 405; covers convoy, 409-10; 477, 503, 512, 517-18, 522, 531, 547, 560
—— 'K', inflict heavy enemy losses, 419-20; 423, 424; 425; successes, 426; 429; activities diminished owing to losses, 432-3; 441
—— 'Q', causes enemy holocaust, 505; 510, 512-3, 517
—— 'V', 560, 571
Ford, Vice-Admiral (now Admiral Sir) Wilbraham T. R., 236, 296, 308, 309;

perturbed at submarine crews getting no rest, 341, 364, 417, 432, 439; leaves Malta, 439-40
—— Captain, 656
Foreign Legion, 540
Formosa, 636
Fort Capuzzo, bombed, 271; captured, Dec. 1940, 295
—— Koudiat, Bizerta, 529
—— Southwick, Hampshire, 603
Forteau Bay, Labrador, 129
Foster, Montague, 14
—— Mrs., 14
Fournet, General D'Artige de, 84
Fox, Capt. Cecil H., 51
France capitulates, 240-1
—— south of, invaded (Operation 'Dragoon'), 608-9
Franco, General, 185, 188, 189, 191, 470
Fraser, Rear-Admiral (now Admiral of the Fleet Lord) Bruce A., 199, 580, 590, 591, 601; C.-in-C. Eastern Fleet, 608; 614, 615, 629-30, 637, 639-40, 650
—— Lieut. I. E., 631
—— Hon. Peter, Prime Minister of New Zealand, 378, 387, 601, 602
Freeland, Lt.-Commander Harry, R.C.N., 520
Freetown, U-boats operate near, 321
French, General, 25
—— military authorities resist Inter-Allied War Council, 210
—— Fleet, plans for seizure at Alexandria, 243-46; subsequent action, 246-56
—— Forces in Syria resist British, 396-7
—— Fleet resist in N. African landing, 487-8
—— Morocco, American troops land, 491
—— —— at Toulon asked to sail to Gibraltar, 496-7
—— Equatorial Africa, use of to Allies, 502
—— Navy at sixes and sevens, 508
—— mercantile marines work for Allies, 542
—— First Armies land in Southern France, 618
—— President visits Great Britain, 1939, 200
Freyberg, Lieut.-Gen. Sir Bernard, 357, 378, 385, 387, 406
Frendendall, Major-Gen. L. R., U.S.A., 490
Frisian Islands, 642
Fuller, Vice-Admiral Sir Cyril, 136
Fulmar fighters in action, 272-3
Fyler, Capt. H. A. S., 71

Gaeta, Italy, 43
Gallipoli peninsula bombarded, 59; 113; necessity of holding in 1940, 222
Garrett, Major, 392
Gathering Storm, The, by Winston Churchill, 20
Gavdo Island, Crete, 326

'Geddes axe', a lack of foresight and injustice, 112; 152
Gela, Sicily, 537; American landing, 552
Genefra, 461
General Strike, 1926, 120
Genoa bombarded, 316
Gensoul, French Admiral, 249
George V, H.M. King:
  coronation, 49
  Jubilee year, 171
  death of, 177-8
George VI, H.M. King, 97, 472, 603, 643
  at Jamaica, 128
  coronation, 181
  congratulations on crippling Italian Fleet at Taranto, 287
  visits troops and Sea Services, N. Africa, 543-4
  visits Malta, Tunis and Tripoli, 544-5
  present at final 'Overlord' plans, 602
  visits France, 605
  tours South Africa, 659
  at Victory march, 661
  parting audience with, 661
  on final victory, 653
  visits Edinburgh, 656
Georges, French General, 541, 542
German merchant fleet, disposal of, 106
—— pocket-battleships at large, 321
—— battle cruisers in N. Atlantic, 321
—— 'Hipper' class cruiser at large, 322
—— air reconnaissance faulty, 336
—— Afrika Corps, Libya, lack of fuel and transport, 411
—— High Command misled over N. African landing, 483
—— submarines severely punished, 510
—— control Italy, 560-1
—— Navy, lack of fighting spirit, 592-3
—— submarine activity renewed, 625
—— defeat rests on Navy maintaining supplies, 631
—— U-boat casualties, 667
Germans enter S. France, 497
—— produce torpedoes of new type, 607
Germany, 43
—— attacks Russia, 400
—— capitulates, 642-3
—— strained relations with, 1911, 49-50
Gethsemane, 208
Giant's Causeway, 144
Gibbons, Lieut. F. C., 19
Gibbs, Lt.-Commander C. E. I., 427
—— Capt. George, 506
Gibraltar, 33, 86, 110, 113, 116; gala night, 177; spring cruise to, 139; 141, 162, 172, 186; races, 188; patrols and anti-submarine measures, 218; commitments and Spanish attitude, 470; 475; strain on resources and organization, 480; 494, 501; first unopposed through convoy since 1940, 532
Giraud, French General, 478, 480-1, 483, 498, 500, 516, 541, 556
—— lands at Gibraltar, 486

—— proves stubborn, 486-7
—— flies to Algiers, 494
—— asked to use influence, 495
—— insists on being C.-in-C., 495-6
—— Darlan refuses to see him, 496
—— visits Darlan, 497
—— C.-in-C. French Army in N. Africa, 500
—— High Commissioner for N. Africa, 514
—— disliked, 542
Gladiator fighters as spares for Fleet Air Arm, 197
Glasgow Bank, failure of, 11
—— University confers hon. degree LL.D., 656
Glen Martin Flight, No. 431, 283
Glennie, Rear-Admiral I. G., 323, 365, 368, 369, 370, 373
Gloucester, H.R.H. the Duke of, 461, 583
Godesberg, Chamberlain visits Hitler, 194
Godfrey, Capt. (now Admiral) John H., 8, 88, 89, 182
Godfroy, French Vice-Admiral R. E., 225, 234, 235, 237, 238, 243, 244, 246, 397, 479, 500, 501
—— immobilizes French Fleet at Alexandria, 247-54
—— —— joins British Fleet, 256
—— his obstinacy, 502
—— unable to co-operate, 508
—— consents to fight on side of Allies, 541
Godsal, Commander, 92
Godwin-Austen, Brigadier (now Gen. Sir) Alfred, 208
'Gold' Beach, France, 605
Golfe Juan, France, courtesy visit to, 189
Golgotha, 208
Goltz, Gen. von der, 100, 102, 104, 105
Gomez, President (Chile), 134
Gort, Field-Marshal Viscount, 544, 573
Gosport, torpedo carrying and artillery observation base, 114
Goubellat Plain, 528
Gould, Lieut. P. F. S., 525
—— Petty Officer T. W., 445-6
Gouraud, General, 77
Government House, Trinidad, 128-9
—— —— Barbados, 129
—— policy of wait and see, 1939, 200
Gozo, Malta, Americans prepare airstrip, 547
Graham, Commander H. R., 453
—— James (*see* Montrose, Duke of)
Grant, Commander W. L., 22, 30
Grantham, Capt. Guy, 417, 448
Graspan, Battle of, 22
Great Britain no longer first Naval Power, 112
—— —— becomes an armed camp, 594
—— —— why it requires a Navy, 651-2
—— Crocodile River, S.A., 29
—— Pass, Alexandria, mined, 360
Greece, H.M. King George II of, 191
—— landing in the Piræus, 83-4
—— guarantees by British Government, 202

690   INDEX

Greece, southern ports surveyed as anchorages, 212
—— ultimatum presented by Italians, Oct. 28, 1940, 282
—— refuses direct military aid, 307
—— greatest possible help sent, 314
—— hazards of transporting Army, 315, 318-20
—— convoys continually bombed, 319
—— enemy air reconnaissance, 325
—— attacked by Germany, 338
—— Navy evacuate Army with meagre air support, 350, 352-7
—— German air superiority, 352
—— decision to withdraw troops, 352
—— liberation of, 624
—— problem of, 657
Greek Fleet captured, 84
—— Army successes on Albanian front, 289
—— Government seek assistance, 313
—— —— fail to implement agreement, 320
—— Army, signs of disintegration, 352
—— independence, political rivalry, 624
Greenock, 610
Greenwich, 356
Griffiths, Commander L., R.N.R., 359
Gruenther, Brig.-Gen. Alfred, M., 477
Graziani, Italian Marshal, 273
Guards' Brigade, 27
Guatemala, 115; courtesy visit to, 133
Gullane, E. Lothian, 156
Gumishlu bombarded, 82
Gun Cay, H.Q. of rum-running industry, visited, 127
Gunboats, their grand service, 274
Gunnery, progress in, 44
Guayaquil, Ecuador, courtesy visit to, 133
Gyro compasses, supply of, 113

Haggard, Lt.-Commander H. A. V., 347
Hargiss, Brigadier, 406
Haifa, 208, 358, 397
—— slow convoys to, 277
—— threat to oil-fuel supplies, 396
Haining, Lt.-Gen. (now General Sir Robert, 208, 401
Halfaya bombarded, 422
—— Pass, 273
Halifax, Lord, 202, 466
—— Lady, 466
—— Nova Scotia, visit to, 122; 129, 130, 610
Hall, Rear-Admiral John L., U.S.N., 516, 545, 560, 566
Hallifax, Rear-Admiral R. H. C., 409
Halsey, Admiral W. F., U.S.N., 638, 639, 646, 649, 650
Hamanatsu, Honshu, bombarded, 650
Hamblen, Col., 478

Hamburg, 106, 109; R.A.F. devastation, 341, 343, 625, 631, 644
Hamilton, Capt. R. M., 108
—— General Sir Ian, 26, 77
—— Island, 124
—— Ontario, 654
—— Sir Robert, 144
Hampton, Capt. T. C., 370
Handyside, Patrick, naval surgeon, 20
Harcourt, Rear- (later Admiral Sir) C. H. J., 490, 505, 510-11, 517, 531, 547, 650-1, 653
Hare Bay, Newfoundland, 122, 129
Harford, Miss, 13
Harland and Wolff, 45, 660
Harper, Capt. John, 168
Harriman, Averill, 401
Harris, Capt. C. F., R.N., 158
—— Vice-Admiral Sir Robert Hastings, 18
Hartebeestefontein, S.A., 28
Harwich, 49, 106
—— force, 86, 89, 91, 93
Harwood, Admiral, Sir Henry, 459, 521, 522
Haslar Creek, 34
—— Hospital, 660
Havre, 605, 619
Hawke Bay, Newfoundland, 122, 129
Haynes Commander H. J., 300, 310
Hector Spruit, S.A., 30
Heligoland, destruction of, 1920, 108-10, 642; devastated, 644
Heliopolis, 402
Hellenes, H.M. King of the, 352
—— evacuated, 357, 358, 374
Helles, 76-8
Henderson, Capt. Frank Hannam, 19
—— Admiral Sir Reginald G. H., his death, 199
Heneage, Commodore A. W., 70-1, 83
Henry II, 179
Heraklion, Crete, airfield, 289, 358
—— Leinster Regt. landed, 366
—— patrol off, maintained, 373
—— Army win battle, 380
—— evacuation of troops, 382
Hewitt, Vice-Admiral H. Kent, U.S.N., 477, 491, 492, 494, 519, 535, 546, 554, 556, 560, 566, 568, 569, 571, 572, 626, 654, 661
—— in command of Navy for Casablanca landing, 471
—— C.-in-C. U.S. naval forces in Mediterranean, 522-3
—— sore at change of plans for invasion of Sicily, 538
Hickey, Commander W. R., R.N.R., 427
Hickling, Capt. (later Rear-Admiral) Harold A., 307, 602
Hill, master of a collier, 80
—— Professor Sir Leonard, 180
Hillgarth, Alan, 186, 187
Hine, Lt.-Commander J. F. W., 426
Hiroshima receives first atomic bomb, 650
Hitachi, Japan, shelled, 649
Hitler and his Admirals, 513 fn.

INDEX

Hitler in Italy, 189, 190
—— demands Sudetenland, 194
—— visited twice by Neville Chamberlain, 194
—— abrogates clause in Anglo-German Naval Agreement of 1935, 197–8
—— becomes more truculent and grasping, 198
—— rejects President Roosevelt's plea, 202
—— fears Italian collapse, 306
—— displeased, 592
—— last bid for victory, 620
Hodges, Gen. C. H., U.S.A., 634
—— Rear-Admiral (later Admiral Sir Michael), 110, 115, 143
Hodgkinson, Lt.-Commander Hugh, 383
Hodgson, Capt, John C., R.N., 111
Holbrook, Lieut., 66
Holland, invaded, 225
—— Canadian Army advance into, 634
—— enemy surrenders, 642
—— food for, 644
—— John, 664
Hollis, Major-Gen Sir Leslie, 661
Holmes, Col. Julius, 478, 494, 496, 497
Holt, Rear-Admiral R. V., 645
Holyhead, 146
Home and Mediterranean Fleets exercise, 159–62
Home Fleet, 579, 580
—— success, 600–1
—— successful operation off Norwegian coast, 608
Hong-Kong, reoccupation of, 650–1
—— delay in surrender signatures, 653
Honshu, Japan, 646
Hood, Lord, 189, 627
Hope, Capt. George, R.N., 68
Hopkins, Harry, 472, 515, 587, 598
Horan, Capt. H. E., R.N., 158, 163, 164, 226
Horsey, Commander de, 25
Horsley, Capt. A. J., R.N., 40, 41
Horton, Admiral Sir Max, 410, 579
Hoste, Capt. Sir William, exploits of, 168
Hotel St. Georges, Algiers, 495, 500, 503
Hotham, Capt. C. E., 206
House of Keys, Isle of Man, 146
Howell, Squadron-Leader, 367
Huddart, midshipman, 22
Huddleston, Major-Gen. Sir Herbert, 460
Hudson Squadron, Coastal Command, request for American control, 467
Hughes, Capt. Guy D'Oyly, 170
Hull, 89, 90
Human torpedoes penetrate boom defence, Alexandria, 434–5
Hungerford, Viscount Portal of (see Portal, Wing Commander)
'Hunt' class destroyers, 442, 450, 451, 455, 530, 631
Hurricanes at Bermuda, 124–5
'Hurricanes before honour', 318; 320–1
Hutchings, Capt. J. H., 602
Hutchison, Capt. C. A. G., 429, 455, 456
Hyndhope, Kirkhope, Selkirk County, 9

Iachino, Italian Admiral Angelo, mistakes British fleet for Italian, 336
Iceland and Denmark, H.M. King Christian of, 144–5
—— Althing millenary celebrations, 144–6
—— enemy submarines near, 631
Icon of St. Nicholas presented to E. Mediterranean Fleet, 335
Imperial Defence College, 138–9
Indian Medical Service, 44
—— Ocean, communications across, 580
Industrial capacity of Great Britain, 196
Ineunu, General, Turkish Republic President, 214–15
Infra-red detection leads to unfortunate result, 480
Ingersoll, Admiral Royal E., C.-in-C. Atlantic Fleet, 477
Inkerman battlefield visited, 628
Inshore Squadron formed for W. Desert coast, 294
—— —— in action, 307, 339
—— —— praised by C.-in-C., 310
—— —— outstanding service, 359
Instruments of Italian surrender, 560–1, 572–3
Inter-Allied Commissions in Germany, 106
—— War Council resisted by French, 210
—— —— Plans unsatisfactory, 210
Invasion of Continent, preparations, 585–7
Inverchapel, Lord (see Kerr, Sir Archibald C.)
Invergordon, 111, 113, 143, 147; Atlantic Fleet mutiny at, 150–1
Inverkeithing, 119
Inverness, 88
Ionian Islands, 284
—— Sea, enemy forces in, 430; 547
Ipswich, 51
Iran, oil resources, 314
Ireland Island, Bermuda, hurricane, 124–5
Irish Franciscan father conducts tour o Jerusalem, 589
—— Sea, midget submarines in, 625
Iron ore traffic to Germany, 223
Ishigaki, enemy airfields attacked, 636
Isle of Wight, 34
Ismailia bombed by enemy, 408
Ismay, General Lord, 587, 605, 613, 661
Ismet Pasha, 111
Istanbul, 111; Vali of, visit to, 213, 215
It Might Happen Again, 153
Italian Navy and discipline, 162–3
—— —— always royalist, 163
—— transports use Suez Canal, 174
—— squadron visits Malta, June 1938, 190
—— invasion of Albania while British ships visit Italian ports, 201
—— Navy, problem if war declared, 210–11
—— Somaliland, 210, 211
—— Navy in mock attack on British Fleet, 216
—— ships use Suez Canal, June 1940, 233
—— declares war, 235
—— destroyer sunk, 263
—— bombers shot down, 264

Italian Navy attacked, 266
—— —— cease to use Tobruk as supply base, 267
—— attack British Somaliland, 269
—— twelve bombers shot down, 271
—— launch W. Desert offensive, 273
—— Fleet sighted, 258, 259
—— air reconnaissance highly efficient, 258-9
—— Fleet engaged, 260-2; turn away, 262
—— Regia Aeronautica in action, 262, 265
—— Fleet fails to attack, 276
—— ultimatum presented to Greece, 282
—— Fleet attacked at Taranto; half are crippled, 286-7
—— —— move to Naples, 287
—— convoy shot up on way to Tripoli, 295
—— bomber squadrons mauled, 290
—— prisoners, 307
—— 10th Army ceases to exist, 309
—— forces on brink of further collapse, 314
—— naval losses at Battle of Matapan, 335
—— Navy, extraordinary state of unpreparedness, 336-7
—— ships lack radar, 337
—— shipping disorganized, 420, 421
—— convoy turns back, 430
—— use human torpedoes, 434-5
—— enemy meet striking success, no British battle-fleet to oppose, 438-43; 447-8
—— people anxious for peace, 560
—— colonies, problem of disposal, 657
—— U-boat casualties, 668
Italians bomb British ships outside Spanish ports, 190
Italy, King Victor Emmanuel, 43; commands Army, 555
—— futile sanctions for attack on Abyssinia, 175
—— war with, seemed unlikely, 210-11, 217, 218
—— declares war, June, 1940, 235
—— decides to build aircraft carriers, 337
—— peace terms discussed, 560-1, 572
—— Quebec Conference discuss future campaign, 611
Itea Bay, Greece, 170
Ithaca Island, 56; courtesy visit to, 163

Jacob, Major-Gen. Sir Edward, 661
Jamaica, visit to, 127, 128; courtesy visit to, 133
—— Club, 128
James, Capt. P. H. G., R.N., 634
—— Admiral Sir William, 194
Japan attacks Pearl Harbour; British tactics followed, 428-9
—— unconditionally surrenders, 650
—— instrument of surrender signed, 650
Japanese consul hoodwinked, 326
—— surface raiders and submarines, 580
Japanese surface raiders and submarines, 580
—— war, British naval part, 613
—— kamikazes (suicide 'planes), 616, 637, 639
—— submarines in Indian Ocean, 629
—— mainland heavily bombed, 645
—— aircraft losses, 649
—— coast heavily shelled, 649-50
—— battleships sunk, 650
—— U-boat casualties, 669
Jarrett, C. G., 197
Java Sea, 308, 629
Jellicoe, Admiral of the Fleet Earl, J. R., 613
Jerusalem, 208; American colleagues entertained, 588
Jervis, John (Earl of St. Vincent), 627
Jewell, Lieut. N. L. A., 478, 481
Jibouti, 234
Johannesburg, Transvaal, 25
Johore Strait, Singapore, 631
Joughin, J. C., 304
J.U. 88's in venomous attack on convoy, 452
Jubilee Review, Spithead, 172-3
Juin, French General, 478, 488, 496, 497, 498, 499, 500, 540, 541, 658
Juneh harbour, Syria, 398
'Juno' beach, France, 605
Justinian, 215
Jutland, 1914-18, 120; night action avoided, 161

Kaapmuiden, Transvaal, 30
Kairouan, Tunisia, 545
Kaiserhof Hotel, Berlin, 198
Kai Shek, Marshal Chiang, 587
—— Madame, 587
Kalamata, Peloponnesus, 353, 356, 357 365, 368, 369, 370, 397, 385-9, 417
Kamaishi, Japan, bombarded, 650
Kamikazes (suicide bombers) in action, 637, 639
Kano, Nigeria, 461
Kaso Island, operation vetoed, 306
—— Straits, Crete, 358; Italian M.T. boats damaged, 368; 382
Kassala captured by Germans, 267
Keenan, Major, 103
Keighly-Peach, Commander, 264
Keith, Lord, 627
Kelibia, Tunisia, 457, 525; 'regatta' (Operation 'Retribution'), 529-30
Kells, Royal Marine driver, 586, 589
Kelly, Admiral Sir Howard, 224-5
—— Admiral Sir John D., 113

INDEX

Kelsey, Capt. M. H. A., 417
Kemal, Mustapha, wreath laid, 213; 215
Kennedy-Purvis, Vice-Admiral Charles, 200, 578; death of, 659
Kent, H.R.H. the Duke of, 168
Kent-Lemon, Brigadier A. L., 490
Kephalo Bay, Imbros Island, 68, 74
Kephez Point, 62, 64, 66
Keren, Eritrea, captured, 338
Kerkenah Islands, Tunisia, enemy convoy shot up, 296
Kerr, Sir Archibald Clark, 133
Kerry, Eire, 13
Kesselring, German General in Sicily, 421; 595
Keyes, Lt.-Commander Adrian St. Vincent, 54, 68, 74
—— Admiral Lord, 86; 92, 94, 95, 96, 98, 291; death of, 656
Khartoum, conference at, 281; 460
Kiel, bombing of, 343; 625
—— Canal, 644
Kilindini, E.A., 20
Kimberley, S.A., 21, 22
King Alfred establishment, Hove, 656
—— David Hotel, Jerusalem, 588
—— Rear-Admiral (later Admiral) E. L. S., 365, 368, 369, 370, 385-9, 397, 417
—— Admiral Ernest J., U.S.N., 464, 465-6, 468, 469; antipathy to placing U.S. forces under British command, 471; 479, 515, 516, 598; determined to keep Royal Navy out of Pacific, 606, 611; gives way with bad grace, 612; still averse to British Fleet, 613, 628; 641-2, 654
—— Capt. I. E., 533
—— Mackenzie, Premier of Canada, 601, 610, 611
Kingston, Jamaica, visited, 128
Kirk, Lt.-Commander (later Rear-Admiral) Alan, U.S.N., 123, 124, 456, 552; commands American assault on Normandy, 602
Kitcat, Lt.-Commander C. A. de W., 382
Kitchener, Lord, 29
Kithera Island, Crete, surveyed as anchorage, 212
—— Channel, 358
Kitson, Lt.-Commander E. H., 131
Knatchbull-Hugessen, Sir Hughe, 213
Knights of St. John, Malta, 627
Knox, Brig.-General, R.M., 108, 109
—— Frank, U.S. Secretary for the Navy, 464
Kobe, Japan, bombed, 645
Koetz, French General, 497
Kola Inlet, Russia, 618
Komati Poort, 29, 30
Kondia Bay, 59-60
Kos, Gulf of, Dodecanese, 82
—— Island recaptured by Germans, 574, 582-3
Kotor (see Cattaro)

Krithia, 61, 73
Kroonstadt, Orange Free State, 24, 25
Kruger, Oom Paul, 29
Kum-Kale, 61; landing on 64, 72
Kure naval base bombed, 645, 649

La Calle, French N. Africa, supplies to, 506
—— Cateau, France, visited, 139
—— Fosette, France, Gen. Giraud picked up from small boat, 486
—— Senia airfield, N. Africa, bombed, 490
Labour Government elected, July 1945, 647
Labuan airfield, Borneo, captured, 648
Ladysmith, Natal, 21
Laird's shipyard, 38
Lake Tirso dam, Sardinia, attempt to torpedo, 316
Lambe, Commander (later Captain) Charles E., 157, 162, 579
Lambert, Capt. (later Commodore) C. Foley, 39, 51, 53
Lambton, Capt. (later Rear-Admiral) the Hon. Hedworth, 21, 43
Lamington, Lord, 144, 146
Lampedusa Island surrenders, 543; 549; aircraft crash, 626
Lampson, Sir Miles, 226, 274
—— Lady, 274
Lamu, E. Africa, 20
Landing craft, tanks, enter Sfax, 525
—— —— tied down for Army supplies, 555-6
—— —— crews, tributes, 557, 599
Lane, Commander R. H. D., 354
Lang, G. H., midshipman, 21
Lapeyrère, Admiral Boué de, 57
Larken, Capt. (later Commodore) Frank, 79, 90, 92
Latvia, 99; G.H.Q. attacked by Germans, 102
Latvian Republic proclaimed, 100
Layton, Vice-Admiral Geoffrey, 192, 206, 219
Lazaretto Creek, Malta, 441
League of Nations, faith in, 114
—— —— futile contortions with Mussolini, 173, 177
—— —— unenlightened belief in 'Collective Security', 193
Leah, Capt. Henry, R.N., 34
Leahy, Admiral William D., U.S.N., 466, 612, 661
Leatham, Vice-Admiral Sir Ralph, 417, 439, 457, 522
Leathers, Lord, opposes ships for fleet train, 598; 613, 614-15, 626
Lecky, Lt.-Commander A. M., 70
Lee, Lieut. Hugh, 275, 460
Lee, Major, U.S.A., 504; causes consternation, 518-19
Lee-Barber, Lt.-Commander J., 333

INDEX

Leeds University confers honorary degree LL.D., 656
Lees, Capt. D. M., 388
Leghorn, Tuscany, courtesy visit to; an abrupt ending, 162
—— bombarded, 316
Leicester, Paymaster-Lt. Charles, 108
Leigh-Mallory, Air Chief Marshal for Normandy invasion, 594
Leinster Regt. land at Heraklion, Crete, 366
Leith, 120
Lemnitzer, Brig.-General, U.S.A., 478
Lemoine, R., 113, 117
Leros bombed, 279; 574, 575; enemy landing, 582-3
LETTERS, DISPATCHES AND SIGNALS:
  From Admiralty
    their decision to blockade considered inopportune, 341-2
    replies pointing out difficulties of operation and their Lordships' decision queried, 342-5
    ideas as to how enemy convoys to Tripoli should be attacked, 348
  To Admiralty
    report on bombardment of Tripoli and Fleet's risk, 347-8
    Mediterranean Fleet short of anti-aircraft equipment, 363-4
    on outstanding naval examples in frustrating Crete seaborne landing, 371-2
    lack of ammunition and anti-aircraft prevents sea control, 375-6
    officers, men and machinery near exhaustion, 376, 389-90
    an appreciation in which matters are not minced, 395-6
    retention of 22nd S.A. Anti-Submarine Group sought, 427
    Navy's achievement at Tobruk, 427-8
    main objective need of security in Central Mediterranean, 436-7
    every submarine 'worth its weight in gold', 445
    requests for Malta to be adequately protected from air attack, 448
    N. African campaign summed up; deficiencies pointed out, 492-3
    on establishment of Italian beach-head, 571
  To General Eisenhower
    and Eisenhower's greatest memory, 493
  From Admiral Sir Dudley Pound (First Sea Lord)
    anti-aircraft defence for Malta, 216-17
    trend of naval affairs at home, 219
    general naval situation, 223
    Italian entry into the war, 227
    defensive action, 231
    occupation of Crete, 233
    objects to withdrawal of E. Mediterranean Fleet, 241-2
    seizure of French Fleet, 244-6
    effect on Cabinet at news of Taranto, 287
    tart signal reply for Hurricanes for Malta, 321
    suggests Navy will 'let side down' over enemy supplies to Libya, 343; repudiation by C.-in-C. in reply, 343-4
    asking further attempt to evacuate troops in Crete, 388-9
    urges publicity as propaganda, 410
    troubled about interception of enemy supplies to Tripoli, 411
    necessity to interrupt enemy traffic by surface forces and reply thereto, 423-4
    condolence on loss of the *Barham*, 425
    anti-submarine craft sadly out of practice, 425
    intimation to represent First Sea Lord on Combined Chiefs of Staff Committee at Washington, 458
  From C.-in-C. Mediterranean Fleet (Viscount Cunningham) *to Admiral Sir Dudley Pound*
    Prime Minister's fears rejected, 231
    naval strategy in E. Mediterranean, 239-40
    consequences of French Fleet collapse, 241-2
    lack of reinforcements, 268
    concerned with submarine casualties, 269
    intention to attack Italian communications, 288-9
    Operation 'Workshop' disliked, 291
    frank words at action in ordering Court of Enquiry for Force 'H' action, Nov. 27, 1940, 291-4
    counter measures to German dive bombers, 313
    taking and abandonment of Castelorizzo 'a rotten business', 316
    strong comments on air situation, loss of many ships and questions policy of helping Greece, 318-19
    signal for Hurricanes for Malta meets tart reply, 321-3
    a mollifying message, 322
    suggestion that Navy 'will let side down' hotly repudiated, 343-4
    deprecates sacrifice of ship to block Tripoli; reasons for, 344
    concerning gruelling time of officers and ratings, 360
    complains of waste of time through lack of tank filters, 363
    on enemy's vast air superiority, 364
    signals inability to evacuate all troops from Crete, 389
    physical and mental exhaustion of officers and men in battle for Crete, 390
    suggests Admiralty would like to change fleet commands, 390
    concerning heavy air raids on Alexandria, 399-400

INDEX

LETTERS, DISPATCHES AND SIGNALS (*contd.*)
  opposed to moving to Cairo, 400
  suggests convoy to Malta be run from west, 404–5
  on delay in W. Desert offensive, 406
  publicity is anathema to naval officers; an injudicious example, 410
  disputes assertion on increase of enemy forces in Libya, 411
  on inability to provide cruisers for Malta, 411–12
  advice on replacement of troops at Tobruk turned down, 414
  steps to ensure air position in E. Mediterranean is understood, 415–16
  Operation 'Whipcord' (suggested attack and capture of Sicily) premature, 417
  Prime Minister's speech on supplies at Tobruk angers Navy, 428
  points out all battleships out of action, 434
  Alexandria boom defence penetrated by enemy human torpedoes, 434–5
  grim bleakness of Malta and hazards of running convoys, 441–2
  deplores loss of the *Naiad*, 448
  condition of Fleet desperate; only two destroyers serviceable, 454
  offers to continue command of Mediterranean Fleet on receiving another appointment, 458–9
  on American aerial anti-submarine war; considers 'they are in a mess', 467
  American lack of keenness about N. African Operation 'Torch', 468
  urges one naval commander, 470
  lack of radar warning at Algiers, 503
  on state of deadlock over plans to invade Sicily, 536–7
  on acceptance of the final 'Husky' plan, 538
  concern at unjustified optimism in Army circles over assault on Italy, 546
Leuchars, Fifeshire, 114
Lewis, Rear-Admiral Spencer S., U.S.N., 522
Leyte, Philippines, 638
Libau, Latvia, 99, 100, 101; tense situation, 102–5
Libya, 210, 211, 216, 234, 235, 258
—— offensive postponed, 218
—— Mussolini dissatisfied, 290
—— stopping of supplies to enemy, 343–4, 408
Libyan coast bombed, 274
—— offensive, 77, 277
—— —— our convoys heavily bombed through lack of air protection, 350
Licata, Sicily, 537; American landing, 552
Life of Nelson, The, 190, 262
Lima, Peru, 133, 134
Limerick, 129
'Limpet' attacks at Mers-el-Kebir, 524
Linosa Island, 539; surrenders, 543

Lisbon, Portugal, 159, 160, 560
Lissa Island (*see* Vis)
Lithuania, 99
Little, Admiral Sir Charles, 15, 101, 102, 200, 458, 462, 464, 603
—— Lady, 464
Liverpool, visited by Royal Navy, 117; 137, 660
Livno, Dalmatia, primitive accommodation 184
Ljubac, Yugoslavia, courtesy visit to, 165–6
Llewellin, Col. J. J., 209
Lloyd, Air Vice-Marshal Sir Hugh, 523
Lloyd George, Rt. Hon. David, 97
Loch Erribol, 644
Lodge, Rev. N. B., naval instructor, 16
'Logberg', or Law Rock, Iceland, 146
London Gazette supplement, 640
London, German bombers attack, 596
Longley-Cook, Capt. E. W. L., R.N., 505, 512
'Longer Instrument, The', Italian surrender terms, 572
Longmore, Air Chief Marshal Sir Arthur, 225, 281, 282, 287, 305, 314, 317–18, 320, 322, 338–9, 352, 359, 364–5, 402
Long-term policy, Admiralty's decision, 210
Loraine, Sir Percy, 221
L'Orient isolated by Eighth Army Corps, 608; 619
Lough Carlingford, 45
Love, a leading torpedo man, 61
Lowe, Ernest, gunner, R.N., 24
L.S.T.s, 607
Ludendorff Bridge over Rhine seized intact, 634
Lussin Piccolo, Italian island, courtesy visit to, 165
Luxemburg invaded, 225
Luzon, Philippines, occupied, 648
Lyme Regis, Dorset, 147
Lyne, Rear-Admiral Sir Thomas J. S., 52
Lynes, Commodore Hubert, 90
'Lyon, General' (H.M. King George VI) visits the Services in N. Africa, 543; Tunis and Tripoli, 544; Malta, 544–5
Lyttelton, Oliver, 398, 401
Lyster, Rear-Admiral A. L. St. G., 273, 283 285, 296, 323, 477

MacArthur, General Douglas, 402, 628, 648
Macbeth, 38
Macedonia, Greeks fail to withdraw troops, 320
Machadodorp, S.A., 28
Mack, Capt. (later Rear-Admiral) Philip, 253, 329, 333, 334, 341, 345, 359, 404; an appreciation, 448–9
Mackenzie, Lieut. H. S., 445
—— Rear-Admiral, K. H. L., 522

MacLeod, Capt. Kenneth, R.N., 118
MacMichael, Sir Harold, 208
Macmillan, Harold, 514, 540, 541, 573
Macready, Major-General, 466
Macrorie, Capt. Arthur, R.N., 39
Madden, Admiral Sir Charles, 132
—— Capt. Sir Charles, 660
Mafeking, S.A., 21
Magennis, Leading Seaman J. J., 631
Magnetic mines used by Germans, 219
Mahon, Commander Richard F. H., 46
Mainz, 634
Maison Blanche aerodrome, Algiers, captured, 488, 494; 500, 518
Maisky, M. (Russia), praises British Fleet, 618
Majorca, 185
Malacca, Straits of, 629, 631, 649
Malakoff, Crimea, visited, 628
Malaya, Japanese unhindered campaign, 429
—— employment of British Fleet, 598
—— Prime Minister on, 611
—— coast bombarded, 649
—— Japanese surrender, 651
Malcolm, Vice-Admiral Sir Pulteney, 521
Maleme, Crete, 321, 329
—— airfield, 289, 358; captured by Germans, 367; bombarded, 373
—— -Suda area, Crete, troops evacuated, 382
Malete, Italian General, 294
Massigli, M., 542
Malta, 43, 54, 55, 56, 60, 77, 85, 86, 113, 128, 157, 159, 170, 171, 172, 185, 208, 219, 230, 301
—— festivities, 186-7
—— anti-aircraft equipment, its unpreparedness, 196, 197, 226
—— Gladiator fighters in crates used as spares for Fleet Air Arm, 197
—— desire for increased air defences, Aug., 1939, 211
—— heavy scale anti-aircraft defence approved, 216-17
—— use of, not to be relied upon, 231, 233
—— bombed day and night, 236
—— its poor defences, 240
—— its importance again stressed, 241
—— the Services situation and advice to hold it at all costs, 257-8
—— 72 raids in 29 days, 264
—— fighters for its defence, 268
—— supplies become necessary, 277
—— R.A.F. reconnaissance, 283
—— Convoys to, 284, 316; no interference, 322; 409-10; successful, 440; faced with enemy aerodromes on each flank, 441; a commitment for all three Services, 444, 449; efforts of the Services to get convoys through, 449-58
—— touching reception, Dec. 20, 1940, 296-7
—— back to normal in repair work, 298
—— dockyard recoveries following air attacks, 308-9
—— in a very bad state, 304, 319
—— further demand for aircraft and a tart reply, 321-3
—— ample oil fuel required, 340
—— attention again drawn to serious situation, 340-1
—— R.A.F. assist the Royal Navy, 348
—— fuel situation precarious, 348
—— disagreement as to primary duties of R.A.F., 350
—— continuous air attacks, 350
—— virulent mine-laying attacks, 359
—— completely mined in and all sweepers lost, 361
—— heavily bombed, 361, 362, 426, 438, 441
—— many fighters on the ground lost, 364
—— supplies shelved, 394
—— acute anxiety, 404
—— unable to supply surface force, 411-12
—— attempts to reduce it to rubble, 421
—— vivid picture of affairs, Jan. 1942, 439
—— submarines spend most of day submerged, 441
—— drastic steps to retain island put forward, 443-4
—— placed under command of C.-in-C. Middle East, 444
—— an evil time, 447
—— dockyard a shambles of rubble, 457
—— end of trial in sight, 473
—— visited by H.M. King George VI, 544-5
—— H.Q. set up for assault on Sicily, 545; preparations, 547-8
—— returns to full activity, 555
—— Italian Fleet surrender, 562
—— *en fête*, 564
—— presented with 'Presidential Citation' by President Roosevelt, 589
—— preparations for Yalta Conference, 626
—— 'there is antiquity', 627
Maltby, Commander Henry Bradford, 121, 124, 126
Maltizana, Stampalia Island, 79
Manchester Guardian, 144
Manchester, visited by Royal Navy, 117
—— Luncheon Club, 659
Manchuria, Russian action in, 646
Mandalay occupied, 630
Mandelyah, Gulf of, 81
Manoel Island, Malta, 170, 172; hit by bombs, 441
Manstein, German General, 627
Manual of Anatomy, by Daniel John Cunningham, 11
Manus, Admiralty Islands, 614, 635-6, 637, 639
Marchant, Major, 25
'Marchesa Graziani', a sewing machine, 308
Mareth Line broken through, March 1943, 525
Margaret, H.R.H. Princess, 653, 659, 661
—— Queen, 179
Marittimo, Sicily, bombarded, 547
Marks, Lord, 144

INDEX

Marmora, Sea of, 66, 112, 113, 212
Marrakesh, Morocco, Mr. Churchill at, 589
Marriott, Capt. J. P. R., R.N., 97
Marsala, Sicily, bombed, 547
Marseilles, 192, 609, 618
Marshall, General George C., U.S.A., 464, 466-7, 516, 541, 585, 605, 609, 612, 619; disagrees with General Brooke, 626; 627, 646
Marshall-A'Deane, Commander W. R., 333
Martienssen, Anthony, 513 *fn.*
Martin, Kingsley, 144
Mason-Macfarlane, Lt.-General Frank, 482
Massawa, Eritrea, 227
—— Italian destroyer at, 234
—— —— destroyers and submarines lethargic, 267
—— captured, 338
Massingberd, General Sir A., 139
Mast, French General René, 478
Matapan, Battle of, 15, 324, 326-37; result of battle, 341
—— Cape, patrols established, 218
Mateur occupied, 502
Maturba airfield shelled by Army, 450
Maynard, Air Commodore, 236
McCall, Capt. H. W. U., 384, 452
McCarthy, Capt. E. D. B., 278
McCreery, Major-General, 569, 570
McCrum, Capt. C. R., 513
McGregor, Commander E. G., 384
McGrigor, Rear-Admiral (later Admiral Sir) Rhoderick R., 540, 545, 554, 559, 572, 660
McKendrick, Lt.-Commander G. W., 563
Mechili, British armour captured, 339
Mediterranean Cruiser Squadron, 43
—— Fleet, 91-2, 110, 157
—— —— exercises, 117
—— —— dispersed, 152
—— —— 1934, strength of, 157, 158
—— —— and the Abyssinian crisis, 173
—— —— move to Alexandria, 174
—— —— Chiefs of Staff defeatist views, 173-4
—— —— strengthened, 174-5
—— —— ready to strike at Italians, 175-6
—— —— visit Italian ports when Albania invaded, 201; ordered to leave, 202
—— —— criticized by Mr. Churchill as to its disposition April 1939, 201; the facts, 201-2
—— —— appointed C.-in-C., 202
—— —— ordered to assemble south of Malta, April 1939, 202
—— —— problem if Italy declared war, 210
—— —— gradually melts away, Oct. 1939, 218
—— —— operations during Second World War, 230-532
—— —— serious deficiencies, 239, 374-5
—— —— maintenance of, 241-2
—— —— constant advice and interference causes annoyance, 348-9

—— —— Prime Minister enters controversy and no reply is sent, 349
—— —— men and machinery nearing exhaustion, 375, 388-90
—— —— restricted operations in central Mediterranean, 316
—— —— enemy attacks back-door route, 408
—— Fleets, combined exercises, 159-62, 171-2
—— service in, 87, 157-78, 191-2, 202-460, 521-60
—— U-boats greatly increased, 509-10
—— the war in the, 671-4
Medjez-el-Bab, 528
Megera, Athens, 353
Mehdia, French Morocco, American landing, 491-2
Memorial to *Valerian* casualties, Bermuda, 127
Mena House Hotel, Cairo, 586
Mendalia (*see* Mandelyah)
Mendere River, Dardanelles, 64
Mendigal, French General, 496, 497, 514
Merchant vessels, arming of, 196
—— —— in convoy slows up reinforcements, 268-9
—— Navies, fine discipline and fighting qualities, 520
—— Navy at Algiers visited by H.M. King George VI, 544
Mersa Matruh, 273, 413; supplies for Army, 422; occupied by enemy, 465
Mers-el-Kebir, Oran, base for French ships, 225, 243; 503, 512, 517; attacked by limpeteers, 524; 546
Mersin, Asia Minor, 280
Messina, Sicily, 56, 537; entered, 556
—— Straits of, 237, 263; nightly raids, 533; 555, 556, 634; 'Regatta', 559
Metaxas, Greek General, death of, 313
Methuen, Lord, 22
Metz, France, 619
Meuse, 620
Michelier, French Admiral, 542
Michell, Commander K., 353
Micklethwait, Capt. St. J. A., 452, 453
Midget submarines, 580; penetrate Aaltenfiord, 600; 622, 625
'Middle Class Union', the, 117
Middle East Defence Council, 401, 443
—— —— War Council, 405-6
—— —— unsatisfactory situation, 220
—— —— unwelcome reinforcements, 221
—— —— left practically staffless, 222
—— —— bomber squadrons wanted, 227
—— —— Home authorities ignorant of affairs, 340-1
Middleburg, Cape Colony, 27, 28
Miers, Commander A. C. C., 446
Milford Haven, 45
Miller, Capt. F. S., 41
Milligan, Lieut. Patrick, 460
Milne, Admiral Sir Archibald Berkeley, 54

Milos, 83
—— preparations to occupy, 230
Mine-laying policy not commendable, 608
Minefields of length laid by enemy off Bizerta, 511
—— clearance of shortens 6,000 miles, 531-2
—— defensive, laid, 625
Mines a menace round many coasts, 321; 605
Minesweepers, shortage of, June 1949, 233
—— keep channel to Tobruk clear, 339
—— congratulatory message to officers and men, 532
—— good work, 557
Ministry of Marine, France, in England for defence talks, April 1939, 202
Minorca, 43, 185
Mittelhauser, French General, 238
Miyako Island, enemy airfields attacked, 636; 638
Mobile Naval Base Defence Organization, 358, 389
Molotov, M., at Teheran, 587, 588; 627, 647
Mombasa, East Africa, 20
Monckton, Sir Walter, 460
Monemvasia, Peloponnesus, 353
Monnet, M., 542
Monte Camino, Italy, 589
Montecorvino airfield, Italy, captured, 571
Montenegro coast blockaded by Austrian Fleet, 57
Montgomery, General (later Field-Marshal Viscount) Sir Bernard, 483, 519, 528, 535, 536, 545, 570; appointed G.O.C. British Army for Normandy invasion, 594; 605; diverse views with General Eisenhower, 619-20; seeks unified command, 620; responsibilities increased, 620; 634, 642, 647
Montreal, visits to, 122-3, 130
Montrose, Duke of, 29
Moore, Admiral Sir H. R., 206, 219, 600-1, 656
Moray Firth, 50
Moreau, French Admiral, 497, 500
Morena, Spanish Admiral Francesco, 186
Morgan, Capt., R.N., 435
Morley's School, Dublin, 13
Morocco, 49
—— Sultan of, presents Orders to Allied Commanders, 541
Morse, Capt. (later Rear-Admiral) J. A., 358, 366, 374, 377, 385, 387, 398, 503, 533, 572
Morto Bay, 62, 67
Motor torpedo-boats lamentably slow, 521
—— —— success, 524
—— —— prove a menace to enemy, 525
—— —— lads in Sicily, 555
—— —— in spirited encounters, 605
Mountbatten, Commander Lord Louis, 171, 360, 373; appointed Supreme Commander S.E. Asia, 561
Mount Etna, 554
—— of Olives, 208
—— Olympus, Greece, 315

Mozambique, 20
Mudros, Lemnos, 60, 65, 68, 70, 76, 78, 84, 88
Muirhead-Gould, Rear-Admiral G. C., 644
'Mulberry', building of, at 'Gold' beach, France, 605
'Mulberries', building of, 595-6, 599; a partial demolishment, 619
Muller, Lt.-Commander A. G., 70
Munich, Neville Chamberlain meets Hitler, 194; agreement criticized, 195
Munn, Lieut. James, 181, 182
—— Lt.-Commander W. J., 383
Murphy, Robt. D., U.S.A., 478, 488, 495, 496, 497, 500, 514, 541, 573
Murray, Susan Porteous (see Cunningham, Mrs. John)
—— William, 9
Mussolini, designs on Abyssinia and action thereon, 173-5
—— efforts in Spanish Civil War frustrated, 186
—— mistrust of, 190, 223
—— not committing himself to war, 217
—— dissatisfied with campaign in Libya and Albania, 290
—— on brink of a further collapse, 314
—— and the Battle of Matapan, 337
—— his downfall, 555
Mustafa Kemal Pasha, 111
Mutiny in the Royal Indian Navy, 659
Myres, Professor Sir John L., 79-80
Mytilene Island, 79

Nagara, 66, 113
Nagasaki, Japan, bombed, 645
Nagoya, Japan, bombed, 645, 650
Namur, France, 620
Naples, 43, 54, 189; Italian Fleet moved to 287; 559, 566; occupied, 572; 595
Narrows, Dardanelles Straits, 62-3, 67-8, 113
Narvik, iron ore traffic to Germany, 223; battles, 224; second battle of, 578
Nassau, Bahamas, visited, 127-8, 133
Nauplia, Greece, 353, 354
Naval Academy, U.S.A., 123-4
—— —— Leghorn, harsh discipline, 162-3
Naval Air Arm, criticized, 115
—— Air Squadron, No. 826, 450
—— Brigade in S. African war, 1899-1902, 21-31
—— Co-operation Group, No. 201, set up, 416; praised, 440; 448, 583
—— demobilization, 658
—— Estimates drastically shorn, 143; 'fast escort vessels', 194; in 1939 largest on record, 199
—— exercises in 1938, 188
—— Inter-Allied Commission of Control in Germany, appointed president of Sub-Commission 'C', 108

INDEX

Naval long-term policy, 209–10; short-term policy accepted, 217
—— personnel greatly reduced, 143
—— post-war problem, 655
—— Reserves, expansion of, 199
—— Review at Spithead, 15–16; Coronation Review, 1911, 49; 1935, 171, 172–3; 1937, 181
—— treaties on disarmament disastrous to Royal Navy, 193
—— War Memorial, Dover, 98
Navarin, Greek island, courtesy visit to, 163; regattas, 164, 191; supplies to Derna, 426
Navigation School, Portsmouth, 36, 49
Navy Department, Washington, averse to use of British Fleet in the Pacific, 613
Neame, Capt. D. M. L., 450
—— General, captured by Germans, 339
Nelson, Horatio, and Antigua, 128; 627
Netherlands, civilians on verge of starvation, 634; problem of, 657
—— East Indies, 648; Japs surrender, 651
New Brunswick, Canada, 130
—— Guinea, offensive, 629; 635, 648; Japs surrender, 651
—— Mexico, atomic bomb test, 646
—— Zealanders in Crete, 379
—— —— show gratitude to Royal Navy, 406–7
—— —— at Tobruk, 425–6
—— —— evacuated from Crete, 602
New Statesman, 144
Newcastle-upon-Tyne, visited by Royal Navy, 116, 118
Newfoundland, visit to, 122, 129; visit to, 130; enemy submarines near, 631
Newton, Lord, 144
Nibeiwa Camp, near Sidi Barrani, 294
Nichan Iftikhar, Tunisian Order presented to Allied Commanders, 541
Nicholas, Capt. John, R.N., 45
Nicholl, Capt. A. D., R.N., a difficult decision, 432; 458
Nicholson, Rear-Admiral D. R. L., 76–7
Nicobar Islands attacked, 649
Nicolas, Sub-Lieut. (later Capt.) John G., 75–6, 266
Nieuport, Germans evacuate, 95
Night fighting problems, 142
—— actions vindicated, 161
—— exercises, collision avoided, 161–2
Nikaria, Ægean, 79
Nimes, France, visit to, 189
Nimitz, Admiral Chester W., U.S.N., 402, 614; commands British Fleet in Pacific, 615; 622, 630, 635, 642, 650; on use of naval forces, 651
Noble, Lt.-Commander Delorest J. D., 99, 103, 104
—— Admiral Sir Percy, 601, 610
Noguès, French General, 238, 499, 500, 518, 541
Noon, Sir Firozkhan, 601–2

Norfolk House, St. James's Square, London, 475
Norman, Capt. (now Rear-Admiral) H. G., 281
Normandy, preparations for invasion, 587
—— C.-in-C.s appointed, 594
Norway invaded, 224, 608
North African campaign operations, 468–532
—— America and W. Indies Station appointment, 120–31
—— Atlantic, enemy submarines in, 631
—— Borneo, 611
—— France, Americans favour a landing in 1942, 468
Notes on Handling Ships, 41
Nova Scotia, enemy submarines near, 631
Nyon Conference, 1937, 185; patrols, 186

Oban, 46
O'Connor General (now Sir) Richard, 294; captured by Germans, 339
O'Conor, Capt. Rory, R.N., 253, 260, 431
Ofot Fiord, Norway, 578
Ogilvie-Forbes, Sir George, 198
O.G.P.U., 628
Ogulin, Yugoslavia, visit to, 164–5
Oil fuel for ships, 47–8
—— resources, Iran, a problem to Hitler, 314
Okinawa, Ryukyu Islands, 628; seizure of, 636; 650
Old Manor House, Fareham, 156
O'Leary, Gunner Michael, 100–1
Oliphants River, Cape of Good Hope, 28
Oliva, Italian Admiral, 563
Oliver, Lt.-Commander (later Rear-Admiral) Geoffrey N., 143, 171, 480, 504, 512, 529, 531, 560, 566, 569, 570, 571, 572, 602, 603, 630, 649
—— Admiral Sir Henry, 118, 120
—— Mrs. (Sarah Churchill), 586
Ollive, French Admiral C.-in-C., suggests naval operations, 211; attacks on Italian seaboard approved, 212
Operations:
  'Hats', reinforcement of Mediterranean Fleet, 271–2
  'Judgment', half Italian Fleet crippled, 284–7
  'Workshop', to capture Pantellaria intensely disliked, 290–1
  'Excess', passing a convoy, 301
  'Lustre', transporting Army to Greece, 320, 338
  'Demon', evacuation of Army in Greece, 352–7
  'Tiger', convoy through Mediterranean, 360–3; Admiralty congratulations, 363
  'Battleaxe', counter offensive in Western Desert, June 15, 1941, 399, 402–3, 408

INDEX

Operations (*contd.*)
  'Substance', convoy to Malta from the west, 405
  'Torch', a dead secret, 481; 501
  'Husky', invasion of Sicily, 519, 527, 534-58
  'Retribution', 'sink, burn or destroy, let nothing pass', 529-30
  'Baytown', guns around Messina to cover landing in Italy, 559-60
  'Avalanche', Salerno landing, 556, 572
  'Overlord', 587, 595
  'Shingle', the landing at Anzio, 595
  'Anvil', landing in south of France, 597-8; divided views, 606; renamed 'Dragoon', 606, 608-9
  'Neptune' (naval part of Operation 'Overlord'), greatest amphibious operation in history, 602
  'Dragoon' (*see* Operation 'Anvil')
  'Argonaut', preparations for Yalta Conference, 625-6
  'Octagon', Quebec Conference, 630
  'Iceberg', seizure of Okinawa, 636
Oran, action against French Fleet, July 3, 1940, 246; 471, 475, 477; attack on French ships criticized by U.S. Rear-Admiral, 479; landing at, 487; 498, 503, 507, 545
Orders by sign only, 43
—— duplicated by means of a tray of jelly, 81
Orkanie Fort, Dardanelles, 64
Orr-Ewing, Capt. David, 511
Osaka bombed, 645, 650
Oslo, visit to, 99
Ostend, 89, 90, 93, 94, 98
—— attempted blockade of, 92
—— Germans retire from, 95
—— T.M. the King and Queen of the Belgians land, 1914, 96
—— captured, 619
—— supplies landed, 634-5
Oswin, Paymaster-Captain H. C., 481
Otago University, New Zealand, 11
Otranto, Straits of, patrols established, 218; raid on, 285
—— decision to attack Italian communications, 288-9
Ouissam Alaouite, Moroccan Order presented to Allied Commanders, 541
Ouistreham, France, 605
Outer Gabbard Yacht Club, 49
Overseas Press Club lunch, outspoken remarks, 467
Owen, Capt., 46
Oxford University confers honorary degree D.C.L., 656

Paardeburg, Orange Free State, 23
Pachino peninsula, Sicily, 536
Pacific, strong naval claims, 596

—— British Fleet train for, 598, 613, 614-15, 635, 636, 639, 645
Paestum, Italy, 566
Paget, Capt. Sir James, 374
Paine, Capt. Godfrey, 39
Painted Hall, Greenwich, 476
Palace House, Bishop's Waltham, 179, 182, 192, 193, 195, 196, 201, 203, 208, 463, 570; a 'scrambler' telephone installed, 581-2; 597, 599, 603, 605, 607, 622, 627, 628, 657, 660, 661, 663
Palais D'Etè, Algiers, 556
Palembang, Sumatra, Fleet aircraft attack, 622
Palermo, Sicily, suggested operation against, Aug. 1939, 212; 535, 537; captured, 554
Palestine, 397
Palliser, Vice-Admiral Sir Arthur, 655
Palma, Majorca, 142, 189
—— British Squadron at, 185
—— remonstrance with Spanish Admiral, 186
—— Italian Admiral entertained at, 187
Panama Canal zone, courtesy cruise to, 133, 135
Pantellaria Island, 271, 301
—— —— idea of its capture intensely disliked, 290-1
—— —— cruise to, and convoy shot up, 296
—— —— plans for capture, 539
—— —— bombarded and bombed, 542
—— —— M.T.B's close harbour entrance, 542-3
—— —— surrenders to Allies, 543
Papen, von, introduced to, 213
Paramythia, Greece, 321
Pares, Bip, 8
Parry, Commodore W. E., 480
Patch, Capt. Olivier, R.M., 271
—— General Alexander M., U.S.A., 634
Patras, Gulf of, 38, 170
Patriarch of the Orthodox Greek Church, Alexandria, sends congratulations, 334-5
Patterson, Rear- (later Vice-) Admiral Sir Wilfred, 462, 465, 472, 659
Patton, General George, U.S.A., commands N. African expedition, 471, 491, 519, 523, 535; sore at change of plans, 538; 554, 587, 620, 634
Pavlov, Russian interpreter, 589
Pearl Harbour attacked by Japanese, 428-9; 630, 651
Pearse, A. W. (3rd officer), 18
Pearson's Holiday Fund, 76
Pegram, Rear-Admiral F. H., 578
Peile, Major, 22-3
Pelly, Group Captain C. B. R., 380, 382
Peña, Lieut. (Chile), 135
Penang, Malay pensinsula, 629, 631
Penzance, Cornwall, 45
Peru, courtesy visit to, 133
Pétain, Marshal, 237, 479, 496; disowns Darlan, 497; 499; orders resistance to Allies, 501; civil population's loyalty to, 502

INDEX

Peter of Yugoslavia, H.M. King, 184, 338.
Peters, Capt. Frederic Thornton, 489
Peyrouton, N., 518
Philadelphia, courtesy visit to, 123
Philippe, André, 542
Philippines, Japanese unhindered campaign, 429; 636; liberated, 648
Phillimore, Capt. Valentine, R.N., 39
Phillips, Capt. G. C., R.N., 510
Physical fitness endurance test, 51
Piers Hill, Edinburgh, 44
Pieta Creek, Malta, 157, 183
Pieto Curassiers, Chile, 134
Pilotless aeroplane rumour, 600
Pipon, Vice-Admiral Sir James, 312
Piræus, Greece, 343
—— campaign, 83
—— landing in the, 83-4
—— convoys to, 283
—— disembarkation port for troops, 315
—— heavily attacked by enemy, 339-40; wrecked and disorganized, 352
Pisa bombarded, 316
Plaka Bay, Crete, 380; troops evacuated, 382, 387
Platea Island, courtesy visit to, 163
Platt, General, 307, 338
Plumbe, Major, 22
Plunkett-Ernle-Erle-Drax, Rear-Admiral Hon. Reginald A., 142
'Pluto', pipe-line for petrol, 602
Plymouth, 83, 86, 147, 646
Point Amour, Strait of Belle Isle, 129
Poland, British Government guarantees, 202; 209; invaded, 217
—— Capt. A. L., R.N., 448, 452, 453
Ponte Olivo airfield, Gela, 535
Poplar Grove, S.A., 23
Porchester, 172
Portal, Wing-Commander (now Air Chief-Marshal) Charles, 139, 578, 586, 589, 605, 611, 612, 626, 643; becomes Viscount, 657; awarded Order of Merit, 662; receives Freedom of London, 662
—— Rear-Admiral R. H., 615
Port Blair, Andaman Islands, 629
—— defences, a stubborn problem, 196-7
—— Edgar, Firth of Forth, 98, 99, 111, 113, 115; a destroyer base, 119, 153
—— House, Alexandria, 207
—— Itea, Gulf of Patras, 38
—— Laki, Leros, 79
—— Lyautey, French Morocco, 491-2
—— Tewfik bombed, by enemy, 408
Portland, 34, 50, 116, 141
Portrush, N. Ireland, visited, 117; 144
Port Said, 55, 174, 397
—— —— inadequate defences, 208
—— —— minor repair facilities, 230
—— —— anti-aircraft defences, 230
—— —— preparedness for embarking troops, 230
—— —— convoys to, 238, 277

—— —— lack of repair facilities, 270
—— —— heavy air raids, 403, 408
—— —— Vathi, Isle of Ithaca, 56
—— —— Samos, 57
Portsdown Hill, Hampshire, 603
Portsmouth, 33, 34, 35, 36, 45, 51, 110, 111, 113, 118, 139, 143, 153, 646
—— Technical School, 260
Post-war defence organization, 657
Potsdam Conference, 646-7
Pound, Admiral Sir Dudley (*see also* Letters), 140, 190, 191, 209, 216-17, 219, 220, 221, 223, 227, 231, 239, 241, 255, 277, 324, 463, 476, 516, 561, 581
—— C.-in-C. Mediterranean Fleet, 177, 178, 182, 183, 186, 187
—— First Sea Lord, 202, 203
—— shares dislike of 'Workshop' operation, 291
—— cruel and unjust attacks made on, 299
—— on appointment of a Naval C.-in-C., 469-70
—— at Casablanca, 515
—— his illness, 573, 574
—— death of, 583
—— a tribute, 583-4
—— Lady, 183, 461; death of, 561; 581, 583
Powell, Commander Bingham, 42
Power, Capt. Manley L. (later Capt.), R.N., 8, 207, 301; takes a bet, 326; and wins, 327; 331, 475; high praise, 493; 532, 631
—— Rear-Admiral, (later Admiral Sir Arthur), 527, 547, 564, 660, 629, 630, 649, 655
Praise for officers and men, 240, 282-3, 335, 372, 379, 394, 428, 449, 456, 526, 530, 533, 663-4
Prentis, Commander O. J., 54, 70
'Presidential Citation' presented to Malta by President Roosevelt, 589
Press criticisms over agreement with Darlan, 501-2
Press interview, 467
Pretoria, Transvaal, 24; battle for, 25; 30
Pretty, Capt. F. C., 272
Prien, German submarine commander, 219
Prince Rupert's Bay, Dominica, 41
Princeton University, visit to and a football match, 123-4
Pridham, Capt. Arthur F., R.N., 182
Pridham-Wippell, Rear-Admiral (later Admiral Sir) H. D., 263, 264, 280, 285, 286, 301, 313, 326, 327, 328, 329, 330, 331, 333, 334, 347, 353, 356, 360, 365, 367, 376, 377, 400, 416, 425, 459
Prothero, Capt. Reginald, R.N., 18, 19, 21, 22, 23, 24, 37
Publicity anathema to naval officers, 410
Pugsley, Capt. A. F., R.N., 634
Puerto Cabello, Venezuela, courtesy visit to, 133, 135-6
—— Barrios, Guatemala, courtesy visit to, 133
Puttick, Brigadier, 406

INDEX

Quebec, visit to, 122, 123, 130
—— Conference, 560, 561, 609, 610–12
Queenstown, 42

Raby, Admiral James, 16
Radar, in its infancy, 196
—— ships fitted with, 272
—— proves invaluable, 369
—— R.A.F. lack of, 409
—— useless for enemy Schnorkel boats, 607–8, 625
—— improvements, 616
Radio-controlled bomb used by Germans, 566
Raeder, German Admiral, 197, 198, 513
Ragusa (*see* Dubrovnik)
Raikes, Rear-Admiral R. H. T., 174, 177
Ramree Island occupied, 630
Ramsay, Capt. R. B., 138
—— Admiral Sir Bertram, 471, 474, 481; high praise, 493; 519, 535, 545, 547, 554, 585; naval C.-in-C. for invasion of Normandy, 594; 599, 602, 603, 604, 607, 609; on the 'Battle of the Bulge', 621; death of and a tribute, 624–5; 644
Rangoon occupied, 630
Raphina, Athens, 353
Raphtis, Athens, 353
Rathmines, district of, Dublin, 9
Ravenstein, German General von, rescued, 427
Raw, Capt. S. M., R.N., 238, 445
Rawlings, Rear-Admiral (later Admiral Sir) H. B., 294, 297, 365, 367, 370, 374–5, 382, 383; wounded, 384; 424; an appreciation, 444–5; 614, 615, 636, 637, 638, 639, 640, 650
Rawson, Vice-Admiral Sir Harry, 32
Rearmament programme, pressing need, 195–6; pushed forward, 198
Reconnaissance over sea fitful, and fleet without air protection, 267
—— aircraft in M. East insufficient, 448
Redan, Crimea, visited, 628
Red Cross gifts, 660
—— Sea, complications, 234
—— —— convoys never in serious danger, 338
—— —— mined, 364
—— —— attacks on shipping, 364
—— —— command problem settled, 409
Rede, Commander Roger, 95, 96
Reed, Petty Officer, 93–4
Reggio area bombarded, 559
Regia Aeronautica (Italy), an unknown quantity, 173; 212; forced on defensive, 238; has its teeth drawn, 298
Renouf, Rear-Admiral E. de F., 240, 301, 302, 303, 323
Reserve Flotilla, cruise for boys, 120

Retimo, Crete, 358; evacuation of troops, 382
Reval, Estonia, 105
Reykjavik, Iceland, 144, 145
Reynveld, General Pierre van, 320
Rheims heavily bombed, 226
Rhine crossing a formidable obstacle, 634; crossed, 635
Rhodes, Cecil, 18
—— Island, 79, 216, 296, 336
—— —— airfields attacked, 273, 344
—— —— attack on, 307
—— —— bombarded, 448
Riccardi, Italian Admiral, 190, 262, 290; and Battle of Matapan, 337
Richard I, 179
Richards, Engineer-Lieut., 84
Richmond, Admiral Sir Herbert, 651
Riga liberated, 1918, 99
Rimington, Lt.-Commander M. G., 269
Ritchie, Rear-Admiral J. S. M., 645
Rivalries and jealousies in American inter-services, 466–7
Riviera, 190
'River' Class destroyers, 58, 60
River Plate, 278
Robeck, Rear-Admiral (later Admiral Sir) John de, 39, 60, 63, 65, 68–9, 111, 116
Roberts, Field-Marshal Lord, 11, 22–4, 26, 27, 28, 35
—— Lieut. P. S. W., 445–6
Robertson, Sir William, 129
—— Lady, 129
Robinson, Lt.-Commander E. G., 64, 67
Robson, Commander W. G. A., 171, 372, 386, 432
Rocket bomb rumour, 600
—— and flying bombs, casualties in London, 616
Roman Life in the Days of Cicero, 14
Rome, 189
Romer, Lord Justice, 29
Rommel, German General, 399; forced to a standstill, 421; 426, 525; hands over Tunisian command, 528
Roodevaal, S. Africa, 25
Roosevelt, President Franklin, 586, 587, 606, 609, 610, 611, 612, 661
—— his plea for no further aggression by dictators rejected, 202
—— enquiries about N. Russian convoy losses, 471
—— discusses Operation 'Torch', 472
—— support for agreement with Admiral Darlan, 502
—— at Casablanca, 515
—— at Quebec Conference, 561
—— presents 'Presidential Citation' to Malta, 589
—— at Yalta Conference, 619, 622
—— 'looked frail and worn out', 627, 628
—— death of, a tribute, 641–2
—— Mrs., 610, 611
Rose, Capt. (later Rear-Admiral) Frank F., 112, 157

Rosetta, Egypt, 435
Rosyth, 46; dockyard, 108, 119
Rotherham, Commander (later Capt.) Eustace, 149, 151, 175
Rothesay, 144
Rothiemay, near Huntley, 462
Rotterdam opened for shipping, 644
Rough seas round Capt St. Vincent, 86; off Ushant, 132
Roumania, guarantees by British Government, 202
Rowlands Castle, Hampshire, 144, 148
Rowley, Capt. Henry Aubrey, 371
Royal Air Force:
  formation of, 114
  Base at Leuchars, 114
  bomb Italian targets, June 1949, 238
  excellent work, 267
  support Greek Army, 289
  deal heavy blows on Tripoli, 298
  Coastal Command short of aircraft, 299
  fighters take heavy toll, 304
  scantiness of, in the Mediterranean, 317
  maintenance personnel used by Fleet Air Arm, 321
  bombers in action, 329, 346, 361
  gallant struggle in Greece, 352
  at evacuation of Crete, 386, 388
  undeserved odium and criticism, 406
  relations with Navy not easy, 406
  gratifying results from Malta, 408
  defence of shipping beyond their resources, 408-9
  co-operation pressed for, 415
  outstanding work in N. African campaign, 482
  efficient support for landings in N. Africa, 488
  hampered by weather in N. Africa, 504
  dispose of the *Tirpitz*, 618
  attack Japanese shipping, 629
  and assault on Japan, 645
Royal Australian Navy, gallant work, 635, 648
—— Canadian Navy, 121; tribute to, 520-1
—— Dublin Society, 11-12
—— Engineers at Benghazi, 441
—— Flying Corps merged, 114
—— Horse Artillery, comparison with, in S. African war, 28
—— Indian Navy mutiny, 659
—— Marine Commandos land in Sicily, 552
—— Marines assist on Naval Inter-Allied Commission in Germany, 108
—— —— in Crete, 388, 389
—— Naval Academy, 36
—— —— Air Service merged, 114; 287
—— —— Barracks, Portsmouth, 98
—— —— —— Chatham, Commodore of, 149-56
—— —— —— College, Greenwich, 35, 36, 180, 601
—— —— —— Dartmouth, 203
—— —— force required at Malta, 340-1
—— —— losses at end of 1940, 299
—— —— responsibilities increased, 299
—— —— Volunteer Reserves, new divisions formed, 199; a tribute, 551; training establishment, 656
—— —— reaction to reductions in pay causes rebellion, 150-2
—— —— reduction in personnel due to Geddes 'Axe', 152
—— —— improved conditions, 152-3
—— —— local manning of warships unfair; mixed companies advocated, 153
—— —— difficulty of recommissioning a ship, 153
—— —— sail training, 153-4
—— —— spring exercises, 1933, 159-62
—— —— night action question vindicated, 161
—— —— committee to study ventilation in ships, 180
—— —— fights for its own Air Arm, 180
—— —— committee investigates effect of 'A' cordite on men, 180
—— —— orders for mobilization and cancellation Sept. 1938, 195
—— —— personnel increase, March 1939, 199
—— —— fleet under construction, March 1939, 199
—— —— stretched almost to breaking point, 299, 318, 319
—— —— tangible gratitude from Dominion troops, 406-7
—— —— help in driving enemy from Tunisia, 529-31
—— —— congratulated by General Eisenhower, 558
—— —— in Indian Ocean, 629-30
—— —— support Fourteenth Army, Arakan coast, 630
—— —— final operations against Japan, 650
—— —— why it is required, 651-2
—— —— post-war problems, 655
—— —— new pay code, 658
—— —— a tribute, 663
—— —— no Service or profession in comparison, 664
—— Netherlands Navy, 430
—— Thames Yacht Club, 107
—— Tournament, Olympia, 1931, 142
—— Zoological Society of Ireland, 11
Ruhr, advance into the, 619
Rundstedt, Marshal von, 499
—— offensives, 620, 627
—— his defeat, 624
Russia, convoys to, 580; temporarily suspended, 616; total losses, 617; weather conditions, 617; a 'Northern Saga' of heroism, 618
—— heavy losses in P.Q. 17, 471
—— counter-offensive starts, 508; gathers weight, 515, 624
—— ex-prisoners of war escorted home, 618

INDEX

Russia, hospitality, 628
Russian allies, a lack of sea sense, 580
—— Bolshevik armies and the Baltic, 100
—— forces penetrate Poland, 594
Ryder, Major-Gen. C. W., U.S.A., 488, 494
Ryukyu Islands, 628, 636

Saarbrucken, 618
Sabang, north of Sumatra, attacked, 608; 629
Sackett, chief steward, 465
Safi, French Morocco, American troops land at, 491-2
Sagami Bay, near Tokyo, 650
Sail training, 33
Sailors' circumstances, enquiry into, 152
St. Andrews, Fife, 13
—— New Brunswick, 130
—— University, 10; confers hon. degree of LL.D., 656
St. Florent, Corsica, 189
—— George's Bay, Newfoundland, 129; visit to, 122, 130
—— George's Hotel, Algiers, 522, 575
—— Lawrence River, 122
—— Lucia, Georgetown, British Guiana, visit to, 128
—— Mary's, Scillies, 146
—— Nazaire isolated by Eighth Army Corps, 608, 619
—— Paul's School, Hammersmith, 602
—— Sophia's Church, Istanbul, 215
—— Vincent, Earl of, 581
—— —— B.W.I., visit to, 128
Sakishima Islands bombed, 636, 638
Salamis, Greece, 83
Saldanha Bay, Cape of Good Hope, 52
Salerno, 275, 566, 569; success in landing, 572; 602
—— Gulf of, decision to land on toe of Italy, 556; the landing, 566-70
Salmon fishing in Newfoundland, 129
Salonika, 77, 79; French suggest landing forces, 222; 315, 353
Samos Island, 574, 575; evacuated by British, 582
Samson, Lieut. C. R., 41
San Anton Palace, Malta, 522, 626
San Francisco, 655
San Pedro Roads, Leyte, 637
Sans Souci, Potsdam, 198
Santiago, Chile, courtesy visit to, 134
Saragoglu, M., Turkey, 214
Sarawak liberated, 648
Sardinia, Italian Fleet in full flight towards, Nov. 1940, 290; enemy mass aircraft, 486; 519, 563
Sasebo, Japan, naval base, bombed, 645
Saseno Island, 296
Saunders, Admiral Sir Charles, 122

"S" class destroyer impressions, 193-4
Scaletta, Sicily, troops landing, 554
Scapa Flow, 88, 89, 113, 144; made safe as air base, April 1940, 224
Scarlett-Streatfield, Group Captain, 416
Scarpanto airfield, Crete, shelled, 273, 368, 376, 383; 306
Scheer, German Admiral, 198
Scheldt, the, 90; approaches heavily mined, 609; 622, 625
Schniewind, German Admiral, 198
'Schnorkel' ('Snort') boats, enemy's development of, 579; in Normandy invasion area, 607; 625
Schreiber, General Sir Edward, 626
Schultze, French Admiral Otto, 513
Scoglitti, Sicily, American landing, 552
'Scoop' by American naval officer, 562
Scott, Capt. Percy, 21, 22
Scutari, 57
Sea communications, control of in E. Mediterranean, 230
Seaplane carriers, development of, 114
Seath, Lieut. Gordon, R.M., 74
Second World War, 210-652
Sedd-el-Bahr, nr. Cape Helles, 61, 62, 67, 71; V beach, 72
Seehundes (midget submarines), 625
Sele River, Agropoli, Italy, 566, 568
Selsey, Sussex, 603
Senglea, Malta, parish priest of, 564
Sephton, Petty Officer A. E., 372
Seria oilfields, Sarawak, captured, 648
Servaes, Rear-Admiral R. M., 615
Setif, Algeria, occupied by Allies, 502
Sevastopol visited, 628
Seymour, Lieut, Michael, 207
Sfax, French units at, 254; occupied, April 1943, 525
Sham landings by Navy on W. Desert coast, 419
Shatt-el-Arab, mined, 364
Shaw, Capt. (later Paymaster-Capt.) A. P., 8, 116, 153, 156, 203, 207, 481, 532, 660
Sheerness, 90, 94, 138
Sheffield University confers hon. degree LL.D., 656
Shelley, Capt. Richard, 301, 460
Sherman tanks sent to W. Desert, 465
Sherwood, Robert E., 598
Ship Canal, trip through, 118
Ships, list of, 711
Shipping losses diminish, 579
—— problems, 596
—— many good ones scrapped, 143; due to the Geddes 'Axe', 152
'Shorter Instrument' surrender terms for Italy, 560-1, 572-3
Shotley, Harwich, 138
Showing the flag, 121-37
Sicily, 275, 310
—— inability to attack aircraft on ground, 211
—— attack on contemplated, 418, 519

Sicily, Luftwaffe heavily reinforced, 420, 486
—— airfields and defences heavily bombed, 548
Sicilian Channel, air cover necessary for convoys, 509
—— heavily mined, 510
—— night sweeps, 517
—— Narrows penetrated, 271-2
Sidi Barrani occupied by enemy, 273, 280, 465; bombarded, 283; fall of, 295; R.A.F. base, 413
Sidi-bel-Abbes, 527
Sidi Resegh, 422; 426
Siebel ferries used by enemy, 525
Sierra Leone, 460; heavy Allied convoy losses, 483
Signal School, 157
Signals (*see under* Letters)
Sikorski, Polish General, 421, 422
Silver, Capt. Mortimer L'Estrange, 47
Silverton, Pretoria, 27
Sim, Capt. E. W. B., R.N., 430
Simmons, Lieut. E. T., R.C.N., 520
Simonstown, S.A., 12, 19, 21, 30
Simplon Express, 111
Simpson, Capt. G. W. G., 445
Singapore, Japanese cruisers at, 580; 611, 629, 649
'Sink, burn or destroy. Let nothing pass.'— signal by Admiral of the Fleet, May 1943, 529
Sirte, Battle of, one of most brilliant naval actions, 449-58
'Six Mile Drift', S.A., 25-6
Slatter, Air Commodore L. H., 416
Sliema Creek, Malta, 157
Smith, Sir Aubrey, 645
—— General Bedell, U.S.A., 466, 468, 469, 472, 521, 541, 560, 573, 599, 607, 626
—— Capt. Frank M., R.N.R., outstanding gallantry, 415
—— Dr. Temple, 12
—— Miss Cookie, 141
Smuts, General, 281, 320, 476, 601
Smyrna, 68, 223
Socotra, 629
Sollum occupied by enemy, 273, 465; captured, 295; 297, 307; preparations to open port, 399; 403
Somaliland successes, 320
Somervell, General B. B., U.S.A., 465
Somerville, Admiral of the Fleet Sir James, 139, 176, 178, 188, 243, 246; forced to fire on French Fleet, 250; 271, 316, 410, 580, 594, 601, 626, 629, 643
—— Lt.-Commander Philip, 372, 458
Sousse occupied, April 1943, 525
South Africa, Royal visit to, 659
—— African War, 1899-1902, 21-3
—— Beveland Island, Netherlands, 609
—— Queens ferry, 117, 119
—— Staffordshire Regt., signals sympathy to R. Navy, 363
—— Sudan campaign held up, 297

Southern Attack Force in Italy, 566
Southwick Park, 599-600
Spaatz, General Carl, 511-12, 642
Spahis, the Seventh, 556
Spain, U.S.A. Chiefs of Staff nervous of attitude, 470
Sphakia, Crete, retreat to, 380; evacuation, 382, 384, 386, 387, 388, 392
Spanish Civil War, 181, 185-8, 195
—— —— —— British squadron at Palma, Majorca, 185
—— —— —— British ships sunk by Italian submarines, 185
—— —— —— merchant traffic routed, 185-6
—— —— —— Mediterranean Fleet reinforced, 186
—— —— —— R.A.F. flying-boats at Arzeu, near Oran, 186
—— —— —— Italian bombing, 186
—— —— —— blockade relaxed, 188
—— Morocco, 470
Spithead, naval review, 15-16; coronation review, 1911, 49; 1935, 171, 172-3; 1937, 181
Split, regatta, 167; 168; courtesy visit to, 183
Sporades, the (islands), 79
Spruance, Admiral R. A., U.S.N., 628, 636
Stalin, Marshal Joseph, at Teheran, 587; receives King's Sword of Stalingrad, 588; at Yalta, 622, 627, 628; 642, 647
Stalingrad, 508, 515, 588
Stampalia Island, 79
Stanhope, Lord, causes a Press furore, 200-1; 202
Stark, Admiral Harold R. ('Betty'), U.S.N., 467; his work for Anglo-American harmony, 476-7; 602, 626; a tribute, 654
Starkie, Lieut. Walter A., 203, 220, 221; 224, 275; killed, 368
—— Mrs. (*see* Bramwell, Hilda)
—— (Starkey), Sir Oliver, 221
Statesman and Sea Power, 651
Ste. Maxime, Gulf of Ste. Tropez, courtesy visit to, 162
Stettinius, Edward R., U.S.A. Secretary of State, 626, 628
Stimson, Henry L., U.S.A. Secretary of State for War, 464
Stokes, Commander G. H., 430
Stone, Lieut. R. G., 48
Stormberg, S. Africa, 21
Strada Mezzodi, Malta, 208
Straits, Dardanelles, 71, 78
—— of Taranto, Italian Fleet concentrate April 1939, 201
Strasbourg, 618
Strong, Brigadier Kenneth, 560
Stubbington School, Fareham, 14
Submarines, exercises against, 176
—— casualties cause concern, 269
—— exact heavy toll against enemy in Mediterranean, 361
—— gratifying results from Malta, 408

INDEX

Submarines play havoc on enemy supply line to Libya, 420
—— force return of Italian convoy, 430
—— excellent work, 445-6, 510, 523, 557-8
—— midget, 580
—— successful operations off Norway, 608
Suda Bay, Crete, courtesy visit to, 163 164; 301, 304, 353, 358 (*see also* Crete)
—— —— a refuelling base, 230
—— —— advanced base, 282, 289
—— —— heavy air raids, 283
—— —— convoys to, 284
—— —— commando troops landed, 290
—— —— attacked by fast enemy explosive motor-boats, 323
—— —— cruisers help Malta convoy, 323
—— —— lack of air protection, 350
—— —— poor unloading facilities, 366
—— —— no use as a base, 366, 368
—— —— our Army pressed back, 374
—— —— Royal Marines man defences, 389
Sudan, activity in the, 280; southern advance in, 307
Suez Canal and use of by Italians, 174, 177
—— —— lack of repair facilities, 230, 270
—— —— Italian ships pass through, 233
—— —— Egyptians ordered to release Italian vessel, 233
—— —— attacked, 306, 408, 447
—— —— mined by enemy, 312-13, 403, 408
—— —— susceptible to acoustic mine-laying, 318
Suicide bombers (kamikazes) in action, 637, 638, 639
Sukegawa, Japan, shelled, 649
Sullivan, Commodore W. A., U.S.N., 531
Sumatra, 622
Summerfield, Sub-Lt. Ronald, 127
Supreme H.Q. Allied Expeditionary Force set up, 599
Surabaya project, 606; attacked 608; 629
Surface enemy raiders far afield, 299
Susa, French units at, 254
Sutton, an observer, 368
Suvla operations, 76-8
Sweden, Crown Prince of, 144, 145
Swift, Charles Clement, 15
Swordfish fighters, 300, 321, 329, 330, 517
—— —— sink three ships and a submarine, 271
—— —— four lost, 273
—— —— blow up part of enemy convoy, 296
—— —— squadrons, 321, 524
—— —— sink three enemy ships, 338
—— —— make name for themselves, 416
Sydney, Australia, 638
Symonds-Tayler, Sub-Lt. R. V., 84, 93
Syfret, Vice-Admiral (later Admiral) Sir Neville, 477, 503, 512, 517, 579, 596, 655
Syracuse, Sicily, 537; Allied landing, 551
Syria, 79, 314
—— German penetration forestalled, 396-8
—— enemy U-boats in strength, 408

Tabarka, French N. Africa, 502; supplies to 506
Tactical School, Portsmouth, a tribute, 260
Tactical, Technical and War Courses, 1936, 180
Tafaraoui airfield, N. Africa, bombed, 490
'Taffrail' (*see* Dorling)
Talbot, Rear-Admiral A. G., 602
Talliana, Maltese P.O. steward, 405
Tangier, visit to, 186
Tank landing craft used on supply run to Tobruk, 413
—— reinforcements for Egypt, 360
Tarakan Island liberated, 648
Taranto, Italy, 217, 259
—— harbour, preparations for attack on Italian fleet, 273, 283-5
—— enemy air attack beaten off, 284
—— half Italian fleet crippled, 284-7
—— congratulations to Royal Navy by H.M. the King, 287
—— a much-needed stimulus at home, 287
—— effect of defeat, 290
—— the attack copied by Japanese, 428-9
—— occupation of, 563-4
Tassigny, General de Lattre de, 642
Taylor, Brig.-General Maxwell D., U.S.A. 561, 620
—— Capt. L. A., R.N., 533
Tchakmak, Turkish Marshal Fevzi, 213; visit to, 214; 222, 223; doubtful of British help, 226
Tedder, Air Chief Marshal Sir A. W., 378, 385; cannot allot aircraft solely for naval co-operation, 406; his resources strained to breaking point, 415; 460, 516, 519, 535, 536, 540; invested with Moroccan Order, 541; 543, 573, 575, 589, 594, 622 642, 657, 660
Teheran Conference, Nov. 1943, 587-8
Tenedos Island, 58, 60, 65
Tenedos Times, 58
Tennant, Rear-Admiral W. G., 602
Thanksgiving Service, 653
Thingvellir, Iceland, celebrations, 145, 146
Thomas, Commander Mervyn 171, 237, 238, 311
Thorneycrofts, 111
Thorrowgood, Gunner W. W., 64-5, 66-7
Times, The, 144, 146
Tinos, Cyclades, 282
Tirailleurs in victory march, Tunis, 540
Tmimi, 450
Tobruk, 235, 266
—— bombed, 267
—— Italians cease use as supply base, 267
—— its capture an asset to Royal Navy, 297-8, 307
—— British troops retreat to, 338
—— views on holding, 338-9
—— enemy heavily mine channel, 339
—— air force withdrawn, 339
—— decision to hold, 339

INDEX

Tobruk, supplies to, a costly undertaking, 394, 445
— relief of, attempted, 399
— one ship sent at a time due to lack of fighter protection, 350
— forces evacuated and fall back, 359, 441
— supplies fly to meet increased enemy opposition, 408
— 'a running sore' to the enemy and the Royal Navy, 412
— demand to replace Australian Brigade, 413
— greatly damaged by Navy, 419
— Army supplies, 422
— relieved, 427
— details of Royal Navy's achievements, 427-8
— under continuous air attack, 457
— discussed at Washington, 464-5
— falls to enemy, 465
Tokyo bombed, 645, 649
Tolon, Greece, 353
Tomkinson, Capt. Wilfred, R.N., 96
'Torch' area, total tonnage landed, 520
Torpedo-carrying air base, Gosport, 114
—— —— aircraft attack fleet, 270
Torpedoes, Germans produce new type, 607
Toulon, 43, 159
— base for French ships, 225, 501, 609
— French Fleet asked to sail for Gibraltar, 496-7
— occupied by Germans, and French ships scuttled, 507
Tovey, Capt. (later Admiral of the Fleet, Lord), John C., 120, 153, 206, 219, 238, 240, 260, 265, 272; appointed C.-in-C. Home Fleet, 280; 449, 475
Towing exercises, failure of, 142-3
Training Squadron formed, 40-1
Trew, Lt.-Commander S. A. S.A.N.S., 427
Trewly, Lieut. George, 16
'Tribal' class destroyers built, 47
Trincomalee floating dock buckled, Ceylon, 608; 629
Trinidad, visit to, 128, 133, 136; 139
Trinity College, Dublin, tercentenary, 12
Tripoli, 310, 516
— mounting enemy convoy losses, 290, 298
— suggestion to bombard strongly resisted, 341
— orders to block and bombard, 341-2; order considered inopportune, decision queried and counter-proposals made, 342-5
— bombarded, 346-7
— enemy supplies being built up, 411
— constantly bombed, 420
— enemy succeed in running large convoy, 438
— enemy convoy attacked, 447
— visited by Mr. Churchill, 518
Troubridge, Capt. (later Vice-Admiral Sir) Thomas, 56, 57, 197, 477, 478, 479, 545-6

Troup, Vice-Admiral Sir James A. G., 32, 130, 156
Truk, Caroline Islands, bombarded, 649
Truman, President, agrees on use of atomic bomb, 646, 647
Tunis, 502, 545, 561
— Germans fly into, 499
— occupied, 528
— victory march of Allies, 540-1, 662
— Bey of, presents highest Tunisian Orders to Allied Commanders, 541
— Mr. Churchill develops pneumonia, 589
Tunisia, 470, 477, 515, 516
— military and air forces, 218
— reaction of French if N. Africa invaded, 469
— move to forestall Germans, 494
— occupied by German airborne troops, 507
— First Army being built up, 507
— Army reverses, 519
— defeat of Axis, 528
— the Royal Navy's rôle, 529-31
Turkey, dealings with after First World War, 111-13
— not enthusiastic, 218
— aid to, 221
— authorities in 1940 prove difficult, 222-3
Turkish Government remain neutral, 315
— soldiers, 213-14
— waters, visit to, 213-15
Turner, Professor (Sir William), 11, 12
Tymbaki, Crete, 374, 377
— Argyle and Sutherland Highlanders landed, 366
— evacuation of troops, 382
Tyrwhitt, Capt. (later Admiral of the Fleet) Sir Reginald, 46, 86, 119; Commander-in-Chief at the Nore, 149, 151; 154
— Lady, 148
— Commander L. R. K., 432; an appreciation, 457
— Commander St. John, 275

U-boats range farther afield, 299
— menace, 321
— on Tobruk route, 412
— enter the Mediterranean, 422
— counter-offensive against, 436
— busy along Libyan coast, 438, 445, 457
— off east coast U.S.A., and in Caribbean, 467
— bases bombed, 482
— heavy losses, 520-1, 579, 607, 617, 621-2
— high submerged speed, 579
— shadow convoy to N. Russia, 590
— menace held, 593, 631
— ascendancy over, 594

INDEX

U-boats, ordered to take all risks, 604
—— menace to convoys to N. Russia, 616
—— successes, 621-2
—— in Indian Ocean, 629
—— increased activity, 631
—— surrender, 643-4
—— total destroyed, 644
—— casualties: German, Italian and Japanese, 667-9
U-class submarines success against enemy Libyan convoys, 341
Uganda Railway, E. Africa, 20
Uhlmanis, M., Latvia, 103
Ulgin, Turkish Admiral, 280
Ulithi, Palau Islands, 614, 636
Unilateral disarmament disastrous to Royal Navy, 193
United Nations Organization, Americans show little faith, 655; 657
Unknown Warrior's tomb, Arlington, visit to, 131
U.S.A. and bases required at close of war, 655
—— 101st Airborne Division surrounded, 620
—— Army Air Force, heavy demands, 482
—— —— —— —— hampered in N. Africa, 504
—— —— —— —— persistent good work, 510
—— —— —— —— inability to deal with enemy supply ships, 511-12
—— —— —— —— blow enemy out of the sky, 528
—— —— —— —— headquarters, near Tunis, 545
—— —— —— —— in Europe, 631
—— —— and Navy, courtesy visits to, 122, 131
—— —— intolerant of naval control of aircraft 467
—— —— 1st Division land in Sicily, 552
—— Armies:
   First in France, 619; partly overrun, 620
   Second Corps in Tunisia, 528
   Third, in France, 619, 620, 634
   Fifth in Italy, 566, 570, 589; 594
   Sixth Corps in Italy, 566, 569
   Seventh, attack on Sicily, 537 545, 555; enter Messina, 556; in France, 618, 634
   Eighth Corps overrun Brittany peninsula, 608
   Ninth in France, 619, 620
   cautious about landing in N. Africa, 470
   Chiefs of Staff visit England and return dissatisfied, 468; 605
—— Fleets:
   Third, 638, 639, 649
   Fifth, 628, 636
   —— Task Force, 639
   Seventh, 648

—— at Pearl Harbour, 651
—— Marine Corps entertain Royal Marines, 131
—— Naval authorities strive to keep British Fleet from Pacific, 598, 635
—— Navy at Algiers visited by H.M. King George VI, 544
—— —— Dept. and 'Torch' operation, 469-70
—— —— praised by General Eisenhower, 558
—— —— helpful to British Fleet, 614
—— —— welcomes British Fleet, 635-6
—— place high value on naval bombardment, 596
—— Super-Fortresses bomb Japan, 645
—— troops land in French Morocco, 491-2
—— visits to ports, 122, 123-4
Ushant, rough weather, 132

V-1's worse than the blitz over London 606
—— casualties in London, 616
V-2's, 616
Vaal, Transvaal, 25
Valencia, 185, 186, 187, 189; refugees and crews of British ships taken off, 191
Valetta, Malta, 555
Valona, enemy convoy heavily damaged, 286; bombarded, 296; 321
Valparaiso, 133, 134
Vansittart, Lord, 202
Vardar River, Greece, 315
Vaudreuil, Governor of Quebec, 122
V.E.-Day celebrations, 642-3
Venezuela, courtesy visit to, 133
—— visit to President Gomez, 135-6
Venice, 185
Verdala Palace, Malta, 544
Vereeniging, Transvaal, 25
Versailles, 625
Vian, Capt. (later Admiral Sir) Philip, 175, 417, 430, 431, 442, 443, 447, 448; a fine performance, 450-5, 545, 560, 571; commands Navy in assault on Normandy, 602; 603, 605, 615, 636, 637, 640, 649
Vichy, France, 501
Vickery, Gunner A. V., R.M., 142
Victoria, H.M. Queen, diamond jubilee naval review, 15-16; death of, 32
Victory march in London, 661-2
Vietri sul Mare, Italy, 566
Vis (Lissa) Island, Adriatic, 168
V.J.-Day, 650; celebrations, 653
Viljoen's Drift, S. A., 25
Villa Kleine, Algiers, 503-4
Vincent, Lord St., 287

INDEX 709

Volo, Greece, disembarkation port, 315
von Arnim, German General, 528
Vorontsov, Prince, 627
Voroshilov, Russian Marshal, 587-8
Vourlah, Gulf of, Smyrna, 58-9

Waistell, Rear-Admiral Arthur, 115
Wake-Walker, Vice-Admiral Sir Frederic, 578; death of, 655
Walcheren Island, Netherlands, 609, 610
Waller, Capt. H. M. L., R.A.N., 294, 307; enters Tobruk, 308; 333
—— Capt. J. W. A., R.A.N., 265
Walters, Leading Seaman J., 432
Waltham Chase, Bishop's Waltham, 179
Walther, German Dr., 647
Wanklyn, Lt.-Commander Malcolm D., 361-2, 445
Warburton-Lee, Commander (later Capt.) B. A. W., 171; death of, 224
War College, Portsmouth Dockyard, 156
Wardman Park Hotel, Washington, 464, 465
Warhirst, H., 144
Warren, Capt. Guy L., R.N., 173
—— Surgeon-Commander Leonard, 108
—— Colonel, R.M., 108
Warwickshire Regt., 26
Washington, U.S.A., visit to, 130-1, 134
—— Conference, 541
—— Treaty, 1922, 112, 114
Waterlow, Lt.-Commander (later Commander) J. B., 58, 64, 75
Waterval Onder, S.A., 28
Watkins, Lieut. G. R. G., 333
Watson, Commander F. Burges, 99
Watts, Chief P.O. Percy, 465, 504, 581, 586, 589
Wavell, General, 77, 225, 267, 269, 281, 295, 306, 314, 320, 352, 358, 374, 378, 380, 385, 387, 417
—— dealings with French Generals in Morocco, 238
—— his opinion on holding Egypt, 241
—— called upon to help Greece, 282, 314-15
—— sympathetic about lack of anti-aircraft defences at Alexandria, 288
—— Western Desert offensive, Dec. 1940, 294
—— gratitude to Royal Navy, 390-1
—— Syrian operations, 396
—— counter-offensive, W. Desert, 399
—— appointed C.-in-C. India, 401-2
Weisacker, Baron von, 198
Wells, Vice-Admiral Sir Gerald A., 207
Welsh, Air Marshal Sir William, 477
Wemyss, Capt. (later Admiral Sir) Rosslyn, 42, 43, 44, 65, 96, 97
West Indian Islands, cruises and visits to, 121-9
—— Indies hospitality, 128-9

—— Point, U.S.A., 466
—— Scheldt, 634
Western Desert coast road; naval assistance not asked for, 271
—— —— Italians launch offensive, 273
—— —— offensive preparations without naval co-operation, 289; final plans, 294
—— —— offensive opens, 295
—— —— Tobruk captured, 307
—— —— Derna captured, 309
—— —— Benghazi captured, 309
—— —— British troops retreat, 338
—— —— counter-offensive fails, 399, 402-3
—— —— large reinforcements, 403
—— —— preparations for further offensive, Nov. 1941, 419-20
—— —— offensive opens, 421
—— —— Tobruk relieved, 427-8
—— —— Derna captured, 428
—— —— Benghazi captured, 428
—— —— Army's rapid progress, 428
—— —— things go badly, 441-2
—— Task Force, N. Africa, 494, 538
Weston, Major-General E. C., R.M., 358, 382, 387, 388, 389
Weygand, General, 222, 224, 225; appointed C.-in-C., France, 226; 237
Whale Island, 36, 75
Whitamore, Professor, 215
White, General, 21
—— Bear River, Newfoundland, 129
—— Ensign, showing of, valuable policy, 122
White House Papers of Harry Hopkins, The, 598
Whitfield, Commander Paul, 45
Whitworth, Capt. (later Admiral Sir) William J., 174, 578, 599
Wilhelm, King Friedrich, 49
Wilhelmshaven bombed, 631; 644
Wilkinson, Capt. J. B. H., R.N., 328
Willan, Capt. Leonard L. P., 108
William IV and Antigua, 128
William-Powlett, Capt. P. R. B. W., 371
Williams, Hamilton, 15
—— Lieut. Wilfred Joe, 93, 97
Willis, Rear-Admiral (later Admiral of the Fleet) Sir Algernon U., 8, 56, 206, 247, 251, 301, 323-4, 331, 522, 546, 547, 573, 574, 586, 599, 655
Wilson, Admiral of the Fleet Sir A. K., 32-3
—— Lt. - General Sir Henry Maitland ('Jumbo') (now Field-Marshal Lord Wilson of Libya), 294, 353, 397; appointed Supreme Commander, Mediterranean, 589; prepares Operation 'Anvil', 598; 626
Winant, John G., U.S. Ambassador, 586, 598, 656-7, 661
Windau, 100, 101
Winn, Capt. C. R. B., R.N.V.R., 579
Wodehouse, Lt.-Commander P. G., 70
Wolfe, General James, 122
Wolsey, Cardinal, 179

2 s*

Women's Royal Naval Service at Algiers, 518
Wonderfontein, Transvaal, 28
World 'scoop' by American naval officer, 562
Wright, Capt. Gerauld, U.S.A., 477, 478, 481, 494, 497
Wrottesley, Lieut. F. R., 39
Why Britain requires a Navy, 651-2
Wykeham, William of, 179
Wyld, Lt.-Commander H. W., 70

Yorkshire Regiment, 26
Yugoslavia, murder of King Alexander of, 167; his funeral, 168-9
—— warm admiration for the British, 168
—— primitive methods, 164-5
—— birthday celebrations of King Peter II, 184
—— visit of Mediterranean Fleet cancelled, 190
—— attacked by Germany, 338
—— crown jewels taken to safety, 357
—— fighting ends, April, 1941, 352

'X' lighters, 77; of 1914-18 war, 294-5

Yalta Conference, 619-20, 622-3, 627-9
Yap Island, 636
Yemen, 234
Yokohama bombed, 645
Yokosuka naval base bombed, 645, 649
York, T.R.H. the Duke and Duchess of (their present Majesties), in Jamaica, 128

Zambesi River, 20
Zand River, Orange Free State, 25
Zanzibar, 19, 20
Zara, Italian port, 165
Zara, Italian Admiral da, 564-5
Zhukov, Russian Marshal, 642
Zeebrugge, 89; blockade of, 90; 91, 96, 98, 342
Zeppelin raid over Hull, 89
Zouaves in victory march at Tunis, 540

II—SHIPS INDEX

BRITISH BATTLESHIPS

Agamemnon, 60, 61, 71, 73
Albion, 60
Barham, 140, 142, 185, 186, 206, 276, 284, 300, 326, 329, 332, 335, 342, 346, 347; 377, 389, 400, 410, 424, 425
Canopus, 60, 63
Centurion, used as a 'gooseberry', 599
Cornwallis, 60, 63
Duke of York, 477, 590, 591, 650
Empress of India, 140
Exmouth, 74
Glory, 83, 84
Goliath, sunk, 67; 68
Hannibal, 32, 33, 39
Howe, 531, 544, 546, 547, 564–5, 630, 635, 636, 639
Implacable, 37, 38
Inflexible, 54, 55, 60, 65, 66
Iron Duke, 112
Irresistible, 60, 61; sunk, 65
King George V, 199 449, 531, 544, 546, 547, 564, 565, 635, 636, 637, 649, 650
Magnificent, 33
Lord Nelson, 60
Majestic, 33, 60, 73, 74
Malaya, 140, 207, 224, 225, 234, 235, 258, 260, 263, 265, 270, 271, 284, 287, 297
Marlborough, 140
Nelson, 120, 140, 142, 143, 147, 206, 322, 405, 410, 512, 517, 531, 546, 555, 559, 568, 573
Ocean, 60; sunk, 65
Prince George, 60
Prince of Wales, 199; sunk, 436
Queen Elizabeth, 61, 68, 158, 177, 178, 300, 360, 365, 376, 394, 400, 410, 421, 424, 425; 433–4, 435, 460, 580, 629
Ramillies, 206, 224, 225, 226, 234, 235, 239 253; boilers worn out, 270; 271, 287, 297, 580
Resolution, 158, 244
Revenge, 118, 158
Rodney, 119; appointed in command of, 139; excessive executive officers, 140; 141, 142, 143, 144, 145, 146, 147, 148, 152, 171, 182, 196, 477, 478, 490, 512, 517, 531, 546, 547, 555, 559, 568, 573
Royal Oak, 219
Royal Sovereign, 120, 158, 224, 234, 239, 258, 259, 260, 263, 365, 270; loaned to Russia, 642
Swiftsure, 60, 93, 94, 96
Triumph, 52, 60; sunk, 73–4
Valiant, 244, 268, 272, 277, 280, 284, 290, 296, 300, 302; casualties, 303; 326, 328, 331, 332, 334, 335, 346, 347, 367, 370, 371, 394, 424, 425, 433, 435, 546, 547, 559, 562, 563, 568, 570, 580, 608, 629
Vanguard, 577, 659
Vengeance, 60, 64
Warspite, 190–1, 206, 207, 208, 212–13, 215, 218, 219; at Narvik, 224; 225, 234, 235, 238, 247, 250, 258, 259, 260–2, 263, 265, 270, 271, 280, 281, 284, 290, 296, 300, 301, 302, 303, 305, 306, 324, 326, 327, 328, 330, 331, 332, 333, 334, 335, 346, 347, 352, 363, 367, 370, 389, 400, 449, 522, 546, 547; congratulated, 552; 555, 559, 562, 568; damaged and sunk, 570; 578; White Ensign laid up, 656

BATTLE CRUISERS

Hood, 168, 169, 181, 182, 183, 185, 186, 187, 188, 189, 190, 191, 243–4, 262, 323, 383
Indefatigable, 54, 58, 59, 60
Indomitable, 54, 58, 59, 60
Renown, 37, 128, 140, 477, 580, 586, 629
Repulse, 35, 140, 151, 182, 188, 191; sunk, 436
Tiger, 140, 142

CRUISERS

Cruiser Squadrons, Mediterranean Fleet, reduced to two ships, 239
1st, 158, 206
3rd, 158, 206, 234
7th, 234, 235, 238–9, 240, 260–2, 296, 365
12th, 547
15th, 365, 417, 429, 527, 531, 547
Achilles, 649
Ajax, 278–9, 326, 340, 353, 357, 361, 367, 368, 370, 373, 377, 382, 394, 397, 424, 425, 433, 441, 517
Amethyst, 62, 64
Antenor (merchant), 221
Arethusa, 206, 605
Argonaut, 477, 505, 512–13, 638
Argyll, 43
Aurora, 412, 419, 430, 431, 432, 457, 489, 490, 503, 505, 531, 542, 545, 547, 563
Belfast, 589, 590, 591, 592, 603
Bermuda, 477
Berwick, 175, 284, 287, 288, 610
Birmingham, 221
Black Prince (new), 638, 649

INDEX

Black Prince (old), 42, 54, 55, 58
Boadicea, 47, 48, 51
Bonaventure, 302, 309, 322; sunk, 338
Cairo, 130, 131
Calcutta (anti-aircraft), 121, 124, 125, 127, 128, 130, 131, 132, 137, 268, 272, 273, 309, 320, 340, 346, 353, 362, 369, 385, 386; sunk, 388, 611
Caledon, 234, 235, 238, 344
Calypso, 234; torpedoed, 235
Capetown, 122, 124, 125, 126, 127, 234, 238
Carlisle (anti-aircraft), 265, 309; damaged, 320; 353, 362, 369; hit, 370; 389, 409, 430, 431, 440, 442, 450, 454, 452, 455, 456, 457
Carnarvon, 43
Centaur, 140
Charybdis, 568; sunk, 580
Chatham, 54, 55
Coventry (anti-aircraft), 106, 110, 115, 117, 158, 161, 162, 163, 164, 165, 167, 168, 169, 170, 172, 173, 181, 187, 268, 272, 273, 309, 310; torpedoed, 320; 353, 372, 374, 377, 385, 386, 388, 394, 397, 409
Cleopatra, 447–8, 450, 451, 453, 531, 547, 558
Curaçoa, 99, 101, 105, 106
Curlew, 126, 127
Dauntless, 136–7, 158
Defence, 54, 56, 57
"Delhi" Class, 206
Delhi, 158, 223, 234, 531
Despatch, 132, 133, 136, 137, 158, 172, 173, 174, 611
Devonshire, 158, 206, 610
Diadem, 34, 35, 40
Dido, 362, 365, 368; blown up, 369; 370, 377, 382, 384, 389, 390, 429, 442, 448, 450, 452, 547, 563, 589
Diomede, 175
Doris, 19, 21, 22, 30, 32, 33, 37, 79, 90
Dublin, 54, 55, 56, 58, 59, 113
Duke of Edinburgh, 54
Durban, 158; used as a 'gooseberry', 599
Edgar, 41, 76, 79
Endymion, 76
Enterprise, 592–3
Euryalus, 424, 425, 430, 442, 448, 450, 451, 453, 531, 547, 560, 568, 638, 649
Exeter, 175, 265
Fiji, 360, 370, 371; sunk, 389
Fox, 12, 17, 19–21, 32
Frobisher, 140
Galatea, 176, 177, 206, 287, 409; sunk, 430
Gambia, 649
Glasgow, 284, 288, 289, 583, 592–3, 659
Gloucester (old), 54–6, 58, 59
Gloucester, 235, 239, 258–9, 263, 265, 270, 296, 301, 302, 303–5, 326, 327, 346, 347, 348, 360, 370, 371, 373, 394; sunk, 389
Grafton, 76
Hawke, 40, 41, 42
Highflyer, 41
Hobart, 650
Isis, 41
Jamaica, 490, 590, 591, 592

Kent, 270, 271, 274, 289, 610
Lancaster, 43
Leander, 400
Leviathan, 43
Liverpool, 234, 235, 239, 240, 258, 260, 263, 264, 268, 279
London, 158
Manchester, 219, 500
Mauritius, 547, 559
Naiad, 360, 362, 365, 369, 370; sunk, 371; 372, 373, 389, 409, 411, 417, 424, 425, 430, 442, 447; sunk, 448
Natal, 25
Neptune, 234, 236–7, 253, 258, 260, 263, 424, 425, 431; sunk, 432
Newfoundland, 531, 547, 558, 649
Norfolk, 590, 591, 592
Northampton, appointed to, 39, 40, 41
Orion, 234, 236–7, 258, 260, 263, 279, 285, 326, 353, 357, 368, 369, 370, 373, 382, 384, 389, 400, 531, 547, 559, 626
Penelope, 203, 206, 412, 419, 425, 430, 431, 432, 433, 441, 443, 455, 456, 457, 458, 531, 547, 563
Perth, bombed, 304, 326, 369, 385, 386, 389
Phœbe, 346, 353, 369, 385, 386, 387, 394, 397, 406, 407, 411, 413, 417
Powerful, 21, 22
Raleigh, 129
Ranpura (merchant), 221
St. George, 41
Scylla (old), 42
Scylla, 481, 568, 605
Sheffield, 196, 490, 590, 591, 592
Shropshire, 158, 206, 650
Sirius, 477, 505, 531, 547, 563, 626
Southampton, 301, 302, 303, 304
Suffolk, 42–4, 65
Sussex, 158, 206
Swiftsure, 638
Sydney, 234, 236–7, 258, 260, 263, 273, 285, 288
Talbot, 74, 75
Terrible, 21, 22, 32
Theseus, 76
Topaze, 45
Uganda, 547, 568
Vindictive (old), 37, 92, 94, 206
Vindictive (new), 140
Warrior, 54, 55
Weymouth, 54, 55
York, 175, 265, 278, 288, 296, 323, 353

MINELAYING CRUISERS

Abdiel, 375, 377, 403–4, 413, 419, 429, 444, 511, 552, 555, 564
Latona, 400, 403–4, 413–14
Welshman, 458, 494, 511, 520

INDEX

DESTROYERS

Flotillas:
  1st, 111–13, 115, 116, 117, 157, 159, 170, 171
  2nd, 116, 235, 266
  3rd, 112, 157, 159, 162, 164, 170, 172, 175
  4th, 157, 162, 164, 168, 170, 175
  5th, 175, 362, 373
  6th (appointed captain of), 110
  10th, 605
  14th, 88, 448
  26th, 631
Albatross, 50
Avon Vale, 450, 457
Banshee, 39
Barfleur, 650
Basilisk, 75
Beagle, 56, 75
Beaufort, 450
Bicester, 520, 530
Blanche, 172
Boreas, 189
Broke, 479
Bulldog, 56, 75
Chelmer, 58, 73
Cleopatra, 101
Colne, 58
Coquette, 39
Cossack, 212
"D" Class, 234
Dainty, 237, 311; sunk, 318
Decoy, 235, 287, 374, 382, 384, 389, 403, 444
Defender, 307, 354, 357, 374, 386, 403; sunk, 394; 404
Delight, 162
Diamond, 304; sunk, 354
Douglas, 95, 96
Dulverton, 450
Easton, 520
Encounter, 414
Eridge, 450, 456
Eskimo, 544
Farndale, 430; damaged, 445
Gallant, mined, 302, 303
Garry, 58
Grampus, 70
Grasshopper, 58, 60, 70
Greyhound, 326, 332, 333; sunk, 370; 371; praised, 372; 389
Griffin, 322, 326, 333, 355, 414, 422, 444
Gurkha, sunk, 440, 445
Hambledon, 563
Hardy, 224
Harpy, 55, 58
Hasty, 258, 326, 346, 368, 385, 450, 457
Havock, 278, 326, 333, 389, 431, 432, 440, 453, 455, 457, 500
Hereward, 302, 326, 354, 368, 382; sunk, 383; 389
Hero, 354, 356, 374, 377
Heythrop, 445

Hostile, lost, 272
Hotspur, 326, 382, 383, 387, 397
"Hunt" Class, 106, 194, 199, 234
Hurworth, 450
Hyperion, 266; sunk, 297
"I" Class, 234
Ilex, 237, 297, 326, 398
Imperial, 278, 382; sunk, 383, 389
Isis, 356, 397, 398
Ithuriel, 505, 517
"J" Class, 234
Jackal, 360, 373, 382, 387, 397, 426
Jaguar, 374, 377, 386, 414
Janus, 326, 341, 345–6, 368, 385, 397, 398
Jersey, mined, 360
Jervis, 275, 326, 329, 333, 341, 345–6, 385, 404, 433, 448, 449, 450, 452, 544
Juno, sunk, 368, 370, 389
"K" Class, 234
Kandahar, 356, 369, 370, 371; praised, 372, 384, 386, 397, 431, 432
Kangaroo, 45
Kashmir, 360; sunk, 373, 374, 389
Kelly, 360; sunk, 373, 374, 389
Kelvin, 360, 373, 384, 386, 389, 450
Kempenfelt, 189
Keppel, 171
Kimberley, 356, 368, 382, 387, 397, 425, 444, 445, 455, 458, 609
Kingston, 356, 369, 370, 371; conduct praised, 372; 389, 425, 447, 450, 453; destroyed, 458
Kipling, 360, 373, 389, 421, 448, 450
Laforey, 526
Lamerton, 491, 520
Lance, 412, 419, 431, 432
Legion, 430, 450, 451, 453, 455, 456
Lightning, 517; sunk, 523
Lively, 412, 419, 425, 431, 448, 450, 453
Locust, 38, 39, 170
Lookout, 517, 544
Loyal, 517
Malcolm, 479, 487
Maori, 212, 430; sunk, 441
Mohawk, 285, 302, 326, 329, 341, 345; sunk, 346
Mosquito, 59, 70, 73
Napier, 384, 386, 389, 650
Nizam, 377, 384, 385, 386, 389, 650
Nubian, 212, 280, 285, 326, 329, 341, 345–6, 369, 376–7, 389, 526, 527, 544
Offa, 570
Ophelia, 88, 89
Orwell, 39, 50
Pakenham, sunk, 526
Paladin, 526
Pathfinder, 518
Penn, 518
Petard, 526
Pincher, 70
Quality, 650
Quentin, sunk, 505, 520
Quiberon, 520
Racoon, 70, 73, 75

714   INDEX

Rattlesnake, 70, 83, 84
Renard, 50, 70, 75, 77
Ribble, 58
Roebuck, 46, 47
Rowena, 175
"S" Class, capabilities, 106, 193–4
Saumarez, 631
Scorpion, 47, 48, 49, 50, 52, 53, 54, 56, 58, 59, 60, 64, 66, 67, 68, 69, 70, 72, 73, 74, 75, 77, 79, 80, 81, 82, 83, 84, 86, 87, 88, 90, 93, 113, 128, 132, 135, 157, 203
Scotsman, 99, 102, 103, 104, 105
Sea Bear, 99
Seafire, transfer to, 98; 99, 100, 101, 102, 104, 105; farewell to, 106; 193
Shakespeare, 99, 111
Sikh, 430, 450, 452
Solebay, 660
Southwold, 450, 452; sunk, 456
Stuart, 234, 265, 307 308, 326, 333, 377, 386, 413
Tartar, 526, 559
Tenacious, 650
Termagant, appointed to, 89; 90, 91, 93, 94, 95, 96, 97, 98, 650
Terpsichore, 650
Thruster, 175
Torrid, 175
"Tribal" Class, 234
Troubridge, 650
Ulster, damaged, 637
Usk, 58
"V" and "W" Classes, 141, 170, 171, 175; Australian flotilla, 234
Vampire, 307, 308
Vendetta, 308, 326, 413
Venus, 631
Verulam, 631
Veteran, 171
Vigilant, 631
Virago, 631
Voyager, 308
Vulture, 46, 47
Wager, 650
Wakeful, 650
Wallace, 111, 113, 114, 115, 118
Warramunga, 650
Warwick, 118
Waterhen, 308
Wear, 58
Wheatland, 491, 520
Whelp, 650
Wild Swan, 171
Wishart, 171, 483
Witch, 171
Witshead, 171
Wizard, 650
Wolverine, 54, 57, 59, 64, 67, 68, 70, 73, 74, 75, 76, 77, 78, 79, 80, 82, 84, 186
Wrangler, 650
Wryneck, sunk, 354
Zetland, 488, 530
Zulu, 212, 443, 450, 452, 453

BRITISH AIRCRAFT CARRIERS
(Including Escort Carriers)

Activity, 617
Argus, 114, 140, 268
Ark Royal, 200, 244, 321, 420
Attacker, 560
Battler, 560
Campania, 617
Chaser, 617
Courageous, 175
Eagle, 114, 234, 235, 239, 258–60, 263–4, 266–8, 271, 273, 279, 284, 290, 304–5, 313, 338, 340; sunk, 473; 660
Fencer, 617
Formidable, 305, 312, 313, 321, 322, 323, 326, 327, 328, 329, 330, 332, 333, 334, 335, 346, 361, 362, 367, 376–7, 389, 400, 477, 517, 638, 639, 649
Furious, 114, 140, 158, 477, 478, 601
Glorious, 182, 206, 217, 218
Hunter, 560
Illustrious, 231, 265, 268, 272–3, 277, 278, 279, 280, 283, 284, 285, 287, 290, 296, 300, 301, 302; badly hit, 303; 304, 305, 312, 313, 578, 580, 629, 635, 637, 638
Implacable, 649
Indefatigable, 635, 637, 650
Indomitable, 546, 547, 558, 635, 637, 638; 639
Ruler, 650
Speaker, 650
Stalker, 560
Tracker, 617
Unicorn, 560
Victorious, 477, 601, 635, 637, 638, 639
Vindex, 617

AUXILIARY A.A. SHIPS

Alynbank, 503
Tynwald, sunk, 491

BRITISH SUBMARINES

Submarine Flotillas, 1st, 170, 445
—— —— 8th, 510, 526, 542–3
—— —— 10th, 410, 411; high praise, 445, 510, 526
B2, 67
B11, 66
Cachalot, 395, 458
Cyclops (depot ship), 186
E15, 66, 67, 68
Grampus, sunk, 237; 269
Heythrop (anti-submarine sweeper), sunk, 450
"O" Class, 234, 269

Odin, sunk, 237, 269
Orpheus, sunk, 237, 269
Oswald, sunk, 269
Otus, 425
"P" Class, 234, 269
P36, 450
P219, 478, 481, 483, 486 (later *Seraph*)
Parthian, 269, 458
Phoenix, 258; sunk, 269
Porpoise, 442, 458
"R" Class, considered too large and old, 269
Regent, 458
Rorqual, 395, 458, 511
Rover, 444
Safari, 526, 557
Sahib, sunk, 526
Seraph, 557 (*see also* P219)
Shakespeare, 557
Splendid, sunk, 526
"T" Class, many successes, 401
Thrasher, 392, 393, 445–6
Thunderbolt, lost, 523–4
Tigris, lost, 523–4
Torbay, 446
Trenchant, 631
Truant, 347, 444
Trusty, 444
Turbulent, lost, 523–4
"U" Class, 400–1
Unison, 557
Unrivalled, 557
Unruffled, 557
Unseen, 557
Upholder, 362, 445
Upright, 430
Urge, 430
Utmost, 430

MISCELLANEOUS VESSELS
(H.M. Ships)

Abercrombie (Monitor), 552
Abingdon (Minesweeper), 439
Aphis (Gunboat), 274, 283, 294, 300, 557, 559
Auckland (Sloop), 394
Blenheim (Destroyer Depot Ship), 54, 55, 58, 64, 73–5, 81, 85, 88
Boston (Minesweeper), 553
Breconshire (Naval Fuel Carrier), 429, 430–1, 441, 443, 449, 455, 456

Britannia (Training Ship), 14–17, 39, 42, 64, 101, 176, 203
Chakdina (Supply Ship), 427
Chantala (Supply Ship), 427
Cricket (Gunboat), 394, 404
Cromarty (Minesweeper), 553
Erebus (Monitor), 559
Fantome (Minesweeper), 532
Flamingo (Sloop), 394, 404, 427
Glenearn (Landing Ship), 354, 403
Glengyle (Landing Ship), 385, 392, 397, 440–1
Glenroy (Landing Ship), 374, 377, 422, 428
Gnat (Gunboat), 274, 294, 414–15
Grimsby (Sloop), 354, 394, 404
Hartland, 479, 489
Hilary (H.Q. Ship), 566, 569, 571, 572
Huntley (Minesweeper), 320
Ladybird (Gunboat), 274, 283, 294, 300, 307, 316, 362–3
Largs (H.Q. Ship), 526, 562
Maidstone (Submarine Depot Ship), 206, 510, 518, 542–3, 575
Martin (Brig), 33–4
Medway (Submarine Depot Ship), 234, 238, 270
Monarch (Depot Ship), 21
Parramatta (Sloop), 400, 422
Poole (Minesweeper), 553
Port Arthur (Corvette), 520
Princess Beatrix, 506
Queen Emma, 506
Regina (Corvette), 520
Roberts (Monitor), 559
Royal Scotsman, 506
Royal Ulsterman, 506
Scarab (Gunboat), 557, 559
Seaham (Minesweeper), 553
Terror (Monitor), 274, 289, 300, 307, 310, 311
Valerian (Sloop), 126–7
Ville De Quebec (Corvette), 520
Walney, 479, 489

HOSPITAL SHIPS

Aba, bombed, 372
Dorsetshire, bombed, 310
Karapara, bombed, 364
Leinster, bombed, 568
Newfoundland, bombed and sunk, 568
Talamba, bombed and sunk, 557